DOMESTIC VIOLENCE

ASPEN CASEBOOK SERIES

DOMESTIC VIOLENCE

Legal and Social Reality

D. KELLY WEISBERG
Professor of Law
Hastings College of the Law
University of California

Printed in the United States of America.

1 2 3 4 5 6 7 8 9 0

ISBN 978-0-7355-0863-7

Library of Congress Cataloging-in-Publication Data
Weisberg, D. Kelly.
    Domestic violence : legal and social reality / D. Kelly Weisberg.
        p. cm.—(Aspen casebook series)
    ISBN 978-0-7355-0863-7 (casebound)
    1. Family violence—Law and legislation—United States. 2. Casebooks I. Title.

KF9322.W45 2012
344.7303'28292—dc23

                                                                                    2011050122

SUSTAINABLE
FORESTRY
INITIATIVE

Certified Sourcing
www.sfiprogram.org
SFI-01234

SFI label applies to the text stock

About Wolters Kluwer Law & Business

Wolters Kluwer Law & Business is a leading global provider of intelligent information and digital solutions for legal and business professionals in key specialty areas, and respected educational resources for professors and law students. Wolters Kluwer Law & Business connects legal and business professionals as well as those in the education market with timely, specialized authoritative content and information-enabled solutions to support success through productivity, accuracy and mobility.

Serving customers worldwide, Wolters Kluwer Law & Business products include those under the Aspen Publishers, CCH, Kluwer Law International, Loislaw, Best Case, ftwilliam.com and MediRegs family of products.

CCH products have been a trusted resource since 1913, and are highly regarded resources for legal, securities, antitrust and trade regulation, government contracting, banking, pension, payroll, employment and labor, and healthcare reimbursement and compliance professionals.

Aspen Publishers products provide essential information to attorneys, business professionals and law students. Written by preeminent authorities, the product line offers analytical and practical information in a range of specialty practice areas from securities law and intellectual property to mergers and acquisitions and pension/benefits. Aspen's trusted legal education resources provide professors and students with high-quality, up-to-date and effective resources for successful instruction and study in all areas of the law.

Kluwer Law International products provide the global business community with reliable international legal information in English. Legal practitioners, corporate counsel and business executives around the world rely on Kluwer Law journals, looseleafs, books, and electronic products for comprehensive information in many areas of international legal practice.

Loislaw is a comprehensive online legal research product providing legal content to law firm practitioners of various specializations. Loislaw provides attorneys with the ability to quickly and efficiently find the necessary legal information they need, when and where they need it, by facilitating access to primary law as well as state-specific law, records, forms and treatises.

Best Case Solutions is the leading bankruptcy software product to the bankruptcy industry. It provides software and workflow tools to flawlessly streamline petition preparation and the electronic filing process, while timely incorporating ever-changing court requirements.

ftwilliam.com offers employee benefits professionals the highest quality plan documents (retirement, welfare and non-qualified) and government forms (5500/PBGC, 1099 and IRS) software at highly competitive prices.

MediRegs products provide integrated health care compliance content and software solutions for professionals in healthcare, higher education and life sciences, including professionals in accounting, law and consulting.

Wolters Kluwer Law & Business, a division of Wolters Kluwer, is headquartered in New York. Wolters Kluwer is a market-leading global information services company focused on professionals.

Table of Contents

Preface   *xxiii*
Acknowledgments   *xxvii*

PART I: INTRODUCTION

I.   SOCIAL AND HISTORICAL PERSPECTIVE: EVOLUTION OF
      THE RIGHT OF PRIVACY   3

      A.   Social-Historical Context   3
                 Reva B. Siegel, "The Rule of Love": Wife Beating as
                     Prerogative and Privacy   3
                 Susan Schechter, The Roots of the Battered Women's
                     Movement: Personal and Political   7
                 Nadine Taub & Elizabeth Schneider, Women's
                     Subordination and the Role of Law   10
                 Notes and Questions   12
      B.   Legal Historical Context   16
           1. Common Law View of Marital Roles and Responsibilities   16
                 1 William Blackstone, Commentaries
                     of the Laws of England   16
                 Notes and Questions   17
           2. Judicial Doctrine of Nonintervention in the Marital
               Relationship   19
                 McGuire v. McGuire   19
                 Notes and Questions   22

3. Interspousal Immunity Doctrine: Tort Actions Between
    Spouses   23
    Thompson v. Thompson   23
    Notes and Questions   26

II. CHARACTERISTICS OF DOMESTIC VIOLENCE   29

A. Extent of the Problem   29
    Centers for Disease Control and Prevention, National
        Intimate Partner and Sexual Violence Survey: 2010
        Summary Report, Executive Summary   29
    Notes and Questions   34
B. Dynamics of Abusive Relationships   36
    Angela Browne, Violence in Marriage: Until Death Do Us
        Part?   36
    Judith A. Wolfer, Top Ten Myths About Domestic
        Violence   38
    Clare Dalton, Domestic Violence, Domestic Torts and
        Divorce: Constraints and Possibilities   42
    Lundy Bancroft, Understanding the Batterer in Custody
        and Visitation Disputes   44
    Notes and Questions   46
C. Causes of Intimate Partner Violence   47
    1. Theories of Intimate Partner Violence   47
    2. Cycle Theory of Violence   53
        Lenore E. A. Walker, The Battered Woman Syndrome   53
    3. Duluth Model: Power and Control Wheel   56
        Notes and Questions   59
D. Lethality Assessment   59
    Neil Websdale, Assessing Risk in Domestic Violence Cases   60
    Jacquelyn C. Campbell, Danger Assessment Instrument   62
    Notes and Questions   64
E. Consequences of Abuse   66
    Centers for Disease Control and Prevention, Costs of
        Intimate Partner Violence Against Women in the
        United States   66
    Centers for Disease Control & Prevention, Intimate
        Partner Violence: Consequences   68
    Notes and Questions   69

III. INFLUENTIAL FACTORS   71

A. Age   71
    1. Teen Dating Violence   71
        Neilson ex rel. Crump v. Blanchette   71
        Notes and Questions   73

Carrie Mulford & Peggy C. Giordano, Teen Dating
Violence: A Closer Look at Adolescent Romantic
Relationships   77
    Problems   78
  2. Elder Abuse   79
    Gdowski v. Gdowski   79
    Notes and Questions   82
    Problems   86
    New York Socialite Brooke Astor is a Victim of Elder
    Abuse   86
B. Sexual Orientation   87
    Stephen White, Guilty of Britain's First Gay Domestic
    Murder   87
    Sharon Stapel, Falling to Pieces: New York State Civil
    Legal Remedies Available to Lesbian, Gay, Bisexual,
    and Transgender Survivors of Domestic Violence   88
    Tara R. Pfeifer, Comment, Out of the Shadows:
    The Positive Impact of Lawrence v. Texas on Victims of
    Same-Sex Domestic Violence   89
    Notes and Questions   89
C. Disability   92
    Jennifer Nixon, Domestic Violence and Women with
    Disabilities: Locating the Issue on the Periphery of
    Social Movements   92
    Jane K. Stoever, Stories Absent from the Courtroom:
    Responding to Domestic Violence in the Context of
    HIV and AIDS   93
    Notes and Questions   95
D. Race and Ethnicity   97
    Callie Rennison & Mike Planty, Nonlethal Intimate
    Partner Violence: Examining Race, Gender, and
    Income Patterns   98
    Lisa M. Martinson, Comment, An Analysis of Racism and
    Resources for African-American Female Victims of
    Domestic Violence in Wisconsin   98
    Mary Ann Dutton et al., Characteristics of Help-Seeking
    Behaviors, Resources and Service Needs of Battered
    Immigrant Latinas: Legal and Policy Implications   100
    Sujata Warrier, (Un)Heard Voices: Domestic Violence in
    the Asian-American Community   102
    Notes and Questions   103
E. Religion   105
    Adam H. Koblenz, Jewish Women Under Siege: The Fight
    for Survival on the Front Lines of Love and the Law   105
    Kenneth Lasson, Bloodstains on a "Code of Honor":
    The Murderous Marginalization of Women in the
    Islamic World   108

			Kathleen A. McDonald, Battered Wives, Religion, and Law: An Interdisciplinary Approach	109
			Notes and Questions	110
	F.	Social Class		110
			Karl Vick, Case of John Michael Farren Seen as Refresher Course on Domestic Violence	111
			Claire M. Renzetti & Vivian M. Larkin, Economic Stress and Domestic Violence	112
			Notes and Questions	115
	G.	Substance Abuse		118
			Monica L. Zilberman & Sheila B. Blume, Domestic Violence, Alcohol, and Substance Abuse	118
			Notes and Questions	119
	H.	Special Contexts		119
		1.	Military	120
			Simeon Stamm, Note, Intimate Partner Violence in the Military: Securing Our Country, Starting with the Home	120
			Notes and Questions	121
		2.	Police-Perpetrated Domestic Violence	124
			Alex Roslin, Batterer in Blue	124
			Notes and Questions	125
			Safe Haven by Nicholas Sparks	129
		3.	Sports	130
			Joan Ryan, O. J. Case Changed Rules for Cox	130
			Bethany P. Withers, Comment, The Integrity of the Game: Professional Athletes and Domestic Violence	131
			Family Violence Prevention Fund, Domestic Violence and the Super Bowl	132
			Notes and Questions	133
IV.		SPECIFIC TYPES OF ABUSE		135
	A.	Physical Abuse		135
		1.	Strangulation	135
			Carter v. State	135
			Notes and Questions	138
			Problem	140
		2.	Murder-Suicide	140
			Clark v. Office of Personnel Management	140
			Notes and Questions	142
			Famous Murder-Suicide: World-Famous Wrestler Chris Benoit	144
		3.	Separation Assault	144
			Crawford v. Commonwealth	144
			Martha R. Mahoney, Legal Images of Battered Women: Redefining the Issue of Separation	148
			Sarah M. Buel, Fifty Obstacles to Leaving, A.K.A. Why Abuse Victims Stay	151
			Domestic Violence: A Personal Safety Plan	154

		Notes and Questions	156
		Problem	158
		Sondra Burman, Stages of Leaving Abusive Relationships	159
B.		Sexual and Reproductive Abuse	161
	1.	Sexual Assaults: Marital Rape	162
		S.D. v. M.J.R.	162
		Notes and Questions	165
		Famous Case of Marital Rape: Mary Murphy	167
	2.	Pregnancy-Related Abuse	167
		Smith v. Martin	167
		Notes and Questions	169
	3.	Birth Control Sabotage	170
		Family Violence Prevention Fund, 1 in 4 Hotline Callers Report Birth Control Sabotage, Pregnancy Coercion	170
		Ann M. Moore et al., Male Reproductive Control of Women Who Have Experienced Intimate Partner Violence in the United States	171
		Notes and Questions	172
		Problem	173
	4.	Interference with Abortion Decisionmaking	174
		Planned Parenthood of Southeastern Pennsylvania v. Casey	174
		Notes and Questions	177
C.		Psychological Abuse	179
	1.	Background	179
		Evan Stark, Coercive Control	179
	2.	Stalking	182
		Weiner v. Weiner	182
		Notes and Questions	186
		Problems	191
		Long Term Case of Stalking	192
	3.	Cyber Harassment	193
		In re Marriage of Nadkarni	193
		Notes and Questions	195
	4.	Financial Abuse	197
		Jackson v. United States	197
		Notes and Questions	198
		Financial Abuse: Tax Implications	200
	5.	Pet Abuse	201
		Cat Killer Denied Parole	201
		Notes and Questions	201
		Problems	204
		"A Jury of Her Peers" and Pet Abuse	206
	6.	Other Forms of Psychological Abuse	206
		Anique Drouin, Comment, Who Turned Out the Lights?: How Maryland Laws Fail to Protect Victims of Domestic Violence from Third-Party Abuse	207
		Problems	208

PART II.   CRIMINAL JUSTICE RESPONSE

V.   LAW ENFORCEMENT RESPONSE   213

A.   Police   213
  1.   Traditional Response to Intimate Partner Assaults   213
       Joan Zorza, The Criminal Law of Misdemeanor Domestic
         Violence, 1970-1990   213
       Notes and Questions   215
  2.   The Road to Mandatory Arrest   217
       State v. Farrow   217
       Notes and Questions   220
  3.   Evaluation of Mandatory Arrest: Benefits and
       Shortcomings   224
       Arthur L. Rizer III, Mandatory Arrest: Do We Need to
         Take a Closer Look?   224
       Emily J. Sack, Battered Women and the State; The Struggle
         for the Future of Domestic Violence Policy   225
  4.   Unintended Consequences: Dual Arrest   225
       David Hirschel et. al., Nat'l Inst. of Justice, Explaining the
         Prevalence, Context, and Consequences of Dual Arrest
         in Intimate Partner Cases   226
       Postscript   227
  5.   Primary Aggressor Statutes   228
       Iowa Code Ann. §236.12   228
       S.C. Code Ann. §16-25-70   228
       Wash. Rev. Code §10.31.100   229
       Notes and Questions on Mandatory Arrest   229
  6.   Victims' Experience with the Police   234
       Marsha E. Wolf et al., Barriers to Seeking Police Help for
         Intimate Partner Violence   234
  7.   Statutory Expansion of Police Powers to Ensure Victims'
       Safety   237
       Mass. Gen. Laws Ann. Ch. 209A §6   237
       N.H. Rev. Stat. §173-B:10   238
       Note: Introduction to the Violence Against Women Act
         (VAWA)   239
       Remarks of Senator Joseph R. Biden, Jr.: Introducing
         the Violence Against Women Act Before
         Congress   239
B.   Prosecutors: No-Drop Policies   242
  1.   Background   243
       Cheryl Hanna, No Right to Choose: Mandated
         Victim Participation in Domestic Violence
         Prosecutions   243
  2.   Constitutional Issues   244
       McClure v. Rehg   244
  3.   Victims' Reluctance to Prosecute: The Battered Woman's
       Dilemma   245

Donna Wills, Domestic Violence: The Case for Aggressive
    Prosecution   245
William Glaberson, Abuse Suspects, Your Calls Are Taped,
    So Speak Up   247
4. Criticisms of Mandatory Interventions   249
    Leigh Goodmark, Autonomy Feminism: An Anti-
    Essentialist Critique of Mandatory Interventions in
    Domestic Violence Cases   249
    Notes and Questions   250
    Note: Criminal No-Contact Orders   253
5. An Innovative Approach to Criminal Behavior:
    Restorative Justice   254
    Joan Zorza, Restorative Justice: Does It Work for DV?   254
    Notes and Questions   257
C. Suits Against Law Enforcement   258
    1. Victim's Constitutional Rights   258
        Town of Castle Rock v. Gonzales   258
        Testimony of Jessica Lenahan (Gonzales) v.
            United States   261
        Notes and Questions   264
        Problem   269
    2. Legacy of Lawsuits: Improvements in Police Training   269

VI. DOMESTIC VIOLENCE AS A CRIME: STATE LEGISLATIVE
     RESPONSE   271

A. Criminal Sanctions   271
    1. Traditional Response: Assault and Battery   271
        Bradley v. State   272
        Notes and Questions   273
    2. Modern Response: Domestic Violence
        Statutes   275
        Eve S. Buzawa et al., Responding to Domestic Violence:
            The Integration of Criminal Justice and Human
            Services   276
        Statutory Comparison: Traditional Criminal Assault
            Statutes Versus New "Domestic Violence" Statutes   277
        Model Penal Code §211.1   277
        Colo. Rev. Stat. §18-6-800.3   277
        Ind. Code §35-41-1-6.3   278
        N.J. Stat. Ann. §2C:25-19   278
        N.M. Stat. Ann. §§30-3-11, 30-3-12   279
        S.C. Code Ann. §§16-25-10, 16-25-20   279
        Notes and Questions   280
        Problems   283
B. Constitutional Challenges to State Laws   284
    1. Vagueness   284
        People v. Johnson   284
        Notes and Questions   286

2.   Defense of Marriage Act   287
     State v. Carswell   287
     Notes and Questions   290
     Problem   293

VII.   JUDICIAL RESPONSE   295

   A.   Defenses   295
        1.   Historical Background   295
             Garthine Walker, Crime, Gender and Social Order in
                  Early Modern England   295
        2.   Battered Woman Syndrome: The Role of Expert
             Testimony   297
             Hawthorne v. State   297
             Lenore Walker, Terrifying Love: Why Battered Women
                  Kill and How Society Responds   298
             Notes and Questions   300
        3.   Self-Defense   305
             State v. Harden   305
             Notes and Questions   310
        4.   Duress   314
             Dixon v. United States   314
             Keshia Dixon's Story, Brief for the United States   318
             Notes and Questions   319
             Natalie's Story, Avon Global Center for Women & Justice,
                  From Protection to Punishment: Post-Conviction
                  Barriers to Justice for Domestic Violence Survivors-
                  Defendants in New York State   323
             Marti Tamm Loring & Pati Beaudoin, Battered Women as
                  Coerced Victim-Perpetrators   324
             Problem   324
        5.   Cultural Defense   325
             People v. Benitez   325
             Notes and Questions   327
             Problem   330
        6.   Provocation   330
             Murray v. State   330
             Notes and Questions   331
             Problems   333
   B.   Evidentiary Issues   334
        1.   Spousal Testimonial Privilege   334
             State v. Taylor   334
             Notes and Questions   337
             Problems   340
        2.   Marital Rape Exemption   340
             People v. Liberta   340

		Notes and Questions	344
		Problems	346
	3.	Prior Act Testimony	346
		People v. Brown	346
		Notes and Questions	351
	4.	Confrontation Clause	353
		Davis v. Washington	354
		Note: O. J. Simpson Trial and Its Legacy for Domestic Violence Law	359
		Janet Gilmore, Jurors Hear Frantic 911 Calls, Tape Captures Nicole Simpson Pleading for Aid	361
		Police Chief Ass'n of Santa Clara County, 911 Call-Taker/ Dispatcher Response	362
		Notes and Questions	363
		Problems	368
		Note: Interfering with a 911 Call	368
	5.	Forfeiture by Wrongdoing	369
		Giles v. California	369
		Notes and Questions	375
		Problem	378
	6.	Victim Recantation	379
		People v. Santiago	379
		Notes and Questions	383
		Problem	385
VIII.	**FEDERAL CRIMINAL RESPONSE**		**387**
A.	Introduction		387
	1.	Setting the Stage: A Story of Interstate Violence	387
	2.	VAWA's Federal Criminal Provisions	388
		18 U.S.C. §2261, 2261A, 2262(a)	389
B.	Interstate Domestic Violence as a Crime		391
		United States v. Larsen	391
		Notes and Questions	395
		Problems	399
C.	Firearm Regulation: Punishing Possession of Firearms		400
		Andrew R. Klein, Office on Violence Against Women, Enforcing Domestic Violence Firearm Prohibitions: A Report on Promising Practices	400
		United States v. Skoien	406
		Notes and Questions	409
		Problem	414
D.	Federal Indian Law and Domestic Violence		415
		Jacqueline P. Hand & David C. Koelsch, Shared Experiences, Divergent Outcomes: American Indian and Immigrant Victims of Domestic Violence	415

PART III.   CIVIL LAW RESPONSE

IX.   PROTECTION ORDERS   421

    A.   Introduction: Traditional Approach   421
        Keller v. Keller   421
        Notes and Questions   422
        Peter Finn, Statutory Authority in the Use and
          Enforcement of Civil Protection Orders Against
          Domestic Abuse   424
    B.   Modern Approach: Scope of Protection   425
        1.   An Overview of Modern Protection Orders   425
            Sally F. Goldfarb, Reconceiving Civil Protection Orders
              for Domestic Violence: Can Law Help End the Abuse
              Without Ending the Relationship?   428
        2.   Who Is Eligible as a Petitioner?   430
            Evans v. Braun   430
            Notes and Questions   433
            Eve S. Buzawa & Carl G. Buzawa, Domestic Violence:
              The Criminal Justice Response   435
        3.   What Conduct Gives Rise to a Protection Order?   436
            Cloeter v. Cloeter   436
            Alaska Stat. §18.66.100   440
            Notes and Questions   441
            Problem   442
        4.   How Long Does It Last?: Duration of an Order of
            Protection   442
            Dyer v. Dyer   442
            Sinclair v. Sinclair   444
            Notes and Questions   446
        5.   Where Is Jurisdiction Over the Defendant?   447
            Hemenway v. Hemenway   447
            Notes and Questions   450
            Problem   451
        6.   Termination of an Order of Protection   452
            Freeman v. Freeman   452
            Notes and Questions   456
    C.   Procedural Issues   457
        1.   Standard of Proof   457
            Crespo v. Crespo   457
        2.   Right to Jury Trial   460
            Blackmon v. Blackmon   460
        3.   Right to Discovery: The Problem of Discovery Abuse 462
            Depos v. Depos   462
            Notes and Questions on Procedural Issues   465
    D.   Enforcement   467
        1.   Contempt: Criminal, Civil, and Private Actions   467
            ABA Comm'n on Domestic Violence, The Domestic
              Violence Civil Law Manual: Protection Orders and
              Family Law Cases   467

		In re Robertson	468
		Notes and Questions	470
	2.	Violations of Restraining Orders: Criminal Sanctions	474
		Report from the Attorney General's Task Force on Local Criminal Justice Response to Domestic Violence, Keeping the Promise: Victim Safety and Batterer Accountability	475
	3.	Interstate Enforcement of Protection Orders: Full Faith and Credit	480
		Emily J. Sack, Domestic Violence Across State Lines: The Full Faith and Credit Clause, Congressional Power and Interstate Enforcement of Protection Orders	481
E.	Victim's Actions		484
	1.	Mutual Restraining Orders	484
		Williams v. Jones	484
		Notes and Questions	486
		Lundy Bancroft et al., The Batterer As Parent: Addressing the Impact of Domestic Violence on Family Dynamics	488
	2.	Victim's Violation of Order	489
		State v. Branson	489
		Notes and Questions	491
	3.	Victim's Request to Withdraw	492
		James C. Roberts et al., Why Victims of Intimate Partner Violence Withdraw Protection Orders	492
F.	Effectiveness		493
		Andrew R. Klein, Nat'l Inst. of Justice, Special Report: Practical Implications of Current Domestic Violence Research	493
		Sally F. Goldfarb, Reconceiving Civil Protection Orders for Domestic Violence: Can Law Help End the Abuse Without Ending the Relationship?	494
		Notes and Questions	496

X.	**TORT REMEDIES**		499
A.	State Causes of Action		499
	1.	Against the Abuser	499
		Feltmeier v. Feltmeier	499
		Notes and Questions	502
	2.	Against Third Parties	507
		McSwane v. Bloomington Hospital & Healthcare System	507
		Colo. Rev. Stat. §12-36-135	510
		Notes and Questions	511
B.	Defenses		514
	1.	Interspousal Immunity	514
		Thompson v. Thompson	514
		Notes and Questions	514
	2.	Statutes of Limitations	517
		Pugliese v. Superior Court	517
		Notes and Questions	520

		3.	Procedural Barriers: Res Judicata	522
			Chen v. Fischer	522
			Notes and Questions	524
	C.	Social Reality: Victims' Reluctance to Use Tort Remedies		526
			Jennifer Wriggins, Domestic Violence Torts	526
			Notes and Questions	529
	D.	Federal Tort Liability: VAWA's Civil Rights Remedy		530
			United States v. Morrison	530
			Patrick Tracey, Christy's Crusade	537
			Brooke A. Masters, "No Winners" in Rape Lawsuit: Two Students Forever Changed by Case That Went to Supreme Court	538
			Joseph Shapiro, Myths That Make It Hard to Stop Campus Rape	540
			Notes and Questions	541

XI.	FAMILY LAW: MARRIAGE AND DIVORCE			551
	A.	Marriage		551
		1.	Introduction: Online Dating	551
			Phyllis Coleman, Online Dating: When "Mr. (or Ms.) Right" Turns Out All Wrong, Sue the Service!	551
			Notes and Questions	552
			Problem	553
			N.J. Stat. Ann. §56:8-171	553
		2.	Mail-Order Brides and Domestic Violence	555
			Fox v. Encounters International	555
			Notes and Questions	559
	B.	Divorce		566
		1.	Modern Fault-Based Grounds	566
			Peters v. Peters	566
			Notes and Questions	568
			Problem	570
		2.	What Role for Fault in a No-Fault System?	570
			Feltmeier v. Feltmeier	570
			Notes and Questions	570
		3.	The Relationship of Divorce and Tort Law: Joinder	572
			McCulloh v. Drake	572
			Notes and Questions	574
			Problem	577
		4.	Role of Domestic Violence in Spousal Support	578
			In re Marriage of Cauley	578
			Notes and Questions	580
		5.	Role of Domestic Violence in Property Division	582
			Havell v. Islam	582
			Ira Mark Ellman, The Place of Fault in a Modern Divorce Law	584

	Notes and Questions	585
	Problem	589
C.	Name Changes	590
	In re E.F.G.	590
	Notes and Questions	593

XII.	FAMILY LAW: PARENTING	597
A.	Introduction	597
	Peter G. Jaffe et al., Custody Disputes Involving Allegations of Domestic Violence: Toward a Differentiated Approach to Parenting Plans	597
	Lundy Bancroft et al., The Batterer as Parent: Addressing the Impact of Domestic Violence on Family Dynamics	600
B.	Standards to Award Custody	602
	1. Fitness	602
	Custody of Vaughn	602
	Notes and Questions	606
	2. Rebuttable Presumptions	609
	Peters-Riemers v. Riemers	609
	Leslie Joan Harris, Failure to Protect from Exposure to Domestic Violence in Private Custody Contests	611
	Notes and Questions on *Vaughn* and *Peters-Reimer*	613
C.	Conditions on Visitation: Supervised Visitation	617
	In re Marriage of Fischer	617
	Kim Barker & Arthur Santana, Slain Woman Was "Very Afraid"	620
	Maureen Sheeran & Scott Hampton, Supervised Visitation in Cases of Domestic Violence	621
	Nat'l Council of Juvenile & Family Court Judges, Model Code on Domestic and Family Violence	623
	Notes and Questions	624
	Problem	630
D.	Role of Special Participants	630
	1. The Child's Preference and Traumatic Bonding	630
	Wissink v. Wissink	630
	Notes and Questions	633
	2. Role of Child's Representative	637
	Richard Ducote, Guardians Ad Litem in Private Custody Litigation: The Case for Abolition	637
	Notes and Questions	638
	3. Role of the Custody Evaluator	642
	Lundy Bancroft et al., The Batterer as Parent: Addressing the Impact of Domestic Violence on Family Dynamics	642
	Notes and Questions	643
	Note: Parental Alienation Syndrome	645
E.	Fleeing with Children	646
	Desmond v. Desmond	646
	Schultz v. Schultz	648

	Notes and Questions on *Desmond* and *Schultz*	651
	Problem	656
F.	International Child Abduction	656
	Simcox v. Simcox	656
	Notes and Questions	660
	Problem	665
G.	Children's Exposure to Domestic Violence: A Novel Approach	665
	Bevan v. Fix	665
	Notes and Questions	669
H.	Domestic Violence and the Child Protection System	672
	1. Background: Fundamental Tensions in the Law's Response to Domestic Violence and Child Protection	672
	Susan Schechter & Jeffrey L. Edleson, In the Best Interests of Women and Children: A Call for Collaboration Between Child Welfare and Domestic Violence Constituencies	673
	2. Failure to Protect	677
	Nicholson v. Scoppetta	677
	Jill M. Zuccardy, Nicholson v. Williams: The Case	679
	Note: The Green Book Initiative	682
	Notes and Questions	683
	3. Termination of Parental Rights	685
	State ex rel. C.J.K.	685
	Notes and Questions	689
	Problem	692
XIII.	DISCRIMINATION AGAINST VICTIMS	693
A.	Housing Discrimination	693
	Bouley v. Young-Sabourin	693
	Notes and Questions	695
	Problem	698
	Note: Domestic Violence and Homelessness	699
	National Alliance to End Homelessness	700
B.	Employment Discrimination	701
	Danny v. Laidlaw Transit Services, Inc.	701
	Joan Zorza, New Study on Domestic Violence in the Workplace	705
	Notes and Questions	706
	Problems	713
	Note: Discrimination in Insurance Coverage	714
PART IV.	LEGAL AND SOCIAL SERVICES	
XIV.	LEGAL SERVICES	719
A.	Representing the Victim	719
	1. Constitutional Issues: What Is Effective Assistance of Counsel?	719
	Dando v. Yukins	719
	Notes and Questions	723

		2.	Ethical Issues of Representing Victims of Domestic Violence	728
			Leigh Goodmark, Going Underground: The Ethics of Advising a Battered Woman Fleeing an Abusive Relationship	728
			ABA, Commission on Domestic Violence, Standards of Practice for Lawyers Representing Victims of Domestic Violence, Sexual Assault and Stalking in Civil Protection Order Cases	731
		3.	Effective Representation in Practice	735
			Sarah M. Buel, Effective Assistance of Counsel for Battered Women Defendants: A Normative Construct	735
			Joan S. Meier, Notes from the Underground: Integrating Psychological and Legal Perspectives on Domestic Violence in Theory and Practice	737
			Deborah M. Goelman, Safety Planning	741
	B.	Mediation		744
			Adolphson v. Yourzak	744
			Jessica Pearson, Nat'l Inst. of Justice, Divorce Mediation and Domestic Violence	745
			Alexandria Zylstra, Mediation and Domestic Violence: A Practical Screening Method for Mediators and Mediation Program Administrators	748
			Association of Family and Conciliation Courts, Model Standards of Practice for Family and Divorce Mediation	752
			American Law Institute, Principles of the Law of Family Dissolution	754
			Nat'l Council of Juvenile & Family Court Judges, Model Code on Domestic and Family Violence	754
			Notes and Questions	755
	C.	Specialized Domestic Violence Courts		762
			Judge Amy Karan et al., Domestic Violence Courts: What Are They and How Should We Manage Them?	763
			Allison Cleveland, Specialization Has the Potential to Lead to Uneven Justice: Domestic Violence Cases in the Juvenile and Domestic Violence Courts	765
			Robyn Mazur & Liberty Aldrich, What Makes a Domestic Violence Court Work? Lessons from New York	768
			Notes and Questions	772
XV.	SOCIAL SERVICES			777
	A.	Shelters		777
		1.	Constitutional Issues	777
			Woods v. Horton	777
			Notes and Questions	780
			Problem	783
		2.	Confidentiality	784
			Shelter Sues for Breach of Confidentiality	784
			Frigm v. Unemployment Compensation Board of Review	785

		Ga. Code Ann. §19-13-23	787
		Kelly White, A Safe Place for Women: Surviving Domestic Abuse and Creating a Successful Future	787
		Notes and Questions	788
		Problem	789
	3.	What Services Do Shelters Provide?	789
		Safe Horizon, Tour a Domestic Violence Shelter	789
		Kelly White, A Safe Place for Women: Surviving Domestic Abuse and Creating a Successful Future	790
		Eleanor Lyon et al., Nat'l Inst. of Justice, Meeting Survivors' Needs: A Multi-State Study of Domestic Violence Experiences, Summary of Findings	791
	4.	Benefits of Advocacy Services	792
		Deborah Epstein, Procedural Justice: Tempering the State's Response to Domestic Violence	792
		Notes and Questions	793
		Problem	795
B.	Batterers' Intervention Programs		796
	1.	Court-Ordered Treatment	796
		D.O.H. v. T.L.H.	796
	2.	Effectiveness	800
		Shelly Jackson, Nat'l Inst. of Justice, Batterer Intervention Programs: Where Do We Go From Here?	800
		Notes and Questions	803

| *Table of Cases* | *807* |
| *Index* | *813* |

Preface

This book provides a comprehensive treatment of the law of domestic violence. It integrates legal and social science perspectives on the nature of domestic violence and the law's response to it. This approach derives from the author's orientation as a sociologist, feminist legal theorist, and family law professor. The book interweaves theory, social science research, and practice in an effort to enhance students' understanding of the multiple ways that domestic violence influences victims' experiences and their legal claims. It views intimate partner violence through a wide-angle lens that focuses on the family, gender roles, and societal inequality between men and women. It also takes into account the historical perspective, recognizing that violence against female intimate partners, until far too recently, has long been condoned by social institutions.

The theme of the book is the conflict between two imperatives: the need for state intervention to protect family members from victimization by intimate partners versus the responsibility of the state to respect the individual (specifically, individual rights and values). The field of domestic violence ineluctably pits these imperatives against each other. That is, the right of vulnerable family members to state protection conflicts with state deference to such values as autonomy and family privacy and the need to respect the offender's constitutional rights. An examination of this conflict calls for a broad focus on the complex nature of domestic violence as well as a narrow focus on the individual perspective.

This book adopts a unique approach to the study of domestic violence. It emphasizes a fundamental belief that underlies the feminist movement that gave birth to the field of domestic violence—the importance of the inclusion of women's voices and social science research findings to enhance the understanding of victims' experiences. The treatment of the Supreme Court case of United States v. Morrison, 529 U.S. 598 (2000), illustrates this unique approach.

Morrison involves the issue of the constitutionality of the Violence Against Women Act (VAWA)'s civil rights remedy for gender-based violence in terms of whether the law exceeded the scope of Congressional authority under the Commerce Clause. The case is typically presented in legal casebooks as a dry exegesis of federalism and the principles underlying the Supreme Court's Commerce Clause jurisprudence.

In the course of that academic exercise, regrettably, the plight of Plaintiff Christy Brzonkala (a student at Virginia Polytechnic Institute who was gang raped by members of the varsity football team) is lost. This book sets forth the traditional pedagogical exegesis. However, the treatment of *Morrison* herein goes far beyond that approach, first elucidating the victim's experience through an account of the events surrounding Christy's sexual assault. The book then integrates social and psychological research on rape to enhance the understanding of Christy's experience and the law's response. For example, an exploration of Rape Trauma Syndrome clarifies the reasons for Christy's delay in reporting and thereby dictates her choice of available legal remedies. At the same time, social science research on date rapists sheds light on the actions of one of Christy's rapists (that is, his bragging in the dorm dining room about his "conquests") and explains, in part, the reason for his eventual conviction on a charge of "using abusive language" rather than "sexual assault." In addition, social science data on educational institutions' response to campus violence reveal the shortcomings in their processing of claims of sexual assaults, thus confirming that the institutional response to Christy's rape was not unusual. This treatment of *Morrison* concludes by setting forth recent federal guidelines and pending legislative provisions that represent a new approach to campus sexual assault. Thus, the book's approach emphasizes that social reality (that is, the application of social science research) breathes life and meaning into legal reality.

The field of domestic violence currently represents "second-stage" scholarship. This feature is attributable to two developments. In the past two decades, an explosion of social science research has occurred, including several national, comprehensive, federally funded studies. This spate of research calls for a paradigm shift in our understanding of intimate partner violence by shedding new light on the nature of this social problem and challenging formerly authoritative findings. Moreover, both theory and practice have benefited from the proliferation of significant federal and state legislation over the past two decades on a wide variety of relevant topics. This book mines these treasure troves of information by applying the findings of social science research to such cutting edge issues as teen dating violence; children's exposure to domestic violence; workplace violence; pregnancy abuse; cyber harassment, "new" crimes of strangulation and stalking, and "new" forms of victimization (such as financial abuse, pet abuse, litigation abuse, third-party abuse). The book also includes key findings from the federally funded National Intimate Partner and Sexual Violence Survey of 16,000 women and men that was released as this book was going to press.

In addition, the book's Notes and Questions provide in depth treatment of issues that are sometimes minimized: teen dating violence and elder abuse; police-perpetrated domestic violence; domestic violence in the military and professional sports; intimate partner violence among the affluent; the full range of psychological abuse; innovative methods of enforcement (such as private suits for contempt for violation of restraining orders); and practical topics such as screening, safety planning, emergency dispatch, discovery abuse, and identity change. Stemming from the author's family law orientation, the book devotes considerable attention to the role of intimate partner violence in family law, focusing not only on issues of child custody/visitation but also on the role of domestic violence in online dating; the international marriage broker industry; covenant marriage; divorce grounds and procedure; the financial incidents of marriage, domestic partnerships, and dissolution (that is, spousal support, property distribution, bankruptcy, and inheritance issues); and issues of sexual and reproductive control (that is, pregnancy abuse, birth control sabotage, interference with abortion decision-making, and marital rape).

Further, the book explores some issues that are traditionally ignored, such as murder suicide, suicide by cop, lethality assessment, and intimate partner violence in youth gangs, to name a few. Problems drawn from recent events (such as the rape case of WikiLeaks' editor Julian Assange and the new French law on emotional abuse) deepen students' understanding of the issues. To accommodate fully the victim's perspective, the book takes into account the unique needs of victims from diverse cultures and backgrounds, thereby emphasizing the role of gender, race, ethnicity, social class, and sexual orientation in both individual and institutional responses to domestic violence. Provisions of the pending reauthorization of the Violence Against Women Act are discussed throughout the book.

The book aims for comprehensive treatment that is not overlong. Therefore, only some international issues are covered here, such as mail order brides and regulation of the international marriage broker industry; honor killings; the cultural defense; the rights of battered immigrant spouses; asylum; international child abduction and the Hague Convention on the Civil Aspects of International Child Abduction; and the Inter-American Commission on Human Rights case of Lenahan (Gonzales) v. United States of America. Spatial constraints dictated omission of some issues of international human rights law, such as international human rights documents and reports.

The organization of the book highlights the dynamics of intimate partner violence in various legal contexts. Part I presents essential background on the history of the battered women's movement; the characteristics and consequences of abusive relationships; influential factors in intimate partner violence (that is, gender, age, disability, sexual orientation, race, religion, ethnicity, social class); the spectrum of abuse (that is, physical, sexual, psychological); and intimate partner violence in specific settings (such as the military, police, sports).

Part II begins a searching inquiry into the full range of legal contexts in which domestic violence materializes. The book considers the criminal justice system by examining the state legislative response, law enforcement response (that is, police and prosecutors), and judicial response (that is, criminal defenses and evidentiary issues). Part III turns its attention to the civil law response in the form of orders of protection; family law (specifically, the role of domestic violence in marriage, divorce, child custody, visitation, spousal support and property distribution); and discrimination against victims (that is, illegal practices in the areas of housing, employment, and insurance). Students are urged to assess the benefits and shortcomings of the law's response in all of these legal contexts.

Part IV concludes with a study of legal representation and social services. It covers the issues of attorneys' legal and ethical obligations; the alternative dispute resolution process (that is, mediation, collaborative law); battered women's shelters and batterers' intervention programs.

Readings from case law, state and federal statutes, legal commentary, and social science research illuminate all the preceding topics. Informative and provocative Notes and Questions constitute the heart of this book and are intended to stimulate student thinking about the issues. Also, the presentation of narratives serves to deepen understanding of the subject matter while enlivening student interest.

The book is intended for a one-semester course that meets three hours per week. However, the format allows instructors considerable flexibility in designing courses or seminars of varying lengths and emphasis.

Editorial matters

A mention of editorial matters is necessary. The cases and excerpts in this book have all been edited, often quite extensively. Most deletions are indicated by ellipses and brackets, with some exceptions: Some concurring and dissenting opinions have been eliminated; citations have been modified or eliminated; some footnotes and references have been omitted; and paragraphs have been modified, and sometimes combined, to save space and to make the selections more coherent. When retained, footnotes in reprinted materials have the original footnote numbers. Original footnotes in the cases and excerpts are reprinted non-consecutively throughout the book. In contrast, the author's textual footnotes are numbered consecutively and are indicated throughout the chapters by the placement of brackets around footnote numbers.

Terminology in the field of domestic violence has evolved in the past few decades. This book reflects that evolution. For example, the terms "wife beating" and "battering" have been replaced by the broader term "intimate partner violence" (sometimes shortened to "IPV") to reflect the ideas that (1) violence occurs not only to wives, but also to single women, men, and same-sex partners who may or may not be living together; and (2) abusive conduct encompasses a far wider range of conduct than "beating." The terms "intimate partner violence" and "domestic violence" are used interchangeably, although the book tends to avoid the term "family violence" because that term generally includes child abuse. Finally, the book utilizes the term "survivor," as well as "victim," in an effort to avoid some of the negative implications of victimization.

Acknowledgments

I would like to thank many people who contributed to this project. Colleagues at several institutions provided valuable suggestions, including Sarah Buel, Teresa Drake, Eugene Hyman, Robin Runge, Julie Saffren, Jane Stoever, and Merle Weiner. I also gratefully acknowledge Academic Dean Shauna Marshall, Hastings College of the Law, for her generous research support, Divina Morgan for her exceedingly capable help with manuscript production and administrative tasks, and Tony Pelczynski for his endless cooperation with library requests.

Special thanks for research assistance are merited by Rebecca Licavoli Adams, Edward Beeby, Ari Cover, Cory Hammon, Bhavit K. Madhvani, Robert Philbrook, Jacqueline Ravenscroft, and Millie Yan. I am particularly indebted to former student Kristen M. Driskell whose help was invaluable at virtually every stage of this project. I would also like to thank Susan Frelich Appleton for her agreement to allow me to use material from our co-authored casebook, *Modern Family Law: Cases and Materials.* I also extend my appreciation to John Devins at Aspen Publishers, for his helpful criticisms, suggestions, and support.

Finally, I would like to thank the following copyright holders for permission to excerpt their materials:

American Bar Association, Commission on Domestic Violence, Standards of Practice for Lawyers Representing Victims of Domestic Violence, Sexual Assault and Stalking in Civil Protection Order Cases (2007). Reprinted with permission of the American Bar Association.

American Law Institute, Principles of the Law of Family Dissolution §§2.06, 2.07 (2002). Reprinted with permission of the American Law Institute.

Association of Family and Conciliation Courts, Model Standards of Practice for Family and Divorce Mediation (2000). Reprinted with permission of the Association of Family and Conciliation Courts.

Bancroft, Lundy, et al., The Batterer as Parent: Addressing the Impact of Domestic Violence on Family Dynamics 141-150 (2d ed. 2012). Reprinted with permission.

Barker, Kim, & Arthur Santana, Slain Woman Was "Very Afraid," Seattle Times, Dec. 12, 1998, at A1. Reprinted with permission.

Browne, Angela, Violence in Marriage: Until Death Do Us Part?, in Violence Between Intimate Partners: Patterns, Causes, and Effects 48, 56-58 (Albert P. Cardarelli ed., 1997). Printed and electronically reproduced by permission of Pearson Education, Inc., Upper Saddle River, New Jersey.

Buel, Sarah M., Effective Assistance of Counsel for Battered Women Defendants: A Normative Construct, 26 Harv. Women's L.J. 217 (2003). Reprinted with permission.

_____, Fifty Obstacles to Leaving, A.K.A. Why Abuse Victims Stay, Colo. Law., Oct. 1999, at 19. Reprinted with permission.

Burman, Sondra, Stages of Leaving Abusive Relationships, in Encyclopedia of Domestic Violence 675, 676-679 (Nicky Ali Jackson ed., 2007). Reprinted with permission.

Buzawa, Eve S., & Carl G. Buzawa, Domestic Violence: The Criminal Justice Responses 234, 241-242 (3d ed. 2003). Reprinted with permission.

Buzawa, Eve S., et al., Responding to Domestic Violence: The Integration of Criminal Justice and Human Services 221, 223 (2012). Reprinted with permission.

Campbell, Jacquelyn C., Danger Assessment Instrument, © Jacquelyn C. Campbell (2003). Reprinted with permission of Jacquelyn C. Campbell.

Cardarelli, Albert P., Violence Between Intimate Partners: Patterns, Causes, and Effects, 1st ed., ©1997. Printed and electronically reproduced by permission of Pearson Education, Inc., Upper Saddle River, New Jersey.

Cleveland, Allison, Specialization Has the Potential to Lead to Uneven Justice: Domestic Violence Cases in the Juvenile and Domestic Violence Courts, 6 Mod. Am. 17 (2010). Reprinted with permission.

Coleman, Phyllis, Online Dating: When "Mr. (Or Ms.) Right" Turns Out All Wrong, Sue the Service!, 36 Okla. City U. L. Rev. 139 (2011). Reprinted with permission.

Dalton, Clare, Domestic Violence, Domestic Torts and Divorce: Constraints and Possibilities, 31 New Eng. L. Rev. 319 (1997). Reprinted with permission.

Domestic Abuse Intervention Project, Power and Control Wheel. Reprinted with permission of Domestic Abuse Intervention Project, 202 East Superior Street, Duluth, MN 55802, 218-722-2781, www.theduluthmodel.org.

Drouin, Anique, Comment, Who Turned Out the Lights? How Maryland Laws Fail to Protect Victims of Domestic Violence from Third-Party Abuse, 36 U. Balt. L. Rev. 105 (2006). Reprinted with permission.

Ducote, Richard, Guardians Ad Litem in Private Custody Litigation: The Case for Abolition, 3 Loy. J. Pub. Int. L. 106 (2002). Reprinted with permission.

Dutton, Mary Ann, et al., Characteristics of Help-Seeking Behaviors, Resources and Service Needs of Battered Immigrant Latinas: Legal and Policy Implications, 7 Geo. J. on Poverty L. & Poly. 245 (2000). Reprinted with permission of the publisher, Georgetown Journal of Poverty Law and Policy © 2000.

Ellman, Ira Mark, The Place of Fault in a Modern Divorce Law, 28 Ariz. St. L.J. 773 (1996). Reprinted with permission of the author.

Epstein, Deborah, Procedural Justice: Tempering the State's Response to Domestic Violence, 43 Wm. & Mary L. Rev. 1843 (2002). Reprinted with permission of William & Mary Law Review.

Family Violence Prevention Fund, 1 in 4 Hotline Callers Report Birth Control Sabotage, Pregnancy Coercion (Feb. 15, 2011), http://www.futureswithoutviolence.org/content/features/detail/1674/. Reprinted with permission.

_____, Domestic Violence and the Super Bowl (Jan. 31, 2011), http://www.futureswithoutviolence.org/content/features/detail/1659/. Reprinted with permission.

Finn, Peter, Statutory Authority in the Use and Enforcement of Civil Protection Orders Against Domestic Abuse, 23 Fam. L.Q. 43 (1989). Reprinted with permission.

Glaberson, William, Abuse Suspects, Your Calls Are Taped, Speak Up, N.Y. Times, Feb. 26, 2011, at A1. Reprinted with permission.

Gilmore, Janet, Jurors Hear Frantic 911 Calls: Tape Captures Nicole Simpson Pleading for Aid, Daily News (L.A.), Feb. 3, 1995, at N1. Reprinted with permission.

Goelman, Deborah M., Safety Planning, in The Impact of Domestic Violence on Your Legal Practice 11-15 (ABA Commission on Domestic Violence 1996). Reprinted with permission of the American Bar Association.

Goldfarb, Sally F., Reconceiving Civil Protection Orders for Domestic Violence: Can Law Help End the Abuse Without Ending the Relationship?, 29 Cardozo L. Rev. 1487 (2008). Reprinted with permission.

Goodmark, Leigh, Autonomy Feminism: An Anti-Essentialist Critique of Mandatory Interventions in Domestic Violence Cases, 37 Fla. St. U. L. Rev. 1 (2009). Reprinted with permission of Florida State University Law Review, original publisher and copyright holder.

_____, Going Underground: The Ethics of Advising a Battered Woman Fleeing an Abusive Relationship, 75 UMKC L. Rev. 999 (2007). Reprinted with permission.

Hand, Jacqueline P., & David C. Koelsch, Shared Experiences, Divergent Outcomes: American Indian and Immigrant Victims of Domestic Violence, 25 Wis. J.L. Gender & Soc'y 185 (2010). Reprinted with permission.

Hanna, Cheryl, No Right to Choose: Mandated Victim Participation in Domestic Violence Prosecutions, 109 Harv. L. Rev. 1849 (1996). Reprinted with permission.

Harris, Leslie Joan, Failure to Protect from Exposure to Domestic Violence in Private Custody Contests, 44 Fam. L.Q. 169 (2010). Reprinted with permission.

Jaffe, Peter G., et al., Custody Disputes Involving Allegations of Domestic Violence: Toward a Differentiated Approach to Parenting Plans, 46 Fam. Ct. Rev. 500 (2008). Reprinted with permission of Wiley-Blackwell.

Karan, Amy, et al., Domestic Violence Courts: What Are They and How Should We Manage Them?, 50 Juv. & Fam. Ct. J. 75 (1999). Reprinted with permission of Wiley-Blackwell.

Koblenz, Adam H., Jewish Women Under Siege: The Fight for Survival on the Front Lines of Love and the Law, 9 U. Md. L.J. Race, Religion, Gender & Class 259 (2009). Reprinted with permission.

Lasson, Kenneth, Bloodstains on a "Code of Honor": The Murderous Marginalization of Women in the Islamic World, 30 Women's Rts. L. Rep. 407 (2009). Reprinted with permission.

Loring, Marti Tamm, & Pati Beaudoin, Battered Women as Coerced Victim-Perpetrators, 2 J. Emotional Abuse 3 (2000). Reprinted with permission.

Mahoney, Martha R., Legal Images of Battered Women: Redefining the Issue of Separation, 90 Mich. L. Rev. 1 (1991). Reprinted with permission.

Martinson, Lisa M., Comment, An Analysis of Racism and Resources for African-American Female Victims of Domestic Violence in Wisconsin, 16 Wis. Women's L.J. 259 (2001). Reprinted with permission.

Masters, Brooke A., "No Winners" in Rape Lawsuit: Two Students Forever Changed by Case That Went to Supreme Court, Wash. Post, May 19, 2000. Reprinted with permission.

Mazur, Robyn & Liberty Aldrich, What Makes a Domestic Violence Court Work? Lessons from New York, 42 Judges' J. 5 (Spring 2003). Reprinted with permission of the American Bar Association.

McDonald, Kathleen A., Note, Battered Wives, Religion, and Law: An Interdisciplinary Approach, 2 Yale J.L. & Feminism 251 (1990). Reprinted with permission.

Meier, Joan S., Notes from the Underground: Integrating Psychological and Legal Perspectives on Domestic Violence in Theory and Practice, 21 Hofstra L. Rev. 1295 (1993). Reprinted with permission.

Moore, Ann M., et al., Male Reproductive Control of Women Who Have Experienced Intimate Partner Violence in the United States, 70 Soc. Sci. & Med. 1737 (June 2010). Reprinted with permission.

National Alliance to End Homelessness, Fact Sheet: Domestic Violence (Jan. 11, 2010), http://www.Endhomeless.Org/Content/Article/Detail/1647. Reprinted with permission.

National Council of Juvenile and Family Court Judges, Model Code on Domestic and Family Violence (1994), §§405, 406 & cmt., 407, 408. Reprinted with permission of the National Council of Juvenile and Family Court Judges.

Nixon, Jennifer, Domestic Violence and Women with Disabilities: Locating the Issue on the Periphery of Social Movements, 24 Disability & Soc'y 77 (2009). Reprinted with permission.

Pfeifer, Tara R., Comment, Out of the Shadows: The Positive Impact of *Lawrence v. Texas* on Victims of Same-Sex Domestic Violence, 109 Penn St. L. Rev. 1251 (2005). Reprinted with permission.

Rennison, Callie, & Mike Planty, Nonlethal Intimate Partner Violence: Examining Race, Gender, and Income Patterns, 18 Violence & Victims 433 (2003). Reprinted with permission.

Renzetti, Claire M., & Vivian M. Larkin, Economic Stress and Domestic Violence, National Online Resource Center on Violence Against Women, Applied Research Forum (Sept. 2009). Reprinted with permission.

Rizer, Arthur L., III, Mandatory Arrest: Do We Need to Take a Closer Look?, 36 UWLA L. Rev. 1 (2005). Reprinted with permission.

Roslin, Alex, Batterer in Blue, Georgia Straight (Canada), July 24, 2003. Reprinted with permission.

Ryan, Joan, O.J. Case Changed Rules for Cox, S.F. Chron., May 10, 1995, at D2. Reprinted with permission.

Sack, Emily J., Battered Women and the State: The Struggle for the Future of Domestic Violence Policy, 2004 Wis. L. Rev. 1657. Reprinted with permission.

Safe Horizon, Tour a Domestic Violence Shelter, http://www.safehorizon.org/index/get-help-8/dealing-with-domestic-violence-35/tour-a-domestic-violence-shelter-3.html. Reprinted with permission.

Schechter, Susan, The Roots of the Battered Women's Movement: Personal and Political, in Women and Male Violence: The Visions and Struggles of the Battered Women's Movement 29, 29-38, 43 (1982). Reprinted with permission.

Schechter, Susan, & Jeffrey L. Edleson, In the Best Interests of Women and Children: A Call for Collaboration Between Child Welfare and Domestic Violence Constituencies (1994). Reprinted with permission.

Shapiro, Joseph, Myths That Make It Hard to Stop Campus Rape, NPR News Investigation, Mar. 4, 2010. Reprinted with permission.

Sheeran, Maureen, & Scott Hampton, Supervised Visitation in Cases of Domestic Violence, Juv. & Fam. Ct. J., Spring 1999, at 13. Reprinted with permission.

Siegel, Reva B., "The Rule of Love": Wife Beating as Prerogative and Privacy, 105 Yale L.J. 2117 (1996). Reprinted with permission.

Stamm, Simeon, Note, Intimate Partner Violence in the Military: Securing Our Country, Starting with the Home, 47 Fam. Ct. Rev. 321 (2009). Reprinted with permission of Wiley-Blackwell.

Stapel, Sharon, Falling to Pieces: New York State Civil Legal Remedies Available to Lesbian, Gay, Bisexual, and Transgender Survivors of Domestic Violence, 52 N.Y. L. Sch. L. Rev. 247 (2008). Reprinted with permission.

Stark, Evan, Coercive Control, in Encyclopedia of Domestic Violence 166, 166-171 (Nicky Ali Jackson ed., 2007). Reprinted with permission.

Stoever, Jane K., Stories Absent from the Courtroom: Responding to Domestic Violence in the Context of HIV and AIDS, 87 N.C. L. Rev. 1157 (2009). Reprinted with permission.

Taub, Nadine, & Elizabeth Schneider, Women's Subordination and the Role of Law, in The Politics of Law 328-332 (David Kairys ed., 1998). Reprinted with permission.

Tracey, Patrick, Christy's Crusade, Ms. Magazine, Apr. 1, 2000, at 53. Reprinted by permission of Ms. Magazine, ©2000.

Vick, Karl, Case of John Michael Farren Seen as Refresher Course on Domestic Violence, Wash. Post, Feb. 25, 2010, at 24. Reprinted with permission.

Walker, Garthine, Crime, Gender and Social Order in Early Modern England 138-143 (2003). Reprinted with permission of Cambridge University Press.

Walker, Lenore, The Battered Woman Syndrome 71-72, 91, 94-95 (3d ed. 2009). Reprinted with permission.

_____, Terrifying Love: Why Battered Women Kill and How Society Responds 23-41 (1989). Reprinted with permission.

Warrier, Sujata, (Un)Heard Voices: Domestic Violence in the Asian-American Community 5, 10-11 (2002). This material was reprinted and/or adapted from the Family Violence Prevention Fund's publication entitled "(Un)heard Voices: Domestic Violence in the Asian American Community." The report was authored by Sujata Warrier, Ph.D. Production was made possible by a grant from the Violence Against Women Office, Office of Justice Programs, U.S. Department of Justice.

Websdale, Neil, Assessing Risk in Domestic Violence Cases, in Encyclopedia of Domestic Violence 38, 38-40 (Nicky Ali Jackson ed., 2007). Reprinted with permission.

White, Kelly, A Safe Place for Women: Surviving Domestic Abuse and Creating a Successful Future 130-131, 180-181, 186-188 (2011). Reprinted with permission.

White, Stephen, Guilty of Britain's First Gay Domestic Murder, Mirror (UK), May 7, 2010, at 39. Reprinted with permission.

Wills, Donna, Domestic Violence: The Case for Aggressive Prosecution, 7 UCLA Women's L.J. 173 (1997). Reprinted with permission.

Withers, Bethany P., Comment, The Integrity of the Game: Professional Athletes and Domestic Violence, 1 Harv. J. Sports & Ent. L. 145 (2010). Reprinted with permission.

Wolf, Marsha E., et al., Barriers to Seeking Police Help for Intimate Partner Violence, 18 J. Fam. Violence 121 (Apr. 2003). Reprinted with permission.

Wolfer, Judith A., Top Ten Myths About Domestic Violence, 42 Md. B.J. 38 (May/June 2009). This article originally appeared in the Maryland Bar Journal and is reprinted with permission from the Maryland State Bar Association.

Wriggins, Jennifer, Domestic Violence Torts, 75 S. Cal. L. Rev. 121 (2001). Reprinted with permission.

Zilberman, Monica L., & Sheila B. Blume, Domestic Violence, Alcohol, and Substance Abuse, 27 Revista Brasileira de Psiquiatria 51 (Oct. 2005). Reprinted with permission.

Zorza, Joan, The Criminal Law of Misdemeanor Domestic Violence, 1970-1990, 83 J. Crim. L. & Criminology 46 (1992). Reprinted with permission.

_____, New Study on Domestic Violence in the Workplace, 3 Fam. & Intimate Partner Violence Q. 217 (2011). Reprinted with permission.

_____, Restorative Justice: Does It Work for DV?, 16 Domestic Violence Rep. 33 (Feb./Mar. 2011). Reprinted with permission.

Zylstra, Alexandria, Mediation and Domestic Violence: A Practical Screening Method for Mediators and Mediation Program Administrators, 2001 J. Disp. Resol. 253. Reprinted with permission.

DOMESTIC VIOLENCE

PART ONE

INTRODUCTION

I

Social and Historical Perspective: Evolution of the Right of Privacy

Domestic violence is a serious and pervasive social problem. Only in the nineteenth century was "wife beating" first recognized as a social issue. The more recent "discovery" of this social problem dates to the 1960s when the women's liberation movement shed light on the ills afflicting the modern family. Of course, domestic violence has far deeper roots in history owing to women's subordinate status to men.

Why was domestic violence hidden from public view for so long? The answer lies, in part, in the idea of the family as a private social institution. This paradigm, with its accompanying notion of family privacy, led to a long-standing noninterventionist governmental policy that condoned violence in the family. How did the paradigm of the private family develop? What were the implications of this paradigm for the family and its members? These issues are addressed in the following materials.

A. SOCIAL-HISTORICAL CONTEXT

■ REVA B. SIEGEL, "THE RULE OF LOVE": WIFE BEATING AS PREROGATIVE AND PRIVACY
105 Yale L.J. 2117, 2122-2134, 2136-2141 (1996)

Until the late nineteenth century, Anglo-American common law structured marriage to give a husband superiority over his wife in most aspects of the relationship. By law, a husband acquired rights to his wife's person, the value of her paid and unpaid labor, and most property she brought into the marriage. A wife was obliged to obey and serve her husband, and the husband was subject to a reciprocal duty to support his wife and represent her within the legal system. According to the doctrine of marital unity, a wife's legal identity "merged" into her husband's, so that she was unable to file suit without his participation, whether to enforce contracts or to seek damages in tort. The husband was in turn responsible for his wife's conduct—liable, under certain circumstances, for her contracts, torts, and even some crimes.

As master of the household, a husband could command his wife's obedience, and subject her to corporal punishment or "chastisement" if she defied his authority. In his treatise on the English common law, Blackstone explained that a husband could "give his wife moderate correction" [reprinted infra pp. 16-17]. As Blackstone suggested, the master of the household might chastise his wife (or children or servants), but the prerogative was a limited one. A husband was not allowed to do violence to his wife, except as a means of "ruling and chastising" her. . . . [Blackstone] also took pains to qualify the prerogative, describing it as an antiquated practice that persisted primarily among the British lower classes. . . .

Blackstone's *Commentaries* played an important role in shaping American legal culture; and the law treatises that began to appear in the United States during the early nineteenth century displayed a similar ambivalence about the chastisement prerogative. . . . Yet cases in a number of states, particularly in the southern and mid-Atlantic regions, recognized a husband's prerogative to chastise his wife.

There were, however, a variety of social forces in antebellum America that combined to draw the legitimacy of the chastisement prerogative into question. Perhaps most prominently, corporal punishment was the subject of widespread social controversy in this period, with campaigns against the practice developing in a variety of contexts [such as prisons, the navy, slavery, and childrearing]. . . . Yet, for all the public discussion of corporal punishment, talk about wife beating during the antebellum era, and after, remained circumspect.

The first organized protest against wife beating did not challenge the husband's legal prerogative to inflict marital chastisement. . . . [Rather, it came from the antebellum temperance movement.] As temperance advocates demonstrated the social evils of alcohol, they drew attention to the violence that drunken husbands so often inflicted on their families. The movement's conventions, newspapers, poems, songs, and novels featured vivid accounts of women and children who had been impoverished, terrorized, maimed, and killed by drunken men. Temperance protest was simultaneously radical and conservative in tenor. Condemning alcohol provided reformers an outlet for criticizing the social conditions of family life, in the name of protecting the sanctity of family life. Initially, at least, temperance activists preached one remedy for the family violence they so graphically depicted: prohibiting the sale of alcohol.

Soon thereafter, a very different kind of challenge to wife beating was mounted by the woman's rights movement that grew out of temperance and abolitionist protests of the antebellum era. Although membership in this new reform initiative was relatively small, the group was well connected to social elites both within and outside government. In 1848, when the woman's rights movement held its first convention, it denounced the common law doctrines of marital status in a formal *Declaration of Sentiments*:

> He has made her, if married, in the eye of the law, civilly dead.
> He has taken from her all right in property, even to the wages she earns.
> . . . In the covenant of marriage, she is compelled to promise obedience to her husband, he becoming, to all intents and purposes, her master—the law giving him power to deprive her of her liberty, and to administer chastisement. . . .

The woman's rights movement differed from the temperance movement, both in its diagnosis of family violence and in the social remedies it proposed. As the *Declaration of Sentiments* illustrates, the chastisement prerogative figured prominently in the feminist movement's first challenge to the marital status rules of the common law. Woman's rights advocates protested the hierarchical structure of marriage; and, as they did so, they attacked the chastisement prerogative as a practical and symbolic embodiment of the husband's authority over his wife. The woman's rights movement thus broke with the temperance movement by depicting wife beating as a symptom of fundamental defects in the legal structure of marriage itself. The movement's 1848 *Declaration of Sentiments* identified chastisement as part of a political system of male dominance, an analysis that feminists continued to elaborate in the ensuing decades. . . .

Over time, the American legal system did respond to these criticisms of wife beating. Decades of protest by temperance and woman's rights advocates, combined with shifting attitudes toward corporal punishment and changing gender mores, together worked to discredit the law of marital chastisement. By the 1870s, there was no judge or treatise writer in the United States who recognized a husband's prerogative to chastise his wife. Thus, when a wife beater was charged with assault and battery, judges refused to entertain his claim that a husband had a legal right to strike his wife; instead they denounced the prerogative, and allowed the criminal prosecution to proceed. In several states, legislatures enacted statutes specifically prohibiting wife beating; three states even revived corporal punishment for the crime, providing that wife beaters could be sentenced to the whipping post.

But it would be misleading to look to the repudiation of the chastisement doctrine as an indicator of how the legal system responded to marital violence. [D]uring the Reconstruction Era, jurists and lawmakers vehemently condemned the chastisement doctrine, yet routinely condoned violence in marriage. And when the legal system did prosecute wife beating, it treated the crime as a deviant social act rather than as conduct recently condoned by law, selecting men for prosecution in ways that suggest that concerns other than protecting women animated the punishment of wife beaters [as we shall see]. . . .

[As an illustration,] Massachusetts was a stronghold of woman's rights advocacy, yet the [women's movement there] was unsuccessful in persuading authorities to adopt reform legislation protecting battered wives from abusing husbands. For example, after publicizing various "crimes against women" in the *Woman's Journal* during the 1870s, Lucy Stone led the editors of this Boston-based suffrage paper in a petition campaign to persuade the Massachusetts legislature to adopt a bill—modeled after recent legislation in England—that would have given battered wives protection from their husbands. The proposed bill provided that when a husband was convicted of aggravated assault, his wife could apply to the court for an order "forbidding her husband to visit her without her permission, and giving her the custody of her minor children, and directing the officer of the court or the overseers of the poor to collect from the husband and pay to her a reasonable weekly allowance for support of the family." The Massachusetts legislature rejected the petition, on the grounds that such legislation "'would be granting to police and district courts the power of decreeing divorce.'" . . . [T]he Massachusetts legislature [thereby] made explicit its hostility to remedies for domestic violence that might assist wives in separating from their husbands. . . .

[Gradually, divorce became the accepted remedy for abused wives. State legislatures became more sympathetic to victims' requests to separate from their abusive husbands. However, divorce law had its limitations.] In the decades after the Civil War, legislatures were expanding the statutory grounds for divorce, and judges charged with applying these statutory norms interpreted them ever more liberally. In most jurisdictions, a wider range of somatic harms now supplied evidence of "cruelty" as a grounds for divorce; but . . . courts gave sense to the concept in ways that drew upon gender- and class-based understandings of the marriage relationship. To demonstrate that she was entitled to a divorce, a battered wife typically had to prove that her husband acted with "extreme" and "repeated" cruelty. A husband in turn could defeat his wife's divorce petition either by showing that she misbehaved in some way that "provoked" his violence, or by showing that she delayed petitioning for divorce and so forgave and "condoned" his violence. In other words, nineteenth-century judges developed a body of divorce law premised on the assumption that a wife was obliged to endure various kinds of violence as a normal—and sometimes deserved—part of married life. Furthermore, . . . judges reasoned about the propriety of violence in the marriage relationship with attention to the economic status of the married couple, with the result that the evidence required to prove "extreme cruelty" varied by class, on the doctrinally explicit assumption that violence was a common part of life among the married poor.

The class-based assumptions about marital violence that shaped divorce law in this era also shaped the criminal law, but with very different regulatory consequences. . . . During the Reconstruction Era, public interest in marital violence rose as wife beating began to shift in political complexion from a "woman's" issue to a "law and order" issue. Wife beating now attracted the interest of groups not known for their commitment to temperance or woman's rights causes. During this period, the Ku Klux Klan took an interest in punishing wife beaters (both white and black), and began to invoke wife beating as an excuse for assaults on black men. . . . By the 1880s, prominent members of the American Bar Association advocated punishing wife beaters at the whipping post, and campaigned vigorously for legislation authorizing the penalty. Between 1876 and 1906, twelve states and the District of Columbia considered enacting legislation that provided for the punishment of wife beaters at the whipping post. The bills were enacted in Maryland (1882), Delaware (1901), and Oregon (1906).

With this surge of interest in wife beating, the wife beater was demonized as a deviant character, whose criminal or licentious propensities authorities needed to control in order to secure social stability. . . . As wife beating emerged as a "law and order" issue, class- and race-based discourses about marital violence became even more pronounced. . . . [C]ommentators increasingly depicted wife beating as the practice of lawless or unruly men of the "dangerous classes." Statistics on arrests and convictions for wife beating in the late nineteenth century suggest that while criminal assault law was enforced against wife beaters only sporadically, it was most often enforced against immigrants and African-American men. In Northern states, members of immigrant ethnic groups (e.g., German- and Irish-Americans) were targeted for prosecution; in the South, African-Americans were singled out for prosecution in numbers dramatically exceeding their representation in the population. . . .

Thus, as the American legal system repudiated the husband's prerogative to chastise his wife, it did begin to respond differently to wife beating—yet did not adopt policies calculated to provide married women much relief from family violence. Women of the social elite might escape husbands who beat them by obtaining a divorce, if they were not deemed blameworthy, and if they were willing to subject themselves and their children to the economic perils and social stigma associated with single motherhood. Women of poorer families might have a husband fined, incarcerated, or perhaps even flogged, if they were willing to turn him over to a racially hostile criminal justice system. The law thus provided relief to some battered wives, but the majority had little recourse against abusive husbands. . . .

The "second stage" of the women's rights movement in the late 1960s again brought domestic violence to public attention, as the excerpt below reveals. However, this time, different social forces and social movements were at work.

■ **SUSAN SCHECHTER, THE ROOTS OF THE BATTERED WOMEN'S MOVEMENT: PERSONAL AND POLITICAL**
in Women and Male Violence: The Visions and Strategies of the Battered Women's Movement 29, 29-38, 43 (1982)

. . . In the 1950s and 1960s, the civil rights, anti-war, and black liberation movements challenged the nation. Although not all women who would become feminist activists were involved directly in these struggles, the movements of the 1960s deeply affected the development of feminism. Efforts to win equality for blacks set precedents for women's struggle for equality. As in the nineteenth century, women working against racial oppression came to question their own position—and gained political experience that would help them in building a feminist movement. . . .

There were, however, many other influences operating upon those who would start or join the feminist movement. Published in 1963, Betty Friedan's *The Feminine Mystique* captured the discontent of a whole generation of middle-class women, caught between aspirations for fulfillment and an ideology that consigned them to the home. Feminism was influenced, too, by women's participation in the paid work force. . . . Low salaries, limited opportunities, and dead end jobs—juxtaposed to a rhetoric of equality and social justice and their families' economic problems—compelled many to scrutinize their own situation as women. From another direction, thousands of women, committing themselves to fight against poverty through welfare rights organizations and government agencies like the Office of Economic Opportunity or the Peace Corps, began to apply newly acquired political insights personally. As women saw others define the solutions to their life problems as political, they were inspired to act.

By the late 1960s and early 1970s, feminism itself had developed into two major branches, a women's rights feminism, embodied by organizations like NOW, and a women's liberation movement, embodied in socialist feminist and radical feminist groups, and small, autonomous organizing projects working on issues like abortion, women's schools, day care, and prisoners' rights. Women's rights activism [the former group] focused mainly on gaining access to the rights and opportunities held by men. Women's liberation encompassed this goal, but went far beyond it, exploring the unequal gender division of labor and women's lack of control over their bodies, sexuality, and lives. . . .

In addition to fighting discrimination, the women's liberation branch of the feminist movement declared that the private and the social were no longer separable categories. By claiming that what happened between men and women in the privacy of their home was deeply political, the women's liberation movement set the stage for the battered women's movement. Through small consciousness-raising groups, women, often in fear or shame and then exhilaration, found that what they felt was "petty" or "private" was widely shared. Some of the most energizing topics for consciousness raising focused on previously discussed "personal" problems. . . . In the early women's liberation anthologies and newsletters, articles proliferated on the unequal division of labor within the household, women's responsibilities for child care, the maintenance of rigid sex roles, the internalization of oppression expressed as women's self-hatred, low-esteem and the need for male affirmation, the socialization of women for passivity and caretaking, the continual and degrading sexual objectification by men, and the repression of female sexuality.

Although many political, strategic, and ideological differences were evident in the developing women's liberation movement, women agreed that men held power and privilege over women in personal life. Domination was uncovered operating, not only in the public political world, but also in the private political sphere of the family. This analysis moved women closer to a collective realization about violence. If women were dominated by men both outside and inside the family, women and men no longer had identical interests even within the family unit. Claiming conflicting interests, husband and wife were no longer "one." The importance of this message was twofold. First, women had rights as autonomous human beings which meant that their psychological and physical dignity could be asserted. Secondly, no longer could women be blamed for their own vague sense of dissatisfaction or for their husbands' unhappiness. Women's right to verbalize their pain without self-blame created an environment in which discussing violence was less shameful. . . .

The influence of the women's liberation movement on the battered women's movement is illustrated concretely in hundreds of shelters and women's crisis centers in the United States. In St. Paul, Minnesota, Women's Advocates, one of the oldest shelters solely for battered women, began as a consciousness-raising group in 1971. . . . The first Boston shelter, Transition House, was also influenced by women's liberation ideas. Although the two women who started the shelter were former battered women, they were soon joined by two former members of Cell 16, one of Boston's earliest radical feminist groups. Women using the house were encouraged to explore their personal lives, learning the political parameters of "private" problems. For the activists at Transition House, physical abuse was not an isolated fact of daily existence. Battering was an integral part of women's oppression; women's liberation its solution. . . .

[The anti-rape movement served as a model for the battered women's movement.] In some cities, like Chicago, women active in anti-rape work formed part of the group that would later demand help for battered women. In Boston, close personal contact without organizational affiliations existed between feminists in the anti-rape and battered women's movements. In still other places, women's crisis centers that originally provided rape counseling and anti-rape education added battered women's concerns to their tasks.

[T]he battered women's movement maintains a striking and obvious resemblance to the anti-rape movement and owes it several debts. The anti-rape movement articulated that violence is a particular form of domination based on social relationships of unequal power. Through the efforts of the anti-rape movement, it became clear that violence is one mechanism for female social control. Today this sounds obvious; [then] it was a revelation. The anti-rape movement changed women's consciousness and redefined the parameters of what women would individually and collectively tolerate. . . .

Susan Brownmiller, the first author to document the history of rape, described how unaware people were of the magnitude and significance of rape, noting that "few outside its victims thought it might be an important subject to explore." No one considered that it might have a history, and only a handful believed that it was going to become an issue of international feminist concern. Yet, in 1971-72, Bay Area Women Against Rape formed; in June 1972, the first emergency rape crisis line opened in Washington, D.C. Soon after, rape crisis centers appeared all over the country, started by former rape victims and active feminists. . . .

The anti-rape movement unearthed the multitude of ways in which victims historically had been blamed for the crime and silenced. Hundreds of articles about rape . . . detailed this discovery, describing how, "the vast majority of victims fail to report the crime out of fear—fear of vengeance, of police, of publicity, of courtroom hassles—and out of shame. . . ." Recognizing victims' needs for emotional and legal support and the movement's need to document and change sexist abuses in police stations and courts, rape crisis centers trained women to become legal advocates. . . .

Based on its understanding of how institutions re-victimize women, the anti-rape movement demanded legal and institutional reforms. . . . Throughout the United States, women worked to overthrow laws that required corroboration of evidence by someone other than the victim. They focused on improving police arrest and evidence gathering procedures and some worked legislatively to change criminal sentencing procedures. . . .

In addition to replacing a sexist ideology with a feminist one and pushing for institutional reform, the anti-rape movement brought together thousands of women who continually developed new skills. Activists educated themselves and others politically. The Feminist Alliance Against Rape (FAAR) newsletter, started in 1974, was the movement's political sounding board and brought inspiration to hundreds of women, often working in isolated groups. Later it played a role in encouraging the battered women's movement to engage in the same kind of political and skill exchanges. . . .

The feminist anti-rape movement has not only laid the foundation to change public consciousness, but also has built organizations and networks of politically sophisticated and active women. The anti-rape movement has unmasked the domination that violence maintains, has torn away a veil of shame, and shown that women can aid one another, transforming individual silence and pain into a social movement. Such work handed ideological tools, collective work structures, and political resources to the battered women's movement. Without this precedent, the new movement might have faced far greater resistance and hostility from bureaucracies, legislatures, and the general public. By 1975, it was clear that since rape and battering had the same effects upon their victims and depended upon similar sexist mythology, battering had to be declared socially, not privately, caused.

Challenges to the private family paradigm continued in the twentieth century. What were the implications of this paradigm for the legal regulation of the family and its members? The following excerpt addresses these issues.

■ NADINE TAUB & ELIZABETH SCHNEIDER, WOMEN'S SUBORDINATION AND THE ROLE OF LAW
in The Politics of Law 328, 328-332 (David Kairys ed., 1998)

The Anglo-American legal tradition purports to value equality, by which it means, at a minimum, equal application of the law to all persons. Nevertheless, throughout this country's history, women have been denied the most basic rights of citizenship, allowed only limited participation in the marketplace, and otherwise denied access to power, dignity, and respect. Women have instead been largely occupied with providing the personal and household services necessary to sustain family life. . . .

Excluded in the past from the public sphere of marketplace and government, women have been consigned to a private realm to carry on their primary responsibilities, i.e., bearing and rearing children, and providing men with a refuge from the pressures of the capitalist world. This separation of society into the male public sphere and the female private sphere was most pronounced during the nineteenth century. . . .

The most obvious exclusion of women from public life was the denial of the franchise. . . . This initial exclusion gained even greater significance in the 1820s and 1830s when the franchise was extended to virtually every white male regardless of property holdings. Even after the Civil War, when black men gained the right to vote, women of all races continued to be denied the ballot. The Nineteenth Amendment, giving women the vote, finally became law in 1920 after what has been described as a "century of struggle." . . . The amendment's passage, however, did not mean that women were automatically accorded the rights and duties that generally accompanied elector status, for example, the exclusion of women from jury duty was upheld as late as 1961. . . .

. . . Under English common law, not only were [women] barred from certain professions (such as law), but, once married, they were reduced to legal nonentities unable to sell, sue, or contract without the approval of their husbands or other male relatives. Although these disabilities were initially rigidified by codification of laws, which began in the 1820s, they were gradually lifted in the middle and latter part of the nineteenth century [by the Married Women's Property Acts]. The enactments were, however, repeatedly subjected to restrictive judicial interpretations that continued to confirm male dominance in business matters.

Even as women moved into the paid labor force, they were limited in their work opportunities and earning power by the ideological glorification of their domestic role reflected in the law. Women have been consistently excluded from certain occupational choices and denied equal earning power by statute and other governmental action. . . .

While sex-based exclusionary laws have joined with other institutional and ideological constraints to directly limit women's participation in the public sphere, the legal order has operated more subtly in relation to the private sphere to which women have been relegated. On the one hand, the legal constraints against women retaining their earnings and conveying property—whose remnants endured well into the twentieth century—meant that married women could have legal relations with the outside world only through their husbands. In this sense, the law may be viewed as directing male domination in the private sphere. On the other hand, the law has been conspicuously absent from the private sphere itself.

[Traditionally, the law refused to interfere in ongoing family relationships. For example,] tort law which is generally concerned with injuries inflicted on individuals, has traditionally been held inapplicable to injuries inflicted by one family member on another. Under the doctrines of interspousal and parent-child immunity, courts have consistently refused to allow recoveries for injuries that would be compensable but for the fact that they occurred in the private realm. In the same way, criminal law declined to punish intentional injuries to family members. Common law and statutory definitions of rape in many states continue to carve out a special exception for a husband's forced intercourse with his wife. Wife beating was initially omitted from the definition of criminal assault on the ground that a husband had the right to chastise his wife. . . .

The state's failure to regulate the domestic sphere is now often justified on the ground that the law should not interfere with emotional relationships involved in the family realm because it is too heavy-handed. Indeed, the recognition of a familial privacy right in the early twentieth century has given this rationale a constitutional dimension. The importance of this concern, however, is undercut by the fact that the same result was previously justified by legal fictions, such as the woman's civil death on marriage. More importantly, the argument misconstrues the point at which the law is invoked. Legal relief is sought when family harmony has already been disputed. Family members, like business associates, can be expected to forgo legal claims until they are convinced that harmonious relations are no longer possible. Equally important, the argument reflects and reinforces powerfully myths about the nature of family relations. It is not true that women perform personal and household services purely for love. The family is the locus of fundamental economic exchanges, as well as important emotional ties.

Isolating women in a sphere divorced from the legal order contributes directly to their inferior status by denying them the legal relief that they seek to improve their situations and by sanctioning conduct of the men who control their lives. For example, when the police do not respond to a battered woman's call for assistance or when a civil court refuses to evict her husband, the woman is relegated to self-help, while the man who beats her receives the law's tacit encouragement. . . .

But beyond its direct, instrumental impact, the insulation of women's world from the legal order also conveys an important ideological message to the rest of society. . . . [T]he law's absence devalues women and their functions: women simply are not sufficiently important to merit legal regulation. . . . By declining to punish a man for inflicting injuries on his wife, for example, the law implies she is his property and he is free to control her as he sees fit. . . . These are important messages, for denying women's humanity and the value of her traditional work are key ideological components in maintaining women's subordinate status. . . .

Finally, isolating women in a world where the law refuses to intrude further obscures the discrepancy between women's actual situation and our nominal commitment to equality. Like other collective ideals, the equality norm is expressed predominantly in legal form. Because the law as a whole is removed from women's world, the equality norm is perceived as having very limited application to women. . . .

Notes and Questions

1. *Stages of law reform.* Widespread recognition of domestic violence as a social problem is linked to two stages of the women's rights movement. From 1874 to 1890, first wave feminists agitated against domestic violence as part of a larger agenda focusing on equal rights for women, particularly in the areas of divorce, married women's property rights, child custody, child support, and the right to vote. Elizabeth Pleck, Domestic Tyranny: The Making of American Policy against Family Violence from Colonial Times to the Present 4 (2004). Second wave feminists in the 1960s and 1970s again called attention to the issue of wife beating as part of a larger agenda within the context of women's rights.

Of course, violence in the family has existed long before the nineteenth century. But, battering first became recognized as a social issue that evoked a *public policy response* only in the nineteenth century. For a study of the deeper roots of battering, see Virginia H. Murray, A Comparative Survey of the Historic Civil, Common, and American Indian Tribal Law Responses to Domestic Violence, 23 Okla. City U. L. Rev. 435 (1998).

2. *Related social movements.* The history of the women's rights movement is linked, both ideologically and politically, to other social movements. In the nineteenth century, these included the anti-slavery movement, temperance movement, child protection movement, and the movement against corporal punishment generally. What did these social movements have in common? How did they contribute to the fight for women's rights generally and, specifically, recognition of wife battering as a social problem? How did the goals of the various social movements influence the way domestic violence was viewed? How did each social movement characterize the source of the social problem and frame the appropriate remedy?

3. *Twentieth-century parallels.* What role did the modern civil rights and anti-war movements play in modern recognition of domestic violence as a social problem? How did the anti-rape movement serve as a model for the modern battered women's movement? How were domestic violence shelters influenced by ideas from the women's liberation and the anti-rape movements?

4. *Changes in family structure.* How did family structure and gender roles change in the nineteenth century? How did those changes influence societal views about

wife beating? Industrialization and urbanization led to major economic, cultural, demographic, and social changes in society, and also in family life and family structure. Rapid societal changes fueled middle-class fears that family life was disintegrating. Such fears triggered a new notion of the home that took root in the nineteenth-century psyche. The city, with its slums, immigrants, gambling dens, brothels, and saloons, came to symbolize all that was evil in the larger society. The remedy to these social problems was a retreat from the city to the sanctuary of the home. Accompanying this belief was a predominant nineteenth-century literary theme of perfectionism that led to a glorification of womanhood, housework, and childcare. The emergence of this "cult of domesticity" reinforced traditional women's roles. These views contributed to, and reinforced beliefs in, family privacy and nonintervention in the family. "The cult of domesticity and beliefs in family harmony and bliss made the idea of outside intervention in domestic affairs seem a needless violation of the sanctity and privacy of the home." R. Emerson Dobash & Russell Dobash, Violence Against Wives: A Case Against the Patriarchy 7 (1979). See also Nancy F. Cott, The Bonds of Womanhood: "Woman's Sphere" in New England, 1780-1835 (2d ed. 1997); Richard Sennett, Families against the Cities: Middle Class Homes of Industrial Chicago 1872-1890 (1984).

5. *Husband's right of chastisement.* What was the husband's "right to administer chastisement"? Why was the husband responsible for his wife's conduct? For which aspects of her conduct was he responsible? How did Blackstone articulate the husband's right of chastisement? How influential were Blackstone's views? Did the husband have an *absolute* right of chastisement? If not, how was his right limited? Why does Siegel state, supra, that American legal culture displayed an "ambivalence about the chastisement prerogative"?

6. *Feminist legacy.*

a. *Women's roles as reformers.* The first wave of feminism began when prominent feminists were refused seats in the World Anti-Slavery Convention in 1840 because of their sex. In response, the women decided to hold a women's rights convention to give women the opportunity to voice their views about oppression. They chose Seneca Falls, New York, as the site of their convention in 1848. See Kathryn Kish Sklar, "Women Who Speak for an Entire Nation": American and British Women Compared at the World Anti-Slavery Convention, London, 1840, 59 Pacific Hist. Rev. 453 (1990) (describing the influence of this convention on the development of the suffrage movement). The feminists' work product, the *Declaration of Sentiments* modeled after the Declaration of Independence, listed numerous grievances, and set an agenda for the women's rights movement. Declaration of Sentiments (1848), *available at* http://www.usconstitution.net/sentiments.html. Their grievances specified that women had been historically and collectively oppressed and denied equal rights. They advocated changes in society and its institutions, starting with marriage and the family. They protested that a wife is compelled to promise obedience to her husband because he was "to all intents and purposes, her master—the law giving him power to deprive her of her liberty, and to administer chastisement." Dobash & Dobash, supra, at 66. Feminists sought control of their property and earnings as well as the rights to divorce and custody of their children.

b. *Feminists' role in reframing the problem.* How were nineteenth- and twentieth-century feminists' views of wife beating similar? How were they different? One significant contribution of feminism was the conceptualization of wife beating as a *social*, rather than individual, problem. As Siegel explains, legal policy in the nineteenth century publicly condemned, but private condoned, the practice of wife beating. Battering was regarded as an individual problem of dysfunctional families. If a husband beat his wife, the wife was treated as if she provoked the violence (i.e., "victim blaming").

Nineteenth-century and twentieth-century feminists reconceptualized wife beating as a social problem—a malady of the patriarchal social order. As Professor Linda Gordon explains:

> The basis of wife beating is male dominance—not superior physical strength or violent temperament [but] social, economic, political, and psychological power. . . . [I]t is male dominance that makes wife beating a social rather than a personal problem. Wife beating is not comparable to a drunken barroom assault or the hysterical attack of a jealous lover, which may be isolated incidents. Wife beating is the chronic battering of a person of inferior power who for that reason cannot effectively resist.

Linda Gordon, Heroes of Their Own Lives: The Politics and History of Family Violence 251 (2002). What are the implications for the legal system of this reconceptualization? Do vestiges of "victim blaming" persist in our views of intimate partner violence? See Jane Aiken & Katherine Goldwasser, The Perils of Empowerment, 20 Cornell J.L. & Pub. Pol'y 139, 139-141 (2010) (recounting story of a woman, slain by her abusive husband, who was posthumously criticized in the media for not having purchased a gun to protect herself).

7. *Divorce.* Divorce was rare until the twentieth century. In the mid-nineteenth century, only a few states permitted divorce on the ground of extreme cruelty. Nineteenth-century feminists Elizabeth Cady Stanton and Susan B. Anthony were unable to persuade the New York legislature to add physical cruelty as a ground for divorce. Pleck, supra, at 6. States slowly began liberalizing the grounds for divorce in the nineteenth century. In England, cruelty was a ground for only judicial separation until the Matrimonial Causes Act of 1857, 20 & 21 Vict., c. 85 §16 (allowing civil divorce for adultery). However, this remedy was limited to cases of the most extreme cruelty and required high levels of proof. Dobash & Dobash, supra, at 68. See generally Norma Basch, Framing American Divorce: From the Revolutionary Generation to the Victorians 99-120 (2001); Homer H. Clark, Jr., The Law of Domestic Relations in the United States §11, at 281, 282 (1968).

8. *Twentieth-century reforms.* The second wave of reform regarding domestic violence began with the women's liberation movement in the late 1960s. The National Organization for Women (NOW), established in 1966, created an agenda for women's rights, emphasizing equal opportunity in the public and private arenas. By 1976, feminist reformers were lobbying state legislatures to pass laws addressing wife beating and to provide funding for domestic violence shelters. They filed class action lawsuits against police departments for their refusal to respond to women's calls for help from abusive partners. Congress enacted the first federal legislation in 1984, the Family Violence Prevention and Services Act and the Victims of Crime Act, 42 U.S.C. §10401 (as amended), to provide funding for shelters and related services for victims of domestic violence. A decade later, in 1994, Congress enacted the Violence Against Women Act (VAWA), Pub. L. No. 103-322, §§40001-40703, 108 Stat. 1902 (codified throughout 42 U.S.C.). (VAWA is discussed throughout this

book. The federal criminal provisions are explored infra Chapter 8 and the gender-based tort provision infra Chapter 10.)

9. *Race and class.* How did race and social class characterize the origins and orientation of feminist reformers of the nineteenth and twentieth centuries? The portrayal of batterers? How did these factors influence assumptions about marriage and family, and especially the acceptance of domestic violence? For a study of sexism in the nineteenth-century anti-slavery movement and racism in the woman suffrage movement, see Angela Y. Davis, Women, Race and Class (1983).

10. *Remedy.* How did ideas about the appropriate remedy for wife beating differ in the nineteenth and twentieth centuries? How did these ideas evolve? What role does the "public" nature of punishment serve? What role did "public" punishments play in the nineteenth versus twentieth centuries? What historical remedies were most effective, in your view, to address domestic violence?

11. *Family harmony.* The policy of nonintervention into marriage was justified by the desire to preserve family harmony. Does nonintervention promote family harmony? Does it promote respect for the rights of all family members? Or does it preserve the freedom of more powerful family members at the expense of weaker members? What light do the above excerpts shed on these questions?

12. *The public-private dichotomy.* What are the differences between the public and private spheres of life? Why did nineteenth-century feminists, and later, twentieth-century feminists, view the public-private dichotomy as a major contributing factor to women's oppression?

The public-private sphere applied not only to married women, but also to single women as well. A classic statement of separate spheres ideology, Bradwell v. Illinois, 83 U.S. (16 Wall.) 130 (1872) (denying married women the right to practice law), sheds light on this issue:

> It is true that many women are unmarried and not affected by any of the duties, complications, and incapacities arising out of the married state, but these are exceptions to the general rule. The paramount destiny and mission of woman are to fulfill the noble and benign offices of wife and mother. This is the law of the Creator. And the rules of civil society must be adapted to the general constitution of things, and cannot be based upon exceptional cases. . . .

Id. at 141-142 (BRADLEY, J., concurring). On the public-private dichotomy in feminist theory, see Joan B. Landes ed., Feminism, the Public, and the Private (Oxford Readings in Feminism ser. 1998).

13. *Implications of privacy for domestic violence.* What are the various meanings of privacy? To what extent is domestic violence viewed as a public and/or private issue today? What are the modern consequences of viewing domestic violence as public or private—for the individual, the family, and society? Professor Elizabeth Schneider suggests:

> By seeing woman-abuse as "private," we affirm it as a problem that is individual, that only involves a particular male-female relationship, and for which there is no social responsibility to remedy. . . . Focusing on the woman, not the man, perpetuates the power of patriarchy.

Elizabeth M. Schneider, The Violence of Privacy, 23 Conn. L. Rev. 973, 983 (1991).

What is the meaning of the phrase, "The personal is political"? How does it apply to the battered women's movement? See generally Kimberly D. Bailey, Lost in Translation: Domestic Violence, "The Personal is Political," and the Criminal Justice System, 100 J. Crim. L. & Criminology 1255 (2010).

A basic tenet of classical liberalism that was given shape by seventeenth-century British philosopher John Locke was the belief that limiting the power of government is essential for the achievement of individual liberty and freedom. How does this philosophical belief advance or impede individual rights? How do contemporary political interest groups that promote the private family and private "family values" influence the public response to domestic violence?

14. *Paradox.* How can legal policy best address an important paradox in family law, that is, how to reject privacy for the purpose of combating domestic violence yet embrace it to enhance reproductive rights? See Suzanne A. Kim, Reconstructing Family Privacy, 57 Hastings L.J. 557 (2006) (advocating reconstructing privacy to enable intervention to protect battered spouses but to respect the privacy of the parent-child relationship in other family conflicts).

How do the concepts of individual privacy and family privacy conflict, for purposes of protecting members' legal rights? Can they be reconciled? In formulating public policy on domestic violence, how can society balance the need for public intervention to protect individual family members and still promote respect for individual autonomy? See generally Martha Albertson Fineman & Roxanne Mykitiuk, eds., The Public Nature of Private Violence (1994).

B. LEGAL HISTORICAL CONTEXT

1. *Common Law View of Marital Roles and Responsibilities*

■ 1 WILLIAM BLACKSTONE, COMMENTARIES
*442-445

. . . By marriage, the husband and wife are one person in law: that is, the very being or legal existence of the woman is suspended during the marriage, or at least is incorporated and consolidated into that of the husband: under whose wing, protection, and *cover,* she performs everything; and is therefore called in our law-french a *feme-covert;* is said to be *covert-baron,* or under the protection and influence of her husband, her baron, or lord; and her condition during her marriage is called her *coverture.* Upon this principle, of a union of person in husband and wife, depend almost all the legal rights, duties, and disabilities, that either of them acquires by the marriage. . . . For this reason, a man cannot grant anything to his wife, or enter into covenant with her: for the grant would be to suppose her separate existence; and to covenant with her, would be only to covenant with himself: and therefore it is also generally true, that all compacts made between husband and wife, when single, are voided by the intermarriage. . . . The husband is bound to provide his wife with necessities by law, [and] if she contracts debts for them, he is obliged to pay them: but for anything besides necessaries, he is not chargeable. . . . If the wife be indebted before marriage, the husband is bound afterwards to pay the debt; for he has adopted her and her circumstances together. If the wife be injured in her person or her property, she can bring no action for redress without her husband's concurrence, and in his name, as well as her own: neither can she sue or be sued, without making the husband a defendant. . . . In criminal prosecutions, it is true, the wife may be indicted and punished separately; for the union is only a civil union. But, in trials of any sort, they are not allowed to be evidence for, or against, each other: partly because it is impossible their testimony should be indifferent; but principally because of the union of person. . . .

But, though our law in general considers man and wife as one person, yet there are some instances in which she is separately considered; as inferior to him, and acting by his compulsion. And therefore all deeds executed, and acts done, by her, during her coverture, are void, or at least voidable; except it be a fine, or the like matter of record, in which case she must be solely and secretly examined, to learn if her act be voluntary. She cannot by will devise lands to her husband, [because] she is supposed to be under his coercion. And in some felonies, and other inferior crimes, committed by her, through constraint of her husband, the law excuses her: but this extends not to treason or murder.

The husband also (by the old law) might give his wife moderate correction. For, as he is to answer for her misbehavior, the law thought it reasonable to entrust him with this power of restraining her, by domestic chastisement, in the same moderation that a man is allowed to correct his servants or children; for whom the master or parent is also liable in some cases to answer. But this power of correction was confined within reasonable bounds; and the husband was prohibited to use any violence to his wife [other than what is reasonably necessary to the discipline and correction of the wife]. . . .

[I]n the politer reign of Charles the Second, this power of correction began to be doubted, and a wife [might] have security of the peace against her husband; or, in return, a husband against his wife. Yet, the lower rank of people, who were always fond of the old common law, still claim and exert their ancient privilege: and the courts of law will still permit a husband to restrain a wife of her liberty, in case of any gross misbehavior.

These are the chief legal effects of marriage during the coverture; upon which we may observe, that even the disabilities, which the wife lies under, are for the most part intended for her protection and benefit. So great a favorite is the female sex of the laws of England.

Notes and Questions

1. *Coverture.* The common law reflected the doctrine of *coverture*, the legal fiction that the husband and wife were one person. When the wife came under the husband's "cover" or protection, her legal identity merged with that of her husband. This theory, also called the doctrine of "marital unity," regulated women's legal relationship vis-à-vis their husbands, third parties, and the state. What were the consequences of this legal fiction for wives, husbands, and our views of marriage and the family? Why did the doctrine endure for so long?

2. *Blackstone's views.* The eighteenth-century British jurist, Sir William Blackstone, articulated the influential view that, based on the doctrine of *coverture*, the common law gave husbands the authority to chastise their wives so long as the corporal punishment did not cause permanent injury. This view had ramifications

for married women in terms of the law's response to battering as well as married women's lack of autonomy. As one legal commentator explains:

> [L]egal authorities continued . . . to treat wife beating more favorably than other instances of assault and battery and remained extremely reluctant to enforce criminal or civil penalties for marital violence. A husband could also, with only modest limitations, legally restrict his wife's movements in the nineteenth century—could conclusively determine where the couple would live, could physically restrain his wife to prevent her from leaving that household, and could retrieve her if she did stray, particularly if she had left to go to another man.

Jill Elaine Hasday, Contest and Consent: A Legal History of Marital Rape, 88 Calif. L. Rev. 1373, 1390-1391 (2000).

According to Blackstone, why did the law give the husband the right of "moderate correction"? Was the man allowed to "correct" anyone else in this manner? What are the implications of analogizing wives to other subservient persons? Blackstone adds that in some circumstances, the law regarded the wife as under the husband's "coercion." What were those circumstances?

3. *Married women's legal disabilities. Coverture* imposed a broad range of legal disabilities on married women. The husband acquired an estate in the wife's real property for the duration of the marriage, entitling him to sole possession and control of any real property that she owned in fee whether acquired by her before or after the marriage. He could alienate her real property without her consent, and her property was subject to the claims of her husband's creditors. A wife had no right to possess personal property either. Whatever personal property that she owned before marriage, or might acquire thereafter, became her husband's. She also lacked the right of testamentary disposition over any property. During the marriage, the wife could not enter into contracts except as her husband's agent. The husband was liable for the wife's premarital debts, as well as for torts she committed before or during the marriage. The legal status of married women changed little until the mid- to late-nineteenth century when many states passed "married women's property acts." See generally, Norma Basch, In the Eyes of the Law: Women, Marriage and Property in Nineteenth Century New York (1982); Peggy A. Rabkin, Fathers to Daughters: The Legal Foundations of Female Emancipation (1980); Marylynn Salmon, Women and the Law of Property in Early America (1986).

4. *Early criminal statutes on wife beating.* From 1640 to1680, Massachusetts Puritans enacted the first American laws against wife beating as part of a criminal code that encompassed their religious and humanitarian beliefs about the proper treatment of women and children. Pleck, supra, at 4-5. The next major change in legal policy occurred in the late nineteenth century. Feminists in the temperance movement argued that flogging laws should apply to wife beaters. Several states enacted such laws. Maryland was the first state in 1882 to make wife beating a crime punishable by flogging. Similar bills were introduced in many state legislatures. Pleck, supra, at 249 n.4. Why was flogging viewed as an appropriate punishment? Why did it lose its favor? How effective do you think it was?

5. *Early criminal case law.* During the nineteenth century, American courts occasionally adjudicated cases involving domestic violence. Some courts upheld a husband's right to beat his wife, but subjected the right of chastisement to limitations. What were these limitations? By the end of the nineteenth century, judicial policy

generally rejected the husband's right of chastisement. See, e.g., Fulgham v. State, 46 Ala. 143, 147-148 (1871) (abolishing husbands' legal right to beat their wives); Harris v. State, 71 Miss 462, 462 (1894) (overruling husband's right to administer moderate chastisement).

6. *British law on wife beating.* Significant law reforms about wife beating also occurred in England in the nineteenth century. In fact, British law underwent a parallel evolution. Parliament abolished the husband's right to chastise his wife in 1829. In 1853, Parliament enacted legislation (Act for Better Prevention and Punishment of Aggravated Assaults upon Women and Children) that provided a punishment of £20 or six months imprisonment for wife beaters. The criminal law was not the only remedy for spousal abuse. Parliament enacted legislation in 1895 that permitted a conviction for assault as a ground for divorce. Dobash and Dobash, supra, at 63.

7. *Origin of "Rule of Thumb."* Case law and commentary sometimes cite Blackstone's "doctrine of reasonable chastisement" as the origin of the expression "rule of thumb," that is, the idea that the husband was permitted to beat his wife with a stick that was not bigger than his thumb. A heated controversy exists about the origins of the term and its actual acceptance by nineteenth-century judges. Some scholars contend that nineteenth-century judges *erroneously* attributed the "rule of thumb" to Blackstone because, at the time of his *Commentaries,* the rule was no longer law in England. See, e.g., Henry Ansgar Kelly, Rule of Thumb and the Folk-law of the Husband's Stick, 44 J. Legal Educ. 341, 364 (1994); Reva B. Siegel, "The Rule of Love": Wife Beating as Prerogative and Privacy, 105 Yale L.J. 2117, 2123-2124 (1996).

Other scholars argue that, despite doubts about the origins of the term, the "rule of thumb" did play an important role in nineteenth-century case law. See Letter from Professor Joan Meier, George Washington University Law School, cited in William Safire, No Uncertain Terms 189 (2003). For a lively contemporary debate about the origins of the term, see Myths or Facts in Feminist Scholarship? An Exchange Between Nancy K. D. Lemon & Christina Hoff Sommers, The Chronicle Review, Online Edition, Aug. 10, 2009, *available at* http://chronicle.com/article/Domestic-Violence-a/47940 (disagreeing about whether the term can be traced to Romulus, the first king of Rome in 753-717 BC).

2. *Judicial Doctrine of Nonintervention in the Marital Relationship*

■ McGUIRE v. McGUIRE

59 N.W.2d 336 (Neb. 1953)

MESSMORE, Justice.

The plaintiff, Lydia McGuire, brought this action ... against Charles W. McGuire, her husband ... to recover suitable maintenance and support money. [A] decree was rendered in favor of the plaintiff.

The record shows that the plaintiff and defendant were married in Wayne, Nebraska, on August 11, 1919. At the time of the marriage the defendant was a bachelor 46 or 47 years of age and had a reputation for more than ordinary frugality, of which the plaintiff was aware. She had visited in his home and had known him for about 3 years prior to the marriage. [P]laintiff had been previously married. Her first husband ... died intestate, leaving 80 acres of land in Dixon County. The plaintiff and each of [their two] daughters inherited a one-third interest therein. At the time of the marriage of the plaintiff and defendant, the plaintiff's daughters were 9 and 11 years of age. By working and receiving financial assistance from the parties to this action, the daughters received a high school education in Pender. One daughter attended Wayne State Teachers College for 2 years and the other daughter attended a business college in Sioux City, Iowa, for 1 year. [Both] are married and have families of their own. [At trial] plaintiff was 66 years of age and the defendant nearly 80 years of age. No children were born to these parties. ...

The plaintiff testified that she was a dutiful and obedient wife, worked and saved, and cohabited with the defendant until the last 2 or 3 years. She worked in the fields, did outside chores, cooked, and attended to her household duties such as cleaning the house and doing the washing. For a number of years she raised as high as 300 chickens, sold poultry and eggs, and used the money to buy clothing, things she wanted, and for groceries. She further testified that the defendant was the boss of the house and his word was law; that he would not tolerate any charge accounts and would not inform her as to his finances or business; and that he was a poor companion. ... On several occasions the plaintiff asked the defendant for money. He would give her very small amounts, and for the last 3 or 4 years he had not given her any money nor provided her with clothing, except a coat about 4 years previous. ... The defendant had not taken her to a motion picture show during the past 12 years. They did not belong to any organizations or charitable institutions, nor did he give her money to make contributions to any charitable institutions. ... For the past 4 years or more, the defendant had not given the plaintiff money to purchase furniture or other household necessities. Three years ago he did purchase an electric, wood-and-cob combination stove which was installed in the kitchen, also linoleum floor covering for the kitchen. [T]he house is not equipped with a bathroom, bathing facilities, or inside toilet [or kitchen sink]. Hard and soft water is obtained from a well and cistern. She has a mechanical Servel refrigerator, and the house is equipped with electricity. ... She had requested a new furnace but the defendant believed the one they had to be satisfactory. She related that the furniture was old and she would like to replenish it, at least to be comparable with some of her neighbors; ... that one of her daughters was good about furnishing her clothing, at least a dress a year, or sometimes two; that the defendant owns a 1929 Ford coupe equipped with a heater which is not efficient, and on the average of every 2 weeks he drives the plaintiff to Wayne to visit her mother; and that he also owns a 1927 Chevrolet pickup which is used for different purposes on the farm. The plaintiff was privileged to use all of the rent money she wanted to from the 80-acre farm, and when she goes to see her daughters, which is not frequent, she uses part of the rent money for that purpose, the defendant providing no funds for such use. ... At the present time the plaintiff is not able to raise chickens and sell eggs. [P]laintiff has had three abdominal operations for which the defendant has paid. [P]laintiff further testified that ... use of the telephone was restricted, indicating that defendant did not desire that she make long distance calls. ...

It appears that the defendant owns 398 acres of land with 2 acres deeded to a church, the land being of the value of $83,960; that he has bank deposits in the sum of $12,786.81 and government bonds in the amount of $104,500; and that his income, including interest on the bonds and rental for his real estate, is $8,000 or $9,000 a year. . . .

[Defendant appeals, alleging that the decree is not supported by sufficient evidence, and is contrary to law.] The plaintiff relies upon the following cases. [In] Earle v. Earle, 27 Neb. 277, 43 N.W. 118 [(1889)], the plaintiff's petition alleged, in substance, the marriage of the parties, that one child was born of the marriage, and that the defendant sent his wife away from him, did not permit her to return, contributed to her support and maintenance separate and apart from him, and later refused and ceased to provide for her support and the support of his child. The wife instituted a suit in equity against her husband for maintenance and support without a prayer for divorce or from bed and board. The question presented was whether or not the wife should be compelled to resort to a proceeding for a divorce, which she did not desire to do, or from bed and board. On this question, in this state the statutes are substantially silent and at the present time there is no statute governing this matter. The court stated that it was a well-established rule of law that it is the duty of the husband to provide his family with support and means of living—the style of support, requisite lodging, food, clothing, etc., to be such as fit his means, position, and station in life—and for this purpose the wife has generally the right to use his credit for the purchase of necessaries. The court held that if a wife is abandoned by her husband, without means of support, a bill in equity will lie to compel the husband to support the wife without asking for a decree of divorce. . . .

In the case of Brewer v. Brewer, 79 Neb. 726, 113 N.W. 161 [(1907)], the plaintiff lived with her husband and his mother. The mother dominated the household. The plaintiff went to her mother. She stated she would live in the same house with her husband and his mother if she could have control of her part of the house. The defendant did not offer to accede to these conditions. The court held that a wife may bring a suit in equity to secure support and alimony without reference to whether the action is for divorce or not; that every wife is entitled to a home corresponding to the circumstances and condition of her husband over which she may be permitted to preside as mistress; and that she does not forfeit her right to maintenance by refusing to live under the control of the husband's mother. . . .

In the instant case the marital relation has continued for more than 33 years, and the wife has been supported in the same manner during this time without complaint on her part. The parties have not been separated or living apart from each other at any time. In the light of the cited cases it is clear, especially so in this jurisdiction, that to maintain an action such as the one at bar, the parties must be separated or living apart from each other.

The living standards of a family are a matter of concern to the household, and not for the courts to determine, even though the husband's attitude toward his wife, according to his wealth and circumstances, leaves little to be said in his behalf. As long as the home is maintained and the parties are living as husband and wife, it may be said that the husband is legally supporting his wife and the purpose of the marriage relation is being carried out. Public policy requires such a holding. It appears that the plaintiff is not devoid of money in her own right. She has a fair sized bank account and is entitled to use the rent from the 80 acres of land left by her first husband, if she so chooses. . . . Reversed and remanded with directions to dismiss.

Notes and Questions

1. *Doctrines of support and nonintervention.* *McGuire* illustrates two doctrines. First, *McGuire* reflects the common law duty of support: A husband had the duty to provide support to his wife. The wife had a correlative duty to render domestic services. Second, the case illustrates the common law *doctrine of nonintervention*: The state rarely will adjudicate spousal responsibilities in an ongoing marriage. That is, marital support obligations are enforceable only *after* separation or divorce. The doctrine of nonintervention stems from judicial reluctance to disrupt marital harmony and family privacy by interference with the husband's authority. Was there any marital harmony in the McGuires' marriage to disrupt?

2. *Necessaries doctrine.* The common law *doctrine of necessaries* was the basis of the lower court opinion in Mrs. McGuire's favor. This doctrine imposed liability on a husband to a merchant who supplied necessary goods to a wife. "Necessaries" generally include food, clothing, shelter, and medical care, although case law sometimes extends the term. See, e.g., Jewell v. Jewell, 255 S.W.3d 522, 523-524 (Ky. Ct. App. 2008) (funeral expenses for child); In re Hofmann, 823 N.Y.S.2d 397, 398 (App. Div. 2006) (legal fees). Many American jurisdictions codified the common law duty of support of dependents via so-called family expense statutes that render both spouses liable for support of family members. Such statutes are broader than the common law doctrine (that is, applying to "family expenses" rather than merely "necessaries"). Equal protection challenges to the gender-based common law necessaries doctrine led to a gender-neutral rule for interspousal liability for debts. See, e.g., Va. Code Ann. §55-37; St. Luke's Episcopal-Presbyterian Hosp. v. Underwood, 957 S.W.2d 496 (Mo. Ct. App. 1997).

3. *Third-party interests.* Why should the state permit a creditor, but not a spouse, a remedy for support? Professor Marjorie Shultz argues that "the presence of third party interests, even though minimal compared to the spouses' duties to one another, has been viewed as sufficient to allow disruption of the domestic harmony that could not be disturbed for the sake of resolving the spouses' own problems." Marjorie Maguire Shultz, Contractual Ordering of Marriage: A New Model for State Policy, 70 Calif. L. Rev. 204, 238 (1982). Further, Shultz points out, the necessaries doctrine encourages a spouse to deal with a creditor behind the other spouse's back (by purchasing necessaries for which the other spouse will be liable). Does this approach promote marital harmony?

4. *Criticisms.* Feminist commentators have been especially critical of the doctrine of nonintervention, as we have seen. Many of these scholars argue that nonintervention in the family has had a disproportionately negative effect on women, pointing to "doctrines like interspousal tort immunity, parental tort immunity, and the marital rape exemption in criminal law [which] ensured that the law historically provided little or no recourse for wife battering, incest, and marital rape." Sally F. Goldfarb, Violence Against Women and the Persistence of Privacy, 61 Ohio St. L.J. 1, 22 (2000). Feminist scholars also criticize nonintervention because it "devalues women and their functions" by implying that "women are not important enough to merit legal regulation." Elizabeth M. Schneider, The Violence of Privacy, 23 Conn. L. Rev. 973, 978 (1991).

While many scholars criticize the negative implications of nonintervention for women and children, a few scholars suggest that perhaps the family should still be protected from state intervention. See, e.g., Martha Albertson Fineman, What Place for Family Privacy?, 67 Geo. Wash. L. Rev. 1207 (1999). Professor Fineman criticizes feminists for opposing nonintervention, advocating a quasi-presumption of the family's entitlement to autonomy unless the family grossly fails to perform its responsibilities. *Id.* at 1223-1224. Contra Barbara Bennett Woodhouse, The Dark Side of Family Privacy, 67 Geo. Wash. L. Rev. 1247 (1999) (disputing Professor Fineman's claims about the costs and benefits of constructing the family as an autonomous entity to prevent inappropriate state intervention). Which argument do you find most persuasive?

5. *Civil and criminal remedies for nonsupport.* What additional remedies might Mrs. McGuire have? Civil remedies include a suit for separate maintenance if the couple is living apart. Criminal remedies also exist for nonsupport of a child and spouses. What purposes do criminal remedies serve? Would you have advised Mrs. McGuire to pursue these?

3. Interspousal Immunity Doctrine: Tort Actions Between Spouses

■ THOMPSON v. THOMPSON
218 U.S. 611 (1910)

Mr. Justice DAY delivered the opinion of the court:

This case presents a single question, which is involved in the construction of the statutes governing the District of Columbia. That question is: Under that statute may a wife bring an action to recover damages for an assault and battery upon her person by the husband? [Plaintiff Jessie Thompson] charges diverse assaults upon her person by her husband, [Charles Thompson], for which the wife seeks to recover damages in the sum of $70,000. [The trial court] held that such action would not lie under the statute. . . .

At the common law the husband and wife were regarded as one—the legal existence of the wife during *coverture* being merged in that of the husband; and, generally speaking, the wife was incapable of making contracts, of acquiring property or disposing of the same without her husband's consent. They could not enter into contracts with each other, nor were they liable for torts committed by one against the other.

In pursuance of a more liberal policy in favor of the wife, statutes [i.e., Married Women's Property Acts] have been passed in many of the states looking to the relief of a married woman from the disabilities imposed upon her as a *feme covert* by the common law. . . . It is unnecessary to review these statutes in detail. Their obvious purpose is, in some respects, to treat the wife as a *feme sole*, and to a large extent to alter the common law theory of the unity of husband and wife. These statutes, passed in pursuance of the general policy of emancipation of the wife from the husband's control, differ in terms, and are to be construed with a view to effectuate the legislative purpose which led to their enactment.

It is insisted that the Code of the District of Columbia has gone so far in the direction of modifying the common law relation of husband and wife as to give to her an action against him for torts committed by him upon her person or property. The answer to this contention depends upon a construction of §1155 of the District of Columbia Code:

> . . . Married women shall have power to engage in any business, and to contract, whether engaged in business or not, and to sue separately upon their contracts, and also to sue separately for the recovery, security, or protection of their property, and for torts committed against them, as fully and freely as if they were unmarried. . . .

By this District of Columbia statute the common law was changed, and . . . [m]arried women are authorized to sue separately for the recovery, security, or protection of their property, and for torts committed against them as fully and freely as if they were unmarried. That is, the limitation upon [the wife's] right of action imposed in the requirement of the common law that the husband should join her was removed by the statute, and she was permitted to recover separately for such torts, as freely as if she were still unmarried. The statute was not intended to give a right of action as against the husband, but to allow the wife, in her own name, to maintain actions of tort which, at common law, must be brought in the joint names of herself and husband.

This construction we think is obvious from a reading of the statute in the light of the purpose sought to be accomplished. It gives a reasonable effect to the terms used, and accomplishes, as we believe, the legislative intent, which is the primary object of all construction of statutes.

It is suggested that the liberal construction insisted for in behalf of the plaintiff in error in this case might well be given, in view of the legislative intent to provide remedies for grievous wrongs to the wife; and an instance is suggested in the wrong to a wife rendered unable to follow the avocation of seamstress by a cruel assault which might destroy the use of hand or arm; and the justice is suggested of giving a remedy to an artist who might be maimed and suffer great pecuniary damages as the result of injuries inflicted by a brutal husband.

[T]his construction would, at the same time, open the doors of the courts to accusations of all sorts of one spouse against the other, and bring into public notice complaints for assault, slander, and libel, and alleged injuries to property of the one or the other, by husband against wife, or wife against husband. Whether the exercise of such jurisdiction would be promotive of the public welfare and domestic harmony is at least a debatable question. The possible evils of such legislation might well make the lawmaking power hesitate to enact it. But these and kindred considerations are addressed to the legislative, not the judicial, branch of the government. . . .

Had it been the legislative purpose not only to permit the wife to bring suits free from her husband's participation and control, but to bring actions against him also for injuries to person or property as though they were strangers, thus emphasizing and publishing differences which otherwise might not be serious, it would have been easy to have expressed that intent in terms of irresistible clearness. We can but regard this case as another of many attempts which have failed, to obtain by construction radical and far-reaching changes in the policy of the common law, not declared in the terms of the legislation under consideration. . . .

[The wife is not] left without remedy for such wrongs. She may resort to the criminal courts, which, it is to be presumed, will inflict punishment commensurate with the offense committed. She may sue for divorce or separation and for alimony. The court, in protecting her rights and awarding relief in such cases, may consider, and, so far as possible, redress her wrongs and protect her rights. She may resort to the chancery court for the protection of her separate property rights. . . .

We do not believe it was the intention of Congress, in the enactment of the District of Columbia Code, to revolutionize the law governing the relation of husband and wife as between themselves. We think the construction we have given the statute is in harmony with its language, and is the only one consistent with its purpose. [A]ffirmed.

Mr. Justice HARLAN, dissenting [joined by Justices Holmes and Hughes]:

This is an action by a wife against her husband to recover damages for assault and battery. The declaration contains seven counts. The first, second, and third charge assault by the husband upon the wife on three several days. The remaining counts charge assaults by him upon her on different days named—she being at the time pregnant, as the husband then well knew. . . .

The court below held that [the applicable] provisions did not authorize an action for tort committed by the husband against the wife. In my opinion these statutory provisions, properly construed, embrace such a case as the present one. . . . Now, there is not here, as I think, any room whatever for mere construction, so explicit are the words of Congress. Let us follow the clauses of the statute in their order. The statute enables the married woman to take, as her own, property of any kind, no matter how acquired by her, as well as the avails of her skill, labor, or personal exertions, as absolutely *as if she were unmarried*. It then confers upon married women the power to engage in any business, no matter what, and to enter into contracts, whether engaged in business or not, and to sue separately upon those contracts. If the statute stopped here, there would be ground for holding that it did not authorize this suit. But the statute goes much farther. It proceeds to authorize married women "also" to sue separately for the recovery, security, or protection of their property; still more, they may sue separately "for *torts* committed against *them*, as fully and freely *as if they were unmarried*." No discrimination is made, in either case, between the persons charged with committing the tort. No exception is made in reference to the husband, if he happens to be the party charged with transgressing the rights conferred upon the wife by the statute.

In other words, Congress, by these statutory provisions, destroys the unity of the marriage association as it had previously existed. It makes a radical change in the relations of man and wife as those relations were at common law in this District. In respect of business and property, the married woman is given absolute control; in respect of the recovery, security, and protection of her property, she may sue separately in tort, as if she were unmarried; and in respect of herself, that is, of her person, she may sue separately as fully and freely as if she were unmarried, "for *torts* committed against *her*." So the statute expressly reads. But my brethren think that, notwithstanding the destruction by the statute of the unity of the married relation, it could not have been intended to open the doors of the courts to accusations of all sorts by husband and wife against each other; and therefore they are moved to add, by construction, to the provision that married women may "sue separately . . . for torts committed against them, as fully and freely as if they were unmarried," these words: "*Provided, however, that the wife shall not be entitled, in any case, to sue her husband separately for a tort committed against her person.*"

If the husband violently takes possession of his wife's property and withholds it from her, she may, *under the statute*, sue him, separately, for its recovery. But such a civil action will be one in tort. If he injures or destroys her property, she may, *under the statute*, sue him, separately, for damages. That action would also be one in tort. If these propositions are disputed, what becomes of the words in the statute to the effect that she may "sue separately for the recovery, security, and protection" of her property? But if they are conceded—as I think they must be—then Congress, under the construction now placed by the court on the statute, is put in the anomalous position of allowing a married woman to sue her husband separately, in tort, for the recovery of her property, but denying her the right or privilege to sue him separately, in tort, for damages arising from his brutal assaults upon her person. I will not assume that Congress intended to bring about any such result. . . .

My brethren feel constrained to say that the present case illustrates the attempt, often made, to effect radical changes in the common law by mere construction. On the contrary, the judgment just rendered will have, as I think, the effect to defeat the clearly expressed will the legislature by a construction of its words that cannot be reconciled with their ordinary meaning. . . .

Notes and Questions

1. *Interspousal immunity.* Interspousal immunity was a common law doctrine that barred one spouse from maintaining an action against the other to recover damages for spousal abuse. What was the rationale for the doctrine? Recall Blackstone's explanation (supra, pp. 16-17). The interspousal immunity doctrine was first recognized by American courts during the 1860s. The doctrine endured until the 1970s.

2. *Married Women's Property Acts.* Married women's property legislation, enacted in many states during the nineteenth century, resulted in significant liberalization of the rules to which married women had been subject for centuries. This legislation conferred upon a married woman a separate legal identity and a separate legal estate in her own property. Although state laws differed in their scope, they generally enabled married women to acquire and control real and personal property, to sue and be sued, to retain their own earnings, to make contracts, and to execute wills.

Several factors contributed to the widespread legislative reform: (1) economic antebellum conditions that led to a desire to protect family property (particularly to protect the wife's slaves from her husband's creditors), (2) the codification movement in law reform, and (3) the desire to improve women's status (stemming from the first stage of the women's rights movement). Married women's property legislation started a trend in the erosion of the common law interspousal immunity doctrine. See generally Basch, In the Eyes of the Law, supra, at 27; Lawrence M. Friedman, A History of American Law 113, 147 (2005).

3. *Significance of* Thompson. In a sharply divided decision in *Thompson*, the U.S. Supreme Court upheld the interspousal immunity doctrine. The famous dissent by Justice Harlan signified "the first substantive break with immunity, marking the commencement of its erosion, a process that continued throughout the twentieth century." Carl Tobias, Interspousal Tort Immunity in America, 23 Ga. L. Rev. 359, 399 (1989). Following *Thompson*, courts and legislatures slowly abrogated the

doctrine. After 1970, on the heels of the second stage of the women's rights movement, the doctrine finally became a minority rule. *Id.* at 422.

The majority in *Thompson* distinguishes the case of a seamstress or artist who might be able to sue for injuries inflicted to her hands or arms by an abusive husband. What distinguishes those victims from other battered wives? How do the majority and dissent differ in terms of their views of the law as an agent of social change?

4. *Rationale: family harmony.* In *Thompson*, the U.S. Supreme Court held that the common law interspousal immunity doctrine was *not* abrogated by the District of Columbia's enactment of married women's property legislation. One of the primary rationales for the persistence of the doctrine was the need to protect family harmony. See, e.g., Logendyke v. Logendyke, 44 Barb. 366 (N.Y. Sup. Ct. 1863) (interspousal lawsuits would lead to "destructi[on] of that conjugal union and tranquility which it has always been the object of the law to guard and protect"). What reasons support and refute this rationale? Which is more destruction to family harmony—spousal abuse or interspousal lawsuits?

5. *Interspousal immunity and the public-private distinction.* Many feminist legal theorists (such as Nadine Taub and Elizabeth Schneider, supra) criticize the interspousal tort immunity doctrine as an illustration of the lack of legal protection for women in the "private sphere" of family life. What are the implications of *Thompson* for abused partners? What light do Taub and Schneider shed on this question?

What are the consequences of the public-private dichotomy for victims in terms of *equality*? One commentator summarizes the feminist criticism as follows:

> [I]f serious wrongs mounting to the level of marital domestic physical or emotional abuse are not punished at all, it is women, who are usually the victims of serious physical and emotional abuse in the home, that are left without recourse.

Pamela Laufer-Ukeles, Reconstructing Fault: The Case for Spousal Torts, 79 U. Cin. L. Rev. 207, 255 (2010). Does the interspousal immunity's guarantee of different treatment for spouses and nonspouses violate equal protection? See, e.g., Moran v. Beyer, 734 F.2d 1245, 1247-1248 (7th Cir. 1984) (holding that statute is not rationally related to maintenance of marital harmony).

Is there a way to permit interspousal tort claims while still protecting family privacy? Professor Benjamin Shmueli suggests reconciling these interests by allowing tort litigation when family harmony is not relevant but advocating mediation in other cases. See Benjamin Shmueli, Tort Litigation Between Spouses: Let's Meet Somewhere in the Middle, 15 Harv. Negot. L. Rev. 195, 200-201 (2010). What do you think of his proposal? For a debate on reconciling state intervention and respect for individual autonomy, compare Jeannie Suk, Criminal Law Comes Home, 116 Yale L.J. 2 (2006) (contending that state control of the home undermines individuals' decisions to live as intimate partners), with Cheryl Hanna, Because Breaking Up Is Hard to Do, 116 Yale L.J. Pocket Part 92, 98 (2006) (arguing that the benefits of state intervention far outweigh the costs for survivors). For additional discussion of the interspousal tort immunity doctrine, see Chapter 10. Mediation is discussed in Chapter 14.

II

Characteristics of Domestic Violence

A. EXTENT OF THE PROBLEM

Knowledge of the nature of domestic violence is essential to understanding the law's response to this social problem. This chapter highlights various characteristics of domestic violence, including its prevalence, dynamics, causes, and consequences.

■ CENTERS FOR DISEASE CONTROL AND PREVENTION, NATIONAL INTIMATE PARTNER AND SEXUAL VIOLENCE SURVEY: 2010 SUMMARY REPORT, EXECUTIVE SUMMARY (2011) [hereafter NISVS, Executive Summary]

[The National Intimate Partner and Sexual Violence Survey (NISVS) was a random telephone survey of 16,507 adults (9,086 women and 7,421 men) that collected information about the experiences of sexual violence, stalking, and intimate partner violence among English and/or Spanish speaking women and men aged 18 or older in the United States.][1]

[1]. The Centers for Disease Control, with the support of the National Institute of Justice, conducted the NISVS in 2010 to describe the prevalence and characteristics of sexual violence, stalking, and intimate partner violence; the persons most likely to experience such violence; the patterns and impact of the violence; and the health consequences of these forms of violence. NISVS also studied various types of intimate partner violence that had not been previously measured in a national survey, such as sexual violence other than rape, expressive psychological aggression and coercive control, and control of reproductive or sexual health.

Sexual Violence by Any Perpetrator

- Nearly 1 in 5 women (18.3%) and 1 in 71 men (1.4%) in the United States have been raped at some time in their lives, including completed forced penetration, attempted forced penetration, or alcohol/drug facilitated completed penetration.
- More than half (51.1%) of female victims of rape reported being raped by an intimate partner and 40.8% by an acquaintance; for male victims, more than half (52.4%) reported being raped by an acquaintance and 15.1% by a stranger.
- Approximately 1 in 21 men (4.8%) reported that they were made to penetrate someone else during their lifetime; most men who were made to penetrate someone else reported that the perpetrator was either an intimate partner (44.8%) or an acquaintance (44.7%).
- An estimated 13% of women and 6% of men have experienced sexual coercion in their lifetime (i.e., unwanted sexual penetration after being pressured in a nonphysical way); and 27.2% of women and 11.7% of men have experienced unwanted sexual contact.
- Most female victims of completed rape (79.6%) experienced their first rape before the age of 25; 42.2% experienced their first completed rape before the age of 18 years.
- More than one-quarter of male victims of completed rape (27.8%) experienced their first rape when they were 10 years of age or younger.

Stalking Victimization by Any Perpetrator

- One in 6 women (16.2%) and 1 in 19 men (5.2%) in the United States have experienced stalking victimization at some point during their lifetime in which they felt very fearful or believed that they or someone close to them would be harmed or killed.
- Two-thirds (66.2%) of female victims of stalking were stalked by a current or former intimate partner; men were primarily stalked by an intimate partner or an acquaintance, 41.4% and 40.0%, respectively.
- Repeatedly receiving unwanted telephone calls, voice, or text messages was the most commonly experienced stalking tactic for both female and male victims of stalking (78.8% for women and 75.9% for men).
- More than half of female victims and more than one-third of male victims of stalking indicated that they were stalked before the age of 25; about 1 in 5 female victims and 1 in 14 male victims experienced stalking between the ages of 11 and 17.

Violence by an Intimate Partner

- More than 1 in 3 women (35.6%) and more than 1 in 4 men (28.5%) in the United States have experienced rape, physical violence, and/or stalking by an intimate partner in their lifetime.
- Among victims of intimate partner violence, more than 1 in 3 women experienced multiple forms of rape, stalking, or physical violence; 92.1% of male victims experienced physical violence alone, and 6.3% experienced physical violence and stalking.
- Nearly 1 in 10 women in the United States (9.4%) has been raped by an intimate partner in her lifetime, and an estimated 16.9% of women and

8.0% of men have experienced sexual violence other than rape by an intimate partner at some point in their lifetime.

- About 1 in 4 women (24.3%) and 1 in 7 men (13.8%) have experienced severe physical violence by an intimate partner (e.g., hit with a fist or something hard, beaten, slammed against something) at some point in their lifetime.[2]
- An estimated 10.7% of women and 2.1% of men have been stalked by an intimate partner during their lifetime.
- Nearly half of all women and men in the United States have experienced psychological aggression by an intimate partner in their lifetime (48.4% and 48.8%, respectively).
- Most female and male victims of rape, physical violence, and/or stalking by an intimate partner (69% of female victims; 53% of male victims) experienced some form of intimate partner violence for the first time before 25 years of age.

Impact of Violence by an Intimate Partner

- Nearly 3 in 10 women and 1 in 10 men in the United States have experienced rape, physical violence, and/or stalking by an intimate partner and reported at least one impact related to experiencing these or other forms of violent behavior in the relationship (e.g., being fearful, concerned for safety, post traumatic stress disorder (PTSD) symptoms, need for health care, injury, contacting a crisis hotline, need for housing services, need for victim's advocate services, need for legal services, missed at least one day of work or school).[3]

Violence Experienced by Race/Ethnicity

- Approximately 1 in 5 Black (22.0%) and White (18.8%) non-Hispanic women, and 1 in 7 Hispanic women (14.6%) in the United States have experienced rape at some point in their lives. More than one-quarter of women (26.9%) who identified as American Indian or as Alaska Native and 1 in 3 women (33.5%) who identified as multiracial non-Hispanic reported rape victimization in their lifetime.
- One out of 59 White non-Hispanic men (1.7%) has experienced rape at some point in his life. Nearly one-third of multiracial non-Hispanic men (31.6%) and over one-quarter of Hispanic men (26.2%) reported sexual violence other than rape in their lifetimes.

[2]. The first comprehensive national telephone survey on intimate partner violence (called the National Violence Against Women (NVAW) Survey) was conducted by the Centers for Disease Control and Prevention and the National Institute of Justice in 1995-1996 (also based on approximately 16,000 women and men). That earlier study, like the recent NISVS, noted a marked gender disparity in the rate of physical abuse: 22.1 percent of women and 7.4 percent of men reported they were physically assaulted by an intimate partner at some time in their lifetime (or, one out of every 5 women compared with 1 out of every 14 men). Patricia Tjaden & Nancy Thoennes, Nat'l Inst. of Justice, Women's and Men's Risk of Intimate Partner Violence, in Full Report of the Prevalence, Incidence, and Consequences of Violence Against Women 10 (2000).

[3]. According to the 1995 NVAW survey, female intimate partners experience more chronic and injurious physical assaults than do men. That is, female intimate partners averaged 6.9 physical assaults by the same offender, whereas men averaged 4.4 assaults. Moreover, 41.5 percent of the women who were physically assaulted by an intimate partner were injured during their most recent assault, compared with 19.9 percent of the men. Id. at iv.

- Approximately 1 in 3 multiracial non-Hispanic women (30.6%) and 1 in 4 American Indian or Alaska Native women (22.7%) reported being stalked during their lifetimes. One in 5 Black non-Hispanic women (19.6%), 1 in 6 White non-Hispanic women (16.0%), and 1 in 7 Hispanic women (15.2%) experienced stalking in their lifetimes.
- Approximately 1 in 17 Black non-Hispanic men (6.0%), and 1 in 20 White non-Hispanic men (5.1%) and Hispanic men (5.1%) in the United States experienced stalking in their lifetime.
- Approximately 4 out of every 10 women of non-Hispanic Black or American Indian or Alaska Native race/ethnicity (43.7% and 46.0%, respectively), and 1 in 2 multiracial non-Hispanic women (53.8%) have experienced rape, physical violence, and/or stalking by an intimate partner in their lifetime.
- Nearly half (45.3%) of American Indian or Alaska Native men and almost 4 out of every 10 Black and multiracial men (38.6% and 39.3%, respectively) experienced rape, physical violence and/or stalking by an intimate partner during their lifetime.

Number and Sex of Perpetrators

- Across all types of violence, the majority of both female and male victims reported experiencing violence from one perpetrator.
- Across all types of violence, the majority of female victims reported that their perpetrators were male.
- Male rape victims and male victims of non-contact unwanted sexual experiences reported predominantly male perpetrators. Nearly half of stalking victimizations against males were also perpetrated by males. Perpetrators of other forms of violence against males were mostly female.

Violence in the 12 Months Prior to Taking the Survey

- One percent, or approximately 1.3 million women, reported being raped by any perpetrator in the 12 months prior to taking the survey.
- Approximately 1 in 20 women and men (5.6% and 5.3%, respectively) experienced sexual violence victimization other than rape by any perpetrator in the 12 months prior to taking the survey.
- About 4% of women and 1.3% of men were stalked in the 12 months prior to taking the survey.
- An estimated 1 in 17 women and 1 in 20 men (5.9% and 5.0%, respectively) experienced rape, physical violence, and/or stalking by an intimate partner in the 12 months prior to taking the survey.

Health Consequences

- Men and women who experienced rape or stalking by any perpetrator or physical violence by an intimate partner in their lifetime were more likely to report frequent headaches, chronic pain, difficulty with sleeping, activity limitations, poor physical health and poor mental health than men and women who did not experience these forms of violence. Women who had experienced these forms of violence were also more likely to report having asthma, irritable bowel syndrome, and diabetes than women who did not experience these forms of violence.

State-Level Estimates

- Across all types of violence examined in this report, state-level estimates varied with lifetime estimates for women ranging from 11.4% to 29.2% for rape; 28.9% to 58% for sexual violence other than rape; and 25.3% to 49.1% for rape, physical violence, and/or stalking by an intimate partner.
- For men, lifetime estimates ranged from 10.8% to 33.7% for sexual violence other than rape; and 17.4% to 41.2% for rape, physical violence, and/or stalking by an intimate partner.

Implications for Prevention

The findings in this report underscore the heavy toll that sexual violence, stalking, and intimate partner violence places on women, men, and children in the United States. Violence often begins at an early age and commonly leads to negative health consequences across the lifespan. Collective action is needed to implement prevention approaches, ensure appropriate responses, and support these efforts based on strong data and research.

Prevention efforts should start early by promoting healthy, respectful relationships in families by fostering healthy parent-child relationships and developing positive family dynamics and emotionally supportive environments. These environments provide a strong foundation for children, help them to adopt positive interactions based on respect and trust, and foster effective and non-violent communication and conflict resolution in their peer and dating relationships. It is equally important to continue addressing the beliefs, attitudes and messages that are deeply embedded in our social structures and that create a climate that condones sexual violence, stalking, and intimate partner violence. For example, this can be done through norms change, changing policies and enforcing existing policies against violence, and promoting bystander approaches to prevent violence before it happens.

In addition to prevention efforts, survivors of sexual violence, stalking, and intimate partner violence need coordinated services to ensure healing and prevent recurrence of victimization. The healthcare system's response must be strengthened and better coordinated for both sexual violence and intimate partner violence survivors to help navigate the health care system and access needed services and resources in the short and long term. One way to strengthen the response to survivors is through increased training of healthcare professionals. It is also critically important to ensure that legal, housing, mental health, and other services and resources are available and accessible to survivors.

An important part of any response to sexual violence, stalking, and intimate partner violence is to hold perpetrators accountable. Survivors may be reluctant to disclose their victimization for a variety of reasons including shame, embarrassment, fear of retribution from perpetrators, or a belief that they may not receive support from law enforcement. Laws may also not be enforced adequately or consistently and perpetrators may become more dangerous after their victims report these crimes. It is important to enhance training efforts within the criminal justice system to better engage and support survivors and thus hold perpetrators accountable for their crimes. . . .

Notes and Questions

1. *Extent of the problem.* The National Intimate Partner and Sexual Violence Survey (NISVS) (above) reports findings based on a survey of persons who experienced intimate partner violence. Surveys are research methods that are useful to collect information on social phenomena that are difficult to observe directly. What factors make domestic violence so difficult to observe?

Survey researchers attempt to study a "representative" population. What was the NISVS sample? Is it representative of victims and abusers, in your view? Why or why not? Do you think that the study accurately determined the extent of intimate partner violence? Can you think of a better method (or methods) to study the problem of domestic violence?

2. *Methodological issues.* How might a particular methodology influence research findings? For example, what homes would a *telephone* survey reach? What homes might it fail to reach? Might certain respondents be eliminated based on the languages spoken by the interviewers? See Kathleen Malley-Morrison & Denise A. Hines, Family Violence in a Cultural Perspective: Defining, Understanding, and Combating Abuse 87 (2003) (suggesting the omission of poor Native Americans who lack telephones as well as those who speak only their tribal language).

How might the definition of offenses influence research findings? What offenses were included in the NISVS study? See Diana E. H. Russell & Rebecca Morris Bolen, The Epidemic of Rape and Child Sexual Abuse in the United States 115 (2000) (criticizing prior NVAW study for asking only one question on attempted rape and omitting other questions on the rape of incapacitated women). How might other definitional problems influence research findings?

3. *Self-report vs. police data.* NISVS relies on self-report data. The collection of self-report data depends on respondents' willingness to disclose their experiences. Might victims and abusers be particularly reluctant to disclose their abuse? Why? Might the gender of the interviewer influence the respondent's willingness to disclose violence? Might problems of memory recall distort self-report data? What other problems might affect such data?

How might another methodology (for example, police reports) yield different findings? On the other hand, what factors might discourage victims from reporting their experiences to the police? Are self-report data and/or police reports more likely to lead to underreporting or overreporting? Are both methods likely to lead to underreporting or overreporting? See generally Stephanie Riger et al., Evaluating Services for Survivors of Domestic Violence and Sexual Assault 62 (2002) (criticizing arrest records for their failure to measure accurately the incidence of domestic violence and reporting research findings suggesting that three "assaultive actions" occur for every reported arrest).

4. *Stereotypes.* What images come to mind when you picture a victim of domestic violence? How does the media portray victims? To what extent do the NISVS data validate (or fail to validate) these stereotypes? How might these stereotypes affect institutional responses to intimate partner violence?

5. *Gender and intimate partner violence.* Women are significantly more likely than men to experience intimate partner violence. The above empirical study documents this reality. Why are females more likely to suffer from intimate partner violence? Why might women be more likely to experience such violence regardless of the *type* of abuse—rape, physical assault, or stalking?

To what extent are the reasons attributable to biology? Gender-based differences? Race, ethnicity, culture, and/or socioeconomic status? Societal attitudes? Women's subordination? Other factors? See generally Walter S. DeKeseredy & Martin D. Schwartz, Theoretical and Definitional Issues in Violence Against Women, in Sourcebook on Violence Against Women 8 (Claire M. Renzetti et al., 2d ed. 2011).

6. *Gender symmetry debate.* Several prominent social scientists claim that female intimate partners are as violent as males. See, e.g., Donald G. Dutton, Rethinking Domestic Violence (2006); Murray A. Straus et al., Behind Closed Doors: Violence in the American Family (1981). These scholars also contend that feminist researchers minimize evidence to the contrary. See Donald G. Dutton & Tonia L. Nicholls, The Gender Paradigm in Domestic Violence Research and Theory: Part 1—The Conflict of Theory and Data, 10 Aggression & Violent Behavior 680 (2005); Murray A. Straus, Processes Explaining the Concealment and Distortion of Evidence on Gender Symmetry in Partner Violence, Eur. J. Crim. Pol'y Res. 227 (2007).

However, other social scientists counter that proponents of gender-symmetry arguments omit measures of context and also rely on narrow definitions of violence that fail to account for multiple forms of victimization. That is, opponents of gender symmetry suggest that surveys that simply count the *number of physical assaults* are misleading because such surveys (1) ignore the fact that women use violence in intimate relationships in self-defense whereas men use violence to control their partners; (2) include only limited forms of victimization and therefore fail to recognize that men perpetrate a greater *range* of aggressive acts; (3) neglect to include violence by *former* spouses and partners; and (4) fail to consider the *extent* of injuries suffered by victims, thereby ignoring the fact that women are more likely to be seriously injured during the violence. See DeKeseredy & Schwartz, supra, at 8; Claire Renzetti, The Challenge to Feminism Posed by Women's Use of Violence in Intimate Relationships, in New Versions of Victims: Feminists Struggle with the Concept 43-46 (Sharon Lamb ed., 1999); Daniel Saunders, Wife Abuse, Husband Abuse, or Mutual Combat? A Feminist Perspective on the Empirical Findings, in Feminist Perspectives in Wife Abuse 90 (Kersti Yllo & Michele Bograd eds., 1990); Kersti Yllo, Political and Methodological Debates in Wife Abuse Research, in id. at 28; Russell P. Dobash et al., The Myth of Sexual Symmetry in Marital Violence, 39 Soc. Probs. 71 (1992); Suzanne C. Swan et al., A Review of Research on Women's Use of Violence with Male Intimate Partners, 23 Violence & Victims 301 (2008). What do you think about the gender symmetry argument?

7. *Role of age.* According to NISVS, more than 1 in 5 female victims of intimate partner violence experience some form of victimization for the first time between the ages of 11 and 17 years, and nearly half between the ages of 18 and 24. CDC, National Intimate Partner and Sexual Violence Survey: 2010 Summary Report 49 (2011) [hereafter NISVS, 2010 Summary Report], http://www.cdc.gov/Violence-Prevention/pdf/NISVS_Report2010-a.pdf. What are the policy implications of these findings? The role of age in intimate partner violence is explored further in Chapter 3.

8. *Multiple victimization.* Many victims experience several forms of violence. The NISVS reports that among women, 12.5 percent experience all three forms of violence with an intimate partner during their lifetime, 8.7 percent experience rape plus physical violence, and 14.4 percent experience physical violence plus stalking. Among male partners, approximately 92 percent experience physical violence

alone, while 6.3 percent experience both physical violence and stalking. NISVS, 2010 Summary Report, supra, at 41, http://www.cdc.gov/ViolencePrevention/pdf/NISVS_Report2010-a.pdf.

9. *Role of race.* How does the rate of intimate partner violence vary among different racial and ethnic groups, based on the above research? Might other factors, such as socioeconomic status, play a more important role? The role of race, ethnicity, and social class is explored further in Chapter 3.

10. *Sexual orientation.* How does sexual orientation play a role in intimate partner violence, according to the above research? The role of sexual orientation is explored further in Chapter 3.

B. DYNAMICS OF ABUSIVE RELATIONSHIPS

■ ANGELA BROWNE, VIOLENCE IN MARRIAGE: UNTIL DEATH DO US PART?

in Violence Between Intimate Partners: Patterns, Causes, and Effects 48, 56-58 (Albert P. Cardarelli ed., 1997)

Onset of Violence

[T]he onset of physical aggression is often preceded by nonviolent verbal abuse and restrictions, as well as by attentive and loving behavior. Many women who have lived with violent and threatening mates report that—early in their relationships—these men were the most attentive and romantic partners they have ever had.

Warning signs of a potential for future violence are often found in the very behaviors that initially seemed so attentive and caring. Early and intense interest, a constant concern with the women's whereabouts and activities, wanting to do everything together, jealousy over any activity or relationship outside of the relationship with the partner, and pressure for an early commitment are frequently mentioned as characterizing relationships in which the male partner later becomes violent toward his partner. Women, however, often interpret a new partner's intensity or pressure for early commitment as indications of love, and fail to recognize the warning signs of future trouble embedded in these behaviors. . . .

Early Warning Signs

Intrusion. A constant desire by a male partner to know a woman's whereabouts and activities—which at first makes the woman feel valued and cared for—is often described by women with violent mates as escalating over time into an insistence that they account for every hour, with violent reprisals if their explanations are not believed. Women with abusive partners report being followed to or from work or school, receiving frequent phone calls to make sure they are where they said they would be, intensive questioning about daily activities, and sudden appearances to check up on them. Arriving home a few minutes late, insisting on going out alone, or being seen talking with someone (especially a man) becomes triggers for suspicion and assault, regardless of the explanation.

Isolation. Early in romantic relationships, a partner's desire to spend every moment alone together may seem understandable and endearing. However, the tendency of abusive men to discourage their partners from maintaining relationships with others frequently leads to severe restrictions in later contacts and activities. Women involved with violent mates may increasingly isolate themselves from friends and family even before the onset of physical aggression, in an effort to avoid upsetting their partners. Sometimes such women quit their jobs or leave school because of their partners' negative reactions; or else in later stages of the relationship, they are ordered or forced to quit activities outside the home. In many of these cases, however, prior warnings are evident. The man may have shown little interest in, or even expressed jealousy of, friends and family; he may have seemed to resent the woman's involvement in work or school. However, this discomfort with the woman's involvement in a larger network is often overlooked in the initial intensity of being together.

Possession. Belief that a girlfriend or wife "belongs" to the man with whom she is involved is supported by the cultural traditions of romance and marriage. . . . In the early stages of a relationship, a woman may experience a man's belief that she is "his" as more protective than controlling. However, beliefs of ownership underlie the justification of many acts of violence by men toward their woman partners. Abusive men insist that they have the right to tell their wives what they may or may not do, to punish them for misbehavior, to force sexual activity on them if they choose to, to violently retaliate if they believe their wives have been with another man, and—sometimes—to murder their wives if they leave.

Jealousy. Jealousy is another warning sign imbedded within our romantic tradition. People expect jealousy to be a by-product of infatuation and love and often mistake it as a yardstick by which to gauge affection. However, in abusive relationships, jealousy typically far exceeds the bounds of reason and, except for attempts to end the relationship, tends to underlie the most violent and life-threatening assaults. Jealousy fuels [many] intrusive behaviors and contributes to the severity of retaliation for imagined misdeeds during times of physical separation or estrangement. Women with violent and jealous mates describe extreme situations such as being unable to shop at the supermarket because of the presence of male employees or having to keep their eyes lowered while riding in the car with their partner to avoid the appearance of making eye contact with people on the street. As with other warning signs, there are often early indications. Constant jealous reactions by a male partner that generalize to all types of relationships—or to all contacts with men, regardless of relationship—are particularly serious, and suggest that reasoning or increasing the level of commitment will not be enough to reduce the threat of violence and isolation that extreme jealousy presents.

Prone to Anger. Retrospective analyses of relationships in which men physically assault their wives suggest other early warning signs less confounded with the conception of romantic love, although supported by cultural stereotypes of acceptable male behavior. Even before the onset of violence, many women noticed that their partners not only were easily angered, but that their moods could change without warning and what might set them off was difficult to predict. More importantly, the anger was often completely out of proportion to the circumstance that occasioned it. This pattern of out-of-proportion rage later puts a woman at risk of physical attack for something as minor as forgetting to buy beer or leaving the checkbook in the car.

History of Violence. Finally, although other warning signs may be hard to separate from more typical romantic interactions, a prior history of aggression should never be ignored. Some women become involved with men with known histories of violence and believe that, with them, it will be different. Yet aggressive responses in one area of life often spill over into another. Although initially this aggression may be directed against other people or against objects, women whose partners have a past or current history of reacting violently to their environments should consider themselves at risk for similar actions. A potential for violence also may become evident in driving behaviors. Women survivors recount occasions during which the man seemed to deliberately put both of their lives in danger; abusive partners deliberately ran into stop signs or parked cars, drove the car toward pedestrians or cyclists, or over curbs and lawns to frighten them. Such behaviors demonstrate a willingness to endanger and do damage; they are an indication that a potential mate may someday direct this destruction against his partner. . . .

■ JUDITH A. WOLFER, TOP TEN MYTHS ABOUT DOMESTIC VIOLENCE
42 Md. Bar J. 38, 38-41 (May/June 2009)

. . . This list of 10 myths discusses common assumptions about domestic violence and what the latest research has to say about those assumptions.

MYTH #1:

Domestic violence happens when a batterer loses control of himself.

Many of us hold the view that individuals who batter their partners simply lose control of themselves and their emotions; that, in an excess of anger or passion, batterers lose their reason and lash out at their partners. These outbursts are seen as unpredictable and, therefore, almost impossible to prevent. After interviewing, surveying, studying and representing millions of abused women, however, domestic violence researchers and advocates have roundly rejected this explanation for domestic violence. We now know that domestic violence arises from a batterer's desire to control and dominate his (usually) female partner because he feels entitled to do so, not because he is suddenly angry.

Batterers utilize a wide array of coercive tactics to cement their control of their partners, such as isolating them from sources of help; humiliating them privately and in public; controlling their access to money, food, community and transportation; and micro-regulating their personal lives and those of their children. Physical violence only punctuates these coercive tactics—not the other way around. . . .

MYTH #2:

Men and women beat one another in equal numbers.

The rates of domestic violence for both men and women have been studied regularly over the past 20 years with remarkably consistent results. Domestic violence continues to be the number one health and safety issue affecting women, but not men, in the United States. In a 2007 study, female victims of violent assaults by their intimate partners made up 22 percent of all violent assault victims compared to only 3.6 percent male victims.

In 2006, the Centers for Disease Control and Prevention (CDC) reported an annual rate of 4.8 million incidents of intimate partner violence against women over the age of 18 compared to only 2.9 million incidents against men. Not only are women beaten more by male partners, but they are injured more: 39 percent of female physical assault victims, compared with 24.8 percent of male physical assault victims, reported being injured during their most recent physical assault.

Women die at the hands of their intimate partners more often than men do. Of all the women killed annually in the United States, 40 to 50 percent of them are killed by an intimate partner. Only 3 percent of all men who are killed die at the hands of female intimate partners. In summary, domestic violence continues to be more frequent, more injurious and more lethal for women than for men.

Myth #3:

If a woman doesn't leave her abuser, she must not really be afraid of him.

Research demonstrates that a woman is most at risk of serious injury or death when she leaves her abuser than if she stays with him, so a battered woman's fear that leaving might be worse for her safety is an objectively reasonable fear. [For example,] Veronica Williams was so afraid of being hurt by Cleaven Williams that she refused to name him to Frederick police when she reported being beaten. She was killed as she attempted to leave him. . . .

In a Department of Justice study, 75 percent of the domestic assaults reported to law enforcement agencies were perpetrated on victims who were either divorced or separated from their assailants. Subsequent studies have only underscored these findings that a woman is most at risk of serious injury or death if she leaves her abuser.

Despite this grim reality, studies have also found that battered women often make multiple attempts to leave their abusers before they are finally successful in leaving their abusers permanently. A battered woman is often forced to weigh a staggering number of conflicting needs and realities against her fear of being abused again: she may have no other place to live, she may depend upon her partner's financial support to make ends meet, she may still care for him or feel responsible for him, she may stay with him for the sake of minor children, she may be too embarrassed to ask for help or too afraid to go out on her own, she may be isolated from family and friends and have no other source of help, or she may be simply too tired to move. These reasons are all highly rational and do not negate her fear of her abuser.

Myth #4:

Getting a protective order does no good—it's just a sheet of paper.

In fact, a protective order is much more than a mere piece of paper. It is quite clear now from the research that protective orders make a significant positive difference in victims' long-term experiences of safety and security. In a large study, researchers discovered that victims who had obtained protective orders experienced an 80 percent reduction in police-reported physical violence 12 months following the first reported incident. In statistical language, this is an extraordinarily large effect [citing Victoria L. Holt et al., Civil Protection Orders and Risk of Subsequent Police-Reported Violence, 288 JAMA 589 (2002)].

This same effect did not occur, however, for victims who only obtained temporary orders but did not obtain final protective orders. The research may suggest that victims who only obtained temporary protective orders, then dismissed them or failed to appear for the final hearing, may be at an increased risk of future battering. (One hypothesis for this is that the batterer may perceive her failure to complete the legal action as indecision or weakness on her part and feel more emboldened by it to continue his behavior.)

MYTH #5:

When a man threatens to kill his spouse or girlfriend, he doesn't really mean it—he's just blowing off steam.

Statistically, it is more likely that he does mean it. In a large study involving 12 different cities across the country, researchers found that battered women who had been threatened with being killed were 15 times more likely to be killed than battered women who had never been threatened by their partners. The second highest predictor of whether a woman will be killed by an intimate partner is his threat to kill her. What this means in practice is that lawyers and judges must start taking batterers at their word—if a batterer says that he will kill his partner, we should believe him rather than dismissing the statement.

MYTH #6:

There is no way to predict if a particular man will kill or seriously injure his partner.

Actually, there is. Over the last few years, a group of public health researchers have disseminated the results of carefully designed, rigorous studies that looked for factors that were predictive of death from domestic violence. These lethality studies found 15 discrete factors that were highly predictive of lethality in domestically violent relationships. The most predictive factor was the use or threatened use of a weapon. [Lethality Assessment is explored further infra this chapter, Section D.]

The second most predictive factor was the batterer's threat to kill his partner. Other factors include the batterer's abuse of alcohol or drugs, an increase in the frequency or severity of battering, a report of choking or strangulation, forced sex, the presence of a child in the home from a previous relationship, abuse while pregnant, his unemployment, previous separations by the victim, stalking behavior, the existence of a new intimate partner for the victim, and the victim's subjective belief that the batterer could kill her.

Judges and lawyers should take note of the implications of this research—if a batterer has access to a gun during the period of separation, it increases the victim's risk of death significantly. If the batterer has threatened to kill his victim, engages in any type of stalking behavior once separated, has a history of choking her, and is obsessively jealous of a new partner in the victim's life, this is a prescription for a violent death.

MYTH #7:

Just because a father abuses the mother of his children doesn't mean that he's not a good parent.

Many members of the legal profession try to draw this distinction between how an abusive partner treats his intimate partner and what kind of parent he is. This distinction may be a false one in a majority of families. One study analyzed 36 separate studies that all looked at the risk of abuse of children where the mother reported being abused by the father. These studies revealed that 30 to 60 percent of those children whose mothers had been abused were themselves likely to be abused.

Even if children are not themselves physically abused, it is well settled in the field that living in a domestically violent home creates four distinct types of physical and emotional harms: the risk of exposure to traumatic events, the risk of neglect, the risk of being directly abused, and the risk of losing one or both of their parents. . . .

MYTH #8:

Women apply for protective orders to get a leg up on a custody case.

[Most] victims apply for protective orders simply to get the abuse to stop. But they need a custody order to insure that there is no child snatching back and forth between the victim and abuser, and that exchanges can be safe and regulated. Without a custody order, a victim cannot avoid interactions with her abuser and loses whatever protection the protective order gives her.

MYTH #9:

[Most state laws do not address domestic violence.]

[In fact, most states have a variety of civil and criminal laws that address domestic violence. For example, most] states have protective orders that last at least two years, and require proof of abuse at a preponderance of the evidence standard. . . . [Protective orders are explored further in Chapter 9, and state criminal laws in Chapters 5 and 6.]

MYTH #10:

Rape or sexual assault really doesn't happen in a marriage.

No act communicates domination and control better than rape or sexual assault. Rape and sexual assault occur in approximately 40 to 45 percent of all battering relationships, whether the parties are married or not. The notion that a woman "owes" sexual services to her husband as part of the marriage contract is no longer viable and a husband may be convicted of raping his wife.

■ CLARE DALTON, DOMESTIC VIOLENCE,
   DOMESTIC TORTS AND DIVORCE:
   CONSTRAINTS AND POSSIBILITIES
31 New Eng. L. Rev. 319, 333-338 (1997)

HOW ABUSIVE RELATIONSHIPS WORK

Because it has been the strategy of battered women's advocates to stress the extreme physical violence that is involved in all too many abusive relationships, and because it is the physical violence that has been criminalized, it is easy to equate "abusive" relationships with "violent" relationships. But in fact, abusive relationships are about coercion and control, and while physical violence is certainly one way of asserting control over another human being, it is by no means the only way. Thus, even the most physically abusive batterer is likely to employ a range of controlling behaviors. Some will use physical violence quite rarely, relying for the most part on those other behaviors, with an occasional threat, or beating, thrown in for good measure. . . .

What are some of the other strategies of control? One is the systematic undermining of a partner's sense of herself as an intelligent, attractive and competent person, a good parent, and caring spouse. Put downs, ridicule, constant criticism and complaints, delivered sometimes only in private, but sometimes in public too, are standard fare. She is fat, ugly, stupid, clumsy, dirty, a bad cook, a neglectful parent, a slut. She could never hold down a job, or hold up her end of a conversation. Her failure to respond to the sex he forces on her proves that she is frigid. She lies. If she told someone about the abuse that she suffers, no one would believe her.

Another strategy is isolation. Batterers often systematically undermine their partners' relationships with others. An abusive mate may forbid his partner outright from visiting with or calling family or friends; may routinely become verbally abusive and threatening if she seeks company outside the relationship, or may make scenes in the presence of others so embarrassing that she will forgo the relationships rather than suffer the consequences of trying to maintain them. He may refuse to share house or car keys. He may "check" frequently in the course of the day to ensure that his partner is in place, and then may become irrationally suspicious and angry if she is not at home or if the phone line is busy.

Some isolating strategies are also ways of ensuring economic dependence. Batterers often mount fierce campaigns to keep their partners from attending school or taking a job. Many women have had their professional wardrobes destroyed by an abusive mate. A black eye may be enough to keep her at home. Embarrassing surveillance or intrusion into her workplace or classroom may be enough. Simply failing to show up to mind the children, as promised, can sabotage an important test or compromise a job.

Much terrorizing behavior falls short of physical abuse. A great deal can be accomplished without an abuser actually laying hands on his partner. Batterers often rely on slashed tires, torn photos and broken furniture; cruelty toward family pets; threats leveled at the children or behavior that puts them at risk; threats leveled at family members or friends; stalking; monitoring phone calls; and threats of violence toward a partner who acts in forbidden ways, fails to act in prescribed ways, or ever suggests she might leave.

For many battered women sexual abuse is a routine aspect of their relationship. They are required to have sex on demand, and to engage in whatever sexual practices please their partners, no matter how painful or degrading. They may not themselves conceive of this forced sex as rape or sexual assault—so relatively novel in our culture is the idea that nonconsensual sex, within a marriage, can be rape.

Children play a special part in the drama of domestic violence. First, there is significant overlap between partner abuse and child abuse, so that in any family in which a partner is being abused the chances are great that the minor children in the household are also suffering physical or sexual abuse. The evidence increasingly shows that merely living in a household in which one parent is abusing the other, and witnessing that abuse, causes significant emotional harm to the children. This emotional harm produces the symptoms of post-traumatic stress disorder, affects children's capacity to problem-solve without resorting to violence, limits their capacity to build trusting relationships, and increases the chances that they will be abusive or abused in their own adult relationships. Sometimes children become the inadvertent victims of violence intended for a parent, especially when they seek to intervene. And sometimes they suffer the anguish and disruption of being withheld from one parent by the other, as part of a strategy of control or intimidation.

Why Doesn't She Leave?

For those with relatively little experience or understanding of the dynamics of abusive relationships, confronted with a situation involving prolonged and serious abuse, the first question is often "Why doesn't she leave?" Indeed, expert testimony on battered woman syndrome in self-defense cases was in large measure designed to answer this question—to explain how a woman who reasonably feared for her life could still be living in an intimate relationship with her batterer. The explanations preferred today still draw from that earlier testimony, but in the years since, our understanding both of battered woman syndrome, and of the many other aspects of women's situations that keep them in battering relationships has become more sophisticated and more complicated.

First, women do not fall in love with batterers, but with individuals who often treat them with an almost exaggerated respect and attention, and can be extraordinarily appealing. Often, by the time the abuse begins, the woman has already made a strong emotional commitment to the relationship, which is not easy to abandon. It is commonplace for women to decide that the first acts of violence are aberrational, and that the batterers' contrition and vows that the violence will not be repeated are sincere. It is also sometimes easier for women to take responsibility for "provoking" the violence, because then they can imagine that they can control it by making changes in their own behavior, rather than demanding change from their partners. This is all the easier because the batterer, although remorseful, may also be telling her that she caused his outburst.

By the time a woman acknowledges to herself that she cannot control the violence, and that it is not an aberration, but a permanent aspect of her relationship with her partner, she may be in too deep to make an easy escape. She may have made efforts to seek help, and found little response, whether from police, the courts, her doctor, her priest, pastor or rabbi, or even other members of her family. Those efforts may have elicited threats from her partner about what he will do if she discloses his violence to others, or seeks to leave him—threats that are perfectly credible given his past behavior. She may have children by now, locking her in to a co-parenting relationship from which she fears, with justification, that the legal system will not allow her to withdraw unless she abandons her children to her abuser. Her batterer is likely to reinforce those fears, telling her that if she tries to leave she will lose her children. She may be daunted by the economic realities of escape—how to find shelter, food, a job, or child care—when she has no separate funds, and cannot even use a check or credit card without revealing her whereabouts to her batterer. She may also, if the abuse has been prolonged and severe, be in a state of psychological depletion and paralysis that makes it almost impossible for her to take charge of her life in such new and risky ways. In this situation, she may marshal all the resources at her disposal to control the violence as best she can from within the relationship, and keep herself and her children safe from day to day, without triggering the explosive rage she knows from experience is associated with any attempt on her part to challenge her partner's control, or set limits with him.

If, despite all these obstacles, she does seek to leave her relationship with her batterer, the risks to her and her children are not a figment of her disordered imagination, as some judicial interpretations of battered woman syndrome have appeared to suggest. Rather, it is a stark reality that taking steps to leave an abusive relationship, or to confront the abuser and end the violence, is likely in the short term to increase the woman's danger. In one study, 75 percent of reported domestic incidents involved women who were already separated from their abusers. Which is to say that one answer to the question "Why didn't she leave?" is another question: "What makes you think that would have made her safer?" . . .

■ **LUNDY BANCROFT, UNDERSTANDING THE BATTERER IN CUSTODY AND VISITATION DISPUTES**

(1998), **http://www.lundybancroft.com/?page_id=279**

PROFILE OF THE BATTERER

. . . Batterers come from all socioeconomic backgrounds and levels of education. They have the full range of personality types, from mild and mousy to loud and aggressive. They are difficult to profile psychologically; they frequently fare well in psychological testing, often better than their victims do. People outside of a batterer's immediate family do not generally perceive him as an abusive person, or even as an especially angry one. They are as likely to be very popular as they are to be "losers," and they may be visible in their communities for their professional success and for their civic involvement. Most friends, family, and associates in a batterer's life find it jarring when they hear what he has done, and may deny that he is capable of those acts.

The partner and children of a batterer will, however, experience [the following general] characteristics, though he may conceal these aspects of his attitude and behavior when other people are present:

The batterer is *controlling*: he insists on having the last word in arguments and decision-making, he may control how the family's money is spent, and he may make rules for the victim about her movements and personal contacts, such as forbidding her to use the telephone or to see certain friends.

He is *manipulative*: he misleads people inside and outside of the family about his abusiveness, he twists arguments around to make other people feel at fault, and he turns into a sweet, sensitive person for extended periods of time when he feels that it is in his best interest to do so. His public image usually contrasts sharply with the private reality.

He is *entitled*: he considers himself to have special rights and privileges not applicable to other family members. He believes that his needs should be at the center of the family's agenda, and that everyone should focus on keeping him happy. He typically believes that it is his sole prerogative to determine when and how sexual relations will take place, and denies his partner the right to refuse (or to initiate) sex. He usually believes that housework and childcare should be done for him, and that any contributions he makes to those efforts should earn him special appreciation and deference. He is highly demanding.

He is *disrespectful*: he considers his partner less competent, sensitive, and intelligent than he is, often treating her as though she were an inanimate object. He communicates his sense of superiority around the house in various ways.

The unifying principle is his attitude of *ownership*. The batterer believes that once you are in a committed relationship with him, you belong to him. This possessiveness in batterers is the reason why killings of battered women so commonly happen when victims are attempting to leave the relationship; a batterer does not believe that his partner has the right to end a relationship until he is ready to end it.

Most abusers do not express these beliefs explicitly: they are more likely to deny having them, or even to claim to have opposite convictions that are humane and egalitarian. An experienced batterers' counselor may have to spend several hours with the abuser before the underlying attitudes begin to show. These attitudes are generally evident to victims, however, who often feel frustrated at the batterer's ability to present a markedly different face to the outside world. This dual aspect to his personality also helps to keep the victim confused about what he is really like, and can contribute to her blaming herself for his abusive behaviors.

SPECTRUM OF VIOLENCE AND OTHER FORMS OF ABUSE

The level of physical violence used by batterers is on a wide spectrum. Some use violence as much as a few times per month, while others do so once or twice a year or less. A significant proportion of batterers required to attend counseling because of a criminal conviction have been violent only one to five times in the history of their relationship, even by the victim's account. Nonetheless, the victims in these cases report that the violence has had serious effects on them and on their children, and that the accompanying pattern of controlling and disrespectful behaviors are serving to deny the rights of family members and are causing trauma.

Thus the nature of the *pattern* of cruelty, intimidation, and manipulation is the crucial factor in evaluating the level of abuse, not just the intensity and frequency of physical violence. In my decade of working with abusers, involving over a thousand cases, I have almost never encountered a client whose violence was not accompanied by a pattern of psychological abusiveness.

THE PERCEPTUAL SYSTEM OF MEN WHO BATTER

Because of the distorted perceptions that the abuser has of rights and responsibilities in relationships, he considers himself to be the victim. Acts of self-defense on the part of the battered woman or the children, or efforts they make to stand up for their rights, he defines as aggression *against* him. He is often highly skilled at twisting his descriptions of events to create the convincing impression that he has been victimized. He thus accumulates grievances over the course of the relationship to the same extent that the victim does, which can lead professionals to decide that the members of the couple "abuse each other" and that the relationship has been "mutually hurtful."

Although a percentage of batterers have psychological problems, the majority do not. They are often thought to have low self-esteem, high insecurity, dependent personalities, or other results from childhood wounds, but in fact batterers are a cross-section of the population with respect to their emotional make-up. Certain labels such as "control freak" or "self-centered" have the appearance of accuracy, but even these overlook the fact that the battering problem is very context-specific; in other words, most batterers do not have an inordinate *need* for control, but rather feel an inordinate *right* to control under family and partnership circumstances. Thus unlike other problems with violence, battering behavior is mostly driven by culture rather than by individual psychology. Many batterers are "in touch with" their feelings and skilled in the language of therapy and recovery, which throws evaluators off the track. They may use their childhoods and emotions as an excuse, to divert attention from their entitled and possessive attitudes.

Battering is a learned behavior, with its roots in attitudes and belief-systems that are reinforced by the batterer's social world. The problem is specifically linked to how the abuser formulates the concepts of *relationship* and *family*; in other words, within those realms he believes in his right to have his needs come first, and to be in control of the conduct (and often even of the feelings) of others. . . .

Each batterer has his own mix of controlling and entitlement. Some monitor every move their partners make like a prison guard, but at the same time are somewhat lower in entitlement, contributing more to housework and childcare than other batterers (though still less than nonbatterers). Other batterers don't control their partners' freedom as severely, but become irate or violent when they are not fully catered to, or when victims remind them of responsibilities that they are shirking. The levels of manipulativeness and overt disrespect also vary, so that each batterer has a particular style.

Because batterers are typically charming and persuasive, and are often kind and attentive early in relationships, [they do not] necessarily need to seek out a special kind of woman to victimize. Efforts to find common ground among battered women from the point of view of background or personality type have been largely unsuccessful, just as they have been with batterers. . . .

Notes and Questions

1. *Early warning signs.* What are some early warning signs of intimate partner violence? Why might a potential victim fail to recognize these signs? What are the conflicting messages that are reflected in some of these signs? How are early warning signs "embedded in our romantic tradition"?

2. *Myths about domestic violence.* What are the "top ten" myths about domestic violence? On what basis do domestic violence advocates reject these myths?

3. *Characteristics of abuse.* Are abusive relationships always violent? What are some of the controlling behaviors of abusers? Why are these controlling behaviors so effective?

4. *Children.* How does an abuser use children to control an intimate partner? Can living in a household in which abuse occurs harm a child—even if the child is never physically abused? Exposure to domestic violence is considered in Chapter 12.

5. *Women's exit.* Why don't victims of intimate partner violence leave once the abuse occurs? Why is leaving more difficult for those victims who have children? How do economic factors militate against victims' being able to exit? Does leaving the relationship end the abuse? If not, how do the victim's steps to leave the relationship increase the danger? The issue of women's exit from abusive relationships is explored further in Chapter 4.

6. *Level of violence.* What is the spectrum of *physical* violence inflicted by batterers? Why does Lundy Bancroft assert in the above excerpt that "the nature of the *pattern* of cruelty, intimidation, and manipulation is the crucial factor in evaluating the level of abuse, not just the intensity and frequency of physical violence"?

7. *Abusers' characteristics.* What are some common characteristics of batterers, according to Bancroft? Given these common characteristics, what explains Bancroft's assertions that batterers often perform better than victims on psychological tests, and are viewed as kind and popular to family and friends? How might such perceptions affect the legal response to domestic violence? For example, how might such perceptions play a role in child custody litigation, criminal prosecutions, or proceedings for restraining orders? See generally Erin Street Mateer, Comment and Note, Compelling Jekyll to Ditch Hyde: How the Law Ought to Address Batterer Duplicity, 48 How. L.J. 525, 532 (2004) (describing how and why batterers achieve a positive public image).

Bancroft also explains that "[b]ecause of the distorted perceptions that the abuser has of rights and responsibilities in relationships, he considers himself to be the victim." How can the abuser consider *himself* to be a victim? What other attitudes does the abuser project to others? How might these attitudes contribute to the victim's "blaming herself" for the abusive conduct? Bancroft adds that the "unifying principle in [the batterer's] attitude is *ownership.*" How does the batterer manifest this attitude? What role does it play in the batterer's criminal conduct?

C. CAUSES OF INTIMATE PARTNER VIOLENCE

1. Theories of Intimate Partner Violence

What are the causes of family violence? Various theories have been proposed. As you read the following analysis, consider how each theory characterizes the cause of, and solution to, domestic violence. Which theory do you find most helpful in understanding the causes of domestic violence?

a. Biological Theories

Biological theories focus on the genetic or organic roots of behavior. These theorists identify head injury (from accidents, falls, and sports injuries) as the cause of aggression in the family. Early research in the late 1980s and 1990s reported that men who batter tend to manifest a significantly higher percentage of head injuries.[4] Subsequent research confirmed the prevalence of this medical condition in a large percentage of batterers.[5] Researchers theorize that head injury leads to neurological impairment that contributes, in turn, to batterers' poor impulse control, communication difficulties, and substance abuse.

Another biological theory posits a neo-Darwinian gene-based evolutionary explanation. Male aggression is seen as a solution to specific evolutionary adaptive problems.[6] Intimate partner violence is a "mate retention strategy" that aims to control the sexual behavior of females in order to resolve men's concern about the paternity of children.[7] Male sexual proprietariness serves to deter women from engaging in sexual infidelity.[8] Domestic violence occurs when the man perceives a threat (real or imagined) by a rival—an event that provokes intense sexual jealousy and evokes a violent reaction to counter the threat.[9]

b. Psychopathology Theories

Psychopathology theories suggest psychodynamic factors as the cause of intimate partner violence. This perspective suggests that batterers are characterized by personality disorders (that is, borderline personality and antisocial personality disorders) that interfere with the development of normal inhibitions.[10] These disorders manifest themselves in immaturity, impulsivity, dependency, manipulation, rage, intense jealousy, egocentrism, undermining of the significant other, demanding behavior, and abandonment anxiety. The source of the psychopathology is a disruption in the batterer's early childhood attachment to a mother figure.

One type of personality disorder is borderline personality organization (BPO). Research reveals that this disorder is especially common among batterers.[11] Psychologist Donald Dutton posits a connection between BPO and the learned behavior theory of violence.[12] He suggests that BPO is the personality-based explanation for Lenore Walker's three-stage cycle of violence (described infra). Like Walker's theory, borderline personality disorder also has a three-phase structure marked by

[4]. See Alan Rosenbaum, The Neuropsychology of Marital Aggression, in Neuropsychology of Aggression (Joel S. Milner ed., 1991); Alan Rosenbaum & Steven K. Hoge, Head Injury and Marital Aggression, 146 Am. J. Psychiatry 1948 (1989) (finding that 61.3 percent of men referred for evaluation for marital violence had histories of severe head injury).

[5]. Alan Rosenbaum et al., Head Injury in Partner-Abusive Men, 62 J. Consulting & Clinical Psychol. 1187 (1994) (finding that half of batterers had experienced a severe head injury compared to 25 percent of unhappily married nonviolent men and 16 percent of happily married nonviolent men).

[6]. David M. Buss & Todd K. Shackleford, Human Aggression in Evolutionary Psychological Perspective, 17 Clinical Psychol. Rev. 605 (1997).

[7]. Margo I. Wilson & Martin Daly, Lethal and Nonlethal Violence against Wives and the Evolutionary Psychology of Male Sexual Proprietariness, in Rethinking Violence Against Women 199, 200 (R. Emerson Dobash & Russell P. Dobash eds., 1998).

[8]. Id. at 200-201.

[9]. Id. at 202.

[10]. Psychologist Donald Dutton is the leading theorist who espouses this view. See Donald G. Dutton & Susan K. Golant, The Batterer: A Psychological Profile 140-155 (1995); Donald G. Dutton, Trauma Symptoms and PTSD-like Profiles in Perpetrators of Intimate Abuse, 8 J. Traumatic Stress 299 (1995); Donald G. Dutton, The Origin and Structure of the Abusive Personality, 8 J. Personality Disorders 181 (1994); Donald G. Dutton & Andrew J. Starzomski, Borderline Personality in Perpetrators of Psychological and Physical Abuse, 8 Violence & Victims 327 (1993).

[11]. Dutton & Starzomski, supra note [10], at 334 (identifying batterers' rates of psychopathology in the 80 to 90 percent range).

[12]. Id. at 327-328.

sudden shifts in behavior. Dutton applies the three-phase personality disorder to the three-stage battering cycle. In the first stage (analogous to Walker's "tension-building" phrase), "the BP exists in a 'dysphoric stalemate,' where intimacy needs are unmet and the requisite motivation, insight, and skills to assert those needs are nonexistent."[13] The batterer expects his "significant others" to meet his unmet needs, but, at the same time, he resents his dependency on them.

In Stage 2 (corresponding to Walker's "acute battering incident"), the individual perceives a threat to the relationship with his significant other. He is afraid of expressing his needs because he fears the possibility of abandonment. "The defense structure at this stage expresses itself as anger, devaluation of the significant other, or open rage."[14] By means of acts of violence, the batterer succeeds in rejecting the significant other and warding off the imagined threat of abandonment.

In Stage 3 (analogous to Walker's "loving contrition" stage), the batterer attempts to deal with the strong feelings associated with being alone. He resorts to various coping mechanisms, including substance abuse, promiscuity, and "the exaggerated 'appeasement' behaviors that assaultive husbands engage in after their wives have emotionally and/or physically left the relationship."[15] However, because the batterer fears the precise outcome that he professes to desire—intimate attachment—the cycle begins again.

Both biological and psychopathological theories reveal provocative insights on the sources of violence. Nonetheless, feminists are staunch critics of the philosophical underpinnings of these theories. Feminists criticize these perspectives for focusing on the traits and characteristics of aberrant perpetrators, claiming that such a focus diverts attention from more important issues—"understandings of the patriarchal social context, of the unequal distribution of power, and the socially structured and culturally maintained patterns of male/female relations."[16]

c. Family Systems Theory

Family systems theorists explain intimate partner violence as a product of the family system. These theorists believe that family members cannot be understood in isolation, but rather that families must be seen as systems of interconnected and interdependent individuals.[17] The behavior of one family member is affected by the responses and feedback of other family members.

Family system theorists study domestic violence by exploring the communication patterns and problem-solving skills of the parties in relationships in which violence occurs. According to this theory, the family is a "goal-seeking system," in which each member tries to meet his or her own needs. All family members play a

[13]. Id. See also Dutton & Golant, supra note [10], at 140-155.
[14]. Dutton & Starzomski, supra note [10], at 327-328.
[15]. Id.
[16]. See Michele Bograd, Feminist Perspectives on Wife Abuse: An Introduction, in Feminist Perspectives on Wife Abuse 11, 17 (Kersti Yllo & Michele Bograd eds., 1990) (identifying and examining these perspectives); Walter S. DeKeseredy & Molly Dragiewicz, Understanding the Complexities of Feminist Perspectives on Woman Abuse, 13 Violence Against Women 874 (2007).
[17]. Herta A. Guttman, Systems Theory, Cybernetics, and Epistemology, in 2 Handbook of Family Therapy 41 (Alan S. Gurman & David P. Kniskern eds., 1991); Michael P. Nichols & Richard C. Schwartz, The Essentials of Family Therapy: Concepts and Methods (2d ed., 2005).

role in the construction of the violence. When one family member resorts to violence as a means of communication and problem solving, a feedback process occurs that reinforces the violence.[18] If aggressive acts result in positive feedback (that is, the aggressor attains his desired end), then the aggression will continue. In this manner, abusive family dynamics are created, maintained, and lead to future aggressive behavior.

Feminist scholars also have been extremely critical of the application of family systems to domestic violence.[19] They criticize the assumption that all family members share equal power. And, they emphatically reject the implication that all family members share responsibility for the violence, believing that the batterer should be solely accountable for his conduct.

d. Sociological Theories

Sociological theories broaden the focus from the individual to the social context. Although many sociological theories of criminal behavior exist, the social learning theory is most frequently cited as an explanation for family violence. Social learning theory is based on the theory of psychologist B. F. Skinner[20] in which learning occurs when a behavior is reinforced. This theory was later applied to explain aggression,[21] and still later to domestic violence.

According to social learning theory, intimate partner violence is a learned behavior that works through modeling and reinforcement. Children identify their parents as their most important role models and then imitate their behavior. If a powerful parent engages in violent behavior toward other family members, the child will imitate the aggressor's behavior. Reinforcement creates the potential for reabuse when the child perceives that the violence achieves its desired effect.

This perspective postulates a causal link between exposure to violence in the family of origin and intimate partner violence in adulthood. Childhood abuse contributes to low self-esteem, lack of trust, a tendency to link intimacy with violence, depression, and substance abuse. These factors lead to the individual's propensity to seek abusive relationships.[22] This perspective is known as the "intergenerational transmission of abuse" theory.[23]

The learned behavior theory is the predominant approach to domestic violence today. Unlike some theories of family violence, this theory has been empirically tested. High levels of childhood exposure to, and the experience of, abuse have

[18]. Murray A. Straus, A General Systems Theory Approach to a Theory of Violence Between Family Members, 12 Soc. Sci. Info. 105 (1973).

[19]. Michele Bograd, Family Systems Approach to Wife Battering: A Feminist Critique, 54 Am. J. Orthopsychiatry 558 (1984); Christine E. Murray, Controversy, Constraints, and Context: Understanding Family Violence through Family Systems Theory, 14 Fam. J. 234 (2006).

[20]. B. F. Skinner, Science and Human Behavior (1953).

[21]. Albert Bandura, the leading proponent of social learning theory, refined Skinner's theory of behaviorism and applied social learning theory to the study of aggression. See Albert Bandura, Aggression: A Social Learning Analysis (1973).

[22]. Glenda Kantor Kaufman & Jana L. Jasinski, Dynamics and Risk Factors in Partner Violence in Partner Violence: A Comprehensive Review of 20 Years of Research 1-43 (Jana L. Jasinski & Linda M. Williams eds., 1998) (reviewing literature).

[23]. Murray Straus et al., Behind Closed Doors: Violence in the American Family (1980); Debra Kalmuss, The Intergenerational Transmission of Marital Aggression, 46 J. Marriage & Fam. 11 (1984); Diana Doumas et al., The Intergenerational Transmission of Aggression Across Three Generations, 9 J. Fam. Violence 157 (1994).

been found among offenders who abuse other family members and among criminal offenders generally.[24] However, this theory fails to explain why *some* children who are exposed to intimate partner violence do not manifest these outcomes and also why many abusive adults do not report these childhood experiences.[25]

Social-psychological theories of family violence have also produced typologies of batterers that enhance our understanding of the violence. Psychologist Donald Dutton identifies the following typology based on his research in batterers' treatment programs: (1) men who are violent solely or primarily in their relationships with women; (2) antisocial psychopathic batterers who display high levels of anger and jealousy and have extensive criminal records; and (3) sociopathic batterers who manifest high levels of violence in many different contexts, suffered severe child abuse, and have extensive criminal records.[26]

Psychologists Amy Holtzworth-Munroe and Gregory Stuart, based on a review of the literature, identify another typology with three descriptive dimensions: (1) "family-only batterers" who engage in the least severe partner violence, show little psychopathology, and are least likely to engage in violence outside the home or to have related legal problems; (2) "dysphoric/borderline batterers" who engage in moderate to severe partner abuse, have the most psychopathology, have substance abuse issues, and commit extrafamilial violence and criminal behavior; and (3) "generally violent/antisocial batterers," who engage in moderate to severe partner violence, commit the most violence outside the family and have extensive criminal histories, are most likely to have substance abuse problems, and have the most psychopathology (including antisocial personality disorder).[27]

Sociologist Michael P. Johnson, based on another review of the literature, delineates a typology of *relationships* rather than a typology of batterers. He labels these relationships: "Coercive Controlling Violence" (also called "Intimate Terrorism"), "Violent Resistance," and "Situational Couple Violence."[28] According to Johnson, the first type, "Coercive Controlling Violence," is characterized by a partner's efforts to exert power and control over the partner, and is more likely to escalate over time, less likely to be mutual, and more likely to involve serious injury. "Violent Resistance" consists of violence that generally takes the form of self-defense. "Situational Couple Violence" arises in the context of a specific argument and may be driven by personality-based factors.

These typologies are useful for broadening our understanding of the types of abusers and the types of partner abuse. In addition, such theories add important new insights by suggesting that different interventions are necessary for different types of batterers.

[24]. A considerable amount of research confirms this point. For a sampling of the literature, see Robin Malinosky-Rummell & David J. Hansen, Long-Term Consequences of Childhood Physical Abuse, 114 Psychol. Bull. 68, 75 (1993) (reporting a strong relationship between childhood abuse and nonfamilial and family violence); Cathy S. Widom & Michael G. Maxfield, NIJ Report, Research in Brief: An Update on the "Cycle of Violence" 1 (2001) (reporting that childhood abuse increased the likelihood of arrest as an adult by 28 percent, and for a violent crime by 30 percent), available at http://www.ncjrs.gov/pdffiles1/nij/184894.pdf

[25]. See Mildred Daly Pagelow, Family Violence 225-228, 244-249 (1984) (reviewing literature on whether abused children become abusers); Joan Kaufman & Edward Ziegler, Do Abused Children Become Abusive Parents?, 57 Am. J. Orthopsychiatry 186 (1987) (same).

[26]. Dutton & Golant, supra note [10], at 122.

[27]. See Amy Holtzworth-Munroe & Gregory L. Stuart, Typologies of Male Batterers: Three Subtypes and the Differences among Them, 116 Psychol. Bull. 476, 481-482 (1994).

[28]. Michael P. Johnson, A Typology of Domestic Violence: Intimate Terrorism, Violent Resistance, and Situational Couple Violence (2008).

e. Feminist Theories

Feminist theory explores the gender-based aspects of social institutions (that is, political, economic, and social) and their implications for women's equality. Although feminist theories incorporate a diversity of views, these perspectives share a fundamental theoretical assumption that society is a patriarchal social order.[29] Patriarchy is a pervasive influence in the formation and maintenance of societal institutions. Structural factors in patriarchal society impede women's equal participation in the public sphere. Women's inequality in the public sphere parallels that of the private sphere, and women experience male subordination of women in each sphere.

The early battered women's movement highlighted the role of patriarchy in domestic violence.[30] "The reality of domination at the social level is the most crucial factor contributing to and maintaining wife abuse at the personal level."[31] According to feminist theory, patriarchal society supports traditional gender roles and cultural beliefs that promote the normative acceptance of the male as an authoritarian and dominant partner. Society engenders violence through its institutions (such as the military) and its popular culture (such as the media), thereby reinforcing violence in attitudes and practices that contribute to victimization in the home.

Feminist theorists identify four perspectives that are common to all feminist perspectives on battering, including: (1) a focus on gender and power and their role in explaining intimate partner violence ("Men as a class wield power over women"); (2) the historical importance of the family as a social institution ("wife abuse is not a private matter but a social one"); (3) the importance of including women's voices and validating their experiences ("a basic step toward understanding the factors contributing to wife abuse is illuminating experiences of women from their own frames of reference"); (4) the use of family violence research findings to help women (feminist scholarship "is dedicated to advocacy *for* women").[32]

Feminist theory is composed of different schools of thought. Liberal feminists played an important role in the women's movement in both theory and practice. Although early liberal feminists (such as those in the National Organization for Women) sought formal equality for women in the public sphere (that is, employment, education, and politics), subsequent liberal feminists addressed the private sphere. The concern of these later liberal feminists with privacy led them to focus on the need for reform of laws regulating contraception and abortion before they turned their attention to domestic violence.

Radical feminists were the most influential group in focusing public attention on domestic violence. In large part, this resulted from their traditional concern with theories about male violence toward women. Broadening their original focus from rape to battering, radical feminists characterized battering as one of the many forms of sexual violence in society ("female sexual slavery"),[33] along

---

[29]. R. Emerson Dobash & Russell P. Dobash, Violence Against Wives: A Case Against the Patriarchy (1979) (exploring the historical origins of patriarchal beliefs that support domestic violence).

[30]. Id. at 1-13 (discussing the case against patriarchy).

[31]. Bograd, Feminist Perspectives: Introduction, supra note [16], at 14 (identifying and examining these perspectives).

[32]. Id. at 13-17.

[33]. Kathleen Barry, Female Sexual Slavery (1984).

with prostitution, incest, and pornography.[34] These feminists believe that genuine equality for women can only be achieved by a restructuring of social relationships as well as a major overhaul of the patriarchal social order. Unlike liberal feminists whose quest for "equal treatment" concentrates on women's treatment in the public arena, radical feminists challenge the meaning of "equal treatment" and reconceptualize equality as the elimination of subordination in both the private and public spheres.[35]

Feminist perspectives enhance our understanding of family violence by highlighting the link between patriarchy, family violence, and inequality. In the past several decades, feminist activists and advocates have been largely responsible for bringing the issue of domestic violence to public attention and, in the process, contributing to significant law reforms.

Two additional theories of domestic violence (explained below) emerged from the efforts of battered women's advocates: the Cycle Theory of Violence, and the Power and Control Wheel. The former theory has revolutionized the law of self-defense. The latter model is used extensively in battered women's shelters and support groups, and also batterers' intervention programs.

2. Cycle Theory of Violence

The "Battered Woman Syndrome" was introduced by psychologist Lenore Walker in her book *The Battered Woman* (1979). Her research and clinical practice with battered women led her to the conclusion that these women shared common personality characteristics.[36] She designated these commonalities as a "syndrome" (Battered Woman Syndrome) consisting of two components: (1) learned helplessness and (2) the cycle of violence. Walker has since refined her theory to characterize Battered Woman Syndrome as a component of Post-Traumatic Stress Disorder.[37]

■ LENORE E. A. WALKER, THE BATTERED WOMAN SYNDROME
71-72, 91, 94-95 (3d ed., 2009)

The theoretical concept of learned helplessness was adapted in this research to help explain why women . . . found it so difficult to escape a battering relationship. [It was based on the research of psychologist Martin Seligman involving random shocks to laboratory animals.] Seligman and his colleagues discovered that when

---

[34]. Andrea Dworkin, Pornography: Men Possessing Women (1991).

[35]. For a prominent proponent of this view of equality, see Catharine A. MacKinnon, Women's Lives, Men's Laws (2005) (conceptualizing equality in terms of the elimination of subordination rather than "equal treatment").

[36]. Walker conducted interviews with over 400 "self-referred" battered women (solicited from community mental health clinics and media advertisements). Lenore E Walker, The Battered Woman Syndrome 41 (3d ed. 2009).

[37]. Id. at 70-71 ("And while Battered Woman Syndrome has been similarly criticized for making it easier to continue to pathologize battered women, it is my opinion that as a subcategory of PTSD, it is the most useful diagnostic category to use for battered women when it is necessary to use a diagnostic formulation").

laboratory animals (usually dogs, in their early experiments) were repeatedly and noncontingently shocked, they became unable to escape from a painful situation, even when escape was quite possible. . . . Seligman likened what he labelled, *learned helplessness*, to a kind of human depression, and showed that it had cognitive, motivational, and behavioral components. The inability to predict the success of one's actions was considered responsible for the resulting perceptual distortions. . . . Seligman's theory was further refined and reformulated, based on later laboratory trials with human subjects to determine how attributional styles and expectancies were connected and how hopelessness related to the original theory of helplessness.

For example, depressed humans were found to have negative, pessimistic beliefs about the efficacy of their actions and the likelihood of obtaining future rewards; helpless animals acted as if they held similar beliefs. Both depressed humans and helpless animals exhibited motivation deficits in the laboratory. Both exhibited signs of emotional distress with illness, phobias, sleep disturbances, and other such symptoms similar to those described as part of the Battered Woman Syndrome as a subcategory of PTSD. . . .

On the basis of clinical work with battered women, it was hypothesized that the women's experiences of [their attempts] to control the violence would, over time, produce learned helplessness and depression as the "repeated batterings, like electrical shocks, diminish the woman's motivation to respond." If a woman is to escape such a relationship, she must overcome the tendency to learned helplessness. . . .

[T]here are three distinct phases associated with a recurrent battering cycle: (1) tension-building accompanied by a rising sense of danger; (2) the acute battering incident, and (3) loving-contrition. The cycle usually begins after a courtship period that is often described as having a lot of interest from the batterer in the woman's life and usually filled with loving behavior. . . .

PHASE I

During the first phase, there is a gradual escalation of tension displayed by discrete acts causing increased friction such as name-calling, other mean intentional behaviors, and/or physical abuse. The batterer expresses dissatisfaction and hostility but not in an extreme or maximally explosive form. The woman attempts to placate the batterer, doing what she thinks might please him, calm him down, or at least, what will not further aggravate him. She tries not to respond to his hostile actions and uses general anger reduction techniques. Often she succeeds for a little while which reinforces her unrealistic belief that she can control this man. It also becomes part of the unpredictable noncontingency response/outcome pattern that creates the *learned helplessness*. . . .

PHASE II

The tension continues to escalate, the woman becomes more fearful of impending danger, and eventually she is unable to continue controlling his angry response pattern.

"Exhausted from the constant stress, she usually withdraws from the batterer, fearing she will inadvertently set off an explosion. He begins to move more oppressively toward her as he observes her withdrawal. . . . Tension between the two becomes unbearable" (citing Lenore Walker, The Battered Woman 59 (1979)).

The second phase, the acute battering incident, becomes inevitable without intervention. Sometimes, she precipitates the inevitable explosion so as to control where and when it occurs, allowing her to take better precautions to minimize her injuries and pain. Over time she may learn to predict the point in the cycle where there is a period of inevitability—after that point is reached, there is no escape for the woman unless the man permits it.

"Phase two is characterized by the uncontrollable discharge of the tensions that have built up during phase one" (Walker, Battered Woman, supra, at 59). The batterer typically unleashes a barrage of verbal and physical aggression that can leave the woman severely shaken and injured. The woman does her best to protect herself, often covering parts of her face and body to block some of the blows. In fact, when injuries do occur they usually happen during this second phase. It is also the time police become involved, if they are called at all. The acute battering phase is concluded when the batterer stops, usually bringing with its cessation a sharp physiological reduction in tension. This in itself is naturally reinforcing. Violence often succeeds because it works.

PHASE III

In phase three that follows, the batterer may apologize profusely, try to assist his victim, show kindness and remorse, and shower her with gifts and/or promises. The batterer may himself believe at this point that he will never allow himself to be violent again. The woman wants to believe the batterer and, early in the relationship at least, may renew her hope in his ability to change. This third phase provides the positive reinforcement for remaining in the relationship, for the woman. Many of the acts that he did when she fell in love with him during the courtship period occur again here. [R]esearch results demonstrated that phase three could also be characterized by an absence of tension or violence, with no observable loving-contrition behavior, and still be reinforcing for the woman. Sometimes the perception of tension and danger remains very high and does not return to the baseline or loving-contrition level. This is a sign that the risk of a lethal incident is very high.

Walker's theory is the most widely known explanation of domestic violence. Nonetheless, it has received considerable criticism from legal scholars and social scientists. Critics contend that her theory characterizes only some battering relationships; fails to recognize that not all abusive relationships evidence a cycle with three distinct phases; disadvantages women who deviate from the standard (that is, minority women, lesbians); pathologizes battered women as mentally unstable and passive; fails to provide an adequate explanation for women's agency and survival strategies; deflects blame from the offender onto the victim; and fails to recognize the range of the partner violence (for example, psychological abuse).[38] Despite these

[38]. For a review of these criticisms, see Brenda L. Russell, Battered Woman Syndrome as a Legal Defense: History, Effectiveness and Implications (2010); David Faigman et al., 2 Modern Scientific Evidence: The Law and Science of Expert Testimony §13:25, at 348-386 (2010-2011). See also Hillary

criticisms, Walker's theory has had a profound influence on the criminal justice system, particular on the law of self-defense. The Battered Woman Syndrome is explored in Chapter 7.

3. Duluth Model: Power and Control Wheel

The Domestic Abuse Intervention Project (DAIP) was established in Duluth, Minnesota, in 1980 by sociologist Ellen Pence and other activists in the battered women's movement in response to a specific incident of partner homicide.[39] The group formed a model for intervention in cases of domestic violence consisting of: (1) a batterers' treatment program based on the "Power and Control Wheel," and (2) strategic principles of interagency intervention. The model aimed to place the burden for responding to domestic violence on the community rather than on the victim.

DAIP's initial task from 1980 to 1981 was to convince law enforcement agencies, the courts, and social service providers to conduct a comprehensive overhaul of their agency's practices. DAIP secured an agreement among the different agencies to coordinate their interventions "through a series of written policies and protocols that limited individual discretion on the handling of cases and subjected practitioners to minimum standards of response."[40] The implementation of new policies resulted in an escalation in arrests and prosecutions, leading to the unanticipated problem of how to deal with the increasing number of first-time offenders who were rarely jailed. In response, DAIP formulated a model batterers' intervention program based on input from leading battered women's activists.[41]

The Power and Control Wheel, the theoretical framework of the batterers' treatment program, is derived from interviews with over 200 battered women who participated in over 30 educational sessions at Duluth's battered women's shelters in 1984.[42] There, survivors challenged the conventional wisdom that battering is cyclical (that is, Lenore Walker's cycle-of-violence theory), believing instead that abuse was a constant dynamic of their intimate relationships. These interviews led to the creation of the Power and Control Wheel that describes the behavior of men who are physically and emotionally abusive. "It illustrates that violence is a pattern of behaviors rather than isolated incidents of abuse or cyclical explosions of pent-up anger, frustration, or painful feelings."[43] Although the batterer's use of physical or sexual violence may be infrequent, it "reinforces the power of the other

---

Potter, Battle Cries: Black Women and Intimate Partner Abuse 122 (2008) (criticizing Walker's theories as applied to Black women).

A new paradigm that rejects Walker's learned helplessness theory is a model of "survivorship," in which victims actively, but unsuccessfully, seek help. See Edward W. Gondolf & Ellen R. Fisher, Battered Women as Survivors: An Alternative to Treating Learned Helplessness (1988). This model shifts blame from the individual to the social structure that prevents access to needed resources.

[39]. Ellen Pence & Michael Paymar, Education Groups for Men Who Batter: The Duluth Model xiii (1993). On the history of the Domestic Violence Intervention Project, see the DAIP website at http://www.theduluthmodel.org/history.php (last visited June 12, 2011).

[40]. Melanie F. Shepherd & Ellen Pence, Coordinating Community Responses to Domestic Violence: Lessons from Duluth and Beyond 4 (1997).

[41]. Pence & Paymar, supra note [39], at xiii.

[42]. Id. at 2.

[43]. Id.

tactics on the wheel (for example, emotional abuse, isolation, threats of taking the children) that are used at random and eventually undermine his partner's ability to act autonomously."[44]

The Power and Control Wheel sets forth the organization's feminist philosophy premised on the belief that domestic violence is a male-specific form of power and control analogous to other forms of domination (for example, racism). According to this theory, men batter women based on patriarchal ideology as a means of ensuring female subordination.

The batterers' treatment program attempts to educate batterers through cognitive-behavioral methods that help them recognize their abusive behavior and to adopt alternative methods of dealing with conflict. The educational curriculum attempts to refocus the batterer's ideology and includes support groups that discuss relationship issues (for example, respect, negotiation, support, and partnership). The program aims to keep victims safe, hold perpetrators accountable, and provide offenders an opportunity to change.

The Duluth Model sets forth principles for interagency intervention, including: (1) the establishment of standards, practices, and protocols for the various agencies and stages of intervention; (2) an emphasis on victim safety that enhances victim advocacy at all stages of intervention; (3) promotion of ongoing interagency cooperation; and (4) an approach that holds offenders accountable (emphasizing mandatory arrest for primary aggressors, evidence-based prosecution, increasingly harsh penalties for repeated acts of violence, court-ordered batterers' programs, and a tracking system of offenders to ensure victims' safety).

The Power and Control Wheel and its philosophical basis, similar to other theories of domestic violence, has received its share of criticism.[45] Among these criticisms are: the group's feminist ideological basis; its singular approach to domestic violence that fails to address other causes (for example, substance abuse, histories of childhood abuse); and its neglect of female-perpetrated violence or mutual violence.[46] Despite these criticisms, DAIP has had significant influence on the legal system because of its pioneering work regarding proactive arrest and prosecution polices,[47] creation of the first batterers' intervention program,[48] and the adoption of a coordinated community approach to domestic violence. Batterers' treatment programs and their effectiveness (including the Duluth Model) are explored further in Chapter 15.

---

[44]. Id.

[45]. For some of these criticisms, see Samuel R. Aymer, Beyond Power and Control: Clinical Interventions with Men Engaged in Partner Abuse, 36 Clinical Soc. Work J. 323 (2008); Donald G. Dutton & Kenneth Corvo, Transforming a Flawed Policy: A Call to Revive Psychology and Science in Domestic Violence Research and Practice, 11 Aggression & Violent Behavior 457 (2006); Edward W. Gondolf, Theoretical and Research Support for the Duluth Model: A Reply to Dutton and Corvo, 12 Aggression & Violent Behavior 644 (2007).

[46]. Johnna Rizza, Comment, Beyond Duluth: A Broad Spectrum of Treatment for a Broad Spectrum of Domestic Violence, 70 Mont. L. Rev. 125, 129-136 (2009).

[47]. DAIP is credited with the establishment in Duluth of the first mandatory arrest policy for misdemeanor assaults. Jan Hoffman, When Men Hit Women, N.Y. Times, Feb. 16, 1992, §6 (Magazine), at 23, available at http://www.nytimes.com/1992/02/16/magazine/when-men-hit-women.html.

[48]. By 2001, 43 states had established batterer intervention programs based on the Duluth model. Dutton & Corvo, supra note [45], at 459. The Duluth model has also been adopted in other countries.

POWER AND CONTROL WHEEL

Physical and sexual assaults, or threats to commit them, are the most apparent forms of domestic violence and are usually the actions that allow others to become aware of the problem. However, regular use of other abusive behaviors by the batterer, when reinforced by one or more acts of physical violence, make up a larger system of abuse. Although physical assaults may occur only once or occasionally, they instill threat of future violent attacks and allow the abuser to take control of the woman's life and circumstances. The Power and Control diagram is a particularly helpful tool in understanding the overall pattern of abusive and violent behaviors, which are used by a batterer to establish and maintain control over his partner. Very often, one or more violent incidents are accompanied by an array of these other types of abuse. They are less easily identified, yet firmly establish a pattern of intimidation and control in the relationship.

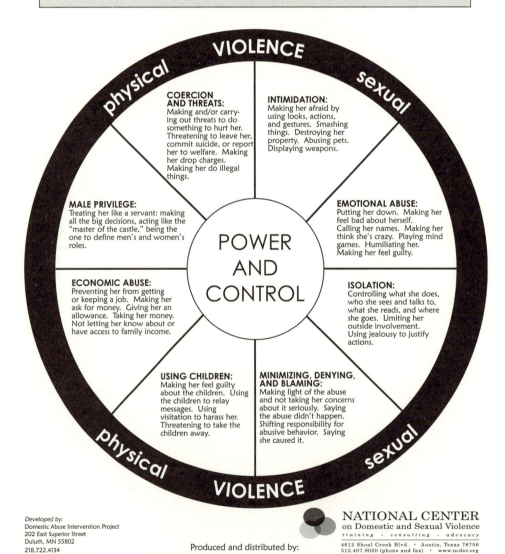

Developed by:
Domestic Abuse Intervention Project
202 East Superior Street
Duluth, MN 55802
218.722.4134

Produced and distributed by:

NATIONAL CENTER
on Domestic and Sexual Violence
training · consulting · advocacy
4612 Shoal Creek Blvd. · Austin, Texas 78756
512.407.9020 (phone and fax) · www.ncdsv.org

Notes and Questions

1. *Causes of domestic violence.* Explain the following theories of domestic violence: (1) biological theories, (2) psychopathology theories, (3) family systems theory, (4) sociological theories, (5) feminist theories, (6) the Cycle Theory of Violence, and (7) the Duluth Model. What is the focus of each theory? How does each theory explain the cause(s) of domestic violence? How does each theory view the victim? The abuser? What are the similarities between the theories? Differences? Has each theory evolved over time? If so, how?

On the recent resurgence of interest in biological theories of criminality, see Steven K. Erickson, Blaming the Brain, 11 Minn. J.L. Sci. & Tech. 27 (2010); J. W. Looney, Neuroscience's New Techniques for Evaluating Future Dangerousness: Are We Returning to Lombroso's Biological Criminality?, 32 U. Ark. Little Rock L. Rev. 301 (2010).

2. *Factors.* In each theory, what is the role of the following factors: the individual, couple, family, and society? Internal factors? External factors? Socioeconomic class? Unemployment? Race and ethnicity? Substance abuse? Mental illness? Patriarchy?

3. *Methodology.* How was each theory formulated? Do particular academic disciplines provide the source for each theory? What research methods are used to gather data on each theory? Which theory or theories can be empirically tested?

4. *Solution.* How does each theory conceptualize the solution to domestic violence? To what extent is the solution located in the individual, family, and/or society? To what extent can each theory protect victims? Deter abusers? Reduce domestic violence? How easily can the proposed solution(s) be achieved?

5. *Criticisms.* What are the strengths of each theory? Weaknesses? Do you agree with the criticisms of each theory? Why or why not? Additional criticisms of the Cycle Theory of Violence are explored in Chapter 7.

6. *Evaluation.* Which is the most popular theory? Least popular? Which theory is most helpful, do you think, to explain the causes of domestic violence? The responses of victims? Of abusers? The types of abuse? The dynamics of abuse? Which theory is the best predictor of which persons will become victims? Become abusers? The possibility of behavioral change? Which theory is most useful in suggesting helpful interventions to address intimate partner violence by the helping professions? By the legal profession?

7. *Policy.* Based on the above theories, what should be the focus of domestic violence policy? To what extent should domestic violence policy focus on prevention? Treatment? Individual change? Institutional change? Which institutions? Should policy be based on a multidimensional model that integrates several of the above theories? If so, which theories?

D. LETHALITY ASSESSMENT

Risk factors have been identified that help to predict cases in which intimate partner violence is most likely to be fatal. Criminologist Neil Websdale developed risk markers that identify the risk of death based on his work with domestic violence fatality review teams. In addition, Professor of Nursing Jacquelyn Campbell developed a special diagnostic tool (called the "Danger Assessment Instrument") to measure a victim's risk of death from intimate partner homicide. These risk factors are discussed below.

■ NEIL WEBSDALE, ASSESSING RISK IN DOMESTIC VIOLENCE CASES

in Encyclopedia of Domestic Violence 38, 38-40 (Nicky Ali Jackson ed. 2007)

Risk assessment procedures seek to identify the most dangerous perpetrators. . . . [I]dentifying cases that will escalate to the occurrence of the abuse victim's death is an inexact science at best. Nevertheless, risk assessment and management are integral and important aspects of the delivery of all kinds of services to victims. . . .

RED FLAGS OR RISK MARKERS

Researchers appear to have identified characteristics of cases in which domestic violence victims die. Digging deeply into that population of domestic violence homicides uncovers a number of factors that do not seem to surface as frequently or with the same level of intensity in everyday (nonlethal) cases. . . . Certain red flags loom large in both the research literature and in risk assessment instruments. These red flags are outlined below.

A PRIOR HISTORY OF INTIMATE PARTNER VIOLENCE

The first and most important red flag is a prior history of intimate partner violence. Under this broad umbrella of "prior history," some researchers note the predictive significance of particular forms of violence such as "choking" and "forced sex." Using data from the Danger Assessment Instrument, Campbell et al., found that compared with the control group of abused women, murdered women were forced to have sex 7.6 more times and were 9.9 times more likely to be choked.[49]

"Stalking" appears as a prominent correlate in a number of works. According to the research of McFarlane et al., "Stalking is revealed to be a correlate of lethal and near lethal violence against women and, coupled with physical assault, is significantly associated with murder and attempted murder."[50] A prior history of intimate partner violence may include the use of a weapon. According to Campbell et al.'s Danger Assessment study, abused women who were threatened or assaulted with a gun or other weapon were 20 times more likely than other women to be murdered. "The mere presence of a gun in the home meant that an abused women "was six times more likely than other abused women to be killed."[51] Although prior intimate partner violence in many of its guises powerfully informs the debate on risk, it is also the case that significant numbers of women who die report no prior history of violence that researchers are able to later identify. For example, the

[49]. Jacquelyn C. Campbell et al., Assessing Risk Factors for Intimate Partner Homicide, 250 NIJ J. 14, 17 (2003).
[50]. Judith M. McFarlane et al., Stalking and Intimate Partner Femicide, 3 Homicide Stud. 300, 300 (1991).
[51]. Campbell et al., Assessing Risk Factors, supra note [49], at 16.

Chicago Women's Health Risk Study reports that in one in five cases of men killing female intimates, researchers uncovered no evidence of prior intimate partner violence.[52]

PENDING OR ACTUAL SEPARATION OR ESTRANGEMENT

The extant research literature contends that women experience an increased risk of lethal violence when they leave intimate relationships with men. More recent research from Campbell et al.'s eleven-city case control study found, "Women who separated from their abusive partners after cohabitation experienced increased risk of femicide, particularly when the abuser was highly controlling."[53]

OBSESSIVE POSSESSIVENESS OR MORBID JEALOUSY

The research literature consistently identifies obsessive or morbid jealousy as central to intimate partner homicides. For example, [some researchers point to the role of male sexual proprietariness in homicides cross-culturally, particularly obsessive or pathological jealousy in terms of the perpetrator seeing his partner as part of his own identity].[54] Consequently, any threat of the female's leaving threatens the man's identity. The emphasis with this red flag is firmly on "extreme" or "morbid" forms of jealousy.

MAKING THREATS TO KILL

Threats to kill constitute one of the most consistent correlates of intimate partner homicide when compared with abused women in general. "Women whose partners threatened them with murder were 15 times more likely than other women to be killed."[55] Batterers' threats to take their own lives, perhaps as a means of gaining some control in the relationship, also appear as risk indicators for homicide. [B]atterers' suicidal threats, ideation, and plans [are] very significant risk markers. . . .[56] [Campbell et al.'s eleven-city control study found] ". . . there was an increased risk of homicide when the man is suicidal and there has not been any physical abuse."[57]

ALCOHOL AND DRUG USE

It is a widely held belief that excessive alcohol and, to a lesser extent, drug use accompany intimate partner violence. In predicting dangerous and lethal outcomes, these variables figure prominently on nearly all risk assessment forms. Campbell et al. found that women whose partners became "drunk every day or almost every day" were 4.1 times more likely to die than battered women whose partners did not engage in this behavior.[58]

[52]. Carolyn R. Bloch, How Can Practitioners Help an Abused Woman Lower Her Risk of Death?, 250 NIJ J. 4, 5 (2003).

[53]. Campbell et al., Risk Factors for Femicide in Abusive Relationships: Results from a Multisite Case Control Study, 93 Am. J. Pub. Health 1089, 1092 (2003).

[54]. Martin Daly & Margo Wilson, Homicide 202-205 (1988).

[55]. Campbell et al., Assessing Risk Factors, supra note [49], at 16.

[56]. Barbara Hart, Beyond the Duty to Warn: A Therapist's Duty to Protect Battered Women and Children, in Feminist Perspectives on Wife Abuse 234 (Kersti Yllo & Michele Bograd eds., 1988).

[57]. Campbell et al., Assessing Risk Factors, supra note [49], at 16.

[58]. Id. at 17.

UNEMPLOYMENT

Recent research reveals a clear association between unemployment and intimate partner homicide. One group of researchers comments that the "abuser's lack of employment was the only demographic risk factor that significantly predicted femicide risks after we controlled for a comprehensive list of more proximate risk factors, increasing risks 4-fold relative to the case of employed abusers."[59] This statistical research is a fine start, but more research is needed that indicates what being unemployed means to victims, perpetrators, and others.

STEPCHILDREN

[T]he presence of children of other unions [also] constitutes "a major risk marker for violence against wives."[60] Campbell et al. note that "instances in which a child of the victim by a previous partner was living in the home increased the risk of intimate partner homicide." . . . [61]

An important tool for measuring a victim's risk of homicide or severe physical violence in an intimate relationship is the Danger Assessment Instrument. Developed by Professor Jacquelyn Campbell of Johns Hopkins University School of Nursing after consultation with victims and professionals, the test assesses severity and frequency of battering by the use of a calendar to increase recall, raise the consciousness of the victim, and reduce the victim's denial and minimization of the abuse. The test includes a "yes/no" response format of risk factors.

The tool is one of the few evidence-based measures of lethality. As such, its predictive value rests on the fact that it has been scientifically validated. Campbell's multi-city case study of over 600 femicide and attempted femicide cases (cited in note [53]) found that the risk factors are significant predictors of intimate partner homicide.

A fascinating finding of Campbell's research is the inaccuracy of women's own perceptions of the risk of lethality. That is, fewer than half of the women who were eventually killed by their partners accurately perceived their risk of death.[62] The Danger Assessment Instrument is presented below.

■ JACQUELYN C. CAMPBELL, DANGER ASSESSMENT INSTRUMENT

© *Jacquelyn C. Campbell (2003)* **http://www.dangerassessment.org/ WebApplication1/pages/da/DAEnglish2010.pdf**

Several risk factors have been associated with increased risk of homicides (murders) of women and men in violent relationships. We cannot predict what

[59]. Campbell et al., Risk Factors for Femicide, supra note [53], at 1092.
[60]. Wilson & Daly, supra note [54], at 226.
[61]. Campbell et al., Risk Factors for Femicide, supra note [53], at 1092.
[62]. See Jacquelyn C. Campbell et al., The Danger Assessment: Validation of a Lethality Risk Assessment Instrument for Intimate Partner Femicide, 24 J. Interpersonal Violence 653, 669 (2009) (pointing out that slightly more women were able to perceive the risk of near-lethal violence than those who could accurately perceive their risk of death, i.e., 54 percent compared to 45 percent).

will happen in your case, but we would like you to be aware of the danger of homicide in situations of abuse and for you to see how many of the risk factors apply to your situation. Using the calendar, please mark the approximate dates during the past year when you were abused by your partner or ex-partner. Write on that date how bad the incident was according to the following scale:

_____1. Slapping, pushing; no injuries and/or lasting pain
_____2. Punching, kicking; bruises, cuts, and/or continuing pain
_____3. "Beating up"; severe contusions, burns, broken bones
_____4. Threat to use weapon; head injury, internal injury, permanent injury
_____5. Use of weapon; wounds from weapon

(If any of the descriptions for the higher number apply, use the higher number.) Mark Yes or No for each of the following. ("He" refers to your husband, partner, ex-husband, ex-partner, or whoever is currently physically hurting you.)

_____1. Has the physical violence increased in severity or frequency over the past year?
_____2. Does he own a gun?
_____3. Have you left him after living together during the past year?
_____3a. (If have never lived with him, check here_____)
_____4. Is he unemployed?
_____5. Has he ever used a weapon against you or threatened you with a lethal weapon? (If yes, was the weapon a gun?_____)
_____6. Does he threaten to kill you?
_____7. Has he avoided being arrested for domestic violence?
_____8. Do you have a child that is not his?
_____9. Has he ever forced you to have sex when you did not wish to do so?
_____10. Does he ever try to choke you?
_____11. Does he use illegal drugs? By drugs, I mean "uppers" or amphetamines, speed, angel dust, cocaine, "crack," street drugs or mixtures.
_____12. Is he an alcoholic or problem drinker?
_____13. Does he control most or all of your daily activities? For instance: Does he tell you who you can be friends with, when you can see your family, how much money you can use, or when you can take the car? (If he tries, but you do not let him, check here: _____)
_____14. Is he violently and constantly jealous of you? (For instance, does he say "If I can't have you, no one can.")
_____15. Have you ever been beaten by him while you were pregnant? (If you have never been pregnant by him, check here: _____)
_____16. Have you ever threatened or tried to commit suicide?
_____17. Has he ever threatened or tried to commit suicide?
_____18. Does he threaten to harm your children?
_____19. Do you believe he is capable of killing you?
_____20. Does he follow or spy on you, leave threatening notes or messages on answering machine, destroy your property, or call you when you don't want him to?
_____ Total "Yes" Answers

Thank you. Please talk to your nurse, advocate or counselor about what the Danger Assessment means in terms of your situation.[63]

The Danger Assessment tool has been widely adopted by medical personnel and domestic-violence service providers. In addition, many states now require or encourage its use by police, prosecutors, court personnel, and service providers.[64]

Notes and Questions

1. *Definition.* What is lethality assessment? How does it differ from risk assessment? What are the objectives of each form of assessment?

2. *Origins of risk assessment.* The use of risk assessment in legal policy has proliferated in the past few decades. Risk assessment became popular because of several legal developments: (1) the adoption of the "dangerousness to others" criteria for involuntary hospitalization of persons with mental disorders in the 1960s; (2) the imposition of tort liability on clinicians in the 1970s for their failure to predict patients' violence toward third parties; and (3) the mandate of explicit risk assessments of violence during the 1990s pursuant to the Americans with Disabilities Act (ADA). John Monahan, Violence Risk Assessment: Scientific Validity and Evidentiary Admissibility, 57 Wash. & Lee L. Rev. 901, 901-902 (2000).

What developments might have influenced the development of lethality assessment in cases of domestic violence? What academic disciplines were influential in the development of lethality assessment? How did those disciplines influence the field?

3. *Methods of risk assessment.* Two different approaches exist to determine risk assessments of human behavior: (1) subjective predictions of experienced decision-makers (such as mental health or legal professionals); and (2) statistical predictions that rely on measures of various risk factors. John Monahan, A Jurisprudence of Risk Assessment: Forecasting Harm among Prisoners, Predators, and Patients, 92 Va. L. Rev. 391, 405-406 (2007). What are the advantages and disadvantages of each type of risk assessment?

4. *Assumptions.* What assumptions underlie risk assessment generally? Which assumptions underlie risk assessment in the context of domestic violence? See Margaret E. Johnson, Balancing Liberty, Dignity, and Safety: The Impact of Domestic Violence Lethality Screening, 32 Cardozo L. Rev. 519, 522-523 (2010) (identifying underlying assumptions in the context of domestic violence).

5. *Benefits and shortcomings.* What are the benefits of risk assessments? What are the disadvantages of risk assessments?

---

[63]. See Jacquelyn Campbell, Assessing Dangerousness: Violence by Batterers and Child Abusers (2007); Campbell et al., Risk Factors for Femicide, supra note [53], at 1089.

[64]. See generally Amanda Hitt & Lynn McClain, Stop the Killing: Potential Courtroom Use of a Questionnaire that Predicts the Likelihood that a Victim of Intimate Partner Violence Will be Murdered by Her Partner, 24 Wis. J.L. Gender & Soc'y 277 (2009); Margaret E. Johnson, Balancing Liberty, Dignity, and Safety: The Impact of Domestic Violence Lethality Screening, 32 Cardozo L. Rev. 519 (2010).

6. *Professionals.* Who should conduct risk assessments? When should assessments be conducted? How is risk assessment important in safety planning? The delivery of services? What are the legal uses to which risk assessment should be put? The nonlegal uses?

7. *Risk Factors.* The field of risk assessment has identified various factors that predict violence in general. These include: (1) individual factors (that is, violence decreases with age, women commit fewer violent acts than men, African-Americans are more likely than Whites to be arrested for violent crime, and hyperactive and impulsive persons are more likely to commit violent acts); (2) clinical risk factors (that is, the presence of a major mental disorder, personality disorder, and substance abuse disorder); (3) historical risk factors (that is, the existence of a prior criminal history and prior crimes of violence); and (4) experiential risk factors (that is, exposure to a pathological family environment as well as physical abuse in childhood). Monahan, Jurisprudence of Risk Assessment, supra, at 414-427. What factors identify the risk of death from intimate partner violence? How are these factors similar to those that predict the risk of violence generally?

8. *Diagnostic tools.* The field of risk assessment has moved in the direction of statistical measures. Monahan, Violence Risk Assessment, supra, at 910. In the past few years, researchers have developed several violence risk assessment tools (even risk assessment software) and statistical instruments have been developed for special populations (that is, mentally disordered offenders in both prisons and psychiatric facilities). See Monahan, Jurisprudence of Risk Assessment, supra, at 410-413 (describing instruments). What is the diagnostic tool that is used in the context of domestic violence? How was it developed? What does it measure? How does it work?

9. *Accuracy.* Which do you think is more accurate—statistical assessments or decisionmakers' subjective risk assessments? See id., supra, at 408 (explaining that "the general superiority of actuarial assessment . . . has been known for half a century"). Why? How accurate, do you think, are risk assessments and lethality assessments? See Jan Roehl & Kristin Guertin, Intimate Partner Violence: The Current Use of Risk Assessments in Sentencing Offenders, 21 Just. Sys. J. 171, 191 (2000).

In the past two decades, the predictive ability of actuarial instruments has significantly improved. How accurate, according to Professor Campbell, is the predictive ability of the Danger Assessment Instrument?

10. *Groups.* Risk assessment is common in regard to the civil commitment of people with serious mental disorders and the commitment of sexually violent predators. How are these subgroups similar to, and different from, perpetrators of domestic violence? How might these similarities and differences affect the accuracy of predictions of violence for perpetrators of domestic violence?

11. *Admissibility.* Should danger assessments be admissible as scientific evidence generally? See generally Monahan, Violence Risk Assessment, supra, at 910-915. Should risk assessments be admissible in cases of domestic violence? If so, in what legal proceedings? Would character evidence rules preclude the admissibility of evidence of danger assessment? See Roehl & Guertin, supra, at 294. (Character evidence is explored further in Chapter 7.) Would evidence of lethality assessments for abuse victims be admissible under the widely adopted test for the admission of scientific evidence of Daubert v. Merrell Dow Pharmaceuticals, Inc., 509 U.S. 579 (1993)?

E. CONSEQUENCES OF ABUSE

The two excerpts below shed light on the health-related consequences of intimate partner violence for the victim and the ultimate economic cost to society. The impact of children's exposure to abuse is explored in Chapter 12.

■ **CENTERS FOR DISEASE CONTROL AND PREVENTION, COSTS OF INTIMATE PARTNER VIOLENCE AGAINST WOMEN IN THE UNITED STATES**
13-15, 18-21 (2003) available at http://www.cdc.gov/violenceprevention/ pub/IPV_cost.html

[The Centers for Disease Control and Prevention (CDC) conducted a study, based on the National Violence Against Women Survey (NVAWS) of 8,000 women and 8,000 men, to measure both the magnitude of IPV and the resulting economic costs. Data reveal that an estimated 201,394 women are raped; 1.3 million women are physically assaulted, and 503,485 women are stalked by intimate partners annually.]

Injuries Among Victims of Intimate Partner Violence

. . . The NVAWS found that 36.2 percent of the women who were raped by an intimate partner sustained an injury (other than the rape itself) during their most recent victimization, and 41.5 percent of physical assault victims were injured. . . . Of the women injured during their most recent intimate partner rape, 31 percent received some type of medical care, such as ambulance/paramedic services, treatment in a hospital emergency department (ED), or physical therapy. A comparable proportion (28.1 percent) of IPV physical assault victims who were injured received some type of medical care.

More than three-quarters of the rape and physical assault victims who received medical care were treated in a hospital setting (79.6 percent and 78.6 percent, respectively). Among women seeking medical care, 51.3 percent of rape victims and 59.1 percent of physical assault victims were treated in an ED (Emergency Department), while 30.8 percent of rape victims and 24.2 percent of physical assault victims received some other type of outpatient service. Of those who were treated in a hospital, 43.6 percent of rape and 32.6 percent of physical assault victims were admitted and spent one or more nights in the hospital.

National Estimates of Medical Care Service Use

Of the estimated 322,230 intimate partner rapes each year, 116,647 result in injuries (other than the rape itself), 36,161 of which require medical care. And of the nearly 4.5 million physical assault victimizations, more than 1.8 million cause injuries, 519,031 of which require medical care. Nearly 15,000 rape victimizations and more than 240,000 physical assault victimizations result in hospital ED visits.

Multiple medical care visits are often required for each IPV victimization. For example, victims of both rape and physical assault average 1.9 hospital ED visits per victimization, resulting in an estimated 486,151 visits each year to hospital EDs resulting from rape and physical assault victimizations. Consequently, the total number of medical service uses exceeds the total number of victimizations resulting in medical care.

Victims' Use of Mental Health Services

. . . One-third of female rape victims, 26.4 percent of physical assault victims, and 42.6 percent of stalking victims said they talked to a mental health professional, most of them multiple times. Among these women, rape victims averaged 12.4 visits, physical assault victims averaged 12.9 visits, and stalking victims averaged 9.6 visits.

National Estimates of Mental Health Care Service Use

Of the estimated 5.3 million rapes, physical assaults, or stalking incidents by intimate partners each year, nearly 1.5 million result in some type of mental health counseling. The total number of mental health visits by female IPV victims each year is estimated to be more than 18.5 million.

Victims' Lost Productivity

The NVAWS asked IPV victims whether their most recent victimization caused them to lose time from routine activities, including employment, household chores, and childcare. . . . Of adult female IPV victims, 35.3 percent who were stalked, 21.5 percent who were raped, and 17.5 percent who were physically assaulted lost time from paid work. Women stalked by an intimate partner averaged the largest number of days lost from paid work. Women raped by an intimate partner lost an average of 8.1 days from paid work, and victims of IPV physical assault lost 7.2 days on average per victimization.

Among IPV stalking victims, 17.5 percent lost days from household chores; IPV rape and physical assault victims lost 13.5 percent and 10.3 percent respectively. Victims of IPV rape lost the largest average number of days from household chores, followed by stalking and physical assault victims.

According to NVAWS estimates, U.S. women lose nearly 8.0 million days of paid work each year because of violence perpetrated against them by current or former husbands, cohabitants, dates, and boyfriends. This is the equivalent of 32,114 full-time jobs each year. An additional 5.6 million days are lost from household chores. . . .

Summary

Nearly 5.3 million intimate partner victimizations occur among U.S. women ages 18 and older each year. This violence results in nearly 2.0 million injuries and nearly 1,300 deaths. Of the IPV injuries, more than 555,000 require medical attention, and more than 145,000 are serious enough to warrant hospitalization for one or two nights. IPV also results in more than 18.5 million mental health care visits each year. Add to that the 13.6 million days of lost productivity from paid work and household chores among IPV survivors and the value of the IPV murder victims' expected lifetime earnings, and it is clear to see that intimate partner violence against women places a significant burden on society.

■ CENTERS FOR DISEASE CONTROL AND PREVENTION,
    INTIMATE PARTNER VIOLENCE: CONSEQUENCES
    (Oct. 28, 2010) available at http://www.cdc.gov/ViolencePrevention/
    intimatepartnerviolence/consequences.html

I. Cost to Society

Costs of intimate partner violence (IPV) against women in 1995 exceeded an estimated $5.8 billion. These costs included nearly $4.1 billion in the direct costs of medical and mental health care and nearly $1.8 billion in the indirect costs of lost productivity. This is generally considered an underestimate because the costs associated with the criminal justice system were not included. When updated to 2003 dollars, IPV costs exceeded $8.3 billion, which included $460 million for rape, $6.2 billion for physical assault, $461 million for stalking, and $1.2 billion in the value of lost lives. . . .

II. Consequences

In general, victims of repeated violence over time experience more serious consequences than victims of one-time incidents. The following list describes some, but not all, of the consequences of IPV.

A. PHYSICAL

In 2007, intimate partners committed 14 percent of all homicides in the U.S. The total estimated number of intimate partner homicide victims in 2007 was 2,340, including 1,640 females and 700 males. As many as 42 percent of women and 20 percent of men who were physically assaulted since age 18 sustained injuries during their most recent victimization. Most injuries, such as scratches, bruises, and welts, were minor. More severe physical consequences of IPV may occur depending on severity and frequency of abuse. Physical violence by an intimate partner has also been associated with a number of adverse health outcomes. Several health conditions associated with intimate partner violence may be a direct result of the physical violence (for example, bruises, knife wounds, broken bones, back or pelvic pain, headaches).

Studies have also demonstrated the impact of intimate partner violence on the endocrine and immune systems through chronic stress or other mechanisms. Examples include: fibromyalgia, irritable bowel syndrome, gynecological disorders, pregnancy difficulties like low birth weight babies and perinatal deaths, sexually transmitted diseases including HIV/AIDS, central nervous system disorders, gastrointestinal disorders, [and] heart or circulatory conditions. . . .

B. PSYCHOLOGICAL

Physical violence is typically accompanied by emotional or psychological abuse. IPV—whether sexual, physical, or psychological—can lead to various psychological consequences for victims: depression, antisocial behavior, suicidal behavior in females, anxiety, low self-esteem, inability to trust others, especially in intimate relationships, fear of intimacy, symptoms of post-traumatic stress disorder, emotional detachment, sleep disturbances, flashbacks, [and] replaying assault in the mind.

C. SOCIAL

Victims of IPV sometimes face the following social consequences: restricted access to services, strained relationships with health providers and employers, [and] isolation from social networks.

D. HEALTH BEHAVIORS

Women with a history of IPV are more likely to display behaviors that present further health risks (e.g., substance abuse, alcoholism, suicide attempts) than women without a history of IPV. IPV is associated with a variety of negative health behaviors. Studies show that the more severe the violence, the stronger its relationship to negative health behaviors by victims. . . .

See also Ann Coker et al., Physical Health Consequences of Physical and Psychological Intimate Partner Violence, 9 Archive Fam. Med. 451 (May 2000) (addressing physical health consequences); Wendy Max et al., The Economic Toll of Intimate Partner Violence Against Women in the United States, 19 Violence & Victims 259 (2004) (explaining expenditures for medical care and mental health services as well as lost productivity from injury and premature death).

Notes and Questions

1. *Extent of injuries.* What are the health-related consequences of intimate partner violence in terms of physical, psychological, and social factors? What proportion of victims of assault suffers injuries? How severe are their injuries? Why do victims of repeated violence over time experience more serious consequences?

2. *Medical services.* What percentage of victims receives medical care for injuries? In what medical settings do these victims tend to be treated? How frequently do victims experience multiple medical visits for each victimization?

3. *Medical screening.* How can medical screening increase the safety of abuse victims? The federal government is encouraging improved screening of domestic violence by means of guidelines for health insurance reform legislation enacted by Congress in 2010. The Department of Health and Human Services (HHS) recently adopted guidelines for women's preventive health services pursuant to the Patient Protection and Affordable Care Act, Pub. L. No. 111-148, sec. 2713(a), §2733, 124 Stat. 119, 131-132 (2010). These guidelines require health plans to cover domestic violence screening and counseling (as of August 2012) without cost sharing (that is, co-payments or deductibles) from patients. What is the likely impact of these new federal guidelines? Issues regarding medical screening for domestic violence are explored further in Chapter 10.

4. *Mental health services.* How often do victims use mental health services? What type of services? How does the use of mental health services vary by the *type* of abuse? What might explain this fact?

5. *Lost productivity.* What is the meaning of the term *lost productivity*? How does intimate partner violence contribute to lost productivity for victims? What role does the *type* of intimate partner violence play in their loss of productivity? What explains this fact? Why might the rate of lost productivity constitute an underestimate?

6. *Cost to society.* What is the cost of intimate partner violence to society? What are direct costs? Indirect costs? What costs are included in those estimates? What costs are excluded?

III

Influential Factors

Various social factors play an important role in the law's response to domestic violence. This chapter explores a number of these factors, including age, sexual orientation, disability, race, ethnicity, religion, social class, and substance abuse. Moreover, intimate partner violence occurs in many special social contexts—contexts that, in turn, influence the law's response. Some of these contexts (for example, the military, police, and sports) are examined here. As you read the materials that follow, consider the role of each of these factors and contexts in defining the nature of domestic violence as well as the law's response.

A. AGE

Domestic violence affects persons of all ages. Two common forms of intimate partner violence are teen dating violence and elder abuse. How does age matter in terms of the nature of the abuse and the law's response?

1. Teen Dating Violence

■ **NEILSON EX REL. CRUMP v. BLANCHETTE**
201 P.3d 1089 (Wash. Ct. App. 2009)

Jacob Michael Blanchette, a minor, appeals the trial court's domestic violence protection order issued under chapter 26.50 RCW to protect 14-year-old Kendra Diane Crump at the request of her mother, Jamie Crump Neilson. . . . Ms. Crump, whose date of birth is May 29, 1993, and Mr. Blanchette, whose date of birth is August 26, 1990, had a dating relationship. After the relationship ended, Ms. Crump's mother, Ms. Neilson, filed a petition for a domestic violence protection order on Ms. Crump's behalf, pursuant to chapter 26.50 RCW, against Mr. Blanchette. The petition alleged Mr. Blanchette hit Ms. Crump on one occasion, and sexually assaulted her on one occasion. . . . The trial court concluded that Mr. Blanchette and Ms. Crump had a dating relationship and that domestic violence occurred between them. The trial court then entered a domestic violence protection order, effective until April 3, 2010. Among other items, the protection order restrained Mr. Blanchette from attending East Valley High School. . . . At both the time the incidents of domestic violence occurred and the time the protection order was entered, Mr. Blanchette was 17 years old and Ms. Crump was 14 years old. . . .

The dispositive issue is whether the trial court erred in issuing the domestic violence protection order. Mr. Blanchette contends, for the first time on appeal, that the trial court lacked authority to issue the protection order, because he and Ms. Crump did not have a relationship covered by chapter 26.50 RCW. . . .

Under the Domestic Violence Protection Act (the Act), chapter 26.50 RCW, a victim of domestic violence may petition for an order of protection. "Domestic violence" is defined, in relevant part, as "[p]hysical harm, bodily injury, assault, or the infliction of fear of imminent physical harm, bodily injury, or assault, *between family or household members* [or] sexual assault *of one family or household member by another.*" RCW 26.50.010(1)(b)(c) (emphasis added). "Family or household members" are defined, in relevant part, as "persons sixteen years of age or older with whom a person sixteen years of age or older has or has had a dating relationship." RCW 26.50.010(2). . . .

Here, Ms. Neilson, on behalf of Ms. Crump, sought a domestic violence protection order. Mr. Blanchette contends the trial court lacked authority to enter such an order, because there was no "domestic violence" between him and Ms. Crump, as defined by RCW 26.50.010(1) and (2).

RCW 26.50.010(1) and (2) are not ambiguous. Accordingly, the "meaning is to be derived from the plain language of the statute alone." Under RCW 26.50.010(1), domestic violence includes the incidents enumerated therein, "between family or household members" or "of one family or household member by another." Plainly, [however,] the statutory definition of "family or household members" does not apply here, as Ms. Crump was not a "person [ ] sixteen years of age or older with whom a person sixteen years of age or older has or has had a dating relationship." RCW 26.50.010(2). At the time the protection order was entered, Ms. Crump was 14 years old. None of the other definitions of "family or household members" apply. . . . Accordingly, the acts committed by Mr. Blanchette against Ms. Crump were not "domestic violence," because they were not committed "between family or household members" or "of one family or household member by another." The trial court lacked authority to issue the domestic violence protection order.

Ms. Neilson contends the trial court had the authority to issue the protection order, as RCW 26.50.010(1) allowed her to petition for a protection order on behalf of Ms. Crump. . . . The plain language of RCW 26.50.020(1) allows a victim of domestic violence to file a petition for a protection order "on behalf of *minor* family or household members." . . . Because Ms. Crump was 14 years old, pursuant to RCW 4.08.050, Ms. Neilson was required to file the petition for the protection order on her behalf. [Washington Revised Code 26.50.020 (2)] provides an exception to the general rule in RCW 4.08.050, but it does not apply here. See RCW 26.50.020 (2) (providing "[a] person under eighteen years of age who is sixteen years of age or older may seek relief under this chapter and is not required to seek relief by a guardian or next friend."). Even so, the fact that Ms. Neilson filed the petition does not eliminate the requirement of "domestic violence" between Mr. Blanchette and Ms. Crump.

This is not a situation where Ms. Neilson, as a victim of domestic violence herself, petitioned for relief "on behalf of minor family or household members." Rather, Ms. Neilson sought relief for Ms. Crump because she had not yet reached the age where she could file for relief on her own behalf. Here, a showing of "domestic violence" between Mr. Blanchette and Ms. Crump was required. . . . But, under the plain language of RCW 26.50.010(2), such a relationship between Mr. Blanchette and Ms. Crump could not exist. In sum, we cannot modify the Act to encompass the incidents between Mr. Blanchette and Ms. Crump. . . .

Notes and Questions

1. *Background.* The alleged act of dating violence occurred at a party after the end of the relationship between the high school freshman and senior. Kendra alleged that Jacob raped her; he alleged that their sexual encounter was consensual. Following the encounter, he repeatedly harassed and threatened Kendra by means of text messages, phone calls, and Internet posts. Kendra became distraught and was afraid to return to school. In response, her mother petitioned for the order of protection. Telephone Interview with Gerri M. Newell (petitioner's attorney), Wee & Newell PLLC, June 18, 2010.

2. *Social reality.* Recognition of domestic violence as a social problem initially focused on abuse of *adults.* Soon, it became apparent that partner violence affects teenagers as well. Approximately one in four adolescents annually report verbal, physical, emotional, or sexual abuse from a dating partner. Centers for Disease Control and Prevention, Understanding Teen Dating Violence Fact Sheet 1 (2010), available at http://www.cdc.gov/violenceprevention/pdf/TeenDating-Violence_2010-a.pdf. Although both boys and girls are victims, girls inflict minor physical and psychological abuse, whereas boys inflict more severe physical abuse. Judith W. Herrman, There's a Fine Line . . . Adolescent Dating Violence and Prevention, 35 Pediatric Nursing 164, 165 (2009).

Teen dating violence contributes to substance abuse, eating disorders, risky sexual activity, pregnancy, and suicide. See generally Jay G. Silverman et al., Dating Violence Against Adolescent Girls and Associate Substance Use, Unhealthy Weight Control, Sexual Risk Behavior, Pregnancy, and Suicidality, 286 JAMA 572 (2001). In addition, violence in teen dating relationships may develop into adult partner violence. What are the alleged acts of abuse in *Crump*? Are those forms of abuse covered by the Washington statute?

3. *Statutory remedy: order of protection.* Kendra's mother seeks an *order of protection* against her daughter's abuser. If you were a parent of a victim, what factors would influence you to file for a protective order for your child? What other remedies might you seek?

a. *Meaning of order of protection.* What is an order of protection, and how does it work? An order of protection (sometimes called "a restraining order") is a legal document, sought by a victim and awarded by a judge, which is intended to prevent abusive behavior. Orders of protection can be emergency, temporary, or permanent. Which was the order of protection requested by the mother in *Crump*?

b. *Conditions on contact.* The protection order specifies the ways in which the abuser must refrain from contacting the victim. For example, a protection order can require an abuser (1) to stay away from the victim, as well as the victim's home, school, or place of employment (sometimes, even specifying the distance in yards); (2) to refrain from making any contact with the victim or members of her household/family by mail, phone, electronic means, or even via third parties, and (3) to surrender any firearm. An order of protection can also require an abuser to move out of the home; award child custody, visitation, and child support; and require the batterer's participation in a batterer's intervention or substance abuse treatment program.

What conditions on contact would you advise Kendra's mother to request? Do such conditions differ for teenage and adult victims? Should they? What conditions did the trial court order? What difficulties might such orders entail for the petitioner and respondent, respectively? How might these difficulties differ for youth compared to adults?

"Textual harassment" has become an important feature of dating violence. Such harassment includes demands by the abuser—by cell phone or text messaging—that partners "check in" multiple times per day to say where they are and with whom. See, e.g., Donna St. George, Text Messages Become a Growing Weapon in Dating Violence, Wash. Post, June 21, 2010, available at http://www.washingtonpost.com/wp-dyn/content/article/2010/06/20/AR2010062003331.html. Can an order of protection address this type of harassment?

c. *Temporary versus permanent orders of protection.* Three different types of restraining orders exist: emergency orders, temporary restraining orders, and permanent orders. The criteria for each differ.

Emergency protective orders are issued through the police upon exigent circumstances. These orders have an immediate-danger standard, and last a short period (perhaps only days). A *temporary* restraining order requires reasonable proof of past acts of violence (based on state law) and lasts a somewhat longer period (perhaps weeks). A *permanent* order requires a preponderance standard of proof of past acts of violence (based on state law) and can be issued for a longer period (perhaps years, although it is not really "permanent"). Emergency and temporary orders are generally ex parte. The risk-of-immediate-harm standard overcomes the respondent's due process rights in the ex parte proceeding. On the other hand, a permanent order requires constitutional safeguards of notice and an opportunity to be heard (i.e., an adversary proceeding).

Depending on the jurisdiction, a hearing for an order of protection may take place in family court or criminal court. Often family and criminal courts share concurrent jurisdiction, thereby enabling a victim to bring a civil action for an order of protection in family court but simultaneously pursue a criminal complaint in criminal court. Proof of abuse consists of written or oral statements, testimony by the victim and witnesses, police reports, school reports, and medical records (including photos of the victim's injuries or damage). After the judge issues a temporary or permanent order of protection, any violation of that order by the abuser (such as an attempt to contact the victim) may result in the arrest of the perpetrator. Orders of protection are explored more fully in Chapter 9.

d. *Representation*. At the initial hearing, Kendra and her mother are represented by counsel. Jacob appears pro se. Both petitioners and respondents in protection proceedings have the right to counsel. Should courts routinely provide counsel to teenagers in such proceedings? In the vast majority of civil matters, there are no attorneys on either side. However, are special procedural safeguards necessary in the context of teen dating violence?

4. *Disclosure of teen dating violence*. Kendra disclosed the abuse to her mother. Yet, many teens hide dating violence. What explains the secrecy? Signs of teen dating violence include extreme jealousy; controlling behavior; rapid involvement in the relationship; unpredictable mood swings; alcohol and drug use; explosive anger; threats of violence; verbal abuse; use of force during arguments; attempts at isolation from friends and family; hypersensitivity; belief in rigid sex roles; blame of others for problems or feelings; cruelty to animals or children; and abuse of former partners. See Alabama Coalition Against Domestic Violence, Dating Violence, available at http://www.acadv.org/dating.html (last visited June 26, 2011). What should a parent do if she or he recognizes these signs? How does a parent tell the difference between the signs of dating violence and the volatile behavior that characterizes adolescence?

5. *Parental consent*. A minor has direct access to the court in some contexts, such as abortion decisionmaking. Can abused minors, on their own behalf, petition for an order of protection? Could Kendra? See generally Pamela Saperstein, Note, Teen Dating Violence: Eliminating Statutory Barriers to Civil Protection Orders, 39 Fam. L.Q. 181 (2005) (criticizing those statutes that require an adult to petition on the minor's behalf). Should the same procedures apply for minors in the teen dating violence and abortion decisionmaking contexts? What procedures should apply if a child needs a protection order against a parent? Should the child be required to obtain the consent of the other parent? See Allie Meiers, Comment, Civil Orders of Protection: A Tool to Keep Children Safe, 19 J. Am. Acad. Matrim. Law. 373 (2005).

6. *Professional responsibility issues*. Kendra's mother seeks the order of protection against her daughter's abuser. In such a case, who is the client? Kendra? Her mother? Her mother, on Kendra's behalf? Both? Does this situation pose a conflict of interest because the parties' interests might diverge? For example, suppose the mother wants the order, but Kendra is too embarrassed to pursue the legal action or wants to vacate the order. Does the attorney have a duty to seek Kendra's wishes, in confidence from the mother? Is the attorney able to discuss the case with Kendra's mother and seek the protective order against Kendra's wishes? Does it matter if the parent is paying the bill?

7. *Statutory application*.

a. *Age of victim*. How does the Washington statute define persons who are eligible to petition for temporary orders of protection? Why do you think legislators chose that age? Why wasn't Kendra covered?

At what age should statutory protection extend to teens? Does it alter your view to learn that "surprising, significant levels of abusive behavior" in dating relationships involve youth aged 11 to 14 and aged 15 to 18? See Tween/Teen Dating Relationships Survey 2008, available at http://www.ncdsv.org/images/

LoveIsNotAbuse_TweenTeenDatingRelSurvey_Summ_2008.pdf (last visited June 21, 2011). See also Christine N. Carlson, Invisible Victims: Holding the Educational System Liable for Teen Dating Violence at School, 26 Harv. Women's L.J. 351, 366 (2003) (advocating a lower age of protection); Herrman, supra, at 165 (reporting data on dating violence that occurs among middle school students). Based on the above research, what ages should be covered?

Respondent's attorney in *Crump* supports higher age thresholds. "There are sound policy reasons for age thresholds in these statutes. Very young teenagers in that stage of life, when going through conflicts, often fabricate accounts. They're unaware of the tremendous impact that such accounts can have on others' lives." Telephone Interview with Aaron Rasmussen, Rasmussen Law Offices PLLC, June 18, 2010. How should a legislature balance these interests?

b. "*Same household.*" Some domestic violence statutes address victims who are members of the offender's "family or household." What explains this limitation? How does it provide unique problems for teen victims, such as Kendra?

c. *Definition of "dating relationship."* What is the meaning of "dating relationship"? In many jurisdictions, the term is not specifically defined. The Washington statute in *Crump* provides:

> "Dating relationship" means a social relationship of a romantic nature. Factors that the court may consider in making this determination include: (a) The length of time the relationship has existed; (b) the nature of the relationship; and (c) the frequency of interaction between the parties.

Wash. Rev. Code §26.50.010(3). What does "a social relationship of a romantic nature" mean? What problems might occur in applying the term to teenagers? To younger teens? What factors affect a teen's definition of a "date"? See, e.g., J.S. v. J.F., 983 A.2d 1151, 1153 (N.J. Super. Ct. App. Div. 2009) ("'Dating' is a loose concept undoubtedly defined differently by members of different socioeconomic groups and from one generation to the next"). How relevant should be the manner in which the parties, themselves, define the relationship—that is, whether they label their conduct as "dating"?

8. *Remedies.* Was Kendra left without any remedy? What alternative remedies might have been available to her?

9. *Attitudes.* Certain attitudes contribute to the acceptability of teen dating violence. For example, some teenagers cannot differentiate abuse from caring, have traditional views of gender roles, and believe that sexual betrayal or disclosure of sensitive information justifies abuse. Herrman, supra, at 164. Can such attitudes be changed? See generally Corinne M. Graffunder, et al., Through a Public Health Lens: Preventing Violence Against Women: An Update from the U.S. Centers for Disease Control and Prevention (2004) [hereinafter CDC Update], available at http://www.vawnet.org/Assoc_Files_VAWnet/CDC-PublicHealth.pdf (discussing media campaign to change attitudes).

10. *Other community-based responses.* How can professionals (health care personnel, educators) better address teen dating violence? What can family members and friends do? See Tiffany J. Zwicker, Note, Education Policy Brief: The Imperative of Developing Teen Dating Violence Prevention and Intervention Programs in Secondary Schools, 12 S. Cal. Rev. L. & Women's Stud. 131 (2002); ABA, Teen Dating Violence

Prevention Recommendations (2006), available at http://www.americanbar.org/content/dam/aba/migrated/unmet/teenabuseguide.authcheckdam.pdf.

11. *Teen abuse in gang settings.* Girls who are partners of youth gang members experience a unique form of partner violence. "In the gang world 'the most desirable position is to be the steady girlfriend or wife' of a gang member." Videtta A. Brown, Gang Member Perpetrated Domestic Violence: A New Conversation, 7 U. Md. L.J. Race, Religion, Gender & Class 395, 404 (2007). Girls may be physically and sexually abused whether they are partners of gang members or members themselves. Id. at 405. Abuse occurs when the girls join or leave a gang or are elevated in rank. Id. at 405-406. Further, for the male partners, violence toward women is part of gang culture. Id. at 408. If a girlfriend of a gang member wants to end her intimate relationship, she is faced "with the increased danger of deadly violence because she may be privy to gang secrets." Id. at 408. How can legal and social services address these problems?

12. *Epilogue.* In the principal case, the trial court ruling required Jacob to transfer to another school. His attorney later successfully petitioned to modify the protective order to enable Jacob to return to Kendra's high school to complete one course that he needed for graduation. Upon his return to school, Kendra withdrew. She re-enrolled after he graduated. Telephone Interviews with Newell, supra, and Rasmussen, supra. Does the school have a duty to take action to keep Kendra safe? Does the school's duty differ if the setting is a high school or college/university? The topic of acquaintance rape on college campus is explored in Chapter 10.

The following excerpt examines the differences between teen and adult intimate partner violence, as well as the implications of these differences for prevention and treatment.

■ CARRIE MULFORD & PEGGY C. GIORDANO, TEEN DATING VIOLENCE: A CLOSER LOOK AT ADOLESCENT ROMANTIC RELATIONSHIPS

261 NIJ Journal (Oct. 2008), available at **http://www.ojp.usdoj.gov/nij/journals/261/teen-dating-violence.htm**

How Teen Dating Violence Differs: Equal Power

One difference between adolescent and adult relationships is the absence of elements traditionally associated with greater male power in adult relationships. Adolescent girls are not typically dependent on romantic partners for financial stability, and they are less likely to have children to provide for and protect. [In contrast, a majority of seventh, ninth and eleventh graders] said they had a relatively "equal say" in their romantic relationships. In cases in which there was a power imbalance, they were more likely to say that the female had more power in the relationship. Overall, the study found that the boys perceived that they had less power in the relationship than the girls did. . . .

Lack of Relationship Experience

A second key factor that distinguishes violence in adult relationships from violence in adolescent relationships is the lack of experience teens have in negotiating romantic relationships. Inexperience in communicating and relating to a romantic partner may lead to the use of poor coping strategies, including verbal and physical aggression. A teen who has difficulty expressing himself or herself may turn to aggressive behaviors (sometimes in play) to show affection, frustration or jealousy. . . .

As adolescents develop into young adults, they become more realistic and less idealistic about romantic relationships. They have a greater capacity for closeness and intimacy. Holding idealistic beliefs about romantic relationships can lead to disillusionment and ineffective coping mechanisms when conflict emerges. . . .

The Influence of Peers

[Peer attitudes and behaviors are critical influences on teens' attitudes relating to dating violence.] Not only are friends more influential in adolescence than in adulthood, but they are also more likely to be "on the scene" and a key element in a couple's social life. In fact, roughly half of adolescent dating violence occurs when a third party is present. Relationship dynamics often play out in a very public way because teens spend a large portion of their time in school and in groups. For various reasons, a boyfriend or girlfriend may act very differently when in the presence of peers, a behavior viewed by adolescents as characteristic of an unhealthy relationship. For example, boys in one focus group study said that if a girl hit them in front of their friends, they would need to hit her back to "save face." . . .

Problems

1. Mother files a petition for an order of protection for her daughter Cassandra, a high school junior. She alleges that a schoolmate, Matt, drove Cassandra and one of her friends to his parents' home for a party. Later, Cassandra wanted to leave. Matt refused to drive her home and refused to let her call her parents. Cassandra was so tired that she fell asleep on the living room couch. She was awakened by Matt who, allegedly, sexually assaulted her. She immediately sought treatment at the hospital. A month later, Cassandra's mother seeks an order of protection because Cassandra is afraid to return to school.

The court issued a temporary ex parte order. At the hearing for a permanent order, the court focuses on whether Cassandra and Matt had a "dating relationship." The statute defines "dating relationship" as a "social relationship of a romantic nature." It sets forth the following factors to consider in the determination: (1) the nature of the relationship, (2) its length, (3) frequency of interaction between the parties; and (4) length of time since the relationship was terminated, if applicable. At the hearing, Cassandra testifies that she has known Matt for about two or three years. She alleges that she "dated" Matt when she went with him during freshman year to a party, and during sophomore year when she watched a movie at his house. Since then, they have "talked on the phone and we have talked in school." Matt's father testifies that Matt had another "serious" 18-month "dating relationship" with another girl during the same time frame. The new girlfriend came to the house, according to the father, "at least once a day." Does a "dating relationship" exist between Cassandra and Matt that entitles her to the order of protection? See Wright v. Bradley, 910 A.2d 893 (Vt. 2006).

2. The day after her sixteenth birthday, Demi Cuccia, a Gateway High School cheerleader in Pittsburgh, Pennsylvania, is stabbed 16 times by her boyfriend, John Mullarkey. John, who just graduated from their high school, was feeling depressed when he came to see Demi to talk about their relationship. She was trying to break up with him. In the previous two days, John sent Demi countless desperate text messages, including threats to harm her. At Demi's house, they exchanged angry words. Then, John stabbed Demi in the chest and shoulder with a 3.5-inch pocket knife. Demi staggered out of the house and into the arms of a neighbor. She died about 45 minutes later.

Demi's friends reported that the relationship had been volatile. "He was very jealous of her. She wasn't allowed to do anything," said one friend. "He always yelled at her and told her that he didn't want her to have friends at all." Still another friend said, "He was always threatening he was going to hurt her." John is charged with first-degree murder. At trial, his attorney contends that the homicide was a crime of passion that was aggravated by depression resulting from John's cessation of the acne drug Accutane. Specifically, the attorney argues that John's conduct should be excused because the prescription medication interfered with the development of the requisite intent to kill. What should the jury decide? See Jim McKinnon, Ex-Boyfriend to be Tried in Gateway Student's Death, Pittsburgh Post-Gazette, Sept. 15, 2007, at B1, available at http: //www.post-gazette.com/pg/07258/817747-56.stm

2. Elder Abuse

■ GDOWSKI v. GDOWSKI
95 Cal. Rptr. 3d 799 (Ct. App. 2009)

FYBEL, J.

. . . On June 12, 2008, 83-year-old Michael filed a request for a protective order against his adult daughter, 56-year-old Diana, pursuant to Welfare and Institutions Code section 15657.03. In a declaration attached to his request, Michael claimed Diana had physically and emotionally abused him, and had caused caregivers for 88-year-old Frances Gdowski, Michael's wife and Diana's mother, to quit. Specifically, Michael claimed Diana had punched him on six occasions between October 2007 and February 2008. Michael also stated that Diana had yelled at him several times during March 2008, causing Frances to cry. Michael and his other daughter, Sandra Schulz, disagreed with Diana regarding Frances's medical care. Michael declared that Frances's caregiver had quit because Diana's harassment and threats were causing the caregiver too much stress. (Michael also made numerous hearsay statements about Diana's threats to kidnap Frances and take her to Italy, her desire that Michael and Schulz were dead, and references to her lawyer's friends in the Mafia.) Based on Michael's declaration, a temporary restraining order was issued against Diana on that same day, without notice or a hearing. . . .

An evidentiary hearing was conducted [at which] Michael and Diana testified. Michael admitted he had filed a petition to be appointed conservator for Frances. He was seeking a protective order against Diana because of "[t]hreat of bodily harm, and threats of kidnapping. And stabilizes [sic] the family." Michael testified Diana had struck his back with her fists in February or March 2008. Michael said this was the first time Diana had hit him, and it occurred "spontaneously" and not in response to an argument. Michael and Diana were always having disagreements, during which Diana would get excited and scream at him; Michael claimed his hearing problems were the result of Diana screaming "right up close to my ear." Michael also testified Diana created confusion and disrupted the order of the household. A full-time caregiver provided care for Frances. Michael testified two caregivers had quit, although no testimony was offered for the reasons they left. Michael felt Diana posed a threat to the health and safety of himself, Frances, and other members of his family.

On cross-examination, Michael admitted he reported the February or March 2008 incident of physical abuse only after he had filed a petition in the probate court to be appointed Frances's conservator. Michael also testified on cross-examination that, although he had only identified one incident of physical abuse on direct examination, there were actually multiple incidents; Michael did not provide any testimony as to the nature or timing of those other incidents.

Diana testified she had never struck Michael, and they had never had "heated" arguments. Diana claimed she and her father agreed about everything other than his investments and the care to be provided for Frances. Diana had concerns about Frances's welfare, objected to Michael's conservatorship petition [of her mother], and filed her own petition asking that a professional conservator be appointed. Before the temporary restraining order was issued, Diana had almost daily contact with Frances, and made her dinner every night. Diana denied ever threatening Michael or suggesting to anyone she would harm him. Diana testified that when she expressed her belief that the money Michael was investing should be used to provide care for Frances, Michael replied, "he didn't have a wife anymore," and Frances "was not worth spending any money on." Diana believed Michael's investments were very risky because too much of his and Frances's portfolio was tied up in oil, gas, and gold, and because he traded on margin. Diana testified Frances's former caregiver quit because caring for Frances was too physically demanding, and the caregiver "was not happy about the situation there." Diana claimed that Michael's hearing loss was due to his age, diet, and circulatory problems, not to her yelling at him.

After the parties completed their testimony, the trial court made the following ruling:

[*The Court*]: What I have here, is simply a rather close call. It's one person's word against the other. The court has observed carefully the demeanor of this process. Frankly, the court is affected by the manner in which [Michael] was examined, and that [Diana] allowed that to happen.

[*To Diana's Counsel*]: I assume that your rather aggressive and confrontational cross-examination of [Michael] was consistent with your client's desire to treat her father in such a fashion.

[*Diana's counsel*]: That is an unfair characterization.

[*The Court*]: I'm speaking, counsel. I'm the one that sat and watched you beat up on this fellow. And speak to him in such a way. There is a problem here. It's an elderly man that is having difficulty. His wife is disabled, and in need of a conservatorship. He has concern about her. He has come to this court to ask for relief. What he has got in response is an allegation that he is a bad person, and in some fashion that he is out for some evil motive and that he does not have the best interest of his wife.

[*The Court continues*]: The examination of him I think was abusive to him. We're in a court of families that go through these difficult times. And they need to be treated with respect. And I compared that to how [Michael's counsel] cross-examined [Diana]. With respect, without raising his voice, without being confrontational. This is a family in trouble. It's not a war we're fighting . . . in this courtroom. This is a family. *The court observed that happening and your client didn't tap you on the shoulder and say to you "this is my father you are speaking to." That was the straw that made the difference in tipping the scale as to whether or not [Michael] has been treated in an abusive way.*

[*The Court continues*]: . . . The Elder [Abuse] statute provides that causing emotional distress or mental suffering to an elder person is elder abuse. So it's not the same as domestic violence, where you have to hit, where you have to commit something equivalent to a crime in order to have a restraining order issued. We treat our elderly with respect. We don't yell at them, we don't treat them rudely, we don't tell them I have a right to come in your house whether or not you want me here or not. They have rights.

So it's a very close call. I can only judge it on a preponderance of the evidence. Has [Michael] been yelled at, treated rudely, to the point that would cause him emotional [di]stress or mental suffering? Pursuant to the elder abuse statutes, the court believes that he has.

I don't have an opinion as to whether he's been hit or how many times he might have been hit. I'm not making a finding on that. But I'm quite sure that he's been treated in an abusive fashion on an emotional level.

And on that basis the court will grant the order that [Diana] will not contact, molest, attack, strike, threaten or assault or otherwise disturb the peace of [Michael]. She is to stay 100 yards away from his place of residence and . . . his automobile. (Italics added by the appellate court.)

[The court issued the protective order. Diana appealed.] Diana argues the trial court erred in issuing the protective order because there was no threat of ongoing abuse. . . .

[T]he relevant language regarding issuance of a protective order under the Elder Abuse Act reads as follows: "An order may be issued under this section, with or without notice, to restrain any person for the purpose of preventing a recurrence of abuse, if an affidavit *shows, to the satisfaction of the court, reasonable proof of a past act or acts of abuse of the petitioning elder or dependent adult.*" (Welf. & Inst. Code, §15657.03, subd. (c), italics added.) The legislation enacting Welfare and Institutions Code section 15657.03, and thus creating the right to seek a protective order to prevent elder abuse, was intended to "set forth procedures under which an elder or dependent adult in immediate and present danger of abuse may seek protective orders." . . .

Family Code section 6300, part of the Domestic Violence Prevention Act (Fam. Code, §6200 et seq.) (DVPA), uses language which is almost identical to that in Welfare and Institutions Code section 15657.03. . . . Both Family Code section 6300 and Welfare and Institutions Code section 15657.03 require a showing of past abuse, not a threat of future harm. Family Code section 6300 has been interpreted to permit a trial court "to issue a protective order under the DVPA simply on the basis of an affidavit showing past abuse." The DVPA and the Elder Abuse Act therefore permit issuance of protective orders on a different, broader basis than permitted under Code of Civil Procedure sections 527.6 and 527.8 [that requires that great or irreparable harm would result without issuance of the prohibitory injunction]. Additionally, a lower level of proof is required for issuance of a protective order under the DVPA and the Elder Abuse Act—a preponderance of the evidence, rather than clear and convincing evidence.

We hold that a protective order under the Elder Abuse Act may issue on the basis of evidence of past abuse, without any particularized showing that the wrongful acts will be continued or repeated. This holding is consistent with the language, legislative intent, and history of the Elder Abuse Act in general.

Diana [next] argues the trial court abused its discretion in issuing the protective order because its findings were not based on substantial evidence. She argues the trial court instead based its findings on her counsel's behavior, and her alleged failure to control that behavior. Diana's argument has merit. . . .

Because Diana was represented by counsel, she was not able to appear in her own behalf in court, or control the court proceedings. . . . The manner in which cross-examination will be conducted is another matter of trial strategy which is within the control of counsel. Additionally, because the attorney-client relationship is a fiduciary one, the client properly cedes to his or her counsel the right to act in a manner that will protect the client's best interests. To require a client to correct his or her counsel's behavior during the examination of a witness in order to avoid inferences as to the client's prior actions outside the courtroom would go against all these accepted principles of the attorney-client relationship. . . . Therefore, Diana's counsel's questions of Michael could not have been evidence on which the trial court could rely. . . . [T]he court's decision was demonstrably based on an impermissible reason, namely, the manner of Diana's counsel's cross-examination and Diana's failure to intervene. [Therefore] [t]he order is reversed. . . .

Notes and Questions

1. *Social reality.* Some elderly persons are mistreated, neglected, or exploited by a person on whom they depend for care. See Nat'l Research Council, Elder Mistreatment: Abuse, Neglect, and Exploitation in an Aging America xiii (2003) (estimating 1 to 2 million persons age 65 and older are abused). Many cases are not reported. See Dept. of Health & Human Servs., Nat'l Ctr. on Elder Abuse, National Elder Abuse Incidence Study (NEAIS), Executive Summary 4 (1998) (only 20 percent are reported). Women and the *most* senior elders (80 years and older) are the most likely victims. Id. at 1. Abusers are spouses in one-fifth of the cases, and adult children in about half of the cases. Id. at 4-28. See also Derrick Thomas, Note, Chapter 152: Abusers Beware: Legislators Up Penalty for Violating a Protective or Stay-Away Order Involving Elder or Dependent Adults, 40 McGeorge L. Rev. 503, 505-506 (2009) (citing data). Most elder abuse consists of physical abuse (62 percent), followed by abandonment (56 percent), psychological abuse (54 percent), financial abuse (45 percent), and neglect (41 percent). NEAIS, supra, at 5. What explains the gendered findings? How does the familial nature of the abuse explain the lack of reporting? What factors place an elderly person

at risk? See Nat'l Research Council, Elder Mistreatment, supra, at 91. What characteristics of elder abuse apply to Michael Gdowski? How did his alleged abuse come to light?

2. *Identifying elder abuse.* Problems arise in identifying elder abuse. For example, how does one differentiate normal bruises? Treatment sores? Medication sensitivity? See Nat'l Inst. of Justice, Identifying Elder Abuse (2009), available at http://www.nij.gov/topics/crime/elder-abuse/identifying.htm (noting bruises are more common among abused versus nonabused elderly adults). What types of abuse and/or neglect were alleged in *Gdowski?* Whose version of events is most convincing? Why?

3. *Case holding.* What is the standard of proof for issuance of a protective order, according to Diana? What difference does it make if there was "ongoing" or "past" abuse? How did the appellate court respond? Do the standards in the Elder Abuse and Domestic Violence Prevention acts differ from that of the Code of Civil Procedure for injunctions? Should they?

Note that the appellate judge appears to be mistaken about the domestic violence standard applicable to the issuance of protection orders for elder abuse. The judge implies that the elder abuse statute (Welf. & Inst. Code §15657.03(c)) contains a lower standard for issuance of a restraining order, permitting a protective order for "causing emotional distress or mental suffering," whereas the Domestic Violence Protection Act (Cal. Fam. Code §6203) requires physical abuse ("you have to hit") or a criminal act ("commit something equivalent to a crime") as the basis for a restraining order. But cf. Cal. Fam. Code §6203 (defining abuse as causing or attempting to cause bodily injury; placing a person in reasonable apprehension of imminent serious bodily injury; and engaging in the same nonviolent abusive behavior that is specified by Welf. & Inst. Code §15657.03(c)).

Why did the appellate court reverse the issuance of the protective order? What explains the respondent's attorney's trial strategy? Why did it backfire?

4. *Conditions of contact.* Michael Gdowski sought a protective order against his daughter. What are the different types of protective orders in *Gdowski?* What were the conditions on contact requested by the petitioner? What types of conditions did the trial court issue? For additional discussion of restraining orders, see Chapter 9.

5. *Protection orders for elders.* How might age and infirmity affect elders' access to protection orders? Should courts make special procedures available in such cases? For example, should telephonic appearances by elders be allowed? Should hearings be held in elders' homes? How might such accommodations affect the constitutional rights of the responding party?

6. *Financial abuse and exploitation.* Financial abuse of elders is probably more common than physical abuse. See Melissa Repko, Risks of Elderly Financial Abuse Increase, Buff. News, Oct. 10, 2010, at D1 (noting 60 percent of Adult Protective Services cases involve financial abuse). What explains this? Financial abuse of intimate partners is explored in Chapter 4.

a. *Traditional versus modern approach.* Guardianships and/or conservatorships are the traditional approach to adult protective services. In contrast, the modern approach criminalizes financial exploitation involving elderly or dependent adults, or enhances sentences based on victims' age or vulnerability. Carolyn L. Dessin, Should Attorneys Have a Duty to Report Financial Abuse of the Elderly?, 38 Akron L.

Rev. 707, 708 (2005). Which persons are in a position to identify financial abuse? See Repko, supra (naming health care providers, bank officials, religious officials, neighbors, and mail carriers).

b. *Criticisms.* Although most state statutes target "misuse" or "misappropriation" of assets, financial abuse of vulnerable adults often takes more subtle forms, such as persuasion to transfer title to an asset or to create a testamentary instrument. Such acts easily could be construed as gifts. See Carolyn L. Dessin, Financial Abuse of the Elderly: Is the Solution a Problem?, 34 McGeorge L. Rev. 267, 269 (2003). How can this form of abuse be addressed? See id. at 274-275; Joseph A. Rosenberg, Regrettably Unfair: Brooke Astor and the Other Elderly in New York, 30 Pace L. Rev. 1004, 1026 (2010) (discussing statutory definitions).

7. *Stereotypes of the elderly.* "Ageism" is prejudice or discrimination against the elderly. Stereotypes of the elderly include senility, rigidity in thought and manner, and being old-fashioned. Linda S. Whitton, Ageism: Paternalism and Prejudice, 46 DePaul L. Rev. 453, 456 (1997). Other stereotypes are "golden-agers," "work horses put to pasture," "Gray Panthers" (aggressive, self-interested), "cranky despots," "repositories of wisdom and experience," and "parasites feeding at the public trough" (collectors of Social Security). Alvin M. Laster, Debunking Stereotypes on the Elderly, N.Y. Times, Nov. 13, 1988, at 36. Ageist attitudes reflect envy for elders' affluence as well as resentment for their being burdens. Whitton, supra, at 457. Which stereotypes of the elderly are reflected in *Gdowski*? See generally John Macnicol, Age Discrimination: An Historical and Contemporary Analysis (2006).

8. *Federal versus state responses.*

a. *Federal law.* Federal legislation on elder abuse was first proposed in 1981. See Prevention, Identification, and Treatment of Elder Abuse Act, H.R. 769, 97th Cong. (1st Sess. 1981) (modeled after the Child Abuse Prevention and Treatment Act of 1974). Thirty years later, Congress finally enacted legislation as part of recent health care reform. See Elder Justice Act and the Patient Safety and Abuse Prevention Act, Pub. L. No. 111-148 §§6701-6703, 124 Stat. 119, 782-804 (2010). The Act (1) provides federal funding for adult protective services for the prevention, detection, assessment, and treatment of, and intervention in, elder abuse; (2) encourages coordination of federal, state, and local authorities; (3) authorizes grants to demonstration projects, forensic centers, and training for long-term care providers; (4) targets volunteer and compensated caregivers (including family members who provide compensated or uncompensated support services); and (5) mandates creation of a federal office of elder abuse, as well as Centers of Excellence to specialize in research, clinical practice, and training. What explains the delay in the federal response? See James H. Pietsch, Who's Afraid of Protecting Older Persons?—Addressing the False Illusion of Having to Keep "Elder" Out of Elder Abuse Laws, 16 Geo. J. on Poverty L. & Pol'y 391 (2009).

Critics contend that the Elder Justice Act does not go far enough because it fails to reform the criminal justice system. The ABA advocates the Elder Abuse Victims Act, S. 462, 112th Cong. (2011), that would authorize funding for prosecutorial training and research programs to enhance the ability to investigate and prosecute abuse. See Rhonda McMillion, Fending for the Elderly; ABA Sees Elder Justice Act as Partial Solution, 97 A.B.A. J. 57 (May 2011). What do you think of this criticism?

b. *State laws.* All states have civil and criminal laws addressing the physical maltreatment of the elderly. Recent innovations include protective orders specifically targeting abuse of elderly or dependent adults, special prosecution units, elder fatality review teams, and mandatory reporting. However, statutory definitions of both abuse and victims vary considerably. Some jurisdictions protect elderly persons generally; some also protect vulnerable persons; some jurisdictions protect only disabled elders. Some jurisdictions address only physical, but not financial, abuse. Finally, some statutes target only caregivers with an affirmative duty. Arthur Meirson, Note, Prosecuting Elder Abuse: Setting the Gold Standard in the Golden State, 60 Hastings L.J. 431, 439-440 (2008). Are these restrictions well tailored to the problem?

9. *Mandatory reporting.* Most elderly victims, unlike Michael Gdowski, rarely seek assistance. Nat'l Research Council, Elder Mistreatment, supra, at 88. Their reluctance stems from "shame, stoicism, recalcitrance, [and] diminished mental faculties" and their dependence on abusers. Meirson, supra, at 432. See also Georgia Akers, Elder Abuse and Exploitation: The Ethical Duty of the Attorney, 47 Houston Law. 10, 13 (July/August 2009) (citing the "fear of being institutionalized"). Because of this reluctance, detection depends on effective screening. Who would be the most likely to report elder abuse? See NEAIS, supra, at 5 (noting family members, hospitals, police, in-home service providers, friends/neighbors, and medical personnel).

Although all states mandate reporting of elder mistreatment, laws vary considerably. Some states limit the duty to specific professionals (for example, health care professionals), whereas other states provide that anyone can report. States impose different consequences for failure to report (that is, civil versus criminal liability, loss of professional licenses). And, different factors (that is, age, disability, vulnerability) trigger a report. A few states include "self-neglect" as a factor. Finally, some states provide exceptions if reporting is not in the victim's best interests. Nina A. Kohn, Outliving Civil Rights, 86 Wash. U. L. Rev. 1053, 1059-1065 (2009). How effective are these statutes? Do professionals comply? See Seymour Moskovitz, Golden Age in the Golden State; Contemporary Legal Developments in Elder Abuse and Neglect, 36 Loy. L.A. L. Rev. 589, 611 (2003) (suggesting statutes often are ignored). How can these laws be improved? See Akers, supra (suggesting methods to improve attorneys' duty). Who should be mandatory reporters? See Charles Pratt, Comment, Banks' Effectiveness at Reporting Financial Abuse of Elders, 40 Cal. W. L. Rev. 195, 202 (2003) (suggesting the inclusion of bank employees).

Critics point out that mandatory reporting laws discourage vulnerable elders and their caregivers from seeking medical attention, increase health care providers' investigatory obligations, impede providers' ability to meet the needs of their elderly clients, and undermine the autonomy of elderly adults. Kohn, supra, at 1065-1067. Do you agree with these criticisms? Should states abolish such laws? Note that all states have laws that require reporting of institutional abuse at residential facilities (such as nursing homes). See id. at 1059.

10. *Child abuse analogy.* Elder abuse laws were modeled on child abuse laws based on the rationale that some professionals are in a position to identify at-risk groups. Is this a persuasive comparison? Or, should statutory treatment differ because the elderly are more socially isolated and more deserving of respect and

autonomy? See generally Joseph W. Barber, Note, The Kids Aren't All Right: The Failure of Child Abuse Statutes as a Model for Elder Abuse Statutes, 16 Elder L.J. 107, 120-126 (2008).

Problems

1. Some caretakers and financial advisers persuade their clients to enter into sham marriages in order to exploit the elders financially. A possible remedy is a "marital capacity test" for anyone 65 years or older who desires to marry. The ten-minute test evaluates memory, comprehension, and attention. It is administered by a physician or mental health professional, in private, and at least three months before marriage. See Ashley E. Rathburn, Comment, Marrying Into Financial Abuse: A Solution to Protect the Elderly in California, 47 San Diego L. Rev. 227, 261-269 (2010) (making this proposal). Should this proposal be enacted?

2. Ninety-year-old Mickey Rooney is a box-office star who appeared in countless films and TV shows and was nominated four times for an Academy Award. In 2011, he testified before the Senate Committee on Aging that he was a victim of elder abuse. A court granted him a temporary restraining order based on his allegations that his stepson and daughter committed verbal, emotional, and financial abuse; withheld food and medicine; and interfered in his personal finances. His attorneys obtained a temporary conservatorship over his finances.

Rooney said that he felt "trapped, scared, used and frustrated." "For years I suffered silently. I didn't want to tell anybody. I couldn't muster the courage. . . . I needed help, and I knew I needed it. Even when I tried to speak up, I was told to shut up and be quiet." Rooney's stepson and Rooney's wife both deny the claims.

The Senate Committee is holding hearings to address issues of elder abuse and to coordinate federal, state, and local efforts to combat it. If you were a legislative aide, what recommendations would you make? What images of the elderly are conveyed by Rooney's testimony?

On Rooney's allegations, see Katie Moisse & Courtney Hutchison, Mickey Rooney Takes Stand Against Elder Abuse, ABC News, Mar. 2, 2011, available at http://abcnews.go.com/Health/Wellness/mickey-rooney-speaks-senate-committee-elder-abuse/story?id=13037126; Stephen M. Silverman, Mickey Rooney: Elder Abuse Made Me Feel Trapped, People Mag., Mar. 3, 2011, available at http://www.people.com/people/article/0,,20470562.00.html; Associated Press (AP), Mickey Rooney Tells Congress About Abuse, Mar. 3, 2011, available at http://www.accesshollywood.com/actor-mickey-rooney-testifies-to-congress-about-abuse-against-elderly-says-hes-a-victim_article_44701.

New York Socialite Brooke Astor is a Victim of Elder Abuse

A recent scandal focused public attention on elder abuse. New York socialite philanthropist Brooke Astor died at age 105, leaving an estate of $185 million. According to family and friends, as Mrs. Astor was suffering from Alzheimer's disease, her son Anthony physically neglected her. She reportedly slept on a urine-soaked couch in a torn nightgown. Anthony refused to allow her to visit her beloved Maine summer home. He reportedly sold her valuable art work by misrepresenting her financial status to her; charged excessive commissions and paid himself well for managing her affairs; stole assets from her art collection; improperly used her funds to provide upkeep of his property and pay the captain of his yacht; and isolated her by firing her staff and attorney. The charges were brought to light by Anthony's estranged son, Philip, who petitioned for a court-appointed guardian for his grandmother.

Witnesses testified that Anthony conspired to inflate his inheritance in order to appease his wife, Charlene. Also convicted was a lawyer, Francis X. Morrissey, Jr., who was chosen by Anthony to do estate planning for Mrs. Astor. Morrissey was convicted of fraud, conspiracy, and forgery of her signature on a codicil to her will that bequeathed $60 million to Anthony rather than to those charities that were beneficiaries of earlier wills. Marshall was convicted on 14 charges of fraud and conspiracy, and sentenced to 1 to 3 years in prison. Morrissey received a similar sentence.

See generally Meryl Gordon, Mrs. Astor Regrets: The Hidden Betrayals of a Family beyond Reproach (2008); Joseph A. Rosenberg, Regrettably Unfair; Brooke Astor and the Other Elderly in New York, 30 Pace L. Rev. 1004 (2010).

B. SEXUAL ORIENTATION

What is the role of sexual orientation in domestic violence? How does the legal system respond to same-sex intimate partner violence?

■ **STEPHEN WHITE, GUILTY OF BRITAIN'S FIRST GAY DOMESTIC MURDER**
The Mirror (UK), May 7, 2010, at 39

A gay man who stabbed his partner to death has been convicted of Britain's first domestic violence murder within a same-sex marriage. Michael Edwards, 32, knifed John Edwards in the heart after a late-night row over a heating bill. The pair, who had just celebrated their second wedding anniversary, were described as a "lovely couple" but their stormy marriage was blighted by domestic violence. Edwards admitted often beating up or trying to strangle John, 35, as a "means of relieving stress." It has since emerged that the killer, who was jailed for life, had a conviction for stabbing an ex-partner during an argument.

The couple, both bartenders, had worked together on the day of last November's murder before drinking with friends and returning home at 1:15 a.m. After arguing, Edwards grabbed a knife and fatally stabbed John as he tried to protect himself behind a door. Edwards then called an ambulance claiming John had "stabbed himself." . . . Edwards, from Manchester, admitted the murder. He wept in the city's crown court as he was ordered to serve at least 13 years.

■ SHARON STAPEL, FALLING TO PIECES: NEW YORK STATE CIVIL LEGAL REMEDIES AVAILABLE TO LESBIAN, GAY, BISEXUAL, AND TRANSGENDER SURVIVORS OF DOMESTIC VIOLENCE

52 N.Y. L. Sch. L. Rev. 247, 254-257, 259 (2008)

. . . [D]omestic, or intimate partner, violence occurs within the LGBT communities with the same statistical frequency as in the heterosexual community. The prevalence of domestic violence among gay and lesbian couples is approximately 25 to 33 percent. . . . As in the heterosexual community, domestic violence in the LGBT communities is generally defined as a pattern of behavior in which one partner coerces, dominates, or isolates the other partner. It is the exertion of any form of power that is used to maintain control in a relationship. The violence can be physical, emotional, sexual, psychological, or economic. Same-sex batterers use tactics of abuse similar to those of heterosexual batterers. However, some forms of battering are unique to the LGBT communities. Batterers in same-sex relationships have an additional social weapon in their arsenal. Same-sex batterers are able to successfully exploit their victims' internalized, or the community's externalized, homophobia, biphobia, or transphobia, simply by threatening to "out" their partners' sexual orientation or gender identity to family, friends, employers, landlords, or other community members. . . .

Same-sex survivors of domestic violence faced with custody battles worry that their sexual orientation will negatively impact their cases, and decide to stay with their abusers rather than risk losing custody or visitation rights. Batterers who abuse their transgender partners often tell their partners that no one will understand or love them because of their gender identity or transition process; or they may threaten to evict their transgender partners, leaving the survivors homeless and facing dangers on the streets, in homeless shelters, and in a discriminatory job market. Survivors face further isolation because they are reluctant to access services that are not perceived as LGBT-friendly. For LGBT survivors, their batterers are often the first or the only persons to accept their sexual orientation or gender identity, and batterers use this knowledge to keep survivors isolated.

Legal, social, and academic responses to domestic violence in the LGBT communities are largely acknowledged to be inadequate. Theories for this inadequacy include homophobia within the legal system, lack of knowledge of agencies and organizations that would otherwise respond to the violence, the reluctance of LGBT community members to discuss domestic violence, and the lack of attention the issue has received from LGBT rights and anti-domestic violence advocates.

LGBT survivors [in New York] cannot access the commonly used legal protection of civil orders of protection, however, because they lack standing under the Family Court Act. Although bisexual and transgender individuals who marry opposite-sex partners and same-sex partners who adopt children in common may be able to use this remedy, the definition of family prevents the majority of LGBT people in long-term, committed relationships, most of whom are not married and do not have children in common, from obtaining this relief in family courts. . . .

. . . [The police often misperceive incidents of intimate partner violence as discrete arguments.] Even if the police acknowledge and understand the intimate nature of the relationship between the parties, the officers often fall victim to stereotypes that interfere with the proper implementation of the mandatory arrest law. For example, an officer may assume that the primary aggressor is the more masculine-identified partner, or that an incident of domestic violence between gay male partners does not require police intervention because, as men, each partner can handle himself.

Although the criminal justice system is available to LGBT survivors, LGBT survivors view this system with trepidation. Many survivors of domestic violence have themselves had past homophobic or transphobic interactions with the police and do not view law enforcement as available to the LGBT communities. Survivors who would otherwise call the police are often afraid to do so because of a fear of what the police will do to their partners once the partners are in custody. . . .

■ TARA R. PFEIFER, COMMENT, OUT OF THE SHADOWS: THE POSITIVE IMPACT OF LAWRENCE v. TEXAS ON VICTIMS OF SAME-SEX DOMESTIC VIOLENCE
109 Penn St. L. Rev. 1251, 1255-1256 (2005)

. . . Oftentimes domestic violence shelter programs and workers are unprepared and ill-equipped to handle cases of same-sex domestic violence. Domestic violence shelters have been slow and late in providing services to battered gays and lesbians, with many shelters refusing to admit GLBT victims or expressing homophobic attitudes when those individuals do elicit support. A lesbian victim of domestic violence in Minnesota reported that she felt like an outcast at her local domestic violence shelter, often hearing anti-gay remarks being made by fellow victims.

Reporting their abusive partners forces closeted gay and lesbian victims to out themselves, a significant decision that may adversely affect other important aspects of the victim's life. The homophobia of society and victim apprehension about revealing his or her sexual orientation provides batterers with the reassurance that their abuse will continue in secrecy. . . .

Even the gay community has been reluctant to confront the problem. Members of the community are often afraid that recognition of same-sex domestic violence will provide right-wing conservatives with ammunition to counter the community's political progress and damage the image of positive, egalitarian gay and lesbian relationships. . . .

Notes and Questions

1. *Social reality.* How does same-sex intimate partner violence compare to that of opposite-sex partner violence, according to the excerpts? Although intimate partner violence among same-sex couples occurs with the same approximate frequency as intimate partner violence in the heterosexual community, lesbian couples report significantly *less* intimate partner violence than women in opposite-sex relationships (11 versus 30 percent), whereas gay men experience *more* such violence than men in opposite-sex relationships (15 versus 8 percent). See Patricia Tjaden & Nancy Thoennes, Nat'l Inst. of Justice, Extent, Nature, and Consequences of Intimate

Partner Violence iv, v (2000). What are the possible implications of these findings for policy formulation?

2. *Similarities.* How is same-sex partner violence similar to that of opposite-sex couples, according to the excerpts? The Danger Assessment Tool (discussed Chapter 2) identifies factors that predict the risk of death by partners. Although the Danger Assessment Tool was developed for opposite-sex relationships, might the same factors be predictive of lethality in same-sex relationships? See Nancy Glass et al., Risk for Reassault in Abusive Female Same-Sex Relationships, 96 Am. J. Pub. Health 1021 (2003) (confirming that the Tool accurately predicts such risk). See generally Diane Hiebert-Murphy et al., The Meaning of "Risk" for Intimate Partner Violence among Women in Same-Sex Relationships, in Intimate Partner Violence in LGBTQ Lives 37 (Janice L. Ristock ed., 2011).

3. *Differences.* How is same-sex partner violence different from that of opposite-sex couples, according to the excerpts? Specifically, what role does sexual orientation play in disclosure, help-seeking behavior, social service intervention, and legal intervention? Another difference is that abusive partners may threaten to reveal their partners' HIV/AIDS status. Janice Ristock & Norma Timbang, Moving Beyond a Gender-Based Framework: Relationship Violence in Lesbian/Gay/Bisexual/Transgender/Queer Communities 5, available at http://www.mincava .umn.edu/documents/lgbtqviolence/lgbtqviolence.html (last visited June 14, 2011) (reporting findings of interviews with lesbians and service providers); Stoever, supra.

4. *Stereotypes.* What stereotypes (gender-based or LGBT-related) affect beliefs about the role of sexual orientation in domestic violence? What stereotypes influence the legal response? See generally Marc A. Fajer, Can Two Real Men Eat Quiche Together? Storytelling, Gender-Role Stereotypes, and Legal Protection for Lesbians and Gay Men, 46 U. Miami L. Rev. 511(1992); Nancy J. Knauer, Same-Sex Domestic Violence: Claiming a Domestic Sphere While Risking Negative Stereotypes, 8 Temp. Pol. & Civ. Rts. L. Rev. 325 (1999); Sheila M. Seelau & Eric P. Seelau, Gender-Role Stereotypes and Perceptions of Heterosexual, Gay and Lesbian Domestic Violence, 20 J. Fam. Violence 363 (2005).

5. *Reasons to seek help.* Why might a same-sex partner be reluctant to seek help? Lesbian mothers seek help for many of the same reasons as other mothers (that is, severity of the violence and worries about the effect of the violence on children). However, they also fear the potential infringement of their legal rights (that is, loss of child custody, eviction, etc.) due to homophobic attitudes. See Jennifer L. Hardesty et al., Lesbian/Bisexual Mothers and Intimate Partner Violence: Help Seeking in the Context of Social and Legal Vulnerability, 17 Violence Against Women 28, 39-40 (2011) (reporting research findings).

6. *Same-sex partners of color.* Same-sex partners of color are subject to racism as well as homophobia. See generally Valli Kanuha, Compounding the Triple Jeopardy: Battering in Lesbian of Color Relationships, in Diversity and Complexity in Feminist Therapy 169 (Laura S. Brown & Maria P. P. Root eds., 1990); Amorie Robinson, "There's a Stranger in This House": African American Lesbians and Domestic Violence, in Violence in the Lives of Black Women: Battered, Black, and Blue 125 (Carolyn M. West ed., 2002). How might this factor affect their experience of, and response to, domestic violence?

7. *LGBT community's response.* Why has the LGBT community been slow to acknowledge the problem of intimate same-sex partner violence?

8. *Law's response.* Although all states have civil and criminal legislation addressing domestic violence, not all statutes apply to same-sex partners. A few states limit protection to opposite-sex or married partners. Ruth Colker, Marriage Mimicry: The Law of Domestic Violence, 47 Wm. & Mary L. Rev. 1841, 1858 (2006). Should statutory protection be circumscribed in this manner? Professor Ruth Colker criticizes the "marriage-mimicry" model, noting:

> [T]he marriage-mimicry model is not necessarily the correct framework, because it was developed without lawmakers asking the fundamental questions of who is most in need of legal recourse and how the law can best provide that recourse. A more functional approach would permit the legal system to disentangle privileges and benefits from marital status rather than reflexively extend privileges and benefits under a marriage-mimicry model.

Id. at 1845. Do you agree? What policy rationales explain expansive versus narrow definitions?

Another critic, Professor Ruthann Robson, contends that legal sanctions are often directed more at sensationalism than censuring the violence. She charges that judges, who frequently mischaracterize the abuse as "mutual combat," tend to deny restraining orders or issue a mutual restraining orders (leading to negative ramifications for the genuine victim). Ruthann Robson, Lesbian (Out)Law: Survival Under the Rule of Law 161-162 (1992). Why might a judge make this assumption? How should the legal and social service systems address these criticisms? The doctrine of mutual combat is discussed in Chapter 5.

9. *Lawrence v. Texas.* What is the likely impact of Lawrence v. Texas, 539 U.S. 558 (2003) (invalidating state sodomy laws) on the legal protections available to victims of same-sex domestic violence? See Pfeifer, supra, at 1254.

10. *State DOMAs.* Many states have statutes or constitutional amendments that ban recognition of same-sex marriage or recognition of those same-sex relationships in which the partners are "living as spouses." The application of these "baby DOMAs" to domestic violence prevention laws is discussed in Chapter 6.

11. *VAWA.* Do VAWA's criminal provisions (that is, prohibitions on interstate domestic violence, stalking, and the interstate violation of a state order of protection) apply to partners in same-sex relationships? A recent Opinion of the Justice Department's Office of Legal Counsel explains that, although the statute is entitled the "Violence Against *Women* Act," its provisions apply to violence perpetrated against male, as well as female, victims and also apply regardless of sexual orientation. See Whether the Criminal Provisions of the Violence Against Women Act Apply to Otherwise Covered Conduct When the Offender and Victim Are the Same Sex, 34 Op. O.L.C. 1, 2010 WL 2431395 (2010). Interstate orders of protection are discussed in Chapter 8.

12. *Same-sex marriage.* In June 2011, the New York legislature legalized same-sex marriage, making New York the sixth state to allow such marriages. See Nicholas Confessore & Michael Barbaro, New York Allows Same-Sex Marriage, Becoming Largest State to Pass Law, June 25, 2011, at A1 (identifying states as Connecticut, Iowa, Massachusetts, New Hampshire, Vermont, as well as the District of Columbia). How might these laws change the protections against domestic violence that are available to same-sex couples?

C. DISABILITY

How does disability affect the way an individual experiences domestic violence? How does the legal system respond to intimate partner violence among the disabled?

■ **JENNIFER NIXON, DOMESTIC VIOLENCE AND WOMEN WITH DISABILITIES: LOCATING THE ISSUE ON THE PERIPHERY OF SOCIAL MOVEMENTS**
24 Disability & Society 77, 79-82 (2009)

[D]isabled women are at "disproportionately high risk for multiple forms of abuse in diverse settings." Women with disabilities report experiencing abuse of longer duration and feeling as though they have fewer alternatives for escaping or ending the abuse. Moreover, disabled women can experience forms of abuse that non-disabled women do not.

Because disabled women are frequently more dependent on partners or care-givers than non-disabled women, their experiences of violence can be more diverse. An additional layer of complexity involves recognizing that the abuse of disabled women is not limited to those acts that are normally recognized as intimate partner violence. Acts of abuse can include isolation, withholding medication or medical aids, the denial of necessities or simple neglect. Disabled women who require personal care are vulnerable to a range of forms of abuse, including verbal abuse and ridicule related to the impairment, physical abuse or threat of it, financial abuse, forced isolation, withholding of medication or equipment and being left in physical discomfort or embarrassing situations for long periods of time. Additionally, abuse can be impairment-specific, such as refusing access to mobility aids or communication equipment or encouraging fears or paranoia in women with mental health difficulties. . . .

Common perceptions of disabled women also figure in efforts to understand the dynamics of the violence and abuse they can experience. The construction of disabled women as helpless and passive has implications for their vulnerability to abuse. Disabled women in particular may be encouraged to be endlessly compliant, especially with doctors and healthcare professionals. Additionally, people with disabilities are frequently portrayed as non-sexual or as incapable of having intimate relationships with either non-disabled or disabled people. The sexuality of disabled women in particular has frequently been denied or controlled, as has their capacity for motherhood.

The denial of disabled women's sexuality, however, has not translated into an immunity from male violence. The construction of a passive and nonsexual identity may, in fact, create opportunities for abuse. A non-sexual identity has been linked to an increased risk of sexual abuse due to fewer boundaries that can discourage others from perpetrating abuse. The perceived silence, invisibility and asexuality of disabled women, while not the cause of violence against them, can make it much more difficult to disclose or escape the violence.

All women experiencing domestic violence face a number of obstacles in their attempts to escape or end the violence. These barriers can include emotional and financial dependency on the abuser, an unwillingness to be stigmatized, worries about being a single parent or fear of losing contact with children and concerns that they will not be believed or helped when they disclose abuse. Women may also be reluctant to take any action that will escalate the violence. These fears and uncertainties contribute to the under-reporting of domestic abuse and can prevent women from disclosing, seeking help from service providers or taking steps to build lives free from abuse. Women with disabilities confront all of these issues and may face additional barriers to help-seeking. These can include increased dependence (physical, financial or both) on the abuser for care, difficulty in making contact with refuges or other intervention services, lack of access to information about available services, difficulties in accessing transportation and fear of being institutionalized.

Additionally, disabled women may choose not to disclose abuse because they fear they will not be believed, either because some professionals do not recognize disabled women's capacity for sexual and intimate relationships or because care-givers are regarded as being beyond reproach. Inappropriate responses to disclo-sures or requests for help can have disabling effects. Disabled women disclosing abuse or attempting to leave a violent relationship may find that others do not understand the many forms that abuse can take. Attitudes of police and other professionals can be problematic if allegations of abuse are not taken seriously or are minimized. Professionals may fail to understand and identify forms of abuse that disabled women experience and instead shift the focus to the impairment, thereby obscuring the abuse. These are all forms of disbelief and raise very real barriers to disabled women constructing lives free from violence. . . .

■ JANE K. STOEVER, STORIES ABSENT FROM THE COURTROOM: RESPONDING TO DOMESTIC VIOLENCE IN THE CONTEXT OF HIV AND AIDS
87 N.C. L. Rev. 1157, 1162-1163, 1168, 1171-1179 (2009)

. . . In the last decade, those in public health and medical professions have begun to recognize the connection between domestic violence and HIV/AIDS. While Dr. Antonia C. Novello was the U.S. Surgeon General, she wrote, "Today, we face two major public health epidemics that represent particular dangers to women. One is the human immunodeficiency virus (HIV) epidemic, and the other is domestic violence. Although these two epidemics might seem unrelated, they are intertwined in ways that pose serious challenges to the health care community." . . . [This article explores the ways in which one intimate partner uses the other partner's HIV/AIDS status as an effective form of control.]

Use of Knowledge of a Partner's HIV Status to Exert Control

. . . As a way of exerting control over an intimate partner and coercing her to stay in a relationship, the abusive partner may threaten to publicize the woman's HIV status if she breaks off the relationship. One woman reported that her abusive partner told her, "No one else will want you now, so you'll have to stay," and, when she tried to end the relationship, he threatened that if she left, "I'll tell the world what you got." Because of societal bias and prejudice, a survivor may fear the social and professional ramifications of having her HIV status become public knowledge.

She is faced with choosing between safety and the potential repercussions of the abuser's retaliatory act of revealing her status to her employer, her children's school, daycare providers, friends, neighbors, and others. . . .

Interference with Medical Care

A client revealed that she was HIV positive and that she took numerous medications to maintain her health. Her boyfriend had been physically abusive for some time, but the most hurtful incident, the event that finally caused her to seek help, was related to her HIV status. After her boyfriend gave her a black eye and bruised her arm, he flushed all of her HIV medications down the toilet, saying, "You're going to die anyway." An abusive partner may prevent the HIV-positive partner from obtaining medical care and from following a doctor's prescribed medical regimen. It is common to hear that a batterer destroyed medication to control a partner's health and keep her sick. . . .

[S]ome clients are literally locked inside their homes by their abusers and are unable to leave for any reason, including medical appointments. The frequency of medical appointments may fuel suspicion and tension in the home, as an abusive partner may not believe the HIV-positive partner actually has a medical need for the appointments, suspecting she is going elsewhere. Thus, it is important for health care providers to understand the ways in which intimate partner abuse can prevent and interfere with treatment. . . .

Sexual Assault

. . . The high rates of sexual abuse in intimate partner violence put victims at greater risk for contracting HIV. Research shows that women who are physically and sexually assaulted face an increased risk of HIV infection. One woman reported her experience with her HIV-positive husband: "[H]e forced me to have sex whether I liked it or not, even up until the time he died." Sexual violence often accompanies other forms of physical violence in battering relationships. During a relationship in which there is domestic violence, at least sixty percent of abused women are sexually assaulted by their partners, and almost half of all battered women are raped by their partners. The majority of women who are raped by an abusive partner experience multiple sexual assaults by this partner during the relationship, and women are particularly at risk for HIV infection from HIV-positive perpetrators.

Infidelity

. . . In both violent and nonviolent relationships in which one partner is not monogamous, there are risks of HIV infection; however, a battered woman may fear the repercussions of confronting her abusive partner about his fidelity. She may continue to have sexual intercourse with her partner because she fears that if she refuses, asks that he be tested for sexually transmitted diseases, or insists on using protection during sexual intercourse, he may respond with physical violence. If her partner admits to having been unfaithful, he may maintain that it was an isolated event and that he used protection, and her fears about potential violence may inhibit her ability to express concern about his truthfulness and about her own health. Research further indicates that, even in the face of concerns about HIV transmission, "she may feel certain that if she confronts her husband, the physical and emotional consequences will be serious and immediate."

Intentional Infection with HIV

In some cases, HIV transmission may result from rape and the refusal to use a condom, but the infecting partner may not intend the result of HIV infection. In other cases, the context and surrounding words make it clear that infection was intentional. One HIV-infected woman reported that her partner confessed to infecting her deliberately, explaining to her, "I only did it because I love you so much." An abusive partner may engage in many actions to keep the survivor from leaving. Willfully infecting a partner with HIV is an extreme attempt to lock the other partner into the relationship by making the partner ostensibly undesirable to others. Intentionally infecting a partner in a relationship that has power and control dynamics is the ultimate expression of control. . . .

Notes and Questions

1. *Social reality.* Disabled women face a higher risk of domestic violence than women without disabilities. See Douglas A. Brownridge, Violence Against Women: Vulnerable Populations 236 (2009) (based on a large Canadian study, finding that 21 percent of disabled women report partner violence compared to 14 percent of other women); Nat'l Coalition Against Domestic Violence (NCADV), Fact Sheet: Domestic Violence and Disabilities 1 (reporting that women with disabilities face a 40 percent greater risk of violence than women without disabilities), available at http://www.leanonus.org/images/Domestic_Violence_and_Disabilities.pdf   (last visited June 16, 2011).

In addition, disabled women suffer abuse by multiple partners and for longer periods of time. Dena Hassouneh-Phillips and Elizabeth McNeff, "I Thought I was Less Worthy": Low Sexual and Body Esteem and Increased Vulnerability to Intimate Partner Abuse in Women with Physical Disabilities, 23 Sexuality & Disability, 227, 229 (2005). Also, they are more likely to suffer severe abuse and more types of abuse. See Douglas A. Brownridge, Partner Violence Against Women with Disabilities: Prevalence, Risk, and Explanations, 12 Violence Against Women 805, 813 (2005). What might account for these facts?

2. *Federal legislation.* Although VAWA originally did not provide services for victims with disabilities, VAWA 2000 provided funding for education and technical assistance to improve services to these survivors. Pub. L. No. 106-386, 114 Stat. 1491, 1508-1509 (codified as amended at 42 U.S.C. §§3796gg, 3796hh, 14041a). In VAWA 2005, Congress provided even more funds to support education, training, and direct services for disabled victims of sexual assault, domestic violence, dating violence, and stalking. Pub. L. No. 109-162, 119 Stat. 2960, 3000-3001 (codified as amended at 42 U.S.C. §§3796gg). See also National Coalition Against Domestic Violence, Comparison of VAWA 1994, VAWA 2000, and VAWA 2005 Reauthorization Bill (2006) (summarizing VAWA provisions), available at http://www.ncadv .org/files/VAWA_94_00_05.pdf

In addition, the Federal Sentencing Guideline §3A1.1, authorizes sentence enhancements for federal crimes if the victim was unusually vulnerable due to age or physical or mental condition (provided that the defendant knew or should have known about the victim's vulnerability). The Americans with Disabilities Act of 1990 (codified in relevant part at 42 U.S.C. §12182(a)) (guaranteeing equal opportunity in public accommodations, governmental services, and telecommunications) does not address domestic violence.

3. *State laws.* Legislation in many states offers special protection to dependent adults against abuse.

a. *Adult protective services laws.* All states have "adult protective services" laws. See, e.g., Mont. Code Ann. §§52-3-201 et seq. The term *protective services* signifies services provided by the state to prevent the maltreatment or self-neglect of "at-risk" adults. Conservatorships and guardianships protect both disabled and elderly persons against physical and financial abuse. See generally Lawrence A. Frolik & Melissa C. Brown, Advising the Elderly or Disabled Client (2d ed. 2002); Dorothy Thomas, Protecting the Elderly and Vulnerable Adults from Financial Fraud and Exploitation, 30 Wyo. Law., Dec. 2007, at 24.

b. *Criminal laws.* Some states have special criminal provisions addressing abuse of dependent adults. See, e.g., Md. Code Ann., Crim. Law §3-604(b) (establishing new crime for abuse of "vulnerable" adult, defined as "an adult who lacks the physical or mental capacity to provide for the adult's daily needs"). How do these laws differ from guardianships?

c. *Mandatory reporting laws.* Many states have laws that mandate reporting of abuse of dependent adults. For further discussion of these laws, see supra this chapter, p. 85.

d. *Tort claims.* Some state legislatures provide civil, as well as criminal, penalties for financial exploitation of vulnerable adults. See, e.g., Ariz. Rev. Stat. Ann. §46-455 and §46-456 (authorizing a private right of action by the victim).

4. *Risk.* How does the fact that many caregivers are simultaneously partners compound the risk of abuse? See Brownridge, Partner Violence, supra, at 809.

5. *Types of disability.* Does the *type* of disability play a role in the experience of intimate partner violence? How is abuse "impairment-specific"? Consider the following:

> Sally has been battered by her husband for years. Since she is blind, when he hits her, she cannot usually anticipate where the strikes will come from. . . . He has accidentally bumped her into things, or left her standing on the street in a strange place to teach her a lesson. . . . He reads all the family mail, and she has only his word of what that mail contains.

Cathy Hoog, Enough and Yet Not Enough: An Educational Resource Manual on Domestic Violence Advocacy for Persons with Disabilities in Washington State 12 (2003). Can you think of other disability-specific difficulties of a survivor? What are the ways in which a partner uses the other partner's HIV/AIDS status as a form of abuse? How is abuse in the context of HIV/AIDS similar to, and different from, other forms of abuse of disabled victims? How can legal and medical responses to disabled victims of domestic violence be improved?

6. *Stereotypes of disability.* What stereotypes complicate the legal and service delivery responses to disabled victims? See Brownridge, Partner Violence, supra, at 807; Doug Jones, Comment, Domestic Violence Against Women with Disabilities: A Feminist Legal Theory Analysis, 2 Fla. A. & M. U. L. Rev. 207, 217 (2007). What can be done to counter these attitudes?

7. *Perceptions of self.* The disabled internalize stereotypes of disability, thereby increasing their vulnerability to abuse. Because women with disabilities may grow up

in protected atmospheres, they may be inclined to "accept the dictates of authority figures, making them particularly attractive to men who seek vulnerable women to control." Karen Nutter, Note, Domestic Violence in the Lives of Women with Disabilities: No (Accessible) Shelter from the Storm, 13 S. Cal. Rev. L. & Women's Stud. 329, 339 (2004). In addition, women with disabilities often want to partner with non-disabled men, and, for that reason, may be more willing to remain in abusive relationships. Hassouneh-Phillips & McNeff, supra, at 234-236; Marlene F. Strong et al., Caregiver Abuse and Domestic Violence in the Lives of Women with Disabilities 8 (1997). How can service providers address these attitudes?

8. *Additional barriers to leaving.* Unique barriers affect disabled victims who want to leave abusive relationships.

a. *Disclosure.* Abuse of the disabled is often not reported. NDADV, Domestic Violence and Disabilities, supra, at 1 (reporting that 70 to 85 percent of cases are not reported). What make disclosure so difficult? How does isolation contribute to reporting problems? See Nutter, supra, at 340.

b. *Investigation.* Many disabled victims face difficulties because of professionals' misconceptions. How might this factor affect law enforcement officers' response to disabled victims? See Hoog, supra, at 15 (suggesting that officers may believe that disabled persons are intoxicated or not credible); Jones, supra, at 215 (reporting that people are more inclined to disbelieve abuse or sympathize with the perpetrator); Strong, supra, at 9 (noting police officers' difficulties communicating with victims).

How can the law enforcement response be improved? If disabled victims have to testify, what difficulties might they encounter in court? How can the judicial system better respond to their needs? See Mark Dubin, Serving Women with Developmental Disabilities: Strategies for the Judicial System 12-13, in Impact: Feature Issue on Violence Against Women with Developmental or Other Disabilities (Wendie Abramson et al. eds., 2000).

c. *Services.* Disabled victims may have difficulty accessing social services. Conversely, shelters may not be familiar with the needs of disabled victims. How can access to services be improved? See Int'l Network, supra, at 11-12; Jones, supra, at 218-219; Lisa McClain, Women, Disability and Violence: Strategies to Increase Physical and Programmatic Access to Victims' Services for Women with Disabilities, Center for Women's Policy Studies 6-10 (2011). Legal issues pertaining to domestic violence shelters are explored in Chapter 14.

9. *Intersectionality.* How do race, ethnicity, and poverty explain the experiences of disabled victims? Disabled women are more likely to live in poverty and be unemployed. See Margaret A. Nosek et al., Disability, Psychosocial, and Demographic Characteristics of Abused Women with Physical Disabilities, 12 Violence Against Women 835 (2006); Strong et al., supra, at 8. How might this increase their vulnerability to intimate partner violence?

D. RACE AND ETHNICITY

Domestic violence affects members of all racial and ethnic groups. How does race and/or ethnicity play a role in a person's experience of intimate partner violence? How does legal policy take race and/or ethnicity into account?

■ **CALLIE RENNISON & MIKE PLANTY, NONLETHAL**
INTIMATE PARTNER VIOLENCE: EXAMINING RACE,
GENDER, AND INCOME PATTERNS
18 Violence & Victims 433, 436-440 (2003)

[Data are based on the National Criminal Victimization Survey (NCVS) of 336,295 households and 651,750 individuals.] Focusing on females only, the NCVS demonstrates that IPV rates differ by victim's race. Specifically, Black women experienced IPV at higher rates than White women, and women of other races (10.7, 7.8 and 4.5 victimizations per 1,000 respectively). Further, Black women suffered serious violence and assault at the hands of an intimate partner at rates higher than White women and women of other races. Thus, even after controlling for victim's gender, the analyses suggest that the victim's race is significant.

Research consistently shows that while IPV exists across the spectrum of household incomes, it occurs most often among persons with lower annual household incomes. [P]ersons living in households with an annual income less than $7,500 experienced 13.4 intimate partner victimizations (per 1,000), while persons in households with an annual income of $50,000 or more experienced 2.3 victimizations (per 1,000).

When the relationship between income and IPV is further refined by controlling for victims' race, the picture changes dramatically. *IPV rates become differentiated along income rather than racial lines for White and Black victims* (italics in the original). . . . Among female victims, IPV rates continued to differ based on income, not race, for White and Black victims. In general, the higher the annual household income, the lower the rate of IPV. For example, considering all female victims, IPV rates were highest (20.0 victimizations per 1,000) in households with an income of less than $7,500 annually. In contrast, IPV rates were lowest (3.6 victimizations per 1,000) for females in households with incomes of greater than $50,000 annually. This pattern existed for White and Black females as well. . . .

These findings are inconsistent with a racial explanation of crime—a Black subculture of violence. [Rather,] these findings support the notion that violence is largely associated with populations characterized by social and economic isolation. Blacks are disproportionately represented in communities with extreme levels of social and economic dislocation. Associations demonstrating high rates of victimization of Black individuals—without controlling for economics—are confounded by the fact that a large segment of the underclass is Black. Failure to account for the role of income leads to the use of race as an oversimplified proxy. . . .

■ **LISA M. MARTINSON, COMMENT, AN ANALYSIS**
OF RACISM AND RESOURCES FOR AFRICAN-
AMERICAN FEMALE VICTIMS OF DOMESTIC
VIOLENCE IN WISCONSIN
16 Wis. Women's L.J. 259, 264-273 (2001)

. . . African-American women hesitate to report abuse by African-American men because of the readiness of the outside society to label or blame these acts of violence as racially predictable. Not only must African-American women be concerned about the public as a whole, but also the effects of reporting abuse within their race community.

The African-American woman "may be ostracized within [her community] for contributing to racial stereotypes by reporting domestic violence by an African-American man." This fact creates a dilemma for African-American women because "[p]reserving cultural identity often requires strong allegiance to the community as a whole, causing women to choose between fear of rejection or continued violence." . . . This concern is described by African-American women as one arising from the belief that racism always trumps sexism, and that the hierarchy of interests within the Black community assigns a priority to protecting the entire community against the assaultive forces of racism. [Therefore,] the lack of reporting, in part, is a result of the victim balancing the abuse against the fear that the community will not support her decision to report and/or leave the abuser. . . .

Another major concern connected to racism and domestic violence is the status of the African-American man within the United States. Unfortunately, African-American victims of abuse receive the message that to report abuse by an African-American man is to feed the stereotype of African-American men as violent. Research [reveals] that an African-American woman was more likely to feel protective of her abuser than a white woman. The reason for this reaction is a manifestation of the effects of discrimination and the hard times the African-American male has faced in the United States. Some African-American women feel that incidents of violence against African-American women by African-American men should not be reported because they would be putting another brother in prison. . . . The victim is forced to make a choice between the violence she experiences and the racism that her batterer may experience. Racism, when considered a more serious problem, can keep African-American women from trying to end the violence.

Along with the concerns about the African-American race and the status of African-American men, the family is another reason that prevents African-American women from reporting or seeking out resources for domestic violence. . . . African-American women face pressure to keep the family together to combat racist views concerning the African-American family, thus ignoring the abuse for the sake of others. This concern again forces the African-American woman to place societal perceptions of her and her family above the reality of the violence within the home. . . .

To understand the plight of the African-American domestic violence victim, we must recognize her economic position in our society. Over half of homeless families nationally are African-American, while African-Americans only make up 12 percent of the total population. [T]he U.S. Census Bureau found while 28 percent of white female-headed households [were] below the poverty line, 40 percent of black female-headed households were below the poverty line. . . . African-American women of lower socioeconomic status (as well as all women of lower socioeconomic status) who are victims of domestic violence are more likely than middle- and upper-class white women who are victims of domestic violence to need extensive services and support in order to leave an abusive relationship. Therefore, while the option of calling the police offers immediate safety for the victim of domestic violence, the victim may not see this as an option when the abuser is needed to support the family financially.

The alarming rate of poverty among African-American women is evident and has significant effects on African-American domestic violence victims. More than half the African-American women interviewed in [one study] stated that they stayed with their batterers because they did not think they could support themselves and their children alone. . . .

Racism affects African-American victims within the informal structures of society and economics, as well as within our formal infrastructures of the police and judiciary. . . . Evidence shows that many within the African-American population do not have a trusting relationship with the police. . . . The result is that many women of color simply will not call the police for fear of what will happen to themselves or their abusive partner in the hands of law enforcement officers. . . .

Along with distrusting the police, a general distrust of the court system and its actors also exists for many African-Americans. . . . The obstacles of a historically founded distrust of the court system and documented discrimination against African-American women can lead African-American victims of domestic violence to turn away from state resources [when attempting to get out of a violent relationship].

. . . To effectively provide solutions to help African-American victims, the problems that victims and African-American women face must be considered together. Racism and domestic violence are not separate entities. Viewed together, they are a part of a larger social issue of all people not treated equally in our legal system. . . .

■ MARY ANN DUTTON ET AL., CHARACTERISTICS OF HELP-SEEKING BEHAVIORS, RESOURCES AND SERVICE NEEDS OF BATTERED IMMIGRANT LATINAS: LEGAL AND POLICY IMPLICATIONS
7 Geo. J. on Poverty L. & Pol'y 245, 248-255 (2000)

Latinas, like other battered women, make attempts to avoid, escape, and resist their batterers and protect themselves and their children. [However, certain factors influence their conduct.] [I]n general, battered women often fail to escape from a battering relationship because of social obstacles such as lack of social support, expectations based on sex roles, and past family history of abuse. Battered Latinas often marry younger, have larger families, are more economically and educationally disadvantaged, have been victims of violence for longer periods of time, and stay longer in the relationship than Caucasian or African-American battered women. They are also unlikely to classify such actions as pushing, shoving, grabbing, and throwing things at them as physical abuse. Latinas experience more conflict with their abusers over decision making, housekeeping money, the woman's going out, and her pregnancies. They report more unpredictability in the episodes of abuse and are more frequently hit in front of their children and relatives.

These social disadvantages, combined with difficulties in obtaining secure financial status without relying on the partner's economic help after separation, force some battered women to choose between enduring the violence and living in poverty. For many battered immigrant Latinas, economic factors pose a significant barrier to their escape from the domestic violence; these factors include financial dependence on the batterer, lack of formal education, and lack of employment skills. . . .

For immigrant Latinas, the issues inherent in their immigration and residency status in the U.S., together with their having fewer personal resources and limited access to community resources as new arrivals, add to their disadvantage and entrap them further in the intimate violence. [One study of immigrant Latina and Filipina women] reported that 34 percent of Latinas surveyed admitted experiencing domestic violence, 48 percent indicated that the level of violence increased with their immigration to the U.S. . . . Forty-eight percent of the Latinas interviewed spoke no English. . . . Sixty percent of the immigrant Latina women had from one to three children and 17 percent had from four to eight children. These findings suggest that the personal resources and socioeconomic conditions for battered immigrant Latinas are a challenge to the self-reliance which often accompanies successful strategies to escape, avoid or resist a violent partner. . . .

Given the importance of social support to victims of violence in general, it is likely that for battered Latinas, the establishment and response of their social and cultural milieu is a crucial issue as well. [T]he research literature has identified reliance on nuclear and extended family members as the main source of emotional support for Latinos. However, the research literature suggests that this general conclusion is more complex for Latinas. . . . The immigration process often leads to the fragmentation of the extended family which Latina women could traditionally rely upon to resolve conflict. In addition, the presence of relatives who witness the violence may not deter the batterer, as research has found that family members in Latino cultures may ignore or condone intimate violence. . . . Social isolation, exacerbated by lack of social contacts, geographic isolation, and limited mastery of English or cultural alienation, increases the risk for family violence because it interferes with detection and accountability, makes it easier for the batterer to ignore social sanctions, promotes increased marital dependence and increases intrafamilial exclusivity and intensity. . . .

[Latinas] tend to use formal strategies less often. Immigrant battered women may be reluctant to report the violence due to the lack of understanding of their legal rights and their undocumented immigrant status, resulting in fear of detection and deportation. A study of battered Caucasian, African-American, and Latina women living in a shelter found that of all groups Latinas were the least likely to contact a friend, minister, or social service agency for help. [B]urdened by language differences, discrimination, and limited mobility, Latinas' ability to seek help was also hindered by the fact that a substantial number of them were undocumented immigrants and therefore their eligibility for formal supports from government services was more limited than for other survey participants. Immigrant status may deter a Latina from seeking assistance from community institutions, as Latinas who are undocumented or have unstable legal residency status may mistakenly believe that seeking help from social services will lead to their deportation. . . .

. . . Another important cultural issue to take into consideration when understanding help-seeking behavior is that some Latinas turn for help first from the healing arts, rather than the justice or social service system. This is not surprising, given the significant value spirituality and religiosity have in the Latino culture. . . .

. . . Evidence suggests that social service agencies themselves may unwittingly create barriers, for some of their organizational characteristics, such as location, professional background of staff, Spanish-speaking capabilities, ethnicity of staff and planning board, are not responsive to or reflective of the unique needs of Latinas. Battered women also often encounter weak or negative responses from the criminal law enforcement system when they ask for help in stopping the violence. Prosecutors, courts, and even shelters are often slow to respond or are insensitive to the special needs of immigrant and refugee women, which can lead to further frustration. . . .

■ SUJATA WARRIER, (UN)HEARD VOICES: DOMESTIC VIOLENCE IN THE ASIAN-AMERICAN COMMUNITY

5, 10-11 (2002) available at **http://endabuse.org/userfiles/file/ ImmigrantWomen/UnheardVoices.pdf**

[D]omestic violence occurs in all the communities that comprise Asian America. . . . [It] stems from a legacy of patriarchy and sexism that is widespread in many Asian American communities. As a result, woman are socialized to believe and accept that violence in a relationship is acceptable, that male power expressed abusively is part of the cultural milieu, and therefore batterers are not held accountable for their behavior in their own communities. Also, women continue to believe that they are worthless, and that revealing the situation to anyone can be a cause of great shame to their families and communities. . . .

In some ethnic groups, such as South Asians, the issue of dowry—its payment or non-payment—and its variants in the U.S. can escalate domestic violence. For many battered Asian women, immigration concerns and status can be a serious cause for concern. [I]n some immigrant and refugee communities, such as the Vietnamese, stress of immigration—uncertain status and often changing roles, especially role reversals—can force men to become violent as they feel their power and position being eroded.

Additionally, religion and associated belief structures can exert a strong influence in some communities. For example, the long history of Spanish colonization in the Philippines left behind the "Jesus Syndrome," which exacts women to sacrifice for the family and achieve martyrdom by submitting to abuse. The more one submits, the more one is idealized. Interestingly, the share of the sacrifice falls disproportionately on women and is predominantly encouraged by the priests. . . .

Asian battered women deal with barriers on the individual and institutional levels as well as on a cultural level within the community. [T]hese barriers interact in different ways in different Asian communities. At the individual level, two of the most important barriers are fear and shame. These are followed by a lack of fluency in English and not knowing the cultural parameters of the U.S. Age and a lack of marketable skills are also barriers for the individual Asian woman.

The cultural values of a community can perpetuate a woman's isolation and sometimes force her to leave her community in order to live free from violence. Leaving a violent relationship may not be a choice without community and family support. In many Asian American communities, the hierarchical structure of the family may lead to violence from family members as well as from the spouse, which can further demoralize the woman in ways the outside world cannot understand.

Intricately linked to this is the fact that seeking help from outside agencies is usually not acceptable, but women are forced to seek such help when faced with a very difficult choice. Community members can place additional burdens by shaming the woman, especially if she is in an inter-racial or same-gender relationship. Additionally, the isolation created by the community and the batterer can make it difficult for a woman to know what resources are available and what the legal system can and cannot do for her.

When battered Asian women do seek help from outside agencies, the hurdles they face are tremendous. The primary institutional barriers are racism and xenophobia and its variant expressions in the U.S. system. Racism is particularly problematic for Asian women. The attitude that immigrants don't belong and shouldn't ask for help or cause trouble is just one variant of racism. Another is the myth of the "model minority," which assumes that Asian women don't have issues with domestic violence. Yet another involves the xenophobic belief that people from colonized parts of the world are inferior to Americans. . . .

Immigration policy [and] the current welfare policy have additional barriers for battered Asian women. When a woman seeks services she encounters a number of barriers including lack of sensitivity of service providers; the need to justify accessing services; the lack of services overall; lack of documents (restraining or protection orders, multilingual signs in the courtrooms, multilingual brochures) in the woman's language; and the judicial system process. Once a woman decides to seek help but cannot get help because of problems with the service delivery system or the criminal justice system, it becomes harder for her to think about seeking assistance again. . . .

Notes and Questions

1. *Social reality.* Although domestic violence occurs among all racial and ethnic groups, Native American women and African-American women are at particularly high risk. Hillary Potter, Battle Cries: Black Women and Intimate Partner Abuse 8 (2008) (citing government data that reports a rate of 18.2 per 1,000 victimizations for Native American women and 8.2 for Black women). Do these findings suggest a racial or ethnic explanation of crime? Or, do other reasons explain the overrepresentation of some groups?

a. *Alternative risk factors.* High victimization rates among certain minority groups appear to be attributable to "multiple marginalization factors." Potter, supra, at 8. For example, socioeconomic factors are largely responsible for the disproportionately high rate of domestic violence in African-American communities. See Angela Browne, Violence in Marriage: Until Death Do Us Part?, in Violence between Intimate Partners: Patterns, Causes, and Effects 48, 52-53 (Albert P. Cardarelli ed., 1997); Robert L. Hampton et al., Domestic Violence in African American Communities, in Domestic Violence at the Margins 127, 132-138 (Natalie J. Sokoloff & Christina Pratt eds., 2008) (attributing disproportionate rate of victimization to persistent and concentrated poverty; racial, economic, and social isolation; chronic unemployment; social disorganization; and family disruption). See also Eve S. Buzawa & Carl G. Buzawa, Domestic Violence: The Criminal Justice Response 41-43 (3d. ed. 2003) (citing factors of societal oppression, high cohabitation rates, and gender-based income inequality in some subgroups).

b. *Explanation.* Might high victimization rates also reflect sample bias? See Angela M. Moore, Intimate Partner Violence: Does Socioeconomic Status Matter?, in Violence between Intimate Partners, supra, at 91 ("Studies that utilized police, shelter, social service agency, or court records oversampled the poor, who are more likely to use such services"). See also Rennison & Planty, supra, at 440 (accord).

2. *Similarities.* As the excerpts reveal, race and ethnicity influence the willingness to report abuse. What reasons explain the reluctance to report abuse for all victims?

3. *Immigration status.* How do immigration and residency status affect victims' willingness to seek intervention? See Leslye Orloff et al., Battered Immigrant Women's Willingness to Call for Help and Police Response, 13 UCLA Women's L.J. 43, 43 (2003) (reporting that disclosure depends on the victim's duration in U.S., presence of children who witness abuse, previous disclosures to others, and immigration status). For example, some immigrants fear that their abusive partners will jeopardize the victim's immigration status. Can a battered immigrant spouse prevent her non-immigrant spouse from contacting immigration authorities? See In re Marriage of Meredith, 201 P.3d 1056 (Wash. Ct. App. 2009) (holding that a protective order restraining the husband in this manner violated his right to free speech and to petition the government). See generally David P. Weber, (Unfair) Advantage: Damocles' Sword and the Coercive Use of Immigration Status in a Civil Society, 94 Marq. L. Rev. 613 (2010). Another problem facing immigrant victims is their attitude about the acceptability of domestic violence in their countries of origin.

4. *Family.* How do family-related issues prevent victims of racial and ethnic groups from seeking help? How does family size influence disclosure? What role does the extended family play? Why might some victims be "least likely to contact a friend, minister, or social service agency for help"? To whom would these victims turn instead? See also Michelle DeCasas, Comment, Protecting Hispanic Women: The Inadequacy of Domestic Violence Policy, 24 Chicano-Latino L. Rev. 56, 70 (2003) (discussing the cultural belief that Latinas should be self-sacrificing and put their family's needs above their own, and the influence of Catholicism).

5. *Attitudes toward the legal system.* How do race and ethnicity affect the likelihood of seeking assistance from police? Prosecutors? Courts? What explains victims' distrust of the legal system? See Zanita E. Fenton, Domestic Violence in Black and White: Racialized Gender Stereotypes in Gender Violence, 8 Colum. J. Gender & L. 1 (1998).

6. *Economic concerns.* How do economic concerns influence victims' experience of, and response to, domestic violence? Their disclosure of the abuse? Ability to exit? Intervention-seeking behavior? How are these concerns similar for members of the various racial and ethnic groups? How are they different?

7. *Stereotypes.* The early stereotype of victims of domestic violence was passive, white, middle-class, and heterosexual. Leigh Goodmark, When Is a Battered Woman Not a Battered Woman? When She Fights Back, 20 Yale J.L. & Feminism 75, 82-92 (2008) (discussing "paradigmatic victim"). How do such stereotypes disadvantage victims? See generally Martinson, supra.

8. *Language barriers.* Many non-English-speaking abused immigrants face unique difficulties. What are the different ways in which language barriers affect victims' experiences of violence? One solution is for courts and social service

agencies to provide interpreters. Yet, qualified interpreters are expensive and not always available. See generally Nancy K. D. Lemon, Access to Justice: Can Domestic Violence Courts Better Address the Needs of Non-English-Speaking Victims of Domestic Violence?, 21 Berkeley J. Gender, L. & Just. 38 (2006). How can courts and social service agencies meet the needs of non-English-speaking clients?

9. *Social services.* Why is help seeking from outside agencies not acceptable to victims of some racial and ethnic groups? When battered African-American, Latina, or Asian women do seek help from outside agencies, what barriers do these victims face? How do social service agencies "unwittingly create barriers" to victims of the various racial and ethnic groups? See also DeCasas, supra, at 69-70 (discussing shelter issues).

10. *Community response.* What explains victims' concerns about the effects of reporting on their racial or ethnic communities? See e.g., Kimberlee Crenshaw, Mapping the Margins: Intersectionality, Identity Politics, and Violence Against Women of Color, 43 Stan. L. Rev. 1241, 1256 (1991) (addressing intracommunity concerns for African-American women); Marilyn Yarbrough & Crystal Bennett, Cassandra and the "Sistahs": The Peculiar Treatment of African-American Women in the Myth of Women as Liars, 3 J. Gender Race & Just. 625, 643 (2000) (noting that failure to prioritize the community over racism jeopardizes a victim's support from the community).

Many battered women's advocates are committed to increasing community awareness of domestic violence. For example, the "Brides' March" was created in the wake of the murder of a Latina by her former boyfriend on her wedding day. This march from Miami to New York by women in wedding dresses brought attention to domestic violence in the Latino community. See Candice Hoyes, Here Comes the Brides' March: Cultural Appropriation and Latina Activism, 13 Colum. J. Gender & L. 328 (2004). How effective are such methods of community activism?

E. RELIGION

What is the role of religion in intimate partner violence? Do members of various religions experience intimate partner violence similarly to, and differently from, other persons? How does the law respond to domestic violence in different religious communities?

■ **ADAM H. KOBLENZ, JEWISH WOMEN UNDER SEIGE: THE FIGHT FOR SURVIVAL ON THE FRONT LINES OF LOVE AND THE LAW**

9 U. Md. L.J. Race, Religion, Gender & Class 259, 259-264, 266-267, 269-270, 294-295 (2009)

A myth persists in contemporary American society that domestic violence is virtually nonexistent in the Jewish community. This falsehood subsists both within and outside the Jewish population. . . . However, studies show that domestic violence occurs in Jewish households at a comparable rate to other ethnic and religious groups. . . .

[A study by the Jewish Women International and Baltimore's Counseling, Helpline and Network for Abused Women, reported that] battered Jewish women were the least likely of any ethnic or religious group to utilize available resources or implement self-help remedies such as women's shelters, support groups, or social services. This finding is alarming considering that Jewish women often stay in violent relationships longer than women in the non-Jewish community. [T]he tendency of Jewish women to remain in violent relationships is due in large part to the often cited attempt of Jewish women to maintain *shalom bayit*, also known as peace in the home. . . . Jewish women stay in abusive relationships for 7–13 years, whereas women in non-Jewish homes stay in such relationships for 3–5 years. Abused Jewish women, embarrassed by their plight, are less inclined to seek public assistance, especially because society perceives Jewish women as well-educated and financially secure. . . .

The stigmatization of Jewish women as being inferior to Jewish men has endured for centuries. In evaluating the American secular courts' treatment of battered Jewish women, it is imperative to understand the origin of this stigmatization. From a historical context, rabbis living between 200 and 500 B.C.E. created most of the existing body of Jewish law in the Mishnah and Talmud; any other additions came from medieval scholarship. This body of religious law was codified between the Twelfth and Sixteenth Centuries. . . .

Marriage is a prime example of gender inequality within the Jewish community. Historically, marriage in Judaism serves two fundamental purposes: (1) the satisfaction of the spouses; and (2) the procreation of children. Within traditional Jewish law (*Halakhah*) and culture, Jewish women were historically treated as inferior to Jewish men in most facets of Jewish life. Over time, a patriarchy evolved from the teachings of *Halakhah*, the core of which established Jewish men as the focal point in the Jewish community. Based on these teachings, Jewish women were essentially treated as second-class citizens. In some instances, women were even viewed as their husband's property. Essentially, a Jewish woman's main purpose on earth was to be at their husband's disposal and to bear his children. Accordingly, the disparate role of Jewish women was apparent within familial relationships, religious practices and cultural traditions. . . .

[S]exism plays a critical role in the perpetuation of domestic violence in the Jewish community. The pervasiveness of sexism varies depending on the denomination of Judaism at issue. . . . [S]exism is most prevalent in the Ultra-Orthodox and Orthodox communities. This deeply rooted sexism reinforces traditional gender roles and creates a culture that accepts domestic violence against women. . . . [T]raditional Jewish law also bars Orthodox Jewish women from participating in many important daily religious ceremonies. These rituals include the listening to Torah reading and the reciting of sacred prayers. In fact, the Orthodox do not allow Jewish women to become rabbis or lead a religious service. Orthodox Jewish women are also excluded from reciting the Mourner's *Kaddish*, a sacred prayer specifically recited in honor of the dead. In effect, these exclusionary practices have unnecessarily isolated Jewish women and deprived them of a vital opportunity to pray at a time when they needed spiritual solace the most. The fact that Jewish women are excluded from certain religious practices and obligations commanded by God provides further evidence of the inequity and contempt for women that underlie the Orthodox community's stance on domestic violence. . . .

Anti-Semitic stereotypes play a critical role in spawning societal antipathy towards Jewish women. For example, the typical stereotype that Jewish women are almost always catered to by their fathers and dominant of their husbands engenders a false reality that is dangerous to the security of Jewish women. Likewise, the modern societal perception endures that Jewish women are unlikely to become victims of domestic violence based on imperfect notions of empowerment or dominance in relation to men (within their faith) than their non-Jewish counterparts. Stamped as an abrasive, emasculating, and overbearing mother or a pampered, demanding, and self-centered shrew, a Jewish woman hardly evokes sympathy from the public or a court of law. As a result, Jewish women are mistakenly viewed as unsympathetic figures that possess great power over the men in their lives.

It is often the case that Jewish women are simply afraid to report domestic violence directly to the authorities because they believe that law enforcement will fail to protect them. Thus, domestic violence in Jewish households remains virtually undetected by the outside public. As a result, Jewish women tend to succumb at the hands of their abusers due to the absence of viable options or preemptive recourse. The reporting of domestic violence can also create animosity within the Jewish community itself, often polarizing Jewish women from one another within the faith. Abused Jewish women often face the unsympathetic scorn of other Jewish women, as well as the Jewish community at large, who frown upon those who dare accuse abusive Jewish men of such heinous and immoral crimes. As one scholar aptly noted, "[t]o some Jews, [the abused Jewish woman] is nothing short of a traitor who undermines efforts to combat the more pressing issue of anti-Semitism. . . ."

Depending on the denomination of Judaism, the role of rabbis and community leaders and their underlying attitudes towards the issue of domestic violence varies. Among the three most popular denominations of Judaism, the Reform Movement tends to be the most progressive, flexible, and active denomination when it comes to the prevention of domestic violence. Reform Judaism promotes gender equality while encouraging participation of women in religious customs. Moreover, rabbis within the Reform community struggle to counter the inherent inequity that Jewish women face in other denominations of Judaism by seeking to rewrite antiquated Jewish law that is detrimental to Jewish women today. . . .

Similarly, Conservative Judaism is less rigid than Orthodox, but not nearly as sensitive or inclusive in its treatment of women as Reform Judaism. While the modern Conservative Movement has allowed for active participation of women in certain religious rituals and practices, the ultra-right Conservative Rabbinate is more closely aligned with the Orthodox Rabbinate in its stance on domestic abuse issues impacting the Jewish community today. Unfortunately, domestic violence within the ultra-Orthodox Jewish community remains unaddressed. Orthodox rabbis strictly adhere to Jewish religious doctrine and traditions, and consequently many do not acknowledge domestic violence. . . .

The following excerpt addresses the social practice of "honor killings" in the Islamic Muslim world. Yet the custom of punishing women for real and suspected sexual impropriety has longstanding roots in many cultures outside this context.

■ **KENNETH LASSON, BLOODSTAINS ON A "CODE OF HONOR": THE MURDEROUS MARGINALIZATION OF WOMEN IN THE ISLAMIC WORLD**

30 Women's Rts. L. Rep. 407, 407-408, 415-418, 425-426, 440-441 (2009)

. . . In early February of 2009, the decapitated body of Aasiya Zubair Hassan was found in Orchard Park, New York, an upstate suburb of Buffalo. The dead woman had recently filed for divorce from her husband, Muzzammil Hassan—whom police promptly arrested and charged with murder. There was widespread speculation that the gruesome death was an honor killing based on Islamic religious or cultural beliefs.

As unfathomable as it is to Western minds, honor killings occur frequently. A vestige of traditional patriarchy, its condonation can be traced largely to ancient tribal practices. Justifications for it can be found in the codes of Hammurabi and in the family law of the Roman Empire. In the real world of the twenty-first century, deep biases against women are prevalent in much of Muslim society. Although there is no explicit approval of honor killing in Islamic law (Sharia), it remains part of the fundamentally patriarchal culture. . . .

Unfortunately, honor killings in the twenty-first century are not isolated incidents, nor can they be regarded as mere relics of a primitive past. Instead they are part and parcel of an ancient culture with strong roots and an ever-increasing population—a tribal custom where family honor is determined largely by its women's compliance with accepted standards of propriety. Their pre-marital virginity is considered to be the property of their male relatives, who are duty-bound to guard it. Even suspicions of infidelity—whether consensual or coerced—may be punished by beatings, torture, or execution. Usually the punishment is meted out by a male member of the family who, like the alleged paramour, seldom faces recrimination.

Thus, grounded in religion and involving sexual relationships, the sensitivities brought to bear in honor killings are so great and nuanced that the slightest offense to an exceptionally strict norm elicits harsh responses. Many honor killings occur based on suspicion or rumor of illicit sexual relations. . . . "[T]he true number of honor killings occurring worldwide remains unknown, largely because they often remain a private family affair." Most take place in predominantly Muslim countries. In Jordan, for example, honor killings may account for one-third of all violent deaths each year. Since 1998 more than 2,000 cases of honor killings have been reported in Pakistan. But such murders have also occurred in Australia, Brazil, Britain, Canada, Ecuador, Italy, Sweden, and the United States. . . . [Furthermore, it is unknown] how many women are maimed or disfigured for life in attacks that fall short of murder. . . .

If we are to accept the fact that honor killings violate international law and should be considered repugnant to modern civilization, what meaningful and effective responses can be provided by Western democracies? A number of social, economic, and political issues complicate and limit the range of options. Countries with large Islamic communities—such as, Australia, Britain, Canada, Germany, Italy, and the United States—are often constrained by domestic considerations. For example, a recent wave of honor killings in Germany, accompanied by extremist preaching in German mosques, has led government officials to speak out against various multi-cultural initiatives, and there have been moves in the Legislature to expel Islamic extremists who condone such activity. However, the high concentration of Islamic migrant workers, combined with their poor economic conditions, make the situation tense and fluid. . . . Other international issues—above all, the oil trade—likewise serve to deny Western nations the full political and economic leverage required to deal most effectively with human rights abuses in the Islamic world. . . .

There is no justification for honor killings. Yet the practice, which can be traced to ancient tribal traditions, continues unabated to this day in much of the world. Though there is a clear moral imperative to combat violence toward women, local, national, and international responses to these atrocities have been largely muted and ineffective.

The best approach to combat honor killings worldwide would be to substantially raise public consciousness about it, to enact meaningful measures to prevent and punish it, and to enforce such laws swiftly and with certainty. . . .

■ KATHLEEN A. McDONALD, NOTE, BATTERED WIVES, RELIGION, AND LAW: AN INTERDISCIPLINARY APPROACH
2 Yale J.L. & Feminism 251, 253, 290 (1990)

. . . Religions wield considerable power and influence in modern society; thus, their pronouncements regarding women take on momentous significance, especially when justified as "the word of God." Furthermore, millions of women choose to develop themselves spiritually in organized religion. Not only does religion affect how a woman perceives an appropriate husband-wife relationship, but it also influences her decision to seek legal assistance should that relationship founder. . . .

Religion seems to pervade the lives of women in one of three primary ways: through a woman's direct and active practice in a particular sect, through childhood inculcation of religious values even if active practice is subsequently abandoned in adulthood, or through the influence of religion on attitudes and mores that imperceptibly shape the structure of husband-wife interactions. Although followers of Judeo-Christian traditions do not have a monopoly on "traditional" beliefs and customs that affect a battered wife's choices and behaviors, these beliefs and customs take on increased significance because they are grounded in "God's will." Wives influenced by men's selective and skewed interpretation of Judeo-Christian scriptures typically believe in the correctness of submitting to their husbands and forgiving their offenses "seventy times seven." These women are committed to their families, which occupy a high, if not the highest, priority in their lives. Judeo-Christian teachings can lead women to consider divorce an anathema. The women themselves may feel stigmatized by the specter of a "failed marriage"; moreover, their churches may either expressly condemn divorce or make the process for obtaining an ecclesiastical marital dissolution long and difficult.

The importance of religious doctrines to so many battered wives requires serious and constructive treatment of religious experiences. When forced to choose between religious beliefs or assistance in escaping from abusive relationships, these battered wives are likely to select the former. . . .

Notes and Questions

1. *Role of religion.* What role do religious beliefs play in domestic violence? See generally Robbin G. Todhunter & John Deaton, The Relationship between Religious and Spiritual Factors and the Perception of Intimate Personal Violence, 25 J. Fam. Violence 745 (2010).

2. *Differences in responses to domestic violence.* How do the different denominations of Judaism regard domestic violence? Why do Jewish women stay in abusive relationships longer? Why are they unlikely to utilize social services? See also Beverly Horsburgh, Lifting the Veil of Secrecy: Domestic Violence in the Jewish Community, 18 Harv. Women's L.J. 171 (1995); Yuval Sinai & Benjamin Shmueli, Changing the Current Policy Towards Spousal Abuse: A Proposal for a New Model Inspired by Jewish Law, 32 Hastings Int'l & Comp. L. Rev. 155 (2009) (comparative study of spousal abuse in religious law and modern Israeli law).

3. *Judeo-Christian principles.* How do Judeo-Christian beliefs contribute to domestic violence? How do religious teachings about women's roles, marriage, and divorce provide support for domestic violence? Some abusers use religious beliefs to justify their abuse. How? See Heidi M. Levitt et al., Male Perpetrators' Perspectives on Intimate Partner Violence, Religion, and Masculinity, 58 Sex Roles 435, 446 (2008) (finding that 24 percent of abused women report that their partners used religion to justify their abuse).

4. *Islamic beliefs.* What is "honor killing"? How do views of women, sexuality, and gender roles contribute to the practice? How can honor killings be addressed by the legal system? What social, economic, and political issues impede the development of public policy condemning honor killings? See generally Nooria Faizi, Comment, Domestic Violence in the Muslim Community, 10 Tex. J. Women & L. 209 (2001); Lisa Hajjar, Religion, State Power, and Domestic Violence in Muslim Societies: A Framework for Comparative Analysis, 29 Law & Soc. Inquiry 1 (2004).

5. *Clergy.* How do some clergy impede women's exit from abusive relationships? See Sarah M. Buel, Access to Meaningful Remedy: Overcoming Doctrinal Obstacles in Tort Litigation Against Domestic Violence Offenders, 83 Or. L. Rev. 945, 970 (2004) (criticizing that clergy often advise battered women to be more compliant, rather than "addressing the importance of the batterer's ceasing his conduct").

How can religious leaders help members of their congregation who are experiencing domestic violence? See generally Jewish Women International, Resource Guide for Rabbis on Domestic Violence (1996); United States Conference of Catholic Bishops, When I Call for Help: A Pastoral Response to Domestic Violence Against Women (2002). See also Nancy Nason-Clark, When Terror Strikes at Home: The Interface between Religion and Domestic Violence, 43 J. Sci. Study Religion 303 (2004) (exploring the experience of victims who turn to their faith).

F. SOCIAL CLASS

Does social class affect the likelihood of being victimized by an intimate partner? How does an intimate partner's social class play a role in the law's response to domestic violence?

■ **KARL VICK, CASE OF JOHN MICHAEL FARREN SEEN
AS REFRESHER COURSE ON DOMESTIC VIOLENCE**
Wash. Post, Feb. 25, 2010, at 24

[W]hat mattered to Mary Margaret Farren in the darkness [was] that lights were on inside [the large Cape Cod-style house nearby]. The 43-year-old lawyer swung the BMW into the drive of a family she didn't know, leaned on the horn, pounded on the front door. When it opened, she collapsed, bleeding, in the airy stillness of a New Canaan, Connecticut, foyer.

"She made several remarks implying that she did not think she was going to live," New Canaan police Sgt. Louis Gannon noted in his report. Summoned by the owners of the house[,] the officer found Farren on her side, inside the front door of the dumbfounded family's house, shivering and pale under a pile of blankets in an expanding pool of blood.

She said her husband had tried to kill her, first with his hands, then with a metal flashlight, according to the police report. She said his plan was to kill her and then himself. She said that he was still at home, a mile away, and that there was a gun somewhere in the house.

The sergeant relayed the information to the squad cars screaming toward the house she had fled. And so what appeared before J. Michael Farren a year after leaving the White House were four police officers, two with shotguns, one with an assault rifle, one with a shield held across the other three, advancing toward the $4 million home of a man last employed as deputy counsel to the president of the United States.

Mike Farren came out with his hands up. After he was handcuffed, the officers photographed the blood on the floor of the master bedroom, where his wife said he erupted over divorce papers that would cite "long-term verbal, emotional and, in at least one instance, physical abuse." They photographed ligature marks around Mike Farren's neck that matched the pattern of his braided belt. They photographed blood on his hands. "He said to me, 'I am killing you' as he was strangling me," Mary Farren wrote in an affidavit from her hospital bed, private guards posted in the corridor. . . .

[Farren, who was the son of a nurse and a police captain, earned a master's degree in public policy and a law degree. He worked for the Republican National Committee, President George H. W. Bush's transition team and re-election campaign, and then became Undersecretary for International Trade in the Commerce Department. After Bill Clinton become president, Farren became general counsel for the Xerox Corporation.] "He was a hot commodity," said a friend of two decades. . . . "His powers of analysis and memory are astounding. He's somebody who can remember a fact from 20 years ago and how it relates to policy both then and now." "Having said that, he definitely was—is—a very intense guy. Had a temper. He could get extremely angry, in a way that would stand out from other people."

[When Farren was 44, he married Mary Margaret Scharf, who was 31] "a very chipper, upbeat, happy person who is also a very meticulous lawyer," said the friend. "Both of them are very meticulous, organized people." She was a lawyer, too, also out of the University of Connecticut but raised in Pennsylvania, the daughter of a management consultant and a school nurse. . . . [She was employed as an attorney in the Washington, D.C., office of Skadden, Arps, Slate, Meagher & Flom.]

[They bought a large home in New Canaan], a five-bedroom, seven-bath pile tucked well away even by local standards. The iron gate separates its private driveway from the private road. . . . "But you know what?" said Sue Delaney, who counsels victims of domestic violence in the area. "Nobody can hear you scream." "Whether you're in a 2.5 or in subsidized housing, the dynamic is surely the same," Delaney said. "It's only the furniture that's different." . . .

Mary Margaret was at the home of a friend, police wrote, when the process-server [served her husband with divorce papers two days before the attack]. "I could no longer remain married and live in a marital relationship where I was in a state of almost constant anxiety as a result of the Defendant's temper, volatility and personality," she later wrote. It's unclear whether the couple saw each other before that Wednesday night, when, according to police accounts, Mike Farren said he wanted her to drop the proceedings and stay together. She said she could not. He walked toward her.

When she said, "Do not approach me," he "exploded in rage," she told police. She has flowing brunette hair. Her husband pulled out "gobs" of it, she said. She said he threw her across the room and began hitting her with a metal flashlight. On the floor, she passed out for a time, she told police, and went briefly blind when he strangled her. Then she remembered the alarm button on the security system, which automatically summoned police. "Don't hit the alarm button," Mike Farren warned, according to the police account. When she managed to do so, "he went nuts" at the sound. . . . [He began hitting her again with the metal flashlight.]

At this point, according to the affidavit, she pleaded with him to stop, saying they could work it out. He paused for a moment, she wrote, then decided: "You're just saying that because you're scared." Mike Farren then announced he was going to slit his wrists, his wife said. She told police he took a kitchen knife into the bathroom and made an effort to get her in as well. Instead she scrambled to her daughter's room screaming, "Daddy's trying to kill me," got the startled barefoot girl and her infant sister down to the garage, into the BMW sedan and past the gate.

The bloody BMW keys were photographed as evidence. So was Mary Margaret's lacerated face, broken nose, broken jaw, bruised arms, legs, torso. In an image now attached to the divorce action, she leans forward in the emergency room, the entire chair behind her black with blood. Police ended the interview the second time she began vomiting blood.

"Generally in the more affluent areas, the level of violence is far more severe," said Kucera Mehra [director of the Domestic Violence Crisis Center]. . . . [Mary Margaret filed a civil suit against her husband for $30 million. Farren remains in a maximum security prison.]

■ CLAIRE M. RENZETTI & VIVIAN M. LARKIN, ECONOMIC STRESS AND DOMESTIC VIOLENCE

National Online Resource Center on Violence Against Women, Applied Research Forum (Sept. 2009)

The claim is often made that domestic violence affects individuals in all social classes. This assertion has been critical in raising awareness about DV by reminding the public that wealth does not protect against victimization. . . . Nevertheless, various types of research show a strong relationship between financial status and a woman's risk for domestic violence victimization. Although it is certainly the case that middle-class and affluent families do experience domestic violence, studies consistently indicate that as the financial status of a family increases, the likelihood of domestic violence decreases. . . . [Data from the National Crime Victimization Survey report] DV rates five times greater in households with the lowest annual incomes compared with households with the highest annual incomes.

Economic Hardship, Employment, and Domestic Violence

[The relationship between employment and DV is a complex one.] DV appears to substantially affect women's employment. . . . [C]ompared with women who have not experienced DV, women who report DV victimization also report more days arriving late to work, more absenteeism from work, more psychological and physical health problems that may reduce their productivity, and greater difficulty maintaining employment over time. . . .

Still, employment can have a protective effect for women. Employment provides not only important financial resources, but also may raise a woman's self-esteem, thereby providing her with psychological resources to cope with or end an abusive relationship. Research also shows that abused employed women who received social and tangible support from co-workers and supervisors experienced less social isolation, improved health, and fewer negative employment outcomes.

Several studies have documented how batterers often deliberately try to sabotage their partners' efforts to obtain and maintain paid employment. Such tactics are often referred to as economic abuse and include damaging or destroying women's work clothes or books and other items associated with their jobs or job training, inflicting facial cuts and bruises or other visible injuries to keep them from going to work, promising to care for their children but not showing up or becoming unavailable at the last minute, and stalking women while they are at work. . . . Employed women who experience DV, especially stalking at work, may consequently lose their jobs or give them up with the hope of increasing their safety, resulting in another pathway from DV victimization to lower financial stability and even poverty for some women. . . .

. . . [M]en who experience unemployment are at greater risk of DV perpetration. [A]mong couples where the male partner was consistently employed, the DV rate was 4.7 percent; [however,] it increased to 7.5 percent for couples where the male partner experienced one period of unemployment, and rose to 12.3 percent for couples where the male partner experienced two or more periods of unemployment. Thus, the research on employment and DV indicates that cultural norms of masculinity that prescribe male dominance in intimate relationships and families may affect the employment—DV relationship. . . .

Social Support Networks

Norms of male dominance have also been used to explain why domestic violence rates are higher in communities and neighborhoods characterized by economic disadvantage compared with more economically stable or affluent communities and neighborhoods. The social and structural contexts in which people live help shape their values and norms, including gender norms. This observation has led some researchers to hypothesize that unemployed and underemployed men who live in neighborhoods of concentrated economic disadvantage may experience high levels of stress because they cannot achieve the type of masculine success most valued in our patriarchal culture, i.e., financial success. But while these men may not be successful in the breadwinner role, they may measure masculine success in other ways. For example, they may assert dominance through violence, be it violence against one another, against those who disrespect them or cross them in some way, and against women. Some studies indicate that economically disenfranchised men often associate with one another in male peer support networks that collectively devalue women and regard them as legitimate victims who deserve physical and sexual abuse. While some studies indicate that sexual conquest and asserting social and physical control over women may be a source of power and a measure of success for powerless men who are unsuccessful by traditional patriarchal success markers, such as wealth, there is also considerable research that shows similar attitudes and behaviors among more privileged men, including members of college fraternities. Male peer support networks supportive of violence against women, then, are prevalent across social classes. . . .

Public Assistance and Domestic Violence

[I]mpoverished women who are battered and battered women who become poor as a result of leaving abusive relationships may have no choice but to work, given requirements of public assistance (commonly referred to as welfare) passed by Congress in 1996.

The Personal Responsibility and Work Opportunity Reconciliation Act (PRWORA) replaced the former means-tested federal entitlement program, Aid to Families with Dependent Children (AFDC) with Temporary Assistance to Needy Families (TANF) (PL 104-193). TANF established time limits and low family caps on aid receipt. Lifetime receipt of cash assistance is limited to five years, although states may choose to impose even lower limits or, conversely, to extend the five-year limit under certain circumstances. Quotas were also imposed on states for establishing paternity and enforcing child support orders, since child support is considered an important source of income for TANF applicants. TANF applicants who are single parents are required to cooperate with child support agencies by assisting them in establishing paternity, locating the absent parent, and obtaining a child support order. Such requirements are dangerous for DV survivors, as they put them at further risk of DV by, for instance, making abusers aware of their location or angering the abuser with a child support order.

Congress was made aware of the particular barriers to work that DV survivors face and that trying to meet TANF requirements could jeopardize their safety. In response, Congress included in the PRWORA the Family Violence Option (FVO), which was designed to ensure that women would not be unfairly denied public assistance because DV prevents them from meeting TANF requirements. The FVO allows state welfare offices to grant DV survivors temporary waivers or exemptions from TANF requirements and to waive time limits on the receipt of benefits, as well as provide referrals to battered women's services when appropriate. Adoption of the FVO was optional for the states and although most have adopted it, only a minority (.5 percent-3 percent out of an estimated 20 percent-30 percent of applicants who are eligible) of TANF clients disclose DV to their caseworkers, request an FVO waiver or exemption, or utilize DV victim services. To some extent, this discrepancy is due to the failure of TANF caseworkers to adequately and sensitively screen TANF applicants for DV. Another barrier to full DV disclosure is fear among women, especially women living in poverty, that reporting DV may trigger an automatic report to child protection authorities, and potentially result in losing custody of their children.

[M]any DV survivors do not see the waivers as the best way to meet their multitude of needs. In fact, DV survivors living in poverty often report that DV is not the most serious problem they face. Of greater concern to them are the challenges posed by living daily life in unrelenting financial hardship: getting a job that pays enough for them to support themselves and their children; access to safe, reliable and affordable child care; safe and reliable transportation to and from work; and safe and affordable housing. Thus, effectively meeting the needs of low-income and impoverished battered women and women who are forced into financial hardship because of DV requires multidimensional, collaborative strategies that simultaneously address the intersecting problems and consequences of poverty and DV. . . .

Notes and Questions

1. *Universal risk theory.* The "universal risk theory" suggests that all women are equally victimized by intimate partner violence. Angela M. Moore, Intimate Partner Violence: Does Socioeconomic Status Matter?, in Violence between Intimate Partners, supra, at 93. This theory marshaled widespread appeal early in the battered women's movement. By rejecting the view that intimate partner violence was confined to the lower classes, the theory avoided charges of classism and racism. The theory also "mobilized women of diverse backgrounds to take a stand against a problem that is common to all women." Id. However, the role of socioeconomic class in intimate partner violence soon became impossible to deny.

2. *Income and domestic violence rates.* The relationship of income and domestic violence is multifaceted. The rate of domestic violence decreases as household income level increases. That is, women in low-income households experience a higher rate of nonlethal violence from an intimate partner than do women in households with higher incomes. Lawrence A. Greenfeld et al., U.S. Dept. of Justice, Violence by Intimates: Analysis of Data on Crimes by Current or Former Spouses, Boyfriends, and Girlfriends 14 (1998), available at http:// www.ojp.usdoj.gov/bjs/pub/pdf/vi.pdf

Other studies substantiate the findings of Renzetti and Larkin in the excerpt that couples experiencing financial strain have significantly higher rates of violence. In addition, women whose partners are unemployed are three times as likely to suffer abuse. Women living in economically disadvantaged neighborhoods suffer the greatest risk of violence, and women living in these communities are more likely to suffer repeated abuse than women living in more affluent communities. Michael L. Benson & Greer Litton Fox, Nat'l Inst. of Justice, When Violence Hits Home: How Economics and Neighborhood Play a Role, Research in Brief ii (Sept. 2004), available at http://www.ncjrs.gov/pdffiles1/mij/205004.pdf

3. *Criticism of correlation.* Advocates and commentators are critical of data emphasizing the correlation between poverty and domestic violence. Some authorities point out that this emphasis obscures the nature and extent of domestic

violence because certain factors that are *associated* with poverty (that is, unemployment, substance abuse) also contribute to domestic violence. See Hillary Potter, Battle Cries: Black Women and Intimate Partner Abuse 8 (2008) (citing "multiple marginalization factors"). Moreover, critics note the many subtle ways that abusers keep women in poverty by preventing them from working and/or isolating them. Jody Raphael, Battering Through the Lens of Class, 11 Am. U. J. Gender Soc. Pol'y & L. 367, 373 (2003).

4. *Reciprocal nature.* Renzetti and Larkin point out that the relationship between poverty and domestic violence is "reciprocal in nature." Other commentators explain the reciprocity as follows: "Violence affects poor women in two critical ways: it makes them poor and it keeps them poor." Martha F. Davis & Susan J. Kraham, Protecting Women's Welfare in the Face of Violence, 22 Fordham Urb. L.J. 1141, 1144 (1995). How does domestic violence "make" and "keep" women poor?

5. *Vicious Cycle.* Abusers use power and control to keep victims dependent. Many victims stay in abusive relationships because they are financially dependent. Also, victims may be kept isolated from financial resources. See Raphael, supra. See also Mary Ann Dutton et al., Characteristics of Help-Seeking Behaviors, Resources and Service Needs of Battered Immigrant Latinas: Legal and Policy Implications, 7 Geo. J. on Poverty L. & Pol'y 245, 250 (2000). One method of breaking the cycle is for victims to obtain employment. Employment provides financial independence and also raises self-esteem—both effects counter abusers' control. See Davis & Kraham, supra, at 1151. However, victims face other difficulties in obtaining and maintaining employment. See generally Nina W. Tarr, Employment and Economic Security for Victims of Domestic Abuse, 16 S. Cal. Rev. L. & Soc. Just. 371, 375 (2007). The role of employment and domestic violence is explored further in Chapter 13.

6. *Welfare.* As Renzetti and Larkin point out, there is a strong correlation between domestic violence and welfare recipients. How does victims' need to satisfy welfare requirements (that is, cooperating with child support agencies in establishing paternity, locating an absent parent, and obtaining a child support order) jeopardize their safety? In recognition of this dilemma, Congress included the Family Violence Option (FVO) in 1997 in welfare reform legislation, 42 U.S.C. §602(a)(7), to prevent welfare reforms from adversely impacting those welfare recipients who are victims of domestic violence. How does the FVO ensure that intimate partners who are victims of domestic violence are not unfairly denied public assistance? Why do so few eligible applicants utilize the Family Violence Option when applying for public assistance? How can this problem be remedied?

On the relationship of domestic violence and the welfare system, see Jody Raphael, Saving Bernice: Battered Women, Welfare, and Poverty (2000) (recounting story of welfare recipient who was a survivor); Andrea Hetling & Catherine E. Born, Examining the Impact of the Family Violence Option on Women's Efforts to Leave Welfare, 15 Soc. Work Practice 143, 151 (2005) (reporting "disturbing prospects" for victims whose experiences are not administratively documented); Shelby A. D. Moore, Understanding the Connection between Domestic Violence, Crime, and Poverty: How Welfare Reform May Keep Battered Women from Leaving Abusive Relationships, 12 Tex. J. Women & L. 451 (2003) (concluding that FVO does not eliminate all obstacles to receipt of welfare). For additional discussion of different states' implementation of the FVO, see Katie Scrivner, Comment, Domestic

Violence Victims after Welfare Reform: Looking Beyond the Family Violence Option, 16 Wis. Women's L.J. 241 (2001).

7. *Social reality: affluent victims.* How is abuse of affluent victims *similar* to that of other victims? How was the experience of Mary Margaret Farren similar to that of other victims? The experiences of abused affluent women also reflect several differences from the experiences of other women. For example, affluent women fail to recognize abuse because they never experienced it previously or witnessed it; they are more likely to blame themselves for the abuse and resolve to try harder to make their marriages work; and their abusers are less likely to be remorseful after the abuse, stemming from their sense that they are the wronged party. Susan Weitzman, Not to People Like Us: Hidden Domestic Violence in Upscale Families, 46 Soc. Work Networker 3, 5 (2008). See also Susan Weitzman, Not to People Like Us: Hidden Abuse in Upscale Marriages (2001). What policy reforms might address these barriers to women's exit from abusive relationships?

8. *Incidence of abuse among the wealthy.* What difficulties arise in gathering data on domestic violence among the affluent? For example, data on domestic violence is collected generally from emergency rooms, shelters, and law enforcement sources. Do upper-class women tend to use these services? Why or why not? What alternative services might they use?

9. *Shelter services.* Suppose that Mary Margaret Farren sought shelter services earlier in her relationship. What difficulties might she have faced? Weitzman reveals that upper-class women are rarely believed by service providers. When service providers discover that a victim owns a house and has a career, they become less helpful, believing that these women have other resources. Weitzman, Hidden Abuse in Upscale Marriages, supra, at 8-10. Other professionals, such as doctors and lawyers, discredit the victim's account, stemming from their reluctance to believe that violence happens to people "like them." Id. at 11. Some professionals believe that the poor are more deserving of social work and advocacy services. Id. at 7. What might be the effect of these attitudes for the victim? Might they enhance her isolation and self-doubt?

10. *Reluctance to disclose.* Upper-class women are often reluctant to disclose their victimization. They remain silent because of a desire to maintain their lifestyle and identity, as well as a reluctance to jeopardize their husbands' position, income, and social standing. Weitzman, Hidden Abuse in Upscale Marriages, supra, at 26-27. How can social service personnel and other professionals address these attitudes? See also Kathleen Waits, Battered Women and Family Lawyers: The Need for an Identification Protocol, 58 Alb. L. Rev. 1027, 1035 (1995).

11. *Special types of abuse.* Victims of affluent abusers are particularly vulnerable to "litigation abuse." Litigation abuse is defined as batterers' "engage[ing] in prolonged, frivolous, and repetitive use of the legal system for their own purposes . . . not to further the case, but to maintain the harassment and drain their partner's finances." Kara Bellew, Silent Suffering: Uncovering and Understanding Domestic Violence in Affluent Communities, 26 Women's Rts. L. Rep. 39, 44-45 (2005). For example, abusers can be very litigious in protective order proceedings, divorce, and child custody proceedings. Id. Why are victims of affluent abusers so vulnerable to this type of abuse? What are the implications of these findings for policy formulation? Litigation abuse is explored further in this Chapter and in Chapter 10.

G. SUBSTANCE ABUSE

■ MONICA L. ZILBERMAN & SHEILA B. BLUME, DOMESTIC VIOLENCE, ALCOHOL, AND SUBSTANCE ABUSE

27 Revista Brasiliera Psiquiatria 51-55 (Oct. 2005)

. . . Substance use (by the perpetrator, the victim or both) is involved in as many as 92 percent of reported episodes of domestic violence. Alcohol frequently acts as a disinhibitor, facilitating violence. Stimulants such as cocaine, crack cocaine and amphetamines are also frequently involved in episodes of domestic violence by reducing impulse control and increasing paranoid feelings. Alcohol use seems to be involved in up to 50 percent of the cases of sexual assault. Violent married men have higher rates of alcoholism when compared to their non-violent counterparts. Studies report rates of alcoholism of 67 percent and 93 percent among wife batterers. Among male alcoholics in treatment, 20 to 33 percent reported having assaulted their wives at least once in the year prior to the survey, their wives reporting even higher rates. The American Medical Association reports that rape represents 54 percent of cases of marital violence. Rape and other forms of victimization are disproportionately frequent among women with substance use problems in comparison to other women in the general population. Substance use may also be involved in domestic violence in more subtle ways, such as arguments over financial matters (the substance user takes money from the spouse, or diverts money that should be used to pay household bills to buy drugs, for example).

On the other hand, alcohol and other drugs are often used to medicate the pain involved in situations of domestic violence and trauma by women. Women injured by a male partner are twice to three times as likely to abuse alcohol and to have used cocaine. . . .

Domestic violence and substance use disorders in women often go undetected by health care professionals. Professionals do not feel comfortable asking women about domestic violence and substance problems, and patients do not feel comfortable reporting them. These are painful conditions and experiences associated with shame and stigma. Feelings that they are the guilty parties, that they somehow provoked the violence, also contribute to underreporting. Both patients and professionals may feel it is not worthwhile to raise these issues, feeling powerless to fix the situation and afraid of creating even more difficulties. . . .

The association of violence and substance use problems tends to complicate and to impose challenges in providing treatment for women with both conditions. Physical consequences of substance use may complicate victimization-linked medical conditions. Likewise, physical and psychological consequences of violence, such as head injuries, pain, and reduced self-esteem may make it difficult for many women to attend addiction treatment. Concentration and memory problems may interfere with treatment. Medications used to alleviate physical and psychological injuries associated with violence also impact the treatment of alcohol and other drug problems. Moreover, victimized women may find it particularly difficult to build a trusting, working relationship with health care professionals.

Recent research has clarified health care professionals' understanding of domestic violence and its connections with substance use, abuse and dependence, offering the opportunity for us to use that understanding to improve the care of affected patients. These issues impact not only patients, but also their partners, children, and the elderly, influencing the physical and psychological well-being of the whole family. Screening is critical, and, once the problems are identified, interventions must be directed towards both domestic violence and substance abuse, so as to reduce further victimization and its impact on the health of future generations.

Notes and Questions

1. *Prevalence.* What is the prevalence of substance use by the abuser? By the victim?

2. *Types of abuse.* What *types* of intimate partner victimization are frequent among those persons with substance use problems?

3. *Cause or correlation.* Does substance abuse cause domestic violence? Or, is it merely correlated with domestic violence? Or both? What light does the above excerpt shed on these questions? See also Kathryn Graham et al., Alcohol May Not Cause Partner Violence But It Seems to Make It Worse: A Cross National Comparison of the Relationship Between Alcohol and Severity of Partner Violence, 26 J. Interpersonal Violence 1503 (2011) (finding that severity of abuse was higher if both parties had been drinking).

4. *Roles.* How does substance abuse play a role in domestic violence, according to the excerpt? Additional ways that substance abuse affects the abuser include: (1) causing a lack of inhibition that leads to acting on impulse and a disregard for the consequences; (2) serving as a "catalyst, excuse or justification" for violence; and (3) serving as a source of marital conflict. See John Nicoletti & Sally Spencer-Thomas, A Cognitive Processing Model for Assessing and Treating Domestic Violence and Stalking by Law Enforcement Officers, in Domestic Violence by Police Officers 273 (Donald C. Sheehan ed., 2000). How does it affect the victim?

5. *Screening.* Why does the link between substance abuse and domestic violence often go undetected by health care professionals? How might these professionals screen better? What other professionals might detect the link between substance abuse and domestic violence?

H. SPECIAL CONTEXTS

Intimate partner violence occurs in many contexts. Some of these contexts (e.g., the military, police, and sports) are explored here. What are the unique characteristics of these social contexts that influence the law's response?

1. Military

■ **SIMEON STAMM, NOTE, INTIMATE PARTNER VIOLENCE IN THE MILITARY: SECURING OUR COUNTRY, STARTING WITH THE HOME**
47 Fam. Ct. Rev. 321, 322, 324-326 (2009)

... Domestic violence in the U.S. Military is a growing concern. Research shows that the rates of domestic violence in the U.S. Military are two to five times higher than among the civilian population. [The] Army has demonstrated the highest rates of domestic violence out of any other military sector. ... The typical victim of military domestic violence is a female, civilian spouse of an active duty military soldier. On average, the victim is under the age of twenty-five years old. Most victims are also parents and more than half of the victims have been married two years or less. In most cases, when domestic violence involving members of the military has been substantiated, the perpetrator is predominantly a male serving on active duty.

There are many known risk factors in both the civilian population and the military population that can lead a person to commit acts of domestic violence. ... Individual risk factors may include young age, low self-esteem, low income, drug abuse, alcohol abuse, unemployment, and low academic achievement. The relationship risk factors may include a desire for power and control in the relationship, poor family functioning, exhibiting anger and hostility toward a partner, and marital conflict. Finally, the community risk factors may include poverty, low social capital, and factors associated with poverty such as overcrowding, hopelessness, stress, and frustration.

[S]tatistics show that military families are substantially more vulnerable to domestic violence than others. A high percentage of military personnel have prior experiences of domestic violence. For example, among Navy recruits, 54 percent of women and 40 percent of men witnessed parental violence prior to enlistment. Moreover, 30 percent of active duty military women report lifetime intimate partner physical or sexual assault, and 22 percent report some form of intimate partner sexual assault during their time of military service. ...

The constant relocation of military families may also make them more vulnerable to domestic violence than others. Military families frequently move from place to place, sometimes to locations with unfamiliar cultures and values. This can lead to isolation for the victims by cutting them off from family and other familiar support systems. Deployments and military personnel returning to the family also create unique stresses on military families. When a soldier is deployed, the partner who is left at home (usually the wife) needs to assume new roles, such as running the household and becoming more independent. There may be issues related to this role reversal upon the soldier's return home. For example, when the husband is deployed, the wife will bear the brunt of the economic decision-making responsibilities. Upon the husband's return, there may be a power struggle in the family. Furthermore, long separations can also foster distrust between the couple, and uncertainty about their future.

Military domestic violence victims experience the same barriers to reporting domestic violence that their civilian counterparts experience. [F]eelings of shame, isolation, fear of retaliation from the abusive partner and economic concerns are just a handful of them. However, there are issues unique to the military that make military victims even less likely to report an incident of intimate partner violence.

Underreporting in the military may be due to the limited confidentiality of domestic violence reports in military cases, as the confidentiality of disclosed information cannot be guaranteed. Currently, new policies allow for restricted reports to be made by victims to a Health Care Provider or Victim Advocate. . . .

Another possible reason that reporting is low is that victims fear what will happen to the abuser's career. "Many survivors fear reporting domestic violence because they believe the report will affect their husbands' chance for promotions and pay increases or will result in their husbands' discharge." This can have a significant impact on the family. For instance, if the husband loses his job, then there will be a loss of money coming into the family, which can be the cause of even more violence. Furthermore, for many military members, being in the military is more than just a career; it is their identity. The loss of this identity can lead to higher risks of violence, because the abuser may feel like he has nothing left to lose now that he has lost his identity and career.

Similarly, victims who are military members show low rates of reporting domestic violence for fear of career consequences. Many women in the military are fearful that if they report their abuse, their fellow soldiers will no longer trust them and will no longer want them in their company. . . . In conclusion, all of these factors contribute to the low reporting rates of intimate partner violence in the military.

Notes and Questions

1. *Prevalence.* How does the prevalence of domestic violence in the military compare to that of the civilian population? See also Amy D. Marshall et al., Intimate Partner Violence among Military Veterans and Active Duty Servicemen, 25 Clinical Psych. Rev. 862 (2005) (reporting rates of 13.5 to 58 percent of intimate partner violence in military families).

2. *Common characteristics.* What are the characteristics of victims who experience intimate partner violence in the military? The characteristics of abusers?

3. *Risk factors.* What are the risk factors in the military context that contribute to domestic violence? How does relocation contribute to these risks?

4. *Reporting.* What are barriers to reporting domestic violence in the military context? How are these barriers similar to those experienced by civilians? How are they different? How do the consequences of disclosure differ in the military context? See also Riccobene v. Scales, 19 F. Supp. 2d 577 (N.D. W. Va. 1998) (defamation claim by army officer against attorney representing officer's wife in domestic violence proceedings, in response to disclosure that jeopardized his career).

5. *Severity.* Data suggest a higher rate of *severe* intimate partner violence among military personnel. See James E. McCarroll et al., Characteristics of Domestic Violence Incidents Reported at the Scene by Volunteer Victim Advocates, 173 Military Med. 865 (2008). The military relies on a Department of Defense "Incident Severity Index" to categorize the severity of intimate partner violence—requiring that for an incident to be categorized as severe, it must result in major physical injury requiring inpatient medical treatment or causing temporary or permanent disability or disfigurement. Stamm, supra, at 328-329. How does this definition complicate the military's response to domestic violence?

6. *Deployment.* Deployment also increases the risk of domestic violence among military families. See Andra L. Teten et al., Intimate Partner Aggression Perpetrated

and Sustained by Male Afghanistan, Iraq, and Vietnam Veterans With and Without Posttraumatic Stress Disorder, 25 J. Interpersonal Violence 1612 (2010) (comparing marital aggression by male Afghanistan or Iraq veterans and Vietnam veterans). Since 2001, nearly 2 million men and women have been deployed for service in the war in Iraq and Afghanistan. Many returning veterans suffer from mental health disorders, including anxiety, depression, and PTSD. Suicide rates are also high. See Cost of War—Part 2, Cong. Testimony, Oct. 1, 2010 (statement of Prof. Joseph Steiglitz) (reporting that 30 to 40 percent of veterans are diagnosed with mental health issues), available at 2010 WLNR 19513866 (last visited June 21, 2011).

Soon after the first veterans of the war in Afghanistan began returning in 2002, the media began reporting numerous incidents of fatal domestic violence in military families. See Elaine Thompson, Returning Veterans Get Help, Telegram & Gazette (Worcester), Nov. 6, 2010, at A6 (reporting that 12 to 50 percent of returning vets are involved in domestic violence). See generally Marshall et al., supra. How can the military address this problem?

7. *Military regulations regarding domestic violence.* The military's response to domestic violence is a mixture of military regulations, federal statutes, and state law. The response depends on whether the abuser is a civilian or a member of the armed services, and whether the incident occurs on or off the base. If the abuser is a civilian or if the incident occurs off the base, the military has no jurisdiction and the matter will be handled by state authorities. A service member who is convicted of a state domestic violence offense (for example, occurring off the base) by the civilian justice system may face discharge and even court martial depending on the seriousness of the offense. For this reason, many victims are hesitant to report abuse because of the impact of the disclosure on their partner's military career.

8. *Family Advocacy Programs.* If military authorities are informed of a report of domestic violence (e.g., by the victim, offender, civil law enforcement, and/or medical personnel), the military commander has a choice of pursuing the matter through the military's Family Advocacy Program and/or the military justice system. The former program addresses the identification and treatment of domestic violence rather than its punishment.

A report to the Family Advocacy Program prompts: (1) the assignment of a Victim Advocate to ensure the development of a safety plan for the victim and the provision of medical and mental health services; (2) the assignment of a caseworker to interview the parties and present the case to a Case Review Committee (CRC); (3) an assessment by the CRC as to the sufficiency of the evidence (i.e., whether the case is "substantiated, suspected, or unsubstantiated"); and (4) a determination by the CRC of a recommendation regarding the appropriate military response. This response may range in severity from an order that the abuser undergo treatment to disciplinary procedures pursuant to the Uniform Code of Military Justice, 10 U.S.C. §§801-950.

9. *Military orders of protection.* The Victim Advocate (who is assigned as part of the Family Advocacy Program) may suggest that the victim apply for a military protection order (MPO). Such orders, similar to civilian restraining orders, constitute conditions on a service member's liberty. The requirements for issuance of a MPO include a "reasonable belief" that the person to be restrained committed an offense triable by court martial and the restraint is required by the circumstances. For example, in the case of an assault on an intimate partner, a military official might order the abusive service member to sleep in the barracks and refrain from contact with the intimate partner. Violation of such a condition subjects the

offender to punishment under the Uniform Code of Military Justice, 10 U.S.C. §§801-950. See generally Mark E. Sullivan, The Military Divorce Handbook: A Practical Guide to Representing Military Personnel and Their Families (2011).

10. *Enforcement of civil protection orders on military bases.* Enforcement of civil protection orders on military bases posed a problem until 2002. Orders of protection are a valuable mechanism to protect victims of domestic violence. A protection order can prohibit a person from harming the victim; coming to the victim's home or work; and purchasing or owning firearms (among other conditions). The Violence Against Women Act (VAWA) (codified as amended and in relevant part at 18 U.S.C. §2265) requires states to give full faith and credit to any valid state protection order. However, when Congress enacted VAWA in 1994, VAWA did not apply to military bases, which are subject to exclusive federal jurisdiction. Congress remedied this shortcoming with the Armed Forces Domestic Security Act (AFDSA) of 2002, Pub. L. No. 107-311, §2, 116 Stat. 2455 (codified in relevant part at 10 U.S.C. §1561a). The AFDSA mandates that a "civilian order of protection shall have the same force and effect on a military installation as such order has within the jurisdiction of the court that issued such order." 10 U.S.C. §1561a(a).

11. *Military support payments for family members.* What financial resources are available to a victim of abuse if the abusive service member is discharged? A federally-authorized program, Transitional Compensation for Abused Family Members (TCAFM), 10 U.SC. §1059, provides one to three years of support payments to family members of service members who are "separated" from active duty due to domestic violence. These support payments are designed to assist family members to establish a life apart from an abusive service member. The program applies to family members of service members who have been on active duty for more than 30 days and who have been: (1) convicted at a court-martial and sentenced to be separated from active duty for a dependent-abuse offense; or, (2) administratively separated from active duty when the basis for separation includes a dependent-abuse offense. A "dependent-abuse offense" involves abuse of the spouse or a dependent child that is considered a criminal offense under state, federal, or military law.

12. *Male culture of violence.* Does the male culture of violence contribute to domestic violence in the military? Some theorists posit the existence of a "cultural approval of violence," that manifests itself in sports, media, movies, and the military. Mildred D. Pagelow, Family Violence 127-133 (1984). According to culture-of-violence theorists, society educates boys to become violent and provides them with violent role models. See also Karel Kurst-Swanger & Jacqueline L. Petcosky, Violence in the Home: Multidisciplinary Perspectives 47-48 (2003) (discussing culture-of-violence theorists). Feminist scholars introduce the notion of "hypermasculinity" to denote the convergence of violence and masculinity, and its hostility to femininity and homosexuality. On "hypermasculinity" in the military, see Valorie K. Vojdik, Sexual Abuse and Exploitation of Women and Girls by U.N. Peacekeeping Troops, 15 Mich. St. J. Int'l L. 157, 158 (2007).

The field of "masculinities theory," an outgrowth of feminist theory, examines male behavior and practices to provide a better understanding of the use of male power in the subordination of women. See generally Nancy E. Dowd, Asking the Man Question: Masculinities Analysis and Feminist Theory, 33 Harv. J.L. & Gender 415 (2010); Nancy E. Dowd, Masculinities and Feminist Legal Theory, 23 Wis. J.L. Gender & Soc'y 201 (2008); Ann C. McGinley, Masculinities at Work, 83 Or. L. Rev. 359 (2004). How might this theory shed light on the interaction of privilege and harm

in intimate relationships in the military? See Jamie R. Abrams, The Collateral Consequences of Masculinizing Violence, 16 Wm. & Mary J. Women & L. 703, 742-744 (2010).

How are stereotypical gender roles transformed by deployment that might play
a part in intimate partner violence? See Angela P. Harris, Gender, Violence, Race,
and Criminal Justice, 52 Stan. L. Rev. 777, 791 (2000) (explaining that men resort to
violence when their masculinity is threatened). The authors of the above excerpt
explain that victims are hesitant to report abuse because they fear the career consequences of disclosure not only for their partners but also for themselves. What
stereotypical gender traits are associated with being a "victim" that might impede a
military service member's career?

2. Police-Perpetrated Domestic Violence

■ ALEX ROSLIN, BATTERER IN BLUE
Georgia Straight (Canada), July 24, 2003

On the afternoon of April 26, Crystal Brame was driving to a tanning salon as she
spoke on her cell phone with her mother. "Oh, I think I see David," she said,
referring to her estranged husband, David Brame, the police chief in Tacoma,
Washington. "I gotta go; I gotta go," Brame said, ending the call.

Crystal's mother tried to call her daughter back as Crystal and David pulled into
the parking lot of a shopping mall in their separate vehicles. Minutes later, according to local newspaper reports, David shot his wife in the head with his police-issue
.45-caliber Glock handgun. He then killed himself with the pistol as the couple's
two young kids sat in his car a few meters away. Crystal was taken to hospital but never
recovered, dying of her injuries a week later. . . .

Evidence emerged that senior city officials had covered up for Brame for years
and refused to heed warning signs or take action that may have averted the tragedy.
As part of the screening process that accompanied Brame's hiring, two psychologists
had deemed him unfit because he was overly "defensive" and "deceptive." Yet he
made the cut and rose through the ranks to become chief of police, even after a rape
complaint and an allegation that he pointed a gun at a [former] girlfriend.

The day before the shooting, local media reported that Crystal Brame had filed
divorce papers alleging that her husband had tried to choke her, threatened to snap her
neck, and pointed a gun at her, saying, "Accidents happen." City officials didn't investigate these claims or follow a recommendation from their human-resources director
that Brame's gun and badge be taken away. In an interview with [a Seattle newspaper],
Mayor Bill Baarsma dismissed Crystal Brame's allegations as a "private matter."

The FBI and state authorities have now stepped in to investigate what went
wrong. Crystal Brame's family has filed a $75-million suit against the city of Tacoma,
alleging it is responsible for her death. . . .

When most people think of domestic violence, they imagine police to be the
ones breaking it up, not committing it. In fact, [the story of Crystal Brame is not
isolated.] Research shows that a staggering amount of domestic violence is hidden
behind the walls of police officers' homes. . . . In the vast majority of cases, the abuse
remains a secret and the victims are isolated. They rarely make a complaint, criminal
charges are rarer still, and an abusive officer's chances of losing his badge and gun
are virtually nil, even if the woman comes forward.

The average abused woman goes through nine violent incidents before she calls police, said legal advocate Sheryl Burns [of] Battered Women's Support Services in Vancouver. But spouses of violent cops face worse barriers to stopping the attacks and getting justice. . . . These women are usually too afraid to call 911 because it might be a coworker of their partner who comes to the door. They have to confront the infamous blue wall of silence: the strict omerta-like code that protects officers from investigation or arrest. When women do complain, said Amy Ramsay, executive director of the International Association of Women Police, police departments often cover up the case. . . . Ramsay explained that they opt for a closed-door, internal-affairs disciplinary process rather than an embarrassing public trial.

"These types of batterers know where to hit you where other people can't see," said Capt. Dottie Davis, director of training at the police academy in Fort Wayne, Indiana. . . . These men have guns and often bring them home. And if a cop's wife runs, where will she hide? Staff at women's shelters admit they are often powerless to offer protection.

"What stands out is the intensity of their fear," said Laurie Parsons, coordinator of the Mission Transition House in Mission [British Columbia] who regularly gets calls from abused partners of cops. . . .

How widespread is police spousal assault? [A] survey from 1992, coauthored by Albert Seng of the Tucson, Arizona, police department, found [that] 41 percent of 385 male police officers and 37 percent of 115 female spouses reported that there had been physical violence in their relationship in the previous year. Eight percent of officers reported "severe" violence, including strangulation, use of a knife, and threats with a gun. The worst problems were among officers in their 20s—64 percent of whom reported violence—as well as narcotics officers and those working the midnight and swing shifts. The authors added that the numbers could actually be even higher, "given the tendency to under-report socially undesirable events" . . .

Why do so many cops abuse their partners? . . . [According to Carol-Ann Halliday, former president of the International Association of Women Police], a lot of the male officers are in love with the power of being a cop, and this causes strife in their homes. "The job brings it out. It gives this license, and all of a sudden they realize all the power they have," she said. "I can see how that spills over a lot. They just think, 'I am the man; I am the boss. I am the power; I can do whatever I like.' . . . I am sure that's what breaks up a lot of the marriages."

Although some people point to the stress of police work as a reason for the torrent of abuse, counselors of abusive men say that's just an excuse. "Many people experience extreme stress without becoming violent," said registered clinical counselor Dale Trimble. . . . At the root, Trimble said, is a need for power and control over others, traits that are required and fostered among cops, prison guards, and other law-enforcement personnel. Albert Seng, former Tucson detective, concurs. "I think it [policing] attracts the kind of personality that likes to be in control," he said. "In counseling we often tell officers they're control freaks. . . . Domestic violence is in fact a control issue." . . .

Notes and Questions

1. *Frequency.* How widespread is domestic violence among the police? Which officers are the most serious offenders? What explains the low enforcement rate?

What obstacles might Crystal Brame have experienced because her ex-husband was in the police? Because of his rank? See Diane E. Wetendorf, The Impact of Police-Perpetrated Domestic Violence 378 in Domestic Violence by Police Officers (Donald C. Sheehan eds., 2000) ("The higher the abuser's rank, the fewer the number of people willing to help her").

2. *Severity of violence.* David Brame killed his wife and then committed suicide. Law enforcement officers have higher murder-suicide rates than the general population. Violence Policy Center, American Roulette: Murder-Suicide in the United States 8 (2006). What might explain this phenomenon? What event triggered Crystal Brame's murder? What warning signs suggested that her husband posed a lethal threat to her? How did her husband rise to become police chief with his history of domestic violence? How did officials respond to Crystal's allegations that her husband had threatened her? What might officials have done differently? Was there anything else Crystal might have done to protect herself?

3. *Causes: culture of violence.* How does police culture and training predispose some officers to commit domestic violence? One commentator elaborates:

> A conspicuous feature of that culture is the tendency of officers to think of themselves as separate and apart from the citizens whom they serve. In addition, the dangerous nature of the job, the authority to use force, and the close bonds between officers who rely on each other for safety and support may help to strengthen a "code of silence" among the ranks. Some researchers believe that common police skills and techniques such as use of weapons, exercise of authority, and imposition of control can become ingrained in officers' behavior, and thus spill over into their home lives. These practices can combine to create a formidable abuser.

Karen Oehme et al., Protecting Lives, Careers, and Public Confidence: Florida's Efforts to Prevent Officer-Involved Domestic Violence, 49 Fam. Ct. Rev. 84, 85 (2011).

Police work is accompanied by high stress and unstable working hours. Police officers are also known for their substance abuse, personality disorders, post-traumatic stress, and poor anger management. In response to these characteristics, one commentator notes acerbically: "[A]ll of these beg the question as to why they appear only in the presence of others who are powerless against the abuser. Rarely do we hear of police officers using violence against a superior officer. . . ." Wetendorf, Impact of Police-Perpetrated Domestic Violence, supra, at 380. Is police work uniquely stressful or are the types of people who become police officers more prone to commit domestic violence? Recently, researchers have found that the nature of policing involves physical and psychological domination ("authoritarianism") that conflicts with non-work-related roles and creates a "negative spillover of occupational stress." See Anita S. Anderson & Celia C. Lo, Intimate Partner Violence within Law Enforcement Families, 20 J. Interpersonal Violence 1176, 1178 (2011).

4. *Dynamics of police perpetrated domestic violence.* The following dynamics characterize intimate partner violence by police: The officer batterer uses his "command presence" to intimidate his victim in verbal and nonverbal ways; he informs his partner that she is (or can be) under surveillance at all times; he is able to (and does) access multiple sources of confidential and personal information about his partner; he has keen observational and interrogation skills that he uses to detect a partner's deception; he applies his expertise and credibility to influence third

parties (neighbors, co-workers) in adverse ways regarding his partner; he perceives any conflict in his personal life as a challenge to his authority; he uses his familiarity with force to injure his partner in a manner that is not easily visible; and he uses his personal relationships in the criminal justice system to his benefit. Diane Wetendorf, Battered Women's Justice Project, When the Batterer is a Law Enforcement Officer: A Guide for Advocates 14-18 (2004).

Wetendorf adds that police abusers differ from other abusers because they are "tougher and more dangerous." She adds that a police batterer reinforces the victim's sense of "isolation and hopelessness" by frequently reminding her that there is no escape.

> He tells her she can call the police, but asks her who she thinks has more credibility, him, or her? He tells her she can leave, but wherever she goes he can find her. She can press charges against him, but she does not have enough evidence or credibility to make them stick. If she does manage to get him convicted, she loses financial support for their children because of the loss of his job. If he faces the loss of his job, he threatens her life.

Wetendorf, Impact of Police-Perpetrated Domestic Violence, supra, at 378.

5. *Obstacles for victims.* How does the "law enforcement culture" create difficulties for *victims*? In terms of reporting the abuse to 911? In terms of reporting abuse to a partner's supervisor? In terms of disclosure to other officers' intimate partners? What response might the victim expect from responding officers? See, e.g., Arnett v. Wills, 2008 WL 8238957 (Ga. Super. Ct. 2008) (several police officers, who are investigating a domestic dispute, arrest ex-wife based on statements of her abusive former husband). What response from hospital personnel? How might these problems be compounded in small towns or rural areas? See generally Walter S. DeKeseredy & Martin D. Schwartz, Dangerous Exits: Escaping Abusive Relationships in Rural America (2009).

6. *Shelters' response.* Why are the intimate partners of police officers unable to flee to battered women's shelters? Some of the reasons include: Shelter clients may see the batterer as the officer who rescued them from their intimate partner violence. Staff may resent the victim because her presence (specifically, her husband's position) poses a danger to them and the other residents. Finally, staff may blame her for jeopardizing the agency's relationship with the police. Wetendorf, When the Batterer is a Law Enforcement Officer, supra, at 30.

7. *Female police officers.*

a. *Female police officers as victims.* What unique obstacles does a victim face if she is police officer? A police officer-victim "defies everyone's stereotype of a victim and image of a police officer; her colleagues question her professional competence." Wetendorf, Impact of Police-Perpetrated Domestic Violence, supra, at 379. How might disclosure of abuse by a police officer-victim affect her career? Her safety?

b. *Female police officers as perpetrators.* Are female police officers more likely to be abusive to their partners? Research suggests that this pattern occurs. See Anderson & Lo, supra, at 1183, 1187 (based on self-report data of a survey of over 1,000 officers). What might explain this finding? What are the implications of this finding for policy formulation? For improving the institutional response to domestic violence?

8. *Similarities and differences.* How is intimate partner violence among police similar to, and different from, such abuse committed in the military? Are the police analogous to "paramilitary organizations"? One commentator agrees, noting "Power and authority are distributed along a chain of command. . . . An officer who has been trained to give and receive orders without argument may expect compliance at home and react poorly to not being able to get it." Ellen Kirschman, I Love a Cop: What Police Families Need to Know 35 (revised ed., 2006). Kirschman adds that if a police officer fails to get immediate compliance, that failure raises his anxiety because he perceives noncompliance as a threat to his safety. Id.

9. *Firearms.* How does easy access to firearms contribute to domestic violence among the police? In 1996, Congress enacted legislation (called the "Lautenberg Amendment") that prohibits persons (including police officers) from owning or using a firearm if they have been convicted of a domestic violence misdemeanor. 18 U.S.C. §922(g)(9). The bill expanded federal law that formerly barred gun ownership only by those convicted of a felony offense. 18 U.S.C. §922(g)(1). The 1994 Violent Crime Control & Law Enforcement Act, Pub. L. No. 103-322, 103 Stat. 2014, also prohibits individuals from possessing a firearm if they are subject to a protective order, restraining order, or harassment order. 18 U.S.C. §922(g)(8).

Pursuant to an "official use" exemption, police and military personnel, who are subject to a restraining order, may possess their government-issued firearms while on duty. 18 U.S.C. §925(a)(1). However, police and military personnel may *not* possess their government-issued firearms, even while on duty, if they have been convicted of a domestic violence misdemeanor. Id.

How does the "official use" exemption jeopardize the safety of the intimate partners of police? See Lisa D. May, The Backfiring of the Domestic Violence Firearms Ban, 14 Colum. J. Gender & L. 1, 1-2 (2005) (recounting instance of judge who expunged officer's conviction for a misdemeanor assault because the judge did not want the officer to lose his job). How does this exception discourage reporting? See Wetendorf, When The Batterer is a Law Enforcement Officer, supra, at 5 (suggesting that victims were opposed to a zero-tolerance policy because they feared that if their spouse lost his job, he would hold them accountable). For further discussion of firearms and domestic violence, see Chapter 8, pp. 400-414.

10. *Community response.* Given the formidable obstacles to relief that are faced by victims of police-perpetrated intimate partner violence, it is not surprising that reported cases are rare. In one case, the victim obtained relief against her husband only after citizens submitted a petition to the state law enforcement commission. Their petition stemmed from an attempted strangulation by state trooper, Steven Hauser, of his wife that resulted in a 911 call when his wife became unresponsive. Hauser then submitted a false police report, contradicting his wife's testimony and the physical evidence. The citizens' petition led to an investigation that ultimately resulted in the revocation of his certification as a law enforcement officer for "neglect of duty" pursuant to the state patrol code of conduct and oath of office. Hauser v. Nebraska Police Standards Advisory Council, 694 N.W.2d 171, 177 (Neb. 2005). See also Burella v. City of Philadelphia, 501 F.3d 134 (3d Cir. 2007).

11. *Masculinities theory.* How would a masculinities theorist analyze policing? One theorist speculates as follows:

> The short answer is that officers may get "macho" with civilians. Specifically, they may
> enact a command presence in situations where it only serves to boost the officer's

masculine esteem. To enact command presence is to take charge of a situation. It involves projecting an aura of confidence and decisiveness. It is justified by the need to control dangerous suspects. A situation that does not justify enacting command presence is what I call a "masculinity contest." A masculinity contest is a face-off between men where one party is able to bolster his masculine esteem by dominating the other. A prototypical masculinity contest is a bar fight. Men will glare at each other and ratchet up their challenges until one party backs down or is subdued. Male police officers may sometimes be tempted to turn encounters with male civilians into masculinity contests.

Frank Rudy Cooper, "Who's the Man?": Masculinities Studies, Terry Stops, and Police Training, 18 Colum. J. Gender & L. 671, 674 (2009). How does this analysis apply to police-perpetrated intimate partner violence? See also Harris, supra, at 793-794; Anastasia Prokos & Irene Padavic, "There Oughtta Be a Law Against Bitches": Masculinity Lessons in Police Academy Training, 9 Gender, Work & Org. 439 (2002).

12. *Zero-tolerance policy.* How can police training be improved? Should law enforcement adopt a zero-tolerance policy to domestic violence by police? The International Association of Chiefs of Police (IACP) developed such a policy. See IACP, National Law Enforcement Policy Center: Domestic Violence Model Policy 4, 8-10 (June 2006), available at http://www.theiacp.org/LinkClick.aspx?fileticket=-tYPpynChP%2bE%3d&tabid=392. Is it likely to be effective? See Nat'l Center for Women and Policing, Police Family Violence Fact Sheet, http://www.womenand-policing.org/violenceFS.asp (last visited June 20, 2011) (criticizing that "there is no evidence that police departments across the country are doing anything other than including the policy in their manuals").

13. *VAWA Reform.* VAWA 2005 (amending 42 U.S.C. §3796gg) authorized the Crystal Judson [Brame] Domestic Violence Protocol Program (after the slain wife of the Tacoma police chief) to develop law enforcement protocols to respond to police-perpetrated domestic violence and to fund victim services personnel (known as Crystal Judson Victim Advocates) to provide supportive services and advocacy for those victims. Evaluate this approach to intimate partner violence.

Safe Haven by Nicholas Sparks (2010)

A mysterious young woman named Katie Feldman appears one day in the small North Carolina town of Southport. The arrival of this beautiful, quiet young woman triggers many questions for the townspeople. On her part, Katie seems determined to avoid forming personal relationships. Despite her reservations, Katie slowly begins to let down her guard and put down roots in the close-knit community. As she falls in love with a widowed store owner who is father to two children, she struggles with a dark secret that haunts her.

Katie has come to the safe haven of Southport to escape from her former husband, an abusive Boston cop, Kevin Tierney. Kevin started beating his wife "Erin" on their honeymoon. Katie twice tried to escape from Kevin before fleeing to Southport. There, she changed her name and tried to hide from her "control freak" former husband. But Kevin uses all his skills as a detective to track her down and shatter her sense of safety.

> For another fictional account of police-perpetrated intimate partner violence, see Anna Quindlen, Black and Blue (2010) (recounting the story of Fran Benedetto, an emergency room nurse, who flees with her son from her police officer-husband).

3. Sports

There is a popular belief of a link between sports and domestic violence. Newspapers often publicize cases of famous athletes who commit intimate partner violence. The following materials explore the nature and existence of the relationship between sports and domestic violence.

■ JOAN RYAN, O. J. CASE CHANGED RULES FOR COX
S.F. Chron., May 10, 1995, at D2

In the Georgia home of Pamela and Bobby Cox, last Sunday night unfolded like so many nights in so many homes across America. Friends came over for cocktails. Bobby Cox, the manager of the Atlanta Braves, spilled a drink on the carpet. Pamela Cox made a remark. When the friends left, he went after her. She called the police. According to the police report, Pamela Cox said her husband punched her and pulled her hair and that it had happened many times before. But she didn't want the police to arrest him and take him to the station. She just wanted him to stop. But the police took him anyway, ignoring her objections and ignoring Bobby Cox's star status. He was hauled downtown like any other man accused of assault.

At a press conference the following afternoon, Cox and his wife denied he ever hit her, though Cox admitted he pulled her hair. They said the police overreacted. The dispute was strictly a private matter, something that had been brewing for several months. Pamela Cox did not press charges.

In years past, the police probably would have told the couple to talk it out and then would have spent the next 10 minutes asking Bobby Cox about the Braves' chances in the NL East. And the story of the assault would have been buried in the newspaper the next day, if it appeared at all. When O. J. Simpson was charged in 1989 with beating his wife and admitted the abuse in court, the story passed through the news media so lightly that Simpson went right on making more than $1 million a year as a broadcaster and Hertz spokesman.

Not this time. Cox's arrest landed on the front pages of sports sections across the country this week. TV stations, despite their fleeting two- and three-minute sportscasts, played it prominently, even though it was not a local story. ESPN ran it in the first few minutes of SportsCenter.

When Darryl Strawberry, Barry Bonds, Jose Canseco, Sugar Ray Leonard, John Daly, Roy Tarpley, Michael Cooper, Ken Stabler, Moses Malone, et al., were accused of domestic violence, they didn't become top national stories. If Bobby Cox feels he's being unfairly scrutinized, he can blame O. J. Simpson. The Simpson trial, with its tape-recorded 911 calls from a terrified Nicole Simpson, has dramatically changed the way the sports media covers domestic violence and, it seems, the way the police respond to it. . . .

[The O. J. Simpson case is explored more fully in Chapter 7.]

■ BETHANY P. WITHERS, COMMENT, THE INTEGRITY OF THE GAME: PROFESSIONAL ATHLETES AND DOMESTIC VIOLENCE

1 Harv. J. Sports & Ent. L. 145, 146-149 (2010)

[The issue of domestic violence by athletes] has been largely ignored by professional sports leagues. . . . Although [Major League Baseball, the National Basketball Association, and the National Football League] do not release information regarding player arrests or player punishment by teams or leagues, some external studies were conducted in the late 1990s as a result of public attention to domestic violence during the O. J. Simpson murder trial, which concluded with his acquittal for the murders of his ex-wife, Nicole Brown Simpson, and her friend, Ronald Goldman in 1995. One comprehensive study conducted by Jeff Benedict, former director of research at the Center for Sport in Society, [concluded] that 150 athletes had domestic violence criminal complaints filed against them between 1990 and 1996, yet only twenty-eight resulted in convictions and the majority of cases were not prosecuted.

The O. J. Simpson trial and the attention that studies such as Benedict's brought to the issue of domestic violence had a direct effect on NFL policy. Within weeks of the murders, the NFL sent counselors to twenty-eight team training camps to discuss domestic violence with the players. In addition, then-Commissioner Paul Tagliabue adopted the Violent Crime Policy in 1997, which was further revised in 2000, becoming a version of the current Personal Conduct Policy. It was, and is, the only policy of its kind among major U.S. sports.

Regardless of the attention given domestic violence in the 1990s and the studies and policies that resulted therefrom, it remains difficult to go even one week without hearing of an athlete involved in some sort of domestic altercation. For instance, at the start of the broadcast of the 2008 NFL season playoff game between the Arizona Cardinals and Atlanta Falcons, television commentator Cris Collinsworth stated that, in the week leading up to the game, Larry Fitzgerald's girlfriend obtained a restraining order against him and Michael Turner was involved in a domestic dispute with the mother of his child. Fitzgerald and Turner were two of the most celebrated players on the field that day.

Some argue that athletes are predisposed to commit acts of domestic abuse and sexual assault because they are trained to use violence and intimidation for a psychological edge during their games and because sports create a "macho subculture" that equates masculinity with violence. . . . [Despite] the perceived prevalence of such activity in professional sports, evidence is inconclusive regarding whether athletes are more likely to commit violent acts against women. The San Diego *Union-Tribune* reviewed news reports and public records from January 2000 to April 2007 and concluded that the biggest problems for NFL players were the same as those of the general population: drunken driving, traffic stops, and repeat offenses. . . . It is indeed quite possible that the rate of domestic violence involving professional athletes mirrors the violence against women that occurs in society at large, but when committed by professional athletes and splashed across the sports page, the prevalence of such abuse in our society simply becomes more noticeable.

Nonetheless, there is evidence that professional athletes are not punished by the leagues, teams, or criminal justice system as harshly or consistently as their general public counterparts. "One study indicates that, out of 141 athletes reported to police for violence against women between 1989 and 1994, only one was disciplined by league officials." While this number has increased since 1994 . . . the number remains remarkably low. Similarly, conviction rates for athletes are astonishingly low compared to the arrest statistics. Though there is evidence that the responsiveness of police and prosecution to sexual assault complaints involving athletes is favorable, there is an off-setting pro-athlete bias on the part of juries. For example, in 1995, domestic violence cases involving athletes resulted in a 36 percent conviction rate, as compared to 77 percent for the general public. . . .

Does domestic violence escalate on Super Bowl Sunday? The following excerpt explores this common belief.

■ FAMILY VIOLENCE PREVENTION FUND, DOMESTIC VIOLENCE AND THE SUPER BOWL
(Jan. 31, 2011) available at **http://endabuse.org/content/features/ detail/1659**

On Sunday, February 6, millions of people will tune in to watch the Super Bowl. In the past, Super Bowl Sunday has brought a public conversation about domestic violence because of now-discounted decades-old claims that domestic violence escalates on Super Bowl Sunday. There is no hard evidence that Super Bowl Sunday is a "day of dread" for women, or has measurably more incidents of domestic violence than other days. "We have spent years dispelling that myth," said Family Violence Prevention Fund President Esta Soler. "Domestic, sexual and dating violence are serious problems every day, and are not tied to the Super Bowl." . . . The Super Bowl and domestic violence likely became entwined in Americans' minds in 1993, when advocates helped convince NBC to broadcast a public service announcement on abuse during the Super Bowl. It featured a well-dressed man sitting in a jail cell saying, "I didn't think you'd go to jail for hitting your wife." Afterward, the announcer said, "Domestic violence is a crime." While many commentators applauded NBC's decision to air the [public service announcement], others claimed the network had been coerced by inflated claims about Super Bowl Sunday being "a day of dread" for battered women—a day when abuse increases. . . . Domestic violence and the Super Bowl emerged again several years ago when columnist and commentator George Will raised the issue on ABC's *This Week*, criticizing "feminists" for spreading false information about a link between the Super Bowl and domestic violence.

Some research exploring a link between domestic violence and football has received recent media attention. In 2009, the National Bureau of Economics released a working paper from economists Gordon Dahl and David Card which found that losses in professional football games—specifically when the home team suffers an upset—can lead to an eight percent spike in the number of police reports of spousal abuse within a short time of the game. [Their report] also found that the spikes in domestic violence reports were greater if the game was especially important (for instance, if it pitted the home team against a key rival or determined who got a playoff spot). The working paper did not examine police reports on Super Bowl Sunday. . . . [N]o rigorous national studies have firmly established a rise in violence on Super Bowl Sunday.

Notes and Questions

1. *Prevalence.* Does evidence establish that athletes are more likely than others to commit violent acts against their partners?

2. *Prosecutions.* Why has domestic violence by athletes largely been ignored by professional sports leagues? Why are rates of arrests and convictions so low? What is the significance of this indifference—for the athletes and their partners, and society?

3. *Research.* The economics study by Dahl and Card (cited above) analyzes police reports of violent incidents during the professional football season for over 750 police agencies and compares those findings with data on Sunday NFL games played by 6 teams over 12 years. The study finds that a home team's "upset loss" (a loss when the team is expected to win by at least four points) led to approximately a 10 percent increase (not 8 percent as erroneously claimed in the above excerpt) in police reports of at-home opposite-sex intimate partner violence. David Card & Gordon B. Dahl, Family Violence and Football: The Effect of Unexpected Emotional Cues on Violent Behavior, 126 Q. J. Econ. 103 (2011).

How should legal and social service providers respond to these findings? Should police have more officers on duty when the home team is playing—or only if it is expected to lose? Should victims take safety precautions on those days? Might the same result occur for other sports? What other factors might contribute to higher risks during professional sports games? Alcohol consumption?

4. *Super Bowl.* Does the rate of domestic violence escalate on Super Bowl Sunday, based on the data? What light do the findings of Card and Dahl, supra, shed on this correlation?

5. *Male culture of violence.* Is there a "male culture of violence" in sports? If so, what are its characteristics? See Michael Messner, When Bodies are Weapons: Masculinity and Violence in Sport, 25 Int'l Rev. for Soc. Sports 203 (1990). Are these characteristics similar to, and different from, those that exist in the military and police contexts? How do sports reinforce attitudes about "maleness"? How do sports condone violence? One commentator responds:

> [M]any experiences at school reinforce gender role stereotypes and attitudes that condone violence against women and may contribute to socialization supportive of violent behavior. Participation in athletic teams may also be a factor, particularly when coaches deride their players as "girls" when they do not play aggressively enough.

Margi Laird McCue, Domestic Violence: A Reference Handbook 17 (2d ed. 2008). How would a masculinities theorist analyze the relationship between athletics and domestic violence? See Julie A. Baird, Playing It Straight: An Analysis of Current Legal Protections to Combat Homophobia and Sexual Orientation Discrimination in Intercollegiate Athletics, 17 Berkeley Women's L.J. 31, 33 (2002).

IV

Specific Types of Abuse

A. PHYSICAL ABUSE

The paradigmatic type of domestic violence is physical abuse—"battering" in common parlance and "assault" for purposes of the criminal law. Yet, domestic violence encompasses a broader range of victimization. Our increased understanding of this social problem has led to the recognition of many new crimes and new forms of abuse. This chapter explores the unique nature of these types of abuse as well as the law's response to them.

1. Strangulation

■ CARTER v. STATE

235 P.3d 221 (Alaska Ct. App. 2010)

MANNHEIMER, Judge.

The question presented in this case is whether a police officer (called as a witness on behalf of the State) should have been allowed to testify concerning the physical indications that someone has been subjected to strangling. . . .

On March 8, 2006, Romanda Lee contacted the police and reported that her then boyfriend, Lorenzo Carter, had assaulted her by grabbing the back of her head, hitting her, and choking her. Lee's two daughters told the police that they had witnessed the assault. Based on this incident, Carter was charged with second-degree assault (as well as interfering with a report of domestic violence, for unplugging Lee's telephone when she initially tried to call 911).

However, at Carter's trial, Lee denied that Carter had assaulted her. Lee testified that she and Carter had argued, that they had accused each other of infidelity, and that Lee became so angry that she told her daughters to call 911 and falsely accuse Carter of assault. Lee further testified that, when the police arrived, she repeated her false story of assault because she was afraid that she would be in trouble for lying to the 911 operator. Lee's daughters testified that they did not witness any argument between their mother and Carter, and they did not remember any assault.

In the face of these recantations, the State relied on the prior statements made by Lee and her daughters, as well as the testimony of the Anchorage police officers [including that of Officer Earl Ernest] who responded to the scene. . . . Before Officer Ernest took the stand, Carter's attorney asked the trial judge to bar the prosecutor from questioning any of the police officers about [the] signs and symptoms of strangulation. The defense attorney asserted that this would be expert testimony that the officers were not qualified to give. . . .

[T]he prosecutor called Officer Ernest to the stand. Ernest testified that he had received training in the investigation of domestic violence, both at the police academy and in later training sessions during his twelve years with the Anchorage Police Department. Ernest also testified that he had received training specifically focused on the investigation of strangling. When the prosecutor asked Ernest how many cases of domestic violence he had investigated during his police career, Ernest answered "thousands." The prosecutor then asked Ernest to describe [the] things . . . to look for when investigating a reported strangling. The defense attorney did not object to this question. The following colloquy then ensued:

Ernest: [T]he evidence that would probably be present in a strangulation . . . are [such things as] bruising, *petechiae* [a star-burst of red dots created by the bursting of blood vessels within the eyeball], raspy voice, or difficulty swallowing. There may be defensive wounds. . . .

Prosecutor: All right. And . . . how frequently do you see bruising in [strangulation] cases . . . ?

Ernest: Well, . . . not as often as you would think. The fairer the skin, the more likelihood that you'll be able to see red marks, at least. Bruising tends to show up a little bit later, depending on how long it's been since. . . .

At this point, the defense attorney objected. The defense attorney told Judge Volland that the officer was now embarking on the kind of testimony that the defense attorney previously objected to—in particular, the mechanisms of bruising, [and the] conclusions [that the officer] would draw from [the presence or absence of] bruising. . . . [The judge overruled the objection.] Ernest testified (without further objection) that, when investigating a case of strangulation, one would often see red marks or scratches in the area of the throat as well as *petechiae.* . . . The prosecutor then asked Ernest to describe Romanda Lee's physical condition at the time of the reported assault. Ernest testified that Lee had blood on her forehead (from an injury to her forehead), *petechiae* in both of her eyes, and fresh scratch marks on her neck and lower face. . . .

On appeal, Carter acknowledges that Officer Ernest could properly testify concerning his observations of Lee's physical condition—for example, the fresh scratches to her neck and face, and the *petechiae* in her eyes. But Carter contends that it was improper to allow Ernest to testify concerning the *significance* of these observations—that these were some of the signs or symptoms he was trained to look for as part of any investigation into a potential strangling. . . .

The State responds that Ernest's testimony was not expert testimony, but rather lay testimony—simply a description of his own observations of Lee's physical condition, coupled with a description of the training he received as a police officer. The State points out that the prosecutor at Carter's trial never asked Ernest to offer an opinion as to whether Lee's physical condition was consistent with her report of being strangled, or tended to show that her report of being strangled was truthful. But even though the prosecutor may never have asked such questions of the officer, the officer's testimony implicitly rested on the premise that the things he had been trained to look for were, in fact, signs or symptoms of a strangling. Without this foundational premise, Ernest's testimony about his training would have had no relevance. Indeed, [t]he prosecutor explicitly relied on this premise in his summation to the jury. The prosecutor openly argued that the fresh scratches and the *petechiae* were signs or symptoms that Lee had been strangled—and, thus, the presence of these injuries corroborated the State's allegation that Carter strangled Lee.

The real questions presented here are (1) whether the prosecutor's premise was the type of assertion that needed to be supported by expert testimony; and (2) if so, whether Ernest had the requisite expertise to offer that testimony. . . . Carter claims that Ernest was improperly allowed to give expert opinion on three subjects: (1) Ernest's testimony that the fresh scratches on Lee's neck and lower face were indications that she had been strangled; (2) his testimony that the *petechiae* in Lee's eyeballs were also an indication that strangulation had occurred; and (3) his testimony that, often, the victim of a strangling will not exhibit bruising until later.

With regard to the first aspect of Ernest's testimony (the significance of the fresh scratches on Lee's neck and face), this was lay opinion. The jurors did not need specialized training or experience to understand the basis for this inference. With regard to the second aspect of Ernest's testimony (the significance of the fact that Lee exhibited *petechiae*), we agree with Carter that this was expert testimony. Most jurors would likely not be aware of the tie between *petechiae* and strangulation; in other words, it would require scientific, technical, or other specialized knowledge to understand the significance of this observation in the context of an investigation into a reported strangling. However, Judge Volland [the trial judge] concluded (based on Ernest's foundational testimony) that Ernest had sufficient experience investigating cases of strangling to be aware of the connection between *petechiae* and strangulation, and thus to offer an opinion that the presence of *petechiae* was an indication that a strangling had occurred. Based on our review of the record, we conclude that Judge Volland's ruling on Ernest's level of expertise was reasonable, and not an abuse of discretion.

As this Court has previously observed, "[t]here is no requirement that a witness possess a particular license or academic degree . . . to qualify as an expert. The criterion . . . is whether the fact-finder can receive appreciable help from that [witness]." Officer Ernest may not have had the expertise to offer a meaningful opinion on the precise physiological mechanism that causes *petechiae*, and he may not have been aware of all the potential alternate causes of *petechiae*. [However,] Ernest had sufficient experience in criminal investigations to be aware that strangling victims often exhibit *petechiae*. Thus, Ernest could validly offer an opinion that the presence of *petechiae* tended to corroborate Lee's initial report that she had been strangled. . . .

For much the same reasons, we conclude that it was not error for Ernest to testify that strangling victims often will not exhibit bruising until later. . . . [W]e conclude, based on our review of the record, that Judge Volland's ruling on this question was reasonable, and not an abuse of discretion. . . .

Notes and Questions

1. *Background.* Strangulation, a life-threatening form of domestic violence, consists of external pressure applied to the neck that results in a lack of oxygen. It leads to loss of consciousness in 10 seconds and death within 4 to 5 minutes. Center on Family Violence (CFV) (U. Penn), Fact Sheet: Strangulation Assaults in Domestic Violence Cases 1, www.sp2.upenn.edu/ortner/docs/factsheet_strangulation.pdf. Manual strangulation involves pressure to the neck by means of a hand or forearm, or by kneeling or standing on the neck. Ligature involves an implement (for example, phone cord, electrical wire, shoe lace, belt, etc.). Id.

a. *Relationship to domestic violence.* Strangulation is a predictive factor for fatal domestic violence. Almost 60 percent of women who are killed by their partners were victims of attempted strangulations. Id. at 1. Episodes of strangulation tend to occur at late stages in intimate relationships and serve as an indication that the violence is escalating in frequency and severity. Id. See also Archana Nath, Survival or Suffocation: Can Minnesota's New Strangulation Law Overcome Implicit Biases in the Justice System?, 25 Law & Ineq. 253, 269 (2007) (citing research).

b. *Frequency and prevalence.* Attempted strangulation occurs with surprising frequency in abusive relationships. Many victims report several prior attempts. See CFV Fact Sheet, supra, at 1 (noting that most victims who seek shelter services or prevention services report 5.3 attempts).

2. *Injuries.* Physical injuries from strangulation include dizziness, nausea, hoarseness, sore throat, breathing problems, swallowing difficulties, ringing in ears, voice or vision changes, redness, bruises, scratches, swelling, voice change, internal bleeding, larynx fracture, and paralysis. Neurological problems include: eyelid droop or facial droop, left or right side weakness, loss of sensation or memory, and paralysis. Psychological problems also result, including amnesia, depression, psychosis, PTSD, suicidal ideation, and insomnia. Id.

Strangulation is difficult to discover because it often leaves no marks. See Allison Turkel, Understanding, Investigating and Prosecuting Strangulation Cases, Prosecutor, Dec. 2007, at 20 (finding that the police report no visible injuries in half of the cases).

If bruises do occur, they may not appear until several days after the event. In fact, some victims, without visible symptoms, may die 36 or more hours later resulting from internal swelling and undetected internal injuries. Id. at 21. According to the police investigator in *Carter*, what are the physical indicators? Which did he observe? How can evidence of strangulation be discovered if it leaves no marks, according to *Carter*?

3. *State law reform.* Many states recently enacted statutes designating felony liability or enhancing sentences for strangulation attempts. See, e.g., Idaho Code Ann. §18-923 (nonfatal strangulation of household member punishable by up to 15 years in prison); Minn. Stat. §609.2247 (strangulation of family or household member

punishable by up to three years in prison or fine up to $5,000, or both). Before such laws, strangulation either was not charged or was charged as a misdemeanor (felony liability required use of a weapon or visible injuries). Despite the law reform movement, however, many prosecutors still charge strangulation attempts as misdemeanors. See Kelly Francis, Minnesota's New Domestic Abuse Strangulation Statute, Bench & Bar Minn. Sept. 1008, at 26, 28.

Prosecutions are more likely if evidence of injuries exists from other acts of violence, independent corroboration of the strangulation exists, the defendant has a prior history of abuse, the victim uses the word "strangle," the victim receives medical care, and documentation exists of the injuries. Francis, supra, at 28; Turkel, supra, at 21.

Should any incident in which a person places hands around someone's neck and applies pressure be treated as attempted strangulation? What efforts can be taken to encourage prosecutions?

a. *Statutory definition of strangulation.* Some statutes define strangulation as "intentionally, knowingly, or recklessly impeding normal breathing or . . . blood circulation" by applying pressure on the throat or neck or by blocking the nose or mouth of a person. See, e.g., Tex. Penal Ann. Code §22.01. Other states have more general definitions. See, e.g., Idaho Code Ann. §18-923 ("chokes or attempts to strangle" a household member, or a person occupying a dating relationship). What statute is preferable? Who should be protected, that is, "persons," "household members," "dating" partners?

b. *Physical harm requirement?* Should strangulation statutes require "substantial bodily harm"? In *Carter*, would the victim's attempted strangulation meet a definition that requires disfigurement, or loss or impairment of the function of any bodily member or organ? See, e.g., Minn. Stat. §609.02 subd. 7a. Does the loss of consciousness qualify? See Nath, supra, at 271 (jurors often disagree whether this constitutes substantial bodily harm).

c. *Intent to kill?* Must the jury find that the defendant intended to kill the victim? Or, caused her to be "completely" unable to breathe? See State v. Braxton, 643 S.E.2d 637, 642 (N.C. Ct. App. 2007) (holding that it was sufficient that victim had difficulty breathing).

d. *Sanctions.* What is an appropriate penalty? Compare Idaho Code Ann. §18-923 (up to 15 years) with Minn. Stat. §609.2247 subd. 2 (up to three years or a fine of $5000, or both).

4. *Victim recantation.* Victims frequently recant their accounts. Did Romanda Lee? How did the prosecutor respond? Victim recantation is discussed in Chapter 7.

5. *Mutual combat.* Abusers sometimes claim that they were acting in self-defense. Such claims are especially likely in cases of strangulation. See Turkel, supra, at 22. How can police determine whether certain injuries (i.e., scratches, bruises, kicks, bite marks) to the aggressor were inflicted defensively by the victim? See id. Mutual combat is discussed in Chapter 5.

6. *Sadomasochism.* For some people, the fear of sudden death serves to increase sexual pleasure. Sadomasochistic sexual acts sometimes result in accidental death. How do law enforcement officials distinguish between a strangulation attempt and a sadomasochistic encounter? See generally Sung-ook Baik & Justin M. Uku, Ligature Strangulation of a Woman During Sadomasochistic Sexual Activity, 9 Am. J. Forensic Med. Pathology 249 (1988).

Problem

Ashley and her boyfriend, Michael, have lunch at a bar. They spend the afternoon drinking. Late in the afternoon, Michael leaves the bar, saying that he will return soon. When he fails to return, Ashley goes looking for him. She finds him and accuses him of having left to take drugs. They start yelling at each other. People in a nearby coffee shop hear the couple arguing and come outside. They witness Michael put his hands around Ashley's throat and shake her. Michael flees when people approach to help Ashley. A police officer arrives. He takes Ashley to the police station to make a statement and to photograph the red marks on her neck.

Michael is charged with attempted second-degree assault by strangulation. A jury finds him guilty. On appeal, Michael argues that he did not intend to strangle Ashley. He contends that the trial court erred by excluding Ashley's opinion that, in her view, Michael did not intend to strangle her. The definition of attempt requires that a person "with intent to commit a specific crime, does any act which is a substantial step toward the commission of that crime."

The state penal code defines strangulation as follows: "to compress a person's neck, thereby obstructing the person's blood flow or ability to breathe, or doing so with the intent to obstruct the person's blood flow or ability to breathe." Wash. Rev. Code §9A.04.110(26). Further, lay opinion testimony (such as Ashley's) is admissible if it is "rationally based on the perception of the witness, and helpful to a clear understanding of the witness's testimony or the determination of a fact in issue, and not based on scientific knowledge." What result? Did Michael intend to strangle Ashley? Should Ashley's lay testimony have been admitted? State v. Pellegrini, 2008 WL 4838841 (Wash. Ct. App. 2008).

2. Murder-suicide

■ CLARK v. OFFICE OF PERSONNEL MANAGEMENT
256 F.3d 1360 (Fed. Cir. 2001)

MICHEL, Circuit Judge.

[Melonie Clark, a Department of Defense civilian employee was married to Michael Clark]. The couple had two children together. On August 19, 1994, allegedly in the midst of a child custody dispute, Michael traveled to the home of Melonie's parents, where Melonie and the children were temporarily staying. While the details of what occurred that day are not entirely clear, there was an exchange of gunfire that left Michael, Melonie and both of Melonie's parents dead. The two children, ages three and seven, apparently witnessed the events. . . . Melonie's death certificate states that her death was a "homicide" caused by a "gunshot to face," and lists her time of death as 5:10 p.m., August 19, 1994. Michael's death certificate states that his death was a "suicide" caused by a "gunshot to head," and lists his time of death as 5:14 p.m., August 19, 1994.

. . . Phillip Clark, Michael's brother, is the executor and conservator of Michael's estate, as well as the guardian of the two children. As executor of Michael's estate, Clark submitted an application to [the Office of Personnel Management or OPM] in order to obtain the [Basic Employee Death Benefit or BEDB] to which he claims Michael was entitled as a result of Melonie's participation in [the Federal Employees Retirement System or FERS].

. . . OPM is a federal agency charged with the distribution of the BEDB, pursuant to 5 U.S.C. §8442(b) and 5 C.F.R. §843.309(a). The statute and its implementing regulation provide in relevant part that if an employee dies after completing at least 18 months of civilian service and is survived by a spouse, that spouse will receive a benefit. However, neither the statute nor its implementing regulation explicitly addresses whether a survivor benefit should be given to one who has become a widow or widower by intentionally killing his or her spouse. . . .

. . . OPM [previously] determined that Alabama state law prohibits killers from profiting from their crimes. . . . Alabama's intent to preclude killers from profiting from their crimes is further evidenced through the Slayer Statute. In enacting the Slayer Statute, the Alabama Legislature decided that one who "feloniously and intentionally" kills his or her spouse is deemed to have predeceased the decedent and is thus ineligible to receive "surviving spouse" benefits [for purposes of state law]. See Ala. Code §43-8-253(a). . . .

[OPM first determined that Michael had intentionally and feloniously caused the death of his wife. OPM then concluded that it should follow the principle of Alabama law in the instant case, and that therefore Michael's intentional killing of Melonie prevented his estate from obtaining the BEDB.] While neither OPM nor the Board was bound by the conclusions of the state authorities, both reasonably concluded, based on the content of the documents before them, that the principle of Alabama law should be followed to deny Clark's BEDB application. . . .

Clark argues to this court that he is entitled to the BEDB because, in the absence of a conviction, the Slayer Statute requires a finding by an Alabama probate court that Michael intentionally killed Melonie. Clark asserts that absent such a finding, the Slayer Statute is inapplicable and consequently he is entitled to the BEDB from OPM. On the other hand, OPM argues that Clark is not entitled to the BEDB because the Code of Alabama does not limit the term "court" in the Slayer Statute to only include an Alabama probate court, and that therefore OPM and the [Merit Systems Protection Board that reviews decisions of the administrative judge who, in turn, reviews OPM decisions] can constitute "courts" for purposes of the statute.

We disagree with both contentions. The plain language of the Code of Alabama clearly contemplates that, absent a conviction, determinations of intentional killings for purposes of the Slayer Statute will be made by an Alabama "court." See Ala. Code §43-8-253(e). However, merely because the Slayer Statute is technically inapplicable to the instant case does not preclude OPM, nor the Board, from relying on the state law principle behind the statute. [T]he Slayer Statute codified a long-standing Alabama state principle, which is also found in virtually all other states, as well as in federal common law. If there had been a conviction or an Alabama court finding, OPM would have been required to apply the Slayer Statute. However, the absence of a conviction and of a probate court finding did not necessarily preclude OPM from lawfully relying on the Slayer Statute's underlying principles. . . .

[W]e hold [that] because the federal statute in question was silent on the subject of killers obtaining the BEDB earned by their victims, OPM was entitled to look to Alabama state law to determine that the estate of a slayer may not obtain "surviving spouse" benefits. [B]ecause there was substantial evidence that Michael did indeed intentionally cause the death of his wife, we hold that OPM lawfully concluded that the principle of Alabama's "slayer's rule" applied to the instant case, and consequently OPM correctly denied Clark's BEDB application. . . .

Notes and Questions

1. *Prevalence.* Murder-suicides comprise a small percentage of homicides of intimate partners. Although no federal agency tracks such offenses, some studies estimate that 1,000 to 1,500 such deaths occur annually. Cited in Violence Policy Center (VPC), American Roulette: Murder-Suicide in the United States 2 (April 2008) [hereafter VPC study], http://www.vpc.org/studies/amroul2008.pdf.

2. *Social reality.* Most persons who commit murder-suicides are male and use a firearm. Id. at 4, 5. Most victims are intimate partners, and the most frequent precipitating factor is the breakdown of the relationship. Id. at 5. Most murder-suicides occur in the home. Id. at 7. Children frequently witness the events. Id. at 7. Which of these characteristics applies to the Clarks?

3. *Family annihilators.* Slayers who kill intimate partners as well as other family members, such as children and/or other relatives, are called "family annihilators." See Catharine Skipp, Inside the Minds of Family Annihilators, Newsweek, Feb. 11, 2010, http://www.newsweek.com/2010/01/10/inside-the-minds-of-family-annihilators.html. Was Michael Clark a "family annihilator"?

Slayings involving the death of an intimate partner and children, followed by suicide, are called "familicides." Common characteristics for familicides (similar to those of murder-suicides generally) include a prior history of abuse, access to a gun, escalating threats, and poor mental health or substance abuse. Nat'l Inst. of Justice (NIJ), Murder–Suicide in Families 1 (April 7, 2011) [hereafter NIJ Murder-Suicide Report], available at http://www.ojp.usdoj.gov/nij/topics/crime/intimate-partner-violence/murder-suicide.htm.

What is the motivation for familicides? Some researchers suggest that these slayers, who have often had abusive childhoods, respond by striving to create an idealized family life. They exert strict control over family members to maintain that image, and respond violently when that image is threatened. See Bernie Auchter, Men Who Murder Their Families: What the Research Tells Us, NIJ Journal 10, 11-12 (June 2010). Some family annihilators suffer from depression and financial problems. Id. The murder is "altruistic," stemming from a misguided belief that their victims are better dead than experiencing current problems. VPC Study, supra, at 6. See also Auchter, supra, at 11-12 (explaining that killers "overenmesh" their identities with those of their family members, such that they perceive that their family members experience their mental anguish); James Alan Fox & Jack Levin, Extreme Killings: Understanding Serial and Mass Murder 166 (2005) (family massacres are a "perverted act of love"). See generally Neil Websdale, Familicidal Hearts: The Emotional Styles of 211 Killers (2010).

4. *Separation as motivation.* Separation is a risk factor for intimate partner violence and also for murder-suicides. One researcher suggests that murder-suicide is the ultimate reflection of the abuser's refusal to allow his intimate partner to start a new life after a separation. Murder suicides result because it "was the killers who wanted to be united in death with their wives." Sandra McNeill, Woman Killer as Tragic Hero, in Femicide: The Politics of Woman Killing 178, 179 (Jill Radford & Diana E. H. Russell eds. 1992). What role might separation have played in the Clark murder-suicide? The role of separation is explored later in this Chapter.

5. *Elderly.* Some murder-suicides take place among the elderly. What factors might predispose older persons to commit such offenses?

6. *Inheritance.* Murder-suicides often evoke inheritance issues. What is Phillip Clark's argument regarding his deceased brother's right to inherit Melonie's federal death benefits? Melonie's employee benefit plan provided for death benefits (similar to Social Security Survivors' benefits) for each of her children (pursuant to 5 U.S.C. §8443) and also for her "surviving spouse" (pursuant to 5 U.S.C. §8442(b)). Upon Melonie's death, if Michael had survived her, he would have been entitled to her federal death benefits. Then, on his death, his share would have passed to his children if he died without a will. Thus, Phillip's motivation (as executor and guardian) is to acquire additional benefits for the Clark children.

7. *Slayer disqualification.* All states now prevent a slayer from inheriting from the victim, generally by "slayer disqualification" statutes. Allison Bridges, Marital Fault as a Basis for Terminating Inheritance Rights: Protecting the Institution of Marriage and Those Who Abide by Their Vows—'Til Death Do Them Part, 45 Real Prop. Trust & Estate L.J. 559, 564 (2010) (surveying jurisdictions). What did the federal statute specify in *Clark* about the right of a slayer to inherit federal death benefits if the slayer intentionally kills a covered employee-spouse? How did state law become relevant? What does the Alabama's slayer statute provide? Who made the determination that Michael's conduct satisfied the statute in *Clark?*

8. *Requirement of conviction.* Some slayer disqualification statutes require that the slayer must have been "convicted" of murder to be barred from inheritance. Does the Alabama slayer statute contain this requirement? Can a court "convict" Michael of murder if he committed suicide? See, e.g., Cal. Prob. Code §254 (providing that, in the absence of a conviction, a slayer can be disqualified if a court determines by a preponderance of the evidence that the murder was felonious and intentional). What is Phillip's argument about the fact that Michael was never convicted? What does OPM respond? If no court made that determination, on what basis does OPM disqualify Michael from inheriting Melonie's death benefits? On what basis does the circuit court determine that Michael should be disqualified?

9. *Result of disqualification.* If a slayer is disqualified, any property of the slayer is distributed as if the slayer predeceased the victim. William M. McGovern, Jr. & Sheldon F. Kurtz, Wills, Trusts and Estates Including Taxation and Future Interests §2.7 at 80 (3d ed. 2004). That means, in the *Clark* murder-suicide situation, Melonie's federal death benefit would not pass to Michael's estate. Who takes the death benefit instead? Who inherits the rest of Michael's property? Does the rationale underlying slayer disqualification statutes (a murderer should not profit from his wrong) apply in this case?

> **Famous Murder-Suicide: World-Famous Wrestler Chris Benoit**
>
> Professional wrestler Chris Benoit married his second wife Nancy. They had a son, Daniel. Three years later, Nancy filed for divorce, alleging that the marriage was "irretrievably broken" because of her husband's "cruel treatment." Nancy claimed that her husband broke and threw furniture when he was angry. She alleged that he was subject to insomnia, mood swings, depression, and alcohol abuse. Nancy also filed for a restraining order, but later dropped both that request as well as her suit for divorce.
>
> On June 25, 2007, police entered the Benoit home. Relatives had requested police to check on the family because Benoit had missed several appointments. There, law enforcement discovered the bodies of Benoit, his wife Nancy, and 7-year-old son Daniel. Law enforcement officials determined that Benoit had bound his wife before he killed her and had sedated his son before strangling him. Then, Benoit committed suicide by hanging himself with a weight machine.
>
> Several theories were offered to explain the double murder and suicide. After a toxicology report revealed Benoit tested positive for steroids, some authorities pointed to "roid rage"—aggression stemming from high doses of anabolic steroids. Others, including Benoit's father, claimed that years of repeated blows to the head had resulted in severe brain damage.
>
> See Ethan Nelson & Roxanna Sherwood, Chris Benoit's Murder, Suicide: Was Brain Damage To Blame?, ABC News, *Nightline*, Aug. 26, 2010, available at http://abcnews.go.com/Nightline/chris-benoits-dad-son-suffered-severe-brain-damage/story?id=11471875.

3. Separation Assault

A popular misconception about domestic violence is that the victim's ending the relationship will end the violence. "Why didn't she leave?" is a common question. Yet, when victims leave their abusers, often the violence escalates, as the following case reveals.

■ CRAWFORD v. COMMONWEALTH
704 S.E.2d 107 (Va. 2011)

Lemons, Justice:

. . . On Thursday, November 18, 2004, John and Irene Powers had dinner with their thirty-three-year-old daughter, Sarah Crawford at a local restaurant in Manassas, Virginia. When they left the restaurant that night at about 8:30 p.m., it would be the last time that they would see their daughter alive. Twelve hours later Sarah would be dead, and her husband, the appellant, Anthony Dale Crawford would be wanted for her murder.

The Powers had a "very close" relationship with their daughter and saw her frequently. Sarah and her mother talked on the phone often. During dinner, Sarah told her parents of the latest events in her life, including her job as an office manager for a television production company. Sarah mentioned to her mother that she had a hair appointment on Saturday and that, on Saturday afternoon, she had plans to go to a concert with a man she recently met. Sarah was, according to her mother, "really very happy" that night.

Sarah had every reason to be happy. She had a good job with a small company that she enjoyed and found fulfilling. She had gastric bypass surgery in the summer of 2002 and reached her goal of losing one hundred and fifty pounds. In addition, Sarah had just gotten a raise and moved into her own apartment. And, most significantly, Sarah had recently decided to end her relationship with her abusive husband, Crawford.

Sarah and Crawford had been married since 1999, and had been together for several years before that. The couple had a troubled history, and Sarah was growing increasingly fearful of her husband. In October of 2004, Sarah and Crawford separated. Following their separation, Sarah expressed to a number of friends and co-workers that she was afraid that Crawford might physically harm her. This concern caused Sarah to make a number of significant changes in her life. Sarah found a new apartment in a rural area that her mother described as "wooded, desolate, and well-hidden." Sarah chose the apartment because it had a long driveway, so that she "could make a phone call" or "get out" if she saw someone coming.

On October 29, 2004, Sarah and the Powers went to Crawford's apartment to pick up a few of Sarah's things. . . . [Crawford was present in the apartment.] As Sarah expected, Crawford was hostile toward her, refused to allow her to take any of her belongings, and, ultimately, called the police. When the police arrived, they asked Crawford to calm down and to allow Sarah to take her things. However, despite the police officer's request, Crawford's hostile behavior toward Sarah continued. According to the police officer, as Sarah packed up her belongings, Crawford approached her and whispered something in her ear. The officer could not determine what Crawford said to Sarah, but the officer testified that "it was something that obviously upset [Sarah]," because she "immediately stood up and stepped back away from [Crawford]." Sarah then asked Crawford to repeat what he said and asked if Crawford was threatening her. The officer ordered Crawford to back away from Sarah; however, he had to repeat this command several times before Crawford complied. At one point, Mrs. Powers heard Crawford tell Sarah, "You'll pay for this."

Eventually, the police officers left the apartment, but, sensing that things might not remain peaceful, they remained nearby. After the officers left, Sarah mentioned that she wanted a side table that her parents had given her, and she asked Crawford to unlock the bedroom door so she could retrieve it. Instead of unlocking the door, Crawford said that he would get the table. Mr. Powers was packing up some of Sarah's belongings, when he heard Crawford say, "Here's your god-damned table" and the table "came flying over [Mr. Powers'] right shoulder and . . . landed near the sofa and broke. . . ." At that point, the Powers called the police and the same officers immediately responded. The police stayed until Sarah and her family finished packing her things, and then followed them for about a mile to make sure that they got away safely.

Following her encounter with Crawford at the apartment, Sarah went to the Prince William County Juvenile and Domestic Relations District Court (JDR court) and requested a preliminary protective order. . . . [The affidavit] recounted past incidents in which Crawford forcibly raped her, threatened her life, and physically and verbally abused her. In the affidavit, Sarah also stated

> [o]n October 30, 2004, [Crawford] called me and told me that I must want to die. He also said he understands why husbands kill their wives. He told me that he would find me and would come to my work. . . . I am afraid of [Crawford]. I fear he may physically hurt me or even kill me. I want him to stay away from me and my family.

The JDR court granted Sarah's request for a preliminary protective order.[3] . . . As Sarah began to settle into her new life, she tried to take precautions for her own safety. Sarah chose the location of her desk at work because it overlooked the parking lot and allowed her to see if Crawford's vehicle was parked there. In addition, Sarah took a new route home every night after work. According to her supervisor, "[Sarah] would never go home the same way two days in a row because she didn't want someone to be able to follow her or know where she was going to be at any particular time, so she would always choose a new way." Sarah also spoke to her parents several times each day. On November 1, 2004, Sarah sought help from a domestic violence intervention program in Prince William County.

. . . Sarah never made it to work on Friday, November 19, 2004. . . . Later that day, the Powers received a telephone call from a person who found Sarah's cell phone lying in the grass near his driveway in Manassas. Worried for their daughter's well-being, the Powers made the first of several trips to Sarah's apartment. . . . [The last time, they found] a bottle of wine at the door with a note that said, "Sarah, sorry I missed you. Call me to let me know you're okay." Sarah had missed her Saturday afternoon date. . . .

In the early morning hours of November 22, 2004, the night manager of a motel in Charlottesville, Virginia, found Sarah dead in one of the motel's rooms, her body positioned in a particularly gruesome and suggestive manner. A motel towel concealed a fatal gunshot wound to the right side of her chest. . . . [I]nvestigators found Crawford's clothing, personal belongings, and fingerprints in the motel room. Cigarette butts in the motel room's ashtray contained Crawford's DNA, and a pill bottle bearing Crawford's name was also found in the room. The motel's clerk testified that Crawford arrived at the motel at 11:00 a.m. on November 19, 2004. Crawford was driving Sarah's car at the time. . . .

Given the abundance of evidence linking him to the murder scene, the Charlottesville police began to search for Crawford. [He was later found in Jacksonville, Florida, where he was driving Sarah's car.] The driver's window of the vehicle was broken, and police found Sarah's blood on both the driver's and rear seats. The police found gunshot residue in the car and a box of ammunition in the trunk.

---

3. The protective order prohibited Crawford from having any contact with his wife. At a court hearing on November 16, 2004, Sarah appeared in the JDR court and asked that the protective order be dismissed. The record does not establish why she made this request.

Crawford waived his *Miranda* rights and made a statement to the Florida police during a custodial interview [in which he] claimed that Sarah had picked him up early Friday morning at his house. He said they had planned to go to Charlottesville for the weekend to attempt to reconcile. After an hour to an hour and a half drive, they arrived in Charlottesville at about 8:30 in the morning. Sarah was driving, and he was in the passenger's seat. Crawford said they drove directly to a McDonalds and got breakfast. Without any explanation as to why, Crawford then stated that he pulled out his .38 caliber revolver planning to commit suicide. Crawford said he had the gun cocked and his finger on the trigger when Sarah grabbed for the weapon. While they were wrestling over the gun, it went off and the bullet hit Sarah. Crawford claimed the shooting was an accident, telling the police "she basically did it to herself."

Crawford then said that he pulled Sarah into the back seat and drove to a nearby hotel and rented a room. He left Sarah's body on the bed and her clothing in the room and "took off and headed south." Significantly, Crawford never offered any explanation for leaving Sarah's body undressed in the position in which it was found, nor for failing to seek medical help for Sarah. Likewise, he offered no explanation as to why his semen was found in her vagina and sperm was found in her mouth and anus.

Prior to trial, Crawford made a motion to suppress the affidavit executed by Sarah in support of the protective order, arguing that the document was testimonial hearsay and, therefore, inadmissible under Crawford v. Washington, 541 U.S. 36 (2004). . . .

In this case, Sarah executed an affidavit for use in an ex parte court proceeding, and given the nature of the statements themselves, which describe violent, criminal acts, an objective witness would reasonably "believe that the statement would be available for use at a later trial." [Additionally,] Sarah's affidavit described past events that had taken place days, weeks, and even months previously—the very purpose of which was to "establish or prove past events potentially relevant to later criminal prosecution." . . . Despite the fact that the immediate purpose of the affidavit was to obtain a protective order in a civil case, the facts recited were, nonetheless, "potentially relevant to later criminal prosecution." . . .

Given the Supreme Court's definition and examples of testimonial statements [in *Crawford*, supra], we hold that the affidavit in support of Sarah Crawford's petition for a preliminary protective order is testimonial in nature and should not have been admitted against Crawford at trial. Because Sarah was unavailable to testify at Crawford's trial and Crawford did not have a prior opportunity to cross-examine Sarah concerning these statements, Crawford's Sixth Amendment right to confrontation was violated when the affidavit was admitted into evidence against him at trial. Accordingly, the Court of Appeals erred when it held the affidavit to be nontestimonial and upheld its admission at Crawford's trial.

However, this conclusion does not end our analysis. The Commonwealth argues that the admission of the affidavit in Crawford's trial, if error, was harmless. We agree with the Commonwealth. . . .

The overall strength of the Commonwealth's case against Crawford, and the quantum, character, and quality of the other evidence introduced at trial, independent of the affidavit, is overwhelming. The affidavit is simply cumulative of other evidence relating to these charges properly before the jury. [W]e hold that the admission of the affidavit constitutes harmless error beyond a reasonable doubt in relation to Crawford's convictions. [Crawford was convicted of capital murder, abduction with intent to defile, rape, grand larceny, use of a firearm in the commission of a murder, and use of a firearm in the commission of abduction.]

■ MARTHA R. MAHONEY, LEGAL IMAGES OF BATTERED WOMEN: REDEFINING THE ISSUE OF SEPARATION
90 Mich. L. Rev. 1, 64-69 (1991)

Law assumes—pretends—the autonomy of women. Every legal case that discusses the question "why didn't she leave?" implies that the woman could have left. We need to challenge the coercion of women's choices, reveal the complexity of women's experience and struggle, and recast the entire discussion of separation in terms of the batterer's violent attempts at control.

[T]he recently developed term "postseparation woman abuse" begins to grapple with the problem of revealing the issue of power and control in women's experience of violence. At least half of women who leave their abusers are followed and harassed or further attacked by them. In one study of interspousal homicide, more than half of the men who killed their spouses did so when the partners were separated; in contrast, less than ten percent of women who killed were separated at the time. Power and control are crucial here in several ways. Men who kill their wives describe their feeling of loss of control over the woman as a primary factor; most frequently, the man expresses the fear that the woman was about to abandon him, though in fact this fear may have been unfounded. The fact that marital separation increases the instigation to violence shows that these attacks are aimed at preventing or punishing the woman's autonomy. They are major—often deadly—power moves.

However, the term "postseparation woman abuse" fails to capture the many cases where violence occurs in response to the decision itself: the essential attack is on the woman's autonomy. Barbara Hart notes that "[t]he decision by a battered woman to leave is often met with escalated violence by the batterer." When the decision, rather than actual separation, triggers the attack, the circumstances of the violence may not reveal the assault on separation: the couple may still have been living together, and the attack may have taken place inside their mutual home—yet the attack may have been a direct response to her assertion of the will to separate or her first physical moves toward separation.

DEFINING SEPARATION ASSAULT

To expose the struggle for control, we should recognize the assault on the woman's separation as a specific type of attack that occurs at or after the moment she decides on a separation or begins to prepare for one. I propose that we call it "separation assault." The varied violent and coercive moves in the process of separation assault can be termed "separation attacks." Separation assault is the attack on the woman's body and volition in which her partner seeks to prevent her from leaving, retaliate for the separation, or force her to return. It aims at overbearing her will as to where and with whom she will live, and coercing her in order to enforce connection in a relationship. It is an attempt to gain, retain, or regain power in a relationship, or to punish the woman for ending the relationship. It often takes place over time.

Attacks on separation pervaded the stories of [battered women]. The announcement of intent to separate may be fraught with grave danger:

> He was on strike for the second time in a year. I was pregnant with the second baby in a row. There was absolutely no money. Every day, he yelled at me for a long time—an hour, two hours—about how awful I was. . . . I remember how desperate I felt and how much I needed it to stop.
>
> [One day, when he seemed receptive, she told him it had to stop.] He wouldn't listen. I said *I couldn't live like that anymore and would leave if he didn't stop. He kept saying I couldn't leave because we didn't have enough money to support two households. I said that only his failure to listen could make me leave—I couldn't live like that anymore.* . . .
>
> Suddenly he lost his temper. . . . He stormed upstairs, and I heard him pushing around in the closet. I thought, "That's funny. It sounds like he's getting the gun." And I didn't sit down or move—I stood in the middle of the living room floor and waited. He came down the stairs shouting and I saw that he really did have the shotgun. I knew it was fully loaded. I remember making the conscious decision that this was different than waiting through other outbursts, and that any argument would be deadly.
>
> I turned around and ran out the front door screaming that I was pregnant and ran up the landlady's front steps. I was going to call the police. But I realized that I had heard the baby crying upstairs. All the noise had wakened her from her nap. I couldn't believe he would shoot his child, but I didn't know why he'd gotten the gun, how well he actually knew what he was doing . . . how irritating her crying might be. I turned around and went back into the house. I could hear him putting the gun away in the closet. We got to the baby at the same moment.
>
> I dressed her, put on my own clothes, and left. I had $1.60 and no more money coming for several days. I took the better car. I drove away without knowing where I was going to go. (Emphasis added.)

Although women's stories recount many attacks triggered by separation, the nature of the attack *on separation itself* generally goes unrecognized. . . . Women describe protracted and inventive attacks on their moves to separate:

> Well, leaving took months. When I first left, I really didn't even know I was leaving the marriage. I was just going to California to get the car that he had left there. But being on my own again, and away from him, I began to regain some of my self-confidence, and I liked it. And people liked me.
>
> But then he came out to California to reclaim me. And totally humiliated me in front of my friends. ["Humiliation" including forcing her to have sex—essentially committing marital rape—in the back of a Volkswagen van while two other men were in the vehicle.] I was scared of him, I was still scared of his violence. As strong as I had been when he wasn't around, as soon as he came around, I would fall back into the baby talk, I would fall back into the patterns.
>
> Then we got back to Michigan, and I left again and went to stay with my friends. I was in Ann Arbor, and I had a fever. And he came to check on me. . . . He got my heirloom ring off my finger that night. The ring that all my life I felt separated me from poor white trash. The ring that my great-great-grandmother brought over from Germany when she fled the failed revolution of 1848. I never saw that ring again. He threatened to burn down the house I was staying in, but he was satisfied when I gave him the ring because he knew I would come back for it.

> I went back again [because he promised to return the ring]. I never got it. And then when it was time for my friends to leave town, they came to our house in Detroit, en masse, and said it was time to go. And I picked up, and I walked out. . . .

Some of these attacks on separation will go unnoticed until we begin identifying them specifically:

> I felt guilty, so I went back. That lasted a month, until Valentine's Day. . . . Finally, on Valentine's Day, he was throwing things. He was throwing glass—I was barefoot—it was totally absurd. I was being held prisoner in my bed by glass!
> I picked the kids up, scrunched my feet so they were under the glass, dragged my feet over the floor so they weren't getting cut too much, and made it out of the house.

One of the best-known battered women in America is Francine Hughes, whose story was told in *The Burning Bed*. The trial and movie brought the atrocities against her to public attention, but there was little cultural attention to the lessons of her search for autonomy:

> Hughes' entire marriage—and her life after divorce—was a search for the exit. [Family], in-laws, friends, social services, police, sheriff's office, county prosecutor—she tried them all. And even when Mickey Hughes came within moments of choking her to death or cutting her throat, no one helped.

We already recognize the danger of the attack on separation pragmatically and intuitively. This is a major reason for the existence of shelters, which protect women against attacks while giving them a place to live. It is the main reason that shelter numbers and addresses are not listed in telephone directories. It is the main reason women seek protective orders. It fills the pages of our newspapers with accounts of attacks on women by their separated husbands. Although we see this attack everywhere, we cannot analyze it until it has a name.

NAMING SEPARATION ASSAULT AND UNDERSTANDING BATTERING

Naming women's experience is an important component of feminist struggle for social and legal change. Naming separation assault has the potential to change consciousness in a manner comparable to the concept of "date rape." "Date rape" and "separation assault" name phenomena women know from our own experience, but which remain invisible without names. These terms do more, however, than merely identify hitherto unnamed experience. Each term identifies one aspect of a common attack on women in a way that illuminates the whole picture. Date rape is not all rape; separation assault is not the whole story of battering. Yet in each case, the act of identifying and describing the formerly invisible part transforms our understanding of the formerly misunderstood whole. . . .

Naming and recognizing separation assault will make women's experience more comprehensible to ourselves as well as to the legal system: We know it when we hear it. Attacks on our autonomy are one point at which women can— without stereotyping or invoking the likelihood of denial—locate our own experiences [on a continuum of control attempts]. . . . Exposing control attempts reveals the woman's struggle, rather than defining her according to the behavior of her assailant.

The name "separation assault" also helps women understand our own long-term reactions to violence or to the threats accompanying the end of relationships. Shelters and counseling provide short-term separation assistance, but the impact of separation assault goes on: Fear of an ex-husband becomes part of a woman's life. . . .

■ **SARAH M. BUEL, FIFTY OBSTACLES TO LEAVING, A.K.A. WHY ABUSE VICTIMS STAY**
Colo. Law., Oct. 1999, at 19

Domestic violence victims stay for many valid reasons. . . .

1. **[Lack of an] Advocate:** When the victim lacks a tenacious advocate, she often feels intimidated, discouraged, and, ultimately, hopeless. . . .
2. **[Batterer Characteristics]:** If the batterer is wealthy, a politician, famous, a popular athlete, or otherwise a powerful player in his community, he can generally afford to hire private counsel and pressure the decision-makers to view his case with leniency. . . .
3. **Believes Threats:** The victim believes the batterer's threats to kill her and the children if she attempts to leave. . . .
4. **Children's Best Interest:** Some victims believe it is in the children's best interest to have both parents in the home. . . .
5. **Children's Pressure:** Children's pressure on the abused parent [to let "Daddy" come home] can be quite compelling. . . .
6. **Cultural and Racial Defenses:** Cultural defenses may be cited by offenders, victims, and other community members. . . . Issues of race and culture can impact the victim's decision because she may be more worried about how the police will treat a man of color than she is about her safety. . . .
7. **Denial:** Some victims are in denial about the danger, instead believing that if they could be better partners, the abuse would stop. . . .
8. **Disabled:** Victims who are disabled or physically challenged face great obstacles, not only in gaining access to the court and social services, but because they also are more likely to be isolated from basic information about existing resources.
9. **Elderly:** Elderly domestic violence victims tend to hold traditional beliefs about marriage. They believe they must stay, even in the face of physical abuse. Others are dependent on the batterer for care. . . .
10. **Excuses:** The victim may believe the abuser's excuses to justify the violence, often blaming job stress or substance abuse. . . .
11. **Family Pressure:** Family pressure is exerted by those who either believe that there is no excuse for leaving a marriage or have been duped into denial by the batterer's charismatic behavior.
12. **Fear of Retaliation:** Victims cite fear of retaliation as a key obstacle to leaving. . . .
13. **Fear of Losing Child Custody:** Fear of losing child custody can immobilize even the most determined abuse victim. . . .
14. **Financial Abuse:** Financial abuse is a common tactic of abusers, although it may take different forms, depending on the couple's socioeconomic status. . . .

15. **Financial Despair:** Financial despair quickly takes hold when the victim realizes that she cannot provide for her children without the batterer's assistance. . . .

16. **Gratitude:** The victim may feel gratitude toward the batterer because he has helped support and raise her children from a previous relationship. Additionally, a victim who is overweight or has mental health, medical, or other serious problems often appreciates that the abuser professes his love, despite the victim's perceived faults. . . .

17. **Guilt:** Guilt is common among victims whose batterers have convinced them that, but for the victims' incompetent and faulty behavior, the violence would not occur. . . .

18. **Homelessness:** Homeless abuse victims face increased danger, as they must find ways of meeting basic survival needs. . . .

19. **Hope for the Violence to Cease:** A victim's hope for the violence to cease is typically fueled by the batterer's promises of change. . . . Many victims are hopeful because they want so desperately to believe that *this* time the batterer really has seen the error of his ways and intends to change, not realizing that, without serious interventions, chances are slim that the abuse will stop.

20. **Isolation:** [I]solating the victim increases the likelihood that she will stay, for without safety plans and reality checks, it will be more difficult for her to assess her level of danger.

21. **Keeping the Family Together:** Wanting to keep the family together motivates many abuse victims to stay. . . .

22. **Illiterate Victims:** Illiterate victims may be forced to rely on the literate batterer for everyday survival. . . .

23. **Incarcerated or Newly Released Abuse Victims:** Such victims often have few, if any, support systems to assist them with re-entry to the community. . . .

24. **Law Enforcement Officer:** If the perpetrator is a law enforcement officer, the victim may fear, or may have had past experiences of, other officers refusing to assist her. . . .

25. **Lesbian and Gay Victims:** Such victims may feel silenced if disclosing their sexual orientation (to qualify for the protective order) could result in their losing job, family, and home [or they fear] reinforcing negative stereotypes and increasing homophobia. . . .

26. **Low Self-Esteem:** Victims with low self-esteem may believe they deserve no better than the abuse they receive. . . .

27. **Love:** A victim may say she still loves the perpetrator, although she definitely wants the violence to stop. . . . [T]hey tend to try harder to please the abuser, whether because they need or love the job or the person, or hope that renewed effort and loyalty will result in cessation of the abuse. Since many batterers are charismatic and charming during the courtship stage, victims fall in love and may have difficulty in immediately altering their feelings with the first sign of a problem.

28. **Mediation:** Mediation, required in some jurisdictions even with evidence of domestic violence, puts the victim in the dangerous position of incurring the batterer's wrath for simply disclosing the extent of the violence. . . .

29. **Medical Problems:** Medical problems, including being HIV- or AIDS-positive, may mean that the victim must remain with the batterer to obtain medical services. . . .

30. **Mentally Ill Victims:** Such victims face negative societal stereotypes in addition to the batterer's taunts that the victim is crazy and nobody will believe anything she says. . . .

31. **Mentally Retarded or Developmentally Delayed Victims:** These victims are particularly vulnerable to the batterer's manipulation and are likely to be dependent on him for basic survival. . . .

32. **Military:** If the victim or the perpetrator is in the military, an effective intervention is largely dependent on the commander's response. . . . Many commanders believe that it is more important to salvage the soldier's military career than to ensure the victim's safety. . . .

33. **No Place to Go:** Victims with no place to go understand the bleak reality that affordable housing is at a premium in virtually every community in this country. . . .

34. **No Job Skills:** Victims with no job skills usually have no choice. . . .

35. **No Knowledge of Options:** Victims with no knowledge of the options and resources logically assume that none exist. Few communities use posters, brochures, radio and television public service announcements, and other public education campaigns to apprise victims of available resources. . . .

36. **Past Criminal Record:** Victims with a past criminal record are often still on probation or parole, making them vulnerable to the batterer's threats to comply with all of his demands or be sent back to prison. . . .

37. **Previously Abused Victims:** Sometimes previously abused victims [blame themselves]. . . .

38. **Prior Negative Court Experiences:** Those victims with prior negative experiences with the court system may have no reason to believe that they will be accorded the respect and safety considerations so desperately needed.

39. **Promises of Change:** The batterer's promises of change may be easy to believe because he sounds so sincere. . . .

40. **Religious Beliefs and Misguided Teachings:** Such beliefs may lead victims to think they have to tolerate the abuse to show their adherence to the faith. . . .

41. **Rural Victims:** Such victims may be more isolated and simply unable to access services. . . .

42. **Safer to Stay:** Assessing that it is safer to stay may be accurate when the victim can keep an eye on the batterer. . . .

43. **Students:** . . . If the perpetrator is also a student, the victim often does not want him to be expelled from school. . . .

44. **Shame and Embarrassment:** Shame and embarrassment about the abuse may prevent the victim from disclosing it or may cause her to deny that any problem exists. . . .

45. **Stockholm Syndrome:** The victim may experience the Stockholm Syndrome and bond with the abuser, making her more sympathetic to the batterer's claims of needing her to help him.

46. **Substance Abuse or Alcohol:** Either the victim's or offender's substance abuse or alcoholism may inhibit seeking help. . . .

47. **Teens:** Teens, especially those pregnant and who are already parents, are at greater risk for abuse in their relationships than any other age group. . . .

48. **Transportation:** For many victims, a lack of transportation condemns them to a choice between welfare and returning to their abusers. . . .

49. **Unaware that Abuse is a Criminal Offense:** The victim may be unaware that the abuse constitutes a criminal offense. . . .

50. **Undocumented Victims:** Undocumented victims facing complex immigration problems if they leave. . . .

■ DOMESTIC VIOLENCE: A PERSONAL SAFETY PLAN

(Attorney General of Texas website, 2011), *available at* **https://www.oag.state.tx.us/AG_Publications/pdfs/domestic_pf.pdf**

DURING AN EXPLOSIVE INCIDENT

• If there is an argument, try to be in a place that has an exit and not in a bathroom, kitchen, or room that may contain weapons.
• Practice getting out of your home safely. Identify which doors, windows, elevator, or stairwell to use.
• Pack a bag and have it ready at a friend's or relative's house.
• Identify one or more neighbors you can tell about the violence and ask them if they can call the police if they hear a disturbance coming from your home.
• Devise a code word to use with your children, family, friends and neighbors when you need the police.
• Decide and plan where you will go if you ever have to leave home.
• Use your instincts and judgment. In a dangerous situation, placate the abuser if possible, to keep him or her calm.

REMEMBER: You Do Not Deserve to be Hit or Threatened

WHEN PREPARING TO LEAVE

• Open a checking account or savings account in your own name.
• Leave money, an extra set of keys, copies of important documents, and extra clothes and medicines in a safe place or with someone you trust.
• Get your own post office box.
• Find a safe place where you and your children can go or a person who can lend you money.
• Always keep the shelter phone number and some change or calling card on you for emergency phone calls.
• If you have pets, make arrangements for them to be cared for in a safe place.

REMEMBER: Leaving Your Batterer is the Most Dangerous Time

WITH A PROTECTIVE ORDER

• If you or your children have been threatened or assaulted, you can request a Protective Order from your local District or County Attorney.
• Always keep your Protective Order with you.
• Call the police if your partner violates the Protective Order.
• Inform family members, friends, and neighbors that you have a Protective Order in effect.

- Think of alternative ways to keep safe if the police do not respond immediately.

IN YOUR OWN RESIDENCE

- If you stay in your home, lock your windows and change locks on your doors.
- Develop a safety plan with your children for when you are not with them.
- Inform your child's school, day care, etc., about who has permission to pick up your child.
- Inform your neighbors and the landlord that your partner no longer lives with you, and that they should call the police if they see him/her near your home.
- Never call the abuser from your home; he/she may find out where you live. Never tell the abuser where you live.
- Request an unlisted/unpublished number from the telephone company.

ON THE JOB AND IN PUBLIC

- Decide who at work you will inform of your situation.
- Include the office building security (if possible, provide them with a picture of your batterer).
- When at work, if possible, have someone screen your telephone calls.
- Have someone escort you to and from your car, bus, or train.
- If at all possible, use a variety of routes to come and go from home.

WHAT YOU NEED TO TAKE

IDENTIFICATION

- Driver's License
- Birth Certificate
- Children's Birth Certificates
- Social Security Cards

FINANCIAL

- Money and/or credit cards (in your name)
- Checking and/or savings account books

LEGAL PAPERS

- Protective Order
- Lease, rental agreement, house deed
- Car registration and insurance papers
- Health and life insurance papers
- Medical records for you and children
- School records
- Work permits/Green Card/Visa
- Passport
- Divorce and custody papers
- Marriage license

OTHER

- Medications
- House and car keys
- Valuable jewelry
- Address book
- Pictures and sentimental items
- Change of clothes for you and your children.

Notes and Questions

1. *"Separation assault."* The term *separation assault* was coined by Professor Martha Mahoney to describe the abuse suffered by victims when they choose to end an abusive intimate relationship. Martha R. Mahoney, Legal Images of Battered Women: Redefining the Issue of Separation, 90 Mich. L. Rev. 1 (1991). What forms does separation assault take? Why does it occur?

Mahoney's article was influential in refuting the conceptualization (derived largely from the learned helplessness theory) that battered women are passive victims of their circumstances. Mahoney rebuts the commonly asked question of "why didn't the woman leave?" by contending that women *repeatedly try* to leave abusive relationships, but their abusers sabotage their departure. See also Edward W. Gondolf & Ellen R. Fisher, Battered Women as Survivors: An Alternative To Treating Learned Helplessness 11-18, 20-24 (1988) (similarly recognizing, based on a study of 6,000 women in 50 battered women's shelters, that battered women persistently and assertively resort to strategies to protect themselves).

2. *Evidentiary issues.* In the principal case, the defendant attempts to exclude evidence in Sarah's affidavit in support of the restraining order. What evidence does he wish to exclude? Why does he wish to do so? What is his legal argument? Is he successful? The evidentiary issues in the U.S. Supreme Court case of Crawford v. Washington are explained in Chapter 7.

3. *Factor of escalation.* Violence often escalates at separation. In fact, the threat of separation or actual separation is frequently the precipitating event for the victim's murder. Carolyn Rebecca Block, How Can Practitioners Help an Abused Woman Lower Her Risk of Death, NIJ Journal, Nov. 2003, at 6 (revealing that an attempt to leave is the primary factor in almost half of intimate partner murders).

The escalation in abuse often takes the form of sexual assaults. In fact, the most likely time for sexual assaults to occur in an intimate relationship is at, or after, separation. Walter S. DeKeseredy & Martin D. Schwartz, Dangerous Exits: Escaping Abusive Relationships in Rural America 65 (2009) (revealing that 74 percent of victims were sexually assaulted when they expressed a desire to leave, 49 percent while they were leaving, and 33 percent after they left).

4. *Victims' motivation.* Which of the above factors may have influenced Sarah Crawford to remain in the relationship? What might have influenced her to leave? See also Margi Coggins & Linda F. C. Bullock, The Wavering Line in the Sand: The Effects of Domestic Violence and Sexual Coercion, 24 Issues in Mental Health Nursing 723, 732 (2003) (some women adopt a "line in the sand" approach to leaving that provides them an illusion of control over a powerless situation);

DeKeseredy & Schwartz, supra, at 3 (suggesting that some women are too afraid to leave, believing "that they will be beaten if they stay but killed if they try to leave").

Many victims suffer from denial, thereby enabling them to remain in the relationship. "The most striking and pervasive [thought process] was the persistent denial to themselves of what was happening. . . . Denial and minimization of reality is probably a survival tactic." Coggins & Bullock, supra, at 733. For additional discussion of motivations, see Jessica J. Eckstein, Reasons for Staying in Intimately Violent Relationships: Comparisons of Men and Women and Messages Communicated to Self and Others, 26 J. Fam. Violence 21 (2011); Alyce D. LaViolette & Ola W. Barnett, It Could Happen to Anyone: Why Battered Women Stay (2d ed. 2000); Jinseok Kim & Karen A. Gray, Leave or Stay?: Battered Women's Decision after Intimate Partner Violence, 23 J. Interpersonal Violence 1465 (2008).

5. *Victims' financial situation.* Some research suggests that financial independence is an important factor in enabling women successfully to navigate separation. Allstate Foundation, Economic Abuse Fact Sheet (May 16, 2009), http://livearchive.org/2011/pdf/economic-abuse-fact-sheet-5-16-09-vxv3 ("evidence has shown that women with financial skills have an increased chance of leaving an abusive situation and sustaining themselves" on a long-term basis). Did this factor apply to Sarah?

6. *Abusers' motivation at separation.* What evidence supports the view that Sarah's murder was retaliation for her departure? What evidence reveals that Crawford felt justified in killing her? Was the murder premeditated?

Jealousy is the motive in a significant number of cases of intimate partner homicides. "Jealousy of women is a by-product of male attempts to control and possess the women with whom they are (or want to be) intimate. In short, jealousy connotes ownership." Jacquelyn C. Campbell, If I Can't Have You, No One Can, in Femicide: The Politics of Woman Killing 99, 103-104 (Jill Radford & Diana E. H. Russell eds., 1992). Some researchers explain the murder of intimate partners as a manifestation of the killer's "sexual proprietariness." Margo Wilson & Martin Daly, Til Death Do Us Part, in Femicide, supra, at 83, 87. See also DeKeseredy & Schwartz, supra, at 38 (proprietariness is reflected in the slayer's sense of entitlement). Many abusers express this sense of entitlement as, "If I can't have her, no one can." Campbell, supra, at 99. See also People v. Taylor, 86 P.3d 881 (Cal. 2004). Did jealousy play a role in Sarah Crawford's murder? Did the sexual nature of the homicide shed light on Crawford's sense of sexual entitlement? See also McCray v. State, 2010 WL 5130747 (Ala. Crim. App. 2010).

7. *Negotiating departure.* What difficulties did Sarah face in negotiating her departure? How did she navigate those difficulties? What did she disclose and to whom? What additional precautions could she have taken? See also Tina Bloom et al., Intimate Partner Violence During Pregnancy, in Family Violence and Nursing Practice 155, 171 (Janice Humphreys & Jacquelyn C. Campbell eds., 2d ed. 2011) (providing advice on safety precautions). Many clinicians encourage a domestic violence victim to develop an exit plan. "She should have knowledge of where to go, phone numbers, and transportation plans. If possible, a bag with clothing, rent and utility receipts, birth certificates, toys, money, and extra car keys should be kept in a safe place." Ursula A. Kelly et al., Theories of Intimate Partner Violence, in Family Violence, supra, at 51, 65.

8. *Lethality assessment.* Two points in time present the most risk of death for victims of abuse: as they prepare to leave their abusers, and after they have left. See Mahoney, supra, at 5-6. Lethality assessments are helpful for evaluating the

potential risk of death to a victim. Review the Danger Assessment Tool, Chapter 2, pp. 62-63. How would you measure Sarah's risk of death? Did Crawford ever threaten to kill Sarah? Did he have a gun? Was there evidence of substance abuse? Was Sarah a victim of marital rape?

9. *Victim's perception of danger.* Some victims are unable to perceive their risk of danger accurately. Jacquelyn C. Campbell et al., Assessing Risk Factors for Intimate Partner Homicide, NIJ Journal, Nov. 2003, at 16 (finding that almost half of murdered women did not recognize the high level of their risk). Did Sarah accurately perceive the risk?

10. *Safety plans.* Advocates strongly urge that victims formulate safety plans. What measures in the above excerpt on safety plans did Sarah adopt? How well does the above safety plan address the relevant issues and concerns? What additional measures would you recommend? See generally Jill M. Davies et al., Safety Planning with Battered Women: Complex Lives, Difficult Choices 113-128 (1998).

11. *Restraining orders.* Professor Mahoney suggests that a separation assault often triggers the victim's petition for a restraining order. Mahoney, supra, at 68. What induced Sarah Crawford to petition? What evidence did she present? Did the judge issue the restraining order? Sarah later requested that the restraining order be dismissed. Why do you think she did so? Do you think that her petition enhanced the danger? Do you think that her withdrawal of the petition enhanced the danger? Should all lawyers who institute proceedings for protective orders counsel their clients about the advisability of safety plans?

What additional safety measures could the judge have taken at the restraining-order hearing? For example, should judges be more conscientious about inquiring about gun ownership and seizure of firearms? Should Sarah Crawford's protection order have included a firearms search-and-seizure provision and a prohibition on gun ownership? Would those steps have prevented her ex-husband from killing her? The effectiveness of restraining orders is explored in Chapter 9.

Problem

The state legislature in the jurisdiction of Blackacre is considering legislation to protect victims of intimate partner violence by removing abusers from the home after a severe incident of domestic violence. The legislation would authorize a court to issue a "go order," by which the court could ban an abuser from the home for 48 hours, even if the victim has not petitioned for a restraining order. The orders would enable victims to have a safe haven in which they can determine their next course of action. The "go order" would be issued by a judge after an ex parte hearing. It would be served by police. The court would hold an adversary hearing (normally within 14 to 28 days) to determine the appropriateness of a longer period of removal from the home.

You are an aide to a state legislator. How would you weigh the benefits and shortcomings of implementation of the proposed legislation? See Alan Travis, Police to Have Power to Order Violent Partners to Leave Home for 48 Hours, Guardian (U.K.), Nov. 25, 2010, available at http://www.guardian.co.uk/society/2010/nov/25/domestic-violence-police?INTCMP=ILCNETTXT3487.

The Transtheoretical Model of behavior change (or "stages-of-change" model) brought a new level of understanding to the dynamics of domestic violence by identifying the exit from abusive relationships as a *process*. The model explains that, even if a victim decides to remain in an abusive relationship, she may be making life-altering decisions and changing her behavior in imperceptible ways. The following excerpt explains the different stages of exit from an abusive relationship.

■ SONDRA BURMAN, STAGES OF LEAVING ABUSIVE RELATIONSHIPS

Encyclopedia of Domestic Violence 675, 676-679 (Nicky Ali Jackson ed., 2007)

. . . People can (and do) begin the process of change long before excessive pain and suffering might arise. . . .

PRECONTEMPLATION STAGE

It is not unusual for people (family, friends, neighbors, coworkers, etc.) who observe and/or interact with an individual to notice that the person is experiencing problems. Yet the one who is experiencing the problem may personally lack awareness of it, deny its existence, minimize its influence, or consider the problem too hopeless to improve or change. Under these conditions, it is not surprising that there would be no incentive to attempt to make changes that will make life safer and less threatening, and no willingness to take risks to make it happen, at this point in time.

In an abusive relationship, several identifying features are characteristic of the precontemplation stage. The battered woman refrains from viewing her spouse or partner realistically, preferring to recall good times together and the "honeymoon," stage when, after a beating she was showered with gifts and affection. Yearning to believe promises that the battering will never happen again places her in a compromising position. She deludes herself into thinking that if she changes to please him and stops provoking his anger, the assaults will stop. She becomes defensive and will always have excuses when her injuries, bruises, and burns are noticed, even in the emergency room: "I'm accident prone and always falling." . . .

Yet if the victim is not totally entrenched in this stage, a window of opportunity can open to new insights. With this enlightenment, there is a possibility that the seeds of change will be sown. Whether on her own or in treatment, the victim must begin to doubt that her abuser will change in order to begin pondering the risks of remaining in the relationship. The probability of increasing abuse, leading to numerous hospitalizations, even death, must be faced directly. The gravity of this impending possibility can no longer be ignored. Safety is the key component to consider, for herself and her children.

CONTEMPLATION STAGE

During the contemplation stage, battered women are ready to acknowledge the severity of problems and deficits that earlier were minimized or denied. However, even as they begin facing the probability of disastrous consequences, they still are for the most part unable to make decisions to take action and make constructive change. Ambivalence is prominent in this stage. Not ready to make a change, battered women find their feelings frequently shifting back and forth; the resulting dilemmas create high anxiety. Lingering feelings toward husbands/partners, who once provided loving concern and security (whether real or imagined) become difficult to relinquish.

When pondering leaving versus staying, at first the choices may be bewildering. It appears that there may be much to gain and much to lose either way. . . . [Victims must be able to contemplate the advantages and disadvantages of leaving in order to move forward.] For example, advantages of leaving might include: safety/surviving for self and children, feeling empowered and gaining self-confidence in taking charge and control of critical decisions, having a second chance at finding peace and happiness, being a positive role model in protecting the children, and breaking the cycle of violence. Disadvantages might include: fears of continued harassment, stalking and abuse, not being able to obtain a satisfactory job that will provide financial security, depending on educational and employment background, fears of starting over and independently making a new life, and possibly having to move to a distant area and stay hidden for an indefinite period of time.

It can take many months, even years, of weighing how life would change for better or worse. . . . As the intensity of violence escalates to life-threatening proportions, the benefits of staying lessen. Research findings have shown that as children are threatened and also become targets of the abuse, the desire to stay becomes even more narrow. In this way, the decisional balance is tipped, establishing necessary, even crucial, reasons to change. Once this is accomplished, the move toward the preparation stage takes effect.

PREPARATION STAGE

. . . For a woman who realizes that sustaining the status quo is fraught with peril, there is a perceptible awareness that she has no other recourse, excepting more of the same punishing injuries and possible death. . . . [S]afety concerns eventually take precedence as reminders of the agony of the abuse take hold.

Being committed to action, she is ready to make a viable escape and safety plan for her children and herself, including an assessment of the degree of danger in each step taken. Consideration of supports and resources that can be tapped, while utilizing various sources to ensure safety and protection, are important to include in a safety plan. Phone numbers, identifying items (driver's license, Social Security card, children's birth certificates), and money saved are just a few items to gather. Having isolated herself due to years of making excuses and covering up evidence of the battering, a woman reaching out for help hopes she will receive positive responses to her appeals. . . . The greater the strategic planning and corresponding resources and supports, the more opportunities there will be for finding safety and well-being. This necessitates careful and methodical preparation in planning to accomplish well-constructed goals.

ACTION STAGE

Taking action involves challenging fears, facing intermittent uncertainties about having made the right decision and experiencing doubts about moving forward with the plan. It means affirming the necessity and ability to take action, after a great deal of deliberation in earlier stages. Having built up the momentum and made preparations for many months or even years, not proceeding toward the goals of stopping the beatings and ending the relationship can be even more anxiety producing than doing so. Nonetheless, it often takes another horrendous incident (possibly after a lull in the battering and a promise that it will not happen again) to drive the will to immediately take action to leave and end the abuse. This is often described as the final incapacitating attack, the proverbial straw that breaks the camel's back, and strategies already developed are implemented. . . .

MAINTENANCE STAGE

[W]omen are next challenged to maintain the gains they made in leaving behind a life filled with injuries, pain, and fears. . . . This is the time when relapse prevention should be stressed. Unknowingly, when distant distressful memories fade, a longing for the affection and attention once shown can emerge and create a desire to regain the positive parts of the relationship that were lost.

This is a danger zone, where fragile emotions reign and rational thought processes plunge almost spontaneously. Feeling lonely and not having reinvested socially in acceptable outlets, the temptation to reconnect with the abuser can be hasty and very risky. Without contemplating ominous consequences, a re-enactment of the past and a cycle of violence can be repeated. . . .

TERMINATION STAGE

One may wonder whether it is ever possible to terminate an abusive relationship, mourn the loss, and start life anew, safely and securely. Women do it, with varied emotions, numerous uncertainties about what lies ahead, and frequently a feeling of relief that the horror is ending. If achieved under their own actions, an empowering reaction and enhanced self-confidence can emerge. . . .

See generally Jessica G. Burke et al., The Process of Ending Abuse in Intimate Relationships: A Qualitative Exploration of the Transtheoretical Model, 7 Violence Against Women 1144 (2001) (explaining why women end abuse in their intimate relationships); Jessica Griffin Burke et al., Defining Appropriate Stages of Change for Intimate Partner Violence Survivors, 24 Violence & Victims 36 (2009) (same). For application of the model to legal issues, see Jane K. Stoever, Freedom from Violence: Using the Stages of Change Model to Realize the Promise of Civil Protection Orders, 72 Ohio St. L.J. 303 (2011).

B. SEXUAL AND REPRODUCTIVE ABUSE

Intimate partner violence can infringe on victims' sexual and reproductive autonomy in many ways, including sexual assaults, pregnancy-related abuse, sabotage of birth control, and interference with abortion decisionmaking. This section explores these types of intimate partner violence.

1. Sexual Assaults: Marital Rape

■ S.D. v. M.J.R.

2 A.3d 412 (N.J. Super. Ct. App. Div. 2010)

Payne, J.A.D.:

. . . S.D., and defendant, M.J.R., are citizens of Morocco and adherents to the Muslim faith. They were wed in Morocco in an arranged marriage on July 31, 2008, when plaintiff was seventeen years old. [Afterwards, they moved to New Jersey, accompanied by defendant's mother, where defendant found a job as an accountant.] [T]he acts of domestic abuse . . . commenced on November 1, 2008, after three months of marriage. [D]efendant requested that plaintiff, who did not know how to cook, prepare three Moroccan dishes for six guests to eat on the following morning. Plaintiff testified that she got up at 5:00 a.m. on the day of the visit and attempted to make two of the dishes, but neither was successful. . . . Defendant, angry, said to plaintiff, "I'm going to show you later on. . . ."

[When the visitors left, defendant came to her room and said that he was going to punish her. He began to pinch her on her breasts, under her arms, and around her thighs. The pinches left bruises, some of which remained three weeks later when they were photographed by a detective from the prosecutor's office. The punishment continued for approximately one hour, during which time plaintiff was crying.]

An additional incident took place [two weeks later]. At approximately 3:00 p.m., defendant announced that he planned to have guests who were to arrive at approximately 9:00 or 10:00 that night, and he asked plaintiff to prepare a supper for them. Plaintiff responded that she did not know how to cook. Defendant then left the apartment, returning at 6:00 p.m. with his mother and stating that she would do everything. The mother-in-law refused plaintiff's offers of help, so plaintiff went to her room. At some time thereafter, plaintiff, in anger and frustration, pushed papers that defendant had placed on a desk in the bedroom to the floor. [After the guests left, defendant came into the bedroom and saw the papers on the floor.]

> [H]e took off all my clothes and he said the first [thing] "before we start punishing you, now you're nude. You have no clothes on." Even my underwear wasn't on. So I felt I was an animal, like an animal. So he said "first of all, you better go and pick [up] everything from the floor." Then he said, "now we're going to start punishing you." Then he started to pinch my private area [her breasts and chest area, and he pulled her pubic hair].

Plaintiff stated that her vaginal area was very, very red and that it was hurting. Although she attempted to leave, defendant had locked the door. As a consequence, she attempted to lie on the other side of the bed. Plaintiff testified:

> He said to me . . . "You're still my wife and you must do whatever I tell you to do. I want to hurt your flesh, I want to feel and know that you're still my wife." After that, he had sex with me and my vagina was very, very swollen and I was hurting so bad.

The judge then asked: "You told him that you did not wish to have . . . intercourse, is that correct?" Plaintiff responded: "Of course because I was—I had so much pain down there." According to plaintiff, the entire episode took approximately two to three hours. . . .

An additional incident occurred [about a week later when plaintiff had locked herself in a bedroom]. Defendant, having been refused entry, removed the latch from the door, entered the bedroom, and engaged in nonconsensual sex with plaintiff. . . . [After defendant left, plaintiff started to break everything in the bedroom, including one of its two windows. When defendant returned, plaintiff attempted to leave the apartment.] However, defendant pulled her back into the bedroom and assaulted her by repeatedly slapping her face, causing her lip to swell and bleeding to occur. He then left the room, and plaintiff escaped without shoes or proper clothing through the unbroken window. [She went to a hospital where her injuries were treated and photographed. She took up residence with a Moroccan nurse who, after learning that plaintiff was pregnant, arranged a meeting with the Imam of their mosque. He persuaded the couple to reconcile, provided that defendant stop abusing her and that they obtain a separate apartment from defendant's mother.]

However, on the night of the reconciliation, defendant again engaged in nonconsensual sex three times, and on succeeding days plaintiff stated that he engaged in further repeated instances of nonconsensual sex. According to plaintiff, during this period, she was deprived of food, she lacked a refrigerator and a phone, and she was left by her husband for many hours, alone. She responded to her plight by breaking dishes. . . . On January 22, 2009, defendant took plaintiff to a restaurant for breakfast. Upon their return to the apartment, defendant forced plaintiff to have sex with him while she cried. . . .

[Soon thereafter, defendant and his mother took plaintiff to the home of the Imam where defendant verbally divorced plaintiff. Three days later, plaintiff filed a complaint against defendant and sought a temporary restraining order. A parallel criminal action against defendant was also pending. At trial, testimony was offered by an Imam regarding Islamic law as it relates to sexual behavior.] The Imam confirmed that a wife must comply with her husband's sexual demands, because the husband is prohibited from obtaining sexual satisfaction elsewhere. However, a husband was forbidden to approach his wife "like any animal." The Imam did not definitively answer whether, under Islamic law, a husband must stop his advances if his wife said "no." However, he acknowledged that New Jersey law considered coerced sex between married people to be rape.

[The trial judge found that defendant had engaged in harassment and assault, but that defendant lacked the requisite criminal intent for sexual assault based on defendant's view that his religion permitted him to act as he did.] As the judge recognized, the case thus presents a conflict between the criminal law and religious precepts. In resolving this conflict, the judge determined to except defendant from the operation of the State's statutes as the result of his religious beliefs. In doing so, the judge was mistaken.

Early law in this area arose out of prosecutions of Mormons who practiced polygamy. In Reynolds v. United States, 98 U.S. 145 (1878), the Supreme Court considered an appeal from a Mormon's conviction under a Congressionally passed bigamy statute applicable to the Utah territory. . . . [T]he Court found that the First

Amendment's guaranty of religious freedom was not intended to preclude the prohibition of polygamy. . . . [According to the Supreme Court:]

> . . . Laws are made for the government of actions, and while they cannot interfere with mere religious belief and opinions, they may with practices. . . . Can a man excuse his practices to the contrary [of law] because of his religious belief? To permit this would be to make the professed doctrines of religious belief superior to the law of the land, and in effect to permit every citizen to become a law unto himself. . . . [Id. at 166-167.]

[The Supreme Court also held, in Employment Division v. Smith, 494 U.S. 872 (1990), that valid, generally applicable, and neutral laws may be applied to religious exercise even in the absence of a compelling governmental interest.]

Because it is doubtlessly true that the laws defining the crimes of sexual assault and criminal sexual contact are neutral laws of general application, and because defendant knowingly engaged in conduct that violated those laws, the judge erred when he refused to recognize those violations as a basis for a determination that defendant had committed acts of domestic violence.

In this context, we note, as well, the Legislature's recognition [in the enactment of the state Prevention of Domestic Violence Act] of the serious nature of domestic violence, the responsibility of the courts to protect victims of such violence and its directive that the remedies of the PDVA be broadly applied. The Legislature's findings and declaration provide an additional basis for the rejection of the judge's view of defendant's acts as excused by his religious beliefs, and for a recognition of those acts as violative of New Jersey's laws.

Following a finding that a defendant has committed a predicate act of domestic violence, the judge is required to consider whether a restraining order should be entered that provides protection to the victim. . . . In the present matter, the judge properly found that defendant had assaulted and harassed plaintiff in violation of the PDVA. However, he declined to enter a final restraining order, determining that the domestic violence constituted merely a "bad patch" in a short-term marriage and did not result in serious injury to plaintiff, and that plaintiff and defendant had separated, a divorce proceeding was pending in Morocco, and the parties had no reason for further contact. Nonetheless, the judge recognized that contact between the parties would necessarily occur upon the birth of their child. The judge additionally appeared to be sufficiently concerned about the likelihood of renewed domestic violence to instruct defendant to have no contact with plaintiff. In this regard, he also relied upon the likelihood that a no contact order had been put in place as a condition of defendant's bail in the pending criminal proceedings against him arising from the acts of domestic violence that formed the basis for the civil action.

The judge's ruling raises several areas of concern that we regard as warranting reversal and a remand to permit the entry of a final restraining order. We construe the judge's characterization of the violence that took place as a "bad patch" in the parties' marriage and plaintiff's injuries as not severe as manifesting an unnecessarily dismissive view of defendant's acts of domestic violence. Although it is true that the November episodes spanned only three weeks, that period constituted approximately one-fourth of the parties' marriage. Moreover, we find it significant to the issue of whether a final restraining order should have been granted that the violence resumed on the very first night of the parties' reconciliation, and after defendant had assured the Imam that he would not engage in further such acts. . . .

Additionally, we are troubled by the judge's seeming acknowledgment [that a restraining order] might be appropriate and his reliance on a no-contact order that he presumed had been put in place in the pending criminal proceeding as affording adequate protection to plaintiff in the civil domestic violence matter. As a preliminary matter, we note that the judge did not verify the existence, terms or duration of the presumed order. Further, we have previously recognized that a complaint brought under the PDVA and a criminal proceeding brought for the same conduct "are separate and distinct matters." [We have observed] that "[t]he legislative history demonstrates that the Act 'anticipates and provides for simultaneous or subsequent criminal proceedings' unimpacted by the other, except for a contempt proceeding." . . . We find it inappropriate, when restraints are civilly required, for a Family [Court] judge to rely on restraints issued in a parallel criminal proceeding. This is particularly the case because the need to protect the victim-spouse may outlive the termination of the criminal action. . . .

Viewing the evidence as a whole, we are satisfied that the judge was mistaken in determining not to issue a final restraining order in this matter in order to protect plaintiff from future abuse and in dismissing plaintiff's domestic violence complaint. . . .

Notes and Questions

1. *Prevalence.* Sexual assaults occur with frequency in intimate relationships. Estimates of women raped by an intimate partner range from 8 to 10 percent. Jennifer A. Bennice & Patricia A. Resnick, Marital Rape: History, Research, & Practice, 4 Trauma, Violence, & Abuse 228, 234 (2003); NISVS, 2010 Summary Report, supra, at 39 (10 percent). For early studies, see David Finkelhor & Kersti Yllo, License to Rape: Sexual Abuse of Wives (1987); Diana E. H. Russell, Rape in Marriage (1990).

Physical abuse often accompanies marital rape. See Bennice & Resnick, supra, at 234 (revealing that from one-third to one-half of battered women report sexual assaults); NISVS, 2010 Summary Report, supra at 41 (reporting that 8.7 percent of female partners experience rape and also physical violence). Did S.D. in the principal case experience marital rape alone or was it accompanied by physical violence? Did the abuse escalate when S.D. sought to terminate the relationship?

2. *Abusers' motivation.* Sexual assaults in physically abusive relationships are an exercise of the abuser's domination and control. Sexual victimization can be an alternative form of attack during a physically violent incident, a form of punishment, or a reconciliation tactic. See Bennice & Resnick, supra, at 237; Logan et al., supra, at 89. Sexual victimization stems from the abuser's sense of entitlement to the partner's sexual and reproductive services. Offenders "exhibit a tendency to think of women as sexual and reproductive 'property' that they can own and exchange." Margo Wilson & Martin Daly, Til Death Do Us Part, in Femicide: The Politics of Woman Killing 83, 85 (Jill Radford & Diana E. H. Russell eds., 1992). What evidence suggests the defendant's desire to control his victim, his sense of entitlement, his use of violent sex as punishment, and his use of forced sex to reconcile with her?

3. *Victims' voluntary "consent."* Many victims of sexual assaults "consent" to forced sexual activity with their partners because they are afraid of retaliation by their partners if they refuse. Logan et al., supra, at 82. See also Bennice & Resnick, supra, at 237 (reporting that almost half of victims were threatened with beatings for refusing to engage in sex, and 36.7 percent did suffer beatings after refusing). Other women "consent" in order to deescalate a confrontation. Logan et al., supra, at 82.

4. *Spectrum of sexual assaults.* Sexual assault of an intimate partner spans a spectrum of acts, including coercion to have sex or engage in particular sexual acts; degrading and/or humiliating tactics before, during, or after sex; forcing sex on a sleeping partner; forcing sex on a physically ill partner or one who has recently given birth; hitting, kicking or burning a partner during sex; coercing substance abuse during sex; using sex acts as punishment; nonconsensual insertion of objects; holding a partner captive during sex; forcing the partner to have sex in public (for example, in a parked car); and coercing the partner to involve others in sexual activity. Bennice & Resnick, supra, at 237; Logan et al., supra, at 75, 81-82, 89. Which acts did the defendant commit?

5. *Severity.* A commonly held belief, sometimes reflected in judicial decisions, is that intimate partner rape is not as serious as stranger rape. What is the basis for this belief? Did the trial judge reveal this view? What does the appellate court respond? In fact, relationships accompanied by physical violence and rape are marked by *more* severe violence and include *repeated* sexual victimizations. Bennice & Resnick, supra, at 238-239; Logan et al., supra, at 71. Further, victims suffer more *medical and psychological* consequences than victims of stranger rapes. Bennice & Resnick, supra, at 238 (reporting a "more profound sense of betrayal and trauma at a more basic level of trust, which may ultimately lead to severe feelings of powerlessness, isolation, and anger").

6. *Intent.* Why did the trial judge determine that the defendant lacked the requisite criminal intent for sexual assault? How did the appellate court respond?

7. *Marital rape exemption.* At common law, a husband was exempt from prosecution for raping his wife. This legal principle was termed the "marital rape exemption." How does New Jersey define marital rape? The marital rape exemption is explored in Chapter 7.

8. *Parallel proceedings.* S.D. filed for a restraining order under the state Prevention of Domestic Violence Act. A parallel criminal action against her husband was also pending. What is the purpose of each action? The trial judge ruled that, because a criminal proceeding was pending, there was no need to issue the restraining order. Why does the appellate court reverse this ruling?

9. *Willingness to seek legal intervention.* Victims of marital rape are particularly reluctant to report it and seek services. Bennice & Resnick, supra, at 240. Why?

10. *Defenses.* Some abusers, like the husband in *S.D.*, rely on religious or cultural beliefs to justify partner violence. The defendant believed that it was appropriate to react with physical and sexual assaults when a wife fails to fulfill her marital duties. Cultural beliefs sometimes also support the use of force in marriage to protect the family's reputation. See generally John Alan Cohan, Honor Killings and the Cultural Defense, 40 Cal. W. Int'l L.J. 177 (2010). See also Myrna Oliver, Immigrant Crimes: Cultural Defense—a Legal Tactic, L.A. Times, July 15, 1988, Pt. I, at 1 (explaining views of recent Vietnamese immigrants who express disbelief that they can be punished for spousal abuse because they regard their wives as their property). How did the court respond to the husband's defense? The cultural defense is explored in Chapter 7.

> ### Famous Case of Marital Rape: Mary Murphy
>
> Mary Murphy, a champion ballroom dancer and a judge of Fox's hit show "So You Think You Can Dance," endured beatings and rapes throughout her marriage. She met her Jordanian husband when they were both students at Ohio University. She explains, "The honeymoon phase didn't last long." The first time he raped her was about three months into the marriage. She recounts, "We'd had another jealous fight, screaming, crashing over furniture, and he said, 'I want to have sex.'" Murphy replied, "*Are you kidding me*?! We're fighting here!" Her husband responded, "You're my wife, and you'll do what I tell you!" Murphy then describes how she pulled out a kitchen knife and screamed at him. "You're going to have to stab me, because I'm *not* having sex with you!" She continues, "He knocked [the knife] out of my hands, held me down and raped me. It was like a light switch: He became a different person. I fought back, but it was [hopeless]."
>
> Murphy explains that her neighbors called the police. When the police arrived, they saw Murphy's ripped clothes and bruises. They asked if she wanted to press charges. She replied, "I look[ed] over at my husband and his eyes had this look, like he'd kill me if I said yes. I said, 'No.'" Her husband later apologized profusely and took her shopping. That became the pattern," she explains. First, there would be a fight, then rape, then gifts (perhaps a dress, a diamond bracelet, or earrings). "In the first year or two, I'd fight back, but eventually, I'd just lie there. Get it over with, I thought. It'll be quick anyway. But I had such hatred inside. I never did want to have sex with him again after that first rape. He might as well have had sex with a corpse—there was zero response from me. . . ."
>
> After nine years, when Murphy discovered that her husband was having an affair, she obtained a divorce. See Mary Murphy, How I Survived Abuse, US Weekly, Oct. 26, 2009, at 48, 49-50.

2. Pregnancy-Related Abuse

Pregnant women experience many forms of intimate partner violence. How does the law respond to such abuse? How should it respond?

■ SMITH v. MARTIN
2009 WL 2028403 (Ohio Ct. App. 2009)

Tyack, J.

Gabrielle Smith is appealing from the ruling of the Franklin County Court of Common Pleas, Division of Domestic Relations. She assigns two errors for our consideration: (1). The trial court erred when it denied Petitioner's request for a Civil Protection Order to include her unborn child as a designated protected person. (2). The trial court erred when it did not afford Gabrielle Smith's unborn child equal protection under the law.

On July 16, 2008, a civil protection order ("CPO") was granted to protect Smith from her boyfriend who had abused her. Smith was pregnant by her boyfriend and asked that the CPO be modified to specifically protect the unborn child. The trial court refused the additional relief, but effectively addressed the problem by ordering the boyfriend to stay away from Smith and to avoid contact with Smith. The boyfriend obviously could not harm the child without having contact with the mother as long as the child was in utero.

R.C. 3113.31 sets forth the procedure for obtaining a CPO because of domestic violence. The statute defines domestic violence [to include the occurrence of designated acts against a "family or household member." Those terms are defined to include a spouse, parent, or "child." R.C. 3223.31(A)(3)]. The issue of when an unborn child becomes a person within the meaning of various laws is a complex issue, and not easily resolved. Ohio has taken different approaches when considering how the unborn are to be treated under the law. There are certain statutes in the revised code that are meant to protect the unborn and to punish an offender who harms an unborn child. For example, a person can be convicted of felonious assault if the offender knowingly caused serious physical harm to another or to another's unborn. R.C. 2903.11. In that instance, the term "unborn" is specifically used in the statute. . . .

Other cases have held that if a child is born alive, there may be a relation back in civil actions to prenatal injuries [citations omitted]. More recently, in In re Baby Boy Blackshear, [736 N.E.2d 462 (Ohio 2000)], the Supreme Court of Ohio held that a newborn child who tests positive for illegal drugs due to prenatal maternal drug abuse is, for purposes of R.C. 2151.031(D), per se an abused child. That case turned primarily upon the language of the statute [that defined a child as a "person" who is under 18 years of age but did not define "person"].

Obtaining a CPO is distinguishable from these cases by virtue of the fact that a CPO for a respondent to stay away from a pregnant petitioner protects the unborn child to the same extent that it protects the mother. In order to harm the unborn child, the boyfriend would of necessity have to violate the order with respect to the mother. Moreover, the controlling statute does not specifically include the unborn child within its protection. Amendments made by the General Assembly to specifically include the unborn with the purview of a statute lead us to infer that the legislature is fully aware of the situations in which it desires to protect the unborn or punish those who harm them. Under the plain language of R.C. 3113.31, a viable fetus is outside the statutory definition of persons entitled to seek relief.

Smith argues that a construction of R.C. 3113.31 that expands the definition of household or family member to include a viable fetus advances the safety and protection of family and household members. Smith has directed our attention to Roe v. Wade, 410 U.S. 113 (1973), in which the United States Supreme Court held, among other things, that the state has a legitimate interest in protecting potential life.

Smith posits a situation in which a newborn infant would be unprotected if separated from the mother. She asserts that it would be a hardship for the mother to return to court to obtain a civil protection order for the child immediately after giving birth. Clearly a newborn infant could qualify as a family or household member within the meaning of the statute and entitled to a CPO under R.C. 3113.31. However, until such time as the legislature sees fit to grant such protection to an unborn, we conclude that the court made an order that protected the child in the only effective way available. . . .

Notes and Questions

1. *Social reality.* Pregnancy is a particularly vulnerable time for victims of intimate partner violence. Homicide is the second most frequent cause of death for pregnant women as well as new mothers in the first year after birth. Donna St. George, CDC Explores Pregnancy-Homicide Link, Killings Cited Among Top Causes of Trauma Death for New, Expectant Mothers, Wash. Post, Feb. 23, 2005, at A5. Approximately 156,000 to 332,000 pregnant women experience violence annually. Tina Bloom et al., Intimate Partner Violence During Pregnancy, in Family Violence and Nursing Practice 155, 156 (Janice Humphreys & Jacquelyn C. Campbell eds., 2011). See also Ibn-Tamas v. U. S., 407 A.2d 626, 629-631 (D.C., 1979) (account of severe abuse during pregnancy); Donna St. George, Tracking Pregnancies That End in Homicide, Violence Surprisingly Likely Cause of Death, Data Shows, Lexington (Ky.) Herald, Dec. 26, 2004, at A1 (reporting results of study of 1,300 homicides).

2. *Orders of protection.* Orders of protection do not normally include conditions protecting a fetus. Why do you think the petitioner in *Smith* requested such a protective order? Why did the judge deny it? Do you think that the judge made the correct decision? In light of the above research, should judges routinely issue orders of protection that protect the woman *and* her fetus? What might be the implications of such orders? How else might states protect pregnant women? Should they criminalize assaults against pregnant women? See, e.g., Or. Rev. Stat. §163.160(3)(d) (defining assault in the fourth degree as a Class C felony if "[t]he person commits the assault knowing that the victim is pregnant").

3. *Effect of pregnancy on occurrence of violence.* For some victims of intimate partner violence, pregnancy serves a protective function. Yet, for the majority of victims, the violence simply continues during the pregnancy. For other victims, the pregnancy triggers or intensifies the violence. St. George, Tracking Pregnancies, supra (reporting that for more than 70 percent of abused women, the pregnancy does not change the status quo; but for 27 percent of victims, the abuse starts during the pregnancy). See also National Coalition against Domestic Violence (NCADV), Reproductive Health and Pregnancy 1, http://www.ywca.org/atf/cf/%7B3b450fa5-108b-4d2e-b3d0-c31487243e6a%7D/FACT_REPRODUCTIVE.PDF (last visited June 27, 2011).

4. *Motivations.* What motivates an abuser to harm a pregnant partner? Explanations include the following: jealousy of the fetus; resentment of the partner's increased social contacts; increased feelings of insecurity, possessiveness, and sexual jealousy; financial concerns; resentment of the partner's disabilities and decreased emotional availability; resentment about a partner's wish to abstain from substance abuse; and the conscious or unconscious desire to terminate the pregnancy. Bloom et al., supra, at 157-158. See also Ann M. Moore et al., Male Reproductive Control of Women Who Have Experienced Intimate Partner Violence in the United States, 70 Soc. Sci. & Med. 1737 (2010). Might the motivation differ in *pregnancy*-related homicides versus *new-mother* homicides?

5. *Influential factors.* Does age play a role in the likelihood of pregnancy-related abuse? See St. George, CDC Explores, supra (reporting that pregnant women younger than 20 had the highest homicide risk).

6. *Obstacles to disclosure.* Pregnancy presents an obstacle to disclosure—a factor that leads to women delaying prenatal care until the last trimester. Victims' delay results from their desire to avoid health care providers' observation of their injuries.

See Margi Coggins & Linda F. C. Bullock, The Wavering Line in the Sand: The Effects of Domestic Voilence and Sexual Coercion, 24 Issues in Mental Health Nursing 723, 725-726 (2003). Are medical personnel required to report intimate partner violence among pregnant women? See generally Rebekah Kratochvil, Comments and Notes, Intimate Partner Violence During Pregnancy: Exploring the Efficacy of a Mandatory Reporting Statute, 10 Hous. J. Health L. & Pol'y 63 (2009). Mandatory reporting issues are explored in Chapter 10.

7. *Fetal homicide laws.* How does the law respond to fetal homicides, that is, those homicides that result in the death not only of the woman but also her fetus? Does the law treat the homicide as a single count of murder, or two counts? How should the law treat such a homicide?

A majority of states now follow the federal Unborn Victims of Violence Act (UVVA) of 2004, 18 U.S.C. §1841, by imposing dual criminal liability for the death of a fetus during the commission of certain crimes. See Mary Beth Hickcox-Howard, Note, The Case for Pro-Choice Participation in Drafting Fetal Homicide Laws, 17 Tex. J. Women & L. 317, 318 (2008) (reporting that 36 states follow this approach). State statutes vary in terms of the stage of pregnancy at which criminal liability attaches.

UVVA exempts consensual abortions and medical treatment. The Act was named "Laci and Connor's Law" after a pregnant woman and unborn child who were killed by her husband Scott Peterson. See Dean E. Murphy, At Peterson Sentencing, a Family's Anger, N.Y. Times, Mar. 17, 2005, at A20, available at http://www.nytimes.com/2005/03/17/national/17peterson.html?_r=1&ref=scottpeterson. Should a defendant be subject to dual criminal liability if he is unaware of the pregnancy? See People v. Taylor, 86 P.3d 881 (Cal. 2004) (holding defendant liable). Do fetal homicide laws expand or restrict women's rights?

3. Birth Control Sabotage

Some intimate partner violence takes the form of coercion of a partner's reproductive decisionmaking, such as sabotage of the access to birth control. What is the law's response to this form of abuse?

■ FAMILY VIOLENCE PREVENTION FUND, 1 IN 4 HOTLINE CALLERS REPORT BIRTH CONTROL SABOTAGE, PREGNANCY COERCION

(Feb. 15, 2011), available at **http://endabuse.org/content/features/detail/1674/**

What may be the first national survey to determine the extent of "reproductive coercion" was released [recently] by the National Domestic Violence Hotline and the Family Violence Prevention Fund (FVPF). The survey found that 25 percent of [3,000] callers to the National Domestic Violence Hotline reported that they had experienced this form of domestic and dating violence.

Reproductive coercion is defined as threats or acts of violence against a partner's reproductive health or reproductive decision-making. It includes forced sex, a male partner pressuring a woman to become pregnant against her will and interference with the use of birth control. The women who reported this form of abuse said that their male partners either would not allow them to use birth control or sabotaged their birth control method (such as poking holes in condoms or flushing pills down the toilet). Some of the women said they had to hide their birth control.

"Birth control sabotage is a serious form of control that leads to unintended pregnancy and sexually transmitted infections," said FVPF President Esta Soler. "While there is a cultural assumption that some women use pregnancy as a way to trap their partner in a relationship, this survey shows that men who are abusive will sabotage their partner's birth control and pressure them to become pregnant as a way to trap or control their partner." (In the words of one caller, "keep me in his life forever"). . . .

[P]atterns included pressure to become pregnant early in the relationship or before the victim felt ready and, in some cases, pressure to become pregnant followed by pressure to have an abortion. These abuse patterns were apparent in callers' comments, such as: "I better be pregnant, or I'm in trouble with him." "He refuses to use a condom. I've bought them and he throws them out." "He has tried to talk me into having a child. He told me he wanted to keep me from leaving him." "He admitted to me and the psychologist that he intentionally got me pregnant to trap me." . . .

"Survivors of domestic violence don't always recognize reproductive coercion as part of the power and control their partner is exerting over them in their relationship," said National Domestic Violence Hotline Operations Manager Mikisha Hooper. "This form of abuse can be shrouded in secrecy and may be uncomfortable for people to talk about it. By asking the right questions, we help victims identify and understand the abuse. . . ."

■ ANN M. MOORE ET AL., MALE REPRODUCTIVE CONTROL OF WOMEN WHO HAVE EXPERIENCED INTIMATE PARTNER VIOLENCE IN THE UNITED STATES
70 Soc. Sci. & Medicine 1737, 1737-1741 (2010)

[Women who had experienced reproductive control explain the ways that their partners verbally threatened and coerced them to become pregnant.]

> He [said], "I should just get you pregnant and have a baby with you so that I know you will be in my life forever." . . . It's just like, for what, you want me to not go back to school, not go to college, not want me to do anything just sit in the house with a baby while you are out with friends.
> —*Respondent 1, 19 years of age at time of interview. This partner refused condoms and tried to convince the respondent not to use birth control, accusing her of being unfaithful if she tried. He denied paternity when she became pregnant. She had two abortions with him, both of which he refused to pay for.* . . .

Women [explained] their partners' blatant disregard for their own pregnancy intentions. When women objected to being told they were going to be impregnated, women reported being ignored, belittled or abused.

[One woman told her partner that they were not ready for children. He replied:] "That's not true. It's never the right time to have a kid. You just don't want to be a part of me. You just don't want me to be around forever." And I will have to, like, coerce him into believing that I wanted to be with him and that wasn't the reason why. . . .

—Respondent 2, 28 years of age at time of interview. This partner repeatedly flushed her birth control pills down the toilet and refused to use condoms. When she did become pregnant, she had a miscarriage but her partner accused her of having a covert abortion. Years later he raped her and she became pregnant and did have an abortion.

[I]n some situations, men interpreted women's protests to being made pregnant as emotional rejection, this set into play complex dynamics which often led to the woman reassuring her partner of her feelings for him to avoid abuse and this sometimes included having unprotected sex. . . .

[Some women report their partner's active interception of contraceptive use.] The most common ways contraceptive sabotage occurred was either when men failed to withdraw even though it was understood by the woman to be the agreed-upon method of contraception or when men refused to use condoms. When men did consent to use condoms, many respondents said that their partners manipulated the condoms to render them ineffective, including taking them off surreptitiously before or during sex, biting holes in them, and not telling their partners when the condom came off or broke. Another way that respondents experienced contraceptive sabotage was when their partners tried to dissuade them from using hormonal contraception by citing exaggerated side effects that scared the respondent into non-use. This dissuasion often took place in combination with verbal threats of pregnancy or direct physical interference so that there was no doubt about the man's intentions. . . . When a pregnancy occurred, women were vulnerable to further reproductive control to bring about the pregnancy outcome he desired. . . . [The subject of interference with abortion decisionmaking is explored infra.]

Notes and Questions

1. *Social reality.* What are the various ways in which an abusive partner sabotages the other partner's efforts to use birth control? What is the "gamut of behaviors ranging from surreptitiously deceptive to violent"? What are the various motivations for birth control sabotage? See also Coggins & Bullock, supra, at 729 (suggesting that men's refusal to use contraception "did not necessarily mean they wanted their partners to become pregnant, but reflected the deeper implications birth control seems to hold for them . . . as license for infidelity"). Why do victims of domestic violence often fail to recognize birth control sabotage as part of a pattern of domestic violence?

2. *Consequences of birth control sabotage.* Not surprisingly, sabotage of birth control leads to a large number of unintended pregnancies and that, in turn, leads to frequent abortions. See Moore et al., supra, at 1741-1742 (reporting that one respondent had eight abortions of unwanted pregnancies with one partner). See also Jay G. Silverman et al., Male Perpetration of Intimate Partner Violence and Involvement in Abortions and Abortion-Related Conflict, 100 Am. J. Pub. Health 1415 (2010) (finding that the risk of being involved in three or more abortions was greater in a sample of batterers).

3. *Medical intervention.* How can health care professionals assist women whose partners engage in birth control sabotage? Should health care providers routinely

inquire about any interpersonal obstacles to their patients' use? Is there any form of birth control that might not be subject to the abuser's control? Should health care providers always discuss birth control without a partner being present?

4. *Legal intervention.* What, if anything, can the legal system do to address birth control sabotage? Should rape law be revised to take this form of coercion into effect? If so, how?

5. *Sterilization.* What can women do to counteract their partners' efforts to sabotage their access to birth control? Is sterilization a viable alternative? Not surprisingly, female sterilization rates are higher among couples with abuse histories. See Coggins & Bullock, supra, at 730.

6. *Women's sabotage of birth control.* Men are not the only intimate partners who sabotage birth control. "Contraceptive fraud" consists of cases in which a woman stops taking birth control pills because she wants to get pregnant, but does not inform her partner of her decision. Should a man's child support obligation be affected by the deception? See Wallis v. Smith, 22 P.3d 682 (N.M. Ct. App. 2001); L. Pamela P. v. Frank S., 449 N.E.2d 713 (N.Y. Ct. App. 1983). Should the deceived man have a tort action for fraud or infliction of emotional distress? See Day v. Heller, 653 N.W.2d 475 (Neb. 2002). See generally Michelle Oberman, Sex, Lies, and the Duty to Disclose, 47 Ariz. L. Rev. 871 (2005).

Problem

Julian Assange, the 39-year-old Australian founder of the whistleblowing website WikiLeaks that released secret American documents on the Internet, was arrested in Britain on a Swedish warrant. He faced a request by the Swedish government to extradite him on charges of sexual misconduct with two Swedish women stemming from sexual encounters there in August 2010. A 68-page confidential Swedish police report reveals that Mr. Assange described the encounters as "consensual" sexual relationships.

However, the accounts of the two women differ from his. Each woman claims that her respective encounter began consensually, but became nonconsensual when Mr. Assange persisted in having unprotected sex in defiance of her insistence that he use a condom. The first woman, Ms. A., was Mr. Assange's point of contact when he flew from London to Stockholm to give a speech. She claims that, after dinner with Mr. Assange, he pulled off her clothes and snapped her necklace. She then "tried to put on some articles of clothing as it was going too quickly and uncomfortably but Assange ripped them off again." According to Ms. A., he pinned her arms and legs to stop her from reaching for a condom. Eventually he put one on, but, she explained, he appeared to have "done something" with it, resulting in its tearing.

The second complainant, Ms. W., attended the same lecture by Mr. Assange. After the speech, she was seated next to him at a dinner. Two days later, she invited him to her apartment. The pair had sex using a condom. She woke up later to find him on top of her again, having sex with her, but this time without a condom. Subsequently, the two women insisted that Mr. Assange have a test for sexually transmitted diseases. He refused. At that point, each woman went to the police. Prosecutors immediately issued an arrest warrant. Mr. Assange claims that the prosecution is politically motivated as an American-initiated vendetta to punish him.

Swedish law specifies three categories of lesser offenses of rape. When men use threats or mild degrees of force to have sex against their partners' will, the maximum penalty is four years of imprisonment. The offense of having consensual sex without use of a condom, in disregard of the woman's request (also a less severe form of rape), is punishable by a minimum of two years of imprisonment.

What should the British court decide on the extradition request? What should the Swedish court decide regarding his liability for rape? How would you respond to Mr. Assange's defense attorney that "Sexual encounters have their ebbs and flows. What may be unwanted one minute can, with further empathy, become desired." Do you think that this prosecution will make Sweden's justice system "the laughingstock of the world," as another defense lawyer contends? See generally John F. Burns & Ravi Somaiya, Confidential Swedish Police Report Details Allegations Against WikiLeaks Founder, N.Y. Times, Dec. 19, 2010, at A8; Ravi Somaiya, Definition of Rape at Issue as Assange Hearing Closes, N.Y. Times, Feb. 11, 2011, at A5; Daniel Tencer, Lawyer: Sweden Investigating Assange for Sex Without Condom, The Raw Story, Dec. 2, 2010, available at http://www.rawstory.com/rs/2010/12/sweden-assange-sex-without-condom/.

4. Interference with Abortion Decisionmaking

■ PLANNED PARENTHOOD OF SOUTHEASTERN PENNSYLVANIA v. CASEY
505 U.S. 833 (1992)

Justice O'CONNOR, Justice KENNEDY, and Justice SOUTER announced the judgment of the Court and delivered the opinion of the Court [for Part V-C].

. . . Pennsylvania's abortion law provides, except in cases of medical emergency, that no physician shall perform an abortion on a married woman without receiving a signed statement from the woman that she has notified her spouse that she is about to undergo an abortion. The woman has the option of providing an alternative signed statement certifying that her husband is not the man who impregnated her; that her husband could not be located; that the pregnancy is the result of spousal sexual assault which she has reported; or that the woman believes that notifying her husband will cause him or someone else to inflict bodily injury upon her. A physician who performs an abortion on a married woman without receiving the appropriate signed statement will have his or her license revoked, and is liable to the husband for damages.

The District Court heard the testimony of numerous expert witnesses, and made detailed findings of fact regarding the effect of this statute. These included:

- The vast majority of women consult their husbands prior to deciding to terminate their pregnancy. . . .
- Studies reveal that family violence occurs in two million families in the United States. This figure, however, is a conservative one that substantially understates (because battering is usually not reported until it reaches life-threatening proportions) the actual number of families affected by domestic violence. In fact, researchers estimate that one of every two women will be battered at some time in their life. . . .

- A wife may not elect to notify her husband of her intention to have an abortion for a variety of reasons, including the husband's illness, concern about her own health, the imminent failure of the marriage, or the husband's absolute opposition to the abortion. . . .
- The required filing of the spousal consent form would require plaintiff-clinics to change their counseling procedures and force women to reveal their most intimate decision-making on pain of criminal sanctions. The confidentiality of these revelations could not be guaranteed, since the woman's records are not immune from subpoena. . . .
- Women of all class levels, educational backgrounds, and racial, ethnic and religious groups are battered. . . .
- Mere notification of pregnancy is frequently a flashpoint for battering and violence within the family. The number of battering incidents is high during the pregnancy and often the worst abuse can be associated with pregnancy. . . . The battering husband may deny parentage and use the pregnancy as an excuse for abuse. . . .
- Secrecy typically shrouds abusive families. . . . Battering husbands often threaten [the wife] or her children with further abuse if she tells an outsider of the violence and tells her that nobody will believe her. A battered woman, therefore, is highly unlikely to disclose the violence against her for fear of retaliation by the abuser. . . ."

These findings are supported by studies of domestic violence. . . . In well-functioning marriages, spouses discuss important intimate decisions such as whether to bear a child. But there are millions of women in this country who are the victims of regular physical and psychological abuse at the hands of their husbands. . . . Many may fear devastating forms of psychological abuse from their husbands, including [abuse of their children,] verbal harassment, threats of future violence, the destruction of possessions, physical confinement to the home, the withdrawal of financial support, or the disclosure of the abortion to family and friends. These methods of psychological abuse may act as even more of a deterrent to notification than the possibility of physical violence, but women who are the victims of the abuse are not exempt from [the statute's] notification requirement. And many women who are pregnant as a result of sexual assaults by their husbands will be unable to avail themselves of the exception for spousal sexual assault, because the exception requires that the woman have notified law enforcement authorities within 90 days of the assault, and her husband will be notified of her report once an investigation begins. If anything in this field is certain, it is that victims of spousal sexual assault are extremely reluctant to report the abuse to the government. . . . We must not blind ourselves to the fact that the significant number of women who fear for their safety and the safety of their children are likely to be deterred from procuring an abortion as surely as if the Commonwealth had outlawed abortion in all cases.

Respondents attempt to avoid the conclusion that [the notification provision] is invalid by pointing out that it imposes almost no burden at all for the vast majority of women seeking abortions. . . . Legislation is measured for consistency with the Constitution by its impact on those whose conduct it affects. . . . The unfortunate yet persisting conditions we document above will mean that in a large fraction of the cases in which [the notification requirement] is relevant, it will operate as a substantial obstacle to a woman's choice to undergo an abortion. It is an undue burden, and therefore invalid. . . .

We recognize that a husband has a "deep and proper concern and interest . . . in his wife's pregnancy and in the growth and development of the fetus she is carrying." [Planned Parenthood of Central Mo. v. Danforth, 428 U.S. 52, 69 (1976).] With regard to the children he has fathered and raised, the Court has recognized his "cognizable and substantial" interest in their custody. Stanley v. Illinois, 405 U.S. 645, 651-652 (1972). . . . Before birth, however, the issue takes on a very different cast. It is an inescapable biological fact that state regulation with respect to the child a woman is carrying will have a far greater impact on the mother's liberty than on the father's. The effect of state regulation on a woman's protected liberty is doubly deserving of scrutiny in such a case, as the State has touched not only upon the private sphere of the family but upon the very bodily integrity of the pregnant woman. The Court has held that "when the wife and the husband disagree on this decision, the view of only one of the two marriage partners can prevail. Inasmuch as it is the woman who physically bears the child and who is the more directly and immediately affected by the pregnancy, as between the two, the balance weighs in her favor." *Danforth*, supra, at 71. This conclusion rests upon the basic nature of marriage and the nature of our Constitution: "The marital couple is not an independent entity with a mind and heart of its own, but an association of two individuals each with a separate intellectual and emotional makeup. If the right of privacy means anything, it is the right of the *individual*, married or single, to be free from unwarranted governmental intrusion into matters so fundamentally affecting a person as the decision whether to bear or beget a child." Eisenstadt v. Baird, 405 U.S. at 453 (emphasis in original). . . .

There was a time, not so long ago, when a different understanding of the family and of the Constitution prevailed. In Bradwell v. State, 83 U.S. (16 Wall.) 130 (1872), three Members of this Court reaffirmed the common-law principle that "a woman had no legal existence separate from her husband, who was regarded as her head and representative in the social state. . . ." Id., at 141 (Bradley, J., joined by Swayne and Field, JJ., concurring in judgment). Only one generation has passed since this Court observed that "woman is still regarded as the center of home and family life," with attendant "special responsibilities" that precluded full and independent legal status under the Constitution. Hoyt v. Florida, 368 U.S. 57, 62 (1961). These views, of course, are no longer consistent with our understanding of the family, the individual, or the Constitution.

[T]he Court held in *Danforth* that the Constitution does not permit a State to require a married woman to obtain her husband's consent before undergoing an abortion. . . . For the great many women who are victims of abuse inflicted by their husbands, or whose children are the victims of such abuse, a spousal notice requirement enables the husband to wield an effective veto over his wife's decision [contrary to *Danforth.*]

The husband's interest in the life of the child his wife is carrying does not permit the State to empower him with this troubling degree of authority over his wife. . . . A husband has no enforceable right to require a wife to advise him before she exercises her personal choices. . . . After all, if the husband's interest in the fetus' safety is a sufficient predicate for state regulation, the State could reasonably conclude that pregnant wives should notify their husbands before drinking alcohol or smoking. Perhaps married women should notify their husbands before using contraceptives or before undergoing any type of surgery that may have complications affecting the husband's interest in his wife's reproductive organs. And if a husband's interest justifies notice in any of these cases, one might reasonably argue that it justifies exactly what the *Danforth* Court held it did not justify—a requirement of the husband's consent as well. A State may not give to a man the kind of dominion over his wife that parents exercise over their children. . . .

Chief Justice REHNQUIST, with whom Justice WHITE, Justice SCALIA, and Justice THOMAS join, . . . dissenting in part. . . .

. . . The question before us is therefore whether the spousal notification requirement rationally furthers any legitimate state interests. We conclude that it does. First, a husband's interests in procreation within marriage and in the potential life of his unborn child are certainly substantial ones. The State itself has legitimate interests both in protecting these interests of the father and in protecting the potential life of the fetus, and the spousal notification requirement is reasonably related to advancing those state interests. By providing that a husband will usually know of his spouse's intent to have an abortion, the provision makes it more likely that the husband will participate in deciding the fate of his unborn child, a possibility that might otherwise have been denied him. This participation might in some cases result in a decision to proceed with the pregnancy. Judge Alito observed in his dissent below, "the Pennsylvania legislature could have rationally believed that some married women are initially inclined to obtain an abortion without their husbands' knowledge because of perceived problems—such as economic constraints, future plans, or the husbands' previously expressed opposition—that may be obviated by discussion prior to the abortion." 947 F.2d at 726 (opinion concurring in part and dissenting in part).

The State also has a legitimate interest in promoting "the integrity of the marital relationship." [T]he spousal notice requirement is a rational attempt by the State to improve truthful communication between spouses and encourage collaborative decision-making, and thereby fosters marital integrity. . . .

Notes and Questions

1. *Social reality.* Interference with a woman's abortion decisionmaking takes two forms: (1) the woman wants the abortion, but her partner *prevents* her; or (2) the woman does not want the abortion, but her partner *forces* her to have it. Which does *Casey* address?

Abusers resort to many forms of interference to deny their partners' access to abortion: withholding funds to pay for the abortion or transportation to the medical facility; sabotaging appointments for abortions; and "coming into the clinic and 'breaking things up' so that the woman [leaves] with the man to stop him for making more of a scene." Moore et al., supra, at 1741. Some abusers threaten to harm or kill their partners if the latter undergoes an abortion. Id.

Conversely, some abusers force their partners to have abortions against the latter's wishes. Jeanne E. Hathaway et al., Impact of Partner Abuse on Women's Reproductive Lives, 60 J. Am. Med. Women's Ass'n 42, 44 (2005) (reporting that more than half of those battered women who disclose their partners' interference with reproductive decisionmaking report that they were pressured or forced to have abortions). Some abusers threaten to hurt the woman in order to cause a miscarriage. For example, one woman reported that her partner threatened to throw her down the steps or to punch her in the stomach if she didn't have an abortion. She terminated the pregnancy to avoid the possibility of harm. Moore et al., supra, at 1741 (recounting event).

2. *Empirical basis.* To what extent does Justice O'Connor rely on empirical data to invalidate the spousal notification requirement? What evidence does she cite to support her belief that "in a large fraction of the cases in which [the notification requirement] is relevant, it will operate as a substantial obstacle to a woman's choice to undergo an abortion"?

3. *Disclosure.* Most women (married and single) inform their partners about their abortion plans. Marcelle Christian Holmes, Reconsidering a "Woman's Issue": Psychotherapy and One Man's Postabortion Experiences, 58 Am. J. Psychotherapy 103 (2004). Do such data support or undermine the *Casey* dissent's view of the notification requirement as a valid means of furthering the state's interest in promoting marital integrity and spousal communication?

4. *Rationale.* Why did the Court strike down the spousal notification provision? What are the respective rationales of the majority and dissent? How does a requirement of spousal notification differ from one of spousal consent (invalidated by Court in Planned Parenthood v. Danforth, 428 U.S. 52, 67-72 (1976))?

5. *Undue burden.* Why do Justices O'Connor, Kennedy, and Souter conclude that spousal notification constitutes an undue burden but that a 24-hour waiting period does not? See *Casey*, 505 U.S. at 881-887 (upholding the 24-hour waiting period).

6. *Whose privacy?* Does privacy emerge from *Casey* as protection for the individual? The family unit? What role does privacy doctrine play when the family unit is divided about the outcome of a pregnancy? See David D. Meyer, The Paradox of Family Privacy, 53 Vand. L. Rev. 527, 554-558 (2000) (in "splintered" families, privacy does not keep the state out but locates in the Constitution "a substantive rule for resolving a family's internal conflict").

7. *Who decides?* Who should make the abortion determination when women's and men's rights conflict? Should the state provide pre-abortion hearings at which an impartial arbiter decides? Can you imagine circumstances in which the male should prevail? Suppose that the man seeks to avoid having a child but the woman chooses to carry to term. Must he pay child support under all circumstances? See Dubay v. Wells, 506 F.3d 422 (6th Cir. 2007) (unsuccessful challenge in case dubbed "Roe v. Wade for men"); Christopher Bruno, Note, A Right to Decide Not to Be a Legal Father: Gonzales v. Carhart and the Acceptance of Emotional Harm as a Constitutionally Protected Interest, 77 Geo. Wash. L. Rev. 141 (2008).

8. *Vision of marriage.* What vision of marriage does the majority and dissent in *Casey* reflect? What vision of abusive intimate relationships? Does the rejection of traditional gender-based roles provide a better explanation for the outcome than the empirical data?

9. *Father's interest.* What do you think of Justice Rehnquist's reasoning that the spousal notification requirement rationally furthers a legitimate state interest in protecting the husband's interests in procreation within marriage and in the potential life of his unborn child? Does the state have a legitimate interest in protecting this interest of the father's and the potential life of the fetus? Does the spousal notification requirement reasonably advance those state interests?

10. *Gender stereotypes.* What are the gender stereotypes that *Casey* promotes? Does it buttress the belief that men have an entitlement to women's sexual and reproductive capacities?

11. *Law reform.* Some states recently adopted measures addressing coerced abortions. A handful of states now require health care providers who furnish abortions to post signs informing women that they cannot be coerced into having the procedure and encouraging them to contact the authorities or the clinic staff if they feel pressured to have the procedure. Guttmacher Institute, Laws Affecting Reproductive Health and Rights: 2009 State Policy Review, http://www.guttmacher.org/statecenter/updates/2009/statetrends42009.html (last visited June 28, 2011). Is this an effective strategy to address the link between domestic violence and abortion decisionmaking? Do state legislatures pass such notification requirements to empower reproductive decisionmaking or to increase the administrative costs of abortion clinics and/or expose them to liability for failure to post such notifications? What should be the pregnant woman's redress for a coerced abortion? Should she be able to bring a civil suit for damages against her partner who coerced her to have an abortion? See, e.g., Idaho Code §18-615(2) (authorizing civil suit). If so, how should the law measure damages?

12. *Criticisms.* Some critics of coerced abortion laws contend that coerced abortion laws enhance the danger to victims of intimate partner violence. These critics argue:

> [I]f women are unable to get an abortion demanded by their partners, some may be at risk of experiencing physical violence from the partner. Some of this violence might be perpetrated with the intention of inducing an abortion. Denying such a woman a safe abortion can therefore endanger her health.

Moore et al., supra, at 1742. Do you agree?

C. PSYCHOLOGICAL ABUSE

A common misconception is that domestic abuse consists only of physical abuse. Yet, because intimate partner violence fundamentally consists of coercion and control, psychological abuse is pervasive. The following section explores the various forms of psychological abuse in intimate partner violence.

1. Background

■ EVAN STARK, COERCIVE CONTROL
in Encyclopedia of Domestic Violence 166, 166-171
(Nicky Ali Jackson ed., 2007)[citations omitted]

[C]oercive control describes the pattern of sexual mastery by which abusive partners, typically males, employ different combinations of violence, intimidation, isolation, humiliation, and control to subordinate adult victims. In marked contrast to the incident-specific definition of physical assault that dominates domestic violence research and intervention, coercive control is ongoing, extends through social space as well as over time, exploits persistent sexual inequalities, and focuses its regulatory tactics on enforcing stereotypic sex role behaviors. [I]ts harms tend to be cumulative rather than incident specific and include the suppression of autonomy and basic liberties as well as violations of physical integrity. . . . The discrepancy between the pattern of abuse for which most women seek help and the prevailing equation of battering with incidents of physical violence helps explain why such current polices as arrest, court protection orders, batterer intervention programs, and emergency shelter have largely failed to reduce the prevalence and incidence of woman battering.

THE THEORY OF COERCIVE CONTROL

The coercive control model developed from applications of learning theory to the experiences of persons undergoing severe restraint in nonfamilial settings, particularly hostages, prisoners of war (POWs), inmates, mental patients, and members of religious cults. . . . In their efforts at "thought reform" with American prisoners during the Korean War, the Chinese Communists used "coerced persuasion," a technique by which a person's self-concept and resistance was broken down [and a new view of reality was installed] through "random, noncontingent reinforcement by unpredictable rewards and punishments." In the late 1970s, two feminist psychologists, Camella Serum and Margaret Singer, noticed that batterers employed these same or similar techniques, placing their partners in a "coercive control situation" of childlike dependency on the controllers. Psychologist Steven Morgan labeled wife abuse "conjugal terrorism" and noted the "remarkable" resemblance between the attitudes and behaviors of the violent husband and those of the political terrorist.

Building on this work, another psychologist, Lewis Okun wrote what remains the definitive chapter on the coercive control theory of woman battering. Drawing an extended analogy between coerced persuasion, the experience of women being conditioned to prostitution by their pimps, and the experiences recounted to him in his counseling work with abusive men and abusive women, Okun emphasized the "breakdown" of the victim's personality in the face of severe external threats and isolation and highlighted the extreme emotional and behavioral adaptations to this process, ranging from guilt, loss of self-esteem, identification with the controller's aggressiveness, and fear of escape to difficulty planning for the future, detachment from violent incidents, and overreaction to trivial incidents. Importantly, Okun shifted the explanation for victim's reactions from her predisposing personality or background characteristics to the power dynamics mediated by the violent interaction. Although he stressed that any "normal" person would respond to coercive control tactics in a similar way, he emphasized the systemic nature of the oppression, not the extraordinary nature of the violence itself. . . .

COMPONENTS OF COERCIVE CONTROL

Coercion includes acts of physical or sexual assault, threats, or other acts of intimidation used to directly compel or dispel a particular response by inducing pain, injury, and/or fear. . . . Control encompasses forms of regulation, isolation, and exploitation that limit a victim's options, transfer her resources to the controller, ensure her dependence on him, and maximize the benefits of personal service. . . .

Intimidation in coercive control achieves the desired levels of fear, compliance, "loyalty," and dependence primarily through threats, surveillance, and degradation. Intimidation may properly be termed "psychological abuse" because it reduces the victim's sense of worth and psychological efficacy, often inducing an image of the perpetrator as bigger than life. Threats run the gamut from holding a gun to a woman's head and detailing how she will be killed to signals of impending harm that are recognized only by the victim, such as a raised eyebrow or a tapping of the foot. . . . [Threats include the use of force against property or other persons that communicate what a partner is capable of doing if a woman disobeys, and threats directed at the woman through her children.]

Surveillance, a second form of intimidation, makes coercive control portable, allowing it to extend through social space, making physical separation relatively ineffective as a way to end abuse. Stalking is the most prominent of a range of surveillance tactics designed to deprive the person of the right to privacy or to freely negotiate public and private spaces. . . . The range of tactics batterers employ to watch their partners and intrude on their social and private lives goes far beyond anything currently considered criminal. For instance, an important intimidation technique involves micro-surveillance, where the controlling partner may subdivide ordinary behaviors such as sleeping, eating, cleaning, or making love into component parts, set performance rules for each component, and monitor their enactment. Controllers may steal or read diaries; search drawers for "sexy" clothes; measure the toilet paper, the breakfast cereal, or the height of the bed cover off the floor; and inspect underwear to detect disloyalty.

Another facet of intimidation involves chronic insults and shaming. Typically introduced as a test of loyalty, a sign of ownership, a form of discipline, or a means of isolation, shaming involves demonstrating a victim's subservience through public humiliating [and] denying her self-respect. . . .

Isolation, the third tactical component of coercive control, is designed to prevent disclosure, instill dependence, express exclusive possession, monopolize a victim's skills and resources, and keep the victim from mustering the help or resources needed for independence. Controllers isolate victims within and from those arenas that provide the moorings of social identity, including friends, family, coworkers, and professional helpers, eviscerating a woman's selfhood and constraining her subjectivity. By cutting women off from alternative sources of information and support and inserting themselves between victims and the "world," batterers become their primary source of interpretation and validation. . . .

The Gendered Nature of Coercive Control

[T]here is no evidence that any substantial population of men are victims of the same pattern of coercive control by female partners or suffer comparable harms to their liberty. This is because women's vulnerability to entrapment in personal life is due to the larger status inequalities they bring to relationships. . . . Since men cannot be unequal to women the same as women are disadvantaged relative to them, they can exploit inequality in relationships in ways that women cannot. Thus, even though many women hit, intimidate, control, or demean men, the substance, meaning, and consequence of these tactics are completely different when they are used in combination to oppress women. It is this fusion of social and personal constraint that gives coercive control its gendered theme and organizes its delivery around stereotypic sex roles.

For additional discussion of coercive control, see Evan Stark, Coercive Control: How Men Entrap Women in Personal Life (2009); Evan Stark, Re-Presenting Woman Battering: From Battered Woman Syndrome to Coercive Control, 58 Alb. L. Rev. 973(1995).

2. Stalking

■ **WEINER v. WEINER**
899 N.Y.S.2d 555 (Sup. Ct. 2010)

COOPER, J.:

For close to three years, plaintiff Edie Weiner finally felt safe and secure in her country house. Nestled in the mountains of Northeastern Pennsylvania and surrounded by tall woods, the house is in a private vacation community called the Hideout. The reason she felt safe, though, was not because the community is gated or has its own security force. Instead, it was because her ex-husband, defendant Jay Weiner, was barred by an order of protection from entering the Hideout and coming near her home.

Everything changed for plaintiff this past summer. That is when she learned that defendant had rented a house in the Hideout on the very same day that the order of protection expired. What scared her even more is that the house defendant rented is directly behind her house. A short walk through the woods would bring him to the edge of her back lawn where he could stand and stare into her home—under the cover of darkness or hidden by the trees—seeing what she is doing, what she is wearing, who she is with.

Plaintiff contends that her ex-husband, by moving into the Hideout as soon as the order of protection expired, is engaged in a campaign to intimidate and threaten her, and, in his own insidious way, seeking once again to exert control over her life. Although she does not allege that he has tried to have any direct contact with her, she maintains that his mere presence within the gates of her community causes her fear and anxiety. As a result, plaintiff has moved for a new order of protection to again prevent defendant from entering the Hideout. . . .

The major issue before the court is whether it has the power to issue a new order of protection where the ex-husband has had no contact with his ex-wife—and has made no effort to contact or communicate with her—but has simply rented a house in close proximity to her. . . . This is the second time since the parties' divorce that plaintiff has had to return to court seeking post-judgment relief against her ex-husband with regard to her vacation home. The first was in 2007, when she obtained the order of protection that barred defendant from going to the Hideout. . . . The judgment of divorce, which was entered on July 17, 2001, incorporated by reference the terms and provisions of a [standard stipulation of settlement that appears in matrimonial agreements and is referred to as a "no-molestation clause," as follows:]

> Neither party shall in any way molest, disturb or trouble the other, or interfere with the peace and comfort of the other, or compel or seek to compel the other to associate, cohabit or dwell with him or her by any action or proceeding for restoration of conjugal rights or by any coercive means whatsoever.

[The stipulation of settlement provided that wife would have "exclusive and sole ownership" of the Hideout vacation residence. Wife later agreed to allow defendant brief periods of exclusive occupancy at the Hideout when she would not be present.]

As it turns out, defendant had no intention of letting his ex-wife live happily without him. Almost from the moment the divorce was granted, he began barraging her with telephone calls, letters and cards. All of these communications—bitter, mocking and nasty in tone—were to the effect that he would never let her go and that she would always be under his control. A prime example of this is a card he sent to her in which he wrote:

> I tried to stop loving you, by not calling you, not giving you the mail, and hopefully by not seeing you. All for nothing. . . . I haven't lost my love for you in 3 years + 4 months of separation. However, at the same time, strangely, I have grown to hate you for what you have done to my life.

In this same vein, defendant would send letters to his ex-wife addressed "Dear Bitch." In one letter, he referred to her and their grown son as being "perfectly suited for each other—the bitch and the son-of-a-bitch." In another letter, he again demonstrated his twisted obsession with her when he wrote:

> Lady Get Off My Back! You have been bitter, vicious, vengeful, vindictive and menopausal to me since Nov. 16, 1998. You feel uncomfortable about my leaving notes at your building. Too bad! As I told you, I will always love you—always. For some strange reason, I still want you. However I don't need you any longer.

Plaintiff felt defendant's unwanted presence most acutely when it came to the house in the Hideout. Not content to simply enjoy his periods of exclusive occupancy, he would use those periods as a kind of Trojan horse to launch assaults at his ex-wife from within the confines of her own home. One of the most disturbing things he did was to completely violate her sense of privacy. When plaintiff requested that he not enter her bedroom during the times he had use of the house, defendant wrote her this chilling response:

> You told me on the phone and in your letter, there is no need for me to go into your bedroom. Your bedroom, like all the other rooms in the house, is part of the house. I have exclusive use of the house for 10 weeks a year through 2013. I could, if I want, sleep in your bed, open the venetian blinds, play with your underwear, but I don't.

After enduring this torment for a number of years, plaintiff decided she could take no more. Her breaking point came when defendant left a message on her home answering machine threatening to break the locked glass door leading to her bedroom in the house in the Hideout. She then made a motion to terminate his use of the Hideout and for an order of protection to keep him away from her and her home. [The judge granted her a temporary order of protection, requiring defendant to stay away from her and the Hideout, that was subsequently made permanent for a two-year period until July 30, 2009. Here, the wife moves for a new order of protection to prevent the husband from again entering the vacation residence.]

[The standards for determining when an application for an order of protection should be granted are found in section 812 of the Family Court Act (F.C.A.), requiring that the petitioner prove, by a preponderance of the evidence, that the other party has committed one or more of the designated crimes that constitute a "family offense." These offenses include stalking.]

Any meaningful analysis as to whether defendant has committed a family offense upon which the issuance of an order of protection can be predicated [includes] the various degrees of stalking, and in particular stalking in the fourth degree. The crime of stalking in the fourth degree, which the legislature created and included as a family offense in 1999, is defined under P.L. §120.45, in relevant part, as follows:

> A person is guilty of stalking in the fourth degree when he or she intentionally, and for no legitimate purpose, engages in a course of conduct directed at a specific person, and knows or reasonably should know that such conduct:
>
> 1. is likely to cause reasonable fear of material harm to the physical health, safety or property of such person, a member of such person's immediate family or a third party with whom such person is acquainted.

Thus, in order to establish that defendant has committed the crime of stalking in the fourth degree, there are two things that must be proved. The first is that his presence in the Hideout is without legitimate purpose. The second is that he knows or should know that his presence there is likely to cause plaintiff fear for her physical health, safety or property.

Plaintiff testified credibly and compellingly at the hearing held in this matter as to her ex-husband's purpose for being in the Hideout. When asked why she believes he rented a house there as soon as the order of protection expired, she responded, "I feel that he did it ultimately to be near me, to intimidate me." She went on to describe defendant as a stalker who "refuses to stay away from me."

The point was made that there are untold number of vacation communities similar to the Hideout in the Poconos and other rural areas surrounding New York City. Nevertheless, defendant has chosen to rent only in the Hideout—the community in which his ex-wife lives and where he had been prevented from entering because of his long pattern of "egregious" behavior towards her. According to plaintiff, it is clear that his act of moving to the Hideout—compounded by his renting the house directly behind hers—is just a continuation of that same abusive pattern and is absolutely devoid of any "legitimate purpose."

In his testimony, defendant sought to explain why it was so important that he live in his ex-wife's vacation community as opposed to any other place. His testimony, however, was neither credible nor compelling. In fact, with his extended diatribes on such matters as his volunteer work at a blood bank, his prowess as a long-distance runner, and his displeasure over his adult son drinking beer, what he had to say was often bizarre. Perhaps the most peculiar aspect of his testimony was his attempt to tie the irresistible lure that the Hideout has for him to the fauna and flora of Northeastern Pennsylvania. While defendant went on at great length about the joys of seeing deer and wild turkeys on the front lawn, as well as being able to witness the spectacle of the autumn colors, he seemed immune to the notion that deer and turkeys and trees with bright leaves abound just about everywhere in this part of the country.

The only time defendant even approached giving a credible reason for why he had to rent in the Hideout was when he said he knew people there and that this made the community familiar to him. Yet he gave no names and no information as to who these people may be or what type of contact, if any, he has had with them over the past few years. The distinct impression this left was that defendant has no real relationships with anyone in the community and that he returned to the Hideout because of the presence of one person and one person alone: his ex-wife . . .

Plaintiff also testified credibly and convincingly as to what might be called the fear factor. This is the second element of the crime of stalking in the fourth degree, which requires that the conduct at issue be such that it can reasonably be expected to cause fear for one's health, safety and property. The fear on plaintiff's part as she confronted her ex-husband in the courtroom was actually palpable. Asked if she was afraid of him, she responded as follows:

> Yes. He has in the past threatened me, my son, my boyfriend, my property . . . He instigates things. He is a stalker. He just likes to bully people. He is extremely threatening of everyone and I can just—I can never predict what he is going to do. He is capable of almost anything because he is really not all there.

When viewed in the context of defendant's past actions . . . plaintiff has every reason to continue to fear for her health, safety and property. This fear is in no way lessened by the fact that at least to this point there has been no direct contact or communication. Defendant's presence alone in the Hideout is more than enough to make plaintiff feel the way she does.

The crime of stalking in the fourth degree does not require that the offender actually intend to cause harm, or even the fear of harm, to the victim. All that is required is "that the offender know or reasonably know that his conduct is likely to cause reasonable fear of material harm to the victim's physical health, safety or property." Here, it is inconceivable that defendant could be unaware of the effect his presence in the Hideout would have on plaintiff. In fact, every indication is that his insistence on returning there was largely fueled by the knowledge that it would have such effect.

Plaintiff has proved by a fair preponderance of the credible evidence both of the elements of stalking in the fourth degree. . . . Accordingly, the court finds that defendant Jay Weiner has committed the family offense of stalking in the fourth degree. . . .

[T]he provision governing the issuance of orders of protection in the Family Court, D.R.L. §252 does not provide for a maximum term for an order. . . . In order to allow plaintiff to live her life in peace, both in the city and the country, and not have to return to court yet again in the near future, the order of protection that the court is granting her will have a term of 20 years. This means that it will expire on

April 5, 2030. By then defendant will be 85 years old and, one would hope, no longer pose a threat to his ex-wife. . . .

Notes and Questions

1. *Stalking behavior.* One in 6 women report stalking (feeling very fearful or believing someone would be harmed or killed). NISVS, Executive Summary, supra, at 2. Stalking often takes the form of unsolicited phone calls, letters, emails, presents, or flowers; being followed; being spied upon; having the stalker show up or wait at places; and being subject to rumors. Katrina Baum et al., Dept. of Justice (DOJ), Bureau of Justice Statistics, Stalking Victimization in the United States (2009). Which of these behaviors did Mr. Weiner commit? What was the nature of the danger he posed to Mrs. Weiner?

2. *Severity.* Stalking can sometimes lead to murder. Of women who are murdered by intimate partners, 90 percent were stalked. Melinda Beck et al., Murderous Obsession, Newsweek, July 13, 1992, at 60, 61 (citing data).

3. *Statutory requirements.* What are the elements of stalking, according to the statute in *Weiner*? What is a "course of conduct"? "Legitimate purpose"? How did Mrs. Weiner prove the requisite elements of the crime? Did Mr. Weiner have a "legitimate purpose" to be at the Hideout?

a. *Credible threat.* Some statutes require that the stalker make a "credible threat" of violence against the victim, the victim's family, or the victim's property. See, e.g., Cal. Penal Code §646.9; Fla. Stat. §784.048. What is a "credible threat"? What explains this requirement? How does it differ from "a reasonable fear for one's safety"? Should statutes focus on the specific *acts* of the stalker or the *nature* of the threat, or both?

b. *Intent requirement.* Must the stalker *intend* to cause the victim to be afraid? What does the statute in *Weiner* require? Some stalkers might not "intend" to cause fear because they mistakenly believe that their victim returns (or eventually will return) their affection. How relevant should the stalker's motivation be?

c. *Fear requirement. Must* the victim experience fear? Suppose the victim is not easily frightened? See Sparks v. Deveny, 189 P.3d 1268 (Or. Ct. App. 2008) (holding that relentless pursuit was insufficient to support permanent protective order where victim did not fear for her safety). Fear of what? How high should be the threshold of fear? Is the standard subjective or objective? See, e.g., Smith v. Martens, 106 P.3d 28 (Kan. 2005). Who determines whether a victim's fear is "reasonable"? What does the statute in *Weiner* require?

4. *Temporary restraining order.* Penalties for stalking may be enhanced if the stalker is already subject to a restraining order. See, e.g., Fla. Stat. §784.048(4). However, many stalking victims fail to seek a restraining order. David Crary, Survey Shows Scope of Stalking in U.S., Virginian-Pilot (Norfolk, Va.), Jan. 14, 2009, at A6. What explains victims' reluctance?

a. *Particular conditions.* What were the limitations on Mr. Weiner's conduct ordered by the trial judge? By the appellate judge? Why did Mrs. Weiner seek a new order of protection? What is a no-molestation clause in a divorce action? How does it differ from a temporary restraining order? Did Mr. Weiner breach the no-molestation clause in the stipulation settling the Weiners' divorce action? If so, how?

b. *Duration.* How long should restraining orders last? As we have seen, three types of restraining orders exist: emergency protection orders, temporary restraining orders, and permanent orders (the last are not really "permanent"). How long do you think each of these orders should last? Should the duration be statutorily defined or determined on a case-by-case basis? Should there be "good cause" extensions? What factors should enter into the determination of "good cause"? What was the period ordered by the trial court in *Weiner*? Was the appellate court's modification appropriate?

c. *Permanent order.* How can *past* behaviors (such as those by Mr. Weiner) constitute grounds for a permanent order of protection? See also Ritchie v. Konrad, 10 Cal. Rptr. 3d 387 (Ct. App. 2004) (holding that a protection order may be renewed permanently upon a finding of a "reasonable apprehension of future abuse," thereby rejecting an "imminent danger" standard because it failed to fulfill the legislative purpose of preventing future acts of abuse).

5. *Characteristics of victims.* Most stalking victims tend to be former intimate partners, neighbors, friends, or roommates. Only about 10 percent of victims are stalked by a stranger. Baum, supra, at 4. As *Weiner* illustrates, divorced or separated persons have a high rate of victimization, and stalking may persist for a long time. Id. at 1 (reporting that 11 percent of victims say stalking lasted more than 5 years). Acts of stalking occur with considerable frequency. Id. (reporting that about half of stalking victims experience at least one unwanted contact per week).

6. *Characteristics of stalkers.* Stalkers consist of several types: (1) those who target a stranger (often a celebrity) based on a delusional disorder that they are loved by the victim whom they were stalking; (2) those who harass a person with whom they have either no prior relationship or perhaps a brief contact (such as a stranger or acquaintance) based on the belief that they can convince the victim to fall in love with them (these stalkers generally are aware of the bothersome nature of their actions unlike the first group of stalkers); and (3) the most common and most dangerous stalkers who stalk someone with whom they had a prior relationship and who are motivated by a particular circumstance (such as the deterioration of a relationship) or a perception of mistreatment. Approximately one in six victims attribute the stalking to coercion of the victim to remain in the relationship. Baum, supra, at 5. For another typology, see Paul E. Mullen & Michele Pathe, Stalking, 29 Crime & Just. 273, 279-281 (2002) (characterizing stalkers as either "affectionate/amorous" or "persecutory/angry"). What do you think was Mr. Weiner's motivation?

7. *Psychological consequences of stalking.* Stalking victims experience a sense of powerlessness and a fear of bodily harm and death (sometimes for themselves and sometimes for other family members). They are intensely concerned about the unpredictability of the stalker's intrusions. They live in a "charged atmosphere in which attack often seemed imminent, even if it never eventuated." Troy E. McEwan et al., A Study of the Predictors of Persistence in Stalking Situations, 33 Law & Hum. Behav. 149, 150 (2009). Some victims exhibit post-traumatic stress symptoms. Id.

Victims respond to stalking by changing their usual activities; quitting their jobs; changing their names and appearance; moving; installing caller ID or call blocking; and losing time from work (either because they fear for their safety or to obtain a restraining order). Often victims spend considerable money to respond to stalking such as incurring expenses for lost pay, property damage, moving, changing phone numbers, and attorneys' fees.

8. *Harassment distinguished.* How does stalking differ from harassment? What is the line between bothersome, irritating behavior and stalking? Between persistence and obsession?

9. *State and federal stalking laws.* Both state and federal laws (described below) address stalking.

a. *State laws.* Prior to the enactment of stalking laws, victims of stalking had limited legal recourse absent physical injury or conduct involving specified offenses (such as being the recipient of annoying or obscene phone calls). California was the first state to enact a stalking law in 1990 after an obsessed fan stalked and killed Rebecca Schaeffer, the star of a television sitcom "My Sister Sam," following his acquisition of her home address from the Department of Motor Vehicles. Naomi Harlin Goodno, Cyberstalking, A New Crime: Evaluating the Effectiveness of Current State and Federal Laws, 72 Mo. L. Rev. 125, 127 (2007). Within three years, all states enacted stalking laws. The murder also led to the enactment of the Driver's Privacy Protection Act of 1994, Pub. L. No. 103-322, 108 Stat. 2009, 2099-2102 (codified as amended at 18 U.S.C. §§2721-2725), prohibiting the non-consensual disclosure of personal information about a driver.

In most states, stalking is a misdemeanor. States enhance the penalty if the defendant (1) is a repeat offender; (2) violated a protective order or conditions of probation, pretrial release, or bond; (3) commits stalking while in possession of a deadly weapon; or (4) physically harms or restrains the victim. Carol E. Jordan et al., Stalking: Cultural, Clinical and Legal Considerations 38 Brandeis L.J. 513, 560 (2000). Some states also enhance the penalty if the victim is a minor. See, e.g., Tenn. Code Ann. §39-17-315(c)(1)(B).

Statutes underwent several stages of revision, such as the expansion of victims to include family and household members; increase in penalties; expansion of "actionable threat" to include a threat that could be implied by a pattern of conduct; revision of the intent requirement; revision of the scope of fear requirement (from a narrow definition of a threat of *death or great bodily harm* to a threat intended to place the victim in reasonable fear for his/her *safety* or the safety of a family member); notification of victims prior to stalkers' release; provisions enabling prosecution of those stalkers who threaten victims from jail or prison; requirement that stalkers register as sex offenders; and requirement that stalkers participate in counseling as a condition of probation.

Are stalking laws an infringement of the constitutional right to travel and freedom of speech? See, e.g., State v. Elliott, 987 A.2d 513 (Me. 2010) (right to travel); State v. Holbach, 763 N.W.2d 761 (N.D. 2009) (same); Crop v. Crop, 188 P.3d 364 (Or. Ct. App. 2008) (freedom of expression). Are stalking laws vague and overbroad? See, e.g., People v. Richardson, 181 P.3d 340 (Colo. Ct. App. 2007); Bouters v. State, 659 So. 2d 235 (Fla. 1995). Do stalking laws violate the Double Jeopardy Clause, for example if the defendant is convicted of assault as well as stalking? See, e.g., State v. Johnson, 676 So. 2d 408 (Fla. 1996). Mr. Weiner contends that he has a constitutional right to live where he wishes. How does the court respond?

b. *Federal interstate stalking law.* Federal legislation also addresses stalking. Congress enacted the Interstate Stalking Punishment and Prevention Act (Pub. L. No. 104-201, 110 Stat. 2655) in 1996 and subsequently amended it, as part of the Violence Against Women Act (VAWA) (codified as amended at 18 U.S.C. §2261A) in 2000 and 2006. The Act prohibits travel across state lines to stalk, makes restraining orders that are issued in one state valid in other states, and prohibits stalking on federal property (for example, post offices, national parks, military bases). The stalker must have the intent to kill, injure, harass, or intimidate the victim; and, in addition, the victim must be placed in reasonable fear of death or serious bodily injury. Victims' family members, spouses, or intimate partners are also protected. The penalty for violation ranges from 5 to 20 years imprisonment for violations that result in injury or acts stemming from use of a dangerous weapon, and life imprisonment if stalking results in the victim's death. The federal interstate stalking law is explored further in Chapter 8.

10. *Effectiveness.* Are stalking laws an effective deterrent? Are protective orders effective against stalkers or are they merely likely to incite further harassment? What other remedies might deter stalkers? For example, should stalking be characterized as a felony, even as a first offense? Should victims be able to seek civil damages from their abusers? Should stalkers be referred to counseling? Required to register as sex offenders? Required to submit to an electronic tracking device, with the cost of the device and monitoring to be paid by the defendant? Should they be subject to higher bail and/or pretrial detention?

11. *Cyberstalking.* A large percentage of stalking victims experience cyberharassment (that is, stalking by means of electronic communications devices such as the Internet, email, instant messaging, texting). Baum, supra, at 5 (reporting that 25 percent of victims experience cyberstalking). Prior to the growth of the Internet, abusers who wanted to track a partner were limited to the use of car odometers to measure mileage and monitor activities. See also T.R. v. F.R., 2011 WL 242030 (N.J. Super. Ct. App. Div. 2011) (finding harassment, for purposes of protective order, where husband monitored wife's mileage constantly). Now, however, stalkers are able to install monitoring software and/or hardware in computers to harass and locate victims. Other stalkers use online databases (for example, email, chat rooms, bulletin boards, or instant messages), or create websites to threaten victims. Some abusers use Global Positioning Systems (GPS) to follow their victim's movements. Stalkers can remotely activate the pre-installed GPS on phones and also attach GPS trackers to cars. See generally Cindy Southworth & Sarah Tucker, Technology, Stalking and Domestic Violence Victims, 76 Miss. L.J. 667 (2007).

a. *Types of cyberstalking.* Two types of cyberstalking exist: cyberstalking that occurs only in the "virtual world" in which the stalker never makes physical or visual contact with the victim, and cyberstalking that occurs both on-line and off-line. The latter stalker is generally more dangerous. Symposium, A Survey of Cyberstalking Legislation, 32 UWLA L. Rev. 323, 325 (2001).

b. *Similarities and differences.* What are the similarities between off-line and on-line stalking? Women are more likely to be victimized in both cases. Stalkers have similar motivations (to exert control), and also manifest a similar "course of conduct" (that is, repetitive harassing or threatening acts to induce fear) in both cases. Goodno, supra, at 128-132. On the other hand, cyberstalkers can harass victims instantly, inexpensively, and widely; they victimize persons from an unknown locale; they remain anonymous; they can easily impersonate the victim; they can encourage third-party harassment of the victim. Id. Do these differences call for different legal treatment of cyberstalking and off-line stalking?

c. *Psychological effect.* Cyberstalking engenders a sense of terror. "[Uncertainty as to the presence of the stalker] can cause a greater sense of panic among victims who are left to wonder if the cyberstalker is in another state, down the block, or in the next cubicle at work. Victims seldom know if the cyberstalker is a former lover, a total stranger met in a chat room, or simply a random prank from a twisted mind." Harry A. Valetk, Mastering the Dark Arts of Cyberspace: A Quest for Sound Internet Safety Policies, 2004 Stan. Tech. L. Rev. 2, 55 (2004).

12. *State cyberstalking laws.* Stalking laws originally were not sufficiently broad to cover cyberstalking. Almost all states now include electronic forms of communication within their stalking or harassment laws. Nat'l Conf. of State Legislatures, State Cyberstalking, Cyber Harassment and Cyberbullying Laws (2011), available at http://www.ncsl.org/default.aspx?tabid=13495. In addition, first-generation stalking statutes required that the stalker place tracking devices "on property owned or occupied" by the victim, or required the stalker's "physical presence." Many second-generation statutes, however, merely prohibit placing another person "under surveillance" or "recording a person's whereabouts." Laura Silverstein, The Double Edged Sword: An Examination of the Global Positioning System, Enhanced 911, and the Internet and Their Relationship to the Lives of Domestic Violence Victims and Their Abusers, 13 Buff. Women's L.J. 97, 106-107 (2005).

Critics point out that some cyberstalking laws do not cover electronic harassment that stops short of a threat to bodily harm. Kimberly Wingteung Seto, Note, How Should Legislation Deal with Children as the Victims and Perpetrators of Cyberstalking?, 9 Cardozo Women's L.J. 67, 85 (2002). Other critics note that many police departments lack proper training and resources to address cyberstalking. "As a result, a police officer might suggest that a victim contact their Internet Service Provider (ISP) for technical assistance or 'shut off' their computers." Valetk, supra, at 57. Are these effective strategies for victims of cyberstalking? Should GPS devices be regulated, like firearms, to require purchasers to submit to a screening process that would deny access to anyone with a history of domestic violence or subject to an order of protection for domestic violence? Silverstein, supra, at 109 (so suggesting). What do you think of this proposal?

13. *Federal cyberstalking laws.* Four federal laws address cyberstalking. First, the Interstate Communications Act, 18 USC §875, makes it a crime to transmit in interstate commerce any communication (for example, by telephone, email, or other means) containing a specific threat of harm. Second, the Telephone Harassment Act, as amended by the 2000 Violence Against Women Act (VAWA), 47 U.S.C. §223 & 223(a)(1)(C), makes it a crime anonymously and knowingly to use a telephone or the Internet to transmit in interstate or foreign commerce any message "to annoy, abuse, harass, or threaten a person." A major limitation of this law is that it applies only to direct communications (such as phone or email) by the stalker to the victim and does not apply, for example, to messages that are posted or that encourage third-party harassment.

Third, Congress amended the aforementioned Interstate Stalking Punishment and Prevention Act, 18 U.S.C. §2261A (amended by Violence Against Women and Department of Justice Reauthorization Act of 2005, Pub. L. No. 109-162, 119 Stat. 2960, 2987-2988 (2006)), to punish those who, "with the intent to kill, injure, [or] harass," use the "mail, any interactive computer service, or any facility of interstate or foreign commerce to engage in a course of conduct that causes substantial emotional distress [or] reasonable fear of the death of, or serious bodily injury" to another person. The pending VAWA Reauthorization Act would amend 18 U.S.C. §2261A by broadening the above definition to "any interactive computer service or electronic communication service or electric communication system of interstate commerce" and expanding the prohibited acts to include "causes or attempts to cause or would be reasonably expected to cause substantial emotional distress to any person."

Finally, the Prosecutorial Remedies and Other Tools to End the Exploitation of Children Today Act (PROTECT Act), 18 USC §2425, makes it a federal crime for anyone to transmit information about a minor (such as the minor's name, address, telephone number, social security number, or email address) by means of interstate or foreign commerce (such as a telephone line or the Internet) with the intent to entice, encourage, offer, or solicit the minor into unlawful sexual activity.

Problems

1. After Joy separates from Thomas after an 11-year marriage, Thomas begins harassing her. He telephones many of her friends to tell them disparaging stories about her, he goes to her job to watch her, he rummages through her dresser drawers and garbage and confiscates various papers, he makes frequent hang-up calls, and he screams obscenities at her in the presence of their son. One night he telephones her and describes what she is wearing (leading her to believe that he is watching her). Another night, he taps on her window (a method of communication they had occasionally used in the past but never so late). Thomas's behavior frightens Joy badly. Her fear is enhanced by an episode nine years earlier in which Thomas had shared his obsession with her about his fantasy of killing his former employer. Joy also is worried that, because Thomas resides with his brother who is a police officer, Thomas has access to weapons. Joy seeks a restraining order. In response, Thomas alleges that he had never committed any actual or overt threat of physical violence to Joy and that his actions amount merely to "unwanted contact." He adds that he never owned a firearm. He alleges also that the incident regarding his employer was too remote in time to be relevant to the issuance of a present restraining order.

The state Family Abuse Prevention Act provides that a court may issue a restraining order on a showing that the petitioner "has been the victim of abuse committed by the respondent within 180 days preceding the filing of the petition and that there is an immediate and present danger of further abuse to the petitioner." "Abuse" is defined as the occurrence of one or more of the following acts between family or household members: (a) attempting to cause or intentionally, knowingly, or recklessly causing bodily injury; (b) intentionally, knowingly, or recklessly placing another in fear of imminent serious bodily injury; or (c) causing another to engage in involuntary sexual relations by force or threat of force. Should the judge issue the restraining order? See Lefebvre v. Lefebvre, 996 P.2d 518 (Or. Ct. App. 2000).

2. Cynthia obtains a protective order against her husband Daniel. That order prohibits him, for a six-month period, from committing, or threatening to commit, acts of domestic violence, stalking, or harassment against her and her children. The order also prohibits him from being in the "physical presence of, telephoning, contacting, or otherwise communicating directly or indirectly" withCynthia or her children. On the day after the issuance of the protective order, Cynthia sees Daniel

at the local mall. She alleges that he was staring at her in the houseware department and that later that day she saw him outside the mall pet store. Daniel admits that he was at the mall on the day in question, but denies having seen Cynthia. Two months later, Cynthia claims that Daniel slowly drove past her and her son as they came out of a barber shop and that he made eye contact with her. She also asserts that shortly thereafter, Daniel saw her while she was driving; he then slowed down his car and "paced" behind her car for about 50 feet.

Three months later, Cynthia, who is a lawyer, attends the morning session of the Alaska Bar Association Annual Convention. Cynthia notices that Daniel, who is also a lawyer, is also attending the session. Cynthia calls the police and has him arrested for violating the protective order. Daniel contends that he had the right to be at the mall and outside the barber shop. He also argues that his attendance at the bar convention was justified. He maintains that he did not violate the protective order because he never attempted to communicate with Cynthia.

According to the statute, stalking may constitute the independent crime of violating a protective order. A person commits stalking "if the person knowingly engages in a course of conduct that recklessly places another person in fear of death or physical injury." To be a "course of conduct" there must be "repeated acts of nonconsensual contact." Nonconsensual contact specifically includes "following or appearing within the sight of a person." Further, the violation of a protective order requires that the court finds that respondent has committed a crime involving domestic violence against the petitioner. Crimes involving domestic violence include stalking. Cynthia argues that the definition of "contact" that applies to the stalking statute (that is, "following or appearing within the sight of a person") should apply to the "contacting" prohibition in the previous protective order. Daniel argues that the term *contact*, as used in the violation-of-a-protective-order statute requires physical touching or communicating. Did Daniel violate the restraining order? See Cooper v. Cooper, 144 P.3d 451 (Alaska 2006).

Long Term Case of Stalking

Cameron Wallace was a 15-year-old high school sophomore when she found herself seated next to Ryan Clutter in art class. They never became friends, but over the next 11 years, he seemed to be present everywhere. "[H]e appeared at her house or at the mall, sat behind her at the movies, sent demands by email and threatened her life. He described how he would kill her."

At first, Cameron just found Ryan's actions creepy. But years later, after she married, when the threats to her and her husband continued, she decided to obtain a protective order. Even the restraining order did not stop Ryan from stalking. "Three years later, he broke into her house and then, by e-mail, sent her a photograph he had taken of her sleeping. When the police searched his apartment, they found a kind of shrine to [her], with stolen articles of her clothing." They also found a handgun and a computer containing threatening email messages and child pornography. Ryan was convicted of stalking and sentenced to 13 years in prison. Elizabeth Olson, Though Many Are Stalked, Few Report It, Study Finds, N.Y. Times, Feb. 15, 2009, at A22, A23.

3. Cyber Harassment

■ **IN RE MARRIAGE OF NADKARNI**
   93 Cal. Rptr.3d 723 (Ct. App. 2009)

BAMATTRE-MANOUKIAN, Acting P.J.

. . . During their long-term marriage, Darshana [Wife] and Datta [Husband] had a son and a daughter. Darshana filed a petition for marital dissolution on June 21, 2002. [T]heir divorce was final in May 2005 and a child custody order awarding joint legal and physical custody of the children was entered on May 2, 2006. [The couple continued to fight over child custody and child support. On August 31, 2007, the husband filed a supplemental declaration to a custody motion] in which he accused Darshana of "gross negligence" in leaving their children, aged 14 and 16, alone while she was in India during March and April of 2007 without informing him of her absence or providing him with contact information.

Datta attached to his August 31, 2007, supplemental declaration copies of several emails between Darshana and third persons, including her family law attorney and the children, that were sent in March and April of 2007. Datta stated in his supplemental declaration that he "had no choice" but to access Darshana's emails because his "kids' safety was at stake." He further stated that "in sheer panic and desperation I tried to access the email accounts which I had myself set up for [Darshana] and my son several years ago, to see if I had missed any emails from her regarding her international travel plans."

According to Datta, the emails showed that when Darshana was contacted by Child Protective Services (which had begun an investigation of the children's welfare at Datta's request), she falsely stated that she had arranged for her brother to look after the children in her absence. Datta also asserted in his supplemental declaration that the emails showed that Darshana had instructed the children to lie to him regarding her whereabouts. Additionally, Datta claimed that he had "procured more evidence from the above-mentioned email accounts, which could be considered inflammatory and sensitive to certain others. I have no intention to share these emails other than as evidence in future legal proceedings."

On October 17, 2007, Darshana filed [a request] for a temporary restraining order under the Domestic Violence Prevention Act (DVPA), Fam. Code §6200 et seq. [Her supporting declaration stated] that she became aware in August 2007 that Datta had accessed her email account when he attached copies of her email messages to documents that he filed in their child custody matter. She asserted that she had created the email account after the parties separated and she had never authorized Datta or any third party to use the account or given them the password. According to Darshana, she used the email account for several confidential matters, including communicating with her family law attorney, communicating with her clients in her executive search and employment counseling business, storing her financial records, storing her mother's financial and medical records, communicating with third parties regarding her mother's finances, and communicating with third parties regarding potential job candidates.

[She] further asserted in her October 17, 2007, declaration that "I am also quite disturbed by [Datta's statement in his August 31, 2007, supplemental declaration] that 'I have procured more evidence from the above-mentioned email accounts, which could be considered inflammatory and sensitive to certain others. I have no intention to share these emails other than as evidence in future legal proceedings.' Given that the information was in my email account, I believe this statement is a direct threat that unless I succumb to his demands in the family law case, he will interfere and directly impact my business relationships. I also believe he will file my personal emails in the family court action in order to embarrass me, and to injure my relationships with my family members and third parties, including professional clients."

Additionally, Darshana claimed that Datta had used the information obtained from her email account to subpoena the records of third parties, including her business contacts, and to find out what social events she would be attending. She stated that Datta "has told others that he knew which social events I would be attending within the past three months. I was unable to determine . . . how [he] became aware of my schedule until learning of his access to my email account. His knowledge of my attendance at these activities has caused me fear for my safety based on his prior treatment of me during our marriage. [Datta] repeatedly abused me physically during our marriage. The most recent incident was in November, 1999, when he beat me viciously and repeatedly in front of our children. He was convicted and sentenced to 20 days in jail" [for misdemeanor spouse abuse pursuant to Cal. Penal Code §273.5].

Based on these allegations, Darshana requested an ex parte temporary restraining order that, with respect to the emails, barred Datta from "(1) engag[ing] in any behavior that has been or could be enjoined such as blackmail, slander, stalking, threatening, harassing, and disturbing the peace of [Darshana] or third parties through the use of personal information accessed through [Darshana's email]"; (2) "using, delivering, distributing, printing, copying, or disclosing the message or content of [Darshana's] email account to others"; and (3) attempting to access or "otherwise interfere with [her] internet service provider accounts." . . .

[The trial court issued a temporary restraining order that restricted the husband's conduct as requested and set a date for a hearing on the permanent restraining order.] Darshana sought a permanent restraining order for a 10-year period, an order sealing her email messages that Datta had filed in court, and an award of attorney fees and monetary sanctions. The trial court dismissed her application for a restraining order, contending that the husband's conduct did not rise to the requisite level under the DVPA.]

We will begin our evaluation of Darshana's claims of trial court error with an overview of the DVPA (§6200 et seq.). . . . To be facially sufficient under the DVPA, an application for a restraining order must allege abuse within the meaning of the DVPA. . . .

[S]ection 6320 provides that "the requisite abuse need not be actual infliction of physical injury or assault." To the contrary, section 6320 lists several types of nonviolent conduct that may constitute abuse within the meaning of the DVPA, including two types of conduct relevant to the present case. First, section 6320 provides that contacting the other party "either directly or indirectly, by mail or otherwise" may constitute abuse. . . . Datta's alleged conduct of viewing Darshana's private email, learning her social schedule, and communicating this information to third persons who then told Darshana that Datta was aware of her schedule, could constitute indirect and threatening contact with Darshana, and thus abuse within the meaning of section 6320.

Second, section 6320 broadly provides that "disturbing the peace of the other party" constitutes abuse for purposes of the DVPA. The DVPA does not provide any definition for the phrase "disturbing the peace of the other party," and we therefore turn to the rules of statutory construction to determine the meaning of the phrase and whether Datta's conduct, as alleged by Darshana in her declaration, may constitute abuse within the meaning of the DVPA.

. . . The ordinary meaning of "disturb" is "[t]o agitate and destroy (quiet, peace, rest); to break up the quiet, tranquility, or rest (of a person, a country, etc.); to stir up, trouble, disquiet." (Oxford English Dictionary Online (2d ed.1989) <http:// www. oed. com> [as of Apr. 24, 2009].) "Peace," as a condition of the individual, is ordinarily defined as "freedom from anxiety, disturbance (emotional, mental or spiritual), or inner conflict; calm, tranquility." (Ibid.) Thus, the plain meaning of the phrase "disturbing the peace of the other party" in section 6320 may be properly understood as conduct that destroys the mental or emotional calm of the other party.

Our interpretation of the phrase "disturbing the peace of the other party" in section 6320 also comports with the legislative history of the DVPA. . . . [A]s originally enacted, the DVPA reflected the Legislature's goal of reducing domestic violence and its recognition that "[i]t is virtually impossible for a statute to anticipate every circumstance or need of the persons whom it may be intended to protect. Therefore, the courts must be entrusted with authority to issue necessary orders suited to individual circumstances, with adequate assurances that both sides of the dispute will have an opportunity to be heard before the court."

Accordingly, we believe that the Legislature intended that the DVPA be broadly construed in order to accomplish the purpose of the DVPA. Therefore, the plain meaning of the phrase "disturbing the peace" in section 6320 may include, as abuse within the meaning of the DVPA, a former husband's alleged conduct in destroying the mental or emotional calm of his former wife by accessing, reading and publicly disclosing her confidential emails. . . . Since "disturbing the peace" of the party is a form of abuse within the meaning of the DVPA, we find that Darshana's application and supporting declaration are facially sufficient for a showing of abuse under the DVPA and require a hearing on the merits. Therefore, we will reverse the trial court's [order] dismissing the application [to extend the restraining order]. . . .

Notes and Questions

1. *Definition.* Cyber harassment and cyberstalking are different forms of cyber abuse (that is, intimate partner violence by electronic means). Cyber harassment is the use of a broad range of electronic technology to harass victims, such as by accessing their private email accounts, social networking accounts, and cell phones logs. Sean Kane, Rise in Domestic Violence as Men Turn to Technology, Daily Mail (UK), June 24, 2010, available at 2010 WLNR 12744311. Concerns about a partner's electronic surveillance prevent many women from seeking help, stemming from their fear that a partner will take note of a call to a hotline, a search of a domestic violence website, or an email or text message about the abuse. Id.

What acts of cyber harassment did the husband commit in *Nadkarni?* What acts of cyberstalking did he commit?

2. *Direct versus indirect harassment.* Cyber harassment can be direct (that is, by means of communications with the victim) as well as indirect (that is, by means of communications with third parties). The latter involves instrumental use of third parties to harass the partner or damage her reputation. In what way did the husband in *Nadkarni* engage in *direct* acts of cyber harassment? *Indirect* acts?

Other examples of *indirect* acts of cyber harassment by intimate partners include the following: (1) a man who seeks revenge against a former girlfriend by assuming her identity at an online dating service and contacting 70 men to invite them for a date at the woman's home; (2) a man sends threatening messages to himself from his ex-wife's email account, and then requests that the police arrest her for threatening him; and (3) an abuser sets up a website to encourage other men to contact the victim by telling them that his former partner enjoys being raped. See Cindy Southworth & Sarah Tucker, Technology, Stalking and Domestic Violence Victims, 76 Miss. L.J. 667, 669-670 (2007) (citing these examples). See also Silverstein, Double Edged Sword, supra, at 107 (citing the example of a man who engages the police to harass his wife by forwarding all her cell phone calls to 911 and rewiring her home security system so that her alarm calls the police at random intervals).

3. *Law reform.* Virtually all states have laws prohibiting harassment through the Internet, email, or other electronic means. Valetk, supra, at 71. However, these laws vary significantly. Some states make cyber harassment part of their general stalking or harassment laws. Other states incorporate new provisions in their computer crime legislation. Id.

Some laws prohibit the creation of a web page on a social networking site in another person's name without permission, and also the transmission of an electronic communication (that is, email, instant message, text) in another person's name without permission and with intent to harm or defraud someone. See, e.g., Tex. Penal Code Ann. §33.07; David Hector Montes, Note, Living Our Lives Online: The Privacy Implications of Social Networking, 5 J.L. & Pol'y for Info. Soc'y 507, 520 (2010) (citing examples).

4. *First Amendment defense.* Are state cyber harassment laws unconstitutional? Might Mr. Nadkarni defend against the imposition of a temporary restraining order under the state Domestic Violence Prevention Act by claiming that his harassment was protected by the First Amendment? Was his conduct "speech"? Evaluation of the constitutionality of any such governmental restriction would call for strict scrutiny review and require that the conduct constitute a designated exception. Did the husband's actions constitute criminal threats, hate speech, or "fighting words"? See generally Merritt Baer, Cyberstalking and the Internet Landscape We Have Constructed, 15 Va. J.L. & Tech 153 (2010) (discussing First Amendment rationales).

5. *Tort liability.* A civil action for damages is another possible avenue of redress for a victim of cyber harassment. Such actions might encompass claims for intentional infliction of emotional distress. Can a victim maintain a suit against Internet service providers (ISPs)? See Communications Decency Act of 1996, 47 U.S.C. §230(c)(1) (providing broad immunity for ISPs for any content on their sites, thereby precluding civil as well as criminal liability).

6. *Teenage cyberbullying distinguished.* State legislatures were motivated to enact cyber harassment laws in response to media attention to a teen victim who responded to cyberbullying by committing suicide. In 2006, Megan Meier, a 13-year-old girl,

hanged herself after a former friend's mother created a fake Myspace profile of a teenage boy who later cruelly rejected Megan. The mother escaped criminal liability because existing laws were inadequate. See United States v. Lori Drew, 259 F.R.D. 449 (C.D. Cal. 2009). See also Montes, supra, at 513-519.

7. *Teen dating violence and cyber harassment.* Cyber harassment is a prominent feature of teen dating violence. Teenagers engage in frequent daily use of cell phones, email, social networking sites, and personal computers. Not surprisingly, abusers access this same technology to harass and monitor their partners' activities and communications. See Teen Dating Violence Technical Assistance Center, Technology and Teen Dating Violence 2-3 (2008) (reporting that one in three teenagers say "they are text messaged up to 30 times an hour by a partner or ex-partner inquiring where they are, what they are doing, or who they are with"), available at http://www.vaw.umn.edu/documents/technologytdv/technologytdv.pdf. How can teenagers protect themselves from cyber harassment? How can schools address this problem?

8. *Proposed federal legislation.* Congress considered legislation to address cyber harassment, but the bill never became law. The Megan Meier Cyberbullying Prevention Act, H.R. 1966, 111th Cong. §3 (2009), would have amended the federal criminal code to impose criminal penalties on any person who transmits in interstate or foreign commerce a communication intended to coerce, intimidate, harass, or cause substantial emotional distress to another person, using electronic means to support severe, repeated, and hostile behavior. The proposal called for a penalty of up to two years imprisonment. What are the benefits and shortcomings of the bill as a remedy to address intimate partner cyber harassment?

4. Financial Abuse

■ JACKSON v. UNITED STATES
819 A.2d 963 (D.C. 2003)

WASHINGTON, Associate J.

The questions presented in this case are: (1) whether a co-owner of property can be found guilty of malicious destruction of that property and (2) if yes, whether there was sufficient evidence presented in this case to find appellant guilty of destruction of property. . . .

Appellant, Ronald Jackson, became a co-owner of a house located in Washington, D.C., when his wife, Mrs. Jackson, added his name to the deed of her house. Subsequently, in January 1998, the couple became estranged and appellant moved out. However, Mrs. Jackson continued to live in the house. On June 13, 1998, Mr. Jackson called his wife and stated he wanted to stop by the house to pick up a pair of sunglasses he had left. Although Mrs. Jackson informed appellant that he could not retrieve the sunglasses at that time, appellant nevertheless came to the house. Upon seeing him, Mrs. Jackson went inside and locked the door. However, appellant gained entry into the house by applying force to the locked door. [Upon entering, he threatened to burn the house down and was later charged with threats to do bodily harm, pursuant to D.C. Code §22-407 (2001).]

After a bench trial, appellant was found guilty of malicious destruction of property, D.C. Code §22-303 (2002), for damaging the front door of the house that appellant and Mrs. Jackson co-owned. The statute makes it a crime to "maliciously injure or break or destroy or attempt to injure or break or destroy, by fire or otherwise, any public or private property, whether real or personal, not his or her own." . . . Appellant appeals his conviction because he interprets the phrase "not his or her own" as precluding the prosecution of anyone with any ownership rights, either full or partial, in the damaged property. . . .

The parties contend, and we agree, that the phrase "not his or her own" is ambiguous because it could either refer to property that is fully owned by an individual or property that is at least partially owned. Thus, we must look beyond the plain language of the statute to determine whether the legislature intended for the statute to apply to individuals who have an ownership interest in the damaged property. . . . Unfortunately, the legislative history of the Act provides no assistance in interpreting the language "not his or her own." Given the ambiguity of the language and the lack of any helpful legislative history, we have looked to other jurisdictions with similar statutes to determine whether their interpretations provide any guidance on how to interpret the phrase not his or her own. [The survey reveals that a significant number of states permit prosecution of joint owners of property for destruction of jointly owned property.] . . .

This issue has particular relevance in domestic violence situations, where spouses co-own property. When a family has domestic violence problems, one manifestation of the violence is often destruction of co-owned property. Others also acknowledge the connection between domestic violence and criminal liability for destruction of co-owned property. The Domestic Violence Unit Chief in San Diego, California stated: "the single biggest advance in domestic violence intervention in this jurisdiction occurred when California's vandalism laws were interpreted to apply to a batterer's destruction of community property." Victoria L. Lutz & Cara A. Bonomolo, My Husband Just Trashed Our Home; What Do You Mean That's Not a Crime?, 48 S.C. L. Rev. 641, 654 (1997). . . . The court in People v. Kheyfets, 665 N.Y.S.2d 802, 805 (Sup. Ct. 1997), stated that holding individuals liable for destruction of property they own jointly with another "would be in tune with the spirit of the recent Federal and State domestic violence legislation." Id. at 806. These considerations are not insubstantial given the number of legislature initiatives that have been passed to address issues of domestic violence in the District of Columbia. Our conclusion, that D.C. Code §22-303 applies to individuals who destroy jointly owned property, is certainly consistent with the intent of those legislative initiatives. . . . Mrs. Jackson's testimony provided sufficient evidence for the trial court to find appellant guilty of malicious destruction.

Notes and Questions

1. *Multidimensional nature of abuse.* Financial abuse is a common form of intimate partner violence. See Walter S. DeKeseredy, Nat'l Inst. of Justice, Sexual Assault During and After Separation/Divorce: An Exploratory Study 46 (2007) (reporting that 70 percent of battered women had experienced financial abuse). What forms of abuse did Mrs. Jackson suffer?

2. *Property destruction.* Property damage is inflicted as a form of abuse, an act of retaliation, or an act of psychological abuse (for example, the destruction of a prized

possession) intended to cause emotional anguish. If the property is jointly owned, the legal issue concerns whether the offender can be prosecuted for damaging property that is partly "his" property. How does the *Jackson* court resolve this question? What is the rationale? See also People v. Sullivan, 53 P.3d 1181 (Colo. Ct. App. 2002) (rejecting husband's defense, based on his joint ownership interest, for burning his wife's clothes). See generally John M. Leventhal, Spousal Rights or Spousal Crimes: Where and When Are the Lines to Be Drawn?, 2006 Utah L. Rev. 351, 364 (2006); Victoria L. Lutz & Cara M. Bonomolo, My Husband Just Trashed Our Home; What Do You Mean That's Not a Crime?, 48 S.C. L. Rev. 641 (1997).

3. *Types of financial abuse.* Financial abuse involves a broad range of conduct, including:

a. *Forgery, fraud, theft.* Some abusers forge a partner's signature on legal documents. DeKeseredy, supra, at 46. Some abuse involves outright theft. See, e.g., People v. Wallin, 167 P.3d 183, 186 (Colo. Ct. App. 2007) (abuser stole $60 from victim's purse during an assault); State v. Nam, 150 P.3d 617, 619 (Wash. Ct. App. 2007) (during an assault, defendant stole ex-girlfriend's purse containing her money, credit cards, and phone). Often, abusers damage the victim's car. See, e.g., People v. Lo Kuan Saechao, 2008 WL 344231 (Cal. Ct. App. 2008).

b. *Credit.* Some abusers ruin the victim's credit. They may appropriate the victim's credit cards and run up large debts, or destroy her credit rating by paying bills late or failing to pay them. See, e.g., People v. Henry, 2004 WL 2538138, at 3 (Cal. Ct. App. 2004) (describing characteristics of abusers); Meade v. Chambliss, 2010 WL 1814963 (Ky. Ct. App. 2010) (woman entered partner's apartment when he was absent, accessed his email, and took his credit card numbers). See generally D. R. Follingstad et al., The Role of Emotional Abuse in Physically Abusive Relationships, 5 J. Fam. Violence 107 (1990).

4. *Abusers' isolating techniques.* Financial abuse is sometimes used to increase the victim's dependence. Financial abuse can preclude partners' ability to take part in social activities, thereby isolating the victim from other persons. Kara Bellew, Note, Silent Suffering: Uncovering and Understanding Domestic Violence in Affluent Communities, 26 Women's Rts. L. Rep. 39, 42 (2005) (explaining characteristics of financial abuse among affluent victims). Financial abuse also creates an obstacle to exit from the relationship.

5. *Bankruptcy.* Congress recently amended the federal bankruptcy code to offer protection for victims of intimate partner violence. A person who files for bankruptcy (the "debtor") must report necessary household expenses, such as the cost of basic needs like food and shelter, because the debtor is required to pay all disposable monthly income—minus necessary monthly expenses—toward settling the debtor's debts. The Code now permits a victim to exempt (as "necessary" expenses) those expenses that are "incurred to maintain the safety of the debtor and the family of the debtor from family violence." 11 U.S.C. §707(b)(2)(A)(ii)(I). Such expenses might include the costs associated with obtaining an order of protection or a subscription to a security service to protect personal safety. See Eugene R. Wedoff, Means Testing in the New §707(b), 79 Am. Bankr. L.J. 231, 265 (2005) (explaining provisions).

Federal bankruptcy law also provides protection to a victim if the abuser files for bankruptcy. When debtors file for bankruptcy, they are protected by an "automatic stay" of any other legal action against them until the bankruptcy is final. However, the bankruptcy code exempts from the "automatic stay" any civil suit against the debtor that involves domestic violence. 11 U.S.C. §362(b)(2)(A)(v). In addition, bankruptcy courts are becoming more sensitive to the interrelationship between bankruptcy and domestic violence. See, e.g., In re Minton, 402 B.R. 380 (Bankr. M.D. Fla. 2008) (finding that victim-debtor did not abandon her home, in order to claim a homestead exemption, when she fled from domestic violence); In re Young, 346 B.R. 597 (Bankr. E.D.N.Y. 2006) (allowing discharge to a victim of abuse in a bankruptcy proceeding even though she could not produce requisite paperwork as a result of her physical and financial abuse).

Financial Abuse: Tax Implications

Mona Lisa Herrington, the owner of an H&R Block franchise, lives with her partner, John, who has an extensive criminal record and a violent temper. Once, John threw Mona from a moving car. Another time, he hit her in the head with a beer bottle and threw her from a boat into a lake. When she threatened to leave, he gave her a picture of her daughter with her face shot out, saying that that would happen to her if she left him.

John opens a video poker business. When he loses his license for selling liquor to a minor, he convinces Mona to open two new video poker businesses. He sets his own compensation by writing checks to himself and taking cash. Over a two-year period, he withdraws over $200,000 that he uses to pay personal expenses, including his child support obligation from a previous relationship. Mona knows that John is taking money from her business accounts, although she does not know the amounts. John falsely tells Mona that he has filed federal tax returns for the businesses for two years. After this omission comes to light, Mona pleads guilty to willful failure to file tax returns. When she eventually files the late returns, she claims, as deductible business expenses, the losses attributable to John's withdrawals. She argues that these amounts are deductible either as compensation for personal services rendered by her partner to the business or as thefts.

The tax court disagrees that the payments are reasonable compensation for John's personal services. However, the court concludes that the $200,000 constitutes theft within the meaning of state law and that Mona is entitled to deduct them as business-related theft losses. The court reasons that Mona was unaware of these payments and did not consent to them. The court explains:

> [E]ven if petitioner might be thought in some general way to have consented to the boyfriend's compensating himself with her business funds, we do not believe that it was effective consent, but rather that it was induced by force and threats by the boyfriend, who had on more than one occasion threatened to kill petitioner and her children. For similar reasons, we assign little significance to the fact that she did not report the thefts to the authorities.

Herrington v. Comm'r, 101 T.C.M. (CCH) 1336 (2011).

5. *Pet Abuse*

■ CAT KILLER DENIED PAROLE

Russell Swigart has a long history of stalking women. He also has a long history of torturing and killing their pets. In 1997 he was convicted of a series of attacks on a girlfriend. When she left him, he went to her apartment, placed her cat in a shoebox, taped it shut, and killed the cat by blasting the box with a shotgun. He then forced the girlfriend to look at her dead cat and threatened to do the same to her. Another former girlfriend says that after their relationship ended, he broke into her house and nearly tortured her dog to death.

Ten years later, Swigart was working at a medical equipment company when he hired Bridgett Wright as a sales representative. They dated a few times. When the relationship ended, Swigart started sending her threatening text messages. One day, armed with an 11-inch Buck Knife, Swigart broke into her condo. When he saw that she wasn't home, he took out his rage on her cats. He then texted her: "*You should get home and clean up the mess. Piggy & Frank have seen better days. I just stabbed your cats to death. Piggy put up a good fight, but Frank went out like a b****" Bridget called the police who found the dead cats. "Bridgett Wright is likely alive today only because she took a last minute, out-of-town business trip," commented former Kenton County Assistant Commonwealth Attorney Justin Sanders.

Swigart pleaded guilty to two counts of animal torture and one count of second-degree burglary. He is thought to be the first person prosecuted under a Kentucky law that makes it a felony to kill a domesticated animal. When Swigart came up for parole after serving two years of his 12-year sentence, the Parole Board denied his request based on 15,000 signatures gathered by Wright. Attorney Sanders had urged the parole board to order Swigart to serve out his entire sentence. "It is imperative that Kentucky's citizens feel free and safe to end bad relationships . . . without fear of revenge or retribution." . . . Swigart "has left a trail of emotionally devastated and frightened women in his wake," Sanders concluded. See Cat Killer Up for Parole, Cincinnati (Ohio) Enquirer, Jan. 26, 2011, available at 2011 WLNR 1585503; Kentucky "Cat Killer" Russell Swigart's Parole Denied, available at http: sites.google.com/site/mrfrankpiggy (last visited Nov. 13, 2011).

Notes and Questions

1. *Social reality.* Pet abuse is a common form of intimate partner violence. More than half of victims report violence toward their animals. Am. Humane Assoc., Facts about Animal Abuse and Domestic Violence 1, http://www.americanhumane.org/about-us/newsroom/fact-sheets/animal-abuse-domestic-violence.html (last visited June 29, 2011). See also Melissa Trollinger, The Link among Animal Abuse, Child Abuse, and Domestic Violence 30 Colo. Law. (Sept. 2001), at 29, 30 nn.12, 13 (citing research findings, based on study of the largest battered women's shelters in 48 states, that 85.4 percent of the shelters report adult residents' acknowledgment of incidents of pet abuse).

Moreover, many victims delay leaving because they fear the abuser's retaliatory violence to pets or livestock. Id. (reporting that 25 to 40 percent of women delay leaving for this reason). See also Catherine A. Faver & Elizabeth B. Strand, To Leave or To Stay? Battered Women's Concern for Vulnerable Pets, 18 J. Interpersonal Violence 1367 (2003).

Pet abuse includes threats of harm as well as actual harm to animals. See Miranda Sherley, Why Doctors Should Care About Animal Cruelty, 36 Australian Fam. Physician 61, 62 (2007) (reporting that 46 percent of battered women report threats of pet abuse, 53 percent report harm to pets, and 17.3 percent report that the abuser killed their pets). See also Celinkski v. State, 911 S.W.2d 177 (Tex. App. 1995) (affirming conviction for poisoning cats with acetaminophen and torturing them by placing them in the microwave oven).

2. *Abusers' motivations.* Abusers threaten to harm or commit harm to a family pet for the purpose of terrorizing, retaliating against, or controlling family members. Abusers are aware how strongly attached their partners are to their animals. Harming pets is "the dynamic of preying on the love and affection that women often have for the animals in their lives, which may be their only source of solace, their only source of unconditional love." Pam Belluck, New Maine Law Shields Animals in Domestic Violence Cases (April 1, 2006), available at http://www.nytimes.com/2006/04/01/us/01pets.html (quoting Frank A. Ascione, Psychologist, Utah State University). Abusers are also motivated by jealousy if they perceive the pet as competition for their partner's devotion. Amy J. Fitzgerald, Animal Abuse and Family Violence: Researching the Interrelationships of Abusive Power 152 (2005). What acts of cruelty did Russell Swigart commit to terrorize his partners? What was his motivation?

3. *Police assistance to remove personal effects.* Some state statutes authorize police to accompany victims of domestic violence who have fled from abusers for the purpose of returning home to collect "personal effects." See, e.g., Wyo. Sta. Ann. §35-21-107(b)(iii). Some of these statutes specify the meaning of "personal effects." See, e.g., Miss. Code Ann. §93-21-28 ("food, clothing, medication, and such other personal property as is reasonably necessary . . . to remain elsewhere pending further proceedings"). Should statutes provide for police assistance to remove a companion animal? See Dianna J. Gentry, Including Companion Animals in Protective Orders: Curtailing the Reach of Domestic Violence, 13 Yale J.L. & Feminism 97, 107 (2001) (so suggesting).

4. *Differences.* Abusers who harm pets tend to be more controlling and more dangerous because they use multidimensional forms of violence compared to other abusers. Catherine A. Simmons & Peter Lehmann, Exploring the Link Between Pet Abuse and Controlling Behaviors in Violent Relationships, 22 J. Interpersonal Violence 1211, 1218 (2007).

5. *Law reform.* All states have laws that ban cruelty to animals. Until recently, pet abuse in the domestic violence context was prosecuted under animal cruelty laws. Darian Ibrahim, The Anticruelty Statute: A Study in Animal Welfare, 1 J. Animal L. & Ethics. 175, 176 (2006). However, these laws have several limitations when applied to domestic violence, including: Animal cruelty is usually investigated by humane societies rather than law enforcement; only severe cases result in prosecutions and, even then, the penalties are light; and, offenses, if prosecuted, are considered misdemeanors, thereby precluding conditions on firearm possession, pet ownership, and psychological counseling.

This approach changed in 2006 in Maine after one victim of domestic violence shared her experience of pet abuse with state legislators. Susan Walsh explained that she was terrified to leave her abusive husband because she feared he would harm the animals on their 32-acre farm. Belluck, supra. Her husband had previously run over her blind and deaf Border collie, shot two of her sheep, and wrung the necks of her prized turkeys. In response, Maine became the first state to include animals in domestic violence protection orders and to award custody of animals to victims. See Me. Rev. Stat. Ann. tit. 19-A, §4007(1)(N). See also Belluck, supra (describing law reform movement).

6. *Statutory approaches.* States take three modern approaches to pet abuse.

a. *Animal cruelty laws.* Some state legislatures have enacted or revised existing animal cruelty laws to provide felony status for abuse of "companion animals." Deborah J. Challener, Protecting Cats and Dogs in Order to Protect Humans: Making the Case for A Felony Companion Animal Statute in Mississippi, 29 Miss. C. L. Rev. 499, 507 (2010).

b. *Orders of protection.* A new trend is inclusion of animals in protection orders. These statutes: (1) enjoin the abuser from injuring, threatening, or harming an animal; (2) require that the abuser stay a certain distance away from an animal; (3) subject the abuser to seizure or forfeiture of an animal; (4) require the abuser to pay the costs of caring for an animal and/or restitution to the owner; (5) subject the abuser to future restrictions on pet ownership; and (6) impose criminal penalties (that is, criminal contempt, fines, damages, and/or imprisonment) for violation of these orders. Joshua L. Friedman & Gary C. Norman, Protecting the Family Pet: The New Face of Maryland Domestic Violence Protective Orders, 40 U. Balt. U.F. 81, 94-95 (2009).

c. *Possession.* Some statutes place a pet in the custody of the victim, thereby enabling her to take the pet with her when she leaves. See, e.g., Cal. Fam. Code §6320 (authorizing a court, on a showing of good cause, to include in a protective order "a grant to the petitioner of the exclusive care, possession, or control of any animal owned, possessed, leased, kept, or held by either the petitioner or the respondent or a minor child residing in the residence or household of either the petitioner or the respondent").

If a pet belongs to the abuser, do such statutes raise constitutional problems? What is the purpose of the various animal protection laws? To protect property rights? To provide affirmative rights for animals? To protect animals from suffering? To protect the most vulnerable in society as a moral imperative? To protect victims of domestic violence? To protect the "transmission" of violence to the next generation of abusers and victims?

What are the best legal approaches to address the link between pet abuse and domestic violence? Should any of the above approaches be adopted? How should "cruelty" to animals be defined? Compare Colo. Rev. Stat. §18-6-800.3 (defining domestic violence as violence against an animal "when used as a method of coercion, control, punishment, intimidation or revenge"), with N.C. Gen. Stat. §50B-3(a) (authorizing a court to order a party to refrain from "[c]ruelly treating or abusing an animal owned, possessed, kept, or held as a pet by either parent or minor child residing in the household"). If pets are included in protection orders, which animals should be included? Should mice, rats, birds, gerbils, and fish be included? Which activities should be exempt? Should laboratory animals for medical research purposes be excluded? Should veterinarians be excluded?

7. *Federal law.* Federal law does not address the link between domestic violence and pet abuse.

8. *Pet-friendly shelters?* Most domestic violence shelters do not accommodate pets, thereby discouraging victims from leaving abusers. Tara J. Gilbreath, Where's Fido: Pets Are Missing in Domestic Violence Shelters and Stalking Laws, 4 J. Animal L. 1, 7 (2008). In recognition of the need for services, a few states establish shelters that take pets in emergencies, or allow placement of a pet with a veterinary hospital, foster family, animal shelter, or private kennel. See Jennifer Golson, A Hidden Peril for Animals: Domestic Rage, Star-Ledger [Newark N.J.] 1 (May 30, 2010). Should more funding be provided for this purpose?

9. *Effects on humans of animal cruelty.* What is the effect on children of exposure to animal cruelty? The link between domestic violence and animal cruelty has been known since the late 1990s. See Frank R. Ascione, Battered Women's Reports of Their Partners' and Their Children's Cruelty to Animals, in Cruelty to Animals and Interpersonal Violence 290 (Randall Lockwood & Frank R. Ascione eds., 1998). In response to witnessing abuse or being abused, some children begin to harm animals themselves. As one researcher explains, "This can stem from a range of reasons including, but not limited to, killing an animal to protect it from ongoing abuse, imitation, identification with the abuser, and post-traumatic play." Sherley, supra, at 63. See also Judith Lewis Herman, Trauma and Recovery 33 (1992) (explaining the trauma caused by witnessing cruelty to individual animals).

Animal cruelty is an indicator of child abuse and suggests that some children may subsequently commit violence toward others. See Arnold Arluke et al., The Relationship of Animal Abuse to Violence and Other Forms of Antisocial Behavior, 14 J. Interpersonal Violence 963 (1999); Cheryl L. Currie, Animal Cruelty by Children Exposed to Domestic Violence, 30 Child Abuse & Neglect: The Int'l J. 425, 429 (2006); Joseph G. Sauder, Enacting and Enforcing Felony Animal Cruelty Laws to Prevent Violence Against Humans, 6 Animal L. 1 (2000). Should children who abuse animals be screened? Should teachers be required to report such students?

10. *Proposals for reform.* Should efforts be made to improve the safety of pet-owning victims of intimate partner violence? If so, how? Should shelter staff question victims about the presence of pets and their welfare? Should law enforcement officials be trained to take pet abuse into account? Should veterinarians be encouraged to report pet abuse? Be required to do so? Compare Idaho Code Ann. §24-3514A (exempting veterinarians from civil and criminal liability for good faith reporting of known or suspected cases of animal abuse), with Minn. Stat. Ann. §346.37 (mandating reporting of animal abuse by veterinarians). Should states allow victims to recover damages for emotional distress stemming from harm to their pets? Should states require cross-reporting between animal protection organizations, social welfare agencies, and law enforcement officials? What other reforms should be made?

Problems

1. Emelie is living with Michael and her children (Juan, age nine; Crystal, age eight; and Emma, age five) from a previous marriage, as well as an assortment of pets

(two dogs, a cat, and three goldfish named after each of the children). One evening, Emelie wakes up to find Michael standing over her, holding the fish tank. He throws the tank into the television, saying "That could have been you." The tank breaks, as does the television. Juan and his sisters come running out their rooms, crying. Michael turns to Juan and says, "You want to see something awesome?" and stomps on the fish, killing them. Emelie has to calm down her hysterical children before she can clean up the mess.

The next day, Michael attacks Emelie in her bedroom. He flings her against the bed, punches her head and face with closed fists, and begins choking her. While he is choking her, he reaches into his pocket and pulls out a small knife. Emelie breaks free and calls for her son to help. Michael drops the knife, but the assault escalates to the point where Michael attacks nine-year-old Juan. The police arrest Michael later that day and charge him with attempted assault in the first degree (that is, intent to cause serious physical injury by means of a deadly weapon or a dangerous instrument), and aggravated cruelty to animals (both felonies).

The jurisdiction's felony animal cruelty statute provides:

> A person is guilty of aggravated cruelty to animals when, with no justifiable purpose, he or she intentionally kills or intentionally causes serious physical injury to a companion animal with aggravated cruelty. [A]ggravated cruelty shall mean conduct which: (1) is intended to cause extreme physical pain, or (2) is done or carried out in an especially depraved or sadistic manner.

N.Y. Agric. & Mkts. §353-a(1). Michael argues that the evidence is insufficient to charge him with the crime of aggravated cruelty to animals and that the animal-cruelty statute is unconstitutionally vague. What result? See People v. Garcia, 812 N.Y.S.2d 66 (App. Div. 2006). Would the result differ if defendant killed the fish without the accompanying acts of domestic violence? Would the result differ if the defendant had merely swallowed the goldfish?

2. The following proposal addresses the relationship between family violence and pet abuse. Whenever an investigating officer of an Animal Humane Society observes a child at the home of a person reasonably suspected of animal abuse, the officer shall prepare a "Child Presence Report," directed to Child Protective Services, who will then investigate whether child abuse has occurred in that home. Following the investigation, a child protective services social worker must prepare a "Suspected Abuse Report" or "Animal Presence Report" whenever the social worker "has knowledge of or observes an animal whom she knows or reasonably suspects has been the victim of cruelty, abandonment, or neglect." These reports will be directed to the Animal Humane Society which will investigate them as complaints of animal abuse.

What are the benefits and shortcomings of this proposal? What other recommendations would you make to improve agency cross-reporting to improve the law's response to animal abuse, domestic violence, and child abuse? Should child abuse laws be amended to require psychiatric assessment of any children accused of animal cruelty in order to determine the cause of their behavior? See Joan E. Schaffner, Linking Domestic Violence, Child Abuse, and Animal Cruelty, ABA-

TIPS Animal Law Committee Newsletter (Fall 2006) (suggesting this reform proposal), available at http://ssrn.com/abstract=1001255.

"A Jury of Her Peers" and Pet Abuse

The classic feminist tale by Susan Glaspell, "A Jury of Her Peers," illustrates the harm of battering though the use of an evocative analogy to pet abuse. In the story, Mrs. Martha Hale, who is making bread at home, is interrupted by her husband Lewis, who asks her to accompany him and several others to investigate the murder of neighbor John Wright. The Hales, together with the sheriff and his wife (Mr. and Mrs. Peters), and the county attorney, travel to the home of Minnie and John Wright. Minnie is currently being held at the jail as a suspect in the murder of her husband. Another neighbor, the first to arrive, recounts how he found Minnie in her rocking chair looking "queer." Minnie told the neighbor that her husband upstairs had been strangled to death. She suggests that someone killed him while they were sleeping. The investigators are suspicious of Minnie's story, wondering why she did not awaken during the murder.

The women visitors (Mrs. Hale and Mrs. Peters) remain inside the kitchen, keeping each other company, while the men search fruitlessly for a motive—in the bedroom, the barn, and outside the house. The women, looking around the kitchen, find themselves wondering why Minnie left her tasks half done and why her quilting is so jagged. They notice a bird cage with a broken door. Mrs. Hale notes, "Looks as if someone must have been rough with it," suggesting a parallel with Minnie's lifetime of abuse. Inside, a dead canary had its neck wrung. The dead bird is wrapped in silk, lying in a pretty box, a symbol of something that was precious to Minnie. Thinking of Minnie's brutish husband, Mrs. Hale remarks, "Wright wouldn't like that bird, a thing that sang. She [Minnie] used to sing. He killed that, too."

The two women gradually reach the conclusion that Minnie was subject to severe emotional and physical abuse. Sympathizing with Minnie's plight, they are drawn into a conspiracy to hide any evidence of Minnie's murder of her husband. See Susan Glaspell, A Jury of Her Peers, in Lifted Masks and Other Works 279 (Eric S. Rabkin ed., 1993). For critical feminist analyses of this short story, see Marina Angel, Teaching Susan Glaspell's A Jury of Her Peers and Trifles, 53 J. Legal Educ. 548 (2003); Orit Kamir, To Kill a Songbird: A Community of Women, Feminist Jurisprudence, Conscientious Objection and Revolution in a Jury of Her Peers and Contemporary Film, 19 Law & Literature 357 (2007).

---

6. Other Forms of Psychological Abuse

Many forms of psychological abuse exist. One common type, "domestic violence by proxy" (also called "third-party abuse" or "instrumental abuse by third parties"), consists of the abuser's *use of third parties* to harass, intimidate, and harm the victim. The following excerpt explores this form of abuse. What is the law's response to this form of abuse? Another form of psychological abuse, "litigation abuse," is examined in Chapter 11.

■ **ANIQUE DROUIN, COMMENT, WHO TURNED OUT
    THE LIGHTS?: HOW MARYLAND LAWS FAIL TO
    PROTECT VICTIMS OF DOMESTIC VIOLENCE
    FROM THIRD-PARTY ABUSE**
    36 U. Balt. L. Rev. 105, 106, 121-125, 131 (2006)

[Abusers sometimes use] third parties such as landlords or utility, telephone
and insurance companies to continue harassing and in some instances harming,
their victim. A judge may order an abuser to vacate the residence the abuser shares
with his victim in either a temporary or final protective order. Upon being ordered
to vacate the residence, the abuser may contact any of the above mentioned third
parties and discontinue services, thus leaving their victims on the streets, in the cold,
uninsured or all of the above. . . .

Third parties that do not know of the domestic abuse situation in a household
may cause further harm to the victim through manipulation by the abuser. Abusers
can find creative ways to punish their victims that are not physical per se, but that will
hurt the victims nonetheless. One of these ways is through terminating the victim's
insurance. Abusers can use all varieties of insurance as a means of controlling their
victims, medical insurance being the most common. Abusers have also been known
to terminate their victim's car insurance to prevent them from driving and have
threatened to take the children off of the medical insurance policy and then hurt
them.

In Maryland, there are no laws prohibiting one spouse from removing the other
spouse, or their children-in-common, from a medical insurance policy. The only
ways a victim can avoid being left without coverage is to submit to her abuser's
demands, or to file for divorce and ask the court to enjoin her spouse from removing
her or the children from his medical insurance policy. It is within the court's equitable powers to make such an order, and a judge may be inclined to make such a
ruling when either children are involved or the petitioning spouse has a serious
medical condition.

After a victim obtains a protective order, her abuser may attempt to control her
emotionally in less obvious ways. For example, an abuser can shut off the utilities or
telephone services. Often, these bills are set up in the abuser's name (as yet another
means of control). When a woman receives a protective order from the court, there
is often an order directing the abuser to vacate the shared home. [In nearly every
state in the nation], the abuser can legally have the services shut off if he chooses to
do so in retaliation, and it is possible for the overdue payments or the reconnection
fees to be too expensive for the victim. . . .

For a victim, having the telephone service shut off can be extremely distressing,
especially if that victim has used the telephone to call for help or support in the
past. . . . [A] court in New Jersey held that shutting off a phone service was not
domestic violence when proof of other violence did not exist. . . . Mrs. Corrente
filed a domestic violence complaint against the defendant, her husband, from
whom she was separated, stating that he called her at work "threatening
drastic measures if [she] did not supply [him] with money to pay bills." When
Mrs. Corrente returned home that afternoon, her phone service was disconnected
and she later discovered her husband had his sister shut the service off for him.
The trial court found that domestic violence had occurred based on the plaintiff's

fear and called the defendant's behavior harassment. The appellate court overturned the decision on the grounds that the behavior "was neither repeated nor a course of conduct" as is required by the state's statute. The appellate court stressed that neither Mrs. Corrente's complaint nor the trial judge's finding asserted any history of domestic violence. [Corrente v. Corrente, 657 A.2d 440 (N.J. Super. Ct. 1995)]. . . .

A legal advocate at the House of Ruth Maryland Domestic Violence Legal Clinic estimated that at least one victim per week calls and reports that her utilities have been disconnected by her abuser. More often than not, the victim cannot afford the expense of past-due payments or the reconnection fee and will have to borrow money from a relative or apply for emergency aid at the Department for Social Services. . . . Currently, only one state has a statute that specifically forbids the defendant in a civil protective order case from shutting off any utilities. Massachusetts' definition section of the Abuse Prevention chapter [Mass. Gen. Laws Ann. ch. 209A, §1 (West 1998)] states that when a court gives a vacate order, the defendant "shall not shut off or cause to be shut off any utilities . . . to the plaintiff." This is not to say that the abuser should be required to pay for utilities when he no longer lives on the premises, but instead of having them shut off, he could have the bill transferred over to the victim's name. . . .

Women who are victims of domestic violence continue to face adversity when dealing, not only with their abuser, but with third parties as well. There are viable options available to law makers that would make a victim's transition from an abusive environment safer and more successful. These options must be explored to guarantee [victims] protection from harm and equality of treatment.

Problems

1. The French National Assembly has proposed to amend the law of intimate partner violence by the addition of the new offense of "psychological violence." The law would impose criminal liability and provide for civil protective orders. It would be applicable to both male and female partners; and would include repeated verbal abuse, threats of violence, insults, and other forms of harassment. Specifically, the bill provides that letting a wife, husband, partner, or concubine "act or repeatedly say things that could damage the victim's life conditions, affect his/her rights and his/her dignity or damage his/her physical or mental health is subject to a three-year jail term and a 75,000 euro fine" (about $100,000). The law would also provide for a temporary order of protection to evict a violent partner. Another aspect of the law would authorize an electronic bracelet with a GPS unit so that police can track an offender's movements. Prime Minister Francois Fillon stated that the proposed law "will allow people to take into account the most insidious situations, which don't leave a mark to the naked eye but can mutilate the victim's inner self."

Would you recommend enactment of such a law in the United States? What enforcement problems might you anticipate? Would the law be subject to constitutional challenges? See Steven Erlanger & Maia de la Baume, France May Make Mental Violence a Crime, N.Y. Times, Jan. 26, 2010, at A10; Marlise Simons, France: Bill Would Outlaw Harassment by Partners, N.Y. Times, Jan. 14, 2010, at A16.

2. Psychologist Evan Stark suggests that a new law is necessary to criminalize coercive control. The new crime would address "a course-of-conduct crime much like harassment, stalking, or kidnapping, rather than as a discrete act, and highlight its effects on liberty and autonomy." Evan Stark, Coercive Control: How Men Entrap Women in Personal Life 382 (2009). Acts of coercive control could be identified by their "intent, consequence, and their functional role in the overall pattern of criminal conduct regardless of where they occur or the proximity of the perpetrator and victim when they occur." Id. Stark concedes that assaults, threats, stalking, and harassment are already crimes. "But these crimes take on new significance when woven into the larger pattern of entrapment." Id. at 383.

Sociologist Neil Websdale disagrees. He believes that society should protect victims and hold perpetrators accountable. However, Websdale opines that "[t]he fact that the anti-domestic violence movement has aligned itself so closely with the criminal-justice arm of the state ought to be grave cause for concern." Websdale, supra, at 281. He explains that "We can lock up offenders for as long as we like, but until we address the reasons for their anger, fear, anxiety, and shame, we will not move toward more egalitarian intimate relationships." Id. at 281-282. He urges greater expenditures on the "importance of community, of caring for others," as well as on the social, political, and economic conditions that generate violence and abuse. Id. at 281.

Suppose that you are a legislative intern for a state legislator who is considering adopting the following statute criminalizing coercive control. The new offense of "Domestic Violence Assault" would constitute a Class A felony, and be defined as follows:

> "Domestic violence assault" means the threat of the infliction of physical injury, any act of physical harm or the creation of a reasonable fear thereof, or the intentional inflic-tion of emotional distress by a spouse or former spouse, intimate partner or former intimate partner, or a present or former member of the household, including acts of coercive control and controlling behavior that involve physical, sexual, psychological, emotional, economic, or financial abuse.

Discuss the advantages and disadvantages of this approach. What do you advise the legislator?

PART TWO

CRIMINAL JUSTICE RESPONSE

V

Law Enforcement Response

This chapter explores the law enforcement response to domestic violence, specifically the role of police and prosecutors. Traditionally, police and prosecutors adopted a policy of nonintervention in cases of domestic violence. What explains this policy? What factors influenced it to change? The following materials explore the traditional policy and its transformation.

A. POLICE

1. Traditional Response to Intimate Partner Assaults

■ **JOAN ZORZA, THE CRIMINAL LAW OF MISDEMEANOR DOMESTIC VIOLENCE, 1970-1990**
83 J. Crim. L. & Criminology 46, 47-63 (1992)

. . . In most communities police officers may be the only meaningful contact citizens have with "the law." The evidence suggests, however, that police are largely indifferent to domestic violence, and that they attach to it a very low priority. Throughout the 1970s and early 1980s, officers believed and were taught that domestic violence was a private matter, ill suited to public intervention. Police departments also consider domestic violence calls unglamorous, non-prestigious, and unrewarding. [P]olice frequently ignored domestic violence calls or purposefully delayed responding for several hours. Even when they eventually arrived on the scene, police rarely did anything about domestic violence, and some actually responded by laughing in the woman's face. Other officers talked to the abuser, possibly removing the batterer from the home temporarily to cool off. Some police officers removed the abused woman from "his" home. Yet, in conformity to traditional practice, police virtually never arrested the abuser. . . .

Indeed, those police departments that had policies on handling domestic calls in the 1970s had a clear non-arrest policy. The Oakland Police Department's 1975 *Training Bulletin on Techniques of Dispute Intervention* explicitly described

> [t]he police role in a dispute situation [as] more often that of a mediator and peacemaker than enforcer of the law. . . . [T]he possibility that . . . arrest will only aggravate the dispute or create a serious danger for the arresting officers due to possible efforts to resist arrest . . . is most likely when a husband or father is arrested in his home. . . . Normally, officers should adhere to the policy that arrests shall be avoided . . . but when one of the parties demands arrest, you should attempt to explain the ramifications of such action (e.g., loss of wages, bail procedures, court appearances) and encourage the parties to reason with each other.

. . . [I]t is hardly surprising that the police who did respond to domestic violence calls almost always took the man's side. And because abusers, when they did not or could not deny their abuse, tried to shift the blame onto others, especially their victims, the police frequently joined in blaming the victim. The responding officer often admonished the woman to be a better wife or asked, or at least wondered, why she did not leave. Some officers concluded that she must enjoy the beatings, or at least not mind them. These officers conveniently ignored the fact that their failure to protect the woman, her lack of money, and the far greater risk of being beaten or killed if she tried to separate herself from her abuser all combined to make her decision logical. Women's fears of retaliation for leaving are rational. . . .

Police frequently rationalized their refusal to intervene in domestic violence cases on the ground that domestic violence work was highly dangerous. . . . Restoring peace while maintaining control was seen as the best way to minimize the risk to the responding officer with an emphasis on maintaining control. . . . The reality, however, is that domestic disturbance incidents, which account for 30 percent of police calls, account for only 5.7 percent of police deaths, making domestic disturbances one of the least dangerous of all police activities. In addition, training police to better handle domestic violence incidents can reduce assaults against officers. Nevertheless, the myth that domestic violence work is dangerous is still used to justify police discrimination against battered women. Another factor makes police education and training difficult. Beyond dismissing woman battering as a real crime, far too many police officers either engage in it themselves or tolerate it within their ranks. . . .

[Beginning in the 1970s, reformers initiated suits against law enforcement officials who failed to protect battered women. Realizing that such lawsuits] were time-consuming and that judgments were difficult to enforce, battered women's advocates soon turned to other approaches to changing police handling of woman abuse cases. . . .

[I]n most, but not all, jurisdictions police could not make an arrest for a misdemeanor assault unless the assault occurred in the police officer's presence. Because most police charge domestic violence offenses only as misdemeanors, the law, in order to enable an officer to arrest the abuser when the offense was not committed in the officer's presence, has to permit the arrest without a warrant. Changes [needed to] be made. . . .

[Empirical research on police response to domestic violence also influenced law reform. In 1982, in a study of recidivism rates for misdemeanor domestic violence cases in Minneapolis, researchers concluded that arresting abusers put the victims at considerably lower risk for repeat victimization.] By 1984, the Minneapolis police domestic violence experiment was widely cited as proof that arrests had a deterrent effect on men who beat their wives. The movement to expand police arrest powers was already well established [by that time]. . . . The enactment of domestic violence legislation had actually begun in the 1970s. By 1976, the District of Columbia and Pennsylvania had each enacted such legislation. In 1978, Pennsylvania amended its domestic violence act to permit warrantless arrests if the officer had probable cause to believe that a protection order had been violated. . . .

The Oregon Coalition Against Domestic and Sexual Violence took a different approach. It proposed a bill imposing a mandatory duty on the police. The bill required police officers to arrest anyone in a domestic violence incident whom the officer had probable cause to believe had committed an assault or had placed a victim with an order of protection in fear of imminent serious physical injury. This bill was enacted in 1977, making Oregon the first state to *require* police to arrest. . . .

Notes and Questions

1. *Rationale for nonarrest policy.* How did police traditionally respond to cases of domestic violence? How did they treat the victim? The abuser? What explains this policy of nonintervention?

2. *Lack of seriousness.* Police, historically, treated abusers differently from strangers who perpetrated assaults. Why did police regard violence by a *known* abuser as less serious than that perpetrated by a stranger? Data from the 1980s reveal that domestic violence cases were characterized by low arrest rates (from 3 to 14 percent) until the 1990s. Eve S. Buzawa & Carl G. Buzawa, Domestic Violence: The Criminal Justice Response 82 (3d ed., 2011).

3. *Policy statements.* Policy statements of major police organizations reflected the traditional nonintervention policy. For example, in 1967, the International Association of Chiefs of Police (IACP) advised its law enforcement officers that "in dealing with family disputes, the power of arrest should be exercised as a last resort." Lawrence W. Sherman, Influence of Criminology on Criminal Law: Evaluating Arrests for Misdemeanor Domestic Violence, 83 J. Crim. L. & Criminology 1, 10 (1992) [hereafter Sherman, Influence of Criminology](quoting IACP "Training Key 16: Handling Disturbance Calls" (1967)). Even the American Bar Association endorsed this approach. The ABA's Project on Standards for Criminal Justice, Standards for the Urban Police Function, maintained that police should "engage in the resolution of conflict such as that which occurs between husband and wife . . . without reliance upon criminal assault or disorderly conduct statutes." Cited in id.

4. *Delay in response.* Zorza contends that police sometimes "purposefully delayed responding." Why? Early research in three cities confirmed that police took longer to respond to domestic disturbances (4.65 minutes) than others (3.86 minutes). "Police in these areas openly told observers it was the officers' policy (not the department's) "to proceed slowly in the hope that the problem would be resolved or that a disputant would have left before they arrived." Sherman, Influence of

Criminology, supra, at 10-11 (citing research in 1977). What are the implications of this delay?

5. *Blaming the victim.* Why did the police blame the victim for the violence? How did they manifest this blame? What is the possible consequence of this attitude?

6. *Mediation approach.* Mediation was a traditional alternative to arrest for domestic violence. This approach stemmed from recommendations in the 1960s by psychologists who trained police in conflict mediation. Psychologists urged police to adopt the role of emergency marriage counselor—to separate the parties and permit each party to give an uninterrupted version of the events. If one of the parties would not calm down, the officers would advise that person to leave to "cool off." Id., at 13. What are the advantages and disadvantages of this approach?

7. *Fear of escalation.* Police also preferred the nonintervention policy based on their belief that an arrest did not resolve the underlying conflict and instead might aggravate the situation. Why did battered women's advocates reject this approach?

8. *Police perception of their law enforcement role.* Another reason for the noninterventionist policy was police perception of domestic violence cases as less prestigious than other cases. What cases are most prestigious? Why? Why are domestic violence cases "unglamorous, nonprestigious, and unrewarding," according to Zorza? See also Buzawa & Buzawa, Criminal Justice Response, supra, at 78-80 (discussing police views of "real policing").

9. *Victim preferences.* Yet another reason for the failure to arrest abusers was, according to police, the victim's opposition to the arrest. The victim's reluctance still plays a role in preventing arrest of abusers. A large federally funded study reports that one of the primary reasons for police failing to make an arrest when responding to an incident of assault is "victim refused to cooperate." David Hirschel et al., Nat'l Inst. of Justice, Explaining the Prevalence, Context, and Consequences of Dual Arrest in Intimate Partner Cases 55 (2007) [hereinafter NIJ Dual Arrest Report]. What explains this reluctance? Victim's reluctance is discussed infra this chapter and in Chapter 7.

10. *Danger to police.* Police also justified their policy of nonintervention by claiming that domestic violence was a leading cause of police homicides. Just how dangerous is domestic violence to law enforcement personnel? What does Zorza believe? A contemporary of Zorza's, criminology professor Lawrence Sherman, disagrees. He maintains that, although domestic violence is not a large source of police deaths, it constitutes a frequent source of *injury* to police. See Sherman, Influence of Criminology, supra, at 12 n.56 (citing research).

Does current research support either view? A recent national study confirms that almost one-fourth of firearms-related police deaths in 2009 involve domestic disturbance calls. See National Law Enforcement Officers Memorial Fund, Research Bulletin, Circumstances of Fatal Law Enforcement Shootings—2009, 2 (Dec. 2009), available at http://www.nleomf.com/assets/pdfs/2009_end_year_fatality_report.pdf. Moreover, domestic disturbances also result in a high rate of *injuries* to police. See Dean MacLeod, Museum Developing Domestic Violence Prevention Programs, NLEM Insider, Nov. 2009, at 3 (revealing that 32 percent of almost 60,000 assaults on police in 2007 occurred during domestic disturbance calls, compared to the next highest category "attempting other arrests" that resulted in only 15 percent of total assaults against police), available at http://www.nleomf.com/assets/pdfs/newsletters/museum_insider/nlem_insider_vol_1_issue_2_november_2009.pdf.

11. *Victims' likelihood of calling police.* Several factors appear to influence a victim to call police during acts of domestic violence: a previous history of abuse, the severity of the abuse, the use of weapons, and the offender's alcohol consumption during the incident. David Hirschel & Ira W. Hutchison, The Voices of Domestic Violence Victims: Predictors of Victim Preference for Arrest and the Relationship Between Preference for Arrest and Revictimization, 49 Crime & Delinquency 313, 315 (2003). What additional factors might influence a victim to contact the police for assistance?

2. The Road to Mandatory Arrest

The policy of nonarrest characterized the traditional police response to domestic violence, as we have seen. However, another important obstacle stood in the path of aggressive enforcement of the criminal law: the common law prohibition on arrests of misdemeanants without a warrant. The following materials explore this legal obstacle, its modification, and the subsequent reform movement that led to the policy of mandatory arrest of abusers.

■ **STATE v. FARROW**

919 P.2d 50 (Utah Ct. App. 1996)

BILLINGS, Judge:
. . . On November 5, 1994, a Beaver City Police Officer, Cameron Noel, received a telephone call from a Cedar City Police Officer informing him that an instance of "spousal abuse" had occurred in Beaver and that the victim, A.F., was staying at a "safe house" in Cedar City. That same day, Officer Noel drove to Cedar City and interviewed A.F. at the Cedar City Police Department.

A.F. informed Officer Noel of three separate instances of violence. The first instance occurred on April 14, 1994, in front of the Beaver City Tri-Mart, defendant's [Gregory Farrow's] employer. . . . [D]efendant's mother was taking A.F. [who was pregnant] to a doctor's appointment and wanted to stop by the Tri-Mart to see defendant. A.F. and defendant were then separated, and defendant was angry because A.F. had applied for public assistance. . . . Defendant "leaned into the car . . . about two inches from [A.F.'s] face" and told her she "couldn't have [her] child" and threatened to take A.F.'s money. A.F. stated defendant grabbed her purse and tried to pull it from her shoulder. When A.F. resisted, defendant "grabbed [her] arm, . . . threw her to the ground onto [her] stomach, and began hitting [her] in the back of the head." A.F. stated defendant was about to strike her in the stomach when his mother told him she was going to call the police if he did not stop. . . .

The couple's baby was born on April 22, 1994, and they attempted a reconciliation. . . . A.F. then described a second incident occurring on October 10, 1994. A.F. was in the couple's apartment when defendant arrived home from work. She informed defendant "things just weren't working out and [that they would] probably be better off apart." A heated argument ensued. Defendant threatened to kill himself, pulled out a gun, and placed the muzzle to his head. [This act caused A.F. to fear for her safety because defendant had threatened to kill her and the baby in the past, so A.F.] decided it would be best if she "backed down."

By October 21, 1994, A.F. had decided their marriage was over. While defendant was at work, she packed her belongings and the things she needed to take care of the baby. [While A.F. was waiting to be picked up by her mother, brother, and a friend], defendant entered the apartment. Defendant told A.F., "You're not taking nothing. You're not going to take baby blankets, you're not taking nothing." Defendant tore a gold necklace from around her neck. [Defendant wrestled the baby from A.F.'s hands and ran outside to his car.] A.F. ran back into the apartment to call 911. Defendant [ran back] into the apartment where he ripped the phone cords from the wall. . . . Defendant grabbed A.F. around the neck and hit her in the mouth hard enough to give her a "fat lip." A.F. began to plead as defendant held her down on the couch, choking her.

[When A.F.'s friend arrived and intervened, A.F. was able to convince defendant to let her leave with the baby. She moved first to her mother's home and later to the battered women's shelter where she reported the abuse to Officer Noel.] Based upon the information Officer Noel had gathered, he concluded he had probable cause to believe defendant had committed several counts of assault. He also believed defendant posed an ongoing threat of violence to A.F. . . . [On] November 6, 1994, Deputy Chambers saw defendant in front of the Beaver post office [where] Deputy Chambers arrested him and informed him that Officer Noel wished to speak to him about an assault charge. . . . [The police later conducted an inventory search of the car incidental to defendant's arrest and found a handgun and methamphetamine.] Defendant was charged with one count of aggravated assault, two counts of assault, one count of possession of a controlled substance, and one count of possession of a handgun by a convicted felon. . . .

[On appeal] Defendant contends the trial court erred in finding Officer Noel was "respond[ing] to a domestic violence call" when he arrested defendant sixteen days after the last incident of abuse. He concedes [that Utah Code Ann. §77-36-2] provides law enforcement with warrantless arrest powers in domestic violence cases and, in fact, requires arrest in certain circumstances, but argues the statute only applies in emergency situations occurring during or immediately after an incident of domestic violence.

Section 77-36-2 (3)(a) provides:

> In addition to the arrest powers described in Section 77-7-2, *when a peace officer responds to a domestic violence call and has probable cause to believe that a crime has been committed, the peace officer shall arrest without a warrant or issue a citation* to any person that he has probable cause to believe has committed any of the offenses described in Subsection 77-36-1(2)(a) through (i).
>
> *If the peace officer has probable cause to believe that there will be continued violence against the alleged victim, or if there is evidence that the perpetrator has either recently caused serious bodily injury or used a dangerous weapon in the domestic violence offense, the officer shall arrest and take the alleged perpetrator into custody, and may not utilize the option of issuing a citation* under this section.

Id. (emphasis added).

[In interpreting a statute, we examine the statute's plain language]. The plain language of section 77-36-2 (3)(a) does not require a response to an emergency situation for the warrantless arrest provisions to apply. The statute contains no temporal requirement. We refuse to read a temporal requirement into the language of this statute where the legislature easily could have provided for a time requirement had it so desired. Only four states have chosen to require a temporal element in their domestic violence statutes, and each state has done so explicitly. Further, our plain reading of section 77-36-2 is supported by the entire domestic violence statutory scheme, its legislative history, and sound public policy.

. . . [T]his court must harmonize subsection (3)(a) with the balance of the domestic violence legislation [which makes clear] "[t]he primary duty of peace officers responding to a domestic violence call is to protect the parties and enforce the laws allegedly violated." Utah Code Ann. §77-36-2 (2) (1995) (repealed 1995). Likewise, subsection (1) requires that "[a]ll training relating to the handling of domestic violence complaints by law enforcement personnel shall stress *protection of the victim, enforcement of criminal laws* in domestic situations, and availability of community resources." (emphasis added). Finally, when read in its entirety, the Spouse Abuse Procedures Act, Utah Code Ann. §77-36-1 through -9 (1995), stands for the proposition that because domestic violence is serious in nature and has a high likelihood of repeated violence, incidents of domestic abuse require the mandatory and immediate attention of law enforcement. Thus, the Act as a whole demonstrates the legislature's desire to grant law enforcement broad authority to make warrantless arrests and even to require arrest in some cases of domestic violence, such as the one presented in this case.

Likewise, a "primary rule of statutory interpretation is to give effect to the intent of the legislature." By enacting [Utah Code Ann. §77-36-2], the Utah State Legislature expressed, in statutory form, a public policy to arrest perpetrators of domestic violence. In part, the legislature observed that domestic violence is cyclical and often does not end with a single occurrence or incident. Rather, "[w]omen do not seek [intervention] after a single beating, but after several." Because of fear for the victim's safety and that of the victim's children, "[i]n many cases, . . . women will endure years of abuse before [leaving their homes.]" Moreover, the legislature deemed the expanded arrest procedures included in section 77-36-2 necessary to "ensure that law enforcement officers will understand what their responsibilities are and rights in making arrests and assisting [domestic violence] victims." Finally, allowing law enforcement to make arrests upon finding probable cause to believe that an incident of domestic violence has occurred permits officers to "[p]rotect victims from further domestic [abuse]."

Again, in 1991, when the mandatory arrest provisions of subsection (3)(a) were added, the legislature provided that when notified of "a domestic violence situation, . . . wherever the arresting officer sees . . . evidence of . . . domestic violence . . . , [the officer] *must arrest* [the perpetrator] and take him into the judicial system." The legislature expressly recognized that domestic violence is often not reported immediately, and therefore that police officers often are not able to respond to domestic violence calls when the abuse is then in progress. This legislative history supports our reading of the warrantless arrest power as not limited to emergency situations.

Finally, we look to related case law and "'relevant policy considerations'" for guidance in construing section 77-36-2 (3)(a). In Strollo v. Strollo, 828 P.2d 532, 534 (Utah Ct. App. 1992), this court liberally construed [protective order legislation]. [We] found that a party seeking entry of a protective order need not establish "immediate peril." Rather, the court stated, the plain language of "[t]he statute clearly protects those who are reasonably in fear of physical harm resulting from past conduct coupled with a present threat of future harm." "Otherwise, the prophylactic purpose of the statute would be defeated. We do not think the legislature intended such a result." Thus, this court found that so long as the statute is applied as to effectuate the legislative purpose, temporal proximity is not an express element of the statute. In light of the plain language of the statute buttressed by the entire statutory scheme, relevant legislative history, and the foregoing policy considerations, we conclude the trial court's refusal to limit application of subsection (3)(a)'s mandatory arrest procedures to require temporal proximity to the alleged abuse was correct.

We further determine the court's conclusion that Officer Noel properly arrested defendant under this warrantless arrest statute was proper. In the instant case, the parties were involved in an abusive relationship, wherein defendant physically assaulted A.F. on at least three occasions. . . . Defendant does not challenge the trial court's findings that Officer Noel had probable cause to believe defendant had committed an incident of domestic violence, that he had used a dangerous weapon during an incident, and that there was an ongoing threat of future violence to A.F., thus triggering the mandatory arrest provisions. . . . Furthermore, when A.F. reported the alleged incidents of domestic violence, Officer Noel drove to Cedar City to interview A.F. that same day, and he arrested defendant within twenty-four hours of receiving A.F.'s complaint. There was simply no undue delay in law enforcement's response. Based upon these facts, we conclude the trial court correctly determined Officer Noel was "respond[ing] to a domestic violence call" when he arrested defendant without a warrant. . . .

Notes and Questions

1. *Law reform objectives.* One of the top priorities of the battered women's movement in the 1970s was to increase the responsiveness of the police. The first step in that battle was to change the *common law warrant rule.* When that reform proved inadequate to curb police discretion, reformers fought for *mandatory arrest* laws to require police to arrest abusers.

2. *Common law warrant rule.* When police are called to the scene of violence, they face the decision whether to arrest the suspected offender. The common law had different rules for the arrest of suspected felons and suspected misdemeanants. A police officer could make a warrantless arrest for a misdemeanor *only* in cases in which the suspect committed the criminal act in the officer's presence (the "in-presence restriction"). That is, a law enforcement officer did not have the discretion to arrest a person for misdemeanors that were committed outside the arresting officer's presence.

In contrast, the common law gave police considerably more power when the arrest involved a felony. When a police officer believes a person has committed a felony, the officer does not actually have to witness the felonious act. Rather, the officer may arrest the suspected felon without a warrant based on probable cause that the suspect had committed the felony. See Carroll v. U.S., 267 U.S. 132, 156-157 (1925).

The rationale for these different rules is that officers are granted more latitude when arresting felons because felonies present more danger to the public safety. The prohibition on misdemeanor warrantless arrests for crimes outside the officer's presence was to minimize the harm to defendants that was associated with lengthy custodial detentions for less important crimes. The rule developed to rein in the historical practice of "arrests [being] made by private citizens," and "when years might pass before the royal judges arrived for a jail delivery." Cave v. Cooley, 152 P.2d 886, 890 (N.M. 1944).

Obviously, most abusers do not commit acts of domestic violence in a police officer's presence. How, then, can a police officer arrest an abuser in the frequent case of a misdemeanor assault? Because the warrant requirement was a common law rule, battered women's advocates pressured state legislatures to change that rule.

3. *Warrantless arrest statutes.* By the 1980s, reformers had convinced many state legislatures to enact legislation conferring warrantless arrest powers on police in cases of misdemeanors. These statutes authorize a law enforcement officer to arrest an alleged misdemeanant without a warrant, provided that the officer has probable cause to believe that domestic violence has occurred and that the suspect is the perpetrator. The effect of the statutory reform was to expand the arrest authority of the police which, formerly, had allowed probable cause to justify arrests only for felonies. "By 1988, all but 2 states had created an exception to the in-presence requirement to permit warrantless arrest when the officer has probable cause to believe that someone has committed a misdemeanor or violated a restraining order. All 50 states now provide for warrantless misdemeanor arrests in domestic violence cases." Cheryl Hanna, No Right to Choose: Mandated Victim Participation in Domestic Violence Prosecutions, 109 Harv. L. Rev. 1849, 1859 (1996).

4. *Range of applicable discretion.* The enactment of warrantless arrest laws, however, was not sufficient to alter the police response of non-intervention. As a result, reformers called for an even stronger policy to limit police discretion: mandatory arrest that would *require* police to arrest a domestic violence offender when police have probable cause to believe the offender has committed a crime. Statutes do not explicitly use the term *mandatory.* They provide, instead, that an officer "shall," "will," or "must" arrest a suspect.

Instead of mandatory arrest statutes, some states enacted *preferred arrest* (or "pro-arrest") statutes providing that police *should* make an arrest in designated circumstances. Such legislation generally provides that arrest is the "preferred" response or action, or that the officer "shall presume" that arrest is the appropriate response. In contrast to both mandatory and preferred arrest policies, other states have discretionary (sometimes called "permissive") arrest policies that confer discretion on the police to decide to arrest. Statutory provisions authorize such discretion by use of the word *may* or *can.* See NIJ Dual Arrest Report, supra, at 32 n.1 (explaining the subjectivity in classifying state statutes). As of 2000, 22 states and the District of Columbia had mandatory arrest statutes. Another 6 states had preferred arrest statutes. The remaining 22 states had discretionary arrest statutes. Id. at 15-19. Mandatory arrest policies have been upheld against constitutional challenges. See, e.g., Hedgepeth v. Washington Metro. Area Transit, 284 F. Supp. 2d 145, 159 (D.D.C. 2003).

Which of the above approaches do you favor? Why? See generally Donna M. Welch, Mandatory Arrest of Domestic Abusers: Panacea or Perpetuation of the Problem of Abuse?, 43 DePaul L. Rev. 1133, 1148-1155 (1994) (discussing various approaches).

5. *Statutory variations.* Mandatory arrest provisions differ in the various jurisdictions. Some statutes apply to both felonies and misdemeanors, whereas others are limited to felonies. NIJ Dual Arrest Report, supra, at 15. Some statutes target only

some but not all perpetrators (for example, current or former spouses, current or former cohabitants, or couples with a child in common); some of these statutes fail to include dating relationships. Id. at 17.

6. *Mandatory arrest for violations of restraining orders.* Subsequent reforms led to the expansion of mandatory arrest provisions to include not only crimes of domestic violence but also violations of protection orders. Many states adopt a stricter stance toward violation of restraining orders than they do toward domestic violence offenses generally. See id. at 22 (33 states mandate arrest for violations of restraining orders compared to 23 jurisdictions that mandate arrest in domestic violence cases). What explains this approach?

7. *Implications for arrest rate.* Do mandatory arrest policies result in an increase in arrests? The impact of mandatory arrest on arrest rates is controversial. For an early examination of this controversy, see Sherman, Influence of Criminology, supra, at 23-25. Recent research, based on a large representative sample, confirms that the odds of arrest for abusers are higher among those police agencies with mandatory and preferred policies compared to agencies with discretionary policies. NIJ Dual Arrest Report, supra, at 69.

8. *Validity of defendant's arrest.* Did the police officer in *Farrow* have probable cause to believe that a crime had been committed when he made the warrantless arrest? Why or why not? Could the officer have obtained a warrant? Should he have done so? What additional factors in *Farrow* contributed to the decision to charge the defendant with domestic violence?

9. *Abusers who have fled the scene.* In *Farrow*, when the police officer went to the battered women's shelter to investigate the domestic violence involving A.F., the defendant Farrow was no longer at the scene. Abusers who have fled or who are absent from the scene of the crime pose special dilemmas for law enforcement. Estimates suggest that from one- to two-thirds of domestic violence offenders flee by the time law enforcement arrives. Andrew R. Klein, The Criminal Justice Response to Domestic Violence 109, 110 (2004). Those abusers who flee may be significantly more dangerous than those who remain. Id. at 111.

Many police departments do not aggressively pursue suspects who leave the scene. Police often fail to issue warrants for these offenders. Or, if they do issue warrants, they do not serve the warrants. Huge warrant backlogs are common in many police departments. Often, "[u]nless the subject is stopped for another reason, little effort is made to arrest them." Id. at 110. How was the defendant in *Farrow* arrested? What can be done to improve warrant service?

10. *Temporal requirements.* What is the defendant's argument in *Farrow* about the requisite proximity of his arrest to the incident of abuse? How does the appellate court respond? Why does the appellate court determine that the police officer had the authority to make the warrantless arrest, despite the fact that two weeks had elapsed since the last incident of abuse?

Some statutes do require proximity of the arrest to the incident of abuse. For example, some states' mandatory arrest laws limit their application to arrests within a specified time ranging from 4 to 24 hours after the crime. See, e.g., Nev. Rev. Stat. §171.137(1) (within 24 hours); Wash. Rev. Code §10.31.100(2)(c) (within previous 4 hours). What explains these temporal requirements? What interest do they serve? In light of *Farrow*, do you think states should have temporal requirements? If so, what time should be required? If not, why not? Note that if the police do seek a warrant, they have to execute that warrant in a timely manner.

11. *Impetus for law reform: research study.* Many states enacted mandatory arrest statutes in the 1970s and 1980s. As Zorza explains, support for mandatory arrest legislation stemmed in part from: (1) a landmark study of various police responses to misdemeanor domestic assaults, and (2) class-action lawsuits against police departments for failure to respond to calls from battered women. The latter issue is discussed subsequently in this chapter.

In 1984, criminologists Lawrence Sherman and Richard Berk conducted the first major study of the deterrent power of arrest. The Minneapolis Domestic Violence Experiment (MDVE) studied the effects of different police responses to domestic violence (that is, arrest followed by one night in jail; separation of the parties for eight hours; and on-the-spot mediation). Researchers compared the effect of these approaches on future acts of domestic violence over the next six months (based on police records and victim interviews). The authors concluded that arrest was the most effective deterrent to future acts of domestic violence. See Lawrence W. Sherman & Richard A. Berk, The Specific Deterrent Effects of Arrest for Domestic Assault, 49 Am. Soc. Rev. 261 (1984). See also Lawrence W. Sherman & Ellen G. Cohn, The Impact of Research on Legal Policy: The Minneapolis Domestic Violence Experiment, 23 Law & Soc. Rev. 117 (1989).

The MDVE findings had a profound effect on social policy. Buzawa & Buzawa, Criminal Justice Response, supra, at 96-97. The U.S. Attorney General issued a report afterwards that recommended arrest in all cases of misdemeanor domestic assault. William L. Hart et al., U.S. Att'y General's Task Force on Family Violence, Final Report 16-17 (1984). In response, by 1989, police practices had changed significantly. Most large metropolitan police agencies adopted mandatory arrest polices. See Sherman, Influence of Criminology, supra, at 23-24.

12. *Deterrent effect: differential effects.* Criticisms of the methodology and findings of the MDVE study led the National Institute of Justice (NIJ) to fund five replication studies. These studies, differing significantly in their case selection criteria and outcome measures, did not substantiate the original findings. Christopher D. Maxwell et al., The Effects of Arrest on Intimate Partner Violence: New Evidence from the Spouse Assault Replication Program, Nat'l Inst. of Justice Research in Brief, July 2001, at 1, 2. The studies found that arrest has a deterrent effect for *some* offenders (that is, employed, married, and white) but backfires when used against other offenders, particularly poor and minority offenders, for whom arrest may actually increase domestic violence. Sherman, Influence of Criminology, supra, at 25, 32, 37. Faced with inconclusive results, NIJ funded yet another replication study. This study, based on consistent measures across sites, found a modest deterrent effect of arrest. Maxwell et al., supra, at 9, 13. However, researchers also found that arrest does not deter all batterers: A small number of chronically aggressive batterers continue to commit acts of intimate partner violence regardless of the type of intervention they received. Id. at 1, 9, 13. Why might deterrence work better for only some offenders? How should policymakers respond to these findings?

13. *Role of VAWA.* VAWA also played a role in the enactment of mandatory arrest legislation (although the law reform movement was well underway by the time Congress enacted VAWA in 1994). VAWA requires that state and local governments receiving federal funding follow either a mandatory or preferred arrest policy. Specifically, VAWA provides grants to encourage states, local courts, and governmental units to treat domestic violence as a serious crime by requiring grantees to "certify that their laws or official policies . . . encourage or mandate arrests of domestic violence

offenders based on probable cause that an offense has been committed." Pub. L. No. 103-322, 108 Stat. 1932 (codified as amended at 42 U.S.C. §3796hh(c)(1)(a)).

14. *Change in arrest rates.* Has mandatory arrest changed law enforcement's response to domestic violence? The traditional police approach to domestic violence treated domestic violence as less serious than stranger-perpetrated violence. How has the current response to intimate partner violence changed? And, how do arrest rates for domestic violence compare to those for stranger-perpetrated violence? A recent federally funded study suggests that the passage of domestic violence laws has resulted in an increased likelihood of arrest. In a study of 577,862 incidents of simple assault, aggravated assault, and intimidation, 49 percent of the intimate partner cases resulted in an arrest compared to 31 percent of stranger cases. See NIJ Dual Arrest Report, supra at 68. Arrests for domestic disturbances in the 1970s and 1980s, in comparison, ranged from 7 to 15 percent. Id. at 7. See also Klein, supra, at 90-91 (comparing arrest rates).

15. *Objectives of mandatory arrest laws.* Support for mandatory arrest was based on several aims: the deterrent effect of police involvement, the hope that arrest would empower victims, and the importance of societal condemnation of domestic violence. Does mandatory arrest accomplish these purposes? Consider that question as the read the following materials.

3. Evaluation of Mandatory Arrest: Benefits and Shortcomings

Mandatory arrest is a controversial practice. The following excerpts explore the benefits and shortcomings of mandatory arrest laws.

■ **ARTHUR L. RIZER III, MANDATORY ARREST: DO WE NEED TO TAKE A CLOSER LOOK?**
36 UWLA L. Rev. 1, 11-14 (2005)

THE ADVANTAGES OF MANDATORY ARRESTS

. . . Advocates of mandatory arrest contend that the policy of mandatory arrest ensures that those that commit this crime are labeled and treated as criminals. Such criminals are put in jail because it serves as a deterrent. Therefore, another benefit for putting batterers in jail is that it will send a message not only to them, but also to society at large. When a batterer is put in jail, society is saying that what he is doing is not okay and that it will not accept his behavior. . . . Put simply, criminals should be treated as criminals. . . .

[Another benefit is that mandatory arrest, by limiting police discretion, serves to empower women.] Evan Stark wrote, "The absence of a standard for police practice increased women's sense of powerlessness and thus posed a major obstacle to their empowerment." In essence, he argues that mandatory arrest promotes the autonomy and empowerment of women.

A positive effect on police is that mandatory arrest clarifies their role as law enforcers. . . . "Mandatory arrest would clarify the role of police in domestic violence cases and would help guarantee each victim an appropriate response from the criminal justice system." Furthermore, it would avoid forcing police officers to play the role of family counselors. . . .

Another positive aspect of mandatory arrest is that it redistributes resources, giving women's issues more attention. "The message is that the police are a resource and that battered women have just as much right to that resource as any other segment of society." One theory is that mandatory arrest encourages victims to report violence because there are guaranteed results.

One of the most acclaimed benefits to mandatory arrest is that it provides protection from immediate violence. Dave Mather, a Cheney, Washington, police officer, agrees with that position. He claims that there is an immediate payoff by arresting one of the parties in that there is an instantaneous separation. "If the perpetrator is not there, he can't hit her." . . .

■ EMILY J. SACK, BATTERED WOMEN AND THE STATE; THE STRUGGLE FOR THE FUTURE OF DOMESTIC VIOLENCE POLICY
2004 Wis. L. Rev. 1657, 1678-1680 (2004)

. . . While battered women's advocates are concerned about the effectiveness of mandatory policies, their fundamental interest is the impact of these policies on the safety and the autonomy of battered women. Although the push for mandatory criminal justice policies came from the battered women's movement, some within that movement argue that women have been revictimized by these policies. These critics argue that when the arresting officer and prosecutor have no discretion, domestic violence victims lose the opportunity to make choices about whether they want the abuser arrested or prosecuted, and they are placed at greater risk. These critics argue that battered women are the best predictors of the severity of risk they face from their abusers, and their desire not to press charges may be motivated by the knowledge that this will aggravate the violence. When victims realize that they have no choice once police and prosecutors get involved, they are less likely to initiate calls for help, and mandatory policies thus have an effect contrary to that which was intended. More broadly, they argue that these policies disempower victims, and some analogize this taking of power and control from the victim to the dynamic of the battering relationship itself.

Critics from within the movement have also argued that certain groups of women, including immigrants and racial minorities, may be particularly harmed by the imposition of these mandatory state policies. For example, if the abuser is an immigrant, he may be subject to deportation if convicted of a domestic violence crime; this can be a powerful disincentive for a woman to pursue criminal charges. African American women may resist calling the police or pursuing prosecution because they are hesitant to expose African American men to a criminal justice system that they perceive as racist. For these reasons, the benefits of mandatory policies may be outweighed by their costs, particularly for poor, immigrant, or minority women. . . .

4. Unintended Consequences: Dual Arrest

Do mandatory arrest laws lead to an unintended consequence: punishment of victims who protect themselves? The following excerpt explores this question.

■ **DAVID HIRSCHEL ET AL., NAT'L INST. OF JUSTICE,
EXPLAINING THE PREVALENCE, CONTEXT, AND
CONSEQUENCES OF DUAL ARREST IN INTIMATE
PARTNER CASES**
4, 8-10, 12-13 (2007)

. . . Current research indicates that the passage of mandatory and preferred arrest domestic violence laws has resulted in an increased likelihood of arrest in cases of domestic violence. This research also suggests that the increased arrest rate is in part attributable to a disproportionate increase in arrests for females either as a single offender or as part of what is known as a "dual arrest," the situation that arises when both parties involved in an incident are arrested. . . .

. . . Research conducted in Washington State after the enactment of a mandatory arrest law in 1984 showed that women were now being arrested in 50 percent of all cases in which an arrest was made for domestic violence offenses. In California, a state with a preferred arrest law, [researchers] observed that, while women constituted 5 percent of felony domestic violence arrests in 1987, they made up 18 percent of such arrests in 2000. In Delaware, where police departments tend to operate under pro-arrest policies, [research] found that the proportion of female arrests for domestic assault grew from 5 percent in 1987 to 17 percent in 1999. . . .

There are several possible explanations for [the increase in the arrest of females following passage of mandatory arrest legislation]. First, police may find themselves in a situation where the admissions of the involved parties, evidence, and/or witnesses identifies the female as the primary aggressor. Thus, while officers may be inclined to assume that adult male against female violence typically involves a male primary aggressor, they believe the evidence necessitates an arrest of the female. [Research] suggests that women do in fact commit a considerable number of violent acts in intimate relationships that do not constitute self-defense, although the researchers emphasize that women's rates of violence are considerably lower, and their acts are less severe, than those perpetrated by males. Therefore, women may not be the sole victims of domestic violence.

Second, officers may be attempting to implement a gender-neutral policy and believe that in order to implement the law fairly, they must arrest all violent parties. Thus, the officer makes a decision regarding an assault in the context of a specific incident, rather than in the context of the victim-offender relationship.

Third, legislation directed at changing an organization's response can be expected to limit the influence of non-organizational variables. Specifically, domestic violence legislation directed at limiting discretion in the decision to arrest can be expected to limit the influence of situational variables and result in a more legalistic response.

Fourth, police may be more likely to arrest women as part of an overall increase in arrests out of concern for the perceived or real threat of lawsuits. The increased concern by departments to reduce liability and officer perceptions about civil liability may result in a decreased likelihood to use discretion. In the case of domestic violence, this may create an unwillingness to attempt the identification of a primary aggressor and result simply in the arrest of "any and all violent parties."

Fifth, there has been a historic concern regarding the police propensity to arrest in cases of domestic assault compared to incidents of non-domestic assaults.

In domestic violence cases, arrest has generally been infrequent and considered a last resort. Statutes mandating arrest in cases of domestic assault are likely to result in an increase in a more "legalistic" approach to domestic assault resulting in a greater likelihood for arrest in a domestic compared to a non-domestic assault. Since the vast majority of domestic violence incidents involve a female as one of the parties while the majority of non-domestic assaults involve males only, there may be a disproportionate increase in the proportion of females arrested for assault overall as a result. . . .

In some cases, dual arrests may be the result of legislation and/or department policies failing to require officers to identify the primary aggressor. [A] majority of states do not have primary aggressor statutes on the books. In addition, when such provisions are present, there may be a lack of sufficient police training and/or a lack of information needed when responding to a domestic assault in order to identify the primary aggressor. This situation may be compounded by the allegation that batterers have become increasingly adept at manipulating the criminal justice system in an effort to further control or retaliate against their victim and may make efforts to "preempt" victims from notifying police.

Even in those cases where officers are asked to select a primary aggressor, current political and/or organizational pressure, and cultural norms may discourage officers from identifying women as "aggressors," and, unsure what to do, the officers may arrest both parties. This observation is supported by some of the existing research. . . .

Some research has suggested that the dual arrest of a female may be the result of specific behaviors and traits. Females who were unmarried cohabitants were reported to have higher rates of dual arrest than females in other intimate relationships. . . . In addition, female use of alcohol and possession of a weapon has been reported to increase the likelihood of dual arrest. This substantiates [some researchers'] longstanding position regarding the more punitive treatment of women who deviate from the "good woman" image. The male failure to conform to expected social norms and behavior is more likely to be tolerated than is similar behavior by females. . . .

Postscript

The above findings of the National Institute of Justice are based on a comprehensive study of dual arrest involving cases of intimate partner violence. The sample consisted of 577,862 incidents of aggravated assault, simple assault, and intimidation, reported in the National Incident-Based Reporting System (NIBRS), involving 2,819 jurisdictions in 19 states. NIJ Dual Arrest Report, supra, at iii.

The NIJ study sheds light on the concern that mandatory arrest leads to an increase in the rate of dual arrests and constitutes discrimination on the basis of gender. Findings reveal that dual arrests are not occurring as often as previously suggested. Although dual arrests do occur, the actual rate of dual arrest is quite low. Id. at 172 (reporting a dual arrest rate of 1.3 percent). Not surprisingly, among the different arrest policies, mandatory and preferred are more likely to result in dual arrests than discretionary polices. Id. Moreover, the researchers found no evidence of gender discrimination in arrest rate. "Several of our findings indicate that officers appear to execute their duties without considering the extra-legal characteristic of the sex of the involved parties. We found that sex exerted no significant effect on the response to intimate partner cases." Id. at 174.

5. Primary Aggressor Statutes

Primary aggressor statutes emerged following the widespread implementation of mandatory arrest legislation. Criticism of mandatory arrest policies (specifically, the resulting increase in dual arrests) prompted state legislatures to reform the law by enacting primary aggressor statutes. Consider the following statutes in order to determine the statutory guidelines that assist law enforcement in the identification of the primary aggressor.

■ IOWA CODE ANN. §236.12. PREVENTION OF FURTHER ABUSE, ARREST

[T]he peace officer shall arrest the person whom the peace officer believes to be the primary physical aggressor. The duty of the officer to arrest extends only to those persons involved who are believed to have committed an assault. Persons acting with justification . . . are not subject to mandatory arrest. In identifying the primary physical aggressor, a peace officer shall consider the need to protect victims of domestic abuse, the relative degree of injury or fear inflicted on the persons involved, and any history of domestic abuse between the persons involved. A peace officer's identification of the primary physical aggressor shall not be based on the consent of the victim to any subsequent prosecution or on the relationship of the persons involved in the incident, and shall not be based solely upon the absence of visible indications of injury or impairment. . . .

■ S.C. CODE ANN. §16-25-70. WARRANTLESS ARREST

. . . (D) If a law enforcement officer receives conflicting complaints of domestic or family violence from two or more household members involving an incident of domestic or family violence, the officer must evaluate each complaint separately to determine who was the primary aggressor. If the officer determines that one person was the primary physical aggressor, the officer must not arrest the other person accused of having committed domestic or family violence. In determining whether a person is the primary aggressor, the officer must consider the following factors and any other factors he considers relevant:

(1) prior complaints of domestic or family violence;
(2) the relative severity of the injuries inflicted on each person taking into account injuries alleged which may not be easily visible at the time of the investigation;
(3) the likelihood of future injury to each person;
(4) whether one of the persons acted in self-defense; and
(5) household member accounts regarding the history of domestic violence.

. . .

(F) A law enforcement officer who arrests two or more persons for a crime involving domestic or family violence must include the grounds for arresting both parties in the written incident report, and must include a statement in the report that the officer attempted to determine which party was the primary aggressor pursuant to this section and was unable to make a determination based upon the evidence available at the time of the arrest. . . .

■ WASH. REV. CODE §10.31.100. ARREST WITHOUT WARRANT

. . . When the officer has probable cause to believe that family or household members have assaulted each other, the officer is not required to arrest both persons. The officer shall arrest the person whom the officer believes to be the primary physical aggressor. In making this determination, the officer shall make every reasonable effort to consider: (i) The intent to protect victims of domestic violence under RCW 10.99.010; (ii) the comparative extent of injuries inflicted or serious threats creating fear of physical injury; and (iii) the history of domestic violence of each person involved, including whether the conduct was part of an ongoing pattern of abuse. . . .

Notes and Questions on Mandatory Arrest

1. *Advantages and disadvantages.* What are the benefits of mandatory arrest for the victim? For society? What are the shortcomings? See generally Buzawa & Buzawa, Criminal Justice Response, supra, at 127-138 (exploring advantages and disadvantages).

2. *Role of race.* Critics contend that mandatory arrest is discriminatory because it results in higher arrest rates for racial and ethnic minorities. Such claims were based on early studies and those that yielded inconsistent results. Recent comprehensive research on arrest rates (involving over 500,000 incidents in 2,819 jurisdictions in 19 states) among various racial and ethnic groups (that is, white, Black, Asian/Pacific Islander, American Indian, and Hispanic) fails to substantiate those claims. Although mandatory and preferred arrest laws, but not discretionary arrest laws, produce higher arrest rates based on the offender's race, *white* offenders are most likely to be arrested. See NIJ Dual Arrest Report, supra, at 81. Researchers speculate that police are *less* likely to arrest minority offenders because police view violence in such communities as "normal behavior." Id. at 92. See also Hirschel & Hutchison, supra, at 330 (2003) (pointing out that Black women are *more* likely than white women to desire the arrest of their partners).

3. *Role of sexual orientation.* Do mandatory arrest laws adversely affect same-sex partners? The NIJ study reveals that same-sex couples are particularly susceptible to dual arrest. See NIJ Dual Arrest Report, supra, at 86 (reporting dual arrest rate of 26.1 percent of female same-sex cases and 27.3 percent of male same-sex cases, compared to 1.3 percent dual arrest rate for all intimate partner violence cases). The researchers speculate that "sex role stereotyping may play a part in the arrest decision [for female same-sex couples]; while some level of violence may be regarded as 'normal' between two males, such violence may be regarded as

intolerable between two females." Id. at 172-173. The law enforcement response to same-sex violence is explored in Chapter 3.

4. *Factors that increase likelihood of arrest.* The NIJ research reveals that certain factors increase the likelihood of arrest: the seriousness of the offense, presence of children, and presence of the offender at the scene. NIJ Dual Arrest Report, supra, at 141. The probability of arrest also increases when a third party (as opposed to the victim) calls the police (id. at 129), and when an offender presents an angry demeanor to police (id. at 133). What explains the impact of these specific factors on the police response?

5. *Dual arrests.* Dual arrests may occur when police confront conflicting accounts of abuse or equivocal physical evidence (such as injuries inflicted on the abuser by the victim in an act of self-defense).

a. *Determination of self-defense.* How can police determine whether the alleged aggressor in fact acted in self-defense? Does the extent of the injuries help in this determination? How can the police make such a determination if both parties have injuries?

Criminologist Eve Buzawa criticizes that police sometimes fail to correctly assign offender status because police focus on the concrete incident rather than the pattern of physical and psychological abuse. Buzawa & Buzawa, Criminal Justice Response, supra, at 136. Cf. Donna Coker, Shifting Power for Battered Women: Law, Material Resources, and Poor Women of Color, 33 U.C. Davis L. Rev. 1009, 1045 (2000) (suggesting that a victim's conduct sometimes fails to meet the legal definition of self-defense because the victim initiated the immediate hostilities, but did so in reaction to a long pattern of abuse). The self-defense doctrine is explored in Chapter 7.

b. *Consequences of dual arrest.* What are the consequences for victims if they are arrested? Dual arrest means that the victim is treated as a criminal and also denied necessary social and legal services. Moreover, arrest may affect mothers' right to child custody and subject their children to social service intervention. Joan Zorza & Laurie Woods, Mandatory Arrest: Problems and Possibilities 23-24 (1994). A criminal record adversely affects employment. And, victims' arrests serve a symbolic function "as a means of batterers' use of the state to punish and intimidate their victim partners." Coker, supra, at 1044-1045. Finally, arrest of the victim may enhance "her own sense of guilt and responsibility for the abuse, while contributing to the batterer's denial of accountability and blame of the victim." Machaela M. Hoctor, Comment, Domestic Violence as a Crime Against the State: The Need for Mandatory Arrest in California, 85 Calif. L. Rev. 643, 685 (1997). What other messages does the practice of dual arrest send—to the victim, the abuser, and society?

c. *Written reports.* Some states require written reports if police make dual arrests. See, e.g., Mass. Gen. Laws Ch. 258E §8 ("if a law officer arrests both parties, the law officer shall submit a detailed, written report in addition to an incident report, setting forth the grounds for arresting both parties"). What is the purpose of this requirement? Is it a beneficial development?

d. *Effect of mandatory arrest on dual arrest rate.* Early research suggests that the enactment of mandatory arrest laws produced high rates of dual arrest. What light does the above excerpt shed on this issue? See also Zorza & Woods, supra, at 18-19. Assuming that the passage of mandatory arrest laws did result in an increased rate of dual arrests, does that effect still exist? See NIJ Dual Arrest Report, supra, at 172 (reporting a low dual arrest rate of 1.3 percent). What factors might have contributed to this change in law enforcement practice?

e. *Criticism.* Some domestic violence advocates criticize the legal system for its failure to recognize that mutual battering is an infrequent occurrence. Professor Sarah Buel remarks that "An isolated incident often does not accurately reflect who is the true victim and who is the abuser. . . . A survivor's use of force in response to certain situations does not make her a batterer." Sarah M. Buel, Access to Meaningful Remedy: Overcoming Doctrinal Obstacles in Tort Litigation Against Domestic Violence Offenders, 83 Or. L. Rev. 945, 958-959 (2004). Buel notes that charges of mutual battering often arise because a common tactic of batterers is to claim that the victims are either mutually combative or the sole aggressors. Id. at 958.

6. *Fighting back.* Dual arrests may result because police cannot determine, in a "mutual combat" situation, which of the participants is the "offender" and which is the "victim." Why are some victims more likely to fight back? What are the characteristics of those who fight back? What are consequences of fighting back?

a. *Reasons why victims fight back.* Victims may use force against their abusers for many reasons. Obviously, they desire to protect themselves and/or their children. However, victims may also fight back in order to "stand up for themselves in an attempt to salvage their self-worth, to get their partners' attention, to earn their partners' respect, to retaliate for threats against their families, and to retaliate for their partners' abusive behavior." See Leigh Goodmark, When is a Battered Woman Not a Battered Woman? When She Fights Back, 20 Yale J.L. & Feminism 75, 92 (2008).

b. *Characteristics of victims who fight back.* A large proportion of women who fight back are Black and/or lesbian. Research has found that Black women fight back at higher rates than white women. Hillary Porter, Battle Cries: Black Women and Intimate Partner Abuse 116 (2008). Commentators speculate that African-American women, as well as lesbians, are particularly likely to fight back based on their perception that they must defend themselves because the legal system is unlikely to assist them. Id. at 137 (Black women); Goodmark, supra, at 96-99, 104 (lesbians). In addition, as Potter explains, Black women who fight back are more likely to have been exposed to childhood abuse and to reject characterizations of themselves as victims. Porter, supra, at 125-126 (exposure to child abuse), 127-129 (rejection of victim label).

Resistance, of course, can be passive as well as active. See Margaret Abraham, Fighting Back: Abused South Asian Women's Strategies of Resistance 253, in Domestic Violence at the Margins (Natalie J. Sokoloff & Christina Pratt eds., 2008) (identifying South Asian women's resistance strategies of silence, hiding, challenging the abuser's fiscal control, and contemplating suicide).

c. *Consequences of fighting back.* The consequences for victims if they fight back may be severe. Not surprisingly, victims' use of force may contribute to escalation of the violence and may subject them to more serious injury. Goodmark, supra, at 93-94.

d. *Gender-based meaning of fighting back.* Is women's use of force against their partners similar to, and/or different from, men's use of force? See Goodmark, supra, at 93 (explaining that men use violence to exert control and induce fear in their partners, but women use violence either defensively or expressly to voice their frustration about their inability to control the violent situation). See also Susan L. Miller, Victims as Offenders: The Paradox of Women's Violence in Relationships 116-120 (2005) (presenting findings from her empirical study of women arrested for domestic assaults).

7. *Primary aggressor.* Primary aggressor statutes respond to law enforcement's inability and/or unwillingness to distinguish victims from offenders. Primary aggressor laws authorize police to arrest only the "primary" aggressor. Such statutes attempt to reduce dual arrests by recognizing that, although both parties may be participants in the violence, one party may be more culpable.

a. *Prevalence.* Washington was the first state to enact such legislation in 1985. Wash. Rev. Code. §10.31.100. Currently, 22 states have primary aggressor laws. Buzawa & Buzawa, Criminal Justice Response, supra, at 136.

b. *Statutory variations.* A few state statutes direct police officers to arrest the "primary aggressor" but fail to provide guidelines for identifying this offender. See, e.g., R.I. Gen. Laws §12-29-3 ("The officer shall arrest the person whom the officer believes to be the primary physical aggressor"). However, most primary aggressor laws do contain statutory guidelines based on either the Washington statute above or the Model State Code for Family Violence §205(A), drafted in 1991-1994 by the National Council of Juvenile and Family Court Judges, under the auspices of the Conrad N. Hilton Foundation. The Family Violence Model Code was developed by a committee of battered women's advocates, medical and health care professionals, law enforcement personnel, legislators, family law practitioners, and educators. See National Council of Juvenile and Family Court Judges, Family Violence: A Model State Code §205(A), 6-7 (1994), available at http://www.ncjfcj.org/images/stories/dept/fvd/pdf/modecode_fin_printable.pdf.

The Family Violence Model Code provides that a police officer shall consider the following factors in the determination of primary-aggressor status: (1) prior complaints of domestic violence; (2) the relative severity of injuries; (3) the likelihood of future injury to each person; and (4) whether one person acted in self-defense. Id. at 7. How does the Model Code differ from the Washington statute above? How does it differ from the other statutes above?

What is the difference between "a peace officer shall consider the need to protect victims of domestic abuse" and the police should consider the "intent of the law to protect victims of domestic violence"? Is there a difference between the factors of "any history of domestic abuse between the persons involved," and "prior complaints of domestic or family violence"?

What guidelines might be more helpful to police in their determination? What additional factors might be relevant? See Mont. Code Ann. §46-6-311(iv), (vi) (including "the relative sizes and apparent strength of each person"; "the apparent fear or lack of fear between the partners or family members"; and "statements made by witnesses"). How relevant are the visible injuries, victim's history of prior complaints, or the party who requested police assistance? See generally Klein, supra, at 100 (describing different primary aggressor statutes).

c. *Primary versus dominant.* The California legislature clarified its primary aggressor statute by addition of the word *dominant*. In situations when a court has issued mutual protective orders, the statute provides that liability for arrest applies only to persons "who are reasonably believed to have been the dominant aggressor." The statute defines "dominant aggressor" as "the person determined to be the most significant, rather than the first, aggressor." Cal. Penal Code §836. Is this new terminology an improvement? What is the difference between "primary" aggressor and "dominant" aggressor? Which designation is more helpful to law enforcement? What is the role of provocation in the determination of "primary aggressor"? Is the person who struck the first blow in this incident necessarily the primary aggressor? How relevant are nonphysical acts in the determination?

d. *Excluded factors.* Some statutes exclude certain factors from consideration in the identification of the primary aggressor. Why does the Iowa statute (above) provide that the identification of the primary physical aggressor shall *not* be based on: (1) the victim's consent to prosecution, (2) the relationship of the parties, and (3) the absence of visible indications of injury or impairment?

e. *Expansion.* Some states consider the relevance of primary aggressor status in other legal proceedings, such as child custody determinations. See ALI Principles of the Law of Family Dissolution §2.11 (Criteria for Parenting Plan—Limiting Factors) cmt. c. ("[I]n situations of mutual domestic violence, when one parent's aggression is substantially more extreme or dangerous than the other's, it may be appropriate for the court to impose limits on the primary aggressor but not on the primary victim").

8. *Effectiveness of primary aggressor statutes.* Do primary aggressor statutes accomplish their purpose of reducing dual arrests? The NIJ study suggests that such statutes do have this result. NIJ Dual Arrest Report, supra, at 173. Should more states enact such statutes?

9. *Victims' preferences.* What role do victim preferences play in arrest? The NIJ study found that when police do not make an arrest, 43.2 percent of the time their decision stems from victim "declined prosecution" and 49.7 percent of the time their decision stems from "victim refused to cooperate." Id. at 56.

What role *should* victim preferences play in arrest? Victims' preferences appear to be related to their likelihood of revictimization. Victims who exhibit a strong preference for the arrest of the offender are more likely to suffer subsequent abuse than victims who do not want arrests. Hirschel & Hutchison, supra, at 330 (based on sample of 419 battered women). What explains this result? Might these victims be particularly aware of their partners' dangerousness? How should these research findings influence social policy? Victim non-cooperation is explored further in Chapter 7.

Should *some* victims' preferences be disregarded? Psychologist Evan Stark suggests that reliance on victim preference is "problematic" for certain victims: women whose "entrapment prevents their expressing a preference for arrest," minorities who view arrest as a "betrayal of cultural norms," and women who do not understand the nature of the risk. Evan Stark, Mandatory Arrest of Batterers: A Reply to Its Critics, in Do Arrests and Restraining Orders Work? 115, 143 (Eve S. Buzawa & Carl G. Buzawa eds., 1996). Do you agree that these victims' preferences should be disregarded?

10. *Empowerment debate.* The above excerpts suggest that mandatory arrest paradoxically serves to empower as well as disempower victims. How does it accomplish

both these objectives? One commentator identifies the opposing views as "protagonist" feminists and "antagonist" feminists:

> The Protagonists view mandatory practices [referring to both mandatory arrest and prosecutorial no-drop policies as necessary for women's safety] because battered women are incapable of making a "rational" choice while being traumatized by the violence. Mandatory practices then serve as a necessary shield—not just from the violence of individual males, but from what is perceived as survivor powerlessness. [This position is problematic because it reifies] the cultural stereotypes of the incapacitated and irrational woman—stereotypes that confine women to, rather than liberate women from, oppressive homes.
>
> At the opposite end of the spectrum are the Antagonists. . . . The state is perceived as a replacement for the individual-as-oppressor in its usurpation of women's decision-making power. Such practices are significant in the continued regulation of women rather than as a means to liberation. Mandatory practices, then, operate as a sword, severing women from personal and social power. . . .

G. Kristian Miccio, A House Divided: Mandatory Arrest, Domestic Violence, and the Conservatization of the Battered Women's Movement, 42 Hous. L. Rev. 237, 241-242 (2005). See also Hirschel & Hutchison, supra, at 316 (explaining that proponents of removing discretion from victims assert that victims are unable to decide and that no-drop policies lessen the likelihood of intimidation by the abuser; opponents assert that no-drop policies disempower women, provide only a temporary solution, and lead to retaliation).

Which view do you find more persuasive? Do the benefits of mandatory arrest outweigh the infringement on women's autonomy? See Hanna, supra, at 1886-1188 (so arguing).

6. Victims' Experiences with the Police

The police response can be effective only if acts of domestic violence come to the attention of law enforcement. Such disclosure can stem from victims' reports of the abuse or reports of third parties, such as neighbors, friends, relatives, etc. Unfortunately, many barriers exist that prevent victims from contacting police to ask for help. The following excerpt highlights some of these barriers.

■ MARSHA E. WOLF ET AL., BARRIERS TO SEEKING POLICE HELP FOR INTIMATE PARTNER VIOLENCE
18 J. Family Violence 121, 124-126 (2003)

[Victims' reluctance to disclose abuse stems from fear of retaliation, cultural attitudes about marriage and gender roles, low self-esteem, and economic dependence on the abuser. Another important factor, explained below, is victims' past experiences with the police.]

Batterer Not Arrested

[In some cases, the police failed to arrest the batterer.] Some victims who called the police expecting that the batterer would be arrested have felt that their efforts were wasted or left them in a more dangerous environment had they not called the police. As a result, they are reluctant to call again. This was especially true in cases where women called because their batterers violated a protection order but received no punishment. . . .

Mistaken Identification of Victim as Batterer (or Failure to Identify the Primary Aggressor)

Prior experience caused some women to express hesitation in calling the police because they feared arrest if police misidentify them as the abuser. Misidentification may occur when victims leave marks on the batterer in the course of self-defense. Victims voiced the concern that police may not take a statement from them and therefore not recognize that the victim was acting in self-defense.

> I had no physical (marks) like on my face or whatever, my hair was pulled . . . but he was bleeding because I'd hit him with the chair (after being choked and beaten by her batterer) and the police seemed to be more concerned why he was bleeding . . . well, I was defending myself. . . . We both ended up going to jail.

Batterers sometimes attempt to make the victim appear drunk or as the aggressor with the intent of manipulating the police into misidentifying the "drunk" person as the alleged perpetrator. . . .

Victim Not Listened To or Situation Trivialized

Women stated that when they are in contact with the police for domestic violence, it is for a crisis situation. Thus, police responses that seemed to trivialize their experience have left some women feeling that the police do not understand the profound impact of domestic violence on their lives. Slow police response to IPV incidents also conveyed the message that IPV is not a serious crime. . . .

Batterer Manipulation and Apparent Bonding with Officer

Victims viewed their batterers as very smart and manipulative in being able to convince others, including the police, that they had not committed any abuse or that the victim had been at fault. The victim's fear that she would not be believed is further aggravated by a perception that the police may identify and bond with their abuser. As a result, victims perceive calling the police as a gamble that they would sometimes rather not take.

> [H]e (batterer) just puts on the drama and (says), "I do this for her and I buy the baby this," and take them in the room and will show them all the stuff . . . and (says), "She pushed me to do this . . . she keeps nagging me and I don't know what to do, officer."

Race, Socioeconomic Status, and Homophobic Stereotyping

[W]omen expressed concern that police biases about race, neighborhoods, or sexual orientation affected response time, how seriously a situation was taken, and the correct identification of the batterer. Participants who were White and staying in more affluent neighborhoods reported they received prompter responses to calls for help and that officers were more courteous and took time to listen to them.

> . . . I was staying at my mom's house and the police came out there and like they were so cool, I mean he (batterer) kept calling and threatening me, they were like, "He calls (you) . . . call us." . . . and I called . . . they showed up in like a minute . . . they were just so nice to me . . . my mom lives in a nice condo . . . lot of money out there. . . . I've never had it (treatment by police) like that.

. . . Victims also expressed concerns of how police discrimination might cause batterers to be unduly punished. When victims seek help from the police, they want the violence to stop and expect to have their batterers punished for the abuse that they committed. However, victims sometimes hesitate to seek police help because they believe their abusers may be subjected to excessive punishment or police brutality because of their race, class, or sexual orientation.

> . . . [W]hen there's domestic violence, they be giving these black men years. . . . Sometimes with the police, you're damned if you do (call) and you're damned if you don't.

Language Barrier and Lack of Adequate Interpretation

Limited knowledge of English or an inability to speak English was an evident barrier for victims to communicate their experience to the police. Some non-English-speaking women felt very disadvantaged by their language skills and felt that because of this the police dismissed them. Their sense of alienation and despair was worsened when police would speak only to the batterer, who is often the only one to speak English.

> (She) says that because of her limited English, she thinks that the police won't listen to her, instead (they) listen to other people who can speak English better. So whatever she says, it doesn't matter . . . they are more likely to listen to other people's side. . . .

Batterer: Retaliation on Victim

Women saw the potential costs of calling the police as greater than the benefits. Some women anticipated their batterers becoming more enraged as a result of police contact and eventually punishing the victim, whereas some women reported experiencing violent beatings after the abuser was released from jail. Several women reported their batterer threatening to kill them if they ever called police. . . .

Children: Child Protective Services (CPS) Involvement and Removal of Children

Many women did not contact the police for fear that their children would be removed from the home as a result of domestic violence. They believed that once CPS was contacted, they would lose control of the situation and subsequently, their children. It is important to note that Native American women were especially concerned regarding this issue and mentioned removal of Native American children from their families when they were growing up. Consequently, they are even more reluctant to enlist police assistance. . . .

7. Statutory Expansion of Police Powers to Ensure Victims' Safety

The law reform movement that led to mandatory arrest also resulted in the statutory expansion of other police powers. Virtually all states prescribe a range of victim-assistance actions that police can take at the scene of an incident of partner violence. The following statutes illustrate these police powers. What forms of assistance do these statutes prescribe? What additional police actions might enhance victims' safety?

■ MASS. GEN. LAWS ANN. CH. 209A §6. POWERS OF POLICE

Whenever any law officer has reason to believe that a family or household member has been abused or is in danger of being abused, such officer shall use all reasonable means to prevent further abuse. The officer shall take, but not be limited to the following action:

(1) remain on the scene of where said abuse occurred or was in danger of occurring as long as the officer has reason to believe that at least one of the parties involved would be in immediate physical danger without the presence of a law officer. This shall include, but not be limited to remaining in the dwelling for a reasonable period of time;

(2) assist the abused person in obtaining medical treatment necessitated by an assault, which may include driving the victim to the emergency room of the nearest hospital, or arranging for appropriate transportation to a health care facility, notwithstanding any law to the contrary;

(3) assist the abused person in locating and getting to a safe place; including but not limited to a designated meeting place for a shelter or a family member's or friend's residence. The officer shall consider the victim's preference in this regard and what is reasonable under all the circumstances;

(4) give such person immediate and adequate notice of his or her rights. Such notice shall consist of handing said person a copy of the statement which follows below and reading the same to said person. Where said person's native language is not English, the statement shall be then provided in said person's native language whenever possible.

> "You have the right to appear at the Superior, Probate and Family, District or Boston Municipal Court, if you reside within the appropriate jurisdiction, and file a complaint requesting any of the following applicable orders: (a) an order restraining your attacker from abusing you; (b) an order directing your attacker to leave your household, building or workplace; (c) an order awarding you custody of a minor child; (d) an order directing your attacker to pay support for you or any minor child in your custody, if the attacker has a legal obligation of support; and (e) an order directing your attacker to pay you for losses suffered as a result of abuse, including medical and moving expenses, loss of earnings or support, costs for restoring utilities

and replacing locks, reasonable attorney's fees and other out-of-pocket losses for injuries and property damage sustained.

For an emergency on weekends, holidays, or weeknights the police will refer you to a justice of the superior, probate and family, district, or Boston municipal court departments.

You have the right to go to the appropriate district court or the Boston municipal court and seek a criminal complaint for threats, assault and battery, assault with a deadly weapon, assault with intent to kill or other related offenses.

If you are in need of medical treatment, you have the right to request that an officer present drive you to the nearest hospital or otherwise assist you in obtaining medical treatment.

If you believe that police protection is needed for your physical safety, you have the right to request that the officer present remain at the scene until you and your children can leave or until your safety is otherwise ensured. You may also request that the officer assist you in locating and taking you to a safe place, including but not limited to a designated meeting place for a shelter or a family member's or a friend's residence, or a similar place of safety.

You may request a copy of the police incident report at no cost from the police department."

The officer shall leave a copy of the foregoing statement with such person before leaving the scene or premises.

(5) assist such person by activating the emergency judicial system when the court is closed for business;

(6) inform the victim that the abuser will be eligible for bail and may be promptly released; and

(7) arrest any person a law officer witnesses or has probable cause to believe has violated a temporary or permanent vacate, restraining, or no-contact order or judgment . . . or similar protection order issued by another jurisdiction. When there are no vacate, restraining, or no-contact orders or judgments in effect, arrest shall be the preferred response whenever an officer witnesses or has probable cause to believe that a person:

(a) has committed a felony;

(b) has committed a misdemeanor involving abuse as defined in section one of this chapter;

(c) has committed an assault and battery in violation of section thirteen A of chapter two hundred and sixty-five.

The safety of the victim and any involved children shall be paramount in any decision to arrest. Any officer arresting both parties must submit a detailed, written report in addition to an incident report, setting forth the grounds for dual arrest. . . .

■ N.H. REV. STAT. §173-B:10. PROTECTION BY PEACE OFFICERS

Whenever any peace officer has probable cause to believe that a person has been abused, as defined in RSA §173-B:1, that officer shall use all means within reason to prevent further abuse including, but not limited to:

(a) Confiscating any deadly weapons involved in the alleged domestic abuse and any firearms and ammunition in the defendant's control, ownership, or possession.

(b) Transporting or obtaining transportation for the victim and any child, to a designated place to meet with a domestic violence counselor, local family member, or friend.

(c) Assisting the victim in removing toiletries, medication, clothing, business equipment, and any other items determined by the court.

(d) Giving the victim immediate and written notice of the rights of victims and of the remedies and services available to victims of domestic violence. The written notice shall include a statement substantially as follows:

> "If you are the victim of domestic violence and you believe that law enforcement protection is needed for your physical safety, you have the right to request that the officer assist in providing for your safety, including asking for an emergency telephonic order for protection. You may also request that the officer assist you in obtaining from your premises and curtilage, toiletries, medication, clothing, business equipment, and any other items as determined by the court, and in locating and taking you to a local safe place including, but not limited to, a designated meeting place to be used as a crisis center, a family member's or friend's residence, or a similar place of safety. If you are in need of medical treatment, you have the right to request that the officer assist you in obtaining an ambulance. You may request a copy of the report filed by the peace officer, at no cost, from the law enforcement department." . . .

Note: Introduction to the Violence Against Women Act (VAWA)

The Violence Against Women Act, introduced by former Senator Joseph Biden, Jr., and enacted by Congress in 1994, was landmark legislation that addressed intimate partner violence. A major objective of the legislation was to improve the response of law enforcement. The Act had many other important provisions, however, including the creation of federal crimes (for example, interstate stalking, interstate travel to commit domestic violence, interstate travel to violate an order of protection); regulation of firearms in connection with domestic violence offenses; interstate recognition of orders of protection; a self-petitioning process for immigrant battered spouses to enable them to apply for visas without the cooperation of their abusive spouses; and amendment of civil rights laws, among others. Some of these provisions, which are explored more fully throughout this book, are summarized below.

■ REMARKS OF SENATOR JOSEPH R. BIDEN, JR.: INTRODUCING THE VIOLENCE AGAINST WOMEN ACT BEFORE CONGRESS
136 Cong. Rec. 14,563, 14,563-14,564 (June 19, 1990)

Mr. President, I rise today to introduce the first ever comprehensive legislation specifically geared toward combating violent crime against women: the Violence Against Women Act of 1990.

Violent crime against women is a serious problem in America—a serious problem and a growing one, too. We are all familiar with the sensational well-publicized cases of horrifying brutality against women—indeed, as I speak now, underway in New York is the trial of the young men who brutally beat and raped an investment banker on an evening jog in Central Park. While such stories rivet our attention, we must understand that this is not a problem of one or two horrible incidents. Violent crime against women happens every day in this country—every day, every hour, every minute. Indeed, every 6 minutes, a woman is raped in this country; and every 18 seconds, a woman is beaten. As tragic as these facts are, there is one truth even more troubling: violence against women is not only widespread—it is growing.

Over the last 10 years, the rape rate has risen four times faster than the national crime rate—four times faster. That means that rape is increasing not 50 percent more, or 100 percent more, but 400 percent faster than other crime in the United States.

Young women are victims of epidemic increases in violent crimes. Over the past decade and a half, while assaults against men in their early 20s have fallen 12 percent, assaults against young women have risen almost 50 percent. . . . While the [overall] rate of murder of men has fallen 5.6 percent, [t]he rate of murder of women has climbed almost 30 percent. This epidemic of violence against women must be stopped. And the need for urgent action becomes clearer still when we realize that many, many serious crimes against women are never even reported.

Experts estimate that less than half of all rapes are ever reported to the police. Crimes in the home—affecting as many as 3 to 4 million women a year—have an even lower reporting rate. And let's make no mistake about how serious these beatings at home are: Experts tell us that at least one-third of these crimes would be labeled as felonious rapes or felonious assaults if they did not fall into the category of domestic disputes. We all know the consequences of this epidemic. Our wives, our mothers, and our colleagues are afraid to walk in grocery store parking lots, to jog in public parks, or to ride home from work late at night in city buses. They are losing a fundamental human right—the right to be free from fear.

I believe that the legislation I am introducing today will help in the fight against violent crime against women. It attacks the problem in all forms—from rape cases to domestic violence, from every day assaults to murder. And it attacks the problem at all levels of our society: From the home to the streets, from the criminal justice system to the prison system.

The Violence Against Women Act of 1990 is best summarized by the names of its three major titles: Title I—Safe Streets for Women; Title II—Safe Homes for Women; and Title III—Civil Rights for Women. The bill contains many significant legislative proposals. . . . I would like to explain a few of the bill's key provisions in more detail.

Title I: Safe Streets for Women

Title I of the bill recognizes that any concerted effort to reduce violent crime against women must target the areas where women are most often victimized. Thus, the bill provides $200 million in grants to the 40 areas in the country found by the Justice Department to be the most dangerous for women. In addition, $100 million is provided for the Nation's remaining State and local governments. These grants will significantly boost the number of police officers on the streets and prosecutors in the courts—police and prosecutors targeting violent crimes against women. Title I also helps prevent street crime against women by providing grants for lights and cameras in public transit, and punishes these crimes more severely by doubling the penalties for rape and aggravated rape tried in Federal court.

TITLE II: SAFE HOMES FOR WOMEN

The second major title of the bill deals with the crisis confronting millions of women every year who are the victims of violent crimes in their own homes. Despite its name—domestic violence—these incidents are by no means tame; 1 million women a year require medical attention for injuries inflicted by abusing spouses.

Title II provides new laws, encourages new policies, and adds new funds to help in the fight against domestic violence. For example, the bill protects women who flee their abusers, by making protective court orders issued by any State valid in the 49 others. This way, when a woman crosses a State line, she does not lose the benefit of a judge-issued order aimed at keeping her abusive spouse away from her.

In addition, the bill uses Federal grant programs to encourage States to arrest abusive spouses—particularly in cases of repeated abuse. Right now, in some States, a man can be arrested on sight if he has two outstanding speeding tickets, but police won't arrest him when they arrive—for the second or third or fourth time—on the scene where he has abused his spouse. This sort of discrimination must end.

Title II contains other provisions as well, including increased funding for shelters that house battered women, and funds for training prosecutors and courts in handling spouse abuse cases.

TITLE III: CIVIL RIGHTS FOR WOMEN

Finally, and perhaps most importantly, Title III of the Violence Against Women Act addresses the issue of civil rights.

For too long, we have ignored the right of women to be free from the fear of attacks based on their gender—97 percent of all sex assaults in this country are against women. We all know this; indeed, we assume it; but we ignore the obvious implication of the fact: A rape or sex assault should be deemed a civil rights crime, just as hate beatings aimed at blacks or Asians are widely recognized as violations of their civil rights. This bill attempts to fill a gap in our civil rights laws by defining gender-motivated crimes as bias or hate crimes and amending Federal civil rights laws to say that such attacks violate a woman's civil rights.

Such protections can never blunt the pain to a victim of a sex crime; but they do say that we as a nation—as a whole nation—will not tolerate these crimes of hate. We will not tolerate them because they cause physical and emotional injuries; and we will not tolerate them because they deprive a woman of the freedom from fear that she will be attacked because—and simply because—she is a woman. Sex crimes are crimes of hate and discrimination—bias crimes—and it is time that Federal law treated them as such. [*This provision was declared unconstitutional in United States v. Morrison, discussed in Chapter 10.*]

In closing, Mr. President, the Violence Against Women Act contains all of these provisions and more. I ask unanimous consent that the text of the bill be printed in the [Congressional Record]. I hope my colleagues will join me in supporting this legislation which aims at putting an end to this problem of violence—a problem that puts more women in the hospital today than breast cancer, auto accidents, plane crashes, and strokes combined.

VAWA was re-authorized in 2000 as part of the Victims of Trafficking and Violence Protection Act of 2000, Pub. L. No. 106-386, 114 Stat. 1464, to increase funding for law enforcement, shelter services, and legal services for victims (regarding protection orders, family court matters, housing, and immigration). The bill reauthorized existing programs and added funding initiatives addressing dating violence, transitional housing, protection of children during visitation, and protection of elderly and disabled victims. VAWA 2000 expanded protections for victims of sexual assault and dating violence. In addition, VAWA 2000 addressed residual immigration law obstacles for battered immigrant spouses seeking to exit from abusive relationships, and also clarified and expanded federal jurisdiction over interstate stalking and other interstate crimes of violence against women. For a comprehensive summary of VAWA 2000, see Bill Summary: Violence Against Women Act of 2000, available at www.acadv.org/VAWAbillsummary.html.

Congress authorized VAWA again in 2005 (Pub. L. No. 109-162, 119 Stat. 2960) to provide additional funding for services to elderly victims, disabled victims, Native American women, and children exposed to domestic violence; to improve health care and legal services to victims of domestic violence; to expand transitional housing options, target housing discrimination (that is, denial of applications, eviction, lease termination) against victims, and protect the confidentiality of homeless victims receiving services; to create a National Resource Center on Workplace Responses to help make the workplace safer and provide support for employees who are being victimized; and to make technical corrections to existing immigration law (that is, VAWA 1994 and 2000 provisions that enabled battered immigrant spouses to leave their partners without jeopardizing their immigration status) by resolving inconsistencies in the eligibility for immigrant victims. For a comprehensive summary of VAWA 2005, see National Network to End Domestic Violence, Violence Against Women Act of 2005: Summary of Provisions, available at www.nnedv.org/docs/Policy/VAWA2005FactSheet.pdf. VAWA is scheduled for re-authorization in 2011. VAWA 2011 would enhance workplace protections for victims and improve the health care system's response to domestic violence (among other provisions). These provisions are explored in subsequent chapters.

VAWA's federal criminal provisions are explored in Chapter 8. Interstate recognition of orders of protection is explored in Chapter 9. VAWA's civil rights remedy is explored in Chapter 10. The right of immigrant spouses to self-petition for independent legal residency is discussed in Chapter 11. Workplace protections are explored in Chapter 13.

B. PROSECUTORS: NO-DROP POLICIES

The role of the prosecutor has evolved considerably since the beginning of the battered women's movement. What factors influenced this evolution? What are the consequences of this policy transformation?

1. Background

■ CHERYL HANNA, NO RIGHT TO CHOOSE: MANDATED VICTIM PARTICIPATION IN DOMESTIC VIOLENCE PROSECUTIONS

109 Harv. L. Rev. 1849, 1857-1865 (1996)

Police response to domestic violence has recently undergone enormous change. Aggressive arrest policies are now in place throughout the country. . . . Once police started to arrest alleged batterers, advocates began to focus reform efforts on prosecution practices. Prosecutors often fail to initiate charges and to follow through with criminal prosecution in domestic violence cases. Victim non-cooperation, reluctance, or outright refusal to proceed are often cited as the major reasons for this lack of criminal prosecution. Prosecutors may also resist pursuing cases because they believe that battering is a minor, private crime. Within the past ten years, domestic violence advocacy groups have urged prosecutors to follow through with legal intervention. . . .

Although policies vary among jurisdictions, many offices now have pro-prosecution or "no-drop" policies. . . . Pro-prosecution policies check prosecutorial discretion and actively encourage women to proceed through the criminal justice system. Prosecutors cannot routinely dismiss charges at a woman's request, but are required to pursue cases and elicit the victim's cooperation. Moreover, the prosecutor usually signs the charge, relieving the woman of responsibility. Thus, pro-prosecution policies treat domestic violence as a serious crime and recognize the ambivalence that abused women bring to the process. These policies also provide guidelines on how to handle cases in which the victim is reluctant to proceed. Policies range from formal protocols requiring that all victims be subpoenaed to informal practices against routinely dismissing cases at the victim's request.

The term "no-drop" is something of a misnomer. Pro-prosecution policies are often characterized as either "hard" or "soft" no-drop policies. Under "hard" policies, cases proceed regardless of the victim's wishes when there is enough evidence to go forward. . . . Many more cases are prosecuted as a result of this hard no-drop policy. The San Diego approach is to pursue every provable felony case, regardless of the victim's wishes. Under this city's hard no-drop policy, the prosecutor can request a continuance and a bench warrant when a victim fails to appear or cooperate if the case cannot be proved without her testimony.

[L]imited available research suggests that most jurisdictions that give special attention to domestic violence cases employ "soft" no-drop policies. Under soft policies, prosecutors do not force victims to participate in the criminal process; rather, victims are provided with support services and encouraged to continue the process. . . .

Numerous state programs employ or work closely with victim advocates. In Alexandria, Virginia, for example, a victim can drop charges after appearing before a counselor or a judge to explain her refusal. In other soft no-drop jurisdictions, a victim who fails to appear, refuses to testify, or recants her testimony is not sanctioned or forced to participate. Thus, if a woman still refuses to cooperate after counseling and support—and there is not enough evidence to proceed without her testimony—then the prosecutor is likely to dismiss the case rather than request a warrant and a contempt hearing, despite the no-drop policy.

No-drop policies are difficult to assess. . . . [I]t is difficult to measure the difference between written policies and practice. Even in model jurisdictions that follow strict guidelines mandating participation by the victim, prosecutors still maintain broad discretion over whether to pursue cases. . . . [In addition,] there is no clear consensus on how to determine whether a policy is successful. Conviction rates, recidivism rates, deterrence, effective communication of strong symbolic messages, and meaningful protection of victims are all possible criteria for measuring the success of a prosecution strategy. . . . Although advocates have lobbied for better prosecutorial response, they remain ambivalent about the use of state power, such as subpoenas, in prosecution strategy. Just how far the state should go in forcing women to participate before dismissing charges remains an issue of intense debate. . . .

2. Constitutional Issues

■ McCLURE v. REHG
2007 WL 3352389 (E.D. Mo. 2007)

Rodney W. Sippel, United States District Judge.

[Plaintiffs bring this action, pursuant to 42 U.S.C. §1983, for alleged violations of their constitutional rights. They seek monetary relief and the removal of a state criminal action to this court. Defendants include the mayor, prosecutor, judge, police chief, and police officials.]

The complaint alleges that plaintiff [Alice] Ingram called 911 and claimed that plaintiff [Walter] McClure, who is her husband, abused her. Plaintiffs claim that Ingram called 911 a second time and told them that nothing had happened. Plaintiffs say that despite Ingram's second call to 911, the police continued their response to plaintiffs' home. Plaintiffs allege that McClure was arrested as a result of the 911 call. Plaintiffs claim that defendants are continuing to prosecute criminal charges against McClure despite Ingram's wishes. Plaintiffs claim that the prosecution is continuing because the City of Jennings has a "no-drop" policy.[1]

. . . Plaintiffs allege that McClure was arrested and prosecuted because of the City of Jennings' "no-drop" policy. The Court need not reach the constitutionality of the policy, however, because the alleged facts do not rise to the level of a constitutional violation. Plaintiffs are responsible for the police activity in this case because plaintiff Ingram called 911 and requested help. Plaintiffs cannot state a claim for unconstitutional warrantless entry into their home when they voluntarily gave the police officers probable cause to think that there was dangerous activity in their home. As a result, plaintiffs have failed to state a prima facie case under §1983.

---

1. A "no-drop" policy is one that ensures domestic violence cases will be prosecuted irrespective of the wishes of the victim. . . . "No-drop" policies work hand-in-hand with "evidence based prosecution" or "victimless prosecution," which rely "on the use of out-of-court statements to establish the guilt of the defendant when the complaining witness either refuses or is otherwise unable to cooperate with the prosecution." Rather than the victim's testimony, the prosecutors rely on "statements the complainant may have made to a third party, such as a 911 operator or a police officer at the crime scene. These statements often are introduced as 'excited utterances' under an exception to the general rule against hearsay and are offered up 'for the truth,' i.e., as a factual account of the alleged assault."

Additionally, even if the Constitution is implicated by the alleged facts, defendants are immune from this lawsuit. [The court first explains that the trial judge and prosecutor have *absolute* immunity. Then, the court turns to address the issue of the liability of the remaining defendants.] "Qualified immunity protects state actors from civil liability when their conduct does not violate clearly established statutory or constitutional rights of which a reasonable person would have known." The Court is not aware of any constitutional prohibition of "no-drop" policies, and a reasonable state actor could believe that the aggressive prosecution of domestic violence thorough the use of "no-drop" policies is lawful. As a result, the remaining defendants are entitled to qualified immunity. For each of these reasons, the complaint will be dismissed. . . .

3. Victims' Reluctance to Prosecute: The Battered Woman's Dilemma

■ DONNA WILLS, DOMESTIC VIOLENCE: THE CASE FOR AGGRESSIVE PROSECUTION
7 UCLA Women's L.J. 173, 177-182 (1997)

. . . People v. Houston, [No. A569469 (Cal. Super. Ct. 1987)] illustrates the battered woman's dilemma. . . . Donna [Houston] reported escalating attacks by her jealous husband on three separate occasions. Early in the marriage, Donna's ten-year-old son witnessed the defendant push his mother into a bookshelf, causing a heavy statue to fall and lacerate her head. Donna later "minimized" this incident by telling police that her injury was an accident and no charges were filed. Months later, after another argument, Donna's husband stabbed her in the face with scissors, causing a serious jagged laceration. Only after she pleaded with him for medical help and promised not to report his behavior to authorities did he take her to the emergency room for sutures to close the gaping wound. When Donna told the hospital staff what had happened, they called the police who arrested the defendant when he returned to the hospital to pick her up. The defendant had no prior record, but due to the seriousness of Donna's injury, the stabbing incident was filed as a felony spousal assault.

A few days before the preliminary hearing, Donna came to the District Attorney's Office and insisted that she wanted to drop the charges. She had reconciled once again with the defendant and wanted to give their marriage another chance. When told that the prosecution would not be dismissed, Donna made herself "unavailable" to testify by going to New Jersey for an unscheduled "family visit." The case was dismissed for insufficient evidence to proceed.

Donna's girlfriend later testified that the parties subsequently separated and that when Donna refused to talk to him, the defendant tried to run Donna and the girlfriend off the road. Donna did not report this incident. Later, the defendant went to the babysitter's residence, grabbed their five-month-old daughter from Donna's arms, and then led the police on a high-speed chase, with the baby unrestrained in his van. He was apprehended and arrested and the child was safely returned to her terrified mother. Despite Donna's pleas, the defendant's wealthy family promptly posted his bail.

On the same day he was released, the defendant bought a 12-gauge shotgun and ammunition from the local gun store. The next morning, he waited in the parking lot where Donna worked. As she walked out the back door, [he] shot Donna, delivering a fatal wound to her neck, in broad daylight, at close range, in front of six horrified co-workers. . . .

The defendant's escalating attacks on his wife and her initial refusal to cooperate with his prosecution demonstrate a classic scenario in domestic violence cases. Regrettably, many battered women fail to see that criminal intervention can assist in the shared goal of getting their abuser to stop the violence. Too often, they will seek to jettison prosecution of their batterer in favor of concerns inconsistent with their safety and the safety of their children. Too frequently, they are desperate to forgive and forget and to placate the abuser. Instead of criminal intervention, they dare hope to ease the violence by well-learned methods of coping. However, prosecutors have learned from the carnage and despair we have witnessed in domestic violence cases that victims cannot afford to forgive and forget and that the only thing worth negotiating is how much incarceration and how much mandated counseling is necessary to stop the batterer.

Cases like Donna Houston's remind prosecutors that while we wait for the battered woman to garner her "inner strength" to decide whether to press charges, harm continues to occur. Children are psychologically damaged from witnessing the battering, a child is placed in danger of physical injury or death, hospital emergency rooms are filled by injured women, and innocent third parties are endangered by assaults intended for someone else. Domestic violence prosecutors are haunted by tragedies like Donna Houston's. We need to be able to say that despite a battered woman's ambivalence, we did everything within our discretion to reign in the batterer, to protect the victim and her children, and to stop the abuser before it was too late.

Batterers are "master manipulators." They will do anything to convince their victims to get the prosecution to drop the charges. They call from jail threatening retaliation. They cajole their victim with promises of reform. They remind her that they may lose their jobs and, hence, the family income. They send love letters, pledging future bliss and happiness. They have their family members turn off the victim's electricity and threaten to kick the victim and her children out into the street. They pay for the victim to leave town so that she will not be subpoenaed. They use community property to pay for an expensive lawyer to try to convince the jury that the whole thing was the victim's fault and that she attacked him. They prey on the victim's personal weaknesses, especially drug and alcohol abuse, physical and mental disabilities, and her love for their children. They negotiate financial and property incentives that cause acute memories of terror and pain to fade dramatically. Prosecutors watch with practiced patience as these vulnerable victims succumb to their batterers' intimidation and manipulation. Then, "no-drop" prosecutors try to hold the batterers responsible regardless of the victims' lack of cooperation by using creative legal maneuvering.

Supporters of "no-drop" domestic violence policies realize that empowering victims by giving them the discretion to prosecute, or even to threaten to prosecute, in actuality only empowers batterers to further manipulate and endanger their victims' lives, the children's lives, and the safety and well-being of the entire community. By proceeding with the prosecution with or without victim cooperation, the prosecutor minimizes the victim's value to the batterer as an ally to defeat criminal prosecution. A "no-drop" policy means prosecutors will not allow batterers to control the system of justice through their victims.

Some critics of aggressive prosecution worry that "no-drop" policies endanger victims by angering already volatile batterers. They argue that "jail doesn't do the batterer any good." However, arrest and prosecution of batterers does not endanger victims; batterers who attempt to control their mates through threats and violence endanger victims. . . .

Prosecutors are aware of complaints that "no-drop" policies make battered women feel "powerless" to keep the government, specifically the courts, from "interfering" in their lives. Some object to the court "dictating" what will happen to the case and the abuser in the aftermath of reporting the abuse. However, prosecutors must seize the "window of opportunity" given to us by the report of violence to get the batterer's attention. Working closely with victim advocates, prosecutors try to convince battered women to see the wisdom of criminal justice intervention. We tell the victims that we proceed with the prosecution because we cannot allow the batterer to believe that physical abuse is acceptable. We tell them that left without intervention, the violence may increase both in frequency of occurrence and severity of injury, often leading to the tragic scenario where he kills her or she kills him while defending herself against his aggression. We tell victims that the children suffer when they see their mother hurt and that the children need their mother to stay alive and well. . . .

Aggressive prosecution of domestic violence offenders rejects the notion that victims should be given the choice of whether to press or drop charges. No humane society can allow any citizen, battered woman or otherwise, to be beaten and terrorized while being held emotionally hostage to love and fear or blackmailed by financial dependence and cultural mores. As guardians of public safety, prosecutors must proceed against domestic violence offenders with or without victim cooperation as long as there is legally sufficient evidence. This policy of aggressive prosecution adopts the wisdom that "[t]here is no excuse for domestic violence." . . .

The following excerpt reveals some of the ways in which abusers influence victims to drop charges.

■ **WILLIAM GLABERSON, ABUSE SUSPECTS,
YOUR CALLS ARE TAPED, SPEAK UP**
N.Y. Times, Feb. 26, 2011, at A1

The men charged with beating, stabbing or burning their wives or girlfriends have plenty to say. Lately, their words have been used against them in New York courts as never before. . . . [E]very prisoner telephone call at every New York City jail, except calls to doctors and lawyers, has been recorded. And prosecutors have been mining the trove in all kinds of cases. . . . But there is one area where the tapes are beginning to play a central role: cases of domestic violence.

The reason is simple. Once those accused in domestic violence crimes get on the jailhouse telephone, it turns out, many of them cannot seem to stop themselves from sweet-talking, confessing to, berating and threatening those on the other end of the line, more often than not the women they were charged with abusing.

The tapes overcome one of the biggest hurdles prosecutors face in such cases: that 75 percent of the time, the women who were victimized stop helping prosecutors, often after speaking to the men accused of abusing them.

Scott E. Kessler, the domestic violence bureau chief in the Queens district attorney's office, said the recordings "revolutionized the way we're able to proceed." In the Queens Boulevard courthouse where Mr. Kessler's assistant district attorneys handle more than 6,000 domestic violence cases a year, the jailhouse recordings have become an appalling kind of reality radio, a fly-on-the-wall guide to the chilling intimacies of domestic violence. "We have the ability now," Mr. Kessler said, "to prove what we've always suspected, which is that the defendants in domestic violence cases are in constant contact with their victims, and they use various means and methods to try to have the case dropped."

The jailhouse calls are almost always flagrant violations of court orders directing men charged with domestic violence not to contact the women who were attacked. Deirdre Bialo-Padin, the domestic violence bureau chief in the Brooklyn district attorney's office, said the tapes gave jurors a vivid understanding of men who can be masters of manipulation. . . . In the cases in which victims stop cooperating with prosecutors, the recordings plug crucial holes. District attorneys use the recordings partly to explain why injured women are not testifying for the prosecution. . . . "When you're talking about domestic violence cases," [former California prosecutor Casey Gwinn said], "this policy of monitoring every jail call is probably the single most important investigative procedure put in place in the last decade anywhere in the country."

On the recordings used in Queens cases, the men proclaim their love. They tell the women to disappear when it is time for the trial. They beg and plead.

The Queens courthouse tapes . . . include one of Mohamed Khan, who was charged with slicing his wife's head and shoulder with a meat cleaver. He was recorded from Rikers Island telling her that he was a "brand new" man and had been under the spell of a "passion of love." She ended up testifying that she did not remember who her attacker was. Because the recordings showed what the prosecutors called "a campaign of coercion," they were able to introduce her statements at the hospital and to the police. . . . [Khan was convicted and sentenced to seven years in prison.]

The men have been heard complaining to the women about what they see as unfair charges. "I need you right now in my corner," begged Eric Persaud, the man charged with branding his girlfriend's cheeks with [an] iron. He had a strategy, he said: she should vanish for the trial. "I'm smarter than you," he said in one of what prosecutors have said were 437 calls from Rikers Island. On Wednesday, he pleaded guilty, and he is to be sentenced next month to 13 years in prison. . . .

And the tapes have caught the men trying gentle charms. Ishaaq Rahaman, a 28-year-old with big brown eyes, kept saying "baby" to the woman he was charged with scratching with keys, urging her not to tell the prosecutor anything useful. "Basically tell him things like this: 'It was just a misunderstanding. I love him. We want to get married and we want to have children together,'" he suggested. "Say something nice like that, anything like that, you know what I'm saying, baby?"

Then, forlornly, Mr. Rahaman added: "Even though you probably don't want to marry me and you don't want to have kids. But it's all right. It's all right. It's no big deal. We're not going to talk about that now." He pleaded guilty this month.

Over the objection of prisoners' groups and defense lawyers, the city jails changed policy in 2007 to permit the recording, which was already routine in some New York State and federal prisons. . . . Defense lawyers around the city . . . rail about prosecutors' use of the recordings. "The whole system is patently unfair," Mr. Khan's lawyer, Warren M. Silverman, said. He called it a trap for men who were cut off from the world. The Queens district attorney, Richard A. Brown, argued, "There really is no issue of fairness." He noted that inmates were told that their phone calls would be taped.

4. Criticisms of Mandatory Interventions

■ LEIGH GOODMARK, AUTONOMY FEMINISM: AN ANTI-ESSENTIALIST CRITIQUE OF MANDATORY INTERVENTIONS IN DOMESTIC VIOLENCE CASES
37 Fla. St. U. L. Rev. 1, 12-14, 45 (2009)

Advocates of no-drop prosecution strategies offer three justifications for the policies. First, they argue that no-drop prosecution in domestic violence cases is good for society in that the purpose of the criminal system is not to bend to the wishes of individual victims, but rather to punish offenders and to deter others from committing similar crimes. The role of the prosecutor in the American criminal system is to reinforce the state's conception of the boundaries of acceptable behavior by ensuring compliance with the laws that define and regulate what individuals are and are not permitted to do. The failure to prosecute domestic violence cases, whether attributable to prosecutorial diffidence or victim unwillingness, sends the message that violence against one's intimate partner is acceptable, in direct contravention of the criminal laws. . . .

The second justification proffered for no-drop prosecution is victim safety. Prosecuting those who commit domestic violence increases safety both for the individual victim by removing the immediate threat to her, and for future victims of the same perpetrator. The victim's inability to thwart the process is a particularly important guarantor of her safety. Because the victim no longer has the ability to stop the prosecutor from bringing the case to court, her abuser has no motivation to pressure her to do so. Shifting the burden of deciding whether to prosecute the abuser from the victim to the prosecutor was thought to significantly safeguard the victim from further coercion and violence.

The final justification for no-drop prosecution policies was, ironically, victim empowerment. Women who had been battered, the argument went, would derive strength and validation from the experience of participating in the prosecution. This argument assumed successful prosecution of the case and positive treatment of the victim throughout the process. . . .

At their core, these policies reflect a struggle over who will control the woman who has been battered—if the state does not exercise its control over her by compelling her testimony, the batterer will, by preventing her from testifying. Hard no-drop policies express the state's belief that it has a superior right to intervene on behalf of the woman who has been battered in service of both the woman's needs and the state's objectives. [H]ard no-drop policies clearly prioritize safety over all other aims, including fostering the agency of the woman who has been battered. . . .

Mandatory policies assume that all women who have been battered are "victims," stereotyping them as meek, afraid, and easily manipulated and controlled, rather than seeing the complexity of and differences among them. These policies deny women the ability to define themselves, distilling every woman down to the stereotypical victim in need of the system's protection, unable to make rational choices. Mandatory policies ignore that women experiencing violence may have multiple goals, assuming instead that all women prioritize safety and accountability. . . .

Defining all women as victims allowed the legal system to narrow the available options, depriving women who had been battered of the ability to pursue possibilities beyond the range of those deemed acceptable by the legal system. [W]omen who have been battered [should] be treated as individuals with different identities and capacities, and . . . given the opportunity to make choices consistent with their own goals and priorities. [W]omen who have been battered should not be told by the state that they have no choice about arrest, prosecution, or mediation. Instead, domestic violence law and policy should respect the rights of individual women to choose whether and how to use the criminal and civil legal systems. . . .

Notes and Questions

1. *Traditional failure to prosecute.* Prosecutors, traditionally, either refused to prosecute cases of domestic violence or followed an "automatic drop" approach. See Naomi R. Cahn & Lisa G. Lerman, Prosecuting Woman Abuse, in Woman Battering: Policy Responses 95, 96 (Michael Steinman ed., 1991); Deborah Epstein, Effective Intervention in Domestic Violence Cases: Rethinking the Roles of Prosecutors, Judges, and the Court System, 11 Yale J.L. & Feminism 3, 15 (1999). In the 1980s and 1990s, only 2 to 4 percent of arrestees in some jurisdictions were ever prosecuted. Andrew R. Klein, The Criminal Justice Response to Domestic Violence 131 (2004). The automatic drop policy was common too. "Typically, prosecutors would drop charges in anywhere from 50 percent to 80 percent of cases in which the victim requests it, refuses to testify, recants, or fails to appear in court." Emily J. Sack, Battered Women and the State: The Struggle for the Future of Domestic Violence Policy, 2004 Wis. L. Rev. 1657, 1664 (2004). What are the effects of automatic drop policy for victims? For offenders? See Epstein, supra, at 15 ("This 'automatic drop' policy ceded to perpetrators an enormous degree of control over the criminal justice process. All a batterer had to do was coerce his victim—through violence or threats of violence into asking the prosecutor to drop the charges.")

2. *Factors affecting impact of mandatory arrest laws.* Enactment of mandatory arrest laws increased the pressure on prosecutors' offices to file charges in domestic violence cases. Several class action lawsuits against prosecutors also fostered aggressive prosecution policies. See Klein, supra, at 131 (discussing lawsuits against prosecutors in Cleveland, Ohio, in 1975, and Los Angeles, California, in 1979). However, increasing case loads did not automatically result in higher conviction rates because of the influence of institutional factors (i.e., budgetary constraints, agency priorities to target high-profile offenses, and the need to achieve high rates of felony convictions as the measure of evaluating prosecutors' performance). Another factor, of course, was victims' reluctance to prosecute. See Buzawa & Buzawa, Criminal Justice Response, supra, at 178-181 (discussing factors).

3. *Source of no-drop policies.* Many jurisdictions currently have some form of no-drop. Laurie S. Kohn, The Justice System and Domestic Violence: Engaging the Case But Divorcing the Victim, 32 N.Y.U. Rev. L. & Soc. Change 191, 220 (2008). See, e.g., Fla. Stat. §741.2901(2) ("The filing, nonfiling, or diversion of criminal charges, and the prosecution of violations of injunctions for protection against domestic violence by the state attorney, shall be determined by these specialized prosecutors over the objection of the victim, if necessary. . . .") Both statutes and prosecutorial practice are the sources of no-drop policies. See generally Miccio, supra, at 266 (discussing sources).

4. *Type of no-drop policies.* What is the difference between "soft" versus "hard" no-drop policies? What are the advantages and disadvantages of each? Note that the prosecutor or the judge may be the ultimate decisionmaker in whether to drop charges. See, e.g., People v. Alexander, 769 N.E.2d 802, 806 (N.Y. 2002) (refusing to allow defendant to withdraw guilty plea to criminal contempt for violation of a protection order, even after victim decided to drop charges for assault).

5. *Victims' preferences.* How far did the court in *McClure* delve into the reasons that the plaintiff might want the case dropped? Victims' refusal to cooperate is a primary reason why prosecutors refuse to prosecute or drop cases. Studies during the 1970s to 1990s reveal that attrition rates for victim-initiated cases were 60 to 80 percent. Buzawa & Buzawa, Criminal Justice Response, supra, at 182 (citing research). Despite considerable reform efforts, victim non-cooperation remains problematic.

Victims' motives for failure to cooperate consist of concerns about retaliation (for themselves and their children), financial issues, and loss of child custody. Id. Other victims may not be interested in prosecution because they have reconciled with the offender or are satisfied with the impact of the arrest. Some victims simply want the abuse to stop, rather than to end the relationship, and may want to use the criminal justice system as leverage. Hirschel & Hutchison, supra, at 316.

Available research confirms the legitimacy of victims' fear of retaliation. See Buzawa & Buzawa, Criminal Justice Response, supra, at 183 (reporting that nearly half of victims who pursue restraining orders report physical threats by their abusers if the victims continue court proceedings).

6. *Judicial determination.* How can a judge determine if the request to drop the charges stems from fear of retaliation? How can the judge make that determination if an abuser's efforts are subtle? See Tamara L. Kuennen, Analyzing the Impact of Coercion on Domestic Violence Victims: How Much Is Too Much?, 22 Berkeley J. Gender L. & Just. 2, 4-5 (2007). Should judges use an objective or subjective test to evaluate the victim's fears? See, e.g., Stevenson v. Stevenson, 714 A.2d 986 (N.J. Super. Ct. Ch. Div. 1998) (applying an objective test to determine level of victim's fear in consideration of her motion to vacate an order of protection).

Some jurisdictions have adopted guidelines for judges to determine if a victim's reluctance is coerced. Kuennen, supra, at 12-13. For example, Alabama's Domestic Violence Benchbook suggests that judges should consider defendants' past violent behavior; the seriousness of the allegations; the existence of pending criminal charges against the defendant; the duration of time between the request for dismissal and the filing of the petition; the fact whether the plaintiff-victim makes a personal appearance to file the request for dismissal; and the reasons for the request for dismissal. Judicial Benchbook Committee, Alabama's Domestic Violence Benchbook 40 (2005), available at http://www.acadv.org/2005benchbook.pdf. How else might a judge determine the reasons for victims' non-cooperation? Are there legitimate, noncoercive reasons why a victim might want to drop a case?

7. *Prosecutorial strategies.* Prosecutors have employed a number of strategies to address victim non-cooperation, including having the prosecutor: (1) sign the criminal complaint rather than the victim; (2) subpoena victims to appear; (3) require the victim who wants to drop charges to appear on the day of trial to discuss the case with the prosecuting attorney; (4) advise victims that if they do not appear, a judge may assess court costs against them; (5) permit victims to drop charges but only after they see a counselor; and (6) use victim advocates as contacts for victims (to explain the criminal process and counsel victims while charges are pending, and to accompany victims to court). Cahn & Lerman, supra, at 101-103. Which is preferable? Most effective?

8. *Victimless prosecutions.* If the victim refuses to cooperate, can the prosecutor try the case without her testimony? Law reformers lobbied legislatures to enact legislation authorizing prosecutors to pursue "victimless prosecution" (also called "evidence-based prosecution"). Such strategies allow the prosecutor to prove the charges without the victim's testimony, provided that there is sufficient alternative evidence of the defendant's criminal conduct. What alternative evidence would be helpful? See generally Erin Leigh Claypoole, Evidence-Based Prosecution: Prosecuting Domestic Violence Cases Without a Victim, Prosecutor, Jan./Feb. 2005, at 18, 20 (describing use of photographs; observations of visible injuries; and observations of physical evidence such as torn clothing, broken furniture, or broken telephones); John M. Leventhal & Liberty Aldrich, The Admission of Evidence in Domestic Violence Cases After Crawford v. Washington: A National Survey, 11 Berkeley J. Crim. L. 77, 80-81 (2006). Victim non-cooperation is explored further in Chapter 7.

9. *Prosecution rates.* How have prosecution rates changed over time? While prosecution rates, formerly, for partner violence were lower than for stranger assaults, intimate partner violence today results in *higher* prosecution and conviction rates in comparison with other assault cases. See NIJ Report, supra, at 145, 147. Ironically, however, the existence of a mandatory arrest policy, although it increases the likelihood that police will arrest offenders, appears to *reduce* the likelihood of conviction. States with mandatory arrest provisions are more likely to have cases that do *not* result in conviction when compared with cases in states with discretionary arrest policies. NIJ Dual Arrest Report, supra, at 152. Because mandatory arrest policies result in increased caseloads, prosecutors respond by choosing cases with the best chance of conviction. "Thus, it appears that prosecutors in mandatory arrest states may be compensating for the increase in caseload generated by the higher number of police arrests by dismissing more cases." Id. Cf. Robert C. Davis & Barbara Smith, Domestic Violence Reforms: Empty Promises or Fulfilled Expectations?, 41 Crime & Delinq. 541, 546 (1995) (suggesting that mandatory arrest merely moves discretion from the police, in terms of the arrest decision, to the prosecutor, in terms of screening evidence for sufficiency to file charges).

10. *Civil "no-drop" policies.* Victims may also wish to drop petitions for *civil* orders of protection. If the request occurs at the petition stage, victims do not need to file a motion—they simply fail to show up and their request will go off calendar. On the other hand, if victims wish to drop their *order* of protection, they must file a motion to vacate that order. Should the same factors enter into decisionmakers' determinations to allow the victim to drop the case for orders of protection and criminal charges? Orders of protection are explored in Chapter 9.

11. *Sanctions for victims.* Are sanctions that are imposed on the victim ever appropriate when a victim refuses to cooperate? If so, what types of sanctions and in what circumstances? If not, why not? Should the victim be jailed for her refusal to testify? See John Riley, Spouse-Abuse Victim Jailed After No-Drop Policy Invoked, Nat'l L.J., Aug. 22, 1983, at 4 (victim jailed for contempt for her refusal to testify). Today, many states have "DV shield" laws that explicitly provide that victims will not be jailed for contempt. For example, California law (Cal. Civ. Proc. Code §1219) protects a domestic violence victim from the threat of incarceration if the victim refuses to testify by conferring on her the same protections as those conferred on rape victims who refuse to testify against their attackers. See generally David Wiksell, Chapter 49: No Jail for Victims of Domestic Violence, 40 McGeorge L. Rev. 333 (2009) (explaining history of statute).

12. *No-drop policies: Do they insulate victim?* One of the arguments for no-drop policies is that they insulate the victim from pressure by the abuser to convince the prosecutor to drop the charges. Do such policies accomplish that objective? What policies might be more effective?

13. *Debate.* No-drop policies have been criticized for revictimizing the victim, as the excerpt by Professor Goodmark reveals. In contrast, as the Willis excerpt explains, no-drop policies are lauded as essential to the administration of justice. See also Hanna, supra, at 1907 (contending that mandated victim participation policies keep women safer because such policies minimize the abuser's ability to intimidate the victim as well as reinforce the public interest). Which view do you find most persuasive?

Note: Criminal No-Contact Orders

Another weapon in the criminal justice arsenal for combating domestic violence is the no-contact order. A criminal no-contact order is a *criminal* protection order that is issued as a condition of bail, pretrial release, or sentence. Similar to a civil protection order, a criminal no-contact order prohibits the offender from contacting the victim, returning to the home, or approaching the victim in designated locations (for example, home, business, employment, etc.) When the no-contact order is a condition of bail or pretrial release, the judge may issue the order at the offender's first appearance before the court (that is, at the arraignment). Unlike a civil protection order where the moving party is the victim, however, the state is the moving party for issuance of the criminal no-contact order. The purpose of such an order is to vindicate the interest of the state. For this reason, the victim does not have the ability to request that the judge vacate the order.

Commentators criticize no-contact orders for the same reasons as mandatory arrest and no-drop policies—that is, they fail to respect victims' wishes. See Robert F. Friedman, Note, Protecting Victims from Themselves, But Not Necessarily from Abusers: Issuing a No-Contact Order Over the Objection of the Victim-Spouse, 19 Wm. & Mary Bill Rts. J. 235, 247-248 (2010); Christine O'Connor, Note, Domestic Violence No-Contact Orders and the Autonomy Rights of Victims, 40 B.C. L. Rev. 937 (1999). In addition, commentators charge that criminal no-contact orders may run afoul of constitutional requirements regarding bail determination (that is, courts should make case-by-case determinations of the reasons for the denial or revocation of bail). Christopher R. Frank, Comment, Criminal Protection Orders in Domestic Violence Cases: Getting Rid of Rats with Snakes, 50 U. Miami L. Rev. 919, 924-925 (1996).

Another criticism of criminal no-contact orders is that they function as a form of "state-imposed de facto divorce" that leads to restrictions on autonomy and privacy. Jeannie Suk, Criminal Law Comes Home, 116 Yale L.J. 2, 8 (2006). Professor Suk contends that the no-contact order is a form of state-mandated divorce in terms of its prohibition against all contact by either party, sometimes against the parties' wishes. Suk explains that violation of the no-contact order results in criminal liability for the abuser, even if the victim initiates the contact. As a result, the no-contact order, according to Suk, lamentably shifts the goal "from punishment to control over the intimate relationship in the home." Id. at 49-50. This transformation, she theorizes, presages a breakdown of the traditional boundaries between public and private space. See also Jeannie Suk, At Home in the Law: How the Domestic Violence Revolution is Transforming Privacy (2009). What do you think of these criticisms?

5. An Innovative Approach to Criminal Behavior: Restorative Justice

Many advocates criticize the criminal justice system for not giving sufficient attention to the needs and desires of the victim. Restorative justice, an innovative approach to conflict resolution, holds out the potential for giving voice to the victim's wishes. What are the benefits and shortcomings of this new approach?

■ JOAN ZORZA, RESTORATIVE JUSTICE: DOES IT WORK FOR DV?
16 Domestic Violence Rep. 33, 33, 38, 42-44 (Feb./Mar. 2011)

WHAT IS RESTORATIVE JUSTICE?

Restorative justice is an approach to criminal behavior that can take many forms. However, all of them are informal and generally include some kind of encounter between the offender and the victim, with the aim of repairing the harm that the offender did to the victim and sometimes the community, but by decreasing the role of the state. The encounter between the victim and the perpetrator can be direct or indirect (i.e., in some models it is left to the victim, and even the offender, to decide whether they should participate directly, or even at all). RJ has been used for any number of different types of crimes and different types of victims, particularly those involving youth.

RJ is a very old, traditional means of resolving conflicts that dates back thousands of years, and is primarily seen as a way to restore someone who has been the victim of an injustice. While it has been used in many communities, it has been especially present in aboriginal ones, where it is a traditional way of dealing with crimes. . . .

A PROMISING APPROACH

There is much that attracts people to RJ, the most obvious appeal being deficiencies in our current retributive justice approach, which has not shown itself to be all that effective either in preventing interpersonal crimes against women or in preventing recidivism by offenders. . . . RJ, with a name that combines two admirable concepts—restorative and justice—has much appeal and promise. Many victims, and especially battered women, feel they get far too little justice and usually no restoration from the current criminal justice system (CJS), making many hope that they will do better outside of it.

RJ Is Liked by Criminal Defense Attorneys

While RJ holds out much promise to battered women, RJ is almost universally supported and greatly preferred by criminal defense attorneys, and by offenders who are familiar with the concept. First, RJ is usually far easier for the attorneys, both in absolute terms and emotionally, as it eliminates time-consuming trial preparation, the trial itself, and the distress that accompanies an unfavorable verdict, particularly if the defendant receives a harsh sentence. RJ is far less likely than any traditional engagement with the criminal justice system to result in incarceration (or at least any significant length of incarceration) or lasting legal repercussions for their clients, such as having a criminal record. By making incarceration unlikely or not even a consideration, RJ generally also spares offenders from the myriad harms that result from incarceration. These include: damage to reputation; lower economic status (from loss of education opportunities, lost jobs, fewer job opportunities after release, loss of access to certain public benefits, sometimes for the rest of the offender's life); emotional distress . . . ; harsher treatment by the criminal justice system if the offender later reoffends; and possible later deportation if the offender is not a U.S. citizen. This list, which is hardly complete, ignores the harms that befall the families of incarcerated offenders. . . .

By sparing clients all of these things, the attorneys are also far less likely to feel pressure or guilt; they may feel very positive about keeping the clients out of jail. . . . The community can claim that RJ holds the defendant accountable since it often requires him to admit to a crime, and at least encourages him to apologize for it and, in some manner, make amends for the crime.

RJ Is Victim-Based

RJ uses much of the language of human rights, including the importance of restoration and self-empowerment, language still foreign to our criminal justice system or civil courts. As such, it seems to offer much promise, particularly when coupled with the notion of finding solutions that are specific to the two people involved. . . . RJ gives a real voice to the victim, enabling her to participate in the entire proceeding and tell her story in her own words, of how she was wronged, what it did to her and perhaps others in her family and community, and what she needs to be made whole. . . . In contrast to the criminal justice system, which makes her only a witness with relatively little voice, the RJ system holds out the promise that it makes her needs the central focus. . . .

Problems with, and Concerns about, RJ

[P]articularly as it is practiced in American courts, RJ tends to be very event specific, looking to right only the immediate crime that brought the case to the attention of the criminal justice system, showing that its restorative aspect is illusory. At most, the system will address this latest abuse, and not try to deal with all of the wrongs, particularly not when the redress involves monetary restitution or anything else that has significant tangible costs. Many RJ advocates note that RJ regards victims as only "alleged victims," until they prove in an investigation that they really were victimized, and that the offender was the one who did it. This effectively duplicates one of the worst failings of the criminal justice system for victims . . . a presumption that the alleged offender is innocent until proven guilty. . . . Since RJ cases are often negotiated without the prosecutor, there are probably far more instances when the case is dropped because the victim is unable or unwilling to help prove the crime, or because the RJ facilitator, who is probably somewhat sympathetic to the defendant to begin with, concludes that this is a meritless, unprovable, or trivial case, and so either lets or encourages it to lapse or, in other instances, effectively negotiates such a minimal slap on the offender's wrist that it is meaningless and incapable of holding him accountable. Yet with ongoing interpersonal crimes, particularly those involving DV, when an offender gets away with the crime, he only takes it as proof that he is right, that society disbelieves his victim and supports him, and that he is free to continue abusing his victim. That is to say, by not holding the offender sufficiently accountable (and, if truth be told, even the retributive justice system seldom holds him really accountable), the offender's power is increased and the victim's lessened, leaving her less safe and less likely to heal. . . .

RJ proponents put much emphasis on the importance of [the offender's] apologizing. They assume that an abuser's apology means he is sorry and will probably stop being abusive. However, as Lenore Walker found, over half of abusers (54.5 percent) repeatedly put their victims through a cycle of violence in which the abusers first build up tension, then attack their victims, and only after each abusive episode apologize and act loving and contrite. The men apologized as needed to entrap their victims into remaining in their coercive control. Their apologies and promises to never do it again were seldom genuine, [nor were their apologies and promises any indication that the abusers would stop being abusive]. . . . [W]hen confronted by his own attorney telling him that he faces going to jail if he does not apologize and act at least a little contrite, most abusers (who use a cost benefit analysis to determine what they can get away with), quickly grasp the benefit of their apologizing for their abuse.

RJ invests great significance not only in having the abuser apologize, but also in having the victim forgive the offender. Given that batterers' apologies are seldom made with any sincerity or translate into ending their violence, it is unfair to hold this out as constructive to battered women. . . .

A related problem with RJ is that many practitioners and proponents of it believe that there is often little distinction in culpability between the victim and perpetrator, that the victim, and sometimes society, is partially or even equally at fault for the abuser's wrongful actions. The result is that some RJ facilitators can become highly victim blaming, effectively siding with the offender, and thereby further empowering him against his victim and making him feel justified. . . . Anything that focuses on the victim's role in the wrongdoing or in not stopping him only exacerbates the power differential and increases her chance of being worse harmed in the future. . . .

[The second part of the article explains that restorative justice lacks the ability to enforce any agreement unless that agreement is entered into a court order.

However, by its nature, restorative justice rarely leads to judicial involvement. In addition, advocates of restorative justice laud its confidentiality (that is, lack of public record). However, according to Zorza, such confidentiality results in the lack of evidence that might be admissible in court, thereby jeopardizing the victim's safety. Zorza, Restorative Justice: Does It Work for Domestic Violence?, 16 Domestic Violence Rep. 51, 52 (Apr./May 2100).]

Notes and Questions

1. *Definition.* What is restorative justice? What are its origins? How is it different from mediation? From therapy?

2. *Advantages and disadvantages.* What are the advantages of restorative justice for the victim of criminal behavior generally? The offender? Defense attorneys? Prosecutors? What are the disadvantages of restorative justice for these parties? What are the special hazards that arise when restorative justice is applied to cases of domestic violence?

3. *Objectives.* What are the objectives of restorative justice? How is restorative justice different from retributive justice? Do you think that restorative justice accomplishes its objectives? How does restorative justice hope to transform the role of the state in the response to domestic violence? Do you think that this is a sensible approach?

4. *Safety.* Is restorative justice likely to lead to decreased recidivism in domestic violence and ensure the victim's safety? Why or why not? See Loretta Frederick & Kristine C. Lizdas, The Role of Restorative Justice in the Battered Women's Movement, in Restorative Justice and Violence Against Women 39, 41-42 (James Ptacek ed., 2010); Julie Stubbs, Domestic Violence and Women's Safety: Feminist Challenges to Restorative Justice, in Restorative Justice and Family Violence 42-61 (Heather Strang & John Braithwaite eds., 2002).

5. *Different practices of restorative justice.* Three common practices of restorative justice are victim-offender mediation, family group conferencing, and peacemaking circles. James Ptacek, Resisting Co-optation: Three Feminist Challenges to Antiviolence Work, in Restorative Justice and Violence Against Women, supra, at 8. Victim-offender mediation includes face-to-face interactions between victims and offenders with the assistance of mediators. It emphasizes victim empowerment, offender accountability, and restoration of losses. Family group conferencing address youth crimes and involves meetings of victims, offenders, family members, and supporters with the help of a coordinator. Peacemaking circles provide a forum for addressing crime in indigenous populations. Id. at 8-9. How does restorative justice differ in each of these settings in terms of the benefits and disadvantages for the parties?

6. *Critical commentary.* Why might restorative justice have particular application to minorities? Compare Donna Coker, Enhancing Autonomy for Battered Women: Lessons from Navajo Peacemaking, 47 UCLA L. Rev. 1 (1999); Laurie S. Kohn, What's so Funny About Peace, Love, and Understanding? Restorative Justice as a New Paradigm for Domestic Violence Intervention, 40 Seton Hall L. Rev. 517 (2010) (both advocating application of restorative justice to domestic violence), with C. Quince Hopkins et al., Applying Restorative Justice to Ongoing Intimate Violence: Problems and Possibilities, 23 St. Louis U. Pub. L. Rev. 289, 302-304 (2004); Meghan

Condon, Note, Bruise of a Different Color: The Possibilities of Restorative Justice for Minority Victims of Domestic Violence, 17 Geo. J. on Poverty L. & Pol'y 487, 504-506 (2010).

C. SUITS AGAINST LAW ENFORCEMENT

1. *Victim's Constitutional Rights*

■ TOWN OF CASTLE ROCK v. GONZALES
545 U.S. 748 (2005)

Justice SCALIA delivered the opinion of the Court.

We decide in this case whether an individual who has obtained a state-law restraining order has a constitutionally protected property interest in having the police enforce the restraining order when they have probable cause to believe it has been violated.

The horrible facts of this case are contained in the complaint that respondent Jessica Gonzales filed in Federal District Court. [At] about 5 or 5:30 p.m. on Tuesday, June 22, 1999, respondent's [ex-]husband took [their] three daughters [ages 10, 9, and 7] while they were playing outside the family home. No advance arrangements had been made for him to see the daughters that evening. When respondent noticed the children were missing, she suspected her husband had taken them. At about 7:30 p.m., she called the Castle Rock Police Department, which dispatched two officers. The complaint continues: When [the officers] arrived . . . , she showed them a copy of the TRO [that had been issued to her in conjunction with her divorce proceedings that ordered her ex-husband not to "molest or disturb the peace of [respondent] or of any child," and to remain at least 100 yards from the family home at all times.] [She] requested that it be enforced and the three children be returned to her immediately. [The officers] stated that there was nothing they could do about the TRO and suggested that [respondent] call the Police Department again if the three children did not return home by 10:00 p.m.

At approximately 8:30 p.m., respondent talked to her husband on his cellular telephone. He told her "he had the three children [at an] amusement park in Denver." She called the police again and asked them to "have someone check for" her husband or his vehicle at the amusement park and "put out an [all points bulletin]" for her husband, but the officer with whom she spoke "refused to do so," again telling her to "wait until 10:00 p.m., and see if" her husband returned the girls.

At approximately 10:10 p.m., respondent called the police and said her children were still missing, but she was now told to wait until midnight. She called at midnight and told the dispatcher her children were still missing. She went to her husband's apartment and, finding nobody there, called the police at 12:10 a.m., she was told to wait for an officer to arrive. When none came, she went to the police station at 12:50 a.m. and submitted an incident report. The officer who took the report "made no reasonable effort to enforce the TRO or locate the three children. Instead, he went to dinner."

At approximately 3:20 a.m., respondent's husband arrived at the police station and opened fire with a semiautomatic handgun he had purchased earlier that evening. Police shot back, killing him. Inside the cab of his pickup truck, they found the bodies of all three daughters, whom he had already murdered.

[Gonzales brought a civil rights action against the municipality and police officers under 42 U.S.C. §1983, claiming that she had a property interest in enforcement of the restraining order; and that the town deprived her of this property interest without due process by having a policy that tolerated nonenforcement of restraining orders.]

[W]e left a similar question [whether a statute conferred an entitlement to due process protection] unanswered in DeShaney v. Winnebago County Dept. of Social Servs., 489 U.S. 189 (1989), another case with "undeniably tragic" facts: Local child-protection officials had failed to protect a young boy from beatings by his father that left him severely brain damaged. We held that the so-called substantive component of the Due Process Clause does not "requir[e] the State to protect the life, liberty, and property of its citizens against invasion by private actors." Id., at 195. We noted, however, that the petitioner had not properly preserved the argument that—and we thus "decline[d] to consider" whether—state "child protection statutes gave [him] an 'entitlement' to receive protective services in accordance with the terms of the statute, an entitlement which would enjoy due process protection."

The procedural component of the Due Process Clause does not protect everything that might be described as a "benefit." . . . Our cases recognize that a benefit is not a protected entitlement if government officials may grant or deny it in their discretion. The Court of Appeals in this case determined that Colorado law created an entitlement to enforcement of the restraining order because the "court-issued restraining order . . . specifically dictated that its terms must be enforced" and a "state statute command[ed]" enforcement of the order when certain objective conditions were met (probable cause to believe that the order had been violated and that the object of the order had received notice of its existence). . . .

[The Tenth Circuit based its reasoning primarily on] language from the restraining order, the statutory text, and a state legislative hearing transcript. . . . The critical language in the restraining order [came from] the preprinted notice to law enforcement personnel that appeared on the back of the order. That notice effectively restated the statutory provision describing "peace officers' duties" related to the crime of violation of a restraining order [that is, *A peace officer shall use every reasonable means to enforce a restraining order. . . . A peace officer shall arrest, or, if an arrest would be impractical under the circumstances, seek a warrant for the arrest of a restrained person. . . . A peace officer shall enforce a valid restraining order whether or not there is a record of the restraining order in the registry.* Colo. Rev. Stat. §18-6-803.5(3) (Lexis 1999) (emphases added).]

The Court of Appeals concluded that this statutory provision [about police officers' duties regarding enforcement of TRO's]—especially taken in conjunction with a statement from its legislative history, and with another statute restricting criminal and civil liability for officers making arrests—established the Colorado Legislature's clear intent "to alter the fact that the police were not enforcing domestic abuse restraining orders," and thus its intent "that the recipient of a domestic abuse restraining order have an entitlement to its enforcement." Any other result, it said, "would render domestic abuse restraining orders utterly valueless."

This last statement is sheer hyperbole. Whether or not respondent had a right to enforce the restraining order, it rendered certain otherwise lawful conduct by her husband both criminal and in contempt of court. The creation of grounds on which he could be arrested, criminally prosecuted, and held in contempt was hardly "valueless"—even if the prospect of those sanctions ultimately failed to prevent him from committing three murders and a suicide.

We do not believe that these provisions of Colorado law truly made enforcement of restraining orders *mandatory.* A well-established tradition of police discretion has long coexisted with apparently mandatory arrest statutes [in the criminal law generally]. [A] true mandate of police action would require some stronger indication from the Colorado Legislature than "shall use every reasonable means to enforce a restraining order" (or even "shall arrest . . . or . . . seek a warrant"), §§18-6-803.5(3)(a), (b). That language is not perceptibly more mandatory than the Colorado statute which has long told municipal chiefs of police that they "shall pursue and arrest any person fleeing from justice in any part of the state" and that they "shall apprehend any person in the act of committing any offense . . . and, forthwith and without any warrant, bring such person before a . . . competent authority for examination and trial." Colo. Rev. Stat. §31-4-112 (Lexis 2004). It is hard to imagine that a Colorado peace officer would not have some discretion to determine that— despite probable cause to believe a restraining order has been violated—the circumstances of the violation or the competing duties of that officer or his agency counsel decisively against enforcement in a particular instance. The practical necessity for discretion is particularly apparent in a case such as this one, where the suspected violator is not actually present and his whereabouts are unknown. Cf. Donaldson v. Seattle, 831 P.2d 1098, 1104 (Wash. Ct. App. 1992) ("There is a vast difference between a mandatory duty to arrest [a violator who is on the scene] and a mandatory duty to conduct a follow up investigation [to locate an absent violator]. . . . A mandatory duty to investigate . . . would be completely open-ended as to priority, duration and intensity").

The dissent correctly points out that, in the specific context of domestic violence, mandatory-arrest statutes have been found in some States to be more mandatory than traditional mandatory-arrest statutes. . . . Even in the domestic-violence context, however, it is unclear how the mandatory-arrest paradigm applies to cases in which the offender is not present to be arrested. As the dissent explains, much of the impetus for mandatory-arrest statutes and policies derived from the idea that it is better for police officers to arrest the aggressor in a domestic-violence incident than to attempt to mediate the dispute or merely to ask the offender to leave the scene. Those other options are only available, of course, when the offender is present at the scene. . . .

Respondent does not specify the precise means of enforcement that the Colorado restraining-order statute assertedly mandated—whether her interest lay in having police arrest her husband, having them seek a warrant for his arrest, or having them "use every reasonable means, up to and including arrest, to enforce the order's terms," Brief for Respondent 29-30. Such indeterminacy is not the hallmark of a duty that is mandatory. Nor can someone be safely deemed "entitled" to something when the identity of the alleged entitlement is vague. The dissent, after suggesting various formulations of the entitlement in question, ultimately contends that the obligations under the statute were quite precise: either make an arrest or (if that is impractical) seek an arrest warrant. The problem with this is that the seeking of an arrest warrant would be an entitlement to nothing but procedure—which we have held inadequate even to support standing; much less can it be the basis for a property interest. . . .

Even if the statute could be said to have made enforcement of restraining orders "mandatory" because of the domestic-violence context of the underlying statute, that would not necessarily mean that state law gave *respondent* an entitlement to *enforcement* of the mandate. Making the actions of government employees obligatory can serve various legitimate ends other than the conferral of a benefit on a specific class of people. The serving of public rather than private ends is the normal course of the criminal law. . . .

Respondent's alleged interest stems only from a State's *statutory* scheme. . . . She does not assert that she has any common law or contractual entitlement to enforcement. If she was given a statutory entitlement, we would expect to see some indication of that in the statute itself. . . .

Even if we were to think otherwise concerning the creation of an entitlement by Colorado, it is by no means clear that an individual entitlement to enforcement of a restraining order could constitute a "property" interest for purposes of the Due Process Clause. Such a right would not, of course, resemble any traditional conception of property. Although that alone does not disqualify it from due process protection . . . , the right to have a restraining order enforced does not "have some ascertainable monetary value." . . . Perhaps most radically, the alleged property interest here arises *incidentally*, not out of some new species of government benefit or service, but out of a function that government actors have always performed—to wit, arresting people who they have probable cause to believe have committed a criminal offense. . . . We conclude, therefore, that respondent did not, for purposes of the Due Process Clause, have a property interest in police enforcement of the restraining order against her husband. . . .

EPILOGUE

In December 2005, Jessica Gonzales filed a petition with the Inter-American Commission on Human Rights (IACHR), alleging that the actions of the police and the decision of the Supreme Court violated her human rights. Below is her testimony before the Commission.

■ TESTIMONY OF JESSICA LENAHAN (GONZALES) v. UNITED STATES

Case 12.626, Inter-Am. Comm'n H.R. (Mar. 2 2007), available at **http:// www.aclu.org/human-rights-womens-rights/jessica-gonzales- statement-iachr**

[M]y name is Jessica Lenahan. My former married name was Jessica Gonzales. . . . I am a Latina and Native American woman from Pueblo, Colorado. I met my previous husband, Simon Gonzales, while still in high school. I married Simon in 1990 and we moved to Castle Rock, Colorado, in 1998. We lived together with our three children—Rebecca, Katheryn, and Leslie—and my son Jessie, from a previous relationship.

Throughout our relationship, Simon was erratic and abusive toward me and our children. By 1994, he was distancing himself from us and becoming more and more controlling, unpredictable, and violent. He would break the children's toys and other belongings, harshly discipline the children, threaten to kidnap them, drive recklessly, exhibit suicidal behavior, and verbally, physically, and sexually abuse me. He was heavily involved with drugs. Simon's frightening and destructive behavior got worse and worse as the years went by. One time I walked into the garage, and he was hanging there with a noose around his neck, with the children watching. I had to hold the rope away from his neck while my daughter Leslie called the police. Simon and I separated in 1999 when my daughters were 9, 8, and 6. But he continued scaring us. He would stalk me inside and outside my house, at my job, and on the phone at all hours of the day and night.

On May 21, 1999, a Colorado court granted me a temporary restraining order that required Simon to stay at least 100 yards away from me, my home, and the children. The judge told me to keep the order with me at all times, and that the order and Colorado law required the police to arrest Simon if he violated the order. Having this court order relieved some of my anxiety. But Simon continued to terrorize me and the children even after I got the restraining order. He broke into my house, stole my jewelry, changed the locks on my doors, and loosened my house's water valves, flooding the entire street. I called the Castle Rock Police Department to report these and other violations of the restraining order. The police ignored most of my calls. And when they did respond, they were dismissive of me, and even scolded me for calling them. . . .

Simon had at least seven run-ins with the police between March and June of 1999. He was ticketed for "road rage" while the girls were in the truck and for trespassing in a private section of the Castle Rock police station and then trying to flee after officers served him with the restraining order.

On June 4, Simon and I appeared in court, and the judge made the restraining order permanent. The new order granted me full custody of Rebecca, Katheryn, and Leslie, and said that Simon could only be with our daughters on alternate weekends and one prearranged dinner visit during the week. Less than 3 weeks later, Simon violated the restraining order by kidnapping my three daughters from our yard on a day that he wasn't supposed to see the girls. When I discovered they were missing, I immediately called the police, told them that the girls were missing and that I thought Simon had abducted them in violation of a restraining order, and asked them to find my daughters. The dispatcher told me she would send an officer to my house, but no one came.

I waited almost two hours for the police, and then called the station again. Finally two officers came to my house. I showed them the restraining order and explained that it was not Simon's night to see the girls, but that I suspected he had taken them. The officers said, "Well, he's their father, it's okay for them to be with him." And I said, "No, it's not okay. There was no prearranged visit for him to have the children tonight." The officers said there was nothing they could do, and told me to call back at 10 p.m. if the children were still not home. I was flustered and scared. Unsure of what else I could say or do to make the officers take me seriously, I agreed to do what they suggested.

Soon afterwards, Simon's girlfriend called me and told me that Simon called her and was threatening to drive off a cliff. She asked me if he had a gun and whether or not he would hurt the children. I began to panic. I finally reached Simon on his cell phone around 8:30 pm. He told me he was with the girls at an amusement park in Denver, 40 minutes from Castle Rock. I immediately communicated this information to the police. I was shocked when they responded that there was nothing they could do, because Denver was outside of their jurisdiction. I called back and begged them to put out a missing child alert or contact the Denver police, but they refused. The officer told me I needed to take this matter to divorce court, and told me to call back if the children were not home in a few hours. The officer said to me, "At least you know the children are with their father." . . .

I called the police again and again that night. When I called at 10 p.m., the dispatcher said to me that I was being "a little ridiculous making us freak out and thinking the kids are gone." Even at that late hour, the police were still scolding me and not acknowledging that three children were missing. . . . [After midnight] I drove to the police station and told yet another officer about the restraining order and that the girls had been gone for seven hours. After I left, that Officer went to a two hour dinner and never contacted me again. I asked the police for help nine separate times that night—two times in person and seven times on the phone. . . .

At 3:25 a.m., Simon's girlfriend called me to tell me that she had been on the phone with Simon when she heard shooting, and that she believed he and the girls were dead. . . . I later learned that Simon had driven up to the Castle Rock Police station at 3:20 a.m. and opened fire with a semi-automatic handgun he had purchased earlier that evening, after he had abducted the children. The police returned fire, spraying the truck with bullets. After Simon was killed, they searched his truck and found the bodies of my three little girls inside. I was told that Simon had killed them earlier that evening.

After hearing about the shooting, I drove to the police station. As I attempted to approach Simon's truck, I was taken away by the police and then to the local sheriff's office. . . . They detained me in a room for 12 hours and interrogated me throughout the early morning hours, as if I had a role in the children's deaths. . . .

I never received an explanation for why Simon was approved in the FBI's background check system when he went to purchase the gun that night. Under federal law, gun dealers can't sell guns to people subject to domestic violence restraining orders. . . . So why did the police ignore my calls for help? Was it because I was a woman? A victim of domestic violence? A Latina? Because the police were just plain lazy? . . .

I brought this petition to the Inter-American Commission on Human Rights because I have been denied justice in the United States. It's too late for Rebecca, Katheryn, and Leslie but it's not too late to create good law and policies for others. Police have to be required to enforce restraining orders or else these orders are meaningless. . . .

EPILOGUE

In July 2011, the Inter-American Commission on Human Rights concluded that the American Declaration of the Rights and Duties of Man (the source of legal obligation for the Commission's member states) imposes an affirmative duty upon the Commission's member states to protect their citizens from private acts of domestic violence. The IACHR ruling provided that

> "the systemic failure of the United States to offer a coordinated and effective response to protect Jessica Lenahan and her daughters from domestic violence, constituted an act of discrimination, a breach of their obligation not to discriminate, and a violation of their right to equality before the law under Article II [that is, the right to equal protection pursuant to the American Declaration]. The Commission also finds that the State failure [sic] to undertake reasonable measures to protect the life of Leslie, Katheryn and Rebecca Gonzales, and that this failure constituted a violation of their right to life established in Article I of the American Declaration, in relation to their right to special protection [as female children] contained in Article VII of the American Declaration."

Jessica Lenahan (Gonzales) v. United States of America, Inter-American Commission on Human Rights Report No. 80/11, Para. 170, available at http://www.legalmomentum .org/our-work/vaw/gonzales-v-usa-decision.pdf.

In addition, the Commission issued recommendations regarding the resolution of Jessica Lenahan's case in particular, and the treatment of domestic violence generally. The Commission recommended that the United States (1) undertake an investigation to ascertain the cause, time, and place of the deaths of Lenahan's children and the imparting of that information to Lenahan and her next of kin; (2) conduct an investigation into the "systemic failures" that took place related to the enforcement of Lenahan's protection order "in order to guarantee their non-repetition," including a determination of the responsibility of public officials for violating state and/or federal laws, and holding those responsible accountable, and (3) offer "full reparations" to Lenahan and her next-of-kin.

More generally, the Commission recommended the adoption of (1) state and federal legislation making mandatory the enforcement of protection orders and the creation of effective implementation mechanisms, including training programs and protocols for law enforcement and justice system officials; (2) state and federal legislation to improve protection measures for children in the context of domestic violence; (3) public policies aimed at restructuring stereotypes of domestic violence victims, and eliminating "socio-cultural patterns that impede women and children's full protection from domestic violence"; and (4) state and federal protocols for law enforcement investigations of reports of missing children in the context of reports of restraining order violations. Id. at Para. 215. What do you think will be the impact of these recommendations?

Notes and Questions

1. *Background. Castle Rock* is one of several cases that were instituted to force local police departments to treat victims' complaints seriously. Beginning in the 1970s, lawyers, grassroots organizations, and battered women joined forces to sue the police departments in several major cities. This impact litigation was designed to bring about social change that would improve the police response to domestic violence.

2. *Early suits.* The first class action suit, Scott v. Hart, No. C-76-2395 (N.D. Cal. filed Oct. 28, 1976), targeted the police department in Oakland, California. The lawsuit had two objectives: (1) to improve police protection for battered

women by reversing the departmental policy of nonarrest, and (2) to educate both the criminal justice system and the public about the problem of domestic violence. Pauline W. Gee, Ensuring Police Protection for Battered Women: The Scott v. Hart Suit, 8 Signs 554, 554 (1983).

A subsequent class action suit, Bruno v. Codd, 396 N.Y.S.2d 974 (Sup. Ct. 1977), rev'd, 407 N.Y.S.2d 165 (App. Div. 1978), aff'd 393 N.E.2d 976 (N.Y. 1979), charged the New York City Police Department with a failure to enforce the law. Plaintiffs sought declaratory and injunctive relief against the City Police Department, Department of Probation, and Family Court, alleging a pattern and practice of discriminatory enforcement against victims of domestic violence who were predominantly women. The trial court allowed the suit to continue against the police, suggesting that the departmental policy against arrest presented a colorable equal protection claim.

Both Scott v. Hart and Bruno v. Codd resulted in settlements that changed police policy regarding the arrest of domestic violence offenders and improved police training in response to domestic violence. See Susan Schechter, Women and Male Violence: The Visions and Struggles of the Battered Women's Movement 160 (1982) (describing *Bruno* settlement: police must respond to all domestic violence calls, arrest men for felonious assaults and misdemeanors, arrest men who violate protection orders, assist women to receive medical help, and search for husbands who flee).

In the most famous lawsuit, Thurman v. City of Torrington, 595 F. Supp. 1521 (D. Conn. 1984), a victim of domestic violence was attacked by her abusive husband despite repeated requests for police assistance over an eight-month period. Her estranged husband stabbed her repeatedly; and, in the presence of police, kicked her in the head twice. Police failed to arrest him. While she was waiting on a stretcher to be put into an ambulance, her husband continued his attack. Only then, did police take him into custody. She contended that the police's failure to respond constituted a denial of equal protection (that is, treating battered women differently from male victims of non-domestic assault). A federal district court agreed. A jury awarded her $2.3 million in damages. See Machaela M. Hoctor, Comment, Domestic Violence as a Crime Against the State: The Need for Mandatory Arrest in California, 85 Cal. L. Rev. 643, 654 n.83 (1997) (recounting the subsequent appeal by the city and the settlement of $1.9 million).

3. *Next wave of reform.* Advocacy groups subsequently instituted a second wave of reform in the 1980s to challenge police officers' failure to enforce orders of protection. See, e.g., Nearing v. Weaver, 670 P.2d 137 (Or. 1983) (holding that police officers who knowingly fail to enforce an order of protection are potentially liable for resulting harm to intended victims); Sorichetti v. City of New York, 482 N.E.2d 70, 76-77 (N.Y. 1985) (holding that a special relationship existed between plaintiff and the city that arose out of the order of protection and from the police department's knowledge of husband's violent history).

4. *Impact.* Although few lawsuits were filed, this litigation spearheaded enormous change in the institutional response to domestic violence. Lawsuits contributed to the passage of mandatory arrest legislation, no-drop policies, and improvements in police training. "The final major force that changed the police response to domestic violence was that individual officers as well as entire police departments as organizations were exposed to substantive risks of liability awards, fines, and injunctions if they failed to make an arrest for domestic assault." Buzawa & Buzawa, Criminal Justice Response, supra, at 104. See also Susan Schechter, Women

and Male Violence: The Visions and Struggles of the Battered Women's Movement 160 (1982) (discussing impact of early lawsuits).

5. *Constitutional theories.* Many suits, like *Castle Rock*, were brought pursuant to the Civil Rights Act, 42 U.S.C. §1983, which requires a plaintiff to show a deprivation under color of law of a constitutional right. Domestic violence victims seeking damages from police departments based their claims on several constitutional theories, such as substantive due process, procedural due process, and equal protection.

6. *Special relationship doctrine.* Generally, no right to police protection exists for private acts of violence absent the existence of the state's "special relationship" to a victim. Courts first applied the special relationship doctrine to battered spouses in Balistreri v. Pacifica Police Department, 855 F.2d 1421 (9th Cir. 1988), which upheld application of the doctrine to impose a duty of protection by law enforcement. The court reasoned that the police had repeated notice of the husband's assaults and of plaintiff's restraining order. However, after the U.S. Supreme Court severely limited the special relationship doctrine in DeShaney v. Winnebago County Department of Social Services, 489 U.S. 189 (1989), the Ninth Circuit reheard *Balistreri* and found no substantive due process violation for failure to protect. 901 F.2d 696 (9th Cir. 1990).

7. *The impact of* DeShaney. *DeShaney*, cited in *Castle Rock*, had significant implications for victims of domestic violence despite its child abuse context. *DeShaney* held that, absent a special relationship, state social workers did not violate a child's *substantive* due process rights by the former's failure to intervene to protect the child from his father's abuse. As applied to victims of domestic violence, *DeShaney* barred plaintiffs from challenging police officers' failure to protect them under §1983 based on the theory that police inaction violated plaintiffs' substantive due process rights.

8. *Post-*DeShaney *litigation options.* Post-*DeShaney*, domestic violence plaintiffs were limited to different theories, by claiming: (1) an exception to *DeShaney* pursuant to one of two doctrines—the "custodial relationship" doctrine (providing that police have an affirmative duty to protect a victim who is in state custody) or the "state-created danger" doctrine (providing that police have an affirmative duty to protect a victim if the state either creates or increases the risk that an individual will be exposed to private acts of violence); (2) a violation of *procedural*, rather than substantive, due process (that is, the claim of an entitlement to procedural safeguards); (3) a violation of equal protection; or (4) liability under state tort theories.

9. *Procedural due process.* Castle Rock addressed whether state actors violated plaintiffs' *procedural* due process rights (the second theory above). Because *DeShaney* raised the procedural due process claim for the first time before the Supreme Court, the Court had refused to consider it. What was the nature of plaintiffs' claim in *Castle Rock*? How did the U.S. Supreme Court rule? What was the Court's rationale?

10. *Mandatory nature of restraining order.* What does "mandatory" mean in the context of the enforcement of restraining orders, according to Justice Scalia? Why does Justice Scalia conclude that the function of police pursuant to mandatory arrest statutes is not mandatory? Why does he conclude that Jessica Gonzales was an "*indirect*" beneficiary of the mandatory arrest statute? Why did he determine that the entitlement to a restraining order is different from other property interests? How is it similar to other property interests? How does the statutory grant of immunity to officers for the arrest of a person for violating a restraining order promote the legislature's goal of mandatory enforcement of restraining orders? What do the dissenting justices respond to each of these arguments?

11. *Mandatory language.* What was the language that was allegedly "mandatory" in the restraining order? Is there a difference between statutory language that provides that police "*shall use every reasonable means* to enforce" a restraining order and language that provides that the police "*shall arrest* a defendant for violating an order"? See Burella v. City of Philadelphia, 501 F.3d 134, 143-146 (3d Cir. 2007) (addressing plaintiff's attempt to distinguish the Pennsylvania Protection from Abuse statute from the Colorado statute at issue in *Castle Rock*).

12. Castle Rock: *dissent.* In a sharp dissent in *Castle Rock,* Justice Stevens (joined by Justice Ginsburg) charged that the majority failed to take seriously (1) the purpose and nature of restraining orders, and (2) authority from other states recognizing that mandatory arrest statutes and restraining orders create an individual right to police action. 545 U.S. at 788-789 (Stevens, J., dissenting). The dissent criticized the majority for ignoring legislative intent in enacting the state mandatory arrest statute as part of a wave of laws designed to redress police reluctance to enforce domestic violence restraining orders. According to the dissent, mandatory arrest statutes "undeniably create an entitlement to police enforcement of restraining orders" (id. at 784) because, under the statute, the police were *required* to provide enforcement; they *lacked the discretion to do nothing* (id. at 784-785) (emphasis in the original). Finally, the dissent noted that cases have found "property" interests in other state benefits and services (welfare benefits, disability benefits, etc.) and, therefore, reasoned that police enforcement of a restraining order is a government service that is "no less concrete." Id. at 791 (Stevens, J., dissenting). Whose views do you find more persuasive? Why? How much discretion should law enforcement officials have in the enforcement of domestic violence restraining orders, in your view?

13. *State-created danger.* The state-created danger doctrine, an exception to *DeShaney,* allows victims to seek redress from state actors who condone or increase the harm. The Second Circuit Court of Appeals recently made it easier for victims to prove their §1983 claims by liberalizing the requirement that police *explicitly* enhance the danger. The Second Circuit permitted an affirmative act to qualify instead if it communicates *implicit* sanction of the violence and also allowed repeated sustained inaction to suffice as condoning the violence, thereby providing for a broader interpretation of conscience shocking actions in domestic violence cases. Okin v. Village of Cornwall-On-Hudson Police Dept., 577 F.3d 415 (2nd Cir. 2009). How would *Okin* have helped Jessica Lenahan?

14. *"Suicide by cop."* Did Simon Gonzales's criminal acts fit the characteristics of a "family annihilator" type of suicide (see Chapter 4)? Did he commit suicide? In firing on the police station with a semiautomatic handgun, Simon Gonzales may have been attempting to commit "suicide by cop" (SBC). By this act, an individual who is bent on self-destruction provokes police officers to shoot him in self-defense or defense of others. A significant number of persons who commit SBC have a history of domestic violence. H. Range Hutson, et al., Suicide by Cop, Annals Emergency Med., Dec. 1998, at 665 (finding that SBC accounts for 11 percent of 437 officer-involved shootings and that 39 percent of perpetrators have a history of domestic violence). See also Vivian B. Lord & Michael W. Sloop, Suicide by Cop: Police Shooting as a Method of Self-Harming, 38 J. Criminal Justice (2010).

15. *Restraining orders: effectiveness.* How effective are restraining orders—before and after *Castle Rock?* How likely are victims to continue to seek restraining orders after *Castle Rock?* Restraining orders and their effectiveness is discussed more fully in Chapter 9.

16. *Other remedies.*

a. *State tort theories.* Victims of domestic violence sometimes seek to recover damages by arguing that police departments were *negligent* in the performance of their duties. However, these negligence claims can only succeed if the "special relationship doctrine" imposes a duty to protect the victim. Courts have been exceedingly reluctant to recognize such claims for intimate partner violence for the same reasons as explained above. Moreover, law enforcement agencies can defend themselves based on their immunity from civil liability pursuant to state tort immunity laws. See, e.g., Lacey v. Village of Palatine, 904 N.E.2d 18 (Ill. 2009).

State and local governmental entities (such as law enforcement agencies, hospitals, etc.) have extraordinary protection when it comes to being sued. This protection may include the necessity for plaintiffs to file a written "notice of claim," a shorter statute of limitations than those applicable to nongovernmental defendants, and immunity from certain types of lawsuits as well as from punitive damages.

On the other hand, such immunity does not apply to intentional torts. Occasionally, plaintiffs pursue such intentional torts against the police. Cf. Burella ex rel. Burella v. City of Philadelphia, 2003 WL 23469295 (E.D. Pa. 2003) (permitting action for intentional infliction of emotional distress for police's failure to enforce restraining order against another police officer), *rev'd on other grounds*, 501 F.3d 134 (3d Cir. 2007) (rejecting theories of procedural due process, substantive due process based on state-created danger doctrine, and equal protection).

b. *Contempt.* In *Castle Rock*, the Tenth Circuit Court of Appeals found liability for the police's failure to enforce the restraining order based on the statutory language and the legislative history. The appellate court said that any other result would render "domestic abuse restraining orders utterly valueless." Justice Scalia, however, disagrees by saying that "This last statement is sheer hyperbole." He counters that the restraining order had value because Jessica Gonzales had another alternative—an action for contempt. The Colorado statute allowed a victim of domestic violence to request that the state initiate such contempt proceedings for violation of a restraining order. Do you find his reasoning persuasive? Explore the benefits and shortcomings of a remedy for contempt in this case.

17. *Reform after* Castle Rock. What strategies should reformers adopt to improve the enforcement of restraining orders? Should they target state legislatures? If so, how? Should they strive to make mandatory arrest statutes "more" mandatory? In response to this question, Professor Kristian Miccio comments cynically:

> After *Castle Rock*, advocates believed that if we did what Scalia told us to do, specifically go back to the legislative drawing board and make our laws "more mandatory" the promise of the Fourteenth Amendment Due Process Clause would be attainable in our lifetime. Remember, Scalia told us that "shall," meant "maybe or maybe not," dismissing out of hand the legislative history of thirty-two states and the plain statutory meaning of the word. I guess to the good Justice, the Ten Commandments are merely the ten suggestions. From a policy standpoint, I cannot envision how one makes "a peace officer shall arrest, or . . . seek a warrant," more mandatory.

G. Kristian Miccio, The Death of the Fourteenth Amendment: *Castle Rock* and Its Progeny, 17 Wm. & Mary J. Women & L. 277, 293 (2011).

Should reformers address their efforts, instead, to state tort law reform by pressuring legislators to craft an exception to governmental immunity for police officers' failure to protect victims of domestic abuse? What is the likelihood of this strategy? See *Burella*, supra, 501 F.3d at 153-154 (Ambro, Circuit Judge, concurring in part, suggesting that such a reform may "prove to be a Potemkin village").

VAWA 2005 authorized the use of STOP grants to fund the appointment of Jessica Gonzales Victim Assistants to serve as liaisons between victims and law enforcement personnel in order to improve the enforcement of protection orders and to ensure that victims receive referrals for services in addition to police assistance. VAWA 2011 would revise that program to encourage these victim assistants to undertake risk assessments and to prioritize potentially lethal cases (amending 42 U.S.C. §3796gg). Evaluate this approach to intimate partner violence.

Problem

Shala is trying to leave her abusive husband Dwayne. One Sunday, she tells Dwayne that she wants to attend church. Dwayne threatens to kill her two children if she does not return. Instead of going to church, Shala goes to the police. She informs them that Dwayne has violated an order of protection. She explains that she fears imminent harm because he has beaten her and threatened to kill her in the past, and that he possesses at least one handgun. She pleads with them to escort her home, so that she can remove her personal belongings and take the children. Two officers accompany her to her home. When the officers encounter Dwayne, they do not separate him from Shala or search him. While Shala is retrieving some of her personal belongings in the third-floor bedroom in preparation for leaving, Dwayne draws a revolver from a pocket (which he had in his possession since the officers arrived), kills Shala, and then turns the gun on himself. The personal representative of Shala's estate brings a §1983 claim, claiming that the city violated Shala's due process rights stemming from the city's alleged failure to properly train its police officers in handling domestic violence. What result? Did police action or inaction enhance the danger? See Simmons v. City of Inkster, 323 F. Supp. 2d 812 (E.D. Mich. 2004). See also Zelig v. County of Los Angeles, 45 P.3d 1171 (2002). Cf. Freeman v. Ferguson, 911 F.2d 52 (8th Cir. 1990).

See generally Atinuke O. Awoyomi, The State-Created Danger Doctrine in Domestic Violence Cases: Do We Have a Solution in Okin v. Village of Cornwall-on-Hudson Police Department?, 20 Colum. J. Gender Law 1 (2011); Laura Oren, Some Thoughts on the State Created Danger Doctrine: *DeShaney* is Still Wrong and *Castle Rock* is More of the Same, 16 Temp. Pol. & Civ. Rts. L. Rev. 47 (2006).

2. Legacy of Lawsuits: Improvements in Police Training

The pressure of lawsuits altered the response of police agencies to domestic violence. "Between 1985 and 2000, many police departments mandated that training sessions on family violence should be part of their police academy curricula." Albert R. Roberts & Karel Kurst-Swagner, Police Responses to Battered Women: Past, Present, and Future, in Handbook of Domestic Violence Strategies: Policies, Programs and Legal Remedies 101, 105 (Albert R. Roberts ed., 2002). By 1998, state legislators had enacted laws in 30 states and the District of Columbia to encourage or require police training on the subject of domestic violence. Id. at 106.

The first specialized police unit to address domestic violence was created in San Diego, California, in 1989. Klein, supra, at 112. Many large cities subsequently followed suit. Id. Specialized units include officers with special knowledge and expertise to respond to domestic violence. Currently, most law enforcement agencies have implemented procedures that emphasize police accountability in responding to domestic violence. Meg Townsend et al., Nat'l Inst. of Justice, Law Enforcement Response to Emergency Domestic Violence Calls for Service 3 (2005) (reporting that 88 percent of departments require an incident report for all domestic violence calls, 68 percent require written justification when no arrest is made, and 86 percent require written justification when both parties are arrested).

Federal funding spurred the development of these training initiatives. An amendment to the Victims of Crime Act (VOCA), Pub. L. No. 100-690, 102 Stat. 4420 (codified at 42 U.S.C. §10605), in 1988 established the Office for Victims of Crime (OVC) and charged it with administering the funds to provide programs and services to help victims in the immediate aftermath of crime. Beginning in 1991, OVC expanded its mandate by providing federal funding to develop and implement training programs to improve the police response to incidents of domestic violence.

Then, in 1994, VAWA authorized Law Enforcement and Prosecution Grants to provide funding to state and local governments "to develop and strengthen effective law enforcement and prosecution strategies to combat violent crimes against women, and to develop and strengthen victim services in cases involving violent crimes against women." Pub. L. No. 103-322, 108 Stat. 1190 (codified as amended at 42 U.S.C. §3796gg). VAWA mandated that at least 25 percent of "Services, Training, Officers, Prosecutors" (STOP) grants had to be distributed to law enforcement, another 25 percent to prosecution, and another 25 percent to victim services (and allowed considerable latitude regarding how the remaining 25 percent could be spent). Id. at 1912 (codified as amended at 42 U.S.C. §3796gg-1). The legislation permitted grants to be used for police training; establishment and expansion of specialized units on domestic violence and sexual assault; and the development and implementation of policies, protocols and procedures.

Pending federal legislation, the Violence Against Women Reauthorization Act of 2011, authorizes grants to assist state and local governments to strengthen law enforcement, prosecution strategies, and victim services, and also to encourage a coordinated community response to domestic violence (Sec. 201, amending 42 U.S.C. §3796hh). Grants may be used for the following purposes (among others): (1) implementation of pro-arrest programs in police departments, including policies for protection order violations, including enforcement against state and tribal lines; (2) development of policies, educational programs, protection order registries, and training in police departments to improve tracking of cases; (3) provision of training and education about domestic violence, dating violence, sexual assault, and stalking; (4) strengthening legal advocacy service programs and other victim services; and (5) education of judges and court personnel in criminal and civil courts (including juvenile courts) about domestic violence and to improve judicial handling of such cases.

Proposed revisions would clarify the definition of domestic violence to make it consistent across categories (that is, to include dating violence, sexual assault, and stalking); emphasize the interstate aspect of enforcement; clarify the purpose to improve data collection systems and the classification of complaints; improve the response to immigrant victims; enlarge the audience for training purposes to include judges at all levels as well as court-based and court-related personnel; and encourage the development of prosecutorial training programs "regarding best practices to ensure offender accountability, victim safety, and victim consultation."

VI

Domestic Violence as a Crime: State Legislative Response

The criminalization of domestic violence law reflects a major policy shift. Today, the criminal justice system mandates intervention in cases of intimate partner violence on the state, as well as federal, level. In the last chapter, we witnessed the development of criminal policies that targeted the police and prosecution (that is, warrantless arrest, mandatory arrest, and pro-prosecution policies). In this chapter, we explore the statutory creation of domestic violence-specific crimes. As you read these materials, consider the reasons for these statutory reforms and the implications of these reforms.

A. CRIMINAL SANCTIONS

1. *Traditional Response: Assault and Battery*

State legislatures define many forms of intimate partner violence as criminal acts. Yet, historically, relief was rarely available for interspousal victimization that stopped short of murder. In part, this shortcoming stemmed from the fact that the common law recognized the "husband's right of chastisement." Early American case law reflected this common law spousal prerogative, as we have seen (Chapter 1). Nonetheless, the doctrine of reasonable chastisement was subject to some restrictions. Did those restrictions enhance women's safety? The case below illustrates the application of the doctrine and its limitations.

■ BRADLEY v. STATE

1 Miss. (1 Walker) 156 (1824)

Opinion of the Court (Hon. POWATTAN ELLIS):

. . . [D]efendant was indicted for a common assault and battery, and upon his arraignment, pleaded not guilty, *son assault demesne*, and that Lydia Bradley was his lawful wife. [A]fter the evidence was submitted, and before the jury retired, the counsel for the defendant moved the court to instruct the jury. If they believed the person named in the bill of indictment, and upon whom the assault and battery was committed, was the wife of the defendant at the time of the assault and battery, [then] in such case they could not find the defendant guilty. The court refused to give the instructions prayed for by the defendant, and charged the jury, that a husband could commit an assault and battery on the body of his wife. . . .

The only question submitted for the consideration of the court, is, whether a husband can commit an assault and battery upon the body of his wife. This, as an abstract proposition, will not admit of doubt. But I am fully persuaded, from the examination I have made, an unlimited license of this kind cannot be sanctioned, either upon principles of law or humanity. It is true, according to the old law, the husband might give his wife moderate correction, because he is answerable for her misbehavior; hence it was thought reasonable, to entrust him, with a power, necessary to restrain the indiscretions of one, for whose conduct he was to be made responsible. Sir William Blackstone says,

> during the reign of Charles the first, this power was much doubted. Notwithstanding the lower orders of people still claimed and exercised it as an inherent privilege, which could not be abandoned, without entrenching upon their rightful authority, known and acknowledged from the earliest periods of the common law, down to the present day.

I believe it was in a case before Mr. Justice Raymond, when the same doctrine was recognized, with proper limitations and restrictions, well suited to the condition and feelings of those, who might think proper to use a whip or rattan, no bigger than my thumb, in order to enforce the salutary restraints of domestic discipline. I think his lordship might have narrowed down the rule in such a manner, as to restrain the exercise of the right, within the compass of great moderation, without producing a destruction of the principle itself. If the defendant now before us, could show from the record in this case, he confined himself within reasonable bounds, when he thought proper to chastise his wife, we would deliberate long before an affirmance of the judgment.

The indictment charges the defendant with having made an assault upon one Lydia Bradley, and then and there did beat, bruise [her], and the jury [did find] the defendant guilty. . . . However abhorrent to the feelings of every member of the bench, must be the exercise of this remnant of feudal authority, to inflict pain and suffering, when all the finer feelings of the heart should be warmed into devotion, by our most affectionate regards, yet every principle of public policy and expediency, in reference to the domestic relations, would seem to require, the establishment of the rule we have laid down, in order to prevent the deplorable spectacle of the exhibition of similar cases in our courts of justice.

Family broils and dissensions cannot be investigated before the tribunals of the country, without casting a shade over the character of those who are unfortunately engaged in the controversy. To screen from public reproach those who may be thus unhappily situated, let the husband be permitted to exercise the right of moderate chastisement, in cases of great emergency, and use salutary restraints in every case of misbehavior, without being subjected to vexatious prosecutions, resulting in the mutual discredit and shame of all parties concerned. Judgment affirmed.

Notes and Questions

1. *Common law crimes.* Most acts of domestic violence are assaults. See Andrew R. Klein, The Criminal Justice Response to Domestic Violence 12 (2004) (citing research findings). Assaults give rise to both criminal and civil liability (that is, tort law). At common law, assault and battery were categorized, for criminal law purposes, as misdemeanors. Today, assault and battery can constitute either misdemeanors or felonies, depending on the seriousness of the offense (that is, the factors of intent to kill and/or use of a firearm). Assault and battery may be categorized as simple or aggravated (the latter is generally more violent and may involve the use of a weapon).

2. *Holding. Bradley* was one of the first American cases to set forth the legality of the husband's power of chastisement of his wife. See Linda Gordon, Heroes of their Own Lives 364 (2002). Justice Ellis in *Bradley* announces the view that the husband's power of chastisement is not absolute ("an unlimited license of this kind cannot be sanctioned"). Why?

The judge then explains that the husband's right is one of "moderate" correction. What is the reason, according to the court, for allowing the husband this power over the wife? What does it mean that the husband is responsible for the wife's "misbehavior"? What significance is conveyed by the court's use of the terms *misbehavior* and *indiscretions* to describe a wife's acts?

Justice Ellis states that the case would have been difficult to decide if the defendant had proven that "he confined himself within reasonable bounds, when he thought proper to chastise his wife." What does "reasonable bounds" mean? What does "when [the husband] thought proper" mean? Did the defendant exceed the scope of his right of "moderate chastisement"?

3. *Husband's defense.* The defendant in *Bradley* asserted a defense to the charge of assault and battery. His defense was in the form of a plea termed *son assault demesne.* The basis of this plea is that the defendant is asserting provocation—that the plaintiff committed an assault on him. That is, the husband in *Bradley* offered as a defense to his wife's charges of assault and battery that he was provoked by her. He claims that he struck his wife after she committed an assault on him—which act, he contends, was within his rights as her lawful husband to correct her behavior. See Melville M. Bigelow, Leading Cases on the Law of Torts Determined by the Courts of America and England 232 (1875) (explaining the plea).

What jury instruction did the defendant want? Why did the trial judge refuse to give it? Was the trial judge's ruling regarding the jury instruction in error? What does the state supreme court rule?

4. *Abrogation.* The husband's right of "reasonable chastisement" was finally abrogated in Mississippi in Gross v. State, 100 So. 177 (Miss. 1924) (holding that

husband has no right of chastisement even if done in moderation). Yet, despite abrogation of the husband's prerogative in case law and statute, legal policy still condoned marital violence. As Reva Siegel remarks: "[I]t would be misleading to look to the repudiation of the chastisement doctrine as an indicator of how the legal system responded to marital violence. . . . [J]urists and lawmakers vehemently condemned the chastisement doctrine, yet routinely condoned violence in marriage." Reva B. Siegel, "The Rule of Love": Wife Beating as Prerogative and Privacy, 105 Yale L.J. 2117, 2130 (1996).

5. *Ambivalence.* Justice Ellis reveals some ambivalence about the husband's right of chastisement. What language reflects this ambivalence? He also refers to Blackstone's views as reflecting a discrepancy between legal and social reality. What is this discrepancy? Despite his ambivalence, Justice Ellis nonetheless announces the rule that spousal abuse is permissible provided that the husband's conduct remains within "reasonable bounds." What does that outer limit mean? Does the court define its parameters? Or, will its determination be made on a case-by-case basis?

6. *Family structure.* What does *Bradley* reveal about nineteenth-century family structure and family life? About marriage? About appropriate gender roles for husbands and wives? See Siegel, supra, at 2145-2150 (exploring demise of the hierarchical view of marriage and the ascendance of the concept of the companionate marriage).

7. *Rationale.* Justice Ellis in *Bradley* determines that husbands may continue to exercise the right of moderate chastisement only in exigent circumstances and subject to limitation ("in cases of great emergency, and us[ing] salutary restraints in every case of misbehavior, without being subjected to vexatious prosecutions . . ."). What is the policy rationale for this holding? How does the court balance the woman's interests, the husband's interests, and the state's interest in cases of spousal assault and battery?

Bradley reflects the evolution of legal policy toward wife beating in the antebellum era. Professor Reva Siegel explains this transformation in the husband's disciplinary prerogative:

> A key concept in the doctrinal regime that emerged from chastisement's demise was the notion of marital privacy. During the antebellum era, courts began to invoke marital privacy as a supplementary rationale for chastisement, in order to justify the common law doctrine within the discourse of companionate marriage, when rationales based in authority-based discourses of marriage had begun to lose their persuasive power.

Siegel, supra, at 2151. She adds that antebellum jurists were particularly likely to invoke the marital privacy rationale in cases involving the middle and upper class. Id. at 2153.

8. *Women's rights.* The judge who authored Bradley v. State was a surprisingly well-educated jurist for his era. At a time when most lawyers and judges learned the law as apprentice clerks in lawyers' offices, Powhattan Ellis (a Virginian and descendant of Pocahontas) graduated from Washington Academy (now Washington and Lee University), attended Dickinson College (Carlisle, Pennsylvania) for two years, and then studied law for two years at William and Mary College. He relocated to Mississippi where he later became a senator and federal judge. See Dickinson (College) Chronicles, Powhattan Ellis, Class of 1810, http://chronicles.dickinson.edu/encyclo/e/ed_ellisP.htm (last visited June 24, 2010).

Despite his holding in the *Bradley* case, Justice Ellis was not indifferent to women's rights. In a prior case, Hackler's Heirs v. Cabel, 1 Miss. (1 Walker) 91 (1821), he upheld a woman's right to dower against her husband's heirs. In flowery language, he expressed his outrage at the heirs' attempt to usurp the widow's property rights and to eject her from her home:

> We cannot perceive without some emotion, an attempt on the part of so many children, whose filial obligations and gratitude to an affectionate mother, were increased by her care and vigilance in securing to them this very property, to turn her out of that mansion, where so much of her life and health had been devoted in maternal tenderness and watchful affection, to cherish, succor and protect them, during the helplessness of infancy and the ignorance and indiscretion of youth. . . .

Id. at 97. What gender stereotypes are reflected in the above case? Are they consistent with the gender-based stereotypes and the view of family privacy that Justice Ellis expresses in *Bradley*? Why might Justice Ellis have been willing to protect a widow's property rights against her husband's heirs but not a wife's safety against her husband?

9. *Blaming the victim.* Traditionally, the attitudes of law enforcement and the courts to the plight of victims of spousal violence have been indifference and "blaming the victim." How are both these attitudes reflected in *Bradley*?

10. *Reforms.* By 1870, most states no longer *officially* recognized the husband's common law prerogative to chastise his wife. See, e.g., Fulgham v. State, 46 Ala. 143 (1871); Commonwealth v. McAfee, 108 Mass. 458 (1971). Yet, the unofficial policy of condonation persisted. Significant law reforms would not occur until the next century.

2. *Modern Response: Domestic Violence Statutes*

Domestic violence encompasses a wide range of criminal behavior. Assault is the most common offense. Homicide is the most serious offense. Acts of sexual violence, including rape and sexual assaults, also occur. Other domestic violence crimes include: stalking, violations of protective orders, kidnapping, firearm-related offenses, harassment, arson, and breaking and entering. Occasionally, prosecutors may charge offenders with lesser offenses, such as disorderly conduct, disturbing the peace, and/or destruction of property.

The traditional criminal response by law enforcement to intimate partner violence was indifference. Assaults in the family were treated differently than assaults involving strangers. Abusers of intimate partners were rarely arrested and rarely prosecuted. Beginning in the 1970s, however, these attitudes began to change. The ensuing widespread reform of the criminal law produced several tangible results. Many state legislatures enacted special criminal statutes that set forth new crimes of "domestic violence." These statutes expanded criminal protections by broadening definitions of offenses and victims. In addition, the new statutes provided for sentence enhancements for the most dangerous batterers (that is, those who used weapons, inflicted very severe injury, or committed successive acts of domestic violence).

This era of legislative reform also addressed other aspects of the criminal justice system, as we have seen, such as police policies (for example, warrantless arrest, mandatory arrest, mandatory police training) and prosecutorial policies (for example, no-drop policies). Subsequent chapters will explore additional areas of reform, such as civil protection orders and family law reforms.

As you read the following materials, consider how these changes came about, the benefits and shortcomings of the new approaches, and the effectiveness of these modern policies.

■ EVE S. BUZAWA ET AL., RESPONDING TO DOMESTIC VIOLENCE: THE INTEGRATION OF CRIMINAL JUSTICE AND HUMAN SERVICES
221, 223 (2012)

THE CREATION OF DOMESTIC VIOLENCE-SPECIFIC CRIMES

[A] major change has been enactment of substantive changes to states' criminal laws. Currently, all states have enacted statutes creating a separate criminal offense for domestic or family violence. At first glance, explicit domestic violence laws may appear superfluous. After all, every state has a lengthy legal history prohibiting assault and battery since their adoption of English common law.

There are, however, several key advantages to a statute specific to domestic violence. These statutes direct law enforcement to types of crimes more common with domestic violence, not the specific requirements of common law assault and battery. Through various amendments during the past 15 years, coercive behavior such as harassment, intentional infliction of emotional distress, or threats other than the threat of assault that were not technically either assaults or batteries could be prosecuted.

Also the existence of one centralized statute that addressed most types of domestic abuse as well as traditional violent assaults could in theory focus law enforcement attention. This happened [in part] because police officers had an enhanced knowledge of the new domestic violence legislation and, somewhat cynically, because they now recognized increased exposure to civil liability for a knowing failure to enforce a specific criminal statute.

[In addition,] the earlier statutes that had simply allowed warrantless misdemeanor arrests often contained major procedural limitations. For example, often there were strict limits on the time between the event and the arrest, requirements of visible injury, or both. The creation of express domestic violence statutes freed the police from such unnecessary restrictions. Similarly, because a domestic violence assault violation was more specific, it was assumed that the legislative intent to mete out punishment appropriate to the crime would influence courts as they imposed sentences. Although difficult to monitor, it was certainly hoped that innovative sentences such as including injunction-type conditions, threatening deferred prosecution, and forcing assignment of a batterer to counseling programs would become the norm. Although these sentences were available in the past and might be undertaken at the initiative of an individual judge, they were not always intuitively obvious because sentencing judges typically only rapidly reviewed a plea bargain on a generalized assault charge.

Finally, most such state statutes now require their agencies to retain accurate records of the occurrence of domestic violence and resultant case dispositions. When such cases were aggregated into the generic category of "assault and battery," it was difficult to determine accurately whether domestic abuse cases were prosecuted with the same vigor as other assault.

How do traditional assault statutes differ from modern domestic violence statutes? Traditional definitions are illustrated below by the Model Penal Code provisions (drafted by the American Law Institute in 1962). (The Model Penal Code consolidates the common law crimes of assault and battery.) Examples of modern state "domestic violence" statutes are included below. How do these modern statutes differ from the traditional approach?

STATUTORY COMPARISON: TRADITIONAL CRIMINAL ASSAULT STATUTES VERSUS NEW "DOMESTIC VIOLENCE" STATUTES

■ MODEL PENAL CODE §211.1. ASSAULT

(1) Simple Assault. A person is guilty of assault if he:

(a) attempts to cause or purposely, knowingly or recklessly causes bodily injury to another; or

(b) negligently causes bodily injury to another with a deadly weapon; or

(c) attempts by physical menace to put another in fear of imminent serious bodily injury.

Simple assault is a misdemeanor unless committed in a fight or scuffle entered into by mutual consent, in which case it is a petty misdemeanor.

(2) Aggravated Assault. A person is guilty of aggravated assault if he:

(a) attempts to cause serious bodily injury to another, or causes such injury purposely, knowingly or recklessly under circumstances manifesting extreme indifference to the value of human life; or

(b) attempts to cause or purposely or knowingly causes bodily injury to another with a deadly weapon.

Aggravated assault under paragraph (a) is a felony of the second degree; aggravated assault under paragraph (b) is a felony of the third degree.

■ COLO. REV. STAT. §18-6-800.3 DEFINITIONS

As used in this part 8, unless the context otherwise requires:

(1) "Domestic violence" means an act or threatened act of violence upon a person with whom the actor is or has been involved in an intimate relationship. "Domestic violence" also includes any other crime against a person, or against property, including an animal, or any municipal ordinance violation against a person, or against property, including an animal, when used as a method of coercion, control, punishment, intimidation, or revenge directed against a person with whom the actor is or has been involved in an intimate relationship.

(2) "Intimate relationship" means a relationship between spouses, former spouses, past or present unmarried couples, or persons who are both the parents

of the same child regardless of whether the persons have been married or have lived together at any time.

■ IND. CODE §35-41-1-6.3. CRIME OF "DOMESTIC VIOLENCE" DEFINED

"Crime of domestic violence," . . . means an offense or the attempt to commit an offense that:

    (1) has as an element the:

      (A) use of physical force; or

      (B) threatened use of a deadly weapon; and

    (2) is committed against a:

      (A) current or former spouse, parent, or guardian of the defendant;

      (B) person with whom the defendant shared a child in common;

      (C) person who was cohabiting with or had cohabited with the defendant as a spouse, parent, or guardian; or

      (D) person who was or had been similarly situated to a spouse, parent, or guardian of the defendant.

■ N.J. STAT. ANN. §2C:25-19. DEFINITIONS

As used in this act:

a. "Domestic violence" means the occurrence of one or more of the following acts inflicted upon a person protected under this act by an adult or an emancipated minor:

    (1) Homicide (N.J.S. §2C:11-1 et seq.)

    (2) Assault (N.J.S. §2C:12-1)

    (3) Terroristic threats (N.J.S. 2C:12-3)

    (4) Kidnapping (N.J.S. §2C:13-1)

    (5) Criminal restraint (N.J.S. §2C:13-2)

    (6) False imprisonment (N.J.S. 2C:13-3)

    (7) Sexual assault (N.J.S. §2C:14-2)

    (8) Criminal sexual contact (N.J.S. §2C:14-3)

    (9) Lewdness (N.J.S. §2C:14-4)

    (10) Criminal mischief (N.J.S. §2C:17-3)

    (11) Burglary (N.J.S. §2C:18-2)

    (12) Criminal trespass (N.J.S. §2C:18-3)

    (13) Harassment (N.J.S. §2C:33-4)

    (14) Stalking (P.L.1992, c. 209; C. §2C:12-10)

    . . .

d. "Victim of domestic violence" means a person protected under this act and shall include any person who is 18 years of age or older or who is an emancipated minor and who has been subjected to domestic violence by a spouse, former spouse, or any other person who is a present or former household member. "Victim of domestic violence" also includes any person, regardless of age, who has been subjected to domestic violence by a person with whom the victim has a child in common, or with whom the victim anticipates having a child in common, if one of the parties is pregnant. "Victim of domestic violence" also includes any person who has been subjected to domestic violence by a person with whom the victim has had a dating relationship. . . .

■ N.M. STAT. ANN. §30-3-11. DEFINITIONS

As used in the Crimes Against Household Members Act [that follows]:

A. "household member" means a spouse, former spouse, parent, present or former stepparent, present or former parent-in-law, grandparent, grandparent-in-law, a co-parent of a child or a person with whom a person has had a continuing personal relationship. Cohabitation is not necessary to be deemed a household member for the purposes of the Crimes Against Household Members Act; and

B. "continuing personal relationship" means a dating or intimate relationship.

■ N.M. STAT. ANN. §30-3-12. ASSAULT AGAINST A HOUSEHOLD MEMBER

A. Assault against a household member consists of:

(1) an attempt to commit a battery against a household member; or

(2) any unlawful act, threat or menacing conduct that causes a household member to reasonably believe that he is in danger of receiving an immediate battery.

B. Whoever commits assault against a household member is guilty of a petty misdemeanor.

■ S.C. CODE ANN. §16-25-10. "HOUSHOLD MEMBER" DEFINED

As used in this article, "household member" means:

(1) a spouse;

(2) a former spouse;

(3) persons who have a child in common; or

(4) a male and female who are cohabiting or formerly have cohabited.

■ S.C. CODE ANN. §16-25-20. ACTS PROHIBITED; PENALTIES

(A) It is unlawful to:

(1) cause physical harm or injury to a person's own household member; or

(2) offer or attempt to cause physical harm or injury to a person's own household member with apparent present ability under circumstances reasonably creating fear of imminent peril.

(B) Except as otherwise provided in this section, a person who violates the provisions of subsection (A) is guilty of the offense of criminal domestic violence and, upon conviction, must be punished as follows:

(1) for a first offense, the person is guilty of a misdemeanor and must be fined not less than one thousand dollars nor more than two thousand five hundred dollars or imprisoned not more than thirty days. . . .

(2) for a second offense, the person is guilty of a misdemeanor and must be fined not less than two thousand five hundred dollars nor more than five thousand dollars and imprisoned not less than a mandatory minimum of thirty days nor more than one year. . . .

(3) for a third or subsequent offense, the person is guilty of a felony and must be imprisoned not less than a mandatory minimum of one year but not more than five years. . . .

Notes and Questions

1. *Legislative intent.* One of the primary purposes of the reform movement that defined the crime of "domestic violence" was the recognition that intimate partner violence deserved to be treated more seriously than previously. This legislative intent is clearly expressed in the following purpose clause of domestic violence legislation that was enacted in 1988:

R.I. Gen. Laws §12-29-1. Legislative Purpose

(a) The purpose of this chapter is to recognize the importance of domestic violence as a serious crime against society and to assure victims of domestic violence the maximum protection from abuse which the law and those who enforce the law can provide.

(b) While the legislature finds that the existing criminal statutes are adequate to provide protection for victims of domestic violence, previous societal attitudes have been reflected in policies and practices of law enforcement agencies, prosecutors, and courts which have resulted in differing treatment of crimes occurring between family or household members and of the same crimes occurring between strangers. Only recently has public perception of the serious consequences of domestic violence to society and to the victims led to the recognition of the necessity for early intervention by law enforcement agencies.

(c) It is the intent of the legislature that the official response to cases of domestic violence shall stress the enforcement of the laws to protect the victim and shall communicate the attitude that violent behavior is not excused or tolerated. Furthermore, it is the intent of the legislature that criminal laws be enforced without regard to whether the persons involved are or were married, cohabiting, or involved in a relationship.

2. *Different labels.* When state legislatures created new offenses to address domestic violence, they adopted a variety of labels. Many adopted the term *domestic violence.* However, some jurisdictions labeled the new offenses as *domestic abuse, domestic assault, domestic battering, domestic battery, spouse abuse,* or *family violence.*

3. *Different approaches.* In the wave of law reform from the 1970s to 1990s, states adopted a number of different approaches to the criminalization of domestic violence. Some states retained their existing criminal statutes (for example, for assault

and battery) but enhanced the penalties if the violence involved familial or household members. See, e.g., Ga. Code Ann. §16-5-21(j) (enhancing simple assault to aggravated assault if committed "between past or present spouses, persons who are parents of the same child, parents and children, stepparents and stepchildren, foster parents and foster children, or other persons excluding siblings living or formerly living in the same household"). This approach was based on the belief that existing laws were adequate to address the problem. Thomson Reuters/West, 50 State Statutory Surveys: Criminal Law: Domestic Violence, 0030 Surveys 7 (Sept. 2010).

However, about half of the states created separately chargeable crimes of "domestic violence." See, e.g., Ala. Code §§13A-6-130 to 132 ("domestic violence" in the first, second and third degree); Ohio Rev. Code §2919.25 (crime of "domestic violence" if a person "shall knowingly cause or attempt to cause physical harm to a family or household member").

In addition, several states mandated longer sentences for repeat offenders of, specifically, domestic violence offenses compared to other recidivists. See, e.g., Nev. Stat. Ann. §200.485(1) (providing penalties for first, second, third offense for "battery which constitutes domestic violence"). [Other differences are discussed in subsequent chapters.]

Review the kinds of offenses, acts, and harm that are covered in each of the above statutes. Which approach does each statute adopt? How are the prohibited offenses defined? Are they limited to specific offenses or do they cover ensuing physical harm or injury? Which additional kinds of abuse or harm *should* be covered by domestic violence statutes? Do "catchall" provisions adequately address offenses, or do they merely provide the courts with excess discretion? If a given statute does not include a particular "act" as "domestic violence," can other criminal provisions be used to prosecute the batterer? Should acts of "coercive control" be included? If so, would such a statute survive a vagueness challenge?

See generally Deborah Tuerkheimer, Recognizing and Remedying the Harm of Battering: A Call to Criminalize Domestic Violence, 94 J. Crim. L. & Criminology 959, 1020 (2004) (contending that the statutory definition of battering should encompass a course of conduct characterized by power and control); Dennis Feeney, Jr., Note, Ensuring the Domestic Violence Victim a Means of Communication: Why Passing Legislation that Criminalizes Impairing Another's Communication is the Next Logical Step in Combating Domestic Violence, 32 Seton Hall Legis. J. 167 (2007) (advocating punishment for "impairing another's communication" as a crime of domestic violence); Steve Mulligan, Comment, Redefining Domestic Violence: Using the Power and Control Paradigm for Domestic Violence Legislation, 29 Child. Legal Rts. J. 33 (2009) (arguing that current criminal domestic violence statutes fail to capture the dynamic of power and control that is uniquely present in domestic violence).

4. *Distinctions.* How do definitions of "domestic violence" differ from the traditional definitions of assault and battery? One difference is that domestic violence covers not only assault and battery but also a broader range of conduct (for example, psychological abuse, stalking, etc.). Another distinction is that the offense of domestic violence is committed by a person who has a special relationship with the victim (as statutorily defined). An assault or battery, in contrast, can occur between complete strangers. Thus, the allegation in a domestic violence case is

that the alleged victim of the harmful act was a "family or household member" or some other designated party as defined by state law.

Punishment also differs. Often, penalties are more severe for an offense of "domestic violence" than for assault. This feature stems from recognition of the fact that, whereas an assault-battery may be an isolated act, an assault on an intimate partner is likely to be one of a continuing series of acts, that is, a "course of conduct" that becomes more frequent and severe with the passage of time. Yet another distinction is that most states provide more forms of protection (both criminal and civil) for victims of domestic violence than for victims of assault and battery. For example, a court might require the domestic violence offender to surrender all firearms and also to attend treatment (in addition to other conditions).

5. *Protected persons.* Domestic violence statutes require that the victim show a designated relationship with the abuser. Early statutes established that relationship by reference to marriage, that is, covering only spouses and former spouses. Gradually, however, legislatures expanded statutes beyond marriage to include such other relationships as: the unmarried "parents" of the partners' child, cohabitants or former cohabitants, former boyfriends and girlfriends. Many statutes currently also cover "dating" relationships.

What relationships should be included in domestic violence statutes? See generally Devon M. Largio, Note, Refining the Meaning and Application of "Dating Relationship" Language in Domestic Violence Statutes, 60 Vand. L. Rev. 939, 954 (2007). Should same-sex intimate relationships be included? See Shannon Little, Note, Challenging Changing Legal Definition of Family in Same-Sex Domestic Violence, 19 Hastings Women's L.J. 259 (2008). Should "cohabitation" be defined? If so, how? Should the term "dating relationship" be defined? If so, how? See Fla. Stat. Ann. §784.042(b)(2) ("'dating relationship' means a continuing and significant relationship of a romantic or intimate nature"). Could protection be extended under the above statutes if the parties are no longer living together and parental rights have been terminated? See, e.g., People v. Mora, 59 Cal. Rptr. 2d 801 (Ct. App. 1996). See generally Orly Rachmilovitz, Bringing Down the Bedroom Walls: Emphasizing Substance over Form in Personal Abuse, 14 Wm. & Mary J. Women & L. 495 (2008) (criticizing statutory definitions).

6. *Criminal and civil overlap.* Many statutes, such as the New Jersey statute above, reflect the interrelationship between criminal and civil law treatment of domestic violence. Sometimes, the same statutory definitions apply to criminal and civil laws, that is, to criminal offenses and protection orders. However, sometimes different definitions apply for criminal and civil codes. What problems does this cause? Given that the underlying acts are criminal in nature, should the criminal standard of proof (beyond a reasonable doubt) apply in civil actions such as those for protection orders? Why or why not? Which standard better protects victims of domestic violence? Which standard better protects the rights of offenders? See Roe v. Roe, 601 A.2d 1201, 1206 (N.J. Super. Ct. App. Div. 1992).

7. *Theory.* Based on the above statutes, what is the modern rationale for the criminal law's response to domestic violence? For example, do criminal laws protect victims of intimate partner violence because such acts are more harmful than assaults committed by strangers? Or do they protect those who face harm in the

setting of the home because violence in the sanctity of the home merits special condemnation? See Ruth Colker, Marriage Mimicry: The Law of Domestic Violence, 47 Wm. & Mary L. Rev. 1841, 1853-1869 (2006) (raising these issues about domestic violence law).

Problems

1. The state of Blackacre has decided to amend its criminal provisions regarding domestic violence. The current statute defines domestic abuse as:

(A) Physical harm, bodily injury, assault, or the infliction of fear of imminent physical harm, bodily injury, or assault between family or household members; or

(B) Any sexual conduct between family or household members, whether minors or adults, that constitutes a crime under the laws of this state.

The statute further defines "family or household members" as "spouses, former spouses, parents and children, persons related by blood within the fourth degree of consanguinity, any children residing in the household, persons who presently or in the past have resided or cohabited together, persons who have or have had a child in common, and persons who are presently or in the past have been in a dating relationship together." [Ark. Code Ann. §9-15-103.]

What recommendations would you make in amending this statute? In your recommendations, consider whom the law currently protects, whom the law should protect, whom the law should punish, and what kind of crimes the law will punish. Also consider how the law will be enforced and who should enforce it and how the prosecution must meet its burden of proof in situations of nonphysical domestic abuse.

2. Johanna and Frank begin a romantic relationship. They live together for almost eight years. When their romantic relationship ends, they continue to live in the same house (but in separate bedrooms) and share financial responsibilities and household duties. One evening, the police are called to the home. They find Johanna with severe bruises on her arms and legs and black eyes. Both Johanna and Frank are intoxicated. Johanna claims that Frank kicked her with his spurred boots and hit her. Frank claims that Johanna injured herself falling down due to her drunken state. The police arrest Frank for "domestic abuse assault" (an aggravated misdemeanor) in violation of the Iowa Code.

The Iowa Code provides: "domestic abuse assault" means an assault, committed under any of the following circumstances: (1) between family or household members who resided together at the time of the assault; or (2) between separated spouses or persons divorced from each other and not residing together at the time of the assault. Iowa Code §236.2(2). The code further defines "family or household members" as "spouses, persons cohabiting, parents or other persons related by consanguinity or affinity, except children under eighteen." Iowa Code §236.2(4).

Frank contends that "cohabitation" under the domestic abuse statute requires proof of a sexual relationship. What result? See State v. Kellogg, 542 N.W.2d 514, 518 (Iowa 1996).

B. CONSTITUTIONAL CHALLENGES TO STATE LAWS

1. Vagueness

■ **PEOPLE v. JOHNSON**
793 N.E.2d 774 (Ill. App. Ct. 2003)

Presiding Justice Gordon delivered the opinion of the court:

. . . The testimony established that around 2 a.m. on May 18, 2001, defendant and Denise Howard were at the intersection of Union and 60th Streets in Chicago loudly arguing and using profanity. Howard was holding an automobile antitheft device called the Club, with which she proceeded to smash the windows in defendant's car. Defendant then started the car, stepped on the accelerator and hit Howard with the car, carrying her approximately 15 feet. When defendant slowed the car, Howard fell to the ground by the passenger side front tire. Defendant then turned the car around and drove back toward Howard, who was lying in the street. Upon approaching Howard, defendant swerved the car and drove away.

Gerard Wilson, who witnessed the altercation, called the police and put a towel over Howard to stop her bleeding. When the police arrived, Wilson provided a description of defendant's car. Howard provided the police with defendant's name, stating her boyfriend, Darren Johnson, ran over her with his car. Chicago police officer Herschel Lewis located defendant and his car at St. Bernard Hospital. . . . Subsequently, at the police station, defendant spoke with Detective Thomas Benoit. At that time, defendant reported that he and Howard had gotten into an argument. He told the detective that Howard did not break any of his car windows with the Club, but that she took a gun from under his front passenger seat, got out of the car and shot at him. The bullet shattered the window and grazed his right shoulder. The next day, defendant told Detective Benoit that he and Howard argued in the car and Howard hit him in the shoulder and face with the Club. She then got out of the car and began breaking his windows with the Club. Defendant drove off, unaware that he had hit Howard with the car. . . .

Howard herself told the detective that she had been drinking heavily at a funeral the day of the incident and the last thing she remembered was defendant hitting her with his car. When asked, Howard testified at trial that she had been "dating" defendant for almost two years. . . . She admitted to hitting defendant with the Club during their altercation, but denied shooting at him. The parties stipulated that, as a result of being run over by defendant's car, Howard required surgery and received blunt trauma injuries, multiple pelvic fractures, fractures to her clavicle and multiple skin contusions. . . .

Defendant also testified, upon being questioned, that Howard was his "girl-friend" and they had been "going together" approximately one year at the time of the incident. . . . [He] testified that [Howard] was intoxicated and attempted to jump out of his car while it was moving. He grabbed her arm to prevent her from jumping and Howard began hitting him and grabbing the steering wheel. After defendant drove onto the sidewalk, Howard got out of the car and began hitting the car windows with the Club. When defendant tried to stop her, Howard hit him with the Club two or three times. Defendant testified that after he got back into the car, Howard broke another window and glass flew into his eye. When he started the car, he heard the Club hit the ground and heard Howard run away. He then pulled away and hit something that he thought was a tree or pole. He backed the car up and drove away.

The trial court found defendant guilty of aggravated domestic battery and aggravated battery. Merging the aggravated battery conviction, the court sentenced defendant to four years in prison for aggravated domestic battery. The sole issue raised by defendant on appeal is the constitutionality of the domestic violence statute, pursuant to which he was convicted of aggravated domestic battery. Defendant contends that the statute is unconstitutionally vague due to the lack of a definition for the term "persons who have or had a dating or engagement relationship," which is included in the category "family or household members." . . .

The Criminal Code of 1961 provides that a person commits aggravated domestic battery if he intentionally or knowingly causes great bodily harm or permanent disability or disfigurement to any family or household member. 720 ILCS 5/12-3.2(a), 3.3(a) (West 2002). The definition of "family or household member," provided in the Code of Criminal Procedure (the Code), includes "persons who have or had a dating or engagement relationship." . . . Defendant contends that, because the term "dating or engagement" relationship is not defined in the Code and is not susceptible to a single commonly understood meaning, the statute is unconstitutionally vague and his conviction thereunder must be reversed.

The constitutionality of a statute is a question of law and is subject to de novo review. There is a strong presumption that a statute is constitutional and the challenging party bears the burden of rebutting that presumption. . . .

[Defendant has] standing to raise the unconstitutionality of the domestic battery statute as it was applied to him. In cases such as this one, which do not involve first amendment freedoms, due process is satisfied where: "(1) the statute's prohibitions are sufficiently definite, when measured by common understanding and practices, to give a person of ordinary intelligence fair warning as to what conduct is prohibited, and (2) the statute provides sufficiently definite standards for law enforcement officers and trier of fact that its application does not depend merely on their private conceptions." These considerations are to be analyzed in light of the particular facts of the case at hand. . . .

Section 112A-3(3) of the Code classifies persons in a "dating or engagement relationship" as "family or household members" for purposes of the domestic battery statute. The section further provides that "neither a casual acquaintanceship nor ordinary fraternization between 2 individuals in business or social contexts shall be deemed to constitute a dating relationship." As defendant argues, a potential difficulty with this term might arise where a relationship is new. Some people might define one date as a "dating relationship," while others may not do so until after several dates. However, a statute is not unconstitutionally vague merely because "one can conjure up a hypothetical dispute over the meaning of some of the act's terms." Defendant's argument in this regard is unavailing as the hypothetical situations he raises are not at issue in this case.

Defendant himself testified that Howard was his "girlfriend." He stated he had been "going with" Howard for one year before the incident, she visited him in jail, and they wrote letters to each other. Defendant admitted that some of his letters contained the sentiment "I love you" or "love you." He also stated that he and Howard were going to live together or get married after he was released from prison. In further support of the existence of their dating relationship, Howard testified that defendant was her "boyfriend" and that she had been dating him for almost two years at the time of trial. She stated that she loved defendant and they were planning on living together or maybe getting married after he was released from prison. Howard visited defendant once a week in prison, called him on the telephone and wrote him letters.

In light of defendant's and Howard's testimony, their relationship was clearly a "dating relationship," which fell squarely within the parameters of the statute; it was not a casual acquaintanceship or ordinary fraternization in a business or social context. Because a person of ordinary intelligence would undoubtedly conclude that defendant's relationship with Howard constituted a "dating relationship," defendant was provided with a reasonable opportunity to determine that his conduct of hitting Howard with his car was prohibited by the domestic violence statute. Furthermore, given that their long-term, romantic relationship was established by defendant's own testimony, the enforcement of the statute in defendant's case was not arbitrary or capricious.

Although defendant argues that "even the [trial] court demonstrated confusion as to the nature of the relationship between [defendant] and Ms. Howard," we agree with the State that the court did not appear confused about the statute or the relationship at issue, but was instead commenting on the credibility of defendant's testimony. The court specifically stated:

> "Mr. Frazin [defendant's counsel] has suggested these letters are innocent. Maybe I would even give that argument some consideration if there wasn't more than one letter. It's just one letter, it's two letters. It's clear to me that the defendant was trying to coach what his girlfriend or ex-girlfriend or alleged girlfriend was going to say here today, and that again I believe affects the defendant's credibility."

The court's comments were directed at defendant's credibility and his attempt to influence Howard's testimony at trial, and do not support defendant's argument that the statute is unconstitutionally vague. . . . Accordingly, the judgment of the circuit court is affirmed.

Notes and Questions

1. *Vagueness.* Defendant challenges the constitutionality of the state domestic violence statute, pursuant to which he was convicted of domestic battery, based on the ground of vagueness. The harm of a vague law is that it violates due process by not providing fair warning of unlawful conduct, thereby promoting arbitrary and discriminatory enforcement of the law. "A conviction fails to comport with due process if the statute under which it is obtained fails to provide a person of ordinary intelligence fair notice of what is prohibited, or is so standardless that it authorizes or encourages seriously discriminatory enforcement." United States v. Williams, 553 U.S. 285, 304 (2008) (finding that the provision of a federal act prohibiting the solicitation of child pornography is not impermissibly vague under the Due Process Clause). What is necessary to satisfy due process concerns here, according to the appellate court?

2. *Definitional issue.* Defendant's challenge addresses the lack of a statutory definition of the phrase "persons who have or had a dating or engagement relationship," which is included in the category "family or household members." What specific aspect(s) of the statute concern(s) him?

3. *Holding.* Why did the appellate court hold that the statute was not unconstitutionally vague as applied to defendant? Did the defendant's relationship with the victim meet the statutory definition of a "dating relationship"? How did the defendant's testimony help establish that their relationship fell within the parameters of the statute? How did the victim's testimony? How might a state statute define the term *dating relationship* more precisely? Should state legislatures do so in order to protect victims of intimate partner violence? What portion of the victim's testimony was credible? What portion was not? What portion of the defendant's testimony was credible? What portion was not?

4. *Credibility.* The trial court raised questions about the credibility of defendant's testimony. In explaining the dynamics of battering, one commentator notes: "Because abusers rarely admit to the full extent of their violence or take responsibility for their violent actions, excuse and justifications are frequently part of their accounts." Molly Dragiewicz, Equality with a Vengeance 72 (2011). How does the defendant excuse and/or justify his physical abuse? See generally Alesha Durfee, "I'm Not a Victim, She's an Abuser": Masculinity, Victimization, and Protection Orders, 25 Gender & Soc. 316 (June 2011) (pointing out that, in proceedings for protective orders, batterers often describe their actions as not "abusive" and focus instead on their power and control over their partner).

5. *Other constitutional challenges.* Courts have upheld state domestic violence statutes against other challenges based on vagueness. See, e.g., State v. Kealoha, 753 P.2d 1250 (Haw. 1988) (upholding the domestic violence statute against a vagueness challenge concerning term *physical abuse,* reasoning that persons of ordinary intelligence would know that they violate the statute by punching someone in the face); State v. Hellickson, 24 P.3d 59 (Idaho 2001) (upholding "felony domestic violence" statute on the grounds of vagueness regarding the term *traumatic injury*). Similarly, courts have upheld stalking statutes against constitutional attack based on vagueness. See generally Robert Batey, Vagueness and the Construction of Criminal Statutes—Balancing Acts, 5 Va. J. Soc. Pol'y & L. 1, 27-28 (1997) (exploring some of these challenges).

2. Defense of Marriage Act

■ **STATE v. CARSWELL**
871 N.E.2d 547 (Ohio 2007)

MOYER, C.J.

[W]e asked to determine whether the domestic-violence statute codified at R.C. §2919.25 violates Section 11, Article XV of the Ohio Constitution [the Defense of Marriage Amendment, providing that:]

> Only a union between one man and one woman may be a marriage valid in or recognized by this state and its political subdivisions. This state and its political subdivisions shall not create or recognize a legal status for relationships of unmarried individuals that intends to approximate the design, qualities, significance or effect of marriage.

Appellant, Michael Carswell, was indicted on one count of domestic violence in violation of R.C. §2919.25(A), which provides: "No person shall knowingly cause or attempt to cause physical harm to a family or household member." [The term *family or household member* was further defined to include: "(i) A spouse, a person living as a spouse, or a former spouse of the offender" who is cohabiting with, or has cohabited with, the offender.] The alleged victim was a female to whom Carswell was not married. The state intended to present evidence that Carswell's alleged victim had been "living as a spouse" with Carswell and that she was therefore a "family or household member" under R.C. §2919.25(F).

The trial court granted Carswell's motion to dismiss the indictment, concluding that the domestic-violence statute violated Section 11, Article XV of the Ohio Constitution, because the statute recognized a legal status similar to marriage for unmarried persons. The court of appeals reversed. . . . We begin our analysis with the established rule that statutes are presumed to be constitutional. . . . In determining whether a statute and a constitutional provision are clearly incompatible, we use the plain and ordinary meaning of the words in question and attempt to reconcile the words of the statute with the terms of the constitution whenever possible.

We consider first the terms of the constitutional provision. The first sentence of Section 11, Article XV, prohibits the state from recognizing as a marriage any union between persons other than one man and one woman. That constitutional prohibition is clear and is not at issue in this case. At issue is the second sentence of Section 11, Article XV, which bars the state from creating or recognizing a legal status for unmarried persons that "intends to approximate the design, qualities, significance or effect of marriage." This appeal requires this court to determine whether the indictment of Carswell for knowingly causing or attempting to cause physical harm to a "person living as a spouse" with him is vitiated because the statute under which he was indicted conflicts with the provision of Section 11, Article XV, that prohibits the state from creating or recognizing a legal status for unmarried persons that approximates marriage.

The term "legal status" is not defined in the amendment, nor is it defined in the case law of this court. A dictionary definition of the term "status" is succinctly stated as "[a] person's legal condition, whether personal or proprietary; the sum total of a person's legal rights, duties, liabilities, and other legal relations." Black's Law Dictionary (8th Ed. 2004) p. 1447. Even more concisely, the term "status" is defined as "[t]he standing of a person before the law." Random House Dictionary of the English Language (2d Ed. 1987) p. 1862.

Under these definitions, being married is a status. Marriage gives individuals a standing before the law. Being married gives a person certain legal rights, duties, and liabilities. For example, a married person may not testify against his or her spouse in some situations (R.C. §2945.42). A married person may inherit property from a spouse who dies intestate (R.C. §2105.06). The definition of "status," our understanding of the legal responsibilities of marriage, and the rights and duties created by the status of being married, combined with the first sentence of the amendment's prohibition against recognizing any union that is between persons other than one man and one woman, causes us to conclude that the second sentence of the amendment means that the state cannot create or recognize a legal status for unmarried persons that bears all of the attributes of marriage—a marriage substitute. . . .

It is clear that the purpose of [the constitutional amendment] was to prevent the state, either through legislative, executive, or judicial action, from creating or recognizing a legal status deemed to be the equivalent of a marriage of a man and a woman. The first sentence of the amendment prohibits the recognition of marriage between persons other than one man and one woman. The second sentence of the amendment prohibits the state and its political subdivisions from circumventing the mandate of the first sentence by recognizing a legal status similar to marriage (for example, a civil union).

In contemplation of the possible effect in Ohio of marriages between the same gender authorized by another State such as Massachusetts, the General Assembly by R.C. §3101.01(C)(2) took the approach that such marriages "shall be considered and treated in all respects as having no legal force or effect in this state and shall not be recognized by this state." Finally, regarding benefits for government employees, R.C. §3101.01(C)(3) provides that recognition or extension by the State of statutory benefits of a legal marriage to non-marital relationships between persons of the same or different genders "is against the strong public policy of this state." In other words, the General Assembly expressed its intent that such benefits for marriage partners should not be conferred upon individuals cohabiting out of wedlock, whatever their gender. To further emphasize its intent in enacting the legislation, the General Assembly passed uncodified law stating that substitutes for marriage such as "civil unions" shall not be recognized in Ohio. . . .

We next consider whether the prohibitions in Section 11, Article XV, prohibit the state from prosecuting an alleged violation of R.C. §2919.25 when an element to be proved is that the accused is "living as a spouse" with the alleged victim. . . . The statute distinguishes domestic violence from assault. The conduct of the accused is the same in both instances. Both crimes prohibit the act of "knowingly caus[ing] or attempt[ing] to cause physical harm," but the accused's relationship with the victim is the determining element. Physical harm caused to another is an assault (R.C. §2903.13); physical harm caused to a family or household member is "domestic violence," (R.C. §2919.25). . . . The distinction between the two offenses is important because of the large class of potential victims created by R.C. §2919.25(F). The General Assembly clearly intended to offer protections to a wide class of persons. In addition to the contested classification of a "person living as a spouse," the statute recognizes at least 11 other classifications of specific victims: spouse, former spouse, a parent, a child, a blood relative (consanguinity), an in-law (affinity), the parent of a spouse or former spouse, the child of a spouse or former spouse, a blood relative or in-law of a spouse or former spouse, and the natural parent of a child who is also the issue of the offender (R.C. §2919.25(F)(1)).

R.C. §2919.25 does not create any special or additional rights, privileges, or benefits for family or household members. Any legal benefits that these persons might possess (such as a right to inherit property through intestacy) are derived from other statutory provisions, not from the person's status as a family or household member in the domestic-violence statute. Additionally, each subset of potential victims has different rights or duties in other statutory provisions. For example, spouses have many other rights and duties, while former spouses do not. By the plain language of the statute, R.C. §2919.25 creates a subset of victims, separate from the generic term "another" in the assault statute; it does not bestow additional rights, duties, or liabilities. The specific statutory category that Carswell argues violates the constitution is the "person living as a spouse" category. The statute says that "person living as a spouse" means "a person who is . . . cohabitating with the offender, or who . . . has cohabitated with the offender within five years" of the alleged crime.

The statute does not define "cohabitation," but we have construed the term in this statute as follows: "The essential elements of 'cohabitation' are (1) sharing of familial or financial responsibilities and (2) consortium." . . . The state does not create cohabitation; rather it is a person's determination to share some measure of life's responsibilities with another that creates cohabitation. The state does not have a role in creating cohabitation, but it does have a role in creating a marriage. See R.C. §3101.01 et seq. The state played no role in creating Carswell's relationship with the alleged victim. Carswell created that relationship. While the intent of the domestic-violence statute is to protect persons from violence by close family members or residents of the same household, the intent of the marriage amendment was to prevent the creation or recognition of a legal status that approximates marriage through judicial, legislative, or executive action. The statute and the constitution are not in conflict.

We hold, therefore, that the term "person living as a spouse" as defined in R.C. §2919.25 merely identifies a particular class of persons for the purposes of the domestic-violence statutes. . . . A person "living as a spouse" is simply a classification with significance to only domestic-violence statutes. Thus, R.C. §2919.25 is not unconstitutional. . . . Judgment affirmed.

Notes and Questions

1. *Background.* Appellant Michael Carswell was indicted on one count of domestic violence for pushing his girlfriend roughly to the floor by her neck and head, resulting in her suffering injuries to her neck, head, and leg. Because the defendant had two prior convictions for the offenses of domestic violence, those prior convictions elevated the offense to a felony of the third degree. Memorandum of the State of Ohio in Response to Memorandum in Support of Jurisdiction, at 1, n.1. State v. Carswell, (871 N.E.2d 547), 2006 WL 4725886 (Ohio 2006). The trial court later reduced the felony domestic violence charge to a lesser-included offense of misdemeanor assault. Id. at 2, n.3.

2. *Statutory definition.* How does the state criminal statute at issue in *Carswell* distinguish domestic violence from assault? If Carswell could not be constitutionally convicted under the domestic violence statute, would he still face prosecution under Ohio's assault statute? See *Carswell*, supra, at 554-556 (Lanzinger, J., dissenting) (arguing that the statute was unconstitutional but that Carswell would still face charges of assault).

The Ohio domestic violence statute provides protection from victimization for specifically "a family or household member." Those terms were subsequently defined to include a person who was "living as a spouse" with the defendant. Domestic violence statutes generally require that a nonmarital abuser fall within the designated categories of persons who are either "cohabitants" or "household members" of the victim. Determining whether persons are "cohabiting" generally requires case-by-case analysis of such factors as sexual relations between the parties, the sharing of income and/or expenses, the joint use or ownership of property, the manner in which the parties hold themselves out, and the continuity and length of the relationship. Elizabeth Trainor, Annot., "Cohabitation" for Purposes of Domestic Violence Statutes, 71 A.L.R.5th 285, 292 (1999 & Supp.). What did the Ohio statute at issue in *Carswell* require?

3. *Defense of Marriage Act (DOMA).*

a. *Federal DOMA.* In the early 1990s, the Hawaii Supreme Court held that the denial of marriage licenses to same-sex couples violates the state constitution's Equal Protection Clause, which explicitly bars sex-based discrimination. Baehr v. Lewin, 852 P.2d 44, 67 (Haw. 1993) (superseded by state constitutional amendment). In reaction, Congress enacted the Defense of Marriage Act (DOMA), Pub. L. No. 104-199, 110 Stat. 2419. DOMA has two parts: (1) it provides a federal definition for the terms *marriage* and *spouse* (for purposes of federal benefits) by specifying that marriage is a union of a man and a woman, and that the term *spouse* refers only to a person of the opposite sex (1 U.S.C. §7); (2) it specifies that states are not required to give effect to same-sex marriage under the Full Faith and Credit Clause (28 U.S.C. §1738C). DOMA purportedly rests on Congress's power (in art. IV, §1) to implement the Full Faith and Credit Clause.

b. *State DOMA.* Many states responded to the same-sex marriage debate by enacting their own bans on the legal recognition of same-sex marriages. Sometimes referred to as "State Baby DOMAs," these prohibitions take the form of either state constitutional amendments or state statutes. What was the Ohio provision in *Carswell* with which, arguably, the state domestic violence statute conflicted? What was the nature of that conflict?

c. *Subsequent developments.* Several federal lawsuits are currently challenging *state* DOMAs. Compare Perry v. Schwarzenegger, 704 F. Supp. 2d 921 (N.D. Cal. 2010) (holding that the state constitutional amendment (Prop. 8), which abrogated the judicial decision permitting same-sex marriage, violated federal due process and equal protection guarantees), with In re Marriage of J.B. and H.B., 326 S.W.3d 654 (Tex. App. 2010) (holding that the state ban on same-sex marriage did not violate federal equal protection guarantee).

Additionally, there have been several successful challenges to the *federal* DOMA on federal constitutional grounds. See, e.g., In re Balas, 449 B.R.567 (Bankr. C.D. Cal. 2011) (holding that DOMA's denial of bankruptcy protection to same-sex couples violates the Equal Protection Clause); Gill v. Office of Personnel Management, 699 F. Supp. 2d 374 (D. Mass. 2010) (holding that DOMA's denial of federal employee health benefits to same-sex couples violates the Equal Protection Clause); Massachusetts v. U.S. Dept. of Health & Human Servs., 698 F. Supp. 2d 234 (D. Mass. 2010) (holding that DOMA's denial of federal veterans' benefits and federal Medicare funds violates the Tenth Amendment and Spending Clause).

In 2011, President Obama instructed the Department of Justice to discontinue its defense of the constitutionality of the definitional section of DOMA in cases that deny federal benefits to same-sex couples who were legally married in states that recognize such unions. Adam Liptak, The President's Courthouse, N.Y. Times, Feb. 27, 2011, at 5. In response, the U.S. House of Representatives hired Paul Clement (former solicitor general under President George W. Bush), to defend the federal statute. Mallie Jane Kim, House Could Spend $1.5M Defending Marriage Act, Congressman Fights Back, U.S. News & World Rep., Oct. 20, 2011, available at 2011 WLNR 21700986. Congress is currently considering legislation that would repeal DOMA. Respect for Marriage Act, S. 598, H.R. 1116, 112th Cong. (1st Sess. 2001).

4. *Holding.* Why did the trial court in *Carswell* conclude that the state domestic violence statute violated the state DOMA? Why did the state supreme court decide that the state domestic violence statute was constitutional? What was the basis of the state supreme court's reasoning?

5. *Same-sex cohabitants.* Can a same-sex relationship give rise to an offense under the statute at issue in *Carswell*, given that one partner cannot be "living as a spouse" in a jurisdiction that does not permit same-sex marriage? A prior Ohio case addressed this question. Joe Fields and Ronnie Yaden lived together as a same-sex couple for approximately four years, sharing expenses and attending social activities together. After they broke up, they continued to live together occasionally. During the course of an argument following the break-up, Yaden ripped the phone from the wall and threw it, striking Fields in the forehead. Yaden then punched Fields in the stomach. Yaden was charged with a violation of the same statute under which Michael Carswell had been charged. The statute defined a victim as a person with whom the defendant is living or has lived with the offender in a "common law marital relationship" or, alternatively, a person who is cohabiting or has cohabited with the offender within one year of the alleged act. In State v. Yaden, 692 N.E.2d 1097 (Ohio Ct. App. 1997), the appellate court upheld Yaden's conviction after determining that he had "cohabited" with the victim within the meaning of the state domestic violence statute. The court accepted a broad definition of cohabitation as "living together in an intimate relationship" and sharing financial support.

Few courts have addressed whether same-sex partners are considered "cohabitants" for purposes of state domestic violence statutes. What policy rationale explains expansive applications of these criminal statutes? Does legislative intent, as explained in *Carswell*, shed any light on this question? See generally Colker, supra; Marc Spindelman, State v. Carswell: The Whipsaws of Backlash, 24 Wash. U. J.L. & Pol'y 165, 179-183 (2007).

6. *Similar cases.* A similar challenge to the constitutionality of a state domestic violence statute in light of a state DOMA arose in State v. Curreri, 213 P.3d 1084, 1088-1090 (Kan. Ct. App. 2009). Anthony Curreri appealed his convictions for aggravated battery, criminal restraint, and domestic battery, resulting from his restraining and attempting to strangle his live-in girlfriend, Silvia Perez. Like the defendant in *Carswell*, Curreri contended that the domestic battery statute was unconstitutional when applied to an unmarried cohabitant because of the state DOMA. In response, the appellate court adopted the reasoning of *Carswell*, as follows:

> Curreri's conviction of domestic violence is not predicated upon the State recognizing his relationship with Perez as bearing all the hallmarks of a conventional marriage. The fact that Curreri and Perez were living together does not entitle them to all the benefits, rights, and obligations of marriage (e.g., spousal support, inheritance rights, or the marital privilege), as well as the right to be protected by Kan. Stat. Ann. §21-3412a [the state battery statute, subsequently repealed]. To the contrary, this statute simply extends to Perez the added protection from being battered that is extended to other persons, married or not, who may be particularly vulnerable to violence due to their close proximity to or relationship with the defendant. . . .

Id. at 1090.

7. *Policy.* Domestic violence advocacy groups filed amici curiae briefs in *Carswell*. What might have been the policy implications if *Carswell* had declared the domestic violence statute unconstitutional—both for domestic violence policy generally as well as the validity of same-sex marriage? See Patrick J. Fazzini, Cases Involving Statutory Interpretation: State v. Carswell, 34 Ohio N.U. L. Rev. 1017, 1022-1024 (2008); Spindelman, supra, at 177-184.

Problem

Mary lives in a small hotel room without kitchen facilities. A friend, Joe, comes to stay during June. In July, Joe rents another motel room, taking his belongings with him. He comes to live with Mary for the last two weeks of August. Joe returns to the hotel room after long days at work only to shower and sleep. Mary and Joe do not cook together and rarely eat together. They have sex occasionally. Mary describes the relationship as that of friends and roommates. Joe admits sleeping in Mary's bed (explaining that there was no other bed) but states that he slept on top of the covers, with his pants on. Joe does not have a key to Mary's room; she leaves the door unlocked. Mary and Joe do not share rent, have a joint bank account, make joint purchases, or hold themselves out as husband and wife.

On August 29, Joe beats and terrorizes Mary. He is charged with inflicting corporal injury on a cohabitant under the following penal code provision:

> Any person who willfully inflicts upon his or her spouse, or any person who willfully inflicts upon any person of the opposite sex with whom he or she is cohabiting, corporal injury resulting in a traumatic condition, is guilty of a felony, and upon conviction thereof shall be punished by imprisonment in the state prison for 2, 3 or 4 years. . . .
> (b) Holding oneself out to be the husband or wife of the person with whom one is cohabiting is not necessary to constitute cohabitation as the term is used in this section.

Joe argues that the provision is void for vagueness by not defining "cohabiting." What result? See People v. Holifield, 252 Cal. Rptr. 729 (Ct. App. 1988).

VII

■

Judicial Response

This chapter explores the role of courts in criminal justice policy regarding domestic violence. The chapter first examines the criminal defenses that are available to battered women who kill their spouses. Next, it turns to evidentiary issues that complicate the prosecution of abusers.

A. DEFENSES

1. Historical Background

How did the common law punish women who killed their husbands? Were they treated more leniently, more severely, or the same as men who killed their wives? The following excerpt provides historical insight on these questions.

■ **GARTHINE WALKER, CRIME, GENDER AND SOCIAL ORDER IN EARLY MODERN ENGLAND**
138-143 (2003)

From 1351 to 1828, the willful murder of her husband by a wife constituted an aggravated form of murder: petty treason, so termed "because there is subjection due from the wife to the husband, but not [the reverse]." The punishment of being "burnt to ashes" made brutally clear that husband-murder was more heinous, more sinful and more treacherous than uxoricide [wife killing]. . . . The construction of husband-killing as treason was based on natural law. As a wife's inferiority and subordination to her husband was ordained by God, in disobeying, let alone killing, their husbands, wives disobeyed God. . . . Killing one's husband directly assaulted godly hierarchies; murdering one's wife did not. Servants who killed their masters or mistresses, and ecclesiastics their prelates, were defined as petty traitors for similar reasons. Female servants were burnt; male servants, like uxoricides, were hanged. . . .

Other than treason, the only crime punishable by burning was heresy, which powerfully reinforced the link with sin. This form of execution undermines the view that law treated women "leniently." . . . Burning for petty treason is hardly explained by Blackstone's oft-cited claim that concerns about modesty made hanging inappropriate for women. Far greater numbers of women were hanged for other felonies. . . .

Spousal murder by wives fulfilled almost all the theoretical requirements of wrongful violence. It was the product and concomitant of disorder and disobedience; it broke moral and natural law as well as the King's peace, and neither motive nor intent fitted any accepted category of excusable or justifiable killing. In short, it defied the principles of hierarchical authority. While the man who murdered his wife was culpable, the degree to which he offended against these principles was extenuated by his position of master of the household. Men who excessively "corrected" their wives were neither encouraged nor condoned, but their actions could be excused and justified. . . . Men's domestic violence was perceived as an extension of their nature and expected role; women's marital violence was a manifestation of *un*naturalness. Whereas male violence was sanctioned to uphold household order, female violence subverted it. Husband-murder was a "radical disobedience to social order"; uxoricide was not. . . .

[S]elf-defense was an inappropriate mitigating concept for women who killed their husbands. Women very rarely invoked it. Indeed, in [two Surrey trials], the women's lethal violence was presented not as self-defense per se, but as the other form of excusable homicide—accident, compounded with the notion that the deceased had slain himself during his attack. Both women ascribed a form of non-action to themselves. One claimed that her husband had "accidentally" run upon the scissors she held in self-defense, he having already struck her with a fire-shovel as neighbors testified, and by then having a frying pan in his hand. The other said that as her husband beat her, "the knife stuck in his leg unknown to me." Neither defense was successful—both women burned at the stake. There was no convenient legal or societal concept of justifiable or excusable homicide for women who killed their husbands. . . .

———————————

Historian Garthine Walker concludes, based on her study of English court records, that women murderers were punished more harshly than men. "[W]omen's homicides characteristically failed to meet the legal criteria for mitigation," she notes. Id. at 136. On the one hand, men who received a verdict of manslaughter were able to invoke "benefit of clergy." Id. at 137-138. According to this practice, clergy who were convicted of designated felonies could escape hanging provided that they were able to read from the Bible. This benefit was gradually extended to all literate men, and permitted ecclesiastical authorities to mete out lighter punishments, such as branding. On the other hand, women were not eligible for benefit of clergy because the relevant statute applied only to men. See 4 William Blackstone, Commentaries *363 n.1. As a result, for several centuries, the prescribed punishment for wives who killed their husbands was burning at the stake. Walker, supra, at 138-140.

2. Battered Woman Syndrome: The Role of Expert Testimony

■ HAWTHORNE v. STATE
408 So. 2d 801 (Fla. Dist. Ct. App. 1982)

PER CURIAM.

[Joyce Hawthorne shot her husband to death in the early morning hours by bullets fired from five weapons. Here, she appeals her conviction of second-degree murder.]

. . . [Appellant argues that] the trial court erred in disallowing the testimony of Dr. Lenore Walker, a clinical psychologist who would have testified as an expert with regard to the battered-woman syndrome. The purpose of such testimony would have been to give the jury a basis for considering whether appellant suffered from the battered-woman syndrome, not in order to establish a novel defense, but as it related to her claim of self-defense. We are aware of the conflicting decisions of various jurisdictions as to the admissibility of this type of expert testimony. The courts that have considered the admissibility of this type of expert testimony have generally analyzed it to see whether it meets three basic criteria: (1) the expert is qualified to give an opinion on the subject matter; (2) the state of the art or scientific knowledge permits a reasonable opinion to be given by the expert; and (3) the subject matter of the expert opinion is so related to some science, profession, business, or occupation as to be beyond the understanding of the average layman. Basically, the same criteria are applicable in the instant case.

The few case authorities which have considered the admissibility of this type of expert testimony disagree primarily with regard to (1) whether the study of the battered-woman syndrome is an area sufficiently developed to permit an expert to assert a reasonable opinion, and (2) whether the battered-woman syndrome is beyond the knowledge and experience of most laymen.

[In Ibn-Tamas v. United States, 407 A.2d 626 (D.C. App. 1979), and Smith v. State, 277 S.E.2d 678 (Ga. 1981)], the courts concluded that the expert testimony should have been allowed, inasmuch as the subject matter was "beyond the ken of the average layman." . . . The *Ibn-Tamas* court determined, however, that the trial court had not ruled on whether the expert, Dr. Lenore Walker, was sufficiently qualified to give an opinion or whether "the state of the pertinent art or scientific knowledge" would permit an expert opinion. The court said that this third criterion depended on "whether Dr. Walker's methodology for identifying and studying battered women" was generally accepted. The question whether the second and third criteria [above] were satisfied was remanded to the trial court. [*Ibn-Tamas*, 407 A.2d at 638] . . .

We agree with the view expressed by the Georgia Supreme Court in Smith v. State insofar as it concluded that jurors would not ordinarily understand "why a person suffering from battered-woman's syndrome would not leave her mate, would not inform police or friends, and would fear increased aggression against herself." . . . 277 S.E.2d at 683. In the instant case, however, there has been no determination below as to the adequacy of Dr. Walker's qualifications or the extent to which her methodology is generally accepted indicating that the subject matter can support a reasonable expert opinion. Our determination that this expert testimony would provide the jury with an interpretation of the facts not ordinarily available to them is subject to the trial court determining that Dr. Walker is qualified and that the subject is sufficiently developed and can support an expert opinion.

Appellee argues that to admit this type of expert testimony would violate the rule [that] "testimony regarding the mental state of a defendant in a criminal case is inadmissible in the absence of a plea of not guilty by reason of insanity." . . . In this case, a defective mental state on the part of the accused is not offered as a defense as such. Rather, the specific defense is self-defense which requires a showing that the accused reasonably believed it was necessary to use deadly force to prevent imminent death or great bodily harm to herself or her children. The expert testimony would have been offered in order to aid the jury in interpreting the surrounding circumstances as they affected the reasonableness of her belief. . . .

Appellant did not seek to show through the expert testimony that the mental and physical mistreatment of her affected her mental state so that she could not be responsible for her actions; rather, the testimony would be offered to show that because she suffered from the syndrome, it was reasonable for her to have remained in the home and, at the pertinent time, to have believed that her life and the lives of her children were in imminent danger. It is precisely because a jury would not understand why appellant would remain in the environment that the expert testimony would have aided them in evaluating the case. . . . Reversed and remanded for a new trial.

■ LENORE WALKER, TERRIFYING LOVE: WHY BATTERED WOMEN KILL AND HOW SOCIETY RESPONDS
23-41 (1989)

I first met Joyce Hawthorne three years after [husband] Aubrey's death. An ordinary-looking woman of forty, about 5′3″ tall, weighing about 150 lbs., she didn't attract much attention. Her smile was rare but sweet; her eyes sparkled when she laughed. She looked just like the church-going mother of five that she was. Judging by her appearance alone, no one would have known that she'd killed a man much larger than herself, firing five guns in the process, even if sometimes her facial expression, at rest, revealed her fear and unhappiness. . . .

Joyce never denied that she'd fired the fatal shots; rather, although she had no memory of it, she claimed that she had been justified in firing them because she had wanted to protect herself and her family from assault, rape, and death. . . . [A]n appellate court had ruled that evidence about the extensive family abuse in this case could be introduced in the upcoming trial; but nothing had been specifically stated about the permissibility of allowing an expert witness to explain what Joyce's behavior had meant. . . .

Battered Woman Syndrome had not previously been used in the state of Florida to support a self-defense argument (although several other states had, by that time, permitted such testimony in courts of law). Before, it would have been much more common for a woman like Joyce to plead insanity, arguing that her husband's terrible abuse had rendered her temporarily insane. . . . Shortly after Aubrey's death, Joyce Hawthorne had been examined by a psychiatrist, who had found that she knew right from wrong, the legal standard for Florida's insanity plea. I, too, would find that Joyce Hawthorne was legally sane—but terrified that she and her family would be slaughtered, just as Aubrey had threatened. In my opinion, her belief that she and her children were in danger that night had been reasonable, and reasonable perception of imminent physical danger is the legal standard for acting in self-defense.

. . . I agreed with [defense attorney] Leo Thomas that a second jury would have to be carefully educated as to how and why this soft-spoken, church-going mother of five had been able to kill the father of her children. . . . Leo knew that, without understanding the long history of marital abuse Joyce had endured, the average person sitting on a jury could not be expected to comprehend why she had believed her husband would kill her when she refused his sexual advances. . . .

But Battered Woman Syndrome would provide the appropriate explanation; it would delineate the perception of imminency, and show how that perception was affected by the woman's state of mind. It would make her state of mind comprehensible, because battered women are always afraid of being hurt; any crisis situation may be perceived as a matter of life or death. . . .

Leo Thomas realized that he would have to educate this second jury . . . to make them understand why Joyce hadn't divorced Aubrey despite the daily horror of their marriage; he would have to corroborate Joyce's reports of domestic violence, even if no one else had seen Aubrey beat her; he would have to introduce convincing evidence to demonstrate that Joyce's fear had been reasonable on the night she finally killed him. All this would mean persuading the jury that Aubrey Hawthorne's repeated abuse of his wife had so affected her state of mind that she'd believed she needed to shoot him, to stop him from hurting her—as she perceived him coming toward her, even before he'd actually touched her—on that night in January 1977. Leo would have to help Joyce persuade the jury that her acute state of terror had induced her to use no less than five guns that night, firing at least nine bullets into her husband's body; that, in fact, her behavior had been a demonstration not of anger but of fear. . . .

. . . Most women are at a serious disadvantage when facing an attack from a man who is not only physically stronger but more ready and willing to fight. And battered women who kill are really like battered women who don't kill—they endure the same harassment, the same psychological torture; they experience the same terror—except that they have partners who are ready, able, and willing to kill them. When a battered woman kills her abuser, she has reached the end of the line. She is absolutely desperate, in real despair. She believes, with good reason, that if she does not kill, she will be killed. . . .

After being sworn in, I [found myself] the silent center of a swirling legal argument. . . . "Dr. Walker is not being presented to testify as to Joyce Hawthorne's mental status," I heard Leo say. "We are not trying to test Florida's insanity standards under the law." . . .

"If Dr. Walker tells the jury what effect the Battered Woman Syndrome had on Joyce Hawthorne's state of mind at the time she killed Aubrey Hawthorne, then she will be testifying as to a mental condition," Ron Johnson countered. "No notice of an insanity plea has been received, and therefore she shouldn't be permitted to testify. The state has the right to examine the defendant if an insanity plea is filed; therefore, we would have been denied that right." . . .

"Judge, this is justifiable homicide we are arguing, not excusable homicide, which would have been a mental health defense. Dr. Walker can testify as to the reasonableness of Joyce Hawthorne's perception that she was in imminent danger when she shot her husband. We say she acted in self-defense, not out of a disturbed mental condition." . . .

Ron Johnson assumed a threatening stance. "If you let her testify, Judge, then she takes away the role of the jury to decide if Joyce Hawthorne's perceptions of danger were reasonable. You'll open the door to allow any woman to kill a man she doesn't like, and get away with it!" . . . "She is a noted feminist," Johnson continued, "she admits to it right here [in] the introduction to her book *The Battered Woman,* so we all know she's biased against men. This woman would have decent people justify the actions of any woman who kills a man, just because he tells her to obey him. It will be open season on killing men, your honor, and you mustn't allow it!" . . .

I knew of no feminists who'd advocated killing men as a way to equalize power. . . . I heard Leo Thomas echo some of my thoughts to the judge. "Dr. Walker will not be invading the jury's province. The appellate court judges in the case of Ibn-Tamas v. United States ruled that they needed a psychologist to explain the defendant's state of mind. This is not a feminist issue, your honor. It is about what happens to a woman when she lives with a man whom she loves and who beats her." . . .

Notes and Questions

1. *Epilogue.* The admissibility of evidence about the nature of battering was at issue in Joyce Hawthorne's three criminal trials. Her first conviction for first-degree murder was reversed based on the improper exclusion of evidence of her prior history of abuse, that is, her husband's prior threats and violence toward her, their children, and third persons (including his sexual assault on their oldest daughter). The reversal was also based, in part, on findings that her confession had been illegally obtained, stemming from police coercion to release her children in exchange for her confession. 377 So. 2d 780 (Fla. Dist. Ct. App. 1979).

The principal case reversed Hawthorne's subsequent conviction for second-degree murder based on, inter alia, the exclusion of expert testimony on the Battered Woman Syndrome (BWS). Upon rehearing, the trial court again rejected BWS evidence, this time reasoning that its scientific basis in the professional community was not sufficiently accepted. The appellate court affirmed. 470 So. 2d 770 (Fla. Dist. Ct. App. 1985). When Hawthorne was again charged with murder, her attorney successfully argued that a fourth trial would constitute cruel and unusual punishment. See Walker, Terrifying Love, supra, at 16-41; Lenore E. A. Walker & David L. Shapiro, Introduction to Forensic Psychology: Clinical and Social Psychological Perspectives 89-90 (2003).

2. Hawthorne: *significance.* The issue of the admissibility of expert testimony is essential to an understanding of the law's response to battered women who kill their abusers. *Hawthorne* was one of the first cases in which defense attorneys sought to

introduce evidence about the dynamics of domestic violence for the purpose of helping a decision-maker determine whether a particular defendant acted reasonably in exercising self-defense against her abuser.

Hawthorne is illustrative of the early judicial climate that was "generally inhospitable to the new form of evidence." Donald Alexander Downs, More Than Victims: Battered Women, the Syndrome Society, and the Law 77 (1996). That climate changed dramatically. Within a few years, case law reflected increased sensitivity to the plight of battered women by accepting the view that BWS was an appropriate subject of expert testimony and was relevant to defendants' self-defense claims. See, e.g., State v. Kelly, 478 A.2d 364 (N.J. 1984). The recognition of the admissibility of BWS evidence "was heralded as a landmark victory for battered women." Regina A. Schuller & Sara Rzepa, Expert Testimony Pertaining to Battered Woman Syndrome: Its Impact on Jurors' Decisions, 26 Law. & Human. Behav. 655, 655 (2002).

In the principal case, the appellate judge explains the divergence of case law regarding the admissibility of BWS. What are those areas of disagreement, according to the judge?

3. *BWS: origins.* BWS derives from the research of clinical psychologist Lenore Walker based on her interviews in the 1970s with over 400 battered women. Walker theorizes that the Battered Woman Syndrome has two components: a three-stage cycle of violence and learned helplessness. The cycle of violence consists of: (1) a tension-building phase; (2) an acute battering incident; and (3) a contrition stage (discussed in Chapter 2). "Learned helplessness" purports to explain why women remain in abusive relationships. According to Walker, BWS is not a mental disorder but rather the psychological reaction of a normal person when exposed to traumatic events.

4. *Reasonable standard and relevance of BWS.* BWS evidence does not negate the requisite mental culpability for murder. Rather, it is introduced because it is relevant to establish a defense, such as self-defense. BWS provides valuable evidence in criminal trials of battered women: (1) to address misconceptions that jurors hold in regard to battering and battered women, and (2) to address gender-based norms of reasonableness and imminence in the law of self-defense. Specifically, it shows the reasonableness of the battered woman's belief, under the circumstances, that the use of deadly force was necessary to protect herself against the imminent risk of death or great bodily injury. Professor Elizabeth Schneider elaborates:

> Evidence of battering [helps] jurors to understand the experiences of battered women as they are relevant to women's understanding of the level of danger they are in and their reactions to the perceived danger. In other words, evidence of battering in a self-defense case is not relevant insofar as it attempts to justify killing in and of itself. It is relevant because it helps the jury to understand the woman's particular experiences with her batterer. It gives the jury insight about the development of her heightened ability to sense that she was in grave danger at the time of the killing. It provides the jury with the appropriate context in which to decide whether her apprehension of imminent danger of death or great bodily harm was reasonable.

Elizabeth M. Schneider, Resistance to Equality, 57 U. Pitt. L. Rev. 477, 511 (1996). Schneider emphasizes that jurors need to hear expert testimony to shed light on the reasonableness of the defendant's belief "precisely because the jury may not understand that the battered woman's prediction of the likely extent and imminence of violence is particularly acute and accurate." Elizabeth M. Schneider, Describing and Changing: Women's Self-Defense Work and the Problem of Expert Testimony on Battering, 14 Women's Rts. L. Rep. 213, 229-230 (1992). The elements and application of the self-defense doctrine are examined later in this chapter.

5. *Various uses of BWS testimony.* Depending on the jurisdiction, evidence of BWS may be introduced to establish proof of self-defense or duress (explored later in this chapter), or as a mitigating factor at sentencing. Many states limit expert testimony on BWS to explain the behavior of battered victims but not to answer the questions of whether a particular defendant suffers from the syndrome or told the truth about the crime. Finally, prosecutors sometimes introduce BWS evidence to bolster the credibility of battered women who change their testimony during prosecutions of abusers by explaining the victims' motivations for recantation.

6. *Prevalence of spouse murders.* Despite the considerable media attention to the issue of battered women who kill, battered women rarely murder their partners. Such homicides consist of only .05 percent of intimate partner-related crimes. See U.S. Census Bureau, Statistical Abstract of the United States: 2011, 200 (Table 314: Violence by Intimate Partner Violence by Sex, 1995-2007, and By Type of Crime, 2007) (reporting 2007 data of 346 male homicide victims compared to 1,185 female victims, of a total of 646,790 victims of intimate partner-related crimes), available at http://www.census.gov/ compendia/statab/2011/tables/11s0314.pdf. Why do you think such cases capture so much media attention? See Ann Jones, Why Are We So Fascinated by the Harris Case, N.Y. Times, Nov. 8, 1981, §11, at 24. What light does Garthine Walker's historical perspective shed on this question?

7. *Confrontational versus nonconfrontation homicides.* Intimate partner homicides occur in confrontational as well as nonconfrontational situations. See Holly Maguigan, Battered Women and Self-Defense: Myths and Misconceptions in Current Reform Proposals, 140 U. Pa. L. Rev. 379, 397-398 (1991) (suggesting most battered women kill during a confrontation, based on her study of 223 appellate cases). Nonconfrontational homicides pose particular problems for the self-defense doctrine, as explored below.

8. *Characteristics of* Hawthorne *homicide.* The threshold question in the principal case concerns the admissibility of expert testimony on BWS. Several facts suggest a need for such testimony in cases of battered women who kill and, in particular, Joyce Hawthorne's case. For example, why does a battered woman kill during *that particular incident*, after enduring so many years of abuse? Hawthorne killed after enduring 18 years of abuse when her husband reached for a gun after she rejected his demand for sex. What leads a battered woman to believe that the risk of death or bodily harm is imminent? Battered women's perception of the risk stems from their experiences of past abuse that endow them with an enhanced ability to assess the seriousness of the risk at the time of the killing. *Hawthorne* is illustrative. During the evening of the homicide, the drunken husband repeatedly threatened to kill the entire family and himself before morning. "[Joyce] noticed something different in his demeanor, something even more violent than before, more uncontrolled, more terrifying." Walker, Terrifying Love, supra, at 22-23.

Why does a battered woman use excessive force? For example, why did Joyce Hawthorne use *five* weapons? In part, the woman recognizes the ineffectiveness of her past defensive measures in the face of the batterer's superior strength. A commentator elaborates:

> A high percentage [of battered women who kill] use guns, which, it can be argued, equals the odds. Men can beat women to death with their fists. Women rarely have such an option. If she chooses to use a gun, she cannot risk a violent husband disarming her. So she may start shooting when he is most vulnerable—asleep, with his back turned, or when he is drunk. . . . She also almost always empties the gun. "They are so afraid, feel so powerless, and believe he is omnipotent and about to rise up at any moment and beat them that they keep shooting, even when it would be clear to most people that the first bullet has killed him". . . .

Kay Bartlett, Battered-Woman Plea Grows More Acceptable, Seattle Times, Apr. 14, 1991, at A5. See also Teresa Carpenter, The Final Self Defense, N.Y. Times, Dec. 31, 1989, §7, at 17 (attributing Hawthorne's use of so many weapons to a battered woman's inability to assess the amount of force required to subdue her attacker stemming from the magnitude of her fear).

9. *Admissibility:* Frye *and* Daubert. The admission of expert testimony lies within the discretion of the judge who has the responsibility of ensuring that experts have proper credentials (that is, knowledge, skill, experience, training), and also that the evidence is relevant and reliable. Courts use different approaches to determine the reliability of expert testimony: (1) the general acceptance, and (2) reliability approaches. Until 1993, the leading case on the admissibility of novel scientific evidence was Frye v. United States, 293 F. 1013 (D.C. Cir. 1923). *Frye* held that novel scientific evidence must have gained "general acceptance" in the relevant scientific community to be admissible. *Frye* was superseded by Daubert v. Merrell Dow Pharmaceuticals, Inc., 509 U.S. 579 (1993), which adopted the reliability approach of Federal Rule of Evidence 702, providing that evidence may be admitted if it is helpful to the trier of fact and if the methodology is scientifically valid. In *Hawthorne*, what does the appellate court rule on the issues of relevance and reliability?

10. *Gender bias in the law of self-defense.*

a. *Paradigm shift:* Wanrow. At the time of the Hawthorne murder, a paradigm shift was occurring in the law of self-defense. In State v. Wanrow, 559 P.2d 548 (Wash. 1977), Yvonne Wanrow, a petite Native American woman, who was disabled by a broken leg, killed a large, intoxicated, known child molester (whom she believed had attempted to molest her son) because she feared that he was threatening her. Wanrow subsequently claimed, based on her perception of danger, that she was justified in acting in self-defense. Although the case did not deal with intimate partner violence, it had significant implications for the law of self-defense, particularly for battered women who kill their abusers.

The law of self-defense is traditionally based on an isolated, sudden episode of deadly force (the prototypical "bar room brawl"). In *Wanrow*, the Washington Supreme Court ruled that jury instructions based on an *objective* standard of self-defense violated the defendant's right to equal protection. The court found that the jury instructions erroneously called for measuring the female defendant's conduct against that of a reasonable male in the same circumstances—applying an equal-force standard (finding self-defense only if the defendant responded with force that was equal to that of the aggressor), and a time-limited perspective (restricted to the circumstances at, or immediately before, the killing). These jury instructions ignored important facts: the parties' different size and strength; the defendant's belief that she could defend herself against a large, intoxicated, dangerous, mentally ill man only by using a weapon; the defendant's knowledge of the aggressor's reputation (that is, suspected criminal conduct and prior mental commitment); and the defendant's mistrust of the police (who had failed to arrest the man, as previously requested). The court recognized that these facts should enter into the determination of whether the defendant had a reasonable belief that the use of deadly force was necessary to protect herself from imminent danger or great bodily harm.

This landmark case recognized the gender bias inherent in the law of self-defense (regarding the elements of reasonableness, imminence, and proportionality). In order to give a woman the same right to a fair trial as a man, according to *Wanrow*, the law must incorporate her individualized perspective. It must judge her conduct in light of her physical limitations and all the facts and circumstances known to her. By recognizing the unique legal problems confronting women who defend themselves against male attackers, *Wanrow* led to major reforms in the doctrine of self-defense and, in addition, "set the stage for the widespread (if not total) acceptance of BWS in the 1980s." Downs, supra, at 77. For a discussion of *Wanrow* and its implications, see Elizabeth Schneider, Battered Women and Feminist Lawmaking 30-32, 132-138 (2000) (Schneider was one of the lawyers at the Center for Constitutional Rights who represented Wanrow on appeal).

b. *Equality. Wanrow* contributed to reframing the self-defense doctrine through the lens of gender equality by its ruling that jury instructions based on an *objective* standard of self-defense a violate women's equal right to a fair trial. However, resistance to this perspective continues. As Professor Schneider explains: "There is deep societal resistance to perceiving the circumstances of battered women, and particularly the circumstances of battered women who kill their assailants, as a problem of gender equality." Id. at 113. How is this "societal resistance" apparent in *Hawthorne* and Walker's excerpt? Does the admissibility of BWS result in equal treatment or special treatment? See id. at 115-116 (explaining how battered women's claims may be perceived as special treatment); Schneider, Describing and Changing, supra, at 232-233.

11. *Modern status of BWS evidence.* All states and the District of Columbia admit BWS evidence, at least to some degree, either by statute or case law. BWS has achieved such widespread acceptance that some courts hold that an attorney's failure to pursue a BWS defense constitutes ineffective assistance of counsel. See, e.g., Paine v. Massie, 339 F.3d 1194 (10th Cir. 2003); Smith v. State, 144 P.3d 159 (Okla. Crim. App. 2006).

12. *Statutory reform.* Many states provide for the admission of BWS evidence by statute (rather than case law). State legislatures acted promptly after *Hawthorne* to enact legislation. See Janet Parrish, Trend Analysis: Expert Testimony on Battering and Its Effects in Criminal Cases, 11 Wis. Women's L.J. 75, 85 (1996) (reporting that, by 1996, 12 state statutes authorized admission of BWS testimony). Political forces, led by a coalition of feminist groups and law-and-order conservatives, influenced the reform movement. See Robert P. Mosteller, Syndromes and Politics in Criminal Trials and Evidence Law, 46 Duke L.J. 461, 485, n.82 (1996).

Statutes vary considerably. Many statutes put to rest concerns about the reliability of BWS evidence by announcing that the scientific validity of BWS is generally accepted (thereby eliminating the need for case-by-case determinations). Other statutes provide parameters for the admission of such evidence: Some statutes limit admissibility of BWS evidence to explain the effects of abuse on beliefs, behavior, and perception, whereas other statutes limit such evidence to the imminence of the threat. See Mosteller, supra, at 484-485, nn. 78-82 (1996) (surveying statutes). Some statutes limit BWS evidence to self-defense claims. Other statutes address procedure, that is, requiring defense counsel to notify the court if it intends to offer BWS evidence in order to allow the state sufficient time to order a psychological examination of the defendant.

13. *Clemency movement.* The reform movement failed to address the dispositions of battered women who were convicted *before* the liberalization of the law. In response to this oversight, advocacy groups urged clemency for these defendants. The governors of two states (Ohio and Maryland) granted pardons and commutations in the early 1990s to many women who had been convicted of murder or assault before the law reform. Other states adopted a more limited case-by-case approach. See Joan H. Krause, Of Merciful Justice and Justified Mercy: Commuting the Sentences of Battered Women Who Kill, 46 Fla. L. Rev. 699, 719-742 (1994) (studying clemency movement).

3. Self-Defense

■ STATE v. HARDEN
679 S.E.2d 628 (W.Va. 2009)

KETCHUM, J.:

[D]efendant was arrested upon her admission to having shot and killed her husband, Danuel Harden. At trial, the defendant asserted a claim of self-defense, arguing that her actions precipitously followed a "night of domestic terror" that ended only when the defendant shot and killed the decedent. . . . An emergency room physician at Cabell Huntington Hospital, who examined the defendant on the morning of the shooting, testified that the defendant "had contusions of both orbital areas, the right upper arm, a puncture wound with a foreign body of the right forearm, contusion of her chest, left facial cheek, the left upper lip" and that "X-rays done at the time demonstrated a nasal fracture." [Defendant was convicted of first-degree murder and sentenced to life imprisonment with the possibility of parole. She appeals.]

. . . It is conceded by the State that the defendant suffered a "night of domestic terror." [T]he State nonetheless argues that the defendant's claim of self-defense is "untenable." . . .

APPREHENSION OF DANGER

A longstanding tenet of our self-defense doctrine is that a defendant's use of deadly force must be based upon a reasonable apprehension by the defendant that he or she was at imminent peril of death or serious bodily injury. . . . [T]he State argues, the defendant did not have a reasonable basis to apprehend any imminent danger from the decedent at the time she used deadly force because the facts suggested that there had been a "cooling off" period after the decedent's violent acts [when the decedent had passed out, drunk]. Therefore, the State argues, because the decedent's violent acts had ended, those violent acts constituted "an apprehension of danger previously entertained" and could not justify the defendant's use of deadly force. . . .

We begin our analysis by noting that our precedent establishes that the "reasonableness" of a defendant's belief that he or she was at "imminent" risk of death or serious bodily injury is a two-part inquiry, with a subjective component and an objective component. . . . Plainly stated, the reasonableness inquiry is as follows. First, a defendant's belief that death or serious bodily injury was imminent must be shown to have been subjectively reasonable, which is to say that a defendant actually believed, based upon all the circumstances perceived by him or her at the time deadly force was used, that such force was necessary to prevent death or serious bodily injury. Second, that the defendant's belief must be objectively reasonable when considering all of the circumstances surrounding the defendant's use of deadly force, which is to say that another person, similarly situated, could have reasonably formed the same belief.

[The court explains that it has previously upheld the admissibility of evidence of prior threats of violence in order to negate criminal intent for murder based on a defendant's claim of self-defense.] In State v. Plumley, 401 S.E.2d 469, 473 (W. Va. 1990), we further noted that:

> the reasonableness of an individual's beliefs and actions in self-defense must be . . . viewed "in [the] light of the circumstances in which he acted at the time and not measured by subsequently developed facts." Moreover, we have explained that the *reasonableness of the conduct may depend upon past actions of the decedent, including threats, violence, and general reputation*. . . . (emphasis added)

It is clear to us [that] the decedent's violent criminal acts and threats of death are relevant to the determination of the subjective reasonableness of the defendant's belief that she was at imminent risk of death or serious bodily injury. This is to say, under the facts of this case, the defendant's subjective belief that death or serious bodily injury was imminent, and that deadly force was necessary to repel that threat, necessarily included the fact that the decedent had, precipitously preceding his death, physically and sexually assaulted the defendant and repeatedly threatened the life of the defendant and the lives of the children. We therefore hold that where a defendant has asserted a plea of self-defense, evidence showing that the decedent had previously abused or threatened the life of the defendant is relevant evidence of the defendant's state of mind at the time deadly force was used. . . .

DUTY TO RETREAT

[T]he State further argues that the ["cooling off" when the victim passed out following his violent attack] provided the defendant the opportunity to retreat from her home so as to avoid further attacks. [D]uring closing arguments, the State advanced this argument, telling the jury that the defendant "could have walked out of that trailer. Period. But she didn't." Implicit in this argument is that the defendant had a duty to retreat from her home.

As a general proposition, our precedent in self-defense cases clearly state that where an unlawful intrusion has occurred in the sanctity of one's home, an occupant of the home has no duty to retreat. Generally described as the "castle" doctrine, "castle" rule or "home" rule, our precedent succinctly states that "[a] man attacked in his own home by an intruder may invoke the law of self-defense without retreating."

The distinction of the present issue is that the decedent was not an intruder, but instead a lawful *co-occupant* having equal entitlement with the defendant to be present therein. . . . Initially we note that West Virginia is in the apparent minority of jurisdictions who impose upon an occupant of a home the duty to retreat from an attack by a co-occupant. . . .

It is now widely recognized that domestic violence "attacks are often repeated over time, and escape from the home is rarely possible without the threat of great personal violence or death." As quoted by the New Jersey Supreme Court:

> Imposition of the duty to retreat on a battered woman who finds herself the target of a unilateral, unprovoked attack in her own home is inherently unfair. During repeated instances of past abuse, she has "retreated," only to be caught, dragged back inside, and severely beaten again. If she manages to escape, other hurdles confront her. Where will she go if she has no money, no transportation, and if her children are left behind in the "care" of an enraged man? . . .
>
> What [the duty to retreat] exception means for a battered woman is that as long as it is a stranger who attacks her in her home, she has a right to fight back and labors under no duty to retreat. If the attacker is her husband or live-in partner, however, she must retreat. The threat of death or serious bodily injury may be just as real (and, statistically, is more real) when her husband or partner attacks her in home, but still she must retreat.

[New Jersey v. Gartland, 694 A.2d 564, 570-571 (N.J. 1997)]. . . .

[W]e see no rational legal basis for imposing upon an occupant of a home the duty to retreat from his or her home and to abandon it to a co-occupant who, by his or her conduct, is engaged in such improper behavior as to place the occupant in danger of death or serious bodily injury. In such circumstances the occupant may use, without retreating, deadly force if the occupant reasonably believes such force to be necessary to prevent his or her death or serious bodily injury presented by the co-occupant's criminal behavior. . . .

ELEMENTS OF SELF-DEFENSE

[The court turns to the sufficiency of the evidence of self defense and sets forth the required elements.] The first required element is that a defendant must show that he or she was not the "aggressor" and did not provoke the attack. This requirement reflects the common law rule that "one who is at fault or who is the physical aggressor can not rely on self-defense." The second and third required elements are that a defendant show that the circumstances of the attack formed a "reasonable" basis to believe, and that the defendant did believe, that he or she was at "imminent" risk of death or serious bodily injury. . . . The fourth required element is that a defendant must show that his or her actions were "proportionate" to the danger. . . . The final element of our self-defense doctrine requires a defendant to present "sufficient evidence" on all of the above elements before being entitled to a self-defense instruction and shifting the burden of proof to the State "[t]o] prove beyond a reasonable doubt that the defendant did not act in self-defense." [The court then applies these elements to the facts.]

Provocation. There is no evidence in the record that the defendant did any deed or act that provoked the attack upon her by the decedent. Accordingly, not only has the defendant established sufficient evidence that she did not provoke the attack, but this element is proven beyond a reasonable doubt as an uncontested issue.

Reasonableness. We next turn to the issue of whether the defendant submitted sufficient evidence that she actually believed and had a reasonable basis to believe that she was at risk of death or serious bodily injury as a result of the decedent's conduct. . . . The defendant testified that the decedent started drinking early in the evening and that the decedent started "getting very, very angry" and as the evening wore on, the decedent became increasingly verbally abusive and started making threats that he was going to kill her. When asked what she thought when the decedent said he was going to kill her, the defendant testified "[i]t was a change in him, and I knew it was going to happen." . . . The defendant further testified that the "beating went on for hours, and it was just a continuous beating and verbal abuse" during which the decedent told the defendant he was going to kill her, that she "wasn't going to live to see the next day" and that "the children wouldn't live." The defendant explained that "I was so scared and I was scared for my life, and not only mine but the three kids that was in my home" and that the decedent even "put the shotgun to my son's head and said he was going to kill him."

When asked what happened after the decedent put the gun to their son's head, the defendant said "I started talking to him so that he would leave B.H. alone and he went back to beating me." The defendant testified that she knew at this point that "none of us was going to walk out of the house."

As the evening wore on, the defendant testified that the decedent "made me have sex with him. (Crying). After he beat me. (Crying)." . . . Following the sexual assault, the defendant testified that the decedent continued to be verbally and physically aggressive, and that the decedent started taunting her, daring her to shoot him or that he would shoot her, and that it was at this point that she got the decedent's shotgun and shot him. The defendant explained that "I thought I was going to die. I knew I was," and that the decedent "would have killed them [the children], too" because the decedent "said that nobody was going to walk out of the house that night." It is clear to this Court that the evidence adduced at the defendant's trial . . . was sufficient evidence that the defendant did believe, and had a reasonable basis to believe, that her life was at risk of death or serious bodily injury.

Imminency. We next consider whether the defendant submitted sufficient evidence that she had reasonable grounds to believe, and did believe, that the danger of death or serious bodily injury was "imminent." The defendant's testimony established that precipitously preceding the defendant's shooting the decedent, that the decedent sexually assaulted the defendant and thereafter continued to threaten the defendant's life and the lives of the children, as well as physically assault the defendant. Considered in context with the evidence discussed above, and that the violence and threats had been ongoing for several hours, it is clear that the defendant submitted sufficient evidence upon which she could have reasonably believed, and did believe, that death or serious bodily injury were imminent.

Proportionality. The next element considered is whether the evidence showed the defendant's actions to be "proportionate" to the danger. [T]he evidence submitted sufficiently established that the decedent had threatened to kill the defendant and the children [and] sexually assaulted the defendant [and] immediately preceding her shooting the decedent, the decedent had again threatened her life, the lives of the children, and physically assaulted her. This evidence, in the context of all the other evidence, would sufficiently warrant the use of deadly force.

Sufficiency. The final element considered is whether the defendant met her burden of proof. Our review of the record [convinces us that] the evidence was clearly sufficient to create a reasonable doubt that the killing resulted from the defendant acting in self-defense. [Therefore,] the burden shifted to the State to prove beyond a reasonable doubt that the defendant did not act in self-defense. . . . [W]e find that the State's evidence failed to prove beyond a reasonable doubt that the defendant did not have a reasonable basis to believe, and did not believe, that she was in imminent danger of death or serious bodily injury at the time deadly force was used against the decedent. The mere fact that the decedent was found on the couch after being shot creates only a "suspicion or conjecture," that the decedent might possibly have been "asleep" or possibly have been "passed out drunk," and that the brutal beatings, sexual assault, and threats to kill the defendant and the children had ended. . . . [T]here is just no evidence, only conjecture, that the defendant's "night of terror" had ended or that the defendant and the children in her care were safe from death or serious bodily injury. . . .

Uncontested evidence also established that the decedent was drinking heavily and had a blood alcohol level of 0.22 percent—nearly three times that where a person would be presumed intoxicated in West Virginia. In this intoxicated state of mind, the uncontested evidence is that the decedent's behavior immediately preceding his death was violent, unpredictable, criminal and placed the defendant at risk of death or serious bodily injury. Under such circumstances the defendant's use of deadly force to protect herself, without retreating, is objectively reasonable. . . .

BENJAMIN, Chief Justice, dissenting:
. . . Here, the defendant resorted to a type of self-help that previously has not been permitted by our law, but that the majority has now vindicated. While there is no doubt that the defendant was brutalized by the decedent, as the jury heard, and that the decedent should have been criminally prosecuted for his actions, I question the wisdom of a self-defense standard in our jurisprudence which sanctions the use of deadly force to defend one's self from a person who is unconscious or incapacitated, and who poses no threat of imminent harm. I also question how such a lessened self-defense standard, which may be seen by some as condoning or even tacitly encouraging the use of self-help violence or vigilantism in a domestic setting, can be seen as a positive advancement in our efforts to reduce domestic violence. . . .

[The law] properly recognizes as a defense to murder that the defendant acted to defend himself or herself from the threat of imminent serious bodily injury or death. Significantly, the threat of serious bodily injury or death must be imminent. An imminent threat of serious bodily injury or death separates a killing in self-defense from a retaliatory killing or a preemptive killing. In other words, the requirement that the threat is imminent distinguishes a killing in self-defense from a killing to redress a previous wrong or to prevent a non-imminent threat. Thus, the law is based on the proper understanding that the recognition of defense of self absent the element of an imminent threat would be to countenance violence and lawlessness. By placing absolutely no limit on the use of evidence of prior abusive conduct to negate an element of the crime charged, the majority unwittingly permits a defendant to claim that the most senseless murder is justified by an allegation that the decedent had wronged the defendant or posed a threat to the defendant. [S]uch a notion was totally foreign to our jurisprudence.

Sadly, the majority opinion disregards the progress that this State has made in recent years in the prevention, treatment, and remediation of domestic violence. Thanks to the diligent efforts of our legislature and courts, our society now works to educate, treat, aid, and prevent the scourge of violence among family members. Spouses who find themselves in abusive or threatening situations now have resources that previous generations of abused spouses did not. In the instant case, no reasonable person believes that the appellant should have quietly endured the abusive actions of the decedent. But once the decedent fell asleep or passed out on the sofa, the threat of imminent harm was over and the appellant had several options available short of resorting to homicide. . . .

Notes and Questions

1. *Social reality.* Why do some battered women kill their abusers? Paradoxically, the answer may lie in an understanding of batterers' behavior. See Martha R. Mahoney, Legal Images of Battered Women: Redefining the Issue of Separation, 90 Mich. L. Rev. 1, 43 (1991) ("Evidence suggests that the batterer's behavior, rather than the battered woman's characteristics, determines her response and predicts whether she will kill in self-defense").

a. *Characteristics.* What characteristics of batterers predict victims' lethal response to the violence? The most significant differences between women who kill and those who do not are that the battered defendants are more likely to report (1) partners' frequent substance abuse; (2) partners' frequent and severe threats, assaults, and abuse of children; and (3) an escalation of their partners' abuse. In response, the women make more attempts to stop the abuse but feel increasingly desperate, hopeless, and trapped. Brenda L. Russell, Battered Woman Syndrome as a Legal Defense: History, Effectiveness ad Implications 108 (2010).

b. *Punishment.* At common law, as historian Garthine Walker reveals (supra pp. 295-296), women who killed their husbands were treated more harshly than men who killed their wives. Does gender bias still result in harsh treatment? Some evidence suggests that the legal system is responding more appropriately to domestic violence. See Patrick A. Langan & John M. Dawson, Bureau of Justice Statistics, Spouse Murder Defendants in Large Urban Counties 21-23 (1995), available at bjs.ojp.usdoj.gov/content/pub/pdf/SPOUSMUR.PDF (reporting results of a national study of 540 spousal murders revealing that battered wives had a lower conviction rate, were less likely to receive prison sentences, and, received shorter prison sentences than their male counterparts). But cf. Elizabeth Dermody Leonard, Convicted Survivors: The Imprisonment of Battered Women Who Kill (2002) (concluding, based on a study of over 40 female prison inmates who killed their partners, that the majority of women serve long, harsh sentences).

2. *Traditional defenses: mental capacity.* Traditional defenses for battered women who kill their abusers were insanity and diminished capacity. However, battered defendants are generally unable to satisfy the requirements for these defenses because they rarely suffer from insanity or diminished capacity at the time of the killing. As a result, insanity and diminished capacity defenses have been largely abandoned in favor of the self-defense doctrine.

3. *Outcome of defenses: justification and excuse distinguished.* The criminal defenses, if successful, have different legal outcomes. A self-defense claim constitutes *justification* for a homicide because the defendant's belief in the need to use deadly force is "reasonable." This justification results in an acquittal (as a "complete defense"). An insanity defense (that is, "not guilty by reason of insanity") is also a complete defense but generally results in the defendant's mental commitment. In contrast, a conviction based on diminished capacity *excuses* the homicide, that is, treats it less harshly and reduces a murder charge to manslaughter.

At common law, if an element of a self-defense claim was lacking, the defense was unavailable. However, some states currently recognize an "imperfect self-defense" rule if a defendant is unable to satisfy the "reasonableness" requirement (that is, if the defendant's belief in the need to use deadly force is honest but unreasonable). This defense, if successful, results in mitigating the crime of murder to manslaughter. Wayne R. LaFave, Other-Extenuating-Circumstances Voluntary Manslaughter, 2 Subst. Crim. L. §15.3(a)(2d ed. 2011).

4. *Self-defense: elements and application.* Self-defense requires: (1) the defendant must use only proportional force; (2) the defendant must reasonably fear that she or he is in imminent danger of death or great bodily harm; (3) the defendant must not have been the aggressor; and (4) in some jurisdictions, the defendant must seek to retreat before using deadly force. Did the defendants in *Hawthorne* and *Harden* use proportional or excessive force? Did they reasonably fear that they were in imminent danger of death or great bodily harm? Were they aggressors? Could they have retreated before resorting to deadly force? Compare the views of the majority and dissent in *Harden* regarding: (1) the significance of the "cooling off" period, (2) the "imminence" of the harm, (3) the admissibility of evidence of prior abusive conduct, and (4) the available options that might have prevented the homicide.

5. *Reasonableness standard as applied.* BWS evidence is relevant, as explained, to shed light on the *reasonableness* of the belief that the use of deadly force was necessary in the face of the risk of *imminent* death or great bodily harm. Expert testimony may help explain to jurors (whose experiences may lead them to misinterpret defendants' actions) that a particular defendant, based on her experiences of past abuse, perceives imminent danger that others might not be capable of recognizing and that she therefore responds reasonably in using deadly force.

What led the defendant in *Harden* to believe that her husband threatened both her and her children with imminent death or great bodily harm? Was her belief reasonable? Could her belief have been unreasonable and/or stemmed from a desire for retaliation? Cf. Whitley R. P. Kaufman, Self-Defense, Imminence, and the Battered Woman, 10 New Crim. L. Rev. 342, 365 (2007) (suggesting that "it is of course equally possible that victims of repeated abuse . . . become hypersensitive to signs of danger even where they do not exist, or become subject to the natural human tendency towards self-serving bias in regards to the use of force").

6. *Imminent versus immediate.* What is the difference between an "immediate" and "imminent" threat? How does the following distinction apply to *Hawthorne* and *Harden*?

> An immediate threat has [a police] officer literally dodging bullets, knives, motor vehicles or any other assortment of instruments likely to cause death or serious bodily injury. An imminent threat is often an anticipatory perception of events that are mentally processed within the context of situation and behavioral cues.

Thomas Aveni, The "Must-Shoot vs. May-Shoot" Controversy, Law & Order 38 (Jan. 2005), available at http://www.theppsc.org/Newsletters/03-17-05/Jan-05.pdf.

7. *Relaxing the imminence requirement.* Why does the criminal law limit defensive force to cases of an imminent threat? Is imminence a proxy for "necessity," that is, the homicide was necessary for defendant's protection? Is imminence a proxy for moral justification? Should necessity prevail over imminence, so that the use of force by a battered woman would be permitted if necessary, even if the threat is not imminent? Or, must the victim wait until the threat of death or great bodily harm becomes imminent before she can protect herself? What difficulty does that pose?

Should the imminence requirement be modified? If so, how? Should it be eliminated? Should it be waived in some circumstances, for example, if the victim of abuse has requested, but been denied, state protection? Or, is the real solution the "unfair application" of existing law rather than reform of the law of self-defense? See Holly Maguigan, Battered Women and Self-Defense: Myths and Misconceptions in Current Reform Proposals, 140 U. Pa. L. Rev. 379, 458 (1991) (so arguing). For reform of the imminence requirement, see Whitley R. P. Kaufman, Self-Defense, Imminence, and the Battered Woman, 10 New Crim. L. Rev. 342 (2007); Jeffrey B. Murdoch, Is Imminence Really Necessity? Reconciling Traditional Self-Defense Doctrine with the Battered Woman Syndrome, 20 N. Ill. U. L. Rev. 191 (2000).

8. *Duty to retreat.* In some jurisdictions, a person who is threatened by deadly force must retreat rather than use deadly force (that is, if a non-aggressor can accomplish retreat safely). If the non-aggressor then fails to retreat, the use of deadly force becomes unjustified and, therefore, the self-defense claim is unavailable. However, according to a widespread exception (called the "castle-doctrine"), a non-aggressor need *not* retreat if attacked at home (or within the immediately surrounding area). *Harden* explores this exception applied to an assailant who is a *co-occupant* of the dwelling. How does *Harden* resolve this issue? How does *Harden* apply the battered woman's perspective to the duty to retreat? Might eliminating the castle doctrine have any negative consequences? See Benjamin Levin, A Defensible Defense?: Reexamining Castle Doctrine Statutes, 47 Harv. J. on Legislation 523 (2010).

9. *Subjective versus objective.* Is the determination of the reasonableness of the defendant's belief that she was at imminent risk of death or serious bodily injury a subjective or objective determination for purposes of a self-defense claim? Or both? What does *Harden* say? See also Schneider, Feminist Lawmaking, supra, at 123 ("[I]n fact, evidence of battering is relevant under both an objective and a subjective standard of self-defense. Under either approach the jury must find that the actor acted reasonably"). Thus, the trier of fact must consider both the individual's subjective perspective as well as the objective reasonableness of that perspective. Id. at 122.

10. *Gender-based stereotypes.* The law of self-defense as applied to battered criminal defendants is complicated by gender-based stereotypes. Commentators criticize that BWS reinforces the same gender-based stereotypes that BWS testimony hoped to dispel. Schneider, Feminist Lawmaking, supra, at 125; Schneider, Describing and Changing, supra, at 216. See also Joan H. Krause, Of Merciful Justice and Justified Mercy: Commuting the Sentences of Battered Women Who Kill, 46 Fla. L. Rev. 699, 716 (1994). What are these stereotypes?

a. *Crazy women.* Battered women who kill their abusers are sometimes characterized as mentally ill. Martha M. Mahoney, Legal Images of Battered Women: Redefining the Issue of Separation, 90 Mich. L. Rev. 1, 42 (1991); Schneider, Describing and Changing, supra, at 234. The term *syndrome,* for example, evokes imagery of a medical disorder. Schneider, Feminist Lawmaking, supra, at 81. What are the consequences of this stereotype for representation of battered criminal defendants? Schneider, Feminist Lawmaking, supra, at 79 ("myths and misconceptions of battered women as 'crazy' or 'provocative' made them particularly unreasonable").

b. *Impact on minorities.* BWS has also been criticized as disadvantaging minorities. See Sharon Angella Allard, Rethinking Battered Woman Syndrome: A Black Feminist Perspective, 1 UCLA Women's L.J. 191 (1991) (advocating inclusion of racial perspective on BWS). BWS was derived from research on predominantly white, middle-class, and married women. As a result, many commentators contend that women who deviate from this paradigm (that is, African-Americans, lesbians, and women who fight back) face difficulty convincing the jury of the reasonableness of their fear of harm. See Linda L. Ammons, Mules, Madonnas, Babies, Bathwater, Racial Imagery and Stereotypes: The African-American Woman and the Battered Woman's Syndrome, 1995 Wis. L. Rev. 1003, 1005-1006 (identifying harm to African-Americans); Phyllis Goldfarb, Describing Without Circumscribing: Questioning the Construction of Gender in the Discourse of Intimate Violence, 64 Geo. Wash. L. Rev. 582, 586-590 (1996) (harm to lesbians); Leigh Goodmark, When is a Battered Woman not a Battered Woman? When She Fights Back, 20 Yale J.L. & Feminism 75, 76-77 (2008) (harm to women who fight back).

c. *Other misconceptions.* Among other misconceptions are the beliefs that battered defendants provoked their partner's violence. Schneider, Feminist Lawmaking, supra, at 79. Because of the perception these women somehow deserved the abuse, jurors may have difficulty believing that they are "innocent" victims. Another prevalent belief is that these women are regarded as particularly heinous criminals because of their commission of an act (spousal homicide) that threatens the fabric of society. See id. at 113-114. What gender-based stereotypes and assumptions can you identify in *Hawthorne, Harden,* and the Walker excerpt above?

11. *Victimization stereotype.* Another problem with the use of BWS evidence is that its imagery of victimization presents a significant obstacle in the representation of these criminal defendants. Id. at 74-86 (criticizing victimization paradigm). Specifically, jurors have great difficulty understanding why a woman who is so passive that she cannot leave her abuser (that is, a person subject to "learned helplessness") suddenly becomes so assertive that she kills. As a result, decision-makers may fail to understand the reasonableness of the defendant's belief and, therefore, conclude that she was not justified in her assertion of self-defense.

Professor Elizabeth Schneider terms this dilemma the "victimization-agency dichotomy." Victimization and agency are "understood to exist as the absence of the other—as if one must be either pure victim or pure agent—when in fact they are profoundly interrelated." Elizabeth M. Schneider, Feminism and the False Dichotomy of Agency and Victimization, 38 N.Y.L. Sch. L. Rev. 387, 396 (1993). In fact, Schneider explains, battered women are both victims and agents. However, an emphasis on one aspect of women's victimization (that is, the failure to exit from an abusive relationship) leads jurors to ignore "all the other active efforts that the woman may have made to protect herself and her children." Id. at 391. Victimization imagery prevents jurors from understanding that the homicide, in fact, may be "a woman's necessary choice to save her own life." Elizabeth M. Schneider, Particularity and Generality: Challenges of Feminist Theory and Practice in Work on Woman-Abuse, 67 N.Y.U. L. Rev. 520, 561 (1992).

How can defense counsel better convey this understanding to jurors? See Mary Ann Dutton, Understanding Women's Responses to Domestic Violence: A Redefinition of Battered Woman Syndrome, 21 Hofstra L. Rev. 1191, 1227 (1993) (advocating reframing the question of "why didn't she leave?" to incorporate greater understanding of the "impressive array of strategies" that battered women use to stop the violence, and explaining these strategies).

12. *Effectiveness of BWS testimony.* Does the admission of BWS evidence influence jury verdicts? Based on juror simulation studies, BWS testimony in confrontational homicides is more likely to lead to leniency (that is, verdicts of manslaughter and self-defense rather than murder verdicts). However, in nonconfrontational homicides (for example, the murder of sleeping husbands), jurors are more likely to impose severe sentences (that is, verdicts of murder compared to manslaughter and self-defense) even after hearing BWS testimony. In these latter cases, jurors are also more likely to view defendants as psychologically unstable. Yet, jurors rendered the harshest sanctions in nonconfrontation homicides when no expert testimony was presented. Regina A. Schuller et al., Rethinking Battered Woman Syndrome Evidence: The Impact of Alternative Forms of Expert Testimony on Mock Jurors' Decisions, 36 Can. J. Behav. Sci. 127, 132 (2004). What are the implications of these findings?

4. Duress

■ DIXON v. UNITED STATES
548 U.S. 1 (2006)

Justice STEVENS delivered the opinion of the Court.

[P]etitioner Keshia Dixon purchased multiple firearms at two gun shows, during the course of which she provided an incorrect address and falsely stated that she was not under indictment for a felony. [At the time of the gun shows, she was under indictment for a check-cashing scheme.] As a result of these illegal acts, petitioner was indicted and convicted on one count of receiving a firearm while under indictment in violation of 18 U.S.C. §922(n) and eight counts of making false statements in connection with the acquisition of a firearm in violation of §922(a)(6) [that is, violations of federal firearm regulations]. At trial, [petitioner's] defense was that she acted under duress because her boyfriend threatened to kill her or hurt her daughters if she did not buy the guns for him. [On appeal] [p]etitioner contends that the trial judge's instructions to the jury erroneously required her to prove duress by a preponderance of the evidence instead of requiring the Government to prove beyond a reasonable doubt that she did not act under duress. . . .

The crimes for which petitioner was convicted require that she have acted "knowingly," §922(a)(6), or "willfully," §924(a)(1)(D). . . . "[T]he term 'knowingly' merely requires proof of knowledge of the facts that constitute the offense." And the term "willfully" in §924(a)(1)(D) requires a defendant to have "acted with knowledge that his conduct was unlawful." In this case, then, the Government bore the burden of proving beyond a reasonable doubt that petitioner knew she was making false statements in connection with the acquisition of firearms and that she knew she was breaking the law when she acquired a firearm while under indictment. [The Government] clearly met its burden when petitioner testified that she knowingly committed certain acts—she put a false address on the forms she completed to purchase the firearms, falsely claimed that she was the actual buyer of the firearms, and falsely stated that she was not under indictment at the time of the purchase—and when she testified that she knew she was breaking the law when, as an individual under indictment at the time, she purchased a firearm.

Petitioner contends, however, that she cannot have formed the necessary mens rea for these crimes because she did not freely choose to commit the acts in question. But even if we assume that petitioner's will was overborne by the threats made against her and her daughters, she still *knew* that she was making false statements and *knew* that she was breaking the law by buying a firearm. The duress defense, like the defense of necessity . . . , may excuse conduct that would otherwise be punishable, but the existence of duress normally does not controvert any of the elements of the offense itself. "[C]riminal liability is normally based upon the concurrence of two factors, 'an evil-meaning mind [and] and evil-doing hand. . . .'" Like the defense of necessity, the defense of duress does not negate a defendant's criminal state of mind when the applicable offense requires a defendant to have acted knowingly or willfully; instead, it allows the defendant to "avoid liability . . . because coercive conditions or necessity negates a conclusion of guilt even though the necessary mens rea was present." . . .

Congress defined the crimes at issue to punish defendants who act "knowingly," §922(a)(6), or "willfully," §924(a)(1)(D). It is these specific mental states, rather than some vague "evil mind," or "'criminal' intent," that the Government is required to prove beyond a reasonable doubt. . . . The jury instructions in this case were consistent with this requirement and, as such, did not run afoul of the Due Process Clause when they placed the burden on petitioner to establish the existence of duress by a preponderance of the evidence. . . .

Having found no constitutional basis for placing upon the Government the burden of disproving petitioner's duress defense beyond a reasonable doubt, we next address petitioner's argument that the modern common law requires the Government to bear that burden. In making this argument, petitioner recognizes that, until the end of the 19th century, common-law courts generally adhered to the rule that "the proponent of an issue bears the burden of persuasion on the factual premises for applying the rule." In petitioner's view, however, two important developments have established a contrary common-law rule that now prevails in federal courts: this Court's decision in Davis v. United States, 160 U.S. 469 (1895), which placed the burden on the Government to prove a defendant's sanity, and the publication of the Model Penal Code in 1962.

[A]t common law, the burden of proving "affirmative defenses—indeed, 'all . . . circumstances of justification, excuse or alleviation'—rested on the defendant." This common-law rule accords with the general evidentiary rule that "the burdens of producing evidence and of persuasion with regard to any given issue are both generally allocated to the same party." And, in the context of the defense of duress, it accords with the doctrine that "where the facts with regard to an issue lie peculiarly in the knowledge of a party, that party has the burden of proving the issue." Although she claims that the common-law rule placing the burden on a defendant to prove the existence of duress "was the product of flawed reasoning," petitioner accepts that this was the general rule, at least until this Court's decision in *Davis* [(reversing a defendant's conviction, based on the insanity defense, for a murder in Indian Territory)]. According to petitioner, however, *Davis* initiated a revolution that overthrew the old common-law rule and established her proposed rule in its place.

Davis itself, however, does not support petitioner's position. [The Court explains that *Davis* established that a defendant under federal law was presumed to be sane until he introduced evidence of insanity, at which point the burden shifted to the government to prove sanity beyond a reasonable doubt. However, that result was overturned by the Federal Insanity Defense Reform Act of 1984, 16 U.S.C. §17, that established insanity as an affirmative defense. This federal legislation placed the burden on a federal defendant to prove insanity by clear and convincing evidence, and not on the government to prove sanity. Although the government is required to prove all the elements of a crime beyond a reasonable doubt, sanity is not an element of a crime.]

It is for a similar reason that we give no weight to the publication of the Model Penal Code in 1962. As petitioner notes, the Code would place the burden on the government to disprove the existence of duress beyond a reasonable doubt. See ALI, Model Penal Code §1.12, p. 88 (2001). Petitioner argues that the Code reflects "well established" federal law as it existed at the time. [However,] no such consensus existed when Congress passed the Safe Streets Act in 1968 [that is, the offenses for which the petitioner was convicted]. And even if we assume Congress' familiarity with the Code and the rule it would establish, there is no evidence that Congress endorsed the Code's views or incorporated them into the Safe Streets Act.

In fact, the Act itself provides evidence to the contrary. Despite the Code's careful delineation of mental states, see Model Penal Code §2.02, at 94-95, the Safe Streets Act attached no explicit mens rea requirement to the crime of receiving a firearm while under indictment, §924(a), 82 Stat. 233. And when Congress amended the Act to impose a mens rea requirement, it punished people who "willfully" violate the statute, a mental state that has not been embraced by the Code. Had Congress intended to adopt the Code's structure when it enacted or amended the Safe Streets Act, one would expect the Act's form and language to adhere much more closely to that used by the Code. It does not, and, for that reason, we cannot rely on the Model Penal Code to provide evidence as to how Congress would have wanted us to effectuate the duress defense in this context.

Congress can, if it chooses, enact a duress defense that places the burden on the Government to disprove duress beyond a reasonable doubt. In light of Congress' silence on the issue, however, it is up to the federal courts to effectuate the affirmative defense of duress as Congress "may have contemplated" it in an offense-specific context. In the context of the firearms offenses at issue—as will usually be the case, given the long-established common-law rule—we presume that Congress intended the petitioner to bear the burden of proving the defense of duress by a preponderance of the evidence. Accordingly, the judgment of the Court of Appeals is affirmed. . . .

Justice BREYER, with whom Justice SOUTER joins, dissenting.

. . . [I]n federal criminal cases, the prosecution should bear the duress defense burden of persuasion. . . . [S]everal factors favor placing the burden on the prosecution. For one thing, in certain respects the question of duress resembles that of mens rea, an issue that is always for the prosecution to prove beyond a reasonable doubt. The questions are not the same. The defendant's criminal activity here was voluntary; no external principle, such as the wind, propelled her when she acted. Moreover, her actions were intentional. Whether she wanted to buy the guns or not, and whether she wanted to lie while doing so or not, she decided to do these things and knew that she was doing them. Indeed, her action was willful in the sense that she knew that to do them was to break the law.

Nonetheless, where a defendant acts under duress, she lacks any semblance of a meaningful choice. In that sense her choice is not free. As Blackstone wrote, the criminal law punishes "abuse[s] of th[e] free will"; hence "it is highly just and equitable that a man should be excused for those acts, which are done through unavoidable force and compulsion." And it is in this "force and compulsion," acting upon the will, that the resemblance to lack of mens rea lies. Davis v. United States, supra, allocated the federal insanity defense burden to the Government partly for these reasons. That case . . . suggests that, even if insanity does not always show the absence of mens rea, it does show the absence of a "'vicious will.'"

For another thing, federal courts (as a matter of statutory construction or supervisory power) have imposed the federal-crime burden of persuasion upon the prosecution in respect to self-defense, insanity, and entrapment, which resemble the duress defense in certain relevant ways. In respect to both duress and self-defense, for example, the defendant's illegal act is voluntary, indeed, intentional; but the circumstances deprive the defendant of any meaningful ability or opportunity to act otherwise, depriving the defendant of a choice that is free. . . . Further, most federal courts, in respect to most federal crimes, have imposed the burden of persuasion in respect to the duress defense upon the Government. . . . Petitioner adds, without contradiction, that the States allocate the burden similarly by a ratio of 2 to 1. . . .

Further, while I concede the logic of the Government's practical argument— that defendants have superior access to the evidence—I remain uncertain of the argument's strength. After all, "[i]n every criminal case the defendant has at least an equal familiarity with the facts and in most a greater familiarity with them than the prosecution." . . .

It is particularly difficult to see a practical distinction between this affirmative defense and, say, self-defense. The Government says that the prosecution may "be unable to call the witness most likely to have information bearing on the point," namely, the defendant. But what is the difference in this respect between the defendant here, who says her boyfriend threatened to kill her, and a battered woman who says that she killed her husband in self-defense, where the husband's evidence is certainly unavailable? Regardless, unless the defendant testifies, it could prove difficult to satisfy the defendant's burden of production; and, of course, once the defendant testifies, cross-examination is possible. . . .

For these reasons I believe that, in the absence of an indication of congressional intent to the contrary, federal criminal law should place the burden of persuasion in respect to the duress defense upon the prosecution, which, as is now common in respect to many affirmative defenses, it must prove beyond a reasonable doubt. . . .

■ KESHIA DIXON'S STORY, BRIEF FOR THE UNITED STATES

at 3-9, Dixon v. United States, 548 U.S. 1 (2006) (No. 05-7053), 2006 WL 907229

[On January 4 and 11, 2003, Keshia Dixon purchased multiple firearms at separate gun shows by providing false information to gun dealers, in violation of federal law.] In defense, petitioner claimed that her boyfriend, Thomas Earl Wright, had coerced her into purchasing the firearms. [He was a convicted felon, so he could not purchase the guns directly.] Petitioner testified that she had been in an abusive relationship with Wright for several months and that the abuse escalated in December 2002 and January 2003. Petitioner testified that on the evening before the January 4 gun show, Wright awakened her and announced that they were going to a gun show and that she was going to purchase some guns for him. According to petitioner, at that time, Wright pointed a gun at her face, threatened to kill her, and split her lip.

Petitioner further testified that the following day, she, Wright, Wright's sister, and two of Wright's companions went to the gun show. She claimed that Wright instructed her on which guns to purchase and how to fill out the forms for the dealers, and he provided her with money to make three purchases. She testified that she complied with his requests because she was afraid that Wright would kill her or her daughters if she did not. She claimed that Wright told her that someone was home with her daughters and that they were only a telephone call away.[3]

Petitioner testified that, after the January 4 gun show, her relationship with Wright deteriorated further. She claimed that, one week after the first gun show, on January 11, Wright again awakened her, pointed a gun at her, and made her go to another gun show with him and one of his companions. She purchased four additional firearms at that gun show, and testified that she did so because she was afraid that Wright would kill her or that something would happen to her daughters. She testified that a fifth attempted purchase failed, but that she persisted in attempting to make the purchase under threats from Wright.

On cross-examination, petitioner admitted (as she had on direct), that she did not believe that Wright would harm her while they were at the gun shows. . . . She further admitted that there were security guards at both gun shows, but that she did not alert them to the fact that she was being forced to purchase firearms. She admitted that she did not tell any of the gun dealers that she was being threatened, nor did she indicate when she filled out the forms that she was under any kind of duress. . . .

---

3. Although petitioner's description of her abusive relationship with Wright was largely corroborated by her daughters Ve'Queshia and Jocelyn, aged 16 and 14 at the time of trial, Ve'Queshia testified that she and her sisters were alone at home while her mother went to the first gun show, and that her mother returned home alone in her car from that show, arriving before Wright.

Petitioner also testified—and her daughters confirmed—that on or around the day of the second gun show, the police had been summoned to her apartment as a result of a disagreement that petitioner was having with one of Wright's associates. Petitioner admitted that she spoke with police at that time, but that she did not report to them that she was being abused by Wright or that she had been forced by him to purchase firearms. Petitioner also admitted that between the first and second gun shows, [she did not] tell her daughters to tell the teachers, counselors, or security personnel at the school to report the dangerous situation that her family was experiencing or to call their grandparents for help. She agreed that she had been negligent in letting her daughters return home [to the abusive situation] and in not calling the police, and that those were options available to her.[5]

During the government's case, the gun dealers who sold firearms to petitioner at the two gun shows testified that while petitioner was accompanied by several young black males, her companions did not appear to be controlling her purchases or advising her on what to purchase. . . .

[T]he government objected to the jury receiving any instruction on the defense of duress on the ground that petitioner had failed to introduce evidence sufficient to warrant an instruction. The district court overruled the government's objection [and] further instructed the jury that "[i]f you conclude that the government has proved beyond a reasonable doubt that the defendant committed the crime as charged, you must then consider whether the defendant should nevertheless be found 'not guilty' because her actions were justified by duress or coercion." The court set forth the elements of the duress defense, and instructed the jury that petitioner had "the burden of proof to establish the defense of duress by a preponderance of the evidence." The jury found petitioner guilty on all counts. . . .

Notes and Questions

1. *Epilogue.* Keshia Dixon was sentenced to almost three years in prison. Gina Holland, U.S. Supreme Court: Court Takes Up Battered-Woman Defense, Miami Herald, April 26, 2006, at A5. After her release from prison, she did not continue her relationship with her abusive boyfriend. Diane Jennings, High Court Agrees to Hear Case of Dallas Gun Buyer, Dallas Morning News, Jan. 14, 2006, at 11A.

2. *Elements of duress.* The duress defense generally requires that: (1) an aggressor threatened to use unlawful force against the defendant or a third party unless the defendant committed the offense; (2) the defendant reasonably believed the threat was genuine; (3) the threatened harm was imminent at the time of the criminal act; (4) there was no legal alternative to prevent the threatened harm, and (5) the defendant was not at fault in creating the threatened harm. See generally LaFave, Duress, 2 Subst. Crim. L., supra, at §9.7.

3. *Issue. Dixon* addresses the burden of proof in federal law involving the duress defense. The sole issue before the Supreme Court was: Should the burden of persuasion rest with the government to prove beyond a reasonable doubt that defendant was not under duress, or the defendant to prove duress by a preponderance of the evidence? Dixon argues that the defendant has the burden of

5. [Petitioner also admitted that she had had telephone and in-person contacts with her attorney in the check-cashing case, as well as several family members, but that she never told any of them she was being abused by Wright or that he had forced her to purchase firearms illegally.]

production—but once the issue of duress is raised, the government has the burden to *disprove* the duress claim beyond a reasonable doubt. In contrast, the government argues (and the Supreme Court agrees) that the accused has the burden of production and also the burden of persuasion by a preponderance of the evidence.

4. *Affirmative defense: significance.* Affirmative defenses limit or excuse a defendant's culpability. In asserting an affirmative defense, the defendant affirms that wrongdoing has occurred but offers a defense that bars, or lessens, criminal liability. An affirmative defense is either a "justification" (for example, self-defense) or an "excuse" (for example, duress, necessity). See LaFave, Defenses Generally, 2 Subst. Crim. L., supra, at §9.1(3), (4) (discussing justification and excuse); LaFave, Due Process and Statutory Presumptions, Defenses, and Exceptions, 1 Subst. Crim. L. §3.4(e) (discussing affirmative defenses). Generally, the party who offers the affirmative defense bears the burden of proof. Sometimes, however, a party must only assert the affirmative defense, and then the burden shifts to the prosecution to prove beyond a reasonable doubt that the defense is not applicable. Most legal scholars and courts treat duress as an excuse (as in *Dixon*) rather than a justification. See LaFave, Duress, 2 Subst. Crim. L., supra, at §9.7. Cf. Peter Westen & James Mangiafico, The Criminal Defense of Duress: A Justification, Not an Excuse—and Why It Matters, 6 Buff. Crim. L. Rev. 833 (2003) (agreeing that most scholars define duress as an excuse but advocating it should be classified as a justification).

How is duress similar to, and different from, necessity? Both involve coercion. The coercion required for duress stems from the action of another human being; the coercion required for necessity (sometimes called the "choice of evils" defense) involves natural forces beyond the control of another human being. "Thus, where A destroyed a dike because B threatened to kill him if he did not, A would argue that he acted under duress, whereas if A destroyed the dike in order to protect more valuable property from flooding, A could claim a defense of necessity." United States v. Bailey, 444 U.S. 394 (1980) (citing Wayne R. LaFave & Austin W. Scott, Criminal Law 406 (2d ed. 1986)).

5. *Burden of proof. Dixon* illustrates the critical importance that attaches to the issue of which party has the burden of proof. The burden of proof has two components: the burden of production and the burden of persuasion.

a. *Burden of production versus persuasion.* The burden of production is the obligation of a party to come forward with sufficient evidence to support the claim. The burden of persuasion is the duty that is required to prevail, that is, to establish a right to judicial relief by *convincing* the trier of fact (the judge or the jury) that the facts asserted are true and support the allegations. See generally 2 McCormick On Evidence §336 (6th ed. 2009) (discussing the burden of producing evidence and the burden of persuasion).

b. *Burden of proof in federal law.* Congress has the authority to determine the defenses to *federal* crimes and to direct whether the burden of proof rests with the defendant or the prosecution. *Dixon* addresses who should bear the burden of proof of duress as a defense to the gun-control provisions of the Omnibus Crime Control and Safe Streets Act of 1968, Pub L. No. 90-351, 82 Stat. 223, 228 (codified as amended at 18 U.S.C. §922, 924)—federal legislation that lacked explicit instructions regarding the duress defense or its burden of proof. How do the majority and dissent in *Dixon* differ regarding the significance of congressional intent on this issue?

c. *Importance and application.* The issue of who bears the burden of proof is important in *Dixon* in terms of the relative ease or difficulty for the defendant to prove duress. Dixon urges the Court to place the burden of persuasion on the prosecution to prove that she did *not* act under duress (after she produced evidence of duress). Had she prevailed on this issue, prosecutors would have faced considerable difficulty disproving duress. The government would have been required to question Dixon's boyfriend about his abuse and coercion. Because his conduct was criminal, he would have asserted his Fifth Amendment right against self-incrimination to refuse to testify. The government might have responded by offering him immunity. Such a course of action was unlikely because he was a joint participant in the crime (and arguably, more culpable than Dixon). The result of the holding in *Dixon* is that the prosecution has the burden of proof beyond a reasonable doubt that the defendant "knowingly" or "willfully" committed the crime (here, the firearms violations). How difficult was this burden in *Dixon*?

d. *Holding.* The majority in *Dixon* places the burden of both production and persuasion on the defendant, defining duress as an "excuse" defense (that is, the defendant committed the crime but the existence of duress excuses her conduct). 548 U.S. at 6. In contrast, Justice Breyer, in his dissent, would have placed the burden of persuasion on the prosecution, analogizing duress to the defenses of insanity or entrapment, for the reason that duress negates the requisite "evil mind" that is necessary for the imposition of criminal liability. 548 U.S. at 24 (J. Breyer, dissenting). Whose argument is more compelling?

6. *Gender and criminal liability.* At common law, a married woman was excused from criminal wrongdoing (except murder and treason) if she committed the act at her husband's coercion. If she committed the act in his *presence*, a rebuttable presumption of duress existed. See 4 William Blackstone, Commentaries *28-29; LaFave, Duress, 2 Subst. Crim. L., supra, at §9.7(f). Should the presumption be resurrected for battered women who commit crimes at their partners' request? What role, if any, should gender play in the duress defense? See Myrna S. Raeder, Gender-Related Issues in a Post-*Booker* Federal Guidelines World, 37 McGeorge L. Rev. 691, 726-730 (2006) (discussing the "girlfriend problem" in federal crimes generally).

7. *Duress and murder.* Suppose Dixon's crime was murder. Could she have asserted duress? At common law, duress was *not* a defense to murder. Most states and the federal courts follow this common law rule. LaFave, Duress, 2 Subst. Crim. L., supra, at §9.7(b); Steven J. Mulroy, The Duress Defense's Unchartered Terrain: Applying it to Murder, Felony Murder, and the Mentally Retarded Defendant, 43 San Diego L. Rev. 159, 172-174 (2006). The policy rationale is that a person does not have the right to value his or her own life over that of another. The Model Penal Code, however, does allow duress as a defense to murder. See Model Penal Code §2.09 cmt. 3, at 376 (1985). See also Mulroy, supra, at 173-174 (explaining why some jurisdictions reject the majority rule). Should duress be a defense to murder for battered women? See, e.g., R. v. Ryan, (2011), 2011 CarswellNS 177, 301 N.S.R.2d 255 (N.S. C.A.) (ruling by a Nova Scotia Court of Appeal that upheld an acquittal of a battered wife, based on the defense of duress, for hiring a "hit man" to kill her husband).

8. *Objective versus subjective standard.* Federal courts determine duress by an objective standard. Mulroy, supra, at 191. Duress requires an objective inquiry into whether a defendant was under an imminent threat that would have induced

a well-grounded apprehension of death or serious bodily injury; defendant had not recklessly or negligently placed herself in a situation of duress; and defendant had no reasonable legal alternative to violating the law. *Dixon*, 413 F.3d 520, 523 (5th Cir. 2005). How would a reasonable person have acted in Dixon's situation?

At trial in *Dixon*, why did the jury find that the defendant's firearms violations were not excused by duress? How might evidence of BWS have helped the defense? The district court in *Dixon* excluded BWS evidence. Affirming, the Fifth Circuit Court of Appeals reasoned that BWS testimony focused on the defendant's subjective perceptions of danger, and therefore "was not relevant to the inquiry at hand—that is, to whether such perceptions were 'well-grounded' or objectively reasonable under the circumstances." 413 F.3d at 524. The issue of the admissibility of BWS evidence was not before the U.S. Supreme Court.

9. *Imminent threat.* The batterer, in the usual duress case, is often absent (or at least not an immediate threatening presence) when the victim commits the crime. How does the batterer's absence present problems in proof of the imminence of the threat? See, e.g., United States v. Homick, 964 F.2d 899, 906 (9th Cir. 1992) (holding that defendant failed to establish duress, reasoning that batterer was out of town when he requested that she lie on an affidavit). How can a court determine if a defendant committed a crime based on her fear of general harm by the batterer versus a fear of his retaliation for her failure to comply?

States vary in terms of whether imminence or immediacy is required in a duress claim. Compare Commonwealth v. Ely, 578 A.2d 540 (Pa. Super. 1990) (finding no immediacy requirement in defense of duress), with *Homick*, 964 F.2d at 906 (duress includes immediacy requirement). In states with an immediacy requirement, how likely is the duress defense to succeed if the defendant commits a crime based on a *previous* fear of her abuser? See United States v. Santos, 932 F.2d 244, 253 (3d Cir. 1991) (six-time cocaine distribution over a year's course-of-conduct not subject to duress defense); Laurie Kratky Dore, Downward Adjustment and the Slippery Slope: The Use of Duress in Defense of Battered Offenders, 56 Ohio St. L.J. 665, 711 (1995) (suggesting that "course-of-conduct" crimes may not have a valid duress defense due to the imminence requirement).

What aspects of Dixon's experience support a finding of imminent threat? What aspects detract from such a finding? Can the duress defense be modified to provide an understanding of imminence that includes the plight of a victim of domestic violence for whom abuse is always imminent, if not immediate?

10. *Reasonable opportunity to escape.* The duress defense requires that the defendant have no "reasonable opportunity for escape," that is, the defendant could not have avoided the threat without harm to herself or others and without committing the crime. LaFave, Duress, 2 Subst. Crim. L., supra, at §9.7(b). Did Dixon have a "reasonable opportunity for escape"? What does "opportunity to escape" mean, in the context of an abusive relationship? See United States v. Ceballos, 593 F. Supp. 2d 1054 (S.D. Iowa 2009) (rejecting consideration of the lapse of time *between* two drug deals committed at abuser's request, looking instead at each transaction at which the abuser was present and threatened to beat her if she failed to continue the criminal act).

11. *Recklessly or negligently placing oneself in a situation of duress.* Does a victim of domestic violence, like Dixon, "recklessly or negligently" cause herself to be in a situation of duress? In *Ceballos*, supra, the court was influenced by expert testimony

in the determination of whether defendant's actions were reckless or negligent. The court reasoned:

> that it is not reckless or negligent for a woman to become involved in an abusive relationship because of the often subtle and effective manipulations of the abuser. Indeed, the mere fact that domestic abuse spans every social and economic layer in our society is an indication of the effectiveness of abusers, not the carelessness of victims. [The expert] also testified that one tactic abusers utilize to gain leverage over their victims is to force them to commit an illicit act, which then allows the abuser to essentially blackmail the victim into compliance. Thus, the Court finds that Defendant has made a prima facie case that it was not negligent or reckless for her to be in an abusive relationship where the abuser would later try to force her to commit a crime.

593 F. Supp. 2d at 1063. But cf. Commonwealth v. Markman, 916 A.2d 586, 607-611 (Pa. 2007) (finding that it was a jury question as to whether defendant acted recklessly in continuing her crime while under duress because she had multiple opportunities to seek police help). When should recklessness be analyzed, at the beginning of the commission of the crime, or at each opportunity for escape?

Natalie's Story

Soon after 16-year-old Natalie started living with her 21-year-old boyfriend, Mark, the abuse began. Emotional abuse was followed by physical violence, and then rape. As the abuse escalated, Natalie became increasingly scared. She was particularly frightened because Mark was involved in selling drugs and had a gun. One night, Mark ordered Natalie to get into the car. He put his gun in his jacket pocket. He told her, "Don't ask me questions. Do what I say. I'll let you know what you need to know." He took Natalie to a building and told her to wait outside. Then, Mark approached a female stranger, pointed his gun at her, and ordered both the stranger and Natalie to get into the car. He told the stranger to sit in the back seat. Natalie was in shock. Mark threatened to kill the stranger if she did not give him her ATM card. Then, he put her in the trunk of the car.

Natalie was terrified. Mark continued to drive, increasingly erratically. The police began pursuing them. Later, Natalie learned that the woman had cut the tail lights from the trunk of the car. When the police arrested them, the police charged both Mark and Natalie with robbery and kidnapping. Mark threatened that, if Natalie testified against him, he would kill her. She pled guilty to robbery in the first degree. She served 10 years in prison.

The above account is a summary of a story in Avon Global Center for Women and Justice, From Protection to Punishment: Post-Conviction Barriers to Justice for Domestic Violence Survivors-Defendants in New York State 16-17 (2011), available at http://www.lawschool.cornell.edu/womenandjustice/Avon-Global-Center-investigates-failures-to-secure-justice-for-domestic-violence-survivor-defendants-in-New-York-State.cfm

■ MARTI TAMM LORING & PATI BEAUDOIN, BATTERED WOMEN AS COERCED VICTIM-PERPETRATORS

2 J. Emotional Abuse 3, 7-10, 13 (2000)

[The authors studied 251 battered women who committed crimes at the request of their intimate partners. The crimes included credit card theft, fraud, drug trafficking, murder or attempted murder, bank robbery (driving the get-away car), and prostitution.]

Numerous anecdotal stories ... were illustrative of the terror experienced by the victims, both long-term and immediately preceding an illegal act on the part of the victim. For example, a 23-year-old mother discussed her belief that the children's father, her husband, would follow through with his threat to kill their child if she did not drive the get-away car during a bank robbery. He had beaten the child frequently, holding a gun to his son's head two weeks prior to the bank robbery. While waiting outside the bank during her husband's robbery, she described gripping the steering wheel in terror while experiencing flashbacks to the gun being held to her son's head. ...

Threats to harm pets were reported by the women as no less important than threats to harm or kill the victim's children or nonfamily members. Actually, harm to pets, children, and/or nonfamily members were described as terrifying by all of the women interviewed. In one case, the woman (a stockbroker) was told by the abuser that she must keep the money invested through her by their friends in stock [so that the husband could take it]. Her husband threatened to cut the dog's head off unless she obeyed him. ...

Each of the 251 women reported that they sometimes refused to commit illegal acts even to protect themselves. However, a majority of the women reported committing crimes to protect pets, children, and/or nonfamily members. ... Each of the 251 victim-perpetrators expressed a sense of horror at her criminal act. She seemed unable to integrate the illegal behavior into her sense of who she was. Each reported sadness and shock at her criminal behavior, some a single act and others serial acts, describing it as alien to her own values. Along with this sadness and alienation from her own value system, a victim-perpetrator experiencing physical and/or emotional abuse often suffers from Post-Traumatic Stress Disorder, resulting in terror and frequent difficulty recalling all aspects of traumatic events. In the mist of fear and confusion, these women may struggle with a diminished capacity to think clearly and solve problems. They may also have tunnel vision born of desperation to survive. ...

Problem

Ann and her husband Jeff are at a bar. When Jeff goes to the bathroom, Greg begins talking to Ann. Jeff returns, becomes jealous and argues with Greg. Jeff leaves with Ann and retrieves two handguns from home. They return to the bar. Greg is shot when he exits. The police charge Jeff with murder. However, the grand jury re-indicts both Ann and Jeff after Ann tells police that she fired the fatal shot accidentally during a struggle between the two men. A jury convicts Ann and Jeff of first-degree murder; they are sentenced to life imprisonment. Ann files an application for postconviction relief, alleging that, as a victim of BWS, she was forced by her husband to relate a false account. She claims that he beat her over an 18-month period whenever she failed to rehearse the story or relate it to his satisfaction. What result? *McMaugh v. State*, 612 A.2d 725 (R.I. 1992).

5. Cultural Defense

■ PEOPLE v. BENITEZ
2002 WL 31009371 (Cal. Ct. App. 2002)

Perren, J.

Pedro Aguilar Benitez appeals from the judgment entered after a jury found him guilty of first-degree murder. . . . He contends that the trial court erred in excluding expert testimony on Mexican culture, which was offered to support his defense that he killed in the heat of passion. . . .

Appellant came to the United States from Mexico in 1989 or 1990. The victim, Sandra Castrejon, was appellant's common law wife and the mother of two of his children. Throughout the relationship, appellant was jealous and controlling of Sandra. He told her what to wear, demanded that she ask his permission to go anywhere, listened in on her telephone conversations, and became angry when she talked to other men. One night about seven years before he killed her, he slapped her and pulled her hair after she refused to cook for him. He also hit her on the face during an argument in 1999.

In the summer of 2000, appellant reluctantly moved out for about a week at Sandra's urging and went to stay with Sandra's sister Maria. Appellant told Maria that his jealousy was "destroying" him and that he wanted to kill himself. His jealousy intensified after he returned to live with Sandra. When she refused his sexual advances, he accused her of having sex with someone else. Sandra denied the accusation, but on another occasion she told him that she was seeing someone else in the hope that it would drive him away. Less than a week after appellant had returned from Maria's house, Sandra asked him to leave again. Appellant then accused Sandra of having an affair with appellant's 19-year-old son Sigifredo, who had been living with them since early 2000. Sandra and Sigifredo both denied the accusation.

On August 19, 2000, Maria and Alicia (Sandra's teenage daughter from a prior relationship) held a surprise birthday party for Sandra. Appellant got drunk at the party and accused Sandra of making him "look bad" by refusing to dance with him. Appellant later insisted that Sandra allow him to read the birthday card that Sigifredo had given her, but she refused. An argument later erupted, during which Sigifredo told appellant that he loved Sandra. Appellant blamed Sandra for Sigifredo's affections, but she denied that she had done anything to encourage him.

The following morning, appellant told Sandra he would forgive her for anything she may have done with Sigifredo. Sandra responded that she was tired of appellant and would call the police if he did not leave. After Sandra left for work, appellant threw Sigifredo's clothes around the house and told him to "[g]et the fuck out of here." Appellant also told Sigifredo that he hated him and that "[y]ou'll be sorry for this." Sigifredo called Maria, who picked him up and took him to her house. Appellant also told Alicia that morning that he was going to Mexico, and that she should take care of Sandra while he was gone.

When Sandra came home from work at about 4:00 p.m., appellant asked her to take him back. Sandra reiterated that she would call the police if he did not leave. Then she left and went to Maria's house. Sandra told Maria that after appellant had treated her like "trash" and called her a "whore" and had repeatedly asked her whether she loved Sigifredo, she had told him in anger that she did.

According to appellant, he had thoughts throughout the day of killing Sandra and committing suicide, and of the different ways he might do it. As soon as Sandra returned from Maria's house, she and appellant began arguing in the bedroom. After appellant realized that Sandra was not going to change her mind about reconciling, he told her that if he could not have her, no one could. He then walked to the kitchen, got a knife from the drawer, and walked back to the bedroom. Appellant later told the police that he had already made up his mind to kill Sandra at that point. When Sandra saw the knife, she told him she would stay in the relationship and that they could work things out. Appellant was not persuaded. He repeatedly stabbed Sandra in the chest as she sat on the edge of the bed, then slashed his wrists and stabbed himself in the chest. Sandra stumbled into the living room and cried for help. Shortly thereafter, the police arrived to find Sandra on the living room floor, covered in blood. Before she died, Sandra told paramedics that appellant had attacked her.

. . . Appellant subsequently told the police that he had killed Sandra because "[i]f I can't have her, no one can have her" and because of the "ridicule," "affront" and "disgrace" he felt as a result of his belief that Sandra and Sigifredo were having an affair.

A defense psychologist testified at trial that appellant was severely depressed, which rendered him more likely to "fly off the handle" and to act impulsively. The psychologist also testified that appellant did not have a normal socialization as a child in Mexico and that his father was a strict authoritarian who inflicted corporal punishment on him. Although appellant had been in the United States for over 10 years, he did not speak much English and remained "mostly involved in the Mexican culture." Appellant also had a drinking problem and had abused cocaine in the past. [T]he Minnesota Multiphasic Personality Inventory (MMPI) orally administered to appellant indicated that he was suffering from stress and anxiety in addition to major depression. The psychologist also cited appellant's history of jealousy and marital discord as evidence that he had suffered from long-term depression. He also referred to studies indicating that the vast majority of spousal murders and suicides are committed by severely depressed men who are motivated by jealousy. . . .

Appellant contends that his constitutional due process and fair trial rights were violated when the trial court precluded him from offering expert psychological testimony on "the effect of appellant's Mexican culture upon his thinking processes." He argues that "[c]ultural testimony could have helped the jury understand how [appellant] was led from male Mexican pride to a consuming jealousy" and that "he acted out of passion aroused by reasonable provocation rather than judgment" in killing her, and was thus guilty of voluntary manslaughter and not first-degree murder. According to appellant, "[t]he judging of the ethnic minority male's state of mind based upon how an Anglo-American male would have reacted in the same circumstances is arbitrary and a violation of the due process rights of the ethnic minority male." We disagree on all points.

[T]he trial court did not abuse its discretion in excluding evidence regarding appellant's purported acculturation problem. Trial courts have broad discretion in determining whether evidence is relevant or in excluding evidence. . . . The court concluded that the proffered evidence was irrelevant to the determination whether appellant had killed Sandra in the heat of passion based on sufficient provocation because "it is not appropriate for a jury to determine whether defendant's belief in response to provocation was reasonable based upon a standard that has been adjusted for his particular background." . . . We thus agree with the trial court that the separate "reasonable person" standard for immigrants advocated by appellant simply does not exist. A personalized standard of reasonableness in this regard would effectively swallow the rule. . . .

Notes and Questions

1. *Definition. Benitez* raises the cultural defense. The cultural defense has different variations: (a) an independent defense, or (b) evidence in support of a standard criminal defense (for example, duress, self-defense, provocation). Kent Greenawalt, The Cultural Defense: Reflections in Light of the Model Penal Code and the Religious Freedom Restoration Act, 6 Ohio St. J. Crim. L. 299, 299 (2008). See also Elaine M. Chiu, Culture as Justification, Not Excuse, 43 Am. Crim. L. Rev. 1317, 1324 (2006) (differentiating "cultural defense" from "cultural evidence"). How does the defendant in *Benitez* invoke the cultural defense?

2. *Rationales.* Primary rationales for the cultural defense include: (1) a new immigrant should not be held responsible for unwitting violations of the law; and (2) the values of individualism and multiculturalism mandate consideration of individuals' different perspectives and different cultural perspectives. Deborah M. Boulette Taylor, Paying Attention to the Little Man Behind the Curtain: Destroying the Myth of the Liberal's Dilemma, 50 Me. L. Rev. 446, 447 (1998). Do these rationales apply to *Benitez*?

3. *Exclusion of the evidence.* Why did the defendant seek to introduce expert testimony? What was his objection to the trial court's exclusion of the testimony? How did the appellate court respond? Do you agree? Is culture ever a justification for breaking the law?

4. *Provocation and the cultural defense.* The defendant contends that cultural evidence is relevant to the determination of whether provocation would cause a reasonable person in his position to have acted upon impulse and committed murder. According to the defendant, how did his Mexican culture contribute to his loss of self-control? What stereotypes are evoked by consideration of cultural evidence in this case? Provocation is explored later in this chapter in Section 6.

5. *Sentencing.* The cultural defense is invoked more often to mitigate sentencing than to excuse or justify criminal conduct. See Myrna Oliver, Immigrant Crimes: Cultural Defense—a Legal Tactic, L.A. Times, July 15, 1988, at 1. As a commentator explains:

> Where evidence of cultural influence on behavior does not substantiate a traditional defense to criminal liability such as duress or necessity, that evidence is not simply eliminated from consideration. Rather, it reappears at the defendant's sentencing hearing, where the defendant's lawyer offers it anew to place the defendant's behavior

in context and show how it is less culpable than similar behavior by a person from the dominant culture. . . . Moreover, such an opportunity should often succeed because a person who harms another in a way common to his foreign culture is, in fact, less culpable than an otherwise similarly situated American who causes the same harm with no cultural support.

Eric L. Muller, Fixing a Hole: How the Criminal Law Can Bolster Reparations Theory, 47 B.C. L. Rev. 659, 693 (2006). Do you agree? How much consideration should be given to a defendant's cultural background in sentencing?

6. *Constitutional issues.* Does the judicial system's failure to accommodate cultural differences result in discrimination against members of cultural minorities in violation of the Constitution? What is the defendant's constitutional argument that requires consideration of the cultural defense? How does the appellate court respond? What societal values are promoted by consideration of the cultural defense? By rejection of the cultural defense? Are these values of constitutional significance?

7. *Battered Woman's Syndrome analogy.* The cultural defense is sometimes analogized to the Battered Woman's Syndrome, in terms of its creation of a subgroup of "reasonable persons" against whose actions the defendant is judged. Compare Sharan K. Suri, A Matter of Principle and Consistency: Understanding the Battered Woman and Cultural Defenses, 7 Mich. J. Gender & L. 107 (2000) (arguing that the defenses are theoretically consistent and should therefore be admitted with some precautions), with Alice J. Gallin, Note, The Culture Defense: Undermining the Policies Against Domestic Violence, 35 B.C. L. Rev. 723, 741-744 (1994) (highlighting the policy rationales behind each defense and indicating starkly different theoretical underpinnings). What justifies treating the defenses similarly? Differently? Does judicial consideration of the cultural defense undermine domestic violence policy, in general? In *Benitez*?

8. *Parent-child suicides.* The cultural defense is commonly invoked in the context of child abuse as well as intimate partner violence. Cases sometimes involve mothers' murders of their children or attempted murder-suicides. For example, in People v. Wu, 286 Cal. Rptr. 868 (Ct. App. 1991), a Chinese woman strangled her son and then tried to kill herself (unsuccessfully). Her acts followed her humiliating discovery that her husband was having an affair and also that he was mistreating their son. She rationalized the murder of her son as necessary so that she could care for him in the afterlife. At trial, she argued that her actions would have been justified in China to ensure that a mother did not leave a child behind to suffer abuse by a husband. Her lawyer sought to introduce the cultural defense to prove diminished capacity.

Should evidence of the mother's cultural beliefs be admissible? Should the case be decided similarly to *Benitez*? Professor Leti Volpp proposes that the cultural defense should not be available to an immigrant male defendant who acts as an agent of oppression against a woman, but should be available to a female defendant who is a victim of oppression, based on the antisubordination principle. Leti Volpp, Talking "Culture": Gender, Race, Nation, and the Politics of Multiculturalism, 96 Colum. L. Rev. 1573, 1612-1613 (1996). Do you agree?

9. *Debate.* The cultural defense has engendered heated debates pitting multiculturalists against feminists regarding whether, and to what extent, cultural evidence should be permitted to exculpate or mitigate culpability. Some multiculturalists advocate the establishment of a new separate cultural defense to allow for

individualized justice. See, e.g., Anh T. Lam, Culture as a Defense: Preventing Judicial Bias Against Asians and Pacific Islanders, 1 Asian Am. Pac. Islands L.J. 49 (1993); Alison D. Renteln, A Justification of the Cultural Defense as Partial Excuse, 2 S. Cal. Rev. L. & Women's Stud. 437 (1993).

Other scholars, although supportive of the cultural defense, propose that cultural evidence should be admissible only for limited purposes. See, e.g., Nancy S. Kim, The Cultural Defense and the Problem of Cultural Preemption: A Framework for Analysis, 27 N.M. L. Rev. 101, 103 (1997) (limiting defense to establishing defendant's state of mind at time of offense); Carolyn Choi, Note, Application of a Cultural Defense in Criminal Proceedings, 8 UCLA Pac. Basin L.J. 80, 90 (1990) (limiting defense to sentence mitigation); Feminist opponents argue that the cultural defense denies justice to women and children because the defense is invoked primarily by men who commit crimes against these victims. See Doriane Lambelet Coleman, Individualizing Justice Through Multiculturalism: The Liberal's Dilemma, 96 Colum. L. Rev. 1093, 1095 (1995); Nilda Rimonte, A Question of Culture: Cultural Approval of Violence Against Women in the Pacific-Asian Community and the Cultural Defense, 43 Stan. L. Rev. 1311, 1321 (1991). These feminists also contend that use of cultural evidence undermines deterrence, results in disparate sentences for similar crimes, and encourages immigrants to remain ignorant of the law. See Julia P. Sams, The Availability of the "Cultural Defense" as an Excuse for Criminal Behavior, 16 Ga. J. Int'l & Comp. L.J. 335 (1986).

Some commentators attempt to find a middle ground. For example, Professor Leti Volpp argues that cultural evidence should not be allowed to reinforce stereotypes about a particular community, but that it should be admissible if "based on accurate descriptions of the pressures that individuals face, both within their communities and without." Volpp, Talking "Culture," supra, at 1612-1613. Volpp contends that the goals of multiculturalism and feminism are not antithetical. Id. at 1576. She advocates adoption of an antisubordination approach (that is, examining whether cultural evidence furthers stereotypes versus subordination) to determine when to allow use of the cultural defense because such an approach seeks to eliminate inequality while remaining race conscious. Id. at 1594-1595, 1612-1613.

Professor Volpp also elaborates on the division within the feminist community regarding the cultural defense. According to Volpp, white feminists oppose the use of cultural evidence in the belief that only one standard of justice should prevail, whereas feminists of color advocate its use in some circumstances in the interests of cultural pluralism. Leti Volpp, (Mis)Identifying Culture: Asian Women and the "Cultural Defense," 17 Harv. Women's L.J. 57, 77-78 (1994). Can these interests be reconciled? See Holly Maguigan, Cultural Evidence and Male Violence: Are Feminist and Multiculturalist Reformers on a Collision Course in Criminal Courts?, 70 N.Y.U. L. Rev. 36, 86 (1995) (attempting to recognize the relevance of culture evidence in a way that combats "pluralistic ignorance without trivializing family violence"). Does the cultural defense present a conflict between other values that feminists cherish? See Taylor, supra, at 453-454 (identifying values of inclusion of nondominant people's perspective versus refusal to condone violence toward women and children).

10. *Reform proposals.* Commentators have proposed a variety of ways to accommodate cultural beliefs in the criminal law. One commentator suggests that the cultural defense should be applicable "only to bona fide newcomers who have not acculturated to the mainstream," but that the court should not permit the

defense after a judicially determined point when these persons should be considered acculturated. Sams, supra, at 347. Another commentator contends that courts should decide whether to allow the cultural defense after conducting a preliminary inquiry into the defendant's background that takes into account the following factors: (1) the defendant's experiences in the home country (that is, socioeconomic status, family integration, and prior criminal activities); (2) the defendant's difficulty coping in the new culture; (3) the defendant's lack of assimilation into mainstream culture such that it would be unfair to inflict punishment for noncompliance with the law; and (4) the role of important societal values (such as faithfulness) in the defendant's culture that deserve to be protected. Lam, supra, at 51. What do you think of these proposals?

Problem

A 23-year-old man (Kong Moua) from a rural tribal Asian ethnic group (Hmong) is living in Fresno, California. One day, Moua kidnaps 19-year-old Seng Xiong, who is a student at Fresno City College and also from Laos. He takes her to his cousin's house and forces her to have sexual intercourse several times. Afterwards, she accuses him of kidnapping and rape. At trial, Moua attempts to introduce evidence that his conduct conformed to the Hmong tribal tradition of "marriage by capture," an accepted form of finding a bride that resembles elopement. According to this practice, a Hmong man takes his future bride from her home to his family home and forces her there to consummate the "marriage." Moua argues that, in light of his cultural background, he honestly and reasonably believed that Xiong consented to the intercourse.

Moua's expert witness, an expert on Southeast Asian culture and customs, is prepared to testify that the defendant's force and the woman's resistance are typical of the cultural practice. That is, according to Hmong tradition, the woman is supposed to protest vehemently during the "elopement" because her resistance reveals that she is chaste. The man has to be forceful if he wants to be considered a proper husband. Should the evidence be admitted? Why or why not? Should this case be treated as rape? As "date rape"? For a discussion of this case, see Cynthia Lee, Cultural Convergence: Interest Convergence Theory Meets the Cultural Defense, 49 Ariz. L. Rev. 911, 954-956 (2007).

6. Provocation

■ MURRAY v. STATE

543 S.E.2d 428 (Ga. Ct. App. 2000)

MILLER, Judge.

Frederick Mashard Murray was indicted for murder and possession of a firearm during the commission of a crime, for the shooting death of Kevin Crumedy. After a bench trial, Murray was found guilty of voluntary manslaughter. . . .

[T]he evidence revealed the following: Murray's girlfriend, Sharon Jones, was separated from her husband and had moved from Florida to Moultrie, Colquitt County, Georgia, to live with Murray. Jones testified that Murray was jealous of her friendship with [Kevin Crumedy, a male co-worker of hers], and that Murray had accosted the victim at work after discovering his telephone number in Jones's coat. After work, Murray hit Jones in the mouth with his fist and threatened her with a gun if she ever disrespected him like that again. Murray also threatened Jones that he would shoot [Kevin] if Murray saw him on the street.

The next morning, Murray told Jones she might as well quit her job because it was going to be her last day and started playing with a gun in front of her, suggesting that he would shoot her when she got home from work. At work, the victim helped Jones to leave town on a bus. Escorted by her estranged husband and a police officer, Jones returned to Moultrie several days later to retrieve her belongings when Murray showed up at their house. Murray told Jones not to be afraid of him, yet displayed to her what appeared to be a new or different gun. Jones finished packing without further incident and departed. On her way out of town, she stopped at the victim's home. Murray drove up, walked over to where Jones, her husband, and the victim were standing, and greeted Jones and the victim. Murray queried whether the victim recalled "all that stuff you [were] saying over there at [work]? And [the victim] said, 'yeah, what's up?' . . . And [Murray] said, 'what?'" [Then he pulled out the gun and shot the victim once in the chest.] Murray then told Jones to come with him and [said] that he did it because he loved her and would do anything to keep her. Jones ran around the corner and never went back.

Murray testified [at trial] that the victim admitted having a sexual relationship with Jones and that Jones told Murray she was pregnant and returning to Florida. When Murray came across Jones at the victim's apartment, the victim was "over her hugging on her." As Murray asked Jones what was going on, the victim intervened, telling Jones "you don't have to talk to that punk. . . ." [In response, Murray shot him].

A person commits the offense of voluntary manslaughter when he causes the death of another human being "under circumstances which would otherwise be murder and if he acts solely as the result of a sudden, violent, and irresistible passion resulting from serious provocation sufficient to excite such passion in a reasonable person." [Ga. Code Ann. §16-5-2(a)]. Adulterous conduct can serve as sufficient provocation authorizing a charge on voluntary manslaughter under [Ga. Code Ann. §16-5-2(a)]. And this rationale of sexual jealousy as provocation applies even though the parties to the relationship are not married to each other.

It is for the trier of fact to determine whether the chain of circumstances and conduct were sufficient to engender irresistible passion. The evidence is sufficient [in this case] to authorize the trial court's findings that Murray is guilty, beyond a reasonable doubt, of voluntary manslaughter and possession of a firearm during the commission of a crime. Judgment affirmed.

Notes and Questions

1. *Common law approach.* At common law, if a husband killed his wife or her lover (or both) when he discovered his wife in the act of adultery, the murder was reduced to manslaughter. According to Blackstone,

> if a man takes another in the act of adultery with his wife and kills him directly on the spot, though this was allowed by the laws of Solon, as likewise by the Roman civil law (if the adulterer was found in the husband's own house), and also among the ancient Goths; yet in England it is not absolutely ranked in the class of justifiable homicide . . .

but it is manslaughter. It is, however, the lowest degree of it; and therefore in such a case the court directed the burning in the hand to be gently inflicted, because there could not be a greater provocation.

4 William Blackstone, Commentaries *191-192. To establish provocation at common law, the defendant had to witness the act of infidelity. Why wasn't knowledge of it sufficient? Would the defendant in *Murray* be entitled to a jury instruction on provocation at common law?

2. *Cross-cultural view.* In many countries, discovery of a wife's infidelity is justifiable provocation for murder. See Margo Wilson & Martin Daly, Lethal and Non-lethal Violence Against Wives and the Evolutionary Psychology of Male Sexual Proprietariness, in Rethinking Violence Against Women 199, 203 (Rebecca E. Dobash & Russell P. Dobash eds., 1998).

3. *Elements of provocation.* At common law, provocation requires: (1) reasonable provocation; (2) actual provocation of the defendant; (3) a reasonable person would not have cooled off in the interval between the provocation and fatal act; and (4) the defendant did not cool off during that interval. LaFave, Heat-of-Passion Voluntary Manslaughter, 2 Subst. Crim. L., supra, at §15.2. Culpability is evaluated by an objective standard. Unlike self-defense, provocation does not provide a complete justification but only mitigates criminal wrongdoing. Provocation is sometimes referred to as the "heat of passion" defense. The "passion" generally consists of rage, although some case law recognizes such other emotions as fright, terror, and desperation. Id.

4. *Model Penal Code (MPC).* The Model Penal Code differs from the common law approach. MPC §210.3(b) defines voluntary manslaughter as follows:

> A homicide which would otherwise be murder is committed under the influence of extreme mental or emotional disturbance for which there is reasonable explanation or excuse. The reasonableness of such explanation or excuse shall be determined from the viewpoint of a person in the actor's situation under the circumstances as he believes them to be.

The MPC is broader than the common law doctrine in several ways: (1) it provides for an "extreme mental or emotional disturbance (EMED)" (rather than a sudden act of provocation); (2) it includes a subjective as well as objective test (determining the reasonableness of the excuse for EMED "from the viewpoint of a person in the defendant's situation under the circumstances as he believes them to be"); (3) it broadens provocation to include an act committed on someone other than the defendant; (4) provocation can be verbal; and (5) it omits the suddenness requirement from an EMED defense. See ALI, Model Penal Code §210.3, cmt (1980).

5. *Application.* Compare the defendant's provocation at common law, the Model Penal Code, and Georgia law. Although the court in *Murray* does not offer its analysis of the elements, was there sufficient provocation? Cf. People v. Chevalier, 544 N.E.2d 942 (Ill. 1989) (holding that verbal communication of adultery was insufficient provocation). When Murray killed the victim, was Murray in the throes of intense emotion? Had there been time for his passion to cool? See, e.g., State v. Massey, 535 So. 2d 1135 (La. Ct. App. 1988) (finding that evidence that defendant caught his ex-girlfriend in bed with another man five months earlier was insufficient provocation).

6. *Sexual jealousy.* Do we know whether the victim actually told Murray that he was having a sexual relationship with Jones? Do we know whether Jones actually told

Murray that she was pregnant? Suppose Murray merely suspected Jones of infidelity. Would such a suspicion constitute legally sufficient provocation? See State v. Ward, 210 S.E.2d 407, 414 (1974) (holding that "a mere suspicion, belief or knowledge of past adulterous affairs . . . will not change the character of murder to manslaughter") (*vacated on other grounds*).

Sexual jealousy (based on real and imagined events) is a primary motivation for battering, as we have seen (Chapter 4). See also Jacquelyn C. Campbell, If I Can't Have You, No One Can, in Femicide: The Politics of Woman Killing 99, 103-104 (J. Radford & D. Russell eds., 1992); Margo Wilson & Martin Daly, Till Death Do Us Part, in id. at 83, 87. Thus, it is no surprise that many men who kill their partners allege that infidelity constituted the provocation. Given the state of knowledge about intimate partner violence, should sexual jealousy still constitute legally sufficient provocation? One commentator criticizes that the

> infidelity paradigm rests on a fundamentally flawed and inadequately examined premise: the provocation defense nonchalantly asserts, and the dominant scholarship regarding the defense accepts, that to a certain extent we cannot expect people to control themselves when faced with the sight of a faithless spouse. This it not true. We should, and in fact do, have more control over our passions than the defense and the prevailing scholarship assume. . . .

Susan D. Rozelle, Controlling Passion: Adultery and the Provocation Defense, 37 Rutgers L.J. 197, 199 (2005). What gender-based stereotypes are evoked by the provocation defense? See generally Donna K. Coker, Heat of Passion and Wife Killing: Men Who Batter/Men Who Kill, 2 S. Cal. Rev. L. & Women's Stud. 71 (1992) (applying social science data to reexamine the heat of passion defense).

7. *Policy rationale.* Why should the legal system treat a wrongdoer more leniently because the wrongdoer's homicide was provoked? One commentator queries: "Does society reduce the defendant's punishment because of his temporary mental or emotional impairment, or does society reduce the punishment because the victim's own wrongful acts render the victim partially responsible for the suffered harm, thus reducing the wrongfulness of the killing?" Vera Bergelson, Justification or Excuse? Exploring the Meaning of Provocation, 42 Tex. Tech L. Rev. 307, 308 (2009). Why should the law take the *victim's sexual* behavior into account when determining the extent of a defendant's culpability? Is victim blaming appropriate if the victim is a victim of defendant's abuse? See generally Vera Bergelson, Victims and Perpetrators: An Argument for Comparative Liability in Criminal Law, 8 Buff. Crim. L. Rev. 385 (2005) (contending that victims' conduct should be relevant to perpetrators' culpability).

Societal views about women as property and the wrongfulness of adultery have evolved. In light of changing attitudes and mores, should we continue to mitigate culpability in cases of provocation based on infidelity? See generally Joshua Dressler, Why Keep the Provocation Defense? Some Reflections on a Difficult Subject, 86 Minn. L. Rev. 959 (2002).

Problems

1. Becky and Randall live together for several months before she agrees to marry him. One night, they go to a bar to celebrate their engagement. They are joined by Randall's sister and several friends. When Becky asks an acquaintance to

dance with her, Randall becomes jealous and goes home. Becky calls him to ask him to return. When he does, he sees Becky dancing with still another man. Randall becomes irate, charges onto the dance floor and knocks Becky down. The proprietor of the bar throws him out. Randall's sister takes Becky home with her. Randall later goes to his sister's house and continues beating Becky, knocking her down several times. Becky hits her head on a coffee table and later on a stereo. The sister's daughter later testifies that Becky had bruises all over her face, her eyes were black, and her nose was bleeding. Randall finally leaves, taking Becky with him. The next morning, he calls an ambulance when he cannot rouse her. Becky dies 12 days later. Randall contends that he killed Becky because he was suffering from a "heat of passion." What result under the common law and Model Penal Code approaches? See Dixon v. State, 597 S.W.2d 77 (Ark. 1980).

2. During Christmas week, Lawrence separates from his wife Lisa. Lisa remains in the apartment with their three children. When Lawrence leaves, he takes the family's digital video recorder (DVR). Lisa bemoans the loss of the DVR to a male friend, Kerry Kessler. Kerry brings Lisa a new DVR. Lawrence discovers the new DVR, accuses Lisa of infidelity, and destroys the DVR. A few hours later, he induces Lisa to call Kerry to come over "to talk." When Kerry knocks at the door, Lisa shouts, "Run, he has got a gun!" Kerry runs down the stairway. Lawrence shoots him, hitting him in the face. Lawrence reloads and shoots again, but misses. When Lawrence is taken into custody by a police officer, he says, "I wish I would have killed the son of a bitch." Lawrence is charged with attempted murder.

The state statute provides for mitigation if a person commits or attempts murder:

> under the influence of extreme emotional disturbance for which there is reasonable excuse. The reasonableness of the excuse must be determined from the viewpoint of a person in his situation under the circumstances as he believes them to be. An extreme emotional disturbance is excusable, within the meaning of this subsection only, if it is occasioned by substantial provocation, or a serious event, or situation for which the offender was not culpably responsible. N.D. Cent. Code §12.1-16-01(2).

Lawrence argues that he is entitled to a new trial based on the judge's failure to give a jury instruction on the effect of "extreme emotional disturbance" as a reasonable excuse to reduce the seriousness of his attempted murder offense. Should the jury instruction have been given? Was the evidence sufficient to support defendant's conviction? See State v. Miller, 466 N.W.2d 128 (N.D. 1991).

B. EVIDENTIARY ISSUES

1. Spousal Testimonial Privilege

■ STATE v. TAYLOR
642 So. 2d 160 (La. 1994)

HALL, Justice

The issue we are called upon to decide in this case is whether there is an exception to the spousal witness privilege [that] allows one spouse to be compelled to testify against the other when the testifying spouse is the victim of the defendant spouse's criminal act and/or when the criminal act takes place before marriage. . . .

[B]eginning at about 7:00 p.m. on May 16, 1993, and continuing until approximately 2:00 a.m. the following morning, Kenneth Taylor, then a New Orleans police officer, assaulted, threatened to kill and brutally beat his then-girlfriend, Glenda Richard. He used his fists as well as his police-issue flashlight and 9mm Beretta semiautomatic service weapon to pummel the victim into a state of semi-consciousness. It is alleged that several times in these hours, Taylor placed his Beretta inside the victim's mouth and threatened to pull the trigger. After the beating, Taylor put Richard and the couple's five-month-old daughter into his car and drove them to the Richard home in Violet, Louisiana. The victim's sister called an ambulance, and Glenda Richard spent several days at Chalmette Medical Center and Charity Hospital recovering from her injuries. . . . She gave a typed statement describing the beating, executed an affidavit setting forth her desire to prosecute, and appeared on videotape. Richard was unable to read her statement because her eyes were swollen shut and because the injuries to her mouth rendered coherent speech difficult, but the video recorded her acknowledgment that the typed statement describing the attack was her own.

[Taylor was arrested and charged with aggravated battery.] On the morning of trial, the victim appeared with her own attorney to advise that she no longer wished to prosecute and, further, that she would not testify against the defendant. [The state first entered a *nolle prosequi* but later reinstituted prosecution.] [F]ollowing Taylor's arraignment in January of 1994, a status hearing was scheduled for February 24. At the hearing, the prosecution learned that the victim and the defendant were married February 14, 1994. . . . The state then filed a motion *in limine* which sought: (1) to bar the victim's assertion of a claim of spousal privilege, and (2) to have her written, oral and video-taped statements declared admissible. The state made an oral motion that the victim be compelled to testify. . . . The trial judge denied the state's motion with the following remarks:

> . . . I think if this woman's crazy enough to want to get beat up by her husband to within an inch of her life, and she wants to go back and marry him, that's her business. And I couldn't stop her if she wanted to get up on a ledge and jump off the building, if I wasn't close to her. It's her life. I've seen the pictures. I think she's crazy. But what am I going to do? . . .

[The state appealed.]

The spousal witness privilege in Louisiana has a long history and can be traced to the common law. . . . The common law provided that the husband and wife were incompetent and disqualified from testifying against one another. . . . One of the exceptions from the disqualification of the spouses to testify for or against one another was where the wife had sustained a personal injury from her husband. [The rationale for the disqualification was respect for marital privacy, but the law holds that when one spouse attempts to harm the other, the necessity for the exception no longer exists.] . . .

[The spousal witness privilege provides]:

> In a criminal case or in commitment or interdiction proceedings, a witness spouse has a privilege not to testify against the other spouse. This privilege terminates upon the annulment of the marriage, legal separation, or divorce of the spouses. [LSA-C.E. art. 505].

This privilege is held by the witness spouse and can be waived by her. . . . On the other hand, the confidential communication privilege is found in LSA-C.E. art. 504 [providing]:

> B. *Confidential communications privilege.* Each spouse has a privilege during and after the marriage to refuse to disclose, and to prevent the other spouse from disclosing, confidential communications with the other spouse while they were husband and wife.
> C. *Confidential communications; exceptions.* This privilege does not apply:
>   (1) In a criminal case in which one spouse is charged with a crime against the person or property of the other spouse or of a child of either. . . .

. . . The fact that the defendant spouse can invoke the confidential communications privilege led the legislature to create a statutory exception in cases where "one spouse is charged with a crime against the person or property of the other spouse or a child of either." . . .

The state contends that the court should establish an exception to the spousal witness privilege in cases where one spouse is the victim of abuse by the other spouse, as is the case with the confidential communication privilege. The state believes that the refusal of this court to [apply such an exception would hinder justice because the testifying spouse could simply invoke the spousal witness privilege.] It is argued that this would contravene the purpose of the evidence statutes "to secure fairness and efficiency in administration of the law of evidence to the end that truth may be ascertained and proceedings justly determined." Additionally, the state argues that the spousal witness privilege should not apply in this case and all cases where the crime occurs before marriage and the marriage between the victim and the defendant is used as a means to foreclose the victim from testifying at the criminal trial. . . .

The spousal witness privilege [was] recently affirmed by the legislature when it was considered and included in the Evidence Code adopted in 1992 without any exception as to victim spouses. As a longstanding and recently affirmed legislative enactment, the court would not be justified in reading into the statute an exception purposely omitted by the legislature, regardless of the court's view as to whether or not such an exception represents better policy.

Similarly, the code article makes no exception for acts occurring prior to marriage. It is generally held that the competency of one spouse as a witness depends on the existence of the relationship at the time he or she is offered as a witness, and not upon whether the relationship existed at the time of the occurrence of the events about which he or she is expected to testify. There is no exception in the governing Louisiana code article making the spousal witness privilege inapplicable to testimony about acts occurring prior to marriage.

However, the dynamics of spousal abuse and domestic violence cannot be ignored. Fear, self-blame, and other emotional factors often leave a battered spouse unable to make a sound judgment as to whether to testify against an abusive spouse. Exercise of the spousal witness privilege may be the result of coercion, fear, subjugation, or undue influence, perhaps not even consciously recognized by the abused spouse in some circumstances.

Recognizing these dynamics, and the barrier the spousal witness privilege erects to the prosecution of criminal offenses which are, after all, offenses against society as a whole, the privilege has been legislatively abolished in many states, and judicially limited in decisions of other state and federal courts.

While we do not feel justified or empowered to impose by judicial fiat a victim spouse exception to the legislatively established spousal witness privilege, we nevertheless feel justified and even compelled to limit exercise of the privilege where facts and circumstances established by proper evidence indicate the privilege is being exercised because of fear, threats, or coercion, especially where the marriage giving rise to the privilege is itself the result of fear, threats, or coercion or a mere sham confected to make the privilege available. We do not believe it was the legislative intent to make the privilege available under circumstances such as these, where sanctity of the marriage and marital harmony are hardly served. Also, a defendant should not be able to prevent the introduction of damaging evidence through threats, fear or coercion of a spouse witness anymore than any other witness.

Thus, in a case where the testifying spouse is the victim of the offense charged, and where the evidence supports a finding that the victim spouse asserting the spousal witness privilege is more probably than not acting under fear, threats or coercion, or that the marriage itself is a sham confected for the purpose of making the privilege available, the purpose of the privilege is not served and may, in the court's discretion, be considered as not applicable.

Applying these precepts to the instant case, we note that the evidence was not fully developed at the hearing held in the district court. Nevertheless, the facts established raise a strong inference of both fear and coercion and a sham marriage. The alleged brutal beating, the initial willingness of the victim spouse to cooperate with the law enforcement authorities, the change of heart on the day of trial, the subsequent marriage after charges were reinstated, and . . . the lack of evidence that the victim and defendant have actually established a genuine marital relationship, create an inference that circumstances exist that would support the non-applicability of the privilege in this case. [W]e deem it in the interest of justice and the development of the true facts upon which a determination of the applicability of the privilege can be made to remand this case to the trial court for reconsideration and the taking of further evidence on the issue of whether the privilege is to be applied in this case and whether the victim spouse can be compelled to testify. . . .

Notes and Questions

1. *Spousal privileges: common law. Taylor* addresses the issue of spousal testimonial privileges and exceptions. At common law, a wife could not testify either for or against her husband. This spousal disqualification rule had medieval origins: (1) an accused was not permitted to testify in his own behalf because such testimony would be self-serving; and (2) because of the doctrine of *coverture*, the husband and wife were one legal entity, as represented by the husband, and "what was inadmissible from the lips of the defendant-husband was also inadmissible from his wife." Trammel v. United States, 445 U.S. 40, 44 (1980) (explaining background). The rule of spousal disqualification evolved from a rule of absolute disqualification to a rule of privilege. Id.

The common law recognized two types of marital privileges. Under the confidential marital communications privilege, private communications between husband and wife are privileged absolutely; either spouse may invoke this privilege.

This rule is independent of the privilege of a spouse to exclude adverse evidence about the other spouse's criminal acts and communications in the presence of third parties. Which privilege was at issue in *Taylor*? Why? The issue of a victim's non-cooperation in explored later in this chapter, Section B6.

2. *Modern view.* All 50 states retain the spousal confidential communications privilege. Thirty-one states recognize the adverse spousal testimonial privilege. Only 4 states vest the latter privilege in the defendant-spouse. R. Michael Cassidy, Reconsidering Spousal Privileges After *Crawford*, 33 Am. J. Crim. L. 339, 364-366 (2006). What explains the wider adoption of the former privilege?

3. *Rationale.* What rationale explains the marital privileges? Cf. State v. Bonaparte, 660 P.2d 334, 336 (Wash. Ct. App. 1983) (differentiating the rationales). Does vesting the privilege in the witness-spouse promote marital harmony? How do these rationales apply in cases of intimate partner violence? In *Taylor*? Are there sound policy reasons to compel an unwilling partner to testify? Or, should the criminal justice system honor the wishes of the victim? How should these considerations apply in *Taylor*?

What is the effect of the government forcing a spouse to testify against her will? Might that compulsion "further inflame domestic differences"? *Trammel*, 445 U.S. at 46 (citing Hawkins v. United States, 358 U.S. 74, 79 (1958)). Is the exercise of such governmental compulsion in a marital relationship appropriate? See Richard O. Lempert, A Right to Every Woman's Evidence, 66 Iowa L. Rev. 725 (1981) (arguing that *Trammel* encourages the government to turn spouses against each other by convincing them to testify against each other).

4. *Holding.* As *Taylor* explains, a statutory exception existed in Louisiana for interspousal crimes for purposes of the confidential communications privilege but not for the spousal disqualification privilege. What explains the different treatment? Why did *Taylor* refuse to read such an exception into the spousal disqualification statute? What circumstances led the court to remand to the trial court to develop facts upon which a determination of the applicability of the privilege could be made? On remand, how might the prosecutor make the necessary showing? How difficult is that task likely to be?

5. *Influence of* Trammel. Law reform regarding the adverse spousal testimonial privilege stems from the U.S. Supreme Court's decision in *Trammel*, supra, concerning the federal common law of marital privilege. In *Trammel*, a man was indicted for conspiracy to import, and for importing, heroin. The indictment also named several unindicted co-conspirators, including his wife. In exchange for a grant of immunity, the wife agreed to testify against her husband. At trial, the husband attempted to prevent her from testifying by asserting the spousal testimonial privilege. Rejecting petitioner's claim, the Supreme Court held that the witness-spouse *alone* has a privilege to refuse to testify adversely. *Trammel* addressed only the spousal disqualification rule and left the confidential communications rule intact.

Trammel had several consequences. First, different rules now apply in federal, and many state, courts concerning the different types of marital privileges. Second, *Trammel* influenced many states to limit a defendant's ability to assert the adverse spousal privilege. Milton C. Regan, Jr., Spousal Privilege and the Meanings of Marriage, 81 Va. L. Rev. 2045, 2060-2061 (1995).

6. *Exception for familial offenses.* At common law, the spousal disqualification privilege was inapplicable in cases of *interspousal* crimes. Many states (but not Louisiana in the principal case) subsequently codified this exception. See, e.g., Cal.

Evid. Code §972. Some states extended the exception to include child abuse by a spouse. See, e.g., W. Va. Code Ann. §57-3-3. What explains the extension?

7. *Legacy of* Trammel *specifically for domestic violence offenses. Trammel* had important implications for the prosecution of domestic violence by encouraging states to adopt exceptions to the marital privileges for intraspousal crimes. As one commentator explains:

> [T]he Supreme Court in *Trammel* suggested in dicta that federal law might support an exception to both the adverse testimonial privilege and the confidential communication privilege for "cases in which one spouse commits a crime against the other." The Advisory Committee [that is, Advisory Committee on Federal Rules of Evidence, 51 F.R.D. 315, 370 (1971)] had recommended an exception to the adverse testimonial privilege for crimes against the spouse or a child of marriage, to prevent the "grave injustice" that would otherwise occur. It had not recommended such an exception to the confidential communication privilege because the Advisory Committee had suggested eliminating that latter privilege entirely. However, with a brief citation to Wigmore, the Court in *Trammel* suggested, without deciding, that "similar exceptions" should be recognized to both privileges.

Cassidy, supra, at 363.

8. *Other exceptions.* The law recognizes additional exceptions to the marital privileges.

a. *Separated spouses.* Some courts have held if the spouses are permanently separated at the time of the communication, the spousal privilege is inapplicable. See, e.g., United States v. Singleton, 260 F.3d 1295, 1299 (11th Cir. 2001). Why? How might this exception apply in the context of domestic violence?

b. *Fraudulent marriage.* A few states adopted a "fraudulent marriage" exception to the marital privileges. See, e.g., Wash. Rev. Code Ann. §5.60.060(1) (specifying that adverse spousal privilege does not apply if marriage occurred "subsequent to the filing of formal charges against the defendant"). Should more states adopt such an exception? Should it be applicable to both marital privileges? See, e.g., Glover v. State, 836 N.E.2d 414 (Ind. 2005) (refusing to engraft "fraudulent marriage exception" to the confidential communications privilege to exclude the testimony of a woman who married a co-worker solely to prevent his deportation). What does *Taylor* hold? If the exception applies, how would a court determine whether a marriage is "fraudulent"?

9. *Abolition?* Because the adverse spousal testimony privilege is riddled with exceptions, it provides many avenues for appeal. Should it be abolished? Should the confidential communications privilege be abolished? What would be the consequences of abolishing them?

10. *Other evidentiary privileges.* All states have an attorney-client privilege, preventing attorneys from revealing private communications, and a physician-patient privilege, preventing a physician from disclosing confidential communications made for the purpose of medical treatment. Many states have similar privileges between clients and social workers, clergy, and psychotherapists. Is it advisable to have a "domestic violence" exception to these particular privileges—particularly in cases in which the victim-witness does not wish to testify against her abuser? For discussion of mandatory reporting laws, see Chapter 10.

Problems

1. Sara, an undocumented immigrant, enters the United States at a border crossing in Texas, where her boyfriend Newton is waiting for her. She is authorized to remain in the country for only 72 hours. Disregarding the restriction allegedly because her pregnancy makes her ill, Sarah and Newton travel for three days in Newton's car to Illinois where their children are residing with a relative. Sara's immigration status is discovered two months later when Newton is arrested for stabbing Sara during a violent argument. Newton is charged with aggravated assault and transporting an undocumented immigrant in violation of federal immigration law. Sara marries Newton one month after his indictment. She is called to testify regarding whether he knowingly violated federal law. Newton appeals his conviction, contending that the trial judge should have excluded Sara's testimony because of the marital privilege.

Which privilege was allegedly violated by Sara's testimony? Should the privilege apply in a "joint criminal enterprise," such as this situation? Should the court apply a fraudulent marriage exception? Does the rationale underlying the marital privilege apply? What is the countervailing interest? How should the judge rule? Compare United States v. Van Drunen, 501 F.2d 1393 (7th Cir. 1974), with Appeal of Maltifano, 633 F.2d 276 (3d Cir. 1980).

2. Robert, his wife Trudy, and his friend Pete formulate a plan whereby Robert plans to steal $3,000 from a drug dealer. Robert changes the plan at the last minute and decides, instead, to kill his landlord and steal the money from him. Shortly after he commits the murder, Robert is arrested and charged with first-degree murder. While awaiting trial, Robert writes a letter to Trudy from jail in which he recites details of the crime and advises Trudy how to testify at trial. The letter is confiscated and introduced as evidence at his trial.

At trial, Trudy testifies that she considered her marriage over when Robert was arrested. She claims that the marriage had been rocky for some time because she was a victim of domestic violence. She asserts that she has not seen Robert since he has been arrested. She explains that, although they are still married, she is waiting for Robert to be sent to prison before she seeks a divorce. After Robert is convicted, he appeals, arguing that the judge should have excluded the letter as well as Trudy's testimony pursuant to marital privilege. Which privilege or privileges does Robert contend was (were) violated? Should the privilege(s) apply? How does the rationale underlying the privilege apply? What is the countervailing rationale? How should the judge rule? See State v. Winters, 137 S.W.3d 641 (Tenn. Crim. App. 2003).

2. Marital Rape Exemption

■ **PEOPLE v. LIBERTA**

474 N.E.2d 567 (N.Y. 1984), cert. denied, 471 U.S. 1020 (1985)

WACHTLER, Judge.

[Defendant charges that the marital rape exemption in New York's rape and sodomy statutes violates the Equal Protection Clause.]

Defendant Mario Liberta and Denise Liberta were married in 1978. Shortly after the birth of their son, in October of that year, Mario began to beat Denise. In early 1980 Denise brought a proceeding in the Family Court in Erie County seeking protection from the defendant. On April 30, 1980, a temporary order of protection was issued to her by the Family Court. Under this order, the defendant was to move out and remain away from the family home, and stay away from Denise. The order provided that the defendant could visit with his son once each weekend.

On the weekend of March 21, 1981, Mario, who was then living in a motel, did not visit his son. On Tuesday, March 24, 1981 he called Denise to ask if he could visit his son on that day. Denise would not allow the defendant to come to her house, but she did agree to allow him to pick up their son and her and take them both back to his motel after being assured that a friend of his would be with them at all times. The defendant and his friend picked up Denise and their son and the four of them drove to defendant's motel.

When they arrived at the motel the friend left. As soon as only Mario, Denise, and their son were alone in the motel room, Mario attacked Denise, threatened to kill her, and forced her to perform fellatio on him and to engage in sexual intercourse with him. The son was in the room during the entire episode, and the defendant forced Denise to tell their son to watch what the defendant was doing to her.

The defendant allowed Denise and their son to leave shortly after the incident. Denise, after going to her parents' home, went to a hospital to be treated for scratches on her neck and bruises on her head and back, all inflicted by her husband. She also went to the police station, and on the next day she swore out a felony complaint against the defendant. On July 15, 1981, the defendant was indicted for rape in the first degree and sodomy in the first degree.

Section 130.35 of the Penal Code provides in relevant part that "A male is guilty of rape in the first degree when he engages in sexual intercourse with a female . . . by forcible compulsion." "Female," for purposes of the rape statute, is defined as "any female person who is not married to the actor" (Penal Law, §130.00, subd. 4). Section 130.50 of the Penal Law provides in relevant part that "a person is guilty of sodomy in the first degree when he engages in deviate sexual intercourse with another person . . . by forcible compulsion." "Deviate sexual intercourse" is defined as "sexual conduct between persons not married to each other consisting of contact between the penis and the anus, the mouth and penis, or the mouth and the vulva" (Penal Law, §130.00, subd. 2). Thus, due to the "not married" language in the definitions of "female" and "deviate sexual intercourse," there is a "marital exemption" for both forcible rape and forcible sodomy. The marital exemption itself, however, has certain exemptions. For purposes of the rape and sodomy statutes, a husband and wife are considered to be "not married" if at the time of the sexual assault they [are living apart pursuant to a court order or a separation agreement].

Defendant moved to dismiss the indictment, asserting that because he and Denise were still married at the time of the incident[1] he came within the "marital exemption" to both rape and sodomy. [He also contended that the rape and sodomy] statutes violate equal protection because they are under-inclusive classifications which burden him, but not others similarly situated. . . .

A. The Marital Exemption

[U]nder the Penal Law a married man ordinarily cannot be convicted of forcibly raping or sodomizing his wife. This is the so-called marital exemption for

---

1. The defendant and Denise were divorced several months after the assault in the motel room.

rape. . . . The assumption, even before the marital exemption was codified, that a man could not be guilty of raping his wife, is traceable to a statement made by the 17th century English jurist Lord Hale, who wrote: "[T]he husband cannot be guilty of a rape committed by himself upon his lawful wife, for by their mutual matrimonial consent and contract the wife hath given up herself in this kind unto her husband, which she cannot retract" (1 Hale, History of Pleas of the Crown, p.629). Although Hale cited no authority for his statement it was relied on by State Legislatures which enacted rape statutes with a marital exemption and by courts which established a common-law exemption for husbands. . . .

We find that there is no rational basis for distinguishing between marital rape and nonmarital rape. The various rationales which have been asserted in defense of the exemption are either based upon archaic notions about the consent and property rights incident to marriage or are simply unable to withstand even the slightest scrutiny. . . .

Lord Hale's notion of an irrevocable implied consent by a married woman to sexual intercourse has been cited most frequently in support of the marital exemption. Any argument based on a supposed consent, however, is untenable. Rape is not simply a sexual act to which one party does not consent. Rather, it is a degrading, violent act which violates the bodily integrity of the victim and frequently causes severe, long-lasting physical and psychic harm. To ever imply consent to such an act is irrational and absurd. Other than in the context of rape statutes, marriage has never been viewed as giving a husband the right to coerced intercourse on demand. Certainly, then, a marriage license should not be viewed as a license for a husband to forcibly rape his wife with impunity. A married woman has the same right to control her own body as does an unmarried woman. . . .

The other traditional justifications for the marital exemption were the common-law doctrines that a woman was the property of her husband and that the legal existence of the woman was "incorporated and consolidated into that of the husband" (1 Blackstone's Commentaries [1966 ed.], p.430). . . . Both these doctrines, of course, have long been rejected in this State. . . .

Because the traditional justifications for the marital exemption no longer have any validity, other arguments have been advanced in its defense. The first of these recent rationales, which is stressed by the People in this case, is that the marital exemption protects against governmental intrusion into marital privacy and promotes reconciliation of the spouses, and thus, that elimination of the exemption would be disruptive to marriages. While protecting marital privacy and encouraging reconciliation are legitimate State interests, there is no rational relation between allowing a husband to forcibly rape his wife and these interests. The marital exemption simply does not further marital privacy because this right of privacy protects consensual acts, not violent sexual assaults (see Griswold v. Connecticut, 381 U.S. 479, 485-486 [(1965)]). Just as a husband cannot invoke a right of marital privacy to escape liability for beating his wife, he cannot justifiably rape his wife under the guise of a right to privacy.

Similarly, it is not tenable to argue that elimination of the marital exemption would disrupt marriages because it would discourage reconciliation. [I]f the marriage has already reached the point where intercourse is accomplished by violent assault it is doubtful that there is anything left to reconcile. . . .

Another rationale sometimes advanced in support of the marital exemption is that marital rape would be a difficult crime to prove. A related argument is that allowing such prosecutions could lead to fabricated complaints by "vindictive" wives. The difficulty of proof argument is based on the problem of showing lack of consent. Proving lack of consent, however, is often the most difficult part of any rape prosecution, particularly where the rapist and the victim had a prior relationship. Similarly, the possibility that married women will fabricate complaints would seem to be no greater than the possibility of unmarried women doing so. The criminal justice system, with all of its built-in safeguards, is presumed to be capable of handling any false complaints. Indeed, if the possibility of fabricated complaints were a basis for not criminalizing behavior which would otherwise be sanctioned, virtually all crimes other than homicides would go unpunished.

The final argument in defense of the marital exemption is that marital rape is not as serious an offense as other rape and is thus adequately dealt with by the possibility of prosecution under criminal statutes, such as assault statutes, which provide for less severe punishment. [T]here is no evidence to support the argument that marital rape has less severe consequences than other rape. On the contrary, numerous studies have shown that marital rape is frequently quite violent and generally has *more* severe, traumatic effects on the victim than other rape. . . . We agree with the other courts which have analyzed the exemption, which have been unable to find any present justification for it. Justice Holmes wrote: "It is revolting to have no better reason for a rule of law than that so it was laid down in the time of Henry IV. It is still more revolting if the grounds upon which it was laid down have vanished long since, and the rule simply persists from blind imitation of the past" (Holmes, The Path of the Law, 10 Harv. L. Rev. 457, 469 [(1897)]). This statement is an apt characterization of the marital exemption; it lacks a rational basis, and therefore violates the equal protection clauses of both the Federal and State Constitutions. . . .

B. The Exemption for Females

Under the Penal Law only males can be convicted of rape in the first degree. [The court then proceeds to examine the sex-based classification to determine whether it is substantially related to the achievement of an important governmental objective.] The first argument advanced by the People in support of the exemption for females is that because only females can become pregnant the State may constitutionally differentiate between forcible rapes of females and forcible rapes of males. This court and the United States Supreme Court have upheld statutes which subject males to criminal liability for engaging in sexual intercourse with underage females without the converse being true (Michael M. v. Sonoma County Superior Court, 450 U.S. 464 [(1981)]). The rationale behind these decisions was that the primary purpose of such "statutory rape" laws is to protect against the harm caused by teenage pregnancies, there being no need to provide the same protection to young males.

There is no evidence, however, that preventing pregnancies is a primary purpose of the statute prohibiting forcible rape, nor does such a purpose seem likely. Rather, the very fact that the statute proscribes "forcible compulsion" shows that its overriding purpose is to protect a woman from an unwanted forcible, and often violent sexual intrusion into her body. Thus, due to the different purposes behind forcible rape laws and "statutory" (consensual) rape laws, the cases upholding the gender discrimination in the latter are not decisive with respect to the former, and the People cannot meet their burden here by simply stating that only females can become pregnant.

The People also claim that the discrimination is justified because a female rape victim "faces the probability of medical, sociological, and psychological problems unique to her gender." This same argument, when advanced in support of the discrimination in the statutory rape laws, was rejected by this court [previously], and it is no more convincing in the present case. . . .

Finally, the People suggest that a gender-neutral law for forcible rape is unnecessary, and that therefore the present law is constitutional, because a woman either cannot actually rape a man or such attacks, if possible, are extremely rare. Although the "physiologically impossible" argument has been accepted by several courts, it is simply wrong. The argument is premised on the notion that a man cannot engage in sexual intercourse unless he is sexually aroused, and if he is aroused then he is consenting to intercourse. "Sexual intercourse" however, "occurs upon any penetration, however slight" (Penal Law, §130.00); this degree of contact can be achieved without a male being aroused and thus without his consent.

As to the "infrequency" argument, while forcible sexual assaults by females upon males are undoubtedly less common than those by males upon females, this numerical disparity cannot by itself make the gender discrimination constitutional. Women may well be responsible for a far lower number of all serious crimes than are men, but such a disparity would not make it permissible for the State to punish only men who commit, for example, robbery. . . .

[Because a gender-neutral law would better serve the state's objective of deterring and punishing forcible sexual assaults,] we find that section 130.35 of the Penal Law violates equal protection because it exempts females from criminal liability for forcible rape. [I]t is now the law of this State that any person who engages in sexual intercourse or deviate sexual intercourse with any other person by forcible compulsion is guilty of either rape in the first degree or sodomy in the first degree. Because the statutes under which the defendant was convicted are not being struck down, his conviction is affirmed. . . .

Notes and Questions

1. *Common law.* At common law, a husband was exempt from prosecution for raping his wife. This legal principle, termed the "marital rape exemption," was first articulated as *Liberta* explains, in an influential statement by the British jurist, Sir Matthew Hale. American legislatures and courts enacted legal policy for centuries that incorporated the marital rape exemption based on Hale's assertion that marriage signified a wife's presumed and irrevocable consent to her husband's sexual demands. Jill Elaine Hasday, Contest and Consent: A Legal History of Marital Rape, 88 Cal. L. Rev. 1373, 1396-1398 (2000) (criticizing Hale's view as grounded in nineteenth-century regulation of marriage and sexuality).

2. *Nineteenth-century law reform movement.* Nineteenth-century feminists waged an active public campaign against the idea of the husband's right to forced sexual intercourse. Feminists demanded women's right to control their own person. This right, they claimed, was essential to redress unwanted childbearing. Only by achieving this objective, feminists contended, could women achieve political and economic equality. Id. at 1417-1433.

Despite nineteenth-century reform of married women's property rights, the early feminist movement met with little success reforming the law of marital rape. However, some courts began to recognize that a husband's excessive sexual demands constituted a ground for cruelty-based divorce—but only if the situation endangered the wife's health. Id. at 1467-1468. How likely was this reform to help nineteenth-century victims of domestic violence?

3. *Privacy rationale.* The marital rape exemption was a stalwart feature of American law until *Liberta.* Both statutes at issue in *Liberta* contained a marital rape exemption. On what basis did the defendant contend that the statutes were unconstitutional? What was the court's response?

A traditional rationale for the marital rape exemption was the protection of the right to privacy. Did *Liberta* address the concept(s) of family privacy, marital privacy, or individual privacy? What arguments supported this rationale, according to the court? Why does the court decide that the marital rape exemption does not accomplish its objective? In opposition to this view, one commentator argues that the marital right to privacy should prevail over prosecution of spousal rapists, to wit:

> [I]t appears unseemly to permit the public to examine the intimacies of a marital relationship. Allowing the public this examination is to encourage a type of public voyeurism. Second, one or both of the spouses may feel embarrassed about having the details of their private marital life exposed to the public view. Furthermore, it is questionable whether the complaining spouse alone has the right to waive the marital privacy right of the couple by presenting the matter before the courts and the public. . . .

Michael Gary Hilf, Marital Privacy and Spousal Rape, 16 New Eng. L. Rev. 31, 34 (1980). Is such reasoning persuasive? Why should the marital right to privacy supersede the individual right to privacy? See also Morgan Lee Wooley, Note, Marital Rape: A Unique Blend of Domestic Violence and Non-Marital Rape Issues, 18 Hastings Women's L.J. 269 (2007) (discussing tension between family privacy and victim protection).

4. *Living apart.* As *Liberta* reveals, prior to the reform movement, a few states permitted prosecution only if the spouses were living apart at the time of the incident or if one spouse had initiated legal proceedings at the time of the rape. Why should it matter whether the husband and wife are living apart? Does this requirement help establish the "legitimacy" of the women as victims? See Susan Carol Randall & Vicki McNickle Rose, Barriers to Becoming a "Successful" Rape Victim, in Women and Crime in America 336, 342 (Lee H. Bowker ed., 1981). What additional factors in *Liberta* establish Denise Liberta's legitimacy as a victim? Should states continue to require that the spouses live separate and apart? See, e.g., Walker v. Commonwealth, 2005 WL 2737510 (Va. Ct. App. 2005) (evidence was sufficient to show that spouses lived separate and apart as required for marital rape conviction).

5. *Modern reforms: criticisms.* Following *Liberta,* courts and legislatures gradually abrogated the marital rape exception. Despite widespread reform, however, many states still treat marital rape differently than stranger rape. Some states impose special procedural requirements (for example, reports to designated professionals or within certain time periods); subject marital rape to less severe sanctions; or criminalize a narrower range of offenses. See Michelle J. Anderson, Marital Immunity, Intimate Relationships, and Improper Inferences: A New Law on Sexual Offenses by Intimates, 54 Hastings L.J. 1465, 1468-1473 (2003); Jill Elaine Hasday, Protecting Them From Themselves: The Persistence of Mutual Benefits Arguments for Sex and Race Inequality, 84 N.Y.U. L. Rev. 1464, 1471-1472 (2009); Emily J. Sack, Is Domestic Violence a Crime? Intimate Partner Rape as Allegory, 24 St. John's

J. Legal Comment. 535, 554-555 (2010). Do special distinctions survive constitutional challenges? See, e.g., People v. Alexis, 828 N.Y.S.2d 793 (Sup. Ct. 2007) (invalidating marital exemption to sexual abuse in the third degree).

6. *Same-sex marital rape.* How can marital rape laws be revised to enhance protections for victims? For example, should they be applicable to same-sex couples? See generally Marc Spindelman, Surviving Lawrence v. Texas, 102 Mich. L. Rev. 1615, 1643-1648 (2004); Conor Berry, Insemination Fight Ends in Wife's Arrest, Berkshire Eagle, Mar. 13, 2009 (recounting arrest of Massachusetts wife for domestic assault for allegedly attempting to artificially inseminate her wife with the former's brother's semen, without the female partner's consent).

Marital rape is also explored, as a special type of domestic violence, in Chapter 4.

Problems

1. Mr. and Mrs. Adair have been married for six years. When marital problems arise, Mrs. Adair begins sleeping in the basement. One evening, she is awakened by her husband who sexually assaults her. He is charged with two counts of third-degree criminal sexual conduct based on her allegations of digital-anal penetration and digital-oral penetration against her will. Defendant attempts to introduce evidence of specific instances of his wife's subsequent consensual sexual relations with him, including the couple's practice of similar sexual activity and their consensual sexual relations within thirty days prior to the alleged assault. The prosecutor seeks to exclude such evidence as barred by a rape-shield statute that precludes admission of the victim's past sexual conduct "unless material to a fact at issue" and "unless its prejudicial effect is outweighed by its probative value." How should the court rule? See People v. Adair, 550 N.W.2d 505 (Mich. 1996).

2. Husband and Wife have been married for more than 20 years. Before marrying, the parties agree, in writing, that they will maintain separate residences. They agree to visit each other on weekends in various locations according to an agreed-on schedule. Following years of emotional neglect and abuse and several occasions of marital rape, Wife files for divorce on the grounds of cruel and inhuman treatment. The court finds sufficient proof that Husband committed marital rape on several occasions. On appeal, Husband argues that it was impossible for Wife to establish that marital rape constituted cruel and inhuman treatment because the parties did not cohabit. What result? See K. v. B., 784 N.Y.S.2d 76 (App. Div. 2004).

3. Prior Act Testimony

■ PEOPLE v. BROWN
121 Cal. Rptr. 3d 828 (Ct. App. 2011)

POOCHIGIAN, J.

Appellant/defendant Eddie Brown was charged and convicted of first degree murder in the homicide of his former girlfriend, Bridget Colmore. . . . As of 2001, Bridget had dated defendant for two years. She was a petite woman and weighed about 112 pounds. Defendant was five feet nine inches tall, and weighed 195 pounds.

Defendant had two years of training in taekwondo, and his family and friends knew he was into martial arts. He had a felony conviction for selling drugs in 1998.

At some point between November 2000 and March 2001, Bridget told her co-worker, Margarita Ibarra, about an argument she had the prior evening with her boyfriend, "Eddie." Bridget told Ibarra that "Eddie" choked her during the argument, and she demonstrated how "Eddie" put his hands around her neck. Bridget said her neck still hurt and Ibarra could see discoloration on her neck. Bridget said she could not believe that "Eddie" put his hands on her. Bridget said that as he choked her, she told him to leave her alone, and she either kicked or pushed him away.

Around July 2001, Bridget and defendant were in the mall together. George Ybarra, who previously dated Bridget, was walking nearby and saw the couple. Ybarra smiled at Bridget and tried to greet her, but Bridget shook her head and looked very uncomfortable. A few days later, Bridget told Ybarra that she could not say hello to him because "'it would have been harmful for me and possibly for you.'"

During the summer of 2001, Bridget told Margaret Ibarra that she was no longer seeing "Eddie." Bridget's family believed they broke up a few months before she disappeared. However, defendant kept calling her home telephone and cell phone, and members of her family testified that she tried to screen her calls to avoid speaking with him.

In July or August 2001, Bridget met Patrick McKinnie and they started dating. Shortly before Bridget disappeared, McKinnie was spending the weekend at Bridget's house when defendant unexpectedly arrived. Bridget and McKinnie were outside, defendant walked up to Bridget, and she told McKinnie that defendant was "Eddie," her former boyfriend. Defendant told Bridget that he needed to talk to her. Defendant said, "What is this[?] What is this [?]" McKinnie asked what the problem was. Defendant replied, "You know what the problem is." McKinnie said he didn't know. Bridget told defendant she was going to call the police, and defendant left. When McKinnie drove away from her house the next day, defendant drove very close behind and then alongside McKinnie's car, and motioned for McKinnie to pull over. McKinnie ignored defendant and drove past him.

A few weeks before her death, Bridget spoke to another former boyfriend, Jesse Gutierrez. Bridget was concerned and said defendant threatened her life because she broke off their relationship. Bridget said that defendant said he was going to kill her and whoever was with her. About a week before she disappeared, Bridget drove her children to a restaurant for dinner, and her young son noticed that defendant was following them in his car. . . .

Around 5:00 p.m. on September 10, 2001, Bridget called George Ybarra. She said she had met a new man and she was excited about their relationship. Ybarra had recently seen Bridget with defendant, and he asked why she was still dating defendant because that relationship was not healthy. Bridget said she had to go to defendant's house that evening and pick up some things. Ybarra urged Bridget not to go, but advised her to take her sister if she did.

Around 5:00 p.m. on September 11, 2001, Bridget received a call while she was cooking dinner for her family at her Visalia home. Her 14-year-old niece heard Bridget refer to the caller as "Eddie," and say, "Eddie, what do you want[?]" Bridget was upset but she stayed on the telephone, went into her bedroom, and closed the door. When Bridget emerged from the bedroom, she was very upset. She told her niece to finish cooking dinner and said she would be right back. Bridget walked out of her house and her family never saw her again. . . . Bridget was later seen walking into defendant's Visalia apartment, just before it was dark. . . . [Defendant later disclosed to his half-sister that he had strangled Bridget and buried her body in a cornfield.]

Defendant was charged with first-degree murder. [At trial,] the prosecution moved to introduce evidence pursuant to section 1109, that defendant committed prior acts of domestic violence against Bridget and four other girlfriends. [The court held that the evidence was admissible.] The four women who previously dated defendant separately testified about a series of domestic violence acts that defendant committed against them. They testified that he followed them when they were out with other people. They testified about specific incidents when defendant beat, kicked, choked, and threatened to kill them. They testified the incidents occurred both during and after they were involved in relationships with defendant, and often as a result of arguments when he was jealous and accused them of seeing other men.

At trial, defendant testified he was still dating Bridget at the time of her death, and insisted he never touched Bridget except on the night that she died. Defendant claimed Bridget unexpectedly arrived at his apartment that night, attacked him with a hammer, he pushed her away, she flipped over his couch, and she died by accident. . . . [He] denied committing the domestic violence acts described by his previous girlfriends and claimed he was never jealous of their relationships with other men. Defendant admitted that he was involved in several altercations with some of the women and their boyfriends but claimed he only intervened when he was concerned about the safety of the children he had fathered with those women. [Defendant was convicted of first-degree murder and sentenced to 25 years to life.]

ADMISSION OF PRIOR ACTS OF DOMESTIC VIOLENCE IN A MURDER PROSECUTION

[The court begins its analysis by setting forth the requirements of California Evidence Code §1109, providing that "in a criminal action in which the defendant is accused of *an offense involving domestic violence*, evidence of the defendant's commission of other domestic violence" may be admitted for the purpose of showing a propensity to commit such crimes. Even if the evidence is admissible, the trial court must still determine whether the probative value of the evidence is substantially outweighed by the probability the evidence will consume an undue amount of time, or create a substantial danger of undue prejudice, confusion of issues, or misleading the jury pursuant to California Evidence Code §352.]

"Evidence of prior criminal acts is ordinarily inadmissible to show a defendant's disposition to commit such acts. However, the Legislature has created exceptions to this rule in cases involving sexual offenses and domestic violence." "[T]he California Legislature has determined the policy considerations favoring the exclusion of evidence of uncharged domestic violence offenses are outweighed in criminal domestic violence cases by the policy considerations favoring the admission of such evidence." . . . "[I]t is apparent that the Legislature considered the difficulties of proof unique to the prosecution of these crimes when compared with other crimes where propensity evidence may be probative but has been historically prohibited."

The admission of prior acts as propensity evidence encompasses both charged and uncharged acts. Moreover, evidence of a prior act may be introduced as propensity evidence even if the defendant was acquitted of criminal charges based upon that act. . . .

ADMISSIBILITY OF SECTION 1109 PROPENSITY EVIDENCE IN A MURDER PROSECUTION

Defendant contends that section 1109 only permits the admission of prior acts of domestic violence in a subsequent prosecution for a domestic violence offense. Defendant argues his prior acts against Bridget and his former girlfriends were inadmissible because he was not charged with committing domestic violence in the instant case, he was charged with murder, and murder is not listed in section 1109 as an offense involving domestic violence. Defendant's contentions raise the question of what is "an offense involving domestic violence" within the meaning of section 1109.

Section 1109 does not contain an enumerated list of offenses which are defined as those "involving" domestic violence. However, section 1109, subdivision (d)(3) provides some guidance on the question:

> "'Domestic violence' has the meaning set forth in Section 13700 of the Penal Code. Subject to a hearing conducted pursuant to Section 352, which shall include consideration of any corroboration and remoteness in time, 'domestic violence' has the further meaning as set forth in Section 6211 of the Family Code, if the act occurred no more than five years before the charged offense."[15]

We thus turn to Penal Code section 13700, which defines "domestic violence" as "*abuse* committed against an adult or a minor who is a spouse, former spouse, cohabitant, former cohabitant, or person with whom the suspect has had a child or *is having or has had a dating or engagement relationship*" (italics added). Bridget was someone with whom defendant had a dating relationship for two years. . . . [Further,] Penal Code section 13700 defines "'[a]buse'" as "*intentionally or recklessly causing or attempting to cause bodily injury, or placing another person in reasonable apprehension of imminent serious bodily injury* to himself or herself, or another." (Cal. Penal Code, §3700, subd. (a), italics added). . . .

The prosecution's theory was that defendant strangled and killed Bridget because he was angry and jealous that she broke up with him and was seeing another man, and that theory was firmly supported by the events leading up to Bridget's death. . . . Based on the prosecution's evidence, defendant was alleged to have "intentionally or recklessly" caused bodily injury to Bridget, and placed her "in reasonable apprehension of imminent serious bodily injury," within the scope of the statutory language, when he fatally strangled her. (Cal. Pen Code, §13700, subd. (a).) Defendant was thus "accused of an offense involving domestic violence" within the meaning of section 1109 when he was charged with the first-degree murder of

---

15. Family Code section 6211 defines domestic violence "more broadly" than the more restrictive provisions of Penal Code section 13700. However, section 1109 limits the Family Code's definitions to domestic violence acts which occurred "no more than five years before the charged offense." (§1109, subd. (d)(3).) The vast majority of defendant's prior acts against his former girlfriends occurred more than five years before Bridget's homicide in 2001. We will thus focus on the domestic violence definitions contained in Penal Code section 13700.

Bridget, and the court properly found that his prior acts of domestic violence were admissible as propensity evidence in this case.

We find support for this conclusion in the legislative history of section 1109:

> [T]he legislative history of the statute recognizes the special nature of domestic violence crime, as follows: "The propensity inference is particularly appropriate in the area of domestic violence because on-going violence and abuse is the norm in domestic violence cases. Not only is there a great likelihood that any one battering episode is part of a larger scheme of dominance and control, that scheme usually escalates in frequency and severity. Without the propensity inference, the escalating nature of domestic violence is likewise masked. If we fail to address the very essence of domestic violence, we will continue to see cases where perpetrators of this violence will beat their intimate partners, even kill them, and go on to beat or kill the next intimate partner. Since criminal prosecution is one of the few factors which may interrupt the escalating pattern of domestic violence, we must be willing to look at that pattern during the criminal prosecution, or we will miss the opportunity to address this problem at all." (Assem. Com. Rep. on Public Safety (June 25, 1996) pp. 3-4.) . . .

"Based on the foregoing, the California Legislature has determined the policy considerations favoring the exclusion of evidence of uncharged domestic violence offenses are outweighed in criminal domestic violence cases by the policy considerations favoring the admission of such evidence." . . .

As applied to the instant case, the facts and circumstances of defendant's relationship with Bridget were indicative of defendant's "'larger scheme of dominance and control'" which he attempted to exercise over Bridget, as he became angry, watched her activities, followed her, and tried to prevent her from having any other relationships. Defendant's prior acts of domestic violence, committed against the four women he dated before Bridget, were also indicative of "cases where perpetrators of this violence will beat their intimate partners, even kill them, and go on to beat or kill the next intimate partner."

Given the legislative history and the language of section 1109, we agree with the trial court's observation in this case that murder is "the ultimate form of domestic violence," and that defendant's prior acts of domestic violence were admissible based on the nature and circumstances of his relationship with and conduct toward Bridget. Defendant was charged with first-degree murder based on strangling Bridget, his former girlfriend, after a lengthy period in which he tried to intimidate her because she chose to break up with him. He was clearly "accused of an offense involving domestic violence" within the meaning of section 1109.

Defendant contends that prior acts of domestic violence are not relevant for any purpose in a murder prosecution because such acts do not permit an inference as to malice or any particular mental state. However, a defendant's propensity to commit domestic violence against a former girlfriend who was murdered, and other prior girlfriends who were assaulted, is relevant and probative to an element of murder, "namely, [defendant's] intentional doing of an act with malice aforethought that resulted in the victim's death." A defendant's pattern of prior acts of domestic violence logically leads to the inference of malice aforethought and culpability for murder. . . . [The appellate court also affirms the trial court ruling that the evidence of defendant's prior acts was more probative than prejudicial.]

Notes and Questions

1. *Prior bad acts: rule.* A longstanding rule of evidence is that prior acts of misconduct (typically, other charged or uncharged crimes and bad acts) are *inadmissible*, except in limited circumstances. This so-called propensity rule, prohibits evidence of prior bad acts (that is, a form of character evidence) to show that a defendant acted in conformity with his bad character. See 1 McCormick On Evidence, supra, at §190. According to the general rule, however, evidence of prior bad acts *is* admissible if it is relevant to a *noncharacter* issue, such as motive, intent, mistake, identity, preparation, and a common scheme or plan. See Fed. R. Evid. 404(b); McCormick, supra. What did California law require for the admission of prior acts of misconduct in *Brown*?

2. *Rationale.* The rationale for the reluctance to admit evidence of prior bad acts is the concern that the judge or jury will be so prejudiced against the defendant that they will convict simply because they find the defendant is a "bad person" and has a propensity to commit similar crimes or similar bad acts. This logic undermines the presumption of innocence as well as the principle that a person is convicted based on proof of the charged crime. Yet, evidence of prior bad acts is especially relevant in partner abuse because of the repetitive nature of the violence. To what extent are the traditional policy arguments that support the propensity rule applicable in the modern context of domestic violence prosecutions? Inapplicable? See Andrew King-Ries, True to Character: Honoring the Intellectual Foundations of the Character Evidence Rule in Domestic Violence Prosecutions, 23 St. Louis U. Pub. L. Rev. 313, 359-365 (2004) (contending that the character evidence rule violates its legitimate purposes in the context of domestic violence).

3. *Holding.* What were the defendant's prior bad acts in *Brown*? Why did the court admit evidence of these acts? Why do you think that the court ruled that these acts were more probative than prejudicial?

4. *California statute: background.* The impetus for passage of the California statute in *Brown* was the O. J. Simpson murder trial. The state legislature enacted the statute in response to public clamor over the trial court's refusal to admit some evidence of Simpson's prior abuse of his ex-wife in an attempt to prove the course of conduct that culminated in her murder. In fact, the statutory exception has been called the "Nicole Brown Simpson law." See Tom Lininger, Evidentiary Issues in Federal Prosecutions of Violence Against Women, 36 Ind. L. Rev. 687, 701-702 (2003). The O. J. Simpson trial is discussed later in this chapter in Section B4.

5. *Domestic violence exceptions in other states.* The California law reform movement influenced passage of similar domestic violence exceptions to the ban on propensity evidence. See id. at 701 n.44 (noting reforms in other states); Jay A. Abarbanel, Comment, In Light of Crawford v. Washington and the Difficult Task of Domestic Violence Prosecutions, Maryland Should Adopt Legislation Making Admissible Prior Acts of Domestic Violence in Domestic Violence Prosecutions, 39 U. Balt. L. Rev. 467, 494-495 (2010) (same).

Should other states enact such exceptions? See generally King-Ries, True to Character, supra, at 315; Pamela Vartabedian, Comment, The Need to Hold Batterers Accountable: Admitting Prior Acts of Abuse in Cases of Domestic Violence, 47 Santa Clara L. Rev. 157 (2007). Does the admission of evidence of prior bad acts in domestic violence cases constitute an impermissible focus on the defendant's character or a focus on the context/pattern of domestic violence? See King-Ries, supra, at 365 (suggesting the latter). Should the rule admitting prior bad act evidence to prove propensity in domestic violence cases be extended to the civil context? See Jane H. Aiken & Jane C. Murphy, Dealing with Complex Evidence of Domestic Violence: A Primer for the Civil Bench, Court Rev., Summer 2002, at 12, 21 (so suggesting).

Some states allow evidence of prior domestic violence involving the defendant and *other victims.* Other states admit evidence of "similar conduct" against the victim or *other family or household members.* See Abarbanel, supra, at 494-495. What are the advantages of broad versus narrow definitions of victims? Would the evidence of prior bad acts have been admissible in *Brown* under each of these statutes?

If the judge rules that prior acts evidence is admissible, should the judge give a limiting instruction advising the jury not to punish the defendant for the past acts but to use such evidence only to show propensity for committing the current crime? See, e.g., Colo. Rev. Stat. §18-6-801.5(5). Are such jury instructions likely to be followed? Should evidence of other acts of domestic violence that a defendant has committed, such as violations of an order of protection, be admissible as evidence of prior bad acts?

6. *Constitutional challenges.* Are statutes constitutional that authorize special domestic violence exceptions to the ban on admission of prior bad acts? What might be the basis of a constitutional challenge? See generally Drew D. Dropkin & James H. McComas, On a Collision Course: Pure Propensity Evidence and Due Process in Alaska, 18 Alaska L. Rev. 177, 179 (2001) (contending that the Alaska exception violates due process by infringing on the presumption of innocence, the standard of proof, and the prohibition against status crimes).

Does balancing the probative value of the evidence against the possible preju-dicial impact surmount the due process challenge? See People v. Cabrera, 61 Cal. Rptr. 3d 373, 379-380 (Ct. App. 2007) (holding that admission of prior acts of domestic violence did not violate defendant's due process rights so long as the trial court was required to balance the probative value of the evidence against its prejudicial impact).

7. *Federal Rules of Evidence.* Most states' evidence codes were influenced by the Federal Rules of Evidence. In the context of federal prosecutions, the Federal Rules of Evidence admit evidence of prior bad acts only for limited purposes (that is, motive, opportunity, intent, preparation, plan, knowledge, identity, or absence of mistake or accident). Fed. R. Evid. 404(b).

a. *Exceptions for sexual assault and molestation.* In 1995, Congress enacted several evidentiary provisions that liberalize the federal ban on prior crimes evidence by means of special exceptions for sexual assault (Fed. R. Evid. 413) and child moles-tation (Fed. R. Evid. 414). What are the justifications for such exceptions? What are the criticisms of such exceptions? See Lininger, Evidentiary Issues in Federal Prosecutions, supra, at 703-704 (criticizing both Rules); Aviva Orenstein, No Bad Men!: A Feminist Critique of Character Evidence in Rape Trials, 49 Hastings L.J. 663 (1998) (criticizing Fed. R. Evid. 413). Might additional constitutional problems arise if these special exceptions disproportionately affect members of various racial or ethnic groups? See Aviva Orenstein, Propensity or Stereotype?: A Misguided Evidence Experiment in Indian Country, 19 Cornell J.L. & Pub. Pol'y 173 (2009) (suggesting that the federal rules disproportionately affect Native American defendants).

b. *Exception for domestic violence?* The Federal Rules of Evidence do not have a special domestic violence exception to the ban on the admission of prior bad acts. Does this combination of federal rules (that is, exceptions for sexual assault and molestation but not domestic violence) make sense? Should the federal rules adopt a new evidentiary exception for cases involving domestic violence? Why or why not? Compare Lininger, Evidentiary Issues in Federal Prosecutions, supra, at 704-708 (contending there is no need for a federal rule), with Lisa Marie De Sanctis, Bridging the Gap Between the Rules of Evidence and Justice for Victims of Domestic Violence, 8 Yale J.L. & Feminism 359 (1996), and Myrna S. Raeder, The Admissibility of Prior Acts of Domestic Violence: *Simpson* and Beyond, 69 S. Cal. L. Rev. 1463, 1505-1506 (1996) (both advocating adoption of a domestic violence character exception to federal rules).

8. *Admissibility of prior bad acts in the civil context.* Courts of limited jurisdiction, such as those that hear protection orders, generally do not strictly apply the rules of evidence. Hence, these courts may follow liberal policies on the admission of evidence of prior bad acts. Often, protection order statutes explicitly or implicitly require consideration of a history or pattern of abuse and may even include a directive to include prior acts of abuse. Aiken & Murphy, supra, at 19 n.65. As one court explained the rationale for liberal admission of such evidence:

> The policy consideration underlying the general prohibition against admission of evidence of prior crimes or bad acts is that such evidence tends to prejudice the defendant because the trier of fact will improperly use the evidence to determine the ultimate issue of guilt. This rationale does not apply in a civil protective order hearing where the ultimate issue is what, if any, remedy is necessary to protect the petitioner based on the likelihood of future abuse. Evidence of past abusive acts is admissible to show that abuse is likely to recur and to help the court determine what remedies will adequately prevent future abuse.

Coburn v. Coburn, 674 A.2d 951, 959 (Md. 1996).

Evidence of prior abuse has also been admitted in limited circumstances for noncharacter purposes. For example, evidence of prior bad acts has been admitted to counter anticipated defenses, such as to rebut a claim in a child custody case that the victim has a motive to fabricate allegations of abuse in order to gain an advantage in the litigation. Aiken & Murphy, supra, at 21.

9. *Policy.* Admission of prior act evidence to show propensity in domestic violence cases will arguably make domestic violence prosecutions easier. How should policymakers balance the interests in facilitating prosecution, enhancing the safety of victims, and protecting the rights of defendants?

4. Confrontation Clause

Domestic violence cases are notoriously difficult to prosecute because victims so often refuse to cooperate. This problem contributed to the practice of "evidence-based, victimless" prosecutions, that is, the liberal admission of victims' hearsay statements that enables prosecutors to present victims' out-of-court pretrial statements in lieu of their testimony. The Supreme Court, however, halted this promising development in Crawford v. Washington, 541 U.S. 36 (2004).

Crawford revolutionized Confrontation Clause jurisprudence by the introduction of a new standard for the admission of hearsay statements. After *Crawford*, a victim's pretrial out-of-court statement (such as a statement to police) would be excluded—as a "testimonial" statement—unless the victim was later available at trial and subject to cross-examination. Because battered victims frequently are unavailable at trial, it becomes critically important to understand the parameters of "testimonial" statements. The following case explores these parameters.

■ DAVIS v. WASHINGTON
547 U.S. 813 (2006)

Justice SCALIA delivered the opinion of the Court.

These cases require us to determine when statements made to law enforcement personnel during a 911 call or at a crime scene are "testimonial" and thus subject to the requirements of the Sixth Amendment's Confrontation Clause.

The relevant statements in *Davis v. Washington* were made to a 911 emergency operator on February 1, 2001. When the operator answered the initial call, the connection terminated before anyone spoke. She reversed the call, and Michelle McCottry answered. In the ensuing conversation, the operator ascertained that McCottry was involved in a domestic disturbance with her former boyfriend Adrian Davis, the petitioner in this case:

911 Operator:	Hello.
Complainant:	Hello.
911 Operator:	What's going on?
Complainant:	He's here jumpin' on me again.
911 Operator:	Okay. Listen to me carefully. Are you in a house or an apartment?
Complainant:	I'm in a house.
911 Operator:	Are there any weapons?
Complainant:	No. He's usin' his fists.
911 Operator:	Okay. Has he been drinking?
Complainant:	No.
911 Operator:	Okay, sweetie. I've got help started. Stay on the line with me, okay?
Complainant:	I'm on the line.
911 Operator:	Listen to me carefully. Do you know his last name?
Complainant:	It's Davis.
911 Operator:	Davis? Okay, what's his first name?
Complainant:	Adrian.
911 Operator:	What is it?
Complainant:	Adrian.
911 Operator:	Adrian?
Complainant:	Yeah.
911 Operator:	Okay. What's his middle initial?
Complainant:	Martell. He's runnin' now."

As the conversation continued, the operator learned that Davis had "just r[un] out the door" after hitting McCottry, and that he was leaving in a car with someone else. McCottry started talking, but the operator cut her off, saying, "Stop talking and answer my questions." She then gathered more information about Davis (including his birthday), and learned that Davis had told McCottry that his purpose in coming to the house was "to get his stuff," since McCottry was moving. McCottry described the context of the assault, after which the operator told her that the police were on their way. "They're gonna check the area for him first," the operator said, "and then they're gonna come talk to you."

The police arrived within four minutes of the 911 call and observed McCottry's shaken state, the "fresh injuries on her forearm and her face," and her "frantic efforts to gather her belongings and her children so that they could leave the residence."

The State charged Davis with felony violation of a domestic no-contact order. "The State's only witnesses were the two police officers who responded to the 911 call. Both officers testified that McCottry exhibited injuries that appeared to be recent, but neither officer could testify as to the cause of the injuries." McCottry presumably could have testified as to whether Davis was her assailant, but she did not appear. Over Davis's objection, based on the Confrontation Clause of the Sixth Amendment, the trial court admitted the recording of her exchange with the 911 operator, and the jury convicted him. . . .

In [the consolidated case of] Hammon v. Indiana, police responded late on the night of February 26, 2003, to a "reported domestic disturbance" at the home of Hershel and Amy Hammon. They found Amy alone on the front porch, appearing "'somewhat frightened,'" but she told them that "'nothing was the matter.'" She gave them permission to enter the house, where an officer saw "a gas heating unit in the corner of the living room" that had "flames coming out of the . . . partial glass front. There were pieces of glass on the ground in front of it and there was flame emitting from the front of the heating unit."

Hershel, meanwhile, was in the kitchen. He told the police "that he and his wife had 'been in an argument' but 'everything was fine now' and the argument 'never became physical.'" By this point Amy had come back inside. One of the officers remained with Hershel; the other went to the living room to talk with Amy, and "again asked [her] what had occurred." Hershel made several attempts to participate in Amy's conversation with the police, but was rebuffed. The officer later testified that Hershel "became angry when I insisted that [he] stay separated from Mrs. Hammon so that we can investigate what had happened." After hearing Amy's account, the officer "had her fill out and sign a battery affidavit." Amy handwrote the following: "Broke our Furnace & shoved me down on the floor into the broken glass. Hit me in the chest and threw me down. Broke our lamps & phone. Tore up my van where I couldn't leave the house. Attacked my daughter."

The State charged Hershel with domestic battery and with violating his probation. Amy was subpoenaed, but she did not appear at his subsequent bench trial. The State called the officer who had questioned Amy, and asked him to recount what Amy told him and to authenticate the affidavit. Hershel's counsel repeatedly objected to the admission of this evidence. At one point, after hearing the prosecutor defend the affidavit because it was made "under oath," defense counsel said, "That doesn't give us the opportunity to cross-examine [the] person who allegedly drafted it. Makes me mad." Nonetheless, the trial court admitted the affidavit as a "present sense impression," and Amy's statements as "excited utterances" that "are expressly permitted in these kinds of cases even if the declarant is not available to testify." . . . [The trial judge found Hershel guilty on both charges.]

The Confrontation Clause of the Sixth Amendment provides: "In all criminal prosecutions, the accused shall enjoy the right . . . to be confronted with the witnesses against him." In Crawford v. Washington, we held that this provision bars "admission of testimonial statements of a witness who did not appear at trial unless he was unavailable to testify, and the defendant had had a prior opportunity for cross-examination." A critical portion of this holding, and the portion central to resolution of the two cases now before us, is the phrase "testimonial statements." Only statements of this sort cause the declarant to be a "witness" within the meaning of the Confrontation Clause. It is the testimonial character of the statement that separates it from other hearsay that, while subject to traditional limitations upon hearsay evidence, is not subject to the Confrontation Clause. . . .

Without attempting to produce an exhaustive classification of all conceivable statements—or even all conceivable statements in response to police interrogation—as either testimonial or nontestimonial, it suffices to decide the present cases to hold as follows: Statements are nontestimonial when made in the course of police interrogation under circumstances objectively indicating that the primary purpose of the interrogation is to enable police assistance to meet an ongoing emergency. They are testimonial when the circumstances objectively indicate that there is no such ongoing emergency, and that the primary purpose of the interrogation is to establish or prove past events potentially relevant to later criminal prosecution. . . .

The question before us in *Davis,* then, is whether, objectively considered, the interrogation that took place in the course of the 911 call produced testimonial statements. When we said in *Crawford* that "interrogations by law enforcement officers fall squarely within [the] class" of testimonial hearsay, we had immediately in mind (for that was the case before us) interrogations solely directed at establishing the facts of a past crime, in order to identify (or provide evidence to convict) the perpetrator. The product of such interrogation, whether reduced to a writing signed by the declarant or embedded in the memory (and perhaps notes) of the interrogating officer, is testimonial. . . . A 911 call, on the other hand, and at least the initial interrogation conducted in connection with a 911 call, is ordinarily not designed primarily to "establis[h] or prov[e]" some past fact, but to describe current circumstances requiring police assistance.

The difference between the interrogation in *Davis* and the one in *Crawford* is apparent on the face of things. In *Davis,* McCottry was speaking about events *as they were actually happening,* rather than "describ[ing] past events," Sylvia Crawford's interrogation, on the other hand, took place hours after the events she described had occurred. Moreover, any reasonable listener would recognize that McCottry (unlike Sylvia Crawford) was facing an ongoing emergency. . . . McCottry's call was plainly a call for help against bona fide physical threat. Third, the nature of what was asked and answered in *Davis,* again viewed objectively, was such that the elicited statements were necessary to be able to *resolve* the present emergency, rather than simply to learn (as in *Crawford*) what had happened in the past. That is true even of the operator's effort to establish the identity of the assailant, so that the dispatched officers might know whether they would be encountering a violent felon. And finally, the difference in the level of formality between the two interviews is striking. Crawford was responding calmly, at the station house, to a series of questions, with the officer-interrogator taping and making notes of her answers; McCottry's frantic answers were provided over the phone, in an environment that was not tranquil, or even (as far as any reasonable 911 operator could make out) safe.

We conclude from all this that the circumstances of McCottry's interrogation objectively indicate its primary purpose was to enable police assistance to meet an ongoing emergency. She simply was not acting as a *witness;* she was not *testifying.* . . .

This is not to say that a conversation which begins as an interrogation to determine the need for emergency assistance cannot . . . "evolve into testimonial statements," once that purpose has been achieved. In this case, for example, after the operator gained the information needed to address the exigency of the moment, the emergency appears to have ended (when Davis drove away from the premises). The operator then told McCottry to be quiet, and proceeded to pose a battery of questions. It could readily be maintained that, from that point on, McCottry's statements were testimonial. . . . This presents no great problem [because] trial courts will recognize the point at which, for Sixth Amendment purposes, statements in response to interrogations become testimonial [and] exclude the portions of any statement that have become testimonial. . . .

Determining the testimonial or nontestimonial character of the statements that were the product of the interrogation in *Hammon* is a much easier task, since they were not much different from the statements we found to be testimonial in *Crawford.* It is entirely clear from the circumstances that the interrogation was part of an investigation into possibly criminal past conduct—as, indeed, the testifying officer expressly acknowledged. There was no emergency in progress; the interrogating officer testified that he had heard no arguments or crashing and saw no one throw or break anything. When the officers first arrived, Amy told them that things were fine, and there was no immediate threat to her person. When the officer questioned Amy for the second time, and elicited the challenged statements, he was not seeking to determine (as in *Davis*) "what is happening," but rather "what happened." Objectively viewed, the primary, if not indeed the sole, purpose of the interrogation was to investigate a possible crime—which is, of course, precisely what the officer *should* have done.

It is true that the *Crawford* interrogation was more formal. It followed a *Miranda* warning, was tape-recorded, and took place at the station house. While these features certainly strengthened the statements' testimonial aspect—made it more objectively apparent, that is, that the purpose of the exercise was to nail down the truth about past criminal events—none was essential to the point. It was formal enough that Amy's interrogation was conducted in a separate room, away from her husband (who tried to intervene), with the officer receiving her replies for use in his "investigat[ion]." [Like the wife's statements in *Crawford,* Hershel's statements] deliberately recounted, in response to police questioning, how potentially criminal past events began and progressed. And both took place some time after the events described were over. Such statements under official interrogation are an obvious substitute for live testimony, because they do precisely *what a witness does* on direct examination; they are inherently testimonial. . . .

Respondents [contend] that the nature of the offenses charged in these two cases—domestic violence—requires greater flexibility in the use of testimonial evidence. This particular type of crime is notoriously susceptible to intimidation or coercion of the victim to ensure that she does not testify at trial. When this occurs, the Confrontation Clause gives the criminal a windfall. We may not, however, vitiate constitutional guarantees when they have the effect of allowing the guilty to go free.

But when defendants seek to undermine the judicial process by procuring or coercing silence from witnesses and victims, the Sixth Amendment does not require courts to acquiesce. While defendants have no duty to assist the State in proving their guilt, they *do* have the duty to refrain from acting in ways that destroy the integrity of the criminal-trial system. We reiterate what we said in *Crawford*: that "the rule of forfeiture by wrongdoing . . . extinguishes confrontation claims on essentially equitable grounds." 541 U.S., at 62. That is, one who obtains the absence of a witness by wrongdoing forfeits the constitutional right to confrontation. . . .

Justice THOMAS, concurring in the judgment in part and dissenting in part.

In Crawford v. Washington, we abandoned the general reliability inquiry we had long employed to judge the admissibility of hearsay evidence under the Confrontation Clause. . . . Today, a mere two years after the Court decided *Crawford,* it adopts an equally unpredictable test, under which district courts are charged with divining the "primary purpose" of police interrogations. . . . Because neither of the cases before the Court today would implicate the Confrontation Clause under an appropriately targeted standard, I [dissent] from the Court's resolution . . .

Neither the 911 call at issue in *Davis* nor the police questioning at issue in *Hammon* is testimonial. . . . [T]he statements were neither Mirandized nor custodial, nor accompanied by any similar indicia of formality. Finally, there is no suggestion that the prosecution attempted to offer the women's hearsay evidence at trial in order to evade confrontation. Accordingly, the statements at issue in both cases are nontestimonial and admissible under the Confrontation Clause.

. . . [T]he Court's *Hammon* holding also reveals the difficulty of applying the Court's requirement that courts investigate the "primary purpose[s]" of the investigation. The Court draws a line between the two cases based on its explanation that *Hammon* involves "no emergency in progress," but instead, mere questioning as "part of an investigation into possibly criminal past conduct," and its explanation that *Davis* involves questioning for the "primary purpose" of "enabl[ing] police assistance to meet an ongoing emergency." But the fact that the officer in *Hammon* was investigating Mr. Hammon's past conduct does not foreclose the possibility that the primary purpose of his inquiry was to assess whether Mr. Hammon constituted a continuing danger to his wife, requiring further police presence or action. It is hardly remarkable that Hammon did not act abusively toward his wife in the presence of the officers, and his good judgment to refrain from criminal behavior in the presence of police sheds little, if any, light on whether his violence would have resumed had the police left without further questioning, transforming what the Court dismisses as "past conduct" back into an "ongoing emergency." Nor does the mere fact that McCottry needed emergency aid shed light on whether the "primary purpose" of gathering, for example, the name of her assailant was to protect the police, to protect the victim, or to gather information for prosecution. In both of the cases before the Court, like many similar cases, pronouncement of the "primary" motive behind the interrogation calls for nothing more than a guess by courts.

Because the standard adopted by the Court today is neither workable nor a targeted attempt to reach the abuses forbidden by the Clause, I concur only in the judgment in Davis v. Washington, and respectfully dissent from the Court's resolution of *Hammon v. Indiana*.

Note: O. J. Simpson Trial and Its Legacy for Domestic Violence Law

On June 12, 1994, an unknown suspect murdered Nicole Brown Simpson and Ronald Goldman outside Nicole's condominium. Goldman was Nicole's acquaintance who stopped by her condo to return a pair of sunglasses that Nicole's mother left at the restaurant where he worked. The murder was particularly violent.[1] The slaying of a wealthy, beautiful, blond, white woman shocked the nation.[2] O. J. Simpson, Nicole's ex-husband, and former professional football player, sports announcer, and actor, was the prime suspect. According to friends and family, Simpson physically and verbally assaulted Nicole since they first began dating in 1977.

The *Simpson* trial, named the "trial of the century,"[3] catapulted the issue of domestic violence into the forefront of public awareness.[4] For almost a year, the media provided extensive daily coverage of the trial.[5] Media accounts explored many aspects of domestic violence, including its prevalence, dynamics, the relationship between domestic violence and murder, and the ineffectiveness of the law's response.[6] The public attention on domestic violence encouraged many battered women to seek help.[7] In addition, the case resulted in law reforms (discussed below).[8]

Legal commentators devoted a considerable amount of attention to analyzing Judge Lance Ito's various evidence rulings regarding prior acts of domestic violence.[9] The judge admitted evidence, including photos, of the battering which resulted in O. J. Simpson's spousal abuse conviction in 1989.[10] The judge also allowed evidence of six prior domestic violence incidents and admitted a 911 call recording, in which O. J. Simpson is heard making loud threats to Nicole Brown Simpson.[11] Further, Judge Ito admitted seven incidents of stalking, though the prosecution decided not to present other evidence of stalking at trial.[12]

---

[1]. Jim Mulvaney, O. J.'s Ex Killed in Her L.A. Home: Police Question Him as Witness, Newsday (New York), June 14, 1994, at A6.

[2]. Seth Mydans, O. J. Simpson's Ex-Wife Slain at Her Condo in Los Angeles, N.Y. Times, June 14, 1994, at B9. The assailant slashed Nicole so viciously that he almost severed her neck from her body. Goldman was stabbed about 30 times.

[3]. Zanita E. Fenton, Domestic Violence in Black and White: Racialized Gender Stereotypes in Gender Violence, 8 Colum. J. Gender & L. 1, 31 (1998).

[4]. Joan Smith, O. J. Wife-Abuse Case Not Unusual, There is No Typical Person who Batters, Experts Say, S.F. Examiner, June 19, 1994, at A6.

[5]. Erwin Chemerinsky & Laurie Levenson, The Ethics of Being a Commentator, 69 S. Cal. L. Rev. 1303, 1303-1304 (1996).

[6]. See Elizabeth M. Schneider, Battered Women and Feminist Lawmaking 206 (2000).

[7]. Sheryl McCarthy, The Role of the Media in Domestic Violence Cases: A Journalist's Perspective, 58 Alb. L. Rev. 1235, 1242 (1995).

[8]. For additional commentary on the legacy of the *Simpson* case, see Nancy S. Ehrenreich, O. J. Simpson and the Myth of Gender/Race Conflict, 67 U. Colo. L. Rev. 931 (1996); Elizabeth L. MacDowell, When Reading Between the Lines is Not Enough: Lessons from Media Coverage of a Domestic Violence Homicide-Suicide, 17 Am. U. J. Gender, Soc. Pol'y & L. 269 (2009); Wayne J. Pitts et al., The Legacy of the O. J. Simpson Trial, 10 Loy. J. Pub. Int. L. 199 (2009); Crystal H. Weston, Orenthal James Simpson and Gender, Class, and Race: In That Order, 6 Hastings Women's L.J. 223 (1995).

[9]. See, e.g., Roger C. Park, Character Evidence Issues in the O.J. Simpson Case—Or, Rationales of the Character Evidence Ban, with Illustrations from the *Simpson* Case, 67 U. Colo. L. Rev. 747 (1996).

[10]. Id. at 752.

[11]. Id.

[12]. Id.

However, Judge Ito refused to admit several statements made by Nicole Brown Simpson about prior abuse on grounds of hearsay.[13] These statements included graphic descriptions of abuse Nicole wrote in her diary, a statement Nicole made to a friend that O. J. would kill her if she left him, a statement Nicole made to a friend that she lived in fear of O. J., and a statement Nicole made to her mother describing how O. J. was following her.[14] Judge Ito also denied the admission of a phone call to a battered woman's hotline made five days before Nicole Brown Simpson's murder.[15] The caller, who only identified herself as Nicole from West Los Angeles, said her ex-husband was stalking her and she was afraid of him.[16]

A jury acquitted Simpson of the double murder on October 3, 1995.[17] The verdict prompted outrage about the response of the criminal justice system to domestic violence and a call for law reform.[18] Commentators attributed the verdict to several facts: (1) prosecutors' filed the case in the racially diverse downtown district of Los Angeles, increasing the probability that a jury composed largely of African-Americans would be more sympathetic to the African-American defendant, rather than filing it in the white upper-class venue of Santa Monica where the crime occurred; (2) prosecutors decided not to seek the death penalty, thereby losing the advantage of having a "death-qualified" jury, thus excluding more liberal jurors opposed to capital punishment, which would have been more likely to convict; (3) the judge excluded some of the domestic violence evidence because of hearsay rules, and (4) the focus of the crime shifted from a criminal act of gender-based violence to the unfair treatment of racial minorities by the criminal justice system, based on the theory that corrupt police officers contaminated and planted evidence.[19]

In response to the *Simpson* trial, the California legislature made several changes to the law of evidence relating to domestic violence. At the time of the trial, most states, including California, prohibited using evidence of prior criminal acts to show the character of a defendant, primarily to avoid the jury's concluding that the defendant is "once a criminal, always a criminal."[20] Legislators proposed Senate Bill 1876, later codified as Cal. Evid. Code §1109, to assist the government in prosecuting domestic violence cases when the victim is unavailable or refuses to testify against her abuser.[21] California Evidence Code §1109, known as the "Nicole Brown Simpson Law,"[22] enacted in 2006, allows this type of propensity evidence (revealing a prior history of abuse) to be introduced in trials relating to domestic

---

[13]. Id.

[14]. Karleen F. Murphy, A Hearsay Exception for Physical Abuse, 27 Golden Gate U. L. Rev. 497, 522 n.175 (1997).

[15]. Id.

[16]. Id.

[17]. USAToday.com, Key Dates in the O. J. Simpson Case, http://www.usatoday.com/news/index/nns171.htm (last visited June 19, 2011).

[18]. See Pitts et al., supra note [8], at 200.

[19]. Doug Linder, Famous Trials: The O. J. Simpson Trial, Jurist Legal Intelligence (Oct. 2000), available at http://www.jurist.law.pitt.edu/trials10.htm.

[20]. Tom Lininger, Evidentiary Issues in Federal Prosecutions of Violence Against Women, 36 Ind. L. Rev. 687, 701-702 (2003).

[21]. See Lisa Marie De Sanctis, Bridging the Gap Between the Rules of Evidence and Justice for Victims of Domestic Violence, 8 Yale J.L. & Feminism 359, 361 (1996). For a discussion of the need for a change of California's Evidence Code to allow character evidence in domestic violence proceedings, using the *Simpson* trial as an example, see Myrna S. Raeder, The Admissibility of Prior Acts of Domestic Violence: *Simpson* and Beyond, 69 S. Calif. L. Rev. 1463, 1488-1506 (1996).

[22]. Lininger, Evidentiary Issues in Federal Prosecutions, supra note [20], at 701-702.

violence.[23] This reform allows the prosecution to make the connection between domestic violence and the violent crime that the prosecutors in the *Simpson* trial were not permitted to make.

Almost two years after the criminal trial, a jury found Simpson liable in a civil suit for the wrongful deaths of his ex-wife and Goldman.[24] The jury awarded compensatory damages of $8.5 million and punitive damages of $25 million.[25] Simpson, however, refused to pay the judgment.[26] Commentators attribute the difference in the jury verdicts in the two trials, in large part, to the lower standard of proof in civil proceedings and the admissibility of more evidence of domestic violence.[27]

In 2007, a jury convicted Simpson of armed robbery and kidnapping for his theft of sports memorabilia from two Las Vegas sports dealers. The judge sentenced Simpson to 9 to 33 years. The Nevada Supreme Court denied his appeal.[28]

The following excerpt highlights some important evidence that was admitted in the *Simpson* murder trial. Would the evidence have been admissible based on Davis v. Washington?

■ JANET GILMORE, JURORS HEAR FRANTIC 911 CALLS, TAPE CAPTURES NICOLE SIMPSON PLEADING FOR AID

Daily News (Los Angeles, CA), Feb. 3, 1995, at N1

Nicole Brown Simpson's frightened voice filled the courtroom Thursday, as jurors listened to a haunting 1993 tape of her frantic phone calls to a 911 operator as O. J. Simpson ranted in the background. . . . The tape captured Nicole Simpson's trembling voice as she pleaded with a 911 operator to send help. . . .

"My ex-husband has just broken into my house, and he's ranting and raving outside in the front yard." . . . "Has he been drinking?" dispatcher Terri Moore asked. "No, but he's crazy," Nicole Simpson replied. "He broke the whole back door down. . . ."

Not played for jurors was a portion of the tape in which Nicole Simpson stated, "He's going to beat the s_____ out of me." Superior Court Judge Lance Ito decided weeks ago that the statement was too prejudicial. But jurors heard other extended passages in which Nicole Simpson, her voice breaking, expressed resignation and fear of her former husband, who could be heard shouting in the background. "He's f_____ going nuts," she said at one point, her voice breaking. . . .

The 911 tape is the latest evidence prosecutors have introduced in an effort to show jurors that Simpson was an obsessive wife batterer. . . .

[23]. See Cal. Evid. Code §1109 (allowing evidence of past acts of domestic violence to be introduced to show the defendant's propensity of violence, provided that the evidence offered is less than ten years old, and the trial is related to domestic violence as defined in California Penal Code §13700).

[24]. Rufo v. Simpson, 103 Cal. Rptr. 2d 492 (Ct. App. 2001).

[25]. Simpson Damage Award Called High But Justified "Jury Thought His Conduct was very Reprehensible," St. Louis Post-Dispatch (Mo.), Feb. 11, 1997, at 08A.

[26]. O. J. Civil Judgment Renewal Upheld by Appellate Court, Times Union (Alb.), Feb. 21, 2008, at A2.

[27]. See William Booth, Legal Experts Cite Many Factors as Making a Difference in Simpson Verdicts, Wash. Post, Feb. 6, 1997, at A6.

[28]. Nevada High Court Won't Hear O. J. Simpson Appeal, Charleston Gazette & Daily Mail [WV], May 18, 2011, at 2B.

Before the tape was played, [police dispatcher Terri Moore] was called as a witness to testify about what she heard that night. [S]he testified that she had been trained to classify calls based on their urgency, and that during the phone call she heard enough to convince her to upgrade the importance of the call from "urgent, not life threatening," to "urgent and potentially life threatening." . . .

_____

The following excerpt reveals police procedures for emergency dispatchers in cases of domestic violence.

■ **POLICE CHIEF ASS'N OF SANTA CLARA COUNTY, 911 CALL-TAKER/DISPATCHER RESPONSE**
in Domestic Violence Protocol for Law Enforcement 11 (2007), available at http://www.sccgov.org/keyboard/attachments/Commission%20Agenda/2011/April%201,%202011/203342002/TMPKeyboard203456160.pdf.

A. The dispatcher who receives a domestic violence incident call shall dispatch officers to every reported incident. The dispatcher should, when warranted, give a domestic violence incident call the same priority as any other life-threatening call and should, whenever possible, dispatch at least two officers to the scene.

B. No dispatcher or 911 call-taker, in speaking with a victim of domestic violence, should inquire as to the victim's desire to "prosecute," or "press charges." Any comment or statement which seeks to place the responsibility for enforcement action with the victim is inappropriate.

C. During the initial call for assistance, the call-taker should ask:

1. Where is the emergency? What address? What apartment number?
2. Who am I speaking to (spell name)?
3. What has happened? Is it occurring now?
4. Has anyone been injured? If yes, is an ambulance needed?
5. Are you the victim? If no, are you a witness?
6. Is the suspect present? Is he/she in the same room? Can he/she hear you? What is his/her name? Please describe the suspect and their clothing, and, if not present, his/her expected whereabouts.
7. Does the suspect have current access to weapons? If yes, what kind? Where are they located?
8. Is the suspect under the influence of drugs, alcohol or prescription medication? If yes, what substance?
9. Are children present? How many? Ages?
10. Are there previous incidents of domestic violence involving the suspect and victim? Have the police been to this address before? If yes, how many times?
11. Does the victim have a current restraining order?
12. Is the suspect on probation or parole?
13. Does the suspect have any mental health issues?

D. The safety of domestic violence victims, whether the threat of violence is immediate or remote, should be the primary concern of 911 call-takers. The 911 call-taker should advise the victim to ensure his/her safety. For example, suggest that a victim wait for officers at a neighbor's house or remain on the 911 line.

Notes and Questions

1. *Background.* State courts routinely relied on the "reliability test" to admit hearsay testimony in domestic violence cases until *Crawford.* Prior to *Crawford,* when a victim who made an out-of-court pretrial statement was not available for cross-examination at trial, the Confrontation Clause required a showing that the declarant's statement bore adequate "indicia of reliability." Ohio v. Roberts, 448 U.S. 56, 66 (1980). *Crawford* abrogated this reliability standard and replaced it with a standard that focused on the "testimonial" nature of the hearsay. How would the victims' statements in *Davis* have fared under the former "reliability" standard?

Crawford involved a plea of self-defense, but not in the context of domestic violence. In *Crawford,* a wife made a statement to police that was adverse to the husband's interest (that is, she contradicted his claim that he stabbed a man in self-defense). Because the wife did not testify based on the state's marital privilege, the prosecutor introduced her prior incriminating statement. In ruling that her statement was inadmissible hearsay, the Supreme Court held that if an out-of-court statement is "testimonial," then the statement is admissible only if there is a showing that (1) the declarant is unavailable to testify, and (2) the defendant had a prior opportunity to cross-examine the declarant about the statement. Beyond giving a few examples, the Court failed to establish definitive guidelines for the definition of "testimonial." Thus, *Davis* clarified unanswered questions about the meaning of those "testimonial" statements that would be deemed inadmissible under the Confrontation Clause.

2. *Social reality. Crawford,* with its insistence on the availability of witnesses for cross-examination purposes, had a devastating effect on prosecutions of domestic violence. A post-*Crawford* survey of over 60 prosecutors' offices reported most prosecutors' assessment that *Crawford* "significantly impeded" prosecution of domestic violence. Tom Lininger, Prosecuting Batterers after *Crawford,* 91 Va. L. Rev. 747, 749-750 (2005). In one jurisdiction alone, half of domestic violence cases set for trial were dismissed because of hearsay problems. Id.

3. Davis: *holding.* In the consolidated cases of *Davis* and *Hammon,* the Supreme Court explains that statements to a 911 operator are nontestimonial (and admissible) because they describe what *is currently happening,* while statements to investigating police officers are testimonial (and inadmissible) because they describe what *has* happened in the context of a police investigation. What is the Court's rationale for this distinction? How do the majority and dissent differ in their views about the admissibility of these statements and the dangers that they pose to the defendants' constitutional rights? In the determination of what is "testimonial," why should the victim's tone of voice matter? Why should the "level of formality" of the interrogation matter? See Gary M. Bishop, Testimonial Statements, Excited Utterances and the Confrontation Clause: Formulating a Precise Rule after *Crawford* and *Davis,*

54 Clev. St. L. Rev. 559, 570 (2006) (arguing that the absence of formal questioning is a significant factor in determining whether a statement is nontestimonial).

Why do you think such a conservative justice as Justice Scalia issued rulings in *Crawford* and *Davis* that were so favorable to defendants' rights? A provocative debate exists on Justice Scalia's historical originalist analysis of the Confrontation Clause. Compare Thomas Y. Davies, Revisiting the Fictional Originalism in *Crawford*'s "Cross-Examination Rule": A Reply to Mr. Kry, 72 Brook. L. Rev. 557, 567 (2007); and Thomas Y. Davies, What Did the Framers Know, and When Did They Know It? Fictional Originalism in Crawford v. Washington, 71 Brook. L. Rev. 105 (2005); with Robert Kry, Confrontation Under the Marian Statutes: A Response to Professor Davies, 72 Brook. L. Rev. 493, 555 (2007).

4. *Police functions. Davis* focuses on the "primary purpose" of the police interrogation. For purposes of the determination of admissibility of hearsay statements, *Davis* distinguishes between two police functions: assessment of an ongoing emergency and gathering of evidence. When police are responding to an ongoing emergency, do they always have only one purpose? If the police have dual purposes, how can a court determine whether any statements that victims make to police constitute inadmissible hearsay? How does Justice Thomas respond? See also Ellen Liang Yee, Forfeiture of the Confrontation Right in *Giles*: Justice Scalia's Faint-Hearted Fidelity to the Common Law, 100 J. Crim. L. & Criminology 1495, 1504-1505 (2010).

Justice Scalia suggests that the purpose of an interrogation can change from emergency assessment to investigative information gathering. However, that transformation "presents no great problem," in his words. What guidelines does the Court give to identify such a shift in purposes? What are Justice Thomas's criticisms of the difficulties of applying the Court's requirements? Whose argument is more compelling about the ease of applying the guidelines?

5. *Excited utterances.* An exception to the hearsay rule exists for excited utterances. This rule stems from the jurisprudence of John Henry Wigmore, who advanced the view in his 1904 treatise that the "stress of nervous excitement . . . stills the reflective facilities" and makes statements during that emotional state "particularly trustworthy." 3 John Henry Wigmore, A Treatise on the System of Evidence in Trials at Common Law §§1745-1747, at 2247-2250 (1904). Such excited utterances, according to Wigmore, warranted a special exemption from the hearsay rule. The Federal Rules of Evidence codified the exception for spontaneous statements made under the influence of an anxiety-provoking event. Fed. R. Evid. 803(2).

Calls to 911 are quite common during violent incidents of domestic violence. Should all statements that are made during 911 calls be deemed admissible as excited utterances? After an assailant has fled, do such statements lose their quality of being "excited" and thereby become "testimonial"? Were McCottry's statements excited utterances? How would a court have treated McCottry's statements before *Crawford*? For a pre-*Crawford* examination of confrontation issues posed by 911 calls, see Richard D. Friedman & Bridget McCormack, Dial-In Testimony, 150 U. Pa. L. Rev. 1171, 1184-1190 (2002).

6. *Statements to medical personnel.* In *Davis* and *Hammon*, the victims made incriminating statements to police. Often, however, victims make incriminating statements to medical personnel. Should those statements be analyzed under the same framework?

Another traditional exception to the hearsay rule applies to statements to medical professionals for the "purpose of diagnosis and treatment." Fed. R. Evid.

803(4); 2 McCormick On Evidence, supra, at §277. Such statements are presumed to be trustworthy based on the assumption that a patient would make truthful statements to ensure proper medical treatment. See Moore v. City of Leeds, 1 So. 3d 145 (Ala. Crim. App. 2008) (holding that patient's testimony about identity of abuser was admissible as pertinent to her effective treatment).

Do medical professionals sometimes have other purposes, such as investigatory forensic purposes? At what point do a victim's statements to medical personnel cease being for "diagnosis and treatment" and become investigatory (hence, testimonial and inadmissible)? See generally Dave Gordon, Note, Is There an Accuser in the House?: Evaluating Statements Made to Physicians and Other Medical Personnel in the Wake of Crawford v. Washington and Davis v. Washington, 38 N.M. L. Rev. 529 (2008) (exploring effect of *Crawford* and *Davis* on statements to medical personnel).

7. *Other persons' statements to police.* In *Davis*, the respective victims made statements to the police. However, often nonvictims, such as neighbors, call the police to report acts of domestic violence. How should those statements be analyzed under the testimonial standard?

8. *Incentives for law enforcement.* Under *Davis*, statements made to police to resolve an "ongoing emergency" are nontestimonial and admissible at trial regardless of whether the victim testifies. What are the implications of *Davis* for law enforcement? See Tom Lininger, *Davis* and *Hammon: A Step Forward, or a Step Back?*, 105 Mich. L. Rev. First Impressions 28 (2006) (suggesting police will adapt their practices to list emergency circumstances); The Supreme Court, Sixth Amendment—Witness Confrontation, 120 Harv. L. Rev. 213, 217 (2006) (accord); Nancee Alexa Barth, Comment, "I'd Grab at Anything, and I'd Forget." Domestic Violence Victim Testimony After Davis v. Washington, 41 J. Marshall L. Rev. 937 (2008) (suggesting that *Davis* incentivizes police to keep victims distraught so victims' statements will be deemed nontestimonial and thereby admissible; criticizing that this result compromises victims' safety). Are police likely to establish new protocols for responding to domestic disturbances? See Kimberly D. Bailey, The Aftermath of *Crawford* and *Davis*: Deconstructing the Sound of Silence, 2009 B.Y.U. L. Rev. 1 (2009) (noting that post-*Crawford*, the Prosecutor's Research Institute created a list of questions for police to ask that avoided the appearance of an interrogation).

9. *Meaning of "ongoing emergency."* What is the meaning of "ongoing"? What is the meaning of "emergency"? Does it matter whether the assailant has fled? Whether a victim and/or police are ignorant of the abuser's present location? Whether the abuser has a weapon? Whether the threat has ended? What other factors should enter into the determination? Does (should) the meaning vary according to whether the victim is an intimate partner? How relevant in the determination is the severity of the victim's injuries? For example, is the emergency still "ongoing" whenever a victim must be transported to a hospital? See Michael Baxter, Note, The Impact of Davis v. Washington on Domestic Violence Prosecutions, 29 Women's Rts. L. Rep. 213, 221-222 (2008) (addressing this question).

When has the threat "ended" for a victim of abuse? Does the context of domestic violence call for a different view of "ongoing emergency"? As one commentator explains:

> [I]n the vast majority of cases [of incidents of domestic violence] confronting law enforcement, the emergency has not yet dissipated and some law enforcement conduct

is required for the exigency to be resolved. Typically, then, it is an abuser's arrest—and not the temporary suspension of his physical attack that likely resulted from a victim's call to police—that brings about a "resolution" of the immediate crisis confronting a battered woman.

Deborah Tuerkheimer, Exigency, 49 Ariz. L. Rev. 801, 818 (2007) (arguing for a redefinition of exigency in the context of domestic violence).

What is Justice Thomas's disagreement with the majority about the meaning of "ongoing emergency"? See Baxter, supra, at 221. From whose perspective should the court consider the meaning of "ongoing emergency"—that of the police or that of the victim? Might their perspectives differ? See Tom Lininger, *Davis* and *Hammon,* supra (criticizing cases on this basis).

10. Bryant's *clarification of "ongoing emergency."* The Supreme Court continued its exploration of the parameters of "ongoing emergency" in Michigan v. Bryant, 131 S. Ct. 1143 (2011). The issue concerned the admissibility of a murder victim's pre-death statements to police that identified the shooter and the location of the shooting (6 blocks away from, and 30 minutes after, the event). The situation in *Bryant* falls between *Davis* and *Crawford* in terms of defining the parameters of an "ongoing emergency." As one commentator explains:

> Unlike *Davis*, the victim was not confronting an immediate threat when making the statements. However, [*Bryant*] also does not closely resemble the nontestimonial statements made [by the victim] hours later in a police station in *Crawford.*

Erwin Chemerinsky et al., The Supreme Court 2009 Term Overview and 2010 Term Preview, 27 Touro L. Rev. 33, 61 (2011). In *Bryant,* in an opinion by Justice Soto-mayor, the Court held that the determination of whether a statement is nontestimonial (therefore admissible) is a highly context-dependent inquiry and the existence of an ongoing emergency is only one factor that informs the ultimate inquiry regarding the primary purpose of an interrogation. What are the implications of *Bryant* for domestic violence cases? Does it facilitate or impede prosecutions?

11. *Special evidentiary rules for hearsay statements?* Should there be separate evidentiary rules for hearsay statements that apply only to domestic violence cases? For example, should states enact a special hearsay exception to allow statements made in petitions for orders of protection to be admissible in criminal prosecutions? See Michael H. Graham, Fostering Domestic Violence Prosecutions after *Crawford/ Davis*: Proposal for Legislative Action, 44 Crim. L. Bull. ART 2 (2008)(so suggesting).

The issue of whether states should establish special rules for hearsay statements for domestic violence cases is controversial. Advocates contend that crimes of domestic violence are notoriously difficult to prosecute and that violence between intimates differs from other assaults. See Aviva Orenstein, Sex, Threats, and Absent Victims: The Lessons of Regina v. Bedingfield for Modern Confrontation and Domestic Violence Cases, 79 Fordham L. Rev. 115, 159-160 (2010). See also John M. Leventhal & Liberty Aldrich, The Admission of Evidence in Domestic Violence Cases After Crawford v. Washington: A National Survey, 11 Berkeley J. Crim. L. 77 (2006) (arguing that domestic violence cases are unique because the defendant and victim-declarant "are connected by a history of intimacy, children, economic necessity, and other issues [and] as a result, the defendant's conduct may more easily affect the availability of the complaining witness).

On the other hand, as Justice Scalia acerbically asserts in Giles v. California (explored in the next section), "Is the suggestion that we should have one Confrontation Clause (the one the Framers adopted and *Crawford* described) for all other crimes, but a special, improvised, Confrontation Clause for those crimes that are frequently directed against women?" 554 U.S. 353, 376 (2008). Would the creation of special evidentiary rules for domestic violence cases prove unworkable? Too burdensome? See generally Eleanor Simon, Confrontation and Domestic Violence Post-*Davis*: Is There and Should There Be a Doctrinal Exception, 17 Mich. J. Gender & L. 175 (2011) (concluding that any potential unfairness is offset by the nature of domestic violence and the particular challenges faced by prosecutors).

12. *Post-*Davis *jurisprudence.* How are courts responding to the limitations on hearsay evidence posed by *Crawford* and *Davis*? One survey of post-*Davis* case law bemoans the "lack of consistency and predictability" as well as the judicial tendency to admit considerable hearsay evidence despite its classification as "testimonial" (sometimes, based on determinations that it is "harmless error"). Id. at 197. Simon concludes that courts seem to be applying a de facto domestic violence "exception." Should state and federal law simply carve out a domestic violence exception to the Confrontation Clause?

13. *Proposals for reform.* Commentators have proposed various suggestions for law reform after *Crawford* and *Davis*. For example, Professor Tom Lininger advocates (1) legislative reforms that create more opportunities for cross-examination in preliminary hearings, depositions, and other pretrial proceedings; (2) liberal admission of expert testimony on the psychological effects of domestic violence to explain the reluctance of prosecution witnesses; and (3) legislative diversification of charges to include charges for which the testimony of battered women is unnecessary. Lininger, Prosecuting Batterers, supra, at 783-818. Another commentator suggests that prosecutors develop better strategies to increase victim cooperation in order to encourage victims' in-court testimony, including: specialized prosecution programs, increased victim advocacy (including better communication and contact with victims), and specialized domestic violence courts to reduce victim's fears. Simon, supra, at 203.

Finally, Professor Myrna Rader suggests the enactment of a domestic violence statute (similar to that of Minn. Stat. §609.185(6)) that defines first-degree murder as causing death "while committing domestic abuse" if the abuser has engaged in a pattern of domestic abuse. The statute would not require premeditation or a specific intent to kill. Raeder, The Admissibility of Prior Acts, supra, at 1485-1487. She also proposes enactment of a hearsay exception for trustworthy statements of a domestic homicide victim who has suffered at least three previous instances of domestic violence by the defendant. Id. at 1516-1517. What do you think of these proposals?

14. *Forfeiture by wrongdoing.* In *Davis*, Justice Scalia scoffs at the risk of defendants' attempting to undermine the criminal justice system by coercing the silence of victims and witnesses. He points to the curative rule that defendants who cause a witness's absence by wrongdoing forfeit the constitutional right to confrontation. Are you as sanguine that the forfeiture doctrine will put brakes on the problem of defendants' coercion? The forfeiture-by-wrongdoing doctrine is explored in the next section.

Problems

1. One night, Wynona calls 911 to report that her boyfriend Randal physically abused her two hours earlier. The police arrive and observe evidence of her injuries. However, they depart at her urging. A few hours later, she again calls police and describes more fully the beating she received. Randal is asleep on the couch during the call. Two months later, Wynona fails to show up for work. Concerned, her mother goes to her apartment where she finds Wynona's body with multiple stab wounds to the chest and abdomen. A broken beer bottle and a bloody knife are nearby. The police locate Randal, who has injuries to his hands and a bandage on his left wrist, and charge him with murder. At trial, Randal testifies that he killed Wynona in self-defense when she met him at the front door armed with two knives. The State seeks to admit a recording of Wynona's 911 call regarding the first domestic violence incident. The court admits the tape of the call under a hearsay exception to show motive, state of mind, and absence of mistake or accident. Randal is found guilty of first-degree murder. On appeal, he argues that the trial court erred by admitting the 911 tape because it denied him the right to confrontation. What result? See Hunt v. Oklahoma, 218 P.3d 516 (Okla. Ct. App. 2009).

2. Late one night, the California Highway Patrol (CHP) receives a 911 call from Tina. The call is routed to the CHP because Tina is calling from her cell phone. After learning Tina's location, the CHP transfer the call to the local Police Department dispatcher. The CHP informs the dispatcher that Tina's husband, Tony, had just shot her and that she is fleeing in her vehicle. When asked to confirm her location, Tina responds, "Now I'm driving. I have to get away. I'm just driving down [street name] right now. Oh, my God. Oh, my God he shot at me." In responding to the dispatcher's question about Tony's current location, Tina says that he is at home, and she describes his physical appearance, the clothes he is wearing, and states his date of birth. Tina also gives the dispatcher the address at which the shooting occurred. Tina describes the gun as "a little small black one, like a .22." The dispatcher tells Tina to meet with nearby police. Officer Apley makes contact with Tina who is crying and hysterical.

Office Ponce obtains a search warrant for the residence where the shooting occurred. The search warrant is for a handgun. He finds a .22-caliber pistol in the pocket of a man's jacket and a spent .22–caliber casing in the front yard. In the search of the residence, Officer Apley finds Tony, who is wearing clothing that matches the description given by Tina during her 911 call. At trial, Tony stipulates that he is a previously convicted felon. Tina does not testify, but her statements during the 911 call are admitted as spontaneous statements. Tony is convicted of possession of a firearm by a felon and possession of ammunition by a felon. On appeal, he argues that the admission of Tina's statements to the 911 dispatcher violated his right to confrontation. What result? See California v. Johnson, 117 Cal. Rptr. 3d 132 (Ct. App. 2010).

Note: Interfering with a 911 Call

Telephone dispatchers at 911 centers are the first responders in case of emergencies (for example, crimes, fire, medical emergencies, and traffic accidents). Such dispatchers provide essential liaisons between victims, witnesses, and emergency respondents (such as police, ambulances, etc.). When a caller calls 911 from a land line, the caller's phone and address appear on the dispatcher's computer screen. However, approximately 70 percent of all 911 calls are made from cell phones.[29] When a 911 call is made from a cell phone, the dispatcher does not receive a callback phone number or the location of the caller.[30] This may present a life-threatening problem if an abuser interferes with the victim's call for help.

The Federal Communications Commission (FCC) has established rules that require wireless service providers to transmit all 911 calls from cell phones to call takers at Public Safety Answering Points (PSAPs). These rules enable call takers to receive the caller's wireless phone number as well as the caller's estimated location.[31] Recently, the FCC initiated plans to revolutionize 911 services to receive and transfer text messages, videos, and photos.[32]

Abusers sometimes interfere with victims' efforts to call 911. In response, several state legislatures enacted laws that criminalize such conduct. Some "interference statutes" criminalize the act of interfering with reports of *any* emergency or crime. See, e.g., Ga. Code Ann. §16-10-24.3; Haw. Rev. Stat. Ann. §710-1010.5. Other "interference statutes" prohibit interference specifically with reports of domestic violence. See, e.g., Alaska Stat. §11.56.745. In addition, some domestic-violence-specific "interference statutes" require that the person committing the interference also must have committed a crime of domestic violence. See, e.g., Wash. Rev. Code Ann. §9A.36.150(1)(b). Which statutes are preferable?

5. *Forfeiture by Wrongdoing*

■ GILES v. CALIFORNIA
554 U.S. 353 (2008)

Justice SCALIA delivered the opinion of the Court, except as to Part II-D-2.

We consider whether a defendant forfeits his Sixth Amendment right to confront a witness against him when a judge determines that a wrongful act by the defendant made the witness unavailable to testify at trial.

On September 29, 2002, petitioner Dwayne Giles shot his ex-girlfriend, Brenda Avie, outside the garage of his grandmother's house. No witness saw the shooting, but Giles' niece heard what transpired from inside the house. She heard Giles and Avie speaking in conversational tones. Avie then yelled "Granny" several times and a series of gunshots sounded. Giles' niece and grandmother ran outside and saw Giles standing near Avie with a gun in his hand. Avie, who had not been carrying a weapon, had been shot six times. One wound was consistent with Avie's holding her hand up at the time she was shot, another was consistent with her having turned to her side, and a third was consistent with her having been shot while lying on the ground. . . .

---

[29]. News Release, FCC Takes First Step to Help Revolutionize America's 9-1-1 Services for Consumers, First Responders, Dec. 21, 2011, http://www.fcc.gov/document/fcc-takes-first-step-help-revolutionize-americas-9-1-1-services-consumers-first-responders.

[30]. Nat'l Emergency Number Ass'n, Cell Phones and 911, http://www.nena.org/cellular-wireless-911 (last visited July 1, 2011).

[31]. Id.

[32]. News Release, supra note [29].

At trial, Giles testified that he had acted in self-defense. . . . [He claimed that Avie was extremely jealous. On the day of the murder, he asserted, she went to his house where she threatened to kill him and his new girlfriend. She then charged at him. Fearing that she had a weapon in her hand, he shot her in self-defense, although he claimed that he never intended to kill her].

Prosecutors sought to introduce statements that Avie had made to a police officer responding to a domestic-violence report about three weeks before the shooting. Avie, who was crying when she spoke, told the officer that Giles had accused her of having an affair, and that after the two began to argue, Giles grabbed her by the shirt, lifted her off the floor, and began to choke her. According to Avie, when she broke free and fell to the floor, Giles punched her in the face and head, and after she broke free again, he opened a folding knife, held it about three feet away from her, and threatened to kill her if he found her cheating on him. Over Giles' objection, the trial court admitted these statements into evidence under a provision of California law that permits admission of out-of-court statements describing the infliction or threat of physical injury on a declarant when the declarant is unavailable to testify at trial and the prior statements are deemed trustworthy. Cal. Evid. Code Ann. §1370 (West Supp. 2008).

A jury convicted Giles of first-degree murder. He appealed. While his appeal was pending, this Court decided Crawford v. Washington. . . .

The Sixth Amendment provides that "[i]n all criminal prosecutions, the accused shall enjoy the right . . . to be confronted with the witnesses against him." The Amendment contemplates that a witness who makes testimonial statements admitted against a defendant will ordinarily be present at trial for cross-examination, and that if the witness is unavailable, his prior testimony will be introduced only if the defendant had a prior opportunity to cross-examine him [according to *Crawford*, 541 U.S. at 68]. The State does not dispute here, and we accept without deciding, that Avie's statements accusing Giles of assault were testimonial. But it maintains . . . that the Sixth Amendment did not prohibit prosecutors from introducing the statements because an exception to the confrontation guarantee permits the use of a witness's unconfronted testimony if a judge finds, as the judge did in this case, that the defendant committed a wrongful act that rendered the witness unavailable to testify at trial. . . .

We have previously acknowledged [a] common-law doctrine, which we will refer to as forfeiture by wrongdoing, permitted the introduction of statements of a witness who was "detained" or "kept away" by the "means or procurement" of the defendant. . . . The manner in which the rule was applied makes plain that unconfronted testimony would *not* be admitted without a showing that the defendant intended to prevent a witness from testifying. In cases where the evidence suggested that the defendant had caused a person to be absent, but had not done so to prevent the person from testifying—as in the typical murder case involving accusatorial statements by the victim—the testimony was excluded unless it was confronted or fell within the dying-declaration exception. Prosecutors do not appear to have even *argued* that the judge could admit the unconfronted statements because the defendant committed the murder for which he was on trial.

[The case of King v. Woodcock, 1789 WL 213 (1789), is illustrative]. William Woodcock was accused of killing his wife, Silvia, who had been beaten and left near death. A Magistrate took Silvia Woodcock's account of the crime, under oath, and she died about 48 hours later. The judge stated that "[g]reat as a crime of this nature must always appear to be, yet the inquiry into it must proceed upon the rules of evidence." Aside from testimony given at trial in the presence of the prisoner, the judge said, there were "two other species which are admitted by law: The one is the dying declaration of a person who has received a fatal blow; the other is the examination of a prisoner, and the depositions of the witnesses who may be produced against him" taken under the Marian bail and committal statutes [that is, sixteenth-century statutes regulating the inquisitorial examination of felony suspects and witnesses that gave rise to the Confrontation Clause]. Silvia Woodcock's statement could not be admitted pursuant to the Marian statutes because it was unconfronted—the defendant had not been brought before the examining Magistrate and "the prisoner therefore had no opportunity of contradicting the facts it contains." . . .

King v. Dingler, [1791 WL 634 (1791)], applied the same test to exclude unconfronted statements by a murder victim. George Dingler was charged with killing his wife Jane, who suffered multiple stab wounds that left her in the hospital for 12 days before she died. The day after the stabbing, a Magistrate took Jane Dingler's deposition—as in *Woodcock*, under oath—"of the facts and circumstances which had attended the outrage committed upon her." George Dingler's attorney argued that the statements did not qualify as dying declarations and were not admissible. . . . Relying on *Woodcock*, the court "refused to receive the examination into evidence." . . .

The State offers another explanation for the above cases. It argues that when a defendant committed some act of wrongdoing that rendered a witness unavailable, he forfeited his right to object to the witness's testimony on confrontation grounds, but not on hearsay grounds. No case or treatise that we have found, however, suggested that a defendant who committed wrongdoing forfeited his confrontation rights but not his hearsay rights. And the distinction would have been a surprising one, because courts prior to the founding excluded hearsay evidence in large part *because* it was unconfronted. As the plurality said in Dutton v. Evans, 400 U.S. 74, 86 (1970), "[i]t seems apparent that the Sixth Amendment's Confrontation Clause and the evidentiary hearsay rule stem from the same roots."

The State and the dissent note that common-law authorities justified the wrongful-procurement rule by invoking the maxim that a defendant should not be permitted to benefit from his own wrong. . . . But as the evidence amply shows, the "wrong" and the "evil Practices" to which these statements referred was conduct *designed* to prevent a witness from testifying. The absence of a forfeiture rule covering this sort of conduct would create an intolerable incentive for defendants to bribe, intimidate, or even kill witnesses against them. There is nothing mysterious about courts' refusal to carry the rationale further. The notion that judges may strip the defendant of a right that the Constitution deems essential to a fair trial, on the basis of a prior *judicial* assessment that the defendant is guilty as charged, does not sit well with the right to trial by jury. It is akin, one might say, to "dispensing with jury trial because a defendant is obviously guilty." *Crawford*, 541 U.S. at 62.

Not only was the State's proposed exception to the right of confrontation plainly not an "exceptio[n] established at the time of the founding," it is not established in American jurisprudence *since* the founding. American courts never . . . invoked forfeiture outside the context of deliberate witness tampering. . . .

In 1997, this Court approved a Federal Rule of Evidence, entitled "Forfeiture by wrongdoing," which applies only when the defendant "engaged or acquiesced in wrongdoing that was intended to, and did, procure the unavailability of the declarant as a witness." Fed. Rule of Evid. 804(b)(6). We have described this as a rule "which codifies the forfeiture doctrine." Every commentator we are aware of has concluded the requirement of intent "means that the exception applies only if the defendant has in mind the particular purpose of making the witness unavailable." . . .

In sum, our interpretation of the common-law forfeiture rule is supported by (1) the most natural reading of the language used at common law; (2) the absence of common-law cases *admitting* prior statements on a forfeiture theory when the defendant had not engaged in conduct designed to prevent a witness from testifying; (3) the common law's uniform exclusion of unconfronted inculpatory testimony by murder victims (except testimony given with awareness of impending death) in the innumerable cases in which the defendant was on trial for killing the victim, but was not shown to have done so for the purpose of preventing testimony; (4) a subsequent history in which the dissent's broad forfeiture theory has not been applied. The first two and the last are highly persuasive; the third is in our view conclusive. . . .

The dissent closes by pointing out that a forfeiture rule which ignores *Crawford* would be particularly helpful to women in abusive relationships—or at least particularly helpful in punishing their abusers. Not as helpful as the dissent suggests, since only *testimonial* statements are excluded by the Confrontation Clause. Statements to friends and neighbors about abuse and intimidation, and statements to physicians in the course of receiving treatment would be excluded, if at all, only by hearsay rules, which are free to adopt the dissent's version of forfeiture by wrongdoing. In any event, we are puzzled by the dissent's decision to devote its peroration to domestic abuse cases. Is the suggestion that we should have one Confrontation Clause (the one the Framers adopted and *Crawford* described) for all other crimes, but a special, improvised, Confrontation Clause for those crimes that are frequently directed against women? Domestic violence is an intolerable offense that legislatures may choose to combat through many means—from increasing criminal penalties to adding resources for investigation and prosecution to funding awareness and prevention campaigns. But for that serious crime, as for others, abridging the constitutional rights of criminal defendants is not in the State's arsenal.

The domestic-violence context is, however, relevant for a separate reason. Acts of domestic violence often are intended to dissuade a victim from resorting to outside help, and include conduct designed to prevent testimony to police officers or cooperation in criminal prosecutions. Where such an abusive relationship culminates in murder, the evidence may support a finding that the crime expressed the intent to isolate the victim and to stop her from reporting abuse to the authorities or cooperating with a criminal prosecution—rendering her prior statements admissible under the forfeiture doctrine. Earlier abuse, or threats of abuse, intended to dissuade the victim from resorting to outside help would be highly relevant to this inquiry, as would evidence of ongoing criminal proceedings at which the victim would have been expected to testify. This is not, as the dissent charges, nothing more than "knowledge-based intent." . . .

The state courts in this case did not consider the intent of the defendant because they found that irrelevant to application of the forfeiture doctrine. This view of the law was error, but the court is free to consider evidence of the defendant's intent on remand.

We decline to approve an exception to the Confrontation Clause unheard of at the time of the founding or for 200 years thereafter. The judgment of the California Supreme Court is vacated, and the case is remanded for further proceedings. . . .

Justice BREYER, with whom Justice STEVENS and Justice KENNEDY join, dissenting. . . .

Under the circumstances presented by this case, there is no difficulty demonstrating the defendant's intent. This is because the defendant here knew that murdering his ex-girlfriend would keep her from testifying; and that knowledge is sufficient to show the *intent* that law ordinarily demands. . . .

[T]he law holds an individual responsible for consequences known likely to follow just as if that individual had intended to achieve them. . . . This principle applies here. Suppose that a husband, H, knows that after he assaulted his wife, W, she gave statements to the police. Based on the fact that W gave statements to the police, H also knows that it is possible he will be tried for assault. If H then kills W, H cannot avoid responsibility for intentionally preventing W from testifying, not even if H says he killed W because he was angry with her and not to keep her away from the assault trial. Of course, the trial here is not for assault; it is for murder. But I should think that this fact, because of the nature of the crime, would count as a stronger, not a weaker, reason for applying the forfeiture rule. Nor should it matter that H, at the time of the murder, may have *believed* an assault trial *more likely* to take place than a murder trial, for W's unavailability to testify at *any* future trial was a *certain* consequence of the murder. And any reasonable person would have known it.

The majority tries to overcome this elementary legal logic by claiming that the "forfeiture rule" applies, not where the defendant *intends* to prevent the witness from testifying, but only where that is the defendant's *purpose*, i.e., that the rule applies only where the defendant acts from a particular *motive*, a *desire* to keep the witness from trial. But the law does not often turn matters of responsibility upon *motive*, rather than *intent*. And there is no reason to believe that application of the rule of forfeiture constitutes an exception to this general legal principle.

Indeed, to turn application of the forfeiture rule upon proof of the defendant's *purpose* (rather than *intent*), as the majority does, creates serious practical evidentiary problems. Consider H who assaults W, knows she has complained to the police, and then murders her. H *knows* that W will be unable to testify against him at any future trial. But who knows whether H's knowledge played a major role, a middling role, a minor role, or no role at all, in H's decision to kill W? Who knows precisely what passed through H's mind at the critical moment?

Moreover, the majority's insistence upon a showing of *purpose* or *motive* cannot be squared with the exception's basically ethical objective. If H, by killing W, is able to keep W's testimony out of court, then he has successfully "take[n] advantage of his own wrong." And he does so whether he killed her *for the purpose of* keeping her from testifying, with *certain knowledge* that she will not be able to testify, or with a *belief* that rises to a *reasonable level of probability*. The inequity consists of his being able to *use* the killing to keep out of court her statements against him. That inequity exists whether the defendant's state of mind is purposeful, intentional (i.e., with knowledge), or simply probabilistic.

[T]he majority's approach both creates evidentiary anomalies and aggravates existing evidentiary incongruities. . . . [C]onsider a trial of H for the murder of W at which H claims self-defense. As the facts of this very case demonstrate, H may be allowed to testify at length and in damning detail about W's behavior—what she said as well as what she did—both before and during the crime. H may be able to introduce some of W's statements (as he remembers them) under hearsay exceptions for excited utterances or present sense impressions or to show states of mind (here the victim's statements were admitted through petitioner's testimony to show her state of mind). W, who is dead, cannot reply. This incongruity arises in part from the nature of hearsay and the application of ordinary hearsay rules. But the majority would aggravate the incongruity by prohibiting admission of W's out-of-court statements to the police (which contradict H's account), even when they too fall within a hearsay exception, simply because there is *no evidence that H was focused on his future trial* when he killed her. There is no reason to do so. . . .

The majority tries to find support for its view in 17th-, 18th-, and 19th-century law of evidence. But a review of the cases set forth in Part I, supra, makes clear that no case limits forfeiture to instances where the defendant's purpose or motivation is to keep the witness away. . . .

Rather than limit forfeiture to instances where the defendant's act has absence of the witness as its purpose, the relevant cases suggest that the forfeiture rule would apply where the witness' absence was the known consequence of the defendant's intentional wrongful act. . . .

. . . The rule of forfeiture is implicated primarily where domestic abuse is at issue. In such a case, a murder victim may have previously given a testimonial statement, say, to the police, about an abuser's attacks; and introduction of that statement may be at issue in a later trial for the abuser's subsequent murder of the victim. This is not an uncommon occurrence. Each year, domestic violence results in more than 1,500 deaths and more than 2 million injuries; it accounts for a substantial portion of all homicides; it typically involves a history of repeated violence; and it is difficult to prove in court because the victim is generally reluctant or unable to testify.

Regardless of a defendant's purpose, threats, further violence, and ultimately murder, can stop victims from testifying. [See Tom Lininger, Prosecuting Batterers after *Crawford*, 91 Va. L. Rev. 747, 769 (2005) (citing finding that batterers threaten retaliatory violence in as many as half of all cases, and 30 percent of batterers assault their victims again during the prosecution).] A *constitutional* evidentiary requirement that insists upon a showing of purpose (rather than simply intent or probabilistic knowledge) may permit the domestic partner who made the threats, caused the violence, or even murdered the victim to avoid conviction for earlier crimes by taking advantage of later ones.

In [Davis v. Washington, supra], we recognized that "domestic violence" cases are "notoriously susceptible to intimidation or coercion of the victim to ensure that she does not testify at trial." We noted the concern that "[w]hen this occurs, the Confrontation Clause gives the criminal a windfall." And we replied to that concern by stating that "one who obtains the absence of a witness by wrongdoing forfeits the constitutional right to confrontation." To the extent that it insists upon an additional showing of purpose, the Court breaks the promise implicit in those words and, in doing so, grants the defendant not fair treatment, but a windfall. I can find no history, no underlying purpose, no administrative consideration, and no constitutional principle that requires this result. . . .

Notes and Questions

1. *Epilogue.* The U.S. Supreme Court vacated Giles's conviction and remanded for reconsideration under the correct standard. Upon reconsideration, the California Court of Appeals reversed the defendant's conviction. Because the prosecutor did not establish at trial that defendant killed Avie with the intent to prevent her from testifying, the court concluded that admission of Avie's "testimonial" statements to the police violated the defendant's right to confrontation. People v. Giles, 2009 WL 457832 (Cal. Ct. App. 2009). Upon retrial, the defendant was again convicted of first-degree murder. Affirming, the California appellate court rejected Giles's due process claim as not timely that the prosecutor committed misconduct by cross-examining him about prior domestic violence that she knew she could not prove and by reading his prior testimony to the jury during rebuttal. People v. Giles, No. B224629 (Cal. Ct. App. Jan. 18, 2012) (not published).

2. *Background.* Prosecutors who seek, at trial, to introduce an abused victim's prior out-of-court statements must overcome challenges based on the hearsay rule and the Confrontation Clause. The prosecutor in *Giles* sought to introduce statements made by Avie to the police three weeks before her death to the effect that the defendant threatened to kill her. The trial court had admitted these statements pursuant to California Evidence Code §1370 (permitting admission of hearsay describing the "infliction or threat of physical injury upon the declarant" if the declarant is "unavailable as a witness," the statement was made "at or near the time" of the prior harm or threat, and the statement was made "under circumstances that would indicate its trustworthiness"). Defendant objected that the admission of this hearsay evidence would violate his rights under the Confrontation Clause. The prosecutor countered with the forfeiture by wrongdoing doctrine, that is, contending that the defendant forfeited his right to object to this violation of the Confrontation Clause based on the defendant's wrongdoing in procuring the unavailability of the victim (that is, killing Avie).

The forfeiture-by-wrongdoing doctrine is a common law exception to the Sixth Amendment right to confront witnesses. It signifies that the defendant forfeits his right to claim a violation of the Sixth Amendment in certain circumstances that involve his wrongdoing. *Giles* examines the following issue: Does a defendant forfeit the right to confrontation upon the mere showing that he or she caused the unavailability of a witness, or must there be a showing that the defendant's actions were undertaken for the specific purpose of preventing the witness from testifying? Prior to *Giles*, the majority of jurisdictions applied an expansive "equitable forfeiture" approach—preventing the defendant from benefiting from the forfeiture doctrine by focusing merely on the defendant's *action* in making the hearsay declarant unavailable (without being concerned about what was going through his mind when he procured her unavailability). That is, in *Giles*, if the defendant made Avie unavailable for trial by virtue of his slaying her, then he could not protest the admission of her prior out-of-court statements (even if they violated the hearsay rule). In contrast, the minority approach required that defendant must have specifically intended to make the witness unavailable ("witness tampering") when he killed her in order to preclude him from benefiting from the doctrine by the exclusion of her prior out-of-court statements. Which view did *Giles* adopt?

3. *Rationale.* The rationale of the forfeiture-by-wrongdoing doctrine is to prevent a wrongdoer from profiting from his wrongful conduct. Does the approach of

the majority or minority best accomplish that purpose in *Giles*? How does the ruling create a "windfall" for defendants, in the words of the dissent? What are the implications of *Giles* for defendants and victims of intimate partner violence, the criminal justice system, and society?

4. *Originalist analysis.* Why do you suppose that a conservative judge, such as Justice Scalia, would author an opinion that is so supportive of defendants' rights? Justice Scalia bases his ruling in *Giles* on a historical analysis of early case law and treatises addressing the right to confrontation and concludes that the "equitable forfeiture" approach was not recognized by the Framers of the Confrontation Clause. How appropriate is that historical analysis as applied to our modern criminal justice system?

For scathing criticisms of the "originalist analysis" in *Giles*, see Thomas Y. Davies, Selective Originalism: Sorting out Which Aspects of *Giles*'s Forfeiture Exception to Confrontation Were or Were Not "Established at the Time of the Founding," 13 Lewis & Clark L. Rev. 605, 607 (2009); Tom Lininger, The Sound of Silence: Holding Batterers Accountable for Silencing their Victims, 87 Tex. L. Rev. 857, 875-879 (2009); Myrna S. Raeder, Being Heard After *Giles*: Comments on the Sound of Silence, 87 Tex. L. Rev. 105, 107 (2009); Myrna S. Raeder, Thoughts About *Giles* and Forfeiture in Domestic Violence Cases, 75 Brook. L. Rev. 1329, 1335 (2010).

More pointedly, how appropriate is an originalist analysis to explore the forfeiture-by-wrongdoing doctrine in the context of domestic violence? What does Justice Souter mean when he says (in an omitted concurrence) that the "historical record as revealed [here] simply does not focus on what should be required for forfeiture when the crime charged occurred in an abusive relationship or was its culminated act"? *Giles*, 554 U.S. at 380. Why does Professor Myrna Raeder suggest that "originalism will never protect domestic violence victims"? Raeder, Being Heard after *Giles*, supra, at 105.

To what extent does Justice Scalia's opinion reflect an understanding of the context and dynamics of domestic violence? To what extent does Justice Breyer's dissent? See generally G. Kristian Miccio, Giles v. California: Is Justice Scalia Hostile to Battered Women?, 87 Tex. L. Rev. 93, 101 (2009) (Justice Scalia's decision "speaks volumes about his attitude toward women, in general, and battered women, in particular"); Deborah Tuerkheimer, Forfeiture after *Giles*: The Relevance of "Domestic Violence Context," 13 Lewis & Clark L. Rev. 711, 731 (2009) (noting that *Giles* was the first time that the Court recognized the "domestic violence context" as a "relevant construct").

5. *Meanings of intent.* Both the majority and dissent address the issue of the defendant's intent. What are their respective views of the terms *intent*, *purpose*, and *motive*? What are Justice Breyer's criticisms of the meaning that Justice Scalia attaches to "intent"?

a. *Subjective vs. objective test.* According to Professor Tom Lininger, *Giles* shifted the proof of "intent" from an objective to a *subjective* test by focusing on the defendant's motive in killing the hearsay declarant. Lininger, Sound of Silence, supra, at 879. How? Does Justice Scalia vacillate between these standards? How? See id. at 864. What are the advantages versus disadvantages of an objective versus a subjective test of intent? How might Dwayne Giles's intent be assessed based on these different tests?

b. *Criticism.* How difficult will it be to prove that a defendant intended specifically to prevent the victim from testifying at the time he killed her? What light does Justice Breyer's dissent shed on this question? Suppose Dwayne Giles claims that his motive, at the time of the homicide, was not to make Avie unavailable at a possible future trial for assault but rather to express his outrage for her alleged infidelity. How can the prosecution prove otherwise?

Suppose a defendant has multiple motives in slaying an intimate partner. Could a court make the requisite finding of intent if a defendant has dual motives for making the victim unavailable at trial but only one motive qualifies as witness tampering? Does a court have to find that witness tampering was the defendant's *primary* motive? See Sarah Buel, Putting Forfeiture to Work, 43 U.C. Davis L. Rev. 1295, 1370-1371 (2010) (surveying state courts' approach to mixed-purpose cases); Lininger, Sound of Silence, supra, at 902-904 (discussing Supreme Court's past consideration of dual motives).

6. *Influential dictum: inferred intent.* Justice Scalia (and Justice Souter in his concurrence) suggest a manner to facilitate proof of the defendant's intent of witness tampering when the victim's unavailability results from the defendant's acts. That is, in dictum, Justice Scalia suggests the possibility for *inferring* the intent of witness tampering (in intimate partner homicides) based on the defendant's intent to isolate the victim from law enforcement and judicial authority.

> Where such an abusive relationship culminates in murder, the evidence may support a finding that the crime expressed the intent to isolate the victim and to stop her from reporting abuse to the authorities or cooperating with a criminal prosecution—rendering her prior statements admissible under the forfeiture doctrine. Earlier abuse, or threats of abuse, intended to dissuade the victim from resorting to outside help would be highly relevant to this inquiry, as would evidence of ongoing criminal proceedings at which the victim would have been expected to testify.

Giles, 554 U.S. at 377. How difficult is such an "inferred-intent standard" (as Professor Lininger calls it) to apply? See Lininger, Sound of Silence, supra, at 888 ("the devil is, as always, in the details").

7. *Federal Rule of Evidence.* Federal Rule of Evidence 804(b)(6) codifies the doctrine of forfeiture by wrongdoing. Justice Scalia suggests in *Giles* that this rule supports his analysis of the constitutional forfeiture doctrine. But cf. Lininger, Sound of Silence, supra, at 884 (criticizing that the Federal Rules of Evidence are narrower than constitutional doctrine and fail to support Scalia's view).

8. *Reform.* What can be done to facilitate domestic violence prosecutions after *Giles?* Professor Lininger suggests that jurisdictions adopt "per se rules" by which courts should find that a defendant had the specific intent to silence the accuser: (1) if the defendant violated a restraining order (either in the present case or another case involving the victim); (2) if the defendant committed any act of violence against that victim-accuser after she had made a police report or initiated any judicial proceedings; (3) if the defendant manifest a prolonged pattern of abuse of the victim-accuser even in the absence of a complaint or petition for a restraining order (per Justice Scalia's suggestion). Lininger, Sound of Silence, supra, 898-903. Cf. Andrew King-Ries, A Response to the Sound of Silence, 87 Tex. L. Rev. 85, 90-92 (2009) (criticizing Lininger's proposals).

Professor Sarah Buel has another proposal: adoption of a totality-of-the-circumstances standard in which certain circumstances evoke a rebuttable presumption of intent to silence. These circumstances include: defendant's termination of the abusive relationship by means of murder, pending legal proceedings or a protective order, a "classic abusive relationship," recantation, the presence of mixed purposes, statements to third parties about the abuse, and the cumulative history of abuse. Buel, supra, at 1359-1381. What do you think of these proposals?

Problem

Late one night, Police Officer Mark Armendariz responds to a call at an apartment and finds Mary there, excited and upset. She tells the officer that her partner Manuel assaulted her earlier that day. After determining that Manuel is no longer in the vicinity, the officer leaves. Minutes later, Mary calls 911 again. The call is interrupted, and the 911 operator records an angry exchange between Mary and Manuel in which Manuel physically assaults her and threatens to kill her if she talks to the police. Officer Armendariz is dispatched again to the apartment, with siren blaring. The officer arrests Manuel. Mary obtains a restraining order against Manuel that is valid for three years.

Six months later, Officer Armendariz and his partner are dispatched to Mary's apartment to investigate a possible violation of the restraining order. They see Manuel walking out of the apartment. He confirms that he violated the restraining order, but explains that he wants to reconcile with Mary. Mary is frightened and nervous. The police arrest Manuel for the second time. Three months later, another officer, Fernando Rojas, is dispatched again by Mary to investigate a 911 call about violation of a restraining order. Manuel is at Mary's apartment. Police arrest him a third time. A hearing on the alleged violation of the protective order is scheduled for the next month.

A few weeks before the hearing, Mary starts dating Manuel's friend, Javier. Nine days before the hearing, Manuel makes three late night calls to Mary's apartment. He discovers Javier there. He breaks into the apartment through a window. As Javier flees, he hears Mary screaming for help. Manuel is arrested later that morning for Mary's murder. The police place Manuel in the back of a patrol car with a friend of his. Unbeknownst to the men, the police are recording their conversation. The recording is introduced into evidence at trial. On the recording, Manuel is saying to his friend: "I got even with that whore, like I wanted to. I'm very happy." Manuel says he used a hammer to "smash her . . . so she'll learn, that fucking whore."

At trial, the State seeks to introduce statements that Mary made to police on the three occasions of Manuel's arrest, as well as the recording of the 911 call. The State argues that Manuel forfeited his Sixth Amendment right to confrontation by killing Mary. A jury finds Manuel guilty of second-degree murder and burglary. Manuel appeals, arguing that Mary's statements and the 911 call are testimonial hearsay and, thus, should have been inadmissible. What result? See People v. Banos, 100 Cal. Rptr. 3rd 476 (Ct. App. 2009).

6. Victim Recantation

■ PEOPLE v. SANTIAGO
2003 WL 21507176 (N.Y. Sup. Ct. 2003)

Atlas, J.

The defendant is charged with Aggravated Criminal Contempt and two counts of Criminal Contempt in the First Degree based on Angela R.'s allegations that he violated an Order of Protection which was issued to protect her. She and the defendant have lived together for many years, and as happens frequently in cases of this kind, prior to trial, Angela R. declared that she no longer wished to press charges, that she would decline to testify at trial, and that if she were made to testify she would declare that all the allegations she previously made to the police, prosecutor, and Grand Jury were fabricated by the police and the District Attorney. In view of that, the People moved for an order permitting them to use Angela R.'s Grand Jury testimony and her other out of court statements during the presentation of their direct case against the defendant. [Defendant opposes the motion.] . . .

[After the prosecution demonstrates the possibility that the defendant engaged in witness tampering, the court conducts a special hearing to test the validity of that claim.] At the hearing, Angela R. testified that she and the defendant are married by common-law and by love, and have been living together, as she put it, for "ten beautiful years." During her testimony, Angela R. professed to being a religious person with a deep faith in God. When confronted with the many reports of abuse she filed against the defendant she testified that all of them were false, notwithstanding the fact that she admitted to having written and/or signed them.

Throughout the course of her brief testimony, when challenged about these discrepancies, Angela R. answered the prosecutor's questions: "I don't remember," "I don't recall," "No, I did not," "I do not understand," and "I do not know" over 100 times. As the record bears out, she often responded so inconsistently as to be virtually irrational, all the while nervously watching the defendant for his approval, as he blew kisses to her from his seat at counsel table. Angela R. claimed that in March 1996, she discovered that the defendant fathered a child by another woman and that for six years thereafter she filed various charges against the defendant solely because she is "making him pay for that." Angela R. testified that she has been jealous and becomes violent with the defendant when he wants to leave her. She testified that since she now has a child of her own, she is no longer hurt by his infidelity. Nonetheless, she still wants to punish him. During her testimony she made the strange claim that she fabricates stories of abuse to get Orders of Protection which are designed to prevent him from living with her because she does not want him to leave her. . . .

[Police were first summoned to Angela's home on January 30, 1996, when she claimed Victor had been harassing her, making threats, and hitting.] On March 17, 1996, in response to another call, Police Officer Eleutice testified that she and a number of other officers climbed to Angela R.'s fifth floor apartment and, while outside, heard a female screaming for help. They sought entry but were denied it. . . . [Sergeant Smith] climbed the fire escape to look inside the apartment and he yelled down that he saw a male on top of a female struggling on the floor. The officers returned upstairs to the fifth floor where Sergeant Smith and Police Officer Zaccari broke down the door to gain access to the apartment. . . . It took four officers to pry the defendant off of the complainant, and even then the defendant continued kicking and spitting. The defendant was so violent that an Emergency Services team was called in to assist in restraining him. [The police took Angela to the hospital for treatment of her injuries.] . . .

Regarding this March 17, 1996, incident, Angela R. testified that she did not tell the police or the hospital staff any of the things attributed to her in their reports, and in fact, it was she who was hitting the defendant. [Defendant testified that] she attacked him, knocked him to the ground and then he was dripping with blood. The next thing he recalled was that they were in the apartment and she was hitting him. At that point, he blacked out [until] he woke up in the hospital handcuffed to the bed. . . .

[The court heard testimony from Dr. Ann Wolbert Burgess who frequently testifies on domestic violence and Battered Woman's Syndrome. She reviewed the law enforcement data, Angela's hearing testimony, and attempted to interview Angela. But she refused.]

Dr. Burgess testified . . . [that] Angela R. is an abused woman whose current behavior is explained by Battered Woman's Syndrome. In support of her opinion, Dr. Burgess noted that over a period of years, in a relationship marked by episodes of violence, Angela R. regularly called the police when attacked, obtained orders of protection from the court, then recanted her allegations and refused to prosecute. Dr. Burgess also noted evidence of the defendant's use of psychological abuse to control the complainant. He threatened to kill her, he blamed her for things that she had not done, he took things that were precious to her, he destroyed things that were important to her, and he acted in ways that enhanced her dependence upon him. While noting that their domestic violence cycle has entered the so-called honeymoon phase, Dr. Burgess also observed that while the defendant is in prison, Angela R. has been placed under tremendous pressure to not testify against him. Dr. Burgess testified that, given the amount of recent contact between the defendant and Angela R., the defendant has played a major role in her recantation and willingness to perjure herself. Dr. Burgess concluded that Angela R.'s behavior as a reluctant witness, her willingness to tell patent lies in court, to rationalize the defendant's behavior, and to accept blame for her current predicament reflects her imposed lack of self-esteem and her level of desperation. This, according to the expert, can only be attributed to the coercion inherent in the honeymoon phase of the cycle of violence and the tremendous pressure that the defendant has placed on Angela R. to relieve him of his current confinement.

. . . The credible evidence at this hearing makes very clear that Angela R.'s current attitude toward testifying is a classic example of a battered woman's reaction to what has been described as the honeymoon phase of the abusive relationship. Angela R. is frightened that separation will leave her isolated and without help in caring for her child and her home. The evidence shows that in the past she has feared, and she continues to fear, that the defendant's violent behavior will be directed toward her again and conceivably toward her child. The evidence establishes the defendant's contribution to the complainant's low self-esteem and sense of helplessness. Her interaction with those seeking to help her demonstrates her lack of confidence in herself and her inability to speak up in her own defense. The evidence shows that in the past the defendant had taken steps to isolate Angela R. from those who tried to assist her and that he prevented her from having access to social support agencies. The evidence reveals that the defendant threatened to hurt her if she sought help, he intercepted phone calls from a counselor and he took her Order of Protection (one of many), leaving the complainant to believe that she could not get the help of the police without it. In general, the defendant's behavior toward Angela R. has been abusive, demeaning and humiliating. According to the testimony, the complainant sought help quite often, but only when she was in acute distress, hurt or terrified. However, the testimony also establishes that she is unwilling to follow through when people try to help her because her feelings of shame and humiliation prevent her from discussing her plight publicly. The record also shows Angela R.'s repeated withdrawal of her complaints to law enforcement. In every case that she initiates, she eventually recants and she takes the blame for incidents in which she has been the wounded party. . . . Over time, the defendant has violated one court Order of Protection after another with impunity because, as he testified, the complainant never testifies against him.

Once again, Angela R. has declined to testify against the defendant. However, in this instance there is clear and convincing evidence that her unwillingness to continue with the prosecution comes after persistent efforts by the defendant to reconcile with the complainant and convince her to do what is necessary to get him out of jail. The defendant, in over 100 conversations with her (each of which seems to have constituted another violation of an Order of Protection), has used the complainant's desires for a normal and loving relationship to his own end. Angela R. fears that continued prosecution will make the defendant suffer in prison, hurt their relationship and likely lead to additional acts of violence. Obviously, the avoidance of any jail time is a tremendous incentive for the defendant to place extraordinary pressure upon the complainant. Indeed, the defendant testified that he has regularly discussed with Angela R. his urgent desire to be out of jail, and his view that it is up to her to get him out of jail and home to her . . .

The defense argument in this case suggests that no matter how frustrating, I should simply accept this as a failed prosecution. . . . However, I do not believe domestic violence cases are of the same character as other kinds of cases and I am unable to be indifferent about the effort of this complainant to withdraw her complaint. . . . Expert studies and our experience in the criminal process have taught us that there is a difference between the dynamics of domestic violence and other types of assault cases adjudicated by our courts. Countless judges have presided in courts through which the devastated victims of domestic violence have come, first to seek protection but later to withdraw their complaints even though it was clear from prior experience that they were likely to be the victims of violence again at the hands of their partners. There was a time when domestic violence cases were taken less seriously than other cases because of the routine withdrawal of such complaints and the frequent inability to prosecute these cases notwithstanding the serious injuries suffered by the complainants. Over the years we threw up our hands in surrender and tolerated domestic violence because we did not have a method by which these cases could be prosecuted over the complainants' objections.

Frustrated by this recurring sequence of events, police policy and the law evolved in ways designed to circumvent the inevitable recantation of the domestic violence victim. . . . Attempts to hold complainants in contempt as a means of compelling their testimony are notably unsuccessful and serve only to abuse the complainants further. Efforts to call the complainants as witnesses and cross-examine them with their prior testimony are of limited usefulness since impeached disclaimers cannot serve as proof of the abuse on the people's direct case. Attempts to simply persuade the complainants to testify fail, as they did in this case, because the negative pressures upon the battered complainants far outweigh any thoughts they might entertain of gaining relief from the abuse by prosecuting the defendant.

We are now aware that domestic violence cases brought by complainants with a long-standing history of abuse are to be viewed differently from other crimes of violence which come through our courts. We are accustomed to injured victims seeking retribution, punishment and protection from society. That, without a doubt, is the norm. It is fair to say that we now recognize that in domestic violence cases repeated abuse followed by repeated withdrawal of prosecution and the repeated grant of forgiveness to the abuser make such cases very different from the norm.

What is evident is that domestic violence cases are different because of the complainant's desire for a stable relationship and the exploitation of that desire by the defendant. The hallmark of such cases is the hope for a brighter future with the abuser held by the complainant who is weakened by past abuse and seduced by untrustworthy gestures of love but, whose expectations are eventually met with repeated abuse to the perverse satisfaction of the abuser. . . . Victims of domestic violence do not have the will to follow through. They lack the self-esteem and strength to seek retribution or permanent safety from their attackers. This is so not only because of the psychological damage done by repeated abuse, but also because there lurks in the mind of such complainants the fear of physical retaliation to themselves and their children at the hands of an offender whose past behavior toward the complainant makes it highly probable that such abuse will occur again. In short, the defendant's pattern of behavior causes the victim of domestic abuse to succumb to the offender's importuning in ways that others might not. Thus, attempts to become unavailable as a prosecuting witness cannot be viewed as we might see voluntary withdrawal in a case where the complainant and the defendant are strangers to one another. . . .

Clearly, the nature of this syndrome and the cost to the families involved, the police, medical professionals, the courts and society in general cry out for a solution. It is simply unacceptable for our process to turn a blind eye to the dangers of such abuse by shrugging our shoulders and saying that nothing can be done within the framework of existing law. . . .

In this case the conclusion is inescapable that this abused complainant seeks to make herself unavailable as a witness because of the pattern of misconduct directed toward her by the defendant. The defense notes that in recent weeks the defendant has not threatened the witness but has spoken to her only in terms of endearment, seeking her forgiveness and expressing his desire to return to a harmonious relationship with her. While that claim may be true to some extent, it is clear that the defendant's promises are not to be trusted and, in any event, always contain the implicit threat that the complainant's unwillingness to cooperate with him will result in dire consequences for her. . . . Thus, in my view, there is clear and convincing evidence that the defendant's misconduct procured the complainant's unavailability as a witness in this prosecution and, as a fitting consequence, the People should be allowed to present evidence of the complainant's prior statements and Grand Jury testimony regarding this incident to the trial jury.

Notes and Questions

1. *Background.* In the pretrial ruling in *Santiago*, the judge permitted the prosecutor, at trial, to introduce Angela's grand jury testimony. What are the special features of the grand jury procedure that enabled the assistant district attorney to obtain Angela's testimony? When the assistant district attorney initially informed Angela that he wanted her to testify before the grand jury, she expressed reluctance, explaining that she felt ashamed to recount her story to others, she didn't want others to judge her, and she was concerned that the defendant would be there. *Santiago*, 2003 WL 21507176 at *9. After he assured her that the accused would not be present, she consented. Emily Jane Goodman, Prosecuting the Batterer Without the Victim's Approval, Gotham Gazette, June 18, 2003, available at http://www.gothamgazette.com/article/law/20030618/13/429; Barbara Ross, Alleged Abuser May Use Wife as His Witness, N.Y. Daily News, May 23, 2003, at 1.

Santiago was in jail for one year prior to trial because he was unable to post $50,000 bail. Jail records revealed that he telephoned Angela more than 100 times between August 25 and October 2, 2003. 2003 WL 21507176, at *11. Four previous cases against him were dropped when she refused to testify. Karen Freifeld, Abuse Allegations to be Aired: Woman Had Declined to Testify, Newsday, May 23, 2003, at A17.

2. *Recantation generally.* Defense counsel or prosecutors who call a witness to testify generally have a good idea of the substance of that witness's testimony. Domestic violence prosecutions, however, contain an element of surprise because of the likelihood that a victim-witness may change her story ("flip"). Victim non-cooperation is a significant barrier to successful prosecutions, especially given the fact that there are generally no other witnesses. When the victim recants or refuses to cooperate, prosecutors often are forced to drop the charges. See Lininger, Prosecuting Batterers, supra, at 772 (reporting a finding from a survey of prosecutors' offices in three states that 76 percent are more likely to drop charges in this case).

3. *Forms of noncooperation.* Victim noncooperation takes several forms: failure to appear at court proceedings; testimony that denies or contradicts prior statements (for example, by denying or minimizing the abuse); or claims of memory loss about prior statements or the assault itself. What forms of noncooperation did Angela manifest?

4. *Prevalence of recantation.* How *frequent* is victim noncooperation in cases of domestic violence? According to prosecutors, it is a common occurrence. See Lininger, Prosecuting Batterers, supra, at 768-769 (reporting prosecutors' estimates that perhaps as many as 80 to 85 percent of victims recant). See also Melissa Hamilton, Expert Testimony on Domestic Violence: A Discourse Analysis 52, 102-112 (2009) (documenting types and frequency of recantation based on study of 62 appellate cases).

5. *Comparison.* Are victims of domestic violence more likely than other crime victims to recant or refuse to cooperate with law enforcement? Some prosecutors believe so. See Lininger, Prosecuting Batterers, *supra*, at 768 (so suggesting). Adult sexual assaults and child sexual abuse cases also entail victim recantation. How is recantation in these contexts similar to recantation in the domestic violence context? How is it different?

6. *Reasons for noncooperation.* Fear of retaliation seems to be the major reason for victim noncooperation. See Lininger, Prosecuting Batterers, supra, at 769

(reporting findings that batterers threaten retaliation in as many as half of all cases, and that 30 percent of batterers abuse victims in the predisposition phrase of prosecution). Additional possibilities include: financial dependence; low self-esteem; being in the "honeymoon phase"; fear for the safety of children, other family members, or pets; loyalty to the abuser; the belief that the abuser is making efforts to stop the violence and should be encouraged in those efforts; determination to solve the problem without outside assistance; discouragement based on prior unsuccessful attempts to get help; distrust of agencies or the courts; shame; and a belief that no one will believe their story. See Clare Dalton, When Paradigms Collide: Protecting Battered Parents and Their Children in the Family Court System, 37 Fam. & Conciliation Courts Rev. 273, 281-282 (1999); Thomas L. Kirsch II, Problems in Domestic Violence: Should Victims Be Forced to Participate in the Prosecution of Their Abusers?, 7 Wm. & Mary J. Women & L. 383, 392-398 (2001). Which of the preceding reasons motivated Angela? What efforts did the accused undertake to persuade the victim not to testify? What motivations of the victim did the accused target?

7. *Prior inconsistent statements.* Recantation raises the issue of the admissibility of prior inconsistent statements. In domestic violence cases, victims typically make incriminating statements to many persons, including the police, medical personnel, friends, and relatives, among others. At trial, the victim often denies having uttered these statements. Her testimony and the prior statements are thus inconsistent.

For what purpose(s) were the victim's prior out-of-court statements admitted in *Santiago*? When a victim claims memory loss, all jurisdictions admit a victim's inconsistent statements for impeachment purposes. However, some jurisdictions admit prior inconsistent statements to prove the truth of the matter asserted, provided that the statements meet the requirements of a state hearsay exception or Rule 801(d)(1)(A) of the Federal Rules of Evidence. See 1 McCormick On Evidence, supra, at §36; John E. B. Myers, 2 Myers on Evidence in Child, Domestic and Elder Abuse Cases §13.03([A], p. 850 (2005). Should more states adopt such exceptions? Should courts establish a feigned memory procedure to facilitate the admission of prior inconsistent statements in domestic violence cases? See Douglas E. Beloof & Joel Shapiro, Let the Truth Be Told: Proposed Hearsay Exceptions to Admit Domestic Violence Victims' Out of Court Statements as Substantive Evidence, 11 Columbia J. Gender & L. 1, 23 (2002) (so suggesting).

8. *Prosecutors' strategies to combat noncooperation.* Victim noncooperation is the primary motivating factor for the development of innovative prosecutorial policies. Prosecutors use a variety of practices, such as "victimless prosecution" that relies on the admission of hearsay statements (for example, the victim's statements to law enforcement personnel, health care professionals, and social workers) and that eliminates the need for the victim's in-court testimony. However, as we have seen, *Crawford* and *Davis* imposed significant restrictions on the admissibility of some hearsay statements. See generally Andrew King-Reis, Crawford v. Washington: The End of Victimless Prosecution?, 28 Seattle U. L. Rev. 301 (2005).

What methods are available to prosecutors after *Crawford* and *Davis* to compel a witness's testimony? One method is by showing sympathy for the victim and her plight, which means spending time with the victim and listening to her story. Kirsch, supra, at 399. As a means of encouraging the victim to testify, some prosecutors emphasize to the victim the danger that the abuser poses to the victim's *children*.

Id. at 400. However, time constraints limit prosecutors' ability to establish good relationships with reluctant witnesses. Id. at 399. Some prosecutors attempt to instill fear in the victim by threatening her with jail or an appearance before a judge to explain her noncooperation. Id. at 402, 404. This method is sometimes used in jurisdictions with hard no-drop policies. Id. at 403.

By far, the most common prosecutorial method is a subpoena of the witness. Despite a subpoena, some witnesses refuse to appear in court, subjecting themselves to contempt. Or, they flee the jurisdiction, making it impossible to serve the subpoena. See Casey G. Gwinn & Anne O'Dell, Stopping the Violence: The Role of the Police Officer and the Prosecutor, 20 W. St. U. L. Rev. 297, 302 (1993) (recounting story of witness who fled to Mexico to avoid being served in a case against her abuser—a judge). What methods did prosecutors use in *Santiago?*

Prosecutors have observed a phenomenon of a delay in victims' response—that is, victims' reluctance sometimes develops not in the immediate aftermath but days after the abuse. Lininger, Prosecuting Batterers, supra, at 771. This may present a "window of opportunity" for cooperation between the victim and law enforcement. Id. What strategies can prosecutors use to benefit from this "window of opportunity" to encourage the victim to testify?

9. *Punishment for noncooperation.* A number of factors influence prosecutors' use of coercive methods to compel a victim to testify, including the seriousness of the injuries, a defendant's criminal record, and the type of relationship between the defendant and the victim. Kirsch, supra, at 406-412. Is imprisoning a reluctant witness ever appropriate as a means of coercing testimony in the domestic violence context? See Maureen O'Hagan, In Baltimore, A Victim Becomes a Criminal: Woman Covered Up Domestic Abuse, Wash. Post, Mar. 30, 2001, at A1 (recounting story of victim who received 30-month sentence for perjury and obstruction of justice after she called 911 but later lied to a grand jury to avoid testifying against her partner).

What does prosecuting a victim of domestic violence accomplish? Does it protect the victim? Prevent domestic violence? What message does it send to the victim and perpetrator? Is such state coercion another form of disempowerment of the victim, similar to the coercion by her abuser? See generally Njeri Mathis Rutledge, Turning a Blind Eye: Perjury in Domestic Violence Cases, 39 N.M. L. Rev. 149 (2009).

Problem

Adolph Valentine and J. K. have been dating on and off for three years. One night, they are fighting in Valentine's car when Valentine drags J. K. out of the car and hits her in the face and neck. When police officers respond to a 911 call by a passing motorist, J. K. tells them that Valentine assaulted her. She repeats her account at the hospital. Police arrest Valentine for domestic assault. At trial, J. K. denies that an assault occurred, says that she got out of the car to swing at Valentine, and fell on the ice when he blocked her punch. She testifies that she called 911 to report the assault to retaliate against him. The motorist, police officers, and doctor contradict her. The prosecution wishes to introduce the testimony of Officer Bruessel who investigated the assault. Bruessel has a bachelor's degree in criminal justice, five years' experience in law enforcement, eight years' experience as a probation officer, has completed numerous domestic violence trainings, and has frequently dealt with domestic violence cases. The state wants Officer Bruessel to testify regarding battered woman's syndrome to explain J. K.'s recantation. How should the court rule on the admissibility of the testimony? What limitations, if any, should the court place on this testimony? See State v. Valentine, 787 N.W.2d 630 (Minn. Ct. App. 2010).

VIII

![black square]

Federal Criminal Response

A. INTRODUCTION

This chapter explores the federal criminal response to domestic violence, including the crime of interstate domestic violence, firearm-related domestic violence regulations, and federal regulation of crimes on tribal lands. The chapter begins with a narrative that sets the stage by highlighting the need for federal criminal legislation.

1. Setting the Stage: A Story of Interstate Violence

In September 2008, Robbie Howell pleads guilty to assault for beating his wife Deanna. The couple continues to live together. On Halloween, Robbie accuses Deanna of cheating on him—a claim that she vehemently denies. Robbie, a long-haul trucker, forces Deanna and their two-year-old daughter into his truck, and then drives them from North Carolina to California. Over the next six days, he repeatedly beats Deanna, sometimes using a large industrial-style flashlight, punching her in the face and body, and smothering her with a pillow. When Deanna has a seizure after being suffocated, he douses her with Mountain Dew. Their toddler begs him to stop beating her mother.

Upon reaching California, Robbie brags to his friends that he had beaten Deanna so badly that he broke his hand and had to use a flashlight to finish the job. Concerned, his friends call police as Robbie leaves for his return trip. Law enforcement pull the truck over in Oklahoma and find Deanna with large bruises on her chest, shoulders, and arms, black eyes, a split lip, swelling throughout her body, and a knot on her forehead. When Robbie is arrested by Ashe County, North Carolina, law enforcement officers, he brags that they cannot prosecute him because he wasn't located in their county when he beat Deanna. One witness testified at trial that Robbie boasted that law enforcement, "Ain't got nothing on me. They don't know what state I was in. They can't do nothing to me."

Robbie is convicted in federal court on kidnapping and interstate domestic violence charges. He is sentenced to 250 months in federal prison.

See Press Release, FBI, U.S. Attorney's Office, Man Sentenced to Serve Over 20 Years in Federal Prison for Interstate Domestic Violence (June 15, 2011), available at http://www.fbi.gov/charlotte/press-releases/2011/man-sentenced-to-serve-over-20-years-in-federal-prison-for-interstate-domestic-violence-crimes; Steve Lyttle, Trucker Convicted of Kidnapping, Charlotte Observer [N.C.], Aug. 31, 2010, available at 2010 WLNR 17322728.

2. VAWA's Federal Criminal Provisions

The following section explores the movement toward federalization of the criminal law and also the nature of the federal criminal provisions that apply to domestic violence.

Congress enacted the Violence Against Women Act (VAWA) as part of massive anti-crime legislation. The enactment of VAWA in 1994, supplemented by amendments to the Gun Control Act (GCA) (codified as amended in scattered sections of 18 U.S.C.), led to the establishment of several federal crimes: (1) the interstate crime of domestic violence, (2) interstate stalking, (3) interstate travel to violate a protection order, and (4) firearm restrictions. Congress enacted the firearm restrictions in two stages. In 1994, Congress amended the GCA to prevent individuals who were subject to protective orders from owning firearms (18 U.S.C. §922(d)(8), (g)(8)). In 1996, Congress amended the GCA with the Lautenberg Amendment to criminalize firearm possession for perpetrators of domestic violence misdemeanors (18 U.S.C. §921(a)(33)(A); §922(d)(8)-(9); §922(g)(8)-(9)).

Prior to the enactment of VAWA, crimes of domestic violence were traditionally subject to state jurisdiction. Jurisdictional gaps often led to interstate offenses going unpunished because of the difficulty of determining in which state a given offense began and/or ended in order to establish which state had jurisdiction over an offender who committed domestic violence in two or more states. Jurisdictional dilemmas also occurred in cases involving Native American women and non-Native American offenders because tribal authority only extended to Native American perpetrators on tribal lands. The federalization of domestic violence crimes had several advantages: federal prosecutors could devote superior resources to the prosecution of interstate offenses and the new federal crimes contained harsher sentences.

a. Violence Against Women Act: Interstate Crimes

(i) Interstate Travel to Commit Domestic Violence

■ 18 U.S.C. §2261. INTERSTATE DOMESTIC VIOLENCE

(a) Offenses.—

    (1) Travel or conduct of offender.—A person who travels in interstate or foreign commerce or enters or leaves Indian country or within the special maritime and territorial jurisdiction of the United States with the intent to kill, injure, harass, or intimidate a spouse, intimate partner, or dating partner, and who, in the course of or as a result of such travel, commits or attempts to commit a crime of violence against that spouse, intimate partner, or dating partner, shall be punished as provided in subsection (b).

    (2) Causing travel of victim.—A person who causes a spouse, intimate partner, or dating partner to travel in interstate or foreign commerce or to enter or leave Indian country by force, coercion, duress, or fraud, and who, in the course of, as a result of, or to facilitate such conduct or travel, commits or attempts to commit a crime of violence against that spouse, intimate partner, or dating partner, shall be punished as provided in subsection (b).

(b) Penalties.—A person who violates this section or section 2261A shall be fined [and/or imprisoned: for life or any term of years if death of the victim results; for not more than 20 years if permanent disfigurement or life threatening bodily injury to the victim results; for not more than 10 years if serious bodily injury to the victim results or if the offender uses a dangerous weapon during the offense; for the period provided by Chapter 109A for sexual abuse; for not more than 5 years in any other case; and for stalking in violation of a temporary or permanent civil or criminal injunction, restraining order, no-contact order for not less than 1 year.]

(ii) Interstate Stalking

■ 18 U.S.C §2261A. STALKING

Whoever—

    (1) travels in interstate or foreign commerce or within the special maritime and territorial jurisdiction of the United States, or enters or leaves Indian country, with the intent to kill, injure, harass, or place under surveillance with intent to kill, injure, harass, or intimidate another person, and in the course of, or as a result of, such travel places that person in reasonable fear of the death of, or serious bodily injury to, or causes substantial emotional distress to that person, a member of the immediate family . . . of that person, or the spouse or intimate partner of that person; or

(2) with the intent—
  (A) to kill, injure, harass, or place under surveillance with intent to kill, injure, harass, or intimidate, or cause substantial emotional distress to a person in another State or tribal jurisdiction or within the special maritime and territorial jurisdiction of the United States; or
  (B) to place a person in another State or tribal jurisdiction, or within the special maritime and territorial jurisdiction of the United States, in reasonable fear of the death of, or serious bodily injury to—
    (i) that person;
    (ii) a member of the immediate family . . . of that person; or
    (iii) a spouse or intimate partner of that person;

uses the mail, any interactive computer service, or any facility of interstate or foreign commerce to engage in a course of conduct that causes substantial emotional distress to that person or places that person in reasonable fear of the death of, or serious bodily injury to, any of the persons described in clauses (i) through (iii) of subparagraph (B);

shall be punished as provided in section 2261(b) of this title.

(iii) Interstate Travel to Violate an Order of Protection

■ 18 U.S.C. §2262(a). INTERSTATE VIOLATION OF PROTECTION ORDER

(a) Offenses.—

  (1) **Travel or conduct of offender.**—A person who travels in interstate or foreign commerce, or enters or leaves Indian country or within the special maritime and territorial jurisdiction of the United States, with the intent to engage in conduct that violates the portion of a protection order that prohibits or provides protection against violence, threats, or harassment against, contact or communication with, or physical proximity to, another person, or that would violate such a portion of a protection order in the jurisdiction in which the order was issued, and subsequently engages in such conduct, shall be punished as provided in subsection (b).
  (2) **Causing travel of victim.**—A person who causes another person to travel in interstate or foreign commerce or to enter or leave Indian country by force, coercion, duress, or fraud, and in the course of, as a result of, or to facilitate such conduct or travel engages in conduct that violates the portion of a protection order that prohibits or provides protection against violence, threats, or harassment against, contact or communication with, or physical proximity to, another person, or that would violate such a portion of a protection order in the jurisdiction in which the order was issued, shall be punished as provided in subsection (b).

(b) Penalties.—A person who violates this section shall be fined [and/or imprisoned: for life or any term of years if death of the victim results; for not more than 20 years if permanent disfigurement or life threatening bodily injury to the victim results; for not more than 10 years if serious bodily injury to the victim results or if the offender uses a dangerous weapon during the offense; for the period provided by Chapter 109A for sexual abuse; and for not more than 5 years in any other case].

VAWA's firearm offenses are discussed later in this chapter.

B. INTERSTATE DOMESTIC VIOLENCE AS A CRIME

■ UNITED STATES v. LARSEN
615 F.3d 780 (7th Cir. 2010)

SYKES, Circuit Judge.

. . . David Larsen brutally attacked Teri Jendusa-Nicolai, his ex-wife, when she came to his home in Racine County, Wisconsin, to pick up their two young daughters. The couple had divorced three years earlier after an abusive marriage, and Jendusa-Nicolai had recently taken Larsen to court for nonpayment of child support. Larsen lured her into his home and began to beat her with a baseball bat, strangle, and smother her. When she did not succumb, he bound her head, ankles, and wrists with duct tape and placed her in a garbage can filled with snow. He then put the garbage can, with Jendusa-Nicolai inside, in the back of his pick-up truck and drove to a self-storage facility in Illinois where he had a rented storage locker. He left her there to die, in a cold storage locker, in the snow-filled garbage can with boxes wedged around it to prevent her from climbing out.

During the drive to Illinois, Jendusa-Nicolai managed to free her hands and call 911 from her cell phone. She gave Larsen's home address, and local law enforcement and rescue personnel broke into Larsen's home around 11 a.m. in an attempt to find Jendusa-Nicolai. They remained inside for about 15 minutes—just long enough to ascertain that she was not there. Jendusa-Nicolai was able to make two more calls from her cell phone: She called her husband at noon and called 911 a second time around 2 p.m. At one point along the route to Illinois, she tried to extend her hand outside the garbage can in an effort to attract the attention of passing motorists. Larsen saw this, hit her again, and confiscated her cell phone.

From the second and third phone calls, the police learned that Jendusa-Nicolai was bound and in the back of Larsen's truck. They also learned that Jendusa-Nicolai's two daughters were missing. At about 3:30 p.m., law-enforcement officers and a rescue team re-entered Larsen's home after the Racine County District Attorney concluded that exigent circumstances existed for a warrantless search. The police searched the house thoroughly for six hours looking for the two missing children as well as clues about Jendusa-Nicolai's whereabouts. They went through papers, played back voice-mail messages, and searched through Larsen's computer files. During this search, they observed a large quantity of blood in the front hall, as well as an overturned chair, a blood-stained bucket, sweatpants with duct tape around the ankles, and blood-stained gloves and socks. In the meantime other officers prepared a search-warrant application.

Police arrested Larsen around 6 p.m. that evening when he reported for work. He told investigators that his daughters were at his girlfriend's house but claimed he did not know anything about Jendusa-Nicolai's disappearance. Police recovered the two girls at about 9:45 p.m. and suspended the search of Larsen's home without any further information about Jendusa-Nicolai's location. The search warrant was issued at about 11 p.m.

The next morning, the police searched Larsen's wallet and found two business cards for a storage facility in Illinois. Police called the storage facility, and an employee checked Larsen's unit and heard moaning inside. Local police immediately responded and recovered Jendusa-Nicolai from inside the garbage can. Doctors later said she was about an hour from death: Her body temperature had dropped to 84 degrees, renal failure had begun, and she was frostbitten about her body. She was hospitalized and suffered a miscarriage two days later while still at the hospital; she estimated that she had been pregnant for about five weeks. All her toes had to be amputated due to frostbite, and her hearing was damaged because of the blows to her head.

[Larsen was charged with state and federal crimes. In federal court, he was convicted of kidnapping in violation of 18 U.S.C. §1201(a)(1), and interstate domestic violence in violation of 18 U.S.C. §2261(a)(2) and (b)(2) (the Interstate Domestic Violence Act). Here, he challenges those convictions.]

COMMERCE CLAUSE CHALLENGE TO THE INTERSTATE DOMESTIC VIOLENCE ACT

Larsen first argues that the Interstate Domestic Violence Act is unconstitutional because it exceeds Congress's legislative power under the Commerce Clause. Specifically, he claims that the Act impermissibly regulates purely local, noneconomic conduct that does not have a substantial effect on interstate commerce. The relevant portion of the Act provides as follows:

> A person who causes a spouse, intimate partner, or dating partner to travel in interstate or foreign commerce . . . by force, coercion, duress, or fraud, and who, in the course of, as a result of, or to facilitate such conduct or travel, commits or attempts to commit a crime of violence against that spouse, intimate partner, or dating partner, shall be punished. . . .

18 U.S.C. §2261(a)(2). We conclude . . . that the Interstate Domestic Violence Act is a proper exercise of Congress's Commerce Clause power.

The Supreme Court's "modern Commerce Clause jurisprudence has 'identified three broad categories of activity that Congress may regulate under its commerce power'" [including] "use of the channels of interstate commerce"; the "instrumentalities of interstate commerce, or persons or things in interstate commerce, even though the threat may come only from intrastate activities"; and "those [intrastate] activities that substantially affect interstate commerce." Congress's legislative authority in the first and second categories is plenary. Congressional power in the third category, however, extends only to economic activity that substantially affects interstate commerce. . . .

Larsen conceptually locates his argument in the third Commerce Clause category. The Act is unconstitutional, he contends, because Congress lacks the authority to punish domestic violence, which is wholly intrastate conduct, noneconomic in nature, and does not substantially affect interstate commerce. This argument is misplaced. The Interstate Domestic Violence Act regulates the channels or instrumentalities of interstate commerce and persons in interstate commerce—not purely intrastate activity—and therefore falls within [the] first and second categories, in which Congress has plenary authority to legislate. The Act punishes only those who cause a spouse or intimate partner to "travel in interstate or foreign commerce" and who commit a crime of violence "in the course of, as a result of, or to facilitate" that interstate travel. It is the victim's movement in interstate commerce—not the intrastate crime of violence—that implicates the Interstate Domestic Violence Act.

The Supreme Court has long held that movement of persons across state lines is sufficient to permit congressional regulation under the Commerce Clause [citing Cleveland v. United States, 329 U.S. 14 (1946) (upholding the Mann Act against a challenge by polygamists who transported their wives across state lines); Caminetti v. U.S., 242 U.S. 491 (1917) (upholding the White Slave Act of 1910 prohibiting the transportation of women in interstate commerce for purposes of debauchery or prostitution)]. . . .

Larsen relies heavily on [United States v. Morrison, 529 U.S. 598 (2000)] (invalidating a provision of VAWA that provided a civil remedy to victims of gender-related violence, reasoning that the statute lacked any jurisdictional element that sufficiently tied it to interstate commerce), but that case hurts rather than helps his argument. . . . There is nothing in *Morrison* that limits Congress's authority to regulate the use of the channels or instrumentalities of, or persons in, interstate commerce. To the contrary, the Court specifically distinguished the civil remedy in the Violence Against Women Act, which regulated wholly intrastate conduct, from §2261(a)(1), the criminal-penalty provision at issue here. The Court took note of the "inter-state travel" element of the criminal offense and the difference that the presence of this element made in the Commerce Clause analysis: "The Courts of Appeals have uniformly upheld th[e] criminal sanction [§2261(a)(1)] as an appropriate exercise of Congress' Commerce Clause authority, reasoning that '[t]he provision properly falls within the first [category] as it regulates the use of channels of interstate commerce.'"

This language, of course, cannot be taken as an explicit endorsement of the conclusion that §2261(a)(1) survives Commerce Clause challenge as a regulation of the channels or instrumentalities of, or persons in, interstate commerce; *Morrison* addressed only the civil-remedy provision in the Violence Against Women Act. But the Court's language undermines Larsen's position that §2261(a)(1) regulates purely intrastate activity and must be analyzed as such under *Lopez* and *Morrison*. Accordingly, we join the Second, Fourth, Fifth, and Sixth Circuits in holding that the Interstate Domestic Violence Act is a valid exercise of Congress's power under the Commerce Clause to regulate the channels or instrumentalities of, or persons in, interstate commerce.

DOUBLE JEOPARDY

Larsen next asserts that his convictions for both kidnapping and interstate domestic violence are multiplicitous in violation of the Double Jeopardy Clause. Kidnapping, he argues, is a lesser-included offense of a violation of the Interstate Domestic Violence Act, and so to punish him for both crimes is to punish him twice for the same offense.

The Fifth Amendment's Double Jeopardy Clause provides that no person shall "be subject for the same offense to be twice put in jeopardy of life or limb." The double-jeopardy principle implicated here is that a court may not impose cumulative punishments for the same act unless the legislature intends it. Accordingly, a person may not be convicted and punished for two separate offenses arising out of the same act unless "each [offense] requires proof of a fact which the other does not." . . .

To obtain a kidnapping conviction, the government must prove that the defendant (1) seized the victim; (2) held the victim "for ransom or reward or otherwise"; and (3) transported the victim in interstate commerce. 18 U.S.C. §1201(a)-(a)(1). The Interstate Domestic Violence Act, on the other hand, requires that (1) the defendant is a spouse, intimate partner, or dating partner of the victim; (2) the defendant caused the victim to travel in interstate commerce by force, coercion, duress, or fraud; and (3) the defendant committed a crime of violence against the victim in the course of, as a result of, or to facilitate the interstate travel. 18 U.S.C. §2261(a)(2).

Larsen acknowledges that the Interstate Domestic Violence Act requires proof of facts that the kidnapping statute does not: The defendant and the victim must be spouses, intimate partners, or dating partners, and the defendant must commit a crime of violence against the victim. He contends, however, that the converse is not true; he maintains that kidnapping has no element not also required by the Interstate Domestic Violence Act. Stated differently, Larsen's argument is that the crime of interstate domestic violence encompasses the crime of kidnapping.

We disagree. The kidnapping statute requires that the defendant "hold[ ] [the victim] for ransom or reward or otherwise."[2] This "holding" requirement is an essential element of kidnapping and must be established in every case. Furthermore, the Supreme Court has said that the "holding" requirement "necessarily implies an unlawful physical or mental restraint for an appreciable period." Chatwin v. United States, 326 U.S. 455, 460 (1946). The Interstate Domestic Violence Act, on the other hand, does not require that the defendant hold the victim. Rather, the defendant must cause the victim to travel in interstate commerce "by force, coercion, duress, or fraud," and commit a crime of violence against the victim "in the course of, as a result of, or to facilitate" the interstate travel.

Thus, if a defendant (for example) induces his spouse to travel across state lines by coercion or false pretenses and then commits a crime of violence against her when she arrives, he would be guilty of interstate domestic violence but not kidnapping because the "holding" element of kidnapping would be missing. . . .

Larsen suggests that even if the two crimes require proof of different elements in theory, in this case the same facts proved both the interstate travel element of interstate domestic violence and the "holding" element of kidnapping. That is, Larsen argues that the government could not prove a violation of the Interstate Domestic Violence Act in this case without also proving that the defendant "held" the victim for purposes of the kidnapping statute. . . .

[I]t makes no difference that the same evidence established that Larsen forcibly caused Jendusa-Nicolai to travel in interstate commerce and also that he "held" her

---

2. "Whoever unlawfully seizes, confines, inveigles, decoys, kidnaps, abducts, or carries away and holds for ransom or reward or otherwise any person . . . when the person is willfully transported in interstate or foreign commerce . . . shall be punished by imprisonment for any term of years or for life. . . ." 18 U.S.C. §1201(a).

as required for conviction of kidnapping. Each of these offenses requires proof of an element that the other does not, and that defeats Larsen's multiplicity argument. His convictions do not violate double jeopardy. . . .

Notes and Questions

1. *Background.* Teri Jendusa-Nicolai's divorce from Larsen in 2001 "angered Larsen greatly." Plaintiff-Appellee's Brief at 6, United States v. Larsen, 615 F.3d 780 (7th Cir. 2009) (No. 08-3088). Teri later remarried. When Larsen ceased paying child support, she petitioned to hold him in contempt. The proceeding took place on January 27, 2004, three days before the attack. On the day of the attack, Teri went to pick up their daughters after a visit with Larsen. Because of Larsen's past abuse, she generally arranged the custody transfer in public. That day, however, because he refused to meet in public, she agreed to go to his home. Larsen lured her into the house, telling her that their daughters were playing hide-and-seek and wanted her to find them. When she entered, he knocked her unconscious with a baseball bat. Id. at 6-7.

Larsen was sentenced to 35 years in prison and 20 years of extended supervision. Following the trial, Jendusa-Nicolai filed a tort action against him for assault, false imprisonment, and intentional infliction of emotional distress. She won a judgment of over $3 million. Larsen filed for bankruptcy but was not permitted to discharge the tort judgment. See Larsen v. Jendusa-Nicolai, 442 B.R. 905 (Bankr. E.D. Wis. 2010) (affirming bankruptcy court holding that state tort judgment regarding a debt incurred for "willful and malicious injury" was not dischargeable in bankruptcy). See Stephanie Brien, Judge Awards Teri Jendusa-Nicolai More than $3 Million, Journal Times [Racine, Wis.], June 23, 2008, available at http://www.journaltimes.com/news/local/article_69067283-3edf-5689-81b3-b4f354577a41.html.

2. *Social reality.* How many federal crimes do federal prosecutors prosecute under VAWA? Most offenders who are referred to federal prosecutors for VAWA violations are suspected of firearm-related domestic violence and not interstate domestic violence. Only about 17 percent of those referred to federal prosecutors for violation of VAWA's crimes are suspected, specifically, of interstate travel to commit domestic violence. Matthew R. Durose et al., Bureau of Justice Statistics, Family Violence Statistics Including Statistics on Strangers and Acquaintances 51 (June 2005) (based on a total of 757 suspects from 2000 to 2002), available at http://bjs.ojp.usdoj.gov/content/pub/pdf/fvs.pdf.

What are the conviction rates and sentences of offenders who are adjudicated on charges of interstate domestic violence? Almost all of these offenders are convicted. Id. at 52 (reporting 90 percent conviction rate, based on study of 52 defendants for whom data were available and whose most serious adjudicated offense was interstate domestic violence). Prison terms range from 1 to 25 years depending on the severity of the harm inflicted on the victim; the mean prison term is 7.5 years. Based on these data, how effective is VAWA's provision on interstate domestic violence? When first proposed, VAWA's criminal provisions faced significant opposition, including opposition by Chief Justice Rehnquist, who expressed concern that the new interstate crimes would overburden federal courts on issues that were generally handled by states. William H. Rehnquist, Chief Justice's 1991 Year-End Report on the Federal Judiciary 3 (1992). Was his concern justifiable?

3. *Purpose.* VAWA criminalized conduct in which an abuser crosses state lines to injure, harass, or intimidate an intimate partner or to violate an order of protection. The law was necessary because a wrongdoer's travel across state lines makes state prosecution difficult (that is, it is sometimes difficult to satisfy the burden of proof that a given act took place in a particular state) and also because state penalties were inadequate. Durose et al., supra, at 51.

4. *Elements of crimes.* The defendant in *Larsen* was indicted on federal kidnapping charges (18 U.S.C. §1201(a)(1)), and interstate domestic violence (the Interstate Domestic Violence Act (IDVA), 18 U.S.C. §2261). The former crime requires that the defendant abduct the victim and then transport her in interstate commerce. The latter crime requires that the defendant cause a spouse or former spouse (or intimate partner) "to travel in interstate or foreign commerce . . . by force, coercion, duress, or fraud, and who, in the course of, as a result of, or to facilitate such conduct or travel, commits or attempts to commit a crime of violence against that spouse, [or] intimate partner." Although these issues were not before the Seventh Circuit Court of Appeals, did Larsen's conduct satisfy the requisite elements of those offenses?

5. *Constitutionality.* Larsen raises two constitutional arguments: The IDVA exceeds Congress's power under the Commerce Clause and also violates the Double Jeopardy Clause.

a. *Commerce Clause argument.* Congress can regulate three categories of activity under the Commerce Clause power: (1) "the use of the channels of interstate commerce"; (2) "the instrumentalities of interstate commerce, or persons or things in interstate commerce, even though the threat may come only intrastate activities"; and (3) "those activities having a substantial relation to interstate commerce" (substantially and economically affecting interstate commerce). United States v. Morrison, 529 U.S. 598, 608-609 (2000) (quoting United States v. Lopez, 514 U.S. 549, 558-559 (1995)). Under which category did the Seventh Circuit Court of Appeals find that Congress could criminalize interstate domestic violence? Was the government required to prove that defendant's actions had economic effects, as Larsen urged?

Larsen contends that the statute regulates local violent conduct with an insufficient nexus to interstate commerce, that is, the statute punishes an *intrastate* crime of violence. He argues that the IDVA "is not so much a regulation of the use of channels of interstate commerce . . . as it is a regulation of local violence that either precedes or follows the use of channels of interstate commerce." In other words, he maintains that his "violence was over before interstate travel, or any travel, began." What does the court respond to his arguments? How is regulation of interstate domestic violence similar to, and different from, regulation pursuant to the Mann Act? See Defendant-Appellant's Brief at 29-30, United States v. Larsen, 615 F.3d 780 (7th Cir. 2010) (No. 08-3088) (discussing differences). Do you agree that Larsen's violence was completed before any travel began? What aspects of Larsen's crime could Congress reach that, at first glance, appear wholly intrastate?

In *Morrison,* supra, the U.S. Supreme Court overturned a provision of VAWA that authorized a *civil* remedy for victims of gender-motivated violence. (*Morrison* is discussed in Chapter 10.) The underlying offense was the gang rape of a college student by two acquaintances. VAWA's civil rights remedy (declared unconstitutional in *Morrison*) provided a private tort action against the alleged rapists. According to Larsen, *Morrison* held that Congress may not "regulate noneconomic, violent criminal conduct based solely on that conduct's aggregate effect on interstate commerce." *Morrison*, 529 U.S. at 615-617. Larsen contends that if "violent but local and non-economic crime provides no occasion for congressional intervention with a federal civil remedy" (as in *Morrison*), then "the government logically cannot insist success-fully that violent, local, and non-economic crimes can invite federal criminal punish-ment, either." Appellant's Brief at 18, *Larsen* (No. 08-3088). How is the conduct in *Larsen* distinguishable? See Appellee's Brief at 17-23, *Larsen* (No. 08-3088).

b. *Double jeopardy.* Larsen also asserts that his convictions for kidnapping and interstate domestic violence violate the Double Jeopardy Clause because, since kid-napping is a lesser-included offense of a violation of interstate domestic violence, the statute punishes him twice for the same offense. How does the court respond? What aspects of interstate domestic violence and interstate kidnapping are statuto-rily distinct? Even though statutorily distinct, are the two crimes *factually* distinct? Do you agree with the court's analysis?

6. *Impact of federalization.* Is there a need for federalization of domestic violence crimes? For example, Larsen, although conceding that "[b]eating people with a baseball bat, or abducting them, or torturing them are very bad things to do," maintains nonetheless that "the states, every one of them, have laws adequate to punish such acts." Appellant's Brief at 35-36, *Larsen* (No. 08-3088). Is his argu-ment persuasive? With so many state statutes directly addressing domestic vio-lence, do VAWA's criminal provisions still serve a valid purpose in deterring domestic violence? Why might criminalizing domestic violence as a federal crime be beneficial to victims of domestic violence? To states? To the federal government?

When should the federal criminal law step in to address a problem such as domestic violence, which is a subject that is traditionally considered to be within the scope of state jurisdiction? Former Deputy Attorney General Jamie S. Gorelick and former Deputy Assistant Attorney General Harry Litman suggest that the federal government should invoke its criminal jurisdiction when:

> (1) there is a pressing problem of national concern; (2) state criminal jurisdiction is inadequate to solve significant aspects of the problem; and (3) the federal government—by virtue of its investigative, prosecutorial, or legal resources—is posi-tioned to make a qualitative difference to the solution of the problem. . . .

Jamie S. Gorelick & Harry Litman, Prosecutorial Discretion and the Federalization Debate, 46 Hastings L.J. 967, 972 (1995). Does domestic violence qualify for federal protection under these factors? What other issues support invoking federal criminal law in cases of domestic violence? What types of domestic violence issues should be left to states to enforce or implement? What are the consequences of criminalizing domestic violence as a *federal* crime?

Professor Myrna Raeder suggests several reasons for the federalization of domestic violence-related crimes, including: (1) the ability to impose more severe federal penalties; (2) the inability of individual state prosecutions to capture "the full tenor of the abuse"; (3) the fact that interstate domestic violence is easier to prove than kidnapping and avoids the problem that juries are prone to acquit defendants on kidnapping charges (stemming from jurisdictional difficulties); and (4) "it is important to have a venue where domestic violence-related charges are consistently viewed as leading to incarceration, rather than to batterers' or anger management treatment." Myrna S. Raeder, Domestic Violence in Federal Court: Abused Women as Victims, Survivors, and Offenders, 19 Fed. Sent. R. 91, 92 (2006), 2006 WL 3912217. What do you think of these reasons?

7. *Cyberstalking.*

a. *Background.* Cyberstalking consists of the use of electronic media, such as the Internet or other electronic devices, to annoy, threaten, or harass. Congress enacted the first federal stalking law, in 1996. The Interstate Stalking Punishment and Prevention Act, Pub. L. No. 104-201, §1069(a), 110 Stat. 2655-2656 (codified at 18 U.S.C. §2261A) (as amended by VAWA), prohibits abusers from traveling across state lines with the intent to injure or harass a person and, in doing so, putting a person in fear of death or serious bodily injury. Congress amended the statute in 2000 via the Victims of Trafficking and Violence Protection Act, Pub. L. No. 106-386, §1107(b)(1), 114 Stat. 1498, to further prohibit the use of "the mail, any interactive computer service, or any facility of interstate or foreign commerce" to engage in a "course of conduct" intended to harass or threaten someone in another state with death or serious bodily injury. The amendment thus criminalized cyberstalking and other forms of remote stalking, punishing a crime that could occur wholly intrastate, such as sending a harassing email from and to people within the same state. The Interstate Stalking Act was amended a third time when VAWA was reauthorized in 2006. The Violence Against Women and Department of Justice Reauthorization Act of 2005 (VAWA), Pub. L. No. 109-162, §114, 119 Stat. 2960, 2987-2988, expanded Section 2261A to criminalize any course of conduct that causes substantial emotional distress through the defendant's use of an interactive computer service.

Other federal laws that also address cyberstalking include: the Interstate Communications Act (codified in relevant part at 18 U.S.C. §875(c)) (making it a crime to transmit any communication in interstate commerce containing any threat to injure another person); and the Federal Telephone Harassment Statute (codified in relevant part at 47 U.S.C. §223) (punishing making a phone call, anonymously and knowingly, or using a telecommunications device, "to annoy, abuse, threaten, or harass" a person).

b. *Constitutionality.* Is the Interstate Stalking Punishment and Prevention Act constitutional? Is it within Congress's power to regulate the channels or instrumentalities of interstate commerce? How is the regulation similar to, and different from, the crime of interstate travel to commit domestic violence? Courts have generally upheld VAWA's interstate stalking provisions as a valid exercise of Congressional power under the Commerce Clause. See, e.g., United States v. Al-Zubaidy, 283 F.3d 804 (6th Cir. 2002).

c. *"Course of conduct" requirement.* Stalking laws sometimes define stalking as a "course of conduct" involving intrusive threatening behavior. See 18 U.S.C. §2261A(B) (requiring a "course of conduct that causes substantial emotional distress"). In United States v. Shrader, 2010 WL 2425900 (S.D. W. Va. 2010), the defendant challenged the federal cyberstalking "course of conduct" language. There, the victim's former boyfriend harassed her and murdered her mother and her friend, in her presence, stemming from his jealousy. Id. at *2. Over the next several decades, from prison and upon release, the defendant sent the victim and her family harassing mail and phone calls. Id. Finally, in 2009, he sent a 32-page letter from West Virginia to the victim in Texas. Id. When he was charged with interstate cyberstalking, he argued that the single interstate letter constituted only a single act of interstate cyberstalking, and not two or more acts necessary for the requisite "course of conduct." Id. at *3. Rejecting the argument, the court found that the statute does not require two or more uses of interstate facilities to establish a "course of conduct," but rather only two or more acts of harassment. Id. at *4.

d. *Effectiveness.* How effective are VAWA's cyberstalking provisions? One commentator criticizes the Federal Interstate Stalking Punishment and Prevention Act for its failure to address third-party harassment (that is, innocent harassment by a third party who has been provided false information by the abuser). See Naomi Harlin Goodno, Cyberstalking, a New Crime: Evaluating the Effectiveness of Current State and Federal Laws, 72 Mo. L. Rev. 125, 132 (2007). Goodno also criticizes other federal legislation addressing cyberstalking—the Interstate Communications Act for its requirement that the communication must contain an *explicit threat* (id. at 136), and the Federal Telephone Harassment Statute for its requirements that the cyber message must be sent *anonymously* and for the purpose of *annoying* another (id. at 150). The legislation thereby precludes prosecution of known abusers and raises questions about subjective interpretations of conduct that constitutes an "annoyance." Stalking and cyberstalking are also explored in Chapter 4.

8. *Proposed federal legislation.* Congress is considering a bill that would enhance federal criminal protections for victims of sexual offenses. Nicole's Law (H.R. 1678, 112th Cong. (2011)) would require states to extend to such victims the same protection that is available to domestic violence victims. The proposed legislation permits a court to issue a no-contact order as a condition of bail to continue a prior order, or issue a new order upon conviction that prohibits a defendant charged with or convicted of a sex offense from having any contact with a victim, including restraining the defendant from entering the victim's residence, place of employment, business, or school, and from harassing or stalking the victim or victim's relatives. The bill applies broadly even to victims who are not in a dating or intimate relationship.

Problems

1. Rita Gluzman asks her cousin, Vladimir Zelenin, to help her murder her estranged husband, Yakov Gluzman. On the appointed day, Rita and Vladimir meet in New Jersey, drive to New York, and hide in Mr. Gluzman's apartment with an ax and a knife. Upon Mr. Gluzman's return, they murder him. Vladimir dismembers Mr. Gluzman's body while Rita erases traces of the crime. They put the body parts in plastic bags in the car, and plan to dispose of the body in a river. Vladimir drops Rita off back in New Jersey, but is arrested before they can dispose of the body. Police find Rita hiding in New York. She is charged with conspiracy to commit interstate domestic violence and the commission of interstate domestic violence under the Violence Against Women Act. What result? See United States v. Gluzman, 154 F.3d 49 (2d Cir. 1998).

2. Linda decides to end her 12-year abusive marriage to James after his behavior becomes increasingly erratic. After she announces her intention to divorce him, he threatens to kill her, telling her that he will "leave [her] body in a pool of blood," and that he found a place "where I could kill you and nobody would hear you scream." She notices that he often follows her in his truck. In New York,

she files for, and obtains, an order of protection prohibiting him from assaulting, stalking, harassing, or intimidating her. After that, she no longer sees him following her.

Unbeknownst to Linda, James has put a GPS device on her car. He has enlisted a friend to track her movements through an Internet website. A few months later, when Linda has a car accident in New Jersey, the repair shop discovers the GPS device and gives it to police. James is charged with two counts of interstate stalking and one count of interstate violation of a protection order in violation of 18 U.S.C. §§2261A and 2262(a)(1). He defends, claiming that the use of the GPS device could not have caused the requisite emotional distress or a reasonable fear of death or serious bodily injury because it was deactivated by the time Linda learned of it. What result? See United States v. Curley, 639 F.3d 50 (2d Cir. 2011) (reversing, based on improper admission of other evidence). See also John Martin, Use of GPS May Support Federal Felony Stalking Charges, DIRT Blog (Apr. 28, 2011), http://www.dirtllc.com/blog/bid/56056/Use-of-GPS-May-Support-Federal-Felony-Stalking-Charges.

C. FIREARM REGULATION: PUNISHING POSSESSION OF FIREARMS

■ **ANDREW R. KLEIN, OFFICE ON VIOLENCE AGAINST WOMEN, ENFORCING DOMESTIC VIOLENCE FIREARM PROHIBITIONS: A REPORT ON PROMISING PRACTICES**
3-4, 5-8, 14-16, 95 (Sept. 2006), available at http://www.bwjp.org/files/bwjp/articles/Enforcing_Firearms_Prohibitions.pdf

Firearms are the weapons of choice among abusers who kill their intimate partners and children. Multiple studies have found that intimate partners are more likely to be murdered with a firearm than by all other means combined. In fact, the mere presence of a firearm makes it six times more likely that a batterer will commit lethal abuse. Women who have been previously threatened or assaulted with a firearm or other weapon are 20 times more likely than other women to be murdered by their abusers.

According to a recent University of California, Los Angeles study, when a firearm is kept in a home with an abuser, nearly two-thirds of the victims report that it is used by the abuser to scare, threaten, or harm them. A study of abusers between 1999 and 2003 found that owning a gun is highly correlated with using it to threaten an intimate partner, typically in one or more of the following ways:

- Threatening to shoot the victim
- Cleaning, holding, or loading the gun during an argument
- Threatening to shoot a person or pet the victim cares about
- Firing a gun during an argument with the victim.

To protect victims of domestic violence, Congress, many states, and a number of tribes have enacted statutes that bar abusers from possessing or purchasing firearms. If enforced, these laws can dramatically reduce domestic homicides. Moreover, enforcement can diminish the power of abusers to terrorize and intimidate their partners.

Federal, state, and tribal firearm prohibitions are not self-implementing. These laws cannot protect victims without the concerted actions of law enforcement officers, prosecutors, courts, probation and parole officers, and advocates to vigorously facilitate their enforcement. The processes involved in enforcing firearm prohibitions—including those prohibitions established by statute or court order outside of the enforcing state or tribe—often require intergovernmental and interagency communication, coordination, and cooperation among multiple state, tribal, and federal agencies.

To accomplish these goals, agencies must develop the capability to work closely with their counterparts in other jurisdictions to enforce firearm prohibitions and protection orders issued in other states or tribes and to investigate and prosecute crimes that involve more than one jurisdiction. . . .

OVERVIEW OF DOMESTIC VIOLENCE FIREARM LAWS—FEDERAL STATUTES

The Gun Control Act (GCA) of 1968 (18 U.S.C. §921 et seq.) regulates firearms at the federal level. Subsection 922(g) of the act lists persons disqualified from possessing firearms and ammunition. Under subsection 922(n), persons under indictment for a crime punishable by imprisonment for up to one year cannot receive firearms or ammunition. Any person disqualified from possessing firearms or ammunition under the Gun Control Act is prohibited from shipping, transporting in interstate or foreign commerce, or possessing in or affecting commerce, any firearm or ammunition. A disqualified person is also prohibited from receiving any firearm or ammunition that has been shipped or transported in interstate or foreign commerce. Subsection 922(d) prohibits firearms or ammunition from being transferred to persons who are not eligible to possess firearms. Nearly all firearms and ammunition meet this requirement, because most include at least one component part that was imported from another country or that was manufactured in another state from the state where it was possessed.

Four subsections added to the GCA since 1994 (18 U.S.C. §922(g)(8) and (g)(9), and 18 U.S.C. §922(d)(8) and (d)(9)) specifically prohibit certain perpetrators of domestic violence from possessing firearms or ammunition and make it a crime to transfer a firearm/ammunition to these prohibited persons. Below are descriptions of these provisions.

18 U.S.C. §§922(g)(1-7)

The 922(g) subsections of the Gun Control Act prohibit certain persons from possessing firearms and ammunition. Persons convicted of a crime punishable by more than one year of imprisonment, fugitives, drug addicts, certain mentally ill persons, illegal and certain immigrant aliens, dishonorably discharged military personnel, and those who have renounced their U.S. citizenship may not possess a firearm or ammunition. Some abusers who are not disqualified under sections 922(g)(8) or 922(g)(9) (see below) may be prohibited from possessing firearms and ammunition pursuant to one of the other subsections of 922(g).

18 U.S.C. §922(g)(8)

This section, enacted in 1994 as part of the Violent Crime and Law Enforcement Act, of which the Violence Against Women Act is also a part, prohibits certain court-restrained abusers from possessing firearms and ammunition. For a person to be disqualified under this statute, a number of conditions must be met:

1. The protection order must have been issued after a hearing of which the respondent (the abuser) had actual notice and an opportunity to participate. Most emergency or temporary ex parte orders do not qualify under this statute because they are typically issued before notice is provided to the respondent.

2. The order must restrain the abuser from harassing, stalking, or threatening an intimate partner of the abuser or a child of the abuser or intimate partner, or engaging in other conduct that would place an intimate partner in reasonable fear of bodily injury to the partner or child.

3. The order must include a finding that the abuser represents a credible threat to the physical safety of the intimate partner or child, or the order must explicitly prohibit the use, attempted use, or threatened use of physical force against the intimate partner or child that would reasonably be expected to cause bodily injury.

4. The petitioner must be an intimate partner of the abuser. The federal statute defines intimate partner as a spouse or former spouse, a person who is a parent of the child of the abuser, or a person who cohabits or has cohabited with the respondent. This definition does not include orders issued against a person who dated the petitioner but with whom the petitioner never cohabited or with whom the petitioner does not share a child in common. If an order meets the above requirements, possession of a firearm or ammunition can subject the court-restrained abuser to federal prosecution. The respondent does not need to have violated any court-ordered provisions in a protection order to violate the federal statute. Additionally, there does not have to be a statement in a protection order that requires the respondent to turn over his/her firearm(s) or ammunition while the order is operative. Language in a protection order that indicates the abuser can have weapons does not negate the applicability of the federal law, and the person is still disqualified from possessing firearms or ammunition during the duration of the protection order. The firearm prohibition under 922g(8) applies only while the protection order is valid.

Law enforcement officers, armed forces personnel, and other local, state, and federal employees who are required to use weapons as part of their official duties have a limited exemption from this statute.

Firearms used in performing official duties are permitted while their possessors are carrying out their official duties. Weapons possessed in a personal capacity, however, are prohibited while a final protection order is enforceable.

18 U.S.C. §922(d)(8)

This section of the Gun Control Act prohibits the transfer of firearms and ammunition to persons who are subject to qualifying protection orders. It is a federal crime to sell or otherwise dispose of a firearm or ammunition to a person while knowing or having reasonable cause to believe that the person is subject to a federally disqualifying protection order. There is no exception for law enforcement and court personnel who return firearms to abusers who are subject to qualifying protection orders. If a third party receives an abuser's firearms to keep in his/her possession for the duration of a protection order, the court should apprise the third party of steps he/she must take before lawfully returning the firearm or weapon to the abuser, such as ensuring the order is no longer in effect. Transferring the firearm or ammunition back to the abuser while the protection order is in effect can subject the third party to federal prosecution.

18 U.S.C. §922(g)(9)

This section—commonly referred to as the "Lautenberg Amendment"—prohibits a person convicted of a "misdemeanor crime of domestic violence" . . . from possessing firearms and ammunition.

Anyone who has ever been convicted of an MCDV is prohibited from possessing firearms or ammunition. An MCDV under this statute is the following:

1. A misdemeanor under federal, state, or tribal law.
2. Includes as an element the use or attempted use of physical force or the threatened use of a deadly weapon.
3. The offender of the crime must have been a current or former spouse of the victim; a parent or guardian of the victim; a person who shares a child in common with the victim; a person who is currently cohabitating with or has cohabited with the victim as a spouse, parent, or guardian; or a person similarly situated to a spouse, parent, or guardian of the victim.
4. The offender must have been represented by counsel or knowingly and intelligently waived counsel and, if the crime with which the abuser was charged allowed the defendant to opt for a jury trial, the defendant must have been afforded a jury trial or made a knowing and intelligent waiver of this option.

To qualify under this statute, the misdemeanor crime need not have consisted of the violation of a statute that is labeled or categorized as a domestic violence crime (e.g., domestic abuse, domestic assault). A crime is covered by this statute if the defendant is convicted under a general misdemeanor statute, provided that the requisite relationship between the perpetrator and the victim exists; if the use of force/deadly weapon is an element of the crime that must be proven in order to obtain a conviction/plea, and the defendant was represented by counsel or waived the right to counsel; and if the offender was entitled to a jury trial, the offender was afforded a jury trial, or waived one.

The disability imposed by this statute is a lifetime prohibition. It applies even if the conviction occurred years before 1996, the year that the statute was enacted. The disability may, however, be lifted if the conviction is expunged or legally set aside, or the abuser is pardoned or has his or her civil rights restored, if the law of the applicable jurisdiction provides for loss of civil rights for conviction of the offense. There is no official use exemption for law enforcement officers or military personnel under this section of the Gun Control Act. Consequently, officers and military personnel who have been convicted of a qualifying MCDV may not carry a duty weapon.

18 U.S.C. §922(d)(9)

This section prohibits the transfer of firearms and ammunition to a person who has been convicted of an MCDV. As with the protection order prohibition (18 U.S.C. §922(d)(8)), it is illegal to sell or otherwise dispose of firearms and ammunition to a person who has been convicted of an MCDV. If a third party is given an abuser's firearms to hold after such a conviction, the third party may not transfer the firearm back to the convicted person. Doing so can subject the third party to federal prosecution.

18 U.S.C. §922(a)(6)

This section makes it a crime for any person to knowingly make false statements or furnish false identification that is intended or is likely to deceive a firearm importer, manufacturer, dealer, or collector regarding the lawfulness of a firearm transfer. Each person who intends to receive a firearm from a federal firearms licensee ("transferee") must fill out ATF Form 4473 (Firearms Transaction Record), which asks a number of questions designed to reveal whether a person is federally disqualified from receiving a firearm or ammunition. A person who fails to answer any question truthfully (e.g., indicating that he/she is not currently subject to a protection order when he/she is in fact the restrained party to a protection order) commits a federal crime. . . .

Pre-Transfer Background Checks

Congress enacted the Brady Handgun Violence Prevention Act to ensure that persons who fall under one or more of the categories of "prohibited persons" listed in the federal Gun Control Act are unable to receive firearms and ammunition from federally licensed firearm dealers ("licensees"). Effective November 30, 1998, the act established the National Instant Criminal Background Check System (NICS) and requires that licensees conduct a NICS background check through the Federal Bureau of Investigation (FBI) or a state point of contact (POC) on every person applying to receive a firearm or ammunition. An NICS check involves a search of federally maintained databases, i.e., the National Crime Information Center (NCIC), III ("Triple I"), a criminal history file, and the NICS that includes federally prohibiting records (including mental health records). When necessary, NICS personnel conduct further inquiries and seek information beyond that available in the searchable databases.

NICS completes most background checks very quickly. For certain applicants, though, it may be unclear as to whether a person is disqualified from receiving a firearm. For this reason, the Brady Act allows NICS up to three business days to complete an investigation. If insufficient information is found to verify that a person is, in fact, disqualified, the transfer may proceed after three days have passed. If a disqualifying record is found after the end of the three business-day period and the transfer has already taken place, the FBI makes a referral to the ATF to investigate whether it can retrieve the firearm.

The accuracy and speed with which NICS checks are conducted depends on whether local, state, and tribal jurisdictions forward complete and accurate criminal history, protection order, and other relevant information to the FBI in a timely manner. NICS checks are currently limited in their ability to identify all prohibited persons because many states and tribes submit incomplete records. For example, only 949 of more than 3,000 domestic violence assault convictions between 2002 and 2003 were properly filed with the FBI. It is vital that state misdemeanor offenses are placed in both state and federal systems for access in background data.

In 2002, NICS checks prevented 19,040 abusers from purchasing firearms. A quarter of those thwarted sales were due to the discovery of an active protection order against the person who wished to purchase a firearm. However, according to FBI statistics, nearly 4,040 domestic violence abusers were able to buy firearms between 2002 and 2006.

A General Accounting Office study found that despite the efforts of some states to make it easier to identify individuals convicted of domestic violence, NICS was still unable to determine that some persons were prohibited from purchasing firearms.

Additionally, nearly 10,000 persons who were later found to be ineligible were allowed to purchase firearms in the first 30 months of NICS operation because their records could not be obtained within the three-day maximum mandated waiting period.

Many states also conduct pre-purchase background checks using their own databases to investigate whether a person is prohibited under state law from possessing a firearm. However, as with the federal NICS, state efforts can be hampered if the information that is needed to conduct accurate and timely checks is unavailable. Automated registries and statewide registries help to make data readily available for background checks. Most states have a system for tracking protection orders, but a handful of states do not access a statewide system as part of the background check process. Six states do not include MCDVs in the criminal history files that they access for background checks. Four other states include MCDVs in their criminal history records that are searched during background checks, but do not flag the records or otherwise distinguish them from other misdemeanors.

Data such as these make it clear that states must improve the quality and increase the quantity of information that they submit to the databases searchable by NICS as well as improve their own systems for storing and accessing information about prohibited persons. Equally important, the data highlight the need for jurisdictions to institute agency, community, and systemic changes that maximize the effectiveness of current state, tribal, and federal firearm laws by using all available resources to ensure that abusers are unable to possess and use firearms. . . .

LESSONS LEARNED

1. The honor system is not sufficient to ensure compliance with state and federal statutes, or court orders. It is not enough to instruct or order abusers to refrain from possessing firearms. There must be a specific, comprehensive effort to enforce such orders over time.

2. Checking federal and state databases to determine if persons are prohibited from possessing firearms represents only a first step in completing full investigations. More investigation is necessary, given the incompleteness of these files.

3. Once firearms are relinquished, they should not be automatically returned to their owners until the owners' eligibility for repossession is determined. Although the firearms may have been surrendered as a result of a protection order filed against the firearm owner, there may be other bases that disqualify the person from possessing firearms.

4. Authorities must act quickly and encourage immediate, voluntary surrender of firearms to police, not to other third parties. Authorities should encourage firearm relinquishment as soon as possible after the presence of domestic violence has been established, and encourage victims to identify and, where authorized pursuant to state joint ownership rules, turn over household firearms for safe storage or destruction.

5. Written procedures are vital. To ensure necessary follow-up and institutionalization of programs and procedures to keep firearms from prohibited persons, agencies must develop specific forms and regulations, accompanied by in-service training of all relevant personnel.

6. Disarming abusers is not antigun. Firearm prohibition enforcement programs should not allow themselves to be perceived as antigun, and should

communicate that they are pro–victim safety. It should be made clear that such efforts are not aimed at law abiding, nonabusive citizens.

7. There is no substitute for federal involvement. Notwithstanding the presence or absence of equivalent state statutes, federal firearm prohibition enforcement has a crucial role to play in educating both the public and local criminal justice officials about the necessity of disarming dangerous abusers as well as effectively removing from society the most dangerous abusers. Adequate federal enforcement requires cross-deputization of local law enforcement officers.

8. Disarming abusers saves lives.

■ UNITED STATES v. SKOIEN

614 F.3d 638 (7th Cir. 2010) (en banc)

EASTERBROOK, Chief Judge.

[Steven Skoien was convicted of two offenses of "misdemeanor crimes of domestic violence." Both state court convictions were for misdemeanor domestic battery: The 2003 offense involved his wife and the 2006 offense his fiancée. Following the 2006 offense, Skoien was sentenced to two years' probation. He was prohibited from possessing firearms both as a condition of his probation and because federal law prohibits any person convicted in any court of a misdemeanor crime of domestic violence from possessing a firearm. 18 U.S.C. §922(g)(9); see also 18 U.S.C. §921(a)(33)(A)(ii) (defining a misdemeanor crime of domestic violence as any offense that "has, as an element, the use or attempted use of physical force, or the threatened use of a deadly weapon"). In 2007, probation officers learned that Skoien had purchased a deer-hunting license. Believing that he had acquired a gun in violation of his probation, they searched his home and found a Winchester 12-gauge shotgun in his truck. Skoien admitted he had used the shotgun to go deer hunting earlier that day. This statement was corroborated by evidence found in the trunk and the deer carcass in his garage. A federal grand jury indicted him for possessing a firearm after having been convicted of a domestic-violence misdemeanor in violation of 18 U.S.C. §922(g)(9). (The preceding summary is derived from United States v. Skoien, 587 F.3d 803 (7th Cir. 2009). In this case, Skoien maintains that prosecuting him under §922(g)(9) for possessing a shotgun violates his Second Amendment right to bear arms pursuant to District of Columbia v. Heller, 554 U.S. 570 (2008)).]

We heard this appeal en banc to decide whether §922(g)(9) comports with that amendment, as interpreted in District of Columbia v. Heller, 554 U.S. 570 (2008). . . . *Heller* concludes that the Second Amendment "protects the right to keep and bear arms for the purpose of self-defense" and that a law "that banned the possession of handguns in the home" violates that right. The United States submits that, before considering how the amendment applies to shotguns and hunting (which is how Skoien contends he used that weapon), we must decide whether Congress is entitled to adopt categorical disqualifications such as §922(g)(9). The prosecutor relies on this passage from *Heller*:

> Like most rights, the right secured by the Second Amendment is not unlimited. . . .
> Although we do not undertake an exhaustive historical analysis today of the full scope
> of the Second Amendment, nothing in our opinion should be taken to cast doubt on

longstanding prohibitions on the possession of firearms by felons and the mentally ill, or laws forbidding the carrying of firearms in sensitive places such as schools and government buildings, or laws imposing conditions and qualifications on the commercial sale of arms.[26]

128 S. Ct. at 2821-2822. To this Skoien replies that his prior offenses were misdemeanors rather than felonies, and that §922(g)(9) is not a "longstanding" prohibition, having been enacted in 1996. . . . *Heller* also observes that the Second Amendment "elevates above all other interests the right of law-abiding, responsible citizens to use arms in defense of hearth and home." Id. at 2821. People convicted of domestic violence are neither law-abiding nor responsible, the prosecutor contends.

We do not think it profitable to parse these passages of *Heller* as if they contained an answer to the question whether §922(g)(9) is valid. They are precautionary language. Instead of resolving questions such as the one we must confront, the Justices have told us that the matters have been left open. . . . Although the passages we have quoted are not dispositive, they are informative. They tell us that statutory prohibitions on the possession of weapons by some persons are proper—and, importantly for current purposes, that the legislative role did not end in 1791. That some categorical limits are proper is part of the original meaning, leaving to the people's elected representatives the filling in of details. . . .

The first federal statute disqualifying felons from possessing firearms was not enacted until 1938; it also disqualified misdemeanants who had been convicted of violent offenses. Federal Firearms Act, c. 850, §2(f), 52 Stat. 1250, 1251. . . . The Federal Firearms Act covered only a few violent offenses; the ban on possession by all felons was not enacted until 1961. Pub. L. 87-342, 75 Stat. 757 (extending the disqualification to all persons convicted of any "crime punishable by imprisonment for a term exceeding one year," the current federal definition of a "felony"). . . .

So although the Justices have not established that any particular statute is valid, we do take from *Heller* the message that exclusions need not mirror limits that were on the books in 1791. . . . This means that some categorical disqualifications are permissible: Congress is not limited to case-by-case exclusions of persons who have been shown to be untrustworthy with weapons. . . .

Categorical limits on the possession of firearms would not be a constitutional anomaly. Think of the First Amendment, which has long had categorical limits: obscenity, defamation, incitement to crime, and others. These categories are not restricted to those recognized in 1791, when the states approved the Bill of Rights. The Justices have held that legislatures may add child pornography to the list [(citing New York v. Ferber, 458 U.S. 747 (1982))]. . . .

The belief underpinning §922(g)(9) is that people who have been convicted of violence once—toward a spouse, child, or domestic partner, no less—are likely to use violence again. That's the justification for keeping firearms out of their hands, for guns are about five times more deadly than knives, given that an attack with some kind of weapon has occurred.

[United States v. Hayes, 129 S. Ct. 1079 (2009)] held that whether a crime is one of "domestic violence" depends on the identity of the victim rather than the

26. We identify these presumptively lawful regulatory measures only as examples; our list does not purport to be exhaustive.

elements of the offense. When describing why §922(g)(9) was enacted, the Court wrote (129 S. Ct. at 1087):

> Existing felon-in-possession laws, Congress recognized, were not keeping firearms out of the hands of domestic abusers, because "many people who engage in serious spousal or child abuse ultimately are not charged with or convicted of felonies." 142 Cong. Rec. 22985 (1996) (statement of Sen. Lautenberg). By extending the federal firearm prohibition to persons convicted of "misdemeanor crime[s] of domestic violence," proponents of §922(g)(9) sought to "close this dangerous loophole." Id. at 22986.
>
> Construing §922(g)(9) to exclude the domestic abuser convicted under a generic use-of-force statute (one that does not designate a domestic relationship as an element of the offense) would frustrate Congress' manifest purpose. Firearms and domestic strife are a potentially deadly combination nationwide.

There are three propositions in this passage: first that domestic abusers often commit acts that would be charged as felonies if the victim were a stranger, but that are charged as misdemeanors because the victim is a relative (implying that the perpetrators are as dangerous as felons); second that firearms are deadly in domestic strife; and third that persons convicted of domestic violence are likely to offend again, so that keeping the most lethal weapon out of their hands is vital to the safety of their relatives. Data support all three of these propositions.

[We shall start with the assertion that prosecutors charge] domestic violence as a misdemeanor when similar acts against a stranger would be a felony (a practice often called "undercharging"). Prosecutors face two major obstacles to obtaining felony convictions: some family members are willing to forgive the aggressors in order to restore harmonious relations, while others are so terrified that they doubt the ability of the police to protect their safety. Either way, victims of domestic violence are less willing to cooperate with prosecutors, who may need to reduce charges to obtain even limited cooperation and thus some convictions. Indeed, either forgiveness or fear induces many victims not to report the attack to begin with. The result is that many aggressors end up with no conviction, or a misdemeanor conviction, when similar violence against a stranger would produce a felony conviction.

That firearms cause injury or death in domestic situations also has been established. Domestic assaults with firearms are approximately twelve times more likely to end in the victim's death than are assaults by knives or fists. Part of this effect stems from the fact that some would-be abusers go buy a gun, and much from the fact that guns are more lethal than knives and clubs once an attack begins. The presence of a gun in the home of a convicted domestic abuser is "strongly and independently associated with an increased risk of homicide." And for this purpose the victims include police as well as spouses, children, and intimate partners. Responding to a domestic-disturbance call is among an officer's most risky duties. . . .

Finally, the recidivism rate is high, implying that there are substantial benefits in keeping the most deadly weapons out of the hands of domestic abusers. For example, a study of persons arrested for misdemeanor domestic violence in Cincinnati concluded that 17 percent of those who remained in the area were arrested again for domestic violence within three years. John Wooldredge & Amy Thistlethwaite, Reconsidering Domestic Violence Recidivism: Individual and Contextual Effects of Court Dispositions and Stake in Conformity vi (1999). The full recidivism rate includes violence that does not lead to an arrest. Estimates of this rate come from survey research and range from 40 percent to 80 percent "when victims are followed longitudinally and interviewed directly." Carla Smith Stover, Domestic Violence Research, 20 J. Interpersonal Violence 448, 450 (2005). Skoien cites, as if it were favorable, a study showing that within three years of conviction 48 percent of domestic abusers "suspended" their abusive conduct—which means that the other 52 percent did not, and that even the 48 percent may have committed new crimes within three years after conviction. John H. Laub & Robert J. Sampson, Understanding Desistance from Crime, 28 Crime & Justice 1, 31 (2001). No matter how you slice these numbers, people convicted of domestic violence remain dangerous to their spouses and partners.

By the time this appeal reached oral argument en banc, Skoien's principal argument had shifted. Instead of denying the logical and empirical basis of §922(g)(9), he contended that Congress overreached by creating a "perpetual" disqualification for persons convicted of domestic violence. This goes too far, according to Skoien, because the propensity for violence declines with advancing age, and people who are not convicted of additional offenses have demonstrated that they no longer pose risks to other members of their households. Applying §922(g)(9) to older persons who have not been in legal trouble for many years cannot be substantially related to an important governmental objective, the argument concludes.

Although the statute provides that expungement, pardon, or restoration of civil rights means that a conviction no longer disqualifies a person from possessing firearms, see 18 U.S.C. §921(a)(33)(B)(ii), Skoien maintains that, as a practical matter, these routes to restoration are unavailable to domestic-battery misdemeanants in Wisconsin. We have our doubts. [The state of Wisconsin] does give misdemeanants an opportunity to seek pardon or expungement. Some of the largest states make expungement available as of right to misdemeanants who have a clean record for a specified time. . . . This means that §922(g)(9) in its normal application does not create a perpetual and unjustified disqualification for a person who no longer is apt to attack other members of the household. . . .

. . . The fact remains that Skoien is poorly situated to contend that the statute creates a lifetime ban for someone who does not pose any risk of further offenses. First, Skoien is himself a recidivist, having been convicted twice of domestic battery. . . . A person to whom a statute properly applies can't obtain relief based on arguments that a differently situated person might present. . . . Whether a misdemeanant who has been law abiding for an extended period must be allowed to carry guns again, even if he cannot satisfy §921(a)(33)(B)(ii), is a question not presented today. There will be time enough to consider that subject when it arises. Affirmed.

Notes and Questions

1. *Background.* Federal law limits the ability of abusers to own firearms by means of two statutes.

a. *Persons subject to restraining orders.* In 1994, Congress enacted legislation in conjunction with VAWA that prohibits firearms sales to, and possession by, a person subject to a domestic violence restraining order, provided that the restraining order meets certain requirements. Violent Crime Control and Law Enforcement Act of 1994, Pub. L. No. 103-322, §110401, 108 Stat. 2014. Those requirements include: (1) the respondent must have received actual notice and had an opportunity to participate at the hearing that led to the restraining order (18 U.S.C. §922(g)(8)(A)); (2) the respondent must have been an intimate partner (that is, spouse or former spouse, present or former cohabitant, or a parent of the same child) of the restraining order petitioner (§922(g)(8)(B)); (3) the restraining order must include language restraining the respondent from harassing, stalking, or threatening an intimate partner (or a child of either petitioner or respondent) or from engaging in conduct that would place an intimate partner in reasonable fear of bodily injury to the partner or child (§922(g)(8)(B)) or the order must include a finding that the respondent represents a "credible threat" to the safety of the partner or child or must explicitly prohibit the use, attempted use, or threatened use of physical force that would reasonably be expected to cause bodily injury to the partner or child (§922(g)(8)(C)).

b. *Persons who have committed misdemeanor crime of domestic violence.* In 1996, Congress enacted the Lautenberg Amendment to the Gun Control Act of 1968, Pub. L. No. 104-208, §658, 110 Stat. 3009-372 (codified in relevant part at 18 U.S.C.). It was enacted as part of the massive Omnibus Consolidated Appropriations Act of 1996. The Lautenberg Amendment makes it unlawful for anyone "who has been convicted in any court of a misdemeanor crime of domestic violence" to possess any firearm or ammunition (18 U.S.C. §922(g)(9)).

A misdemeanor conviction must satisfy several requirements to trigger the federal firearms prohibition: (1) the misdemeanor must have included the use or attempted use of physical force, or the threatened use of a deadly weapon, and also must have been committed by a defendant who was a current or former spouse, parent, or guardian of the victim, or who shared a child in common with the victim, or who was cohabiting with or had cohabited with the victim as a spouse, parent, or guardian, or who was a person similarly situated to a spouse, parent, or guardian of the victim (§921(a)(33)(A)); (2) the defendant must have been represented by counsel or knowingly and intelligently waived that right (§921(a)(33)(B)(i)(I)); and (3) the defendant must have received a jury trial or knowingly and intelligently waived that right (§921(a)(33)(B)(i)(II)).

2. *Lautenberg Amendment: background.* At the time of the Lautenberg Amendment, federal law barred convicted felons, but not convicted misdemeanants, from possessing firearms. This limitation to felons was a serious omission because most domestic violence offenses are misdemeanors. Senator Lautenberg (D–NJ) proposed the legislation to remedy this loophole. See 142 Cong. Rec. S10, 377 (1996) (statement of Sen. Lautenberg).

3. *Importance of* Heller. *Heller* invalidated a District of Columbia law prohibiting private ownership or possession of handguns. 554 U.S. 570. As the first case in which the Supreme Court ever invalidated a gun law, *Heller* constituted a significant departure from previous Supreme Court jurisprudence that had held that the Second Amendment protects the right to gun ownership solely for the purpose of militia service (that is, the "states' rights" or "collective rights" interpretation of the Second Amendment in contrast to the "individual rights" interpretation). In McDonald v. City of Chicago, 130 S. Ct. 3020 (2010), the Supreme Court extended the Second Amendment's protections to prohibit gun regulation by state and local governments.

A case in the context of domestic violence led to *Heller*. In United States v. Emerson, 270 F.3d 203 (5th Cir. 2003), an ex-husband was indicted for possession of a firearm while he was subject to a domestic violence restraining order. In response, he challenged the constitutionality of 18 U.S.C. §922(g)(8). The Fifth Circuit Court of Appeals upheld the federal firearm law, finding that its prohibition of firearm possession by a person considered a threat to a domestic partner was a reasonable regulation. Yet the Fifth Circuit's interpretation of the Second Amendment as protecting an individual right to possess firearms marked the first time that a federal appellate court had adopted this liberal position. See *Heller*, 554 U.S. at 638 n.2 (Stevens, J., dissenting). *Skoien* is one of the first post-*Heller* cases to return the federal judiciary to the issue of the constitutionality of firearm laws in the context of domestic violence.

For a discussion of the events that led to the filing of *Heller*, see Clark Neily, District of Columbia v. Heller: The Second Amendment is Back, Baby, 2007-2008 Cato Sup. Ct. Rev. 127 (2008). For an analysis of the historiography of the Second Amendment, see Sanford Levinson, The Embarrassing Second Amendment, 99 Yale L.J. 637 (1989).

4. Skoien: *rationale*. The Supreme Court in *Heller* emphasized that the right to possession of handguns in the home is not absolute. The Court clearly states that the decision does not alter "longstanding prohibitions on the possession of firearms by felons and the mentally ill." *Heller*, 554 U.S. at 626. Why does *Skoien* determine that these "presumptively lawful" regulations should be extended to persons who commit misdemeanors of domestic violence offenses? What is the relationship between firearms and domestic violence, according to the court? Other federal appellate courts have also upheld the constitutionality of federal firearm laws as applied to misdemeanants who commit crimes of domestic violence. See, e.g., United States v. White, 593 F.3d 1199 (11th Cir. 2010). See generally Elizabeth Coppolecchia et al., Note, United States v. White: Disarming Domestic Violence Misdemeanants Post-*Heller*, 64 U. Miami L. Rev. 1505 (2010) (exploring various challenges to the federal firearm ban on gun possession by domestic violence misdemeanants).

5. *Analogy to First Amendment*. In upholding the constitutionality of the firearms restrictions, the Seventh Circuit in *Skoien* analogizes firearm restrictions to such limitations on First Amendment speech as "obscenity, defamation, incitement to crime, and others." Is the analogy apt? How are these restrictions similar? How are they different? For example, do infringements on the respective restrictions under the First and Second Amendments result in similar harms? See Recent Case, Constitutional Law—Second Amendment—En Banc Seventh Circuit Holds Prohibition on Firearm Possession by Domestic Violence Misdemeanants to be Constitutional—United States v. Skoien, 124 Harv. L. Rev. 1074, 1080 (2011) (distinguishing the First Amendment harm regarding the influence on speech of listeners versus the Second Amendment harm regarding injury or death) [hereafter Recent Case].

6. *Level of scrutiny*. The Supreme Court in *Heller* left open the issue of the standard of review that should apply in future challenges based on the Second Amendment. However, the Court implied that the deferential rational basis review was inappropriate. See *Heller*, 554 U.S. 570 at 628 n.27 ("If all that was required to overcome the right to keep and bear arms was a rational basis, the Second Amendment would be redundant with the separate constitutional prohibitions on irrational laws, and would have no effect").

How does *Skoien* address the issue of the level of scrutiny left open in *Heller*? What standard of scrutiny *should* apply? See Lawrence Rosenthal & Joyce Lee Malcolm, McDonald v. Chicago: Which Standard of Scrutiny Should Apply to Gun-Control Laws?, 105 Nw. U. L. Rev. Colloquy 85 (2010). Is *Skoien*'s analogy to First Amendment limitations helpful in determining the level of scrutiny that should be applied to firearm regulations? See Recent Case, supra, at 1078-1081 (criticizing analogy).

7. *Overbreadth.* Skoien briefly raises the argument that the statute is overbroad as applied to older persons who pose less risk of domestic violence as well as to more recently convicted persons. How does the court address this argument? Do you agree that expungement, pardon, or restoration of civil rights is a meaningful distinction between these two groups? Should domestic violence offenders remain under a permanent firearm ban? How do studies of recidivism of abusers contribute to this analysis? In what way does Skoien's own conduct influence the court?

8. *Predicate offense.* The federal firearm law makes possession of a firearm by a person convicted of a "misdemeanor crime of domestic violence" a federal felony. Violations of 18 U.S.C. §922(g)(8), and 18 U.S.C. §922(g)(9), are punishable by a prison term of up to ten years and a fine of up to $250,000. 18 U.S.C. §924(a)(2). The predicate offense for the imposition of federal felony liability is a "misdemeanor crime of domestic violence." What is the meaning of "crime of domestic violence"?

Until recently, the federal circuit courts split about the meaning and application of the term. Some circuit courts (that is, First, Eighth, and Eleventh Circuits) held that the predicate offense merely requires some offensive contact against a domestic partner. Thus, a simple battery would suffice, provided that the offense was perpetrated against a domestic partner. In contrast, the Ninth Circuit held that the predicate offense must be a *violent act* committed against the domestic partner. See Joshua M. Jones, 18 U.S.C. §922(g)(9) and the Circuit Split: The Case for a Broad Definition of Domestic Violence, 45 Crim. Law Bull. 82 (2009) (describing federal appellate court split).

In the first post-*Heller* case to address firearm regulations in the context of domestic violence, the Supreme Court resolved the split. The Court adopted the view that the defendant's underlying conviction could be a misdemeanor conviction under general battery laws. United States v. Hayes, 555 U.S. 415 (2009). What are the implications of *Hayes*? Does *Hayes* adequately protect the constitutional rights of the accused? See Miguel E. Larios, To *Heller* and Back: Why Many Second Amendment Questions Remain Unanswered after United States v. Hayes, Fed. Law., Sept. 2009, at 58; Tanjima Islam, Note, The Fourth Circuit's Rejection of Legislation History: Placing Guns in the Hands of Domestic Violence Perpetrators, 18 Am. U. J. Gender Soc. Pol'y & L. 341 (2010).

9. *Official use exception.* The prohibition on firearm possession by persons subject to a restraining order contains an "official use exception." 18 U.S.C. §925(a)(1). This exception permits police officers, military personnel, and other government employees who are subject to a restraining order to continue to use a firearm for employment-related duties. Does this exception make sense in light of the high rates of domestic violence among police and the military? (See Chapter 3). Moreover, although the exception applies to persons subject to a restraining order, it does not apply to these same persons who have committed misdemeanor crimes of domestic violence. Does the distinction make sense? See Tom Lininger, A Better Way to Disarm Batterers, 54 Hastings L.J. 525, 571-573 (2003) (criticizing the "asymmetry" and advocating reform).

10. *Brady background checks.* The Brady Handgun Violence Prevention Act of 1993 (Pub. L. No. 103 159, 107 Stat. 1536 (1993)) (codified as amended at 18 U.S.C. §921 et seq.) mandates criminal history background checks for any person who attempts to purchase a firearm from a Federal Firearms Licensee. The Brady Act also establishes the National Instant Criminal Background Check System (NICS),

a national data base that is accessed by the FBI or a state point of contact (POC) prior to the transfer of a firearm, containing information on persons who are prohibited from purchasing or possessing a firearm under either federal or state law.

In addition to persons subject to restraining orders and misdemeanants who commit acts of domestic violence, other disqualified persons include: those who are under indictment for, or have been convicted of, a crime punishable by imprisonment for more than one year; fugitives from justice; unlawful users of, or persons addicted to, a controlled substance; persons who have been adjudicated as mental defectives or been committed to a mental institution; illegal aliens or those who have been admitted to the United States under nonimmigrant visas; those dishonorably discharged from the U.S. Armed Forces; anyone who has renounced U.S. citizenship; and those who are under age 18 for long guns or under age 21 for handguns. Michael Bowling et al., Bureau of Justice Statistics, Background Checks for Firearm Transfers, 2009–Statistical Tables 3 (2010), available at http://bjs.ojp.usdoj.gov/content/pub/html/bcft/2009/bcft09st.pdf.

11. *Effectiveness.* How effective are federal firearm laws in addressing domestic violence? Effectiveness can be measured in various ways. One way is to look at whether the laws have reduced deaths from domestic violence. Since the 1970s, when gun control laws first went into effect, the number of women killed has remained about the same. Jennifer L. Vainik, Note, Kiss, Kiss, Bang, Bang: How Current Approaches to Guns and Domestic Violence Fail to Save Women's Lives, 91 Minn. L. Rev. 1113, 1128 (2007) (citing data). Yet, in 2009, more than 25,000 persons were denied firearm applications because of domestic violence convictions or restraining orders. See Bowling, supra, at 10, 13 (based on extrapolation of data in Tables 2 and 4). Does the gap between the number of victims and the firearm application denials signify that the federal gun ban has made little impact? What factors might explain the gap? See Vainik, supra, at 1136-1142 (suggesting such factors as the lack of incentive to implement the gun ban on the state level, the difficulty in enforcement, and the lack of accountability that complicates enforcement of the federal gun ban).

Another gauge of effectiveness is the number of federal firearm-related domestic violence *prosecutions* under VAWA. During a three-year period from 2000 to 2002, the majority of suspects (a total of 757) who were referred to federal prosecutors for violation of VAWA crimes were referred for firearm-related domestic violence crimes (83.2 percent or 630 suspects were referred for firearm-related domestic violence crimes). Of these suspects, 406 were suspected of violating the prohibition on firearm possession by a person with a prior misdemeanor domestic violence conviction. The remainder (224 suspects) were suspected of violating the prohibition on firearm possession by a person subject to a protection order. Durose, supra, at 51. Case outcomes (sentences, etc.) are not included in available federal data. Id. at 52. What light do these data shed on effectiveness?

How effective is the Brady Act background check system in keeping firearms from abusers? For 2009, more than 25,000 persons were denied applications because of domestic violence convictions or restraining orders. See Bowling, supra, at 10, 13 (based on extrapolation of data in Tables 2 and 4). Domestic violence (that is, the presence of a misdemeanor conviction or a restraining order) was the second most common reason for a denial of a firearm application by a state or local agency. Id. at 2. (The most common reason was a felony conviction or indictment.) Id. Based on the above data, how effective is federal firearm-related legislation?

Other measures of effectiveness also exist. For example, federal firearm laws have an important indirect benefit: They circumvent the problem of victim noncooperation. As Professor Tom Lininger explains, "[F]ederal authorities [do] not need to rely on any assistance from [victims] to obtain a conviction . . . under the Lautenberg Amendment." Lininger, supra, at 527. That is, federal prosecutors have to prove only that a defendant, who has a prior conviction of a misdemeanor domestic violence crime, was in possession of a gun. Id. Moreover, as Lininger notes, perhaps the "greatest promise" of the Lautenberg Amendment is its deterrence effect "as a tool not simply to punish batterers who possess guns, but to dissuade other batterers from possessing guns in the first place." Id. at 528.

12. *Reform proposals.* How might firearm regulation be made more effective? Professor Lininger offers several suggestions: (1) reform the requirement in 18 U.S.C. §922(g)(8) that the proceeding for the restraining order must include a hearing for which the abuser received notice and had an opportunity to participate (in light of the fact that most restraining order hearings are ex parte); (2) broaden the requirement in 18 U.S.C. §922(g)(9) regarding the predicate misdemeanor offense that requires the "use of force" (rather than merely the *threatened* use of force); (3) include (for purposes of 18 U.S.C. §922(g)(9)) indictments, pleas that were made without the benefit of counsel, and pleas in which the defendant did not knowingly waive the right to jury trial in the predicate offense, and (4) allow additional time for law enforcement agencies to check whether purchasers have a history of violence pursuant to the Brady Act. Id. at 598-600. What do you think of these suggestions?

How easy is it for an abuser to evade the federal firearm regulations? See, e.g., Anthony Braga et al., The Illegal Supply of Firearms, 29 Crime & Just. 319, 344 (2002) (pointing out that the effectiveness of the Brady Act is undermined by the secondary market in firearms). How can this problem be remedied?

13. *Policy.* The Lautenberg Amendment remains extremely controversial, pitting advocates for victims of domestic violence against opponents of gun-control laws. What are the arguments on each side? What is the best policy in the face of these opposing interests?

Problem

Three clients, who are either police or military personnel and who have committed acts of domestic violence, solicit advice from an attorney about career decisions. Tom, who is currently in the Army Reserve, is about to be sent on active duty. Tom wants to resolve pending charges against him for domestic assault and harassment before he leaves. John, a married police officer with two children, is going through a divorce and has been served with a restraining order. He wants to contest the restraining order because he will lose his job if he loses the use of his service weapon. Sam, a member of the National Guard, wants to expunge a conviction for harassment, because he has been notified by his superior that he will be discharged unless he does so.

What course of action should the attorney recommend to each of the above clients? Should the attorney seek to have any petition, judgment, or charges framed in such a way as to avoid all mention of domestic violence language? What are the attorney's ethical responsibilities? The above examples were suggested by Velda Rogers, Unintended Consequences, Or. St. B. Bull., July 2006, at 62 (deploring the "draconian" nature of the Lautenberg Amendment).

D. FEDERAL INDIAN LAW AND DOMESTIC VIOLENCE

The federal government has jurisdiction over crimes between family members that occur on Indian reservations (as well as military bases, and other federal property). The federal government has a complex jurisdictional relationship with our tribal nations. American Indian tribes are considered as sovereign nations unless Congress acts to divest tribes of their sovereignty. In 1885, federal law (discussed below) removed tribal jurisdiction over most major crimes, including most crimes of domestic violence. The following excerpt explores the nature of this federal response and the effectiveness of that response for the prosecution of domestic violence.

■ JACQUELINE P. HAND & DAVID C. KOELSCH,
   SHARED EXPERIENCES, DIVERGENT OUTCOMES:
   AMERICAN INDIAN AND IMMIGRANT VICTIMS
   OF DOMESTIC VIOLENCE
   25 Wis. J.L. Gender & Soc'y 185, 188, 196-198, 201-203 (2010)

American Indian women experience domestic violence more frequently than other women in the U.S. . . . In fact, physical assaults, most of which are domestic in nature, are higher among American Indian women than among any other demographic group in the United States. Nearly 40 percent of American Indian women report that they have been victims of domestic violence. . . .

[T]he protection offered to American Indian women under the current criminal justice system is completely inadequate [stemming from] deficiencies of the system operating in Indian Country on lands subject to tribal governance. This problem was created by events which began in the nineteenth century and has accelerated in the last three decades. An Indian tribe's authority and power to govern is inherent by virtue of its sovereignty and remains undiminished unless either of two events occurs [that is, a tribe voluntarily gives up some aspect of sovereignty or Congress acts affirmatively to divest the tribe of a particular aspect of sovereignty]. The second [case] is well exemplified by the Major Crimes Act [18 U.S.C. §1153(a) enacted in 1885], which began the erosion of tribal judicial power. Under this statute, Congress removed tribes' jurisdiction over [eight major crimes, including murder, manslaughter, rape, assault with intent to murder, kidnapping, arson, burglary, larceny], and placed them in the exclusive jurisdiction of the federal criminal system. Jurisdiction was further limited by Congress in 1968 by a law which severely limited the criminal penalties which could be imposed by tribal courts to imprisonment of no more than six months and $500 in fines [later increased to one year in jail and $5,000].

In 1978, the Supreme Court delivered a much more severe blow to the ability of a tribe to protect its people within its own territory. In Oliphant v. Suquamish Indian Tribe [435 U.S. 191 (1978)], the U.S. Supreme Court held that despite the fact that Congress had not acted to so limit tribal jurisdiction, the judiciary could also divest the tribes of a portion of their power if such sovereignty was "inconsistent with their status" as domestic dependent sovereigns. In *Oliphant*, the Court divested the tribes of the power to prosecute non-Indians for any crime, including misdemeanors, such as most domestic violence cases, leaving federal action as the only option. . . .

The one-two punch of the Major Crimes Act and the *Oliphant* decision leaves American Indian women in Indian Country substantially unprotected because they must rely upon federal prosecutors and the Federal Bureau of Investigation (FBI) to investigate and prosecute crimes of domestic violence in Indian Country. Unfortunately, such crimes must compete with many other serious crimes and, as such, are often not a high priority for federal law enforcement officials. This does not reflect a lack of concern for victims of domestic violence, rather the fact that resources are limited and often stretched too thin. In addition, complex jurisdictional issues, such as the status of victim and perpetrator and the distance of the location of the crime from the nearest U.S. Attorneys office, make federal prosecution cumbersome and unappealing.

The complex jurisdictional puzzle is further muddled by Public Law 280 [18 U.S.C. §1162(a)]. This statute allows states to assume the federal jurisdictional role over crimes committed by non-Indians against American Indians in Alaska, California, Minnesota, Nebraska, Oregon and Wisconsin in favor of state prosecution. The enactment of Public Law 280 has had the naive consequence of discouraging the development of tribal legal institutions, including courts and police forces despite the fact that it did not inhibit tribal jurisdiction over Indians. Like their federal brethren, state and local prosecutors often do not have the resources or political will to obtain convictions for non-Indians who commit domestic violence against or rape American Indian women. For example, in 2006, federal and state prosecutors only filed 606 criminal cases involving alleged crimes committed by non-Indians in Indian Country, despite the existence of 560 tribes within the United States. The end result of Public 280 is an uneven playing field with respect to prosecutions of domestic violence, which leaves American Indian women with limited protection in their own communities. . . .

In 1994, Congress enacted the original Violence Against Women Act (VAWA I). VAWA I contained specific provisions aimed at combating and deterring domestic violence against all women in the United States but, in particular, domestic violence against American Indian and immigrant women. Those targeted provisions, while well-intended, have had a mixed legacy. . . .

VAWA I contains provisions aimed directly at the pernicious nature of domestic violence against American Indian women: "[a]ny protection order issued . . . by the court of one . . . Indian tribe . . . shall be accorded full faith and credit by the court of another . . . Indian tribe . . . and enforced . . . as if it were the order of the enforcing . . . tribe." [18 U.S.C. §2265]. Nevertheless, it has a relatively small impact on the broader problems with controlling domestic violence in Indian Country. Under VAWA I, this new "one order" system was intended to protect American Indian women throughout Indian Country. VAWA was amended in 2000 to strengthen the authority of tribes to prevent domestic violence. Congress specified that "tribal court[s] shall have full civil jurisdiction to enforce protection orders, including authority to enforce any orders through civil contempt proceedings, exclusion of violators from Indian lands, and other appropriate mechanisms . . ." [18 U.S.C. §2265(e)].

Despite these provisions requiring cross recognition of personal protective orders, VAWA leaves many gaps. Tribes generally adhere to the VAWA mandate to extend full faith and credit to protection orders issued by other tribes yet the lack of jurisdiction over non-Indians prohibits them from enforcing orders against non-Indians even when issued by a state court. Similarly, while states are obligated under

VAWA to enforce personal protection orders issued by tribes, many state courts fail to do so, leaving a woman who moves off the reservation unprotected. Perhaps the most important contribution of VAWA comes not from its jurisdictional provisions but from financial grants and other infrastructure development mechanisms for which VAWA provides. This is particularly true for the 2005 Act reauthorizing VAWA, which for the first time provided Title IX, solely devoted to the protection of American Indian women. [Pub. L. No. 103-322, §40302, 108 Stat. 1941-1942 (1994); Violence Against Women and Department of Justice Reauthorization Act of 2005, Pub. L. No. 109-162, §§901-909, 119 Stat. 2960 (2006).] Under the 2005 reauthorization of VAWA, the Office on Violence Against Women has begun regular consultations with tribes, as well as seeking recommendations on the administration of grant funds and the development of programs from tribal leaders. In addition, VAWA contains a mandate for research to establish baseline data on domestic violence, dating violence, assault, stalking and murder of native women and projecting the incidence of injury and homicide and the health expenses which these require. While these are of some benefit, they do not deal with the fundamental problem for women in Indian Country—the inability of tribes to assert jurisdiction over non-Indian perpetrators.

The obvious solution has been introduced in the Congress in the context of a broader bill entitled the Tribal Law and Order Act that require[s] that federal law enforcement agencies and U.S. attorneys who decline to pursue an Indian Country case must provide evidence and related reports to the appropriate tribal authorities encouraging cooperation between tribal and federal officials in the prosecution of crimes on the reservation. . . . The best solution, although the most politically unlikely, is reflected in the analysis by the National Congress of American Indians, which suggests that violence against women be addressed directly by an expansion of tribal jurisdiction on all matters related to domestic violence to cover all violence within the tribe's territory [such as by non-Indians who live in the tribal community]. Without a change this drastic, given the large proportion of perpetrators who are non-Indian, efforts short of this approach are likely to merely nibble around the edges of the problem. . . .

POSTSCRIPT

The Tribal Law and Order Act, Pub. L. No. 111-211, §202(a)(7), 124 Stat. 2258, was signed into law in 2011. The Act clarifies the responsibilities of federal, state, and tribal governments with respect to crimes that are committed in Indian country and also strengthens tribes' ability to prosecute such crimes more effectively. Specifically, it provides for the appointment of Special Assistant U.S. Attorneys to prosecute reservation crimes in federal courts (25 U.S.C. §2801 et seq.; 28 U.S.C. §543); requires that federal law enforcement personnel who decline to pursue a case must provide information on such cases to tribal authorities (25 U.S.C. §2809); and requires that the federal government collect information on declinations to prosecute (including the types of crimes alleged and the status of the parties as Indians or non-Indians). (Note, however, that the Act does not confer on an Indian tribe criminal jurisdiction over non-Indians.) The Act also focuses on prevention by reauthorizing and improving programs (such as those addressing substance abuse and at-risk Indian youth) that contribute to domestic violence in tribal nations (amending 25 U.S.C. §§2411, 2412, 2432; 42 U.S.C. §5783).

Further, the Act improves services to Native American victims by means of the Indian Health Care Improvement Act (amending Section 3(c)(9) of the Indian Law Enforcement Reform Act, 25 U.S.C. 2802(c)(9), as amended by section 211(a)(2)) to promote the development of standardized sexual assault policies and protocols in health facilities. It also expands training of tribal enforcement officers regarding interviewing victims of domestic and sexual violence and collecting evidence to improve conviction rates. Evaluate the effectiveness of this new legislation.

PART THREE

CIVIL LAW RESPONSE

IX

Protection Orders

Civil protection orders are an important weapon in the legal arsenal against abusers. All states currently provide for civil protection orders for victims of domestic violence. This chapter explores the nature, procedure, enforcement, and effectiveness of these orders of protection.

A. INTRODUCTION: TRADITIONAL APPROACH

■ KELLER v. KELLER
158 N.W.2d 694 (N.D. 1968)

STRUTZ, Judge.

The plaintiff brings this action for separation from bed and board. [Defendant-husband appeals from] a temporary order requiring the defendant to make certain temporary payments for the support and maintenance of the plaintiff and the minor children of the parties, restraining the defendant from molesting the plaintiff and the children, and ordering the defendant to remove himself and his business from the home of the parties, pending trial of the action on its merits. . . .

The trial court has the power to grant temporary orders for support and main-tenance and temporary restraining orders pending appeal. Sections 14-05-23 and 14-06-02, North Dakota Century Code, specifically authorize temporary-support and suit-money orders in divorce actions and in actions for separation from bed and board. Authority to restrain or enjoin a spouse from molesting or interfering with the other spouse pending trial is exercised by the court under its inherent power to make its decrees and orders effective. . . .

[W]e next will consider whether the order was properly granted in this case on the showing made by the plaintiff. While the trial court has the power to issue temporary orders, including orders which require one of the parties to remove himself or herself from the home of the parties, an order should not be issued which requires one of the parties to remove himself or herself from the home except on a showing that the health, security, and well-being of the other party or the minor children might be endangered by the continued presence of such party in the home. Let us look at the plaintiff's showing on which the order appealed from was issued.

The allegations of the complaint are very general. The plaintiff alleges that the defendant abused, embarrassed, and otherwise mistreated her, causing severe disturbances and disorder in the home, and that the plaintiff has suffered physical abuse and mental anguish and distress, constituting physical and mental cruelty. There is no allegation that the defendant has committed or has threatened to commit acts of harm to the plaintiff or the children.

The supporting affidavits of the plaintiff for such temporary order are somewhat more specific. She says that the defendant threatened the plaintiff with bodily harm; that on many occasions he has demonstrated a violent temper and that the plaintiff is fearful for her own safety; that the defendant has gone into a rage on several occasions; and that on at least one occasion he has struck the plaintiff.

This court has held repeatedly that the granting or the denying of an injunction is within the sound discretion of the trial court, and its ruling will not be reversed by this court on appeal unless there has been an abuse of this discretion evidencing a disregard of the facts. An abuse of discretion never is assumed, but must be affirmatively established.

The trial court should not issue a temporary order requiring the defendant to remove himself from the home of the parties on the unfounded fears or assertions of the petitioner. The court should require a showing of specific prior acts or conduct on the part of the defendant to justify such order. However, while the showing in this case is not as strong as it might be, we cannot say that the trial court abused its discretion in issuing the order. . . .

Notes and Questions

1. *Background.* Historically, state courts were able to issue injunctions against acts of interspousal violence as part of courts' equitable powers in conjunction with divorce proceedings. However, in 1976, Pennsylvania became the first state to provide civil restraining orders to battered women regardless of whether they were getting divorced from their abusers. Elaine M. Chiu, That Guy's a Batterer!: A Scarlett Letter Approach to Domestic Violence in the Information Age, 44 Fam. L.Q. 255, 261 (2010). Within two decades, all states had adopted a similar practice. Id.

In *Keller*, the wife sought a "separation from bed and board." Such a cause of action permitted a married couple to obtain a legal separation, thereby enabling the court to make awards of child custody and financial arrangements regarding spousal support, child support, and property. Separation decrees were common in the pre no-fault era when divorce was difficult to obtain. Before 1969, divorce could be obtained only on fault grounds and based on strict requirements of proof. Even after states began adopting no-fault divorce in the late 1960s and early 1970s, many spouses continued to seek legal separations because of the statutory requirement in many states that the divorcing parties must live separate and apart for a designated period of time prior to filing for divorce.

2. *Injunctive relief generally.* A civil order of protection is a form of injunctive relief. Orders of protection, like injunctions, can be temporary or permanent. Like an injunction, a civil order of protection can order a defendant to refrain from doing, or compel the defendant to perform, a particular act. Courts award injunctive relief to prevent irreparable harm. A civil protection order, although similar to an injunction, has some important differences. An order of protection can be issued immediately, without notice to the opposing party and without a hearing (that is, ex parte). In contrast, a temporary injunction *cannot* be issued ex parte; notice and a hearing are required. Also, temporary injunctions may provide broader relief than temporary restraining orders and even may be binding on third parties (such as employees of the petitioner).

3. *Civil vs. criminal overlap.* Both civil and criminal remedies are available to victims of domestic violence. Historically, as *Keller* illustrates, only divorce-related injunctive relief was available. Today, however, unmarried and married victims have access to civil remedies of orders of protection and tort claims. (Tort claims are discussed in Chapter 10.) Criminal sanctions are available as well, as we have seen.

An abuser may be subject to both civil and criminal liability. Civil protection order proceedings differ from criminal prosecutions in several ways. First, the objective of a proceeding for a protection order is to provide immediate protection to the petitioner rather than to punish the offender for unlawful conduct. Second, because orders of protection are civil, the rules of procedure for ordinary civil litigation apply. Procedural aspects of restraining orders are explored later in this chapter.

4. *Nature of divorce-related restraining orders.* Restraining orders can prevent a party from doing a particular act and also order a party to perform a particular act. What acts did Mrs. Keller wish the court to order Mr. Keller to do and/or refrain from doing? What was Mrs. Keller required to show to obtain the relief that she sought? Did she make the requisite showing, according to the North Dakota Supreme Court? Why or why not? What did the court mean by the statement "There is no allegation that the defendant committed or threatened to commit acts of harm to the plaintiff or the children"?

Currently, orders of protection are sometimes issued in conjunction with a pending dissolution. Although divorce courts frequently issue temporary restraining orders for the purpose of restraining a defendant from disposing of property pending the separation, divorce courts may also enjoin a spouse from interfering with, or annoying, the other spouse pending the dissolution proceedings. The Uniform Marriage and Divorce Act authorizes a divorce court to issue a temporary injunction enjoining a party from molesting or disturbing the peace of the other party or of any child during the proceedings. Unif. Marriage & Divorce Act §304(b)(2). UMDA also authorizes temporary restraining orders ("kick-out orders") that exclude a spouse from the home upon a showing of the likelihood of physical or emotional harm. Id. at §304(b)(3).

5. *Need for law reform.* As *Keller* reveals, divorcing spouses who were victims of domestic violence traditionally had the ability to petition for a restraining order as part of divorce proceedings. Until the battered women's movement, in many states

protective orders were available *only* to women filing for divorce. "As of 1981, twelve states still granted such injunctions pending only divorce, separation, or custody proceedings." Susan Schechter, Women and Male Violence: The Visions and Struggles of the Battered Women's Movement 162 (1982).

This limitation on access to relief posed a significant problem for many victims. Battered women who did not wish to file for divorce (due to religious, economic, moral, or emotional reasons) were left without protection. Moreover, relief was not available to victims who were not married to their abusers. Law reform was necessary. From 1976 until the 1990s, all states enacted legislation authorizing protection orders for victims of domestic violence.

The excerpt below explores the specific benefits provided by civil protection orders.

■ PETER FINN, STATUTORY AUTHORITY IN THE USE AND ENFORCEMENT OF CIVIL PROTECTION ORDERS AGAINST DOMESTIC ABUSE
23 Fam. L.Q. 43, 44-45 (1989)

ADVANTAGES OF PROTECTION ORDERS

Civil protection orders provide the only remedy for abuse that is not yet criminal (e.g., intimidation or harassment) and for behavior that is a misdemeanor crime with insufficient evidence for charging or conviction (e.g., threats or shoving). Civil protection orders alone can provide victims with relief when the victim does not want the batterer charged criminally or jailed for a misdemeanor criminal offense. Due to fear of retaliation, many women do not want their partner arrested. In addition, if he were given a criminal record or jailed, he might lose his job and be unable to support the woman and their children. Moreover, the children might turn against their mother for "throwing dad in jail." Furthermore, most women are interested in stopping the battering, not punishing their partner.

Civil protection orders can end the abuse by evicting the batterer from the residence, whereas the plaintiff in a criminal process usually has to live with the defendant while he is awaiting trial—and even a conviction will not necessarily separate the batterer from the victim, if little or no jail time is ordered. Finally, the specific dynamics of domestic violence create havoc with the criminal justice system because, unlike most other types of violent crime, the offender is motivated to retaliate against a specific victim. In addition, as a cohabitant, he has a unique opportunity both to continue to abuse the victim and at the same time to play on her sympathy ("It won't ever happen again! What will the kids do without me?"). By enjoining any contact and evicting the batterer from the home, civil protection orders can address these unique circumstances.

Petitioning for a protection order does not preclude a victim from bringing criminal charges against the batterer at the same time. . . . Many observers recommend that battered women pursue their cases both civilly and criminally. Some would argue that batterers should always be arrested and prosecuted, at least in cases where there has been aggravated assault and battery or other felonious behavior.

In most jurisdictions a protection order can also be issued as a condition of bail or pretrial release in a criminal case. However, these orders usually provide much less relief than civil protection orders; they do not address issues of visitation, child support, or mandatory counseling for the batterer, and in most cases they do not provide for evicting the defendant from the home. This route is also foreclosed when the abuse is not an "arrestable" offense or presents insufficient evidence to bring criminal charges.

Even if the victim plans to file for divorce, a civil protection order may be needed because women often are not granted all the relief from an action in divorce that they can get from a civil protection order. In any case, about three-quarters of domestic assault victims are already divorced or separated at the time of the incident. Thus, a strong civil protection order system is necessary as an alternative and supplement to both criminal prosecution and divorce proceedings.

B. MODERN APPROACH: SCOPE OF PROTECTION

1. An Overview of Modern Protection Orders

All states and the District of Columbia currently have protection order statutes, as we have seen. This section of the chapter provides a brief overview of the characteristics of such orders. Subsequent sections of the chapter explore each of these characteristics in more depth.

a. Protection orders: What are they?

A protection order is a civil order (that is, a document) issued by a court upon a request by a petitioner (that is, the person seeking the order). The order directs another person (the "respondent") either to do or refrain from doing certain acts. Different terms are used to describe a protection order in the various jurisdictions. It may also be called a "restraining order," "temporary restraining order," "personal protection order (PPO)," "order for protection (OFP)," "civil protection order (CPO)," or "protection from abuse order (PFA)".

(i) What is the objective of a protection order?

A protection order is issued for the purpose of protecting the petitioner from harm by the respondent. It can also be issued to protect the petitioner's children and/or the petitioner's family members.

(ii) Who can obtain an order of protection?

State statutes specify who may petition for an order of protection. All statutes provide that spouses and former spouses are eligible. Additional eligible parties, as defined by state law, include other family members, "household" members, cohabitants, boyfriends, girlfriends, etc. Some statutes have narrow definitions, whereas others have a broad range of eligible persons.

(iii) What acts can a protection order prohibit?

A protection order can prohibit a person from threatening or harming the petitioner; entering the petitioner's home ("kick-out order"); coming within a certain distance of the petitioner and/or her children or coming to the petitioner's home, work, school, or the children's home or school ("stay-away" order); contacting the petitioner (directly or indirectly, in person, by phone, email, texting, mail, or through a third party) ("no-contact" order); purchasing or owning firearms (relinquish firearms order); or prohibiting the transfer or disposal of property.

A protection order can order the abuser to pay rent or mortgage payments. It can grant temporary child custody and award temporary child or spousal support. It can grant the petitioner the use of personal effects. It can prevent a person from removing children from a jurisdiction. It can require the abuser to pay for medical costs or property damage (restitution order). It can order police to help the petitioner remove possessions from the home. The specific conditions of a protection order depend on the circumstances of each case and state law.

(iv) How does the protective order apply to firearms?

A court that issues a restraining order must prohibit the defendant from owning firearms and order those persons who do possess firearms either to relinquish them to law enforcement or sell them to a licensed firearms dealer. Relinquishment must occur within 24 hours after issuance of the order (if the batterer was present at the hearing), or 24 hours after service of the order (if the batterer was not present in court). After the restraining order is entered in the state restraining-order database, a restrained party will be unable to purchase firearms because he or she will fail the mandatory background check. The Brady Handgun Violence Prevention Act, 18 U.S.C. §922 (discussed in Chapter 8), enacted in 1993, requires federal background checks on firearm purchasers. Many states also enacted their own background check laws.

(v) What acts are beyond the scope of protection orders?

An order of protection cannot make final child custody determinations or determine title to property.

(vi) What are the types of protection orders?

An order of protection may be temporary or permanent. Some states have different forms of temporary orders: (1) an *emergency protection order* (EPO) issued upon exigent circumstances when a police officer, who has responded to a domestic violence call, requests the order from a judge, by phone, at any hour of day or night; and (2) a *temporary restraining order* (TRO) issued by a family court upon the victim's petition and affidavit that demonstrates reasonable proof of past acts of domestic violence pursuant to statute. The duration of an emergency order is generally considerably shorter than that of a temporary restraining order. An emergency order gives the victim time to go to court to apply for a temporary restraining order. If the victim fails to do so, the emergency order expires. At the hearing on the temporary restraining order, the court schedules a full adversarial hearing. Proceedings for both types of temporary protective orders are ex parte. In each case, the order must be served on the restrained party to be effective.

A *permanent protection order* is issued after an adversarial hearing on the merits. At the hearing, both parties have the opportunity to present evidence. The petitioner must prove acts of abuse pursuant to statute. Respondent has the opportunity to defend. The term *permanent protection order* is a misnomer because the order is valid only for a fixed period based on state law.

(vii) How does a protection order become effective?

A protection order becomes effective when signed by a judge. The county clerk then provides a copy of the order to the local police department so that the order can be entered into the Law Enforcement Information Network (LEIN). The petitioner is generally advised to keep a copy of the order with her at all times. A protection order is not enforceable until the respondent is served (that is, given notice). The petition, ex parte order, and notice of the hearing date must be served on the respondent. In many jurisdictions, local law enforcement officials serve the respondent. If the respondent's address is unknown, the court can order service by publication in a legal newspaper or by certified mail to an address where the abuser might get mail.

(viii) How long does a protection order last?

The court specifies the duration of the order of protection. The maximum period is designated by statute. Orders of protection may be renewed at the petitioner's request if the abuser has threatened the petitioner, caused her to be in fear for her safety, or violated the order.

(ix) What is the consequence of the violation of a protection order?

Traditionally, civil protection orders were enforced by contempt proceedings. Today, most states make the violation of a protection order a crime. Although violations of protection orders generally are misdemeanors, in some states they are felonies, especially for repeated violations.

(x) How do civil and criminal protective orders differ?

Courts also issue some types of protective orders (called "no-contact orders" or "criminal protective orders") in a criminal proceeding. Criminal protective orders can be issued at any time during prosecution, beginning with pre-trial arraignment, and also as a post-conviction condition of probation. Criminal no-contact orders are explored in Chapter 5.

The most common type of protection order excludes an abuser from the residence. The following excerpt explores whether these orders accomplish their goal.

■ **SALLY F. GOLDFARB, RECONCEIVING CIVIL PROTECTION ORDERS FOR DOMESTIC VIOLENCE: CAN LAW HELP END THE ABUSE WITHOUT ENDING THE RELATIONSHIP?**
29 Cardozo L. Rev. 1487, 1503-1505, 1519-1522 (2008)

Civil protection orders have emerged as the most frequently used and, in the view of many experts, the most effective legal remedy against domestic violence. A prominent battered women's advocate has suggested that in the context of domestic violence, any intervention should be evaluated in light of six major goals: safety for battered women, preventing violence, holding perpetrators accountable, challenging batterers' sense of entitlement to dominate their partners, restoring women's lost resources and opportunities, and enhancing women's agency and control over their lives. Civil protection orders are well positioned to advance all of these goals, but as the following discussion demonstrates, that potential has not yet been fully realized.

At the outset, it is important to note that protection orders can be divided into two types: those that require the parties to separate and those that do not. However, the latter have been almost entirely overshadowed by the former. The prevailing view of civil protection orders is that their fundamental purpose is to prevent future harm by separating the parties. Among the most common features of protection orders are provisions requiring that the abuser end his relationship with the victim. These provisions can take several forms, including ordering the offender to refrain from contacting the victim, to remain a specified distance away from her and places that she frequents, and to vacate a home shared with the victim. Such provisions are considered the norm throughout the country. In some jurisdictions, they are mandatory by law or judicial custom. The National Council of Juvenile and Family Court Judges has issued a blanket recommendation that "civil protection orders should remove the offender from the home," and has stated that the relief granted in a protection order should be "designed to deny the respondent access to the victim." Indeed, the term "stay-away order" is sometimes used as a synonym for protection order.

The widespread assumption that all protection orders require the termination of the parties' relationship masks a more complicated reality. An alternative, in the form of orders forbidding abuse but permitting ongoing contact between the parties, exists in some places and under some circumstances. The exact extent of their availability is impossible to determine, because judicial practices often differ from county to county and even from judge to judge. The result is that a battered woman who wants to obtain a protection order designed to end the violence but not the relationship may be unable to do so.

. . . Orders requiring a batterer to sever contact with a victim are a beneficial resource for women who have already separated from the abuser or want to do so. In the past, when a battered woman asked to have the batterer evicted from a shared home, judges often refused, particularly if the home was owned or rented solely in the batterer's name. This left victims with little recourse other than fleeing to a battered women's shelter. Now that the standard in many places has changed to an expectation that protection orders will include stay-away provisions, it has become substantially easier to persuade judges to grant such relief. If they are adhered to, physical distance requirements create a margin of safety around the victim, prohibitions on contact reduce the abuser's opportunities to harass her, and evicting the abuser from the residence makes the victim's home a safe haven. Furthermore, it may be relatively easy to enforce an order requiring an offender to leave the home, cease all contact with the victim, and remain a specified number of feet away from her and from designated locations, because any violations will be clear and unambiguous. All of these characteristics make stay-away orders a worthwhile option for battered women.

Nevertheless, stay-away orders have a number of disadvantages. These disadvantages suggest that forcing women to choose between getting a stay-away order and getting no protection order at all, as some courts now do, does a disservice to domestic violence victims.

First, the effectiveness of stay-away provisions is routinely undercut by the fact that in most cases where the victim and abuser have children in common, the court permits ongoing contact between the abuser and the children. Batterers often use their access to the children to perpetrate further violence against the mother—for example, when exchanging the children for visitation periods. Thus, a batterer who is in principle barred from continuing his relationship with the adult victim in fact has many opportunities to harass and abuse her. For this reason, women with children are at greater risk than other women for experiencing violence after receiving a protection order.

In addition, battered women face the danger of separation assault, which has been defined as "the attack on the woman's body and volition in which her partner seeks to prevent her from leaving, retaliate for the separation, or force her to return." Women are most at risk after ending, or while trying to end, an abusive relationship. A protection order that purports to terminate contact between the parties may be the trigger for an intensification of abuse. The result is that the relationship is over but the violence continues—the exact opposite of what many women seek. . . .

Aside from the danger of additional abuse, a stay-away order can impose other types of harm on the victim. These include loss of access to the abuser's income and resulting impoverishment, loss of his child care assistance leading to the victim's inability to keep a job, and loss of support from extended family and community. Separation also inflicts the emotional loss attendant on ending an intimate relationship and breaking up a family.

Further problems arise if the woman wants to reconcile or even just communicate with her partner. Voluntary contact between the victim and offender following issuance of a protection order is common. If the abuser has been prohibited from having contact with the victim, any future communication between the parties—even if the victim initiated it—can lead to a finding that he has violated the order and subject him to criminal penalties. [M]any women are reluctant to impose criminal prosecution on their partners for a variety of financial, practical, and emotional reasons. Indeed, for many women, one of the advantages of protection orders is that they are a civil remedy. However, once the order has been violated, criminal proceedings may come into play. When a stay-away order is in place, criminal action against the abuser may be unleashed by contacts that the victim herself desires.

Although protection orders are intended to restrict the behavior of the abuser, some courts have penalized victims for engaging in conduct that violates the terms of the order. A Kentucky judge fined two women for contacting men who had been ordered to stay away from them. The Iowa Supreme Court has twice upheld contempt of court convictions against victims in cases involving similar facts. Thus, an order that was designed as a shield to protect the victim can end up being used as a sword to punish her. . . .

The author advocates giving victims the option of obtaining a protection order with or without stay-away provisions. What do you think of this proposal?

2. Who Is Eligible as a Petitioner?

Who is eligible to petition for an order of protection? The following materials explore this question.

■ EVANS v. BRAUN
12 A.3d 395 (Pa. Super. Ct. 2010)

BENDER, J.:

Appellant, Gordon P. Braun, appeals from the January 21, 2010, order granting Appellee, Christine M. Evans, a final protection from abuse (PFA) order against him. Braun argues that the trial court erred in finding that Evans had standing to seek such an order under the Protection from Abuse Act (PFA Act), 23 Pa.C.S. §§6101-6122. . . .

Evans and Braun work together for a community health care provider. After meeting at work, the two began a stormy dating relationship during the summer of 2009. After an agreeable date, however, Braun came to Evans' home uninvited, causing her to become upset and ask him for space. The two later reconciled at some point prior to December, 2009. Both parties agree that on December 5, 2009, Evans and Braun attended a play in Harrisburg, Pennsylvania. On the way to the performance, Braun informed Evans he was carrying a gun. Later, when the two returned to his home, Braun removed the gun from his waistband, handed it to Evans, remarked on its weight and told her it could put a very big hole in her. Evans testified that she did not know whether Braun was attempting to impress her or intimidate her with the statement, and kept her concerns to herself.

On December 17, 2009, the parties were in the midst of a quarrel. Evans, attending a Christmas party organized by women who were friendly to one another at work, asked Braun to come over to the restaurant-bar, Dilly's, to make amends. When Braun arrived, Evans was standing outside smoking a cigarette with a particularly close friend named Tammy Harnish. Ms. Harnish went inside, knowing the two were fighting and wishing to allow them to speak freely. After Braun became increasingly short-tempered, sarcastic, and aggressive, Evans turned to go back into the establishment. Braun called her name, and Evans halted and turned around to look at him. Braun then proceeded to pull back his jacket and expose his Colt forty-five semi-automatic pistol, held in his waistband. He told Evans to remember he still had the gun, and he was not afraid to use it.

Evans fled inside, feeling threatened, intimidated, and scared of Braun, given his previous comments regarding the gun. Evans testified that Braun has a harsh temper, and she was afraid of him. Although she told the table of women only that the two had fought, Evans reported the entire incident confidentially to Ms. Harnish soon thereafter that same evening, becoming hysterical upon relaying Braun's threatening behavior with the pistol. The next day, Evans reported the incident to her employer, impelled by fear due to their shared workplace. An employee assistance counselor advised her to inform the police, who in turn referred her to the office of Women in Need (WIN). The office responded by scheduling her for the next available appointment. After the appointment, WIN filed a [PFA] action on Evans' behalf, with a temporary order of protection issued ex parte the same date, Friday, January 8, 2010. [The hearing on the permanent order of protection was held January 21, 2010, at which time the court issued the final PFA order and required that Braun surrender his firearms. He appeals, alleging that Evans failed to establish her standing under the PFA Act.]

[W]e must begin by analyzing whether the evidence presented by Evans was sufficient to prove that she is a member of the class of people that the PFA Act seeks to protect. The statute directs that an adult may seek relief "by filing a petition with the court alleging abuse by the defendant." 23 Pa.C.S. §6106(a). "Abuse," as defined in the Act, includes, inter alia:

> The occurrence of one or more of the following acts between family or household members, sexual or intimate partners or persons who share biological parenthood:
> (1) Attempting to cause or intentionally, knowingly or recklessly causing bodily injury, serious bodily injury, rape, involuntary deviate sexual intercourse, sexual assault, statutory sexual assault, aggravated indecent assault, indecent assault or incest with or without a deadly weapon.
> (2) Placing another in reasonable fear of imminent serious bodily injury.

23 Pa.C.S. §6102(a)(1)-(2). "[F]or the Act to apply, the petitioner seeking to invoke it must have standing, which is to say that the petitioner and the intended respondent must be a family or household member." Applicable to the instant case is the fact that "family or household member" is defined as including "current or former sexual or intimate partners." 23 Pa.C.S. §6102(a).

[Here], Evans sought relief under the PFA Act alleging that she and Braun were "sexual or intimate partners." While the PFA Act does not specifically define that phrase, we examined the meaning of this language [previously]. We began by analyzing the intent of the legislators in enacting the PFA Act. [As we stated in Scott v. Shay, 928 A.2d 312, 315 (Pa. Super. Ct. 2007)]:

> [T]heir intent was to prevent domestic violence and to promote peace and safety within domestic, familial and/or romantic relationships.
> . . . [T]he persons who undoubtedly fit the Act's definition of family or household members—e.g., spouses, parents, children, relatives, paramours, and persons who undertake romantic relationships—typically share some significant degree of domestic, familial and/or intimate interdependence. There is often an obvious emotional bond. Frequently, these individuals interface in very practical areas of private life—a mutual residence, common family obligations and/or shared involvement in the affairs of day-to-day living. Even in a dating relationship, where the functional interdependence might not be as substantial as in a family, the participants have elected some measure

of personal interaction. This interaction often involves emotional or private concerns not unlike those found in family settings, albeit not normally as extensive or as intense. In sum, the persons protected by the Act as family or household members have a connection rooted in blood, marriage, family-standing, or a chosen romantic relationship.

Scott, 928 A.2d at 315. With this rationale in mind, we construed the word "partners" "to mean those persons who mutually chose to enter relationships." Id. at 316. This interpretation, we concluded, "give[s] effect to the provisions of the statute in a way that promotes its purpose of preventing violence among people with a domestic, familial or romantic bond, past or present." Id.

Applying our reasoning in *Scott* instantly, we conclude that Evans presented sufficient evidence to prove that she and Braun "mutually chose" to enter a "dating relationship" which involved a "romantic bond," albeit short-lived. Evans testified at the final PFA hearing that she and Braun "dated twice." She stated that after going to a play on their second date, Braun drove her back to his house because he wanted her to meet his son. On the night that Braun threatened her with a gun at Dilly's, Evans stated that she invited him to the bar-restaurant to apologize. She explained why she was apologizing, stating:

> [I was apologizing] [b]ecause I had been very straightforward with him, said some things that he might have interpreted to be unkind. I lost my husband a year and a half ago. I've been going very slow, trying to go very slow in relationships. And he's very pushy and wanted things that I was not ready for.

After Evans testified, she called Ms. Harnish to the stand. Ms. Harnish claimed that on the night Braun threatened Evans at Dilly's, Evans confided in Ms. Harnish about Braun. During this conversation, Evans told Ms. Harnish that Braun had told her that he loved her.

Based on this testimony, we conclude that there was sufficient evidence presented that Braun and Evans mutually chose to enter a dating relationship which, pursuant to *Scott*, qualifies as a "sexual or intimate partnership" under the PFA Act. As noted in *Scott*, dating relationships such as this may not have a "functional independence . . . as substantial as in a family" but, nonetheless, Evans and Braun "elected some measure of personal interaction."[1]

Furthermore, we note that our conclusion is supported by the fact that "the Act was passed because the criminal law was sometimes an inadequate mechanism for dealing with violence that arose in the intimate environs of domestic life." *Scott*, 928 A.2d at 315. In this case, criminal law proved to be an ineffective avenue for Evans to seek protection from Braun. Despite the fact that Braun twice showed Evans a gun

---

1. While we do not rely on it, we note that Braun's own testimony bolsters our conclusion that he and Evans were involved in a "sexual or intimate partnership" as defined in *Scott*. For instance, Braun stated that he and Evans had "dated several times." They first went on a date in the summer of 2009 when Braun went to Evans' house to watch a movie and get Chinese food. He testified that "things got a little close" on that date and, as such, he mistakenly believed that it was acceptable to stop by Evans' house unannounced several days later. However, when Braun stopped by, Evans became upset. Braun stated that at that point, he "broke it off" with Evans. Nevertheless, in December of 2009, Braun asked Evans to go on a second date and the two went to a movie. Braun explained that Evans was "very touchy feel-y" during the movie. He testified that he and Evans went out a third time to see a play in Harrisburg. On another occasion, Braun went to Evans' house because she was upset. Braun sat with Evans and they talked about Braun's prior marriage and divorce.

and made threatening comments like "he could put a very big hole in her," and "he still had the gun, and was not afraid to use it," the police did not pursue a criminal investigation or charges against Braun. Instead, they directed Evans to WIN. Arguably, this is precisely the type of scenario that the Legislature intended the PFA Act to address, which bolsters our conclusion that Evans had standing to seek protection under that statute. . . .

Judge CLELAND files a dissenting statement.

I respectfully note my dissent from the majority's expansive view of the Legislature's intent in enacting the Protection from Abuse Act and [their conclusion that] Evans had standing to bring this action. Evans' testimony established that she and Braun were co-workers who had gone on two dates. She did not testify they were particularly intimate, either sexually or emotionally.[1] Under the facts of this case, I do not agree Evans and Braun can be considered "current or former sexual or intimate partners" as that term is used either in the statute or discussed in our case law. Their relationship simply did not entail the "significant degree of domestic, familial and/or intimate interdependence" the Act is intended to address.

The majority further concludes the "criminal law proved to be an ineffective avenue for Evans to seek protection from Braun" and, therefore, "bolsters our conclusion that Evans had standing to seek protection under the statute." However, arguably it was not the criminal law that proved to be ineffective. The criminal law "already affords protection from harassment, stalking, assault and a multitude of other crimes." If the police failed to recognize the possibility Evans was the victim of criminal acts and afford her the protection of the Crimes Code, their failure does not bolster her into an "intimate partner" as defined by the Legislature in the Protection from Abuse Act.

As we noted in *Scott,* "the Act is concerned with persons who have or have had domestic, familial and/or romantic relationships. It is a domestic relations statute, not a statute governing persons without any such relations." I do not believe the Legislature, given its stated intent, intended to authorize a trial court to grant the expansive relief provided in the Act based on a two-date relationship. That is the realm of the criminal law. Therefore, I respectfully dissent.

Notes and Questions

1. *Types of protection orders.* What kind of protection order(s) did the petitioner request? What was her rationale for requesting that particular relief?

2. *Ex parte proceedings. Evans* initially involved an ex parte proceeding—a summary hearing that does not require the appearance of the respondent (that is, the party who is served with the order). Do ex parte proceedings violate an abuser's right to due process? See Blazel v. Bradley, 698 F. Supp. 756, 768 (W.D. Wis. 1988) (upholding statute but holding that it violated due process, as applied, because of lack of allegation of risk of immediate harm); Marquette v. Marquette, 686 P.2d 990, 995-996 (Okla. Civ. App. 1984) (upholding the constitutionality of ex parte orders). Other due process issues are explored later in this chapter.

---

1. While Braun's testimony, cited by the majority in footnote 1, is arguably to the contrary, the trial court did not find his testimony credible.

3. *Elements. Evans* illustrates the requirements for a domestic violence protective order. All domestic violence protective orders require that the victim show (1) a qualifying relationship and (2) evidence of abuse. What does the specific statute require in *Evans*?

4. *Qualifying relationship.* Domestic violence protective orders are always available for spouses and former spouses. Catherine F. Klein & Leslye E. Orloff, Providing Legal Protection for Battered Women: An Analysis of State Statutes and Case Law, 21 Hofstra L. Rev. 801, 814-816 (1993). What was the qualifying relationship in *Evans*?

a. *Quasi-marital relationships.* Statutes extend the definition of eligible parties to those persons in quasi-marital relationships—"relationships that look like traditional, heterosexual marriages in that they are characterized by two people who have financial interdependence, share an intimate relationship, live in the same household, and have a long-term commitment to the relationship." Ruth Colker, Marriage Mimicry: The Law of Domestic Violence, 47 Wm. & Mary L. Rev. 1841, 1845 (2006) (commending the extension of some protections to same-sex partners but nonetheless criticizing the "marriage mimicry" model for its traditional omission of those partners).

b. *Family members.* Most states also provide protective orders for family members, such as siblings, parents, stepparents, and in-laws. Klein & Orloff, supra, at 816-817.

c. *Household members.* Some states authorize orders of protection for household members. Who qualifies? Must household members share an intimate relationship? See, e.g., Sandoval v. Mendez, 521 A.2d 1168 (D.C. 1987) (refusing to issue a civil protection order to a petitioner who was beaten by her cousin's boyfriend, with whom she had no intimate relationship although they once shared a residence); R.M.W. v. G.M.M., 873 N.Y.S.2d 864 (Fam. Ct. 2009) (protective orders available between mothers of child with common father).

d. *Parents.* Many states define eligible parties as parents of the same child. Do the parents have to married to obtain an order of protection? Who should be permitted to seek a protective order on behalf of a minor? See K.J. v. K.K., 873 N.Y.S.2d 867 (Fam. Ct. 2009) (allowing adoptive mother to seek protective order on behalf of child against child's biological parents); Allie Meiers, Comment, Civil Orders of Protection: A Tool to Keep Children Safe, 19 J. Am. Acad. Matrim. Law. 373, 376 (2005).

e. *Dating relationship.* Some states permit protective orders for persons in a "dating relationship." What is a dating relationship? See Neilson ex rel. Crump, Chapter 3. Does one date qualify? See Alison C. v. Westcott, 798 N.E.2d 813, 816 (Ill. App. Ct. 2003) (finding that one date was insufficient). Many jurisdictions require dating relationships to be long-term, substantial, or exclusive. See Colker, supra, at 1859. See also Jennifer Cranstoun et al., What's an Intimate Relationship, Anyway?—Expanding Access to the New York State Family Courts for Civil Orders of Protection, 29 Pace L. Rev. 455 (2009). For a survey of state standards, see ABA, Domestic Violence Civil Protection Orders (CPOs) By State (June 2009), available at http://www.americanbar.org/content/dam/aba/migrated/domviol/docs/DV_CPO_Chart_8_2007.authcheckdam.pdf.

Were Evans and Braun "current or former sexual or intimate partners"? What evidence supports the petitioner's request? What evidence supports the respondent's view? Because the statute does not define "sexual or intimate partner," how does the court determine whether the petitioner satisfies the requisite requirements? In *Evans*, the majority and dissent disagree regarding whether Ms. Evans is a member of the protected class. What is the nature of their disagreement? Whose opinion do you find more persuasive—the majority or the dissent? Why?

5. *Civil vs. criminal overlap.* Protective orders are useful as an addition to, and alternative to, criminal sanctions. Protective orders may be preferable if difficulties arise in prosecution, for example, if the evidence is insufficient, drugs or alcohol are present, the victim would be a poor witness, or timely relief is necessary. Eve S. Buzawa & Carl G. Buzawa, Domestic Violence: The Criminal Justice Response 237 (3d. ed. 2003). Should the availability of criminal sanctions influence the issuance of an order of protection? How do the views of the majority and dissent in *Evans* differ? Which view do you find more persuasive?

6. *Policy rationale.* What policy reasons support a broad or narrow definition of eligible parties? See, e.g., J.S. v. J.F., 983 A.2d 1151, 1153 (N.J. Super. App. Div. 2009) (evidence supported a finding of a dating relationship despite defendant's characterization of plaintiff as a paid escort); Jessica D. v. Jeremy H., 878 N.Y.S.2d 578, 580 (Fam. Ct. 2009) (refusing to find an intimate relationship on policy grounds because petitioner was married to someone else), *rev'd* 906 N.Y.S.2d 119 (NY 2010) (extending statutory definition of these parties). See generally Klein & Orloff, *supra*, at 814-842.

7. *Need for civil protection order statute.* The *Evans* majority points out that the state statute was passed because "the criminal law was sometimes an inadequate mechanism for dealing with violence that arose in the intimate environs of domestic life." What does the court mean? In this case, was the criminal law an ineffective avenue for protection? Why or why not?

The following excerpt examines some of the characteristics of persons who seek temporary restraining orders and also several factors that play a role in attrition rates.

■ EVE S. BUZAWA & CARL G. BUZAWA, DOMESTIC VIOLENCE: THE CRIMINAL JUSTICE RESPONSE
234, 241-242 (3d ed., 2003)

There is virtually no disagreement that domestic violence victims need protective orders. In one recent study, 68 percent of women seeking a restraining order had been victimized by prior violence. Another study reported that more than 50 percent of women applying for restraining orders had been injured during the incident that led to the issuance of the order.

Research in two Colorado counties reported that women filing for temporary restraining orders experienced an average of 13 violent acts in the year before filing. Similar findings were reported in Dane County, Wisconsin, where approximately one-third of women filing for ex parte orders were assaulted at least 10 times in the 3 months before filing. . . .

WHEN WILL WOMEN USE RESTRAINING ORDERS?

There has also been much research on the conditions under which battered women will be able to use the court system effectively to obtain restraining orders. Women who are economically dependent on their abusers obviously are at greater financial risk than those that are financially independent. Not surprisingly, economic dependence has been found to have a great impact on the victim's perseverance in obtaining a permanent restraining order. Similarly, the extent and frequency of abuse may so terrify women that the most severely impacted victims may paradoxically be the most likely to fail to obtain a permanent order.

There is also a predictable interaction between the demands of court procedures and the crisis attendant to being a victim of battering. It has long been known that to use the courts effectively, as with most criminal justice agencies, it is best to present an appearance of a calm demeanor, remembering exactly what has occurred and the expectations that the person has of the agency. In contrast, battered women, as a corollary of abuse, often develop symptoms of post-traumatic stress disorder (PTSD). They may act forgetful, confused, and indecisive—conditions that directly contribute to being marginalized by many court personnel. Similarly, the unwillingness of many victims to discuss the details of abuse in front of an audience may, along with the time-consuming steps needed to obtain a restraining order, account for attrition by many victims.

3. What Conduct Gives Rise to a Protection Order?

■ **CLOETER v. CLOETER**

770 N.W.2d 660 (Neb. Ct. App. 2009)

MOORE, Judge.

. . . Barbara and Kurt are divorced and have two children: a daughter who was born in 1990 and resides with Kurt and a daughter who was born in 2003 and resides with Barbara. . . . On July 11, 2008, Barbara filed a petition requesting a domestic abuse protection order against Kurt and an affidavit containing allegations supporting the request. Barbara's affidavit described the three most recent incidents of domestic abuse which occurred on June 6, 18, and 20, 2008. Barbara alleged that on June 6 at approximately 6:45 a.m., she received a text message from Kurt with the letters "E," "A," and "D." She sent him a text message which asked what that meant and received no response. Barbara alleged that Kurt then began sending one-letter text messages, and she reported this to the police. A police officer who responded noted that when the letters in the text messages were combined, they spelled out the word "behead." Barbara stated that she was very frightened by this threat and was afraid Kurt would behead her or her children.

Barbara's affidavit alleged the second incident occurred on June 18, 2008, at about 6:15 p.m. Kurt arrived at her home to take the younger daughter for visitation and sent Barbara a text message with the letters "B" and "E." She stated that on June 11, Kurt sent her the text messages which spelled out the word "behead" and she notified the police. . . . Barbara stated again that she feared he would attempt to behead her or her daughter. Barbara also stated that she was concerned that Kurt had abused animals in the younger daughter's presence during visitation and that this was harmful to her.

The final incident that Barbara described in her affidavit occurred on June 20, 2008. She stated that she found a 2-by 4-inch piece of wood (2 by 4) in her driveway. This was significant to her because previously, when she expressed to Kurt her fear that he would hurt her with a baseball bat, he allegedly responded: "'Why would I buy baseball bats when I could do the same with a 2 [by] 4?'" Barbara stated that Kurt had been released from jail the day before she found the 2 by 4 in her driveway and that therefore she viewed this as a threat.

The district court entered an ex parte domestic abuse protection order. The court found that Barbara had stated facts showing that Kurt attempted to cause, or intentionally, knowingly, or recklessly caused, bodily injury to Barbara, or by physical menace, placed Barbara in fear of imminent bodily injury. The order excluded Kurt from Barbara's residence, the hospital where Barbara worked, and a specific church. . . . [On September 22, 2008, the district court held a hearing at Kurt's request allowing him to show cause why the protection order should not remain in effect.] Kurt testified that during the past year when he had visitation with the younger daughter, he would normally pick her up at Barbara's home and would communicate that he had arrived by sending Barbara a text message. Kurt testified that to send Barbara a text message, he would usually select her telephone number and then "hit a couple letters or something." Kurt testified that he was "not an avid text messager," so his text messages had no words in them, "just randomly selected letters." Kurt testified that he never intended to send Barbara a text message, either at one time or in a series over a period of time, which would spell out the word "behead." . . . Kurt testified that there was no significance to the letters "E," "A," and "D," that he would have no reason to send her a text message at 6:45 a.m., that normally he would only send Barbara a text message right before he picked up his younger daughter, and that he would not have picked her up on that date at that time. With regard to the 2 by 4 that Barbara found in her driveway on June 20, Kurt offered into evidence four photographs, taken by the older daughter. Those photographs depict Barbara's home, as well as the home directly across the street from hers, which was undergoing construction and demolition work. Kurt testified that he did not place the 2 by 4 in Barbara's driveway, did not have anything to do with a 2 by 4's being placed in her driveway, and believed that it could have come from the demolition project across the street. Kurt also denied killing animals in front of the younger daughter.

Barbara also testified at the hearing. She testified that she received Kurt's comment, "why would I use baseball bats when I could do the same thing with a [2 by 4]," in an e-mail approximately 2 years earlier. She could not recall what the rest of the e-mail said. Barbara also testified that the house across the street from her had been in that condition for more than a year and that there had been no other incidents in which a 2 by 4 or other spare building materials appeared in her driveway. According to Barbara, the 2 by 4 appeared in her driveway the day after Kurt was released from jail for violating a previous protection order against him. However, she did not see anyone put the 2 by 4 in her driveway. Barbara also testified that Child Protective Services was still investigating her allegation that Kurt killed animals in the younger daughter's presence and that she was still concerned for her and her children's safety. . . . On cross-examination, Kurt's attorney asked Barbara, "[I]s it correct that you didn't know if those text messages even spelled out the word 'behead' until [a police] officer brought it to your attention?" Barbara responded, "I wasn't sure what he was trying to say." . . .

[The court entered an order which affirmed the domestic abuse protection order as amended. Kurt now appeals.]

The Protection from Domestic Abuse Act, Neb. Rev. Stat. §42-901 et seq., allows any victim of domestic abuse to file a petition and affidavit for a protection order pursuant to §42-924. Abuse is defined under §42-903(1) as follows:

> the occurrence of one or more of the following acts between household members:
> (a) Attempting to cause or intentionally and knowingly causing bodily injury with or without a dangerous instrument;
> (b) Placing, by physical menace, another person in fear of imminent bodily injury; or
> (c) Engaging in sexual contact or sexual penetration without consent as defined in section 28-318.

The act defines "household member" to include a former spouse. §42-903(3).

In the present case, . . . Barbara did not allege, nor does the record show, that Kurt had caused her bodily injury. Accordingly, we limit our consideration to whether Barbara has shown that Kurt, by physical menace, placed her in fear of imminent bodily injury as required by §§42-903(1)(b) and 42-924. Kurt argues that there is no credible evidence that he engaged in any conduct constituting abuse as defined in §42-903. He submits that even if Barbara's allegations are assumed to be true, the alleged conduct does not rise to the level of abuse within the meaning of the statute.

The terms "physical menace" and "imminent" as used in §42-903(1)(b) are not defined within the statute. Two other Nebraska statutes contain the same terms as §42-903: Neb. Rev. Stat. §28-323(1)(b), which proscribes third-degree domestic assault, and Neb. Rev. Stat. §29-404.02(1)(c)(ii), which sets forth the instances in which a police officer may make a warrantless arrest; however, our research reveals no Nebraska case law construing the term "physical menace."

Case law construing "menace" is most common in the context of an assault cause of action. . . . Webster's Third New International Dictionary, Unabridged, defines "menace" as "to make a show of intention to harm: make a threatening gesture, statement, or act against." In its noun form, the word "menace" generally means a threat. See Webster's Encyclopedic Unabridged Dictionary of the English Language 894 (1983). However, in §42-903(1)(b) the Nebraska Legislature specifically limited the definition of abuse to instances involving "physical menace." Other courts that have construed "physical menace" in the context of statutes proscribing assault have determined that the term necessarily requires more than words, that is, there must be some physical act on the part of the defendant. We agree and therefore conclude that "physical menace" as used in §42-903(1)(b) means a physical threat or act and requires more than mere words.

The facts presented here also require us to construe the word "imminent," which neither §42-903(1)(b) nor Nebraska case law defines. Black's Law Dictionary defines "imminent danger" as "an immediate, real threat to one's safety that justifies the use of force in self-defense" or "[t]he danger resulting from an immediate threatened injury sufficient to cause a reasonable and prudent person to defend himself or herself." Black's Law Dictionary 421 (8th ed. 2004). . . . A likelihood or a bare possibility of injury is not sufficient to create imminent peril. We conclude that "imminent" bodily injury within the context of §42-903(1)(b) means a certain, immediate, and real threat to one's safety which places one in immediate danger of bodily injury, that is, bodily injury is likely to occur at any moment.

We now turn to the facts to determine whether Barbara suffered abuse within the meaning of §42-903(1)(b), specifically whether Kurt, by physical menace, placed Barbara in fear of imminent bodily injury. Barbara alleges several incidents in which Kurt sent her text messages containing letters that combine to form the word "behead." However, these text messages cannot be construed to be within the meaning of physical menace, as words alone are not a physical threat or act within the purview of the statute. Therefore, the text messages are not instances of abuse which could sustain the entry of a domestic abuse protection order within the meaning of §§42-903 and 42-924.

Barbara also alleges that Kurt placed a 2 by 4 in her driveway to threaten her. We assume without deciding that such allegation satisfies the meaning of "physical menace" within §42-903(1)(b). However, even if we allow Barbara the benefit of that assumption, the record does not support a conclusion that, as a result of this incident, Barbara was placed in fear of imminent bodily injury. Barbara testified that the comment Kurt made regarding a 2 by 4 occurred 2 years prior to the incident and that she did not see anyone place the 2 by 4 in her driveway. Kurt denied placing the 2 by 4 or having anything to do with its appearance in Barbara's driveway. There is no evidence that Kurt was on or near the premises at the time Barbara noticed the 2 by 4; therefore, we cannot conclude that Barbara was placed in fear of an immediate, real threat to her safety which placed her in immediate danger of bodily injury, because bodily injury was not likely to occur at any moment. Barbara testified that she viewed this incident as a threat, but there is no evidence to support that either Kurt or the 2 by 4 was an immediate, real threat to Barbara's safety which placed her in immediate danger of bodily injury. As such, this incident is not an instance of abuse which could sustain the entry of a domestic abuse protection order within the meaning of §§42-903 and 42-924. With regard to the allegations regarding animal abuse, we likewise conclude that the record is insufficient to support that this is an instance of abuse.

We note that in 1998, the Legislature enacted 1998 Neb. Laws, L.B. 218, which created a cause of action for a harassment protection order pursuant to Neb. Rev. Stat. §28-311.09 (Cum. Supp. 1998) separate from a cause of action for a domestic abuse protection order . . . Section 28-311.02 defines "harass" as "to engage in a knowing and willful course of conduct directed at a specific person which seriously terrifies, threatens, or intimidates the person and which serves no legitimate purpose." We do not speculate, however, as to the result in the instant case if Barbara had pursued a harassment protection order pursuant to §28-311.09 instead of a domestic abuse protection order pursuant to §42-924 (Reissue 2008). Rather, we point out this legislative history only to indicate that we are bound by the language contained in the specific statutes under which Barbara sought a protection order.

[W]e find that the facts Barbara alleged in the present case do not constitute abuse within the contemplation of §42-903. . . . [Accordingly,] we direct the district court to enter an order dismissing the domestic abuse protection order against Kurt. . . .

The following statute provides examples of the types of relief that protective orders offer.

■ ALASKA STAT. §18.66.100. PROTECTIVE ORDERS: RELIEF

. . . (c) A protective order under this section may:

(1) prohibit the respondent from threatening to commit or committing domestic violence, stalking, or harassment;

(2) prohibit the respondent from telephoning, contacting, or otherwise communicating directly or indirectly with the petitioner;

(3) remove and exclude the respondent from the residence of the petitioner, regardless of ownership of the residence;

(4) direct the respondent to stay away from the residence, school, or place of employment of the petitioner or any specified place frequented by the petitioner or any designated household member;

(5) prohibit the respondent from entering a propelled vehicle in the possession of or occupied by the petitioner;

(6) prohibit the respondent from using or possessing a deadly weapon if the court finds the respondent was in the actual possession of or used a weapon during the commission of domestic violence;

(7) direct the respondent to surrender any firearm owned or possessed by the respondent if the court finds that the respondent was in the actual possession of or used a firearm during the commission of the domestic violence;

(8) request a peace officer to accompany the petitioner to the petitioner's residence to ensure that the petitioner

(A) safely obtains possession of the petitioner's residence, vehicle, or personal items; and

(B) is able to safely remove a vehicle or personal items from the petitioner's residence;

(9) award temporary custody of a minor child to the petitioner and may arrange for visitation with a minor child if the safety of the child and the petitioner can be protected; if visitation is allowed, the court may order visitation under the conditions provided in AS 25.20.061;

(10) give the petitioner possession and use of a vehicle and other essential personal items, regardless of ownership of the items;

(11) prohibit the respondent from consuming controlled substances;

(12) require the respondent to pay support for the petitioner or a minor child in the care of the petitioner if there is an independent legal obligation of the respondent to support the petitioner or child;

(13) require the respondent to reimburse the petitioner or other person for expenses associated with the domestic violence, including medical expenses, counseling, shelter, and repair or replacement of damaged property;

(14) require the respondent to pay costs and fees incurred by the petitioner in bringing the action under this chapter;

(15) order the respondent, at the respondent's expense, to participate in (A) a program for the rehabilitation of perpetrators of domestic violence that meets the standards set by, and that is approved by, the Department of Corrections under AS 44.28.020(b), or (B) treatment for the abuse of alcohol or controlled substances, or both; a protective order under this section may not require a respondent to participate in a program for the rehabilitation of perpetrators of

domestic violence unless the program meets the standards set by, and that is approved by, the Department of Corrections under AS 44.28.020(b);

(16) order other relief the court determines necessary to protect the petitioner or any household member. . . .

Notes and Questions

1. *Types of protective orders.* *Cloeter* illustrates the procedure for requesting a domestic violence protection order. What type of order was the petitioner requesting?

2. *Elements.* All domestic violence protective orders require the victim to show (1) a qualifying relationship and (2) evidence of abuse. *Cloeter* takes a very narrow definition of the abuse that warrants a protective order. What is required under the Nebraska statute?

All states provide protective orders against assault, battery, threat of physical injury, and other criminal acts against the victim. See Margaret E. Johnson, Redefining Harm, Reimagining Remedies, and Reclaiming Domestic Violence Law, 42 U.C. Davis L. Rev. 1107, 1131-1132 (2009). Fewer states provide protection against other forms of abuse. Only one-third of states provide protective orders against coercive behavior, false imprisonment, or interference with personal liberty as abuse. Id. at 1333. Seventeen states recognize psychological or emotional abuse (not including economic abuse) as the basis for a protective order. Id. at 1334. Only one state provides protective orders for economic abuse. Mich. Comp. Laws §600.2950(1).

A protective order must be based on the victim's subjective feeling of a reasonable fear. In *Cloeter*, the court refused to find that Barbara's fear was reasonable. Why? Do you agree? How should courts assess the "reasonableness" of a victim's fears?

3. *Psychological abuse.* *Cloeter* highlights the difficulties for petitioners who seek orders of protection based on psychological abuse. Which of the following acts would qualify for a protective order under the Nebraska statute in *Cloeter*? Intoxication combined with physical and verbal abuse? See Peters v. Peters, 474 N.Y.S.2d 785 (App. Div. 1984). Access to weapons? See Sherman v. Sherman, 522 N.Y.S.2d 910 (App. Div. 1987). Verbal threats of physical violence against the parties' child or threats to abduct the child? See Wardeh v. Altabchi, 815 N.E.2d 712 (Ohio App. 2004). Fear of a partner's violent reaction to a divorce petition? See Parkhurst v. Parkhurst, 793 S.W.2d 634 (Mo. Ct. App. 1990).

4. *Constitutional issues.* Do protection orders' evoke constitutional concerns? *Cloeter* involved an ex parte proceeding that does not require the respondent's presence. Do such proceedings violate the right to due process? See Blazel v. Bradley, 698 F. Supp. 756 (W.D. Wis. 1988); Marquette v. Marquette, 686 P.2d 990 (Okla. Civ. App. 1984) (upholding ex parte orders). How do the procedures of ex parte proceedings overcome due process concerns?

An order of protection may grant to one party exclusive possession of the family residence, even if title is in the name of the restrained party. Does this order deprive an abuser of property rights? Do "stay-away" orders violate an abuser's constitutional right to the custody of children? In an early challenge, the Missouri Supreme Court addressed the constitutionality of provisions of the state Adult Abuse Act permitting courts to issue ex parte orders of protection to exclude respondents from the home and to prohibit contact with children for a 15-day period. The court explored whether these ex parte orders deprived respondent of his constitutional rights. The court concluded that the Act did not violate respondent's due process rights because the Act was necessary to secure important governmental interests in the protection of victims from abuse, and because existing procedural safeguards were adequate to protect against erroneous deprivation of the respondent's constitutionally protected rights. State ex rel. Williams v. Marsh, 626 S.W.2d 223 (Mo. 1982).

Problem

Anthony Meredith, when he is 37 years old and a Virginia Assistant Attorney General, obtains a foreign bride, 18-year-old Jazmin Muriel from Colombia, on the Internet. Less than a year after the wedding, a pregnant Muriel petitions for divorce to end the violent marriage. The court finds that Anthony has committed domestic violence. Anthony appeals, challenging the domestic violence protection order, including one particular provision. He alleges that the provision prohibiting him from interfering in Muriel's immigration proceedings violates his First Amendment rights. What result? Can a protection order restrain lawful speech? See In re Marriage of Meredith, 201 P.3d 1056 (Wash. Ct. App. 2009). See generally David P. Weber, (Unfair) Advantage: Damocles' Sword and the Coercive Use of Immigration Status in a Civil Society, 94 Marq. L. Rev. 613 (2010). (The relationship of domestic violence and mail-order brides is explored in Chapter 11.)

4. How Long Does It Last?: Duration of an Order of Protection

The following two cases examine the issue of the duration of an order of protection.

■ DYER v. DYER
5 A.3d 1049 (Me. 2010)

Levy, J.

Bruce S. Dyer appeals from a judgment entered in the District Court extending for a second time a protection from abuse order against him related to his former wife, Kathleen L. Dyer. Bruce contends that (1) the plain language of the protection from abuse statute allows the court to extend a protection order only once; (2) the evidence was insufficient to support the court's finding that Kathleen had an objectively reasonable fear of further abuse; and (3) the court abused its discretion by extending the protection order for four years. . . .

Kathleen and Bruce are divorced, and they have one daughter, who was born in 1995. In December 2005, Bruce assaulted Kathleen in the garage of their home. After convincing her to enter the garage, he struck her in the head from behind with a lacrosse stick and struck her again in the face. While she was on the ground, he got on top of her and held his hands over her mouth and nose until she was on the verge of losing consciousness. The assault stopped when their ten-year-old daughter entered the garage and Kathleen was able to tell her to call 911. [Bruce was convicted of aggravated assault.]

In December 2005, the parties agreed to an order of protection from abuse, which the court entered without a finding of abuse. The order prohibited Bruce from having direct or indirect contact with Kathleen or their daughter for two years. Bruce twice violated this order by sending his daughter a Christmas card in December 2005 and by entering Kathleen's home in early 2006. In November 2007, Kathleen moved to extend the protection order pursuant to 19-A M.R.S. §4007(2) (2009). The parties agreed to extend the order for an additional two years without a finding of abuse. The extended order did not apply to their daughter.

In December 2009, Kathleen moved to extend the second protection order. After a hearing on the motion, the court made a finding of abuse and extended the protection order for four additional years, reasoning that the Legislature did not intend "to put a two-year limit on how scared somebody can be from such horrendous conduct." Bruce moved for additional findings of fact and conclusions of law pursuant to M.R. Civ. P. 52(a). The court found that the 2005 assault was "extraordinarily brutal and unprovoked," that Kathleen is still affected by Bruce's violations of the first protection order, and that she "lives in fear of [Bruce] as if the assault happened yesterday." Specifically, Kathleen is fearful when she sees vehicles that are similar to Bruce's, she avoids traveling in the town where Bruce lives, and when she learned that Bruce got a job in the town where she works, she informed the local police and reviewed her workplace's safety plan with her employer. The court also concluded that section 4007(2) allows the court to extend a protective order more than once. [Bruce appeals.]

Bruce contends that the court erred in ordering a second extension of the protection order because a second extension is not explicitly authorized by statute. Whether the statute authorizes a second extension is a question that we have not previously addressed. . . .

The protection from abuse statute provides, in relevant part, that a protection order or consent agreement may be extended as necessary to protect the plaintiff or a minor child from abuse:

> 1. *Protection order; consent agreement.* The court, after a hearing and upon finding that the defendant has committed the alleged abuse . . . , may grant a protective order. . . .
> 2. *Duration.* A protective order or approved consent agreement is for a fixed period not to exceed 2 years. At the expiration of that time, the court may extend an order, upon motion of the plaintiff, for such additional time as it determines necessary to protect the plaintiff or minor child from abuse. . . . Upon motion by either party, for sufficient cause, the court may modify the order or agreement from time to time as circumstances require.

19-A M.R.S. §4007(1), (2) (2009). The statute also provides a general rule of statutory construction and a statement of its underlying purpose:

> The court shall liberally construe and apply this chapter to promote the following underlying purposes: . . . To allow family . . . members who are victims of domestic abuse to obtain . . . effective protection against further abuse so that the lives of the nonabusing family . . . members are as secure and uninterrupted as possible.

19-A M.R.S. §4001(2) (2009).

By its plain language, section 4007(2) provides for a court to extend a protective order when it expires, but it neither authorizes nor prohibits further extensions of a protective order. Because the statute is silent on this matter, we consider other indicia of legislative intent, such as the statutory statement of purpose included in section 4001, to choose between two competing constructions.

A liberal construction of section 4007(2) that does not preclude a second extension of a protective order is in harmony with the underlying purpose of the statute to provide family members "effective protection against further abuse so that [their] lives . . . are as secure and uninterrupted as possible." See 19-A M.R.S. §4001(2). By contrast, a strict construction of section 4007(2) that would prevent more than one extension of a protection order ignores the reality and unpredictability of personal relationships and, in this case, would create a result adverse to the statute's purpose. The Legislature could not have intended the latter construction. Accordingly, we conclude that section 4007(2) does not prohibit a court from extending a protection from abuse order more than once.

Although the court may only extend a protection order by agreement of the parties or upon a finding of abuse, the court has broad discretion to provide relief in a protection order without limitations on the amount of time for which a protection order may be extended. However, because a protection order can impose significant restrictions on a defendant's freedom of movement, and other rights, including the right to possess firearms, see 19-A M.R.S. §4007(1)(A-1), the extension must be supported by a court's determination that "such additional time [is] necessary to protect the plaintiff . . . from abuse." Where the underlying abuse consists of "[a]ttempting to cause or causing bodily injury or offensive physical contact" pursuant to 19-A M.R.S. §4002(1)(A) (2009), this determination must be based on proof of continuing harm or the threat of continuing harm arising out of or related to the abuse that necessitated the protection order in the first instance.[1]

Here, the court made the required finding that the 2005 attack on Kathleen constituted abuse pursuant to 19-A M.R.S. §4002(1)(A). The court also found that the attack demonstrably continues to affect Kathleen based on her subjective fear of Bruce "as if the assault happened yesterday," and that her fear is objectively reasonable based on the "extraordinarily brutal and unprovoked" nature of the "horrendous" attack. We [find that] competent evidence exists in the record to support . . . that a four-year extension of the protection order was necessary to protect Kathleen from abuse. Judgment affirmed.

■ SINCLAIR v. SINCLAIR
914 N.E.2d 1084 (Ohio Ct. App. 2009)

McFARLAND, Judge

Petitioner-appellant, Tracy Sinclair, [contends] that it was error for the trial court to issue a one-year civil protection order against respondent-appellee, Charles Sinclair, instead of a five-year protection order, as she requested. . . . In January 2008, appellant and her husband, appellee, had an argument at a convenience

---

1. Because the order in this case does not apply to the parties' minor daughter and, thus, does not implicate parental rights and responsibilities, we need not consider whether the court found "extraordinary circumstances" to justify a four-year extension of the protection order.

store. The argument escalated into a physical altercation, and appellant called 911. As a result of her call, police arrived at the scene and arrested appellee. Five days later, appellant filed a petition for a civil protection order under R.C. 3113.31 and the trial court immediately granted an ex parte CPO.

Approximately two weeks later, the magistrate of the Athens County Common Pleas Court held a full hearing on the issue. Both parties were represented by counsel at the hearing. During the hearing, appellant testified that appellee had recently committed various acts of domestic violence, including causing her physical injury, intimidating her with a handgun and threats, and having nonconsensual sex with her. . . . After the hearing, the magistrate issued a decision recommending a six-month CPO. The magistrate's fourth finding of fact states: "As Petitioner has vacated the marital residence, and the parties intend to terminate their marriage, there will be little future contact and no need to continue a civil protection order beyond the time of the divorce proceedings."

Partly based upon her belief that the six-month CPO was inadequate, appellant filed an objection to the magistrate's decision. Appellant asked that the trial court issue a full five-year CPO, as permitted by statute, instead of the six-month CPO recommended by the magistrate. After considering appellant's objections, the trial court declined to issue a five-year CPO, but lengthened the duration of the recommended CPO from six months to one year. The trial court's entry states:

> The Court in general agrees with the Magistrate's finding there is no need to continue a civil protection order beyond a divorce proceeding, because to do so is to assume the failure of the divorce proceeding. But an examination of the divorce file does not reveal that Plaintiff sought a temporary order that would supplant the civil protection order, and, therefore, the Court . . . will issue the civil protection order for one year rather than six months, to allow more time for the divorce proceeding to end and the parties to make appropriate plans.

. . . Appellant argues [that] it was error for the trial court to issue a one-year instead of a five-year civil protection order. According to appellant, the trial court abused its discretion by mistakenly concluding that a divorce decree stops the threat of domestic violence. Because the trial court decision improperly limited the duration of the CPO based on a policy that divorce proceedings automatically alleviate the need for a CPO, we find error. R.C. 3113.31(G) states that the CPO remedy is "in addition to, and not in lieu of, any other available civil or criminal remedies." Further, "consideration of evidence outside the record is inappropriate and can constitute reversible error." "[I]t is an abuse of discretion for a court to conduct its own investigation and consider its own observations as evidence in deciding a case." "It is axiomatic that the trier of fact must only consider evidence in the record."

We do note that Evid. R. 201 permits the taking of judicial notice; [however,] the trial court could take judicial notice only from the prior proceedings of the CPO case and not the divorce case. Here, no part of the divorce case was entered into the record in appellant's separate, civil protection case against appellee. Because that evidence was not presented at the hearing, appellant did not have an opportunity to question, examine, or clarify it. Accordingly, the trial court abused its discretion in limiting the duration of the CPO based on a pending divorce and relying upon such evidence in making its decision. . . .

Notes and Questions

1. *Duration.* The maximum duration of a protection order is specified by state law. Wide variation in duration exists. The range for initial orders varies from six months to five years. Carolyn V. Williams, Comment, Not Everyone Will "Get It" Until We Do It: Advocating for an Indefinite Order of Protection in Arizona, 40 Ariz. St. L.J. 371, 379-388 (2008) (surveying jurisdictions). Most states provide for a one-year limit on initial orders. Id. Statutes also differ regarding the duration of renewals. Most renewals have a time limit of one year, although some states permit renewals for an indefinite period. Id.

2. *Unlimited duration?* There is a growing trend to expand the protection for victims by providing for indefinite orders of protection. Id. at 374. The Family Violence Model Code recommends unlimited orders of protection, subject to judicial discretion. See National Council of Juvenile and Family Court Judges, Family Violence: A Model Code §306(5)(1994) ("An order for protection issued ex parte or upon notice and hearing or a modification of an order for protection issued ex parte or upon notice and hearing is effective until further order of the court"), available at http://www.ncjfcj.org/images/stories/dept/fvd/pdf/modecode_fin_printable.pdf. The commentary to the relevant section explains:

> Subsection 5 provides that an order for protection issued pursuant to section 306 or 307 is in effect until a court modifies or rescinds the order. No time limitations are imposed. This does not preclude a court from fixing review hearings to evaluate the continuing need for an order, nor does it preclude a request by either the petitioner or perpetrator to terminate the order. Subsection 5 departs from the duration strictures found in some state statutes because the risk posed to victims is not time limited or certain. The Code seeks to protect victims for as long as that protection is required, which should be determined by the court after hearing; expiration should not occur as a function of the passage of an arbitrary period of time. This provision also limits the unnecessary demand on court dockets required for reissuance or extension of orders when protection is required beyond the time of automatic expiration. This provision also shifts the burden from the victim to the perpetrator who is responsible for seeking court approval to terminate an order that is no longer essential.

What are the key features of this provision? What is its rationale?

3. *Extension and renewal.* Jurisdictions vary on what evidence is required to extend the duration of a civil protective order. In some jurisdictions, a court will grant an extension or renewal where the circumstances for the initial protective order continue to exist, regardless of whether there has been a new act or threat of abuse. See, e.g., Barber v. Barber, 150 P.3d 124 (Wash. Ct. App. 2007). In other jurisdictions, the victim must demonstrate a reasonable fear of imminent physical harm at the time of the extension. See, e.g., Odden v. Rath, 730 N.W.2d 590, 595 (N.D. 2007). Finally, some jurisdictions consider the role of such factors in renewals as: recent abusive conduct, past history, demeanor in court, likelihood of future encounters, past violations of the protective order, and the existence of custody or other litigation between the parties. See, e.g., Cruz-Foster v. Foster, 597 A.2d 927, 930-931 (D.C. 1991); Iamele v. Asselin, 831 N.E.2d 324, 331 (Mass. 2005); Smith v. Jones, 915 N.E.2d 260, 266-267 (Mass. App. Ct. 2009). What evidence should be required?

4. *Choice of time limits.* In *Dyer* and *Sinclair* what was the duration of the respective orders of protection and extensions? What was the rationale for the respective courts' chosen time periods? Were the respective durations appropriate in your view? Why or why not?

5. *Husband's legal theories.* Why does the ex-husband in *Dyer* appeal the second extension of the order of protection? What are his legal theories? What does the court respond?

6. *Application to family members.* Does the order of protection in *Dyer* apply only to the ex-wife or to the couple's child as well? Why? Might an abuser's exercise of his visitation rights jeopardize the mother's safety? If so, how? How can courts balance the interests of the parties in such cases? Child custody issues are explored in Chapter 12. In *Dyer*, the parties agreed to extend the original order for an additional two years "without a finding of abuse." Why was this last provision included?

7. *Legislative intent.* What does the statute in *Dyer* authorize in terms of extensions? Why does the state supreme court have to search for legislative intent? How does it determine such intent? What is the nature of that intent? How does the court apply it to the facts?

8. *Relevant factors.* In *Sinclair*, the trial court declined to issue a five-year protection order, as requested by petitioner and authorized by statute, based on the court's reasoning that there was "no need to continue a civil protection order beyond a divorce proceeding." Does a divorce proceeding end the potential for abuse? What does the appellate court respond? See also "Separation Assault," Chapter 4, Section 3. What is the relevance, if any, of a pending divorce proceeding for the issuance of an order of protection?

9. *Policy.* Should state legislatures enact statutes that provide that an order of protection lasts for the abuser's lifetime? In considering such a policy, how should legislators balance the interests at stake? See generally Jennifer Rios, Note, What's the Hold-Up? Making the Case for Lifetime Orders of Protection in New York State, 12 Cardozo J.L. & Gender 709, 723-728 (2006). Are indefinite orders of protection constitutional? See Spence v. Kaminski, 12 P.3d 1030, 1035-1036 (Wash. Ct. App. 2000) (sustaining the constitutionality of an indefinite order of protection).

5. Where Is Jurisdiction Over the Defendant?

What is required for a state court to assert jurisdiction to issue an order of protection? Suppose the parties live in different states. Where does jurisdiction lie—in the state where the victim or abuser resides, the place of the abuse, or all of these locations?

■ HEMENWAY v. HEMENWAY
992 A.2d 575 (N.H. 2009)

DUGGAN, J.

... The plaintiff, Michelle Hemenway, and the defendant [Edmund Hemenway] were married and have four children. They had lived together in Florida until July 16, 2008, when the wife left Florida with their children and moved to New

Hampshire. They reached a mediated divorce settlement in Florida on May 14, 2009.

At the beginning of August 2008, the wife applied for, and received, a temporary restraining order against her husband in Massachusetts [where she went to visit her parents]. In late August, the wife filed a domestic violence petition pursuant to [N.H. Rev. Stat. Ann. (hereafter RSA) chapter 173-B] in the Derry [New Hampshire] Family Division and obtained a temporary restraining order against him. In her petition, the wife alleged that he committed two acts of criminal threatening, to wit, on July 16, 2008, in Florida, he "became verbally abusive and threatened" her and their children, and, on August 2, 2008, he threatened her at her parents' house in Dracut, Massachusetts.

The family division held a hearing on the petition. The husband did not appear but instead through counsel filed a special appearance to contest jurisdiction. The family division found that it had jurisdiction [and issued a final protective order] prohibiting the husband from threatening or abusing his wife or her family members, contacting her absent special authorization by the family division, coming within a certain distance of her, going to her home or workplace, or taking, converting or damaging her property. The family division also ordered the husband to relinquish "all deadly weapons as defined in RSA 625:11, which may have been used, intended to be used, threatened to be used, or could be used incident to the abuse," "all concealed weapons permits and hunting licenses," and prohibited the husband from "purchasing . . . any firearms or ammunition during the pendency of this order." Finally, the family division awarded custody of the children to the wife, and prohibited visitation with the husband pending further hearing. . . .

The husband argues that the family division lacked subject matter jurisdiction over him because the incidents alleged in the petition occurred in Massachusetts and Florida. He also contends that the family division lacked personal jurisdiction over him under our long-arm statute, and under the Due Process Clause of the Federal Constitution. . . .

We first consider the husband's argument that the family division lacked subject matter jurisdiction. . . . To determine whether the family division had subject matter jurisdiction over the wife's petition, we interpret [two state statutes], which delineate the jurisdiction of the family division. . . . The plain language of RSA 173-B:2, IV and RSA 490-D:2, VI granted subject matter jurisdiction to the family division. [The former] states that the family division has "jurisdiction over domestic violence cases." [The latter grants] exclusive jurisdiction over "[a]ctions under RSA 173-B, relating to protection of persons from domestic violence except for concurrent jurisdiction with the superior and district courts to enter temporary protective orders under RSA 173-B:4." [In addition,] RSA 173-B:3, I, provides that "[a]ny person may seek relief pursuant to RSA 173-B:5 by filing a petition, in the county or district where the [wife or husband] resides, alleging abuse by the [husband]." Moreover, a person who "has left the household or premises to avoid further abuse" may "commence proceedings . . . in the county or district where [he or she] temporarily resides." RSA 173-B:2, II. "The fundamental logic of that statutory provision is unassailable: a victim of domestic abuse who seeks a place of refuge must be able to engage the protections of the law of the jurisdiction in which she is sheltered."

We disagree with the husband's argument that the family division lacked subject matter jurisdiction because [the statute granting subject matter jurisdiction to the family division over domestic violence cases incorporates the definition of criminal threatening, with its territorial limitations, that is found in the Criminal Code]. . . . Because the purpose of [protection] proceedings is to protect the victim from further abuse, and not to punish the abuser, such a finding results in a protective order, but not necessarily a criminal prosecution. As a result, the rules of evidence are relaxed. . . . [T]o incorporate the territorial limitations of the Criminal Code would lead to unjust and absurd results, and we decline to do so.

We next consider the husband's argument that the family division lacked personal jurisdiction. . . . We utilize a two-part test to determine whether the wife has met her burden. "First, the State's long-arm statute must authorize such jurisdiction. Second, the requirements of the federal Due Process Clause must be satisfied." . . .

We first address the wife's argument that the family division had personal jurisdiction because the husband flew to Manchester-Boston Regional Airport, made threatening telephone calls and mailed her a threatening letter while she was in New Hampshire. The wife, in her petition, alleged only that the husband threatened her in Florida and Massachusetts, and made no reference to threatening telephone calls or letters in New Hampshire. . . . Because it would be error to rely on allegations not contained in the petition and considered by the family division, we conclude that, on the record before us, the wife has failed to "demonstrate facts sufficient to establish personal jurisdiction over the defendant." Therefore, we need not consider "whether the exercise of personal jurisdiction over the [husband] would fall within the minimum contacts standard required by the Due Process Clause of the United States Constitution." However, this "conclusion . . . does not end the inquiry."

Courts in several states that have considered the validity of a protective order granted without personal jurisdiction over a non-resident defendant have applied an exception to the personal jurisdiction requirement. See, e.g., [Caplan v. Donovan, 879 N.E.2d 117 (Mass. 2008); Bartsch v. Bartsch, 636 N.W.2d 3 (Iowa 2001); Becker v. Johnson, 937 So. 2d 1128 (Fla. Dist. Ct. App. 2006).]. These courts reason that an order that prohibits abuse but does not require affirmative action by a defendant is valid even without personal jurisdiction. . . . Thus, "a court may adjudicate matters involving the status of the relationship between multiple parties even where personal jurisdiction over all of the parties is not established," and "a State court may grant a divorce to a spouse domiciled within that State without violating the due process rights of an absent spouse over whom it does not have jurisdiction" [citing Williams v. North Carolina, 317 U.S. 287, 298-299 (1942)].

A protective order which "prohibits the defendant from abusing the plaintiff and orders him to have no contact with and to stay away from her . . . serves a role analogous to custody or marital determinations, except that the order focuses on the plaintiff's protected status rather than [the plaintiff's] marital or parental status." Accordingly, an order that prohibits abuse but does not "impose any personal obligations on a defendant" is valid even without personal jurisdiction over the defendant.

A protective order "prohibit[s] acts of domestic violence," providing "the victim with the very protection the law specifically allows," while preventing "the defendant from engaging in behavior already specifically outlawed." A contrary ruling would present a domestic violence victim with two "unpalatable choices . . . either to . . . return to the State in which the abuse occurred . . . or, alternatively, to wait for the abuser to follow the victim to [New Hampshire] and, in the event of a new incident of abuse, seek an order from a [New Hampshire] court." Such a result is at odds with the purpose of RSA chapter 173-B and New Hampshire's "strong interest in providing protection to victims of domestic violence within this State."

Accordingly, we affirm the family division's final protective order to the extent that it protects the wife from abuse, but reverse to the extent that the order requires affirmative action from the defendant. . . .

Notes and Questions

1. *Elements.* A petitioner for a protective order must establish both subject matter and personal jurisdiction. How does the New Hampshire Supreme Court respond to the husband's argument in *Hemenway* that the family court lacked subject matter jurisdiction? How does the court respond to his argument that the court lacked personal jurisdiction? As the court explains, normally, the assertion of personal jurisdiction over a non-resident defendant requires that the state's long-arm statute must authorize the assertion of jurisdiction and that the requirements of federal due process are satisfied. Why does the court conclude that it does not need to consider those requirements? What is the rationale for *Hemenway*'s issuance of a protective order without personal jurisdiction over the defendant?

Why does *Hemenway* analogize the issuance of an order of protection to a court's assertion of jurisdiction over "custody or marital determinations"? See Caplan v. Donovan, 879 N.E.2d 117, 122 (Mass. 2008) (granting protection order without personal jurisdiction over defendant based on a "status determination" finding that state had a legitimate interest in the status of residents domiciled in the state). What is the plaintiff's "protected status"?

The language of most long-arm statutes allows personal jurisdiction when an individual has caused tortious injury or damage within the state. In protective order proceedings, this tortious conduct is threatening or causing fear to a resident of the state. See Robert E. Oliphant, Essay: Jurisdiction in Family Law Matters: The Minnesota Perspective, 30 Wm. Mitchell L. Rev. 557, 583-584 (2003). To satisfy due process requirements, some state courts have ruled that threatening phone calls, letters, emails, and other Internet activities establish the requisite minimum contacts and the purposeful availment requirements. See, e.g., A.R. v. M.R., 799 A.2d 27, 28, 31 (N.J. Super. Ct. App. Div. 2002) (holding that husband's phone calls to residents of New Jersey to locate the wife constituted minimum contacts). See generally Roni G. Melamed, Exercising Personal Jurisdiction over Nonresident Cyberstalkers, Colo. Law., Aug. 2008, at 75, 78.

2. *Interstate issues.* What happens when a victim seeks a protective order in a state that is *different* from the one in which she was abused? In State v. Reyes, 796 A.2d 879 (N.J. 2002), a woman, who was abused in New York, fled to New Jersey where she sought a restraining order after her husband followed her and pounded on the door of her sister's New Jersey home. The New Jersey Supreme Court held that it had personal jurisdiction over the abuser where the predicate act of violence in New York formed the basis of his acts of "harassment" in New Jersey. Id. at 886. In addition, the court found that the state domestic violence statute permitted it to exercise jurisdiction to protect victims who seek refuge in the state. Id.

What happens when *neither* the predicate act of violence occurs in the forum in which the victim seeks a protective order *nor* the abuser is a resident of the forum state? See McNair v. McNair, 856 A.2d 5, 9 (N.H. 2004) (holding that a husband's numerous threatening phone calls and emails from Texas to his wife in New Hampshire established the requisite minimum contacts for personal jurisdiction, and reasoning that, by knowingly making the calls into the state, the husband availed himself of New Hampshire jurisdiction).

3. *VAWA Full Faith and Credit provision.* The Full Faith and Credit provision of the Violence Against Women Act (VAWA) requires that states enforce protective orders from other states as if they were their own. 18 U.S.C. §2265. This provision requires that the issuing state had proper personal and subject matter jurisdiction, and also provided for the defendant's due process rights. 18 U.S.C. §§2265 (b)(1) and (b)(2). Interstate enforcement of protection orders is explored later in Section C(3).

4. *Protective orders and child custody.* In *Hemenway,* the wife flees with her four children. Protective orders can include a child custody order, allowing the victim to retain custody of her children. Child custody issues are explored in Chapter 12.

5. *Imposition of "personal obligations."* The court in *Hemenway* grants the protective order, but expressly states that it could not impose any personal obligations on the defendant in the order. Why? What are the "personal obligations" or "affirmative acts" to which the court was referring? Would surrender of firearms be considered a personal obligation? See generally Emily J. Sack, Confronting the Issue of Gun Seizure in Domestic Violence Cases, 6 J. Center for Families, Child. & Cts. 3 (2005).

6. *Knowledge of out-of-state harassment.* Several courts, as we have seen, find that a nonresident defendant has availed himself of the forum's jurisdiction by knowingly placing calls to a person who is presently residing in the forum state. Consider that mobile phones are now the norm. Many people do not bother to change their cell phone number when they move. If a victim flees for safety, an abuser could conceivably not know she has left the state when he telephones her. In such a case, has he "knowingly" availed himself of the benefits of another jurisdiction? In Becker v. Johnson, 937 So. 2d 1128, 1131 (Fla. Dist. Ct. App. 2006), the court refused to grant a protective order based upon the husband's threatening text messages that he sent to his ex-wife's phone, because he was not aware she had fled to Florida from their Maryland home, and therefore he did not purposefully avail himself of the state's jurisdiction. Does this mean that a victim should ensure that her batterer knows she is leaving the state? Must she tell him to which state she is fleeing? How can this conundrum be solved?

Problem

Stacy and Christopher live together in North Carolina. After Christopher threatens Stacy with physical violence, she moves to Connecticut. Christopher continues living in North Carolina. After Stacy leaves North Carolina, Christopher begins posting videos of himself on an Internet website. In the first video, he is holding a gun, and singing a rap song stating that he wants hurt Stacy, to kill Stacy, and to "put her face in the dirt till she can't breathe no more." He posts another video, again identifying Stacy, and raps about killing and hurting her. Stacy files for a protective order in Connecticut. What result? Does the Connecticut court have personal jurisdiction over Christopher, a North Carolina resident who has never set foot in Connecticut? See Rios v. Fergusan, 978 A.2d 592 (Conn. Super. Ct. 2008).

6. Termination of an Order of Protection

Termination of an order of protection is subject to the court's discretion. Under what circumstances *should* the court exercise its discretion to terminate an order of protection?

■ FREEMAN v. FREEMAN
239 P.3d 557 (Wash. 2010)(en banc)

SANDERS, J.

[During dissolution proceedings in 1998, Robin seeks an ex parte order of protection against her then-husband Rob Freeman. The trial court judge issues a temporary order of protection. After testimony from both parties, the commissioner makes the order permanent. Here, the ex-husband moves to modify or terminate the permanent protection order.]

Two incidents underlie the permanent protection order. First, Rob pushed Robin's 16-year-old daughter, Yasmeen, into her bedroom. While Rob characterized the incident as "escort[ing]" Yasmeen to her room after a "semi-heated" confrontation, he also admitted he physically forced Yasmeen down a hallway and through the threshold to her bedroom. Rob testified:

> I tried to grab [Yasmeen] by the arm and she crouched down right away and I placed my hand openly and tried to go for the shoulder but she kept on moving so it was up on the side of the neck and I pushed her all the way down which was like six[,] seven feet. [I] [o]pened her door and put her inside and then closed the door.

In contrast, Robin claims Yasmeen was "rendered unconscious when [Rob] dragged her down the hall and applied pressure to points on her neck and head."

In the second incident, Rob claims he opened his gun safe to show Robin that he had not hidden her jewelry inside, after Robin accused Rob of stealing it. Robin claims Rob inventoried his guns while telling her he was not going to harm her—acts Robin perceived as threats. . . . The commissioner determined these two incidents placed Robin in a reasonable state of fear—particularly in light of Rob's extensive military training—and warranted the permanent protection order. The order prevented Rob from contacting Robin and her children [from a prior relationship], then aged 10, 12, 16, and 18.

More than eight years later, on May 31, 2006, Rob moved to modify or terminate the permanent protection order. In 2001, doctors had amputated Rob's left hand below the forearm [based on injuries that he sustained after his deployment to Iraq]. In response Rob sought retraining to pursue his career in the military, defense, or security industries, but most jobs required security clearance. The permanent protection order barred Rob from obtaining security clearance.

To support his motion to modify or terminate the permanent protection order, Rob claimed he "has not returned to Washington since he left in 1998." Moreover

Rob claimed he has complied with the permanent protection order and made no contact with Robin or her children since the divorce, lives in another state (Missouri), has no criminal record, and "simply do[es] not pose any kind of danger to anyone at this time." He further asserted, "I continue to have neither the inclination nor the ability to do anything to Robin."

Robin responded that she remains in constant fear of Rob. The basis for her present fear appears to be, in her own words, "ongoing disturbances at her home of unknown cause." Chief among the unexplained disturbances are rattling windows, doors, and walls; repositioning of the driver's seat in her car; receiving Rob's mail at her house; reappearance of a flower vase on her dresser; missing tools; and a hole in her bedroom wall. Robin admits she has never seen Rob do any of these things.

On August 9, 2006, a court commissioner heard [Rob's] motion to modify or terminate. Yasmeen, who was 25 years old at the time of the hearing, testified she saw Rob across the street from her high school six or seven years earlier. Rob's counsel denied the allegation, asserting Rob had not been in Washington State since the permanent protection order and had no intention to return. . . .

We must decide whether the commissioner abused her discretion when refusing to terminate the permanent protection order. [Washington's Domestic Violence Prevention Act (DVPA) authorizes protection orders in cases of domestic violence.] The legislature has authorized courts to make protection orders permanent in some circumstances:

> [I]f . . . the court finds that the respondent is likely to resume acts of domestic violence against the petitioner or the petitioner's family or household members or minor children when the order expires, the court may either grant relief for a fixed period or enter a permanent order of protection.

RCW 26.50.060(2). Such permanent protection orders, however, can be modified or terminated ["upon application with notice to all parties and after a hearing"] RCW 26.50.130(1).

The modification statute fails to spell out grounds, factors, or standards authorizing modification of a permanent protection order. It also fails to mention which party bears the burden of modifying or maintaining the permanent protection order. In this vacuum, we read the DVPA as a whole.

[The Washington Supreme Court concludes that the standard for modification or termination of a permanent order should be the same standard as for renewal of a temporary order of protection—a preponderance of the evidence.] As much as it is possible to prove a negative, Rob (the moving party) bears the burden of proving by a preponderance of the evidence (i.e., more likely than not) that he will not resume acts of domestic violence against Robin or her children.

In this matter of first impression, it is not necessary to reinvent the wheel. In Carfagno v. Carfagno, 672 A.2d 751 (N.J. Super. Ct. Ch. Div. 1995), a New Jersey court embraced 11 factors guiding termination of a permanent protection order: (1) whether the victim has consented to lift the order, (2) the victim's fear of the restrained party, (3) present nature of the relationship between parties, (4) whether the restrained party has any contempt convictions for violating the order, (5) restrained party's alcohol and drug involvement, if any, (6) other violent acts on the part of the restrained party, (7) whether the restrained party has engaged in domestic violence counseling, (8) age and health of the restrained party,

(9) whether the victim is acting in good faith to oppose the motion, (10) whether other jurisdictions have entered any protection orders against the restrained party, and (11) other factors deemed relevant by the court. We believe New Jersey's guidelines provide a sensible framework for analyzing whether the preponderance of the evidence suggests a restrained party will commit a future act of domestic violence. . . .

The relevant analysis [includes] whether Rob proved an unlikelihood of committing future acts of domestic violence and whether the facts support a current reasonable fear of imminent harm. . . . It is not enough that the facts may have justified the order in the past. Reasonable likelihood of imminent harm must be in the present. . . .

Robin cites two Court of Appeals cases, Barber v. Barber, 150 P.3d 124 (Wash. Ct. App. 2007), and Spence v. Kaminski, 12 P.3d 1030 (Wash. Ct. App. 2000), for the proposition that permanent protection orders can be permanent based on "past abuse and present fear" alone. Robin's reliance on these cases is misplaced. These cases stand for the proposition that to renew or make permanent a protection order, the victim does not need to prove a new act of domestic violence if the present likelihood of a recurrence is reasonable. Unlike Robin, the victims in both *Spence* and *Barber* showed a reasonable present likelihood of violence, in addition to past abuse. Notably, the victims had ongoing relationships with their abusers. . . . Robin, on the other hand, shows past abuse but the facts show recurrence of domestic violence is unlikely.

Here, to permit the permanent protection order to continue forever would hold Rob hostage to his decade-old imprudence. There is scant evidence that Rob would subject his former wife and her children to future domestic violence. Through his testimony, deeds, relocation, career ambitions, and now 10-year compliance with the permanent protection order, Rob has met his burden to prove that he will more likely than not refrain from future acts of domestic violence against Robin or her children.

The New Jersey factors weigh in favor of Rob. Namely, (factor 2) Robin's fear of Rob is objectively unreasonable;[5] (factor 3) they have had no contact for ten years; (factor 4) Rob has not violated the permanent protection order, so no contempt orders exist; (factor 5) Rob has no known problems with alcohol or drugs; (factor 6) Rob has no criminal record and has committed no other violent acts; (factor 8) Rob's health has suffered as a result of his war injury and amputation; (factor 10) the record does not reflect any other protection orders against Rob; and (factor 11) other relevant considerations include Rob's career ambitions. . . . As Rob noted, he has "clearly moved on with his life and ha[s] not done anything to support Robin's continued fear of harm from him." [A]ccordingly, the commissioner abused her discretion [when] she based her denial of Rob's motion to modify or terminate the permanent protection order on untenable grounds. . . .

FAIRHURST, J. (dissenting).

[W]e are asked what standard and factors are to be applied when a trial court determines whether a permanent order of protection should be terminated. . . . To guide its analysis, the majority adopts wholly the factors enunciated in Carfagno v. Carfagno, 672 A.2d 751 (N.J. Super. Ct. Ch. Div. 1995). [W]e should

---

5. Robin's perception of unexplained household events is not enough to substantiate a reasonable continuing fear of Rob.

look to the provisions of [our] DVPA first, and use these other authorities to supplement, rather than dictate, our analysis. [T]he party seeking termination of a permanent order of protection must demonstrate by a preponderance of the evidence that conditions have changed such that the restrained party is no longer likely to commit acts of domestic violence against the petitioner or his or her family or household members upon termination of the permanent order of protection. . . . Time alone cannot establish such a change in conditions, because if that were possible, then no permanent order of protection would be truly permanent. A more sensible approach is to look to the "totality of the circumstances" and list examples of factors that can be considered in appropriate circumstances. . . .

While I do not support adopting the *Carfagno* factors wholly, some of the factors may be relevant to determining whether the restrained party is no longer likely to commit future acts of domestic violence. For example, factors that can be considered in appropriate circumstances are: the current nature of the relationship between the parties, whether the respondent has been convicted of contempt for violating the order, whether the respondent has a continuing involvement with drug or alcohol abuse, whether the respondent has been involved in other violent acts with other persons, whether the respondent has engaged in counseling, the age and health of respondent, and whether another jurisdiction has entered a restraining order protecting the victim from the respondent. In appropriate cases, these factors all may directly relate to the question of the respondent's likely future conduct.

I believe the other *Carfagno* factors should not be considered. [For example,] the victim's current fear, which *Carfagno* explicitly states must be evaluated from an objective, rather than subjective, standpoint should not be considered. The fear factor shifts the focus onto the victim and creates the possibility, which was realized in this case, that the court will erroneously, if unconsciously, require the victim to prove his or her current fear is real and objectively reasonable.

. . . This is problematic for several reasons. First, the majority's emphasis on current, objectively reasonable fear elevates that *Carfagno* factor into an element without any justification. Second, contrary to the majority's assertion, it is "enough that the facts may have justified the order in the past." [T]he fact that the permanent order of protection was entered in the first place reflects a finding by the trial court that the restrained party is likely to commit future acts of domestic violence upon the order's termination. It is therefore necessary that the order continues to operate unless and until Rob makes the necessary showing of changed circumstances, regardless of how Robin would feel if she were "reasonable." Third, the [analogous] provision for renewal of orders of protection for a fixed time, which presumably should have a similar standard, does not require objectively reasonable fear; it merely requires petitioner to "state the reasons" for renewal, then shifts the burden of proof onto the respondent to show he or she will not commit future acts of domestic violence if the order is lifted. . . .

The Court of Appeals in this case concluded [that Rob] established "a compelling need for lifting the order and a lack of opportunity for contact." However, Rob's "compelling need" that the order be lifted has absolutely no relevance to whether there is a likelihood of future domestic violence, and the "lack of opportunity for contact" is apparently something the Court of Appeals somehow determined on its own, based on the fact that Rob lives in another state. Such a conclusion ignores the ease of travel within the United States and the fact that domestic violence can occur through phone calls and agents. Whether Rob has actually made any such phone calls or enlisted third parties to commit acts of domestic violence has no relevance to the fact that such avenues of abuse are available to him despite his distance from Robin.

Finally, the Court of Appeals finds that "there is no evidence that Rob had hurt his wife" or her children at "any time." This announcement ignores the unchallenged findings at the 1998 hearing that Rob engaged in domestic violence and that an order of less than one year would be insufficient to prevent further acts of domestic violence. The Court of Appeals on review should not substitute its own conclusion for the unchallenged findings of the commissioner who entered the order.

Like the Court of Appeals, the majority opinion appears to pay short shrift to the 1998 finding of domestic violence when it refers to Rob's actions as "his decade-old imprudence." In its determination that the *Carfagno* factors weigh in favor of terminating the permanent order of protection, the majority considers such irrelevant factors as Rob's nonuse of drugs[10] and his loss of a hand.[11] Such factors do not establish that the situation has changed such that Rob is no longer likely to resume domestic violence in the absence of a permanent order of protection.

There are some relevant *Carfagno* factors that favor termination of the permanent order of protection in this case: Rob has not contacted Robin in at least seven years, Rob lives in another state, he has no convictions for contempt for violating the order, the record contains no evidence that Rob has engaged in other violent acts, and there is no record that Rob is subject to any other restraining orders. While these factors weigh in favor of finding Rob less likely to resume domestic violence, they do not necessitate the conclusion that circumstances have changed such that Rob is no longer likely to commit future acts of domestic violence. On the other side, the record does not show that Rob has sought or received any counseling related to domestic violence. Combined with Rob's affidavit, which reflects a denial of responsibility for the earlier incidents of domestic violence, blames Robin for "any harm she has experienced," characterizes her as vengeful and "manipulative," and characterizes this proceeding as a "whine contest," I cannot say that no reasonable court could find that Rob has failed to meet his burden to terminate the permanent order of protection. Nor can I say that such a determination is based on untenable grounds or reasons. . . .

Notes and Questions

1. *Reasons for petitioner's request.* Courts have discretion to terminate an order of protection. Who is the petitioner in *Freeman*? Why does the petitioner wish to modify or terminate the permanent protection order? What evidence does the petitioner present to support the motion? What evidence does the defendant present?

2. *Statutory provisions.* What does the state statute require in terms of grounds, factors, or standards that authorize the modification or termination of a permanent protection order? Which party bears the burden of modifying or maintaining the

---

10. Drugs were not a factor in the abuse in the first place; therefore, the absence of drugs does not make it less likely that Rob will engage in domestic violence in the future.

11. Rob's injury has not rendered him incapable of engaging in domestic violence, so it is difficult to see how his loss of a hand impacts the likelihood of his resuming acts of domestic violence.

permanent protection order? How does the court respond to the statute's shortcomings?

3. *Burden of proof.* Why does the Washington Supreme Court conclude that the standard for modification or termination of a permanent order should be the *same* standard as for renewal of a temporary order of protection—a preponderance of the evidence? The standard of proof in protection order proceedings is discussed later in this chapter, Section B(1).

4. *Requirement of recent abuse?* The majority in *Freeman* finds that "[i]t is not enough that the facts may have justified the order in the past. Reasonable likelihood of imminent harm must be in the present." What does Robin argue? What does Rob respond? What difficulties does Robin face in proof of "imminent harm"? What does the court respond? Does it violate defendant's constitutional rights to issue a permanent order of protection in absence of a recent act of domestic violence? See Spence v. Kaminski, 12 P.3d 1030 (Wash. Ct. App. 2000) (holding that issuance of permanent order of protection, in absence of recent act of violence, does not violate defendant's constitutional rights to due process, equal protection, or the right to travel).

5. *Reasonableness of victim's fear.* *Freeman* adopts the *Carfagno* factor of "the victim's fear of the restrained party" to determine whether to terminate a permanent protective order. Why does the dissent criticize the use of this factor? How do the majority's and dissent's views differ about the reasonableness of Robin's fears? Should the victim's fear be relevant in the determination to terminate a protective order? If so, should it measured by an objective or subjective standard?

6. *Changed circumstances.* Some jurisdictions require a showing of changed circumstances before modifying or terminating a protective order. See, e.g., Sjomeling v. Stuber, 615 N.W.2d 613 (S.D. 2000). What does *Freeman* require? Was the change in circumstances sufficient to terminate the order, in the majority's view? The dissent's? In your opinion? What type of changed circumstances might justify a modification or termination?

7. *Victim's preference.* Should it make a difference if the abuser or victim requests termination? This issue is explored later in this chapter, Section D(3).

C. PROCEDURAL ISSUES

1. Standard of Proof

■ CRESPO v. CRESPO
972 A.2d 1169 (N.J. Super. Ct. App. Div. 2009)

FISHER, J.A.D.:
The parties were married in 1984 and divorced in 2001. Despite the divorce, they continued to inhabit the same two-family house; defendant lived on the second floor with his parents while plaintiff lived with their three children on the first floor.

In 2004, after a dispute over child support, plaintiff filed a domestic violence complaint alleging present and past verbal and physical abuse. An ex parte temporary restraining order (TRO), which restricted defendant from communicating with or contacting plaintiff, was immediately entered. Defendant was served with the complaint and TRO, and, after a two-day trial, which consisted of the testimony of only the parties, the judge entered a [Final Restraining Order or FRO] in plaintiff's favor. Defendant appealed. . . . [D]efendant moved before a different judge to vacate the FRO, asserting the Act's unconstitutionality. . . .

Defendant argues that the Act's preponderance standard, in light of the consequences of a finding of domestic violence, violates these due process principles by placing an unduly light burden of persuasion on the alleged victims of domestic violence. . . . In considering whether the adoption of a particular burden of persuasion adheres to state constitutional due process principles, our Supreme Court has followed the balancing test articulated in Mathews v. Eldridge, 424 U.S. 319, 335 (1976) [requiring consideration of the private interest that will be affected by the official action, the risk of an erroneous deprivation of such interest, and the governmental interests].

Domestic violence actions, by their very nature, naturally pit the first and third *Mathews* factors, that is, victims' interests in being protected from domestic violence against defendants' liberty interests in being free to say what they wish and go where they please. The Legislature obviously viewed the victims' interests as highly important and of far greater weight than defendants' interests, when it declared in the Act that

> domestic violence is a serious crime against society; that there are thousands of persons in this State who are regularly beaten, tortured and in some cases even killed by their spouses or cohabitants; that a significant number of women who are assaulted are pregnant; that victims of domestic violence come from all social and economic backgrounds and ethnic groups; that there is a positive correlation between spousal abuse and child abuse; and that children, even when they are not themselves physically assaulted, suffer deep and lasting emotional effects from exposure to domestic violence. *It is therefore, the intent of the Legislature to assure the victims of domestic violence the maximum protection from abuse the law can provide.*

[N.J.S.A. 2C:25-18 (emphasis added).]

The New Jersey Supreme Court has also recognized the important societal interest in protecting victims of domestic violence:

> Domestic violence is a serious problem in our society. Each year, three to four million women from all socio-economic classes, races, and religions, are battered by husbands, partners, and boyfriends. The Act and its legislative history confirm that New Jersey has a strong policy against domestic violence. Although New Jersey is in the forefront of states that have sought to curb domestic violence, New Jersey police reported 77,680 incidents of domestic violence in 2000 alone.

[State v. Reyes, 796 A.2d 879, 884 (N.J. 2002).]

In light of these unmistakable expressions of public policy, we recognize that the strong societal interest in protecting persons victimized by domestic violence greatly favors utilization of the preponderance standard. In so holding, we are by no means dismissive of the limitations imposed on defendants in such matters. In cases where the parties resided in the same household when the action was commenced, the restraint on defendant imposes a substantial burden—it bars the defendant from his or her home. However, in cases where the parties were not members of the same household, the relief normally granted poses little more than a minor inconvenience; in those many cases the defendant is merely barred from the victim's residence and place of employment, not his own. In either circumstance, we conclude that the limits imposed upon a defendant's private interests carry far less weight in the *Mathews* analysis than does the governmental interest in eliminating domestic violence and in affording immediate and effective protection to victims of domestic violence.

In considering the second *Mathews* factor, we are not persuaded that the preponderance standard may tend to lead to erroneous adjudications or erode public confidence in the ability of our courts to produce fair and accurate determinations in such matters. In this regard we continue to recognize the truth of what we said in [Roe v. Roe, 601 A.2d 1201, 1206 (N.J. Super. Ct. App. Div. 1992)]: "[t]here are usually few, if any, eyewitnesses to marital discord or domestic violence." Most of the events complained of in such matters happen behind closed doors or during private communications; as a result, most cases turn only on the trial judge's assessment of the credibility of only two witnesses—the plaintiff and the defendant.

The Legislature certainly understood that a clear-and-convincing standard would saddle victims of domestic violence with a burden that would often foreclose relief in many deserving cases. When the testimony of the plaintiff is pitted against the testimony of the defendant, with no other corroborating testimony or evidence, a plaintiff would likely have difficulty sustaining the sterner standard urged by defendant here. . . . [6] [W]e conclude . . . that a standard more demanding than the preponderance standard "would undermine the social purposes of the Act . . ."

Defendant also argues that the Act's requirement that a final hearing be held within ten days of the filing of the complaint deprived him of due process. This argument is utterly without merit. Our Supreme Court has already found that the ten-day provision comports with the requirements of due process. . . .

In this case, the complaint was filed on March 16, 2004, and the final hearing did not commence until April 8, 2004, twenty-three days later. The second and last day of the hearing occurred on April 21, 2004, thirty-six days after the action was commenced. Defendant was provided with more than sufficient time to respond to the complaint. Indeed, he has not referred to anything in the record to suggest he either requested or was denied an adjournment or that he was unable to adequately defend against the complaint as a result of the time between the commencement of the action and the start of the final hearing.

We also reject defendant's argument that he was prejudiced by his inability to depose plaintiff or obtain other discovery. Domestic violence actions are "summary actions," a fact that inherently precludes the right to discovery. However, we note [that] in accordance with Rule 5:5-1(d), a defendant may seek leave to obtain discovery in such a matter upon a showing of good cause. . . . Here, the record reveals that at no time did defendant seek leave to conduct any discovery proceedings. We, thus, reject defendant's bald contention that he was deprived of due process because of the absence of discovery in this case. . . .

---

6. The great majority of domestic violence matters do not involve specialized knowledge or present "circumstances or issues that are so unusual or difficult, that proof by a lower standard will not serve to generate confidence in the ultimate factual determination." By contrast, the imposition of a sterner burden of persuasion has been imposed in circumstances that are "intrinsically complex and not readily amenable to objective assessment," such as cases requiring determinations of mental incompetence, parental unfitness, paternity, and undue influence upon testators.

Defendant argues that a right to counsel attaches in domestic violence matters. Due process principles have been found to require the appointment of counsel in civil or quasi-criminal matters when an indigent party faces imprisonment or some "other consequence of magnitude." Whether the imposition of a restraining order of the scope authorized by the Act constitutes a matter of sufficient magnitude to warrant the appointment of counsel has yet to be resolved by our courts.

We find no cause to further consider the right to counsel at the present time. The record does not reflect that defendant ever sought the appointment of counsel prior to or during the adjudication of this domestic violence matter. Accordingly, in the present setting, the issue is purely academic. The order under review, which concluded that the Act is unconstitutional, is reversed and the matter remanded for reinstatement of the FRO.

2. Right to Jury Trial

■ BLACKMON v. BLACKMON
230 P.3d 233 (Wash. Ct. App. 2010)

Quinn-Brintnall, J.
. . . On June 16, 2008, Tiffany filed a petition in Thurston County Superior Court for a protection order against [her estranged husband] Brian. Attached to the petition was a four-page listing of incidents that set out reasons Tiffany stated for fearing for her safety and for the safety of her seven-year-old son. That same day, the trial court entered a temporary protection order and notice of hearing to be held on June 27, 2008. The parties agreed to continue the hearing several times, each time extending the temporary protection order. The hearing was eventually set for September 9, 2008.

During a pretrial hearing on September 8, Brian's counsel informed the trial court for the first time that he might be requesting a jury trial. The trial court directed him to submit a brief to support such a request. On September 9, Brian's counsel filed a demand for a jury trial. . . . The trial court denied Brian's request for a jury trial and his subsequent continuance motion.

The matter proceeded to a protection order fact-finding hearing at which both parties presented opening arguments, testified on direct and cross-examination, and presented witnesses and evidence. After a full day of testimony, the parties rested. The trial court extended the temporary protection order through September 12, 2008, and recessed for final arguments and resolution of the matter on that date.

On September 11, Brian's counsel filed a motion to reopen his case to present testimony from Lori Harrison, a therapist who had conducted a parenting assessment of Brian. The assessment had a domestic violence component. On September 12, when the parties reconvened before the trial court for closing arguments and rulings, Brian's counsel orally renewed his motion to reopen. The trial court denied the motion to reopen, and the parties continued to closing arguments.

After closing arguments, the trial court reviewed the standard of proof in domestic violence matters and recounted the history of events Tiffany and Brian presented. The trial court found that there was sufficient evidence to support granting a domestic violence protection order. It issued the domestic violence protection order, restricting Brian from having contact with Tiffany for one year. The protection order also required that Brian participate in a domestic violence perpetrator treatment program as described in RCW 26.50.150. Although the protection order required supervised visitation between Brian and his son, it explicitly stated that, after he was in treatment, Brian could request modification of the supervised visitation requirement. Finally, the protection order restricted Brian from possessing a firearm or ammunition, except in his capacity as military personnel carrying government-issued firearms.[2]

. . . Brian argues that he has a constitutional right to a jury trial for domestic violence matters decided under ch. 26.50 RCW and that the trial court erred when it rejected his demand for a jury trial. . . .

The right to a jury trial is guaranteed by article I, section 21 of the Washington Constitution. . . . To determine whether parties have a constitutional right to jury trials in Domestic Violence Prevention Act proceedings, we must determine whether such right existed, either at common law or by territorial statute, when the Washington Constitution was adopted in 1889. Under the common law, there is "a right to a jury trial where the civil action is purely legal in nature, but not where the action is purely equitable in nature." "The distinction between legal and equitable claims is based on the nature of the action, not the form of the action." Thus, if cases similar in nature to the modern domestic violence protection order cases were within the exclusive jurisdiction of equity courts when the state constitution was adopted in 1889, then the parties in a modern protection order proceeding do not have a constitutional right to a jury trial.

Here, Brian urges us to hold that modern domestic violence protection order proceedings are essentially criminal assault actions and, as such, are legal in nature. Although assaultive conduct may lie at the heart of a petitioner's request for a domestic violence protection order, the remedy sought, an order prohibiting contact, is not a massive curtailment of liberty amounting to incarceration and is not criminal in nature.

The only matter at issue is whether or not to grant Tiffany and her son a domestic violence protection order limiting Brian's contact with them. As such, protective orders are essentially a type of injunction. Injunctions are equitable in nature. Thus, when a person petitions the court solely for a domestic violence protection order, as Tiffany did here, neither she nor the party she seeks to have restrained is entitled to have a jury decide whether a judge should issue a protection order.

The rules of evidence applicable to Domestic Violence Prevention Act proceedings further support this conclusion. ER 1101 states that the rules of evidence need not be applied in protection order proceedings. Consequently, competent evidence sufficient to support the trial court's decision to grant or deny a petition for a domestic violence protection order may contain hearsay or be wholly documentary.

Moreover, in [Gourley v. Gourley, 145 P.3d 1185 (Wash. 2006)], our Supreme Court held that, although a trial court has discretion to allow it, the Domestic Violence Prevention Act does not create a right for petitioners and respondents to subpoena or cross-examine witnesses. The primary role of a jury—to observe the demeanor of these witnesses, determine witness credibility, and accord weight to witness testimony—is not essential to a legitimate decision to grant a petitioner's motion for a domestic violence protection order under RCW 26.50.060. Because the

---

2. Brian is a member of the United States Army.

purpose of these proceedings is to provide persons who allege that they are victims of domestic violence with ready access to the protections of the court in allowing them to avoid contact with someone with whom they no longer wish to associate, these proceedings do not include the right to compel and cross-examine witness testimony and without such testimony there is no compelling need for a jury to determine the credibility of witnesses or determine the facts underlying the issuing court's protection order. In short, there is no right to a jury trial in a domestic violence protection order hearing because such proceeding is equitable in nature and may be properly determined by a court on documentary evidence alone. The trial court properly denied Brian's request for a jury trial before issuing the order prohibiting him from having contact with his estranged wife and requiring supervision of his contact with his son. . . .

3. Right to Discovery: The Problem of Discovery Abuse

■ DEPOS v. DEPOS
704 A.2d 1049 (N.J. Super. Ch. Div. 1997)

DILTS, J.S.C.

The question presented is whether the defendant in a domestic violence action should be permitted to take the deposition of plaintiff. . . .

On August 28, 1997, plaintiff, Mrs. Depos, appeared at the Somerset County Court House and filed a complaint pursuant to the Prevention of Domestic Violence Act (the "Act"). She alleges that the defendant, her brother-in-law, made a terroristic threat against her. She contends that defendant threatened to shoot her if she did not have sex with him. She contends that she has, in the past, been the victim of domestic violence committed by her brother-in-law. A temporary restraining order was entered by this court on August 28, 1997.

The parties consented to the adjournment of the final hearing which was ultimately scheduled for October 9, 1997. On September 22, 1997, defendant's attorney entered his appearance with the court and simultaneously served a Notice to Take Oral Deposition of plaintiff, returnable on October 3, 1997. Plaintiff's attorney advised defendant's attorney that Mrs. Depos would not attend the deposition without a court order. On October 6, 1997, application was made for leave to take the deposition of plaintiff in order to take her testimony on whether or not this court had jurisdiction to hear this dispute.

After hearing oral argument and receiving letter briefs, the court denied defendant's application based on the following conclusions of law.

There is no right to take plaintiff's deposition because domestic violence actions are deemed to be "summary actions"

The Act does not authorize the taking of a deposition or any other discovery. Neither does R. 5:7A. The only basis for taking the deposition of a plaintiff in a domestic violence action is R. 5:5-1 [which] provides in pertinent part: "Except for summary actions . . . discovery in civil family actions shall be permitted . . ." Therefore, if proceedings under the Act are deemed to be summary actions, then defendant may not take the deposition of plaintiff as of right.

The court concludes that domestic violence actions are "summary actions." A summary action is one which is short, concise and immediate. Black's Law Dictionary 1435 (6th Ed. 1990). "[S]ummary actions are by definition designed to accomplish the salutary purpose of swiftly and effectively disposing of matters which lend themselves to summary treatment." The court's conclusion stems from two inherent qualities of domestic violence proceedings. First, trial courts are mandated by statute to proceed in a summary manner in such cases. "A hearing shall be held in the Family Part of the Chancery Division of the Superior Court within 10 days of the filing of a complaint . . ." N.J.S.A. 2C:25-29(a). The Act "was enacted with the expressed intent that courts . . . promptly and appropriately offer protection to victims of domestic violence. The legislative intent for such mandates is to assure the victim the maximum protection from abuse the law can provide. N.J.S.A. 2C:25-18. To assure such protection, the court's response must be swift because any delay may pose serious and irreversible consequences to the victim. Thus, domestic violence proceedings are "immediate."

Second, domestic violence proceedings normally require no more than a few hours to conduct. They are "short" and "concise."

Defendant Has Failed to Establish "Good Cause" to Take the Deposition of Plaintiff

Before a deposition may be authorized by the court in a summary action, the party seeking it must establish "good cause." R. 5:5-1(d) provides as follows: "All other discovery in family actions shall be permitted only by leave of court for good cause shown . . ." Therefore, even in a summary action, a deposition may be authorized by the court only when the party seeking it can establish "good cause." Although "good cause" is not defined by the Rule, defendant argues "good cause" exists in this case because a factual inquiry of plaintiff is needed to lay the foundation for his motion to dismiss the complaint for lack of jurisdiction. Defendant contends, among other things, that the parties never lived together.

The "good cause" standard in discovery applications is "flexible and its meaning is not fixed and definite. Each application for discovery . . . must be evaluated upon the circumstances appearing from all of the pleadings and then determined in the sound discretion of the court." It has been observed that good cause takes "its shape from the particular facts to which it is applied." This court finds that the determination as to whether "good cause" exists to take the deposition of the plaintiff in a domestic violence matter must also take into account the nature of domestic violence and the legislative intent of the Act.

The Legislature found that "it is the responsibility of the courts to *protect* victims of violence that occurs in a family or family-like setting by providing sanctions, and by ordering those remedies and sanctions that are available to *assure the safety* of the victims and the public." N.J.S.A. 2C:25-18. (Emphasis added.) The objective of protecting victims pervades the statute not only in these passages but throughout. "The Legislature finds that battered adults presently experience substantial difficulty in gaining access to protection from the judicial system. . . ." Id.

"The court's function is to effectuate legislative intent in light of the language used and the objects sought to be achieved and to construe the Prevention of Domestic Violence Act in a fashion consistent with the statutory context in which it appears." To allow a deposition in this case would not effectuate the legislative intent and purpose. First, to allow the taking of a deposition would prevent compliance with the mandate that the hearing be held within 10 days, given the time it takes to schedule, take and prepare the transcript of a deposition.

Second, domestic violence is a cycle of abuse of power and control. The perpetrator has the power and control and the victim does not. The victim comes to court to change that dynamic and to receive protection. Often, however, victims of domestic violence are not represented by counsel, especially in the pretrial stage before a court is in a position to award counsel fees. Thus, in the pretrial stage, victims often must proceed without representation and without an advocate protecting their interests. The taking of a deposition is an intimidating experience for anyone, especially one who is the victim of domestic violence. Thus, allowing the represented alleged perpetrator to depose a victim, represented or unrepresented, perpetuates the cycle of power and control whereby the perpetrator remains the one with the power and the victim remains powerless. This is inconsistent with the legislative purpose and intent. Therefore, the questioning of victims must be done in the presence of the judge at trial or a pretrial hearing in order to insure that the questioning is done fairly and in order to insure that victims are not revictimized by the very process they turn to for protection.

Finally, mindful of the cycle of domestic violence and the guilt often experienced by victims after they turn to the court for help, the court would expect that after undergoing a deposition, many victims would question their resolve to proceed. Because of the resulting delays, increase in expenses for victims, and the opportunity to attack the resolve of victims, it is not difficult to predict that the taking of depositions could quickly become the strategy of choice for defendants.

Denying Defendant Permission to Take the Deposition of Plaintiff Does Not Offend Due Process

Defendant's counsel makes a due process argument in support of his application to allow the deposition. He contends that not allowing the deposition would be unfair to defendant because it would put him in the position of defending against "things he doesn't know about" at the time of the trial. The court addressed this argument on the record and dismisses it here by pointing out that due process involves "such notice as is in keeping with the character of the proceedings and adequate to safeguard the right entitled to protection." The court finds that it can keep with the character of a summary action and can adequately safeguard defendant's right to notice by affording him the following two opportunities.

First, if a short preliminary hearing is needed on the matter of jurisdiction, it can be held before the domestic violence hearing. Second, due process can be secured by granting to the defendant the right to request a continuance of the trial in order to prepare a defense if and when matters are testified to which go beyond what plaintiff has alleged in the complaint. This right can be exercised by defendant either at the end of plaintiff's direct testimony in order to prepare for effective cross-examination or at the end of plaintiff's case, whichever is determined appropriate by defendant. See Nicoletta v. No. Jersey Dist. Water Supply Comm'n, 77 N.J. 145, 162, 390 A.2d 90 (N.J. 1978) (recognizing that the first prerequisite of due process is fair notice, so that a response can be prepared and the respondent can be heard). Thus, due process is not offended. For these reasons, the application of defendant for leave to take the deposition of Mrs. Depos is denied.

Notes and Questions on Procedural Issues

1. *Background: constitutionality.* All states responded promptly to the "discovery" of domestic violence by enacting legislation authorizing civil orders of protection. Peter Finn, Statutory Authority in the Use and Enforcement of Civil Protection Orders Against Domestic Abuse, 23 Fam. L.Q. 43, 43 (1989) (explaining that, by 1989, almost every state had enacted such statutes). Respondents in restraining order proceedings soon began challenging the constitutionality of these statutes. See, e.g., People v. Forman, 546 N.Y.S.2d 755, 764 (N.Y. Crim. Ct. 1989) (upholding the constitutionality of the statute); Boyle v. Boyle, 12 Pa. D. & C.3d 767 (C.P. Alleg. 1979) (accord). Respondents alleged that the law deprived them of procedural due process and challenged, inter alia, the ex parte nature of the proceedings, the standard of proof, vagueness, and the absence of appointed counsel. Courts routinely denied these claims. Some courts even conferred a presumption of constitutionality on their statutes. See, e.g., State ex rel. Williams v. Marsh, 626 S.W.2d 223, 232 (Mo. 1982); H.E.S. v. J.C.S., 815 A.2d 405, 413-414 (N.J. 2003). On what basis did the husband in *Crespo* challenge the constitutionality of the state domestic violence prevention statute?

2. *Ex parte nature of the proceedings.* An early challenge to temporary-restraining-order statutes was that an ex parte order (for example, a "kick-out" order that excluded a respondent from entering the home) deprived the respondent of property without due process because the ex parte order was granted without a full hearing or notice. In *Boyle*, supra, the trial court judge rejected the respondent's contention, saying that any other alternative would "totally defeat[] the purpose of the act—immediate protection." 12 Pa. D. & C.3d at 774. The court reasoned that property rights are not absolute and are subject to the legitimate use of the state's police power. Id. at 772.

3. *Burden of proof.* The ex-husband in *Crespo* alleges that the preponderance-of-the-evidence standard of proof is unconstitutional. Why does the court disagree? For a comprehensive survey of state standards of proof, see ABA, Standards of Proof for Domestic Violence Civil Protection Orders (CPOs) By State (June 2009), available at http://www.americabar.org/content/dam/aba/migrated/domviol/pdfs/Standards-of-Proof_By_State.authcheckdam.pdf.

4. *Jury trial.* The respondent-husband in *Blackmon* argues that the statute deprives him of his right to jury trial. Is a jury trial constitutionally required? How does the court respond? If the wife had requested damages, would she have had the right to a jury trial?

5. *Right to counsel.* The defendant in *Crespo* raises the issue of the right to counsel. Because the defendant never sought the appointment of counsel, the court does not decide that issue. Is there a due process right to counsel in a proceeding for an order of protection? What are the arguments pro and con? The protection order process facilitates access to the court without the need for representation. However, why might it be advantageous for petitioners to be represented by counsel? See Alesha Durfee, Victim Narratives, Legal Representation, and Domestic Violence Civil Protection Orders, 4 Feminist Criminology 217 (2009).

6. *Discovery: purpose.* The defendant in *Depos* contends that he has the right to depose Mrs. Depos in the order-of-protection proceeding. What is the purpose of taking a party's deposition? Why did the defendant want to take Mrs. Depos's deposition? Why do you think she objected?

7. *Procedural posture.* How did the defendant make his request to take petitioner's deposition? What did plaintiff's attorney respond? What did the defendant respond then?

8. *State statute.* What does the state statute authorize in terms of taking evidence in order-of-protection proceedings? Is the defendant absolutely prohibited from taking the plaintiff's deposition? Or, can he do so if he establishes "good cause"? What circumstances might constitute "good cause"? Is a domestic violence proceeding a "summary action"? Is discovery permitted in summary actions? See Crespo, supra, at 1180 ("where a party's ability to adequately present evidence during a domestic violence action may be significantly impaired, a trial judge may, in the exercise of sound discretion, permit limited discovery in order to prevent an injustice").

9. *Role of discovery in domestic violence proceedings.* The court reasons that the nature of domestic violence actions precludes discovery. Why? How does discovery hold the potential that victims will be "revictimized by the very process they turn to for protection," as the judge in *Depos* asserts? How can a court prevent that result?

10. *Discovery abuse: methods.* Do abusers sometimes use the discovery process to harass petitioners? If so, how? See, e.g., Martinez v. Martinez, 52 S.W. 3d 429, 443 (Tex. App. 2001) (rejecting husband's request for a continuance to conduct discovery, reasoning that "the need to conduct discovery is not one of the statutory bases for continuance" in protective order proceedings). One commentator notes that discovery abuse is a common tactic particularly if a criminal proceeding is pending:

> Some criminal attorneys have sought continuances in the protection order hearings, citing their client's Fifth Amendment privilege not to be forced to testify. Although delays do not leave victims unprotected (the temporary stay-away order is usually extended), the victim is denied other relief that may be necessary for her to sustain separation, such as court-ordered mortgage payments by the perpetrator, child support, and protected visitation.

Jane H. Aiken & Jane C. Murphy, Dealing with Complex Evidence of Domestic Violence: A Primer for the Civil Bench, 39 Court Rev. 12, 18 (2002).

11. *Discovery abuse: remedies.* Some state laws and many courts discourage or preclude discovery in civil protective order proceedings. Ann E. Freedman, Fact-Finding in Civil Domestic Violence Cases: Secondary Traumatic Stress and the Need for Compassionate Witnesses, 11 Am. U. J. Gender Soc. Pol'y & L. 567, 578 (2003). Also, some courts limit continuances that can be granted in protective order proceedings. Aiken & Murphy, supra, at 18. How can legislatures and courts discourage discovery abuse by abusers? Should state legislatures enact statutes that preclude discovery in such cases? Discourage it? Which approach does New Jersey take in *Depos*? Should jurisdictions adopt the approach of the District of Columbia provision below?

> Upon motion by a party or witness, the Court may make any order which justice requires to protect a party from annoyance, embarrassment, oppression, or undue burden or expense, including one or more of the following: (a) that discovery be denied; (b) that discovery be granted only on specified terms and conditions; (c) that certain matters not be inquired into or that the scope of discovery be limited to certain matters.

D.C. Court Rules Ann., Rule 8, Rules Governing Proceedings in the Domestic Violence Unit (2010).

D. ENFORCEMENT

All states have some form of contempt available to enforce civil protection orders. Many states also impose criminal liability for the violation of a protection order. This section explores the enforcement of civil protection orders, including the traditional remedy of contempt, the availability of private actions for contempt, sanctions for violations of restraining orders, and the interstate enforcement of protection orders.

1. Contempt: Criminal, Civil, and Private Actions

■ **ABA COMM'N ON DOMESTIC VIOLENCE,
THE DOMESTIC VIOLENCE CIVIL LAW MANUAL:
PROTECTION ORDERS AND FAMILY LAW CASES**
Post-Trial Issues 1, 4-5 (3d ed. 2007)

Of all the remedies available after trial to enforce court orders and command respect for judicial authority, few are stronger or more valuable than the powers of contempt. Even in the absence of a statute, courts have long recognized that they have inherent authority to enforce their orders by the issuance of fines or incarceration in jail, thereby vindicating judicial authority and the rule of law.

In a contempt proceeding, the movant must show:

(1) the existence of a valid order, in effect at the time of the violation,
(2) that the violating party knew of the order,
(3) failed to comply with its terms, and
(4) did so without just cause.

Once these four elements have been established, the moving party will have made a prima facie showing of contempt. The burden of proof then shifts to the non-moving party to show that she or he was unable to comply with the ordered terms. The non-moving party may also argue that his or her actions or failure to act do not amount to a violation of the order.

The goal of *civil* contempt proceedings is to coerce compliance with a court order, assuming that the alleged violating party has had the opportunity to purge him- or herself of the offense. Civil contempt proceedings are appropriate to address violations of support orders, where the goal is to coerce compliance and give the violating party an opportunity to purge himself of the contempt, perhaps by holding the respondent in jail until he pays his support arrearage. When a respondent is found in contempt of a civil order, the judge may stay the execution of those contempt findings to give the respondent the opportunity to cure the violation of the order. If the conditions for stay of execution are violated by the respondent, the court can revoke the stay without holding a hearing, making a stay of execution a very powerful enforcement tool.

On the other hand, *criminal* contempt is intended to punish the offending persons for violating court orders. Criminal contempt would likely be used to address violations of protection orders, where there is no opportunity for the defendant to purge himself of the contempt. Both types of proceedings raise specific issues [to] consider when representing victims of domestic violence. Criminal contempt must be shown by the highest burden of proof—beyond a reasonable doubt—while civil contempt can be proven by a mere preponderance of the evidence.

The following case explores whether a private person can prosecute a criminal contempt action.

■ IN RE ROBERTSON
19 A.3d 751 (D.C. 2011)

REID, Associate Judge, Retired:

[In March 1999, Wykenna Watson was assaulted by her then-boyfriend, John Robertson.] She alleged that on March 27, 1999, Mr. Robertson repeatedly pursued and hit her on various parts of her body, including her head and face, with his closed fist; kicked her several times in the head with his heavy work shoes; and threatened to kill her while holding a pocket knife. She suffered a black eye and head injuries. At Ms. Watson's request, the Family Division issued a temporary protection order on March 29, 1999. On April 26, 1999, the [Office of the Attorney General for the District of Columbia] entered its appearance on behalf of Ms. Watson in the Family Court, and after a hearing that same day, the Domestic Violence Unit of the Superior Court issued a CPO, effective for twelve months, ordering that Mr. Robertson not assault, threaten, harass, or physically abuse Ms. Watson in any manner; stay away from Ms. Watson's person, home, and workplace; and avoid contacting Ms. Watson in any manner. [At the same time,] Mr. Robertson was charged by complaint in the Superior Court, Criminal Division, with one count of aggravated assault based on the March 27, 1999, incident.

[On June 26, 1999, Robertson violated the protective order by again violently assaulting Watson.] Ms. Watson submitted an affidavit stating, in part, that (1) on June 26, Mr. Robertson "harassed [her] by repeatedly demanding that [she] drop the criminal charges that were pending against him," and he called her names (Count 1); (2) on June 26, Mr. Robertson "pushed [her] and knocked [her] into a wall" and called her names (Count 2); (3) on June 26/27, around midnight, Mr. Robertson harassed her by repeatedly cursing her (Count 3); (4) on June 26/27, after midnight, Mr. Robertson "physically attacked [her] in the living room," and followed her into the bathroom where he "repeatedly punched [her] in the head and face" (Count 4); (5) and on June 27, a short time after the living room and bathroom incident, Mr. Robertson "threw drain cleaner at [her]" and caused "lye burns" resulting in her hospitalization in an intensive care unit (Count 5). . . .

On July 8, 1999, a grand jury indicted Mr. Robertson on one count of aggravated assault and two counts of assault with a dangerous weapon. On July 20, 1999, Mr. Robertson entered into a plea agreement with the United States Attorney's Office in which he agreed to plead guilty to one count of felony attempted-aggravated assault related to the March 27, 1999, incident, and in return the United States agreed that it would "not pursue any charges concerning an incident on June 26, [19]99."

On January 28, 2000, Ms. Watson, assisted by OAG, filed a motion to adjudicate Mr. Robertson in criminal contempt for violations of the CPO, based on incidents between Mr. Robertson and Ms. Watson on June 26 and 27, 1999. . . . [She filed suit based on a District of Columbia law (reprinted below) that permits a private party to bring an action for criminal contempt. After a 2-day bench trial, the court found Robertson guilty on three counts of criminal contempt and sentenced him to three consecutive 180-day terms of imprisonment. Robertson filed a motion to vacate the judgment, which the court denied. Robertson appealed. The United States Supreme Court, in a per curiam order, dismissed the writ as improvidently granted, thereby declining to decide whether an action for criminal contempt may constitutionally be brought in the name of a private person. Robertson v. United States, 130 S. Ct. 2184, 2185 (2010). The Court of Appeals then granted defendant's motion for rehearing.]

We turn now to the law governing that preliminary issue. D.C. Code §16-1005(f) and Super. Ct. Dom. V.R. 12(d) authorize an individual to file a motion to adjudicate criminal contempt in an intrafamily matter.[13] Section 16–1005(f), under which the contempt action in this case was initiated, is a penal statute which addresses a public wrong as opposed to a remedial statute that compensates a civil injury.

The prosecution of penal laws or criminal statutes in the District of Columbia is controlled by D.C. Code §23–101. Criminal contempt actions relating to intrafamily offenses fall under §23–101(c), and hence, "shall be conducted in the name of the United States by the United States attorney for the District of Columbia or its assistants, except as otherwise provided by law." Read together, D.C. Code §6–1005(f) and D.C. Code §23–101 permit Ms. Watson, assisted by the OAG, to initiate a criminal contempt action involving intrafamily offenses in the name of the United States for the purpose of enforcing a Superior Court CPO. We considered criminal contempt and CPO statutory and regulatory provisions, including D.C. Code §16–1005(f), in Green v. Green, 642 A.2d 1275 (D.C.1994) and declared: "Those provisions reflect a determination by the Council [of the District of Columbia] that the beneficiary of a CPO should be permitted to enforce that order through an intrafamily contempt proceeding." Id. at 1279. Thus, so long as the beneficiary's CPO enforcement action is brought in the name of the United States, we discern no

---

13. D.C. Code §§16–1005(f) and (g)(2001) currently provide:

(f) Violation of any temporary or final order . . . shall be punishable as contempt. Upon conviction, criminal contempt shall be punished by a fine not exceeding $1,000 or imprisonment for not more than 180 days, or both.

(g) Any person who violates any protection order . . . shall be chargeable with a misdemeanor and upon conviction shall be punished by a fine not exceeding $1,000 or by imprisonment for not more than 180 days, or both.

Super. Ct. Dom. V.R. 12(d) specifies, in pertinent part:

(d) Motion to adjudicate criminal contempt. A motion requesting that the court order a person to show cause why she/he should not be held in criminal contempt for violation of a temporary protection order or civil protection order may be filed by an individual, Corporation Counsel or an attorney appointed by the Court for that purpose.

statutory impediment. Nor does it matter that the contempt action here was not actually captioned in the name of the sovereign, when Mr. Robertson could have had no doubt that the action was being brought as an exercise of the court's authority to vindicate its order. . . .

We focus now on Mr. Robertson's main argument that his plea agreement with the United States Attorney barred the criminal contempt action against him. . . . It is not obvious that a plea agreement or a contract between Mr. Robertson and the United States Attorney can preclude the Superior Court from vindicating its authority. Criminal and punitive contempt proceedings are designed "to preserve the power, and vindicate the dignity of the courts, and to punish for disobedience of their orders. . . ." Indeed, the Court held in [Young v. United States ex rel. Vuitton et Fils S.A., 481 U.S. 787, 800 (1987)] that the prosecution of criminal contempt in Article III courts need not "be considered an execution of the criminal law in which only the Executive Branch may engage." Id. at 823. It based this conclusion on "the longstanding acknowledgment that the initiation of contempt proceedings to punish disobedience to court orders is a part of the judicial function" and on the Judiciary's "need for an independent means of self-protection." Id. at 795, 796. Thus, provided that prosecution for criminal contempt in a congressionally created court such as the Superior Court is understood as an exercise of sovereign power, it is by no means evident—absent a double jeopardy bar not present here—that a plea agreement by the Executive can tie the hands of a Superior Court judge so as to preclude vindication of that court's authority by an order of contempt.

Moreover, "a plea agreement is a contract." "As a consequence, courts will look to principles of contract law to determine whether the plea agreement has been breached." The plea agreement in this case was signed only by Mr. Robertson, his attorney, and an Assistant United States Attorney. The pertinent handwritten narrative stated: "In exchange for Mr. Robert[son's] plea of guilty to Attempt[ed] Aggravated Assault, the gov't agrees . . . not [to] pursue any charges concerning an incident on 6–26–99." The abbreviated word "gov't" clearly referred only to the United States, and hence, only the United States and Mr. Robertson were bound by the agreement.

While Mr. Robertson may have expected that his plea agreement with the government would prevent him from being charged with anything else related to his actions on June 26, 1999, "[a] defendant's subjective expectations as to how a plea agreement will redound to his benefit are enforceable, if at all, only to the extent that they are objectively reasonable." It is not objectively reasonable for a violator of a CPO to expect that his plea agreement with the United States would shield him by taking away the inherent power and authority of the Superior Court to enforce its CPOs through the sanction of criminal contempt. Nor is it "obvious" that Mr. Robertson's plea agreement bargained away the inherent authority of a Superior Court judge to sanction him for criminal contempt. . . . Accordingly, for the foregoing reasons, we affirm the judgments of the trial court. . . .

Notes and Questions

1. *Background.* Wykenna Watson initiated the case by a motion for criminal contempt, filed by the Office of the Corporation Counsel for the District of Columbia on her behalf. What motivated her to initiate the criminal contempt proceeding?

Following defendant's conviction for criminal contempt in the District of Columbia Superior Court, he appealed, contending (inter alia) that the criminal contempt prosecution violated his due process rights by breaching his plea agreement with the U.S. Attorney's Office for the District of Columbia. Defendant brought a direct appeal, as well as a collateral appeal from the denial of his motion to vacate his conviction. The District of Columbia Court of Appeals affirmed. Defendant then appealed to the U.S. Supreme Court which, following a grant of certiorari, dismissed the writ of certiorari as improvidently granted. Thereafter, the Court of Appeals granted defendant's motion for rehearing (resulting in the decision in the principal case).

Dismissal of a writ of certiorari as "improvidently granted" occurs when the Supreme Court, after initially accepting a case for review, decides not to review a case further (perhaps based on a belief that oral arguments did not clearly frame the constitutional issues or that adjudication of the issues should be deferred for a more suitable case). The Court then dismisses the writ as "improvidently granted," generally in a per curiam decision without explanation, although some justices may issue dissenting opinions (as occurred in this case).

2. *Epilogue.* The D.C. Court of Appeals' decision in the principal case was hailed as a victory by domestic violence advocates who contended that allowing private persons to prosecute criminal contempt actions empowers victims. However, two weeks later, the D.C. attorney general filed a motion noting that several superior court judges interpreted the ruling to mean that private individuals could bring such an action only if a government lawyer was involved. D.C. Superior Court Judges, A.G.'s Office Split on Domestic Violence Ruling, Blog of Legal Times, June 3, 2011, http://legaltimes.typepad.com/blt/2011/06/dc-superior-court-judges-ags-office-split-on-domestic-violence-ruling.htm. What is the likely impact of this restriction?

3. *Civil contempt, criminal contempt, and criminal acts.* Courts have carefully distinguished between civil contempt, criminal contempt, and criminal acts. While each can result in incarceration or fines, each is subject to different due process protections (explored below).

a. *Civil contempt.* Civil contempt applies when a party refuses to act as ordered by the court. Civil contempt is both coercive (designed to force the party to act in the manner directed) and compensatory (compensates the injured party for the failure to act in accordance with the order). Thus, for civil contempt, the contemnor must either comply with the order or compensate the injured party in order to be released.

Because civil contempt is not punitive, it is not subject to due process protections. Nonetheless, many states do require some procedural protections for civil contempt. See, e.g., Zetty v. Piatt, 776 A.2d 631, 638-643 (Md. 2001).

b. *Criminal contempt.* Contempt is criminal in nature when its intent is to punish the contemnor for violating a court order, thereby vindicating the authority of the court. The elements of criminal contempt are a reasonably specific court order and a willful violation of that court order. See, e.g., Carthew v. County of Suffolk, 709 F. Supp. 2d 188 (E.D.N.Y. 2010). Unlike civil contempt, the purpose of criminal contempt is not to compel an action by the contemnor but rather to punish him or her for a past act.

Criminal contempt may be punished by a fine, incarceration, or any other remedy deemed appropriate by the court or under statute. Due to its punitive aspect, a criminal contempt proceeding must satisfy constitutional due process requirements. See, e.g., Gormley v. Judicial Conduct Comm'n, 332 S.W.3d 717 (Ky. 2010). Thus, the accused is entitled to the full range of due process protections, including the right to counsel and the right to remain silent. However, as discussed in the principal case, there is some debate about whether that full range of due process protections includes the right to a disinterested prosecutor.

c. *Criminal actions.* There is also debate about whether criminal contempt is distinct from criminal prosecutions generally. The four Supreme Court justices who dissented from dismissal of the writ of certiorari in *Robertson* resoundingly rejected the idea of criminal contempt proceedings as unique from criminal prosecutions generally, arguing that the contempt prosecution counted as a "crime" for purposes of extending the full protections of due process, including requiring prosecution by a disinterested prosecutor, namely the government. See Robertson v. United States ex rel. Watson, 130 S. Ct. 2184, 2187-2188 (2010) (Roberts, J., dissenting).

Should contemnors in criminal contempt proceedings receive the same due process rights as the accused in criminal prosecutions? In what ways are criminal contempt proceedings inherently different from criminal prosecutions? Who does criminal contempt benefit? What notice does a person facing a criminal contempt charge receive when compared with a person facing a criminal prosecution? What do criminal contempt and criminal prosecutions have in common?

4. *Plea agreement.* The effect of the U.S. Supreme Court's per curiam opinion in *Robertson* dismissing petitioner's writ of certiorari as improvidently granted was to let Watson's victory stand—seemingly validating D.C. laws that allow victims to initiate such prosecutions regardless of defendants' plea agreements with the government. However, the four dissenting justices (Chief Justice Roberts and Justices Scalia, Kennedy, and Sotomayor), who contended that an action for criminal contempt may not be brought in the name of a private person, suggested that the plea agreement was therefore binding as to the U.S. Attorney. To the extent that the U.S. Attorney was acting on Ms. Watson's behalf, she, too, would have been bound.

However, plea agreements, like all contracts, bind only the parties to the agreement, as the D.C. Court of Appeals explains in the principal case. During oral arguments, Justice Sotomayor also focused on this issue as follows:

> We have plenty of plea agreements jurisprudence that say if the Southern District of New York prosecutes someone and they sign a plea agreement and say, we're not going to prosecute you for further crimes, we read that to mean that the Southern District of New York won't prosecute you for further crimes.
>
> We don't read it that no other government agency is bound, who has jurisdiction over that criminal activity, that they are equally bound. So why isn't this case the same?

Transcript, Oral Argument of Jacklyn S. Frankfurt, Robertson v. United States ex rel. Watson, No. 08-6261 (Mar. 31, 2010), available at http://www.oyez.org/cases/2000-2009/2009/2009_08_6261/argument. What is the answer to Justice Sotomayor's question? Why was the Court of Appeals able to uphold the imposed punishment for criminal contempt? Which party was missing from the plea agreement?

5. *Constitutional arguments: sovereign power, due process, and the separation of powers.* *Robertson* addresses the question: Who may prosecute a criminal contempt action?

It is generally accepted that a central assumption of the Constitution is that only the government may prosecute a crime. See Standefer v. United States, 447 U.S. 10, 25 (1980); Note, Permitting Private Initiation of Criminal Contempt Proceedings, 124 Harv. L. Rev. 1485, 1493 (2011) [hereinafter Note, Private Initiation]. The rationale is that a crime is considered an offense against the public good, rather than a private wrong—a tradition stemming from both English and American common law. Note, Private Initiation, supra, at 1494-1495. However, there are exceptions to this rule. In Young v. U.S. ex rel. Vuitton et Fils S.A., 481 U.S. 787, 804 (1987), for example, the court allowed a private, "disinterested" prosecutor to handle a criminal contempt proceeding, distinguishing criminal contempt proceedings from criminal actions generally. Some states have also allowed private persons to prosecute on behalf of the sovereign, as was the case in *Robertson*. What factors might play a role in the sovereign's power to yield to a prosecution by a private person?

Another issue in *Robertson* was whether the defendant's plea agreement with the government barred the criminal contempt action against him. Robertson did not present this claim in the trial court during his criminal contempt proceeding; rather, he filed it three years later. What did the Court of Appeals rule? Although only obliquely discussed in the principal case, the defendant seems to suggest that allowing a private person to prosecute criminal contempt violates his due process rights. Is there a constitutional right to be prosecuted by the sovereign alone? See Note, Private Initiation, supra, at 1498-1499 (noting that the Supreme Court has never declared such a right under the federal Constitution).

Finally, allowing a private prosecutor raises concerns about the separation of powers between the judiciary, the legislature, and the executive. If a court or a statute allows a private party to stand in the place of the government, does this unconstitutionally usurp the role of the executive? See Brief for Respondent at 51-58, *Robertson*, 130 S. Ct. 2184 (No. 08-6261), 2010 WL 740749, at *51-*58 (Mar. 1, 2010).

6. *Other states.* The District of Columbia has a slightly more complex constitutional and judicial structure than other states because of its close relationship to the federal government. For example, although it is an independent jurisdiction, it has yielded its authority to prosecute criminal contempt to the U.S. Attorney.

All 50 states have some form of criminal contempt available to enforce civil protection orders. However, many states additionally allow a misdemeanor prosecution for violating a civil protection order. At least 14 states, and the District of Columbia, allow a private person, such as the victim, to prosecute a criminal contempt action when the state declines to, fails to, or is inadequate in doing so. Brief for Domestic Violence Legal Empowerment and Appeals Project et al. as Amici Curiae Supporting Respondent at 14-15. *Robertson*, 130 S. Ct. 2184 (No. 08-6261), 2010 U.S. S. Ct. Briefs LEXIS 224 at *21-*23. Some jurisdictions expressly forbid such an arrangement. See, e.g., Rogowicz v. O'Connell, 786 A.2d 841, 845 (N.H. 2001). Absent statutory authority, should a victim of domestic violence be able to prosecute an action for criminal contempt?

7. *Advantages and disadvantages.* Most domestic violence advocates have applauded attempts by states and courts to allow a private person, such as the battered woman, the ability to prosecute a criminal contempt action against her abuser, particularly when the state drops the case or fails to achieve an adequate punishment. States have often failed to enforce domestic violence protective orders.

As a group of family law judges and domestic violence advocates explained in their amicus brief before the Supreme Court in *Robertson*:

> Other arms of government have made clear their lack of interest in enforcing these orders. In New York City, it is the policy of the New York Police Department not to enforce custody or visitation provisions in court orders despite the fact that custodial interference is a violation of the New York Penal Code. . . .
>
> Likewise, prosecutors have an institutional disinterest in orders regarding private parties. It is unrealistic to expect prosecutors to pursue all contempt actions arising from alleged violations of civil court orders. As a Florida District Court of Appeal noted in *Gordon* [v. Florida, 960 So. 2d 31 (Fla. Dist. Ct. App. 2007)], "[a]lthough an indirect criminal contempt proceeding in a family law case is vitally important to the parties, such a case often has little interest to a professional prosecutor." This disinterest results in part from the fact that it is not in the organizational mission of prosecutors to pursue such cases. In addition, prosecutors lack the time, the resources, and in some cases the will to prosecute transgressors of civil domestic relations orders.

Brief for Family Law Judges, Practitioners & Scholars as Amici Curiae Supporting Respondent at 22-24, Robertson, 130 S. Ct. 2184 (No. 08-6261), 2010 U.S. S. Ct. Briefs LEXIS 229 at *33-*36.

As the above amicus brief suggests, criminal contempt offers a number of practical advantages. In many states, such proceedings are accorded an expedited hearing by statute. David M. Zlotnick, Empowering the Battered Woman: The Use of Criminal Contempt Sanctions to Enforce Civil Protection Orders, 56 Ohio St. L.J. 1153, 1199 (1995). Criminal contempt hearings also may be resolved faster because such proceedings are tried before a judge rather than a jury. For example, in *Robertson*, in response to defendant's contention that he was denied his right to a jury trial, the D.C. Court of Appeals ruled that his criminal contempt prosecution was for a petty offense rather than a serious offense, and therefore he was not constitutionally entitled to jury trial. *Robertson*, 19 A.3d at 762. In addition, because victims can initiate the actions themselves, they are not required to wait for police to make an arrest or prosecutors to file charges, thereby remedying any unwillingness on the part of police and prosecutors to take violations of protection orders seriously. Criminal contempt orders thus fill a critical gap to protect victims of domestic violence when the state cannot, or will not.

However, given that the contemnor is entitled to counsel and other constitutional protections while the private party often appears pro se, actions brought by victims have a low success rate. See District of Columbia Courts, Final Report of the Task Force on Racial and Ethnic Bias and Task Force on Gender Bias in the Courts, 154 (May 1992). Recognizing this disparity, at least two states require the court clerk to assist pro se victims in filing criminal contempt actions. See, e.g., N.C. Gen. Stat. §50B-4(a); Utah Code Ann. §78B-7-105. How helpful is this reform? Can you think of other methods to improve the system for holding abusers accountable in criminal contempt for violation of protection orders?

2. *Violations of Restraining Orders: Criminal Sanctions*

All states have criminal sanctions for violations of a protection order. Depending on the jurisdiction, abusers who violate a civil protection order may be charged with: (1) criminal contempt, (2) a misdemeanor, or (3) a felony. In some states, subsequent violations of restraining orders enhance the penalties.

The purpose of restraining orders is to prevent abusers from committing additional acts of violence. Effective enforcement consists of prohibitions on a range of contact between the abuser and victim, prohibitions on the possession of a firearm, and prosecutions of violations of protective orders. However, in order for civil protection orders to be effective, they must be enforced. Police cannot enforce a restraining order unless they can determine: (1) an order was issued and is still in effect; (2) the order prohibits the alleged misconduct, and (3) the order was served. Police make these determinations by consulting a statewide computer database (called the Domestic Violence Restraining Order System or DVROS) that was created by the Department of Justice in 1991.

Criminal courts input information from criminal protective orders directly into DVROS or, alternatively, designate a local law enforcement agency to fulfill this task. For civil restraining orders, different state agencies (including law enforcement) may be responsible to input information into DVROS.

How effectively does this system work? A California task force conducted a two-year assessment of state practices to address this question. The task force (consisting of a 26-member group of experts from law enforcement, victim advocacy, public health and legislators) identified a number of "problematic practices" relating to obtaining and enforcing of domestic violence restraining orders. Their findings are set forth below.

■ **REPORT FROM THE ATTORNEY GENERAL'S TASK FORCE ON LOCAL CRIMINAL JUSTICE RESPONSE TO DOMESTIC VIOLENCE, KEEPING THE PROMISE: VICTIM SAFETY AND BATTERER ACCOUNTABILITY 21-45 (2005)** [hereafter REPORT, ATTORNEY GENERAL'S TASK FORCE]
available at **http://www.safestate.org/documents/DV_Report_AG.pdf**

1. Criminal Courts Are Not Meeting Legal Requirements

The Criminal Courts in at least 17 counties have not complied with the statutory mandates that they: 1) issue Criminal Protective Orders (CPOs) whenever sentencing domestic violence offenders to probation, and 2) ensure that those orders are entered into the Domestic Violence Restraining Order System (DVROS). . . .

There appear to be three reasons for noncompliance:

- Some courts did not understand that CPOs were required when domestic violence offenders were sentenced to probation;
- Most courts failed to understand their statutorily required leadership role in ensuring the entry of CPOs into DVROS; and
- In some counties, a lack of cooperation between the courts and other criminal justice agencies hindered CPO data entry into DVROS.

2. Unserved and Unrecorded Criminal Protective Orders

A defendant cannot be arrested or convicted for violating a Criminal Protective Order (CPO) unless he or she was present in court when the Order was issued or otherwise notified of the order. According to the Domestic Violence Restraining Order System (DVROS), however, in many counties there are a significant number of defendants who appear not to have been served with the CPOs issued against them. . . .

3. Victims Are Usually Not Notified When Criminal Protective Orders Are Terminated

Current law does not require that domestic violence victims be notified when a Criminal Protective Order (CPO) is terminated by court action before it is scheduled to end. This leaves the victim believing that protection is being provided by a CPO in force, when it is not. . . .

4. Emergency Protective Orders Are Underused

A victim of domestic violence can seek an Emergency Protective Order (EPO), at any time of day or night, from a police officer who responds to a call for assistance [and contacts a judge, by telephone, to assert that the person is "in immediate and present danger of domestic violence, based on the person's allegation of a recent incident of abuse or threat of abuse."] [T]he judge, through the officer, can issue an order on the spot that prohibits firearm possession and requires no contact or peaceful contact. Though of short duration (five to seven days), this order can provide some temporary protection, and serve as "proof" of abuse if the victim later applies for a Temporary Restraining Order (TRO) and Order After Hearing (OAH). It is important to realize that a victim may need an EPO (and TRO and OAFS) even if the abuser is arrested. If the abuser is released on bail, as happens frequently, the criminal justice system can impose no restriction on the abuser until the first arraignment, which may not take place for many weeks.

Despite the importance of EPOs, they are infrequently issued in most counties. . . . This picture of underuse is consistent with both the interviews in core counties and the testimony presented to the Task Force. Victim advocates in five of the 10 core counties reported that EPOs were rarely issued, and advocates in three others reported that the use of EPOs varied significantly depending on the local law enforcement agency involved. In addition, a number of testifiers spoke about law enforcement agencies that have, or appear to have, a policy of discouraging victims from requesting EPOs. . . .

5. The Numbers and Rates of [Permanent Restraining Orders Called "Orders After Hearing"] Can Be Improved

[The numbers and rates of permanent restraining orders vary significantly by county.] Several factors may contribute to the OAH rate, including:

- how difficult it is for a victim to request a TRO (which a victim must do in order to seek an OAH) and the OAH itself. This will vary, depending on such factors as 1) the legal assistance available to help the victim fill out the numerous forms and navigate the court system, 2) the court's accessibility (e.g., distance from victim, and available transportation), and 3) the judge's attitude;

- whether the victim is required to hand-carry the TRO and OAH to one or more local law enforcement agencies; and
- how difficult it is to have the notice of the OAH hearing served on the batterer. . . .

6. Significant Burdens Are Placed on Victims Seeking Family Court Restraining Orders

Obtaining a Temporary Restraining Order (TRO), and ultimately making that temporary order permanent with an Order after Hearing (OAH), is not an easy process. The victim must fill out forms, which, though recently revised and simplified by the Judicial Council, are lengthy and not always easily understood. One critical form requires a description of the abuse. If there are divorce, child custody, and child visitation matters to be considered along with the restraining order (and there often are), the number of forms increases and the help needed multiplies.

Interviews in the core counties revealed how weighty this burden could be. Advocates in all 10 counties discussed the difficulty of the process in general, which usually required providing several hours of one-on-one paperwork assistance to victims. These burdens were confirmed in testimony at the hearings. Free legal assistance is not available in four of the 10 core counties.

Moreover, there appears to be a small number of judges, scattered across the state, who engage in practices that make it difficult for victims to obtain Family Court restraining orders. Examples of such practices include: 1) refusing to issue TROs if the victim did not call the police to report the abuse, 2) refusing to take up child support and custody issues as part of the process, 3) requiring that victims seeking TROs have experienced a recent emergency, and 4) modifying a no-contact request to allow contact, and crossing out the firearms prohibition. . . .

7. Unnecessary Burdens Are Placed on Victims After They Obtain Family Court Restraining Orders

Traditionally, most counties required victims who obtained a Temporary Restraining Order (TRO) and an Order After Hearing (OAH) to carry the orders from the courthouse to a law enforcement agency for entry in the Domestic Violence Restraining Order System (DVROS). This practice now appears to be diminishing in frequency. In nine of the 10 core counties, court personnel, law enforcement, and others cooperate so that the order is entered into DVROS with little or no help from the victim.

The same cannot be said for another practice: that of requiring the victim to carry a copy of the TRO and OAH to all of the law enforcement agencies that might have to enforce the order. These include agencies that have jurisdiction where the victim lives and works, and where the victim's children attend school and are cared for. In seven of the 10 core counties, victims are expressly advised by the court, court personnel, family law facilitators, and/or advocates that they must deliver the orders to the pertinent law enforcement agencies. The eight police departments contacted in these counties stated that they expected the victim to drop off a copy of the order. These departments did state, however, that they would enforce an undelivered order if 1) the order were in DVROS, and 2) the law enforcement agency that had entered the information into DVROS (usually the Sheriff's Department) could confirm the accuracy of the information. These departments' second choice is in fact the preferred practice contemplated by the legislation that created DVROS. . . . Thus, requiring the victim to deliver a copy of a TRO or OAH is unnecessary for enforcement and creates an unnecessary burden on the victim. . . .

8. Family Court Restraining Orders: Unserved and Unrecorded

A batterer cannot be arrested or convicted for violating a Family Court restraining order unless he or she was present in court when the order was issued or otherwise notified of the order. According to the Domestic Violence Restraining Order System (DVROS), however, there are a significant number of batterers in many counties who have not been served with the [permanent restraining order] issued against them. . . . [Some of the largest counties had 40 percent of permanent restraining orders listed as unserved; some of the smallest counties had 40 to 50 percent of unserved permanent restraining orders]. . . . There was testimony that in one county, service was so slow that approximately 30 percent of hearings for permanent orders had to be rescheduled for lack of service.

9. Firearm Prohibitions: Unissued and Unrecorded

[All criminal protection orders and all permanent protection orders must contain firearm prohibitions. Yet, a number of counties had high percentages of criminal protection orders and permanent protection orders that did not contain firearm prohibitions. The percentages of orders with no firearm prohibitions ranged from 14 percent to 52 percent.]

10. A Legal Loophole Allows Many Charged with Domestic Violence Offenses to Keep Their Firearms

If a Criminal Court exercises its discretion to order that an individual charged with domestic violence must have no contact or peaceful contact with the alleged victim, that order—without exception—must also direct the defendant to relinquish any firearms. If a Criminal Court does not enter such an order, however, the court has no independent basis to issue a firearm prohibition. . . . Our witnesses and interviewees left no doubt that judges frequently decline to issue no contact or peaceful contact orders. Whatever the reasons for this practice—the victim objects, the victim and defendant live together or have children, or there is no prosecutor present to request an order—courts should have the authority to order relinquishment of firearms. But they do not under current law. . . .

11. Firearm Prohibitions Are Rarely Enforced

All domestic violence restraining orders—issued by Criminal or Family Courts are supposed to prohibit a batterer from owning, purchasing, possessing, or receiving firearms. . . . These orders direct the batterer to get rid of any firearms that he or she possesses or controls within 24 hours after learning of the order, either by surrendering them to local law enforcement or selling them to a licensed gun dealer. Finally, these orders direct the batterer to file a receipt with the court within 72 hours of learning about the order, demonstrating that relinquishment has taken place. . . . Despite the heightened dangers that domestic violence victims face when there are firearms in the home, we are aware of few criminal justice agencies in the core counties that have a coordinated policy of proactively enforcing firearm prohibitions in Criminal Protective Orders. We are unaware of any agencies in the core counties that have such a policy when it comes to firearm prohibitions in Family Court. . . .

12. Minimal Enforcement and Prosecution of Family Court "No Contact" and "Peaceful Contact" Orders

The heart of a domestic violence restraining order is its requirement that the batterer either have no contact or have peaceful contact with the victim, not simply that the batterer not commit additional crimes (for which a restraining order would be superfluous). The reason for these orders, as explained above, is that a period of separation or of regulated contact will help "prevent . . . a recurrence of domestic violence. . . ." These orders will have limited impact, however, if violations are rarely punished. That is why the Legislature directed law enforcement to arrest all such violators.

Unfortunately, we found broad agreement among victim advocates, law enforcement, and court personnel in the 10 core counties and numerous other counties, through interviews and testimony at all six regional hearings, that enforcement and prosecution of these types of violations were the exception, not the rule. In testimony, we heard that law enforcement seemed to require a "magic number" of violations before they would respond or consider taking action: in one county, it was seven violations, in another it was five pursuant to District Attorney policy, and in another the District Attorney will not prosecute these violations at all.

Law enforcement and prosecutors advanced a number of reasons to explain their extreme reluctance to prosecute these violations:

- the proof of the violation is often difficult (e.g., when the only witnesses are the batterer and victim);
- the proof of the batterer's intent to violate the order is often not clear (e.g., a batterer, prohibited from coming within 100 feet of the victim's home, approaches to within 50 feet);
- the case will not appeal to a jury or judge when the violations are truly technical (e.g., as above, the batterer comes too close to the victim's home);
- the victim sometimes appears to have invited the violation (e.g., the victim invites the batterer over to the home, resulting in the batterer's violation of the order);
- law enforcement does not have useful guidelines to interpret prohibitions on non-peaceful contact; and
- there is a lack of resources to invest in these difficult-to-win non-violent cases, given that existing resources are already taxed by the domestic violence cases with physical injuries.

While any of these reasons might have merit in any given case, the result appears to be that few violations are prosecuted. . . . A general failure to enforce and prosecute is at odds with the purpose of the restraining order system. Moreover, the resulting lack of enforcement and prosecution has negative and dangerous unintended consequences. For the victim, there is a loss of faith in the system and reluctance to report new violations, even as these violations grow in seriousness. For the batterer, there is a sense of empowerment to commit new violations and more violent crimes. Finally, there are studies that show that batterers who are subject to Family Court restraining orders typically have more serious criminal histories than batterers convicted in the criminal courts without a Family Court order history.

We note that there is an alternative basis to enforce violations of Family Court restraining orders—a criminal contempt action brought under California Code of Civil Procedure §1218 by a "party" (i.e., the victim who obtained the Family Court order) against the alleged violator (i.e., the batterer). This section allows up to five days in jail for every incident. Of course, the victim usually will not have an attorney (though he or she can recover reasonable attorney fees, if the batterer has funds), while an attorney will be appointed to defend the batterer. Moreover, there is no statutory authorization, as there must be, for a District or City Attorney to prosecute under §1218.44. As a result, these actions are rarely, if ever, brought. There is also a serious question as to whether a private party—as opposed to a public prosecutor—could legally prosecute a criminal contempt action under any circumstance.

13. Issues of Culture and Interpretation

Many non-English-speaking victims are immigrants to California, and are often reluctant to call the police. In addition to their cultural aversion to involving outsiders in family matters, prior negative experiences with the police and the justice systems in their countries of origin often result in serious reluctance to involve the authorities in this country. Testifiers at regional hearings confirmed this reluctance. Further, whether they are here legally or not, it is likely they will perceive an increased risk of involving law enforcement because they fear deportation. To complicate matters, their fear of deportation is tied to their fear of losing custody of their children.

This cultural backdrop makes it even harder for domestic violence victims who are not English speakers to feel confident about calling and confiding in law enforcement. Although most counties have interpretation services available, interviews with advocates and law enforcement in some of the ten core counties revealed that needing interpretation services in any language besides Spanish slowed the process down considerably. As a result, according to testimony, police sometimes use batterers or children as interpreters if their English is better, as it often tends to be. Allowing the batterer to interpret for the victim, of course, is fraught with danger, carrying the possibility that the victim will be the one arrested. Finally, when police give out information on restraining orders and shelter programs to victims, the information is usually not available in Asian languages.

3. Interstate Enforcement of Protection Orders: Full Faith and Credit

What happens when a victim of domestic violence crosses state lines? Suppose a victim obtains a restraining order in the state of Blackacre. She then moves to the state of Greenacre. Is the state of Greenacre required to give full faith and credit to the order of protection that was issued in another state? This section explores the interstate enforcement of restraining orders.

◼ **EMILY J. SACK, DOMESTIC VIOLENCE ACROSS
STATE LINES: THE FULL FAITH AND CREDIT
CLAUSE, CONGRESSIONAL POWER, AND
INTERSTATE ENFORCEMENT OF
PROTECTION ORDERS**

98 Nw. U. L. Rev. 827, 838-850, 905-906 (2004)

. . . Section 2265 of the Violence Against Women Act provides that a protection order of one state that meets the requirements of the Act shall be accorded full faith and credit by the court of another state and enforced as if it were the order of the enforcing state. In order to qualify for this full faith and credit protection, an order must meet basic requirements. The issuing state must have had jurisdiction over the parties and subject matter jurisdiction according to its law and must have provided reasonable notice and opportunity to be heard to the accused abuser "sufficient to protect that person's right to due process." Ex parte orders also qualify as long as notice and opportunity to be heard is provided within the time required by the issuing state's law and "in any event within a reasonable time after the order is issued, sufficient to protect the respondent's due process rights."

The VAWA provision follows well-established principles of full faith and credit jurisprudence. The enforcing state must give as much full faith and credit to the issuing state's protection order as would be given in the issuing state. In addition, the enforcing state must accord full faith and credit to the issuing state's protection order if it is valid under the issuing state's law, even if it could not have been issued in the enforcing state. That is the true meaning of full faith and credit, requiring that states recognize and honor judgments from their sister states even when they would not have made such a judgment themselves. The enforcement mechanisms and remedies, however, are those of the enforcing state. While the validity of the order is determined by the law of the issuing state, the definition of what constitutes a violation is determined by the law of the enforcing state. The penalty is also determined by the enforcing state's law. . . .

Implementation of the Violence Against Women Act's Full Faith and Credit Provision

The implementation of the broad language in the VAWA full faith and credit provision proved to be difficult. Protection orders typically must be enforced in emergency situations when a violation is alleged and victims may be subject to or threatened with physical danger. Most frequently it is a law enforcement officer on the scene of a domestic violence incident who must make the first decision about the validity of an out-of-state protection order in order to decide whether there is probable cause to make an arrest based on violation of the order. If an arrest is made and the defendant charged, then a court, frequently at an early stage of the case, must make a finding about the order's validity. Therefore, in very short time frames, enforcing states are faced with several issues. Questions include the expiration date of the order, its validity under the laws of the issuing state, and whether the defendant has been served with the order.

When VAWA was passed, very few states had any infrastructure in place to quickly determine the answers to these and other related questions. There were no procedures for communicating with courts in the issuing jurisdiction, particularly after business hours. Few, if any, states had computerized registries of protection orders, and no national registry existed that law enforcement or court personnel from the enforcing state could access to obtain information about out-of-state orders. Law enforcement officers, faced with an order on an unfamiliar form and of unclear validity, were concerned about making an arrest that could subject them to civil liability if the order later proved invalid. Not only was enforcement of in-state orders problematic, enforcement of out-of-state orders added other layers of difficulty.

Since VAWA's passage, states have moved toward more effective enforcement of the full faith and credit provision. This has included such strategies as the creation of state protection order registries, development of more uniform order forms both within and between states, and enactment of state laws granting immunity to law enforcement officers who make arrests in good faith based on protection orders that later turn out to be invalid. The federal government has worked to facilitate interstate enforcement in a number of ways. In May 1997, the government created a national protection order registry that is part of the National Crime Information Center ("NCIC") database run by the FBI. State protection order registries transmit their information to the national database at NCIC, and law enforcement across the country can access the NCIC database to obtain information on out-of-state orders. Though not all states are transmitting their information to NCIC, a growing number of orders are contained in the national registry. . . .

One strategy in the implementation of the full faith and credit provision has been the movement in each state to pass enabling legislation. While this is not required under VAWA, it has the practical purpose in each state of informing state actors—law enforcement, judges, and court personnel—of the requirements of the federal provision and providing more specific guidance on how to enforce out-of-state orders. . . . Currently all fifty states [and the District of Columbia] have some legislation involving enforcement of out-of-state orders.

As the movement for passage of state laws was underway, however, it became clear that some states were developing legislation that was in direct conflict or inconsistent with the VAWA full faith and credit provision. As of March 2004, eighteen states, the District of Columbia, and one U.S. commonwealth have enabling legislation that does not comply with the federal law. Utah's statute is one that directly contradicts the VAWA provision by stating that full faith and credit will be given to a protection order issued by another state only if the foreign order is similar to an order issued in Utah. . . . This violates the central requirement that an enforcing state must give full faith and credit to an out-of-state order if it is valid in the issuing state, even if it involves parties or contains any terms that would not be valid under the enforcing state's law.

Alaska, Kentucky, [and Louisiana] require that an out-of-state order be filed in a court in the enforcing state in order to be accorded full faith and credit. Filing was never required under the original VAWA provision, and VAWA 2000 explicitly states that no filing or registration is required to trigger full faith and credit.

This is not a trivial difference. Many victims of domestic violence will be unaware of this requirement when they move to a new state. If a domestic violence incident occurs in the new state, the police will not be able to enforce the out-of-state order if it has not been registered. . . . In addition, a victim who does know of the requirement may be fearful of registering the order, because it may become a public record and accessible to her abuser. Thus, a state's filing requirement undermines a central purpose of VAWA. . . .

Some states vary other components of the VAWA provision. For example, Mississippi's statute states that, when no expiration date appears on the face of the order, it shall be deemed to have expired one year from the date of issuance. . . . However, VAWA requires that the enforcing state recognize out-of-state orders as valid for the length of time that they would be valid in the issuing state. In many states, protection orders may last far longer than one year. . . .

The development of a uniform act on the subject by the National Conference of Commissioners on Uniform State Laws ("NCCUSL") has also impacted the progress of state implementation of the VAWA provision. While NCCUSL's involvement has likely encouraged additional states to pass enabling legislation, inconsistencies between the VAWA provision and the NCCUSL uniform act have complicated the process and ultimately increased the number of states that are out of compliance with federal law.

In 2000, NCCUSL passed the Uniform Interstate Enforcement of Domestic Violence Protection Orders Act ("UIEDVPOA") [that] was designed to "establish uniform procedures" for effective interstate enforcement. . . .

Alabama, California, Delaware, Idaho, Indiana, Montana, Nebraska, North Dakota, South Dakota, Texas, West Virginia, and the District of Columbia each have passed versions of UIEDVPOA so that these states are now inconsistent with the federal law. In addition, some jurisdictions have made modifications to UIEDVPOA, meaning that even the states using it are not uniform. Many of the states that enacted UIEDVPOA prior to the 2002 amendments have not updated their laws to make them consistent with the amended act, and even some of the states that passed UIEDVPOA more recently relied on its unamended version. All of these factors have created even greater variations among state-enabling laws. . . . [T]he promulgation of an act that is inconsistent in important ways from the federal law has the ironic effect of making interstate recognition and enforcement of protection orders less uniform. . . .

The Violence Against Women Act of 2000

Congress passed the Violence Against Women Act of 2000 ("VAWA 2000") as part of the Victims of Trafficking and Violence Protection Act. . . . Several provisions in VAWA 2000 were aimed at addressing problems in implementation of the original Act's full faith and credit provision. Section 2265 was amended to add a provision that prohibited the court in the enforcing state from notifying or requiring notification of the party against whom a protection order had been issued that the protection order had been registered in that enforcing state, unless requested to do so by the protected party. In addition, VAWA 2000 made clear that registration in the new jurisdiction was not required for enforcement, notwithstanding any state law to the contrary. . . .

One of the original Act's central grants programs was renamed to expressly include enforcement of protection orders as a focus for grant program funds and add, as a grant purpose, the provision of technical assistance, computers, and other equipment for enforcing orders. VAWA 2000 also required, as a condition of funding, that recipients of state block grants and direct federal grants going to states and governmental units certify that their laws, practices, and policies do not require victims to pay filing or service costs related to protection orders in both civil and criminal cases. VAWA 2000 made the development and enhancement of data collection and sharing systems to promote enforcement of protection orders a funding priority under the grant program and instructed the Department of Justice to identify and make available information on promising practices in protection order enforcement. Furthermore, VAWA 2000 amended the definition of protection order in section 2266 to clarify which support and custody orders were entitled to full faith and credit under the VAWA provision.

Despite VAWA 2000's attempts to encourage greater state compliance with the full faith and credit provision, it has not impacted the states whose laws do not meet the federal law's requirements. . . .

The enforcement of domestic violence protection orders across state lines remains a complex logistical undertaking, requiring nationwide access to information on validity of protection orders; training of law enforcement officers, court personnel, and judges; and interstate cooperation among many diverse government agencies and organizations. However, since the passage of the VAWA's full faith and credit provision, the states have made enormous progress on these fronts in order to achieve effective interstate enforcement.

Yet, in the face of all these efforts, several states have not complied with the protections that the federal law requires. An examination of the Full Faith and Credit Clause of the Constitution and of the authority granted to Congress to enact the VAWA provision demonstrates that the states are not permitted to do so. The Full Faith and Credit Clause itself mandates state compliance. . . . States cannot constitutionally resist the requirements of the Full Faith and Credit Clause and the VAWA legislation. The states must act to bring themselves into compliance with these requirements and remove all unnecessary obstacles to providing the protection that is required both by the Constitution and the federal law to victims of domestic violence.

E. VICTIM'S ACTIONS

1. Mutual Restraining Orders

■ WILLIAMS v. JONES

662 S.E.2d 195 (Ga. Ct. App. 2008)

PHIPPS, Judge.

Quatarsha Williams filed a petition for a protective order charging Curtis Jones with various acts of family violence. At the time of the filing of the petition, Williams and Jones were unmarried but resided in the same household with their infant child. Following an unreported hearing, the court entered a family violence protective order containing a number of provisions mutually binding on the parties. We granted Williams's application for discretionary appeal. . . .

Williams's petition alleged that Jones had verbally and physically abused her shortly before the filing of the petition and on previous occasions, and that he had a rather lengthy arrest record. In the petition, Williams acknowledged that in at least one instance she had reacted to Jones's serious physical abuse of her by criminally damaging his property. Jones was promptly served with a copy of the petition. Without having filed any pleadings, Jones appeared at the hearing on the petition and represented himself pro se.

In its order, the court found that Jones had committed acts of family violence that placed Williams in reasonable fear for her safety and that represented a credible threat to her physical safety. The order, however, enjoins and restrains both Jones and Williams from doing, or attempting or threatening to do, any "act of injury, maltreating, molesting, following, harassing, harming, or abusing the other and/or the minor child/ren in any manner." The order additionally orders both parties not to go within 100 yards of each other; to stay away from each other's residence, workplace, and school; not to have any direct or indirect contact with one another; and not to interfere with each other's travel, transportation, or communication for purposes of harassment or intimidation. And it requires both of them to undergo a batterer's intervention program and alcohol/drug abuse evaluation, follow treatment recommendations, and surrender all firearms. In addition, Williams was awarded temporary custody of the parties' child, and Jones was ordered to pay child support. . . .

[Ga. Code Ann.] §19-13-4(a)(1) authorizes the court to "[d]irect the respondent to refrain from" acts of family violence. Under OCGA §19-13-4(a)(2), the court may "[g]rant to a party possession of the residence or household of the parties and exclude the other party from the residence or household." OCGA §19-13-4(a)(5) permits the court to "[o]rder the eviction of a party from the residence or household and order assistance to the victim in returning to it, or order assistance in retrieving personal property of the victim if the respondent's eviction has not been ordered." Under OCGA §19-13-4(a)(9), the court may "[o]rder the respondent to refrain from harassing or interfering with the victim." And under OCGA §19-13-4(a)(11), the court may "[o]rder the respondent to receive appropriate psychiatric or psychological services as a further measure to prevent the recurrence of family violence." . . .

Here, the superior court entered a mutual protective order concerning paragraphs (1), (9), and (11) of OCGA §19-13-4(a) to the extent that the court enjoined and restrained Williams as well as Jones from harassing or interfering with each other and to the extent that it required both of them to undergo a batterer's intervention program and alcohol/drug abuse evaluation. Because the record shows that Jones did not file a verified counter petition to Williams's petition, OCGA §19-13-4(a) deprived the superior court of the legal authority to include such mutually protective provisions in the order.

Mutual protective orders, i.e., orders entered against both parties to a dispute, have been criticized on grounds that they are based on the misconception that victims of domestic abuse have played a part in provoking it; they encourage people to blame the victim rather than hold the abuser accountable; they reward and empower the abuser; they confuse the police; and they violate the due process rights of the person against whom they are entered when pleadings requesting such orders and stating the basis upon which they are sought are not served on the person before the hearing. One commentator has opined that a mutual order can be more dangerous to the victim than no order at all. [Joan Zorza, What is Wrong with Mutual Orders of Protection? (accessible at http://www.scvan.org/mutual_orders.html).]

Indeed, [it] would appear that Williams's due process rights were violated here because Jones filed nothing to put her on notice that she would have to defend against a claim that the protective order be issued against her.

In fact, her petition alleged that after Jones held her down, beat her, and poured a bottle of bleach into her nose, mouth, and eyes, she broke the windows in his car, thereby resulting in his complaint to the police and her arrest. Williams thereby charged Jones with acts of domestic violence that provided compelling reasons for issuance of a protective order against him for her physical safety. . . . For these reasons, we reverse the order . . . to the extent that it contains provisions rendering it a "mutual protective order." . . .

Notes and Questions

1. *Mutual orders: background.* Judges sometimes issue mutual restraining orders. Such restraining orders are reciprocal—they bind each party. A judge issues such orders in cases in which the judge finds evidence that both parties inflicted abuse. Judges also sometimes issue mutual restraining orders as a prophylactic measure to prevent prospective violations by the victim. See, e.g., Uttaro v. Uttaro, 768 N.E.2d 600 (Mass. App. Ct. 2002) (vacating an order of protection against wife that trial judge had issued in order to prevent wife from contacting abuser).

2. *Prevalence.* Mutual *arrests* enhance the likelihood of the issuance of mutual restraining orders. See Anique Drouin, Comment, Who Turned out the Lights?: How Maryland Laws Fail to Protect Victims of Domestic Violence from Third-Party Abuse, 36 U. Balt. L. Rev. 105, 113 n. 67 (2006) ("Often when a victim has fought back in self-defense and there are marks, cuts or bruises on both parties, the police cannot necessarily tell who was the instigator of the incident and must arrest both parties."). How can police or judges determine whether a victim inflicted harm in self defense or whether an abuser is *falsely* claiming that the victim initiated the violence?

3. *Role of race and sexual orientation.* Are minority victims more likely to be the subject of mutual restraining orders? Are same-sex partners? These topics are explored in Chapter 5, Section A(4).

4. *Consequences.* What are the consequences of the issuance of a mutual restraining order for the victim? A protective order that restrains the victim has the same effect as an order restraining the offender. Depending on the conditions imposed by the judge, the restraining order might order the victim to vacate the home, restrict her access to her possessions, and affect her custody or visitation rights. David H. Taylor et al., Ex Parte Domestic Violence Orders of Protection: How Easing Access to Judicial Process Has Eased the Possibility for Abuse of the Process, 18 Kan. J.L. & Pub. Pol'y 83, 85-87 (2008). Another problem is that police may be reluctant to respond to an emergency call for assistance if the caller is subject to a mutual restraining order. Margaret Graham Tebo, Protective Orders' Power in State's Hands, ABA J. E-Report, July 1, 2005, at 1 (citing Joan Meier's criticism). What are the criticisms of mutual restraining orders by the judge in *Williams*? Why did the judge vacate the protective order against the petitioner?

5. *Law reform.* Accusations of gender bias early in the battered women's movement led many states to adopt a policy disfavoring the issuance of mutual restraining orders. See Mass. Supreme Judicial Court & Gender Bias Study Comm'n., Report of the Gender Bias Study of the Supreme Judicial Court 93-94 (1989). As a result, some

states proscribe the issuance of mutual orders. Fredrica L. Lehrman & Nancy McKenna, Domestic Violence Practice and Procedure §4:36 (2007). Other states circumscribe such remedies. See, e.g., Mass. Gen. Laws ch. 209A, §3 (providing that mutual restraining orders may issue only if the court has made specific written findings of fact and such orders are sufficiently detailed "to apprise any law officer as to which party has violated the order").

6. *Federal law.* Federal law also disfavors the issuance of mutual restraining orders. VAWA sets forth strict limitations for granting full faith and credit to mutual orders of protection: Written pleadings are required that request the mutual protection. Even where a petition has been filed, the court must make specific findings that each party was entitled to such an order in order to grant full faith and credit. 18 U.S.C. §2265(c)).

7. *Perpetrators' abuse of process.* Law enforcement authorities and judges sometimes confront a difficulty in determining the role of each party in the violence. That difficulty is compounded by the fact that many abusers make such effective use, themselves, of the litigation process. This abusive use of the legal process may begin as early as the 911 call that reports the abuse. As one commentator explains:

> In some cases, [there is] a "race" to call 911 by which the perpetrator places the call first and actually secures the arrest of the victim, knowing his call will be used as evidence at trial. This results in recurring and alternating arrests of batterer and victim to the point where the identity of the real victim becomes unclear. Problems like this "race" demonstrate the way in which batterers can manipulate the criminal justice system to their own advantage.

Nancee Alexa Barth, Comment, "I'd Grab at Anything, and I'd Forget," 41 J. Marshall L. Rev. 937, 947-948 (2008).

Protection orders provide another mechanism by which an abuser might use the legal system to continue his power and control over the victim. Statutes facilitate access to these emergency ex parte orders of limited duration by means of lowered standard of proof and liberal rules regarding the admissibility of evidence. The law reform movement has had an unanticipated benefit for abusers, as the following commentator explains:

> [A]s the doors of the courthouse have been opened to actual victims of domestic violence, they also have inadvertently been opened to persons who are not victims of domestic violence. In fact, they have been opened to the actual abuser who seeks relief for improper motives, such as trying to gain a tactical advantage in an anticipated domestic violence proceeding or divorce action. The ease with which ex parte orders can be obtained creates the opportunity for this misuse, allowing an ex parte order of protection to be granted on the basis of flimsy or false allegations. Though a temporary restraining order in any other context is an extraordinary remedy, ex parte orders of protection are granted routinely at an extraordinarily high rate; in some jurisdictions, nearly one hundred percent. The danger is presented by the ease and frequency with which the ex parte orders are entered. The abuser can use an order of protection as another means of abuse. . . . In other words, the judicial remedy that was intended to overcome disparity in power and income can be used as another tool for exploiting such disparities. The courts, instead of providing a mechanism for relief from an abusive relationship, then become yet another tool for effectuating abuse.

Taylor et al., supra, at 85-87. How are these criticisms applicable to the parties in *Williams*? For example, who called the police in *Williams*—Curtis Jones or Quatarsha Williams? What precipitated the mutual arrests?

8. *Abusers' characterizations of victimization.* If abusers do request protective orders, how do they successfully characterize themselves as victims? Empirical research reveals that batterers' descriptions of their victimization (1) focus on their power and control over their partner, (2) recount their active resistance but deny that their actions are "abusive" or that the men were "abusers," and (3) do not express fear of their partner, despite the men's portrayal of themselves as victims of both verbal and physical abuse. Alesha Durfee, "I'm Not a Victim. She's an Abuser": Masculinity, Victimization, and Protection Orders, 25 Gender & Soc'y 316 (2011). Given these characterizations, how can judges identify the actual victim? Consider this questions in light of the following explanation of batterers' characteristics (based on the authors' clinical work with several thousand men in batterer intervention programs).

■ **LUNDY BANCROFT ET Al., THE BATTERER AS PARENT: ADDRESSING THE IMPACT OF DOMESTIC VIOLENCE ON FAMILY DYNAMICS**
20-22 (2d ed., 2012) (citations omitted)

Batterers rarely disclose their violence fully, even in the face of considerable evidence. . . . Even those men who admit to some portions of their violence typically minimize their history of abuse, reporting significantly less violence and threatening behavior than their female partners attribute to them and that is revealed by court and police records. They sometimes will admit to violence but characterize it as necessary self-defense. . . .

In assessment of an alleged or established batterer, minimization by the offender can be more effectively misleading than denial. By expressing remorse while simultaneously portraying his victim as provocative and dishonest, a batterer is sometimes able to persuade a professional that he has been wrongly accused. . . . The batterer who uses this approach often states that his partner is falsely alleging domestic violence because she found out that he was involved with another woman, he refused a reunion that she desired, she was pushed into the accusations by an overzealous advocate, or she is using her claims as a weapon in custody litigation. We have had clients say roughly the following, for example: "I did shove her a couple of times, and one time I hauled off and slapped her when she called my mother a whore, and I really regret it. But now, she's saying I grabbed her by the throat and threatened to kill her, which I would never do, and she knows it."

Our clients often characterize their actions as defensive in nature or as being necessary to prevent more serious harm. The most common explanations that clients of ours provide include claims that his partner was assaulting him and he injured her when he was warding off her blows, that he was enraged by her frequent assaults against him and "finally decided to show her what it's like," that she was assaulting one of the children and he stepped in to protect the child, and that she was attempting to drive while drunk or to act self-destructively in some other way. Further inquiry typically reveals distortions in these accounts. . . .

2. Victim's Violation of Order

■ **STATE v. BRANSON**

167 P.3d 370 (Kan. Ct. App. 2007)

BUKATY, S.J.

Darrell J. Branson appeals his conviction following a bench trial for violation of a protective order. He essentially argues that the victim consented to his contact with her and this constitutes a defense to the charge. . . .

The State charged Branson with violating "a protection from abuse order issued pursuant to K.S.A. 60-3105, K.S.A. 60-3106, [and] K.S.A. 60-3107 . . . in violation of K.S.A. 21-3843(a)(1)." It alleged the crime occurred on or about October 18, 2005. Among the witnesses listed was Pamela Hird. Almost 4 months before the events leading to the charge, Hird had obtained a protection from abuse (PFA) order against Branson. . . .

The PFA order prohibited Branson from having any contact with Hird "except as authorized by the Court in this Order." It provided that Branson "shall not enter or come on or around the premises or the residence or workplace where [Hird] resides, stays or works." An exception, not applicable here, allowed Branson to obtain his personal property from Hird's home one time while accompanied by a law enforcement officer.

By its terms, the order expired at midnight on June 27, 2006. It further warned:

THE DEFENDANT IS HEREBY PUT ON NOTICE THAT VIOLATION OF THIS ORDER MAY CONSTITUTE VIOLATION OF A PROTECTIVE ORDER AS PROVIDED IN K.S.A. 21-3843 . . . AND MAY RESULT IN PROSECUTION AND CONVICTION UNDER KANSAS CRIMINAL STATUTES. VIOLATION OF THIS ORDER MAY ALSO BE PUNISHABLE AS A CONTEMPT OF THIS COURT.

At trial, Hird testified that on the evening in question, she was at home. She received a telephone call from an employee of a business that Hird owned stating that Branson had appeared at the business. The employee apparently knew of the PFA order and did not admit Branson to the business. The employee saw Branson leave in Hird's vehicle and then reported the information to police before telephoning Hird. The police soon contacted Hird, who confirmed the existence of the PFA order. The police stopped Branson in Hird's vehicle. Branson denied that he was at Hird's business, but he admitted to taking the vehicle from Hird's residence. He apparently had taken the keys from a table in Hird's house.

Hird then testified about contact she had with Branson prior to the night in question. She said she had seen him either that morning or the prior evening. She admitted that Branson had been staying in her basement for a week or more, and that she had meals with Branson during the 2 days before his arrest. She explained that he was in the basement most of the time and would sometimes come upstairs. The basement has a separate apartment with an outside entrance. She maintained, nevertheless, that he was staying with her and using her vehicle without her permission. She also admitted that Branson had repaired a toilet and had worked on one of the garbage disposals.

Hird explained that she failed to report these violations of the PFA order to the police because:

> I thought that a protection order applied to both of us that if—that I was not supposed to have contact with him or allow him anywhere around me, and since I had not called the police immediately, that I would be in as much trouble as he was, and when he came—when he showed up, I think one of my biggest problems has always been to feel sorry for him when he is intoxicated and has no place to go, and I just couldn't see making him leave when he was that drunk. He was going to be passed out in the yard. It's gotten to be a joke I think in the neighborhood how many times I have called the police, and I was just tired of it.

After the State rested, defense counsel moved to dismiss the charges based on Hird's allowing Branson to stay on the property and not contacting police. The district court denied the motion, stating that Hird's acquiescence was not a defense to the charge of violating the court order. The defense presented no evidence. The district court then ruled as follows:

"Well, based on the testimony, I do find that Mr. Branson has violated the protection order and I certainly understand the defense's position in this matter. Miss Hird's acquiescence in this certainly doesn't help the situation, but he has clearly violated the order, so I will find he is guilty."

[The district court sentenced Branson to 12 months in the county jail.]

Branson first argues on appeal that consent is a defense to criminal violation of a protective order. . . . [N]owhere in the statute defining the crime is consent mentioned at all. Therefore, if consent is deemed to be a defense, it must find its basis in a source apart from the statute defining the crime. . . .

The district court's ruling suggests that one of its rationales for denying a consent defense was the derogation of the court's authority. The court stated its rationale quite simply: "[Branson] has clearly violated the order, so I will find he is guilty." The State similarly argues on appeal: "[T]here is absolutely no precedent for suspending or nullifying a court order except by seeking a further order of the court." This certainly is a factor worthy of consideration even though the Protection From Abuse Act provides a proper remedy for any derogation of the district court's authority in its provisions allowing criminal contempt proceedings for violation of PFA orders.

In addition to this consideration, however, is consideration of the nature of a criminal act in general as set forth in Kansas statutes and case decisions. A criminal act occurs "against the peace and dignity of the State of Kansas," as was stated in the charging document involved here. Also, "the philosophy of this state has always been that a criminal prosecution is a state affair." The current Kansas Criminal Code begins by defining its scope as "conduct [which] constitutes a crime against the state of Kansas." K.S.A. 21-3102(1). Of further significance in this regard is the chapter of the state criminal code where the crime involved here is found. It is in Article 38, titled "Crimes Affecting Governmental Functions."

The facts here particularly indicate why Branson's actions implicate the State and the public at large. Hird testified that she had essentially given up because of public embarrassment and her feelings of pity for Branson. At sentencing, the State referred to an earlier conviction "in 05 CR 925 . . . of violating the same protective order." The State asserted that Branson was on probation in that case under the condition that he have no contact of any kind with Hird. The trial judge noted that Branson had been before him several times in connection with his lengthy, antagonistic relationship with Hird over the past years.

Such longstanding and intractable conflicts implicate more than a victim's own wishes or even the court's authority. Also, the legislature is presumed to have expressed its intent through the language of the statute. Its decision to criminalize a violation of a PFA order reflects a concern for the public peace. Persons granted a PFA order have already proven "the allegation of abuse by a preponderance of the evidence" on a prior occasion. Nothing in the language of K.S.A.2005 suggests a legislative intent to excuse an abuser just because the victim later consents to contact in violation of the PFA order. The legislature saw fit to provide for court supervision over the parties, and that supervision continues until the PFA order is modified or dismissed. In context, then, we deem Branson's act here that was contrary to the court's supervision to be of sufficient threat to the public peace that the act is criminal regardless of consent. . . .

Notes and Questions

1. *Holding.* What were the provisions of Hird's order of protection? How did Branson violate the order? How did the police discover the violation? Had he violated a protective order in the past? How? How did Hird "consent" to his violation of the order? Why didn't she call the police when he did so? What do you think she should have done? What is Branson's defense?

2. *Rationale.* What is the rationale for the imposition of criminal liability for violation of a protection order *despite* the victim's consent, according to the court?

3. *Statutory treatment.* What did the Kansas statute in *Branson* provide about whether consent was a defense to a violation of a protection order? Some states explicitly provide that the victim's consent is *not* a defense. See, e.g., Alaska Stat. §18.66.130(d)(2) ("an invitation by petitioner to have the prohibited contact . . . does not in any way invalidate or nullify the order"). See also State of Alaska v. Strane, 61 P.3d 1284 (Alaska 2003). In light of *Branson*, should more states enact similar statutes?

4. *Notice.* Does the order of protection in *Branson* provide sufficient notice that the victim's consent will *not* relieve the defendant of liability for violation of the order? Compare the language in the following statute applicable to orders of protection:

> You can be arrested even if the person or persons who obtained the order invite or allow you to violate the order's prohibitions. The respondent has the sole responsibility to avoid or refrain from violating the order's provisions. Only the court can change the order upon written application.

Wash. Rev. Code §26.50.035(1)(c). Should final orders of protection contain the above language?

5. *Policy.* The role of the victim in the law's response to domestic violence policy is a controversial topic. What role should be accorded to victims' preferences in the process of initiation, renewal, vacating, and violation of civil protective orders? Should deference vary according to the respective context? Does giving voice to the victim's preference in each context empower or disempower her? What are other benefits and detriments of giving voice to the victim's preference?

See generally Margaret E. Johnson, Redefining Harm, Reimagining Remedies, and Reclaiming Domestic Violence Law, 42 U.C. Davis L. Rev. 1107 (2009) (suggesting that listening to the woman's narrative would help establish her autonomy from her abuser).

3. *Victim's Request to Withdraw*

■ JAMES C. ROBERTS ET AL., WHY VICTIMS OF INTIMATE PARTNER VIOLENCE WITHDRAW PROTECTION ORDERS
23 J. Fam. Violence 369, 371-373 (2008)

[Sociologists conducted a study of 55 battered women who withdrew orders of protection from 2005-2006 to explore their reasons for withdrawal of the orders.] The most common individual reasons women reported for withdrawing a [Protection from Abuse order or PFA] were: (1) the plaintiff was no longer afraid of the defendant (35 percent); (2) the defendant was attending counseling or some type of treatment program (29 percent); (3) the defendant promised to change (26 percent); (4) the defendant was missed by his (or the plaintiff's) children (15 percent); and (5) the plaintiff needed the defendant for financial reasons (13 percent). Sixteen women reported withdrawing a PFA for other reasons, including: getting married, the desire to resolve the situation without a court order, having a child in common with the defendant, and the desire to "start over again" with the defendant.

The [reason] most frequently cited as a reason for PFA withdrawal was a concrete change in the situation (55 percent), followed very closely by emotional reasons (53 percent). . . . [E]conomic resources was a very distant fourth (13 percent) reason for withdrawal, preceded by family concerns (26 percent). Further, while almost two-thirds of these respondents only cited one [reason] (64 percent), when more than one was cited, the combination of concrete change and emotional attachment was the most frequently cited (14.5 percent of all respondents). . . .

[Concrete changes] involved a victim or defendant moving to another area, separation or divorce between the two parties, and/or the defendant attending counseling or rehabilitation. All of these actions involved either a concrete change in situation (e.g., someone moving), or a concrete, conscientious action on behalf of the defendant to change his behavior (e.g., getting counseling) that lead the victim to no longer feel that the PFA was necessary to protect her. Within the change [reason], the defendant attending counseling or rehabilitation was the individual reason most frequently mentioned (29.1 of the respondents), thereby suggesting a faith in the success of batterer intervention programs or counseling. . . .

[A goal of the study was to determine if resources may have prevented women from withdrawing PFAs.] [T]here is currently a debate as to whether women return to abusers because of emotional attachment or whether they return because they lack various resources (such as money, shelter, etc.) that an abuser may possess. Our results indicate that, overwhelmingly, the women in this sample did not feel that the provision of resources would have altered their decision. . . .

F. EFFECTIVENESS

This section explores the effectiveness of orders of protection. The excerpts explore effectiveness in terms of both deterrence and victim satisfaction.

■ **ANDREW R. KLEIN, NAT'L INST. OF JUSTICE, SPECIAL REPORT: PRACTICAL IMPLICATIONS OF CURRENT DOMESTIC VIOLENCE RESEARCH**
58-59 (June 2009), available at **http://www.ncjrs.gov/pdffiles1/nij/ grants/222319.pdf**

DO PROTECTIVE ORDERS WORK?

. . . [I]n terms of their effectiveness in deterring repeat abuse, before and after studies suggest that protective orders may deter certain abusers. In Travis County, Texas, over a period of two years before and after order issuance, physical abuse dropped from 68 percent to 23 percent after the orders were obtained, if victims maintained the order. If the abusers were also arrested at the time of the order issuance, the physical abuse diminished further; if they had children, it diminished less. These studies cannot reveal whether or not the abuse would have naturally declined over time without the orders because, for example, the victims are more likely to have left their abusers when they obtained the orders.

Several Seattle studies compared women who obtained orders to women who were abused (as indicated by a police incident report) but did not obtain orders. They found that women with permanent orders were less likely to be physically abused than women without them. However, women who had temporary orders that lasted only two weeks were more likely to be psychologically abused than women who did not obtain any orders. The women who did not obtain orders appeared at higher risk for abuse, involvement with alcohol and drugs, more likely to have been assaulted and injured as a result of the study incident, and less likely to have been married to their abuser. The study did not look at violations of protective orders that did not involve physical assaults. The second Seattle study found that the orders were more effective nine months after they were obtained than during the first five-month period, significantly reducing the likelihood of contact, threats with weapons, injuries and the need for medical care. . . .

At least one study suggests that the specific stipulations of the protective orders may make a difference. Specifically, victims are more likely to be reabused if their orders bar abusive contact but not all contact. Compared to women whose orders barred all contact, those that barred only abusive contact were significantly more likely to suffer psychological violence, physical violence, sexual coercion and injuries within one year.

Nonetheless, the research consistently finds that victims largely express satisfaction with civil orders, even if they are violated by their abusers. In the multisite study in Massachusetts, 86 percent of the women who obtained a permanent order said that the order either stopped or reduced the abuse, notwithstanding the fact that 59 percent called police to report an order violation. Upon further questioning, the women expressed the feeling that the order demonstrated to the abuser that the "law was on her side." In a multistate study, victims who obtained orders reported that the orders improved their overall well-being, especially if the abuser had a prior criminal history and was more likely to reabuse. It may be that, even though orders do not stop abuse, they reduce the severity of the reabuse. Alternatively, although they may not affect the extent of reabuse, protective orders make victims feel vindicated and empowered.

Although not studied directly, it appears to be significantly easier for law enforcement to monitor and enforce protective and no-contact orders than to monitor and interrupt abuse in general. This may explain why abusers are significantly more likely to be arrested for protective order violations than other common domestic violence offenses. The rearrest rate for abusers in Rhode Island initially arrested for violation of protection or no-contact orders was 45.6 percent over one year, compared to 37.6 percent for domestic assaults, disorderly conduct or vandalism. Of course, it may also be the case that abusers with orders are generally at higher risk for reabusing than abusers without orders.

Victims should be encouraged to take out protective orders and retain them but should also be advised that the orders do not deter all abusers and may be more effective when accompanied by criminal prosecution of the abuser . . .

■ SALLY F. GOLDFARB, RECONCEIVING CIVIL PROTECTION ORDERS FOR DOMESTIC VIOLENCE: CAN LAW HELP END THE ABUSE WITHOUT ENDING THE RELATIONSHIP?

29 Cardozo L. Rev. 1487, 1510-1515 (2008)

. . . Empirical studies have consistently shown a high level of satisfaction among women who have obtained protection orders. For example, in a study conducted in three jurisdictions by the National Center for State Courts, over eighty-five percent of women who had obtained protection orders six months earlier felt their lives had improved since getting the order, and over eighty percent felt safer. Similarly, a Wisconsin study found a victim satisfaction rate of eighty-six percent, with half of the women reporting that they were very satisfied; ninety-four percent felt that their decision to obtain a protection order was a good one. A study conducted in Colorado reported that one year after receiving a protection order, eighty-four percent of women felt somewhat safe or very safe from physical harm and seventy-two percent felt somewhat safe or very safe from harassment. In a study based on interviews with clients of family violence agencies in four states, seventy-two percent of the women who obtained protection orders rated them as "somewhat effective" or "very effective" in preventing further abuse and violence.

Satisfaction with protection orders is not evenly distributed among all groups of women. Significantly, in the Wisconsin study, satisfaction rates were higher among women who wanted to end the relationship than among those who wanted to continue it or were ambivalent. This indicates that the protection orders examined in that study, which were apparently all stay-away orders, did not meet the needs of women who wanted to maintain their relationships. Indeed, many women who are not ready to end a relationship do not seek a protection order at all or fail to complete the process of obtaining one; they thus opt out of the protection order system before their satisfaction can be measured.

The results of studies measuring continuation of abuse and violations of protection orders are more mixed. . . . Some studies report significantly reduced rates
of violence and/or relatively high rates of compliance following issuance of a protection order. A study based on interviews with battered women in Seattle found a
decrease of seventy percent in the occurrence of physical violence in a nine-month
period among women who received protection orders in comparison to those who
did not receive them. In addition to the reduction in physical violence, this study
also showed that women with orders were less likely than those without orders to
experience all other forms of abuse except unwanted calls. Similarly, a Texas study
showed that women who applied for protection orders reported a significant reduction in average levels of violence during the year following their application, and
those who actually received the order reported less violence than qualified applicants who did not receive an order. The National Center for State Courts study
found that after three months, seventy-two percent of women who had received
protection orders reported having "no problems" with the abuser, and after six
months, sixty-five percent had no problems.

However, in other studies, the reported rates of re-abuse and non-compliance
were higher. For example, in the Colorado study, sixty percent of women who
obtained orders reported abuse by the man named in the order during the
following year; by far the most frequently reported type of abuse was psychological
abuse. A Massachusetts study found that forty-nine percent of offenders re-abused
their victims within two years of issuance of a protection order. In the study of family
violence agency clients in four states, twenty-four percent of the women who had
obtained protection orders experienced physical violence within four months after
obtaining the order and fifty-six percent experienced non-physical abuse.

According to the Wisconsin study, women were at higher risk for non-
compliance with the protection order if they did not want to end the relationship
or were ambivalent about it. Much of the non-compliance took the form of violations of prohibitions on contact. Thus, it appears that protection orders purporting
to terminate contact between the parties are more likely to be violated if the victim is
not sure that she wants to sever ties with her partner.

Characteristics Affecting Compliance with Protection Orders

Empirical research indicates that characteristics of the batterer and the relationship can affect rates of compliance. Batterers are not all the same; some of them
are more likely than others to violate an order. According to the Massachusetts
study, abusers with records of criminal activity re-abused their victims more than
those without criminal records; the probability of re-abuse increased for those with
more recent and more extensive criminal records. Other studies reached comparable results. These findings are consistent with the theory that obedience to the law
is reduced among members of society who have the least to lose from the social
consequences of criminal sanctions. A similar pattern emerged in studies of the
effects of arresting batterers, which found that arrest had a stronger deterrent effect
among men who were married and employed than among those who were
unmarried, unemployed and lived in poor, high-crime neighborhoods. Currently,
a high percentage of batterers who are the subjects of protection orders have prior
criminal records and other characteristics indicating a heightened risk of recidivism. A protection order alone is relatively unlikely to deter these offenders from
further abuse. . . . Another factor that is associated with violations of protection

orders is the history of abuse in the relationship. The Colorado study found that the recurrence of abuse in the year following the granting of a protection order was significantly related to the type and severity of abuse that occurred in the year before the order was issued. In addition, the abuser's level of resistance to the protection order at the time of the hearing was a strong predictor of post-order abuse. These criteria may provide valuable assistance in predicting which cases are most likely to result in non-compliance with the order and therefore most in need of additional safeguards.

Reconciling the Disparity Between Rates of Victim Satisfaction and Batterer Compliance: The Importance of Empowering Battered Women

What can explain the fact that according to these empirical studies, the number of women satisfied with their protection orders exceeds the number whose orders have not been violated? One possible explanation is that even though an order has been violated, the amount and severity of abuse is lower than before the order was issued. Thus, the women's level of satisfaction reflects the fact that while the abuse has not been eliminated, it has been reduced.

Another explanation is that rates of compliance and re-abuse are not the only valid ways to measure the success of protection orders. Although ensuring women's safety from violence is one crucial function of protection orders, enabling battered women to exercise their autonomy is another. For many women, obtaining a protection order is deeply empowering because it entails asserting one's own needs, standing up to the abuser, and enlisting a potent institutional ally. This empowerment can be a major step in the process of ending the abuse. One woman who obtained an order said, "After so long of just taking it and taking it[,] I needed to be able to show myself as much as show him that I was tired of being a victim. . . . [T]hat feeling, of fighting back and speaking out, will never leave me."

By breaking the silence about the abuse and creating a public record of what has been hidden in private, battered women can regain a sense of control, which in turn enables them to take further steps toward improving their lives. In addition to giving the woman a chance to speak out, the protection order operates as an amplifier for her voice; it unequivocally communicates to the batterer that his behavior is unacceptable and that society condemns domestic violence. In light of these considerable benefits, it is not surprising that many battered women find that the process of obtaining a protection order is "its own reward." . . .

Notes and Questions

1. *Early studies.* Early statistics on the effectiveness of domestic violence protection orders tended to cast doubt on their ability to help victims of domestic violence. For example, a study based on 350 women who filed petitions for TROs in 1991 in two jurisdictions found that 60 percent of the protective orders were violated within one year of their issuance. Adele Harrell & Barbara E. Smith, Effects of Restraining Orders on Domestic Violence Victims, in Do Arrests and Restraining Orders Work? 240 (Eve S. Buzawa & Carl G. Buzawa eds., 1996). Such research led some commentators to dub civil protective orders mere "paper protections." Lynn D. Wardle, Marriage and Domestic Violence in the United States: New Perspectives about Legal Strategies to Combat Domestic Violence, 15 St. Thomas L. Rev. 791, 799

(2003). What light do later studies shed on the effectiveness of restraining orders? One major study documenting the effectiveness of restraining orders (referred to by Klein above) involved approximately 2,700 women residents of Seattle, who reported incidents of domestic violence. The study compared women who did *not* obtain a protection order after the incident, those who obtained only a *temporary* order (effective for two weeks), and those who obtained a *permanent* order (effective for one year). The researchers found that women with permanent orders were less likely than those without permanent orders to be physically abused in the six-month follow-up period. They concluded that "permanent, but not temporary, protection orders are associated with a significant decrease in risk of police-reported violence against women by their male intimate partners." Victoria Holt et al., Civil Protection Orders and Risk of Subsequent Police-Reported Violence, 288 JAMA 589 (2002). What do you think explains this result?

2. *Measures of effectiveness.* How can the effectiveness of restraining orders be measured? What are the advantages and disadvantages of using such measures as deterrence, prosecution rates for violations, and victim satisfaction? What other measures might be used? What can you conclude from the above studies about the success of deterrence and the level of victim satisfaction with protection orders? How do the characteristics of abusers affect compliance rates, according to Goldfarb?

3. *Consequences of violation.* The NIJ report above suggests that while protective orders may have some deterrent effect, they are most effective when combined with criminal prosecution. Do you agree? For exploration of the criminal law response to domestic violence, see Chapters 5 to 7.

4. *Terms in a protective order.* The NIJ report does not delve into why protective orders may be effective, although it does suggest that the permanency of the order makes some difference. What aspects of protective orders might make them more or less effective? How should judges take this information into account in framing a protective order?

5. *Enforcement.* How does a victim with a protective order seek criminal enforcement of that order? Is the onus on the victim of abuse or police officers to enforce violations of these orders? What policies help increase enforcement of protective orders? On mandatory arrest and no-drop policies, see Chapter 5. How might legislators help increase the effectiveness of protective orders? What procedures can courts develop to make it easier to for victims to obtain protective orders and for prosecutors to prosecute abusers who violate or repeatedly violate those orders?

6. *Victim perceptions.* How do *victims* perceive the effectiveness of restraining orders, based on the above excerpts? What factors might lead a woman to view a protective order as a positive action, even if it does not necessarily stop the abuse? See Carolyn N. Ko, Note, Civil Restraining Orders for Domestic Violence: The Unresolved Question of "Efficacy," 11 S. Cal. Interdisc. L.J. 361, 368-372 (2002) (considering the impact of obtaining a restraining order on victims' psychological well-being). How do victims perceive the judicial system's handling of protective orders, both in terms of issuing them and prosecuting their violations? What factors might explain a victim's frustration with the legal system in terms of the enforcement of protection orders? How can the legal system's response be improved?

X

Tort Remedies

Victims of domestic violence sometimes resort to tort remedies for the harm that is inflicted upon them by their abusers. This chapter explores the nature of these tort remedies as well as the effectiveness of the tort system as a means of compensation for domestic violence.

A. STATE CAUSES OF ACTION

1. *Against the Abuser*

■ **FELTMEIER v. FELTMEIER**
798 N.E.2d 75 (Ill. 2003)

Justice RARICK delivered the opinion of the court:

Plaintiff, Lynn Feltmeier, and defendant, Robert Feltmeier, were married on October 11, 1986, and divorced on December 16, 1997. [O]n August 25, 1999, Lynn sued Robert for the intentional infliction of emotional distress. . . . The first matter before us for review is whether Lynn's complaint states a cause of action for intentional infliction of emotional distress. . . . According to the allegations contained in Lynn's complaint, since the parties' marriage in October 1986, and continuing for over a year after the December 1997 dissolution of their marriage: "[Robert] entered into a continuous and outrageous course of conduct toward [Lynn] with either the intent to cause emotional distress to [Lynn] or with reckless disregard as to whether such conduct would cause emotional distress to [Lynn], said continuing course of conduct, including but not limited to, the following:

A. On repeated occasions, [Robert] has battered [Lynn] by striking, kicking, shoving, pulling hair and bending and twisting her limbs and toes. . . .

B. On repeated occasions, [Robert] has prevented [Lynn] from leaving the house to escape the abuse. . . .

C. On repeated occasions, [Robert] has yelled insulting and demeaning epithets at [Lynn]. Further, [Robert] has engaged in verbal abuse which included threats and constant criticism of [Lynn] in such a way as to demean, humiliate, and degrade [Lynn]. . . .

D. On repeated occasions, [Robert] threw items at [Lynn] with the intent to cause her harm. . . .

E. On repeated occasions, [Robert] attempted to isolate [Lynn] from her family and friends and would get very upset if [Lynn] would show the marks and bruises resulting from [Robert's] abuse to others.

F. On repeated occasions since the divorce, [Robert] engaged in stalking behavior. . . .

G. On at least one occasion, [Robert] has attempted to interfere with [Lynn's] employment by confiscating her computer. Additionally, [Robert] broke into [Lynn's] locked drug cabinet for work on or about March 23, 1997.

[The court then sets forth the elements for intentional infliction of emotional distress: The conduct must be extreme and outrageous; the actor must either intend that his conduct inflict severe emotional distress, or know that there is at least a high probability that his conduct will cause severe emotional distress; and the conduct must in fact cause severe emotional distress.]

In the case at bar, Robert first contends that the allegations of Lynn's complaint do not sufficiently set forth conduct which was extreme and outrageous when considered "[i]n the context of the subjective and fluctuating nature of the marital relationship." . . .

[O]ur examination of both the law of this state and the most commonly raised policy concerns leads us to conclude that no valid reason exists to restrict such actions or to require a heightened threshold for outrageousness in this context.

One policy concern that has been advanced is the need to recognize the "mutual concessions implicit in marriage," and the desire to preserve marital harmony. However, in this case, brought after the parties were divorced, "there is clearly no marital harmony remaining to be preserved." Moreover, we agree with the Supreme Judicial Court of Maine that "behavior that is 'utterly intolerable in a civilized society' and is intended to cause severe emotional distress is not behavior that should be protected in order to promote marital harmony and peace." [Henriksen v. Cameron, 622 A.2d 1135, 1139 (Me. 1993)]. Indeed, the Illinois legislature, in creating the Illinois Domestic Violence Act of 1986 (Act) (750 ILCS 60/101 et seq. (West 2002)), has recognized that domestic violence is "a serious crime against the individual and society." . . . Thus, it would seem that the public policy of this state would be furthered by recognition of the action at issue.

A second policy concern is the threat of excessive and frivolous litigation if the tort is extended to acts occurring in the marital setting. Admittedly, the likelihood of vindictive litigation is of particular concern following a dissolution of marriage, because "the events leading to most divorces involve some level of emotional distress." *Henriksen*, 622 A.2d at 1139. However, we believe that the showing required of a plaintiff in order to recover damages for intentional infliction of emotional distress provides a built-in safeguard against excessive and frivolous litigation. . . .

Another policy consideration which has been raised is that a tort action for compensation would be redundant. [However,] the laws of this state provide no compensatory relief for injuries sustained [here]. An action for dissolution of marriage also provides no compensatory relief for domestic abuse. In Illinois, as in most other states, courts are not allowed to consider marital misconduct in the distribution of property when dissolving a marriage. See 750 ILCS 5/503(d).

After examining case law from courts around the country, we find the majority have recognized that public policy considerations should not bar actions for intentional infliction of emotional distress between spouses or former spouses based on conduct occurring during the marriage. . . . Further, [in prior case law] this court identified several factors that may be considered in determining whether a defendant's conduct is extreme and outrageous. We find the *McGrath* [v. Fahey, 533 N.E.2d 806 (Ill. 1988)] court's comments regarding one such factor to be particularly relevant when examining, as alleged herein, outrageous conduct in the light of the marital relationship:

> It is thus clear . . . that the degree of power or authority which a defendant has over a plaintiff can impact upon whether that defendant's conduct is outrageous. The more control which a defendant has over the plaintiff, the more likely that defendant's conduct will be deemed outrageous, particularly when the alleged conduct involves either a veiled or explicit threat to exercise such authority or power to plaintiff's detriment. Threats, for example, are much more likely to be a part of outrageous conduct when made by someone with the ability to carry them out than when made by someone in a comparatively weak position.

[*McGrath*, 533 N.E.2d at 809.]

Indeed, Illinois cases in which the tort of intentional infliction of emotional distress has been sufficiently alleged have very frequently involved a defendant who stood in a position of power or authority relative to the plaintiff. While these past cases have generally involved abuses of power by employers, creditors, or financial institutions, we see no reason to exclude the defendant at issue here, a spouse/former spouse, from the many types of individuals who may be positioned to exercise power over a plaintiff. . . .

[W]e now examine the allegations set forth in Lynn's complaint to determine whether Robert's conduct satisfies the "outrageousness" requirement . . . Robert contends that "Lynn's allegations are not sufficiently repeated and pervasive so as to justify a claim for intentional infliction of emotional distress." . . .

The issue of whether domestic abuse can be sufficiently outrageous to sustain a cause of action for intentional infliction of emotional distress is apparently one of first impression in Illinois. Other jurisdictions, however, have found similar allegations of recurring cycles of physical and verbal abuse, wherein the conduct went far beyond the "trials of everyday life between two cohabiting people," to be sufficiently outrageous to fall within the parameters of section 46 of the Restatement (Second) of Torts. In the instant case, we must agree with the appellate court that, when the above-summarized allegations of the complaint are viewed in their entirety, they show a type of domestic abuse that is extreme enough to be actionable. . . .

It combines more than a decade of verbal insults and humiliations with episodes where freedom of movement was deprived and where physical injury was often inflicted. The alleged pattern of abuse, combined with its duration, worked a humiliation and loss of self-esteem. Regardless of the form in which it arrived, violence was certain to erupt, and when seasons of spousal abuse turn to years that span the course of a decade, we are unwilling to dismiss it on grounds that it is unworthy of outrage.

[*Feltmeier*, 777 N.E.2d 1032, 1040 (Ill. App. Ct. 2002)].

Therefore, where we find that a reasonable trier of fact could easily conclude that Robert's conduct was so outrageous as to be regarded as intolerable in a civilized community, we reject his contention that the complaint fails to sufficiently allege this element.

[Next,] Robert does contest the adequacy of the complaint as to the third necessary element, that his conduct in fact caused severe emotional distress. He argues that Lynn's complaint "contains no factual allegations from which the level of severity of the emotional distress could be inferred." We must disagree.

Lynn's complaint specifically alleges that, "[a]s a direct and proximate result of the entirety of [Robert's] course of conduct, [she] has sustained severe emotional distress including, but not limited to[,] loss of self-esteem and difficulty in forming other relationships, and a form of Post Traumatic Stress Disorder sustained by battered and abused women as a result of being repeatedly physically and verbally abused and harassed over a long period of time." The complaint also alleges that Lynn has suffered depression and a "fear of being with other men," and that her enjoyment of life has been substantially curtailed. Finally, it is alleged that Lynn has incurred, and will continue to incur, medical and psychological expenses in an effort to become cured or relieved from the effects of her mental distress.

Emotional distress includes all highly unpleasant mental reactions, such as fright, horror, grief, shame, humiliation, embarrassment, anger, chagrin, disappointment, worry, and nausea. See Restatement (Second) of Torts §46, Comment j, at 77 (1965). "'The law intervenes only where the distress inflicted is so severe that no reasonable man could be expected to endure it. The intensity and duration of the distress are factors to be considered in determining its severity.' Restatement (Second) of Torts §46, comment j, at 77-78 (1965)." . . . Here, we find that Lynn has sufficiently alleged that as a result of enduring Robert's physical and psychological abuse for the duration of their 11-year marriage and beyond, she suffered severe emotional distress. Therefore, where the complaint sets forth sufficient facts which, if proven, could entitle Lynn to relief, we conclude that she has stated a cause of action for intentional infliction of emotional distress. . . .

[The court also considered whether evidence of some abusive acts was barred by the applicable statute of limitations. That issue is discussed later in this chapter, pp. 517-522.]

Notes and Questions

1. *Traditional tort claims.* In *Feltmeier*, Lynn sues Robert for intentional infliction of emotional distress (IIED). A number of traditional torts may be relevant in the

context of domestic violence, including: assault, battery, conversion of property, defamation, false imprisonment, fraud, and IIED.

2. *Influential factors in law reform.* Several factors contributed to the expansion of tort liability for acts of domestic violence, including: the abolition of interspousal immunity, recognition and extension of tort liability for emotional injury generally, growing public awareness of domestic violence, and the demise of fault-based divorce.

3. *Restatement (Second) of Torts.* The Restatement (Second) of Torts facilitated the recognition and extension of tort liability for emotional injury. Most courts follow the Second Restatement's requirements that (1) the abusive conduct must be *extreme and outrageous* and (2) the plaintiff must suffer *severe* emotional distress. See Restatement (Second) of Torts §46 (1965). The former requirement focuses on the tortfeasor's conduct; the latter requirement focuses on the effect of that conduct on the plaintiff. The Restatement (Third) of Torts: Liability for Physical and Emotional Harm (§§45-47), currently in draft form, continues the recognition of pure emotional distress claims. See generally Martha Chamallas, Unpacking Emotional Distress, Sexual Exploitation, Reproductive Harm and Fundamental Rights, 44 Wake Forest L. Rev. 1109 (2009); Geoffrey Christopher Rapp, Defense Against Outrage and the Perils of Parasitic Torts, 45 Ga. L. Rev. 107, 110 (2010) (noting "The universal acceptance of the Restatement version of intentional infliction of emotional distress").

4. *Purposes of tort liability.* What purposes are served by allowing spouses to seek liability for interspousal torts? One commentator suggests the following:

> First, torts provide monetary redress for extraordinary and outrageous harms between spouses that would be recoverable as between strangers. Domestic abuse should not be privileged from litigation. Second, a tort remedy is more appropriate given contemporary societal norms that support a focus on protecting caregivers and children in the divorce process. Third, the power of torts should be wielded to counter gendered harms.

Pamela Laufer-Ukeles, Reconstructing Fault: The Case for Spousal Torts, 79 U. Cin. L. Rev. 207, 254 (2010). Can you think of other reasons to allow interspousal tort claims for acts of domestic violence? See Sarah M. Buel, Access to Meaningful Remedy: Overcoming Doctrinal Obstacles in Tort Litigation Against Domestic Violence Offenders, 83 Or. L. Rev. 945, 948-949 (2004) (discussing purposes of tort system).

5. *Tort liability and intimate relationships.* Should the legal system allow claims for IIED in the context of intimate relationships? What are the implications of allowing tort suits in this context? Does the allowance of tort liability "risk elevating all dysfunctional domestic relationships into potential damages actions"? Lyman v. Huber, 10 A.3d 707, 714 (Me. 2010). *Lyman* suggests that a victim of domestic violence has an adequate *alternative* remedy, a civil protection order. Do you agree? On what basis does *Feltmeier* decide to recognize such tort suits in the marital context? How relevant is it that at the time of *Feltmeier*, Illinois did not offer an independent tort remedy for domestic violence?

Are there arguments for recognition of IIED, but not *negligent* infliction of emotional distress claims, in the context of intimate partner violence? See Twyman v. Twyman, 855 S.W.2d 619, 621-624 (Tex. 1993) (explaining policy rationale for recognition of IIED but not NIED).

6. *Limitation to criminal acts.* Should IIED be recognized only for claims in which the tortious conduct is also a criminal act? Two legal scholars make this proposal, stemming from their belief that broad recognition of spousal-IIED claims interferes with the fundamental policy of no-fault divorce. Ira Mark Ellman & Stephen D. Sugarman, Spousal Emotional Abuse as a Tort?, 55 Md. L. Rev. 1268, 1343 (1996). They elaborate that "our list of actionable spousal torts includes battery, certain assaults (including attempted murder), and false arrest or imprisonment. Our list would not, however, include the most conventional tort of assault—threatened battery." Id. at 1335. Do you agree? Recall the range of intimate partner violence (Chapter 2). What types of conduct should be covered by IIED claims? Cf. Chamallas, supra (arguing for greater recognition of sexual abuse in emotional distress claims).

7. *Absence of physical injury.* For a time, some courts refused to permit suits for emotional distress in the divorce context absent physical injury or physical symptoms. See, e.g., Chiles v. Chiles, 779 S.W.2d 127, 131-132 (Tex. 1989) (subsequently overruled). What is the rationale for this view? Is it persuasive?

Courts gradually abrogated the physical injury requirement for both IIED and NIED claims. Rapp, supra, at 111. Cf. Ruprecht v. Ruprecht, 599 A.2d 604, 606 (N.J. Super. Ct. Chan. Div. 1991) (reasoning that "There is no valid policy interest nor logical reason to allow one spouse to sue the other for physical injury but not for emotional distress absent physical injury. Certainly mental and emotional distress is just as 'real' as physical pain"). However, without physical injury, some courts still require physical symptoms of emotional distress to sustain both intentional and negligent infliction of emotional distress claims. See, e.g., Thomas v. Phone Directories Co., 996 F. Supp. 1364 (D. Utah 1998) (negligent); Langeslag v. KYMN Inc., 664 N.W.2d 860, 868-869 (Minn. 2003) (intentional).

The Restatement (Second) of Torts paved the way for recovery for pure emotional distress claims. According to Restatement commentary:

> k. *Bodily harm.* Normally, severe emotional distress is accompanied or followed by shock, illness, or other bodily harm, which in itself affords evidence that the distress is genuine and severe. The rule stated is not, however, limited to cases where there has been bodily harm; and if the conduct is sufficiently extreme and outrageous there may be liability for the emotional distress alone, without such harm. In such cases, the courts may perhaps tend to look for more in the way of outrage as a guarantee that the claim is genuine; but if the enormity of the outrage carries conviction that there has in fact been severe emotional distress, bodily harm is not required.

Restatement (Second) Torts §46 cmt. k (1965). See also William J. Koch, Psychological Injuries, Forensic Assessment, Treatment and Law 24 (2006) ("until the 1948 supplement to the Restatement (Second) of Torts, recovery for psychological injury was *only* possible through parasitic means," that is, if the psychological injury was caused by another intentional tort, such as battery).

8. *Novel torts.* Beginning in the 1990s, in response to battered women's advocates' concerns about the inadequacy of existing remedies for domestic violence, commentators proposed the creation of new torts. See, e.g., Buel, Access to Meaningful Remedy, supra; Clare Dalton, Domestic Violence, Domestic Torts, and Divorce: Constraints and Possibilities, 31 New Eng. L. Rev. 319 (1997); Heather Tonsing, Battered Women Syndrome as a Tort Cause of Action, 12 J.L. & Health

407 (1998). A few courts and legislatures took up the call and began recognizing "domestic torts." See, e.g., Jewitt v. Jewitt, No. 93-2-01846-5 (Wash. Super. Ct., June 16, 1994); Cusseaux v. Pickett, 652 A. 789 (N.J. Super. Ct. Law Div. 1994). For discussion of these early cases, see Jason Palmer, Eleventh Annual Review of Gender and Sexuality Law: Criminal Law Chapter: Domestic Violence, 11 Geo. J. Gender & L. 97 (2010); Mercedes Fort, Casenote, A New Tort: Domestic Violence Gets the Status it Deserves in Jewitt v. Jewitt, 21 S. Ill. U. L.J. 355 (1997).

9. *Statutorily-created novel torts.* Some states created new domestic violence torts by statute. See, e.g., Cal. Civ. Code §1708.6. In enacting the new tort, the California legislature noted: "It is the purpose of this act to enhance the civil remedies available to victims of domestic violence in order to underscore society's condemnation of these acts, to ensure complete recovery to victims, and to impose significant financial consequences upon perpetrators." Stats. 2002, c. 193, §1 (A.B. 1933). One legal scholar elaborates on the purposes underlying new tort remedies:

> Although the injuries of abuse can be captured quite successfully through existing causes of action . . . , an argument can be made for creating a new tort of "partner abuse," which would allow the entire history of combined physical and emotional abuse to be presented to the court in support of a single claim. Recognition of this cause of action, which would in turn support the presentation of cases not as a collection of unfortunate incidents, but as a coherent narrative of domestic abuse, might advance the goal of improving understanding of domestic violence among both lawyers and judges.

Dalton, supra, at 344-345. The tort of domestic violence is discussed in more detail later in this chapter, pp. 520-521.

10. *Feltmeier Holding.*

a. *Was the abuse "extreme and outrageous"?* In the principal case, Robert first contends that his ex-wife's allegations do not set forth conduct which was sufficiently extreme and outrageous when considered "in the context of the subjective and fluctuating nature of the marital relationship." At trial, Robert had contended that:

> [A]ny objectively reasonable woman could have endured the abuse that he is alleged to have administered, without suffering severe emotional distress. He maintains that his alleged misconduct, having taken place in the context of an 11-year marriage, was neither extreme nor outrageous. At oral argument, in an effort to minimize the abusive conduct that Lynn alleged and in order to demonstrate that it was not extreme, Robert's attorney looked at the number of alleged acts and argued that the abuse claimed occurred only three or four times per year over the course of the marriage. The argument suggested that one beating a year, coupled with an act of physical restraint or an annual pelting from flying missiles, when spread out over an 11-year span, constituted marital conduct that any reasonable wife should be able to endure without suffering emotional distress.

Feltmeier, 777 N.E.2d at 1039. What factors does Robert use to trivialize the abuse? How persuasive are his arguments?

b. *High threshold?* What are the justifications for a high threshold for extreme and outrageous behavior in the marital context? Cf. McCulloh v. Drake, 24

P.3d 1162, 1169-1170 (Wyo. 2001) (setting high standard for recovery precludes "an invasive flood of meritless litigation" and protects defendants from the *possibility* of "long and intrusive trials on frivolous claims"). Is a high standard contrary to public policy? See Recent Development, Interspousal Torts: A Procedural Framework for Hawai'i, 19 U. Haw. L. Rev. 377, 389-390 (1997) (so suggesting). See also Tiffany Oliver, Note, Intentional Infliction of Emotional Distress Between Spouses: New Mexico's Excessively High Threshold for Outrageous Conduct, 33 N.M. L. Rev. 381 (2003).

What strategic difficulties does adoption of a high standard pose for intimate partners? See Kathleen L. Daerr-Bannon, Cause of Action in Tort for Spousal Abuse, 41 Causes of Action 2d 407, §7 (2009) (explaining the subjectivity of the standard, its difficulty of measurement, and its "residual cultural bias minimizing abuse or violence in the marital context, perhaps especially when conduct is directed toward a woman").

c. *Severity of the emotional distress.* In *Feltmeier*, the defendant argues that even if his allegedly abusive conduct caused his wife's emotional distress, his acts did not cause the requisite severity of harm. How does the court respond? How can plaintiffs prove the requisite cause, effect, and severity of the inflicted harm? Can the severity be established without the corroborating testimony of an expert medical or psychological witness? See *Lyman*, 10 A.3d at 713. What physical and/or psychological symptoms reveal the severity of a plaintiff's emotional distress? See Friedman & DiMaure, supra (discussing symptoms of severe depression).

d. *Post-traumatic stress disorder (PTSD).* One of Lynn's experts, a psychologist, testified that Lynn suffered from PTSD. He explained that the PTSD resulted from the entire series of her husband's abusive acts, not just one specific incident. *Feltmeier*, 777 N.E.2d at 1044. How does PTSD affect victims of intimate partner violence? Must PTSD be the result of a long period of violence or can it result from a sudden event? PTSD is also a psychological consequence of military service. See generally Loring Jones et al., Post-Traumatic Stress Disorder (PTSD) in Victims of Domestic Violence: A Review of Research, 2 Trauma Violence, & Abuse 99 (2001).

11. *Comparative contexts. Feltmeier* compares IIED in different relationships that involve power differentials. In the determination of "extreme and outrageous" conduct, how is abuse inflicted by an employer similar to, and different from, abuse by an intimate partner? What level of emotional distress should be acceptable in work relationships? In intimate relationships? What light does *Feltmeier* shed on this comparison?

12. *Continuing tort.* How influential in *Feltmeier* was the court's determination that the "extreme and outrageous" element was the fact that the husband's conduct constituted a *pattern* or a *continuing course of conduct* rather than separate instances of abusive behavior? *Feltmeier* adopted the "continuing tort theory" to hold that the husband's acts constituted a continuous series of acts for purposes of surmounting the two-year limitations period. This theory and the topic of statutes of limitations are discussed later in this chapter, pp. 517-522.

13. *Subjective versus objective standard?* According to the general rule, in the determination of IIED, a tortfeasor's conduct is judged by an objective standard. The conduct must be sufficiently severe as to cause substantial emotional distress to an *average person.* See Howard Friedman & Charles J. DiMaure, Strategies in Litigating Intentional Tort Cases, 4 Litigating Tort Cases §50:40 (2010). How

does the application of this standard work in the marital context? See Dalton, supra (explaining that the determination of the severity of emotional distress is highly discretionary); Merle H. Weiner, Domestic Violence and the Per Se Standard of Tort of Outrage, 54 Md. L. Rev. 183, 188-189 (1995) ("the ubiquity of domestic violence in our society presents a major barrier to labeling such violence 'outrageous' under existing doctrine").

14. *Privacy*. What role, if any, should notions of privacy play in recognition of IIED claims? Cf. Buel, Access to Meaningful Remedy, supra, at 976 ("It is ethically questionable for the state to be the sole arbiter of what should remain private and thus within the discretion of the spouses, and what may be considered by the court as within its purview."). How persuasive is the privacy rationale for disallowing liability for interspousal *sexual* torts? Is there more "privacy" to preserve in this context? See generally Michelle J. Anderson, Marital Immunity, Intimate Relationships, and Improper Inferences: A New Law on Sexual Offenses by Intimates, 54 Hastings L.J. 1465 (2003) (advocating elimination of marital immunity for sexual assaults).

2. Against Third Parties

■ McSWANE v. BLOOMINGTON HOSPITAL & HEALTHCARE SYSTEM
916 N.E.2d 906 (Ind. 2009)

SHEPARD, Chief Justice.

. . . On the morning of November 25, 2002, Malia Vandeneede and Monty Vandeneede, divorced but still living together, arrived at the Bloomington Hospital to request treatment for lacerations on Malia's thigh and hand. She told the hospital staff she had been thrown from a horse into a pile of brush. Triage nurse Jennifer Powell examined Malia in Monty's presence. Malia refused to request an examination of the laceration on her thigh, and the larger circumstances (like the fact that Malia's jeans were not torn) led Nurse Powell to suspect that she might have been the victim of domestic assault.

At some point when Monty's attention was diverted, Powell used the opportunity to point Malia's attention toward a domestic violence form taped to the desk. Malia shook her head violently, so Powell dropped the issue. She did report the incident to the surgery nurse on duty.

After some x-rays and other tests, hospital staff referred Malia to Dr. Jean Eelma, an orthopedic surgeon who was on call that day. Dr. Eelma examined Malia, who told her that the injury was the product of falling off a horse into a pile of brush. Monty was present during this examination, but not present when Dr. Eelma and a nurse took Malia to surgery.

Malia was in the custody of nurses during the early period of her recovery. Later in the recovery period, staff permitted Monty to join her. . . . While Malia was still in recovery, her mother Ava McSwane arrived at the hospital and informed a nurse that she believed her daughter had not been in a horse accident at all but rather that Monty had assaulted her with a fireplace poker. After some consultation, Ava McSwane called the State Police, the Monroe County Sheriff's Department, the

Owen County Sheriff's Department, and hospital security. None of the law enforcement agencies responded.

In the meantime, Malia was preparing for release from the hospital, telling Nurse
Guzik that she was ready to go home. As Guzik, Monty, and Malia left the surgery
area, two security guards asked Monty to join them in a nearby hallway, where they
conducted a search for weapons and a sobriety test. These were both negative.

As Malia was being wheeled out of the hospital, Nurse Jennifer Perantoni told
her that she need not depart with Monty. Malia's mother pleaded with her not to
leave with Monty. Malia responded in no uncertain terms that she wanted to leave
with Monty. "Stay out of our business," she said. Malia and Monty drove away
together. They had gone but a few blocks when Monty shot Malia twice, killing
her, and then killed himself as well.

McSwane filed a complaint for medical malpractice on behalf of Malia's estate
and on behalf of her daughter against Bloomington Hospital and Dr. Eelma.
The complaint alleges that the defendants permitted Malia to leave the hospital
in the custody of Monty even though they had information suggesting the possibility
of further violence. [The trial court granted defendants' motion for summary judgment. The Indiana Court of Appeals reversed.]

[T]he elements of a claim for medical malpractice are the same as for any other
claim for negligence. The claimant must show that the defendant owed her a duty of
care at the time the injury occurred, that the defendant's behavior did not conform
to that standard of care, and that the claimant's injuries were proximately caused by
the breach. . . .

The parties have largely argued this appeal based on the trial court's finding
that there was no duty and that the claim is barred by contributory negligence.
McSwane [counters] that a duty existed on three grounds: that the hospital had
assumed a duty to its patients, that the possibility of injury was foreseeable, and that
public policy supports legal imposition of a duty.

The hospital has argued that its duty to McSwane did not extend to protecting
her from harm caused by Monty off its premises. It counters McSwane's argument
about assumption of duty, which rests on the hospital's implementation of an internal domestic violence policy, by noting that there is no indication McSwane relied
upon or knew about its policy. It cites the downside of imposing duties based on an
actor's adoption of protocols designed to protect patrons, namely, the risk that
doing so will discourage adoption of prophylactic measures.

The parties' debate over assumed duty seems unnecessary. It is straightforward
enough to say that a hospital's duty of care to a patient who presents observable signs
of domestic abuse includes some reasonable measures to address the patient's risk.
The hospital in this instance took several such actions, including direct suggestions
that abuse might be the cause, providing a chance to so indicate outside the earshot
of the abuser, security examinations of the suspected abuser, facilitating telephone
calls to law enforcement, and declarations that Malia need not leave the hospital
with him.

While counsel for McSwane argues that the hospital's failure to separate its
patient from her ex-husband so that she could safely report his attack, the record
reflects that the hospital did keep them apart on multiple occasions. While counsel
does not suggest that the hospital should have physically restrained Malia from
leaving the building, it appears plain that little short of that would have kept her
from leaving with Monty. Holding that the hospital's duty encompassed such

measures obviously bumps right up against patient autonomy and informed consent, two touchstones of medical malpractice law. . . .[1]

A plaintiff's contributory negligence operates as a complete bar to recovery. . . . A court should find a plaintiff contributorily negligent if her conduct falls below the standard to which she is required to conform for her own protection. . . .

Counsel for McSwane contends that having received anesthetic and pain medications Malia could not be contributorily negligent as a matter of law. The materials the hospital tendered on summary judgment describe Malia as "alert and oriented" even during her recovery period. Nurse Guzik said Malia was "very aware [of] what was going on. . . . I mean she followed commands very well. Ask her a question, she'd answer appropriately." The surgeon's conclusion about the debate over pain medication was that Malia "was a person in my opinion that probably was very capable of making her own decisions." Counsel for McSwane does not point to any facts that actually contradict this assessment.

While negligence is generally a question for the finder of fact, where the evidence permits only a single inference, contributory negligence may be a matter of law for the court. The trial court found that Malia's insistence on leaving with Monty in the face of offers by hospital staff and pleas by her own mother was negligence that contributed to her injury. This was not error. We affirm the judgment of the trial court. . . .

RUCKER, J., Dissenting.

I agree with the majority that "a hospital's duty of care to a patient who presents observable signs of domestic abuse includes some reasonable measures to address the patient's risk." Although the existence of duty is a matter of law for the courts to decide, a breach of duty is usually a matter left to the trier of fact. Only where the facts are undisputed and lead to but a single inference or conclusion may the court as a matter of law determine whether a breach of duty has occurred. Unlike the majority, however, I do not believe the question of breach in this case can be determined as a matter of law.

The record establishes a lack of communication about suspected domestic abuse between the ER staff and the treating emergency room physician. Although the triage nurse indicated she informed a charge nurse of her suspicions, the record is void of any evidence of an emergency room charge nurse taking any action or informing the treating physician. The fact that the attending physician states that he was not informed of the suspected domestic abuse indicates that the emergency room support staff did not follow the hospital's adopted domestic violence policies, which requires such communication from staff to the treating physician. This concern is amplified because the attending physician was able to spend time alone with Malia before she was heavily medicated and while the "husband" was out of the exam room. Thus the doctor, had he been properly informed, could have asked appropriate questions regarding domestic abuse during that period, which could have given the patient a reasonable opportunity to seek refuge.

In sum, the facts in this case raise genuine issues as to whether the hospital breached its duty of care by, among other things, discharging a patient to the

---

1. McSwane's central contention about the treating physician was that she failed to report the suspected abuse, relying on Ind. Code §35-47-1. As the Court of Appeals' majority noted, this contention was not made in the trial court and thus is not available on appeal. . . .

custody of a suspected abuser. This is not a matter that can be resolved by summary disposition.

I also disagree with the majority's determination that Malia was contributorily negligent as a matter of law. It is of course the case that in a contributory negligence regime any negligence on the part of the plaintiff, no matter how slight, will bar any action for damages. But contributory negligence is generally a question of fact that is not appropriate for summary judgment if there are conflicting factual inferences to be drawn from the designated evidence. . . .

The medical records indicate that, while Malia was present in the emergency room, she received numerous drugs. . . . It was determined that Malia required general surgery to repair her injuries, which was done in an operating room under general anesthesia, with full intubation. Malia was rendered medically unconscious for over one hour and then given numerous medications, one of which was 10 milligrams of morphine (a narcotic analgesic) for post-operative pain. Although the record indicates that Malia was thereafter alert and oriented, it is unclear what her true decision-making capabilities and mental state were at the time of discharge. Furthermore, from the record before us it appears that Malia was discharged from the hospital approximately 90 minutes after the surgery was completed, which leaves open the likelihood that the she had not fully recovered from the general anesthesia and was thus mentally and/or physically incapable of reasonable decision making, or self-protection, when allowed to leave the hospital. . . .

It is clear to me there are different factual inferences that may be drawn from the evidence concerning Malia's mental, emotional, and physical condition. Thus, a factfinder should determine whether having received general anesthetic, a relaxant, numerous doses of various opiates for pain, and being advised by Hospital not to make any important decisions, Malia was exercising that degree of care that a reasonable person under the same or similar condition would have been expected to exercise when she decided to leave the hospital with her former husband. This is not in my view a matter that can be disposed of by summary disposition. For the foregoing reasons I respectfully dissent and would reverse the judgment of the trial court.

■ COLO. REV. STAT. §12-36-135. INJURIES TO BE REPORTED— PENALTY FOR FAILURE TO REPORT—IMMUNITY FROM LIABILITY

(1)(a) It shall be the duty of every licensee who attends or treats a bullet wound, a gunshot wound, a powder burn, or any other injury arising from the discharge of a firearm, or an injury caused by a knife, an ice pick, or any other sharp or pointed instrument that the licensee believes to have been intentionally inflicted upon a person, . . . or any other injury that the licensee has reason to believe involves a criminal act, including injuries resulting from domestic violence, to report the injury at once to the police of the city, town, or city and county or the sheriff of the county in which the licensee is located. Any licensee who fails to make a report as required by this section commits a class 2 petty offense, . . . and, upon conviction thereof, shall be punished by a fine of not more than three hundred dollars, or by imprisonment in the county jail for not more than ninety days, or by both such fine and imprisonment. . . .

Notes and Questions

1. *Social reality.* A significant number of emergency room visits are attributable to domestic violence. Mary Boes & Virginia McDermott, Helping Battered Women: A Health Care Perspective, in Handbook of Domestic Violence Intervention Strategies: Policies, Programs, and Legal Remedies 257, 257, 260 (Albert R. Roberts ed. 2002) (citing estimates of 22 to 35 percent). Many victims of domestic violence who seek police assistance have extensive medical histories of abuse. See 3 in 4 Domestic Violence Victims Go Unidentified in Emergency Rooms, Penn Study Shows, Mental Health Wkly. Dig., Mar. 28, 2011, available at 2011 WLNR 5779828 [hereafter Penn Study] (reporting that 75 percent of victims seeking police assistance previously sought emergency room treatment, and most victims sought medical help at least seven times).

Hospital staff often are the first professionals who interact with victims of domestic violence. In *McSwane*, Malia Vandeneede sought emergency room assistance for injuries to her thigh and hand. What explanation did she give for her injuries? What led the nurse to suspect that Malia might be a victim of abuse? What actions did the nurse take, based on her suspicions?

2. *Background: federal guidelines.* Beginning in the 1990s, with the increasing public awareness of domestic violence, the federal government called for improved identification of intimate partner victimization. The surgeon general recommended routine assessment of abuse in pregnant women. Federal guidelines called for the training of health care professionals and the implementation of standard protocols in health care settings to promote early identification and intervention in cases of domestic violence. Professional organizations (including the American College of Obstetricians and Gynecologists, the American College of Nurse-Midwives, the American Academy of Family Physicians, and the American Medical Association) echoed the refrain. Boes & McDermott, supra, at 268-269. Why did the guidelines target pregnant women in particular?

3. *Lack of screening.* Federal guidelines appear to have had little impact on the conduct of health care professionals. Few health care professionals screen for domestic violence. See National Coalition against Domestic Violence (NCADV), Reproductive Health and Pregnancy 1 (noting that only 10 percent of physicians screen during new-patient visits and 9 percent during checkups), available at http://www.ywca.org/atf/cf/%7B3b450fa5-108b-4d2e-b3d0-c31487243e6a%7D/FACT_REPRODUCTIVE.PDF (last visited July 12, 2011).

The appearance of abused women in medical settings was visible early in the battered women's movement. See Demie Kurz & Evan Stark, Not-So-Benign Neglect: The Medical Response to Battering, in Feminist Perspectives on Wife Abuse 249 (Kersi Yllo & Michele Bograd, eds., 1990). What explains physicians' inability to perceive the cause of patients' injuries? See Boes & McDermot, supra, at 269-270 (pointing to lack of emphasis in medical schools as well as stereotypes); Mildred D. Pagelow, Battered Women: A Historical Research Review and Some Common Myths, in Violence and Sexual Abuse at Home: Current Issues in Spousal Battering 97, 97-99 (1997) (citing myths); Evan Stark & Ann Flitcraft, Women at Risk: Domestic Violence and Women's Health 13, 166-167 (1996) (citing victim blaming and pathologizing).

What behavioral indicators might alert health care providers? See Tina Bloom et al., Intimate Partner Violence during Pregnancy, in Family Violence and Nursing Practice 155, 169 (Janice Humphreys & Jacquelyn C. Campbell eds., 2011) (reporting following factors: partner who is unwilling to leave the woman, speaks for the woman, makes derogatory comments about her, is oversolicitous with health care providers, is emotionally absent or out of tune with the woman's feelings, and a pregnant woman who is overly fearful of her partner). How could medical and legal personnel improve identification? Medical screening for domestic violence is still not common. See Penn Study, supra (noting that only 28 percent of victims are identified).

4. *Denial of abuse.* In *McSwane*, Malia denied that she was a victim of domestic violence. Why are victims reluctant to disclose injuries to health care providers? Are the reasons for victims' reluctance similar to the reasons for their reluctance to report to law enforcement officials? See Connie Mitchell & Deirdre Anglin, Intimate Partner Violence: A Health-Based Perspective 430-431 (2009) ("The mistrust of the legal system for victims of IPV, unfortunately, extends to the health profession as well"). What should a health care provider do if the patient denies the abuse or refuses to discuss it? See Boes & McDermott, supra, at 266.

5. *Negligence.* Why did the Indiana Supreme Court determine that the defendants were not negligent? How does the dissent evaluate the defendants' duty of care? Which view is more persuasive? Why might the court have been reluctant to hold the defendants responsible? What does *McSwane* require of hospital staff in cases of domestic violence? How would you advise health care providers to act in such cases in the future?

6. *Contributory negligence.* What was the role, according to *McSwane*, of the victim's contributory negligence? Did Malia's conduct fall below the standard to which she was required to conform for her own protection? Plaintiff argues that Malia could not have been contributorily negligent because her pain medications interfered with her decisionmaking. What does the court respond? How does the dissent evaluate the issue of contributory negligence? Are there other factors that might have interfered with the victim's decisionmaking abilities? For example, are most victims aware of the level of risk posed by their abusers? (Lethality assessment is discussed Chapter 2.)

7. *Failure to report.* Plaintiff alleges that the physician's negligence rested, in part, on the failure to report the suspected abuse as required by Indiana law. Similar to many states, Indiana requires that medical providers report gunshot wounds or other wounds "apparently inflicted by a knife, ice pick, or other sharp or pointed instrument" to law enforcement authorities, subject to misdemeanor liability. Ind. Code §35-47-7-1. However, *McSwane* refused to consider this claim because it was not raised in the trial court. If plaintiff had raised the claim in a timely fashion, how should it have been decided? Compare the Indiana statute with that of Colorado, supra. What are the benefits and shortcomings of each approach?

8. *Policy.* Should the health care providers' standard of care include the task of reporting domestic violence to law enforcement? What are the arguments for and against the adoption of such a standard of care? How should legislators strike a balance between patient protection versus respect for patient autonomy? How might existing statutes be made more effective? How might medical intervention in cases of domestic violence be made more effective?

9. *Mandatory reporting for domestic violence.* Mandatory reporting by medical professionals is a central aspect of the governmental approach to child abuse and neglect. Although all states have some form of mandatory reporting for incidents of child abuse, relatively few states mandate reporting of intimate partner or spousal abuse. What explains the different treatment? Does patient confidentiality militate against reporting? See Health Insurance Portability and Accountability Act

(HIPAA), 5 C.F.R. §§160, 164 (restricting disclosure of health information based on concerns about patients' right to privacy).

10. *Benefits and detriments of mandatory reporting.* What are the benefits of mandatory reporting for victims of intimate partner violence? One commentator identifies: (1) an increase the commitment of health care providers to better screening and treatment of injuries resulting from domestic violence; (2) holding the perpetrator accountable; (3) enhancing patient safety by providing an opportunity for early intervention; (4) encouraging education of victims about available resources; and (5) "giv[ing] health care providers an opportunity to respond ethically and professionally to IPV without overburdening them." Rebekah Kratochvil, Comment, Intimate Partner Violence During Pregnancy: Exploring the Efficacy of a Mandatory Reporting Statute, 10 Hous. J. Health L. & Pol'y 63, 88 (2009).

On the other hand, such laws may: (1) fail to respect victims' autonomy and reinforce negative stereotypes; (2) compromise doctor-patient confidentiality; (3) serve as a deterrent to the receipt of proper medical care; (4) jeopardize victims' safety by posing a risk of retaliatory violence; and (5) "produce uncertain results in the quality of patient care due to inconsistencies in reporting and lack of effective enforcement." Id. at 92.

Which of the above arguments are most persuasive? Can you think of other benefits and detriments? Given the above concerns, is mandatory reporting the best method for helping victims escape abuse? What other forms of intervention could help victims of domestic violence who seek medical attention?

11. *Comparison of contexts.* State statutes vary in terms of the types of abuse that must be reported. As explained above, all states mandate reporting of child abuse and neglect, pursuant to federal law. Federal law also requires that certain residential facilities, such as nursing homes, report incidents of elder abuse. See 48 C.F.R. §483.13(c)(2) (requiring reporting by residential facilities). Many states also require reporting of elder abuse and/or abuse of persons with disabilities (see Chapter 3). How is the mandate to report domestic violence similar to, and different from, that of reporting other forms of abuse?

12. *Mandated reporters.* States designate the professionals who are required to report child abuse and neglect, such as physicians, psychologists, nurses, dentists, coroners, police officers, social workers, clergy members, caregivers, attorneys, schoolteachers, and school personnel. Which of these would be likely to identify victims of domestic violence?

13. *Sanctions for failure to report.* In states that mandate reporting, the consequences for failing to report a known or suspected incident of domestic abuse vary greatly. Most states make a failure to report a misdemeanor. See, e.g., Ariz. Rev. Stat. Ann. §46-454(K); Haw. Rev. Stat. §346-224(e); Wyo. Stat. Ann. §35-20-111(b). Some states punish failure to report with a fine, while others impose a jail sentence, usually for a maximum one-year term. See, e.g., Ga. Code Ann., §17-10-3 (imposing either fine or maximum sentence of 12 months); Mass. Gen. Laws ch. 19A, §15(a) (imposing fine of not more than $1,000). Mandatory reporters who fail to make a report may also face civil liability or lose their professional license. See, e.g., Iowa Code Ann. §235B.3(12) (imposing civil liability for damages for failure to report); 320 Ill. Comp. Stats. 20/4 (physician's license can be revoked for failure to report).

Most states decline to hold a mandatory reporter civilly liable for a failure to report child abuse. See Arbaugh v. Bd. of Education, 591 S.E.2d 235 (W. Va. 2003). Should domestic violence reporting follow the precedent set by child abuse law? What light does *McSwane* shed on this question?

14. *Federal legislation.* The Child Abuse Prevention and Treatment Act (CAPTA), 42 U.S.C. §§5101-5107, 5116, 5118A-5118E, mandates reporting of child abuse and neglect. Specifically, CAPTA conditions federal funding on a state's adoption and certification of "provisions or procedures for the reporting of known and suspected instances of child abuse and neglect." 42 U.S.C. §5106a(b)(2)(A)(ii). CAPTA further requires that states provide criminal immunity to good faith reporters. 42 U.S.C. §5106a(b)(2)(A)(vii). In contrast, the Violence Against Women Act (VAWA) has no mandatory reporting requirements. Should Congress mandate reporting for victims of intimate partner violence? Why or why not? See Alexi Nicole Vital, Mandatory Reporting Statutes and the Violence Against Women Act: An Analytical Comparison, 10 Geo. Mason U. Civ. Rts. L.J. 171 (2000).

The pending Violence Against Women Reauthorization Act of 2011 addresses the health care system's response to domestic violence. Title V (amending 42 U.S.C. §280g-4) would authorize grants to develop educational programs for medical, nursing, dental, and other health profession students and to improve the response of diverse health settings. In addition, federal guidelines, issued in conjunction with health care reform legislation, require that all new insurance policies must provide coverage for domestic violence screening and counseling. See U.S. Dept. Health & Human Servs., Health Resources & Servs. Admin., Women's Preventive Services: Required Health Plan Coverage Guidelines, available at http://www.hrsa.gov/womensguidelines/

B. DEFENSES

Several doctrines present obstacles to victims' ability to recover damages in tort suits for domestic violence, including the interspousal immunity doctrine, statutes of limitations, and procedural restrictions. This section explores the nature of these barriers and their implications for tort recovery.

1. Interspousal Immunity

▪ THOMPSON v. THOMPSON
218 U.S. 611 (1910)

Review pp. 23-26.

Notes and Questions

1. *Significance.* The U.S. Supreme Court, in a sharply divided decision in *Thompson*, upheld the interspousal immunity doctrine. However, Justice Harlan's famous dissent marked the beginning of the movement to abrogate the doctrine. Carl Tobias, Interspousal Tort Immunity in America, 23 Ga. L. Rev. 359, 399 (1989). The second stage of the women's rights movement (in the 1970s) contributed to transforming the doctrine into a minority rule. Id.

2. *Defense.* The interspousal tort immunity doctrine constitutes a defense to a civil action between husband and wife. The doctrine derived from the principle of

coverture, that is, the legal fiction that a woman's identity merged with that of her husband upon her marriage. Based on this notion of the spouses as constituting one legal entity, it followed that one spouse could not sue the other because of the impossibility of suing oneself. When state legislatures enacted Married Women's Property legislation in the mid- to late nineteenth century, states expanded married women's legal rights. Afterwards, however, even though a married woman could sue and be sued, many state Married Women's Property Acts (such as that of the District of Columbia in the principal case) did not expressly grant wives the right to sue their husbands for tortious conduct. See Michelle L. Evans, Note, Wrongs Committed During A Marriage: The Child that No Area of the Law Wants to Adopt, 66 Wash. & Lee L. Rev. 465, 478 (2009).

3. *Rationales.* Compare and contrast the views of the majority and dissent in *Thompson* regarding: (1) legislative intent, (2) the respective roles of the legislature and judiciary in legal policy and law reform, (3) the "evils" posed by interspousal litigation, and (4) women's roles in the family and society. How does the dissent respond to the majority's dire forecast of the consequences of imposing interspousal liability? Whose views do you find more persuasive—the majority or the dissent? Why?

4. *District of Columbia.* In *Thompson,* the U.S. Supreme Court held that the common law immunity doctrine was *not* abrogated by the District of Columbia's enactment of married women's property legislation. The District of Columbia subsequently rejected that view. See D.C. Code §46-601 (formerly D.C. Code §30-201) (declaring that "The fact that a person is or was married or registered as a domestic partner shall not impair the rights and responsibilities of such person [including the right] to contract or engage in any trade, occupation, or business arrangement or in any civil litigation of any sort (whether in contract, tort, or otherwise) with or against anyone, including such person's spouse or domestic partner, to the same extent as an unmarried person").

5. *Abrogation movement.* Currently, most states have abrogated the interspousal immunity doctrine, in whole or in part, either by statute or case law. See, e.g., Evans, supra, at 479 n.87 (pointing out that, by 2005, nine states had not completely abrogated the doctrine). Abrogation of the interspousal immunity doctrine occurred first for intentional acts and, subsequently, for negligent acts. See Bozman v. Bozman, 830 A.2d 450, 487 (Md. Ct. App. 2003) (explaining history). What explains these stages of abrogation? Does it make sense to permit one spouse to sue the other for intentional torts, but not negligence? See, e.g., Beattie v. Beattie, 630 A.2d 1096, 1098-1099 (Del. 1993) (abrogating interspousal immunity for negligent torts, reasoning that the preclusion would disrupt, rather than promote, family harmony by promoting divorces to allow one spouse to sue the other to collect insurance proceeds).

6. *Consequences of abrogation.* One rationale for judicial reluctance to abrogate interspousal immunity was the fear that abolition would trigger a flood of litigation. See, e.g., Davis v. Bostwick, 580 P.2d 544, 546 (Or. 1978) ("we see no virtue in basing a rule of law on a speculative fear of increased litigation"). Was this fear realistic? See, e.g., Moran v. Beyer, 734 F.2d 1245, 1247 (7th Cir. 1984) ("the fear of a flood of frivolous suits wasting limited judicial resources is unfounded"). What light does Wriggins's excerpt shed on this rationale?

7. *Fraudulent claims.* Another rationale for courts' reluctance to abrogate interspousal immunity was the fear of collusive lawsuits between the spouses in an effort to obtain insurance. See, e.g., Peters v. Peters, 634 P.2d 586 (Haw. 1981) (refusing to

abrogate interspousal immunity based on legislative intent to prevent marital disharmony and collusive suits); William E. McCurdy, Torts between Persons in Domestic Relation, 43 Harv. L. Rev. 1030, 1052-1053 (1930) ("Indeed, the strongest argument against such actions is not disruption of domestic tranquility, but the danger of domestic collusion"). Concern about fraud also centered on the possibility of spousal attempts to circumvent statutes on equitable distribution, spousal support, and child custody. What gender-based stereotypes form the basis for this latter view?

8. *Escalation of hostility.* Another argument in favor of barring interspousal suits was that the introduction of tort liability in the context of divorce would increase animosity between the spouses. According to Professor Harry Krause, "tort law will reintroduce to the end of marriage more and worse acrimony than no-fault divorce ever eliminated." Harry Krause, On the Danger of Allowing Marital Fault Torts to Re-Emerge in the Guise of Torts, 73 Notre Dame L. Rev. 1355, 1364 (2003). In rebuttal, Professor Pamela Laufer-Ukeles responds:

> But why should that be? If the divorce is already procured, custody and support issues already determined, the dispute becomes a purely financial one, like any other tort. Logically, the acrimony should be lessened as compared to fault divorce, not elevated. The longer process for recovery in torts than there should be for obtaining a divorce should provide distance from the wrongful act, assuming legal doctrines such as res judicata and collateral estoppel are not improperly used to prevent bringing the tort after the divorce. Moreover, the parties will have had recourse to the divorce process to separate from the marriage and move on with their lives without an accusatory component.

Laufer-Ukeles, supra, at 262-263. Whose view do you find more persuasive?

9. *Alternative remedies.* According to the majority, a battered spouse has other remedies available to her, thereby obviating the need to abrogate the interspousal immunity doctrine. What are these other remedies? See also Abbott v. Abbott, 67 Me. 304, 307 (1877) (refusing to abrogate interspousal immunity based on the existence of adequate alternative remedies). Do you agree that these alternative remedies are adequate to address the harm?

10. *Role of divorce.* During the slow erosion of the interspousal immunity doctrine, some courts permitted interspousal recovery only for spouses who were divorced. Tobias, supra, at 422. What was the policy rationale for limitation on tort recovery to the *post*-divorce situation?

11. *Privacy doctrine and sexual torts.* Courts recognized tort liability for transmission of venereal disease since the nineteenth century. Several early cases, however, barred recovery based on the interspousal immunity doctrine. See, e.g., Bandfield v. Bandfield, 75 N.W. 287 (Mich. 1898). See generally Allan M. Brandt, No Magic Bullet: A Social History of Venereal Disease in the United States Since 1880 (1987); Michelle J. Anderson, Marital Immunity, Intimate Relationships, and Improper Inferences: A New Law on Sexual Offenses by Intimates, 54 Hastings L.J. 1465 (2003). Should the "family privacy" rationale serve to preserve interspousal immunity in *some* cases? Are there aspects of marital life that should not give rise to liability, such as sexual torts? See G.L. v. M.L., 550 A.2d 525 (N.J. Sup. Ct. Ch. Div. 1988) (holding that wife's claim for husband's transmission of genital herpes was not barred by "marital privilege").

2. Statutes of Limitations

■ PUGLIESE v. SUPERIOR COURT

53 Cal. Rptr. 3rd 681 (Ct. App. 2007)

Chavez, J.

. . . Michele filed a petition for dissolution of [her 13-year marriage to Dante] on April 22, 2002. On April 2, 2004, Michele sued Dante for assault, battery, intentional infliction of emotional distress and violation of civil rights. Michele alleged Dante had engaged in a pattern of domestic abuse, both physical and mental, which began within a few months of the marriage. . . . Dante filed a motion in limine to exclude evidence of any assaults and batteries alleged to have occurred more than three years prior to the filing of the complaint, [contending that] the statute of limitations set forth in Code of Civil Procedure §340.15 barred such recovery. . . .

Spouses are permitted to pursue appropriate civil remedies against each other, including lawsuits asserting the tort of domestic violence (Cal. Civ. Code §1708.6 (a)). The time for commencement of an action under Civil Code §1708.6 is governed by Code of Civil Procedure §340.15, which provides: "(a) In any civil action for recovery of damages suffered as a result of domestic violence, the time for commencement of the action shall be the later of the following:

(1) Within three years from the date of the last act of domestic violence by the defendant against the plaintiff.
(2) Within three years from the date the plaintiff discovers or reasonably should have discovered that an injury or illness resulted from an act of domestic violence by the defendant against the plaintiff. . . .

The rights and remedies provided in Civil Code §1708.6 are in addition to any other rights and remedies provided by law. Thus, spouses and ex-spouses are entitled to allege, as did Michele, causes of action for assault, battery and intentional infliction of emotional distress. When such counts are alleged, we look to the limitations period applicable to *each* of these causes of action to determine if they are barred by the statute of limitations. Causes of action for assault, battery and intentional infliction of emotional distress are governed by the two-year statute of limitations set forth in Code of Civil Procedure §335.1. Michele alleges the last physical act of abuse occurred in April 2001. Thus, [because she instituted suit three years later, in April 2004,] her assault and battery causes of action are barred by Code of Civil Procedure §335.1. As for Michele's intentional infliction of emotional distress claim, she alleges the last act of emotional abuse occurred in April 2004, less than two years prior to the filing of the complaint. Thus, her intentional infliction of emotional distress claim was timely filed pursuant to Code of Civil Procedure §335.1.

Although the assault and battery causes of action are barred by the applicable statute of limitations, the complaint, taken as a whole, alleges a violation of Civil Code §1708.6 [that is, the tort of domestic violence]. Michele claims that during the period June 1989 to April 2004, Dante shoved, pushed, kicked, hit, slapped, shook, choked and sexually abused her. She also alleges he pulled her hair, pinched and twisted her flesh, threatened to kill her, threatened her with bodily harm, confined her in the family car while driving erratically and drunkenly and infected her with sexually transmitted diseases. Clearly, Michele has alleged that Dante intentionally or recklessly caused or attempted to cause her bodily injury, sexually assaulted her, placed her in reasonable apprehension of imminent serious bodily injury and engaged in behavior that could have been enjoined pursuant to Family Code §6320. . . . Because Michele alleges the last physical act of abuse occurred in April 2001 and the last act of emotional abuse occurred in April 2004, and because the complaint was filed within three years of these dates, Michelle's Civil Code §1708.6 domestic violence claim was timely filed.

Michele [next] contends she is entitled to seek damages for acts of domestic abuse occurring beyond the three-year limitations period set forth in Code of Civil Procedure §340.15(a). . . . Code of Civil Procedure §335.1, the statute setting forth the limitations period for assault and battery between *nondomestic* partners, views each incident of abuse separately and the limitations period commences at the time the incident occurs. By contrast, §340.15 provides that domestic violence lawsuits must be commenced within three years "from the date of the *last act* of domestic violence. . . ." (italics added.) The words "last act" are superfluous if they have no meaning. By adding these words, we believe the Legislature adopted by statute the continuing tort theory, thus allowing domestic violence victims to recover damages for all acts of domestic violence occurring during the marriage, provided the victim proves a continuing course of abusive conduct and files suit within three years of the "last act of domestic violence."

Dante makes little attempt to explain the Legislature's use of the words "last act," focusing instead on the purpose of statutes of limitations, which is to "prevent the resurgence of stale claims after the lapse of long periods of time as a result of which loss of papers, disappearance of witnesses, and feeble recollections make ineffectual or extremely difficult a fair presentation of the case." Dante concludes the situation at hand is precisely the sort in which statutes of limitations must be strictly enforced; otherwise he will be forced to combat evidence that has long since faded in amount, potency, reliability, and relevance.

While we recognize the difficulty a spouse or ex-spouse may have in defending against domestic violence cases, the continuing tort doctrine seems especially applicable in such cases. Generally, a limitations period begins to run upon the occurrence of the last fact essential to the cause of action. However, where a tort involves a continuing wrong, the statute of limitations does not begin to run until the date of the last injury or when the tortious acts cease.

Dante contends that the continuing tort doctrine should not be applied to violations of Civil Code §1708.6. He claims, in essence, that the tort of domestic violence is made up of essentially three separate torts, i.e., assault, battery and the infliction of emotional distress. According to Dante, because a victim knows she or he has been injured at the time of the assault, battery or infliction of emotional distress occurs, the victim must file suit against the abuser within two years of the act or forever lose the right to do so. However, the tort of domestic violence is more complex than Dante concedes. Domestic violence is the physical, sexual, psychological, and/or emotional abuse of a victim by his or her intimate partner, with the goal of asserting and maintaining power and control over the victim. Most domestic violence victims are subjected to "an ongoing strategy of intimidation, isolation, and control that extends to all areas of a woman's life, including sexuality; material necessities; relations with family, children, and friends; and work." Pursuing a remedy, criminal or civil, while in such an environment defies the abuser's control, thus exposing the victim to considerable risk of violence.

We have found no California case applying the continuing tort doctrine to the tort of domestic violence. However, an Illinois case, Feltmeier v. Feltmeier, 798 N.E.2d 75 (Ill. 2003), is instructive [in finding that the ex-husband's actions constituted a "continuing tort," for purposes of the statute of limitations, thereby tolling the statute].

The conduct set forth in Michele's complaint could be considered separate offenses of assault, battery and intentional infliction of emotional distress. However, Michele has alleged continual domestic abuse over a 15-year period, and that Dante's tortious conduct did not completely cease until April 2004 [i.e., almost two years after the dissolution]. Accordingly, Michele's Civil Code §1708.6 cause of action did not accrue until April 2004 and she is entitled to seek recovery of damages for acts occurring prior to that time.

. . . While it is clear the Legislature, in adopting the three-year limitations period [in Code of Civil Procedure §340.15], understood that victims of domestic violence need additional time within which to file suit, nothing contained in the legislative history conclusively establishes whether the Legislature intended courts to treat a Civil Code §1708.6 tort as a continuing wrong. The legislative history of Civil Code §1708.6 is more enlightening.

Civil Code §1708.6 was modeled after the Violence Against Women Act of 1994 (VAWA), which provided a federal civil remedy for victims of gender-motivated violence [providing that all persons shall have the right to be free from "crimes of violence motivated by gender," 42 U.S.C. §1398(b)]. . . . As a result [of United States v. Morrison, 529 U.S. 598 (2000) in which the U.S. Supreme Court declared 42 U.S.C. §13981 unconstitutional], it became the responsibility of individual states to institute civil remedies for victims of rape and domestic violence. In 2002, California enacted Civil Code §1708.6 [and declared]:

(a) Acts of violence occurring in a domestic context are increasingly widespread.

(b) These acts merit special consideration as torts, because the elements of trust, physical proximity, and emotional intimacy necessary to domestic relationships in a healthy society make participants in those relationships particularly vulnerable to physical attack by their partners.

(c) It is the purpose of this act to enhance the civil remedies available to victims of domestic violence in order to underscore society's condemnation of these acts, to ensure *complete* recovery to victims, and to impose significant financial consequences upon perpetrators (italics added).

Clearly our Legislature, like the authors of the VAWA, understood that domestic violence encompasses a series of acts, including assault, battery and intentional infliction of emotional distress, and that when these acts are coupled with an oppressive atmosphere of control, the continuing tort of domestic violence results.

The legislative history of Civil Code section 1708.6 and the plain language of Code of Civil Procedure §340.15 convince us that damages are available to victims of domestic violence, not just for the "last act" of abuse, but for acts occurring prior to the date of the "last act." Accordingly, we conclude the trial court erred in granting Dante's in limine motion to exclude all references to acts of domestic violence alleged to have occurred three years prior to the date Michele filed her domestic violence complaint. . . .

Notes and Questions

1. *Purposes.* Special statutory periods restrict the time in which a victim of domestic violence may bring an action for personal injuries. These limitations periods present a major obstacle to tort recovery for victims of domestic violence. See David E. Poplar, Tolling the Statute of Limitations for Battered Women After Giovine v. Giovine: Creating Equitable Exceptions for Victims of Domestic Abuse, 101 Dick. L. Rev. 161, 172 (1996) ("By far, statutes of limitations pose the greatest barrier to a woman who sues her batterer"). Statutes of limitations serve to preclude both the filing of a lawsuit and also the inclusion of certain acts in that law suit if those acts took place before the limitations period. What are the purposes of statutes of limitations? Whose interests do they protect? See Dan B. Dobbs, The Law of Torts 551-552 (2000) (statutes of limitations emphasize justice and process concerns).

2. *Terminology: accrual and tolling.* Statutes of limitations for torts begin to run when the cause of action "accrues" (that is, when a right to sue begins). A cause of action accrues when the wrongful act is committed. If the wrongful conduct consists of multiple acts, then the cause of action generally accrues upon the occurrence of the *last* of these acts. However, state law provides for certain exceptions that serve to "toll" (that is, suspend, delay) the statute of limitations, thereby giving extra time to file suit. Why should statutes permit extra time?

3. *Duration.* Depending on the jurisdiction, statutes of limitation for assault and battery are generally short, usually one to three years from discovery of injury. See, e.g., Haw. Rev. Stat. §657-7 (two years); N.J. Stat. Ann. §2A:14-2 (two years); N.Y. C.P.L.R. Law §215 (one-year); Vt. Stat. Ann. tit. 12, §512 (three years). Limitation periods for IIED claims are often longer, ranging from one to six years. Dalton, supra, at 357. Statutes of limitations for intentional torts are usually shorter than those involving negligent conduct. See, e.g., Minn. Stat. §541.05 (six years for negligence).

4. *Applicable statutes of limitation.* What are the relevant statutes of limitation in *Pugliese* for assault and battery? For intentional infliction of emotional distress? For the tort of domestic violence? What rationale supports the longer period for the tort of domestic violence?

5. *Motion to exclude evidence.* In *Pugliese*, the husband Dante makes a motion in limine to exclude certain evidence. The purpose of this motion is to prevent the admission of evidence that is irrelevant or prejudicial. What evidence did Dante want to exclude? Why?

6. *New torts.* Beginning in the 1990s, in response to advocacy about domestic violence, courts and legislatures began adopting new torts (called the "tort of domestic violence," or the tort of "battered-woman syndrome") to address intimate partner violence. See generally M. Mercedes Fort, Casenote, A New Tort: Domestic Violence Gets the Status it Deserves in Jewitt v. Jewitt, 21 S. Ill. U. L.J. 355 (1997) (explaining history). How does California's tort of domestic violence (Cal. Civ. Code §1708.6) overcome the traditional tort statutes of limitation in *Pugliese*? Note that the plaintiff did not specifically allege a violation of Civil Code §1708.6, but the court found that her allegations of battery, assault, and IIED met the relevant definition of

abuse for purposes of that statute. See *Pugliese,* 53 Cal. Rptr. 3d at 685 n.6. The federal tort statute is discussed in this chapter, p. 530.

7. *Psychological barriers.* Why do many battered spouses wait so long to file tort suits, thereby incurring problems with the statute of limitations? What dynamics of intimate partner violence explain the delay? See Rhonda L. Kohler, The Battered Woman and Tort Law: A New Approach to Fighting Domestic Violence, 25 Loy. L.A. L. Rev. 1025, 1053 (1992) (suggesting that delay results because victims believe that the violence is an isolated act or that they can change the abuser's behavior).

8. *Continuing tort.*

a. *Background.* To address the preclusion posed by statutes of limitations for tort claims, some jurisdictions adopted a "continuous tort theory." Twyman v. Twyman, 790 S.W.2d 819 (Tex. App. 1989), was the first court to apply this theory to enable a battered wife to sue her husband for IIED, although it was reversed and remanded on other grounds. Other jurisdictions soon followed. See, e.g., Curtis v. Firth, 850 P.2d 749 (Idaho 1993); Giovine v. Giovine, 663 A.2d 109 (N.J. Super. Ct. App. Div. 1995). Feltmeier v. Feltmeier (supra this chapter) also adopted this theory. For discussion of *Twyman,* see Brenda Cossman, The Story of Twyman v. Twyman: Politics, Tort Reform, and Emotional Distress in a Texas Divorce, in Family Law Stories 243, 259-265 (Carol Sanger ed., 2008); Janet Halley, Split Decisions: How and Why to Take a Break from Feminism 348, 348-364 (2006).

b. *Definition of continuous tort.* The continuing tort doctrine tolls the statute of limitations and enables a court to treat the entire course of the defendant's abusive conduct as a single ongoing tort, rather than as discrete isolated acts. If the defendant's conduct is regarded as separate isolated acts, then each separate act would trigger a new statute of limitations—resulting in some of the abusive acts being time-barred as falling outside the statutory period. However, if the conduct constitutes a "continuing tort," then the limitations period does not begin to run until the date of the *last* injury or the date that the tortious acts *cease.* Thus, the continuing tort doctrine enables a victim to recover for injuries that result from the entire span of the defendant's wrongful conduct, not merely those acts that fall within the applicable statutory period.

The husband in *Pugliese* contends that the continuing tort doctrine should not be applied to violations of Civil Code §1708.6. Why? What does the court respond? What light is shed on the application of the statutory bar by the legislative history?

9. *Delayed discovery rule distinguished.* The continuing tort rule is an equitable exception to the statute of limitations. How is it distinguishable from the equitable exception of the delayed discovery rule? Under the latter, a cause of action accrues, and the limitations period begins to run, when the party seeking relief knows or reasonably should know of any injury and that it was wrongfully caused. In contrast, in a continuing tort, the plaintiff's claim accrues, and the statute of limitations begins to run, at the time of the last injury or the cessation of the conduct.

10. *Child sexual abuse.* Many jurisdictions have extended their statutes of limitations (both civil and criminal) for child sexual abuse. The clergy sexual abuse scandal hastened these reforms. See generally Susan Vivian Mangold, Reforming Child Protection in Response to the Catholic Church Child Sexual Abuse Scandal, 4 U. Fla. J.L. & Pub. Pol'y 155 (2003). Child sexual abuse induces psychological

trauma that makes it difficult for victims to confront the perpetrator—the delay subjects victims to the bar of statutes of limitations. See generally William A. Gray, Note, A Proposal for Change in Statutes of Limitations in Childhood Sexual Abuse Cases, 43 Brandeis L.J. 493, 504-507 (2005) (surveying state law).

Does intimate partner violence justify the same extension? How are the dynamics of child sexual abuse similar to, and different from, intimate partner violence so as to justify such statutory extensions? Should state legislatures extend the statutes of limitations based on the disability of domestic violence victims' post-traumatic stress disorder that tolls the running of the statute of limitations? See generally Posttraumatic Syndrome as Tolling Running of Statute of Limitations, 12 A.L.R.5th 546 (1993 & Supp.).

11. *Statutory toll for insanity.* Another theory that results in tolling the statute of limitations is disability. In a famous New York case, a battered woman (Hedda Nussbaum) brought an intentional tort suit for the physical and psychological injuries that were inflicted on her by her companion of 10 years, attorney Joel Steinberg. (Steinberg was a child abuser as well as a batterer; he murdered their adopted six-year-old daughter.) New York has a short one-year tort statute of limitations; however, state law (N.Y. C.P.L.R. Law §208) extends the time to sue for those persons under a disability due to infancy or insanity.

Steinberg moved to dismiss Nussbaum's complaint as time-barred by the statute of limitations. (Most of the abusive acts occurred more than one year before Nussbaum instituted her suit.) Nussbaum offered expert testimony to the effect that, as a result of the long-term abuse, she was so incapacitated that she was incapable of functioning independently and therefore unable to protect her own interests. The court agreed and denied Steinberg's motion for summary judgment, thereby permitting Nussbaum to sue for the entire course of abusive conduct. See Nussbaum v. Steinberg, 618 N.Y.S.2d 168 (Sup. Ct. 1994), *aff'd*, 703 N.Y.S.2d 32 (App. Div. 2000). See also Nussbaum v. Steinberg, 204 N.Y.L.J. 21 (1990).

3. *Procedural Barriers: Res Judicata*

■ **CHEN v. FISCHER**
843 N.E.2d 723 (N.Y. 2005)

CIPARICK, J.

Plaintiff Xiao Yang Chen and defendant Ian Ira Fischer were married on March 11, 2001. Shortly thereafter, Fischer commenced an action for divorce on the ground of cruel and inhuman treatment. Chen counterclaimed for divorce—also alleging cruel and inhuman treatment. . . . [A]s grounds for divorce, Chen alleged that on May 6, 2001, Fischer "grabbed [her] and violently slapped her across the face and ear causing [her] to suffer bruising, pain and swelling" and that he threw her on the ground and attempted to suffocate her. As a result of that incident, each party filed a family offense petition against the other in Family Court and received a temporary order of protection. The parties agreed to consolidate these petitions with the matrimonial action. At the conclusion of the matrimonial trial, they further agreed to withdraw the petitions without prejudice on the record in open court.

On October 15, 2001, prior to trial of the matrimonial action, the parties entered into a stipulation on the issue of fault [agreeing] to withdraw all their fault allegations—including those related to the May 6 incident—save one. [O]n May 8, 2002, a dual judgment of divorce was granted on the ground of cruel and inhuman treatment based on each party's sole remaining fault allegation.

Chen allegedly commenced the instant personal injury action on January 18, 2002, while the matrimonial action was pending. The complaint asserted two causes of action—one for intentional infliction of emotional distress and a second for assault and battery. As to the second cause of action, the complaint alleged [the incident on May 6, 2001]. Fischer answered, raising several affirmative defenses, including res judicata and various theories of estoppel.

The Supreme Court granted Fischer's motion to dismiss [finding that] the allegations in Chen's personal injury action were "virtually identical" to those in her counterclaim for divorce and arose out of the same transaction or series of transactions. Thus, the court determined that the tort action was barred by res judicata.

Typically, principles of res judicata require that "once a claim is brought to a final conclusion, all other claims arising out of the same transaction or series of transactions are barred, even if based upon different theories or if seeking a different remedy." In the context of a matrimonial action, this Court has recognized that a final judgment of divorce settles the parties' rights pertaining not only to those issues that were actually litigated, but also to those that could have been litigated. The primary purposes of res judicata are grounded in public policy concerns and are intended to ensure finality, prevent vexatious litigation and promote judicial economy. However, unfairness may result if the doctrine is applied too harshly; thus "[i]n properly seeking to deny a litigant two 'days in court,' courts must be careful not to deprive [the litigant] of one."

It is not always clear whether particular claims are part of the same transaction for res judicata purposes. A "pragmatic" test has been applied to make this determination—analyzing "whether the facts are related in time, space, origin, or motivation, whether they form a convenient trial unit, and whether their treatment as a unit conforms to the parties' expectations or business understanding or usage."

Applying these principles, it is apparent that personal injury tort actions and divorce actions do not constitute a convenient trial unit. The purposes behind the two are quite different. They seek different types of relief and require different types of proof. Moreover, a personal injury action is usually tried by a jury, in contrast to a matrimonial action, which is typically decided by a judge when the issue of fault is not contested. Further, personal injury attorneys are compensated by contingency fee, whereas matrimonial attorneys are prohibited from entering into fee arrangements that are contingent upon the granting of a divorce or a particular property settlement or distributive award.

[Typically,] a personal injury action is not sufficiently intertwined with the dissolution of the marriage relationship as to allow for its efficient resolution. Thus, the interspousal tort action does not form a convenient trial unit with the divorce proceeding, and it would not be within the parties' reasonable expectations that the two would be tried together. . . .

Here, although the personal injury claim could have been litigated with the matrimonial action—as the facts arose from the same transaction or series of events—it was not, as all of Chen's fault allegations, save one, were withdrawn by stipulation for the salutary purpose of expediting the matrimonial action. She is therefore not precluded from litigating that claim in a separate action. . . .

Notes and Questions

1. *Background.* In *Chen*, the husband filed for dissolution based on cruelty, and the wife counterclaimed on the same ground. While the dissolution was pending, the wife filed a claim for assault and battery as well as IIED. In the IIED, claim, she alleged that "during the marriage Fischer repeatedly accused her of being unfaithful, threatened to lock her out of the marital home, refused to allow her to socialize with friends, physically and emotionally abused her for refusing to engage in sexual relations with him, referred to her as a slave and demanded subservience from her, and filed a false police report against her." The assault and battery claim was based on the May 6th incident of physical abuse. Chen v. Fischer, 783 N.Y.S.2d 394 (App. Div. 2004), *rev'd*, 843 N.E.2d 723 (N.Y. 2005).

The husband interjected the affirmative defense that her claims were barred by res judicata. He argued that the wife alleged substantially the same factual allegations in her counterclaim for divorce based on cruelty, and that she withdrew all but one of those allegations in the stipulation of settlement but without expressly reserving any rights to make those assertions in a later action. The trial court agreed, reasoning that once the wife's claim for divorce became final, all other claims and causes of action arising out of the same series of transactions were barred. In the principal case, the New York Court of Appeals reverses. Note that because New York does not recognize interspousal actions for IIED, the New York Court of Appeals limited its discussion to Chen's cause of action for assault and battery. *Chen*, 843 N.E.2d at 725 n.2.

2. *New York divorce law.* Why did the parties in *Chen* sue for divorce based on fault? At the time, New York permitted dissolution either on fault-based grounds, or, alternatively, living apart for at least one year pursuant to a decree of judicial separation or by written agreement. See N.Y. Dom. Rel. Law §170. Until recent divorce reform, New York had the strictest divorce law in the country. In 2010, the state assembly finally enacted no-fault legislation. See 2010 N.Y. Laws, Ch. 384 §1, effective Oct. 12, 2010, amending Domestic Relations Law §170 to add subdivision 7 (adopting "irretrievably broken" as no-fault divorce ground).

3. *Application to facts.* Res judicata (sometimes called "claim preclusion") precludes the relitigation of a claim or cause of action in a subsequent proceeding between the same parties to an earlier action. That is, the doctrine provides that a final judgment on the merits bars claims by the same parties in a subsequent proceeding not only as to any matter that was *actually* litigated, but as to any other matter that *might* have been litigated. What purpose does the doctrine serve? See Jack H. Friedenthal et al., Civil Procedure 653 (4th ed. 2005) (interest in "preventing relitigation of the same dispute recognizes that judicial resources are finite and the number of cases that can be heard by the courts is limited").

Several questions are relevant in determining the existence of a defense of res judicata: (1) Is the claim that was previously decided the same claim that is presented in subsequent action? (2) Did the court reach a final judgment on the merits? (3) Is the party against whom the res judicata defense is asserted the same party as in the prior suit? How does the doctrine apply in Chen v. Fischer? Which party would it benefit and how?

4. *Same or different claim?* As the court in *Chen* explains, "It is not always clear whether particular claims are part of the same transaction for res judicata purposes." How does a court make that determination? See Roussel v. Roussel, 2003

WL 22951910 (Va. Cir. Ct. 2003) (determining that tort claim for assault and battery was not the same as divorce-based claim because plaintiff agreed to raise only the fault-based ground of adultery in the dissolution, therefore divorce court made no findings regarding defendant's assault and battery).

5. *Collateral estoppel distinguished.* Res judicata and collateral estoppel are sometimes confused. How do they differ? Collateral estoppel (sometimes called "issue preclusion") prevents relitigation of factual *issues actually litigated* and necessary to the outcome of the first action. Thus, collateral estoppel requires an identity of factual issues. The doctrines of res judicata and collateral estoppel apply only if the parties in the subsequent suit are the same as those in the prior suit. Why did the defendant in *Chen* raises the bar of res judicata rather than collateral estoppel? See also *Roussel*, supra (holding that neither res judicata nor collateral estoppel barred wife's tort claim because it would be unfair to preclude her tort claim when she agreed to limit her fault-based ground for dissolution purposes to adultery).

6. *Holding.* Could plaintiff's tort claim have been litigated at the same time as the dissolution? If so, why wasn't it? Why did Chen withdraw all her fault allegations, except one? Why did the New York Court of Appeals hold that Chen was not barred from litigating her tort claim in a separate action? Why did the court suggest that personal injury tort actions and divorce actions are not "a convenient trial unit"? What public policy considerations influenced the result? How does the reasoning take into account the dynamics of domestic violence?

7. *Marital settlement provision as a bar.* Res judicata may serve as a bar to tort recovery in some cases in which a domestic violence victim first pursued a divorce. Another potential bar to tort recovery is the release clause of a marital settlement agreement, such as the agreement executed in *Chen.* Marital settlement agreements are executed to settle issues of property and support. Release clauses are routinely inserted that release the parties from "all claims, rights and duties arising or growing out of the marital relationship." Do release clauses preclude a victim from being able to file a subsequent tort claim? The answer depends on the language and how broadly courts construe it. The following language is illustrative:

> To the fullest extent by law permitted to do so, and except as herein otherwise provided, each of the parties does hereby forever relinquish, release, waive, and forever quitclaim and grant to the other, his or her heirs, personal representatives, and assignees, all rights of dower, inheritance, descent, distribution, community interest, marital property, and all other right, title, claim, tort claims, interest, and estate as husband and wife, widow or widower, or otherwise, by reason of the marital relations existing between the parties hereto, under any present or future law, or which he or she otherwise has or might have or be entitled to claim in, to, or against the property and assets of the other. . . .

Feltmeier, 777 N.E.2d at 1182. What specific language of the above marital settlement agreement might bar a tortfeasor-spouse from tort liability? Would such a contract be unenforceable as a matter of public policy?

Several courts have precluded spousal tort claims based on similar marital settlement agreements. See, e.g., Overberg v. Lusby, 921 F.2d 90, 91-92 (6th Cir. 1990); Coleman v. Coleman, 566 So. 2d 482, 483-485 (Ala. 1990); Slansky v. Slansky, 553 A.2d 152, 153-154 (Vt. 1988). But cf. Feltmeier, 777 N.E. 2d at 1182-1183 (holding that a release with "general boilerplate language" that attempted to extinguish specific claims that arose *after* the agreement's execution would violate public policy, and reasoning also that tort liability for domestic abuse should not be barred because it is not a claim that is "derived from the marital relationship itself").

How can attorneys who represent domestic violence victims address the possibility that a release might preclude a subsequent tort suit? Professor Dalton responds:

> The lesson here for lawyers representing clients in divorce proceedings is that much may ride on the language of release provisions. Those representing marital partners who have been abused must be cautious not to give away too much; those representing partners who may have been abusive have every incentive to make the release as all-inclusive as possible. There is an inherent tension between an abused partner's desire not to signal her intention to bring a later tort suit, and her need to protect that possibility by refusing to accede to language, or insisting on language, that may give her intentions away. The courts will eventually be faced with the question of whether a release that precludes a subsequent suit should be invalidated as "involuntary," when the abused partner's fear of further violence is what prevented her from objecting to its inclusion in the settlement.

Clare Dalton, Domestic Violence, Domestic Torts, and Divorce: Constraints and Possibilities, 31 New Eng. L. Rev. 319, 385 (1997).

The relationship between res judicata and joinder is discussed in Chapter 11, pp. 572-577.

C. SOCIAL REALITY: VICTIMS' RELUCTANCE TO USE TORT REMEDIES

Very few victims of domestic violence seek recovery for their injuries by tort claims. The excerpt below explores the reasons for their reluctance.

■ JENNIFER WRIGGINS, DOMESTIC VIOLENCE TORTS
75 S. Cal. L. Rev. 121, 122-124, 135-144 (2001)

Domestic violence has created a massive epidemic of uncompensated intentional torts. . . . People who commit domestic violence generally are, in theory, liable under intentional tort theories, in addition to whatever liability they may face under criminal law. But despite the frequency with which people are injured by "domestic violence torts," very few tort suits are brought to seek recovery for the harms domestic violence causes. . . . Why are there so few lawsuits, given that injuries are widespread and that interspousal immunity, which in the past would have barred many such cases, no longer pertains? Many forces combine to create the dearth.

1. Lack of Insurance

Insurance (or the lack of it) is extremely important in all aspects of tort litigation. Torts and insurance cannot be understood in isolation from one another.

Litigation for harms from domestic violence is no exception. There is very little third-party liability insurance coverage for defendants accused of domestic violence torts. Lack of insurance is a major contributor to the scarcity of tort claims for domestic violence injuries.

The most common types of liability insurance policies issued to individuals, such as homeowners, renters, and automobile policies, typically exclude coverage for "intentional acts" of the insured. As a result of this "intentional acts exclusion," if a plaintiff brings a claim for intentional torts and the insured is a homeowner or renter with liability insurance, the insurance company is likely to claim (successfully) that the suit is not covered by the policy.

A second common barrier to liability insurance coverage is the "family member exclusion." Often with jointly owned property, homeowners' liability policies name all owners or residents as insureds, and exclude all claims by insureds against one another. Thus, a tort claim of any sort between insureds would not be covered by such a policy. . . .

These insurance barriers limit or in many instances, vitiate, insurance coverage. Even if litigation would likely be successful on the merits, these insurance issues present hurdles that discourage filing lawsuits even in cases of clear liability and serious injury.

2. Asset Limitations

Resource limitations are another reason why there are so few reported lawsuits seeking recovery for harms from domestic violence torts. Financial recovery against a defendant who lacks assets or insurance is not possible. Many persons in the United States are judgment-proof.

A house is often a person's or a family's largest asset. . . . In a domestic violence situation, this asset may be jointly owned by the victim and the perpetrator, complicating the obtaining of the asset. The house may be mortgaged, protected by a homestead exemption, located in another state, or encumbered by preexisting involuntary liens. Moreover, lawyers are likely to be more reluctant to pursue a claim on a contingency basis when the only asset is a house owned by the defendant than if there is insurance. Even when there are significant assets, attorneys prefer to seek funds provided by insurance.

Getting a private attorney to take a case on a contingency basis where there are neither assets nor insurance is difficult, if not impossible. If a plaintiff has funds to pay an attorney, she is more likely to find one, but most potential plaintiffs are not in a position to pay a private attorney to pursue a claim.

3. Statutes of Limitations

Another reason so few tort lawsuits are filed for harm from domestic violence torts is the relatively short statutes of limitations for most intentional torts. Statutes of limitations for assault, battery, and false imprisonment are typically between one and two years. Although statutes of limitations for intentional infliction of emotional distress range from one to ten years, the most common statutes of limitations lengths are two and three years. By contrast, statutes of limitations for negligence and strict liability generally are longer, ranging from two to six years.

The complex dynamics of domestic violence, which often include extensive psychological control, as well as physical violence, can make consideration of filing a tort claim near the time that the injuries are inflicted inconceivable. Abuse and control may last for years, and a victim may only be able to escape from the relationship, at great risk, after a long period of time. By the time a person is able to leave an abusive relationship (whether married or unmarried) and decides to sue, the statute of limitations on some or all of her intentional tort claims may well have run.

4. Procedural Barriers

Existing law makes the conjunction of divorce and tort claims complicated and fraught with potential difficulty for domestic violence tort victims. Various procedural obstacles can make it difficult or impossible for an abused person to bring a tort claim for abuse that occurs during a marriage. To bring a claim for compensation while a marriage continues has obvious problems. A person is unlikely to be able to even consider such a claim until she has decided to seek a divorce. A married person's most immediate legal need at that time may be to end the legal relationship with her spouse. Her most immediate practical needs may be physical and economic survival, and maintaining contact with her children. Asserting tort claims at the time of divorce may jeopardize all those interests. Despite these and other reasons why tort claims should not have to be asserted at the time of divorce, some courts have held that a tort claim for abuse occurring during a marriage must be asserted at the time of the divorce, or it is barred by res judicata. Other courts have held that principles of waiver and equitable estoppel may bar tort actions filed after divorces.

5. Other Issues

Additional factors contribute to the relative dearth of lawsuits for domestic violence torts. In general, for a variety of reasons, relatively few injured people seek compensation for their injuries, whatever the source of those injuries. . . .

One reason people do not bring claims is that they do not know that they have a claim. This likely is a reason so few suits are brought for domestic violence injuries even after a person escapes from an abuser. Moreover, unlike injuries from car accidents, for which people have grown to expect compensation through a highly regulated insurance system, there is no such expectation of compensation for domestic violence injuries.

People sometimes blame themselves for injuries caused by unsafe products. Similarly, persons who are victimized by domestic violence often blame themselves (and are blamed for it by their abusers). Thus, it may not occur to a domestic violence victim to sue for a harm for which she feels responsible.

One might be surprised that there are not more tort suits in connection with divorce, given that divorce is an occasion where a victim would come in contact with the legal system, and might have an attorney. Many people, however, do not have attorneys in divorce; this is particularly true for women. Women are much more likely to be victims of domestic violence than are men. Even when a person injured by domestic violence does have an attorney for her divorce, it is possible that the lawyer dealing with the divorce does not even consider a tort case.

Bringing a claim has costs, which "may include stigma associated with the act of asserting a complaint, keeping the memory of the injury or loss alive, or continued confrontation with the injurer, a distressing prospect for most victims." The costs of domestic violence tort claims to victims are much higher than for other kinds of tort claims. First, the injury is caused by someone known by the victim. Continued confrontation with the injurer is likely to be more distressing than when the injurer is a manufacturer or a heretofore unknown driver. Second, for many domestic abuse victims, there is a real and reasonable fear of violent retaliation for the suit. The end of a relationship is the most dangerous time for victims; filing a lawsuit is a way of demonstrating that the relationship is indeed over and may result in serious and, in some instances, fatal consequences. Third, if the parties are married and are not yet divorced, a victim may rationally fear that the potential defendant will assert retaliatory legal strategies in the divorce. Failure to raise the tort claims in a divorce action may result in those claims being barred later. Thus, victims face a catch-22 and pressure to forego asserting tort claims. Fourth, many people who have been in intimate relationships where they have been victims of domestic violence torts simply wish to end the abusive relationship and move on. Fifth, in civil rape cases in state court, rape shield laws do not apply, which may discourage some injured plaintiffs. The plaintiff might appear unsympathetic to a jury, so a lawyer may advise against pursuing an otherwise meritorious claim. It is also possible that a victim may have injured the abuser, making a tort claim on behalf of one likely to be answered with a valid counterclaim.

Deterrence is one of the important justifications for tort liability. But since so few lawsuits are brought by domestic violence victims compared to the harms committed, tort law is not an effective deterrent. . . .

Notes and Questions

1. *Motivations.* What are victims' concerns in ending a relationship that might take precedence over their desire for compensation? What are the psychological costs to the victim of bringing a tort suit? How might self-blame play a role? How can these problems be addressed?

2. *Insurance issues.* How do the lack of insurance and the type of liability insurance coverage explain the infrequency of tort claims for domestic violence-related injuries? What is the "intentional acts exclusion"? What is the "family member exclusion"? How might the insurance system be reformed to provide compensation for victims' needs?

3. *Financial issues.* Lawyers may be unwilling to institute tort suits for victims of domestic violence because abusers often lack sufficient assets to pay damage awards. In the event that litigation is successful, what problems might lawyers face in their attempts to reach defendants' assets? Despite the fact that many abusers come from the middle- and upper-socioeconomic strata, why might a *victim* who is an intimate partner of these offenders have difficulty accessing funds to pay attorneys' fees and the costs of suit?

4. *Legal personnel.* Attorneys facilitate access to the legal system. What factors militate against victims' familiarity with, and access to, attorneys? For example, many people fail to file tort suits because of ignorance of the availability of the tort system as a remedy. How can this ignorance be addressed?

Professor Sarah Buel identifies additional factors regarding legal personnel. She notes that:

> Those few attorneys who have handled domestic violence tort actions often express a general distaste for these cases, based in large part on their aversion to the grievous nature of the batterer's conduct. Several women lawyers with whom I spoke confided

personal fear of the batterers. One had her office destroyed the night after a case (involving a wealthy doctor who had brutally assaulted his eight-months' pregnant wife) settled for $3 million.

Buel, Access to Meaningful Remedy, supra, at 953. How can these problems be remedied?

D. FEDERAL TORT LIABILITY: VAWA'S CIVIL RIGHTS REMEDY

The Violence Against Women Act (VAWA) of 1994 marked the first comprehensive attempt by Congress to address domestic violence as well as sexual assault. The Act's most controversial provision was a civil rights remedy that allowed a victim of gender-based violence to bring a federal civil suit against her abuser. The following case challenges the constitutionality of this provision.

■ UNITED STATES v. MORRISON
529 U.S. 598 (2000)

CHIEF JUSTICE REHNQUIST delivered the opinion of the Court.

. . . Petitioner Christy Brzonkala enrolled at Virginia Polytechnic Institute in the fall of 1994. In September of that year, Brzonkala met respondents Antonio Morrison and James Crawford [members of the varsity football team]. Brzonkala alleges that, within 30 minutes of meeting Morrison and Crawford, they assaulted and repeatedly raped her. After the attack, Morrison allegedly told Brzonkala, "You better not have any . . . diseases." In the months following the rape, Morrison also allegedly announced in the dormitory's dining room that he "like[d] to get girls drunk and . . ." The omitted portions, quoted verbatim in the briefs on file with this Court, consist of boasting, debased remarks about what Morrison would do to women, vulgar remarks that cannot fail to shock and offend.

Brzonkala alleges that this attack caused her to become severely emotionally disturbed and depressed. She sought assistance from a university psychiatrist, who prescribed antidepressant medication. Shortly after the rape, Brzonkala stopped attending classes and withdrew from the university.

In early 1995, Brzonkala filed a complaint against respondents under Virginia Tech's Sexual Assault Policy. During the school-conducted hearing on her complaint, Morrison admitted having sexual contact with her despite the fact that she had twice told him "no." After the hearing, Virginia Tech's Judicial Committee found insufficient evidence to punish Crawford, but found Morrison guilty of sexual assault and sentenced him to immediate suspension for two semesters.

[After Morrison announced that he intended to sue, the University held a second hearing. It upheld Morrison's suspension but based on the offense of "using abusive language" rather than "sexual assault." When he appealed, the University set aside the suspension as "excessive." After learning that Morrison would re-enroll at Virginia Tech, Brzonkala dropped out of school. Brzonkala sued Morrison, Crawford, and Virginia Tech alleging violations of VAWA, 42 U.S.C. §13981, and Title IX of the Education Amendments Act of 1972. VAWA's civil remedy provision declares that "[a]ll persons within the United States shall have the right to be free from crimes of violence motivated by gender." A "crime of violence" is defined to include actions that would constitute a felony under state or federal law. Further, VAWA makes the perpetrator liable to the victim for compensatory and punitive damages. Injunctive and declaratory relief are also available.]

[M]odern Commerce Clause jurisprudence has "identified three broad categories of activity that Congress may regulate under its commerce power" [including "the use of the channels of interstate commerce," "the instrumentalities of interstate commerce even though the threat may come only from intrastate activities," and "activities having a substantial relation to interstate commerce"]. Petitioners do not contend that these cases fall within either of the first two of these categories of Commerce Clause regulation. They seek to sustain §13981 as a regulation of activity that substantially affects interstate commerce. Given §13981's focus on gender-motivated violence wherever it occurs . . . , we agree that this is the proper inquiry.

[Our decision in United States v. Lopez, 514 U.S. 549 (1995), governs this third category of Commerce Clause regulation.] In *Lopez*, we held that the Gun-Free School Zones Act of 1990, 18 U.S.C. §922(q)(1)(A), which made it a federal crime to knowingly possess a firearm in a school zone, exceeded Congress's authority under the Commerce Clause. Several significant considerations contributed to our decision.

First, we observed that §922(q) was "a criminal statute that by its terms has nothing to do with 'commerce' or any sort of economic enterprise, however broadly one might define those terms." . . . [I]n those cases where we have sustained federal regulation of intrastate activity based upon the activity's substantial effects on interstate commerce, the activity in question has been some sort of economic endeavor. The second consideration that we found important in [*Lopez*] was that the statute contained "no express jurisdictional element which might limit its reach to a discrete set of firearm possessions that additionally have an explicit connection with or effect on interstate commerce." . . . Third, we noted that neither [the statute at issue in *Lopez* nor its legislative history contains] "express congressional findings regarding the effects upon interstate commerce of gun possession in a school zone" [that might] "enable us to evaluate the legislative judgment that the activity in question substantially affect[s] interstate commerce, even though no such substantial effect [is] visible to the naked eye."

Finally, our decision in *Lopez* rested in part on the fact that the link between gun possession and a substantial effect on interstate commerce was attenuated. [The United States had attempted to justify the statute by arguing that the possession of guns leads to violent crime, that the costs of violent crime are substantial and pervasive, and also that the presence of guns at schools poses a threat to the educational process, which in turn threatens to produce a less efficient and productive work force, which will negatively affect national productivity and thus interstate commerce].

We rejected these "costs of crime" and "national productivity" arguments because they would permit Congress to "regulate not only all violent crime, but all activities that might lead to violent crime, regardless of how tenuously they relate to interstate commerce." . . . We noted that, under this but-for reasoning:

"Congress could regulate any activity that it found was related to the economic productivity of individual citizens: family law (including marriage, divorce, and child custody), for example. Under the[se] theories . . . , it is difficult to perceive any limitation on federal power, even in areas such as criminal law enforcement or education where States historically have been sovereign. Thus, if we were to accept the Government's arguments, we are hard pressed to posit any activity by an individual that Congress is without power to regulate." [514 U.S. at 564.]

With these principles underlying our Commerce Clause jurisprudence as reference points, the proper resolution of the present cases is clear. Gender-motivated crimes of violence are not, in any sense of the phrase, economic activity. . . . [T]hus far in our Nation's history, our cases have upheld Commerce Clause regulation of intrastate activity only where that activity is economic in nature.

. . . In contrast with the lack of congressional findings that we faced in *Lopez*, §13981 *is* supported by numerous findings regarding the serious impact that gender-motivated violence has on victims and their families. But the existence of congressional findings is not sufficient, by itself, to sustain the constitutionality of Commerce Clause legislation. . . . [Specifically, Congress found that gender-motivated violence affects interstate commerce by deterring potential victims from traveling interstate and engaging in employment in interstate business; diminishing national productivity; and decreasing the supply of, and demand for, interstate products.] Given these findings and petitioners' arguments, the concern that we expressed in *Lopez* that Congress might use the Commerce Clause to completely obliterate the Constitution's distinction between national and local authority seems well-founded. The reasoning that petitioners advance seeks to follow the but-for causal chain from the initial occurrence of violent crime (the suppression of which has always been the prime object of the States' police power) to every attenuated effect upon interstate commerce. If accepted, petitioners' reasoning would allow Congress to regulate any crime as long as the nationwide, aggregated impact of that crime has substantial effects on employment, production, transit, or consumption. Indeed, if Congress may regulate gender-motivated violence, it would be able to regulate murder or any other type of violence since gender-motivated violence, as a subset of all violent crime, is certain to have lesser economic impacts than the larger class of which it is a part. . . .

We accordingly reject the argument that Congress may regulate noneconomic, violent criminal conduct based solely on that conduct's aggregate effect on interstate commerce. The Constitution requires a distinction between what is truly national and what is truly local. . . . Indeed, we can think of no better example of the police power, which the Founders denied the National Government and reposed in the States, than the suppression of violent crime and vindication of its victims.

Because we conclude that the Commerce Clause does not provide Congress with authority to enact §13981, we address petitioners' alternative argument that the section's civil remedy should be upheld as an exercise of Congress's remedial power under §5 of the Fourteenth Amendment [providing that Congress may enforce by "appropriate legislation" the constitutional guarantee that no State shall deprive any person of "life, liberty, or property, without due process of law," nor deny any person "equal protection of the laws"]. . . .

Petitioners' §5 argument is founded on an assertion that there is pervasive bias in various state justice systems against victims of gender-motivated violence. This assertion is supported by a voluminous congressional record. Specifically, Congress received evidence that many participants in state justice systems are perpetuating an array of erroneous stereotypes and assumptions. Congress concluded that these discriminatory stereotypes often result in insufficient investigation and prosecution of gender-motivated crime, inappropriate focus on the behavior and credibility of the victims of that crime, and unacceptably lenient punishments for those who are actually convicted of gender-motivated violence. Petitioners contend that this bias denies victims of gender-motivated violence the equal protection of the laws and that Congress therefore acted appropriately in enacting a private civil remedy against the perpetrators of gender-motivated violence to both remedy the States' bias and deter future instances of discrimination in the state courts.

[S]tate-sponsored gender discrimination violates equal protection unless it serves "important governmental objectives and . . . the discriminatory means employed" are "substantially related to the achievement of those objectives." However, the language and purpose of the Fourteenth Amendment place certain limitations on the manner in which Congress may attack discriminatory conduct. These limitations are necessary to prevent the Fourteenth Amendment from obliterating the Framers' carefully crafted balance of power between the States and the National Government. Foremost among these limitations is the time-honored principle that the Fourteenth Amendment, by its very terms, prohibits only state action. "That Amendment erects no shield against merely private conduct, however discriminatory or wrongful."

Petitioners alternatively argue that . . . here there has been gender-based disparate treatment by state authorities . . . [E]ven if that distinction were valid, we do not believe it would save §13981's civil remedy. For the [statutory] remedy is simply [not directed] at any State or state actor, but [rather] at individuals who have committed criminal acts motivated by gender bias.

Petitioner Brzonkala's complaint alleges that she was the victim of a brutal assault. . . . If the allegations here are true, no civilized system of justice could fail to provide her a remedy for the conduct of respondent Morrison. But under our federal system that remedy must be provided by the Commonwealth of Virginia, and not by the United States. . . .

Justice SOUTER, with whom Justice STEVENS, Justice GINSBURG, and Justice BREYER join, dissenting.

[O]ur cases [stand] for the following propositions. Congress has the power to legislate with regard to activity that, in the aggregate, has a substantial effect on interstate commerce. The fact of such a substantial effect is not an issue for the courts in the first instance, but for the Congress, whose institutional capacity for gathering evidence and taking testimony far exceeds ours. By passing legislation, Congress indicates its conclusion, whether explicitly or not, that facts support its exercise of the commerce power. The business of the courts is to review the congressional assessment, not for soundness but simply for the rationality of concluding that a jurisdictional basis exists in fact. . . . Applying those propositions in these cases can lead to only one conclusion.

[Congress assembled a "mountain of data"] showing the effects of violence against women on interstate commerce. . . . With respect to domestic violence, Congress received evidence for the following findings:

"Three out of four American women will be victims of violent crimes sometime during their life." "Violence is the leading cause of injuries to women ages 15 to

44. . . ." "[A]s many as 50 percent of homeless women and children are fleeing domestic violence." "Since 1974, the assault rate against women has outstripped the rate for men by at least twice for some age groups and far more for others." "[B]attering 'is the single largest cause of injury to women in the United States.'" "An estimated 4 million American women are battered each year by their husbands or partners." "Over 1 million women in the United States seek medical assistance each year for injuries sustained [from] their husbands or other partners."

"Between 2,000 and 4,000 women die every year from [domestic] abuse." "[A]rrest rates may be as low as 1 for every 100 domestic assaults." "Partial estimates show that violent crime against women costs this country at least 3 billion—not million, but billion—dollars a year." "[E]stimates suggest that we spend $5 to $10 billion a year on health care, criminal justice, and other social costs of domestic violence."

The evidence as to rape was similarly extensive, supporting these conclusions:

"[The incidence of] rape rose four times as fast as the total national crime rate over the past 10 years." . . . "[One hundred twenty-five thousand] college women can expect to be raped during this—or any—year." "[T]hree-quarters of women never go to the movies alone after dark because of the fear of rape and nearly 50 percent do not use public transit alone after dark for the same reason." "[Forty-one] percent of judges surveyed believed that juries give sexual assault victims less credibility than other crime victims."

"Less than 1 percent of all [rape] victims have collected damages." . . .

"Almost one-quarter of convicted rapists never go to prison and another quarter received sentences in local jails where the average sentence is 11 months." "[A]lmost 50 percent of rape victims lose their jobs or are forced to quit because of the crime's severity." . . .

Based on the data thus partially summarized, Congress found that

crimes of violence motivated by gender have a substantial adverse effect on interstate commerce, by deterring potential victims from traveling interstate, from engaging in employment in interstate business, and from transacting with business, and in places involved, in interstate commerce . . . [,] by diminishing national productivity, increasing medical and other costs, and decreasing the supply of and the demand for interstate products. . . . H.R. Conf. Rep. No. 103-711, p. 385 (1994). . . .

[T]he sufficiency of the evidence before Congress to provide a rational basis for the finding cannot seriously be questioned. Indeed, the legislative record here is far more voluminous than the record compiled by Congress and found sufficient in two prior cases upholding Title II of the Civil Rights Act of 1964 against Commerce Clause challenges. . . .

If the analogy to the Civil Rights Act of 1964 is not plain enough, one can always look back a bit further [citing Wickard v. Filburn, 317 U.S. 111 (1942) (holding that Congress could regulate the individual act of a small farmer who cultivated home-grown wheat even though that act lacked a substantial effect on interstate commerce because, when aggregated, similar acts had the requisite relation to interstate commerce.] . . . The Commerce Clause predicate was simply the effect of the production of wheat for home consumption on supply and demand in interstate commerce. Supply and demand for goods in interstate commerce will also be affected by the deaths of 2,000 to 4,000 women annually at the hands of domestic abusers, and by the reduction in the work force by the 100,000 or more rape victims who lose their jobs each year or are forced to quit. Violence against women may be found to affect interstate commerce and affect it substantially. . . .

[The majority today] finds no significance whatever in the state support for the Act based upon the States' acknowledged failure to deal adequately with gender-based violence in state courts, and the belief of their own law enforcement agencies that national action is essential. The National Association of Attorneys General supported the Act unanimously, and Attorneys General from 38 States urged Congress to enact the Civil Rights Remedy, representing that "the current system for dealing with violence against women is inadequate." It was against this record of failure at the state level that the Act was passed to provide the choice of a federal forum in place of the state-court systems found inadequate to stop gender-biased violence. The Act accordingly offers a federal civil rights remedy aimed exactly at violence against women, as an alternative to the generic state tort causes of action found to be poor tools of action by the state task forces. . . . All of this convinces me that today's ebb of the commerce power rests on error. . . .

Justice BREYER, with whom Justice STEVENS joins, and with whom Justice SOUTER and Justice GINSBURG join as to Part I-A, dissenting.

No one denies the importance of the Constitution's federalist principles. . . . The question is how the judiciary can best implement that original federalist understanding where the Commerce Clause is at issue.

The majority holds that the federal commerce power does not extend to such "noneconomic" activities as "noneconomic, violent criminal conduct" that significantly affects interstate commerce only if we "aggregate" the interstate "effect[s]" of individual instances. Justice Souter explains why history, precedent, and legal logic militate against the majority's approach. I agree. . . . [Justice Breyer then reasons that the economic/noneconomic distinction is not easy to apply. He adds that the Commerce Clause, as supplemented by the "necessary and proper" language, does not explicitly mention the local or economic nature of an activity that affects interstate commerce. He also reasons that neither the Constitution nor pre-*Lopez* case law explain "why the Court should ignore one highly relevant characteristic of an interstate-commerce-affecting cause (how "local" it is), while placing critical constitutional weight upon a different, less obviously relevant, feature (how "economic" it is)"]. . . .

[The majority contends that] [t]o determine the lawfulness of statutes simply by asking whether Congress could reasonably have found that aggregated local instances significantly affect interstate commerce [that is, the view based on Wicklund v. Filburn, supra] will allow Congress to regulate almost anything. Virtually all local activity, when instances are aggregated, can have "substantial effects on employment, production, transit, or consumption." Hence Congress could "regulate any crime," and perhaps "marriage, divorce, and childrearing" as well, obliterating the "Constitution's distinction between national and local authority."

This consideration, however, while serious, does not reflect a jurisprudential defect, so much as it reflects a practical reality. We live in a Nation knit together by two centuries of scientific, technological, commercial, and environmental change. Those changes, taken together, mean that virtually every kind of activity, no matter how local, genuinely can affect commerce, or its conditions, outside the State—at least when considered in the aggregate. And that fact makes it close to impossible for courts to develop meaningful subject-matter categories that would exclude some kinds of local activities from ordinary Commerce Clause "aggregation" rules without, at the same time, depriving Congress of the power to regulate activities that have a genuine and important effect upon interstate commerce.

Since judges cannot change the world, the "defect" means that, within the bounds of the rational, Congress, not the courts, must remain primarily responsible for striking the appropriate state/federal balance. . . . [A]s Justice Souter has pointed out, Congress compiled a "mountain of data" explicitly documenting the interstate commercial effects of gender-motivated crimes of violence. After considering alternatives, it focused the federal law upon documented deficiencies in state legal systems. And it tailored the law to prevent its use in certain areas of traditional state concern, such as divorce, alimony, or child custody. Consequently, the law before us seems to represent an instance, not of state/federal conflict, but of state/federal efforts to cooperate in order to help solve a mutually acknowledged national problem. . . .

[Justice Breyer also expresses doubts about the majority's reasoning rejecting Congress's authority under Section 5 of the Fourteenth Amendment to regulate private actors in this case.] [T]he Court held [in prior case law] that §5 does not authorize Congress to use the Fourteenth Amendment as a source of power to remedy the conduct of *private persons*. That is certainly so. The Federal Government's argument, however, is that Congress used §5 to remedy the actions of *state actors*, namely, those States which, through discriminatory design or the discriminatory conduct of their officials, failed to provide adequate (or any) state remedies for women injured by gender-motivated violence—a failure that the States, and Congress, documented in depth.

. . .

The Court responds directly to the relevant "state actor" claim by finding that the present law lacks "'congruence and proportionality'" to the state discrimination that it purports to remedy. That is because the law, unlike federal laws prohibiting literacy tests for voting, imposing voting rights requirements, or punishing state officials who intentionally discriminated in jury selection, is not "directed . . . at any State or state actor."

But why can Congress not provide a remedy against private actors? Those private actors, of course, did not themselves violate the Constitution. But this Court has held that Congress at least sometimes can enact remedial "[l]egislation . . . [that] prohibits conduct which is not itself unconstitutional." The statutory remedy does not in any sense purport to "determine what constitutes a constitutional violation." It intrudes little upon either States or private parties. It may lead state actors to improve their own remedial systems, primarily through example. It restricts private actors only by imposing liability for private conduct that is, in the main, already forbidden by state law. Why is the remedy "disproportionate"? And given the relation between remedy and violation—the creation of a federal remedy to substitute for constitutionally inadequate state remedies—where is the lack of "congruence"?

The majority adds that Congress found that the problem of inadequacy of state remedies "does not exist in all States, or even most States." But Congress had before it the task force reports of at least 21 States documenting constitutional violations. And it made its own findings about pervasive gender-based stereotypes hampering many state legal systems, sometimes unconstitutionally so. . . . Why can Congress not take the evidence before it as evidence of a national problem? This Court has not previously held that Congress must document the existence of a problem in every

State prior to proposing a national solution. And the deference this Court gives to Congress's chosen remedy under §5 suggests that any such requirement would be inappropriate. . . . [I]n my view, the Commerce Clause provides an adequate basis for the statute before us. I would uphold its constitutionality as the "necessary and proper" exercise of legislative power granted to Congress by that Clause.

The following excerpts reveal the events leading up to, and the aftermath of, Christy Brzonkala's rape. They also highlight several legal issues in the regulation of acquaintance rape.

■ PATRICK TRACEY, CHRISTY'S CRUSADE
Ms. Magazine, Apr. 1, 2000, at 53, available at 2000 WLNR 7406320

[Christy] Brzonkala's first chance to stand on her own two feet came in the fall of 1994, when she left her suburban home on a quiet little cul-de-sac in Fairfax, Virginia [to head off to Virginia Tech, four hours south of her home]. . . . [One night, three weeks later] several friends from the women's soccer team invited her to a party off-campus. They were there for "three, four, or five hours," she says, and during that time she had "three, four, or five beers. I was by no means loaded."

After the party, Brzonkala and her friend Hope Handley walked back to their dorm, Cochrane Hall. As they approached, two guys whistled at them from a third-floor window, inviting them up for a nightcap. "So we just go up," says Brzonkala. "We're going up to Hope's room, which is on the same floor, and we decide to drop in on these guys, just to say hello, nothing more. We go down the hall and they say, 'Oh, I'm so-and-so and so-and-so, and we're football players.' I almost cracked up, because I was a jock in high school, so it did not impress me."

What began as small talk soon degenerated into blatant come-ons, at which point Handley left the room. Handley remembered that she'd said good-bye when she left, but Brzonkala says, "It was my impression that she had gone to the bathroom. After a few minutes, she didn't come back. I got up to go, and that's when it all happened." Morrison, a six-foot-one-inch defensive linebacker, weighing over 200 pounds, barred her from leaving and asked her for sex. "I am not that kind of person. I said 'No.' No is no, and that's all you need to hear."

After she refused a second time, he stopped asking, a point upon which she and Morrison both later agreed, with one major distinction. He says that he asked twice and then they fell into each other's arms. She says he pushed her onto his bed, forcefully removed her clothes, pinned her arms and legs, and pushed himself into her.

As soon as Morrison finished, Brzonkala says, his friend Crawford raped her. For about 15 minutes, she says, it was Morrison, then Crawford, then Morrison again. "I was in shock, and I blanked out. When Morrison got off me, Crawford came in. Then Crawford left, and Morrison did the same thing again. The only thing I remember was [Morrison] saying, 'You better not have any fucking diseases.'"

For those who have questioned her judgment in going to the dorm room of two big jocks in the wee hours of the morning, Brzonkala has an answer: "We never learned about rape in high school. They thought they were protecting us." . . .

Afterwards, Brzonkala walked down the long hallway to the stairwell. She says Morrison followed her. "I just walked ahead of him," she recalls. "It was weird. He said, "Oh, maybe I can call you sometime?" And I just remember feeling disgust. I went back to my suite and just sat in the tub for hours. I put it somewhere way in the back of my head. . . .

Brzonkala sank into a paralyzing depression. She rarely left her room for fear of running into Morrison or Crawford. . . . She slept all day, skipping classes. Her failing grades seemed a trivial matter. . . . Uncharacteristically, she started smoking and drinking every day. Alcohol was the easiest way to blot it all out. . . . Three weeks after the alleged rape, Brzonkala swallowed a vial of pills she'd been taking for a hypothyroid condition. . . . Brzonkala was treated at Montgomery Regional Hospital [and] released. The suicide attempt had been a cry for help. . . .

■ **BROOKE A. MASTERS, "NO WINNERS" IN RAPE LAWSUIT: TWO STUDENTS FOREVER CHANGED BY CASE THAT WENT TO SUPREME COURT**

Wash. Post, May 19, 2000, available at **http://www.cir-usa.org/articles/ 115.html**

At 23, Christy Brzonkala has had experiences few people could match in a lifetime: She's been featured on national television, testified before Congress and fought a case all the way to the U.S. Supreme Court. But she lost her childhood dreams along the way. Her long-anticipated "real college experience" at Virginia Tech turned nightmarish because of an alleged rape. . . .

The main defendant in the case, Antonio Morrison, also saw his dreams fade. He had real pro football aspirations, but now can't find a job even as a trainer. "There were no winners in this thing," said Virginia Tech spokesman Larry Hincker. "Two students have become poster children in ways they never could have imagined. One never finished college. The other is lost in the woods. Virginia Tech was maligned and mischaracterized. And a law that was supposed to help women has been declared unconstitutional."

. . . On a September night in 1994, [Brzonkala] says, she was gang-raped [at Virginia Tech] by Morrison and another fellow freshman, James L. Crawford. Neither man was ever charged with a crime—Crawford produced an alibi witness; Morrison said the sex was consensual. And Brzonkala felt betrayed when school officials allowed both to stay in school and continue playing on the highly ranked football team. So she filed suit, becoming the first woman to test the newly passed Violence Against Women Act, which allowed women who believe they have been victims of sex-based violence to sue their attackers in federal court.

"I would have tortured myself if I hadn't done everything I could to get justice," she said this week. "I went to these group sessions [for rape victims] in Fairfax, and I couldn't stand to listen to these women say, 'We were afraid to say anything for 20 years, and now we're in Alcoholics Anonymous and Narcotics Anonymous.'"

Crawford, also a defendant in Brzonkala's suit, always said he left the room before any sexual activity occurred. He was convicted of an unrelated sexual assault and also of disorderly conduct after an altercation in a parking lot. He lost his scholarship at Virginia Tech and moved home to Florida [where he now works in retail].

Morrison, who said he had consensual sex with Brzonkala after she came to his room, got the bulk of the public criticism. Suspended from the football team in 1995 after he was arrested in an unrelated bar brawl, he transferred to Hampton University. After a semester there, he transferred back but did not play football again. The Chesapeake, Va., native finished at Tech last summer, receiving a degree in human nutrition, foods and exercise. [H]is attorney, David Paxton, said Brzonkala's accusations have left a permanent scar. Now 23, Morrison has held several jobs but has not been able to find work as an athletic trainer, Paxton said. "How's he going to get hired by a college once people realize he's the guy all the stuff has been written about? His good name has been completely trashed," Paxton said. "He's been convicted of something he never did."

Both Brzonkala and Morrison are angry at Virginia Tech for the way the school handled her accusations: He and his family have said they believe he was treated unfairly because he is black; she sued the school for sex discrimination. That case was settled in February when Virginia Tech agreed to pay $75,000 [to Brzonkala] but admitted no wrongdoing.

Although the case started as a classic "he said, she said," by the time it reached the Supreme Court, U.S. v. Morrison was all about federalism, not sexual politics. Writing for a 5–4 majority that included Sandra Day O'Connor, Chief Justice William H. Rehnquist found that Congress had overstepped its constitutional bounds when it passed the Violence Against Women Act. "The morning after it came down, I cried. I was thinking it would be such a relief to forget all about it and burn everything," Brzonkala said. "But I cry whenever I think about how much I wish it would have been the other way, to have tangible evidence that we're making progress toward men and women being equal."

In theory, Brzonkala could still sue Morrison and Crawford in state court. But she and her attorney, Eileen Wagner, say they see little point. While the federal case helped test the new law and drew national attention to the issue of acquaintance rape, a state suit would simply be about money. And Crawford and Morrison, though they were once hot football prospects, don't have much now. "As far as the courts, it's over," Brzonkala said. "I've done all I can."

The September 1994 encounter with Morrison and Crawford and all that followed have irrevocably changed Christy Brzonkala, she and her parents say. "It hardened her," said her father, Ken, 60. . . . Christy, an outgoing and bubbly high school basketball player, had plans for a sports-related career and talked about saving sex for marriage—or at least a very serious relationship, said her mother, Mary Ellen Brzonkala, 61, an optician.

[At Tech, Brzonkala initially told no one of the incident. Eventually, she told her roommate about the incident and then pressed charges in a campus disciplinary proceeding. Morrison, although suspended initially for sexual assault, had his suspension overturned. The charge was reduced to "using abusive language." His punishment was probation, plus one hour of counseling with a campus affirmative-action official].

When she learned in a newspaper article that Morrison was coming back to school for their sophomore year, Brzonkala dropped out and eventually went public with her charges, first by giving an interview in the campus newspaper and then by filing suit. She tried going back to college at George Mason University, a 10-minute drive from her parents' home. But it all seemed pointless. . . . [S]he moved to the District [of Columbia] and tried to begin her life anew. After temping and working in customer service for Marvelous Market, she found work as a waitress [and started a romantic relationship. But, she admits:] "It's hard to love and trust somebody."

Brzonkala says she'd like to go back to college—someday, not right now. Her settlement money from Virginia Tech may help pay for it. But for now the cash is just sitting in a bank account. "I'm not the same person," Brzonkala said. "I'd probably be on my way to having a nice little family with kids and a job that requires a degree." "One little thing can change a whole lifetime. I think it happened to me."

The underlying offense in *Morrison* was an acquaintance rape. The following excerpt addresses the nature of acquaintance rape.

■ JOSEPH SHAPIRO, MYTHS THAT MAKE IT HARD TO STOP CAMPUS RAPE

NPR News Investigation, Mar. 4, 2010, available at **http://www.npr.org/ templates/story/story.php?storyId=124272157**

There's a common assumption about men who commit sexual assault on a college campus: That they made a one-time, bad decision. But psychologist David Lisak says this assumption is wrong—and dangerously so. Lisak started with a simple observation. Most of what we know about men who commit rape comes from studying the ones who are in prison. But most rapes are never reported or prosecuted. So Lisak, at the University of Massachusetts, Boston, set out to find and interview men he calls "undetected rapists." Those are men who've committed sexual assault, but have never been charged or convicted.

He found them by, over a 20-year period, asking some 2,000 men in college questions like this: "Have you ever had sexual intercourse with someone, even though they did not want to, because they were too intoxicated [on alcohol or drugs] to resist your sexual advances?" Or, "Have you ever had sexual intercourse with an adult when they didn't want to because you used physical force [twisting their arm, holding them down, etc.] if they didn't cooperate?" About 1 in 16 men answered "yes" to these or similar questions.

Profile of a Rapist

It might seem like it would be hard for a researcher to get these men to admit to something that fits the definition of rape. But Lisak says it's not. "They are very forthcoming," he says. "In fact, they are eager to talk about their experiences. They're quite narcissistic as a group—the offenders—and they view this as an opportunity, essentially, to brag."

What Lisak found was that students who commit rape on a college campus are pretty much like those rapists in prison. In both groups, many are serial rapists. On college campuses, repeat predators account for 9 out of every 10 rapes.

And these offenders on campuses—just like men in prison for rape—look for the most vulnerable women. Lisak says that on a college campus, the women most likely to be sexually assaulted are freshmen.

"It's quite well-known amongst college administrators that first-year students, freshman women, are particularly at risk for sexual assault," Lisak says. "The predators on campus know that women who are new to campus, they are younger, they're less experienced. They probably have less experience with alcohol, they want to be accepted. They will probably take more risks because they want to be accepted. So for all these reasons, the predators will look particularly for those women."

Still, Lisak says these men don't think of themselves as rapists. Usually they know the other student. And they don't use guns or knives. "The basic weapon is alcohol," the psychologist says. "If you can get a victim intoxicated to the point where she's coming in and out of consciousness, or she's unconscious—and that is a very, very common scenario—then why would you need a weapon? Why would you need a knife or a gun?" . . .

Findings of the Center for Public Integrity

The investigative nonprofit news organization, Center for Public Integrity, conducted an inquiry in 2010 into sexual assaults at colleges and universities. The Center interviewed 50 experts on campus disciplinary policies and 33 female victims. In addition, they reviewed a federal database of sexual assault complaints filed against college campuses with the U.S. Department of Education from 2003-2008. Their findings are summarized below:

- Students who are found responsible for sexual assaults on campus often face little or no punishment. The alleged perpetrators traditionally remain on campus, whereas victims often drop out.
- Colleges rarely expel those who were found responsible for sexual assault. Only about 10 to 25 percent of assailants were expelled. Of those few students who are expelled, many had committed multiple offenses on campus.
- The U.S. Department of Education has failed to aggressively monitor institutional responses to sexual assault on campus.
- Local law enforcement authorities are reluctant to pursue campus sexual assault cases because they involve conflicting claims (consensual sex versus rape) that typically involve drugs or alcohol. As a result, students must deal with campus judiciary processes that are ill-equipped to handle their cases and often are shrouded in secrecy.

See Kristen Lombardi, A Lack of Consequences for Sexual Assault, Feb. 24, 2010, available at http://www.publicintegrity.org/investigations/campus_assault/articles/entry/1945.

Notes and Questions

1. *Social reality.* Christy Brzonkala was a victim of an acquaintance rape on a college campus. Approximately 20 percent of female college students are victims of attempted or actual sexual assault on campus. Heather M. Karjane, Nat'l Inst. of Justice, Sexual Assault on Campus: What Colleges and Universities Are Doing About It 2 (Dec. 2005), available at http://www.ncjrs.gov/pdffiles1/nij/205521.pdf. Most campus sexual assaults are committed by an acquaintance of the victim. Id. Surprisingly, half of these victims do not define their experience as rape because of the distinctive factors that are associated with campus acquaintance rapes (that is, the absence of a weapon, lack of visible physical injuries, and the presence of alcohol). Id. "These reasons help explain why . . . [l]ess than 5 percent of completed and attempted rapes of college students are brought to the attention of campus

authorities and/or law enforcement." Id. at 2-3. Which of the above characteristics were present in Christy Brzonkala's case?

2. *Rape trauma syndrome.* Victims of rape typically experience a significant degree of physical and emotional trauma during, following, and for a considerable time after a rape. Ann Wolbert Burgess et al., Victimology: Theories and Applications 244 (2010) (describing the "profound suffering" of victims). "Rape trauma syndrome" (RTS), was the psychological condition discovered by psychiatrist Ann Wolbert Burgess and sociologist Lynda Lytle Holmstrom to describe the impact of sexual assault. Ann W. Burgess & Lynda L. Holmstrom, Rape Trauma Syndrome, 131 Am. J. Psychiatry 981 (Sept. 1974) (based on study of 92 rape victims). RTS has an immediate acute phase and a long-term adjustment phase, and includes symptoms of flashbacks, intrusive thoughts of the rape, fear, anxiety, nightmares, and development of phobias. Burgess et al., supra, at 244. Victims are likely to suffer academically and from depression, post-traumatic stress disorder, substance abuse, and suicidal thoughts. U.S. Dept. Education, Dear Colleague Letter: Sexual Violence Background, Summary, and Fast Facts, Apr. 4, 2011, at 1 [hereinafter Sexual Violence Background], available at http://www.whitehouse.gov/sites/default/files/fact_sheet_sexual_violence.pdf. Some victims experience a "silent response" and either fail to disclose the incident or else delay in disclosing it until years afterwards. Burgess et al., supra, at 245. Which reactions did Christy suffer? How does an understanding of RTS explain her decision to file a VAWA claim rather than criminal charges?

3. *Constitutional guarantees.* Christy brought claims under VAWA's civil rights provision against the students who raped her. Congress specified two constitutional bases for enacting VAWA's federal civil rights cause of action: the Commerce Clause and section 5 of the Fourteenth Amendment. The former furnishes the foundation for the government's regulatory power over the economy, providing that Congress shall have the power "To regulate Commerce with foreign Nations, and among the several States, and with the Indian Tribes." (U.S. Const. art. I, §8, cl. 3). This provision is supplemented by the "necessary and proper Clause" (U.S. Const. art. I, §8, cl. 18), providing that Congress shall have the power "To make all Laws which shall be necessary and proper for carrying into Execution the foregoing Powers, and all other Powers vested by this Constitution in the Government of the United States, or in any Department or Officer thereof." Section 5 of the Fourteenth Amendment provides that Congress may enact "appropriate legislation" to protect the individual rights encompassed by the Fourteenth Amendment ("Congress shall have the power to enforce, by appropriate legislation, the provisions of this article") (U.S. Const. amend. XIV, §5).

4. *Congressional authority under the Commerce Clause.* Why did VAWA's civil rights remedy for victims of gender-motivated violence run afoul of the Court's interpretation of Congress's power to regulate commerce?

a. *Prior permissible regulation: background.* As *Morrison* explains, the Court previously upheld many far-reaching laws under the guise of the Commerce Clause, some of which bear only a loose relationship to commerce. See Hodel v. Virginia Surface Min. & Reclamation, Inc., 452 U.S. 264 (1981) (upholding regulation of intrastate coal mining); Perez v. United States, 402 U.S. 146 (1971) (upholding regulation of "loan sharking," as applied to intrastate extortionate credit practices); Heart of Atlanta Motel, Inc. v. United States, 379 U.S. 241 (1964) (upholding Civil Rights Act of 1964 as applied to intrastate hotel owners serving interstate travelers);

Wickard v. Filburn, 317 U.S. 111 (1942) (upholding federal law regulating wheat prices as applied to a wheat grower who produced wheat to meet his own needs). How is gender-based violence similar to, and different from, these activities?

The dissenters in *Morrison* note that while the Court's restrictive interpretation is certainly defensible, the Commerce Clause could be read to extend beyond mere "economic" activity. See also United States v. Faasse, 265 F.3d 475, 483, n.6 (6th Cir. 2001) ("We do not believe, nor does *Morrison* hold, that all activity regulated by the Commerce Clause must be economic in nature; *Morrison* spoke only to congressional regulation of exclusively intrastate activities.") Do you agree? Can or should the commerce power be limited to "economic" activity?

b. *Lopez*. Prior to *Morrison*, petitioners had been generally unsuccessful in striking down an act of Congress as beyond the scope of federal power. *Lopez*, 514 U.S. 549, on which the Court relies heavily to reaching its holding in *Morrison*, marked the first case since the New Deal to hold that a federal law transgressed the powers that were conferred on Congress by the Constitution. In *Lopez*, the Supreme Court held that the Gun-Free School Zones Act (prohibiting "any individual knowingly to possess a firearm at a place that [he] knows . . . is a school zone") exceeded Congress's Commerce Clause authority because possession of a gun in a local school zone is not an economic activity that substantially affected interstate commerce. How is gender-motivated violence similar to, and different from, the possession of firearms in local school zones?

c. *Interstate aspect*. In enacting VAWA's civil rights remedy, Congress decided not to make enforcement dependent on whether a defendant had crossed state lines stemming from congressional concern with providing a remedy for intimate partner violence that occurs in or near homes. How significant was the absence in *Morrison* of an "interstate hook" in interpreting Congress's power to act under its authority to regulate interstate commerce? See Akhil Reed Amar, Substance and Method in the Year 2000, 28 Pepp. L. Rev. 601, 617 (2001) (discussing the necessity of an interstate aspect to find the statute constitutional).

The incorporation of a jurisdictional element into an offense (for example, "moving in interstate or foreign commerce") has traditionally insulated statutes from Commerce Clause challenges. In fact, Congress subsequently remedied the Gun-Free School Zones Act, challenged in *Lopez*, to include the requirement that the firearm "moved in" or otherwise "affects interstate or foreign commerce." 18 U.S.C. §§922(a)(2)(A). What is the nexus between interstate commerce and gender-based violence, according to Congress? According to the majority in *Morrison*? According to the dissent? Which view do you find most persuasive?

Could an interstate aspect be incorporated into a federal statute that might overcome the constitutional infirmities in *Morrison*? Although some members of Congress have introduced post-*Morrison* civil rights legislation to redress the shortcomings of VAWA's remedy, none of these proposals has yet been enacted.

d. *Solely intrastate activities?* The Court previously permitted some congressional legislation that regulates purely intrastate activities. For example, in Gonzales v. Raich, 545 U.S. 1 (2005), the Court allowed Congress to criminalize private possession of homegrown marijuana, and, in Wickard v. Filburn, supra, the regulation of homegrown production of wheat. Why, then, did the Court balk at permitting congressional regulation of gender-motivated violence even if such violence might arguably be perceived as solely intrastate activities?

5. *Congressional authority under Section 5 of the Fourteenth Amendment.*

a. *Holding.* Brzonkala also argues that the VAWA remedy was properly enacted under Section 5 of the Fourteenth Amendment (enabling Congress to enforce the Fourteenth Amendment "by appropriate legislation") (U.S. Const. amend. XIV, §5). She bases her argument in support of the provision's constitutionality on the distinction between VAWA and the Civil Rights Cases, 109 U.S. 3 (1883) (invalidating an 1875 Civil Rights law aimed at private actors). In contrast to the latter law targeting purely private discrimination, she argued that Congress had enacted VAWA's civil rights provision based on its findings of a statistical connection between private violence against women and the eradication of gender-based discrimination in combating such violence. Why does the Court reject this argument?

b. *Background.* Congress previously relied on Section 5 as authority to enact a number of civil rights laws. In the 1960s and 1970s the Court upheld some civil rights laws under the theory that Section 5 granted Congress the power to uphold the barest minimum of civil rights authorized by the Amendment through direct legislation. See Katzenbach v. Morgan, 384 U.S. 641, 650-651 (1966); South Carolina v. Katzenbach, 383 U.S. 301, 326-327 (1966). The Rehnquist Court then swung back toward earlier interpretations of the Court, placing severe constraints on congressional action under Section 5 on the basis of an "original intent" interpretation of the Amendment. See *Morrison*, supra; Board of Trs. of the Univ. of Ala. v. Garrett, 531 U.S. 356, 374 (2001) (Americans with Disabilities Act); Kimel v. Florida Bd. of Regents, 528 U.S. 62, 86, 91 (2000) (Age Discrimination in Employment Act). How is the VAWA civil rights provision similar to other civil rights legislation, such as laws barring discrimination in employment and in public accommodations? Why, then, was it invalidated?

c. *Regulation of private behavior.* The defendants argued that the Fourteenth Amendment, which governs official action, could not be the basis for a law that applies to strictly private behavior. In contrast, petitioner argues that the federal remedy is aimed at redressing the failure of states to provide adequate remedies for violence against women—an aspect of state action or inaction that arguably is an appropriate subject of legislation under the Fourteenth Amendment. Responding to these arguments, *Morrison* ruled that federal statutes "directed exclusively against the action of private persons, without reference to laws of the State, or their administration by her officers," exceeded Congress's power under Section 5. *Morrison*, 529 U.S. at 621. What explains the Court's reasoning? The Court suggests that holding private discrimination outside the reach of the federal government serves certain values. What are those values? Do you agree?

6. *Terminology.* Was the VAWA provision at issue in *Morrison*, a "civil rights remedy" or a "civil" remedy? What are the implications of the difference in terminology? See Sarah F. Russell, Covering Women and Violence: Mediate Treatment of VAWA's Civil Rights Remedy, 9 Mich. J. Gender & L. 327 (2003) (pointing out that pre-*Morrison* commentary focused on the "civil rights remedy," whereas post-*Morrison* commentary discussed the "civil remedy"). Why do you think this shift in discourse occurred? What effect does it have on the ongoing debate about federal legislation on civil rights?

7. *Dissenting opinions.* The Court split five to four in deciding *Morrison*. Both Justices Souter and Breyer argue that the Court's interpretation of the commerce power is too narrow. What are their respective arguments? Does the fact that a state traditionally regulates violent crime make that crime solely noneconomic or solely

intrastate? Does the result change when a state traditionally *fails* to regulate violent crime, thereby doing nothing in the face of the violation of constitutional rights? Is regulation of inaction the same as regulation of action? In an age of globalization, is any activity outside the scope of the commerce power? Should any activity be outside that power?

8. *Federalism and domestic violence.* The Court in *Morrison* relies heavily on an assertion that states (in contrast to the federal government) have primary authority over laws regulating "family law and other areas of traditional state regulation," presumably including violence against women. *Morrison*, supra, 529 U.S. at 615. Is violence against women properly categorized as a family law issue that would be within the purview of the states, or does it reflect a broader violation of the fundamental civil rights of women which is more properly within the purview of the federal government? See Julie Goldscheid, Elusive Equality in Domestic and Sexual Violence Law Reform, 34 Fla. St. U. L. Rev. 731(2007); Emily J. Sack, The Burial of Family Law, 61 SMU L. Rev. 459 (2008). (Julie Goldscheid, a former attorney at the NOW Legal Defense and Education Fund, argued Brzonkala's appeal.)

Aren't some family law issues considered to be properly within the purview of the federal government? How is violence against women similar to, and different from, those issues? Professor Catharine MacKinnon responds that *Morrison*'s conception of family law as an "inviolable preserve"

> blinkers rulings like Loving v. Virginia and Palmore v. Sidoti, not to mention Orr v. Orr and Kirchberg v. Feenstra, all of which assert the preeminence of constitutional equality over state family statutory and case law. These decisions, although not per se providing precedent for the VAWA under §5, underline the affirmative nature of the decision in *Morrison* to permit unredressed violence against women in the name of what is called the private. The VAWA would hardly have been the first invasion by the Constitution in the name of equality into a state legal regime denominated private. The public, the law, the federal Constitution, the Fourteenth Amendment, are already there.

Catharine A. MacKinnon, Disputing Male Sovereignty: On United States v. Morrison, 114 Harv. L. Rev. 135, 170 (2000). If the states are not doing an adequate job of protecting citizens from gender-based violence, should the federal government step in? Could VAWA's civil rights provision coexist with state laws? Or, is there a satisfactory justification for exclusively state control over crime? See Jay S. Bybee, Insuring Domestic Tranquility: *Lopez*, Federalization of Crime, and the Forgotten Role of the Domestic Violence Clause, 66 Geo. Wash. L. Rev. 1, 82 (1997) (affirming the "primacy of the states as the caretakers of the public peace").

Despite *Morrison*, some federal courts have acknowledged that certain aspects of domestic violence fall within Congress's authority to regulate. See, e.g., United States v. Bayles, 310 F.3d 1302 (10th Cir. 2002) (upholding a federal law (18 U.S.C. §922(g)(1)) that prohibited a person subject to a domestic violence protective order from owning a firearm known by its recipient to have been transported in interstate commerce; U.S. v. Lankford, 196 F.3d 563 (5th Cir. 1999) (holding that a prohibition on interstate domestic violence did not exceed Congress's regulatory authority). Are these cases distinguishable from *Morrison*? From *Lopez*, supra? Do these regulations constitute congressional attempts to regulate purely local activities in a manner contrary to the principles of federalism? What other "traditional" areas of state regulation might be subject to federal regulation?

During congressional hearings on VAWA, Chief Justice Rehnquist expressed a concern about the interrelationship between civil rights remedy and federalism concerns. He explained that the issue focused on whether the federal courts, with their limited resources, should be burdened with the enforcement of these substantive rules. He elaborated:

> [T]he question should be asked as to whether the state courts presently deal, and deal with reasonable effectiveness, with these same matters. If the answer is in the affirmative, it is probably better to follow the maxim "if it ain't broke, don't fix it." To shift large numbers of cases presently being decided in the state courts to the federal courts for reasons which are largely symbolic would be a disservice to the federal courts, and, more importantly, to the whole concept of federalism.

Chief Justice Rehnquist Discusses Long-Range Planning for U.S. Courts, 138 Cong. Rec. E746-01 (Mar. 19, 1992). Do you agree? What insight do these remarks shed on the Court's opinion in *Morrison*?

9. *Domestic violence as gender-based discrimination.* In enacting VAWA's civil rights remedy, many congressional leaders conceptualized the remedy as an equality-based measure that was analogous to federal remedies against race-based discrimination. Responding to critics, one of the lead sponsors of the bill (then-Senator Joe Biden) summed up:

> No one would say today that laws barring violent attacks motivated by race or ethnicity fall outside the Federal courts' jurisdiction. Then why are they saying that violent discrimination motivated by gender is not a traditional civil rights violation?

Violence Against Women: Hearing Before the Subcomm. on Crime & Criminal Justice, Comm. on the Judiciary, 102d Cong., 2d Sess. 42 (1992), at 11. Why didn't the Court uphold *Morrison* as an attempt to address gender equality analogous to other federal remedies addressing race-based discrimination? On the analogy between race and gender-based discrimination, see generally Lawrence G. Sager, A Letter to the Supreme Court Regarding the Missing Argument in Brzonkala v. Morrison, 75 N.Y.U. L. Rev. 150 (2000).

What connection did Congress make between victims of domestic violence and pervasive state-sponsored gender discrimination? See also Amar, supra, at 618 ("VAWA calls certain acts of violence not merely random, private assaults, but parts of a larger historically rooted system of insult and degradation. VAWA labels that system of insult a civil rights issue, an equality issue"). What congressional findings are necessary to support this explicit connection? Why did the Court find Congress's findings insufficient to support legislation under Section 5 of the Fourteenth Amendment?

Domestic violence was first seen as an issue of gender inequality in the 1960s when the feminist movement began to challenge "the prevalent ideology that 'mild' chastisement was necessary to 'keep a woman in line' and that 'women like men who dominate.'" Julie Goldscheid, Domestic and Sexual Violence as Sex Discrimination: Comparing American and International Approaches, 28 T. Jefferson L. Rev. 355, 359 (2006). Despite the movement's remarkable successes (that is, encouraging public dialogue on domestic violence, eliminating formal statutory inequalities, enhancing criminal penalties, expanding social services for victims, and enhancing civil remedies against perpetrators of domestic violence), the focus on sexual discrimination as the root of domestic violence was superseded by a gender-neutral discourse that remains today. What are the implications of this neutralization of gender-based violence in terms of the responses of states and state actors (that is, legislators, police officers, judges) confronting domestic violence? What aspects of the Court's decision in *Morrison* reflect this neutralization?

10. *Antisubordination.* VAWA, as explained above, had two goals: to provide a private cause of action for victims of gender-motivated violence who might not have other remedies under existing law, and to address gender inequality. "The law sought to transform the terms of debate in which violence against women was framed, to bring public attention to its severity and impact, and to counter the historic subordination violence against women both reflects and perpetuates." Julie Goldscheid, The Civil Rights Remedy of the 1994 Violence Against Women Act: Struck Down But Not Ruled Out, 39 Fam. L.Q. 157, 158 (2005).

Anti-subordination theorists criticize that the state is not neutral with respect to gender, but instead functions to reinforce male power over women. For example, Catharine MacKinnon contends that the Court in *Morrison* accomplishes this result by its choice of line drawing between the public and private spheres. She elaborates as follows:

> The *Morrison* majority does not simply respect a preexisting line between what is private and what is public. It draws that line by abandoning women wherever violence against them takes place. *Morrison* effectively defines the private as the location where effective redress for sex-based violence is unavailable, ignoring the destruction of women's freedom and equality in private by the lack of public limits on male violence. The private is thus constructed of public impunity. The jealous guarding of this specific line between public and private acts, under which exercise of state power is accountable to public authority but exercise of so-called private power is not, thus becomes one of the central public means of maintaining a system in which male power over women remains effectively without limit. Christy Brzonkala was away at school when she was raped, paying to attend a public educational institution. She was gang-raped by men she had barely met in a room not her own. Public officials effectively condoned her violation through public legal processes. In what sense was her rape private?

MacKinnon, supra, at 170-171. Do you find MacKinnon's reasoning persuasive? What do you think is the impact of *Morrison* on gender equality?

11. *Deference to congressional findings.* Congress made numerous findings to support VAWA, including a "mountain of data" that showed the impact of violence against women on interstate commerce as well as the existence of gender bias in states' responses to violence against women. What deference did the majority in *Morrison* give to these Congressional findings? What deference did the dissent? Why? Should Congress be given the latitude to enforce a broader interpretation of the reach of the Fourteenth Amendment than the Supreme Court? Or, should the Court be the final arbiter? In all cases? Some?

On the issue of the appropriate level of deference to Congressional findings, the Supreme Court previously stated:

> We agree that courts must accord substantial deference to the predictive judgments of Congress. Sound policymaking often requires legislators to forecast future events and

to anticipate the likely impact of these events based on deductions and inferences for which complete empirical support may be unavailable. As an institution, moreover, Congress is far better equipped than the judiciary to "amass and evaluate the vast amounts of data" bearing upon an issue as complex and dynamic as that presented here.

Turner Broadcasting Sys., Inc. v. Federal Communications Comm'n, 512 U.S. 622, 665-666 (1994). Accord Katzenbach v. Morgan, 384 U.S. 641 (1966) (declining to review Congressional resolution of conflicting testimony). Why did the Court not give "substantial deference" to congressional findings in *Morrison*? What concerns about the separation of powers do cases like *Morrison* present, when the Court may declare an issue one of law and remove Congressional findings from consideration?

12. *Title IX.* In addition to her claims under VAWA, Brzonkala sued Virginia Tech for violating Title IX of the Education Amendments of 1972, codified at 20 U.S.C. §§1681-1688. Title IX is landmark legislation that bans sex discrimination in schools that receive federal funding.

Brzonkala claimed that she was subject to sex discrimination because Virginia Tech failed to respond adequately to her complaint of a hostile sexual environment, and also discriminated against her in its disciplinary proceedings (the "disparate treatment claim"). The District Court dismissed, finding that she failed to state a claim under either theory. Brzonkala v. Virginia Polytechnic Inst. & State Univ., 935 F. Supp. 772 (W.D. Va. 1996). The Fourth Circuit affirmed the dismissal of the "disparate treatment" claim, but vacated the dismissal of her hostile environment claim and remanded with instructions to hold that claim in abeyance pending Davis v. Monroe County Bd. of Ed., 526 U.S. 629 (1999) (holding that sexual harassment claims could be maintained only if the educational institution was deliberately indifferent and the harassment was so severe as to bar the student from access to educational opportunity or benefit). See *Morrison*, 529 U.S. at 629 n.2. That case was settled. The principal case did not address either Title IX claim. What is the likelihood that Brzonkala would have succeeded after *Davis*? Do you think that Virginia Tech violated Title IX? Why or why not?

13. *State civil rights remedies to combat domestic violence.* Prior to VAWA, several states had civil, as well as criminal, remedies for bias-motivated violence. See, e.g., Iowa Code Ann. §§729A.2, 729A.5; N.J. Stat. Ann. §2A:53A-21. States continued to enact such laws after *Morrison*. Many state laws specifically target gender-motivated harm. "Currently, eleven states and the District of Columbia include 'sex' or 'gender' as one of the categories that can give rise to civil recovery under those state bias crime frameworks." Julie Goldscheid, Civil Rights Remedy of VAWA, supra, at 168.

How effective is this approach? Can a state tort remedy protect women from private acts of violence? What might limit the effectiveness of such laws? Are states likely to be more effective than the federal government in enforcing remedial legislation for victims of domestic violence? Less effective? See id. (discussing state and federal remedies and responses to violence against women both before and after *Morrison*); Sarah F. Russell, Covering Women and Violence: Media Treatment of VAWA's Civil Rights Remedy, 9 Mich. J. Gender & L. 327 (2003) (discussing state responses post-*Morrison*).

14. *Implications of* Morrison. What are the implications of *Morrison*—for the victim, and victims of acquaintance rape? Does *Morrison* leave women more vulnerable to gender-motivated violence? Congressional findings, noted in *Morrison*, reported that violence against women had a substantial impact on interstate commerce by deterring women from taking certain jobs or continuing their education. Does Christy's epilogue lend support to those findings?

The Court's failure to uphold the VAWA civil rights provision leaves the task of protecting some constitutional rights to the states. As Justice Rehnquist wrote in *Morrison*: "If the allegations here are true, no civilized system of justice could fail to provide her a remedy for the conduct of respondent Morrison." What remedy did Christy Brzonkala have? Could she have pursued state criminal charges for rape? Why did she pursue a federal, instead of state, remedy? See Brzonkala v. Virginia Polytechnic Inst. & State Univ., 132 F.3d 949, 954 (4th Cir. 1997).

15. *Sexual assaults on campus.* Morrison has had significant implications for campus responses to sexual assaults (explained below). How did Virginia Tech respond to Christy's accusations? What was the outcome of the university's administrative proceedings for Crawford and Morrison? How did Christy learn of the University's decision?

What difference do you think it made that the alleged rapists in *Morrison* were members of the school varsity football team? What light does Professor Lisak's research on date rapists, supra, shed on the events in *Morrison*? For example, an understanding of the characteristics of date rapists helps explain the outcome of the student disciplinary hearing, convicting Morrison of "offensive and demeaning language" (stemming from his bragging in the school cafeteria following the rape). Does Morrison fit the date rape "profile"? How should a student who is a victim of sexual assault respond after *Morrison*? Go to the police? A hospital? The university student health center? File a complaint with the university? A tort claim? Criminal charges?

One of Christy Brzonkala's hopes was that her lawsuit would prevent Virginia Tech from adjudicating another felonious sexual assault. How typical was Virginia Tech's response? Consider the following criticism:

> Many schools often try to keep rape charges involving students under wraps, handling them instead through internal administrative hearings just as they would, say, cheating. Yet with lives and futures at stake, should panels of professors, deans—and sometimes other students—be a law unto themselves?

Richard Jerome, No Justice, No Peace, People Mag., Mar. 11, 1996, available at http://www.people.com/people/archive/article/0,,20102990,00.html. See also Kathryn M. Reardon, Acquaintance Rape at Private Colleges and Universities: Providing for Victims' Educational and Civil Rights, 38 Suffolk U. L. Rev. 395, 398 (2005).

In May 2011, the U.S. Department of Education issued new guidelines, pursuant to Title IX, concerning educational institutions' responsibilities to address student complaints of sexual violence and sexual harassment. The guidelines recommend that once a school learns of possible sexual violence: (1) it must take immediate action to investigate; (2) it must take prompt steps to address the effects of such sexual violence, including interim steps to protect the complainant (for example, ensuring the parties do not attend the same classes or reside in the same residence hall and providing counseling, medical, and academic support services); (3) it must use a preponderance-of-the-evidence standard to resolve complaints; (4) it must provide a grievance procedure for complaints that offers equal opportunity to both parties to present witnesses and evidence, and the same appeal rights; and (5) it must notify both parties of the outcome of the complaint. See Sexual Violence Background, supra. If the guidelines had been in effect at Virginia Tech when Christy was a student, would they have changed the resolution of her case?

The pending VAWA Reauthorization Act reauthorizes funding (amending 42 U.S.C. (§14045b) to combat violent crime on campuses (including dating violence, sexual assault, and stalking) and to strengthen victim services. New provisions authorize grants to institutions of higher education to develop and strengthen prevention education and awareness programs (regardless of whether the services are provided by the institution or in coordination with community victim service providers); expand the definition of crimes to include "the use of technology to commit these crimes"; and also provide for the development of "population specific services" and "culturally appropriate, and linguistically accessible print or electronic materials."

Finally, the program requires that grantees (1) create a coordinated community response including both organizations external to the institution and relevant divisions of the institution; (2) establish a mandatory prevention and education program on domestic violence, dating violence, sexual assault, and stalking for all incoming students; (3) train all campus law enforcement to respond effectively to domestic violence, dating violence, sexual assault, and stalking; and (4) train all members of campus disciplinary boards to respond effectively to situations involving domestic violence, dating violence, sexual assault, or stalking.

If the pending legislation had been enacted, how might it have changed the handling of Christy Brzonkala's case? Evaluate the potential of the above federal guidelines and the pending VAWA reauthorization legislation to effectuate meaningful reform.

XI

Family Law: Marriage and Divorce

This chapter explores the role of domestic violence in courtship, marriage, and divorce law. Specifically, it explores the regulation of online dating and the mail-order bride industry, the interrelationship of tort law and no-fault divorce, and the role of domestic violence in the allocation of the financial incidents of divorce (that is, spousal support and property division.)

A. MARRIAGE

1. Introduction: Online Dating

Online dating has become an important method for people to meet partners. What risks does online dating pose for clients' safety? What additional risks does it pose for foreign clients? How do states and the federal government regulate online dating as well as the marriage broker industry? How effective is such legislation? Consider these questions as you read the following materials.

■ **PHYLLIS COLEMAN, ONLINE DATING: WHEN "MR. (OR MS.) RIGHT" TURNS OUT ALL WRONG, SUE THE SERVICE!**
36 Okla. City U. L. Rev. 139, 139-143 (2011)

Dating websites are big business. More than forty million people log on each month looking for love. Even during an economic downturn, the total number of both users and services continued to increase. There are several explanations for the rising popularity. First, "surfing the net" to meet that perfect person has become socially acceptable. Indeed, people from all age groups, social strata, and sexual orientations eagerly await their next communication from someone they met on the Web. Second, there are limited opportunities and locations for busy singles to gather naturally. This is attributable to such phenomena as urbanization, stressful careers, and diminishing involvement in religious organizations. Finally, perhaps the most important reason is that these services work. In fact, individuals who have never used a computer to search for a soul mate know somebody (or know somebody who knows somebody) who met a partner on the Internet.

Due to the industry's success, experts predict revenues that exceeded $900 million in 2007 will rise to $1.9 billion by 2012. With so many individuals spending this much money on an activity where expectations may be unreasonably high and people tend to stretch the truth, it is foreseeable that some will be dissatisfied, and at least a few will decide to litigate. . . .

Notably, since Match.com revolutionized dating when it launched in 1995, the number of such services has grown rapidly. For example, by 2007 there were 1,378 sites in the United States. An estimated forty-four percent of these were niche groups, representing a thirty-five percent increase over the total in 2006.

To attract subscribers, companies attempt to distinguish themselves from their competitors by demonstrating how successful they are. Because objective marriage researchers do not have statistics on the impact of online dating, and thus no actual measure exists, many use marriages between people who met on their site as the standard. For example, when a 2007 survey commissioned by eHarmony found that two percent of all people who married the previous year met on its website, the figure was included in its advertising. An earlier survey of 4,743 newly married or engaged couples registered on WeddingChannel.com revealed twelve percent met online and nearly one-third of those met through Match.com. Match.com then claimed it had "twice as many marriages as any other site in the world."

In the approximately fifteen years of dating websites, an estimated 2.2 million Americans married people they found online. Sadly, however, meeting and marrying Mr. or Ms. Right might not be enough to ensure living happily ever after. . . .

Notes and Questions

1. *Online dating practices.* How successful are online dating sites? What explains their success? Why are they successful even in economic downturns? See Andrea Cambem & Marcey Goulder, Earnings Yield to Yearnings: Matchmakers Flooded as Folks Feel Loneliness of Hard Times, Columbus Dispatch, May 20, 2009, at A10. How has online dating revolutionized dating practices? See Brad Stone, Love Online, Newsweek, Feb. 19, 2001, at 46; Tim Fountain, Sex at the Click of a Mouse, New Statesman, Aug. 23, 2004, at 21. What are the advantages of such sites to search for an intimate partner? The disadvantages?

2. *Risks of domestic violence.* Online dating poses unique risks of domestic violence. How are these risks different from the risks posed by traditional dating practices? Although comprehensive data are lacking on the prevalence of domestic violence in online dating, sensationalistic media accounts abound. See, e.g., Rick Dumont, Police: Date Rape Drugs Present New Challenges, New Hampshire Union Leader (Manchester, N.H.), Jan. 1, 2007, at B1 (police arrest man for raping a woman he met through an online dating service); Doug McMurdo, Man Indicted in Brutal Attack, Las Vegas Rev.-J., Mar. 12, 2011, at 2B (man indicted in attempted

murder of woman he met on the Internet after she broke up with him). What safety precautions should people take when they want to meet prospective partners via online dating services? How likely are these safety precautions to screen out prospective batterers?

3. *State legislation.* Fewer than a dozen states regulate online dating services. Coleman, supra, at 144. What is the purpose of state legislation? To regulate deceptive consumer practices? To enhance clients' safety? What statutory provisions accomplish each of the preceding purposes?

New Jersey was the first state in 2007 to require online dating sites to disclose whether they perform background checks. See N.J. Stat. Ann. §56:8-171. The legislation passed, despite considerable industry opposition, due to lobbying by the sole online dating service (True.com) that performed background checks at that time. Online Dating Industry Divided over Screenings, Chi. Trib., Feb. 12, 2008, at 10. Note that New Jersey law does not *require* that dating sites actually perform such screening, only that they disclose whether they do. How effective are background checks generally? How might abusers circumvent such screening? See Coleman, supra, at 150 n.80.

4. *Access to state registries.* One proposed safety precaution for online dating service users is permitting their access to state data registries that contain the names of persons who are, or have been, subject to final orders of protection. Elaine M. Chiu, That Guy's a Batterer!: A Scarlet Letter Approach to Domestic Violence in the Information Age, 44 Fam. L.Q. 255 (2010). Theoretically, such access would enable a person to screen prospective partners for a history of domestic violence. Although many states record the issuance of orders of protection in their databases, states differ considerably in terms of public access. In some states, anyone can conduct a free search. However, other states restrict access to authorized personnel (for example, day care employers, law enforcement). How effective do you think this safety precaution would be? What countervailing interests might outweigh public accessibility to criminal justice records? See id. at 270.

Problem

A state representative in the state of Blackacre is concerned about the risks of online dating in terms of exposing customers to the risk of intimate partner violence. The legislator wishes to propose legislation patterned on the New Jersey legislation (below) that requires disclosure of the practice of conducting background checks. You are a legislative aide to the state legislator. Your boss solicits your opinion on the advantages and disadvantages of the New Jersey law. Draft a memo evaluating the merits and shortcomings of the statute, and your recommendations regarding whether your boss should introduce the bill. What additional safety precautions, if any, should the proposed legislation include?

N.J. STAT. ANN. §56:8-171. REQUIREMENTS FOR DATING SERVICE PROVIDERS

An Internet dating service offering services to New Jersey members shall:
a. Provide safety awareness notification that includes, at minimum, a list and description of safety measures reasonably designed to increase awareness of safer

dating practices as determined by the service. Examples of such notifications include:

(1) "Anyone who is able to commit identity theft can also falsify a dating profile."

(2) "There is no substitute for acting with caution when communicating with any stranger who wants to meet you."

(3) "Never include your last name, e-mail address, home address, phone number, place of work, or any other identifying information in your Internet profile or initial e-mail messages. Stop communicating with anyone who pressures you for personal or financial information or attempts in any way to trick you into revealing it."

(4) "If you choose to have a face-to-face meeting with another member, always tell someone in your family or a friend where you are going and when you will return. Never agree to be picked up at your home. Always provide your own transportation to and from your date and meet in a public place with many people around."

b. If an Internet dating service does not conduct criminal background screenings on its members, the service shall disclose, clearly and conspicuously, to all New Jersey members that the Internet dating service does not conduct criminal background screenings. The disclosure shall be provided in two or more of the following forms: when an electronic mail message is sent or received by a New Jersey member, in a "click-through" or other similar presentation requiring a member from this State to acknowledge that they have received the information required by this act, on the profile describing a member to a New Jersey member, and on the website pages or homepage of the Internet dating service used when a New Jersey member signs up. A disclosure under this subsection shall be in bold, capital letters in at least 12-point type.

c. If an Internet dating service conducts criminal background screenings on all of its communicating members, then the service shall disclose, clearly and conspicuously, to all New Jersey members that the Internet dating service conducts a criminal background screening on each member prior to permitting a New Jersey member to communicate with another member. The disclosure shall be provided on the website pages used when a New Jersey member signs up. A disclosure under this subsection shall be in bold, capital letters in at least 12-point type.

d. If an Internet dating service conducts criminal background screenings, then the service shall disclose whether it has a policy allowing a member who has been identified as having a criminal conviction to have access to its service to communicate with any New Jersey member; shall state that criminal background screenings are not foolproof; that they may give members a false sense of security; that they are not a perfect safety solution; that criminals may circumvent even the most sophisticated search technology; that not all criminal records are public in all states and not all databases are up to date; that only publicly available convictions are included in the screening; and that screenings do not cover other types of convictions or arrests or any convictions from foreign countries.

2. Mail-Order Brides and Domestic Violence

■ FOX v. ENCOUNTERS INTERNATIONAL
2006 WL 952317 (4th Cir. 2006)

Per Curiam:

This is a tort case brought by a Ukrainian woman, under Virginia law, against an international match-making agency. . . . [D]efendants are Encounters International (EI) and Natasha Spivack [the agency's owner and founder]. EI is a Maryland corporation with offices in Rockville, Maryland; Moscow, Russia; Yaroslavl, Russia; and Kiev, Ukraine. American male clients of EI pay a membership fee of $1,850 plus additional fees for various matchmaking services. At all times relevant to this case, EI distinguished itself from other matchmaking agencies by claiming a 95 percent success rate with matches and claiming to establish a personal relationship with each woman who joined. EI uses its 95 percent success rate as one of its core marketing tools.

In April 1998, in Kiev, EI introduced then Nataliya Derkach (Plaintiff) to EI member Geoffrey Hermesman. [EI assisted Hermesman in bringing Plaintiff to the United States.] When Hermesman and Plaintiff decided not to pursue a relationship two weeks after she arrived in the United States, Defendants induced Plaintiff to remain an EI member and introduced her to EI member James Fox. EI's website contained Spivack's following description of the events leading to Defendants' introduction of Plaintiff to James Fox:

> Although I introduced James Fox of Virginia and Nataliya Derkach from Kiev a few days before they came to EI Saturday Club, I believe that this event solidified their mutual attraction. A couple of months ago James was briefly engaged to another EI woman client from Kiev but that relationship did not feel right for either one of them when this woman came to the United States. More mature of the two of them, James was determined to work out the differences; therefore he was very disappointed when Lena decided to leave for the Ukraine after a couple of weeks together in order to remain "just friends." Nataliya's story was not a happy one either. She came as a fiancée of one of EI clients who did not feel that she was the right woman for him after spending with her one day in Kiev and a couple of weeks in Virginia. By pure accident she missed the plane which would have taken her back to Kiev. Trying to calm her down when she was crying in my office, I told her that I'll introduce her to other EI clients. "They are the most serious about commitment and family, financially and mentally stable, they are not cheap—the horror stories about cheap Americans do not apply to EI clients—they are the best of the best single men on the 'market'—I told her—because they joined EI showing their trust that we have the best women like you. Don't worry, you are in the right place to be and I'll take care of you." Nataliya raised her big, red from tears, eyes at me and smiled with appreciation.

During the trial in this case, Plaintiff testified as follows regarding Spivack's representations to her about James Fox:

> [James] was her favorite client. He was very good. She said that he will be so good that I was so lucky that I was there at that time, because otherwise he would be married to that other woman, and I would never knew [sic] about him. She said that she has her

favorite other client who [was] going to come from some picture book and she is planning to introduce James, but now that—of course if I'm with him, then of course she wouldn't, but she says that he's her best client, he's the youngest client, and he's— he has everything. He is ready. He's ready to settle down to—he just need[s] a good wife.

According to Spivack, EI's screening process of its male clients consists of her interviewing the male client about his expectations and why previous romantic relationships had failed.

Spivack, on behalf of herself and EI, spoke to Plaintiff in her native tongue and undertook to advise her about many matters including American customs and legal requirements, relationship counseling, prenuptial agreements, and the qualities of the male client to whom EI was introducing her. At all times relevant to this case, Defendants knew that Plaintiff was a Ukrainian national who was unfamiliar with the language, laws, and customs of the United States. Defendants also expressly held themselves out on EI's website as relationship counselors. . . . EI links its counseling services to its 95 percent success rate.

Just two months after James Fox and Plaintiff were married in November 1998, James Fox began to subject Plaintiff to emotional abuse. Such abuse began with small instances of cruel name calling and escalated over time to his angrily throwing a cooked potato past her head and smashing a full glass of Pepsi Cola against the kitchen wall when Plaintiff refused to drink from it after he had spit in it, all resulting in Plaintiff being in an increasingly terrorized state.

In May 1999, James Fox began to physically abuse Plaintiff by chasing her into a bedroom closet, pinning her against the wall, screaming loudly in her ear that she is a stupid idiot, and then biting her finger so hard that her finger showed bite and bruise marks for two weeks. Over time the physical abuse escalated. For example, on the evening of December 29, 1999, James Fox threw Plaintiff, then four months pregnant, on the bed, violently grabbed her leg with both hands in his expressed attempt to break it, and hit Plaintiff in the face causing her lip to bleed when she screamed in pain about her leg.

On three separate occasions, once in January 2000, once in March 2000, and once in April 2000, Plaintiff sought Spivack's counseling and advice with regard to the violent physical and mental abuse that she was suffering at the hands of James Fox. . . . Plaintiff told Spivack about the evening of December 29, 1999; specifically that James Fox had beaten her and terrorized her while pregnant, leaving her with a busted lip and bruises, and that she was so afraid of him beating her again that once he left the apartment for a while, she fled on foot and spent the entire night in a nearby Wal-Mart. [Later,] Plaintiff specifically told Spivack that James Fox was becoming increasingly abusive and had chased her with a broken piece of glass, put it on her neck, and then told her he hated her, causing her to be "really scared."

In response to Plaintiff's repeated reports of abuse and request for advice, Spivack always minimized the abuse Plaintiff suffered, advising her that it was nothing to worry about. With respect to the December 29th beating specifically, Spivack advised Plaintiff that ". . . [A]ll American men are crazy." Spivack continued: " 'Maybe you just listen to him, and do what he says.' " Spivack repeatedly advised Plaintiff that she had only two options, work things out with James Fox or be deported back to the Ukraine. Based upon this advice, Plaintiff remained in the marriage and awaited the birth of her daughter.

[A]pproximately three weeks after Plaintiff gave birth to her daughter Sophia, James Fox subjected Plaintiff to a final violent episode. Specifically, James Fox physically and verbally abused Plaintiff for approximately two hours, including threatening to kill her while holding a gun to her head. Shortly thereafter, Plaintiff called an ambulance because of severe chest pain. The ambulance took Plaintiff to the local hospital where she was treated by Air Force Lt. Col. Marilyn Perry, M.D. Plaintiff had numerous physical injuries including contusions and swelling on her face; hand marks on her arms (indicating that she was violently grabbed and/or shaken); a human bite to her hand; and contusions on her chest. Dr. Perry—board certified with substantial experience with domestic abuse—also testified that it was clear to her that Plaintiff had been terrorized and was a victim of domestic abuse.

Immediately after leaving the hospital, Plaintiff and her baby moved into a battered women's shelter at the urging of the hospital staff [where they remained for approximately seven months]. James Fox obtained a divorce from Plaintiff in Haiti. . . .

Once safe at the battered women's shelter, Plaintiff for the first time learned about the battered spouse waiver. In general, the battered spouse waiver allows an alien who validly resides in the United States based solely upon the sponsorship of her United States citizen spouse to leave an abusive relationship with such spouse without fear of being immediately deported. 8 U.S.C. §§1154, 1229b(b)(2). On April 2, 2001, Plaintiff petitioned for a battered spouse waiver, which the Immigration and Naturalization Service (INS) granted on May 29, 2001. . . . Subsequently, Plaintiff petitioned for adjustment of status as a permanent resident of the United States, which petition was granted. Plaintiff currently lawfully resides in Virginia and is employed as a civil engineer.

The record is undisputed that Spivack knew about the battered spouse waiver during the times that Plaintiff had confided in her about the physical and mental abuse that James Fox inflicted upon her. The record is also undisputed that neither Spivack, nor any other agent or employee of EI, ever informed Plaintiff about the battered spouse waiver. Notably, at all times relevant to this case, EI was governed by the Mail-Order Bride Act (MOBA), 8 U.S.C. §1375. As part of this 1996 legislation, Congress found that there was a heightened risk of domestic abuse in relationships formed by international matchmaking agencies and that women who used such services are "unaware or ignorant of United States immigration law." 8 U.S.C. §1375(a). MOBA required that "[e]ach international matchmaking organization doing business in the United States shall disseminate to recruits, upon recruitment, such . . . information as the [INS] deems appropriate, . . . including information regarding . . . the battered spouse waiver." [MOBA was superseded by the International Mail-Order Brides Act (IMBRA).]

Finally, the record is undisputed that EI's website featured Plaintiff's name and likeness throughout the relevant time period, including through trial. Defendants used Plaintiff's name and likeness to portray her as a happy and satisfied customer even after Defendants had actual knowledge that James Fox physically and mentally abused Plaintiff and that Plaintiff was decidedly not a happy customer. Indeed, Defendants placed a picture of Plaintiff taken when she was either six or seven months pregnant (taken in March or April 2000) on the EI website. . . .

[Plaintiff subsequently sued Encounters International and Spivack based on claims, inter alia, of negligence/breach of fiduciary duty, and actual or constructive fraud.] Plaintiff sought to prove her negligence cause of action on the theory that

Defendants and she had a common law fiduciary relationship under which they owed her fiduciary duties which they breached, proximately causing her injury and resulting in her suffering damages. [The fraud claim was based on EI's alleged misrepresentations to plaintiff, as explained below.]

Under Virginia law, whether a fiduciary relationship exists is a question of fact. A fiduciary relationship exists "when special confidence has been reposed in one who in equity and good conscience is bound to act in good faith and with due regard for the interests of the one reposing the confidence." Based upon this duty, the fiduciary is obligated to tell his principal about "anything which might affect the principal's decision whether or how to act." Critically, Plaintiff did not need to prove that Defendants had a fiduciary relationship with all of EI's female recruits, just Plaintiff.

Here, viewing the evidence in the light most favorable to Plaintiff, as we must, sufficient evidence was before the jury for it to reasonably find that Defendants had a fiduciary relationship with Plaintiff. Spivack testified that she holds herself out as an expert in the field of matchmaking. Specifically, Spivack told Plaintiff that she was a psychologist [although she later testified that she merely took courses in psychology] and screened very carefully the men who EI recommended their foreign female clients marry. Spivack always spoke to Plaintiff in Russian, which comforted Plaintiff. She also undertook, through her actions and words, to advise Plaintiff, as a client of EI, regarding prenuptial agreements, immigration matters, relationship counseling, and American/Eastern Europe cultural/language issues. Finally, EI's website touted that Spivack established a relationship of trust with Plaintiff. . . . Spivack testified that Plaintiff was not her friend, and, therefore, she did not give Plaintiff advice as a friend. [P]laintiff's vulnerabilities while in the United States, including language barriers, being very far from her friends and family in the Ukraine, and being subject to the complexities of immigration laws were all known to Spivack, and, therefore, support the existence of a fiduciary relationship.

We hold that, when all of this evidence is woven together, the reasonable juror could find that Spivack, on behalf of herself and EI, engaged in intentional efforts to gain Plaintiff's trust, confidence, and loyalty in order that Plaintiff would marry James Fox, continue to be married to James Fox, and create another EI success story.

We also hold the jury had sufficient evidence before it to find by a preponderance of the evidence that Defendants breached their fiduciary duties to Plaintiff. Spivack admitted at trial that she knows that some women stay in abusive relationships for fear of being deported. Spivack also testified that she knew about the battered spouse waiver in 1999, prior to Plaintiff confiding in her about James Fox's physical and mental abuse. The record is undisputed that, despite this knowledge, when Plaintiff repeatedly complained to Spivack about such abuse and sought advice about the situation, Spivack never told Plaintiff about the battered spouse waiver. From this evidence, the jury could have reasonably found that Defendants withheld knowledge of the battered spouse waiver from Plaintiff because they wanted to keep up EI's 95 percent matchmaking success rate, which rate happened to be, as Spivack herself testified at trial, one of EI's core promotional selling points. A divorce between Plaintiff and James Fox would have negatively affected EI's 95 percent success rate.

As for the analytically intertwined elements of proximate cause and damages, Plaintiff testified that had she known about the battered spouse waiver prior to James Fox's brutal physical and mental attack in July 2000, she would have left him prior to that time, and, therefore, would not have suffered the physical and mental injuries that she did as the result of such attack. From this testimony, the jury could reasonably find that had Defendants informed Plaintiff of the battered spouse waiver prior to James Fox's July 2000 attack, Plaintiff would not have suffered the physical and mental injuries that she did from the attack. . . .

[The court turns next to plaintiff's allegations of fraud.] . . . Among other misrepresentations, Plaintiff [also] sought to prove that Spivack, on behalf of herself and EI, committed actual or constructive fraud by falsely telling her on several occasions that, in light of her complaints of James Fox's physical and mental abuse, she only had two courses of action available to her: (1) remain married to and living with James Fox; or (2) return to the Ukraine. [A] reasonable jury could find, by clear and convincing evidence, that Spivack, on behalf of herself and EI, intentionally withheld knowledge regarding the battered spouse waiver from Plaintiff [and] that Plaintiff reasonably relied upon Spivack's explanation of her two courses of action to her physical and mental detriment. . . . [The jury also held that Spivack was liable for assuring plaintiff that her husband had been carefully screened.]

Turning to the topic of damages, Defendants [contend] that the punitive damage award is excessive in violation of the Due Process Clause. . . . Here, after considering all of the evidence before it, the jury awarded Plaintiff $92,000 in compensatory damages and $341,500 in punitive damages. . . . [T]he degree of reprehensibility of the defendant's misconduct does not suggest excessiveness. . . . Defendants' knowing allowance of this woman to remain in such a physically and mentally abusive relationship while she was pregnant is highly reprehensible. . . . In the final analysis, we have no basis to hold that the jury's punitive damage award is excessive. . . .

Notes and Questions

1. *Marriages to foreign nationals.* What is the attraction to some men of finding foreign fiancées? To experience an intercultural relationship? To find someone who believes in traditional gender roles? See Suzanne H. Jackson, Marriages of Convenience: International Marriage Brokers, "Mail-Order Brides," and Domestic Servitude, 38 U. Tol. L. Rev. 895, 898-899 (2007) (describing international marriage brokers' advertising portrayals of foreign women).

Based on the description of online dating practices in *Fox*, how well do foreign women know their prospective spouses before they marry? Do they have an adequate opportunity to remain in the United States to explore a potential match?

According to federal immigration law, if a citizen-sponsor desires to obtain a visa for his fiancée, he must file a petition for a "K-1 visa" with the Department of Homeland Security's U.S. Citizenship and Immigration Services. 8 U.S.C. §1184(d). The K-1 visa allows a fiancée to travel to the United States for the purpose of getting married. This visa gives a foreigner 90 days to get married or else she must return home. Do you think 90 days is sufficient? What factors contribute to power differentials between prospective foreign brides and their American sponsors that might play a role in the selection process of a partner?

2. *Extent of domestic violence.* The extent of domestic violence in the mail-order bride industry is unknown. No national data exist, and most reports are based on anecdotal accounts. Only a few empirical studies address the rate of intimate partner violence among clients of the mail-order bride industry (discussed below).

a. *Government data.* Congress enacted the Illegal Immigration Reform and Immigrant Responsibility Act of 1996 (IIRIRA) (codified in relevant part at 8 U.S.C. §1375(c)), to reform immigration laws and set forth procedures for certain lawful permanent residents to apply for relief from deportation or removal. As part of that legislation, Congress requested the Immigration and Naturalization Service (INS) to conduct research on the connection between domestic violence, trafficking, and marriage fraud. 8 U.S.C. §1375(c)(4) (superseded by 8 U.S.C. §1375(a)). The resulting study found that less than 1 percent of the spousal abuse cases brought to INS attention through VAWA's self-petition process (total self petitions = 740) in 1998 were attributable to matches associated with the mail-order bride industry. Commissioner of the Immigration and Naturalization Service and the Director of Violence Against Women Office at the Department of Justice, International Matchmaking Organizations: A Report to Congress 16 (1999), available at http://www.ncsl.org/?tabid=18528 (last visited June 7, 2011).

The report concluded that "the administrative sources of information available to INS for this study failed to establish that the international matchmaking industry contributes in any significant way to these problems [of immigration fraud and domestic violence involving foreign-born spouses]." Id. at 19. (Note, however, that because the research was conducted in the early years of VAWA's self-petition process, the findings were based on a small sample.)

b. *Other data.* Also in 1999, Equality Now (an international human rights organization that promotes civil, political, economic and social rights of women) conducted research to discover the extent to which international marriage brokers (IMBs) provide services to men with violent histories. Equality Now, The Willingness of "Mail-Order Bride" Companies to Provide Services to Violent Men 1 (1999), available at http://www.equalitynow.org/reports/mailorderbride.pdf. The organization sent an email to numerous IMBs requesting an application as a customer. They posed as a potential client who was a physician with a criminal record consisting of assault charges by two ex-wives. Virtually all IMBs responded indicating that they were willing to accept his application. Id.(Such data, of course, do not document the prevalence of intimate partner violence among mail-order spouses but only reflect the likelihood of its occurrence.)

Additional data were gathered by the Tahirih Justice Center, a nonprofit organization dedicated to the protection of immigrant women from gender-based violence. The Tahirih Justice Center conducted a study in 2003 of legal service agencies (unspecified sample size) that provide services to battered immigrant women. The study found that over 50 percent of providers had assisted women who met their abusers through IMBs. Tahirih Justice Center, Frequently Asked Questions: International Broker Regulation Act of 2005 (IMBRA) 2, available at http://www.tahirih.org/site/wp-content/uploads/2009/03/FAQs-IMBRA-11.08.10.pdf (last visited June 7, 2011).

3. *Rationales for regulation.* Marriage fraud in immigration has been a longstanding problem for the Immigration and Naturalization Service (INS) and its

modern-day counterpart, the United States Citizenship and Immigration Services Department (USCIS). Marriage to a U.S. citizen facilitates entry of the alien into the country. Specifically, such a marriage exempts an alien from the quota restrictions of the Immigration and Nationality Act (INA) (codified in relevant part at 8 U.S.C. §1151(a), (b)), thereby avoiding lengthy delays in entering the country. This rule contributes to a strong incentive for aliens to marry U.S. citizens.

In a period of anti-immigrant sentiment, Congress enacted the Immigration Marriage Fraud Amendments (IMFA), Pub. L. No. 99-639, 100 Stat. 3537, in 1986 to address the problem of sham marriages. To make it more difficult for foreign nationals to acquire immigration status through marriage, IMFA restricted an alien spouse to "conditional" status for a two-year period, during which time she had to remain married and living with her U.S.-citizen spouse. 8 U.S.C. §1186a(a). The alien spouse could apply two years later, in a joint petition with the U.S. citizen spouse, to the U.S. Citizenship and Immigration Service, for readjustment of her status to legal permanent resident. 8 U.S.C. §1186a(c). The joint petition and the two-year requirement posed significant obstacles for battered spouses who desired to leave their partners. As a result, in 1990 Congress passed the "battered spouse waiver" (8 U.S.C. §1154) (discussed below). The disclosure of the battered spouse waiver was a critical issue in *Fox.*

Until recently, marriage fraud was the overarching concern of federal immigrant law. However, with the explosive growth of the Internet and the practice of online dating, the emphasis on the regulation of marriages between U.S. citizens and foreign nationals shifted from a concern with marriage fraud to that of protection of foreign nationals from domestic violence. Kirsten M. Lindee, Love, Honor, or Control: Domestic Violence, Trafficking, and the Question of How to Regulate the Mail-Order Bride Industry, 16 Colum. J. Gender & L. 551, 555 (2007).

4. *Federal regulation.* To what federal requirements were defendants subject in *Fox*? How did defendants violate those requirements? Would defendants have incurred any liability in the absence of federal legislation? Considerable federal regulation (explored below) currently addresses the problems experienced by the battered immigrant spouse.

a. *Battered Spouse Waiver.* Congress first addressed the abuse of foreign wives in 1990 by amending the IMFA to include a "battered spouse waiver" to facilitate a battered wife's acquisition of legal residency status. 8 U.S.C. §1186a(c)(4)(C). Formerly, to address the problem of sham marriages, the IMFA required that an alien spouse live with her sponsor-spouse for two years (8 U.S.C. §1186a) and was subject to "conditional" status during that time. The two-year cohabitation requirement posed a hardship for an abused spouse who wanted to leave an abusive marriage. Moreover, the foreign national had to depend on her U.S. citizen-husband to initiate the petitioning process for her—another hardship for battered wives. Failure to meet the requirements of cohabitation and joint petition would result in deportation. 8 U.S.C. §1186a(c).

In recognition of these problems facing battered immigrant spouses, Congress enacted the "battered spouse waiver" to exempt a battered immigrant spouse from the joint petition process, thereby enabling her to request that her "conditional resident" status be adjusted to "lawful permanent resident status" without the need for her husband's sponsorship. 8 U.S.C. §1186a(c)(4)(C). Discretionary waivers from the joint petition process, before the enactment of the "battered spouse waiver," had been restricted to the grounds of "extreme hardship" or "good faith/good cause." However, the INS refused to apply those exceptions to most abused immigrant spouses.

In providing for the "battered spouse waiver," the 1990 legislation specified that the petitioner had to be a victim of "domestic violence" and defined that term to include "battering or extreme cruelty." 8 U.S.C. §1186a(c)(4). See generally Leslye E. Orloff & Janice V. Kaguyutan, Offering a Helping Hand: Legal Protections for Battered Immigrant Women: A History, 10 Am. U. J. Gender Soc. Pol'y & L. 95 (2001) (providing an excellent history of the legislation).

b. *VAWA*. Congressional hearings in 1993 preceding VAWA shed increasing light on the problem of domestic violence in marriages between foreign women and U.S. citizens. H.R. Rep. No. 103-395, 1993 WL 484760, at *31. As a result, VAWA created a unique remedy of a "self-petition" option to allow an abused foreign wife to submit a special petition to immigration authorities for legalization of her residency status. Self-petitioning eligibility requirements include proof that she entered into the marriage in good faith, and also that she, or her children, "has been battered or has been the subject of extreme cruelty." 8 U.S.C. §1154(a)(1)(A)(iii)(I)(aa), (bb). Additionally, the foreign battered wife must be of "good moral character." 8 U.S.C. §1154(a)(1)(A)(iii)(II)(bb). "Battering" and "extreme cruelty" include, but are not limited to, "being the victim of any act or threatened act of violence, including any forceful detention, which results or threatens to result in physical or mental injury." 8 C.F.R. §216.5(c)(1)(vi).

The battered foreign wife no longer has to remain married and living with her abusive husband for two years prior to requesting this adjustment to lawful permanent residency status. 8 C.F.R. §204.2(c)(i). Although she has to prove that she is married at the time of her application and that she resided with her husband for a period of time, no specific time period for the latter is required. VAWA also provided for a "suspension of deportation" or "cancellation of removal" petition for abuse victims without the need for the assistance of their citizen-spouses. 8 U.S.C. §1254(a) (repealed 1997, superseded by 8 U.S.C. §1229b(b)(2)). This last provision was helpful, for example, for divorced spouses. A successful suspension of deportation petition permits such a spouse to gain lawful residency status.

c. *Mail-Order Bride Act (MOBA)*. In 1996, Congress enacted comprehensive regulation of the mail-order bride industry with the Mail-Order Bride Act (MOBA), 8 U.S.C. §1375, §1375(a)(3), (a)(4) (2000) (superseded by the International Marriage Broker Act (IMBRA) of 2005). MOBA required international matchmaking organizations (IMOs) to disseminate information to foreign nationals about (1) conditional and permanent resident status; (2) the battered spouse waiver; (3) marriage fraud penalties; and (4) the unregulated nature of international matchmaking organizations. Congress enforced the disclosure requirements (particularly the foreign national's ability to remain in the United States if she leaves her abusive husband) by the imposition of civil penalties on IMOs that fail to provide such information. 8 U.S.C. §1375.

d. *IMBRA*. In 2006, Congress enacted more extensive regulation of the mail-order bride industry with the passage of the International Marriage Broker Regulation Act (IMBRA)(as part of the Violence Against Women Act (VAWA) Reauthorization Bill of 2005, 8 U.S.C. §1375 (superseding the Mail-Order Bride Act, 8 U.S.C. §1375)). Senator Maria Cantwell (D-Wash) introduced the legislation in response to two highly publicized murders of mail-order brides in Washington State. Holli B. Newsome, Mail Dominance: A Critical Look at the International

Marriage Broker Regulation Act and Its Sufficiency in Curtailing Mail-Order Bride Domestic Abuse, 29 Campbell L. Rev. 291, 292 (2007).

IMBRA effectuated several important reforms in an effort to help foreign brides make better-informed decisions about their prospective U.S. citizen-husbands. First, IMBRA requires the development of an informational pamphlet on the rights and remedies that an immigrant victim of domestic violence has once in the United States, including information on the K-1 fiancée visa; methods of obtaining citizenship status; the fact that domestic violence is illegal in the United States; resources for victims of domestic violence; and, information on the rights of parents with respect to child support. 8 U.S.C. §1375a(a)(1). Second, IMBRA requires IMBs to gather and disclose certain information (that is, criminal and marital histories) about the U.S. husband to the foreign bride. 8 U.S.C. §1375a(d).

Third, IMBRA authorizes U.S. consular officials to share the background information that IMBs have gathered about prospective husbands with the foreign national as well as information about their rights in the United States if they or their children become victims of abuse. 8 U.S.C. §1375a(b). Fourth, IMBRA prohibits IMBs from sharing the contact information, photographs, or information with anyone under the age of eighteen. 8 U.S.C. §1375a(d). And, finally, IMBRA prohibits U.S. citizens from petitioning for more than one K-1 visa within a two-year time frame, thereby ending the practice of some clients who apply for multiple mail-order brides and marry the first woman who is approved for fiancée status. 8 U.S.C. §1184(d).

e. *Other remedies: crime visa.* Other immigration remedies are also available, in limited circumstances, to abused foreign wives. The Violence Against Women Act of 2000 (VAWA 2000), 8 U.S.C. §1101, created a nonimmigrant U-visa to enable a victim of a crime, who cooperates with law enforcement, to petition for a temporary visa (even if her presence in the United States was otherwise illegal). "Congress recognized with the U-visa that it is virtually impossible for state and federal law enforcement, other government enforcement agency officials, and the justice system in general to punish and hold perpetrators of crimes against noncitizens accountable if abusers and other criminals can avoid prosecution by having their victims deported." Orloff & Kaguyutan, supra, at 163. To obtain the temporary visa, the victim must (1) have suffered "substantial physical or mental abuse" as the result of a designated crime (for example, rape, trafficking, domestic violence, sexual assault, felonious assault) (8 U.S.C. §1101(a)(15)(U)); (2) possess information concerning listed criminal activity (id.); and (3) have helped or be likely to help law enforcement investigate or prosecute listed criminal activity. Id. The crime must have occurred in the United States. Id.

VAWA 2000 was passed along with the Victims of Trafficking and Violence Protection Act (codified as amended at 22 U.S.C. §§7101-10, 2151n, 2152d). Both included provisions to combat human trafficking, often referred to as a modern form of slavery. (Traffickers sell women and children into forced labor or into the sex trade, often across international borders.)

f. *Other remedies: asylum.* A victim of domestic violence also may apply for asylum (that is, protection from harm that she would suffer if she returned to her home country by allowing her to stay in the United States). Pursuant to federal immigration law, a person may obtain asylum if she can prove that she is a "refugee," meaning someone who cannot return to her country of origin based on a well-founded fear of persecution by a government (or group that the government is unable or unwilling to control) on account of race, religion, nationality, membership in a *particular social group*, or political opinion. 8 U.S.C. §1101(a)(42) (defining refugee), 8 U.S.C. §1158 (allowing "refugees" to apply for asylum) (emphasis added).

Recent governmental reforms enable victims of domestic violence to qualify for asylum. In April 2009, the United States Department of Homeland Security (DHS) issued a supplemental brief to the Board of Immigration Appeals regarding the asylum petition of an abused Mexican woman ("L.R."). The DHS brief supports granting asylum to people who claim that they are fleeing domestic violence in their home countries, provided that petitioners meet other eligibility requirements. See Supplemental Brief, Dept. of Homeland Sec., available at http://media .npr.org/documents/2009/jul/DHS.pdf (last visited June 8, 2011) (addressing the question whether abused asylum petitioners are members of a "particular social group" within the meaning of the Immigration and Nationality Act, and can otherwise establish eligibility for asylum). The new policy reversed the former U.S. Department of Justice's position of denying asylum to victims of domestic violence. See, e.g., In re R.A., 22 I. & N. Dec. 906, 907-910 (B.I.A. 2001) (holding that a woman who suffered domestic violence in Guatemala that authorities there would not stop was ineligible for asylum).

5. *IMBRA's role in preventing abuse.* The nonprofit organization (Tahirih Justice Center) that was influential in the enactment of IMBRA suggests that IMBRA will help prevent abuse of foreign women in the following ways:

> . . . by providing critical background information that might help to predict abusive behavior by their potential American spouse. IMBRA will also provide them with information about where they can turn for help to escape abuse (including practical information about hotlines, shelters, etc.). . . . In addition, the disclosure requirements imposed up front on IMBs themselves may dissuade those with violent histories from using IMBs to find their next victims, and enable a woman to avoid a relationship with [abusive men]. IMBRA's visa limits will also prevent [such men from finding prospective brides] through serial sponsorship.

Tahirih Justice Center, Frequently Asked Questions, supra, at 3-4. Do you agree with the above assessment of IMBRA's effectiveness? If IMBRA had been in effect at the time when plaintiff met James Fox, would that have changed the result?

6. *Constitutionality of IMBRA.* Fearing that IMBRA would severely curtail its business, an international matchmaking company launched a challenge to the constitutionality of the Act. In European Connections (EC) & Tours, Inc. v. Gonzalez, 480 F. Supp. 2d 1355 (D. Georgia 2007), a matchmaking organization that specialized in matching men with women from Eastern Europe and the former Soviet Republics contended that IMBRA's requirements of data collection and disclosure of male clients' background information infringed the organization's First Amendment right to free speech, constituting an impermissible prior restraint and a content-based restriction on constitutionally protected commercial speech. In addition, it contended that IMBRA's definition of an IMB violated the Equal Protection Clause of the Fifth Amendment.

Rejecting the IMB's claims, a federal district court concluded that IMBRA did not constitute an unconstitutional regulation of commercial speech because it neither banned nor completely suppressed such speech but only imposed disclosure requirements that were not overly burdensome and that bore a reasonable relationship to the legitimate governmental interest in protecting women from fraud and domestic abuse. In response to the equal protection challenge, the court held that EC's rights were not violated by its inclusion in the definition of an "international marriage broker," while religious and cultural matchmaking organizations and organizations that did not target American male-foreign female relationships were not, because Congress had a rational basis for concluding that IMBs contributed more to domestic violence against foreign women than matchmaking services.

7. Fox: *facts and issues.*

a. *Facts.* When did Nataliya's husband start to abuse her? What was the nature of that abuse? Based on the lethality assessment tool (discussed in Chapter 2), how lethal was the abuse? What did Nataliya do in response to the abuse? Why didn't she leave her husband? What induced her to leave him finally? To whom did she disclose the abuse? What advice did she receive? Who informed Nataliya of the "battered spouse waiver"? Why didn't Ms. Spivack inform plaintiff of her rights? How might the defendants have better protected plaintiff?

b. *Issues.* On what grounds did Nataliya sue defendants? Did defendants have a fiduciary relationship with Nataliya? What were defendants' legal obligations to Nataliya? Did they breach their fiduciary duty to plaintiff? Did they make false misrepresentations to plaintiff? If so, were those misrepresentations *material?* Did plaintiff *rely* on these misrepresentations? What *detriment* did she suffer as a result of the alleged misrepresentations? Were the damages excessive, according to the court? Do you think that the case was correctly decided?

8. *Divorce.* In *Fox*, the husband obtained a divorce in Haiti. Yet, many battered immigrant spouses have far more difficulty in obtaining a divorce. "Indigency, access to justice, and cultural beliefs all stand as substantial barriers to divorce for immigrant victims of violence." Mariela Olivares, A Final Obstacle: Barriers to Divorce for Immigrant Victims of Domestic Violence in the United States, 34 Hamline L. Rev. 149, 154 (2011). Cultural beliefs often include misconceptions about the legal system (that is, that it is subject to bribery, that it favors the spouse who remains in the marital home). Cultural beliefs about the impropriety of divorce also provide an obstacle. Battered foreign wives often are hampered by language difficulties and also frightened by batterers' threats to obtain child custody and to report them to immigration authorities. Id. at 147-159. How can these difficulties be addressed to improve immigrant battered women's access to divorce?

9. *Epilogue.* Nataliya also sued her ex-husband in tort. The case was settled for $115,000. Fox was charged with attempted murder for the violent incident described in the principal case; however, the charge was dropped. A charge for assault was expunged from his record following his completion of an anger management course. He subsequently married another Russian bride whom he met on the Internet. Daren Briscoe, Mail-Order Misery: Charging Abuse, Imported Brides are Fighting Back, Newsweek, Feb. 7, 2005, at 54.

10. *Legacy of* Fox. The *Fox* case was instrumental in the passage of IMBRA, according to Nataliya Fox's attorney, Randall Miller, of Arnold and Porter. His law firm helped draft and shepherd IMBRA through Congress with the assistance of the non-profit Tahirih Justice Center. Miller and his firm also represented the respondent in a subsequent case, European Connections & Tours v. Gonzalez, 480 F. Supp. 2d 1355 (N.D. Ga. 2007), defending the constitutionality of IMBRA. Miller

identifies two important consequences of *Fox*: (1) instigating the passage of IMBRA, and (2) providing a lesson to international matchmaking agencies that if they fail to provide information to their clients about the battered spouse waiver, the agencies can face exposure to civil liability. Telephone interview with Randall Miller, Partner, Arnold & Porter, June 6, 2011.

B. DIVORCE

1. *Modern Fault-Based Grounds*

■ **PETERS v. PETERS**
   906 So. 2d 64 (Miss. Ct. App. 2004)

MYERS, J., for the Court.
. . . On June 17, 1977, Catherine and Michael married. They met while working together at Sears. In addition to the job at Sears, Michael at this time also owned several rental properties in Gulfport. After marrying, they acquired several other rental properties, and Catherine left her job at Sears to manage the rental properties. In the years that followed, they continued to purchase rental properties, and Michael began what would become a successful computer business. In the early years of their marriage, Michael and Catherine had two children, Michael Jr., and Stephanie. Some years later, in the early nineties, they had two more children, Alexandra and Thomas. [Catherine filed for divorce on January 18, 2001, on the ground of habitual cruel and inhuman treatment. The court granted the divorce, awarded custody and child support to Catherine, and divided the marital assets. Michael appeals.]

In contrast to their financial growth, Michael and Catherine experienced a gradual decline in their relationship. . . . In the words of the chancellor's [the trial judge's] judgment:

> This 24-year marriage was marked by loud arguments, verbal assaults, cursing, and an increasing escalation of physical violence which culminated in the separation of the parties. . . . The arguments between Mike and Cathy were loud, with each cursing the other. Mike's face would get extremely red and to on-lookers, he appeared to be in a rage. All witnesses agreed that Mike never hit or beat Cathy during these arguments, although he would shove, push and slap her, and Cathy never sought medical treatment as a result of any of the arguments. Following the arguments there were long periods of "the silent treatment" where Mike refused to speak with Cathy. He would, however, shove Cathy into the walls with his shoulders when they would pass in the hallways of their home; all four children witnessed this behavior.

The chancellor detailed a list of incidents beginning in 1984 and proceeding up to and beyond the time of separation [in 2000]. Among these incidents, which were also testified to by Catherine and corroborated by the children, the following conduct is described: Michael choking Catherine on numerous occasions after loud arguments; Michael throwing various objects at Catherine including a baseball, telephones, and television remote controls; Michael threatening to commit suicide, in front of the children; Michael accusing Catherine of committing adultery; Michael referring to his grandchild as a "bastard"; and Michael canceling all of Catherine's credit cards and closing her checking account without any notice or warning. The chancellor's listing goes into more detail, but these are a representative sample of the conduct about which Catherine complained.

While Michael testified to a somewhat different version of several of these events, Michael admits that many of these events happened. Michael's different version of some of the events, however, was uncorroborated and was usually contradicted by the version of events testified to by Catherine and the children. In the end, the chancellor made a credibility determination in Catherine's favor, accepting in substantial part the version of events presented by Catherine and the children. . . .

To be granted a divorce on the grounds of habitual cruel and inhuman treatment, the offended spouse must show: "[C]onduct that either (1) endangers life, limb, or health, or creates a reasonable apprehension of such danger, rendering the relationship unsafe for the party seeking relief, or (2) is so unnatural and infamous as to make the marriage revolting to the non-offending spouse and render it impossible for that spouse to discharge the duties of marriage, thus destroying the basis for its continuance." [Miss. Code Ann §93-5-1]. This showing must be made by a preponderance of the credible evidence, and this showing must demonstrate more than mere incompatibility, lack of affection, rudeness, or unkindness. . . .

We now consider Michael's more specific arguments on appeal, namely that (1) there was no causal connection between Michael's alleged conduct and the separation, and (2) that Michael's alleged conduct did not place Catherine in reasonable apprehension of danger to life, limb or health. Each of these arguments will be examined in turn.

First, Michael tries to make much of the fact that many of the incidents described by Catherine occurred several years in the past, going back to 1994. Because of this remoteness in time, Michael argues, there was no causal connection between his conduct and the separation. . . . We agree that . . . the evidence must establish a rather strict causal connection between the cruel and inhuman treatment and the separation of the parties. However, subsequent case law has somewhat lessened this requirement. . . . The case of Richard v. Richard, 711 So. 2d 884, 890 (Miss.1998) [is illustrative]:

> We no longer require that a specific act must be the proximate cause of a separation before a divorce may be granted on grounds of habitual cruel and inhuman treatment. It is, instead, habitual or continuous behavior over a period of time, close in proximity to the separation, or continuing after a separation occurs, that may satisfy the grounds for divorce.

Therefore, we find no merit in Michael's argument that we should reverse because there was no causal connection between the separation and the cruel and inhuman conduct. . . . Indeed, given what we find in the record, we are at a loss to know what could have caused the separation other than the conduct about which Catherine complains. . . .

Second, Michael argues that the conduct Catherine complains of did not rise to the level of placing her in reasonable apprehension of danger to life, limb or health. This argument overlooks the fact that . . . cruel and inhuman treatment may be shown in one of two alternative ways. . . . [E]ven if Catherine failed to show conduct that created a reasonable apprehension of danger to life, limb or health, she could still be entitled to a divorce on the grounds of habitual cruel and inhuman treatment if she succeeded in showing conduct that was "so unnatural and infamous as to make the marriage revolting to the non-offending spouse and render it impossible for that spouse to discharge the duties of marriage." Thus, we find no merit in Michael's second argument on this issue. Having found no merit in Michael's arguments and having found no manifest error, we affirm the judgment of the chancellor granting Catherine a divorce on the grounds of habitual cruel and inhuman treatment. . . .

Notes and Questions

1. *Fault-based divorce: background.* In the nineteenth century, divorce on the ground of cruelty was often the only remedy available to battered spouses, as we have seen (in Chapter 1). Traditionally, divorce required that one spouse prove that the other spouse committed marital misconduct ("fault"). Beginning in the late 1960s, widespread reform led to all states eventually enacting no-fault divorce statutes. California started the trend in 1969. See Cal. Fam. Code §2310 (setting forth "irreconcilable differences" as the basis for no-fault divorce). On the history of no-fault divorce, see generally Lynne Carol Halem, Divorce Reform: Changing Legal and Social Perspectives (1980); Allen M. Parkman, Good Intentions Gone Awry: No-Fault Divorce and the American Family (2000).

Although all states now have no-fault divorce, "no-fault" does not mean the same thing in all jurisdictions. Only a small number of states are "pure" no-fault states (that is, without any fault-based grounds). Far more states retain traditional fault-based grounds for divorce as an alternative to no-fault divorce. In some of these latter states, the spouses are faced with a choice. They may obtain a no-fault divorce if they both agree to the divorce; but, if one spouse does not agree, then the other spouse must resort to proof of a fault-based ground. Mississippi, the jurisdiction of *Peters*, does not permit unilateral no-fault divorce because both spouses must agree to a divorce based on irreconcilable differences. See Miss. Code Ann. §93-5-2.

In traditional fault-based regimes, the divorce petitioner must be "free from fault" in order to obtain a divorce. Historically, fault also played a role in awards of spousal support, property distribution, and child custody. In some states, today, fault continues to influence awards of spousal support and property distribution. See, e.g., Edwards v. Edwards, 26 So. 3d 1254, 1260 (Ala. Civ. App. 2009) (considering fault for property division); Hutson v. Hutson, 908 So. 2d 1231, 1235 (La. Ct. App. 2005) (considering fault for spousal support).

Why do you suppose Catherine sought a fault-based divorce in *Peters*? Why do you suppose Michael opposed it?

2. *Trend in fault-based divorces.* Adultery was far more widely alleged as a nineteenth-century fault-based ground for divorce than cruelty. By the mid-1960s, however, the trend reversed. What might explain this phenomenon? See Jessie Bernard, No News, but New Ideas, in Divorce and After 16-20 (Paul Bohannon ed. 1970) (suggesting changing views about divorce and the companionate marriage).

3. *Cruelty.* Cruelty, sometimes termed "cruel and inhuman treatment," was a traditional ground for fault-based divorce in most states (and continues to exist as a

ground in those states with mixed fault and no-fault provisions). English ecclesiastic courts required actual or threatened bodily harm. Courts gradually expanded the definition to include mental cruelty.

Jurisdictions often require a "course of conduct" of cruel behavior that creates an "adverse health effect." The determination of whether particular abusive acts constitute legally sufficient grounds for a cruelty-based divorce is highly subjective. See, e.g., Scally v. Scally, 802 So. 2d 128, 131 (Miss. Ct. App. 2001) (awarding a divorce based on husband's moody, controlling, and verbally abusive conduct that caused wife to fear for her safety, although dissent found same conduct evidenced mere unkindness and incompatibility).

Courts traditionally required a high standard of proof of cruelty, stemming from a reluctance to facilitate divorce. How do the requirements of a "course of conduct" and "adverse health effect" address this concern? What is "a course of conduct"? What is "an adverse health effect"? How might these requirements pose problems for victims of intimate partner violence? Note that some courts maintain that a single act of cruelty will not satisfy the "course of conduct" requirement, unless that isolated incident is particularly brutal. See, e.g., Ellzey v. Ellzey, 253 So. 2d 249, 251 (Miss. 1971) (granting divorce based upon an attempted murder).

4. *Case holding.* What does Mississippi law require for a divorce based on cruelty, according to *Peters*? How did Catherine establish the requisite elements? What are Michael's counterarguments? What does the court respond? What explains the state's requirement of a causal connection between the marital misconduct and the parties' separation? How might that requirement present difficulty for victims of intimate partner violence? Does Mississippi's liberalization of the strict proximate cause requirement (extending it to behavior "close in proximity to the separation, or continuing after a separation") adequately address this difficulty?

The trial judge, in his judgment, asserted: "All witnesses agree that Mike *never hit or beat* Cathy during these arguments [and] Cathy never sought medical treatment as a result of any of the arguments" (emphasis added). What does the trial judge signify by his use of the words *hit* and *beat* particularly in light of the other evidence? In your view, does the *implement* with which the offender "hit or beat" the victim make a difference in an assessment of the seriousness of the abuse? Compare Heiser v. Heiser 153 N.W.2d 909, 911 (Neb. 1967) (finding that threats with gun and knives constitute cruelty), with Hastings, supra, at 745-746 (finding that throwing a fork does not constitute cruelty).

5. *Corroboration.* In the fault-based era, corroboration was widely required to prove acts of marital misconduct for purposes of divorce. The corroboration requirement necessitated eye-witness testimony and contributed to the adversarial nature of divorce proceedings. What is the rationale for this requirement? For a relatively recent case recognizing the continued importance of the corroboration requirement, see Dee v. Dee, 258 S.W.3d 405 (Ark. Ct. App. 2007) (dismissing husband's divorce petition even though he admitted to placing Internet ads seeking sexual partners because his admission lacked corroboration).

Does Mississippi law, based on the principal case, require corroboration? If so, how did plaintiff satisfy this requirement? Because intimate partner violence generally occurs in private, corroboration may be difficult. If a given jurisdiction requires corroboration but eye-witness testimony is not available, how can a victim satisfy the corroboration requirement? Will photographic evidence suffice?

See Rawson v. Buta, 609 So. 2d 426, 431-432 (Miss. 1992) (finding that photographs cannot be the sole basis of corroborating evidence).

6. *Long-term vs. short-term marriages.* Some jurisdictions require a higher degree of proof of cruelty for divorce involving a long-term marriage. See, e.g., William M.M. v. Kathleen M.M., 611 N.Y.S.2d 317, 318 (App. Div. 1994) (requiring additional corroboration for long-term marriage based upon case law, not statute). What purpose is served thereby? Is the rule sound—in general? In cases, specifically, of intimate partner violence?

Problem

Suppose Mr. and Mrs. Peters (in the principal case) live in another state. Different states define cruelty differently. Consider the following statutory definitions of cruelty. Could Mrs. Peters obtain a cruelty-based divorce, based on the above abusive acts, in each of the jurisdictions below? Which of the following statutes better serve the interests of victims? How should the statutes be improved for divorce-related purposes?

1. "[E]xtreme cruelty . . . is defined as including any physical or mental cruelty which endangers the safety or health of the plaintiff or makes it improper or unreasonable to expect the plaintiff to continue to cohabit with the defendant; provided that no complaint for divorce shall be filed until after 3 months from the date of the last act of cruelty complained of in the complaint, but this provision shall not be held to apply to any counterclaim." N.J. Stat. Ann. §2A:34-2.

2. "'Marital misconduct' means . . . [c]ruel or barbarous treatment endangering the life of the other spouse." N.C. Gen. Stat. Ann. §50-16.1A.

3. "The court may grant a divorce in favor of one spouse if the other spouse is guilty of cruel treatment toward the complaining spouse of a nature that renders further living together insupportable." Tex. Fam. Code Ann. §6.002.

4. "A divorce from the bond of matrimony may be decreed . . . [w]here either party has been guilty of cruelty, caused reasonable apprehension of bodily hurt, or willfully deserted or abandoned the other, such divorce may be decreed to the innocent party after a period of one year from the date of such act." Va. Code Ann. §20-91.

2. *What Role for Fault in a No-Fault System?*

■ FELTMEIER v. FELTMEIER
798 N.E.2d 75 (Ill. 2003)

Review pp. 499-502.

Notes and Questions

1. *Holding.* The first issue that *Feltmeier* presents is whether courts should permit interspousal actions for intentional infliction of emotional distress in divorce actions. Do you agree with *Feltmeier*'s resolution of this issue? What purposes are

served by allowing spouses, such as Lynn Feltmeier, to seek liability for interspousal torts? Why isn't divorce an adequate remedy?

2. *No-fault divorce.* All states currently offer some form of no-fault divorce, as we have seen. California was the first state to pass a no-fault divorce law in 1969 (which went into effect in 1970). See Cal. Fam. Code §2310 ("irreconcilable differences"). A few years later, the National Conference of Commissioners on Uniform State Laws ratified another model for no-fault divorce, the Uniform Marriage and Divorce Act (UMDA). See UMDA §302 ("irretrievable breakdown").

The objectives of the law reform movement that eliminated fault as a ground for divorce were to accommodate the desire for divorce of many unhappy couples and, in the process, to minimize the hostility, acrimony, and trauma that accompanied fault-based divorce. No-fault divorce promotes amicable dispute resolution and eliminates the need for public vindication to prove the existence of fault-based divorce grounds. The elimination of the adversarial nature of fault-based dissolution is thought to facilitate better post-divorce adjustment.

To what extent are these goals accomplished for divorcing spouses whose relationships are characterized by domestic violence? Consider the following view of Professor Sarah Buel, "One problem in most domestic cases, however, is that the batterer will allow neither an amicable divorce nor a peaceful existence for his ex-spouse, thereby sabotaging important goals of no-fault." Sarah M. Buel, Access to Meaningful Remedy: Overcoming Doctrinal Obstacles in Tort Litigation Against Domestic Violence Offenders, 83 Or. L. Rev. 945, 996 (2004).

3. *Continued role for fault?* Does recognition of emotional distress claims in the context of divorce reintroduce fault into the no-fault system? Does it undermine no-fault divorce law? Does it resurrect the fault-based ground of cruelty? Does it lead to double recovery in cases in which fault still plays a role in property distribution?

Scholars disagree about the extent to which the law should permit tort claims in the dissolution context. Compare Ira Mark Ellman & Stephen D. Sugarman, Spousal Emotional Abuse as a Tort?, 55 Md. L. Rev. 1268 (1996) (arguing against allowing intentional infliction of emotional distress claims between spouses), with Buel, supra at 982-995 (arguing that allowing such claims in the divorce context lends credibility to other interspousal tort claims).

Supporters of allowing interspousal infliction claims in the divorce context argue that the law should provide just compensation for outrageous misconduct, regardless of whether it is caused by strangers or intimate partners. Opponents argue that allowing such claims undermines the theoretical basis of no-fault divorce, because this much-needed reform eliminates recriminations and the invasion of privacy that flows from judicial scrutiny of marital relations. How do you think courts and legislatures should balance these interests?

4. *Causation.* Do problems of causation militate against recovery of tort damages in the divorce context? That is, how can a victim prove that her severe emotional distress was caused by the spouse's abusive conduct and not by other marital difficulties?

5. *Victim's preferences.* Why might a victim of domestic violence prefer to file for divorce based on fault-based grounds when a no-fault divorce is so much easier to obtain?

6. *Judges' preferences.* Why might a judge prefer that a victim of domestic violence file for divorce based on no-fault grounds rather than fault-based grounds?

See Buel, supra, at 966 (recounting story of a battered spouse in the midst of a dissolution proceeding who was pressured by the judge to agree to "irretrievable breakdown" as the basis for the divorce despite longstanding history of severe abuse).

7. *Divorce as "leverage."* May a judge dismiss a tort claim or a criminal charge on the basis that the pending dissolution proceeding solves the "problem"? May a judge in a tort case or criminal case require that the victim pursue a divorce? May a judge decide to grant, refuse to grant, or vacate a restraining order on the basis that the married petitioner must seek a divorce—or that she is currently seeking a divorce? See S.D. v. M.J.R., 2 A.3d 412, 439 (N.J. Super. Ct. App. Div. 2010) (criticizing the trial judge's refusal to enter a final restraining order partly because the parties' divorce was pending) discussed in Chapter 4.

Are judges correct in their assumption that divorce will end the violence? On the other hand, should judges assume that battered married women generally want to divorce their batterers? Cf. Laurie S. Kohn, The Justice System and Domestic Violence: Engaging the Case but Divorcing the Victim, 32 N.Y.U. Rev. L. & Soc. Change 191, 229 (2008) (explaining the reasons that a victim may abandon pursuit of a restraining order petition because "after the trauma of the violent event has receded, she may reconcile with her partner or reconsider involving the legal system in her family life"). These judicial practices are sufficiently common that at least one state legislature enacted the following remedial statute:

R.I. GEN. LAW ANN. §12-29-4

. . . (b) Because of the serious nature of domestic violence, the court in domestic violence actions:

(1) Shall not dismiss any charge or delay disposition because of concurrent dissolution of marriage or other civil proceedings;

(2) Shall not require proof that either party is seeking a dissolution of marriage prior to instigation of criminal proceedings;

Does the above statute adequately address the problem? If not, what revisions would you recommend?

3. The Relationship of Divorce and Tort Law: Joinder

■ McCULLOH v. DRAKE
24 P.3d 1162 (Wyo. 2001)

The marriage of Gerri E. McCulloh (the wife) and John W. Drake (the husband) endured for approximately three-and-a-half years before the wife sought a divorce. . . . The wife had one son from a prior marriage, and the couple had another son in October of 1994. During the marriage, the family lived on a ranch that the husband purchased prior to the marriage. After moving to the ranch, the couple commenced the operation of a Morgan horse business. [The husband's net worth was $4 million at the time of the marriage and $5 million at the time of separation.]

[Gerri brings an action for divorce and tort claims of negligent and intentional infliction of emotional distress.] The wife asserts that, beginning shortly after the marriage, the husband began a pattern of physical and sexual abuse. She maintains that various incidents of abuse led up to an encounter where the husband held a pillow over her face, which ultimately caused her departure from the relationship. The wife left her husband on October 4, 1997, and filed for divorce on December 31, 1997. On October 29, 1998, the wife filed the complaint wherein she asserted the various tort claims and requested a jury trial. The trial court denied the jury trial request and, from July 26, 1999, through July 30, 1999, heard evidence pertaining to child custody, child support, property division, alimony, attorney and guardian ad litem fees, the tort claims, and punitive damages.

At the conclusion of the trial, the trial court awarded shared physical custody of the child but gave primary decision-making power regarding medical and educational issues to the husband. It also awarded $1,200 per month to the wife for child support. [The wife also received a property distribution].

In addressing the various tort claims [the facts of which are unspecified in this opinion], the trial court found, regarding the claims of negligent infliction of emotional distress, intentional infliction of emotional distress (except for the pillow incident), outrageous conduct, and sexual assault, that the wife failed "to state a claim for which relief can be granted; to prove the claim by a preponderance of the evidence; to present sufficient evidence on damages; and/or to timely file some allegations." Specifically with regard to the sexual assault claim, the trial court found that the wife "failed to prove by a preponderance of the evidence that a tortious sexual assault occurred."

The trial court found that the wife did prove a tort occurred in September of 1997 when the husband briefly held a pillow over her face and concluded that, although she did not currently suffer a disability, there was some proof she suffered emotional distress as a result of the incident. Accordingly, the trial court awarded damages of $4,250 and $750 in punitive damages, using the following rationale to arrive at the latter figure:

> Given the incompatibility of these parties, conflict was inevitable. Happily, there were no stitches nor broken bones. Still, court decisions must reflect society's disdain for domestic abuse of any type. Hence, the Court finds punitive damages are appropriate.
>
> . . . The Court finds the September 1997 incident where Defendant covered Plaintiff's head briefly with a pillow most closely resembles a battery under W.S. 6-2-501(b). The maximum criminal fine for violating this statute is $750.00.
>
> Neither party was satisfied with the trial court's final decision, and they each filed an appeal. In the wife's appeal, she takes issue with the divided custody order, the award of primary decision-making authority to the husband, the child support award, and the property settlement. The wife also claims that the trial court should not have denied her request for a jury trial on the tort issues. . . .

JOINDER

The wife complains that the trial court's decision to hear the tort issues along with the divorce issues deprived her of her right to have a jury decide her tort claims. Relying on W.R.C.P. 38(a), the husband replies that the wife was not entitled to a jury trial because her action did not exclusively involve the recovery of money.

A civil action in tort is fundamentally different from a divorce proceeding. The issues involved in each are entirely distinct, and the procedure involved in divorce actions, which are purely equitable, makes joining tort claims impracticable.

> The purpose of a tort action is to redress a legal wrong in damages; that of a divorce action is to sever the marital relationship between the parties, and where appropriate, to fix the parties' respective rights and obligations with regard to alimony and support, and to divide the marital estate.

[Henriksen v. Cameron, 622 A.2d 1135, 1411 (Me. 1993) (quoting Heacock v. Heacock, 520 N.E.2d 151, 153 (Mass. 1988) (citations omitted))].

A most basic procedural difference between tort and divorce actions is the right to a jury trial in tort actions.

> [D]ivorce actions will become unduly complicated in their trial and disposition if torts can be or must be litigated in the same action. A divorce action is highly equitable in nature, whereas the trial of a tort claim is at law and may well involve, as in this case, a request for a trial by jury. The administration of justice will be better served by keeping the proceedings separate.

Simmons v. Simmons, 773 P.2d 602, 604 (Colo. Ct. App. 1988) (quoting Lord v. Shaw, 665 P.2d 1288, 1291 (Utah 1983)).

Moreover, joining the actions risks unacceptable delays:

> Resolution of tort claims may necessarily involve numerous witnesses and other parties such as joint tortfeasors and insurance carriers whose interests are at stake. Consequently, requiring joinder of tort claims in a divorce action could unduly lengthen the period of time before a spouse could obtain a divorce and result in such adverse consequences as delayed child custody and support determinations.

Stuart v. Stuart, 421 N.W.2d 505, 508 (Wis. 1988) (quoting Stuart v. Stuart, 410 N.W.2d 632, 638 (Wis. Ct. App. 1987)).

The goal to promote judicial economy should not be sought at the expense of fair and proper consideration of the parties' issues. "Jurors, many of whom are themselves married, are in the best possible position to determine what behavior between spouses is 'atrocious and utterly intolerable in a civilized community,' [Restatement (Second) of Torts §46 (1965)], and what behavior is within the 'ebb and flow' of married life." *Henriksen*, 622 A.2d at 1139. . . . The wife's tort claims were improperly joined with the divorce action. We reverse the trial court's decision to join the causes of action together in one proceeding and remand for a determination by a jury.

Notes and Questions

1. *Joinder.* McCulloh v. Drake raises the issues whether a tort claim can be and should be joined in an action for divorce when both suits involve allegations of domestic violence. How did the issue arise in *McCulloh*? How does *McCulloh* resolve this issue?

2. *Different views.* Courts that permit interspousal actions for intentional infliction of emotional distress adopt different positions regarding joinder of the tort

and divorce. Some courts prohibit joinder, some mandate joinder, and some adopt a permissive policy of joinder. See, e.g., Twyman v. Twyman, 855 S.W.2d 619, 624 (Tex. 1993) (adopting permissive joinder); Brinkman v. Brinkman, 966 S.W.2d 780, 782 (Tex. App. 1998) (explaining various positions). A majority of jurisdictions permit (but do not mandate) joinder. Chen v. Fisher, 843 N.E.2d 723, 726 (N.Y. 2005). Which approach does *McCulloh* adopt? Which approach do you favor? Why?

Courts permit post-divorce interspousal tort claims based on various theories, including: (1) the issues are not identical, or (2) policy considerations militate against application of res judicata. See generally Clare Dalton, Domestic Violence, Domestic Torts and Divorce: Constraints and Possibilities, 31 New. Eng. L. Rev. 319, 374–378 (1997); Barbara Glesner Fines, Joinder of Tort Claims in Divorce Actions, 12 J. Am. Acad. Matrim. Law 285, 306-308 (1994). Which policies?

3. *Remedy.* If a court (like *McCulloh*) does not permit joinder, is a plaintiff without remedy? May she pursue a separate action? Must she?

4. *Relationship of joinder to res judicata.* If a spouse chooses to pursue a separate tort action post-divorce, can the tortfeasor-spouse raise the affirmative defense of res judicata to bar her claim? That is, in the principal case, suppose Gerri first sues John for a divorce alleging cruelty; then she sues John for assault in a separate proceeding. Suppose that in the divorce proceeding, Gerri also asserted that his cruelty should be the basis for a disproportionate share of the marital property. Can John claim in the subsequent tort proceeding that Gerri's assault claim is barred because of res judicata, that is, that Gerri did (or should have) asserted all her claims for cruelty during the divorce? Res judicata (sometimes called "claims preclusion") is a doctrine based on judicial efficiency and a desire to avoid a multiplicity of suits. It prevents the relitigation of a claim or cause of action that has been finally adjudicated (or that should have been adjudicated) in the prior suit. (Of course, in jurisdictions that preclude joinder of tort claims and dissolution, res judicata does not come into play because the tort claim could not have been litigated in the divorce action.)

What is the relationship between joinder and res judicata? Professor Sarah Buel responds:

> At first glance it would appear that most states are permissive regarding joinder of tort and divorce actions. However, closer scrutiny reveals that many divorce statutes include specific language that, although joinder is not strictly mandatory, if the subject of the subsequent tort action was at all part of the dissolution, the tort action will be disallowed on grounds of res judicata.

Buel, supra, at 1000-1001. Compare *Brinkman*, supra, at 383 (holding that wife's subsequent tort claims were precluded by res judicata), with Roussel v. Roussel, 2003 WL 22951910 (Va. Cir. Ct. 2003) (contra).

How does the general acceptance of no-fault divorce affect the bar of res judicata? See Buel, supra, at 1004 ("In no-fault jurisdictions, considerations of res judicata are intensified as the tortfeasor's conduct often cannot be raised in the divorce"). Will res judicata bar subsequent tort claims if a trial court awards a divorce on grounds unrelated to the abuse? Will res judicata bar subsequent tort claims if a trial court does not specify the grounds on which it awards the divorce? See, e.g., Heacock v. Heacock, 520 N.E.2d 151, 153 (Mass. 1998) (holding that husband's claims of issue and claim preclusion did not bar wife's tort claim because trial court made no findings to permit ruling of law). For additional discussion of res judicata, see Chapter 10, pp. 522-526.

5. *Benefits of joinder.* What benefits follow from joinder? Professor Andrew Schepard responds:

> Divorce litigation comprises a major portion of the caseload of many large state court systems. The policy interest in conserving scarce judicial resources by concentrating all claims between the divorcing couple into a single proceeding is thus great. . . . There is also a related social interest in reducing the private transaction costs (the most significant component of which is legal fees) of settling marital differences. Divorce is generally a zero sum economic transaction: there is not enough money in the marital settlement pot for both spouses to live postdivorce at the same standard of living as before the divorce. Increasing the transaction costs of the divorce settlement by reopening proceedings reduces further the total resources available for the postdivorce family to live on. . . .
>
> Also weighing in favor of [joinder] is the policy of repose that underlies [res judicata]. Divorce is a wrenching, all-consuming emotional experience. [The husband's and wife's] well-being, and their continued productive functioning as members of society, require that their emotional stability be reestablished quickly and firmly by a final settlement of marital differences.

Andrew Schepard, Divorce, Interspousal Torts, and Res Judicata, 24 Fam. L.Q. 127, 131-132 (1990). See also Tiffany Oliver, Note, Intentional Infliction of Emotional Distress between Spouses: New Mexico's Excessively High Threshold for Outrageous Conduct, 33 N. Mex. L. Rev. 381, 392 (2003).

6. *Disadvantages of joinder.* What factors militate against joinder? Do the disadvantages of joinder outweigh the benefits?

7. *Purposes.* Do the different purposes of, or legal theories behind, tort actions and divorce militate in favor of, or against, joinder? Do the different procedural characteristics?

8. *Jury trial.* In *McCulloh*, Linda sought a jury trial on her tort claims against her husband. Jury trials are normally permitted in tort actions but not in divorce actions (because the latter, historically, were subject to chancery jurisdiction that did not have juries). Why did Linda want a jury trial on her tort claims? If a plaintiff must join her tort claims to divorce proceedings to avoid their later preclusion and if family courts forbid jury trials, must a plaintiff waive her right to a jury trial for her tort claims? Clare Dalton, Domestic Violence, Domestic Torts and Divorce: Constraints and Possibilities, 31 New Eng. L. Rev. 319, 387-388 (1997).

How should a court resolve the issue of plaintiffs' access to a jury trial if plaintiff desires to bring a tort action in the dissolution proceeding? See Kinsella v. Kinsella, 696 A.2d 556, 571 (N.J. 1997) (suggesting that "Whether a marital tort claim will be afforded a jury trial depends on whether there are dominant issues in the case, such as child welfare, support, and custody issues, that cannot be resolved adequately if the marital tort claim is severed or whether " 'society's interest in vindicating a marital tort through the jury process is the dominant interest in the matter' ").

If a jury trial is ordered, where shall the claim be litigated—in family court or civil court? If the tort and divorce claims are joined, how should a court resolve the problem of attorneys' fees (because contingent fees are not permitted in dissolution actions)? See *Chen*, 843 N.E.2d at 725-726 (addressing distinctions that militate against mandatory joinder).

9. *Outcome considerations.* After an attorney determines that an abused client has a viable tort claim, what factors should the attorney consider in determining whether to bring the tort claim contemporaneously with, before, or after the divorce proceeding? How does the client's safety affect the choices? What additional factors promote the best outcome? See Dalton, supra, at 374-394.

Problem

Helga and Andrew meet at a church bake sale. After a brief courtship, they enter into a "covenant marriage." Covenant marriage laws were passed at the end of the 1990s in a few states as part of a "return-to-fault" movement. These laws require the parties to execute a statement (a "covenant") that contains their respective promises to take reasonable steps to preserve the marriage if marital problems arise.

After six years of marriage and the birth of one child, Helga returns home one afternoon unexpectedly. She catches Andrew in the act of having sex with another woman. Shocked, she storms out of the house. Andrew follows her. He catches up to her on a crowded city street. A heated argument ensues. In his rage, Andrew pummels Helga with his fists and attempts to strangle her in front of a crowd of people. Bystanders pull him off Helga, but not before she passes out. As a result of the attack, Helga suffers from headaches, blurred vision, slurred speech, and problems with her gait and balance. This incident was the first time that Andrew had resorted to physical violence, although he had frequently been verbally abusive.

Helga has come to your office seeking your legal advice. She would like to sue Andrew for divorce and assault/battery. She desires to resolve the divorce and custody proceedings as quickly as possible. She would also like to recover tort damages to provide for her future medical expenses.

Helga and Andrew reside in the State of Grace. The State of Grace does not allow no-fault divorce for covenant marriages. Rather, state marriage law limits the grounds for divorce in cases of covenant marriage to fault on the part of one spouse or, in the absence of fault, a one-year period of living separate and apart. Both adultery and extreme cruelty constitute permissible grounds for divorce. Helga does not want to wait for one year to secure a divorce. The State of Grace authorizes permissive joinder of tort actions to divorce proceedings. According to state law, fault does not play a role in the determination of spousal support, property division, or child custody. How would you structure Helga's dissolution and tort claims against Andrew? Is she likely to accomplish all her objectives? Why or why not?

What are the implications of "covenant marriage" laws for abused spouses? To address those implications, would you recommend passage by the State of Grace legislature of a statute that permits an abused spouse in a covenant marriage (after obtaining counseling) to secure either a divorce or separation on the basis of domestic violence (specifically, if the "other spouse has physically or sexually abused the spouse seeking the divorce") (La. Rev. Stat. Ann. (§9:307(A)(4) (allowing divorce on this ground), (B)(4)(allowing separation on this ground)). See generally Cynthia M. VanSickle, A Return to the Anti-Feminist Past of Divorce Law: The Implications of the Covenant or Marriage Laws as Applied to Women, 6 J. L. Society 154 (2005).

4. Role of Domestic Violence in Spousal Support

Should abusers face economic consequences in divorce proceedings that stem from their abusive conduct? If so, should the economic consequences pertain to spousal support? Property distribution? Both? The next two sections address these questions.

■ **IN RE MARRIAGE OF CAULEY**
41 Cal. Rptr. 3d 902 (Ct. App. 2006)

MIHARA, J.

[O]n November 25, 2002, respondent [Gerald Cauley] filed a petition for dissolution of marriage. The parties had been married for 18 years. In March 2003, respondent requested a temporary restraining order. His declaration stated that appellant [Eileen Cauley] had threatened his life in numerous telephone messages and calls and had physically attacked him several times during the prior year. The court issued the temporary restraining order, which was due to expire in July 2003.

On June 25, 2003, the parties signed a stipulation for judgment. It provided in relevant part:

> Husband shall pay Wife for her support and maintenance $5,250.00 per month, payable via direct deposit on the 10th day of each calendar month commencing immediately after the effective date of this Agreement. These spousal support payments shall continue until Wife's remarriage or the death of either Husband or Wife, whichever occurs first, or until further order of the court. These payments shall be nonmodifiable with the following exceptions which may form the basis for a modification of the above amount: 1) Wife's cohabitation with a partner; 2) Husband's loss of income either due to disability, or job loss.

The trial court retained jurisdiction as to spousal support until March 31, 2010. Respondent also agreed to take his request for a restraining order off calendar with prejudice. [The judgment of dissolution was filed on August 25, 2003.]

On August 6, 2003, appellant flew to Florida where respondent was living with his girlfriend and her son. During the next couple of days, appellant removed items from the exterior of respondent's house, sprayed herbicide in the garden, ripped out plants, killed his fish, stole personal property, and threw numerous items in the bay behind the house. At some point during appellant's crime spree, respondent opened his door, and she sprayed herbicide in his face. When his girlfriend arrived, appellant sprayed her as well. Appellant was eventually arrested for domestic battery.

On August 12, 2003, respondent obtained a temporary restraining order in Florida [effective for one year]. Appellant [repeatedly] violated the restraining order. She sent written and electronic correspondence to respondent. She made telephone calls, and left messages on his voice mail. Appellant threatened respondent, his wife, members of their families, and his employer. Between September 2003 and March 2004, appellant made more than 1,000 calls, and left nearly 500 messages, which totaled almost 70 hours of recordings. Though respondent changed his home telephone to an unlisted number, appellant was able to obtain his new cell phone number within a few weeks, and the calls continued. In February 2004, appellant threatened the president of the company that employed respondent. On March 22, 2004, appellant left over 52 messages on respondent's voice mail.

[The Florida prosecutor obtained appellant-wife's extradition from California for violations of the restraining order. She pleaded guilty to felony aggravated stalking and was placed on five years' probation. Conditions of probation required her to attend anger management training, receive alcoholic/psychiatric treatment, and not contact her ex-husband and his girlfriend.]

[O]n March 30, 2004, respondent requested a restraining order in California so that California authorities could prosecute her if she continued to harass him. On the same date, respondent filed a motion for modification and termination of spousal support based on appellant's acts of domestic violence.

Meanwhile, on April 26, 2004, the court in California ordered a temporary cessation in spousal support under [California Family Code] section 4325 [and granted respondent-husband's request for a restraining order].

On May 17, 2004, appellant was released from custody in Florida. Less than two weeks later, appellant again began making telephone calls in which she threatened to harm respondent and his coworkers. She made over 91 calls between May 28 and October 11, 2004. . . .

[In October 2004, the trial court] set a hearing for appellant to present evidence to rebut the presumption that she was not entitled to spousal support. . . . [Appellant's attorney argued] that there was a nonmodifiable settlement agreement that provided for spousal support, that appellant was a convicted felon who was an alcoholic with no job and no training, and that appellant made the telephone calls to find out when she would receive her support payments. Respondent's counsel argued that respondent and his family had lived through "two years of sheer hell," that appellant had been in numerous alcohol treatment programs, and that appellant had violated court orders in both Florida and California.

Section 4325, subdivision (a) states:

> In any proceeding for dissolution of marriage where there is a criminal conviction for an act of domestic violence perpetrated by one spouse against the other spouse entered by the court within five years prior to the filing of the dissolution proceeding, or at any time thereafter, there shall be a rebuttable presumption affecting the burden of proof that any award of temporary or permanent spousal support to the abusive spouse otherwise awardable pursuant to the standards of this part should not be made.

Relying on section 3591, appellant contends that the trial court erred in applying section 4325 in the present case. . . . Here the parties agreed that spousal support would not be modified or terminated unless appellant cohabited with a partner or appellant suffered a loss of income. Respondent counters that enforcement of the settlement agreement would violate the public policy against domestic violence. . . .

In resolving the issue before us, we turn to the Restatement on Contracts, which provides that "[a] promise or other term of an agreement is unenforceable on grounds of public policy if legislation provides that it is unenforceable or the interest in its enforcement is clearly outweighed in the circumstances by a public policy against the enforcement of such terms." (Rest. 2d Contracts, §178(1)). . . .

In this case, we conclude that the public policy against enforcement of the nonmodifiable spousal support provision clearly outweighs any interest in its enforcement. Though there is a strong public policy in favor of enforcing the spousal support provisions of the parties' settlement agreement and appellant would forfeit a substantial amount of spousal support if there were no enforcement, the parties could not have reasonably expected that respondent would finance his own abuse by appellant. Balanced against these factors, we note that there is a significant public policy against domestic violence. As was noted in the analysis from the Assembly Judiciary Committee [when the bill was pending],

> granting spousal support to a convicted abuser is unconscionable and constitutes unjust enrichment. . . . [S]pousal support orders in such domestic violence cases potentially force victims of abuse to remain dangerously entangled in the abuser's web of violence and intimidation.

(Assem. Com. on Judiciary, 3d reading analysis of Sen. Bill No. 1221, as amended August 23, 2001 (2001-2002 Reg. Sess.) p. 3.)

Refusal to enforce the spousal support provision will further this policy against domestic violence, because appellant will have fewer financial resources to continue her harassment of respondent. . . . While we acknowledge the fundamental principle that former spouses are free to specify the terms of their settlement agreement, we decline to enforce the spousal support provision in the present case. . . .

Notes and Questions

1. *Statutory provisions.* Some states provide that domestic violence plays a role in awards of spousal support. As *Cauley* explains, California law includes statutory authorization to this effect. According to California Family Code §4320, a court must consider various factors in making an award of spousal support, including

> (i) Documented evidence of any history of domestic violence . . . between the parties, including, but not limited to, consideration of emotional distress resulting from domestic violence perpetrated against the supported party by the supporting party, and consideration of any history of violence against the supporting party by the supported party.

A different statute, California Family Code §4325, provides that a conviction for an act of domestic violence shall affect the burden of proof and also provides for a rebuttable presumption disfavoring awards of spousal support in such cases. Which statute was at issue in *Cauley*? Given that the presumption in California Family Code §4325 is rebuttable, what circumstances might serve to rebut the presumption? What circumstances applied in *Cauley*, according to appellant's counsel? Why did the court reject appellant's argument? What role, if any, should financial needs play in the court's determination in *Cauley*? What is the purpose of the requirement of a "conviction" to preclude imposition of spousal support? Is the requirement sound?

2. *Policy.* What is the rationale of spousal support awards in general? To impose a gender-based duty of support? See Orr v. Orr, 440 U.S. 268 (1979) (invalidating gender-specific alimony rules). To address the economic needs of the dependent spouse? To provide compensation for a spouse's unexpected loss of assets during the marriage? See American Law Institute, Principles of the Law of Family Dissolution: Analysis and Recommendations §5.04 (2002) [hereafter ALI Principles]

(proposing "loss compensation" as a rationale for alimony for those marriages characterized by a sufficiently long duration and income disparity).

What is the policy underlying the California statute in *Cauley*? Does the result in Cauley serve that policy? Given the fact that all states now have some form of no-fault divorce, does *Cauley* undermine the divorce law reform movement?

3. *Role of punishment in divorce law.* Neither Uniform Marriage and Divorce Act (UMDA) §308 (setting forth statutory factors for awards of alimony), nor ALI Principles §5.02 (specifying objectives for allocating financial losses at dissolution), takes domestic violence into account in awards of spousal support. Further, Professor Ira Ellman (the Reporter of the ALI *Principles*) rejects a forfeiture rule for spousal support awards, even in cases of attempted murder. He explains: "[R]ejection of a forfeiture rule does not imply that the victim of attempted murder has no recourse against the person who committed it. It is merely to conclude that the appropriate recourse is the same whether or not the perpetrator is the victim's spouse: the remedies provided by the tort law and the criminal justice system. They are designed to serve this purpose, while dissolution law is not." Ira Mark Ellman, The Place of Fault in A Modern Divorce Law, 28 Ariz. St. L.J. 773, 804 (1996). Do you find this view persuasive? How does this view apply to *Cauley*? (Professor Ellman's views are addressed in more detail in the next section.)

4. *Nonmodifiable agreement.* What was the nature of the parties' nonmodifiable spousal support agreement in *Cauley*? Why was it nonmodifiable? What were the specified exceptions to the nonmodifiability of the agreement? Why did the court in *Cauley* decide that California Family Code §4325 applied despite the parties' nonmodifiable spousal support agreement?

5. *Resort to alternative remedy?* The ex-wife in *Cauley* argued (in an omitted portion of the opinion) that her ex-husband should continue to pay spousal support, in part, because he had access to alternative remedies (such as contempt with its possibility of incarceration) to address her harassment. Do you find her argument persuasive?

6. *Time limit.* What is the statutory limitation that restricts application of the bar on spousal support? Should there be any arbitrary limitation? Why or why not? If yes, what should be the appropriate limitation?

7. *Temporary spousal support.* Should courts be able to consider domestic violence in awards of *temporary* spousal support, based on the statute in *Cauley*? In awards of *past due* spousal support? Should the court take into account the fact that the offender may have been incarcerated on domestic violence charges (and therefore unable to pay) while the support obligation was accruing? See In re Marriage of MacManus, 105 Cal. Rptr. 3d 785 (Ct. App. 2010) (holding that trial court did not abuse its discretion, in light of husband's history of abuse and prior conviction for domestic violence, in reallocating funds earmarked for his child support arrearage, instead, to his past due temporary spousal support obligation).

8. *Res judicata effect.* Should a divorce court's consideration of domestic violence in connection with spousal support mean that the res judicata doctrine bars the injured spouse from filing a separate tort action for the same domestic violence? See Boblitt v. Bobblitt, 118 Cal. Rptr. 3d 788, 796 (Ct. App. 2010) (holding that a judgment in a dissolution where claims of domestic violence were or could have been litigated regarding spousal support does not preclude a later tort action

because the latter is based on the right to be free from personal injury whereas the former is based on circumstances justifying support).

On joinder of tort actions and divorce, see supra pp. 572-577.

5. Role of Domestic Violence in Property Division

■ **HAVELL v. ISLAM**

751 N.Y.S.2d 449 (App. Civ. 2002)

WILLIAMS, P.J.

Plaintiff wife commenced this divorce action in May 1999. The facts elicited at trial show that the parties had been married for 21 years and parented six children, four of whom are minors. Both hold Bachelor of Arts and Masters of Arts degrees; the husband from Cambridge University in England, the wife from Manhattanville College and New York University, respectively. [The couple met while both worked at Citibank. The wife then moved to Lehman Brothers, where she earned $150,000-175,000 per year. The husband's highest annual salary at Citibank was $300,000-350,000. His position was eliminated in 1988, and he remains unemployed.]

Subsequently, the wife was the family's sole economic support. After leaving Lehman Brothers, the wife [eventually started] her own company, Havell Capital Management, specializing in the management of fixed income assets. By the time of trial, December 2000, her company had approximately $250 million of assets under management; she was a 50.5 percent owner receiving a draw of $320,000 per year and an estimated income of $879,167. . . .

[D]espite plaintiff wife's alleged encouragement, defendant declined to seek any business opportunities and instead gardened, read and attempted several writing projects. He claimed to be engaged in running the household and child-rearing. Throughout the marriage, defendant was verbally and/or physically abusive to plaintiff and his children on numerous occasions.

On April 15, 1999, plaintiff advised defendant that she would seek a divorce. Several days later, on April 21, 1999, he broke the locks on the door to her bedroom, where she slept separately from him. On April 22, 1999, their daughter Chloe's birthday, he set his alarm clock to waken him at 4 A.M. and entered his wife's bedroom at approximately 5 A.M. The wife awoke to the sight of him entering her bedroom, taking a seat in a chair at the foot of her bed, and wearing yellow rubber gloves and carrying a barbell. When she sat up, he went over, pinned the wife to the bed with his knee and began beating her viciously on the head, face, neck and hands with the barbell. Plaintiff, who was conscious during the incident, observed her blood, teeth and bone spattering everywhere. Her screams brought their three young daughters, Chloe, Clarissa and Georgina, aged 15, 12 and 10 respectively, into the room where defendant told Chloe that he had killed her mother. As Chloe tried to call 911 for assistance, defendant twice attempted to renew his attack on plaintiff, first with a long piece of pipe and then with a large towel over her face. The daughters held him off her until the police arrived and arrested defendant.

Plaintiff's injuries were severe. She suffered, among other things, multiple contusions, a broken nose and jaw, broken teeth, multiple lacerations, and neurological damage. Her medical treatment included the surgical installation of a titanium plate over her eye, over 20 hours of painful dental procedures, and many other oral and facial surgical procedures over the next several months. Afterwards, she has suffered pain, dizziness, headaches, nightmares, sleeplessness and post-traumatic stress syndrome. Despite these problems plus horrible bruises and scarring, plaintiff was back at work on a part-time basis three weeks after the attack.

Defendant was indicted for attempted murder, pleaded guilty to assault in the first degree [and] was sentenced subsequently to 8-1/4 years in prison. [The wife commenced this divorce action a month after the assault].

The [court] granted plaintiff a divorce, denied defendant counsel fees and equitable distribution beyond the pendente lite award, and distributed all other marital assets to plaintiff. [The net value of the marital assets was approximately $13 million, consisting of real property, cash and securities, pension and retirement accounts, jewelry, and home furnishings.]

The several questions raised on this appeal include: whether or not the trial court erred in holding that defendant's attempted murder of plaintiff was a valid consideration here in awarding plaintiff over 95 percent of the marital estate upon equitable distribution, a matter of first impression before this Court; whether or not the trial court gave proper weight to the other statutory factors in rendering its determination as to equitable distribution; whether or not it was proper for the trial court to conclude that defendant's attack on plaintiff was an attempted homicide rather than the first-degree assault to which he pleaded guilty; whether or not, under the circumstances, the trial court properly denied defendant an award of attorneys' fees; and, whether or not the trial court properly denied defendant a set-off, in the amount of his purported "equitable share," against plaintiff's potential judgment in her personal injury action against him.

The general rule in New York is that marital fault should not be considered in determining equitable distribution [pursuant to N.Y. Dom. Rel. Law §236B(5)(d)]. However, the leading New York cases on when and how marital fault may be considered [hold] that marital fault may be taken into consideration pursuant to the statute's catchall provision, which allows consideration of "any other factor" which may be "just and proper." [Case law provides] that marital fault only be taken into consideration where "the marital misconduct is so egregious or uncivilized as to bespeak of a blatant disregard of the marital relationship—misconduct that 'shocks the conscience' of the court thereby compelling it to invoke its equitable power to do justice between the parties" (Blickstein v. Blickstein, 472 N.Y.S.2d 110 (App. Div. 1984).

[D]efendant contends that subsequent cases regarding the consideration of fault have added a second, economic component to the *Blickstein* test: whether the spouse's misconduct has "such adverse physical and/or psychological effect upon the innocent spouse so as to interfere with her ability to be or to become self-supporting." ... [W]e agree with plaintiff's response to this argument, that these decisions are unsupported by any other authority, do not accord with higher, controlling authorities, are not binding on this Court, and are unpersuasive. ...

It is our view that McCann v. McCann, 593 N.Y.S.2d 917 (Sup. Ct. 1993), best explains what the appellate courts mean [by "egregious" and "shocks the conscience," that is,] ... the cases that have taken marital fault into consideration involved the paramount social values: preservation of human life and "the integrity of the human body." Thus, the *McCann* court . . . does not include impairment of economic independence in the definition of "egregious,". . . .

Defendant further argues on the issue of fault that the court incorrectly considered his fault. He alleges that while the court claims to have given due consideration to all of the 13 factors listed at DRL §236B(5)(d) as is mandated, in reality it based its equitable distribution determination completely upon his marital fault, especially the events of April 22, 1999. While he concedes that his economic contribution was non-existent once he was laid off from his last job in 1990, he argues that his evidence of his contributions to the family, active involvement in child-rearing and education, housekeeping and management, was completely disregarded.

We find that the trial court properly exercised its broad discretion in determining equitable distribution here [by specifically addressing] each of the 13 factors and [setting] forth factual findings that support its conclusions. As for the assault on plaintiff, we find that the trial court gave the incident its due consideration. . . . [I]t is precisely the type of "egregious," "conscience-shocking" conduct defined in *McCann*. . . .

Finally, defendant's objection to the trial court's alleged wrongful characterization of the April 22, 1999, incident as an attempted murder, because he only pleaded guilty to first-degree assault, is without merit. Based upon the evidence of defendant's conduct presented to the court, the court had ample evidence under the preponderance of evidence standard to find that his conduct was an attempted murder. The court was not bound by defendant's generous plea bargain.

On the issue of attorneys' fees, we find that the trial court did not abuse its discretion in denying defendant attorneys' fees after trial based on the "extraordinary circumstances" here. . . . It would hardly be just to require plaintiff to pay defendant's attorneys' fees after his murderous attack on plaintiff and the court properly took this into account. . . .

Defendant's final contention is that the trial court should have granted him a 50 percent set-off in plaintiff's separate tort action in the amount of the equitable share of marital property he was denied. This contention is also without merit. Any such ruling by the trial court in this divorce action would be speculative and amount to an advisory opinion, since the tort matter has yet to go to trial. Moreover, an award and the amount of such a set-off should only be determined by the court in the tort case and only if and when plaintiff prevails.

Accordingly, the judgment of the [trial court] which, inter alia, limited defendant's equitable distribution of the marital assets to 4.5 percent and denied him an award of counsel fees should be affirmed, without costs.

■ IRA MARK ELLMAN, THE PLACE OF FAULT IN A MODERN DIVORCE LAW

28 Ariz. St. L.J. 773, 807-809 (1996)

Approximately half the states follow no-fault principles in awarding alimony; considerably more than half do so in allocating marital property. The reason is that the potentially valid functions of a fault principle are better served by the tort and criminal law, and attempting to serve them through a fault rule risks serious distortions in the resolution of the dissolution action. One possible function of a fault rule, punishment of bad conduct, is generally disavowed even by fault states. It is better left to the criminal law, which is designed to serve it, and in doing so appropriately reaches a much narrower range of marital misconduct than do the marital-misconduct rules of fault states. The second possible function, compensation for the non-financial losses imposed by the other spouse's battery or emotional abuse, is better left to tort law. With the general demise of interspousal immunity, tort remedies for spousal violence are readily available. Most courts have been more cautious in recognizing interspousal claims for emotional abuse unaccompanied by physical violence, but the grounds for their caution apply equally to consideration of emotional distress claims in a dissolution action under the rubric of a marital misconduct standard.

Where valid compensation claims arise, whether for physical violence or emotional abuse, the tort law provides principles to measure and satisfy them, and to determine when they are too stale to entertain. The property allocation and alimony rules of the dissolution law, in contrast, are designed for an entirely different purpose. In the dissolution of a short marriage, the dominant principle is to return the spouses to the premarital situations. As the marriage lengthens the [American Law Institute's Principles of the Law of Family Dissolution: Analysis and Recommendations] provide increasingly generous remedies to the financially more vulnerable spouse in recognition of their joint responsibility for the irreversible personal consequences that arise from investing many years in the relationship. . . . [I]t will be the unusual case in which the fairness of the result will be improved by a judicial inquiry into the relative virtue of the parties' intimate conduct. In some cases, the result will become less fair. And the rules that invite such misconduct claims will surely increase the cost and degrade the process in many other cases, even those in which the claim is ultimately cast aside.

Surely the law must provide a remedy for cases of harm caused by serious misconduct even if they are unusual, but those are the cases to which tort law applies. The alternative of using divorce remedies to provide compensation for tortious injury through the application of a fault principle provides a doubly unsatisfactory result: the dissolution remedies [such as taking fault into account to divide marital property and award alimony] still remain inadequate as a tort substitute, while the introduction of fault impairs their utility in serving their primary purpose. Fault makes the outcome of litigation less predictable, and gives parties an incentive to raise claims of misconduct as leverage in the negotiation process. [Even a fault rule that provides for forfeiture for only serious violence] would be less unpredictable in operation, but [have] its own difficulties. Because it would provide an incomplete compensation structure, tort remedies would still be necessary to obtain adequate compensation for many victims. At the same time it would yield a perverse pattern in those cases to which it applied [by apportioning penalties based on a person's financial status], rather than with his blameworthiness or the damage he inflicted. . . .

Notes and Questions

1. *Epilogue.* The plaintiff's subsequent tort suit was dismissed. The court held that it was barred by New York's one-year statute of limitations. Havell v. Islam, 739

N.Y.S.2d 371, 372 (App. Div. 2002). In another suit, she petitioned to change the children's surname. The court granted her petition, holding that the best interests of the children would be promoted by dissociating the children from the "shame and disgrace" of their father's crime. Havell v. Islam, 760 N.Y.S.2d 407, 408 (App. Div. 2003).

2. *Role of fault: background.* Beginning in the 1980s, many states adopted a system of "equitable distribution" to divide property at the end of a marriage. Most states adopted equitable distribution by statute, often modeled on Uniform Marriage and Divorce Act (UMDA) §307. In making an equitable distribution, a court first determines the property that is subject to division and its value, and then looks to specific statutory factors to apply.

3. *Role of domestic violence.* States take different views in consideration of domestic violence in post-divorce property distribution. Some states, either by case law or statute, take domestic violence into account in the property division either as a specific statutory factor or as a factor of general "marital fault." In these states, "[s]pousal abuse is a relevant factor in and of itself without specifically requiring particularly egregious abuse, and without expressly demanding a connection between the abuse and some other factor." Edward S. Snyder & Laura W. Morgan, Domestic Violence Ten Years Later, 19 J. Am. Acad. Matrim. Law. 33, 53 (2004) (surveying states). Other states refuse to consider marital fault in property distribution. However, some of these restrictive jurisdictions make exceptions in cases of "economic fault" or "egregious circumstances." Courts have treated domestic violence as "economic fault" by finding that the spousal abuse had an economic impact on the victim, for example, in terms of increased medical bills or a decreased ability to work. Other jurisdictions consider domestic violence if it reaches a sufficiently high threshold ("egregious" fault). If a jurisdiction considers domestic violence in property division, the victim is generally awarded a larger portion of the marital or community property. Snyder & Morgan, supra, at 53-54.

Does New York consider domestic violence as a factor in property division, according to *Havell*? Is the rule based on statute or case law? What was *Havell's* rationale for taking into account the husband's violence as a factor in the property division?

4. *Egregious conduct.* How does a court determine what constitutes "egregious conduct"? How subjective is the determination? See Cheryl J. Lee, Case Note, Escaping the Lion's Den and Going Back for Your Hat—Why Domestic Violence Should be Considered in the Distribution of Marital Property Upon Dissolution of Marriage, 23 Pace L. Rev. 273, 281 (2002) (criticizing that the role of domestic violence in equitable distribution often depends "on the conscience of the particular judge before whom the aggrieved spouse is appearing").

a. *Spectrum of abusive conduct.* What level of egregiousness must domestic violence reach for purposes of equitable distribution? For example, must the abuse reach the level of attempted murder? Would victimization that falls short of that be sufficient? Compare Dakota Smith, U.S. Rights: Equitable Distribution Upheld in Wife-Beating Case, IPS-Inter Press Service, Feb. 3, 2003, available at http://www.highbeam.com/doc/1P1-71472937.html (worrying that "Since most domestic violence doesn't fall into the category of attempted murder, but consists of misdemeanor crimes such as hitting, shoving and pushing, how the *Havell* ruling will play out in cases where domestic violence isn't as severe, nor the money pot quite so large, remains to be seen"), with Howard S. v. Lillian S., 928 N.E.2d 399, 402 n.2 (N.Y. 2010) ("[Although Havell v. Islam] generally stated the correct standard, to the extent that it can be read to limit egregious conduct to behavior involving extreme violence, the definition should not be so restrictive").

b. *Economic consequences.* Must the domestic violence have negative *economic* consequences for the victim, such as loss of employment or income, in order to be taken into account in the property division? Why did the husband in *Havell* urge that the court adopt that interpretation of prior case law? What does the appellate court respond to his argument?

5. *Evidence of prior history of abuse.* At trial in *Havell*, the husband moved for an order precluding the wife from offering testimony concerning his conduct during the marriage (that is, prior to the attempted murder), on the basis that such conduct is not a "just and proper" factor to be considered in connection with the equitable distribution of the parties' marital property.

The trial judge denied his motion, thereby permitted the wife to testify as to the following: the husband's use of violence and vulgar language with the wife, children, housekeepers, and visitors; his shaming his wife in front of her father by calling her a "f—ing idiot" because she made a mistake in reading him a road map; his telling his wife that his temper was so violent that his mother would never permit a firearm in the house because she knew he would use it to kill someone; his intimidation of his wife by the "silent treatment" and rude treatment if he didn't get his way; his calling his wife "an old hag" and telling her that her "skin was hanging off her" and that he should discard her for a younger woman; his engaging in such abusive behavior while on vacation that his wife packed up to leave; his telling the children that the wife was a whore because she had previously been married; his threatening his wife with his hand, fist, and with kicks, a telephone, and a book; his habit of walking around the house in drawstring pajamas with the drawstring opened to an extent that his sexual organs were exposed; his belief that it was acceptable to beat children, saying routinely that you should "kick the s—out of them"; his calling his wife a "f—ing idiot" and leaving her to treat herself when she stumbled on a heating duct and sliced open her leg; his twisting her arm in such an "excruciating, painful way" that her housekeeper intervened; his spanking their six-month-old infant for crying; his demeaning their son who had learning difficulties, calling him "stupid" and an "idiot" as well as hitting him on the face and head; his refusal to believe the diagnoses of their oldest child's psychiatrist who indicated that the child suffered from periods of bipolar behavior, and instead calling the child a "spoiled brat" and saying that what he needed was a "good kick and a beating to make him better," and proceeding to do so. *Havell*, 718 N.Y.S.2d at 809-810. Should all this evidence have been admissible, or merely the evidence of the attempted murder? Why?

6. *Prenuptial agreement.* In a jurisdiction that takes domestic violence into account in property distribution, suppose that the spouses executed a premarital agreement providing that each spouse's property shall remain separate property. How shall the court factor that into account when it distributes the couple's property? See Reiser v. Reiser, 621 N.W.2d 348, 350 (N.D. 2001) (adhering to premarital agreement giving each spouse his or her separate property, regardless of a finding of domestic violence).

7. *Effect of tort liability in property distribution.* Suppose a divorcing spouse successfully sues the abuser for tort damages. Against what property shall the tort damages be assessed? From the abuser's separate property? From the abuser's share of the marital property? If damages are assessed against the abuser's property, does the abuser have to exhaust his or her separate property prior to resorting to the marital property?

Few state statutes address this issue. California law provides that if the victim-spouse obtains a judgment for domestic violence damages, the court may deduct the amount of the judgment from the abuser's share of the community property, provided that a proceeding for divorce is pending *prior* to entry of the final judgment in the tort case. Cal. Fam. Code §2603.5. Under prior law, a victim could enforce a judgment for domestic violence damages against the abuser's share of the community property only after the abuser's separate property was exhausted. Following enactment of the statute, however, the court can enforce the judgment against the abuser's share of the community property without regard to the availability of separate property. The provision is intended to protect the financial assets of victims of domestic violence when they leave the abuser. Do you think that the statutory provision will streamline the process of collecting damages for domestic violence judgments? Deter domestic violence? See generally Meredith A. Felde, Strengthening Protections for Domestic Violence Victims, 36 McGeorge L. Rev. 922 (2005) (describing statutory reform).

8. *Attorneys' fees.* Should the victim, if she or he is the wealthier spouse, have to pay the attorneys' fees of the perpetrator-spouse? How does *Havell* resolve that issue? Do you agree with the court's resolution?

9. *Policy: Should compensation be left to tort law?* Should domestic violence be taken into account in the distribution of property following a divorce, in your view? Why or why not? If so, how? That is, should the factor of domestic violence be specifically enumerated in equitable distribution statutes or considered in a "catchall" provision? To what extent should it be taken into account—should it result in an unequal distribution of property or a complete denial of property to the abuser? Do you think the 95 percent distribution of property to the wife in *Havell* was appropriate?

Why does Professor Ellman, in the above excerpt, argue that compensation for a spouse's injuries should be reserved for the tort system? Do you agree with him that tort remedies present an adequate alternative? Was tort law an adequate alternative for the plaintiff-wife in *Havell?* Cf. Lee, Case Note, supra, at 299 (pointing out that "In New York, however, there are virtually no cases in which a spouse has successfully brought an action against her abuser and obtained relief"). Recall too the discussion of the reasons for the dearth of tort law suits in Chapter 10 pp. 526-530.

10. *International perspective.* A number of other countries also consider domestic violence as a factor in property division at divorce. See David Hodson, Spare the Child and Hit the Pocket: Toward a Jurisprudence on Domestic Abuse as a Quantum Factor in Financial Outcomes on Relationship Breakdown, 44 Fam. Ct. Rev. 387 (2006) (noting cases in England, Wales, New Zealand, Australia, France, South Africa, Zimbabwe).

On the role of domestic violence in post-dissolution bankruptcy proceedings, see Chapter 4, pp. 199-200.

Problem

Sarah and Tim have been married for 15 years and have 4 children. They live in the jurisdiction of Blackacre. During the course of the marriage, Tim has been verbally and physically abusive. He has beaten up Sarah on numerous occasions, threatened to kill her, followed her to work, and installed a GPS in her car and spyware on her computer to monitor her movements. She has been hospitalized numerous times because of the abuse. She called 911 for help a half dozen times. Finally, when Tim beats up one of the children very badly, Sarah decides that she had had enough. She obtains an order for protection against Tim and also a legal separation. She moves into a battered women's shelter with the children for one month, and thereafter rents an apartment.

Despite the legal separation, Tim continues to harass Sarah. The last time that he violates the restraining order, Sarah has him arrested. They have been separated for three months when Sarah is killed by a drunk driver. She left no will. How will Sarah's estate be divided according to Blackacre's intestate succession law?

Do state intestacy laws take into consideration family violence? Should they? If so, how? Discuss the merits and shortcomings of the following statute.

PROPOSED STATUTE

Effect of Family Violence on Inheritance Rights

(a) [Definitions.] In this section:

(1) "Abuser" is any family member of the decedent who commits family violence against the decedent as defined herein.

(2) "Family Violence" means: (i) physical harm, bodily injury, assault, or infliction of fear of imminent physical harm, bodily injury or assault, between family members; or (ii) terroristic threats, within the meaning of [relevant state statute(s)], or criminal sexual conduct, within the meaning of [relevant state statute(s)], committed against a family member by a family member.

(b) [Forfeiture of Statutory Benefits.] An individual who commits family violence against the decedent forfeits the following benefits with respect to the decedent's estate: an intestate share, an elective share, an omitted spouse's or child's share, a homestead allowance, exempt property, and a family allowance. The decedent's intestate estate shall pass as if the abuser disclaimed his [or her] intestate share.

(c) [Commitment of Family Violence; How Determined.] Commitment of family violence resulting in forfeiture under section (b) is established:

(1) by a past pattern of family violence committed by the abuser against the decedent within [5] years of the decedent's death when the family violence is committed against the decedent while the decedent was an adult. A pattern can be established only by (i) court documents showing a conviction of the abuser for family violence against the decedent; (ii) arrest of the abuser for family violence against the decedent; or (iii) an issuance of an order for protection on behalf of the decedent against the abuser; and

(2) by court documents when family violence is committed against the decedent while the decedent was a minor. Court documents must show (i) a conviction for family violence by the abuser against the decedent while the decedent was a minor; (ii) action by governmental authorities to protect the decedent from the abuser; or (iii) a tort judgment against the abuser in favor of the decedent for family violence committed by the abuser against the decedent while the decedent was a minor.

(d) [Broad Construction.] This statute shall not be considered penal in nature, but shall be construed broadly to effect the policy of this state to further the decedent's donative intent and to further the state's interest in deterring family violence and providing for surviving family members who have not engaged in abusive behavior.

The above statute was proposed by Robin L. Preble, Family Violence and Family Property: A Proposal for Reform, 13 Law & Ineq. 401, 440 (1995). For a rare statutory framework that takes abuse into account in inheritance law, see Oregon Revised Statutes §112.455 (providing for the effect of a homicide or abuse on intestate succession, life insurance, and beneficiary designations); Oregon Revised Statutes §112.465 (providing the manner in which intestate property is distributed in cases of homicide or abuse).

C. NAME CHANGES

■ **IN RE E.F.G.**

942 A.2d 166 (N.J. Super. Ct. App. Div. 2008)

LYONS, J.A.D.

Plaintiff E.F.G. appeals from an order [denying her application] to assume a new name, her request to waive the requirement to publish notice, and her request that the matter be placed under seal and not be entered in any data base accessible by the public. . . .

[P]laintiff filed an action to assume another name in accordance with N.J.S.A. §2A:52-1. The statute reads as follows:

> Any person may institute an action in Superior Court, for authority to assume another name. The complaint for a change of name shall be accompanied by a sworn affidavit stating the applicant's name, date of birth, social security number, whether or not the applicant has ever been convicted of a crime, and whether any criminal charges are pending against him and, if such convictions or pending charges exist, shall provide such details in connection therewith sufficient to readily identify the matter referred to. The sworn affidavit shall also recite that the action for a change of name is not being instituted for purposes of avoiding or obstructing criminal prosecution or for avoiding creditors or perpetrating a criminal or civil fraud. If criminal charges are pending, the applicant shall serve a copy of the complaint and affidavit upon any State or county prosecuting authority responsible for the prosecution of any pending charges.

A person commits a crime of the fourth degree if he knowingly gives or causes to be given false information under this section.

[N.J.S.A. §2A:52-1.]

[P]laintiff's complaint advised the trial court that she was seeking a new name because she is a victim of domestic violence; her abuser continues to contact her after the entry of a restraining order; she believes that her life is in danger; and that she would like to start a new life. Attached to plaintiff's complaint is a lengthy certification by plaintiff outlining in great detail the history of domestic violence to which she was subjected for many years. Plaintiff's certification has attached to it various police reports, medical records, court records, including protective orders and restraining orders, as well as photographs showing her injuries. A review of the verified complaint, and the certification attached to it, as well as all the exhibits, paint a sad and tragic picture of serious life-threatening domestic violence toward plaintiff.

In order to assume a new name, a plaintiff must not only comply with N.J.S.A. §2A:52-1, but also with Rule 4:72 [which sets forth the procedural requirements] that a verified complaint for a name change must contain the requirements set forth in the statute and that notice of the name change application must be published [once, in a newspaper of general circulation in the county of plaintiff's residence, at least two weeks prior to the hearing].

As with almost all court proceedings, an application for a change of name is conducted in open court. The records of name changes are generally available for public inspection and copying.

Because plaintiff has a well-founded concern that publication of her change of name application would provide her abuser with her address, as well as her new name, she filed a motion with the trial court to waive the requirement of publication, Rule 4:72-3, and to seal the record of her application to change her name pursuant to Rule 1:2-1. [T]he trial court denied plaintiff's application to change her name and to relax the requirement of publication. . . .

The record is clear in this matter that, but for the requirement to publish the application contained in Rule 4:72-3, plaintiff's application was in full compliance with both the statute and the rule. We find that the trial court's reliance on [Basile v. Basile, 604 A.2d 693 (N.J. Super. Ct. Chancery Div.1992)] was mistaken. That case merely holds that a court does not have jurisdiction to grant a name change application [to change a child's surname] as part of a pending domestic violence proceeding [to obtain a restraining order]. [However,] Rule 1:1-2 provides authority to relax rules in the appropriate case.

[The court then clarifies that Rule 1:1-2 relaxes rules in appropriate cases "if adherence to it would result in an injustice."] We are, of course, mindful, that "[c]ase law and common sense, however, demonstrate that Rule 1:1-2 is the exception, rather than the norm." We also recognize that recourse to the rule should be sparing. Accordingly, our Supreme Court has advised that "determining whether relaxation is appropriate . . . requires an examination and balancing of the interests that are at stake."

In this case, therefore, it is necessary to identify and balance the interests that are at stake in relaxing the requirement that a plaintiff who is a victim of domestic violence publish her application for a change of name. In the Act, the Legislature stated that "the Legislature finds and declares that domestic violence is a serious crime against society; that there are thousands of persons in this State who are regularly beaten, tortured and in some cases even killed by their spouses. . . ." N.J.S.A. §2C:25-18.

The Legislature went on to state that "the intent of the Legislature [is] to assure the victims of domestic violence the maximum protection from abuse the law can provide." The Legislature declared "it is the responsibility of the courts to protect victims of violence that occurs in a family or family-like setting by providing access to both emergent and long-term civil and criminal remedies and sanctions, and by ordering those remedies and sanctions that are available to assure the safety of the victims and the public." In addition to those statements of policy from the Legislature, our Supreme Court has spoken eloquently concerning what some have referred to as an epidemic of domestic violence [noting that] "[a]t its core, the [state Prevention of Domestic Violence Act] effectuates the notion that the victim of domestic violence is entitled to be left alone. To be left alone is, in essence, the basic protection the law seeks to assure these victims" [State v. Hoffman, 695 A.2d 236 (N.J. 1997)]. It is abundantly clear, therefore, that affording the victims of domestic violence the maximum protection the law has to offer is a matter of vital and significant public policy in New Jersey.

As to factors which would weigh against relaxation of publication, we have recognized that a court entertaining a change of name must consider whether a waiver of publication would somehow provide an avenue for an applicant to obtain a new name so as to avoid or obstruct criminal prosecution, avoid creditors, or perpetrate a fraud. We note, of course, that the statute requires an affidavit, as was provided here, which requires an applicant to swear that the change of name is not being instituted for purposes of avoiding or obstructing criminal prosecution, avoiding creditors, or perpetrating a civil or criminal fraud. Moreover, a person who gives false information in that regard commits a crime. . . .

[W]e clearly find that in a case such as this, where plaintiff has demonstrated a well-founded concern for her personal safety as a result of prior domestic abuse, and where there is otherwise strict compliance with the change of name statute and rule, that to require adherence to the publication requirements of Rule 4:72-3 would result in an injustice. If we were not to relax the publication rules in this instance, plaintiff would be at grave risk in pursuing a change of name because her abuser could easily locate her, her new name, and her new address from either the publication of her application or the court records. Her application would be totally futile. She would be denied one avenue to obtain peace in her life, and an opportunity to live without fear and constant anxiety. We recognize the foreclosure of that opportunity to result in clear injustice.

The second issue raised by plaintiff is the denial of her request to seal the record of this application. . . . Whether to seal or unseal documents is addressed to the discretion of the trial court. In exercising that discretion, the court must be guided by the good cause standard.

The facts in the matter before us clearly indicate that plaintiff has overcome the strong presumption of public access by establishing by a preponderance of the evidence that her interest in sealing these records outweighs the presumption. At issue is plaintiff's very safety which has been recognized by our public policy as having paramount importance. She has not made a broad unsubstantiated allegation of potential harm, but rather has submitted to the court a tragic and upsetting history, documenting domestic violence which warrants protection. Accordingly, we find that the trial court's failure to seal the record in this case constitutes a mistake in the exercise of its discretion. . . .

Notes and Questions

1. *Methods of name change.* Two methods of name change exist: the common law method of consistent, nonfraudulent use, and a statutorily prescribed judicial procedure. Most women change their name upon marriage by the first method.

2. *Name change procedure.* Jurisdiction for name change proceedings rests in probate and family courts. Petitioners generally apply in the county where they reside. As part of the petitioning process, the petitioner must give notice to the public for the change of name to ensure that any interested party has an opportunity to be heard on the petition. Public notice is generally accomplished by publication in a local newspaper.

3. *Problems for victims.* Victims of domestic violence sometimes change their names in an effort to hide from their abusers. Statutory requirements of publication of name change requests pose the risk of disclosure of the victim's new name and new identity.

4. *State law.* Some state statutes address the role of domestic violence in name changes by providing that records of a name change must be sealed and any publication waived in cases of a threat to safety. See, e.g., N.M. Stat. Ann. §40-8-2(B); N.Y. Civ. Rights Law §64-a. Petitioners must file a motion to waive notice by means of filing affidavits and supporting documentation that explain the danger. Relevant documents can include: police reports, orders of protection, as well as medical and social services records.

How did E.F.G. explain the danger that she faced? What was her supporting documentation? In light of her documentation, why did the trial court deny her request? What is the necessary standard for waiver of notice of a name change? What is the standard for sealing the record of the name change? How did the appellate court balance the relevant interests in deciding whether to waive notice of the name change? How should courts strike the balance between protecting domestic violence victims and preventing fraud? Do the New Jersey statutes in *E.F.G.* adequately protect the safety of domestic violence victims? Should state statutes routinely make an exception for domestic violence victims from publication requirements?

5. *Children.* Fleeing victims sometimes seek name changes for *both* themselves and their children in order to insure all family members' safety. Does the procedure for name change differ when the victim flees with children? Should it? Should it matter if the parents are divorced, married, or cohabiting? Generally, if a custodial parent petitions for a child's name change, many states require notice to the noncustodial parent. Notice by publication may not be sufficient—particularly if the noncustodial parent's location is known or reasonably ascertainable. Again, a petitioner may request a waiver of the notice requirement but must satisfy the good cause standard. How should a court balance the interests when a child's name change is sought? Are the child's interests and the custodial parent's the same?

6. *Other records.* What other identifying records do victims need to change to ensure their safety? Drivers' licenses? Vehicle titles? Passports? Financial records (bank accounts, credit cards)? What other records? (Notice by publication is generally not required for these name changes.)

7. *Address confidentiality.* Some states provide programs for address confidentiality for victims of domestic violence. Would you recommend that E.F.G. in the principal case seek to participate in such a program? Why or why not?

Washington State was the first jurisdiction to initiate an "Address Confidentiality Program" (ACP) to help victims of domestic violence, stalking, and sexual assault to keep their addresses confidential. See, e.g., Wash. Rev. Code Ann. §40.24.020. Washington State passed the law after legislators realized that abusers could access public records to locate their intimate partners. Jeffrey T. Even, Washington's Address Confidentiality Program: Relocation Assistance for Victims of Domestic Violence, 31 Gonz. L. Rev. 523, 525 (1996).

Under ACPs, a victim of domestic violence files an application for a new address with the statutorily designed governmental agency. The application must include a signed, sworn statement that the applicant is a victim of domestic violence and fears for her safety. Once the agency approves the application, the victim is given a substitute address (and an authorization card) that she may use for all purposes. The victim's actual address is kept confidential by the governmental agency. The *substitute* address is listed as a matter of public record. Address Confidentiality Programs can also be used if a victim is a resident of a battered women's shelter.

ACPs have a number of shortcomings: high evidentiary requirements in some states to admit victims into the program (such as the requirement that the victim must have a protective order); a lack of uniformity between the various states; courts' discretion to order disclosure; and the lack of a binding effect of the ACPs on third parties (such as employers and federal agencies). See generally Kristen M. Driskell, Comment, Identity Confidentiality for Women Fleeing Domestic Violence, 20 Hastings Women's L.J. 129, 139-148 (2009) (explaining and criticizing ACP law). In what circumstances should a court order disclosure of the victim's new address?

Does an abusive partner who has visitation privileges have a right to know the address of his children? See Sacharow v. Sacharow, 826 A.2d 710 (N.J. 2003) (reversing trial court's denial of the protection of the ACP to a former wife based on father's "right" to know his son's address).

8. *Social Security numbers.* An identity change may also necessitate the issuance of a new Social Security number in particularly dangerous cases. Abusers sometimes attempt to track victims through the use of the latter's Social Security numbers. Important records (that is, medical and welfare records, court documents, educational and employment records) contain Social Security numbers for identification. For this reason, victims sometimes must change their Social Security numbers as well as their names. The Social Security Administration has established special procedures for issuance of new numbers for those victims of domestic violence and stalking who can show that their lives are in danger. The requirements include: proof of citizenship status, a statement explaining the need for the new number, and corroborative evidence documenting the abuse (that is, police records and reports, photographs, official court documents, and letters from officials with knowledge of the abuse).

If a domestic violence victim flees with children, she may need to change their Social Security numbers too to protect herself. To change children's numbers, she must provide proof of legal custody and visitation. Only applicants with sole legal custody can obtain new Social Security numbers for their children.

Such an identity change is not foolproof. "Clients who in fact change their identities and their SSNs should be advised that these dramatic measures may not adequately protect them from a determined abuser. Although SSA does try to protect the confidentiality of these records, they may still be inadvertently disclosed to a manipulative and resourceful abuser." See Amy Schwartz et al., New Social Security Numbers for Domestic Violence Victims (Empire Justice Center, June 2004), available at http://www.empirejustice.org/issues-areas/domestic-violence/case-laws-statues[sic]/confidentiality/new-social-security-numbers-dv.html. How should these problems be addressed?

XII

Family Law: Parenting

Custody disputes arise in many different contexts, including dissolution of relationships, child maltreatment, adoption, and guardianship. This chapter explores the role of domestic violence in the first of these contexts: dissolution of relationships and child maltreatment.

A. INTRODUCTION

■ **PETER G. JAFFE ET AL., CUSTODY DISPUTES INVOLVING ALLEGATIONS OF DOMESTIC VIOLENCE: TOWARD A DIFFERENTIATED APPROACH TO PARENTING PLANS**
46 Fam. Ct. Rev. 500, 501-504 (2008)

How Is Domestic Violence Relevant to Post-Separation Parenting Arrangements?

Research on parent-child relationships and parenting styles in families where domestic violence occurs [sheds] some insights [about] typical parenting issues relevant to [post-separation parenting arrangements]. . . .

Spousal abuse does not necessarily end with separation of the parties. While in a majority of cases the incidence and risk of violence diminishes once the parties are separated, in a small proportion of cases, especially abusive battering relationships, the intensity and lethality of domestic violence escalates after the victim leaves the relationship. Furthermore, promoting parent-child contact where ex-spouses are prone to become physically violent when in conflict may create opportunities for renewed domestic violence over visitation issues and exchanges of children. In the worst cases, terrorizing control of an ex-spouse is achieved by refusing to return the child after visits, abducting the child, or threatening to do so. . . .

Perpetrators of domestic violence are more likely to be deficient if not abusive as parents. There is a wide range of capacity to parent among high-conflict and violent families, ranging from frankly abusive, to poor or marginal, to adequate or even good-enough parenting. However, common features are lack of warmth, coercive tactics, and rejection of their children. This pattern is especially true for those exhibiting abuse and coercive control of their spouse, probably also true for couples who resort to physical force to resolve conflict, and less likely or time limited if the violence was an isolated event. A review of research, largely based on women in shelters, suggests that children whose mothers had been assaulted by their male partners are more likely to be directly abused. Where there is a pattern of abuse, erratic role reversals, swings from permissive to rigid, authoritarian parenting, and periodic abandonment are also common. Children of such primary abusers are subjected to emotional abuse such as name calling, cruel put-downs, and distortion of their reality by telling false and frightening stories. At times they are made the favorite at the expense of siblings who are isolated or outrightly rejected. At other times they may be encouraged in morally corrupt and criminal behavior. Boundary violations between adult abusers and children are more likely, especially where substance abuse is also involved, with a greater incidence of child sexual abuse being reported.

Individuals who have a pattern of abuse of their partners and those who commonly resolve conflicts using physical force are poor role models for children. Poor role modeling occurs even after the parental separation, whether or not parents mistreat their children directly, because when children witness one parent assaulting the other, their sibling, or other family member, and using threats of violence to maintain control, their own expectations about relationships tend to emulate these observations. Moreover, often very frightened by these scenes, young children tend to identify more intensely with the violent parent (i.e., "I will become powerful and mean like my dad and everyone will be scared of me"). To the extent that there is potential for the abusive parent to be violent in subsequent intimate relationships, children's exposure to poor modeling will continue.

Abusive ex-partners are likely to undermine the victim's parenting role. In a range of obvious and more insidious ways, abusive ex-partners are likely to attempt to alienate the children from the other parent's affection (by asserting blame for the dissolution of the family and telling negative stories), sabotage family plans (by continuing criticism or competitive bribes), and undermine parental authority (by explicitly instructing the children not to listen or obey . . .). This facet of the abuser's parenting needs to be considered when deciding what access, if any, the perpetrator should have to the children, what interventions are needed to address these problems, and the prognosis for change with treatment.

Abusive ex-spouses may use family court litigation as a new forum to continue their coercive controlling behavior and to harass their former partner. Litigation exacts a high emotional and financial price, especially for abused women already overwhelmed with the aftermath of a violent relationship. Some authors have suggested that some perpetrators have the persona and social skills to present themselves positively in court and convince assessors and judges to award them custody. In some of these cases the perpetrators are self-represented, heightening the possibilities for abuse through intimidating or berating a former partner in cross-examination, unless an astute judge intervenes.

Diminished parenting capacities among victims of domestic violence often occurs. Preoccupation with the demands of their abuser, a conflict-ridden marriage, or a traumatic separation may render parents physically and emotionally exhausted, inconsistently available, overly dependent upon, or unable to protect their children from the abuser. For the majority of victims, separation from the perpetrator of domestic violence may provide an opportunity for improvement in both general functioning and parenting capacities. However, those who have been victimized by prolonged abuse and control are likely to suffer sustained difficulties—like anxiety, depression, substance abuse, and post-traumatic stress disorder—all of which can compromise their parenting for some time. Female victims may have been brainwashed by the abuser into accepting their own and their children's abusive treatment, and intimidated and embarrassed male victims tend not to protect the children from their abusive mother's rages. Poor self-esteem, lack of confidence in their parenting, and inability to control their children, especially their older sons, makes the female victim an obvious target of blame by the abusive ex-spouse and may raise the suspicions of family court professionals as to her fitness to parent. During the court process, these parents may present more negatively than they will in the future once the stress of the proceedings and life changes have attenuated.

Victims' behavior under the stress of the abusive relationship and during the aftermath of a stressful separation should not inappropriately prejudice the residential or access decision. In the face of a real threat of violence, victims who live in fear of their ex-partner are not paranoid, nor may it be appropriate for them to promote a relationship between their children and the other parent. [P]arents' voiced concerns about their ex-partner's abusive predispositions and their own refusal to communicate or reluctance to agree to the child's liberal access should not be seen as unwillingness to cooperate or as manifestations of parental alienation. Similarly, victims of abuse who leave the family home without the children should not be viewed as abandoning, neglectful, or irresponsible parents; in these cases, leaving alone may be the only way that they believe that they appease their volatile partner. Likewise, distraught individuals who have suffered a traumatic separation may parent in a less child-centered manner than they would normally, although their compromised functioning is usually time limited.

Victims of abusive relationships may need time to reestablish their competence as parents and opportunity to learn how to nurture and appropriately protect themselves and their children. Time, protection, and support allow an adequate opportunity for a distinction to be made between the majority of victims of spousal abuse who are able to reestablish effective parenting, and the small minority of cases where the victim's mental status will be chronic. . . .

■ LUNDY BANCROFT ET AL., THE BATTERER AS PARENT: ADDRESSING THE IMPACT OF DOMESTIC VIOLENCE ON FAMILY DYNAMICS

140-149 (2d ed., 2012)

Batterers' Motivations for Seeking Custody or Increased Visitation

Studies suggest that batterers are more likely than are non-battering fathers to seek custody. . . . [H]ere we will make some observations on the reasons why batterers exhibit increased likelihood to pursue custody or to use legal action to attempt to expand their visitation schedules.

Distorted Perceptions of Their Victims. Batterers generally have a contemptuous outlook on their partners, which can be sharpened by separation. For example, numerous clients of ours have expressed their conviction that their partner's decision to leave the relationship was evidence of the woman's immaturity, weak commitment to the relationship, or lack of concern for the children, as with the client who told us, "Obviously, it's no big deal to her if our children come from a broken home." Our clients almost universally minimize the role of their abusiveness in causing the end of the relationship.

Distorted Perceptions of Themselves. We find it nearly universal among batterers to have little sense of the seriousness of their own abusiveness and of its effects on their children. Their tendency to self-centeredness can sometimes lead to grandiose or romanticized self-images. Furthermore, we encounter cases where the batterer is in denial about the marked improvement that has occurred in the children's emotional, social, and scholastic functioning following the reduction in their exposure to him.

Desire to Impose Control. For some batterers, custody litigation is an important arena through which they seek to reimpose the control and domination that the end of the adult relationship has weakened. Entitled attitudes can feed this desire for control, as many batterers believe that they should have ultimate authority over decisions involving the children.

The Desire to Retaliate. [M]any of our clients who seek custody of their children reveal under questioning that their motive is to hurt and to frighten their former partners; in our experience, custody actions can be uniquely effective for this goal. Also, the costs of custody litigation can be devastating to a mother's financial position and can eliminate many opportunities for her children to improve their living conditions or to participate in enriching activities.

The Desire for Vindication. Partly to refute claims of abuse, our divorced or separated clients tend to have a strong drive to prove that they are more emotionally healthy than are their former partners. These men sometimes pursue custody as a way to gain social validation. Our clients who win custody do interpret their victories as validation of their perspectives, and children unfortunately appear to interpret an award of custody to the batterer in the same way.

Their View of the Effects of Battering on Their Former Partners. It is common for battered women to suffer from depression, substance abuse, hypervigilance, emotional ability [sic], sleep disturbances, and many other problems. Because batterers almost universally fail to recognize the impact of their actions on their partners, they view these symptoms as inherent problems in the woman and as reasons why she should not be given responsibility to care for the children.

The Desire to Gain Economic or Legal Concessions. A number of our clients have admitted that they filed for custody in order to gain a bargaining chip to trade off against alimony, child support, or conjugal assets. Many battered mothers report to us that they accepted settlements that left them and their children in poor economic circumstances in order to keep custody of their children. Batterers also sometimes may use custody actions to coerce their former partners to drop criminal charges. . . .

Batterers' Advantages in Custody Dispute

Batterers win custody of their children with greater frequency than is generally realized. . . . We review here the central reasons why batterers are so often able to prevail.

The Effects of Domestic Violence on Family Dynamics. [B]attering tends to undermine a mother's parental authority and to create multiple tensions between mothers and children. The difficulty that battered mothers may have in controlling their children's behavior can be exacerbated in the immediate aftermath of a separation by the father's absence from the home; children may target the mother for their anger regarding the parental separation, and they may feel free to behave as they choose now that the batterer's authoritarian presence is gone. Custody evaluators may observe that the mother has trouble controlling her children and may conclude that she lacks parenting skills. At the same time, batterers often can perform well under observation, and children may appear relaxed and comfortable with the batterer in the presence of the evaluator. Children often behave better while in the batterer's care, partly because of conscious or unconscious fear of him. Children also may side with the batterer because they perceive him as the more powerful parent or may request to live with him as a result of traumatic bonding.

The Batterer's Ability to Manipulate or to Intimidate Children's Statements to the Custody Evaluator. It is not uncommon for a batterer to succeed in persuading the children that he is the victim in the adult relationship or that the mother's behavior causes the abusive incidents. A batterer who was previously neglectful of the children may abruptly make his children a high priority as a result of his desire to seek custody, and we have observed that this change can have a powerful emotional effect on children who have been craving more attention from him. Children may have difficulty disclosing domestic violence because of their fear of repercussions for themselves or for their mothers. For these reasons, children's statements to professionals sometimes may obscure the family history or their own present feelings and wishes. For example, in response to questions during a custody evaluation of ours, a teen boy primarily spoke positively about his mother and negatively about his father. At the same time, however, he requested to he placed in his father's home, repeatedly expressing concern that his father had been falsely accused of domestic violence and that the father did not have friends. In other cases, children may request to be in the batterer's custody because of ways in which he has shaped their perceptions of their mother and because of his history of currying favor with them.

We also have seen indications of batterers pressuring or rehearsing their children's statements to the evaluator. In one case, for example, a 3-year-old boy said to the evaluator, "Give my dad a chance," but further questioning revealed that he did not know the meaning of the expression. Finally, in some cases, children exhibit signs of being afraid to express a preference to live with their mother because of concern over the batterer's reaction.

The Batterer's Economic Advantage. Our divorced and separated clients generally have more financial resources than do their former partners, especially in the period immediately following separation. These financial advantages can make it possible not only to hire a more experienced and skilled attorney but also to spend money on discovery, depositions, hearings, and trials. We receive many reports from battered mothers of settling cases on terms that they consider detrimental to their children because they cannot amass the resources to pay for a trial. In addition, we have observed some cases in which the batterer's economic advantages appeared to sway the custody evaluator, who felt that the children would be happier in the more fortunate class circumstances of the father. Finally, courts may grant custody to the father if the mother is homeless, even if her economic position is largely the result of his failure to pay child support or of other economically irresponsible behaviors on his part. . . .

Gender Bias[]. There is important evidence that fathers may be favored over mothers in custody disputes. . . . Courts may assume that a father who seeks custody is unusually caring and concerned (and may be unaware of the frequency with which batterers seek custody). Mothers and fathers sometimes appear to be judged by different standards, with mothers evaluated on the basis of their actual history of performance as parents, and fathers evaluated on the basis of their expressions of emotion and their stated intentions for the future. Mothers also appear to be judged more harshly than are fathers for any period of separation from the children, which can, for example, have negative implications for a battered woman who may have needed to flee without her children at some point.

We also observe the presence of societal ambivalence regarding a mother's appropriate role in protecting her children from their legal father. Prior to separation or divorce, professionals and other community members (including child protective services) may be harshly critical of a mother whom they perceive as guilty of "failure to protect" her children from exposure to a batterer. However, a societal reversal tends to take place once a mother and an abusive father are no longer together. At this stage, we have observed that professionals often become suspicious of a mother's motives for attempting to protect her children and may attribute children's symptoms to the mother's alleged anxiety, overprotectiveness, or vindictiveness against the alleged abuser. Thus, battered mothers sometimes can he caught in a societal contradiction that works to the advantage of batterers. . . .

B. STANDARDS TO AWARD CUSTODY

1. *Fitness*

■ CUSTODY OF VAUGHN
664 N.E.2d 434 (Mass. 1996)

Fried, Justice.

. . . Leslie and Ross met in Maine in 1977. Leslie, who was twice divorced, lived with her two children, a girl (Laura) then age nine years and a boy (John) age five years. Leslie worked as a real estate salesperson during the day and as a cocktail waitress at night. The Probate Court judge found that she "has been an abused person. She was abused as a child, she was divorced twice and has endured abuse because of her relationships." Ross, a former marine engineer, was working odd jobs as a carpenter and painter at the time. Shortly after they met, Ross moved into Leslie's home. They have never married. Ross is a big man, six feet five inches tall and weighing some 285 pounds. Leslie is five feet seven inches tall and weighs 150 pounds. The disparity in their size is relevant, because the relationship was fraught with anger and violence from the start. Ross had a terrible temper. The judge found that he "would fly into rages" and strike out at Leslie, once causing her to lose consciousness and requiring her to be sent to the hospital in an ambulance. According to testimony, he inflicted injuries on her on numerous other occasions. Laura and John witnessed a number of these incidents and were terrified of Ross and his rages. The testimony and findings of fact reflected that Ross was also physically and verbally abusive toward them. Both Ross and Leslie drank heavily and used marihuana. Since Leslie joined "Al-Anon" in 1978, her consumption of alcohol has diminished. The testimony is that she drinks mostly on social occasions. Ross has been alcohol free since 1985 and continues to attend Alcoholics Anonymous meetings once a week. . . .

Ross's rages and violence toward Leslie, Laura, and John continued after Vaughn's birth. There was testimony that the police were called on approximately one dozen occasions. Ross's anger and violence, however, did not cease, and he sought psychiatric help. A psychiatrist prescribed Lithium, and there was testimony that when Ross discontinued taking it (on his own) his moods and behavior worsened. Leslie testified that on several occasions she left the house with her children to escape Ross's behavior, that many times Ross also took Vaughn from the house in the course of arguments, and that Ross used the threat of taking Vaughn from his mother as a way of keeping the mother in the relationship. Vaughn was present at many of the episodes of abuse. There was testimony that the father's disposition to use physical force was played out on the boy as well, with cuffing, pushing, knocking, and poking; he also yelled and lost his temper at the boy, as he did at every other member of the household. Laura, who is now a graduate student, further testified that, when she was a teenager, Ross kissed her on the mouth in an inappropriate manner and touched her body in an inappropriate, sexual manner.

The judge also found that Leslie engaged in taunting, provocative, and violent behavior toward Ross. On several occasions she assaulted him in a sexual and humiliating manner. It appears that for some years the parties had not shared a bedroom, and on at least one occasion Leslie without any immediate provocation taunted Ross for his sexual neglect of her. In 1986, on the occasion that received the most attention, she entered Ross's room nude and proceeded to taunt him in the grossest and most explicit terms within the boy's hearing. In 1988, in another similar incident, the judge found that Leslie, "when rejected after demanding sexual favors from [Ross] followed him from the house to the public road. She was naked and directed foul language at him. This too was done in the presence of [Vaughn]."*

Until Vaughn was five years old his mother was his primary caretaker. Thereafter Ross undertook more and more responsibilities. Apparently he did the shopping and cooking for the household over the five years immediately prior to trial, and he

---

* [The Massachusetts Supreme Judicial Court adopts here the trial court's finding about this event. However, the appellate court opinion contains a different version of the events: The mother and father were arguing in the bedroom when the father decided to awaken, and leave with, the sleeping child. "Fearing that the father intended to take the child away, as he frequently threatened to do, the mother ran into the yard to remove the keys from the ignition of the father's truck." 653 N.E.2d 195, 198 n.1. *Ed.*]

was greatly occupied with his son's activities. Ross followed his son's progress in school, visited his teachers, attended his sporting events, and joined him in target shooting and other activities. Indeed the evidence suggests that Ross was, if anything, overly involved with his son. He embarrassed his son at times by participating in games with him or cheering with excessive enthusiasm at his team sports, and the two would shower together and would give each other massages. Ross has been very generous to Vaughn—the mother complains overly generous—buying him motorbikes and electronic equipment.[6]

The tension and violence between the parents finally led Leslie, on October 1, 1992, to obtain an [order of protection] requiring Ross to vacate the couple's home, to surrender custody of the boy to the mother, and to remain away from the home and the mother. The next day Ross commenced this action in the Probate Court to establish paternity (which is not in dispute) and to obtain custody of Vaughn. The parties promptly entered into a temporary agreement providing for joint legal and physical custody, according to which the boy would spend part of each week with each parent. During this arrangement the father bought out the mother's share of the house in which they had been living, and the mother moved into a new home. The parties also agreed that Dr. Michael D. Abruzzese, a clinical psychologist whom they had previously consulted along with the child, should be appointed guardian ad litem to make an evaluation and report regarding custody of the child. On February 21, 1993, Dr. Abruzzese delivered his report, recommending that joint custody be continued but that the boy's primary home during the week be with his father with weekends to be spent with his mother. Thereupon the Probate Court entered a new temporary order maintaining the joint legal custody but giving the father primary physical custody and visitation rights to the mother, substantially in accord with Dr. Abruzzese's recommendations. After a three-day trial in July, 1993, the Probate Court entered a supplementary judgment on September 7, 1993, in effect continuing this arrangement. [Leslie appeals.]

[The Appeals Court reversed, holding that the award of joint legal custody with primary physical custody to the father was not supported by the evidence, and remanded.] The Appeals Court based its remand to the Probate Court on the failure of that court to make findings regarding the evidence that the father had physically abused the mother throughout the relationship and the effect of this abuse on the child. The Appeals Court gave great weight to this court's Gender Bias Study of the Court System of Massachusetts (1989) and particularly to the recommendation in that study that,

> The legislature and/or appellate courts should make it clear that abuse of any family member affects other family members and must be considered in determining the best interests of the child in connection with any order concerning custody.

---

6. The [trial] judge found: "While the mother has been more strict and the disciplinarian, the father has been more liberal with [Vaughn] and has acted more like a friend and companion. . . . While much of [Ross's] conduct and treatment of [Vaughn] may be questionable (i.e. the scented oil massages they give to each other and their showering together) as well as [Ross's] permissiveness with [Vaughn], the father and son have clearly developed a special relationship. The evidence does not reflect that [Vaughn] has been hurt by this relationship. To the contrary it establishes the very strong bonding between father and son. [Ross] for some five to six years has been [Vaughn's] primary care giver. He has been responsible for most of the cooking, shopping and caring for [Vaughn]. [Vaughn] has been his main involvement, while the mother has been significantly involved in her real estate career."

The Appeals Court's remand order is designed to do just that. We endorse the Appeals Court's commitment to the propositions that physical force within the family is both intolerable and too readily tolerated, and that a child who has been either the victim or the spectator of such abuse suffers a distinctly grievous kind of harm.[9] It might be helpful to emphasize how fundamental these propositions are. Quite simply, abuse by a family member inflicted on those who are weaker and less able to defend themselves—almost invariably a child or a woman—is a violation of the most basic human right, the most basic condition of civilized society: the right to live in physical security, free from the fear that brute force will determine the conditions of one's daily life. . . . [F]or those who are its victims, force within the family and in intimate relationships is not less but more of a threat to this basic condition of civilized security, for it destroys the security that all should enjoy in the very place and context which is supposed to be the refuge against the harshness encountered in a world of strangers. Particularly for children the sense that the place which is supposed to be the place of security is the place of greatest danger is the ultimate denial that this is a world of justice and restraint, where people have rights and are entitled to respect. . . .

The Appeals Court was critical of the Probate Court in a number of related respects. First, the Probate Court judge "fail[ed] to make detailed and comprehensive findings of fact on the issues of domestic violence and its effect upon the child as well as upon the father's parenting ability." [R.H. v. B.F, 653 N.E.2d 195, 201 (Mass. App. Ct. 1995)]. Second, "because [the judge] found the mother and the father to have equally flawed parenting abilities, the relationship between the father and the child and the child's preferences weighed the scales [excessively] in the father's favor." [Id. at 202.] And third, the Appeals Court ruled that the Probate Court failed to consider the special risks to the child in awarding custody to a father who had committed acts of violence against the mother. [Id. at 201.] An important theme of all these statements was that the Probate Court had failed to give sufficient weight to the effects of domestic violence on women and their children. . . .

We agree with the Appeals Court [in its criticism that the] Probate Court failed to consider the special risks to the child in awarding custody to a father who had committed acts of violence against the mother. It is well documented that witnessing domestic violence, as well as being one of its victims, has a profound impact on children. There are significant reported psychological problems in children who witness domestic violence, especially during important developmental stages.

Domestic violence is an issue too fundamental and frequently recurring to be dealt with only by implication. The very frequency of domestic violence in disputes about child custody may have the effect of inuring courts to it and thus minimizing its significance. Requiring the courts to make explicit findings about the effect of the violence on the child and the appropriateness of the custody award in light of that effect will serve to keep these matters well in the foreground of the judges' thinking.

The Legislature reached a similar conclusion in respect to shared legal or physical custody. General Laws c. 208, §31, provides that "[i]f, despite the prior or current issuance of a restraining order against one parent . . . , the court orders shared legal or physical custody, . . . the court shall provide written findings to

---

9. To the same effect, see the definition of "[s]hared physical custody," G.L. c. 208, §31 (1994 ed.): "In determining whether temporary shared legal custody would not be in the best interest of the child, the court shall consider . . . whether any member of the family has been the perpetrator of domestic violence."

support such shared custody order." A [protection] order was outstanding in this case, and the judge made no explicit findings regarding the effect of shared custody on the child. We agree with the Appeals Court that such written findings should also be made attending specifically to the effects of domestic violence on the child and the appropriateness of the joint custody award in light of those effects. Accordingly, we remand the case to the Probate Court for such explicit findings. . . .

Notes and Questions

1. *Custody determinations.* Custody consists of legal and physical custody. Legal custody confers responsibility for major decisionmaking (that is, the child's upbringing, health, welfare, and education). Physical custody determines the child's residence and confers responsibility for day-to-day decisions regarding physical care.

Custody can be sole or joint. Sole physical custody involves the right of one parent to have the child live with him or her while the other parent has visitation rights. Sole legal custody means that one parent has the right to make decisions for the child independently. Joint custody (explored below) means that both parties share responsibility. If both parents share decisionmaking about the child, they have *joint legal* custody. If they share the right to determine the child's residence and day-to-day decisions regarding physical care, both parents share *joint physical* custody.

The American Law Institute (ALI) Principles of the Law of Family Dissolution (2002) (hereafter ALI Principles) (a ten-year law reform project by lawyers, judges, and law professors) made recommendations for family law reform concerning child custody, child support, and the distribution of marital property. Because these proposals for reform are not statements of current law (that is, ALI *Restatements*), they are named "Principles." The ALI Principles suggest use of the term *decision making responsibility* for *legal custody*, and the term *custodial responsibility* for *physical custody*. ALI Principles §2.03(3) (custodial responsibility), (4) (decision-making responsibility). The purpose of the change in terminology was to avoid the traditional "win-lose conceptualization" and to reinforce the view that all forms of physical responsibility "are also important, and custodial in nature." Id. cmt.

2. Vaughn: *form of custody.* What form of custody was the basis of the parents' temporary agreement in *Vaughn*? Why do you think the mother agreed to that type of custody? See R.H. v. B.F., 653 N.E.2d 195, 198 (Mass. App. Ct. 1995) (reporting that the mother feared that, if she refused, the father "would harm her or run off with the child"). What did the guardian ad litem recommend? What type of custody did the trial judge award? What type of custody did the appellate court award? What did the state supreme court hold? What form of custody do you think was appropriate?

3. *Best interests of the child.* The prevailing standard in child custody decision-making is the "best interests of the child." This highly discretionary standard is based on a list of factors (usually statutory) regarding the child's needs. Statutory factors proposed by the Uniform Marriage and Divorce Act (UMDA), ratified by the National Conference of Commissioners on Uniform Laws in 1970, have been very influential in legal policy. Specifically, UMDA lists five factors that courts must consider in the determination of the best interests of the child:

(1) the wishes of the child's parent or parents as to his custody;
(2) the wishes of the child as to his custodian;

(3) the interaction and interrelationship of the child with his parent or parents, his siblings, and any other person who may significantly affect the child's best interest;

(4) the child's adjustment to his home, school, and community; and

(5) the mental and physical health of all individuals involved.

§402, 9A U.L.A. (pt. II) 282 (1998). UMDA does not include domestic violence as a factor in the consideration of the best interests.

4. *Fitness.* Traditionally, courts award child custody based on the best interests of the child, unless parental unfitness is shown. Many states now mandate consideration of domestic violence in their determination of best interests and parental fitness. In most states, domestic violence constitutes one of several factors in custody determinations; however, many states have rebuttable presumptions against custody awards to an abusive parent. At the time of *Vaughn*, Massachusetts followed the "domestic violence as a factor" approach. A few years later, the Massachusetts legislature adopted the rebuttable presumption approach. See Mass. Gen. Laws ch. 208 §31A (enacted in 1998).

5. Vaughn*: sufficiency of evidence.* What evidence was relevant to the custody determination in *Vaughn?* How is that evidence presented (that is, documents, testimony, etc.)? What aspects of the abuse are particularly relevant in the analysis of the trial court, appellate court, and state supreme court? The severity of the injuries? Mother's hospitalization? The fact that the child and siblings were subject to, and/or witnessed, the violence? How relevant was the parents' substance abuse? How relevant was the existence of a restraining order? How relevant should each of these factors be in a custody determination? See also In re Custody of Zia, 736 N.E.2d 449 (Mass. App. Ct. 2000) (awarding custody to father despite his being subject to two restraining orders). How is the mother's conduct in *Vaughn* relevant? Do you agree with the trial court finding that "[b]oth the mother are father are batterers"? Custody of Vaughn, 653 N.E.2d at 199.

In *Vaughn*, the father's abuse constituted a "course of conduct." Should a course of conduct be required or could a single act suffice as evidence of abuse? See Kent v. Green, 701 So. 2d 4 (Ala. Civ. App. 1996) (awarding custody to father where there was evidence of a single incident of choking mother, resulting in her hospitalization, based on testimony of psychologist who posited that father would not commit future acts of violence).

The above excerpts explain the characteristics of a batterer as a parent. (Recall too the excerpts in Chapter 2.) Which of these characteristics does the father manifest in *Vaughn?*

6. *Harm to the child.* What is the nature of the father-son relationship in *Vaughn?* A substantial factor in the trial judge's award of primary physical custody to the father was the father-son relationship. See Custody of Vaughn, 653 N.E.2d at 199. What evidence supports the trial judge's observation that Vaughn has not "been hurt by this relationship? To the contrary [the evidence] establishes the very strong bonding between father and son"? Id.

Consider the rebuttal evidence that was presented at trial by the mother's expert witness, a child and family forensic psychologist with expertise in family violence (Dr. Peter Jaffe). Dr. Jaffe testified that Vaughn had told him that, when he was not with his father, his father would be very sad and unhappy. Vaughn expressed the belief that he could help his father keep his temper by keeping his father happy and calm. Id. at 200. In response, the psychologist opined that Vaughn suffered emotional problems typically experienced by boys who witness abuse of their mother, including depression, sadness, and "an excessive sense of personal responsibility for his father." *Id.*

The Probate Court in *Vaughn* appointed a clinical psychologist to serve as a guardian ad litem (GAL) for the child in the custody proceedings. The parents both agreed to the appointment of a licensed clinical psychologist and to his performing a custody evaluation. What might explain the GAL's opinion that Vaughn suffered "separation and anxiety" when he was absent from his father and that, therefore, a forced separation from his father (such as a custody award to the mother) "would likely cause major psychological problems for both [the child and his father]"? Id. at 199. In light of the above testimony by the different experts, what weight should be given to the boy's custodial preference?

Might other harm result to Vaughn from an award of primary physical custody to the father? See id. at 201 (citing danger of child's learning that "violence and intimidation is a way to get what you want"). Custodial preference is discussed later in this chapter, Section D(1). The role of the child's representative is discussed later in this chapter, Section D(2).

7. Vaughn *findings*. *Vaughn* played a major role in child custody law in the context of domestic violence because of its requirement that the trial court make specific written findings of fact regarding the presence and impact of domestic violence. In fact, such findings are called "*Vaughn* findings." See Philip C. Crosby, Custody of Vaughn: Emphasizing the Importance of Domestic Violence in Child Custody Cases, 77 B.U. L. Rev. 483, 505-508 (1997) (discussing prior Massachusetts law). Many jurisdictions require, by statute rather than case law, that courts enter these specific findings. See, e.g., Ariz. Rev. Stat. Ann. §25-403(B); 750 Ill. Comp. Stat. Ann. 5/610; Ky. Rev. Stat. Ann. §403.270(1)(f). What is the purpose of this requirement of written findings? See Naomi R. Cahn, Civil Images of Battered Women: The Impact of Domestic Violence on Child Custody Decisions, 44 Vand. L. Rev. 1041 (1991) (discussing need to address judiciary's treatment of the role of domestic violence).

8. *Victim as parent*. *Vaughn* remands for a new determination of parental fitness in light of the father's domestic violence. On remand, what aspects of Leslie's behavior should be considered in the determination of her fitness? What aspects of Ross's behavior? What light do the above excerpts shed on the determination of the parents' fitness? See also Peter G. Jaffe et al., Child Custody & Domestic Violence 44-46 (2003) (suggesting that victims often give the appearance of being unstable, angry, indifferent, or depressed). How does the batterer's undermining of the mother's parenting affect her position in custody cases?

9. *Domestic violence as a negative factor for victims?* A few states have statutes that protect against the possibility that evidence of domestic violence could be considered adversely to the *victim* in the determination of a child's best interests. See, e.g., La. Rev. Stat. Ann. §9:364(A) ("The fact that the abused parent suffers from the effects of the abuse shall not be grounds for denying that parent custody").

10. *Policy*. The trial court in *Vaughn* awarded primary physical custody of the 11-year-old boy to the abusive father. According to the excerpts, why are some courts so willing to award custody to an abusive parent? See also Joan S. Meier, Domestic Violence, Child Custody, and Child Protection: Understanding Judicial Resistance and Imagining the Solutions, 11 Am. U. J. Gender Soc. Pol'y & L. 657 (2003) (suggesting that courts adopt a theoretical split between domestic violence cases

and child custody/visitation cases); Amy B. Levin, Comment, Child Witnesses of Domestic Violence: How Should Judges Apply the Best Interests of the Child Standard in Custody and Visitation Cases Involving Domestic Violence? 47 UCLA L. Rev. 813 (2000) (criticizing courts' focus on parents', rather than children's, needs and suggesting additional training for judges on the effects of domestic violence on children).

11. *Bifurcating domestic violence and custody decisionmaking.* An early judicial approach was to refuse to consider domestic violence as a factor in custody determinations unless the batterer also injured the child. See, *e.g.*, Baker v. Baker, 494 N.W.2d 282 (Minn. 1992). Does this bifurcation make sense? What is the relationship between intimate partner violence and child abuse? Are batterers also likely to abuse children physically? Considerable research reveals that batterers are several times more likely than nonbattering men to abuse children. One large-scale study (6,000 subjects) reports that 49 percent of batterers physically abused children compared to 7 percent of nonbattering men. Bancroft et al., The Batterer as Parent, supra, at 55-56. Subsequent studies confirm this finding, and some report even higher rates of victimization. Id. If the child is not actually physically abused by the batterer, might the mere act of witnessing domestic violence prove harmful to the child? What light do the above excerpts shed on these questions? Children's exposure to domestic violence is discussed later in this chapter, Section G.

2. Rebuttable Presumptions

■ PETERS-RIEMERS v. RIEMERS
644 N.W.2d 197 (N.D. 2002)

NEUMANN, Justice.
. . . Roland met Jenese, a non-U.S. citizen, in Belize in 1995 while vacationing there. . . . In early 1996, at Roland's invitation, Jenese left Belize and moved to North Dakota. Roland provided her an apartment in Grand Forks and lived with her there. . . . Jenese became pregnant by Roland, and on June 24, 1997, their son, Johnathan, was born. [O]n March 6, 1999, Roland and Jenese were married. . . . After incurring several instances of physical abuse by Roland, Jenese filed a complaint on March 7, 2000, seeking dissolution of the marriage. [T]he court granted Jenese a decree of divorce from Roland on the grounds of adultery, extreme cruelty, and irreconcilable differences. Upon finding Roland had committed domestic violence, the court awarded physical custody of Johnathan to Jenese and provided Roland "closely supervised" visitation with Johnathan. . . . Roland, acting pro se, has appealed and has raised numerous issues on appeal [including that] the trial court failed to make specific findings in concluding that Roland had perpetrated domestic violence. We disagree.

The trial court made the following specific findings regarding Roland committing domestic violence against Jenese, all of which are supported by the evidence:

In the fall of 1996, Jenese became pregnant with the parties' son. A few months later, in February of 1997, Jenese learned of Roland's physical relationship with [another woman]. A physical argument erupted. During the course of such incident, Roland slapped and punched Jenese. He also kicked her in the stomach. Consequently, Jenese suffered vaginal bleeding and obtained medical treatment. . . .

In October of 1999, Jenese heard Johnathan crying outside. She walked out to discover that Johnathan had fallen down the stairs and had hurt himself. Roland was standing a few yards away from Johnathan, talking on his phone instead of tending to his son. Jenese made an angry comment to Roland about his priorities then went back inside. Roland than came into the kitchen and slapped Jenese in the face.

During the marriage, Roland kept pornographic magazines and videos in the marital residence, sometimes in places where Johnathan would encounter them. In January of 2000, Jenese destroyed one of Roland's pornographic videos. When Roland discovered his destroyed tape, he came up behind Jenese as she was making a bed and kicked her in the back.

On March 4, 2000, after a verbal argument, Jenese attempted to leave the marital residence with the parties' son, Johnathan. Roland refused to allow her to leave with Johnathan, but attempted to force her out of her home alone. He pinned her left arm behind her back as she held Johnathan tight in her other arm. Jenese escaped long enough to call 911, but Roland hung up the phone. He then punched her in the face, knocking her to the ground. He broke a finger in the process. Jenese was later diagnosed with a fractured bone in her face.

On March 6, 2000, Jenese obtained a Temporary Protection Order against Roland. On March 7, 2000, Roland was charged with felony assault as a result of striking Jenese. A No Contact Order issued as a condition of Roland's Pretrial Release. After a fully contested hearing, [a]n Adult Abuse Protection Order issued against Roland on March 14, 2000. . . . [Six months later, he pled guilty to a reduced charge of misdemeanor assault.]

Under N.D.C.C. §14-09-06.2(j) evidence of domestic violence is a specifically enumerated factor for the court to consider in awarding child custody:

> j. Evidence of domestic violence. In awarding custody or granting rights of visitation, the court shall consider evidence of domestic violence. If the court finds credible evidence that domestic violence has occurred, and there exists one incident of domestic violence which resulted in serious bodily injury or involved the use of a dangerous weapon or there exists a pattern of domestic violence within a reasonable time proximate to the proceeding, this combination creates a rebuttable presumption that a parent who has perpetrated domestic violence may not be awarded sole or joint custody of a child. This presumption may be overcome only by clear and convincing evidence that the best interests of the child require that parent's participation as a custodial parent. The court shall cite specific findings of fact to show that the custody or visitation arrangement best protects the child and the parent or other family or household member who is the victim of domestic violence. If necessary to protect the welfare of the child, custody may be awarded to a suitable third person, provided that the person would not allow access to a violent parent except as ordered by the court. If the court awards custody to a third person, the court shall give priority to the child's nearest suitable adult relative. The fact that the abused parent suffers from the effects of the abuse may not be grounds for denying that parent custody. As used in this subdivision, "domestic violence" means domestic violence as defined in section 14-07.1-01. A court may consider, but is not bound by, a finding of domestic violence in another proceeding under chapter 14-07.1.

Under this statutory provision a single incident of domestic violence which results in serious bodily injury or a pattern of domestic violence creates a presumption that the perpetrator may not be awarded custody. With regard to the domestic violence factor, the trial court made clear and specific findings. The court found Roland had a pattern of inflicting domestic violence upon Jenese and that in at least one instance that violence resulted in serious bodily injury to her. The court found that although Jenese may have at times acted violently toward Roland, her actions were "largely in self-defense." Acts of domestic violence are mitigated when committed in self-defense. The trial court did not find Jenese's conduct toward Roland rose to a level of violence triggering the presumption against her receiving child custody. We conclude the trial court's findings are supported by the evidence and are not clearly erroneous.

Roland asserts the trial court's finding that Roland inflicted extreme cruelty on Jenese is clearly erroneous. Extreme cruelty is defined under N.D.C.C. §14-05-05 as "the infliction by one party to the marriage of grievous bodily injury or grievous mental suffering upon the other." The trial court awarded Jenese a divorce on the grounds of adultery, extreme cruelty, and irreconcilable differences. Considering the physical violence perpetrated against Jenese by Roland and his illicit extramarital affairs, there is substantial evidence to support the trial court's conclusion that extreme cruelty, consisting of both grievous bodily injury and grievous mental suffering, was inflicted by Roland upon Jenese during their marriage. The trial court's underlying findings of extramarital conduct and physical abuse are supported by the evidence and are not clearly erroneous. . . .

The following excerpt (despite its focus on children's exposure to domestic violence) provides helpful background on the development of statutes that create a presumption against awards of custody to abusive parents. The topic of exposure to domestic violence is discussed later in this chapter in Section E.

■ **LESLIE JOAN HARRIS, FAILURE TO PROTECT FROM EXPOSURE TO DOMESTIC VIOLENCE IN PRIVATE CUSTODY CONTESTS**
44 Fam. L.Q. 169, 171, 173-178 (2010)

The Emergence of Statutes Requiring Courts to Consider Violence between Parents

. . . The first domestic violence/custody statutes provided that battering was among the factors that should inform a court's determination of a child's best interests. More recent statutes in many states go further, creating a presumption against awarding custody to the violent parent. As of early 2010, twenty-two states had enacted such presumptions, whereas the other twenty-eight states and the District of Columbia had only the former kind of statute. Other relatively recent statutory innovations provide that if both parents have engaged in violence, the parent who is less likely to continue to be violent should receive custody or that the person who was not the primary aggressor should. In a number of states, friendly parent statutes, which favor the parent who is more likely to foster the child's relationship with the other parent, do not apply in domestic violence cases. Similarly, several states provide that a parent's absence or relocation should not be considered negatively if it was a response to the other parent's violence.

Most states' statutes do not discuss specifically what level and frequency of violence triggers the consequences discussed above. The statutory approaches in states that do address these issues vary. At one extreme, the New Hampshire and Nevada statutes define abuse in terms of the state criminal codes, requiring that the allegedly violent person's conduct fit into one of a list of crimes in the statute. At the other extreme, the definition in some state codes is so broad that it could cover a single act of assault. For example, the Arizona statute provides that a person commits domestic violence if he or she "intentionally, knowingly or recklessly causes or attempts to cause sexual assault or serious physical injury, places a person in reasonable apprehension of imminent serious physical injury to any person, or engages in a pattern of behavior for which a court may issue an ex parte order to protect the other parent who is seeking child custody or to protect the child and the child's siblings." The California, Kentucky, and Massachusetts definitions are substantially similar. Some states define abuse both in general terms and by reference to the definitions of certain crimes.

Some states set out what kind of proof is admissible or even required to prove domestic violence, but again, provisions vary. In Arizona, the court must consider findings from other courts, police reports, medical reports, child protective service records, domestic violence shelter records, school records, and witness testimony. In California, a court may require independent corroboration that abuse occurred from records of such entities, and the statutes forbid a court from basing its findings "solely on conclusions reached by a child custody evaluator or on the recommendation of the Family Court Services staff." In Iowa, for purposes of determining whether a "history of domestic abuse" exists, the court must consider whether proceedings to obtain a protective order have been initiated, whether an order has issued, and whether it has been violated. On the other hand, in Massachusetts, the issuance of an ex parte domestic violence restraining order is not admissible to show abuse.

Most states' statutes do not require proof that the child witnessed the violence or that the violence had an effect upon the child. Instead, the statutory consequences of a finding of abuse are triggered automatically; in fact, some statutes go as far as to say that whether the child witnessed the violence is irrelevant.

At least six state statutes, however, require the court to determine whether the violence had an adverse effect on the child. Massachusetts requires the court to make findings regarding the effects of domestic violence on the child. Statutes in Maine, Minnesota, and Connecticut also require the court to consider the effect of violence on the child. The emphasis in the New Hampshire and Kentucky statutes is somewhat different, requiring the trial court to look at the impact of the abuse on the child and on the relationship between the child and the abusing parent.

Advocates for laws requiring courts to consider domestic violence had to overcome the argument that domestic violence directed at an adult is irrelevant to a determination of the child's best interests. They relied on empirical studies showing that men who abuse their mates harm or create risks of harm to children in the household, even if the children have not been abused themselves.

The [argument] is that men who batter children's mothers are also likely to abuse the children physically. Lenore Walker, who is usually credited with having identified the battered woman syndrome, wrote that fifty-three percent of men who abused their domestic partners also abused their children. Put a slightly different way, the estimates of the overlap between children who witness men battering the children's mothers and children who are themselves battered by the men range from thirty to forty percent to sixty percent. In addition, evidence shows that children who witness parental violence have more aggressive, antisocial, and fearful behavior; more anxiety, aggression, depression, and temperamental problems; less empathy and self-esteem; and lower verbal, cognitive, and motor abilities. They may also carry violence and acceptance of violence into their adult relationships. This research has been widely accepted and provides the justification for the statutes that require courts to take domestic violence into account in making custody decisions. . . .

Notes and Questions on *Vaughn* and *Peters-Reimer*

1. *Presumptions.* Presumptions play an important role in custody determinations. Presumptions have the benefit of offering certainty and thereby avoiding the stress of litigation. Beginning in the mid- to late nineteenth century, the *tender years presumption* applied to custody determinations, providing that the biological mother of a young child was entitled to custody unless she was found unfit. In the 1970s and 1980s, many states declared that this presumption violated the Equal Protection Clause. See, *e.g.,* Devine v. Devine, 398 So. 2d 686 (Ala. 1981). The primary caretaker presumption briefly superseded the tender years presumption in a few jurisdictions, resulting in custody awards to the parent who took primary responsibility for the child's care. Only two states adopted this presumption (Minn. Stat. §518.17(1)(a); W. Va. Code §48-9-206). However, both states later abrogated it. Today, primary caretaker status is only one factor in the best-interests determination.

2. *Joint custody.* A nascent fathers' rights movement spearheaded the passage of joint custody legislation in the late 1970s. See Herbert Jacob, The Silent Revolution: The Transformation of Divorce Law in the United States 136-143 (1988). California was the first state to provide statutory recognition of awards of joint custody in 1980. See Cal. Fam. Code §3080 (formerly Cal. Civ. Code §4600.5). The doctrine caught on quickly. Within three years, more than 30 states enacted some form of joint custody. Harris, supra, at 172.

Joint custody is a radical departure from conventional psychological wisdom about childrearing. Professors Joseph Goldstein, Anna Freud, and Alfred Solnit propounded the view in the 1970s that stability and minimization of conflict should guide child placement. They asserted that healthy development requires an "omnipotent" parent on whom the child can rely for all important decisions. To that end, they advocated that custody be awarded to only one parent, who should have power to decide the extent of the other parent's contact with the child (even prohibiting it). See Joseph Goldstein et al., Beyond the Best Interest of the Child 38 (1973).

3. *Domestic violence and joint custody.* When is an award of joint custody appropriate? When is it inappropriate? Many commentators urge that joint custody is particularly inappropriate in cases of domestic violence. Judith G. Greenberg, Domestic Violence and the Danger of Joint Custody Presumptions, 25 N. Ill. U. L. Rev. 403, 411 (2005). A number of influential organizations (including the National Council of Juvenile and Family Court Judges and the American Bar Association) have passed resolutions finding joint custody inappropriate in cases of domestic violence. Annette M. Gonzalez & Linda M. Rio Reichman, Representing

Children in Civil Cases Involving Domestic Violence, 39 Fam. L.Q. 197, 197 (2005). In domestic violence cases, why would joint custody be less appropriate than an award of sole custody plus visitation to the other parent?

Do you agree with one commentator's suggestion that courts should prefer other alternatives (for example, supervised visitation and mandated treatment) to rebuttable presumptions against custody awards to batterers? Levin, Comment, Child Witnesses, supra, at 855. Why or why not?

4. *Friendly-parent doctrine.* The "friendly-parent" doctrine mandates that custody be awarded to the parent most likely to foster the child's relationship with the other parent. The doctrine has been codified as a factor in custody, visitation, and relocation disputes. Marsha Kline Pruett et al., The Hand That Rocks the Cradle: Maternal Gatekeeping After Divorce, 27 Pace L. Rev. 709, 720 (2007). Feminists and battered women's advocates denounce the application of the friendly parent doctrine in cases of domestic violence. See, e.g., Margaret K. Dore, The "Friendly Parent" Concept: A Flawed Factor for Child Custody, 6 Loy. J. Pub. Int. L. 41 (2004); Joan Zorza, "Friendly Parent" Provisions in Custody Determinations, 26 Clearinghouse Rev. 921, 923 (1992). As Professor Harris points out in the above excerpt, some state statutes specifically provide that the friendly parent doctrine does not apply in the context of domestic violence. Why is the doctrine contraindicated in this context?

5. *State variations: problems of proof.* About half the states have a rebuttable presumption against awarding custody to an abusive parent. Each state varies in the standard of proof required to trigger the presumption, and the standard and type of proof necessary to rebut it. As Professor Harris explains, the critical issue is what kind of proof triggers the presumption. Some states have a very high standard, requiring that the abuse must constitute a violation of the state criminal code. In other states, evidence of a single act may be sufficient to establish a "history of domestic violence" so as to trigger the presumption. See, *e.g.*, Alexander v. Rogers, 247 S.W.3d 757 (Tex. App. 2008). Still other states require evidence of a pattern of violence against the victim or child. See, *e.g.*, Simmons v. Simmons, 649 So. 2d 799 (La. App. 1995) (holding that a single past act of violence does not trigger presumption). What does the statute in *Peters-Riemers* require? How does the plaintiff satisfy the statutory requirements? What are the advantages of broad versus narrow definitions of the triggering factors—for the abuser, victim, and child?

6. *Constitutional implications.* Do state statutes creating a rebuttable presumption against a custody award to an abusive parent violate that parent's due process rights? If so, how? If not, why not? See Opinion of the Justices to the Senate, 691 N.E.2d 911 (Mass. 1998).

7. *Evidence to rebut the presumption.* Because the presumption against awarding custody to an abuser in cases of domestic violence is rebuttable, the abuser can introduce evidence to counter the presumption. In *Peters-Riemers*, what does the statute require to rebut the presumption? Should evidence that a perpetrator of domestic violence has completed anger management or a domestic violence treatment program be sufficient to rebut the presumption? See Rahn v. Norris, 820 A.2d 1183 (Del. Fam. Ct. 2001) (finding that the father's completion of several counseling classes and parent education was not sufficient to remove the presumption). Why or why not?

a. *Evidence of conviction or restraining order.* All states that include presumptions have found that evidence of a *conviction* for domestic violence is sufficient to trigger the presumption. See, e.g., In re Marriage of Cloyed, 765 N.W.2d 607 (Iowa Ct. App.

2009). However, only some states consider evidence of a restraining order to trigger the presumption. Compare In re Marriage of Ringler, 188 P.3d 461 (Or. App. 2008) (finding that presence of restraining order obtained in a contested proceeding triggered presumption), with Morris v. Horn, 219 P.3d 198 (Alaska 2009) (holding that a restraining order, obtained without litigation, was not issue preclusive and did not automatically trigger the presumption). Professor Harris, in the above excerpt, also points out the split in authority. Why are courts and legislatures so concerned about allowing restraining orders to establish a presumption against awarding custody to an abuser?

b. *Form of violence that triggers presumption. Peters-Riemers* involved a showing of physical violence toward both the mother and the child. Should *nonphysical* acts of domestic violence be sufficient to trigger the presumption? See DesLauriers v. DesLauriers, 642 N.W.2d 892 (N.D. 2002) (finding that verbal and emotional abuse did not trigger presumption, but that such factors weighed in determination of the best interests of the children). What explains judicial reluctance to permit evidence of nonphysical abuse to trigger the presumption?

c. *Timing of violence.* In *Peters-Riemers,* the domestic violence occurred three days before the mother filed for divorce. Some courts require that the domestic violence must occur within a "reasonable time proximate to the proceedings." See, e.g., Tulintseff v. Jacobsen, 615 N.W.2d 129 (N.D. 2000). What is the basis for this requirement? What period is "reasonable"? What factors might cause a victim of domestic violence to delay filing for divorce and custody?

8. *Effect of presumption.* When a court finds that the domestic violence presumption is triggered (and not rebutted), what custody arrangement does the court order? Does the presumption preclude sole custody? Joint physical as well as legal custody? What result does the statute in *Peters-Riemers* dictate? See also Parks v. Parks, 214 P.3d 295 (Alaska 2009) (abuser may not receive joint physical or legal custody). Does the presumption affect visitation rights? Visitation is discussed later in this chapter, Section C.

9. *Mutual combat.* In *Vaughn,* the defendant claims that Jenese "struck, hit, or scratched" him during their fights. Why does the court treat this as evidence of "self-defense" rather than "mutual combat"? How does evidence of "mutual combat" factor into the application of the rebuttable presumption? One court responds:

> [I]f domestic violence has been committed by both parents, the trial court measures the amount and extent of domestic violence inflicted by both parents. If the amount and extent of domestic violence inflicted by one parent is significantly greater than that inflicted by the other, the statutory presumption against awarding custody to the perpetrator will apply only to the parent who has inflicted the greater domestic violence, and will not apply to the parent who has inflicted the lesser. However, if the trial court finds that the amount and extent of the violence inflicted by one parent is roughly proportional to the violence inflicted by the other parent, and both parents are otherwise found to be fit parents, the presumption against awarding custody to either perpetrating parent ceases to exist.

Krank v. Krank, 529 N.W.2d 844, 849 (N.D. 1995). Is this the best way to resolve claims of mutual combat? How would the *Krank* analysis apply in *Peters-Riemers?* See generally Meier, Domestic Violence, Child Custody, and Child Protection, supra, at 692-696 (criticizing judicial willingness to attribute mutual blame).

10. *Presumption in cases of homicide.* What should be the role of domestic violence in custody determinations when the abuser murders the other parent? See In re James M., 135 Cal. Rptr. 222 (Ct. App. 1976) (finding that the father's second-degree murder of his children's mother does not render him unfit to have custody). Some states have enacted presumptions against awards of custody to such parents. See, e.g., Cal. Fam. Code §3030(c) (establishing rebuttable presumption against custody or unsupervised visitation for a parent convicted of first-degree murder of the other parent). Are custody presumptions appropriate in such cases? See generally Deborah Ahrens, Not in Front of the Children: Prohibition on Child Custody as Civil Branding for Criminal Activity, 75 N.Y.U. L. Rev. 737, 756 n.93 (2000). Similar presumptions apply in the visitation context (explored later in this chapter).

11. *Gender bias?* Gender bias complicates legal responses to domestic violence in custody decision making. Various studies highlight accounts of lawyers and judges who minimize or disbelieve reports of domestic violence. See Linda D. Elrod & Milfred D. Dale, Paradigm Shifts and Pendulum Swings in Child Custody: The Interests of Children in the Balance, 42 Fam. L.Q. 381, 395 n.75 (2008). What explains judicial skepticism about women's credibility? See Bancroft et al., The Batterer as Parent, supra, at 148-150; Molly Dragiewicz, Gender Bias in the Courts: Implications for Battered Mothers and Their Children in Domestic Violence, Abuse, and Child Custody 5-2 (Mo Therese Hannah & Barry Goldstein eds., 2010); Meier, Domestic Violence, Child Custody, and Child Protection, supra, at 690-692. What light do the excerpts shed on this question?

12. *Litigation abuse.* Greenberg suggests that litigated cases are particularly likely to involve domestic violence. Greenberg, supra, at 411. Why? What light is shed on this question by the above excerpt by Bancroft et al.? Commentators have identified the phenomenon of "litigation abuse"—the abuser's use of the *legal system* and *legal personnel* to intimidate, harass, and coerce a victim—and claim that it commonly occurs in custody disputes. See Bancroft et al., The Batterer as Parent, supra, at 157-158; Evan Stark, Re-presenting Woman Battering: From Battered Woman Syndrome to Coercive Control, 58 Alb. L. Rev. 973, 1018 (1995).

13. *ALI.* UMDA and the ALI Principles are two important family law reform models. UMDA does not address domestic violence. However, the ALI Principles rectify this omission. The ALI Principles require that parents disclose battering in the parenting plan that they submit to the court and that the court have a process to identify abuse. ALI Principles §§2.06, 2.11. Batterers may not receive custodial responsibility unless the court orders appropriate measures to ensure protection of family members (for example, by mandated counseling). Id. at §2.11(2)(I). The Principles suggest that courts be aware that the abuse might try to use custody or visitation rights to harass the victim-spouse. Id. at §2.11(c) cmt. Finally, the ALI Principles assert that acts of self-defense do not constitute abuse. Rather, if one spouse's act is more extreme or dangerous, "it may be appropriate for the court to impose limits on the primary aggressor but not on the primary victim." ALI Principles §2.11 (c) cmt. Do these provisions provide sufficient protection?

14. *Modification of child custody.* The paramount concern with child welfare gives courts power to modify custody. What role should the existence of domestic violence in the *post-decree* period play in child custody determinations?

The standard for custody modification is higher than for initial awards of custody based on the rationale that it is important to ensure stability for the child. This emphasis on stability in child placement decisionmaking is a central tenet of the work by Professors Goldstein, Freud, and Solnit, who strongly oppose alteration in child placement based on the child's need for continuity of care. See Joseph Goldstein et al., Beyond the Best Interests of the Child 37 (1973).

Under the prevailing standard, the plaintiff has the burden of showing by a preponderance of the evidence that conditions since the dissolution decree have so materially and substantially changed that the children's best interests require a change of custody. A few states have adopted a more liberal requirement that modification serve the best interests of the child (regardless of any change in circumstances). Several states have more stringent rules, influenced by UMDA §409(b), 9A U.L.A. 439 (1998), requiring endangerment for nonconsensual changes. Absent serious endangerment, UMDA §409(a) provides for a two-year waiting period following the initial decree.

Should the occurrence of an act of domestic violence constitute a material change in circumstances that leads to custody modification? See Meyers v. Sheehan, 880 N.Y.S.2d 96 (N.Y. App. Div. 2009) (finding that a single act of domestic violence warranted a change in sole custody from the mother to the father). Suppose that the domestic violence is being perpetrated by a nonparent against the custodial parent, such as by the mother's new boyfriend? Compare Christopher S. v. Ann Marie S., 662 N.Y.S.2d 200 (Fam. Ct. 1997) (allegations of abuse in child's maternal household support claims of father in petition to modify joint custody), with Anderson v. Hensrud 548 N.W.2d 410 (N.D. 1996) (violence directed against other men who were not the father or child did not qualify as domestic abuse for purposes of presumption).

15. *Exposure to violence.* How does *Peters-Riemers* treat evidence of the child's exposure to the domestic violence between the parents? Exposure to domestic violence is explored later in this chapter, Section D.

C. CONDITIONS ON VISITATION: SUPERVISED VISITATION

■ IN RE MARRIAGE OF FISCHER
2009 WL 2469282 (Wash. Ct. App. 2009)

HUNT, J.

. . . Bruce and Karen were married on June 26, 1992. They have two minor children together. The parties separated on July 25, 2006. They dissolved their marriage on October 30, 2007. During the period between separation and post-dissolution, the trial court entered and renewed domestic violence protection orders [restraining Bruce from contacting Karen or the children]. . . . On August 4, 2006, Karen filed a petition to dissolve the marriage.

[At trial] the major issue was whether the trial court should include domestic violence restrictions in the parenting plan. . . . On October 4, the trial court entered the final parenting plan. The trial court found that Bruce had a history of domestic violence, as defined by RCW §26.50.010(1). Based on this domestic violence finding, the trial court (1) ordered supervised visitation between Bruce and the children, (2) gave Karen sole decision-making authority for the children, and (3) ordered Bruce to complete a domestic violence perpetrator treatment program. Bruce appealed. . . . Bruce contends that the dissolution trial evidence was not sufficient to support the trial court's finding that he had a history of domestic violence, and that the restrictions were not reasonably calculated to address an identified harm. We disagree. . . .

The trial court found that Bruce had engaged in a "history of domestic violence" as defined in RCW §26.50.010(1). In its oral ruling, the trial court explained:

> The history of domestic violence upon which I rely is [Karen's] testimony about her treatment within the marriage; [Bruce's] name calling and belittling behavior, his shoving, his efforts at isolating [Karen] from friends and family, his screaming at home, his isolated but numerous outbursts in public. And I find that this behavior frightened [Karen] and for many years has placed her in fear of being hurt by [Bruce].

The evidence adduced at trial supports this finding.

At trial, Karen testified extensively about Bruce's calling her names. She also testified that he frequently shoved her. She specifically described one incident when he had shoved her into a wall, shoved her out of the home office, shoved her down the hallway, and then swept everything off her desk. She also described an incident later that same morning, during which he ripped the turtleneck sweater she was wearing:

> I remember him saying I'm going to kill you. . . . I don't know if he said, "I'd like to kill you" or "I could kill you," but there was definitely "kill you" in there. And he—he grabbed both of his hands around my neck and just shoved me against a corner of the wall. And I just remember just being completely—completely horrified, like—you know, in the past in our marriage he had said to me, just kind of in passing just, you know, if he was frustrated with me or whatever, he had said to me a few times in our marriage, "I could snap your neck." And it—Bruce has very large hands. And it has always been very clear to me that he's very strong. And he had pushed me and shoved me in our marriage, but that was—that was a whole new experience. And I was terrified.

Karen further testified that, starting years earlier, when she was trying to converse with Bruce and he was done talking, he would "shove [her] out of the room and shove [her] down the hall-way." Bruce generally testified that none of these incidents of violence occurred.

[Bruce testified that he never grabbed or shoved Karen but sometimes that he had to "push by" her because she blocked his path. He further testified that Karen was violent toward him and he felt he was a victim of domestic violence. Several character witnesses testified on Bruce's behalf. Mark Ricci, Bruce's childhood friend, testified that he once saw Bruce with scratches on his arm when Bruce arrived at Ricci's house after having an argument with Karen. No other testimony supported Bruce's assertion that Karen was violent toward him.]

The trial court, however, explicitly found Karen's testimony credible and Bruce's testimony not credible:

> I listened to the testimony of the parties and . . . I find that [Karen's] testimony is very credible, and [Bruce's] testimony on the issue of domestic violence is incredible. [Karen's] testimony appeared from the stand to be genuine. Her description of anger and control was consistent with the behaviors that were described by [three

visitation supervisors who observed Bruce's visits with his children and testified about their observations] during the course of this trial. . . . The testimony was consistent with [Bruce's] demonstrated disrespect for others and disrespect for rules that he disagrees with. It was my observation that when things did not go as [Bruce] wanted them to, he has acted in a way that those he was dealing with felt intimidated and were frightened. We will not disturb the trial court's credibility determinations on appeal.[4]

RCW §26.09.187 provides criteria for establishing permanent parenting plans. RCW 26.09.191 provides applicable restrictions for those plans. RCW §26.09.187(2)(b) requires the trial court to "order *sole decision-making to one parent* when it finds that . . . [a] limitation on the other parent's decision-making authority is mandated by RCW §26.09.191." (Emphasis added.) RCW §26.09.191(1) mandates one-parent decision-making authority when the other parent has a history of domestic violence:

> The permanent parenting plan *shall not* require mutual decision-making or designation of a dispute resolution process other than court action if it is found that a parent has engaged in . . . a history of acts of domestic violence as defined in RCW §26.50.010(1).

(Emphasis added.) Thus, because the trial court found that Bruce had a history of domestic violence, RCW §26.09.187(2)(b) required it to grant Karen sole decision-making authority for the children.

In addition, RCW §26.09.191(2)(a) requires the trial court to consider a parent's history of domestic violence when determining the parenting plan's residential provisions: "The parent's residential time with the child shall be limited if it is found that the parent has engaged in . . . a history of acts of domestic violence as defined in RCW §26.50.010(1)." RCW 26.09.191(2)(m)(i) further provides that such limitations "shall be reasonably calculated to protect the child from . . . emotional abuse or harm" and may include supervised contact between the parent and child or the parent's completion of relevant counseling or treatment. We hold, therefore, that in light of the trial court's supported finding that Bruce had a history of domestic violence, the trial court did not abuse its discretion by requiring supervision of his residential time with the children.

Furthermore, the trial court's parenting plan restrictions, as follows, were reasonably calculated to address a specific harm—the effect on the children of Bruce's acts of domestic violence against Karen:

> The father shall have four hours of professionally supervised visits per week. Both parties shall agree upon the professional supervisor. Once the father enrolls and begins his domestic violence perpetrator treatment program, the professionally supervised

---

4. We will not disturb the trial court's finding as not credible Bruce's testimony that Karen committed domestic violence against him. The trial court explained:

> I guess, [Bruce], that you may have been relying on [Karen's] reactive behavior to you to vindicate you and focus attention on her wrongdoing. I have little doubt that [Karen] threw a glass of water on you once, and she may have even struck back at you. But I cannot conceive that she would have been the physical aggressor. Your public behavior, as reported in this trial, and even the behavior that I have observed in court, belies the truth of these allegations. I do not believe you were ever afraid or felt threatened by [Karen's] behavior, that she controlled your behavior, and in fact that was your testimony. You were never frightened or threatened by her.

visits may [be] in the home of the father. After two months of treatment and a favorable report, unsupervised daytime visits may begin. Once the father successfully completes his domestic violence perpetrator treatment program, the parenting plan shall be revisited upon motion and a normalized pattern of contact with the children, including consecutive overnights in the father's home shall occur.

The trial court explained that it was allowing Bruce supervised visits because he is "truly an engaged parent and a parent who needs to be involved in the lives of these children," but that Bruce needed to participate in the treatment program to learn how his behavior affects his children. RCW §26.50.060 provides that where the trial court finds that a parent has committed acts of domestic violence, it may order that parent to participate in a domestic violence perpetrator treatment program. We hold, therefore, that the trial court did not abuse its discretion when it imposed the challenged parenting plan conditions. . . .

■ **KIM BARKER & ARTHUR SANTANA, SLAIN WOMAN WAS "VERY AFRAID"**
Seattle Times, Dec. 12, 1998, at A1, available at 1998 WLNR 1524073

A court kept Melanie Edwards' husband away from her, but allowed him to visit the daughter he is suspected of killing. . . .

Carlton Lee Edwards left on the morning of Oct. 19 to drive his father to the airport. So Melanie Edwards grabbed her daughter and her husband's pistol and left home. She took the gun, inside its locked case, to the Seattle Police Department because she was afraid of her husband. She filed for an order of protection, and she got a temporary restraining order that afternoon. Then she went into hiding, listing her address as "confidential" in any court documents she signed. At one point, she said she lived at New Beginnings domestic-violence shelter.

Carlton Edwards wasn't supposed to come within 500 feet of his wife, of her work, or of his child, according to the King County Superior Court protection order signed Nov. 2. That protection order, however, granted him regular visits with his daughter.

But Wednesday night, shortly after a visit, Melanie Edwards, 33, and their 2-year-old daughter were shot and killed outside of Common Ground, an agency that offers supervised visitations and a neutral child-exchange spot for estranged parents. Police are still searching for Carlton Edwards, who they suspect killed the two. . . .

The last Common Ground visit was Wednesday, when Carlton Edwards spent time with his daughter during the afternoon and early evening. He dropped off Carli about 6 p.m. Police say he may have waited outside in a rental car. Melanie Edwards picked up Carli about a half-hour later. Then Carlton Edwards allegedly approached his wife and shot her as she sat in the driver's seat, police say. He shot Carli in the back seat, police believe. . . .

[Epilogue: Two weeks later, Carlton Edwards committed suicide. Elaine Porterfield, Suicide Note Says That Slain Wife "Had it Coming" But Edwards Didn't Mean to Shoot Daughter, Seattle Post-Intelligencer, Dec. 24, 1998, at A1, available at 1998 WLNR 1972700.]

■ MAUREEN SHEERAN & SCOTT HAMPTON,
SUPERVISED VISITATION IN CASES OF
DOMESTIC VIOLENCE
50 *Juv. & Fam. Ct. J.* 13-18 (1999)

The ongoing risk perpetrators of domestic violence pose to victims and children after separation has led to the development of new laws and services designed to address one crucial area of concern: facilitating safe contact between perpetrators of domestic violence and their children. Specifically, many states have passed laws giving courts broad discretion to order supervised visitations in cases involving domestic violence. As supervised visitation becomes increasingly recognized as a potential tool for protecting battered women and their children, communities are mobilizing to develop supervised visitation services that are safe and appropriate for cases involving domestic violence. . . .

A key indicator of risk in domestic violence situations is the abuser's access to the victim; and visitation with the children in an unprotected visitation or exchange setting is a guarantee of continued access. Visitation can be a time of particular volatility as it provides the small window of opportunity, maybe the only opportunity, for a batterer to focus his desperate efforts to regain control. Judges and victims agree that visitation holds the greatest potential for renewed violence. Many battered women report threats against their lives during visitation and exchanges, and some, in fact, are killed in those contexts. . . . In addition to the risks of severe or lethal violence, child visitation and exchanges create opportunities for batterers to follow through on their threats to abduct their children. . . . Often abduction of the child, or refusal to return children after the scheduled visits, is a manipulative attempt by the perpetrator to coerce the victim into returning.

Aside from the risks of severe violence or homicide after separation, the risks posed by batterers to their children, alone, is enough to cause acute concerns about how safe children may be in an unprotected setting with a violent parent. Battered mothers often work diligently to protect children from battering parents and worry about the children's safety when they are not able to protect them. The concerns for safety are so great that many battered women contemplate violating a court order, or even fleeing with the child, to avoid the dangers of sending the child on an unsupervised visit with a battering father. . . .

Drafters of the [Model Code on Domestic and Family Violence] also were sensitive to the increased danger victims of domestic violence and their children face during visitation. The Model Code sets forth conditions for awarding visitation in cases involving domestic violence. . . . While states have been slower to act in placing limitations on visitations than they have on requiring the consideration of domestic violence in custody determinations, by December 1998, eight states had passed supervised visitation legislation patterned most or entirely on the Model Code §405. Another 17 states have legislation specifically allowing supervised visitation in custody or protection order proceedings involving domestic violence. Those statutes vary. In Iowa for example, the court is required to consider whether the safety of the child, other children, or the parent will be jeopardized by awarding unsupervised or unrestricted visitation when, determining what custody is best for the child. Much stronger restrictions are placed on visitation with a perpetrator of domestic violence in Louisiana, where the court can allow only supervised visitation to a perpetrator-parent, conditioned upon that parent's participation in and completion of a treatment program. In Louisiana, unsupervised visitation is allowed only if it is shown by a preponderance of the evidence that the perpetrator-parent has met certain conditions and poses no danger to the child, and that such visitation is in the child's best interest. . . .

Even in states without specific legislation addressing supervised visitation in the context of domestic violence, courts generally have broad discretion to fashion visitation arrangements appropriate to a given case and thus the authority to require that contacts between a batterer and his children be supervised. . . .

The growing acknowledgment that in some situations the only safe visitation is supervised visitation has created a great demand for visitation services. These services are an essential element in a coordinated community intervention system designed to protect victims from abuse and eliminate violence. . . .

Acknowledging the need for visitation services, the Model Code requires states to provide for visitation centers throughout the state in order to allow court-ordered visitation which protects all family members. . . . The American Bar Association also supports the establishment of visitation centers. . . .

Supervision of visitation or exchanges is not new. Child protection agencies have been supervising parents and abused or neglected children for some time as a way of maintaining ongoing parent-child contact pending reunification or termination of parental rights. Supervised visitation programs and the concept of supervised visitation as a social service, however, are relatively new.

Also new is the use of visitation centers in the context of domestic violence. The past few years have seen the emergence of new supervised visitation programs around the country, many of which have been established specifically to address the safety needs of battered women and their children. . . .

As more centers develop to respond to the needs of battered women and their children and as existing programs, which developed from various approaches, work increasingly with families experiencing domestic violence, the unique demands domestic violence places on centers are coming into focus. Some special considerations brought on by domestic violence are detailed below.

Need for heightened security. Safety of the children and victim-parent are the over-arching concerns in supervised visitation in the context of domestic violence. The dangers posed by batterers are well documented. Therefore, visitation centers working with cases involving domestic violence require procedures designed to reduce risks brought on by domestic violence.

To enhance safety some centers establish such procedures as:

- Ensuring that facilities and procedures preclude contact between the custodial and non-custodial parent. For example, centers can have parents arrive and leave at separate times, park in separate parking lots, enter though different entrances, and wait in separate areas. Assuming the non-custodial parent is the offending parent, safety can be enhanced by having the non-custodial parent arrive 15 minutes prior to the visit and wait 15 minutes after the visit before leaving the facility; and the custodial parent arrive and leave immediately prior to and after the visit.
- Providing on-site security.
- Screening all cases for domestic violence.
- Refusing cases too dangerous for centers to handle safely.

- Developing policies to enhance confidentiality, such as maintenance of separate files for the perpetrator-parent and the victim-parent.

Need for understanding the dynamics of domestic violence. Given the unique dynamics of domestic violence, visitation supervisors working with perpetrators and victims of domestic violence and their children should have an in-depth understanding of the dynamics of domestic violence. . . . [I]t is recommended that visitation providers receive significant training in domestic violence and that visitation programs develop affiliations with domestic violence victim and perpetrator service agencies.

Need for case oversight. Dependency cases have child protection case workers and case or service plans. In contrast, domestic violence cases involved in supervised visitation programs and not involved in child protection proceedings seldom have case workers or mechanisms for ongoing case oversight other than judicial review. Child protection cases are marked by services designed to move families out of the dependency process. Traditionally, that is not the case in family court case, including those with allegations of domestic violence. Given the lack of service plans and independent evaluations in family violence cases, judges often look to visitation supervisors to make more evaluative determinations than supervisors feel qualified to make. And, given the context of supervised visitation, the information visitation supervisors can provide to courts is of limited value to judges. What a visitation supervisor sees is a "snapshot" of a parent and child together for a brief moment in highly artificial circumstances where the parent is aware of observation. This observation is not an adequate predictor of how the batterer will relate to the child in another setting and under other circumstances.

While visitation centers and services are becoming important pieces in a coordinated response to domestic violence, a number of key considerations remain: visitation centers are not a guarantee of safety for vulnerable family members; they do little to improve the ability of a batterer to parent in a responsible, non-violent way; and funding for supervised visitation centers and services is uncertain. . . .

■ **NAT'L COUNCIL OF JUVENILE & FAMILY COURT JUDGES, MODEL CODE ON DOMESTIC AND FAMILY VIOLENCE (1994)**

SEC. 405. CONDITIONS OF VISITATION IN CASES INVOLVING DOMESTIC AND FAMILY VIOLENCE

1. A court may award visitation by a parent who committed domestic or family violence only if the court finds that adequate provision for the safety of the child and the parent who is a victim of domestic or family violence can be made.

2. In a visitation order, a court may:

(a) Order an exchange of a child to occur in a protected setting.

(b) Order visitation supervised by another person or agency.

(c) Order the perpetrator of domestic or family violence to attend and complete, to the satisfaction of the court, a program of intervention for perpetrators or other designated counseling as a condition of the visitation.

(d) Order the perpetrator of domestic or family violence to abstain from possession or consumption of alcohol or controlled substances during the visitation and for 24 hours preceding the visitation.

(e) Order the perpetrator of domestic or family violence to pay a fee to defray the costs of supervised visitation.

(f) Prohibit overnight visitation.

(g) Require a bond from the perpetrator of domestic or family violence for the return and safety of the child.

(h) Impose any other condition that is deemed necessary to provide for the safety of the child, the victim of domestic or family violence, or other family or household member.

3. Whether or not visitation is allowed, the court may order the address of the child and the victim to be kept confidential.

4. The court may refer but shall not order an adult who is a victim of domestic or family violence to attend counseling relating to the victim's status or behavior as a victim, individually or with the perpetrator of domestic or family violence as a condition of receiving custody of a child or as a condition of visitation.

5. If a court allows a family or household member to supervise visitation, the court shall establish conditions to be followed during visitation.

SEC. 406. SPECIALIZED VISITATION CENTER FOR VICTIMS OF DOMESTIC OR FAMILY VIOLENCE.

1. The [insert appropriate state agency] shall provide for visitation centers throughout the state for victims of domestic or family violence and their children to allow court ordered visitation in a manner that protects the safety of all family members. The [appropriate agency] shall coordinate and cooperate with local governmental agencies in providing the visitation centers.

2. A visitation center must provide:

(a) A secure setting and specialized procedures for supervised visitation and the transfer of children for visitation; and

(b) Supervision by a person trained in security and the avoidance of domestic and family violence.

Commentary

Supervised visitation centers are an essential component of an integrated community intervention system to eliminate abuse and protect its victims. Visitation centers may reduce the opportunity for retributive violence by batterers, prevent parental abduction, safeguard endangered family members, and offer the batterer continuing contact and relationship with their children. This section requires a state to provide for the existence of visitation centers but does not mandate that the state own or operate such centers. . . .

Notes and Questions

1. *Supervised visitation: background.* Courts increasingly take domestic violence into account not only in child custody but also awards of visitation. Although visitation law traditionally emphasizes frequent and continuing contact between children and parents, many state legislatures recognize that courts must take into account the safety of the victims of domestic violence and their children when framing visitation

orders. For that reason, a growing number of courts adopt supervised visitation in appropriate cases.

States have a number of approaches to supervised visitation, including statutory guidelines and procedures for providers as well as the creation of state-sponsored supervised visitation centers. The Model Code on Domestic and Family Violence, developed in 1994 by the National Council of Juvenile and Family Court Judges by an advisory committee of experts, was an early advocate of the need to utilize supervised visitation services in cases of domestic violence.

The practice of supervised visitation began in 1982 with the establishment of a small number of supervised programs. The next two decades witnessed considerable growth in supervised visitation centers, including the formation of an international association of visitation providers (the Supervised Visitation Network or SVN) that developed standards of practice for service providers. See Supervised Visitation Network, Standards for Supervised Visitation Practice (2006), available at http://svnworldwide.org/attachments/standards.pdf

Currently, there are over 100 supervised visitation programs in the United States, as well as a considerable number of persons who provide supervised visitation in private practice. Mary L. Pulido et al., Raising the Bar: Why Supervised Visitation Providers Should Be Required to Meet Standards for Service Provision, 49 Fam. Ct. Rev. 379, 380 (2011).

In what circumstances should judges order supervised visitation? When an order of protection has been issued? The abuse victim is in a shelter? The abuser faces criminal charges? The juvenile court determines that a child has been abused? Whenever domestic violence is present? Supervised visitation, although it offers considerable promise, reveals certain shortcomings, as examined below.

2. *Scope of visitation.* The trial judge has considerable discretion to determine the scope of visitation, including the particular conditions on the noncustodial parent's visitation. Parental conduct may lead to a variety of judicially imposed conditions on visitation. What are typical restrictions in cases of intimate partner violence, as illustrated by the Model Code above?

3. *Parenting plan.* The issue confronting the trial court in *Fischer* was whether to include domestic violence restrictions in the *parenting plan.* Many states, similar to Washington State in *Fischer*, provide that parents seeking custody must file a parenting plan with the court (that is, a written agreement specifying a detailed plan for post-dissolution child caretaking and decisionmaking authority as well as the manner in which future disputes are to be resolved). Statutes sometimes provide for "parenting coordinators" to help parents create or implement parenting plans.

Parenting plans were first proposed by the ALI Principles. ALI Principles §2.05. According to the Principles, "an individual seeking a judicial allocation of custodial responsibility or decisionmaking responsibility under this Chapter should be required to file with the court a proposed parenting plan . . ." Id. at §2.05(1). Approximately half of the states provide for such plans. Katherine T. Bartlett, U.S. Custody Law and Trends in the Context of the ALI Principles of the Law of Family Dissolution, 10 Va. J. Soc. Pol'y & L. 5, 6-7 (2002).

4. *Domestic violence and parenting plans.* Some statutory provisions for parenting plans address the role of domestic violence. See, *e.g.*, Fla. Stat. §61.125(2) (prohibiting court-ordered referral to parenting coordinator, absent parental consent, in cases involving "a history of domestic violence"). How did the statute in *Fischer* take domestic violence into account in parenting plans?

5. *Evolving view.* The Washington court of appeals in *Fischer* imposes custodial restrictions in a case that involves physical violence that is directed solely at the intimate partner and not at the children (as far as we know). Note that the court does not require proof of harm to the children, but implicitly assumes that intimate partner violence results in emotional harm to children. *Fischer* thus adopts a progressive approach toward restrictions on a batterer's custody rights, stemming from an enlightened understanding of the consequences of children's exposure to abuse.

Previously, many courts reflected "the outdated notion that if children have not been physically battered, evidence of domestic violence will be of little import in fashioning orders and agreements." Sarah M. Buel, Domestic Violence and the Law: An Impassioned Exploration for Family Peace, 33 Fam. L.Q. 719, 733 (1999). For example, in Dena Lynn F. v. Harvey H.F., 419 A.2d 1374, 1377 (Pa. Super. Ct. 1980), the court affirmed visitation to an abusive father, saying that "any evidence of the father's violent interludes presents no proof that it was directed at his child. It is only logical for us to decide that the appellant should, under these circumstances, be permitted to continue to have partial custody of his child."

6. *Purpose of supervised visitation.* Many states provide, by statute or case law, for supervised visitation in cases of domestic violence and/or child abuse. What is the purpose of supervised visitation? To evaluate parenting behavior? To reassure the custodial parent? To protect the child's safety? All of these? See generally Elizabeth Barker Brandt, Concerns at the Margins of Supervised Access to Children, 9 J.L. & Fam. Stud. 201 (2007). What did the Washington statute provide in *Fischer*? What evidence did the court consider in determining the need for supervised visitation? What conditions on visitation did the trial court impose? What did the appellate court hold? Why?

7. *Model Code on Domestic and Family Violence.* The Model Code provisions on supervised visitation have been extremely influential in legal policy formulation. The drafters were particularly cognizant of the danger presented by visitation. What are these dangers? Does the Model Code view visitation as a matter of right? How does the Model Code protect the victim and children? Are these protections adequate?

As the excerpt by Sheeran and Hampton explains, states were slower to restrict abusers' visitation than to limit custody rights. What do you think explains this fact?

8. *Visitation procedures.* Supervised visitation gives rise to a host of issues in framing the order. In considering each of the questions below, try to frame the order for the situation explained in *Fischer.*

a. *Where visitation takes place: supervised visitation programs.* Visitation can be supervised either by supervised visitation programs or private parties (generally selected by the parties and approved by the court). What are the advantages and disadvantages of visitation at the home of the abusive parent, the victim, a relative, a friend, or at a neutral location? See Debra A. Clement, Note, A Compelling Need for Mandated Use of Supervised Visitation Programs, 36 Fam. & Conciliation Courts Rev. 294, 298-299 (1998) (discussing advantages of various locations); Ellen K. Solender, Report on Miscommunication Problems Between the Family Courts and Domestic Violence Victims, 19 Women's Rts. L. Rep. 155, 158-159 (1998) (suggesting, in addition to supervised visitation program centers, public places like a shopping mall or fire stations). What was the location specified by the trial court in *Fischer*? Why?

Many states now provide for supervised visitation *programs* that furnish services to parents in custody disputes that involve abuse, neglect, or domestic violence. Services range from supervision by a constant observer to more minimal supervision. Supervised visits might take place at, or away from, the program center. Sometimes, supervision takes place only for the actual transfer of the child between the parents. Because transfers provide opportunities for violence, they are often structured to avoid or minimize contact between the parents.

Federal law provided for funding for visitation and exchange services in domestic violence cases in 2000 through the Office on Violence Against Women (OVW). See Safe Havens for Children Pilot Program, 42 U.S.C. §10420(a) (current version at 42 U.S.C.A. §10420(b), enacted as part of the Violence Against Women Act of 2000, Pub. L. No. 106-386, §1301(a), 114 Stat. 1509 (amended by Pub. L. 109-62, §306(1)).

b. *Who pays for visitation?* Which parent should pay for the cost of supervised visitation? Should the cost be shared? See Bancroft et al., The Batterer as Parent, supra, at 272 (urging that the abusive parent should be responsible for the full cost of supervision unless the court decrees otherwise); Buel, Domestic Violence and the Law, supra, at 737 (contending that "any associated costs should be paid by the battering parent, because the visitation center's services would not be needed but for the batterer's unlawful behavior"). What message does the allocation of costs provide? See Bancroft et al., The Batterer as Parent, supra, at 272 (the policy of imposing financial responsibility on the batterer sends "clear messages to all parties regarding whose behavior has caused the need for supervision"). Suppose cost poses an obstacle to supervised visitation by the abuser. Should the court take that factor into account in awarding supervised visitation? See Leslie Kaufman, In Custody Rights, A Hurdle for the Poor, N.Y. Times, Apr. 8, 2007, at 125.

c. *Who supervises?* Who supervised the father's visitation in *Fischer*? How was that supervisor selected? Who should supervise visitation generally in cases of domestic violence? Or should the supervisor be chosen on a case-by-case basis?

What are the advantages and disadvantages of having the supervisor be: Someone the child knows? A social service worker? A mental health professional? An attorney? A community volunteer? A relative? If the supervisor is a relative, should it be a relative of the abuser? Should it matter if the relative denies that the abuse took place? Compare Peter Jaffe et al., Parenting Arrangements After Domestic Violence, 6 J. Center for Families Child. & Cts. 81, 89 (2005) (suggesting that relatives are appropriate as supervisors particularly when the concern is assistance with childcare skills rather than safety), with Bancroft et al., The Batterer as Parent, supra, at 17 (warning that the batterer may manipulate family members into sympathizing with the batterer and engendering hostility toward the mother). See also Buel, Domestic Violence and the Law, supra, at 737 (suggesting that supervised visitation "must not be conducted by any relative or friend of the batterer, as they are frequently afraid of the perpetrator and certainly unable to control him").

d. *Child's perspective.* Should the child's feelings about visitation be taken into account? See Carla Garrity & Mitchell A. Baris, Custody and Visitation: Is It Safe?, Fam. Advoc., Winter 1995, at 40 (proposing models for supervised visitation, based on the child's age and other factors). The child's custodial preference is discussed later in this chapter, Section D.

Should the child be told the reason(s) for supervised visitation? Should the child be told that the reason is not the child's fault? Not the victim's fault? See Janet R. Johnston & Robert B. Straus, Traumatized Children in Supervised Visitation: What Do They Need?, 37 Fam. & Conciliation Cts. Rev. 135, 148 (1999) (children may assume "that the visits are being supervised because of something they did wrong"). Who should tell the child about the reasons for supervision?

A parent? If so, which? The visitation supervisor? See id. (urging the supervisor to ask the parent what he or she plans to tell the child and to have the supervisor provide the same explanation to the child at the initial visit). How much should the child be told? See id. (suggesting that "many children have been overburdened by being told too much").

9. *Batterer's treatment programs.* What type of treatment program did the court order in *Fischer*? What was the basis of the court's authority to issue such an order? What role does the court specify for the treatment program to play in the defendant's transition from supervised to unsupervised visitation? Should supervised visitation commence only after a parent *seeks* treatment? See, *e.g.*, Mary D. v. Watt, 438 S.E.2d 521 (W. Va. 1992). Only after a parent *completes* treatment? *See, e.g.*, La. Rev. Stat. Ann §9:364(C) (requiring batterer to complete counseling before supervised visitation may commence). Model Code on Domestic and Family Violence §405 recommends that visitation (supervised or otherwise) be prohibited unless the batterer has *completed* a specific batterer's intervention program. What do you think of this recommendation?

Can a court impose a visitation condition requiring a parent's attendance at anger management classes—even if that relief is not requested by the opposing party? See Moncher v. Maine, 892 So. 2d 1147 (Fla. Dist. Ct. App. 2005). Can a court require that visitation be denied until a therapist recommends otherwise? See Carmichael v. Siegel, 754 N.E.2d 619 (Ind. Ct. App. 2001); In re Mark M., 782 A.2d 332 (Md. 2001) (both finding that such a court order was an improper delegation of judicial authority). Should the focus of batterers' treatment programs be on "anger management"? See Bancroft et al., supra, at 259 (pointing out that "anger management programs should not be used in place of specialized batterer intervention programs," because control, rather than difficulty in anger management, is the cause of battering). See also Borchgrevink v. Borchgrevink, 941 P.2d 132 (Alaska 1997) (anger management counseling did not address root issues of domestic violence such as power and control). Batterers' treatment programs are explored later in Chapter 15.

Who should determine the parent's "successful" completion of treatment? See Jaffe et al., Child Custody and Domestic Violence, supra, at 89 ("The difficulty arises when it is not clear who bears the responsibility for assessing the perpetrator's progress or compliance with conditions."). Does a court have continuing jurisdiction to reassess a parent's visitation rights pending completion of the program? What does *Fischer* rule?

10. *Monitoring.* Should batterers' supervised visits be monitored? If so, how? Should the monitor make regular reports to the court about the visitation? What parts of the visitation should be supervised? The visit itself? The transportation of the child from one parent to the other? Telephone calls? Letters or emails? Lundy Bancroft and his colleagues suggest that batterers who visit children at visitation centers should never be out of visual or auditory range of center staff and that all materials brought by the batterer (including gifts) should be carefully examined by staff for appropriateness and safety. Bancroft et al., The Batterer as Parent, supra, at 271. What do you think of such suggestions? A criticism of supervised visitation is that it infringes on family members' privacy and infringes on the parties' ability to maintain close relationships. "Children often feel uncomfortable when they are being watched by the supervisor; as a result, their interaction with their parent is inhibited." Clement, supra, at 299. How should the interests of the child, parents, and the state be balanced in such situations?

11. *Modification.*

a. *From supervised visitation to unsupervised visitation.* When should supervised visitation give way to unsupervised visitation? Suppose the abusive parent contends that supervised visitation is interfering with the establishment of a good relationship with the child? See Grant v. Grant, 1995 WL 136775 (Ohio Ct. App. 1995). After a suspension of visitation, should visitation be phased in gradually? Can a court deny unsupervised visitation even after completion of the evaluation?

b. *From supervised visitation to termination of parental rights.* Cases of severe physical or sexual abuse may lead to termination of visitation. What standard of proof should be required to terminate parental rights after a period of supervised visitation? See In re A.C., 643 So. 2d 743 (La. 1994); Mullin v. Phelps, 647 A.2d 714 (Vt. 1994) (both requiring clear and convincing evidence). Does the termination of parental rights also terminate that parent's duty to support the child? See generally Jason M. Merrill, Note, Falling Through the Cracks: Distinguishing Parental Rights from Parental Obligations in Cases Involving Termination of the Parent-Child Relationship, 11 J.L. & Fam. Stud. 203 (2008).

Courts are reluctant to terminate parental rights altogether, even in cases involving domestic violence. See, *e.g.*, McCauley v. McCauley, 678 N.E.2d 1290 (Ind. Ct. App. 1997) (mother could not rely on predivorce violence as evidence to modify custody order from supervised to no visitation); State v. Sturgeon, 742 N.E.2d 730 (Ohio Ct. App. 2000) (reversing order for father to stay away from child for four years as a de facto termination of parental rights without due process). In these cases, is the court concerned about the child's right to a parent-child relationship? The parent's right to due process? What types of evidence should be sufficient to modify visitation from supervised to termination of parental rights? Evidence of continuing violence? Violations of protection orders? Refusal to comply with restrictions? See generally Dana Harrington Conner, Do No Harm: An Analysis of the Legal and Social Consequences of Child Visitation Determinations for Incarcerated Perpetrators of Extreme Acts of Violence Against Women, 17 Colum. J. Gender & L. 163, 208-209 (2008) (briefly discussing variations in state statutes).

12. *Confidentiality of records.* What are the advantages and disadvantages of admitting records produced by supervised visitation programs into evidence in custody proceedings? Is such evidence too freely admitted? See Nat Stern & Karen Oehme, The Troubling Admission of Supervised Visitation Records in Custody Proceedings, 75 Temp. L. Rev. 271, 280 (2002) (pointing out that nearly 80 percent of visitation programs make reports to the court, and nearly 60 percent offer recommendations about parent contact to the court). See also Nat Stern & Karen Oehme, Increasing Safety for Battered Women and Their Children: Creating a Privilege for Supervised Visitation Intake Records, 41 U. Rich. L. Rev. 499 (2007). What kind of evidence do visitation supervisors gather? How likely is such evidence to be informative on parenting issues?

13. *Lizzie's Law: visitation for a batterer who kills.* Should batterers who kill be entitled to visitation rights? That is, suppose a batterer kills the child's mother. Should the child have to visit him in prison? A famous case based on these facts led Massachusetts to enact a law (Mass. Gen. Laws Ann. ch. 209C §3(a)) prohibiting a parent convicted of murder of the other parent from visiting with the child absent a court order and the consent of the child or guardian. The law was nicknamed "Lizzie's Law" after a five-year-old girl whose father killed her mother and requested visitation rights. New York enacted a broader prohibition on visitation by a person

convicted of murder in the first or second degree of a parent, guardian, or sibling. N.Y. Dom. Rel. Law §240. See also In re H.L.T., 298 S.E.2d 33, 34 (Ga. Ct. App. 1982); In re Lutgen, 532 N.E.2d 976 (Ill. App. Ct. 1988).

14. *Child's refusal to visit.* How should courts respond to a child's refusal to visit a parent? Courts frequently respond by holding the *custodial parent* in contempt. See, *e.g.*, In re Marriage of Charous, 855 N.E.2d 953 (Ill. App. Ct. 2006). In such cases, should courts consider the possibility of domestic violence as an explanation for the child's refusal to visit?

15. *Policy.* Supervision centers play an important role in the legal response to domestic violence. However, as Sheeran and Hampton criticize in the excerpt (p. 621), such centers are not "a guarantee of safety for vulnerable family members; they do little to improve the ability of a batterer to parent in a responsible, non-violent way; and funding for supervised visitation centers and services is uncertain." How should these criticisms be addressed?

Problem

Tasha and Jeffrey are the unmarried parents of a four-year-old girl, Sonia. Both parents file petitions for custody of their daughter. Jeffrey has committed several acts of domestic violence against Tasha, one of which led to issuance of an order of protection. The Family Court awards sole custody of Sonia to Tasha and supervised visitation to Jeffrey. Jeffrey appeals. He challenges (1) the Family Court's finding that supervised visitation is necessary and (2) the Family Court's order that supervision be conducted by Tasha's mother, rather than Jeffrey's sister. Jeffrey claims that it would be easier for his sister to supervise visitation because her home is closer to his home. What result? See Taylor v. Fry, 849 N.Y.S.2d 724 (Sup. Ct. 2008). Of what relevance, if any, is the fact that that Jeffrey failed to cooperate with previous efforts by the local family and children's agency to schedule supervised visitation up until the point that his visitation was suspended?

D. ROLE OF SPECIAL PARTICIPANTS

1. The Child's Preference and Traumatic Bonding

■ WISSINK v. WISSINK
749 N.Y.S.2d 550 (App. Div. 2002)

S. MILLER, J.

This appeal presents a vexing custody dispute over a teenaged girl who has expressed a clear preference to live with her father. While both parents are seemingly fit custodians, the father has a history of domestic violence directed at the mother; yet he has never posed a direct threat to the child. Because of this circumstance, we hold that the Family Court erred in awarding custody to the father without first ordering comprehensive psychological evaluations to ensure that this award of custody was truly in the child's best interest.

The child in controversy, Andrea, born June 21, 1986, is the biological child of the mother and father; the mother also has a daughter, Karin, by a prior marriage. The parties have had a tumultuous relationship marked by numerous episodes of heated arguments, physical violence, police intervention and Family Court orders of protection. It is apparent that when it comes to his dealings with the mother, the father is a batterer whose temper gets the better of him. When it comes to Andrea, however, the father is the favored parent; he has never directly mistreated Andrea.

The parties have lived apart at various times during their marriage, and separated most recently in 1999 following yet another physical altercation. The mother commenced a family offense proceeding and a proceeding for custody of Andrea. The father cross-petitioned for custody. The Family Court assigned a law guardian and ordered a mental health study which was clearly deficient. A hearing was held at which the parties, Karin, and other witnesses testified, and the court examined Andrea in camera; she downplayed the father's culpability and expressed her clear preference for living with him.

The order appealed from awarded custody to the father. In separate orders, the Family Court dismissed the mother's custody petition and sustained the mother's family offense petitions, directing, inter alia, that the father enter and complete a domestic violence program. We now reverse the order awarding custody to the father and remit for a new custody hearing following an in-depth forensic examination of the parties and child.

Andrea's preference for her father and her closely bonded relationship to him were confirmed by her law guardian and the "mental health professional" social worker who interviewed her. Indeed, putting aside the established fact of his abusive conduct toward her mother, Andrea's father appears a truly model parent. He is significantly involved in her school work and her extracurricular activities. They enjoy many pleasurable activities, including movies, shopping, building a barn, and horseback riding. He provides her with material benefits—a television set, clothing, a horse, a trip to Europe. He is loving and affectionate. She is his "princess," his "best girl." In contrast, Andrea's mother has not been significantly involved in her school work or her extracurricular activities, and Andrea does not enjoy her company or their relationship.

Were it not for the documented history of domestic violence confirmed by the court after a hearing, we would have unanimously affirmed the Family Court's award of custody to the father in accordance with Andrea's expressed preference and the evidence documenting their positive relationship. However, the fact of domestic violence should have been considered more than superficially, particularly in this case where Andrea expressed her unequivocal preference for the abuser, while denying the very existence of the domestic violence that the court found she witnessed.

The record is replete with incidents of domestic violence reported by the mother, and by evidence supporting her testimony. The earliest incident that the mother reported was perpetrated when Andrea was merely an infant in 1986. In a fit of anger the father hit and kicked the mother and pulled out chunks of her hair. In the course of the attack she heard him say, "Oh well, she's going to die." On Super Bowl Sunday in 1995, he attacked her, throwing her on the floor, kicking, hitting, and choking her. She sustained marks on her neck and a sore throat causing pain while speaking and inhibiting her ability to swallow.

In March 1995, she obtained an order of protection from the Village Court of Montgomery. In the fall of that year the father allegedly held a knife, approximately 8 to 10 inches long, to the mother's throat while Andrea, then nine, sat on her lap. In February 1996 the mother again obtained an order of protection from the Village Court of Montgomery.

In 1997, the father attacked the mother, hit and kicked her, resulting in her obtaining a permanent order of protection from the Orange County Family Court. The severity of her injuries are documented by a photograph, entered in evidence, showing a large black and blue bruise on her left hip.

In June 1999, the mother left the marital home with Andrea and moved into a shelter where they remained for five days. Upon their return home the father blocked her car in the driveway, yelled at the mother and punched her.

On June 24, 1999, a few days after her return from the shelter, during a dispute over tax returns, the father tried to wrest papers the mother held in her teeth by squeezing her face in his hands, leaving marks and even enlisting the assistance of Andrea; he allegedly directed the child to "hold [the mother's] nose so she can't breathe."

On December 20, 1999, while Andrea was at home, the father attacked the mother, choking her. She had marks on her neck for days.

The latter two incidents were the subjects of the mother's most recent Family Offense petition, which the court sustained. In doing so, the Family Court also noted that a final order of protection had been entered in 1997, stating "based upon the proceeding [of 1997] as well as the succeeding [incidents] . . . Mr. Wissink is guilty of incidents of domestic violence occurring on June 24, [1999] and December 20, [1999]."

Domestic Relations Law §240(1) provides that in any action concerning custody or visitation where domestic violence is alleged, "the court must consider" the effect of such domestic violence upon the best interest of the child, together with other factors and circumstances as the court deems relevant in making an award of custody. In this case the Family Court did not entirely ignore that legislative mandate, and specifically noted that it had considered the effect of domestic violence in rendering its custody determination. However, the "consideration" afforded the effect of domestic violence in this case was, in our view, sorely inadequate.

The court-ordered mental health evaluation consisted of the social worker's interview of Andrea on two occasions (about 45 minutes each) and each parent once (about one hour each). These interviews resulted in the social worker's clearly foreseeable conclusion that Andrea was far more comfortable and involved with her father than her mother, that she did not relate well to her mother, and that she preferred living with her father.

In a case such as this, where the record reveals years of domestic violence, which is denied by the child who witnessed it, and the child has expressed her preference to live with the abuser, the court should have ordered a comprehensive psychological evaluation. Such an evaluation would likely include a clinical evaluation, psychological testing, and review of records and information from collateral sources. The forensic evaluator would be concerned with such issues as the nature of the psychopathology of the abuser and of the victim; whether the child might be in danger of becoming a future victim, or a witness to the abuse of some other victim; the child's developmental needs given the fact that she has lived in the polluted environment of domestic violence all of her life and the remedial efforts that should be undertaken in regard to all parties concerned.

The devastating consequences of domestic violence have been recognized by our courts, by law enforcement, and by society as a whole. The effect of such violence on children exposed to it has also been established. There is overwhelming authority that a child living in a home where there has been abuse between the adults becomes a secondary victim and is likely to suffer psychological injury.

Moreover, that child learns a dangerous and morally depraved lesson that abusive behavior is not only acceptable, but may even be rewarded. In many states a rebuttable presumption that perpetrators of domestic violence should not be eligible for legal or physical custody has been accepted and the courts of those states are required to specify why custody should be granted to an offender and how such an order is in the best interest of the child. We in New York have not gone that far, but the legislature, in enacting Domestic Relations Law §240, has recognized that domestic violence is a factor which the court must consider among others in awarding custody or visitation.

Moreover, the court also erred in limiting the mother's inquiry regarding the father's failure to comply with child support obligations and in finding financial consideration "not relevant at all" to the custody proceeding. The Family Court was required to consider the parties' support obligations and their compliance with court orders and to evaluate each party's ability to support the child. If, as the mother alleged, the father violated the child support order, and if he terminated the telephone and electrical services in the marital residence after he had been ordered to stay away pursuant to an order of protection, these facts would clearly be relevant to the court's custody determination.

Only after considering the complex nature of the issues and the relative merits and deficiencies of the alternatives can the court attempt to determine the difficult issue of the best interest of the child in a case such as this.

For the above reasons we thus reverse the custody order and direct a new custody hearing to be conducted after completion of a comprehensive psychological evaluation of the parties and the child. However, we stay Andrea's return to her mother, permitting her continued residence with her father, pending a final custody determination. . . .

Notes and Questions

1. *Child's preference: background.* Is it appropriate to consider a child's custodial preference as a *general rule*? If so, when? For all children? Some? Most states have statutes that call for consideration of a child's custodial wishes, including (a) those statutes modeled after the Uniform Marriage and Divorce Act, which requires consideration of the child's wishes; (b) those statutes that require consideration of the child's preference after a preliminary finding of maturity; (c) those statutes that require deference to the child's preference for children of a specified age (12 to 14 years); and (d) those statutes that give judges complete discretion as to whether to consider children's wishes. Randi L. Dulaney, Note, Children Should Be Seen and Heard in Florida Custody Determinations, 25 Nova L. Rev. 815, 819-822 (2001). Consider how this general rule (and others explained below) should operate both in the absence and presence of domestic violence.

2. *Older child's preference.* The older the child, the more likely it is that a court will consider the child's wishes. Some states require deference to a child's preference for children of statutorily specified ages. Id. at 821-822 (pointing out the statutorily designed age range from 10 to 16). If no age is specified, what should the age be?

3. *ALI approach.* The ALI permits a departure from its policy of deference to the primary caretaking parent in order to accommodate the custodial preference of those children who have attained a specified age (suggesting 11 to 14 years). ALI Principles §2.08, cmt. f. See also Kathleen Nemecheck, Note, Child Preference in Custody Decisions: Where We Have Been, Where We Are Now, Where We Should Go, 83 Iowa L. Rev. 437, 467 (1998) (concluding, based on a study of developmental theory, that statutes should require that judges allow children age 12 and older to make custody decisions). What do you think of this approach? According to the ALI, "[t]his accommodation assumes that the preferences of older children are more likely to conform to their best interests than those of younger children. . . ." ALI Principles, §2.08, cmt. f.

How old was the daughter in *Wissink*? Based on the aforementioned guidelines, what weight should a court give to her custodial preference in the *absence* of domestic violence? What role might her age have played in the trial court's determination?

4. *Procedure.* What is the proper procedure for soliciting a child's custodial preference in general? For example, who should do so—a judge, child's representative, parent's attorney, mental health professional? Who solicited Andrea's preference in *Wissink*? By what procedure should the child's preference be taken into account—the child's testimony? Other witnesses' testimony? GALs' recommendations? Who testified in *Wissink* about Andrea's preference? Should a child discuss his/her custodial preference with a judge in a *private* interview? See Barbara A. Atwood, The Child's Voice in Custody Litigation: An Empirical Survey and Suggestions for Reform, 45 Ariz. L. Rev. 629, 636 (2003) (reporting judges' reluctance to conduct in camera interviews with children). Should counsel be present when a child's preference is solicited? See Barrett v. Wright, 897 So. 2d 398 (Ala. Civ. App. 2004) (holding unconstitutional an in camera interview absent counsel or waiver of counsel). Should the interview be recorded? See, e.g., Couch v. Couch, 146 S.W.3d (Ky. 2004) (requiring recording and disclosure if court relies on child's private statements). How does the presence of domestic violence affect your answer to the preceding questions?

5. *Custody evaluators.* The appellate judge in *Wissink* remands for a new custody hearing following an in-depth forensic examination of the parties and the child. Why? In a custody evaluation, a custody evaluator (often a mental health professional or social worker) gathers information about the family and makes a recommendation to the court based on that information. What guidance does the appellate court judge give to the custody evaluator? What factors does the judge think should enter into the evaluation? See generally Clare Dalton, National Council of Juvenile & Family Court Judges, Navigating Custody and Visitation Evaluations in Cases with Domestic Violence: A Judge's Guide (suggesting guidelines for judges), available at http://www.afccnet.org/pdfs/BenchGuide.pdf (last visited July 16, 2011). The role of custody evaluators in the context of domestic violence is explored later in this chapter, Section D(3).

6. *Custodial preference in domestic violence cases. Wissink* involves a custody decision in the context of domestic violence. What was the nature and extent of the domestic violence in the *Wissink*? What legal action(s) did the mother take in response?

In *Wissink*, both parents petition for custody of Andrea. The trial court awards custody to the father based, in large part, on Andrea's preference. What is the nature of her relationship with her father? With her mother? Why does the appellate court reverse the trial court ruling?

7. *Lethality assessment.* In terms of lethality assessment, how serious was the husband's abuse? Of what relevance is the fact that the father attempted to elicit the daughter's support in his *physical* abuse of the mother? See Evan Stark, Re-Presenting Woman Battering: From Battered Woman Syndrome to Coercive Control, 58 Alb. L. Rev. 973, 1017-1018 (1995) (identifying the phenomenon of "tangential spouse abuse" in which the abuser implicates the children in the abuse of the mother).

8. *Traumatic bonding: origins.* Psychologists have identified the theory of traumatic bonding to explain a victim's attachment to an abuser. Psychologists Donald Dutton and Susan Painter, who introduced the theory in 1981, explain that powerful emotional attachments ("traumatic bonds") form in those abusive relationships that are characterized by two features: (1) the existence of a power imbalance in which the mistreated person is dominated by the other, and (2) a pattern of intermittent good/bad treatment that is characterized by alternating periods of relief/release and aversive/negative reactions. Donald G. Dutton & Susan Painter, Emotional Attachments in Abusive Relationships: A Test of Traumatic Bonding Theory, 8 Violence & Victims 105, 105-107 (1993); Donald Dutton & Susan Painter, Traumatic Bonding: The Development of Emotional Attachments in Battered Women and Other Relationships of Intermittent Abuse, 6 Victimology 139, 146-147 (1981). Traumatic bonding, according to Dutton and Painter, explains the "paradoxical attachment" of people taken hostage who subsequently develop strong positive attachments to their captors. Dutton & Painter, Emotional Attachments, supra, at 106.

9. *Traumatic bonding and children.* Traumatic bonding can occur in intimate partners' relationships as well as parent-child relationships. Psychologists explain that children exposed to domestic violence experience the cycles of domestic violence as fear and kindness. Those feelings evoke a longing in the child for kindness from the abuser and for a relief from the fear. The child may believe that, through an alliance with the abuser, the child will stay out of harm's way. Children turn to the batterer for relief because the batterer is the person in control of the violence as well as in control of the periods of calm. See Bancroft et al., The Batterer as Parent, supra, at 49-51; Johnston & Straus, Traumatized Children, supra, at 140.

Can traumatic bonding explain Andrea's custodial preference? How might the experience of traumatic bonding be similar for Andrea and her mother? How might it be different? Why do you think Andrea denied the presence of domestic violence?

10. *Batterers' ability to foster traumatic bonds.* What characteristics of batterers contribute to the fostering of traumatic bonds? What light do the excerpts by Bancroft et al., and Jaffe et al., shed on this question? The occurrence of litigation adds another dimension to the picture. Bancroft et al., point out that, as custody proceedings begin, batterers' behaviors may become more pronounced, and batterers

may pay increased attention to children in an attempt to persuade them to "choose" them. Bancroft et al., The Batterer as Parent, supra, at 144.

11. *Denigration of the victim as a parent.* What were Andrea's feelings about her mother at the time of the custody determination? Clinicians point out that abusers often undermine and denigrate the mother. The constant undermining of the mother and her authority can have long-term effects on the child's attitudes toward, and relationship with, the targeted parent. Being exposed to constant abuse of the mother may lead the child to internalize the message that the mother deserves to be abused and degraded. See id. at 38-39. In response, the child may speak to the mother disrespectfully and contemptuously—similar to the manner in which the father does. Id. How might a custody evaluator elicit information about the occurrence of this phenomenon—in particular about whether the child has a developmentally appropriate response to the divorce or is reflecting traumatic bonding?

12. *Favoritism.* One characteristic of abusers is their practice of sowing dissension among family members. Id. at 98-101. A common behavior of abusers is showing favoritism toward one child. If the favored child is a girl, according to Bancroft et al., the father-daughter relationship sometimes takes on "a romantic aspect in which the mother is in part replaced as the father's partner; in these cases, we have heightened concern about the possibility of boundary violations by the father." Id. at 100. Although the daughter in the principal case was an only child, did aspects of this phenomenon occur in *Wissink*? What are the consequences of such favoritism in terms of family dynamics and psychological effects on all family members? See id.

13. *Psychological consequences of alienating behavior.* The father's efforts to alienate Andrea from her mother in *Wissink* constitute a form of emotional abuse. See Amy J. L. Baker, Adult Children of Parental Alienation Syndrome 83 (2007) (identifying parental alienation as emotional abuse of children). What are the likely psychological consequences of this abuse for children *when they become adults*? One psychologist who conducted a study of 40 adults who believed that they had been turned against a parent found that the children suffer low self-esteem, substance abuse, depression, and relationship problems. Id. at 180-190. Did the trial judge and/or appellate judge give adequate consideration to the possibility that Andrea was subject to emotional abuse from exposure to the violence? The Parental Alienation Syndrome is discussed more fully later in this chapter, pp. 645-646.

14. *Countering alienating conduct.* Suppose, on remand, that the custody evaluator recommends that Andrea be returned to the mother's custody and the trial court agrees. How can the mother counteract the daughter's attitudes toward the mother that were engendered by the father? Baker recommends that the targeted parent should take an increasingly active role in the child's life if possible, becoming involved in school and extracurricular activities and spending time together at home, even if met with resistance. Baker, supra, at 268. Other experts recommend that the targeted parent should stop trying to enforce visitation, in the hope that the active attempts at alienation on the part of the other parent will cease and the child will initiate contact himself or herself. Still other experts discourage that approach, suggesting if a parent discontinues visitation, the child may feel abandoned. See Barbara Jo Fidler and Nicholas Bala, Children Resisting Postseparation Contact with a Parent: Concepts, Controversies, and Conundrums, 48 Fam. Ct. Rev. 10, 23, 38 (2010). Which approach do you prefer?

2. *Role of Child's Representative*

■ **RICHARD DUCOTE, GUARDIANS AD LITEM IN PRIVATE CUSTODY LITIGATION: THE CASE FOR ABOLITION**

3 Loy. J. Pub. Int. L. 106, 135-139 (2002)

ENABLERS AD LITEM: CHILD ABUSE AND DOMESTIC VIOLENCE CASES

One of the great paradoxes in the nation's family courts is the role of the guardian ad litem in custody cases involving domestic violence and child abuse. On one hand, the appointment of a GAL in an ordinary situation where the child is not subject to potential harm from such dangers at worse can simply raise the expenses of the parents, increase the arbitrariness already inherent in deciding the amorphous best interest issues, and compromise due process. However, in domestic violence and abuse cases, where courts are even more eager to appoint GALs, children are frequently ending up in the custody of the abusers and separated from their protecting parents. This tragedy does not happen in spite of the GALs, but rather because of the GALs. Professionals across the country are appalled that the GALs are actively and forcefully advocating for the children whose interest they are mandated to protect to be placed with violent child abusers and sexual molesters.

One of the most perplexing failures in family court custody litigation is the lack of protection and support for women and children fleeing violent homes, despite the abundant legal and societal demand for abused women to leave their abusers and protect their children. This "damned if you do, damned if you don't" dilemma causes battered women to risk losing custody in juvenile court for neglect if they stay in the violent home, and to also risk losing custody in family court if they leave and insist on the child's protection. The primary reason for this calamity is the clash between the pervasive statutory emphasis on the parent who will encourage the child's relationship with the other parent, and the domestic violence law and policy that supports parents who insist on proper protection and the separation of the abusive parent and the child. A landmark American Psychological Association report summarizes the situation:

> [Child] custody and visitation disputes appear to occur more frequently when there is a history of domestic violence. Family courts often do not consider the history of violence between the parents in making custody and visitation decisions. In this context, the non-violent parent may be at a disadvantage, and behavior that would seem reasonable as a protection from abuse may be misinterpreted as a sign of instability.

The custodial preference for the parent who encourages the child's relationships with the other parent, often referred to as the "friendly parent," typically trumps the mother and child's protection despite the fact that such "friendliness" is contraindicated.

Since GALs are usually plucked from the family court bar, they bring these same misguided principles to bear on the cases. Any attempt to claim, despite the abundant proof of the reality of the situation, that a father is dangerous is simply dumped into the category of "conflict"—the ultimate anathema in the eyes of the family court judge. In a study undertaken by the National Council of Juvenile and Family Court Judges, GALs were identified as a major problem:

> Participants [in the study] noted that custody evaluators and guardians ad litem were the professionals least trained about domestic violence of any actors in the civil justice system . . . . Evaluators and guardians are heavily influenced by the social and legal policies that facilitate contact with the noncustodial parent with regard to the risks attendant upon contact or relationship. They, like mediators, are not guided much by law as by their training and predilections about appropriate post-separation custodial arrangements. Many appear to marginalize domestic violence as a factor with significant import for abused adults and children in custodial outcomes.

Consequently, the question of whether or not brutal domestic violence or heinous child abuse occurred—a fact subject to proof as any other fact in a civil or custody case—is forgotten, ignored, or completely subjugated to the overriding concern preoccupying the judge and the GAL: "Does Mommy say nice things about Daddy and does she encourage the relationship between the two?" The maiming of the fact-finding process by the GALs circumvents the statutes now found in 48 jurisdictions that either prohibit batterers from obtaining custody or require courts to consider family violence as a custody factor. . . .

Notes and Questions

1. *Guardian ad litem: background.* A guardian ad litem (GAL) is a court-appointed representative for the child. Federal law requires states to appoint GALs in child abuse and neglect proceedings in order for states to receive federal funding for child abuse prevention and treatment. See Child Abuse Prevention and Treatment Act (CAPTA), 42 U.S.C. §5106a(b)(2)(B)(xiii). However, CAPTA does not require that states appoint attorneys as GALs. Most GALs are mental health professionals, social workers, or volunteers (such as the Court Appointed Special Advocates or CASAs). What are the advantages of having GALs who are attorneys? The disadvantages? What are the advantages of having mental health professionals serve as GALs? Social workers? Volunteers? The disadvantages? Note that CAPTA does not mandate GALs in proceedings that address only intimate partner violence.

2. *Statutory requirements.* Appointment of a GAL in custody proceedings *generally* is subject to judicial discretion, although some states mandate the appointment of a GAL in some circumstances. See, e.g., Or. Rev. Stat. §107.425(6) (requiring courts to appoint a GAL in a custody or visitation dispute only if one or more of the children request it); Vt. Stat. Ann. tit. 15, §594(b) (requiring appointment only if the children will be called as witnesses). Cf. Wis. Stat. §767.407 (requiring appointment of a GAL in all family court proceedings involving minor children).

GALs are often appointed in contentious custody cases or, as the excerpt points out, in custody cases involving domestic violence. According to the excerpt, why are courts "even more eager to appoint GALs" in domestic violence cases than in custody cases generally?

3. *Standards of practice.* Two different sets of standards of practice exist for attorneys who represent children. Note that nonattorney GALs do not have to meet these standards of practice, although they may be subject to standards of practice of their respective disciplines.

a. *ABA Standards of Practice.* The ABA approved Standards of Practice for Lawyers Who Represent Children in Abuse and Neglect Cases in 1996, available at http:// www.americanbar.org/content/dam/aba/migrated/family/reports/standards_ abuseneglect.authcheckdam.pdf. The Standards apply in (1) petitions filed for the protection of a child; (2) petitions to change custody, visitation, or guardianship involving allegations of abuse or neglect; and (3) actions to terminate parental rights. The ABA approved separate standards of practice in 2003 for lawyers in custody cases. See Standards of Practice for Lawyers Representing Children in Custody Cases, available at http://www.afccnet.org/pdfs/aba.standards.pdf.

b. *Uniform Act.* The ABA's adoption of two different sets of standards (for abuse, neglect and custody) prompted the Uniform Law Commission to draft uniform standards applicable to both areas of practice. The Uniform Representation of Children in Abuse, Neglect, and Custody Proceedings Act, 9C U.L.A. 33, clarifies the responsibilities of children's representatives and provides guidelines to courts in appointing representatives. The Act differentiates between the "child's attorney," who advocates the child's wishes, and the "best interests attorney," who advocates the child's best interests based on an assessment of the evidence. (The Act does not recognize the hybrid role of attorney-guardian ad litem.) Commentators are particularly critical of the extent of judicial discretion that exists in the appointment of the best interests lawyer, who does not have to follow the child's wishes. See Jane Spinak, Simon Says Take Three Steps Backwards: The National Conference of Commissioners on Uniform State Laws Recommendations on Child Representation, 6 Nev. L.J. 1385 (2006).

4. *Role of GAL.* Few jurisdictions have clear guidelines about the role of the GAL. Typically, GALs have several functions, including lawyer, expert witness, investigator, lay witness, mediator, facilitator, and party. Raven C. Lidman & Betsy R. Hollingsworth, The Guardian Ad Litem in Child Custody Cases: The Contours of Our Judicial System Stretched Beyond Recognition, 6 Geo. Mason L. Rev. 255, 262 (1998). The most common role is investigator. Id. at 277.

Critics charge that, with the appointment of GALs, "[t]raditional role definition is ignored; thus, permitting the performance of a function not appropriate to the role." Id. at 258. Thus, without being qualified as experts, GALs offer personal observations and opinions as evidence. Moreover, GALs have broad powers. Consider the following description:

> A guardian is not barred by rules of discovery or privilege from investigating every nook and cranny of a child's life. Guardians also have a right to determine what relevant facts should be entered into the record, or at the least to provide more credibility to one side's presentation of the facts. GALs' wide de facto power allows them broad discretion akin to a judge's exercise of judicial power. . . . With limited judicial resources, GAL opinions often go unchecked and no independent review board exists to oversee GALs.

Mary Grams, Note, Guardians Ad Litem and the Cycle of Domestic Violence: How the Recommendations Turn, 22 Law & Ineq. 105, 128-129 (2004). See also Cynthia Grover Hastings, Note, Letting Down Their Guard: What Guardians Ad Litem Should Know About Domestic Violence in Child Custody Disputes, 24 B.C. Third World L.J. 283 (2004) (emphasizing the need for uniform guidelines for GALs). Should judges always clarify the role each time they appoint a GAL? See Lidman & Hollingsworth, supra, at 259-260 (so suggesting).

5. *Extent of judicial reliance on GALs.* According to the excerpt, how much do judges rely upon GALs' reports and recommendations? One critic charges that GALs' recommendations have become the factual and legal standards for trial in many custody disputes, leaving the disfavored parent with the burden of disproving these recommendations and findings. Margaret Dore, Court-Appointed Parenting Evaluators and Guardian Ad Litem: Practical Realities and an Argument for Abolition, Divorce Litig., April 2006, at 53, 55. Why do judges place such heavy reliance on these reports?

Numerous appellate decisions find that trial courts' over-reliance on GAL reports constitutes an abuse of discretion. See, e.g., Hastings v. Rigsbee, 875 So. 2d 772, 777 (Fla. Dist. Ct. App. 2004); C.W. v. K.A.W., 774 A.2d 745, 749 (Pa. Super. Ct. 2001). How can this problem be addressed?

6. *Ethical considerations.* Do the different roles of GALs give rise to conflicts of interest? Except when GALs are acting as attorney for the child, they are traditionally described as agents for the court, rather than for the child. See Nancy J. Moore, Conflicts of Interests in the Representation of Children, 64 Fordham L. Rev. 1819, 1823 (1996). Can you think of other ethical considerations engendered by GALs? See generally Roy T. Stuckey, Guardians Ad Litem as Surrogate Parents: Implications for Role Definition and Confidentiality, 64 Fordham L. Rev. 1785, 1792 (1996).

7. *Constitutional issues.* Do GALs' broad powers evoke concerns about potential violations of due process and invasions of family privacy? According to Lidman and Hollingsworth,

> This confusion about guardian ad litem roles is startling. It arises in the legal forum where definitions are important, precision is a virtue, and role responsibilities are highly regulated. Such precision and regulation are essential to provide the parties due process, and are particularly important where the state invades families' constitutional rights of privacy,

Lidman & Hollingsworth, supra, at 259. Do you agree?

8. *Guardians ad litem in the context of domestic violence.* According to Ducote in the above excerpt, what problems arise when GALs play a role in custody disputes involving domestic violence? Consider the following:

a. *Ignorance about domestic violence issues.* GALs frequently have minimal training. Grams, supra, at 112. Moreover, they often lack specialized training on issues of domestic violence. A study by the Family Violence Project of the National Council of Juvenile and Family Court Judges reports that GALs and custody evaluators are "the professionals least trained about domestic violence of any actors in the civil justice system." Merry Noford et al., Family Violence in Child Custody Statutes: An Analysis of State Codes and Legal Practice, 29 Fam. L.Q. 197, 220 (1995). See also Hastings, Note, supra, at 295 (most jurisdictions do not require GALs to have training in domestic violence).

As a result, GALS may believe that domestic violence does not reflect on batterers' parenting ability, may not understand the harm of exposure to domestic violence, disbelieve allegations of abuse, or assume that allegations of abuse are efforts to gain leverage in the custody dispute. See Lynn Hecht Schafran, Evaluating the Evaluators: Problems with "Outside Neutrals," Judge's J., Sept. 2003, at 10. Also, GALs may fail to screen for domestic violence, fail to disclose it to the court, or may report allegations of abuse as evidence of a victim's dishonesty or manipulation. In addition, they may overlook or minimize the existence of a restraining order in particular cases. See Grams, supra, at 122 (providing anecdotal evidence of a GAL who minimized allegations of abuse despite the existence of an order of protection). Might GALs play an important role in custody disputes if they had the proper training in domestic violence?

b. *Batterers' manipulation.* Batterers can be manipulative, charming, and sensitive to their children's needs, as we have seen. Batterers may use these tactics to win the support of a GAL who is unfamiliar with the dynamics of domestic violence. Victims, on the other hand, may appear unstable, emotional, angry, or suffering from post-traumatic stress disorder, prompting the GAL to believe the child would be in a safer environment with the batterer. See Rana Fuller, How to Effectively Advocate for Battered Women When Systems Fail, 33 Wm. Mitchell L. Rev. 939, 953-954 (2007). The children may be attached to the batterer as a result of traumatic bonding, further convincing the GAL that abuse has not occurred. What may be reasonable efforts on the part of the victim to keep herself and her children safe may be interpreted by a GAL as vindictiveness. What other factors affect GALs' understanding of the case? See Joan Zorza, Batterer Manipulation and Retaliation Compounded by Denial and Complicity in the Family Courts, in Hannah & Goldstein eds., supra, at 14-2.

c. *Safety issues.* Guardians ad litem often have to conduct joint interviews or observations with parents, or act as mediators. How does this process implicate safety concerns for victims of domestic violence? How can these safety concerns be addressed by the court or an informed GAL? See Clare Dalton, When Paradigms Collide: Protecting Battered Parents and Their Children in the Family Court System, 37 Fam. & Conciliation Cts. Rev. 273, 288 (1999).

d. *Professional bias for joint custody.* Many GALs and custody evaluators are members of the helping professions, as we have seen. This professional orientation may contribute to GALs' predisposition toward making recommendations of joint custody, regardless of domestic violence. As the Family Violence Project study concluded, "Evaluators and guardians are heavily influenced by the social and legal policies that facilitate contact with the noncustodial parent without regard to the risks attendant upon contact or relationship." Noford et al., supra, at 220. How else does this professional bias present risks to victims?

e. *Friendly-parent mandates and rebuttable presumptions.* How is the friendly parent doctrine, as described by Ducote, harmful to victims? Ducote criticizes that many GALs support the friendly parent doctrine, even as it becomes increasingly disfavored by the courts. See also Dalton, When Paradigms Collide, supra, at 277. Many states have rebuttable presumptions against awards of custody to a parent with a history of domestic violence. According to the excerpt, how do GALs undermine these reforms?

9. *Custody awards to batterers.* Ducote criticizes that, far too often, the deficiencies of GALs lead to awards of custody to batterers. He terms GALs as "enablers ad litem," signifying that, like those persons who are enablers of substance abusers, GALs' recommendations facilitate abusers' perpetuation of harmful behavior. How often do courts grant custody to batterers? Empirical data suggest that trial courts do so with "disturbing" frequency, according to Professor Joan Meier. She notes that

several research studies report a significant number of cases in which abusers obtain sole or joint custody even in states with rebuttable presumptions. Meier, Domestic Violence, Child Custody, and Child Protection, supra, at 662. Her own research reveals that of 38 cases in which mothers alleged abuse and sought to limit fathers' access to children, 36 courts awarded either sole or joint custody to the father. Id. at 662 n.19. See also Hannah & Goldstein eds., supra (especially Chapters 11, 13, 14, and 18) (exploring reasons why courts frequently place children at risk by awarding custody to abusers).

10. *Policy.* What does Ducote believe is the solution to the problems caused by GALs in the context of domestic violence? Do you agree? Are there other alternatives that might address the problems that he identifies?

3. Role of the Custody Evaluator

■ **LUNDY BANCROFT ET Al., THE BATTERER AS PARENT: ADDRESSING THE IMPACT OF DOMESTIC VIOLENCE ON FAMILY DYNAMICS**
145-148 (2d ed. 2012)

PSYCHOLOGICAL TESTING AND EVALUATION

We find that psychological evaluation is widely used to assist in custody determinations, but there are various reasons to question its validity for this purpose. There is little evidence validating the ability of any psychological test to contribute to a better custody recommendation, and in fact, there is a general dearth of evidence connecting performance on any psychological test and one's level of functioning as a parent. . . .

These concerns, thus, become even greater where a history of domestic violence is alleged. Because of the absence of serious psychopathology in most batterers and because of the potent traumatic effects of domestic violence on victims, batterers often outperform their victims in psychological testing. Battered women have higher rates than do non-battered women of symptoms associated with a large range of mental illnesses problems, which can lead to incorrect diagnoses by evaluators not familiar with domestic violence trauma. . . .

The MMPI-2, which is the most commonly used psychological test in custody determinations, includes many questions that, if answered accurately by a battered woman, will contribute to elevated scale scores, such as whether she believes that someone is following her, whether she has trouble sleeping at night, whether she worries frequently, or whether she believes another individual is responsible for most of her troubles. Battered women's profiles on the MMPI-2 [according to one study] on average include elevations on [various scales, leading to the conclusion that] "similar individuals are often seen as maladjusted, guarded, alienated, and emotionally upset." This same study found battered women likely to score low on ego strength and high on desire to escape responsibility for their own lives. An earlier study of the MMPI and battered women had highly similar profile results, finding battered women tending to have quite elevated scores for anger, alienation, and confusion, somewhat elevated scores for paranoia and fearfulness, and low scores for intactness and ego strength, regardless of race. We have reviewed many custody evaluations where such psychological testing results were used to disparage a mother despite the presence of extensive evidence of a history of domestic violence that would have accounted for the findings. For example, we have read two or more dozen evaluations in which a psychological evaluator described the mother as chronically mistrustful and as looking for others to take responsibility for her life, with no reference to the fact that these test results are normative for battered women. . . . No psychological test exists that can determine whether an individual is a batterer or which batterers are most likely to reoffend, nor have we encountered any test that can establish whether a woman's abuse allegations are true. Nevertheless, some prominent evaluators believe that psychological testing should be used routinely any time that abuse allegations are raised.

Psychological tests, including both standardized tests such as the MMPI-2 and projective tests such as the Thematic Apperception Test (TAT) and the Rorschach, are poor predictors of parenting capacity and are commonly given inappropriate weight by custody evaluators. Efforts to detect psychological traits associated with likelihood to abuse children have been unsuccessful. Some individuals with substantial psychopathology parent fairly well because of healthy value systems or because of concerted efforts to insulate the children from the effects of the mental illness. At the same time, some psychologically normal people parent badly, because of abusiveness, selfishness, or unhealthy value systems. It is worth noting that the new version of the American Psychological Association's (APA's) "Guidelines for Child Custody Evaluations in Family Law Proceedings" makes no mention of the words *domestic violence, abuse*, or even simply *violence*, and thus makes no suggestion to psychologists that cases involving reports of abuse may require a specialized approach. In fact, wording in the previous version of the guidelines had stated that psychologists should get consultation from experts in cases involving complex issues such as domestic violence, but that wording has been eliminated from the latest version. . . .

Notes and Questions

1. *Custody evaluations: definition.* Courts frequently appoint mental health professionals to conduct child custody evaluations to help determine the custodial arrangement that accords with the child's best interests. The custody evaluator has the task of "assess[ing] the fit between a minor child's emerging developmental and socioemotional needs and the parents' comparative ability to meet those needs." Mary Johanna McCurley et al., Protecting Children from Incompetent Forensic Evaluations and Expert Testimony, 19 J. Am. Acad. Matrim. Law. 277, 277 (2005). Some courts appoint the same person as custody evaluator and guardian ad litem. (Many courts use the terms *GAL, Custody Evaluator*, and *Parenting Coordinator* interchangeably.) What problems arise if the custody evaluator assumes dual roles?

2. *Importance of custody evaluations.* The custody evaluator has the responsibility of giving a recommendation to the court regarding awards of custody and visitation. Many courts accept evaluators' recommendations without challenge. Judges rely heavily upon custody evaluators in the belief that evaluators have the requisite expertise and are a neutral party. "Courts feel they are more likely to hear a recommendation that truly reflects the children's interests from somebody whose sole obligation is to ascertain those interests and who has no other personal or

professional stake in the outcome." Meier, Domestic Violence, Child Custody, and Child Protection, supra, at 707. See also Janet M. Bowermaster, Legal Presumptions and the Role of Mental Health Professionals in Child Custody Proceedings, 40 Duq. L. Rev. 265, 303 (2002) (explaining reasons for reliance on evaluators).

3. *Behavioral observations of parent-child interactions.* The custody evaluator relies on several sources of data, including behavioral observations of parent-child inter-action, interviews with parents and child, psychological tests, and review of relevant records. Which evaluation methods might be most helpful in custody decision-making that involves domestic violence? Which methods might be least helpful?

4. *Use of psychological testing.* The authors of the above excerpt point out that custody evaluators routinely perform psychological tests to assess parenting abilities. Why? What criticisms do these authors assert about the use of such tests to evaluate parenting in the context of domestic violence? See also Lois A. Weithorn & Thomas Grisso, Psychological Evaluations in Divorce Custody: Problems, Principles, and Procedures, in Psychology and Child Custody Determinations 157, 162-165 (Lois A. Weithorn ed., 1987) (exploring limitations of psychological assessment tech-niques in custody evaluations); Robin Yeamans, Urgent Need for Quality Control in Child Custody Psychological Evaluations, in Hannah & Goldstein eds., supra, at 21-1 (same); Marcia M. Boumil, Ethical Issues in Guardian Ad Litem Practice, 86 Mass. L. Rev. 8, 11 (2001) (criticizing psychological testing in custody decision-making).

5. *Lack of legal knowledge.* Commentators criticize custody evaluators' lack of legal training. Their lack of legal knowledge may result in custody recommenda-tions that fail to follow applicable law. Custody evaluators also typically lack training in evidence requirements. As a result, evidence from parental interviews, conducted without the presence of counsel, is often introduced and considered by the court. The evaluators' lack of a grounding in evidentiary requirements means that they may fail to ensure the reliability of the facts they gather. "[C]ourts cannot make independent decisions where others take off-the-record testimony and weigh the credibility of parties and witnesses before reporting to the court." Bowermaster, supra, at 309.

6. *Lack of training in domestic violence.* Custody evaluators also often lack training on the dynamics of domestic violence. The Family Violence Project of the National Council of Juvenile and Family Court Judges reported that custody evaluators, like GALs, are "the professionals least trained about domestic violence of any actors in the civil justice system." Noford et al., supra, at 220. What explains their lack of training? See Bancroft et al., The Batterer as Parent, supra, at 151 (criticizing that graduate training programs often ignore domestic violence and that evaluators fail to keep abreast of professional literature regarding abuse).

7. *Quality of custody evaluations.* The above authors attribute the poor quality of some custody evaluations to several factors including: (1) custody evaluators fre-quently fail to recognize domestic violence in their evaluations of battered women, (2) they allow themselves to be manipulated by the batterer; (3) they fail to conduct adequate investigations of third-party sources of information or court records; (4) they make recommendations of custody awards to the abuser based on the belief that mothers are prone to bring false allegations of abuse and exaggerate reports of violence; (5) they have a strong bias in favor of contact with both parents, and (6) they sometimes offer conclusions to the court that are not substantiated by their observations and data. Id. at 151-154.

8. *Policy.* How should the legal system address the above criticisms about custody evaluators?

Note: Parental Alienation Syndrome

Parental Alienation Syndrome, or *PAS,* is a term coined by child psychiatrist Richard A. Gardner to signify a parent's conscious or subconscious attempts to alienate a child from the other parent. See Richard A. Gardner, The Parental Alienation Syndrome: A Guide for Mental Health and Legal Professionals (1992). Gardner based the syndrome on personal observations drawn from his work with men who were charged with sexually abusing their children. The syndrome is used to refute children's allegations of sexual abuse by explaining those allegations as fabrications by vindictive custodial mothers. Gardner claimed that the syndrome occurred with high frequency in families involved in custody litigation. His treatment recommendation for serious cases of PAS was to transfer custody to the rejected parent (that is, the abuser) for deprogramming. Richard A. Gardner, Legal and Psychotherapeutic Approaches to the Three Types of Parental Alienation Syndrome Families—When Psychiatry and the Law Join Forces, Ct. Rev., Spring 1991, at 14, 16-17.

Legal scholars and mental health professionals have vehemently criticized PAS. They point out that Gardner: (1) mistakenly ascribes a child's appropriate developmentally related reaction to the high parental conflict of the divorce context instead to psychosis; (2) exaggerates the frequency in which custodial parents assert false allegations of sexual abuse for the purpose of destroying the child's relationship with the noncustodial parent; and (3) shifts attention from the dangerous noncustodial parent to that of the protective custodial parent who is assumed to be deceitful and vindictive. Carol S. Bruch, Parental Alienation Syndrome and Alienated Children—Getting it Wrong in Child Custody Cases, 14 Child & Fam. Q. 381, 383-384 (2002). Scholars charge too that PAS is based on vague, ill-defined diagnostic criteria, lacks recognition by reputable medical or psychological diagnostic organizations, has no support in clinical or empirical evidence, and fails to prove that one parent's behavior is the actual cause of the child's behavior toward the target parent. Andraé L. Brown, Criminal Rewards: The Impact of Parental Alienation Syndrome on Families, 23 Affilia 388, 388-389 (2002).

Despite these criticisms, many courts rely on PAS evidence and award custody to an abusive parent. See Rita Berg, Parental Alienation Analysis, Domestic Violence, and Gender Bias In Minnesota Courts, 29 Law & Ineq. 5, 18-24 (2011) (reviewing use of PAS in Minnesota); Jennifer Hoult, The Evidentiary Admissibility of Parental Alienation Syndrome: Science, Law and Policy, 26 Children's Legal Rts. J. 1 (2006) (reviewing use of PAS in general in the courtroom). What explains the judicial willingness to rely on evidence of the syndrome? The syndrome has particularly harmful implications in cases of domestic violence and sexual abuse in which "all negative statements made by children about the noncustodial parent become evidence of alienation by the custodial parent." Brown, supra, at 388.

For additional criticisms of PAS, see Paul Jay Fink, Parental Alienation Syndrome, in Hannah & Goldstein eds., supra, at 12-1; Robert E. Emery, Parental Alienation Syndrome: Proponents Bear the Burden of Proof, 43 Fam. Ct. Rev. 8 (2005); Janet R. Johnston, Children of Divorce Who Reject a Parent and Refuse Visitation: Recent Research and Social Policy Implications for the Alienated Child,

38 Fam. L.Q. 757 (2005); Alayne Katz, Junk Science v. Novel Scientific Evidence: Parental Alienation Syndrome, 24 Pace L. Rev. 239 (2003); Lenore E. A. Walker et al., A Critical Analysis of Parental Alienation Syndrome and Its Admissibility in the Family Court, 1 J. Child Custody 47 (2004).

E. FLEEING WITH CHILDREN

■ DESMOND v. DESMOND
509 N.Y.S.2d 979 (Fam. Ct. 1986)

GEORGE D. MARLOW, Judge.

This custody dispute [asks] whether, in a custody case, the legal position of a repeatedly and severely abused spouse should be considered weakened as a result of her abrupt, out of state move with the children. Although the answer may seem self-evident, this precise issue has not been judicially treated in any extensive manner. And, while the [custody award] in favor of respondent-mother could be based exclusively upon a consideration of the usual "current best interests" test, the instant facts present this court with an occasion to deal also with one of the many issues raised by the entire subject of domestic violence. . . .

This opinion follows a four-day custody trial initiated by a petition filed by William Desmond, age 31, the father of two children (age 13 and age 7). . . .

The parties had their older child out of wedlock when both were teenagers. They were married about three years later. Their marriage was, to say the least, stormy and often unhappy. It was accompanied by outbursts of rage by both of them; repeated acts of physical, sexual, and emotional abuse by petitioner against respondent (some of which he partially admitted); drug use by the mother which ended several years ago; very frequent (at times daily) drug use by the father which by his own admission continued at least until the start of this trial, and much of it while the children were in or near the household; a nine-month separation from 1977 to 1978 during which petitioner fathered a child by another woman; a flagrant disregard by petitioner of his parental duty to provide financial support for his children; an hysterical, secret escape by respondent from Dutchess County to Hampton, Virginia, with the children; an occasional and inappropriate use of corporal punishment inflicted upon the children by petitioner, and to a lesser, but also inappropriate, extent by respondent; an outrageous, destructive, and illegal future offer of unlawful drugs by petitioner to his daughter which offer he vainly attempts to justify with reasoning too irrational and absurd to be worth describing herein; and a degree of mutual anger shared by these parents which, in varying degrees, has completely undermined their ability to deal civilly with each other in a manner likely to promote their children's best interest.

The court, as an example of the mother's inappropriate conduct toward the father, notes that after she fled the state with the children she secreted them from their father for almost two months. While her reasons for leaving her husband are clear and more than understandable, there was no justification for her depriving the children of any contact with their father for such a long period of time.

On the other hand, the court was most disturbed by, inter alia, petitioner's description of two conversations he had with his son and daughter. In one he admitted drug use to them, failed to discourage them from engaging in such conduct, and, indeed, importuned them to keep his continuing illegal conduct secret. In another he deliberately berated his daughter because she made positive statements to him about her life with her mother. Moreover, during his testimony, he displayed no remorse for his insensitivity toward his daughter's feelings. Finally, the court finds that petitioner has so severely abused his wife physically, emotionally, and sexually that there is little hope that their relationship can, for the foreseeable future, be an umbrella of security necessary for these children's emotional peace.

This court's findings of wrongdoing by petitioner are not intended to ignore some of respondent's parental misconduct. While she quite likely can offer some explanation or justification for her actions, they nonetheless did not promote the needed harmony with petitioner. For example, since August, 1985, she has not sufficiently communicated with the father concerning the children's performance in school, their activities, and their health care. She failed to react appropriately against petitioner's illegal drug use in the marital home. Finally, there is insufficient evidence that respondent has actively encouraged the children to call, write, or visit their father since she left with them in August, 1985.

Petitioner urges that he is entitled to custody because respondent ran away with the children and hid them in Virginia for several weeks. While that behavior cannot be condoned—notwithstanding the reasons given—this court cannot ignore or be insensitive to the circumstances preceding respondent's desperate act. Considering the limited options available to respondent in her emotional, physical, and financial circumstances in August, 1985, this court would deem it unconscionable to award petitioner custody based on this one episode.

While in many cases a sudden, long-distance move might precipitate an award of custody to the parent left behind, the instant situation does not justify such a harsh result. This is so not only because this respondent is clearly the more capable custodian, but also because the court finds that there exist exceptional circumstances which completely militate against any ruling which would penalize this mother in any way for her clandestine and abrupt relocation. Such exceptional circumstances include this court's conclusion that respondent was completely justified in escaping from the marital home, with the children, to protect their respective safety and best interests; that respondent had more than reasonable cause to be frightened by any prospect of her taking up residence locally after the proven history of petitioner's abuse; that petitioner's abusive acts substantially worsened the strife to which the children—to their detriment—were repeatedly exposed; and that her selection of Hampton, Virginia, as a new home for her and the children makes sense because it is the only site which provided her with a strong, familial support network to assist her in creating a new and tranquil environment for her children and herself. For all these reasons, this court will not allow the mother's position in this custody case to be adversely affected by her abrupt, out of state move. This holding is consistent with the settled law of this State which requires a trial court to render custody rulings in accordance with a child's current best interests.

While this holding must be construed in light of the particular facts herein, it is also intended to signal the acceptance by this court of the view that severely and/or repeatedly abused parents ought not to be penalized, in the context of a custody-visitation case, for seeking refuge out of the easy reach of their oppressors. On the other hand, this decision must, under no circumstances, be construed as giving a general license to parents to flee the jurisdiction with their children simply because there is some history of marital abuse. Thus, in order for such an escape to be precluded from reflecting adversely on the position of the parent who leaves the area, the level and quantum of abuse must be carefully considered together with all of the other relevant circumstances which surround the family. Such factors may, inter alia, include the availability of family services locally, the nearby residence of close family members of the abused parent, the severity of the abuse and the length of time it has been ongoing, the age of the children and the quality of their relationship with each parent, the presence of the children during episodes of spousal abuse and their knowledge of such misconduct, the commission of abusive acts toward any of the children, the utterance of any credible threats by the abusive spouse, the economic position of each parent, and any other factors which would significantly bear upon the children's welfare. . . .

Petitioner further urges that respondent is lying about, and exaggerating the extent of his abusive conduct. This court flatly disagrees and finds her testimony to be essentially truthful and most credible. It comes as no surprise that a woman—abused so much, for so long, and in so many ways—would effectively hide her miserable plight from friends and family alike. It calls for little compassion indeed to understand, and to sympathize with respondent's assertion that, out of embarrassment, she told no one of her pain until this case began and progressed. That a woman would feel demeaned and that she would steadfastly conceal the humiliation of forced sex, repeated acts of assault and battery upon her face, back, and buttocks with her husband's fists and feet are understandable realities rather than created tales. . . .

Finally, that petitioner's mother, sister-in-law-to-be, and best friend testified— quite credibly—in support of his contention that his wife never appeared abused and never really complained to them does not persuade this court that Jane Desmond was lying about petitioner's violence. The court believes respondent's testimony that her sustained silence over many years was borne not only of her humiliation, but of her naive belief that the violence would end by itself.

Although this court finds petitioner's conduct completely unacceptable as it relates to his quest for custody, this court still believes that, through it all, he genuinely loves, cares for, and wishes to have meaningful contact with his children. His problem has much more relevance to his inability to deal with issues requiring self-control, *vis à vis* his wife and others who evoke his anger, than an incapacity to effectively care for his children and fulfill many of their needs.

Therefore, the court directs that both parents undergo psychological counseling separately; that they provide for such services for their children by a licensed mental health professional; and that each cooperate by attending sessions as requested by the other's counselor. . . . While the court awards custody to respondent-mother, she and the children have agreed to a visitation award. Therefore, visitation shall occur as outlined in a separate court order issued simultaneously herewith.

■ SCHULTZ v. SCHULTZ

187 P.3d 1234 (Idaho 2008)

BURDICK, Justice.

. . . Kenneth Dean Schultz and Rhonda Rae Schultz were married in Boise on February 25, 2005. Their only child, Sylvia Susan Schultz, was born on May 21, 2005.

Kenneth and Rhonda had a tumultuous relationship, characterized by domestic abuse since before they married and became parents. On February 2, 2007, Kenneth was arrested for domestic violence against his wife; he later pleaded guilty to domestic battery. After this instance of abuse, Rhonda fled to Oregon with Sylvia. Rhonda immediately filed for a restraining order in Oregon, which was granted. A month later, Kenneth filed for divorce in Boise. While that action was pending, the Oregon court granted Kenneth temporary supervised visitation with Sylvia. The Idaho and Oregon courts then agreed jurisdiction was proper in Idaho.

Seven months after Rhonda fled to Oregon, and four months after the Oregon court granted him visitation, Kenneth filed a motion requesting that the Idaho court order Rhonda to return with Sylvia to Boise or surrender custody of the child to Kenneth. Rhonda opposed this motion, arguing it was not in Sylvia's best interest to move from Oregon or to live with her father, whom she had not seen in months. Rhonda also argued, based on Kenneth's pattern of domestic abuse, that she feared for their safety should she and Sylvia be ordered to return. Nonetheless, . . . the magistrate entered an order requiring Rhonda and Sylvia to return to Idaho or requiring Rhonda to relinquish custody of the child to Kenneth. Four days later Rhonda filed a motion for permissive appeal and stay, but this was denied. She then petitioned this Court for permission to appeal. . . . This case presents a single issue: whether the magistrate court abused its discretion by entering an order requiring Rhonda to return to Idaho with her daughter or relinquish custody of Sylvia to Kenneth. . . .

We cannot determine from the order whether the magistrate court looked to Sylvia's best interest when making its decision. A court must consider the best interest of the minor child when making custody determinations, and when analyzing this may consider: "Domestic violence as defined in section 39-6303, Idaho Code, whether or not in the presence of the child." I.C. §32-717(1). The court may also consider whether one parent commits child custody interference and any statutory defenses to that crime as defined by I.C. §18-4506. Additionally, a parent leaving Idaho with a child is a factor in determining the child's best interest, but not a "determinative condition in a child custody determination." . . .

In opposition to Kenneth's motion for a temporary custody order, Rhonda relied on two affidavits. In her first affidavit, filed prior to Kenneth's motion in order to support her motion for temporary support, Rhonda testified:

> During the course of our marriage Kenneth Dean Schultz physically abused me on repeated occasions. . . .
>
> While I lived in marriage with Kenneth Dean Schultz he would not allow me to take Sylvia to the doctor.
>
> While I lived in marriage with Kenneth Dean Schultz he prohibited me from working and would not allow me to collect government assistance for which I believe me [sic] and Sylvia to be qualified.
>
> While I lived in marriage with Kenneth Dean Schultz he did not obtain medical insurance for Sylvia or me even though it was available through his employer. . . .
>
> On February 2, 2007, Plaintiff Kenneth Dean Schultz had been drinking and wanted me to drink with him. When I refused he became angry. He grabbed me by my hair and slapped me, knocking me to the ground. He slapped me again while I was on the ground, then picked me up and physically threw me out the front door. Sylvia ran out the door behind me and we were both locked out of the house. I called the

police and waited at a neighbor's house. Kenneth Dean Schultz was arrested when the police arrived. . . .

Kenneth Dean Schultz has not seen Sylvia or attempted to make arrangements to see Sylvia as provided for in the Court Orders from [Oregon]. . . .

Then, in her affidavit filed in opposition to Kenneth's motion, Rhonda testified about the beginning of her relationship with Kenneth, including living in a van with him while pregnant, his refusal to help her obtain state assistance, his attempts to convince her to abort their unborn child, his refusal to allow her to go on doctor-ordered bed rest, his attempts to cause a miscarriage by hitting her in the stomach, and his telling her he wished she would miscarry. She also details four specific instances of domestic violence, each occurring while Kenneth was drinking. During one, Kenneth slapped Rhonda and then locked her in their bedroom for two days and would not allow her to see Sylvia. During another instance of abuse, Kenneth hit Rhonda, pulled her to the ground by her hair, and threw a beer at her, missing and breaking a nearby lamp. After another instance of abuse where Kenneth threw Rhonda into a wall and slapped her, she left the home to escape the battery and Kenneth threatened that she would be sorry for leaving Sylvia with him. Rhonda fled to a neighbor's home, called the police, and when they arrived, she recovered Sylvia and they left to stay with Kenneth's mother in Oregon for several weeks before returning to Boise. During the final instance of domestic abuse (the same instance detailed in her first affidavit), Kenneth physically threw Rhonda out of their home and Sylvia ran after her. Rhonda called the police, who arrested Kenneth. The following Saturday, February 3, 2007, fearing for her safety and Sylvia's safety, Rhonda again took Sylvia to Oregon. . . .

Finally, Rhonda testified: "I would like for Sylvia to know her father and I think it is important that he have a relationship with her. However, I do not want either of us to be alone with him. I will not feel safe for either of us unless he completes some alcohol rehabilitation program and maybe not even then." . . .

Kenneth refuted none of Rhonda's testimony. . . . [N]owhere in the record does he indicate that he has attempted to visit Sylvia or that he has financially supported her as ordered by the Idaho court.

The magistrate failed to consider numerous factors. It appears from the order that the only factor the court considered was the distance between the father and child created when Rhonda moved to Oregon. Such an over-emphasis of this single factor is an abuse of discretion. Additionally, this Court has made clear that a unilateral move out-of-state by one parent is but one factor to consider when making custody determinations. The magistrate court also failed to consider Rhonda's wishes for Sylvia, the extensive history of domestic abuse between the parents and in the presence of Sylvia, the fact that Kenneth made no attempts to visit his daughter either in Oregon or by having his mother bring Sylvia to Boise, or the stability and community support offered to Sylvia in Oregon. The failure to recognize these factors and use them to evaluate the best interests of Sylvia constitutes an abuse of discretion.

Likewise, although Rhonda argued that Kenneth's habitual domestic violence overcame the presumption that joint custody was in Sylvia's best interest, the magistrate made no findings and did not decide this issue. Under Idaho law, it is presumed that a continuing relationship with both parents is in the child's best interest. However, this presumption can be overcome if the court finds one parent is a habitual perpetrator of domestic violence. I.C. §32-717B(5). In light of the evidence before it, the magistrate court's failure to address this argument, in addition to its failure to address I.C. §32-717(1)(g), was an abuse of discretion; the record does not support that Sylvia's best interests would be served by removing her from a stable home with a support order network and returning her to the custody of a father with a history of domestic abuse. . . .

Notes and Questions on *Desmond* and *Schultz*

1. *Criminal liability: kidnapping and custodial interference.* Both *Desmond* and *Schultz* mention the criminal ramifications of a parent's removal of a child from a jurisdiction, that is, interference with the other parent's custodial rights. Can a parent be liable for kidnapping his/her *own* child? See, *e.g.*, State v. Washington, 690 A.2d 583, 585 (Vt. 1997) (surveying case law). See also Susan Kreston, Prosecuting International Parental Kidnapping, 15 Notre Dame J.L. Ethics & Pub. Pol'y 533, 533 (2001) (explaining that all states criminalize parental kidnapping).

Custodial interference is the modern criminal response to parental abduction. Custodial interference occurs when a parent takes or keeps the child, thereby preventing the other parent from exercising custodial rights. Both federal and state liability attach. See Prosecutorial Remedies and Other Tools To End the Exploitation of Children Today Act of 2003, 18 U.S.C. §1204 (establishing criminal liability for attempting to remove a child from the United States with the intent to interfere with another's custody rights). Many states make the offense a felony. Wayne R. LaFave, Substantive Criminal Law, 3 Subst. Crim. L. §18.3 (2d ed.). Can custodial interference occur if a parent has shared or joint custody? See id. When a victim of domestic violence flees with her children, do you think criminal liability for custodial interference should be imposed?

2. *Defenses.* Many states provide for consideration of domestic violence as a mitigating factor or, alternatively, as a defense to criminal parental kidnapping and custodial interference. Catherine F. Klein et al., Border Crossings: Understanding the Civil, Criminal, and Immigration Implications for Battered Women Fleeing Across State Lines with Their Children, 39 Fam. L.Q. 109, 111 (2005). See also Ariz. Rev. Stat. Ann. §13-1302(C). The federal kidnapping statute (18 U.S.C. §1204) contains a similar exception. What should trigger the defense? A single act? Course of conduct? Any form of abuse?

3. *Consequences of flight without the children.* Does a parent face liability if she flees *without* her children? A parent who flees without her children might be liable for criminal child abandonment or abandonment for purposes of child dependency law. See E. H. Shopler, Jurisdiction and Venue of Criminal Charge for Child Desertion or Nonsupport as Affected by Nonresidence of Parent or Child, 44 A.L.R.2d 886 (1955 & Supp.); Homer H. Clark, Jr., Law of Domestic Relations in the United States 895 (2d ed.1988). What are the reasons that a victim of domestic violence might decide to flee *without* her children?

4. *Civil law response.* Some courts, like *Desmond* and *Schultz*, recognize that a parent's violation of the other parent's custodial rights may be justified in cases of severe abuse. How does each court allocate custodial rights? Does the abusive parent presumptively lose the right to visitation? Can the victim-parent permit

visitation despite the existence of violence? What effect does the victim-parent's flight have on the respective court's allocation of custodial rights?

In general, courts assume that the best interests of the child are served by frequent and continuing contact with both parents. What is the effect of this assumption in cases of domestic violence? See Ericka Domarew, Comment, Michigan Keeps It within Limits: Relocation No More than "100 Miles," 20 T.M. Cooley L. Rev. 547 (2003) (noting that some states exempt victims of domestic violence from restrictions on relocation). See also Merle H. Weiner, Inertia and Inequality: Reconceptualizing Disputes over Parental Relocation, 40 U.C. Davis L. Rev. 1747, 1822 (2007) (urging caution when courts encourage parents to reside near each other in cases of domestic violence).

5. *Disposition.* In *Desmond*, the court awards custody to the mother, even after finding that she fled in violation of the father's custodial rights. Why? *Desmond* seemingly applies a balancing approach to the determination of custodial rights. That is, although the mother's flight was wrongful and would normally justify a custody transfer, the court determines that the father's abuse and severe corporal punishment of the child evokes the "unclean hands" doctrine to preclude the father's equitable relief. However, *Desmond* is careful to note that the father retains visitation rights. Do you agree? Do you think the court would have granted visitation if the mother had not consented to it? Why do you think she did so?

Note that the court in *Desmond* explains that it does not condone flight in the case of "minor" marital violence. How does a court differentiate "minor" from "major" violence?

Schultz disposed of the issues in a different manner. The appellate court reverses the magistrate's decision requiring Rhonda to return to Idaho with the child or to surrender custody. Why? The court remands the case to a different magistrate. Why? What kind of order might a new magistrate issue? How can the subsequent magistrate protect Rhonda and Sylvia from violence while recognizing Kenneth's visitation rights? What suggestions does the appellate court make? Note that the risk, as illustrated in *Schultz*, for a parent who flees with her children is the potential transfer of custody.

6. *Right to travel.* Do relocation restrictions infringe on a parent's constitutional right to travel? Or, only on the parent's right to travel *with* the child? See In re Marriage of Ciesluk, 113 P.3d 135, 142 (Colo. 2005) (holding that trial court abused its discretion in applying child custody relocation statute and thereby infringed on mother's constitutional right to travel).

7. *Tort remedies.* Although the custodial parents prevailed in *Desmond* and *Schultz*, the noncustodial parents may not have exhausted their remedies. Many states provide for *tort* liability for custodial interference. See, *e.g.*, Khalifa v. Shannon, 945 A.2d 1244, 1256 (Md. 2008) (recognizing tort of custodial interference); Plante v. Engel, 469 A.2d 1299 (N.H. 1983). However, other courts refuse to recognize the tort. What policy reasons militate against its recognition? See Larson v. Dunn, 460 N.W.2d 39 (Minn. 1990).

What damages are appropriate for the tort of custodial interference? According to the Restatement (Second) of Torts, possible damages include loss of society, emotional distress, loss of services, reasonable expenses incurred to regain custody (including travel expenses and court fees), and reasonable expenses in caring for the child. Restatement (2d) Torts, §700 cmt. Suppose the fathers in *Desmond* and *Schultz* prevailed on a claim of custodial interference, what damages should a court award? Should the court award "make up" parenting time for the period that the children were unavailable? See Bay v. Jensen, 196 P.3d 753 (Wash. Ct. App. 2008) (trial court awarded make-up parenting time in a relocation dispute).

8. *Effect of abandonment on custody.* Suppose the victim of domestic violence flees the jurisdiction without her children. How is her flight weighed in the determination of the best interests of the child or the application of the rebuttable presumption against custody awards to an abuser? In initial or modification custody determinations, courts will usually consider the length of the child's separation from his or her biological parents and any prior voluntary abandonment or surrender of the child. See, *e.g.*, Montgomery Cty. Dept. of Soc. Servs. v. Sanders, 381 A.2d 1154 (Md. App. 1977). These factors can weigh significantly against a parent. See Janet M. Bowermaster, Relocation Custody Disputes Involving Domestic Violence, 46 U. Kan. L. Rev. 433, 452 (1998); Catherine F. Klein, Leslye E. Orloff & Hema Sarangapani, Border Crossings: Understanding the Civil, Criminal, and Immigration Implications for Battered Women Fleeing Across State Lines with Their Children, 39 Fam. L.Q. 109, 133-134 (2005). What weight should be given to such factors in the context of domestic violence?

9. *Model Code.* In response to potential negative consequences for the parent who flees, the Model Code on Domestic and Family Violence provides, "If a parent is absent or relocates because of an act of domestic or family violence by the other parent, the absence or relocation is not a factor that weighs against the parent in determining custody or visitation." Model Code on Domestic and Family Violence §402(2), available at http://www.ncjfcj.org/images/stories/dept/fvd/pdf/modecode_fin_printable.pdf. The commentary explains:

> Subsection 2 recognizes that sometimes abused adults flee the family home in order to preserve or protect their lives and sometimes do not take dependent children with them because of the emergency circumstances of flight; because they lack resources to provide for the children outside the family home; or because they conclude that the abuser will hurt the children, the abused parent, or third parties if the children are removed prior to court intervention. This provision prevents the abuser from benefiting from the violent or coercive conduct precipitating the relocation of the battered parent and affords the abused parent an affirmative defense to the allegation of child abandonment.

Model Code on Domestic and Family Violence §402, cmt. Does this make it easier for a parent to decide whether to flee from domestic violence without her children? What help can lawyers provide to a parent who flees from abuse, with or without her children? See generally Leigh Goodmark, Going Underground: The Ethics of Advising a Battered Woman Fleeing an Abusive Relationship, 75 UMKC L. Rev. 999 (2007). Ethical issues in the representation of victims of domestic violence are explored later in Chapter 15.

10. *Relocation controversies.* Relocation controversies frequently arise in the post-decree period when one parent who has been awarded custody decides to relocate. Such cases pose particular problems in the context of domestic violence.

a. *Background.* Relocation disputes may arise because a decree, statute, or marital settlement agreement requires a custodial parent to seek permission to leave the jurisdiction. Or, the noncustodial parent may learn of the move and petition to enjoin it and, sometimes, request a custody modification. In addition to safety concerns, other reasons that a parent might want to relocate include remarriage, employment or educational opportunities, and the promise of support from relatives. In relocation disputes, some states place the burden of proof on the relocating custodial parent to prove that the move is in the child's best interests. Other states place the burden of proof on the noncustodial parent to demonstrate the adverse impact of the relocation. Until recently, the trend favored decreasing restrictions on parental moves. However, courts now are moving toward a more fact-specific, case-by-case analysis.

b. *Different state approaches.* Relocation restrictions pose considerable risks for victims of domestic violence by placing limitations on a victim's ability to relocate *with her children.* In some cases of domestic violence, courts are willing to recognize that compelling circumstances warrant relocation despite the impact of the relocation on the noncustodial parent's custodial rights. See, *e.g.*, Sheridan v. Sheridan, 611 N.Y.S.2d 688 (App. Div. 1994). Some state statutes require findings on the presence or absence of domestic violence in relocation cases. See, e.g., Ala. Code §30-3-169.3(a); Ky. Rev. Stat. Ann. §403.340; Mich. Comp. Laws Ann. §722.31; David M. Cotter, Relocation of the Custodial Parent: A State-by-State Survey, Divorce Litig., June 2006, at 89 (noting that seven states include domestic violence as a factor to consider in relocation). Is this a sound policy?

c. *Notice requirements.* Many states require that a relocating parent give notice to the noncustodial parent and the court before moving. See, e.g., Mo. Stat. Ann. §452.377 (requiring 60 days notice absent exigent circumstances); Ind. Code §31-17-2.2-1 (requiring 90 days notice). How do these notice requirements affect a victim of domestic violence who may need to flee from her abuser? Is the victim required to let the abuser know of her new location?

Some states waive or delay notice requirements in cases of domestic violence. See, *e.g.*, Wash. Rev. Code §26.09.460(1) (allowing 21-day delay in notice if relocating parent is entering a domestic violence shelter); Mich. Comp. Laws, §722.31(6) (allowing immediate relocation without notice if necessary to escape domestic violence). However, failure to give notice as required by statute could result in "changed circumstances" sufficient to transfer custody to the noncustodial parent. See, e.g., Willis-Marsh v. Wilkerson, 803 N.Y.S.2d 231 (App. Div. 2005). Is this a sound policy in cases of domestic violence?

d. *Relocation risk assessment.* How can a court determine the level of risk that an abuser poses to a child (or to the adult partner) when a custodial parent seeks to relocate? Should the court request a custody evaluator to conduct a relocation risk assessment? A relocation risk assessment, or RRA, uses research-based factors to help determine the level of risk, or possible harm, that is involved in the potential relocation, and points to one of several model parenting plans to address that risk. Domestic violence is one of many factors considered in an RRA. What are the advantages and disadvantages of an RRA? See generally William G. Austin, Relocation, Research, and Forensic Evaluation: Part II: Research in Support of the Relocation Risk Assessment Model, 46 Fam. Ct. Rev. 347 (2008); William G. Austin, Partner Violence and Risk Assessment in Child Custody Evaluations, 39 Fam. Ct. Rev. 483 (2001).

11. *UCCJEA.* In *Schultz*, the mother flees to Oregon with the daughter while the father remains in Idaho. Which state has jurisdiction to determine custody rights when one parent flees across state lines with the children? Different legislation applies in such circumstances.

a. *UCCJEA.* Virtually all states have adopted the Uniform Child Custody Jurisdiction and Enforcement Act (UCCJEA), 9 U.L.A. (Pt. IA) 649. The UCCJEA encompasses all custody and visitation decrees (temporary, permanent, initial, and modifications) and covers those proceedings related to divorce, separation, neglect, abuse, dependency, guardianship, paternity, termination of parental rights, and protection from domestic violence (but not adoptions).

The UCCJEA gives priority, for jurisdictional purposes, to the child's "home state." For modification, the state that makes the initial custody determination has "exclusive continuing jurisdiction" so long as a child or parent in the original custody determination remains in that state. The UCCJEA specifically addresses cases involving domestic violence. Under the UCCJEA, temporary emergency jurisdiction arises in extraordinary circumstances where a child is present in a state and subjected to, or threatened with, mistreatment or abuse, and allows the court to exercise emergency jurisdiction to protect the child, its siblings, or its parents (*not only the particular child in question*). UCCJEA §204. Does the UCCJEA go far enough to protect the interests of victims? See generally Joan Zorza, The UCCJEA: What Is It and How Does It Affect Battered Women in Child-Custody Disputes?, 27 Fordham Urb. L.J. 909, 917 (2000).

b. *Parental Kidnapping Prevention Act (PKPA).* In 1981 Congress enacted the Parental Kidnapping Prevention Act (PKPA), 28 U.S.C. §1738A. A principal purpose of the PKPA is to ensure that custody decrees issued by states asserting jurisdiction in conformity with the PKPA receive recognition and enforcement in other states through full faith and credit. The PKPA also assists parents in locating an abducting parent by making the federal parent locator service available to state agencies and applying the Fugitive Felon Act to all state felony parental kidnapping cases. The PKPA does not confer a private cause of action, but is intended only to resolve interstate custody disputes. Thompson v. Thompson, 484 U.S. 174 (1988).

c. *Uniform Child Abduction Prevention Act.* In 2006, the National Conference of Commissioners on Uniform State Laws (NCCUSL) enacted the Uniform Child Abduction Prevention Act (UCAPA). UCAPA is designed to address *pre-custody* dispute abductions and to provide guidelines for courts during custody disputes, with a focus on identifying families who are at risk for abduction. See generally Linda D. Elrod, Uniform Child Abduction Prevention Act, 41 Fam. L.Q. 23, 29 (2007). UCAPA allows courts to take action to prevent child abduction, such as restricting travel, requiring the surrender of passports, ordering supervised visitation, requiring the at-risk parent to post bond or security, or even taking physical custody of the child. UCAPA §§8, 9.

UCAPA takes domestic violence into consideration by recognizing that an abuser might use the Act to regain control of a mother and child who fled from abuse. See UCAPA §6, cmt. Thus, UCAPA requires that any petition for a court order or for the return of a child be accompanied by disclosure of allegations of, or convictions for, domestic violence. UCAPA §6(4), (5). UCAPA recommends that courts carefully evaluate whether domestic violence is involved in an abduction case, and points out that in many states and under federal law, fleeing domestic violence is a defense to child abduction or custodial interference. UCAPA §5, cmt. Does UCAPA go far enough to protect the interests of victims? Is it a sound policy to rely on courts to probe sufficiently into a child abduction to determine whether domestic violence is the underlying issue? See generally Patricia M. Hoff, "UU" UCAPA: Understanding and Using UCAPA to Prevent Child Abduction, 41 Fam. L.Q. 1 (2007).

Problem

David is separated from Melissa, who is the mother of his nonmarital son. David refuses to return his son to Melissa after she allows David limited visitation. David conceals the child and keeps him hidden for several months until Melissa is able to discover their location with the assistance of a private investigator. David is charged with criminal custodial interference under a state statute that provides: "A person commits custodial interference if, knowing or having reason to know that the person has no legal right to do so, the person takes, entices, or keeps from lawful custody any child who is entrusted by law to the custody of another person. For a nonmarital child, the mother is the legal custodian until a court establishes paternity and awards custody." David challenges the constitutionality of the statute, claiming that it unfairly discriminates between fathers and mothers by requiring fathers to prove paternity and sue for custody while mothers are automatically conferred custody. What result? See State v. Bean, 851 P.2d 843 (Ariz. Ct. App. 1992).

F. INTERNATIONAL CHILD ABDUCTION

■ SIMCOX v. SIMCOX

511 F.3d 594 (6th Cir. 2007)

BOGGS, Chief Judge.

. . . Joseph and Claire Simcox, both United States citizens, were married in London in 1991. They traveled extensively throughout their marriage and moved frequently, visiting approximately 45 countries. Mr. Simcox is a botanical explorer by trade—he collects and sells exotic plant seeds. Mrs. Simcox assisted him in this business and also cared for the couple's five children, each of whom was born in a different country. . . . [T]hey resided in Mexico since at least the birth of their youngest child there in 2002. . . .

The parties paint a starkly different picture of what family life in Mexico was like. Mr. Simcox describes the children's lives as blissful, filled with exotic travel and wondrous educational and cultural opportunities. Mrs. Simcox, on the other hand, claims that the children's lives were "filled with hard labor, severe physical punishment, exposure to [Mr. Simcox]'s humiliations and violent behavior[,] and long weeks of travel confined to a car." The district court expressed frustration at the "lack of credibility of both [parties]" and noted that the "disparities [in their testimonies are] so broad this Court can only speculate on the truth." [Nevertheless] . . . it is clear that Mr. Simcox was both verbally and physically violent with his wife and children. For example, the oldest child testified that he would call Mrs. Simcox a "f—ing bitch [and] a c—" in the presence of the children, and that "[h]e would maybe grab her jaw and put his finger on her neck, pulling hair." She also stated that her father once while driving banged her mother's head against the passenger window of the vehicle in which they were traveling, and that she often had to intervene by placing herself between them. The other children (with the exception of the youngest, who did not testify) expressed fear of their father and recounted frequent episodes of belt-whipping, spanking, hitting, yelling and screaming, and of pulling their hair and ears. They also witnessed their father strike their mother on numerous occasions. For example, C. Simcox, testifying in camera, recalled an incident in which her father "held [her mother] by the neck against the wall. [Her older sister] tried to stop him but he hit her." Mr. Simcox himself acknowledges that he would "physically discipline" his children, but downplays the seriousness of this "discipline."

While there is no dispute that Mr. Simcox is an ill-tempered and oft-times violent man, it is unclear precisely how grave the abuse in the Simcox household actually was. Mrs. Simcox admits that she never sought medical attention following the assaults, either for her own injuries or for those of her children, and she never reported the abuse to any government officials until the weeks immediately prior to her flight from Mexico, when she contacted the American consulate. There was also some evidence that Mrs. Simcox may have left Mexico not (or, at least, not only) to escape Mr. Simcox's abuse, but to be closer to another man with whom she had become romantically involved.

Ultimately, whether to escape her husband's increasingly violent abuse (as Mrs. Simcox claims), or to be with her adulterous lover (as Mr. Simcox claims), or perhaps some combination of the two motivations, Mrs. Simcox decided to leave Mexico with the children and live with her family in Ohio. . . . On the night of January 31, 2006, after Mr. Simcox had fallen asleep, Mrs. Simcox instructed the four younger children to pack their bags and then left with them in the family car, driving to the Texas border. . . . [The oldest daughter was living in France with her grandmother.]

Mr. Simcox filed this petition seeking return of the children to Mexico on January 12, 2007, nearly one year after the abduction. Preliminarily, the district court concluded that Mr. Simcox had established, by a preponderance of the evidence, that the children were wrongfully removed from Mexico—the country of "habitual residence" within the meaning of the [Hague Convention on Civil Aspects of International Child Abduction]—and thus the burden shifted to Mrs. Simcox to prove one of the defenses against return permitted under Article 13. . . .

[A]lthough concluding that Mrs. Simcox "ha[d] provided evidence of a *serious* risk of harm due to abuse and emotional dependence," the court noted that it could "only consider that evidence 'directly establishing the existence of a *grave* risk that would expose the child to physical or emotional harm or otherwise place the child in an *intolerable* situation.'" The court concluded that the threshold of a "grave risk" was not met. . . . . [The court declined to order the return of the two oldest children, who expressed unequivocal objections to returning, based on the Convention's authorization to consider the view of a child of sufficient age and maturity.].

[On appeal, Mrs. Simcox claims that the district court erred by holding that Mexico was the children's place of habitual residence, by misinterpreting Article 13b of the Convention which permits a court to decline to order return if such return would present a "grave risk" of harm; by adopting undertakings that required Mrs. Simcox to return and that did not sufficiently ameliorate the risk of harm to the children; by holding that Mr. Simcox had not consented to the children's removal; and by determining that the eight-year-old child was not of sufficient age and maturity to consider his objection to returning. The court affirms the district court's judgment to all issues except those regarding Article 13 and the district court's undertakings.]

Under Article 13b of the Hague Convention, a court "is not bound to order the return of the child if . . . there is a grave risk that his or her return would expose the child to physical or psychological harm or otherwise place the child in an intolerable situation." The burden is with the respondent to demonstrate "by clear and convincing evidence" that the exception applies. 42 U.S.C. §11603(e)(2)(A). The "grave risk" exception is to be interpreted narrowly, lest it swallow the rule. . . .

[W]hile all jurists would agree that some level of domestic abuse will trigger the Article 13b exception, the more difficult question is at precisely what level will return expose the child to a "grave risk" of harm or place the child in an "intolerable situation"? There is no clear answer, though this court has favorably cited a State Department report that states, "The person opposing the child's return must show that the risk to the child is grave, not merely serious." The same report also noted that "[a]n example of an 'intolerable situation' is one in which a custodial parent sexually abuses the child" because such circumstances would constitute "a grave risk of psychological harm."

[C]ourts that have confronted abusive situations tend to refuse to order the return of the children, at least where the abuse could be characterized as very serious. See, e.g., Van De Sande v. Van De Sande, 431 F.3d 567, 570 (7th Cir. 2005) (reversing order of return where the father had "beat[en] his wife severely and repeatedly in [the children's] presence," and also threatened to kill them); Rodriguez v. Rodriguez, 33 F. Supp. 2d 456, 459-460 (D. Md. 1999) (refusing return where child had been belt-whipped, punched, and kicked, and where the child's mother had been subjected to more serious attacks, including choking her and breaking her nose).

Nevertheless, even when confronted with a grave risk of harm, some courts have exercised the discretion given by the Convention to nevertheless "return [the] child to the country of habitual residence, provided sufficient protection was afforded." That protection may take the form of "undertakings," or enforceable conditions of return designed to mitigate the risk of harm occasioned by the child's repatriation. The determination of whether any valid undertakings are possible in a particular case is "inherently fact-bound" and the petitioner proffering the undertaking bears the burden of proof. . . .

Many courts and commentators have advocated the use of undertakings in order to "accommodate [both] the interest in the child's welfare [and] the interests of the country of the child's habitual residence." The same courts, however, have viewed undertakings much more skeptically in cases involving an abusive spouse. A particular problem with undertakings—especially in situations involving domestic violence—is the difficulty of their enforcement. See Merle H. Weiner, International Child Abduction and the Escape from Domestic Violence, 69 Fordham L. Rev. 593, 678 (2000) ("[T]here is currently no remedy for the violation of an undertaking. Contrary statements by some courts are simply wrong.") . . .

The State Department, whose comments are frequently cited in case law and are "accord[ed] great weight," has offered guidance on the proper use of undertakings. . . . The State Department recommends that

> undertakings should be limited in scope and further the Convention's goal of ensuring the prompt return of the child to the jurisdiction of habitual residence, so that the jurisdiction can resolve the custody dispute. Undertakings that do more than this would appear questionable under the Convention, particularly when they address in great detail issues of custody, visitation, and maintenance.

[Letter from Catherine W. Brown, Assistant Legal Adviser for Consular Affairs, United States Dep't of State, to Michael Nicholls, Lord Chancellor's Dep't, Child Abduction

Unit, United Kingdom (Aug. 10, 1995), available at http://www.hiltonhouse.com/articles/Undertaking—Rpt.txt)]. . . .

[W]e believe that Hague Convention cases dealing with abusive situations can be placed into three broad categories. First, there are cases in which the abuse is relatively minor. In such cases it is unlikely that the risk of harm caused by return of the child will rise to the level of a "grave risk" or otherwise place the child in an "intolerable situation" under Article 13b. In these cases, undertakings designed to protect the child are largely irrelevant; since the Article 13b threshold has not been met, the court has no discretion to refuse to order return, with or without undertakings. Second, at the other end of the spectrum, there are cases in which the risk of harm is clearly grave, such as where there is credible evidence of sexual abuse, other similarly grave physical or psychological abuse, death threats, or serious neglect. In these cases, undertakings will likely be insufficient to ameliorate the risk of harm, given the difficulty of enforcement and the likelihood that a serially abusive petitioner will not be deterred by a foreign court's orders. . . . Third, there are those cases that fall somewhere in the middle, where the abuse is substantially more than minor, but is less obviously intolerable. Whether, in these cases, the return of the child would subject it to a "grave risk" of harm or otherwise place it in an "intolerable situation" is a fact-intensive inquiry that depends on careful consideration of several factors, including the nature and frequency of the abuse, the likelihood of its recurrence, and whether there are any enforceable undertakings that would sufficiently ameliorate the risk of harm to the child caused by its return. Even in this middle category, undertakings should be adopted only where the court satisfies itself that the parties are likely to obey them. . . .

In applying the above framework to the present case, we believe that it fits in the middle category. The nature of abuse here was both physical (repeated beatings, hair pulling, ear pulling, and belt-whipping) and psychological (Mr. Simcox's profane outbursts and abuse of the children's mother in their presence). Importantly, these were not isolated or sporadic incidents. A psychologist who examined the children presently in Mrs. Simcox's custody found that all but the youngest were suffering from some level of post-traumatic stress disorder. Such psychological trauma could be exacerbated if D. Simcox is returned to Mexico and comes again into contact with his father. Although S. Simcox, presumably due to her young age, appears to have largely escaped the physical and psychological injuries suffered by her older siblings, nothing in the Convention requires that a child must first be traumatized by abuse before the Article 13b exception applies. . . . [W]e conclude that Mrs. Simcox has met her burden of establishing, by clear and convincing evidence, a grave risk of harm in this case.

We are confident that this holding best comports with the purposes for which the Convention was adopted, which was never intended to be used as a vehicle to return children to abusive situations. See [Merle H. Weiner, Navigating the Road Between Uniformity and Progress: The Need for Purposive Analysis of the Hague Convention on the Civil Aspects of International Child Abduction, 33 Colum. Human Rights L. Rev. 275, 278-279 (2002)] ("The Convention drafters adopted a 'remedy of return' . . . to discourage abductions, reconnect children with their primary caretakers, and locate each custody contest in the forum where most of the relevant evidence existed. [But] while the remedy of return works well if the abductor is a non-custodial parent, it is inappropriate when the abductor is a primary caretaker who is seeking to protect herself and the children from the other parent's violence.") Indeed, as the Perez-Vera Report [the official commentary to the Hague Convention] itself recognizes, the Convention's mandate of return "gives way before the primary interest of any person in not being exposed to physical or psychological danger. . . ." Perez-Vera Report at ¶29. Returning the Simcox children to Mexico, absent sufficient protection, risks exposing them to just such danger.

We cannot say, however, that the risk here is so grave that undertakings must be dismissed out-of-hand. . . . Nevertheless, as presently constituted, the district court's undertakings are unworkable. The court specifically conditioned return of the children to Mexico on their "remain[ing] in the custody of [Mrs. Simcox] in the family's residence in Rafael Del Gado, Mexico, until the Mexican Court hears and determines whether a protective order is appropriate." The court further ordered that Mr. Simcox "shall have no contact with [Mrs. Simcox] until the Mexican Court determines access and visitation rights. Upon return to Mexico, [Mrs. Simcox] shall provide [the oldest child, "A. Simcox"] reasonable access to her siblings."

The problem with these undertakings is two-fold. First, the court ordered Mrs. Simcox herself, not just the children, to return to Mexico. Thus, Mrs. Simcox could arguably defeat the order of return by simply refusing to accompany her children to Mexico; since the condition that the children "remain in [her] custody" would be unfulfilled, the children would not be returned. . . . Assuming, as we do, that the district court could not compel Mrs. Simcox to return to Mexico, the court must provide for a contingency to assure the children's safety and care should Mrs. Simcox choose to remain in the United States. Second, there may be doubts as to the enforceability of these undertakings. By the district court's analysis, Mr. Simcox has exhibited "an arrogance, a need to be in control and a tendency to act out violently"; such traits raise questions as to Mr. Simcox's willingness to abide by the court's undertakings, as do his threats to have his wife arrested upon her return to Mexico. . . .

On remand, we leave it to the district court to determine what undertakings, if any, will be sufficient to ensure the safety of the Simcox children upon their return to Mexico pending the outcome of custody proceedings. Any order on remand should be explicit as to the appropriate and efficacious undertakings that will apply should Mrs. Simcox decline to accompany her children. . . . If the district court determines that . . . the only way in which the children may be protected from harm is for them to remain in the custody of their mother, then it may be necessary to deny the petition. . . .

Notes and Questions

1. *Social reality.* International parental abductions pose a vexing legal problem. In 2009, 1,194 children were abducted from the United States. Office of Children's Issues, U.S. Dept. of State, Report on Compliance with the Hague Convention on the Civil Aspects of International Child Abduction 68 (2010), available at http://travel.state.gov/pdf/2010ComplianceReport.pdf. The return of these children to the United States depends on the application of the Hague Convention on the Civil Aspects of International Child Abduction (hereafter Hague Convention). The United States implemented the Convention by enabling legislation, the International Child Abduction Remedies Act (ICARA), Pub. L. No. 100-300, 102 Stat. 437 (codified at 42 U.S.C. §§11601-11610).

The Hague Convention was based on the idea that the likely abductor was a noncustodial father. Weiner, International Child Abduction and the Escape from Domestic Violence, supra, at 599. However, the majority of international parental abductions are carried out by custodial mothers. See Nigel V. Lowe & Katarina Horosova, The Operation of the 1980 Hague Abduction Convention—A Global View, 41 Fam. L.Q. 59, 67-68 (2007) (pointing out that mothers constitute 68 percent of abductors).

This fact raises the possibility that many of these mothers may be fleeing from domestic violence. An empirical study in 1993 of 368 parents whose children were abducted confirms that mothers are the majority of abductors and that their marriages tend to be characterized by domestic violence. (Respondents were drawn from organizations that help parents search for missing children.) The study found that violence was present in 54 percent of these cases involving parental abductions. Geoffrey L. Greif & Rebecca L. Hegar, When Parents Kidnap 36 (1993). The study also reports that the incidence of domestic violence in these relationships was twice as high as that of the general population and higher than the rate for divorcing couples generally. See id. at 30. (The findings are all the more surprising because the source of the data was the left-behind parents.)

2. *Background: the Hague Children's Conventions.* The Hague Conference on Private International Law is an international organization made up of 69 nations. The Hague Conventions, convened by the Conference, are attempts to make uniform international laws for problems that transcend the borders of any single nation. For discussion of the various Hague Conventions, see Ann Laquer Estin, Families Across Borders: The Hague Children's Conventions and the Case for International Family Law in the United States, 62 Fla. L. Rev. 47 (2010). The Hague Conference adopted the Hague Convention on the Civil Aspects of International Child Abduction (applied in *Simcox*) in 1980.

3. *The Hague Convention on the Civil Aspects of International Child Abduction.* The goal of the Hague Convention on the Civil Aspects of International Child Abduction is to secure the return of children who are wrongfully removed from, or retained in, a signatory state and to return them to the country of their "habitual residence" (which must be another contracting nation), where the merits of the custody dispute can be adjudicated (Article 12). Article 13 of the Hague Convention specifies three affirmative defenses: (1) the abducting parent establishes that the child's caretaker was not actually exercising custody rights at the time of removal or retention or had consented to removal or retention; (2) the abducting parent establishes a grave risk that the return would entail physical or psychological harm to the child; and (3) the court in the forum of the abducting parent finds that the child, who has attained an appropriate age and maturity (based on the court's discretion) objects to the return.

Currently, 85 nations have ratified the treaty. See Status Table 28: Convention of 25 October 1980 on the Civil Aspects of International Child Abduction, available at http://hcch.e-vision.nl/index_en.php?act=conventions.status&cid=24 (last updated June 14, 2011).

What are the consequences if a country chooses not to ratify the treaty? See Robin S. Lee, Note, Bringing Our Kids Home: International Child Abduction and Japan's Refusal to Return Our Children, 17 Cardozo J.L. & Gender 109, 109-110 (2010) (explaining that Japan's failure to ratify the Hague Convention signifies that

Japan "serves as a haven for Japanese citizens of international marriages who seek sole-custody by absconding with their children back to Japan").

4. *Defense: grave risk of harm.* Under Article 13(b) of the Convention, the host country need not return the child if the return would present a "grave risk" of harm to the child. Does the existence of domestic violence establish the requisite risk of harm under the Hague Convention, according to *Simcox*? What was the husband's abuse in *Simcox*? Was his *physical* abuse directed toward the wife or was it also directed at the children? Why do you suppose the federal district court in *Simcox* concluded that the threshold of a "grave risk" was not met? On what basis does the Sixth Circuit disagree? The mother alleged another affirmative defense to the Hague Convention: The father consented to the children's removal. What did the district court decide on this issue? How did the Sixth Circuit rule?

5. *Domestic violence and The Hague Convention.* Recent federal case law extends the grave-risk-of-harm exception to protect victims of domestic violence even when the violence is directed solely at the intimate partner and not the child. Noah L. Browne, Note, Relevance and Fairness: Protecting the Rights of Domestic-Violence Victims and Left-Behind Fathers Under the Hague Convention on International Child Abduction, 60 Duke L.J. 1193, 1195 (2010).

Several legal scholars urged a broad interpretation of the grave-risk-of-harm exception to extend it to situations that involved abuse of partners and not merely children. See Carol S. Bruch, The Unmet Needs of Domestic Violence Victims and Their Children in Hague Child Abduction Convention Cases, 38 Fam. L.Q. 529, 532-535 (2004); Weiner, International Child Abduction and the Escape from Domestic Violence, supra, at 611-614. Is this a sensible interpretation?

6. *Habitual residence.* The Hague Convention does not define "habitual residence," leaving the determination to the law of the petitioned country. See Maxwell v. Maxwell, 588 F.3d 245, 250 (4th Cir. 2009). Federal courts developed a two-part framework for determining "habitual residence." First, courts ask "whether the parents shared a settled intention to abandon the former country of residence." Id. at 251. Second, courts ask whether there was an "actual change in geography" as well as the "passage of an appreciable period of time" that has allowed the children to become acclimatized to the new environment. Mozes v. Mozes, 239 F.3d 1067, 1078 (9th Cir. 2001). When parents disagree whether they shared the intent to establish a new country of residence, courts look to a wide range of factors to determine the "habitual residence" of the child, including: employment in the new country, the purchase or sale of a home, marital stability, retention of close ties to the former country, storage and shipment of possessions, citizenship, and the stability of the home environment in the new country. *Maxwell,* 588 F.3d at 252. In an omitted portion of *Simcox,* the Sixth Circuit simply affirms the district court's finding that Mexico was the habitual residence of the Simcox children. On what basis do you think the district court made that determination? What information might the court have considered in its determination?

In *Maxwell,* supra, the Fourth Circuit Court of Appeals also explored the role of domestic violence in the application of the Hague Convention. The court examined whether the Maxwell parents shared an intent to make Australia the children's habitual residence after leaving the United States. There, despite evidence that the mother sold her personal possessions, completed permanent residency applications in Australia, and said farewells, the court found that she did not share the intent with the father to make Australia the habitual residence because there was also evidence that she retained return tickets to the United States, sought to return to the United States just five weeks after arriving in Australia, and testified that she only filled out the permanent residency forms because her husband took measures to prevent her from leaving Australia. Id. at 253. The children had lived in Australia for two months. Why do you think *Maxwell* reached a different result from *Simcox*? Do you think courts would prefer to resolve the issues surrounding domestic violence cases under the analysis of "habitual residence" or under an analysis of Article 13(b)? Why?

7. *Defense: children's preference.* The Hague Convention authorizes a court to decline to order the return of a child who objects to the return. Why did the district court decline to order the return of the two older Simcox children but refused to decline to order the return of the younger children (age eight and four)? On what basis does the mother object? What does the Sixth Circuit Court of Appeals decide?

8. *Custody rights and ne exeat restrictions.* Some custody decrees, especially in international cases, contain ne exeat, or nonremoval, clauses. Under such clauses, the custodial parent is not permitted to remove the child from the jurisdiction of the court issuing the decree. If a parent does remove the child, the removal may interfere with the custody rights of the noncustodial parent, triggering the noncustodial parent's right to petition under the Hague Convention on Child Abduction.

Lower courts have differed on whether ne exeat restrictions confer a "right of custody," thereby allowing a parent to petition for return of the child under the Hague Convention. Compare Croll v. Croll, 229 F.3d 133, 138-139 (2d Cir. 2000) (narrowly reading the Convention to find that ne exeat clauses are not a right of custody), with Furnes v. Reeves, 362 F.3d 702 (11th Cir. 2004) (a broad reading indicates that "ne exeat" clauses are included in "rights of custody"). The debate was settled recently by the United States Supreme Court.

9. *Abbott v. Abbott.* The federal court split about the significance of ne exeat restrictions led the United Supreme Court to grant certiorari in Abbott v. Abbott, 130 S. Ct. 1032 (2009). In *Abbott*, a mother removed a child from Chile to the United States in violation of a ne exeat restriction. The noncustodial father (who had visitation but not custody rights) brought suit under the Hague Convention seeking an order requiring the child's return. He claimed that he had the requisite "right of custody" under the Hague Convention because Chilean legislation prohibited removal of any child without the other parent's permission when a parent had a right of visitation (a ne exeat provision). The United States Supreme Court agreed, holding that the father's ne exeat right granted by the Chilean family court was a "right of custody," under the Hague Convention. The Court reasoned that the Chilean family court granted the father direct and regular visitation rights which automatically gave him the joint right to decide his child's country of residence under Chilean law. The Hague Convention, as the Court explained, defined a "right of custody" to include the right to determine the child's place of residence. Although the father's right to determine the child's place of residence was inchoate, the Court reasoned, he would have exercised it but for child's removal by mother.

Although *Abbott* did not explicitly involve domestic violence, advocates were concerned about its implications for victims of domestic violence who flee with their children. The father's success bodes ill for the argument of domestic violence victims that batterers who merely have visitation rights lack a "right of custody" to defeat the return of children. In dictum, however, the Court recognized the availability of the "grave-risk-of-harm" defense and its application to victims of domestic violence. Justice Kennedy gave the following guidance to the court on remand:

> If, for example, Ms. Abbott could demonstrate that returning to Chile would put her own safety at grave risk, the court could consider whether this is sufficient to show that the child too would suffer "psychological harm" or be placed "in an intolerable situation." . . . The proper interpretation and application of [the exceptions] are not before this Court. These matters may be addressed on remand.

Id. at 1997.

10. *Undertakings. Simcox* spends considerable time discussing the insufficiency of the undertakings ordered by the trial court. Undertakings do not appear in either the Convention itself or in the implementing legislation, but are a part of both British and American common law as an important means to protect the child who is being ordered to return to the country of his habitual residence. This approach, "allows courts to conduct an evaluation of the placement options and legal safeguards in the country of habitual residence to preserve the child's safety while the courts of that country have the opportunity to determine custody of the children within the physical boundaries of their jurisdiction." Danaipour v. McLarey, 286 F.3d 1, 21 (1st Cir. 2002). What undertakings did the district court order in *Simcox*? Why did the Sixth Circuit find those undertakings insufficient? In situations of severe abuse, what undertakings might be ordered that would protect both mother and child?

11. *Simcox's understanding of domestic violence.* In what ways does the Sixth Circuit's opinion reflect an enhanced understanding of domestic violence? In what ways does the opinion reflect a lack of understanding of domestic violence? Note, for example, the court's characterization of the severity of the abuse and the reference to the mother's "adulterous lover."

12. *IPKA.* Congress has also addressed international child abduction. In 1993 Congress enacted the International Parental Kidnapping Crime Act (IPKA) of 1993, Pub. L. No. 103-173, 107 Stat. 1998 (1993) (codified at 18 U.S.C. §1204). IPKA (unlike the Hague Convention) imposes criminal sanctions (making it a federal felony for a parent wrongfully to remove or retain a child outside the United States) and has an explicit affirmative defense for a parent fleeing from domestic violence (18 U.S.C. §1204(c)(2)).

13. *Comparative perspective.* Although federal courts take the position that Article 13(b) provides a viable defense to the Hague Convention for a woman fleeing from domestic violence with her children, courts in several other countries hold that the Article 13(b) exception should be interpreted narrowly. See Merle H. Weiner, Half-Truths, Mistakes, and Embarrassments: The United States Goes to the Fifth Meeting of the Special Commission to Review the Operation of the Hague Convention on the Civil Aspects of International Child Abduction, 2008 Utah L. Rev. 221, 286, n.330 (2008) (citing language from court decisions in Australia, Austria, Ireland, Israel, and Scotland, among others). Why do you think courts in some other countries are reluctant to provide a domestic violence defense to child abduction?

14. *Guardians ad litem.* Who, if anyone, represented the children in *Simcox*? Should the Hague Convention as adopted in the United States be amended to require representation for the children? How important is the appointment of a

child's representative in cases of domestic violence? See generally Merle H. Weiner, Intolerable Situations and Counsel for Children: Following Switzerland's Example in Hague Abduction Cases, 58 Am. U. L. Rev. 335 (2008).

Problem

A mother and father have two children in Cyprus. The father is an avid drinker and habitual drug-user who physically and psychologically abuses the mother. Although the father has never physically abused the children, he does constantly yell at them and threaten to take them away and never let them see their mother again. After seven years of this violent and tumultuous relationship, the mother and children flee to the United States to visit the mother's parents. Once there, the mother seeks a protective order against the father, who remained in Cyprus. One of the children is being treated for post-traumatic stress disorder, including bedwetting and night terrors, as a direct result of witnessing the father's abuse of the mother. The father files a petition under the Hague Convention on the Civil Aspects of International Child Abduction for the return of the children to Cyprus. The mother objects, arguing that the father's abuse presents a "grave risk of harm," triggering Article 13b of the Convention. What result? See Miltiadous v. Tetervak, 686 F. Supp. 2d 544 (E.D. Pa. 2010).

G. CHILDREN'S EXPOSURE TO DOMESTIC VIOLENCE: A NOVEL APPROACH

■ BEVAN v. FIX

42 P.3d 1013 (Wyo. 2002)

Lehman, Chief Justice.

[Two children, Brittany Bevan and Steven Tyler Bevan, through their biological father, Steven Matthew Bevan, sue William R. Fix for intentional infliction of emotional distress. Fix has an intimate relationship with the children's mother, Jenni Jones.] The facts that relate to the Bevan children's claims are as follows. On the evening of March 29, 1998, Jones and her children Brittany and Steven, as well as two teenage babysitters, were invited to Fix's home to spend the night. Jones and Fix left the children in the care of the babysitters and spent the evening drinking in a local bar with various others. . . . . [Later, Fix, Jones, and two guests continued drinking and were soaking in Fix's hot tub.] [A] verbal altercation between Fix and Jones escalated into physical violence [eventually] culminating in the violent physical confrontation that forms the basis for the Bevan children's tort claims.

According to the affidavit of Jones:

> In the early morning hours of March 30, 1998, I was awoken from my sleep by Bill Fix who was in the process of throwing me out of the bed. I landed flat on my back on the floor. I tried to sit up several times and he kept pushing me to the floor. He then grabbed my head and started violently banging it against the wall. At the same time that he was banging my head against the wall he was kicking and punching me.

Although I was barely conscious at this time, I could see my blood spattered on the wall. I finally got free of Fix and made it into the bathroom to call my brother and 911. I was terrified and confused and didn't know what else to do. Fix hung up the phone and screamed he was going to "kill" me several times. Fix then started punching and kicking me again. I managed to get to the phone again and call 911 a second time and was told that help was on the way. Fix then broke into the bathroom and dragged me by my hair out of the bathroom, out of the bedroom and out into the hallway. I believe that I lost consciousness briefly. The next thing I remember is Fix holding me up in the air against the wall, at the top of the stairs, with his hands around my neck, choking me, banging my head against the wall, and him screaming incoherently.

I thought I was going to die at that moment and as I turned my head to the side I saw my three-year-old son looking at me in absolute horror. I will never forget the fear and horror I saw in his face. Fix then looked at my son Steven Tyler Bevan and said "it's okay sweetie, go back to bed." Steven then ran down the stairs and Fix threw me to the floor and kicked me one more time. As I was being thrown to the floor and kicked again I saw my daughter and the two babysitters, Michelle and Chelsey, standing down the hallway also watching. Shortly thereafter the Sheriff's Deputies arrived.[4]

Both Fix and Jones were arrested at the scene; and, in the course of the investigation, police reports were generated which contain interviews with those witnesses present.

Relatively soon after these events, Steven began "acting out" in preschool. His angry behavior included swearing and choking his classmates. Brittany reportedly had difficulty sleeping and was experiencing nightmares. Both Steven and Brittany began seeing a counselor for their behaviors. . . . The counselor, following consultation with Steven's parents, caretakers, and teachers, diagnosed Steven as suffering from post-traumatic stress disorder (PTSD). Some months later, the children began seeing a second counselor [who] also diagnosed Steven as suffering from PTSD and, in addition, diagnosed Brittany as suffering from "dysthmic disorder," a form of depression. . . . [A third clinical psychologist, who had evaluated Brittany] disclosed that Brittany has been very depressed and, while being interviewed, admitted continued suicidal feelings. . . . The psychologist flatly stated, "I think that these children are in significant distress. I'm quite worried about both of them."

[Fix's motion for summary judgment was granted by the district court. This appeal followed.]

[T]his court [previously] adopted the third party intentional infliction of emotional distress cause of action found in Restatement, Second, Torts §46(2) (1965). . . . In its application of the Restatement provision to the instant case, the district court . . . concluded that defendant Fix's conduct was not extreme and outrageous as a matter of law, and thus granted summary judgment to him on that basis. The court determined:

[T]his case involves one isolated altercation. There was no continuing course of abuse of either Jenni or the children, and under the circumstances the conduct the children saw, although deplorable, is not sufficient to support the Plaintiffs' claim. . . .

4. According to his deposition testimony, Fix's version of events is essentially that Jones was the aggressor and instigator of the physical confrontation and that the physical contact between the two was much more mutually combative. He denies hitting Jones or banging Jones' head into a wall and rather describes the events in the hallway as a hair-pulling contest.

We disapprove the above reasoning of the district court and its application of the Restatement provisions to the facts of this case for the following reasons.

> First, no language in Restatement §46 or its accompanying illustrations indicates that "a continuing course of abuse" rather than a single "isolated altercation" is required before an actor is subject to liability for intentional infliction of emotional distress. In fact, none of the Restatement section's twenty-two illustrations, culled from actual cases, constitute a continuing course of conduct; rather, *all* involve isolated incidents. . . .

Clearly, no rule of law announced in Restatement §46 requires that the conduct alleged be repetitive or recurrent before it can be considered extreme and outrageous. . . . The district court was in error by reasoning that simply because the alleged extreme and outrageous conduct of this case constitutes domestic violence among intimates it somehow necessitates that the plaintiffs make a "showing of exceptional circumstances" such as a "continuing course of abuse" by the defendant. . . .

Additionally, we disapprove the district court's reasoning that because appellee Fix's alleged conduct was "properly the subject of criminal and injunctive relief" that fact somehow militates against a determination that the behavior is "beyond all possible bounds of decency, and to be regarded as atrocious, and utterly intolerable in a civilized community." Restatement cmt. d. Rather, the fact that the alleged conduct has been criminalized would appear to weigh in favor of recognition that society has determined the acts to be injurious as beyond "mere insults, indignities, threats, annoyances, petty oppressions, or other trivialities."

Lastly, while we generally agree with the district court's statement that, "not every *domestic altercation* constitutes extreme and outrageous conduct or results in sufficiently severe emotional impact to support a third party claim," (emphasis added) we have also consistently rejected so-called floodgate of litigation arguments to support denial of emotional distress claims. . . . Regrettably, this court must recognize the prevalence, and some argue tolerance, of domestic violence within our society; however, we cannot allow judicial fear of an avalanche of cases due to the ubiquity of the conduct alleged as "extreme and outrageous" to deny a remedy to those individual parties with legitimate claims. . . .

Viewing the evidence in the light most favorable to Brittany and Steven Bevan, we find that Fix's alleged conduct, including beating, kicking, punching, dragging by the hair, and choking Jones while screaming that he wanted to kill her, is behavior beyond mere insults, indignities and petty oppressions and which, if proved, could be construed as outrageous, atrocious, and utterly intolerable in a civilized community. At the very least, reasonable persons could differ in their conclusions as to whether Fix's conduct was extreme and outrageous. Consequently, it is for a jury to determine whether his conduct was sufficiently outrageous to result in liability. . . .

[In addition,] appellee argues that Brittany Bevan was not personally present at the time Fix's alleged outrageous conduct took place because, when questioned by defense counsel in deposition, she indicated that she had not actually *visually observed* him beating her mother. Instead, then eight-year-old Brittany stated in regard to the events two years prior: "Well, I woke up early and I heard screaming and shouting, and then I went back to sleep because I was kind of scared." When asked what happened next, she replied: "When I woke up I saw mom, I heard crying and I walked, I stepped down from the bed with the ladder, and I saw mom crying and Steven [age three] holding her and saying it's okay." When asked what else she remembered, Brittany stated: "Bill Fix slammed her against the wall or the floor. It was either one of those because I heard a bounce."

Appellee essentially urges that we reject Brittany's claim because, according to her remembrance, she was not an eyewitness to the alleged outrageous conduct. First, as a purely factual matter, it is unclear from the record precisely what Brittany Bevan observed of the violent confrontation between Fix and her mother, Jones. Jones' affidavit and sworn complaint for family violence protective order both state that Jones saw Brittany, along with her two sitters, observing the alleged beating.[9] Thus, in any event, a fact question remains as to the events actually visually observed by Brittany. More importantly, however, we do not believe that either the Restatement comment and caveat or our precedent on the issue support the very narrow interpretation of the "presence" element urged by appellee. . . . [The Restatement commentatary states that "*The Caveat is intended, however, to leave open the possibility of situations in which presence at the time may not be required.*" Restatement (Second) of Torts §46 cmt. l (emphasis in the original).]

[W]e hold that in order for a plaintiff to be considered "present at the time" of the outrageous conduct for purposes of an intentional infliction of emotional distress claim, he must simply show his "sensory and contemporaneous observance" of the defendant's acts. Consequently, the claimant is not required to have seen the outrageous acts but may still recover . . . if he gained personal and contemporaneous knowledge of them through the use of his remaining senses. . . . [W]e think the record discloses sufficient facts indicating Brittany's "sensory and contemporaneous" observance of Fix's alleged outrageous conduct directed toward her mother to preclude summary judgment against her on this element. . . .

[Next, appellee challenges the children's claims] that they sustained severe emotional distress as a result of that conduct. [A]ppellee's brief makes many factual arguments regarding the children's memories of the events, the manner in which they describe and attribute their distress, the duration and nature of their counseling, etc. . . .

We conclude sufficient evidence of emotional distress was presented to preclude summary judgment for appellee. The facts alleging the children's changes in behavior, their own deposition testimony, the affidavit of Jones, and the deposition testimony of the two counselors and psychologist who have subsequently interviewed and diagnosed the children's disorders are more than sufficient to give rise to a genuine issue of material fact on the issue of Brittany and Steven's severe emotional distress.

Lastly, we must consider whether the record discloses facts sufficient to allow a jury to reasonably conclude that Fix "intentionally" or "recklessly" caused severe emotional distress to Brittany and Steven. [According to the Restatement, liability attaches where the actor desires to inflict severe emotional distress or knows that such distress is substantially certain to result, and also where he acts recklessly in deliberate disregard of a high degree of probability that the emotional distress will follow.]

We find in the evidence a reasonable basis for expecting, and for Fix to have expected, such results. The assault in question was of a type and of such a nature as would ordinarily cause emotional injury to mere bystanders, even more so if they

---

9. This statement is corroborated by the sitters' witness interviews conducted by the police on the morning in question.

were the family members of the person being assaulted. Additionally, the fact that the witnesses are the young children of the woman assaulted would certainly cause the average person to anticipate that those children may experience severe "fright, horror, grief, shame, humiliation, embarrassment, anger, chagrin, disappointment, worry, and nausea" as a result of the witnessed conduct. [Restatement (Second) of Torts §46 cmt. j]. At a minimum, we think a reasonable jury could find that by his conduct Fix "recklessly" caused severe emotional distress to Brittany and Steven Bevan on March 30, 1998. We conclude that genuine issues of material fact are present on each element of the Bevan children's claims for intentional infliction of emotional distress against Fix. Consequently, we reverse the district court's grant of summary judgment in his favor. . . .

Notes and Questions

1. *Social reality.* A considerable number of children are exposed to domestic violence, perhaps as many as 3.3 million to 17 million children annually. Kristen Kracke & Hilary Hahn, The Nature and Extent of Childhood Exposure to Violence: What We Know, Why We Don't Know More, and Why It Matters, in Children Exposed to Violence: Current Issues, Interventions and Research 27, 27 (Robert Geffner et al., 2009) [hereafter Children Exposed to Violence]. Approximately 35 percent of households that involve domestic violence contain children who are likely to have been exposed to the violence. Shannan Catalano, Bureau of Justice Statistics, Intimate Partner Violence in the United States (2006) (based on over 600,000 victimizations), available at http://bjs.ojp.usdoj.gov/content/pub/pdf/ipvus.pdf. See also Adverse Childhood Experiences Study, Centers for Disease Control and Prevention (reporting that 12.7 percent of 17,000 survey respondents reveal that their mother was treated violently during their childhood), http://www.cdc.gov/ace/prevalence.htm (last visited July 10, 2011).

2. *Effects on children.* Exposure to domestic violence has significant effects on children, including: aggression, phobias, insomnia, low self-esteem, depression, poor academic performance, low levels of empathy, and post-traumatic stress order. See John W. Fantuzzo & Wanda K. Mohr, Prevalence and Effects of Child Exposure to Domestic Violence, Future of Children, Winter 1999, at 21; Steve Stride et al., The Physiological and Traumatic Effects of Childhood Exposure to Intimate Partner Violence in Geffner et al., supra, at 80-97. See also Rosie Gonzalez, The Cycle of Violence: Domestic Violence and Its Effects on Children, 13 Scholar 405, 413-414 (2010) (revealing that children exhibit suicidal ideation, increased levels of fear, unnatural passivity and dependency, impulsivity, and extreme crying).

Further, children who are exposed to domestic violence are more likely to accept violence in their own intimate relationships. Id. at 416-418. The effects on children vary depending on proximity to the event, severity of the event, the child's gender and age, length of exposure, the child's relationship to the victim and abuser, and the presence of additional stressful factors. Kracke & Hahn, supra, at 36. Are the effects suffered by child *witnesses* of domestic violence similar to those of children who are direct *victims* of physical abuse? See U.S. Dept. of Health & Human Servs., Administration for Children & Families, Child Witnesses to Domestic Violence: Summary of State Laws (Nov. 2009) (suggesting that the effects are similar) [hereafter Child Witnesses: Summary], available at http://www.childwelfare .gov/systemwide/laws_policies/statutes/witnessdvall.pdf

What effects did the Bevan children suffer? Were they affected psychologically, or physically as well? How old were they at the time of the incident? Were they both affected the same way? See Gonzalez, Cycle of Violence, supra, at 413-414 ("Younger children [who are exposed to domestic violence] generally suffer from poor health, insomnia, excessive screaming, frequent headaches, stomach aches, diarrhea, asthma, and peptic ulcers").

3. *Background:* Bevan. The abuser in *Bevan*, William Fix, was an attorney who represented the children's father, Steven Matthew Bevan, on a criminal charge of battery against their mother, Jenni Jones. Jones was Bevan's girlfriend at the time of the assault. Bevan and Jones later married. When they divorced, Jones asked Fix to represent her in the dissolution proceeding. When Fix later began an intimate relationship with Jenni, he withdrew from her representation.

In the principal case, the children's biological father sued on behalf of his children for intentional infliction of emotional distress (IIED), but also sued Fix for malpractice based on Fix's representation of Jenni after representing Bevan on the domestic violence charge. The former husband claimed that Fix committed an ethical violation for undertaking representation that was adverse to a former client based on a matter substantially related to that in which the lawyer previously served the client. See Restatement (Third) Law Governing Lawyers §33 (2000) (duties when representation terminates). *Bevan* affirms the summary judgment to Fix on this claim, holding that Fix was not liable for malpractice because Bevan failed to present evidence of damages or injury to him resulting from Fix's representation of Jenni. 42 P.3d at 1032.

4. *Evolving views.* Early understandings of domestic violence generally focused on injuries to the adult target of the abuse. Gradually, however, researchers realized that children, even if they were not physically injured themselves, suffer psychological harm from the violence. This recognition led to law reform, such as the imposition of tort liability (as in *Bevan*), criminal liability for exposure to violence (discussed below), and the definition of exposure to domestic violence as a form of child abuse and neglect (discussed below). The evolving recognition was also accompanied by a change in terminology. For example, the idea of children being passive "witnesses" or "observers" of the violence was replaced with the more active and inclusive term of children's "exposure" to the violence. Fantuzzo & Mohr, supra, at 22.

5. *Intentional infliction of emotional distress: background.* The tort of intentional infliction of emotional distress (IIED) was developed by legal scholars in the 1930s. Daniel Givelber, The Right to Minimum Social Decency and the Limits of Evenhandedness: Intentional Infliction of Emotional Distress by Outrageous Conduct, 82 Colum. L. Rev. 42, 42 n.1 (1982) (citing two influential law review articles in 1936 and 1939). The American Law Institute Restatements contributed to the evolution of the tort. The First Restatement of the Law of Torts in 1934 did not recognize pure emotional injury, even when intentionally inflicted, unless the defendant's conduct constituted a tort. Noted tort scholar William Prosser attacked this view. Prosser, Intentional Infliction of Mental Suffering: A New Tort, 37 Mich. L. Rev. 874 (1939). As a result, the Restatement reversed its position to permit recovery for severe emotional injuries that were intentionally inflicted, in the absence of physical contact. Restatement of the Law, Supplement, Torts §46 (1948). The Second and current Restatement continue this position. See Givelber, supra,

at 42-44; Geoffrey Christopher Rapp, Defense Against Outrage and the Perils of Parasitic Torts, 45 Ga. L. Rev. 107, 125-137 (2010) (both explaining the history of the tort). Under the *original* Restatement, would the Bevan children have been able to recover for IIED? That is, did the defendant commit a traditional tort *toward the children?*

6. *Elements.* The tort of IIED, according to the Restatement, requires "extreme and outrageous conduct" that is perpetrated "intentionally or recklessly" and that causes "severe emotional distress." Restatement (Second) of Torts §46. Each of these elements presents certain issues (examined below).

a. *Extreme and Outrageous.* How does a court determine whether conduct is sufficiently "extreme and outrageous"? How does the court in *Bevan* analyze these elements for purposes of the defendant's motion for summary judgment? Should any type of domestic violence be considered extreme and outrageous? Should the existence of a criminal conviction per se satisfy the extreme and outrageous conduct prong of the IIED test? Should certain types of domestic violence, such as stalking, qualify per se? Must the conduct be repetitive before it can be considered extreme and outrageous, according to the court? How does the Wyoming Supreme Court's ruling on this element differ from that of the trial court?

b. *Presence. Bevan* recognized the possibility that children's exposure to domestic violence might result in tort liability. How does the court define "exposure" for purposes of the tort of IIED? To impose liability, did the children have to observe, visually, the defendant's conduct? Did Brittany and Steven Bevan visually observe defendant's conduct? What does the defendant argue? What do the plaintiffs respond? What does the court conclude? In *Bevan*, Brittany testifies that she observed her "mom crying and Steven [age three] holding her and saying it's okay." Should "exposure" include the situation in which a child might observe *only* the aftermath of domestic violence, such as a child who consoles a distraught and bloodied mother? How long after the abuse occurs can the child receive "contemporaneous" knowledge? Suppose a child does not see or hear the abuse, but sees her mother's bruises the day after the abuse? Or, the mother describes the abuse to the child the next day? Or, the child observes the mother's fear when the batterer enters the room? How should "presence" be defined for purposes of exposure to domestic violence? How does "presence" differ from "exposure"? Does the standard imposed by the court leave lower courts with too much discretion?

c. *Severe emotional distress.* What emotional distress did the children suffer from their exposure to domestic violence? Was it sufficiently "severe," according to the court?

7. *Third-party harm.* The Second Restatement clarifies that the victim's emotional distress can be committed by a third party. Restatement (Second) of Torts §46(2). The Restatement provides that, where the conduct is directed at a third person, liability attaches if the person is a "member of such person's immediate family." Id. at §46(2)(a). The commentary illustrates with the example of the emotional distress of the wife of a man who is murdered in her presence by the defendant. Id. cmt. l. The commentary elaborates that recovery has been extended to plaintiffs who were "near relatives, or at least close associates, of the person attacked," and then adds that "there appears to be no essential reason why a stranger who is asked for a match on the street should not recover when the man who asks for it is shot down before his eyes, at least where his emotional distress results in bodily harm." Id. How far should recovery be allowed in cases of domestic violence? For example, could the two teenage babysitters in *Bevan* have recovered

from the defendant? Should the Bevan children have been able to bring a claim against their *mother* for allowing them to witness domestic violence? For a further discussion of "failure to protect," see this chapter, Section H(2).

8. *Legal approaches to exposure: criminal liability.* As mentioned above, the law takes three approaches to children's exposure to domestic violence: (1) tort liability for IIED (as in *Bevan*), (2) criminal liability, and (3) definition of exposure as a form of child maltreatment. This last approach is discussed later in this chapter, Section H(2).

Some states make it a separate crime to commit an act of domestic violence in the presence of a child. See, *e.g.,* Or. Rev. Stat. §163.160(3)(c) (defining assault in the fourth degree as a Class C felony if it is committed in "the immediate presence of, or is witnessed by, the person's or the victim's minor child or stepchild or a minor child residing within the household of the person or victim"). See Child Witnesses: Summary, supra, at 3. Other states enhance penalties for acts of domestic violence that are committed in the presence of a child. See, *e.g.,* Cal. Penal Code §1170.76 (the fact that the offense "contemporaneously occurred in the presence of, or was witnessed by, the minor shall be considered a circumstance in aggravation of the crime").

Which is a better approach? One commentator urges that criminal liability for exposure should not be implemented if it necessitates children's testifying "against a parent or loved one." Laurel A. Kent, Comment, Addressing the Impact of Domestic Violence on Children: Alternatives to Laws Criminalizing the Commission of Domestic Violence in the Presence of a Child, 2001 Wis. L. Rev. 1337, 1367. What do you think of this proposal?

9. *Objectives of the tort system.* The objectives of the tort system include: allocation of losses in respect of a legally recognized interest, punishment of wrongdoers, and deterrence of wrongful conduct. William L. Prosser, Law of Torts §1 at 6 (4th ed. 1971); Restatement (Second) of Torts §901(c). Does the imposition of liability for the *Bevan* children accomplish these objectives? Does the imposition of liability, generally, for children who are exposed to domestic violence accomplish these objectives? One commentator suggests that, although other tort claims exist, an intentional infliction claim is "the best way for the courts to acknowledge the child's injury and to send a message to the abuser and others similarly situated that the law will not tolerate this kind of conduct." Mary Kate Kearney, Child Witnesses of Domestic Violence: Third Party Recovery for Intentional Infliction of Emotional Distress, 47 Loy. L. Rev. 283, 285 (2001). Do you agree?

How effective is tort recovery for IIED as a remedy generally in cases of domestic violence? See Chapter 10, Section C. What legal remedies do you think should be available to children who are exposed to domestic violence?

H. DOMESTIC VIOLENCE AND THE CHILD PROTECTION SYSTEM

1. Background: Fundamental Tensions in the Law's Response to Domestic Violence and Child Protection

Fundamental tensions exist in the law's response to domestic violence and child protection. Each intervention has a different focus, philosophy, and professional orientation. The battered women's movement prioritizes the needs of adult victims of intimate partner violence. Advocates focus on women's safety by means of engaging legal actors in the criminal justice system to hold batterers accountable.

In contrast, the child protection system prioritizes children. Child protective service workers rely on the social service system to promote child welfare. The child protection system holds the mother accountable for her victimization and for the impact that domestic violence has on her children. Often, the initial response of the child welfare system is removal of the child from the home of the abused mother. Thus, the child protection system can serve as another source of victimization for the adult victims of domestic violence.

Yet, despite their differences, these two systems often serve the same clientele. Considerable overlap exists between these approaches because many families experience both forms of abuse. This section explores the overlap between the different responses. In particular, it examines the negative implications of this tension for victims of domestic violence and their children. The following excerpt highlights the source of the tension and poses some solutions.

■ SUSAN SCHECHTER & JEFFREY L. EDLESON, IN THE BEST INTERESTS OF WOMEN AND CHILDREN: A CALL FOR COLLABORATION BETWEEN CHILD WELFARE AND DOMESTIC VIOLENCE CONSTITUENCIES (1994)

available at *http://www.mincava.umn.edu/documents/wingsp/wingsp.html*

... [S]ome of the most difficult cases [that] both child welfare and battered women's programs confront are ones they confront in common. Some are two-parent households where the father is committing severe violence against both the mother and children, others are single-parent households living under a continued threat of violence from estranged husbands or ex-boyfriends, and still others are families in which the perpetrator is absent but where his legacy lives on in the behavior of the mother and children.

So much common ground might lead one to expect wide agreement and cooperation between child protection, family preservation, and domestic violence services. Yet several factors appear to hamper the ability of organizations to cooperate more fully. These include the fact that the respective movements are at different historical points in their development, they abide by different philosophies, sometimes seek different outcomes, use different professional terminologies, and sometimes compete for funding and recognition. Perhaps the most important factor slowing greater cooperation is the way that the two fields think about key issues:

BEST INTERESTS OF CHILDREN

Child welfare and protection work is commonly focused on the "best interests of children." One of the ways to determine best interest is to ascertain who can keep the child safe. In child abuse investigations, for example, workers must quickly make judgments concerning safety. From this perspective, men who batter and their victims may be equally problematic parents. If a woman is unable to protect herself, the child protective worker asks: "How will she be able to care for this child?" And even though the father may be a batterer, the worker wonders: "Is it not the responsibility of the mother to shield her children from harm?" From this position, it is easy to see why child protection workers are often more angry at abused women than they are at the men who batter them and why battered women frequently are labeled as mothers who fail to protect.

On the other side of this discussion, battered women's advocates argue that concepts like the "best interest of children" are defined too narrowly and that it is in the best interest of children to keep their mothers safe. Data from shelters and projects like AWAKE (Advocacy for Women and Kids in Emergencies) at Children's Hospital in Boston suggests that by protecting mothers who are battered, many abused children are also kept safe. At AWAKE, for example, the mother's advocate and the child's advocate work side by side to protect families. As a result, the AWAKE project reports that few abused children have been placed in foster care. At follow-up the overwhelming majority (80 percent) of battered women report that they and their children are safe. AWAKE is one model that shows how protecting women also provides protection to children.

Some child protection workers might respond that they—and their child clients—do not have the time to wait for mothers to reorganize their lives so that they can protect their children. The worker's job is to help protect children, not adults. According to interviews conducted for this report, this tension between the way many child protection workers define their mandate and the way that domestic violence advocates frame theirs remains unresolved in many communities. In fact, local and state leaders in child welfare and battered women's issues almost never explore these differing perspectives. One result is that the false but powerful assumption that the needs of women and children are in conflict is rarely challenged.

Focus on Women

The language and terms used in the movement to end violence against women often leave out attention to children. Many shelters provide far more services to women than they do to children although, as domestic violence organizations acquire more public and private funding, resources for children's programs increase, in some programs dramatically. Ironically, most battered women's shelters now provide at least minimal programming for children, and some have extensive support, counseling and prevention efforts under way. Many of these services, however, remain invisible to the child welfare community.

Historically, the goal of battered women's organizations has been to empower their clients. As part of their mission, shelters see their role as protecting women from assaultive men and from community agencies that revictimize them. One result is that battered women's programs often offer blistering critiques of child protection agencies (CPS) in their communities. Domestic violence groups have claimed that CPS agencies often blame women for the violence that men perpetrate against children, and hold men and women to different, gender-biased standards of care for children. Some shelters have defined their mandate as protecting battered women from CPS and refused to cooperate with child welfare agencies except in the most extreme cases of child abuse.

For its part, the child protection system in many communities has accused shelter advocates of being unconcerned about children and blindly loyal to women—even to those who expose their children to serious harm. Child protection workers justly accuse shelters of ignoring or minimizing the abuse perpetrated by women and underestimating the harm to children of repeated exposure to domestic abuse.

Stereotypes between the two fields are only slowly giving way. Although domestic violence programs have created hundreds of projects for children and most of them report child abuse and cooperate with local CPS workers, shelters are still frequently defined as unconcerned about children. In turn, many battered women's activists still believe that child welfare programs are uninterested in women, though many of these agencies now express keen interest in learning more about domestic violence.

ROLE OF THE PERPETRATOR

Child welfare and battered women's programs often see their role vis-a-vis the male perpetrator in a very different light. Many child welfare workers view the cause of abuse as stress within the family and focus on providing additional supportive services to "shore up" the family unit so that it may function in a healthier manner. The male perpetrator, along with other family members, is included in the work to create a healthy, functioning unit. Battered women's advocates most often view the perpetrator as using violence to exert coercive power and control over other family members, particularly women, and frame their work as an effort to provide oppressed family members, particularly women, with greater power and more options for safety. Advocates often view separation from the perpetrator, at least until he has become nonviolent, as a desirable outcome.

Both child welfare and battered women's programs might encourage the perpetrator to seek specialized services to help him change his behavior. . . . When they are part of a coordinated criminal justice response to violence, batterers' programs may provide effective assistance to some of the men who complete them, but it is clear that most men neither go to treatment nor finish their prescribed program once there. From the perspective of battered women's advocates, the safety of women and children must depend on much more than the hope that the perpetrator will finish the program he has started.

Unfortunately, leaders in child welfare and in battered women's organizations have had little opportunity to discuss this key sticking point between the fields: the relative optimism of the child welfare system and the extreme pessimism of battered women's groups about work with perpetrators.

In spite of the tensions between child welfare and battered women's programs, the commonalities seem far greater than the differences.

BATTERED WOMEN'S CONCERNS FOR THEIR CHILDREN

Unfortunately, much of the current literature focuses on the negative effects children experience as a result of witnessing violence, and ignores the concern that most abused women have for their children, a concern they share with advocates and child welfare workers alike.

While most studies show that many battered women leave their violent partners, one of the most frequently asked questions about the woman is still, "Why does she stay?" Along with this statement may come the implicit judgment that the battered woman is inadequately protecting her children. Interestingly, only a few studies have focused on the concerns battered women have for their children's safety. Yet, these few studies show that many battered women take active steps to protect their children despite the unpredictability of the violence and the effects such violence has on them.

In her study of 20 battered women, Hilton (1992) found many of the women deeply concerned for their children. In fact, a majority of those she interviewed left their abusers for the children's sake. Several women left after their partners carried out life-threatening attacks and others after their children were threatened or abused. . . . Ironically, it was concerns for their children that led almost one-third of the women in Hilton's study to remain with their abusive partners. Women stayed, despite the violence, in order to ensure necessary financial support for their children or because of threats by their violent partners to harm the children and wage lengthy custody battles if they did leave. . . .

Battered women clearly face great economic, social and safety hurdles when attempting to leave a violent partner. The decision to leave or stay often hinges on the mother's assessment of what will be in the best interests of her children. A sympathetic understanding of her reasoning and the many forces that shape her decision is of critical importance to insuring safety for her and her children.

SUPPORTING THE MOTHER-CHILD UNIT

Family preservation, child welfare, and battered women's programs also find common ground when they agree that preserving the mother-child unit in the aftermath of violence is, in most cases, a desired outcome.

Many battered women and their children face major hurdles as they attempt to create a life that is violence free. As Peled (1993) has pointed out, these changes often include a move to a shelter, a relatives' home, or even to a new city. A move is often accompanied by multiple other adjustments in a child's life including a disruption in friendship networks, a separation (temporary or permanent) from the child's father, loss of pets or belongings, and entrance into a new school. At the same time children confront these challenges, mothers are often facing their own burdens, adding further to the child's stress.

These changes may create additional physical and emotional problems. Studies have shown that the number and frequency of major life changes usually have a direct effect on a person's emotional and physical health. Moreover, the greater the number and the more frequent the changes, the greater is the likelihood of emotional and physical illness. Research studies also show that people with greater social supports adjust better to life changes than do those experiencing the same events but with few such supports. . . .

Maintaining social support for the battered woman and her children through such major life changes is, therefore, critical. The need for supporting the remaining family unit—mother and children—in the aftermath of violence is consistent with current thinking in the area of family preservation. . . .

. . . The time is right to link and expand the constituency of advocates for women and children. Despite their differences, battered women's advocates and those concerned with child welfare have much in common. We share a common and growing client population. Each field has a pressing need for increased public attention, resources, and for policy reform. As allies, rather than competitors, the fields have an enormous potential to mobilize constituencies for each other. Finally, as more and more communities call for coordinated interventions to stop family violence, agencies will be required to work together. A conceptual and practical linking of the needs of women and children would make these collaborations far more fruitful and change the way that we think about families.

2. Failure to Protect

■ NICHOLSON v. SCOPPETTA
820 N.E.2d 840 (N.Y. 2004)

KAYE, Chief Judge.

. . . Sharwline Nicholson, on behalf of herself and her two children [and similarly situated mothers and children], brought an action pursuant to 42 U.S.C. §1983 against the New York City Administration for Children's Services (ACS). . . . Plaintiffs alleged that ACS, as a matter of policy, removed children from mothers who were victims of domestic violence [solely on the ground that the mothers had failed to prevent their children from witnessing acts of domestic violence against the mothers] without probable cause and without due process of law. That policy, and its implementation—according to plaintiff mothers—constituted, among other wrongs, an unlawful interference with their liberty interest in the care and custody of their children in violation of the United States Constitution. . . .

[The District Court granted a preliminary injunction. In re Nicholson, 181 F. Supp. 2d 182 (E.D.N.Y. 2002). The Second Circuit Court of Appeals affirms the finding that ACS's practice of removing children from the home based on parents' failure to prevent their children from witnessing domestic violence amounted to a policy or custom of ACS and that, in some circumstances, the removals raised serious questions of federal constitutional law. However, the court certified questions regarding the scope of the state statutes under which city had acted, in particular the question of whether New York law authorized such a policy and whether the definition of child neglect included a parent's exposure of the child to domestic violence.]

CERTIFIED QUESTION NO. 1: NEGLECT

"Does the definition of a 'neglected child' under N.Y. Family Ct. Act §1012(f), (h)I include instances in which the sole allegation of neglect is that the parent or other person legally responsible for the child's care allows the child to witness domestic abuse against the caretaker?" . . .

Family Court Act §1012(f) is explicit in identifying the elements that must be shown to support a finding of neglect. . . . [A] party seeking to establish neglect must show, by a preponderance of the evidence, first, that a child's physical, mental or emotional condition has been impaired or is in imminent danger of becoming impaired and second, that the actual or threatened harm to the child is a consequence of the failure of the parent or caretaker to exercise a minimum degree of care in providing the child with proper supervision or guardianship. The drafters of article 10 were "deeply concerned" that an imprecise definition of child neglect might result in "unwarranted state intervention into private family life."

The first statutory element requires proof of actual (or imminent danger of) physical, emotional or mental impairment to the child. This prerequisite to a finding of neglect ensures that the Family Court, in deciding whether to authorize state intervention, will focus on serious harm or potential harm to the child, not just on what might be deemed undesirable parental behavior. "Imminent danger" reflects the Legislature's judgment that a finding of neglect may be appropriate even when a child has not actually been harmed; "imminent danger of impairment to a child is an independent and separate ground on which a neglect finding may be based." Imminent danger, however, must be near or impending, not merely possible.

In each case, additionally, there must be a link or causal connection between the basis for the neglect petition and the circumstances that allegedly produce the child's impairment or imminent danger of impairment. [In Matter of Nassau County Dept. of Social Servs. (*Dante M.*) v. Denise J., 637 N.Y.S.2d 666 (N.Y. 1995)], for example, we held that the Family Court erred in concluding that a newborn's positive toxicology for a controlled substance alone was sufficient to support a finding of neglect because the report, in and of itself, did not prove that the child was impaired or in imminent danger of becoming impaired. We reasoned, "[r]elying solely on a positive toxicology result for a neglect determination fails to make the necessary causative connection to all the surrounding circumstances that may or may not produce impairment or imminent risk of impairment in the newborn child" [id. at 669]. . . .

The cases at bar concern, in particular, alleged threats to the child's emotional, or mental, health. The statute specifically defines "[i]mpairment of emotional health" and "impairment of mental or emotional condition" to include

> a state of substantially diminished psychological or intellectual functioning in relation to, but not limited to, such factors as failure to thrive, control of aggressive or self-destructive impulses, ability to think and reason, or acting out or misbehavior, including incorrigibility, ungovernability or habitual truancy

Family Ct. Act §1012[h]. Under New York law, "such impairment must be clearly attributable to the unwillingness or inability of the respondent to exercise a minimum degree of care toward the child." Here, the Legislature recognized that the source of emotional or mental impairment—unlike physical injury—may be murky, and that it is unjust to fault a parent too readily. The Legislature therefore specified that such impairment be "clearly attributable" to the parent's failure to exercise the requisite degree of care.

Assuming that actual or imminent danger to the child has been shown, "neglect" also requires proof of the parent's failure to exercise a minimum degree of care. As the Second Circuit observed, "a fundamental interpretive question is what conduct satisfies the broad, tort-like phrase, 'a minimum degree of care.' [*Nicholson*, 344 F.3d at 169]. The Court of Appeals has not yet addressed that question, which would be critical to defining appropriate parental behavior."

"[M]inimum degree of care" is a "baseline of proper care for children that all parents, regardless of lifestyle or social or economic position, must meet." Notably, the statutory test is "minimum degree of care"—not maximum, not best, not ideal—and the failure must be actual, not threatened.

Courts must evaluate parental behavior objectively: would a reasonable and prudent parent have so acted, or failed to act, under the circumstances then and there existing. The standard takes into account the special vulnerabilities of the child, even where general physical health is not implicated. Thus, when the inquiry is whether a mother—and domestic violence victim—failed to exercise a minimum degree of care, the focus must be on whether she has met the standard of the reasonable and prudent person in similar circumstances.

[F]or a battered mother—and ultimately for a court—what course of action constitutes a parent's exercise of a "minimum degree of care" may include such considerations as: risks attendant to leaving, if the batterer has threatened to kill her if she does; risks attendant to staying and suffering continued abuse; risks attendant to seeking assistance through government channels, potentially increasing the danger to herself and her children; risks attendant to criminal prosecution against the abuser; and risks attendant to relocation. Whether a particular mother in these circumstances has actually failed to exercise a minimum degree of care is necessarily dependent on facts such as the severity and frequency of the violence, and the resources and options available to her.

Only when a petitioner demonstrates, by a preponderance of evidence, that both elements of section 1012(f) are satisfied may a child be deemed neglected under the statute. When "the sole allegation" is that the mother has been abused and the child has witnessed the abuse, such a showing has not been made. This does not mean, however, that a child can never be "neglected" when living in a household plagued by domestic violence. Conceivably, neglect might be found where a record establishes that, for example, the mother acknowledged that the children knew of repeated domestic violence by her paramour and had reason to be afraid of him, yet nonetheless allowed him several times to return to her home, and lacked awareness of any impact of the violence on the children; or where the children were exposed to regular and continuous extremely violent conduct between their parents, several times requiring official intervention, and where caseworkers testified to the fear and distress the children were experiencing as a result of their long exposure to the violence.

In such circumstances, the battered mother is charged with neglect not because she is a victim of domestic violence or because her children witnessed the abuse, but rather because a preponderance of the evidence establishes that the children were actually or imminently harmed by reason of her failure to exercise even minimal care in providing them with proper oversight. . . .

■ **JILL M. ZUCCARDY, NICHOLSON v. WILLIAMS: THE CASE**

82 Denv. U. L. Rev. 655, 657-660, 663-665, 667, 669 (2005)

[The author was co-counsel in Nicholson v. Williams, 203 F. Supp. 2d 153 (E.D.N.Y. 2002).]

[I]n 1999, I met Sharwline Nicholson. Sharwline had been separated from her child's father for some time. He lived in South Carolina. Although he had not been a model partner during the relationship, he was never physically abusive toward her or threatened physical abuse during the relationship.

From time to time [however] after Sharwline and her child's father separated, he came to New York to visit his infant daughter. During one visit, he got into an argument with Sharwline and became enraged. He beat her very badly. She managed to call 911, and he took off. Her son was at school and her infant daughter was asleep in the other room.

Sharwline was very seriously injured. She had a broken arm; she had a concussion; she was bleeding from numerous wounds. Yet, even before the police arrived, her first thought was of her children. She called her neighbor, who was her regular child care provider, and had the neighbor come over, get the baby and pick up the son from school. Sharwline was removed by ambulance, thinking that her children were safely with the babysitter. She provided every piece of information she could think of so that the police could capture the abuser, although she believed that he immediately fled the state.

While Sharwline was in the hospital, the police—and to this day we don't know why—went to the neighbor's home with their guns drawn and took custody of the children. This all sounds incredible, but it's true. They called Sharwline at the hospital and said, "We have your children here at the precinct. We can't allow them to be in the custody of a stranger," which is not an accurate statement of New York law by any means. A fit parent has the right to make child care arrangements for his or her child. In any event, they said, "You have to call a relative to take care of the children."

So, Sharwline called her cousin in New Jersey. By now, it was ten or eleven o'clock at night. Sharwline's cousin went to the hospital, told Sharwline that she would go to the precinct and get the children and everything would be okay. However, when Sharwline's cousin went to the precinct, the police refused to release the children, saying the children could not be taken out of state to New Jersey. Again, this was not a proper statement of the law.

Sharwline received a telephone call early the next morning—and the person on the other end of the line said, "This is ACS. We have your children. If you want to see them, you'll need to go to court. We'll call you back and tell you the date." Sharwline immediately left the hospital against medical advice and went off in search of her children. ACS did not file in court until five days later. So, Sharwline had five days during which she did not know where her children were or whether they were being cared for.

When Sharwline finally had an opportunity to appear in court, she learned that she had been charged with child neglect for "engaging in domestic violence." Make no mistake. Sharwline was not accused of perpetrating any violence. She was accused of being a victim and she was accused of being a neglectful mother because she was a victim. . . .

When I got Sharwline's case, I was blown away. . . . I thought the case was some sort of aberration, some sort of a mistake. But as Sharwline's story unfolded over the next nine months that it took to get the charges against her dismissed, so did the stories of many other survivors. . . . [T]here are a few worth mentioning.

Ekaete Udoh, a Nigerian woman, had five daughters and was married to a very strict and punitive Nigerian man, who believed he had a right to take a second wife because his wife had only produced daughters for him. He was very free in admitting that this was the reason that he would beat her, because she wouldn't consent to his taking of a second wife. . . . She had been to court approximately twenty-three times to try to get him excluded from the home, to try to get child support, and to try to get visitation limited. . . . There was another incident of abuse—and in this incident, he hit the child. Mrs. Udoh reported the incident to the police, but her husband was not arrested. However, a teacher reported the incident to ACS. ACS came to the home and, with no investigation, removed all four of her minor children. Mrs. Udoh was charged with child neglect for "engaging in domestic violence" for twenty-five years. . . .

In the class action which ultimately came to pass . . . the theory in all of [their] cases was that the children were suffering, or in danger of suffering, emotional harm from exposure to domestic violence against their mothers and, therefore, should be removed from their mothers. These were not cases in which the City alleged that the children were in danger of physical harm, or that the mother had failed to protect the child from physical harm. Rather, they all focused on the presumption that exposure to domestic violence, per se, constituted impairment rising to the level of imminent harm and neglect under our child welfare statutes. . . .

[T]he city put forth one defense only, "We don't do this. We don't remove children solely or primarily because of domestic violence, period." The city said, "We employ best practices. Look at our written policies." And, in fact, except for [their] mission statement . . . , the ACS domestic violence policies and guiding principles looked really good on paper. Thus, it made the case simpler for us that ACS actually agreed with us as to what constituted best practices in child welfare cases involving domestic violence. They claimed they already employed them; we claimed that they didn't. . . .

The city [ ] waved its written policies like a banner throughout the case. And, as I mentioned, their written policies were actually pretty good. The problem was the disconnection between the written policies and the actual policies and practices. We illustrated this disconnection. . . . [W]e focused our case on, and called as our witnesses, child protective managers at ACS who were involved in some of the cases of the class members. The child protective managers are third-level supervisors who sign off on all removals.

Deposing them and questioning them at trial might have been fun, if it wasn't so sad. They were naïvely honest, believing that their actions were righteous. Some had not seen the agency's written domestic violence policies or, if they had, were only vaguely familiar with them. The child protective managers' description of the agency's practices with regard to domestic violence supported our contentions. . . .

I think *Nicholson* was a unique case for systemic reform: we believed that due to the nature of the lawsuit, because the safety of children was involved, the case could not just be about proving that the city's practices were unconstitutional or that they violated the civil rights of battered mothers and their children. We firmly believed that in order to prevail, we must educate, and challenge head-on some of society's most deeply held biases and judgments regarding domestic violence and child welfare. And we had to show that what the city was doing was hurting children. . . .

We also felt that we had to challenge the notion that removing children from their parents is erring on the side of safety. You hear that a lot. There is a notion that foster care provides safety for children. This is simply not true. . . . Many of our clients' children suffered in foster care, ranging from the physical abuse of Sharwline's son, to various incidents of medical neglect and emotional harm. The mothers' testimony about their children's experience in foster care was very powerful. But we did not only use the mothers, the literature and the experts to help us establish the trauma and danger of foster care.

We called the older children as witnesses. Listening to one fourteen-year-old describe her experience, Judge Weinstein and everyone in the courtroom, including the city's attorneys, became teary-eyed and Judge Weinstein had to call a ten-minute recess. Listening to her describe her trauma of being taken from her mother and being placed in foster care was one of the most wrenching moments in the trial. . . .

The *Nicholson* decision had a domino effect locally and nationwide. ACS stopped removing children from battered mothers, and the case spurred them to make vast improvements in their child welfare practice . . .

Note: The Green Book Initiative

A collaboration of family court judges and experts in the fields of domestic violence and child welfare produced an influential report in 1999 that contained recommendations for the improvement of child welfare proceedings involving families that experience domestic violence. In recognition of the problems engendered by the co-occurrence of domestic violence and child abuse, the National Council of Juvenile and Family Court Judges published Effective Intervention in Domestic Violence and Child Maltreatment Cases: Guidelines for Policy and Practice (1999), available at http://www.ncjfcj.org/images/stories/dept/fvd/pdf/greenbook%20_final_4-5-07.pdf (popularly known as the "Green Book" because of the color of its cover). The Green Book highlights the traditional problems at the interface of the law's response to child welfare and domestic violence and also poses solutions to those problems.

Domestic violence advocates and child welfare professionals have a longstanding troubled relationship. Child welfare agencies, with their focus on child protection, promoted child welfare at the expense of mothers by removing children from homes allegedly on the basis of the mothers' failure to protect their children from exposure to domestic violence. Domestic violence advocates criticized this approach for placing responsibility for the violence on the abused mother, rather than promoting the batterer's accountability for the effects of his violence on the children. They also charged that this approach reflects gender-bias in the courts (as well as in the larger culture) by blaming problems concerning children on their mothers and thereby absolving fathers of responsibility. In their defense, child welfare workers contended that their focus on child protection meant that they were required to make expeditious decisions about child safety.

Child welfare agencies and domestic violence advocates often conceptualized differently the role of the batterer. Child welfare professionals view domestic violence as a symptom of dysfunctional families and strive to re-establish a functioning family unit. Conversely, domestic violence advocates view separation from the perpetrator as the only option to provide safety for the victim and her children. Domestic violence advocates view child protective agencies as another government institution that ignores or minimizes the plight of battered women. Advocates charge that child protective agencies misunderstand the dynamics of domestic violence and that their ignorance contributes to the legal system's difficulty in responding effectively to domestic violence.

Both sides of the debate rebuke the other. Domestic violence advocates point to mothers who have lost parental rights to abusive fathers because child welfare workers ignored evidence of abuse and refused to recognize the effects of abuse on the children. Child welfare workers castigate victims of domestic violence for contributing to the fate of children who are severely injured or killed in homes afflicted by domestic violence.

Amidst this atmosphere, the National Council launched the Green Book Initiative. The committee drafted recommendations for best practices in the provision of services, addressing topics such as culturally competent practice, batterer accountability, the needs of battered immigrant women, and supervised visitation. The objectives of the Initiative were: a policy disfavoring removal of a child from a nonabusive parent; a priority on the protection of the victim, as well as the child, for all agencies that are involved in a case; and a policy of holding batterers accountable for the damage they inflict on families. Recognizing the need for collaboration between service providers to achieve these goals, the recommendations set forth guidelines for agencies to use when working together.

These recommendations instructed courts and agencies as follows: Multiple points of entry should be created for families needing services, and any gaps in services should be addressed; services should be provided without the need to open a child protection case in all cases; courts and welfare agencies should engage in continuous assessment of the family, offering to those batterers who complete an intervention program an opportunity to continue a relationship with his children, while not penalizing a victim that attempts to sever all of *her own* ties to the batterer, to the greatest extent possible.

The report also provides instructions specific to each type of service provider. It charged domestic violence organizations with educating service providers and courts about the dynamics of domestic violence. It encouraged child protective agencies to develop screening and assessment tools to determine if domestic violence is present in child maltreatment cases, and to provide clients with information on available resources from other service providers in the community. It suggested that agencies develop clear criteria for circumstances in which children are allowed to remain with the nonoffending parent, and establish procedures for developing safety plans for both mother and child. It instructed domestic violence organizations to expand services, and to ensure that existing services can accommodate children. It also encouraged dependency courts (that address abused and neglected children) to remain in continuous close contact with criminal courts to ensure batterers' accountability.

The Green Book had a significant influence on legal policy when the trial court in In re Nicholson, 181 F. Supp. 2d 182 (E.D.N.Y. 2000), relied heavily on its findings. In addition to ruling that the New York City child welfare practice of removing children from abused mothers was unconstitutional, the district court ordered the child welfare agency to revise its practices and to coordinate with domestic violence advocates to craft improvements in the handling of such cases. Together, the Green Book and the *Nicholson* decision fundamentally changed the approach of child protective services to those child welfare cases involving domestic violence.

For additional commentary on the Green Book, see Meier, Domestic Violence, Child Custody, and Child Protection, supra, at 661-664, 715, 718-720, 724-725.

Notes and Questions

1. *Juvenile court jurisdiction for abuse and neglect.* Every state has a jurisdictional statute that authorizes courts to assume jurisdiction over children who are endangered because of parental abuse or neglect. Typically, these statutory standards are

broad and vague. The juvenile court's jurisdiction over child abuse and neglect is called "dependency jurisdiction" because the child victims become "dependents" of the state. The source of that jurisdiction is the doctrine of "parens patriae" ("parent of the country"), that is, the state's power to intervene in cases of abuse or neglect and to act as the parent of any child who is in need of protection. In addition to its dependency jurisdiction, the juvenile court also has jurisdiction over juvenile delinquency and status offenses (that is, acts of noncriminal misbehavior of children).

2. *Constitutional right to family integrity.* The right to family integrity is protected by substantive due process. The U.S. Supreme Court cases of Meyer v. Nebraska, 262 U.S. 390 (1923), and Pierce v. Society of Sisters, 268 U.S. 510 (1925), established broad liberal principles of family autonomy in the face of government intervention. These foundational cases affirm that parents have a constitutional right to the care, custody, and control of their children. However, this parental right is not absolute. In Prince v. Massachusetts, 321 U.S. 158 (1944), the Supreme Court established that the state has the right to intervene to remove children from the home in cases of child endangerment based on the state's parens patriae power. What role does constitutional protection of the parent-child relationship play in the analysis in *Nicholson?* How did the New York child welfare procedures violate the mothers' constitutional rights?

3. *Stages of intervention.* State intervention in cases of child abuse and neglect takes two forms: summary seizure or the assertion of temporary custody. If the court determines that an emergency exists, the court may order (in an ex parte hearing) that the child be immediately removed from the home. On the other hand, the adversarial proceeding regarding temporary custody (termed a "jurisdictional hearing") determines whether the child falls within the statutory definition of an abused or neglected child. The next stage of juvenile court intervention occurs after the jurisdictional determination—when the court conducts a "dispositional hearing." At that time, the court chooses among various dispositions (for example, conditions on custody, foster care, termination of parental rights). What were the various forms of state intervention in Sharwline Nicholson's case?

4. Nicholson: *holding. Nicholson* involved a challenge to the New York child welfare system. Was *Nicholson* a challenge to the constitutionality of New York's child welfare law or practice? What does the New York statute require for a finding of child neglect? How were the children in *Nicholson* allegedly neglected by their mothers? What actions did the state social service workers take in response to their beliefs that the children were neglected? How did the state agencies' written policies differ from their actual practices? How did the plaintiffs' prove the discrepancy? How did these practices violate plaintiffs' rights?

5. *Exposure to domestic violence as neglect. Nicholson* dealt with an interpretation of state law that state social service workers were applying to children who were exposed to domestic violence. Some states responded to the problem of exposure of children to domestic violence by legislation that defines childhood exposure to domestic violence as a form of child abuse and neglect. See Lois A. Weithorn, Protecting Children from Exposure to Domestic Violence: The Use and Abuse of Child Maltreatment Statutes, 53 Hastings L.J. 1 (2001). Various policy rationales support this approach, including that the statutes: (1) bring children who are exposed to domestic violence to the attention of authorities, (2) make available the resources of the child protective system, (3) promote consistency in interagency

handling of domestic violence among children, and (4) send a message to domestic violence perpetrators and the community that domestic violence is harmful. Id. at 26-41. How well do the statutes accomplish these purposes?

6. *Blanket presumptions.* In *Nicholson,* the New York Court of Appeals ruled that exposure to domestic violence does not presumptively establish neglect and that removal requires additional particularized evidence. Other blanket presumptions exist in the context of domestic violence, as we have seen. For example, one presumption prohibits court-ordered visitation to a parent who murdered the other parent (absent the child's consent). Does this last presumption have the same constitutional infirmities as the presumption in *Nicholson?*

7. *Harm resulting from removal.* As noted in *Nicholson,* sometimes the harm from removing a child from the home outweighs harm that the child experiences from being in a home where domestic violence occurs. *Nicholson,* 820 N.E.2d at 849. For example, Sharwline Nicholson's son was physically abused while he was in foster care after the City removed him from her care. Zuccardy, supra, at 667. Other children experience emotional harm or are medically neglected while in foster care. Id. Sudden separation from parents also causes emotional trauma to children. See Sharwline Nicholson, Balancing the Harms (Trailer), Jan. 15, 2007, available at http://www .youtube.com/watch?v=P5ne2rapK9M&feature=player_embedded#at=45.

According to national data, 0.4 percent of the perpetrators of child abuse or neglect are foster parents. U.S. Dept. of Health & Human Servs., Administration on Children, Youth and Families: Child Maltreatment 2006 (Table 5-3, Perpetrators by Relationship to Victims, 2006). See also Randi Mandelbaum, Are Abused and Neglected Children in New Jersey Faring Any Better Since the Tragedies of 2003?, N.J. Law., Oct. 2005, at 9 n.9 (citing estimates that one in ten abused children who are removed from their parents are re-abused while in foster care). Given the co-occurrence of child maltreatment and domestic violence, how can the social service system ensure that foster care placements are not made to homes where domestic violence occurs?

3. Termination of Parental Rights

■ **STATE ex rel. C.J.K.**
774 So. 2d 107 (La. 2000)

Traylor, J.

We granted a writ of certiorari to determine whether the court of appeal correctly reviewed the trial court's ruling in a proceeding to terminate parental rights. . . .

R. K. and J. K. were in a relationship for approximately eight years prior to January 1997, the last five during marriage. C. K., a male child, was born July 21, 1991, and K. K., a female child, was born November 2, 1992. According to J. K., R. K. began to frequently and violently abuse her the day they were married. Unfortunately, the children often witnessed this abuse.

J. K. obtained several restraining and protective orders against R. K. and attempted to have him arrested for the abusive behavior on numerous occasions. However, J. K. testified that R. K. often violated the restraining and protective orders. She further complained that sometimes the sheriff's department would not pick her husband up when he violated the court orders or when she reported his abuse. However, J. K. acknowledged that she repeatedly returned to R. K. after filing the protective orders, and failed to pursue contempt of court proceedings for his violation of the protective orders. Additionally, she acknowledged that no divorce proceedings were initiated.

On January 22, 1997, R. K. again became abusive toward J. K., but she escaped to the Calcasieu Women's Shelter. She left the children with R. K., but when she returned, neither R. K. nor the children were present in the home. Some two weeks later, R. K. telephoned J. K. twice, informing her first that he had hurt the children, and then, that he had killed them. Actually, R. K. had spanked the children with a paint stick sufficiently hard to leave bruises.

Following the spanking incident, the children were returned to J. K. at the Calcasieu Women's Shelter. While at the shelter, the Sheriff's office responded to her complaint and took pictures of the children's injuries. Subsequently, she and the children went to stay with a friend. According to J.K., despite having a restraining order issued against him, three or four times a week R. K. would enter the property where she and the children were staying. Because law enforcement failed to help her keep R. K. away, and purportedly based on law enforcement's advice, J. K. called child protection services in March of 1997 and voluntarily surrendered her children for their protection.

On March 26, 1997, Cheryl James, a Child Protection Investigator for the State's Department of Social Services, Office of Community Services (OCS), sought and obtained an oral instanter order from a judge of the Fourteenth Judicial District Court in Calcasieu Parish to take K. K. and C. K. into protective custody. In her affidavit in support of the instanter order, Ms. James recited the following investigated facts:

> The father, [R. K.] spanked the children with a paint stick and left bruises on their buttocks and he does not have the ability to care for the children due to chemical abuse and/or mental illness.
>
> The mother, [J. K.] is unable to protect the children from further harm by the father and herself. Further, [J. K.'s] mental state has deteriorated drastically in the last few months.
>
> The agency's contacted the paternal grandmother who refused to get involved and the agency was unable to locate relatives in Texas.

[The District Attorney] filed a petition requesting an adjudication that the "children are Physically Abused and Neglected Children in Need of Care. . . ." Attached to the petition [were the social worker's affidavit] and a "parental notice" advising J. K. of the seriousness of the suit and her right to an attorney. J. K. was not represented by counsel at the hearing. When asked by the judge whether she wanted an attorney, she replied, "no sir."

The trial court issued a judgment maintaining custody with OCS, and adjudicating the children as "Physically Abused and Neglected Children in Need of Care, pursuant to Title VI of the Louisiana Children's Code, and by virtue of admission to the allegations in the petition." Subsequently, at the dispositional hearings . . . , the trial court rendered judgment maintaining custody of the two children with OCS and approving the OCS case plan goal of family reunification.

Pursuant to the OCS case plan, J. K. underwent a psychological evaluation by Dr. Sam Williams, a clinical psychologist [who] concluded that she was suffering from chronic depression, present since childhood. According to Dr. Williams, J. K. was abandoned by her mother at the age of seven months and adopted at the age of two years. J. K.'s adoptive father was physically abusive to her, and her mother was mentally and emotionally abusive. Additionally, Dr. Williams believed that J. K. was suffering from a chronic self-defeating personality disorder. According to Dr. Williams, J. K. "[had] come to believe that she kind of deserves the worst in life." In terms of strengths, Dr. Williams found that J. K. was an intelligent, sensitive woman who had a legitimate concern for her children.

Using Dr. Williams' evaluation conclusions, OCS authorized twelve therapy sessions with Dr. Ann Pittman Menou, another clinical psychologist, between July and December of 1997. J. K. missed two of her therapy sessions, and, when the sessions ended, Dr. Menou found that she was making progress in facing her problems. However, Dr. Menou advised OCS that the twelve sessions were not enough. OCS refused to authorize additional therapy, but offered to refer J. K to therapy available at minimal cost for additional treatment. J. K. refused the referral and instead sought psychiatric treatment with Dr. Paul Matthews.

At the third and fourth dispositional review hearings . . . , OCS changed its case plan goal from reunification to relative placement. The trial court approved this new case plan goal and continued the children in the custody of OCS. . . . [OCS issued a summary of the case plan indicating that] J. K. kept OCS informed of her whereabouts, attended visitation with her children, attended domestic violence classes at the Woman's shelter, and provided information on potential placements in compliance with the OCS case plan. However, J. K. failed to attend therapy, take her medication, participate in medication monitoring, attend parenting classes, or attend a Domestic Violence Treatment Program. OCS filed a petition to terminate R. K. and J. K's parental rights [and the trial court agreed. The court of appeal reversed.] . . .

We recently discussed the unique concerns present in all cases of involuntary termination of parental rights. . . .

> In any case to involuntarily terminate parental rights, there are two private interests involved: those of the parents and those of the child. The parents have a natural, fundamental liberty interest to the continuing companionship, care, custody and management of their children warranting great deference and vigilant protection under the law, and due process requires that a fundamentally fair procedure be followed when the state seeks to terminate the parent-child legal relationship. However, the child has a profound interest, often at odds with those of his parents, in terminating parental rights that prevent adoption and inhibit establishing secure, stable, long-term, and continuous relationships found in a home with proper parental care. In balancing these interests, the courts of this state have consistently found the interest of the child to be paramount over that of the parent.
>
> The State's parens patriae power allows intervention in the parent-child relationship only under serious circumstances, such as where the State seeks the permanent severance of that relationship in an involuntary termination proceeding. *The fundamental purpose of involuntary termination proceedings is to provide the greatest possible protection to a child whose parents are unwilling or unable to provide adequate care for his physical, emotional, and mental health needs and adequate rearing by providing an expeditious judicial process for the termination of all parental rights and responsibilities and to achieve*

permanency and stability for the child. The focus of an involuntary termination proceeding is not whether the parent should be deprived of custody, but whether it would be in the best interest of the child for all legal relations with the parents to be terminated. As such, the primary concern of the courts and the State remains to secure the best interest for the child, including termination of parental rights if justifiable grounds exist and are proven.

State in the Interest of J.A., 752 So.2d 806, 810-811 (emphasis added). . . .

[The Louisiana Children's Code governs the involuntary termination of parental rights.] La. Ch. Code art. 1015 provides the specific grounds for involuntary termination of parental rights. The State must only establish one ground under La. Ch. Code art. 1015, but the judge must also find that the termination is in the best interest of the child. Additionally, the State must prove the elements of one of the enumerated grounds by clear and convincing evidence to sever the parental bond.

In this case, OCS sought termination of R. K.'s parental rights under La. Ch. Code art. 1015(5) [(grounds include at least one year of removal from parental custody, no substantial compliance with the case plan, and no reasonable expectation of significant improvement in the parent's condition or conduct]. However, the trial court terminated the parental rights of R. K. and J. K. based on La. Ch. Code art. 1015(3)(i) which provides as a ground for termination:

> (3) Misconduct of the parent toward this child or any other child of the parent or any other child in his household which constitutes extreme abuse, cruel and inhuman treatment, or grossly negligent behavior below a reasonable standard of human decency, including but not limited to the conviction, commission, aiding or abetting, attempting, conspiring, or soliciting to commit any of the following:
>   . . . .
>   i) Abuse or neglect which is chronic, life threatening, or results in gravely disabling physical or psychological injury or disfigurement.

The court of appeal concluded that the only assertion of physical abuse in this case is that committed by R. K., finding no evidence of physical abuse, or knowledge of physical abuse, by J. K until after the incident by R. K. that set in motion the proceedings with OCS. Thus, the court of appeal concluded that the only alleged abuse by J. K. could be the infliction, allowance, or toleration of the infliction of mental injury upon children by a parent as a result of inadequate supervision. The court of appeal appeared to focus on . . . testimony that [J. K.] loves her children and sought to protect them when she perceived that they were in danger.

However, we must continue to stress that the Legislature has expressed its intent that courts shall construe the procedural provisions of Title X of the Children's Code relative to the involuntary termination of parental rights liberally. . . . Although J. K.'s testimony reveals efforts on her part to obtain help for herself through restraining orders and law enforcement, the record also demonstrates her inability to follow through with any attempt to stay away from her husband. In fact, the overwhelming evidence by mental health professionals and her own admissions supports the finding that she sabotaged her own efforts to rehabilitate, for example, by refusing to participate in further therapy to allow OCS to determine compliance with her case plan, and returning to her husband on numerous occasions, including contacts initiated by her, even after the petition to terminate her rights had been filed. . . .

Our review of the record supports the trial court's finding of clear and convincing evidence that J. K. participated in passive abuse, namely that she allowed or tolerated the infliction of mental injury on her children. Whether termed abuse or neglect, the evidence overwhelmingly indicates that the children suffered severe trauma from their repeated exposure to violence perpetrated by R. K. on J. K. We further conclude that the trial court did not err in finding that the children suffered life-threatening and severely disabling psychological injury that in their best interests required termination of J. K.'s parental rights. . . .

We are cognizant that domestic violence and child abuse or neglect are often related problems within the same dysfunctional family. While we recognize that the battered woman in the relationship is the victim, and a pattern of returning to the batterer is common, we must also accept the legislature's mandate that the children are the paramount concern. In the unique facts of this case, the trial court found that because the children had suffered such severe psychological trauma, J. K.'s repeated returns to R. K., and high risk of continuing to do so, constituted neglect that is "chronic, life threatening, or results in gravely disabling physical or psychological injury or disfigurement." La. Ch. Code art. 1015(3)(i). . . .

For the foregoing reasons, [w]e affirm the trial court's termination of J. K.'s parental rights and remand for further expedited proceedings to determine placement in accordance with OCS guidelines. . . .

Notes and Questions

1. *Standard.* The U.S. Supreme Court addressed the minimum standard of proof required in termination of parental rights cases. In Santosky v. Kramer, 455 U.S. 745 (1982), the court held that a "fair preponderance of the evidence" standard used in New York's termination proceedings for permanently neglected children was constitutionally insufficient, and set the standard as requiring clear and convincing evidence. States may require a higher standard. Should they do so? Who benefits from a lower standard of proof? A higher standard of proof?

2. *Stages.* Termination of parental rights proceedings generally involve two stages: (1) an initial stage, at which the court makes a determination of unfitness, and (2) a subsequent stage, at which the court determines whether termination would be in the child's best interests (sometimes called the "best interests stage"). How does *C.J.K.* describe these stages? Does the court clearly differentiate between the two stages?

Although *Santosky* requires the clear-and-convincing standard before termination of parental rights, many states reason that *Santosky* applies only to the initial determination of unfitness and therefore adopt different standards of proof for the best interests stage. Brian C. Hill, Comment, The State's Burden of Proof at the Best Interests Stage of a Termination of Parental Rights, 2004 U. Chi. Legal F. 557, 559 (2004). Is this approach constitutional? See Konrad S. Lee & Matthew I. Thue, Unpacking the Package Theory: Why California's Statutory Scheme for Terminating Parental Rights in Dependent Child Proceedings Violates the Due Process Rights of Parents as Defined by the United States Supreme Court in Santosky v. Kramer, 13 U.C. Davis J. Juv. L. & Pol'y 143 (2009).

What standard of proof does *C.J.K.* require? Why might a state choose to adopt different standards of proof for the different stages?

3. *Grounds for termination.* On what grounds did *C.J.K.* terminate J. K.'s and R. K.'s parental rights? Usually, direct physical or sexual abuse of the child is considered grounds for termination. What was the alleged abuse or neglect in *C.J.K.*? Should a single incident of physical or sexual abuse be sufficient to terminate the parental rights of the abuser?

4. *State's role.* What role should failure to protect play in the determination to terminate the parental rights of the nonabusive parent? Compare P.I. v. Dept. of Children and Families, 14 So. 3d 1173 (Fla. Dist. Ct. App. 2009) (terminating parental rights of mother for failing to protect child from father's abuse), with State *ex rel.* K.G., 832 So. 2d 1035 (La. Ct. App. 2002) (father's failure to discern mother's abuse of infant did not merit terminating his parental rights where he took immediate action to end the abuse upon discovery). Recall Lundy Bancroft et al.'s explanation of the difficulties of conducting custody evaluations in cases of domestic violence earlier in this chapter, Section D(3). How were these difficulties apparent in *C.J.K.*?

5. *Presumptions.* In 1997, Congress enacted the Adoption and Safe Families Act (ASFA), Pub. L. No. 105-89, 111 Stat. 2115 (codified as amended in scattered sections of 42 U.S.C.), as a response to the concerns of legislators and child welfare agencies that the federal emphasis on family preservation and reunification was exposing children to unnecessary risks. ASFA stressed speedier termination of parental rights. In response, many states adopted presumptions of parental unfitness to facilitate termination of parental rights. Thus, for example, a parent is presumed unfit following a conviction for aggravated battery or attempted murder of *any* child (including a sibling). Do these statutory presumptions raise constitutional concerns? See Florida Dept. of Children & Families v. F.L., 880 So. 2d 602 (Fla. 2004) (holding that a statutory rebuttable presumption terminating parental rights when rights to a sibling have been terminated impermissibly shifts the burden of proof to show a lack of substantial risk of harm to the current child); In re D.W., 827 N.E.2d 466 (Ill. 2005) (application of mandatory conclusive presumption of unfitness violates equal protection). How does a policy favoring speedier termination of parental rights play a role in the child welfare system's response to domestic violence?

6. *Policy.* What policy reasons does *C.J.K.* give for terminating the parental rights of J. K. and R. K.? Usually, the policy behind these cases is twofold: first, to protect the child from a dangerous or unhealthy environment without the consent of the parents, and second, to encourage commencement of adoption procedures to give the child a new stable environment. See In re Welfare of Alle, 230 N.W.2d 574 (1975) (stating policy). Does *C.J.K.* implement both of these policies? See generally Elizabeth Bartholet, Nobody's Children: Abuse and Neglect, Foster Drift, and Adoption Alternative (1999) (arguing that the state should be more aggressive in removing children from their biological families and placing them for adoption); Martin Guggenheim, Somebody's Children: Sustaining the Family's Place in Child Welfare Policy, 113 Harv. L. Rev. 1716 (1999) (book review rebutting Bartholet's assumptions and conclusions).

7. *Parent's right to counsel.* The Supreme Court examined the parent's right to counsel in termination of parental rights proceedings in Lassiter v. Department of Social Services, 452 U.S. 18 (1981). The Court rejected the argument that procedural due process requires the appointment of counsel for indigent parents. Applying a case-by-case balancing test, the Court weighed (1) the state's and parent's shared interest in the accuracy of the decision; (2) the cost of providing indigent parents

with counsel; (3) the state's interest in informal procedures; (4) the complexity of the issues; (5) the incapacity of the indigent parent; and (6) the risk of error. The Court held that, although petitioner had not made a sufficient showing of these factors, in a case in which the parent's interests were especially high and the state's interests were particularly low, due process might require the appointment of counsel. Is *Santosky* consistent with *Lassiter*? For further discussion of *Lassiter*'s effect on the right to counsel, see Bruce A. Boyer, Justice, Access to the Courts, and the Right to Free Counsel for Indigent Parents: The Continuing Scourge of Lassiter v. Department of Social Services of Durham, 15 Temp. Pol. & Civ. Rts. L. Rev. 635 (2006).

Despite the Supreme Court's holding in *Lassiter*, many states guarantee indigent parents the right to counsel in parental termination proceedings. Trisha M. Anklam, The Price of Justice: In Light of *LaVallee*, What Should Massachusetts Courts Do When Attorneys Are Not Available to Represent Indigent Parents Involved in Care and Protection Matters?, 32 New Eng. J. on Crim. & Civ. Confinement 111, 112 (2006). See also Brief of American Bar Association Amici Curiae Supporting Petitioners, In re Christian M. and Alexander M., No. 2011–0647 (N.H. Sup. Ct.) (advocating appointment of counsel in parental termination cases). How does Louisiana treat the parent's right to counsel in *C.J.K.*? Was her waiver of counsel a knowing waiver? Why might the right to counsel be particularly helpful for victims of domestic violence? How might counsel have been helpful to J. K.?

8. *Reunification requirements.* Every state has statutory provisions authorizing the permanent removal of an endangered child from the home; however, before termination of parental rights, the state must provide rehabilitation services, including reunification efforts. Federal legislation mandates the provision of these services. Adoption Assistance and Child Welfare Act (AACWA), 42 U.S.C. §§621 et seq., 670 et seq. (2006). Some state statutes contained "reasonable efforts requirements" prior to the enactment of the AACWA, but the AACWA triggered widespread adoption of these requirements.

States adopt different approaches to the "reasonable efforts" requirement. Some states expressly require the child welfare agency to prove that it has made reasonable efforts to rehabilitate the parent as a condition precedent to termination of parent rights. Other states hold that "reasonable efforts" is a factor to be considered in termination determinations. David J. Herring, Inclusion of the Reasonable Efforts Requirements in Termination of Parental Rights Statutes: Punishing the Child for the Failure of the State Child Welfare System, 54 U. Pitt. L. Rev. 139, 172-175 (1992). Significantly, if a given statute requires rehabilitation services, a parent may interpose the defense that the state failed to fulfill its statutory mandate prior to termination of parental rights. Is the "reasonable efforts" requirement constitutionally compelled?

In the context of domestic violence, the ASFA, which expanded on and clarified the AACWA, removed the "reasonable efforts" requirement in cases in which (1) the child was the victim of aggravated circumstances, such as torture, abandonment, or sexual abuse; (2) the parent killed another child or attempted to do so; or (3) the state terminated the parent's rights with respect to a sibling. 42 U.S.C. §671(a)(15)(D)(i), (ii), (iii). What impact do these provisions have on parents who are perpetrators of domestic violence against the child? Against the mother?

9. *Failure to protect.* When is it appropriate to terminate the parental rights of a *victim* of domestic violence, such as J. K.? What evidence does the court consider? The extent of psychological trauma of the children from witnessing the abuse? J. K.'s repeated

returns to her batterer? Her flight to the shelter *without* the children? Her depression? Her childhood history? What weight *should* be given to those factors?

What factors should the court have considered? Should the court have considered letters from family members expressing a willingness to take care of the children? The acts of R. K. and the nature of the abuse that he inflicted? What weight should the court have given to the psychological assessment that "J. K. was an intelligent, sensitive woman who had a legitimate concern for her children"?

To what extent does the case reflect an understanding (or misunderstanding) of the dynamics of domestic violence? The effects of battering on the victim? Do you agree with the result?

Problem

Jane Leon, a single parent, has three children ages three, five, and six. Plagued by problems of homelessness, substance abuse, and domestic abuse by her husband (who is not the father of any of the children), Jane voluntarily places the children in foster care through the Division of Youth and Family Services (DYF). For almost two years, the children remain in foster care with the Johnson family, with whom they develop a very warm relationship. Jane visits the children regularly twice per month. For a short time, Jane enters drug treatment for her substance abuse but drops out of the program after a few weeks. DYF ultimately determines that Jane lacks parental fitness and brings an action to terminate her parental rights in order that the children can be adopted by Mr. and Mrs. Johnson. The family court finds that the children would suffer serious psychological harm if they were removed from the home of the Johnsons and concludes that termination of Jane's parental rights would serve the best interests of the children even if Jane were able to resolve all her other problems. Jane appeals. What result? See In re Guardianship of J.C., 608 A.2d 1312 (N.J. 1992).

Consider the following issues: Is termination of Jane's parental rights justified? Can the children's attachment to their foster parents alone be a sufficient ground for termination of Jane's rights? Would such an approach be constitutional?

XIII

Discrimination Against Victims

Victims of domestic violence face discrimination in housing and the workplace. What are these discriminatory practices? What state and federal laws address these practices? How effective are state and federal remedies? Consider these questions as you read these materials.

A. HOUSING DISCRIMINATION

■ **BOULEY v. YOUNG-SABOURIN**
394 F. Supp. 2d 675 (D. Vt. 2005)

Murtha, District Judge.
The plaintiff in this civil rights action claims the defendant evicted her from an apartment in violation of the Fair Housing Act of 1968, 42 U.S.C. §§3601 et seq. . . . On August 1, 2003, plaintiff Quinn Bouley, her husband, Daniel Swedo, and their two children, rented the apartment upstairs from defendant Jacqueline Young-Sabourin. . . . From August 1, 2003, through October 15, 2003, the plaintiff received no complaints from the defendant related to her tenancy and, in fact, had very little personal contact with the defendant.

On October 15, 2003, at approximately 8:00 p.m., the plaintiff's husband, Daniel Swedo, criminally attacked her. The plaintiff called the police and fled the apartment. St. Albans police arrested her husband and, that night, the plaintiff applied for a restraining order. Swedo eventually pled guilty to several criminal charges related to the incident, including assault.

On the morning of October 18, 2003, the defendant visited the plaintiff's apartment. The plaintiff and defendant dispute the particulars of their conversation; the plaintiff has characterized the discussion as one in which the defendant attempted unsuccessfully to discuss "religion" and "Christianity" with her before declaring "I guess I can't do anything here" and leaving. Later that day, the defendant wrote the following letter, in which she asked the plaintiff to leave the premises by November 30, 2003:

> The purpose of my visit this morning was to try and work things out between you, your agreement in your lease, and the other tenants in the building. I felt very disappointed in the fact that you started to holler and scream, and threaten me, in my efforts to help you. This could only lead me to believe that the violence that has been happening in your unit would continue and that I must give you a 30-day notice to leave the premises.
>
> Agreement #10 on your lease states that "Tenant will not use or allow said premises or any part thereof to be used for unlawful purposes, in any noisy, boisterous or any other manner offensive to any other occupant of the building." Other tenants, and now myself included, feel fearful of the violent behaviors expressed. . . .
>
> Although I did not see the holes in the wall, several sources have told me that holes have been punched in the walls in the unit. . . . I would like to remind you that you signed an Apartment inspection sheet at the time of your rental, and I expect the apartment to be in the same condition when you move out. Daniel has stated that he will work in the apartment after you have moved. Your 30-day notice will mean that you should leave the premises by November 30, 2003. . . .

The Fair Housing Act makes it unlawful, inter alia, "[t]o refuse to sell or rent after the making of a bona fide offer, or to otherwise refuse to negotiate for the sale or rental of, or otherwise make unavailable or deny, a dwelling to any person because of race, color, religion, sex, familial status, or national origin." 42 U.S.C. §3604(a). The plaintiff alleges the defendant unlawfully terminated her lease on the basis of sex and religion. First, she claims the termination was initiated because she was a victim of domestic violence, and second, because she refused to listen to the defendant's attempt to discuss religion with her after the incident. These claims, if proven, could constitute unlawful discrimination under the Fair Housing Act.

Claims of housing discrimination are evaluated using [the following] burden-shifting framework. "[O]nce a plaintiff has established a prima facie case of discrimination, the burden shifts to the defendant to assert a legitimate, non-discriminatory rationale for the challenged decision. . . . If the defendant makes such a showing, the burden shifts back to the plaintiff to demonstrate that discrimination was the real reason for the defendant's action. . . . Summary judgment is appropriate [only] if no reasonable jury could find that the defendant's actions were motivated by discrimination."

The plaintiff has demonstrated a prima facie case. It is undisputed that, less than 72 hours after the plaintiff's husband assaulted her, the defendant attempted to evict her. In addition, the record contains evidence which suggests the eviction also may have been prompted by the plaintiff's refusal to discuss religion with the defendant . . . In response, the defendant has presented little evidence of preexisting problems with the plaintiff, as a tenant. In addition, the timing of the eviction, as well as reasonable inferences which a jury could draw from some of the statements in the eviction letter, could lead a reasonable jury to conclude that the real reason for the defendant's actions was unlawful discrimination. . . .

Notes and Questions

1. *Background.* Discriminatory practices by landlords are a significant problem for victims of domestic violence. Landlords sometimes refuse to rent to them or evict them following a violent incident. Department of Justice Appropriations Authorization Act, Fiscal Years 2006 through 2009, 151 Cong. Rec. H12075, 12094 (2005) (reporting occurrence of 100 housing denials and 150 evictions nationwide in one year). In addition, domestic violence is a leading cause of homelessness. The role of domestic violence in homelessness is explored later in this chapter.

Landlords voice two concerns about domestic violence: the danger that it poses to other tenants and the risk of property damage. What was the landlord's concern in *Bouley*? How serious was the violence? In the landlord's letter, she asserts that "the violence that has been happening in your unit would continue." On what evidence does the landlord base this assertion? After Bouley explains that she is not interested in seeking help through religion, what action does the landlord take?

2. *Bouley's FHA claim.* Bouley involves a suit under the Fair Housing Act (FHA). The FHA (Title VIII of the Civil Rights Act of 1964, codified in relevant part at 42 U.S.C. §3604(a)), applies to any landlord or housing authority receiving federal funding, and prohibits housing discrimination based on "race, color, religion, sex, familial status, or national origin." Because victims of domestic violence are overwhelmingly women, and because women of certain races/ethnicities disproportionately experience such violence, some victims of housing discrimination may have a cause of action under the FHA. What was the basis of Bouley's claim(s)? What did she hope to gain by her suit?

3. *FHA gender-based theories: disparate treatment versus disparate impact.* Bouley holds that the victim presented a prima facie case of sex discrimination under the FHA. To make a claim of gender discrimination, a victim must demonstrate that the landlord's actions or policies result in "disparate treatment" or "disparate impact" based on gender. A showing of disparate treatment requires a showing of intent or motive to discriminate, while showing discriminatory effect is sufficient to maintain a prima facie case for disparate impact. *Bouley* involved a disparate treatment claim. After making out a prima facie case (that is, plaintiff was a woman; she was qualified to rent the housing; she suffered an adverse housing decision; the housing remained available to other renters), the burden shifts to the defendant to prove nondiscriminatory intent. Given the landlord's letter to the plaintiff, will the landlord be able to show a *nondiscriminatory* intent in evicting plaintiff? Is the above analysis different for eviction cases than for initial housing denials?

Unlike disparate treatment claims, a plaintiff making a disparate impact claim need not show discriminatory intent, but must only show that the landlord's actions or policies, although gender neutral, disproportionately harm women. Thus, statistical evidence is the most common method of proof. Plaintiff must make a prima facie showing that women are disproportionately affected by domestic violence, and also that the landlord's action was based on the occurrence of domestic violence. Because discriminatory intent is often difficult to prove, most cases involving housing discrimination against victims rely on a disparate impact theory. How difficult will it be for Bouley to show discriminatory intent?

4. *Federal law's response to housing discrimination against victims.*

a. *Role of HUD's "one strike" rule.* Prior to 2006, federal law permitted the eviction of domestic violence victims by virtue of a "zero-tolerance" approach to any criminal activity. The Low-Income Housing Assistance Voucher Program, 42 U.S.C. §1437d(1)(6)(amended 2006) allowed eviction from federally subsidized housing after a *single incident* of criminal activity that was committed by "a tenant, any member of the tenant's household, a guest or another person under the tenant's control" that threatened the safety or right to peaceful enjoyment of other residents (called the "one strike" rule). Id. HUD policy encouraged such evictions. U.S. Dept. of Hous. & Urban Dev., "One Strike and You're Out" Policy in Public Housing 7 (Mar. 1996). See also §1437d(j)(1)(I). That rule permitted eviction of victims because of the violent acts of their spouses, cohabiting partners, or visitors. See Lenora M. Lapidus, Doubly Victimized: Housing Discrimination Against Victims of Domestic Violence, 11 Am. U.J. Gender Soc. Pol'y & L. 377, 386 (2003); Veronica L. Zoltowski, Note, Zero Tolerance Policies: Fighting Drugs or Punishing Domestic Violence Victims?, 37 New Eng. L. Rev. 1231, 1241-1243 (2003).

b. *VAWA's response.* VAWA 2005 created significant protections against housing discrimination for victims who were tenants in federally assisted housing. VAWA 2005 provided that status as a victim of domestic violence is not a basis for denial of admission to or denial of housing assistance. 42 U.S.C. §1437d(c)(3); 42 U.S.C. §1437f(c)(9)(A); 42 U.S.C. §1437f(d)(1)(A); 42 U.S.C. §1437f(o)(B).

In addition, VAWA 2005 amended 42 U.S.C. §1437d(1)(6) to provide for an exception to the "one strike" rule by prohibiting public housing agencies from considering domestic violence as cause for terminating a tenancy or otherwise affecting "occupancy rights" (such as eligibility for public housing). 42 U.S.C. §§1437d(1)(5)-(6), 1437f(d)(1)(ii),1437f(r)(5). VAWA 2005 was necessary because the original VAWA did not apply to HUD Programs (such as vouchers). See also Metro N. Owners, LLC v. Thorpe, 870 N.Y.S.2d 768 (N.Y. City Civ. Ct. 2008) (dismissing eviction proceeding, reasoning that tenant-victim was entitled to protection pursuant to VAWA 2005). VAWA 2005 also provides that a landlord may evict the abuser but allow the victim, who is a lawful occupant, to remain. 42 U.S.C. §1437d(1)(6)(B) (public housing); 42 U.S.C. §§1437f(o)(7)(D)(ii) (housing choice voucher program); 42 U.S.C. §1437f(c)(9)(C)(ii) and (d)(1)(B)(iii)(II) (project-based Section 8).

Despite the above exception to the "one strike" rule, VAWA 2005 provides that a landlord may still evict a tenant if the landlord can demonstrate an actual and imminent threat to *other* tenants or *property management staff* if a tenant's occupancy is not terminated. 42 U.S.C §1437d(l)(6)(E), 24 C.F.R. §5.2005(d)(2). In such cases, VAWA 2005 requires that eviction be the only action that can be taken to reduce or eliminate the threat. 24 C.F.R. §5.2005(d)(3). Other actions that a landlord might use to reduce the threat include: transferring the victim to a different unit, barring the perpetrator from the property, contacting law enforcement to increase police presence; developing other plans to keep the property safe; or seeking other legal remedies to prevent the perpetrator from harmful activity. Id. See U.S. Dept. Housing & Urban Dev., Memorandum for FHEO Office Directors, Assessing Claims of Housing Discrimination Against Victims of Domestic Violence Under the Fair Housing Act (FHAct) and the Violence Against Women Act (VAWA) 3 n.18 (Feb. 9, 2011). Pending VAWA 2011 provisions provide explicitly for bifurcation of a lease to remove or terminate housing assistance only to the abuser (adding 42 U.S.C §41411(b)(3)(B)); clarify the requisite documentation of domestic violence; and also mandate confidentiality (§41411(c)(4)).

Another housing action that affects some victims is a restrictive housing *transfer* policy. Sometimes, tenant-victims want a landlord to transfer them to another apartment for their safety. Can a tenant *require* the landlord to do so? See Robinson v. Cincinnati Metropolitan Hous. Auth., 2008 WL 1924255 (S.D. Ohio 2008) (holding that a public housing authority is not required to transfer a tenant solely on the basis of a threat of future domestic violence). Neither VAWA 2005 nor the FHA provides such protection. Pending VAWA 2011 provisions remedy this omission by providing for emergency transfers for victims in covered housing programs (adding 42 U.S.C §41411(e)).

c. *Section 8 housing vouchers.* Some victims of domestic violence obtain housing assistance through a federal voucher program. See 24 C.F.R. §960.206(b)(4) ("PHAs should consider whether to adopt a local preference for admission of families that include victims of domestic violence."). That voucher program sometimes presents problems for tenant-victims.

The federal government offers a housing choice voucher program that assists very low-income families to obtain housing in the private market. Housing subsidies are paid directly to the landlord on behalf of the participant. 24 C.F.R. §982.1. The participant then pays the difference between the subsidy and the actual rent charged by the landlord. A participant is not limited to subsidized housing projects but rather may use the voucher to choose housing in the private rental market. Housing choice vouchers are administered locally by public housing agencies (PHAs) that are funded from HUD. 24 C.F.R. §982.1.

Victims of domestic violence who have Section 8 vouchers generally cannot afford to move without continued rental assistance. Traditionally, federal and state law imposed rules about moving with voucher assistance (called "portability") that created difficulties for victims. For example, a voucher tenant might be prohibited from moving without prior notification to the PHA, during the first year of the lease, more than once during a 12-month period, and without first obtaining the landlord's permission. Yet, in order to flee from abuse, a victim may need to relocate on multiple occasions and within a short time frame. In recognition of these problems, Congress amended the law governing federal housing programs. Currently, housing laws provide that for purposes of Section 8 housing vouchers, criminal activity related to domestic violence, dating violence, or stalking may not be grounds for termination of voucher assistance. See 42 U.S.C. §§1437d(l)(6)(A), 1437f(d)(1)(B)(iii), 1437f(o)(7)(D), 1437f(o)(20)(B).

5. *State approaches to housing discrimination.* States take different approaches to housing discrimination against victims of domestic violence. Some states have affirmative bans on such housing discrimination. E.g., N.C. Gen. Stat. §42-42.2; Wash. Rev. Code §59.18.580. Other states adopt more targeted approaches. A few states impose an obligation on a landlord to permit a victim to terminate a lease following an act of domestic violence. E.g., Or. Rev. Stat. §90.453; Tex. Prop. Code Ann. §92.106(b). To obtain this early release, tenants must provide documentation of the abuse (for example, a copy of an order of protection). Other states provide a defense against eviction to victims. E.g., Colo. Rev. Stat. §13-40-107.5. Some states place restrictions on the ability of public housing agencies to terminate leases of victims. E.g., 820 Ill. Comp. Stat. §180/30. Finally, some states prohibit landlords from including rental provisions that waive a tenant's right to call law enforcement in response to domestic violence. E.g., Ariz. Rev. Stat. Ann. §33-1414A(6).

See generally Kristen M. Ross, Note, Eviction, Discrimination, and Domestic Violence: Unfair Housing Practices Against Domestic Violence Survivors, 18 Hastings Women's L.J. 249 (2007); Elizabeth M. Whitehorn, Comment, Unlawful Evictions of Female Victims of Domestic Violence: Extending Title VII's Sex Stereotyping Theories to the Fair Housing Act, 101 Nw. U. L. Rev. 1419 (2007). See also National Coalition Against Domestic Violence, Domestic Violence and Housing, available at http://www.ncadv.org/files/Housing_.pdf (last visited June 7, 2011).

6. *Landlords' liability.* What is the extent of a landlord's duty to protect other tenants from the criminal acts of the *abuser*? Some states hold that a landlord has no such duty of care; others hold that a landlord has to exercise reasonable care in such cases. Still other states hold that a landlord has a duty to exercise reasonable care in such cases only in common areas or areas over which the landlord has control. Tracy A. Batemen & Susan Thomas, Landlord's Liability for Failure to Protect Tenant from Criminal Acts of Third Person, 43 A.L.R.5th 207 (1996 & Supp.).

Does the landlord's duty change if the abuser is a stranger or another tenant? VAWA 2005 permits public housing agencies to require written documentation of a tenant's status as a victim of domestic violence if she claims the landlord cannot terminate her tenancy or housing assistance due to domestic violence. 42 U.S.C. §1437d(u)(1)(A), 42 U.S.C. §1437f(ee)(1)(A). Such documentation may consist of police reports, protective orders, or third-party affidavits. See 24 C.F.R. §5.2007. Could the requirement of written documentation limit the housing protections for those persons who have to flee and therefore are not able to obtain documentation? How would VAWA 2005 protect those who are new or recent victims of domestic violence?

7. *Discrimination under chronic nuisance laws.* Can a tenant be evicted because she makes calls to police to ask for protection? Certain local housing laws require that, after a designated number of calls for police service, the municipality can revoke a rental dwelling permit. These "chronic nuisance laws" (based on public nuisance law) also permit municipalities to seek reimbursement for police services from the owner of property to which police were dispatched. How might such laws adversely affect victims of domestic violence? See Cari Fais, Note, Denying Access to Justice: The Cost of Applying Chronic Nuisance Laws to Domestic Violence, 108 Colum. L. Rev. 1181 (2008). How might federal and/or state law combat the effect of these chronic nuisance laws on victims of domestic violence? See id. at 1205-1224; Alaska Stat. §29.35.125(a) (including a domestic violence exception to its chronic nuisance law).

Problem

You are a legislative aide to a state senator. The state senate is considering proposing a bill that would ban housing discrimination against victims of domestic violence that is modeled on the following statute (Wash. Rev. Code §59.18.580):

(1) A landlord may not terminate a tenancy, fail to renew a tenancy, or refuse to enter into a rental agreement based on the tenant's or applicant's or a household member's status as a victim of domestic violence, sexual assault, or stalking.

(2) A landlord who refuses to enter into a rental agreement in violation of this section may be liable to the tenant or applicant in a civil action for damages sustained by the tenant or applicant. The prevailing party may also recover court costs and reasonable attorneys' fees.

(3) It is a defense to an unlawful detainer action that the action to remove the tenant and recover possession of the premises is in violation of subsection (1) of this section.

(4) This section does not prohibit adverse housing decisions based upon other lawful factors within the landlord's knowledge.

You have been asked to draft a memorandum regarding whether your employer should propose the legislation. What are the benefits and shortcomings of this legislation? What other provisions, if any, would you add to protect victims of domestic violence? To protect landlords?

Note: Domestic Violence and Homelessness

Domestic violence often leads to homelessness. A national study reveals that, in some cities, domestic violence is the *primary* cause of families' homelessness.[1] A victim's decision to leave an abuser enhances the likelihood that she (and her children) eventually will experience homelessness.[2] Victims who leave their abusers face two housing options: (1) informal supports, such as moving in with friends or family, or (2) formal supports, such as emergency shelters, transitional housing programs, and permanent housing programs (that is, federally subsidized or unsubsidized housing).

Victims may be reluctant to move in with friends or family for a multitude of reasons (such as shame or fear of endangering others). On the other hand, formal options "may not be available at the time women need them, or they may have specific eligibility criteria that women do not meet."[3] For low-income victims, housing needs may be acute, stemming from the limited supply of federally funded units as well as long waiting lists for federally funded housing voucher programs.[4] Victims' inability to find housing may force them to return to abusive partners.

Recognizing the need to increase access to temporary housing, Congress authorized funding in VAWA 2000 for transitional housing for victims of domestic and sexual violence.[5] VAWA 2005 continued funding for existing programs and

[1]. U.S. Conference of Mayors, Hunger and Homelessness Survey: A Status Report on Hunger and Homelessness in American Cities: A 27-City Survey 11 (2009), available at http://www.usmayors.org/pressreleases/uploads/USCMHungercompleteWEB2009.pdf. The Conference of Mayors has conducted annual surveys of hunger and homelessness since 1982.

[2]. See Legal Momentum, Understanding the Effects of Domestic Violence, Sexual Assault and Stalking on Housing and the Workplace, http://www.legalmomentum.org/our-work/domestic-violence/statistics-understanding-the.html (last visited June 9, 2011) (pointing out that 57 percent of homeless parents, who had lived with a spouse or partner, left their last residence because of domestic violence).

[3]. Charlene K. Baker et al., A Descriptive Analysis of Transitional Housing Programs for Survivors of Intimate Partner Violence in the United States, 15 Violence Against Women 460, 461 (2009).

[4]. Id. at 461.

[5]. Pub. L. No. 106-386, §319, 114 Stat. 1463, 1506 (2000). See also Baker, supra note [3], at 463 (explaining VAWA provisions). Transitional housing generally consists of grants, rent vouchers, or accommodation in special housing units for durations of one to two years. Id. at 462. Some transitional housing programs also offer social services (counseling, job search programs, etc.).

created new transitional housing programs.[6] VAWA 2005 specifies that victims may not be forced to participate in social services as a condition of housing assistance.[7] Pending VAWA 2011 provisions reauthorize traditional housing assistance grants.

The following excerpt addresses the role of domestic violence and homelessness.

■ NATIONAL ALLIANCE TO END HOMELESSNESS (NAEH)[8]

Fact Sheet: Domestic Violence (Jan. 11, 2010), available at http://www.endhomeless.org/content/article/detail/1647

. . . The consequences of domestic violence can affect a woman's likelihood of becoming homeless. Domestic violence victims are often isolated from support networks and financial resources by their abusers. As a result, they may lack steady income, employment history, credit history, and landlord references. . . .

Homeless Women Experience High Rates of Violence and Victimization

In addition to domestic violence causing homelessness, many homeless women have been victims of domestic violence at some point in their past, even if they do not identify it as the immediate cause of their homelessness. One study in Massachusetts found that 92 percent of homeless women had experienced severe physical or sexual assault at some point in their life, 63 percent had been victims of violence by an intimate partner, and 32 percent had been assaulted by their current or most recent partner.

Housing Is Important

Domestic violence victims have both short- and long-term housing needs that must be met so that they do not need to choose between staying with their abuser and sleeping on the street. Immediately, domestic violence victims need a safe place to stay. Emergency shelters are an important temporary haven for domestic violence victims. Ultimately, domestic violence victims need safe, stable, and affordable housing. An adequate supply of affordable housing is critical to ensuring that survivors of domestic violence can afford to leave the shelter system as quickly as possible without returning to their abuser.

---

[6]. Violence Against Women and Department of Justice Reauthorization Act of 2005, Pub. L. No. 109-162, §602, 119 Stat. 2960, 3038-3040 (2005). VAWA 2005 increased funding for transitional housing programs from $30 to $40 million annually (from 2007 to 2011 subject to congressional authorization); authorized funding for short-term housing assistance (up to 24 months), including rental payments and security deposits, relocation expenses, operational costs, and supportive services to help victims locate and secure permanent housing; and also provided that victims who obtain financial or housing assistance may not be forced to participate in supportive services. 42 U.S.C.A. §13975.

[7]. 42 U.S.C.A. §13975(b)(3)(B) ("Receipt of the benefits of the housing assistance . . . shall not be conditioned upon the participation . . . in any or all of the support services offered"). See also Sargent Shriver National Center on Poverty Law, 9 Woman View: A Look at VAWA Housing Provisions 2 (Mar. 6, 2006), available at http://www.ncdsv.org/images/ALookgatVAWAHousingProvisions.pdf.

[8]. The National Alliance to End Homelessness is a nonprofit, nonpartisan organization committed to preventing and ending homelessness through policy formulation, capacity building, education, and research. The Alliance presently consists of over 10,000 providers and public agencies. Originally established at the National Citizens Committee for Food and Shelter, the Alliance adopted its present name in 1987.

Unmet Needs for Homeless Victims of Domestic Violence

While the basic shelter needs of most people fleeing domestic violence are met, in one 24 hour period, an estimated 3,286 people could not be provided emergency shelter and 1,586 could not be provided transitional shelter. This shows the ongoing need for additional resources to protect adults and children from domestic violence.

B. EMPLOYMENT DISCRIMINATION

■ **DANNY v. LAIDLAW TRANSIT SERVICES, INC.**
193 P.3d 128 (Wash. 2008)

Owens, J.

[Defendant Laidlaw Transit Services, Inc. provides transit services in King County, Washington. They hired Plaintiff Ramona Danny in February 1997. Five years later, in October 2002, they promoted her to scheduling manager.] While she was working at Laidlaw, Danny and her five children experienced ongoing domestic violence at the hands of her husband. She moved out of her house in February 2003 after suffering serious physical abuse but had to leave her children behind. In June 2003, she told [her project manager] about her domestic violence situation. In August 2003, Danny requested time off so she could move her children away from the abusive situation at their home. The project manager initially refused because Danny [was putting together a major transit bid for Laidlaw's largest subcontractor]. On August 20, 2003, Danny's husband beat her 13-year-old son so badly that he had to be hospitalized. Danny immediately moved all five children out of the home. When she returned to work, Danny again requested time off to move her children to a shelter. The project manager approved paid time off between August 25 and September 8, 2003. [During that time], Danny conferred with police regarding protection from her husband and assisted in the prosecution against him for the assault of her son. [She] also used services [to obtain] transitional housing, domestic violence education, counseling and health services, and legal assistance.

[A]bout a month after returning to work, Laidlaw demoted Danny from manager and offered her the position of scheduler, which she accepted. Laidlaw terminated Danny's employment on December 3, 2003. Laidlaw's stated reason for termination was falsification of payroll records.

[Danny filed an action against her employer, alleging a violation of public policy and of Washington's employment discrimination law. Staying a decision on the employer's motion for judgment on the pleadings, the federal district court certified the following question to the state supreme court: Did the state establish a clear mandate of public policy prohibiting an employer from discharging an at-will employee because she experienced domestic violence and took leave from work to take actions to protect herself, her family, and to hold her abuser accountable? Deciding that that particular question would require the state supreme court to make factual inquiries that should be undertaken by the district court, the state supreme court reformulated the question as: Had the state established a clear mandate of public policy of protecting domestic violence victims and their families and holding their abusers accountable?]

Absent a contract to the contrary, Washington employees are generally terminable "at will." An at-will employee may quit or be fired for any reason. The common law tort of wrongful discharge is a narrow exception to the terminable-at-will doctrine. The tort of wrongful discharge applies when an employer terminates an employee for reasons that contravene a clearly mandated public policy. . . . To sustain the tort of wrongful discharge in violation of public policy, Danny must establish (1) "the existence of a clear public policy (the clarity element);" (2) "that discouraging the conduct in which [she] engaged would jeopardize the public policy (the jeopardy element)"; (3) "that the public-policy-linked conduct caused the dismissal (the causation element)"; and (4) "[Laidlaw] must not be able to offer an overriding justification for the dismissal (the absence of justification element)."

[We must] determine whether Danny has met the "clarity" element of wrongful discharge in violation of public policy. . . . To qualify as a public policy for purposes of the wrongful discharge tort, a policy must be "truly public" and sufficiently clear. This court has always been mindful that the wrongful discharge tort is narrow and should be "applied cautiously." Washington courts have generally recognized the public policy exception when an employer terminates an employee as a result of his or her (1) refusal to commit an illegal act, (2) performance of a public duty or obligation, (3) exercise of a legal right or privilege, or (4) in retaliation for reporting employer misconduct. Danny argues that she performed a public duty when she acted to protect herself and her children and that she exercised a legal right to obtain protection from her abuser. . . . Danny points to several [potential] sources of this public policy from the legislative, executive, and judicial branches of government. . . .

As early as 1979, the legislature [created] funding for domestic violence shelters, recognizing that many domestic violence victims are unable to leave violent situations without proper resources. Also in 1979, the legislature enacted the Domestic Violence Act (DVA), requiring law enforcement to respond to domestic violence. [T]he legislature later expanded the DVA to require the mandatory arrest of domestic violence perpetrators. [S]oon after enacting the DVA, the legislature enacted a separate Domestic Violence Prevention Act (DVPA), to provide domestic violence victims with the ability to obtain a civil protection order against their abusers. . . . Significantly, it found that "Domestic violence costs millions of dollars each year in the state of Washington for health care, *absence from work*, services to children, and more. The crisis is growing" (emphasis added).

The legislature has since amended the DVPA several times to improve the protection order process [to eliminate the filing fee, comply with VAWA, and to give full faith and credit to out-of-state protection orders]. In 1991, following enactment of the DVPA, the legislature created an address confidentiality program (ACP), to protect domestic violence victims [by] allowing the secretary of state to provide victims with a substitute address in order to prevent abusers from locating their victim. . . . In 2002, apparently recognizing that fear of losing employment may hinder escape from domestic violence, the legislature enacted laws allowing domestic violence victims to receive unemployment compensation through the state if they must leave employment to protect themselves or their immediate family from violence. RCW §50.20.050(1)(b)(iv).[2] . . .

In 2005, the legislature took another step to encourage victims of domestic violence to escape and prevent further violence by [directing distribution of funds to nonshelter community-based services, including legal services, for victims and their children.] In addition to facilitating domestic violence victims in their escape, the legislature has also emphasized the importance of prosecuting domestic violence perpetrators. . . . In 1996, the legislature [declared it] a gross misdemeanor for a domestic violence perpetrator to interfere in the victim's reporting of the abuse. The legislature has also made violation of a protection order under the DVPA a crime. [Further, the legislature] created domestic violence treatment programs for abusers and provided courts with the ability to order a perpetrator into treatment. . . .

The legislature's consistent pronouncements over the last 30 years evince a clear public policy to prevent domestic violence. . . . The legislature's articulated policy is "truly public" in nature. The legislature has repeatedly and unequivocally declared that domestic violence is an immense problem that impacts entire communities. . . . We find ample evidence of a clear public policy in the legislature's pervasive findings and enactments over the past 30 years.

Washington State's public policy of preventing domestic violence is also expressed in [the governor's] Executive Order 96-05 [that] directs each state agency to create workplace environments that provide "assistance for domestic violence victims without fear of reproach" [and further] directs agencies to "assure[ ] that every reasonable effort will be made to adjust work schedules and/or grant accrued or unpaid leave to allow employees who are victims of domestic violence to obtain medical treatment, counseling, legal assistance, to leave the area, or to make other arrangements to create a safer situation for themselves." Laidlaw contends that the executive order is not a proper source of public policy because it is not a "'constitutional, statutory, or regulatory provision or scheme.'" We disagree. [W]e have recognized that while statutes and case law are "primary sources of Washington public policy," public policy may come from other sources. . . .

This state's policy of preventing domestic violence also finds expression in Washington Constitution's crime victim amendment. Washington Constitution's crime victim amendment acknowledges that "Effective law enforcement depends on cooperation from victims of crime." Wash. Const. art. I, §35. This constitutional expression of public policy encourages crime victims like Danny to cooperate with law enforcement in order to hold their abusers accountable and thus prevent further violence.

The judicial expression of public policy is likewise pervasive. This court has specifically recognized a public policy interest in preventing domestic violence [citing] State v. Dejarlais, 969 P.2d 90 (Wash. 1998) (finding a clear statement of public

---

2. Laidlaw argues that the legislature intended RCW §50.20.050 to provide the sole remedy for victims who lose their jobs as a result of domestic violence. [However,] neither the plain language nor the legislative history characterizes RCW §50.20.050 as the sole remedy. More importantly, Laidlaw's argument ignores the breadth and depth of the legislature's stated commitment to encouraging Washington's domestic violence victims to escape violent situations and then aid in the prosecution of their abusers.

policy to prevent domestic violence and holding that reconciliation may not void a domestic violence protection order); In re Disciplinary Proceeding Against Turco, 970 P.2d 731 (Wash. 1999) (holding that "[t]he Legislature has established a clear public policy with respect to the importance of societal sensitivity to domestic violence and its consequences.") . . .

Laidlaw insists that any evidence of public policy is meaningless unless it directly addresses employers' responsibilities in preventing domestic violence. The dissent and the concurrence/dissent agree . . . that in order to demonstrate a clear public policy and satisfy the "clarity" element, the plaintiff must show that the employer contravened the public policy. This interpretation conflates the elements of wrongful discharge.

The "clarity" element does not require us to evaluate the employer's conduct at all; the element simply identifies the public policy at stake. Other elements of the tort serve to evaluate the employer's conduct in relation to that public policy. [Our court subsequently recognized that] "[w]hereas prior decisions have lumped the clarity and jeopardy elements together, a more consistent analysis will be obtained by first asking if any public policy exists whatsoever, and then asking whether, on the facts of each particular case, the employee's discharge contravenes or jeopardizes that public policy." Because the "clarity" element does not concern itself with the employer's actions, the public policy need not specifically reference employment. . . .

[Moreover, the legislature's recent actions] show that this state's clear and forceful public policy against domestic violence supports liability for employers who thwart their employees' efforts to protect themselves from domestic violence. The 2008 legislature unanimously passed [a new law to increase the safety and economic security of victims of domestic violence.] All 142 legislators who voted on the bill agreed that

> [i]t is in the public interest to reduce domestic violence, sexual assault, and stalking by enabling victims to maintain the financial independence necessary to leave abusive situations, achieve safety, and minimize physical and emotional injuries, and to reduce the devastating economic consequences of domestic violence, sexual assault, and stalking to employers and employees.

Laws of 2008, ch. 286, §1(1). To that end, the new law provides for "reasonable leave" for domestic violence victims to seek legal remedies, law enforcement assistance, treatment for injuries, services from shelters and other agencies, or to relocate themselves or their families, among other things. Though the legislature had not yet considered such a bill at the time of Danny's discharge, the fundamental public policy underlying the bill had long been established at that time. . . . The public policy in this case overwhelmingly requires an affirmative answer to the certified question.

We are mindful of the employer's burden and the need to narrowly construe the public policy exception. . . . Our holding will in no way open the floodgates of litigation. The clarity element is merely one of the elements Danny and future plaintiffs must successfully establish in order to maintain a wrongful discharge claim. Plaintiffs like Danny must also satisfy the jeopardy, causation, and absence of justification elements of the wrongful discharge tort. . . . [W]e return the case to the District Court [for that determination]. . . .

■ JOAN ZORZA, NEW STUDY ON DOMESTIC VIOLENCE IN THE WORKPLACE

3 Fam. & Intimate Partner Violence Q. 217, 217-222 (2011)

[The author reports findings from a study of 500 cases of workplace violence (based on media accounts) conducted by Peace at Work, an organization that addresses workplace violence.]

[Workplace domestic violence] is far more deadly than violence in the home. Half of the assaults resulted in at least one person being killed, and that is without even counting the perpetrators who died, whether they committed suicide, or were killed by responding police officers. While overwhelmingly, it was the abuser's target who was killed, in 42 percent of the cases where someone else was killed, the victim could have been anyone at the workplace, such as a client, co-worker, supervisor/boss, or a bystander. Fifteen percent of the cases involved multiple numbers of victims. . . .

When the time and place of the [workplace domestic violence assault] was recorded, the most common combination (20 percent) occurred in parking lots when the victim was arriving at work, and the second most common place was other locations outside the workplace, places where the victim was particularly vulnerable as they were less likely to be monitored by security or have bystanders easily able to assist them. . . . Often the perpetrator injured her outdoors after starting an argument and luring her outside by shame or embarrassment. Forty-two percent of assault or homicides occurred within the first half hour of the beginning of the victim's work shift. Those occurring at the end of the shift usually took place as the victim was leaving work or getting in her car. . . .

In cases where there was a protection order in existence against the perpetrator, it was violated in 19 percent of the cases, a surprisingly low number. In 29 (6 percent) of the cases, the victim had previously obtained an order of protection, but it had either expired or the victim dropped it.

Overwhelmingly, firearms were used. . . . Firearms were the abusers' choice even for the 67 percent of victims who had orders of protection against their abusers, and despite the fact that federal law should have prevented any of these abusers from having access to firearms.

Forty percent of [workplace perpetrators] made no attempt to flee afterward, and an alarming 30 percent of them either killed themselves or tried to do so, with almost four times as many (120) succeeding as those whose attempts failed (32, or 21 percent of the total). Not all of the suicide events occurred at the workplace; some perpetrators killed themselves on the road or after they returned home. [S]ome of these perpetrators were clearly "suicide by cop" DV cases, killers who had an opportunity to surrender to law enforcement, but forced the police to kill them in a shoot-out. . . .

[Several recommendations follow from what has been learned.]

- Extra security is needed at the beginning and end of workshifts and in parking lots, including police, and patrol requests if resources are limited.
- Reliance on monitoring and detection devices and extra lighting could only provide warning, but could not be relied upon to deter most perpetrators.
- Orders of protection are insufficient, particularly as few perpetrators are mandated to relinquish their weapons.

- Employers should not target employees in an effort to protect others at the workplace, particularly since in the majority of cases only the abuse victim is assaulted. Also, this would discourage other potential victims and co-workers from disclosing potential threats to themselves for fear of termination.
- Employers should use criminal background checks and checks for civil orders of protection. [Businesses should] provide support systems and resources for victim employees, hold abusers accountable for their behavior, train personnel to recognize and respond to warning signs, connect the community DV organizations, and above all, develop a healthy, respectful workplace. . . .

[The author urges better enforcement of federal laws to remove firearms from abusers and suggests that employers be allowed to intervene to protect employees by requesting restraining orders.]

Notes and Questions

1. *Social reality.* Domestic violence impinges on the workplace in many ways. As the above excerpt reveals, workplace violence results in the death of intimate partners and partners' co-workers, or the murder-suicides of victims and abusers. Another consequence, as Ramona Danny discovered, is job loss. See U.S. Gen. Accounting Office, Domestic Violence: Prevalence and Implications for Employment among Welfare Recipients 19 (1998) (reporting that 24 to 52 percent of victims lose their jobs).

2. *Costs.* What are the economic costs of domestic violence in the workplace? According to governmental statistics, (1) women lose 8 million days of paid work annually because of intimate partner violence; (2) the cost of reduced productivity due to injury, mental health, or chronic pain issues stemming from physical abuse or stalking is approximately $727.8 million; and (3) the total costs of intimate partner violence exceed $5.8 billion (that is, the sum of medical and mental health care costs, lost productivity, and lost lifetime earnings from women killed by their partners). Dept. of Health & Human Servs., Centers for Disease Control and Prevention, Costs of Intimate Partner Violence Against Women in the United States 19, 31-32 (Mar. 2003), available at http://www.cdc.gov/ncipc/pub-res/ipv_cost/ipvbook-final-feb18.pdf.

3. *Victims' perspective.* Absenteeism and job loss are not the only work-related problems that victims experience. Victims also report receiving sanctions because of the abuser's work-related harassment. Reprimands may cause the loss of opportunities for advancement. U.S. Government Accounting Office, Report to Congressional Committees, Domestic Violence: Prevalence and Implications for Employment among Welfare Recipients 8 (Nov. 1998), available at http://www.gao.gov/archive/1999/he99012.pdf.

Professor Sarah Buel identifies the various means by which the batterer jeopardizes the partner's employment.

> Realizing that if his partner is employed she is more likely to escape from her abusive situation, a batterer often becomes relentless in his determination to get her fired through frequent phone calls, causing trouble at her workplace, beating

her just before work, destroying her clothes, preventing her from sleeping, and generally interfering with her ability to be a competent employee. [T]he employer usually expects the victim to control the batterer's behavior because it is disruptive to the workplace, and, if the victim does not (or cannot), she is sometimes fired or forced to quit. . . . [S]tudies indicate that [terminations] are not atypical: approximately one-third of battered women lose their jobs as a direct result of abuse, and as many as 57.8 percent do not want to go to work because of threats of future abuse.

Sarah M. Buel, Effective Assistance of Counsel for Battered Woman Defendants: A Normative Construct, 26 Harv. Women's L.J. 217, 244 (2003). Jeopardizing the victim's employment, of course, threatens her economic independence and ultimately her safety because victims facing job loss are less likely to leave an abusive relationship. How did the plaintiff's husband in *Danny* jeopardize her employment?

4. *Public policy exceptions for employment-at-will.* As *Danny* explains, employees generally are terminable "at will," meaning that an employer may fire an employee at any time for nearly any reason. The common law "public policy" exception permits victims of domestic violence to bring wrongful termination suits. What is the nature of that exception? What elements are necessary for a plaintiff to satisfy the exception? Which element(s) does the court address? How does the court establish the existence of Washington State's public policy against domestic violence? What are the defendant's defenses? Why does the court reject those defenses?

What is the plaintiff seeking in *Danny*? What facts make her case particularly compelling? The nature of the abuse? The severity? The injury to her child? The particular legal actions that she took? The social services that she sought?

In the court's determination, how influential is any particular source of the state's public policy against domestic violence? Or, are all sources equally influential? See Apessos v. Memorial Press Group, 2002 WL 31324115 (Mass. Dist. Ct. 2002) (finding a public policy exception in wrongful discharge case based on the state constitution, state statute, and case law, but finding most persuasive the statutory mandate that a victim must appear in court to obtain a protection order). In states without extensive protections for victims of domestic violence, what arguments can plaintiffs make in favor of a public policy exception?

5. *Burden on the employer.* In an omitted portion of *Danny*, the defendant argues that recognition of a public policy exception will result in employers' having to serve as "the functional equivalent of the Department of Social and Health Services" and also require them to address fraudulent claims for wrongful discharge. *Danny*, 193 P.3d at 138. How persuasive are those arguments? How can an employer address these issues?

Responding to defendant's concerns, the Washington Supreme Court counters that the employer's burden is mitigated by the requirements that plaintiffs still must satisfy elements of the wrongful discharge tort (that is, jeopardy, causation, and absence of justification). Id. The court then suggests that Danny must show that the time off was the only available adequate means either to prevent the domestic violence or to hold the abuser accountable. How will she establish that? Defendant Laidlaw fired plaintiff *allegedly* because of her falsification of payroll records. How does a plaintiff establish that the employer's reasoning may be a pretext for its real concern with employee absenteeism or employer's fear of the "spill-over effect" of the violence in the workplace?

6. *Federal legislation.* Limited federal protection is available to victims of domestic violence in the employment context.

a. *OSHA.* The Occupational Safety and Health Act of 1970 (OSHA), 29 U.S.C. §§651 to 678, requires employers to provide safe workplaces "free from recognized hazards that are causing or are likely to cause death or serious physical harm." 29 U.S.C. §654(a)(1). Although the Act does not specifically address domestic violence, it establishes a standard of care that could be used as grounds for assertion of a negligence claim against an employer who fails to take steps to protect an employee or third parties against the acts of a known perpetrator. See Letter from Roger A. Clark, Dir., Directorate of Enforcement Programs, Occupational Safety and Health Admin., to John R. Schuller (Dec. 10, 1992), http://www.osha.gov/pls/oshaweb/owadisp.show_document?p_table=INTERPRETATIONS&p_id=20951 ("In a workplace where the risk of violence and serious personal injury are significant enough to be 'recognized hazards,' [OSHA] would require the employer to take feasible steps to minimize those risks. . . . On the other hand, the occurrence of acts of violence which are not 'recognized' as characteristic of employment and represent random antisocial acts which may occur anywhere would not subject the employer to a citation for a violation of [OSHA].").

Given that abusers often attack their victims at their place of employment, does the risk of domestic violence characterize all workplaces? See Taft v. Derricks, 613 N.W.2d 190, 197-198 (Wis. Ct. App. 2001) (holding that violation of 8 U.S.C. §654(a)(1) could not be used to support claim of negligence per se).

b. *FMLA.* Could Danny have asked for time off pursuant to the Family and Medical Leave Act (FMLA)? The FMLA provides very little protection for victims of domestic violence. The Act requires employers with over 50 employees to allow workers to take 12 weeks of unpaid medical leave for serious health conditions (or to care for family members with serious health conditions) or for the birth/adoption of a child. 29 U.S.C. §2612(a)(1)(D). Given that the FMLA contains no explicit mention of domestic violence, can an employee who suffers injuries from domestic violence take leave pursuant to the Act? One commentator responds:

> [If] a victim of domestic violence suffers a broken wrist or black eye, her injuries may not fall under the definition of a serious medical condition and, therefore, she may not be able to take time off from work to address the problem. Likewise, non-medical needs of domestic violence victims are not covered, such as acquiring restraining orders, filing court actions, or securing new housing. . . . .

Stone, supra, at 737. See also Robin Runge, Double Jeopardy: Victims of Domestic Violence Face Twice the Abuse, 25 Hum. Rts. 19, 20 (1998) (criticizing the FMLA for its failure to address the needs of many victims by not providing for job-protected leaves to attend civil protection order hearings or prohibiting an employer from firing a victim of domestic violence because of her status as a victim).

In a promising development, one court permitted a domestic violence victim who developed post-traumatic stress disorder (PTSD) to take FMLA-related leave to address her health needs. See Municipality of Anchorage v. Gregg, 101 P.3d 181, 189-190 (Alaska 2004) (finding that an employee who suffered PTSD from her abuse, and also had injuries from car accident and was pregnant, met the test for a "serious health condition," but not conferring automatic entitlement to all victims of abuse).

c. *Proposed federal legislation.* Congress is currently considering employment protections for victims of domestic violence. The Domestic Violence Leave Act, H.R. 3151, 112th Cong. (1st Sess. 2011), would expand the Family and Medical Leave Act (FMLA), §§2601-2653, to provide leaves to victims of domestic violence, sexual assault or stalking for the purposes of seeking medical attention for injuries; seeking legal assistance or remedies, including participating in a legal proceeding; attending support groups; obtaining counseling; participating in safety planning; and any other activity necessitated by the abuse. The bill applies to employees as well as their family members (such as adult children) who are addressing these issues, and extends FMLA protections to domestic partners, same-sex spouses, and their children. The terms "domestic violence," "sexual assault," and "stalking" have the same meanings as under the Violence Against Women Act, and the term "domestic violence" includes dating violence. An eligible employee can substitute paid vacation or sick leave for the FMLA 12-week unpaid leave.

The proposed legislation also provides that an employer must keep evidence of domestic violence, sexual assault, or stalking in the strictest confidence, except with the consent of the employee to protect the safety of the employee or a family member or to assist in documenting the violence for a court or law enforcement agency. The bill liberalizes the FMLA certification requirements (that require notice for the leave) to enable a victim who lacks the requisite third-party corroboration to meet the requirements by providing a written statement describing the violence and its effects. The text of the bill has been incorporated into a more extensive leave bill, the Balancing Act of 2011 (H.R. 2346) (1st Sess. 2011).

In addition, Congress is considering the Security and Financial Empowerment (SAFE) Act, H.R. 3271, 112th Cong. (1st Sess. 2011). The SAFE Act would help victims of domestic violence by: (1) allowing 30 days unpaid leave to receive medical attention, seek legal assistance, attend court proceedings and get help with safety planning; (2) requiring employers to provide reasonable accommodations for violence-related needs, such as making safety precautions or job-related modifications (absent an undue burden on the employer); (3) prohibit employment discrimination regarding job termination because of harassment by an abuser, obtaining protective orders, participating in the justice process, or seeking workplace modifications for safety reasons; (4) providing eligibility for unemployment insurance to victims of domestic violence, dating violence, sexual assault, or stalking who leave work as a result of such violence; and (5) reauthorizing the National Resource Center on Workplace Responses (created during the last reauthorization of VAWA) to continue funding for the operation of a national resource center on workplace responses to assist victims. See Press Release, Rep. Lucille Roybal-Allard Introduces the SAFE Act to Ensure Economic Stability for Victims of Domestic Violence, Sexual Assault and Stalking, Oct. 27, 2011, available at http://roybal-allard .house.gov/News/DocumentSingle.aspx?DocumentID=266560

7. *Law reform movement generally.* Currently, more than two-thirds of jurisdictions address the role of domestic violence in the workplace. See Deborah A. Widiss, Domestic Violence and the Workplace: The Explosion of State Legislation and the Need for a Comprehensive Strategy, 35 Fla. St. U. L. Rev. 669, 670-671 (2008). In addition to prohibitions on employment discrimination specifically against domestic violence victims, state laws authorize job-protected leaves for the purpose of securing legal and social services and also unemployment insurance benefits for those persons who leave their employment because of the violence.

Id. Also, almost a dozen jurisdictions permit domestic violence victims to take time off (thereby enabling them to seek medical attention and counseling, and to relocate) without fear of losing their jobs. Elissa Stone, Comment, How the Family and Medical Leave Act Can Offer Protection to Domestic Violence Victims in the Workplace, 44 U.S.F. L. Rev. 729, 740 (2010).

Statutes differ in scope, particularly regarding the persons who are covered; permissible reasons for the leave; type and length of leave; notice requirements; documentation requirements, and confidentiality requirements. Statutes are modeled on several approaches, including: (1) the family and medical leave model (modeled after the Family and Medical Leave Act (FMLA), U.S.C. §§2601-2653); (2) the disability model (modeled after the Americans with Disability Act (ADA), 42 U.S.C. §12112(b)(5)(A)); (3) the unemployment insurance model (modeled after state unemployment insurance systems); and (4) the criminal justice model (modeled after state schemes for crime victims generally). See Widiss, supra (comparing the different models). Consider which of the approaches below best accommodates employers' interests versus victims' interests.

a. *Family and medical leave model.* Some state legislation provides for a leave of a fixed duration for victims of domestic violence. This approach is modeled on the Family and Medical Leave Act, 29 U.S.C. §§2601-2653, that grants leave to employees for "serious health conditions" and/or the birth/adoption of children (although not yet applicable to victims of domestic violence per se). See, e.g., Colo. Rev. Stat. §24-34-402.7 (allowing up to three days leave to seek a protective order, get medical attention, move, change locks, or seek legal assistance). Generally, such legislation applies only to employers with over a certain number of employees. See, e.g., D.C. Code §32-131.02 (requiring employers with at least 25 employees to provide paid leave). Additionally, whether a victim has a right to take such time off may depend upon other conditions, such as how long she has worked for the employer. See, e.g., Fla. Stat. §741.313 (requiring employers of 50 or more employees, to provide 3 days paid or unpaid leave at employers' discretion, to employees who have worked at least 3 months).

b. *Disability model.* The disability model permits victims of domestic violence to take "reasonable leave" similar to that offered by employers to temporarily disabled employees. Disability leave for domestic violence victims generally applies to all employers, rather than only to large employers (like the FMLA-approach). Stone, supra, at 741-742. See, e.g., Cal. Lab. Code §230.

c. *Unemployment insurance model.* Persons who leave work voluntarily for "good cause" may qualify for unemployment insurance (for example, if they quit due to a reasonable fear for their health or safety if they were to remain on the job). E.g., Taylor v. Board of Review, 485 N.E.2d 827, 829 (Ohio Ct. App. 1984). The unemployment insurance model would permit domestic violence victims who leave their jobs to qualify for unemployment insurance. Initially, in the 1990s, courts were divided on whether victims of domestic violence qualified. Compare Hall v. Florida Unemployment Appeals Comm'n, 697 So. 2d 541, 542-543 (Fla. Dist. Ct. App. 1997); and Pagan v. Board of Review, 687 A.2d 328, 329 (N.J. Super. Ct. App. 1997) (both denying unemployment insurance); with Gilbert v. Department of Corr., 696 So. 2d 416, 417 (Fla. Dist. Ct. App. 1997) (granting benefits). In response, many states passed legislation providing unemployment insurance to victims who were forced to quit their jobs. See Press Release, SAFE Act, supra (noting that 40 states and the District of Columbia provide for unemployment insurance laws for victims of domestic violence although not explicitly for victims of sexual assault or stalking).

In evaluating how well the unemployment insurance model accommodates the interests of victims versus employers, consider that many state unemployment insurance systems provide former employees only half their salary (subject to an overall maximum), regardless of the employee's salary prior to quitting, and often only after a specified waiting period. Some victims leave work voluntarily to escape abuse whereas others leave involuntarily when they are discharged, for example, for absenteeism.

d. *Criminal justice model.* Some domestic-violence-leave laws prevent employers from terminating employees who are victims of *any* crime. Such laws also allow victims to miss work to attend criminal trials or confer with the police or the district attorney to prepare for trial. E.g., Alaska Stat. §12.61.017.

8. *Washington State domestic violence work leave.* The same year that *Danny* was decided, the Washington State legislature enacted work leaves for victims of domestic violence. The law provides victims of domestic violence with "reasonable leave from work, intermittent leave, or leave on a reduced leave schedule, with or without pay" in order to:

> (1) seek legal remedies to ensure the safety of the employee or employee's family members including (but not limited to): civil or criminal legal proceeding related to domestic violence, sexual assault, or stalking;
>
> (2) seek treatment for physical or mental injuries caused by domestic violence, sexual assault, or stalking, or to attend to such treatment for a family member;
>
> (3) seek services from a domestic violence shelter, rape crisis center, or other program for relief from domestic violence, sexual assault, or stalking;
>
> (4) seek mental health counseling related to an incident of domestic violence, sexual assault, or stalking; or
>
> (5) participate in safety planning, temporarily or permanently relocate, or take other actions to increase the safety of the employee or employee's family members from future domestic violence, sexual assault, or stalking.

Wash. Rev. Code §49.76.030. The term *reasonable leave* is not defined in the legislation. Wash. Admin. Code §296-135-050 ("The reasonableness of duration of leave must be determined on a case-by-case basis considering the reasons for taking leave"). The employee may elect to take paid sick or vacation leave, compensatory leave, or unpaid leave. Wash. Rev. Code §49.76.030. Pursuant to the statute, an employee has to give advance notice of the intention to take leave (absent "an emergency" or "unforeseen circumstances"). Wash. Rev. Code §49.76.040(1). The employer may request verification in the form of a police report, evidence from the court or a prosecuting attorney that the victim has appeared or is scheduled to appear in connection with an incident of domestic violence, or a written statement of the employee. Wash. Rev. Code §49.76.040(4). The new legislation, more expansive than the tort of wrongful discharge, adds an important remedy—a civil cause of action against employers. Wash. Rev. Code §49.76.100. On which model is the above statute based?

Would the above statute have helped the plaintiff? What statutory provisions best address a victim's needs? For example, what duration is preferable—three days or "reasonable leave"? Can an employer fire an employee who takes off too much time? Does an ill-defined length of time chill the exercise of this right? Which employees are protected? Which employers have the obligation? Is this coverage adequate? How burdensome for the employee and employer, respectively, are the requirements of notice and documentation?

9. *Gender-based remedies.* What employment remedies against gender-based discrimination, specifically, are available to victims of domestic violence? In an omitted footnote in *Danny*, the court mentions, but does not resolve, the argument of the Washington Employment Lawyers Association that the majority of domestic violence victims are women and that terminating Danny under these circumstances would frustrate the policy of providing equal opportunities for women. *Danny*, 165 Wash. 2d at 252 n.6.

Plaintiff in *Danny* alleged that her termination was a violation of public policy and Washington's employment discrimination law. Could she have argued that, because she was a victim of domestic violence, her termination violated Title VII of the Civil Rights Act of 1964, 42 U.S.C. §2000e-2, because it had an impermissible gender-based *disparate impact* due to the disproportionate number of victims of domestic violence who are women? Plaintiffs have faced difficulty proving disparate impact claims in this context because courts often conclude that the adverse employment decision was only an isolated event. See Julie Goldscheid, Disparate Impact's Impact: The Gender Violence Lens, 90 Or. L. Rev. 33(2011) (advocating greater use of disparate impact theory as a remedy for adverse employment decisions for victims of domestic violence); Julie Goldscheid, Gender Violence and Work: Reckoning with the Boundaries of Sex Discrimination Law, 18 Colum. J. Gender & L. 61 (2008) (discussing sex discrimination generally as a remedy for domestic violence in the workplace).

10. *Legacy of* Danny. *Danny* was the first state supreme court case to recognize a common law claim for wrongful discharge of an employee on domestic violence-related grounds. How influential do you think the case will be in light of recent statutory reforms that address domestic violence in the workplace? See Margaret C. Hobday, Protecting Economic Stability: The Washington State Supreme Court Breathes New Life in the Public-Policy Exception to At-Will Employment for Domestic Violence Victims, 17 Wm. & Mary J. Women & L. 87, 132 (2010) (concluding that common law recognition of a public-policy exception for victims provides a "necessary complement" to legislative reform to "implement the clear statutory policies that otherwise fail to provide employees with a cause of action").

11. *Tort liability for employers.* Far too often, acts of violence "spill over" from the home and take place in the workplace. Approximately 1.7 to 2 million violent acts occur in the workplace every year, with 1 percent of all workplace violence being committed by an intimate partner. John E. Matejkovic, Which Suit Would You Like? The Employer's Dilemma in Dealing with Domestic Violence, 33 Cap. U. L. Rev. 309, 309 (2004) (citing data). Intimate partners commit 16 percent of workplace homicides against women. Id. From 35 to 56 percent of battered women also are harassed by their abusive partners while at work. Legal Momentum, Understanding the Effects of Domestic Violence, Sexual Assault and Stalking on Housing and the Workplace, http://www.legalmomentum.org/our-work/domestic-violence/statistics-understanding-the.html (last visited June 9, 2011).

What duty does an employer have to protect an employee from such violence? How should an employer weigh the potential for tort liability against the possibility of a wrongful termination suit brought by a victim of domestic violence who is terminated based on her status? See Nicole Buonocore Porter, Victimizing the

Abused?: Is Termination the Solution When Domestic Violence Comes to Work?, 12 Mich. J. Gender & L. 275, 315-319 (2006).

12. *Workers' compensation benefits.* Employees who are injured in the course of, or arising out of, work are usually entitled to workers' compensation benefits. Can an employee collect benefits if injured at work as a result of domestic violence? Does the injury "arise out of" the employment? Compare Murphy v. Workers' Comp. Appeals Bd., 150 Cal. Rptr. 561 (Ct. App. 1978) (affirming relief, when employer knew of husband's threat and took no precaution), with Colas v. Watermain, 744 N.Y.S.2d 229 (App. Div. 2002) (contra, because death at workplace did not "arise out of" employment). See also Matejkovic, supra, at 340. Should workers' compensation be the exclusive remedy for such cases? Or should the employee also be able to file a tort claim against an employer? What are the advantages/disadvantages of each remedy?

Problems

1. If you were a state legislator, what factors would you consider in drafting legislation to accommodate the workplace-related needs of victims of domestic violence? What accommodations would you suggest for the victim? For the employer? Would you recommend a uniform law or federal legislation? Would you recommend passage of the Domestic Violence Leave Act (discussed above)? If so, what improvements would you suggest?

2. Christine, a supervisor at Manson, Inc.'s manufacturing plant, recently ended a romantic relationship with a co-worker Lee. At that time, Lee attacked her with a bar bell, fracturing her skull. Christine obtains an order of protection. Last week, she informs her superintendent, Taylor, that Lee violated the order by harassing her by phone and email and that his threats are increasing. Taylor chides her to keep her personal problems out of the workplace.

One week later, Lee calls Christine and tells her he is "going to 'off her'" after work. She receives permission to leave early. Taylor takes no safety precautions. As she is leaving, she sees Lee and tells her boss, who calls a security guard to escort Lee off the premises. She goes to a motel instead of to her home. The next day, she asks Taylor for the day off. He refuses, telling her that he really needs her because another employee is sick. As she parks in the company parking lot, Lee shoots her to death and also kills Meredith, a co-worker passing by, who is the sole support of three small children. Is Manson, Inc. liable to Christine's estate? To Meredith's estate? What difference does it make that Christine and Lee both work for Manson? What actions should Manson have taken to ensure Christine's safety and that of other employees?

What policies should employers formulate for preventing workplace violence? How should the policy differ for victims versus innocent bystanders? Should an *employer* be able to seek an order of protection for an employer? Should workplace safety policies be voluntary or mandatory? If state mandated, should states impose criminal liability if employers fail to act? What incentives can states provide to encourage private employers to develop such policies? See, e.g., 20 Ill. Comp. Stat. 605/605-550 (mandating formation of task force to assist businesses in developing policies); N.Y. Lab. Law §27-b (requiring public employers to develop programs); S.C. Code §1-1-1410 (same).

See generally Jessie Bode Brown, The Costs of Domestic Violence in the Employ-
ment Arena: A Call for Legal Reform and Community-Based Education Initiatives,
16 Va. J. Soc. Pol'y & L. 1 (2008); Julie Goldscheid, Elusive Equality in Domestic and
Sexual Violence Law Reform, 34 Fla. St. U. L. Rev. 731 (2007); Marcy L. Karin,
Changing Federal Statutory Proposals to Address Domestic Violence at Work: Creat-
ing a Societal Response by Making Businesses a Part of the Solution, 74 Brook. L.
Rev. 377 (2009); Deborah Weinstein & William Klemick, Who is Liable When
Domestic Violence Invades the Workplace?, 8 Emp. L. Strategist 1 (2000).

3. Mary Smith, the mother of two young children, is hired by the New York State
Corrections Department (NYCD) subject to a probationary period that permits
termination without cause. NYCD has a sick leave policy that requires employees
who report sick to furnish their address and to remain in their residence while on
sick leave. Soon after Mary begins work, she is forced to move into a battered
women's shelter due to abuse by her husband.

When Mary becomes ill, she goes to a doctor who tells her that she needs
surgery. She requests and receives sick leave from her employer. She furnishes
her employer with the address of the shelter office (not its actual location). According to shelter policy, residents are not permitted to divulge the shelter address.
When the employer attempts to verify Mary's sick leave, a shelter staff person tells
NYCD that Mary's residence is confidential. After Mary returns to work, she is terminated for being away from her residence while on leave. Mary files suit, contending that her termination is illegal. New York has a Human Rights Law that prohibits
employers from committing discriminatory employment practices, including "to
refuse to hire or employ or to bar or to discharge from employment, or to discriminate against an individual in compensation or other terms, conditions, or privileges
of employment because of the actual or perceived status of said individual as a victim
of domestic violence." Admin. Code §8-107.1[2]. What result? Reynolds v. Fraser,
781 N.Y.S.2d 885 (Sup. Ct. 2004).

Note: Discrimination in Insurance Coverage

Victims of domestic violence sometimes face discriminatory practices regarding
insurance coverage. Some insurers refuse to issue; cancel; or fail to renew life,
health, disability, property, and casualty insurance coverage to persons with a history
of domestic violence.[9] The insurance companies perceive victims as too costly to
insure because of victims' increased risk of death, injuries, and property damage.
Insurers are able to learn about the abuse from police, medical, or court records.[10]
The mid-1990s saw a rise in publicity concerning insurance company policies that
deny insurance or determine rates on the basis of domestic violence.[11] National
publicity led to several federal and state studies. A survey conducted by the House
Judiciary Committee found that half of the largest insurers in the country used
domestic violence as a factor in coverage.[12] Another survey by a state insurance

[9]. Terry Fromson, Insurance Discrimination Against Victims of Abuse, in ABA, The Impact of
Domestic Violence on Your Legal Practice 10-21 (1996).

[10]. Id.

[11]. See Monica C. Fountain, Insurance Companies Hit Battered Women Too, Chi. Trib., June 4,
1995, at 1; Katharine Q. Seelye, Insurability for Battered Women, N.Y. Times, May 12, 1994, at B10.

[12]. Press Release, Bernard Sanders, Congressman, Discrimination Against Domestic Violence
Victims (Mar. 18, 1997).

commission reported that 24 percent of accident, health, and life insurers took domestic violence into account when deciding on issuance and renewal of insurance.[13]

Some insurance companies defended their discriminatory practices by claiming that victims "chose" to stay in an abusive relationship. Insurers thereby analogized domestic violence to high-risk activities like skydiving or professional boxing that are excluded from coverage.[14] Other companies classified domestic abuse as a "pre-existing condition," like a disease, that justified higher rates.[15] Still other insurance companies justified denying life insurance to battered women because it would provide "a financial incentive . . . for the proceeds to be paid for [the batterer] to kill her."[16]

In response to these discriminatory practices, 41 states adopted laws prohibiting or limiting the use of domestic violence as a factor in health insurance coverage.[17] Some statutes prohibit consideration of domestic violence as the sole factor in denying or limiting coverage (e.g., N.Y. Ins. Law §2612). Some states prohibit using the term *abuse victim* as a classification in underwriting the insurance (e.g., W. Va. Code §33-4-20). Other states go so far as to prohibit any practice that has a discriminatory effect on an abuse victim (e.g., Mass. Gen. Laws §108G).[18]

Congress considered legislation prohibiting insurance discrimination against victims of domestic violence beginning in 1995. See Victims of Abuse Insurance Protection Act, H.R. 2654, 104th Cong. (1995). Initially, bills proposed targeting only health insurance, but later proposals addressed all forms of insurance protection. For example, the Victims of Abuse Insurance Protection Act, H.R. 739, 111th Cong. §403 (2009) prohibited insurers from committing a range of adverse actions (including restricting coverage or charging higher rates in insurance policies and health benefit plans) on the basis that an applicant or insured was in an abusive relationship or might incur abuse-related claims.

Finally, in 2010, Congress enacted important consumer protection provisions as part of health care reform legislation, the Patient Protection and Affordable Care Act (PPACA), Pub. L. 111-148, 124 Stat. 119 (codified as amended in scattered sections of U.S.C.). The PPACA aims to improve affordability of, and accessibility to, health care. It also protects consumers from discriminatory practices based on pre-existing conditions, health status, and gender. The new legislation specifically provides that a health insurance issuer may not impose any preexisting-condition exclusion based on domestic violence. See 42 U.S.C. §300gg-4, §2705(a)(7) ("Prohibiting Discrimination against Individual Participants and Beneficiaries based on

[13]. Id.

[14]. Ellen J. Morrison, Note, Insurance Discrimination Against Battered Women: Proposed Legislative Protections, 72 Ind. L.J. 259, 272 (1996).

[15]. Id. at 275.

[16]. Seelye, supra note [11] (quoting a spokeswoman for State Farm Insurance). State Farm later reversed its policy of denying coverage. See Katharine Q. Seelye, In Shift, State Farm Will Insure Battered Women, N.Y. Times, June 1, 1994, at A19.

[17]. Mary Crossley, Discrimination Against the Unhealthy in Health Insurance, 54 U. Kan. L. Rev. 73, 103 n.151 (2005). See also Catharine Reichert, Michelle Obama Claims that Domestic Violence Counts as a Pre-existing Condition in Some States, St. Petersburg Times, Sept. 21, 2009 (citing eight states and the District of Columbia without statutory protection for victims against insurance discrimination), available at 2009 WLNR 18759500.

[18]. See Crossley, supra note [17], at 103-104; Deborah S. Hellman, Is Actuarially Fair Insurance Pricing Actually Fair?: A Case Study in Insuring Battered Women, 32 Harv. C.R.-C.L. L. Rev. 355, 404-410 (1997) (analyzing existing and proposed legislation).

Health Status" [such as] "Evidence of insurability (including conditions arising out of acts of domestic violence").

In addition, the federal health care reform legislation aims to provide improved preventive coverage by requiring that certain preventive procedures be covered without a co-payment, co-insurance or a deductible. The Obama Administration was charged with determining those services that be classified as "preventive." In August 2011, the Department of Health and Human Services issued guidelines for health insurance coverage by requiring that all new insurance policies must provide coverage for domestic violence screening and counseling (as well as for other women's health issues such as wellness visits, breastfeeding support, and contraception). See U.S. Dept. Health & Human Servs., Health Resources & Servs. Admin., Women's Preventive Services: Required Health Plan Coverage Guidelines, available at http://www.hrsa.gov/womensguidelines/.

PART FOUR

LEGAL AND SOCIAL SERVICES

XIV

Legal Services

This chapter explores some of the dilemmas that emerge in the representation of clients who have been abused. The first section of the chapter explores constitutional issues in the right to counsel. The chapter then turns to ethical issues and practical issues that guide representation. The next section examines the role of domestic violence in the mediation context—an alternative to traditional dispute resolution processes. Finally, the chapter addresses the merits of specialized domestic violence courts that were created to redress the shortcomings of the traditional legal response to domestic violence.

A. REPRESENTING THE VICTIM

1. Constitutional Issues: What Is Effective Assistance of Counsel?

■ DANDO v. YUKINS
461 F.3d 791 (6th Cir. 2006)

MARTIN, Circuit Judge.

[Debra Dando was apprehended following a string of armed robberies and assaults committed with her boyfriend, Brian Doyle.] [S]he waived her *Miranda* rights and confessed to participating in the robberies. She received appointed counsel, who subsequently recommended that she plead no contest to all charges. . . . The plea was entered pursuant to [an agreement], whereby the circuit court agreed to sentence Dando at the low end of the state's sentencing guidelines. [In sentencing her to 10 to 30 years, the circuit court explained:]

Miss Dando's 30, and certainly by sentencing her at the low end of the guidelines we are recognizing the fact that she was apparently misused by Mr. Doyle, but I've indicated on the record already she had several opportunities to remove herself from that and cease in the agreement to perpetrate these crimes. . . .

Sentencing Hr'g Tr. at 13.

On May 22, 2000, Dando obtained new counsel for the appeals process. On January 17, 2001, Dando's appellate counsel moved in the Michigan circuit court for the appointment of an expert on Battered Woman's Syndrome to assist with the appeals process. The motion indicated that Petitioner was considering whether to move to withdraw her plea and enter a duress defense based on Battered Woman's Syndrome. Along with the motion, Dando submitted three affidavits, one from her aunt, Barbara Ditch, one from a friend, Luther Early, and one from herself. The affidavits documented a history of physical and sexual abuse.

The circuit court held a hearing on the motion on January 24, 2001. At the hearing, appellate counsel explained that she needed an expert to assess whether Dando should move to withdraw her no contest plea. The circuit court construed the request as one for an expert to assist with an ineffective assistance of counsel claim, presumably because Dando would need such a claim to withdraw her plea. The circuit court denied this request, holding that Dando had not received ineffective assistance of counsel. The court reasoned that Dando's trial counsel had made a strategic choice to recommend a no contest plea. . . .

[Dando appealed, raising two questions]: (1) whether the sentencing court abused its discretion in denying Dando's motion for an expert witness, and (2) whether trial counsel was ineffective for failing to pursue a duress defense. [H]er request for a mental health expert to help her decide whether or not to withdraw her plea and her claim of ineffective assistance of counsel are one in the same. As presented in her federal habeas claim now before this Court, the issue can be articulated as follows: was it an unreasonable application of federal law to reject Dando's claim of ineffective assistance of counsel based on her trial counsel's failure to consult an expert and otherwise investigate the validity of a duress defense based on Battered Woman's Syndrome? . . .

Dando's claim that her trial counsel's failure to seek a mental health expert and to explore a potential defense based on duress and Battered Woman's Syndrome is governed by the standard set forth in [Hill v. Lockhart, 474 U.S.52, 58 (1985), in which the United States Supreme Court adopted a two-part test to establish ineffective assistance of counsel that "applies to challenges to guilty pleas based on ineffective assistance of counsel"]. Under that test, a defendant must show that counsel's performance fell below an objective standard of reasonableness, and that the defendant was prejudiced by the attorney's error. [T]he defendant must show that "but for counsel's errors, he would not have pleaded guilty and would have insisted on going to trial." Id. at 59. The Supreme Court added that an assessment of prejudice must include a prediction of the likely outcome at trial. In the case of an unexplored affirmative defense or undiscovered evidence, this prediction of the likely outcome at trial is relevant to determine whether or not the potential defense or evidence would have caused counsel to change the recommendation as to the plea.

Dando's counsel failed here to adequately investigate the availability of a duress defense and the related possibility that Dando suffered from Battered Woman's

Syndrome. Dando informed her attorney that she had a long history of violent sexual and physical abuse, that Doyle beat her and threatened to kill her immediately before she participated in the robberies, and even requested a consultation with a mental health expert before entering her plea. The attorney refused to seek assistance from an expert, informing Dando that it would be too costly. This advice was flatly incorrect, as Dando would have been entitled to have the state pay for a mental expert. . . . [2] Investigation of this potential defense was a minimal requirement to providing adequate representation at the plea stage, particularly since Dando herself told her attorney about her history of abuse, and even suggested the need for a mental health expert. Although courts are typically required to show heightened deference to an attorney's strategic decisions supported by professional judgment, where a failure to investigate does not reflect sound professional judgment, such deference is not appropriate. The evidence in this case suggests that the attorney's decision was not an exercise in professional judgment because it reflected a misunderstanding of the law regarding the availability of a mental health expert. The state court's determination that Dando's counsel's performance was not inadequate misapplied clearly established Supreme Court precedent that required counsel to adequately investigate potential defenses.

The fact that Dando received a relatively lenient sentence in exchange for her no contest plea does not render the failure to investigate Battered Woman's Syndrome and duress a sound professional judgment. The state court praised the decision by trial counsel to raise Dando's abuse in obtaining a shorter sentence. However, had counsel investigated the potential defenses and pursued them at trial, Dando would have had a chance to be acquitted altogether, or convicted of only some of the counts charged and acquitted of others (perhaps if the jury found the duress to be more immediate during particular portions of the crime spree). Given this possibility, there is a likelihood that Dando would not have entered a plea, and that the failure to investigate undermined the knowing and voluntary nature of her plea. In showing deference to the decision to seek a plea bargain with a lower sentence, the state courts essentially conflated what were two critical decisions by Dando's attorney into one. Counsel had an obligation both to investigate potential defenses, and to subsequently ensure that Dando's history of abuse was accounted for at sentencing. If the attorney had assessed possible defenses, and still recommended a plea because in his judgment the defenses were long shots, his choice to negotiate a lower sentence based on Dando's history of abuse and to forego the potential defense would be sound, or at least entitled to some deference. However because he simply failed to assess a possible defense, due in part to his incorrect

2. [The U.S. Supreme Court previously held in Ake v. Oklahoma, 470 U.S. 68 (1985), that due process requires a state to pay for a mental health expert who will assist in the preparation of a defense at trial. *Ake* applied a balancing test derived from Mathews v. Eldridge, 424 U.S. 319, 335 (1976), that balances the private interest at stake, the government interest, and the risk of an erroneous result without the safeguard.] These considerations apply with equal, if not greater force, in the guilty plea context. A defendant's decision to plead guilty and waive her right to a jury trial and to put on a defense implicates her significant private liberty interest, and given the relevant consequences, ensuring that a plea is entered knowingly and voluntarily presents as weighty a private interest as ensuring an accurate result at trial. Further, [n]ot only is the financial burden [on the state] less in the plea context, but this burden and the state's interest in prevailing at trial are "necessarily tempered by its interest in the fair and accurate adjudication of criminal cases." Finally, the risk of an inaccurate result in the form of a plea that is not knowing and voluntary presents an issue of significant constitutional concern. In cases where the defendant's mental health is a potential issue at trial, and necessarily could undermine the knowing and voluntary nature of her plea, providing expert consultation would seem almost critical to ensuring a more accurate result. . . .

understanding of the law regarding the provision of a mental health expert, his advocacy at sentencing does not insulate the shortcomings at the plea stage. Given these shortcomings, Dando has met the first requirement [that she show that counsel's performance fell below an objective standard of reasonableness].

The remaining question is whether Dando was prejudiced by the inadequate representation she received in deciding to plead guilty. To meet the prejudice requirement, Dando "must show that there is a reasonable probability that, but for counsel's errors, [s]he would not have pleaded guilty and would have insisted on going to trial." *Hill*, 474 U.S. at 59. This determination depends in part "on the likelihood that discovery of the evidence would have led counsel to change his recommendation as to the plea" and the related inquiry of "whether the evidence likely would have changed the outcome of a trial." Id. Dando argues that she would not have pled guilty had counsel investigated and discussed with her the possibility of presenting a duress defense based on Battered Woman's Syndrome.

The district court rejected this approach based on its determination that evidence Dando was suffering from Battered Woman's Syndrome would not have supported a duress defense. The elements of duress under Michigan law are:

> A) The threatening conduct was sufficient to create in the mind of a reasonable person the fear of death or serious bodily harm;
> B) The conduct in fact caused such fear of death or serious bodily harm in the mind of the defendant;
> C) The fear or duress was operating upon the mind of the defendant at the time of the alleged act; and
> D) The defendant committed the act to avoid the threatened harm.

People v. Lemons, 562 N.W.2d 447 (Mich. 1997). Additionally, "the threatening conduct or act of compulsion must be 'present, imminent, and impending[,][a] threat of future injury is not enough,' and [ ] the threat 'must have arisen without the negligence or fault of the person who insists upon it as a defense.'" Id. The district court found that Dando would have been unable to establish a duress defense because she had several opportunities to escape during the crime spree, and because the requirement for a duress defense that the threat create a fear in the mind of a reasonable person precludes the use of evidence of Battered Woman's Syndrome, which is inherently subjective.

We disagree with the district court's conclusion that evidence of Battered Woman's Syndrome is irrelevant to a duress defense under Michigan law. . . . [T]he theory of Battered Woman's Syndrome is not at odds with a reasonableness requirement—if anything, evidence of Battered Woman's Syndrome can potentially bolster an argument that a defendant's actions were in fact reasonable. Although those of us who are not so unfortunate to have to live with constant, imminent threats of violence might look at the actions of a defendant in Dando's situation from the relative comfort of a judge's chambers or a jury box and wonder what reasonable person would have facilitated Doyle's shocking crime spree, evidence of Battered Woman's Syndrome can explain why a reasonable person might resort to such actions given a history of violent abuse and the imminent violent threats. Additionally, . . . this evidence is relevant to show why a defendant did not leave the company of her abuser. For these reasons, we believe that evidence of Battered Woman's Syndrome could potentially have been relevant to all of the elements of a duress defense under Michigan law.

Dando's experience of abuse is itself shocking, and would present a potentially compelling duress defense based on Battered Woman's Syndrome. Dando's mother was a drug addict, who would "lend out" Dando to drug dealers for months at a time to pay off her drug debts, from the time Dando was six years old until she was twelve. Dando was forced to perform sex acts upon the dealers. Her parents abused her both physically and sexually, and her father took photographs of her which the state court described as shocking and appalling. Dando's first husband seems to have abused her to the point where she was "scared to death of him." Doyle also violently abused Dando, and one of the affidavits submitted by an acquaintance claimed that Doyle said he was "selling" Dando. Doyle threatened and hit Dando on the morning of the offenses, possibly giving her a concussion and requiring her to seek medical attention. Doyle's reckless and violent behavior is also exemplified by his brandishing of a shotgun, repeated robbery attempts, and eventual armed confrontation with the police that resulted in his death.

With help from an expert on Battered Woman's Syndrome, Dando could have introduced evidence of all of the elements of a duress defense. Just prior to embarking on the crime spree, Doyle had threatened her life if she did not cooperate. Given Doyle's propensity for violence, with which Dando had sadly become too familiar, a reasonable person in her situation would likely have feared death or serious bodily harm. Dando's testimony could also support conclusions that the threats in fact caused her to fear death or serious bodily harm, that this fear was operating upon her mind at the time of her cooperation with Doyle, and that she cooperated with Doyle to avoid the threatened harm. Evidence of Battered Woman's Syndrome would also have been relevant to explain why Dando may have felt unable to escape the situation.

[For purposes of evaluating prejudice], we need not determine to an absolute certainty that a jury would have acquitted Dando based on a defense of duress. Rather, we need only find a likelihood of a favorable outcome at trial such that Dando's counsel would not have given the same recommendation and she likely would have rejected the guilty plea. We find there to be a sufficient likelihood here to establish ineffective assistance of counsel. . . . The case is remanded to the district court, with instructions to issue the writ requiring the state to vacate Dando's guilty plea.

Notes and Questions

1. *Right to counsel.* Under the Sixth Amendment, people facing criminal charges and the possibility of jail have a right to the effective assistance of counsel. Gideon v. Wainwright, 372 U.S. 335. Moreover, indigent defendants have a right to have counsel appointed to them. Id. at 343-345.

2. *Effective assistance of counsel: standard.* The right to counsel, in either criminal or civil proceedings, means the right to *effective assistance* of counsel. Although the attorney may not decide for the client certain matters (for example, whether to plead guilty or not guilty, whether or not to testify, or whether to pursue, settle, or drop a lawsuit), the attorney has an enormous influence on those decisions, based on his or her understanding of the courtroom and knowledge of substantive and procedural law.

In *Dando*, the attorney representing the victim was found to have provided ineffective assistance of counsel. Why? What standard did the court apply? At which stage of the criminal proceeding was Dando's counsel considered ineffective? How does the defendant in *Dando* demonstrate that she would not have pled guilty but for defense counsel's ineffective assistance?

The standard for effective assistance of counsel may differ between criminal and civil proceedings. See Turner v. Rogers, 131 S.Ct 2507 (2011) (holding that due process does not require counsel at civil contempt proceedings for nonpayment of child support); Lassiter v. Dept. of Soc. Servs., 452 U.S. 18 (1981) (holding that the Constitution may guarantee counsel to terminate parental rights depending on the circumstances, but that the failure to appoint counsel in this case did not violate due process because counsel would have made no difference). What explains the different standards?

3. *Grounds for ineffective assistance of counsel regarding BWS.* Battered Woman's Syndrome (BWS) is often raised in a self-defense or duress defense, as we have seen (in Chapter 7). For a victim of domestic violence, what actions (or inactions) by an attorney constitute ineffective assistance of counsel? Consider the following:

a. *Failure to investigate BWS as potential defense. Dando* held, in part, that the defendant did not receive the effective assistance of counsel because her attorney did not hire an expert to determine whether the defendant suffered from BWS. Other courts have held, similarly, that counsel must investigate, before trial, whether the defendant suffers from BWS to determine what defenses are available. See People v. Day, 2 Cal. Rptr. 2d 916 (Ct. App. 1992) (overruled on other grounds); Martin v. State, 501 So. 2d 1313 (Fla. Dist. Ct. App. 1986). At what point should the defense counsel's duty to investigate BWS be triggered? Is it a good idea to require counsel to hire an expert to investigate BWS whenever the defendant alleges abuse? Why or why not?

Dando's counsel refused to investigate BWS because of the cost involved in hiring an expert witness. What role does inadequate funding of public defenders play in the effectiveness of counsel? The author of one study responds as follows:

> While some public defender offices have budgeted funds from which to retain such expert assistance, other offices must obtain court approval for such assistance. Surprisingly, almost one-third (30 percent) of the offices reported having difficulty obtaining such approval. Moreover, even when such assistance is approved, there is still a lack of equality in funding between the defender office and the district attorney's office. Over one-half (56 percent) of the institutional public defender offices reported that they are handicapped by the lack of funds sufficient to obtain experts that match the district attorney's experts.

Laurence A. Benner, The Presumption of Guilt: Systemic Factors that Contribute to Ineffective Assistance of Counsel in California, 45 Cal. W. L. Rev. 263, 295-296 (2009). What other institutional factors contribute to the ineffective assistance of counsel? See id.

b. *Failure to present BWS experts.* Criminal, rather than civil, issues generally evoke the need for expert testimony. Experts are permitted to testify when an issue is beyond the ordinary training, knowledge, intelligence, or experience of jurors. In the case of BWS, many state courts have found that understanding the myriad methods of control exerted by an abuser as well as the inability of a domestic violence victim to escape the cycle of violence is beyond the average juror's knowledge and experience, allowing expert testimony on the matter. See, e.g., State v. Borrelli,

629 A.2d 1105 (Conn. 1993); Commonwealth v. Stonehouse, 555 A.2d 772 (Pa. 1989); Dean v. State, 194 P.3d 299 (Wyo. 2008). In the context of the effective assistance of counsel, is introducing and presenting expert testimony *required?* Compare Paine v. Massie, 339 F.3d 1194 (10th Cir. 2003) (failure to call BWS expert was ineffective assistance of counsel) and People v. Day, 2 Cal. Rptr. 2d 916, 924-945 (Ct. App. 1992) (same), with State v. Dulany, 781 S.W.2d 52 (Mo. 1989) (failure to present BWS experts regarding duress defense held appropriate in capital murder case, where duress was not considered defense to murder), and State v. Felton, 803 S.W.2d 1 (Mo. 1991) (failure to present BWS expert held appropriate where expert testimony would counter claim of self-defense). Suppose the defendant does not wish to hire an expert to testify to BWS. Does that relieve the attorney of liability for ineffective assistance of counsel? See Smith v. Oklahoma, 144 P.3d 159 (Okla. Crim. App. 2006) (defendant's decision not to hire expert was result of being ill-informed about BWS defense and resulted in ineffective assistance of counsel). See generally Sarah M. Buel, Effective Assistance of Counsel for Battered Women Defendants: A Normative Construct, 26 Harv. Women's L.J. 217 (2003).

c. *Failure to use appropriate BWS defense.* Evidence of BWS may suggest a number of defenses, including self-defense, duress, heat of passion, or diminished capacity. In addition, the presence of BWS may indicate the merits of pleading to a lesser-included offense. What defense did Dando invoke in the principal case? How would BWS evidence have been relevant to her defense?

When does a defense counsel's choice to pursue one defense rather than another result in the ineffective assistance of counsel? When the choice is informed and a part of the strategy? Compare Meeks v. Bergen, 749 F.2d 322 (6th Cir. 1984) (finding that defense counsel made a permissible strategic claim of self-defense instead of BWS in battered woman's murder trial), and Martin v. State, 712 S.W.2d 14 (Mo. Ct. App. 1986) (choice to use BWS defense instead of diminished capacity was permissible in capital murder prosecution), with State v. Peterson, 857 A.2d 1132, 1154 (Md. 2004) (failure to present BWS defense was ineffective assistance where it resulted from ignorance of the defense rather than strategy), and State v. Felton, 329 N.W.2d 161 (Wis. 1983) (finding that attorney's pursuit of self-defense and ignorance of heat-of-passion defense denied battered woman effective assistance of counsel). When choosing to use BWS as a mitigating defense instead of a complete defense? See United States v. Smith, 113 F. Supp. 2d 879 (E.D. Va. 1999) (finding counsel effective where circuit had not directly ruled on whether BWS was appropriate at trial or at sentencing). Where defendant lacks credibility as a battered woman? Compare Lewis v. State, 457 S.E.2d 173 (Ga. 1995), and Smith v. State, 499 S.E.2d 663 (Ga. Ct. App. 1998) (both finding that defense counsel appropriately analyzed the credibility of the defendant in deciding not to present a BWS defense), with State v. Zimmerman, 823 S.W.2d 220 (Tenn. Crim. App. 1991) (battered woman defendant's inconsistent statements not an excuse for not presenting a BWS defense or allowing her to testify). Where the defense counsel pursues a BWS defense solely to gain publicity and business, despite the defense not being in the client's best interests? See Larson v. State, 766 P.2d 261 (Nev. 1988) (finding counsel ineffective under those circumstances).

d. *Failure to seek BWS jury instructions.* Sometimes defense counsel fails to request a jury instruction on BWS. Does this inevitably result in ineffective assistance of counsel? In Commonwealth v. Stonehouse, 555 A.2d 772 (Pa. 1989), a defendant-police officer sought reversal of her murder conviction after her attorney failed to request instructions on the legal significance of evidence of Battered Woman's Syndrome, either as pertinent to a self-defense instruction or as evidence of the alternative defense of provocation. Prior to his death, the decedent would grow angry when the defendant did not do what he instructed. He destroyed her home and personal belongings, dragged her out of her car and tried to run her over, turned on the gas in her house and threatened to kill her, broke into her house, and relentlessly stalked her. The defendant had sought help from the police and a magistrate, but was told that it was a "domestic" matter. Finally, one night the decedent pointed a gun in the defendant's face and threatened to kill her. After he left, defendant went to her back porch and saw her abuser pointing a gun up at her from outside. Believing she was threatened, the defendant fired her weapon, killing the decedent. The defense presented evidence of BWS to support a claim of self-defense or, in the alternative, provocation for a voluntary manslaughter finding, but failed to request a jury instruction specifically detailing BWS as legally relevant to those defenses. The court agreed with the defendant that this constituted the ineffective assistance of counsel.

However, in McBrayer v. State, 383 S.E.2d 879 (Ga. 1989), the court upheld the defendant's murder conviction, despite her attorney's failure to request a jury instruction on BWS. In that case, the defendant had experienced abuse by her former husband. When she returned home one night to find her child missing, she went to her former husband's house with a shotgun. Both the defendant and her former husband pointed their guns at each other, but the former husband lowered his weapon after convincing the defendant that the child was not there. As the defendant lowered her weapon, it accidentally fired, killing her former husband. Although the defense presented some evidence of BWS, the court agreed that it was appropriate for counsel not to request a BWS jury instruction, as BWS would have been inconsistent with a defense that the death was an accident.

4. *Right to experts.* An issue in *Dando* is whether the defendant had the right to a court-appointed expert before the plea. How did the court resolve this issue? In addressing the issue, the *Dando* court applies a balancing test that weighs: (1) the private interest affected by the State's action, (2) the governmental interest, and (3) the risk of erroneous deprivation without the safeguard. What was the private interest at stake in *Dando*? How important was having a BWS expert to the trial? In other words, how important was having a BWS expert to establish Dando's defense of duress? What interest did the state have in refusing to provide a BWS expert? What was the risk of erroneous deprivation without the safeguard?

Consider other scenarios. Does a defendant have a right to a BWS expert to counter an essential element of the crime? See Dunn v. Roberts, 963 F.2d 308 (10th Cir 1992) (defendant had right to state-funded BWS expert to testify to whether defendant had requisite intent). Is there a right to a court-appointed BWS expert to explain why a defendant might lie? See State v. Dannels, 734 P.2d 188 (Mont. 1987) (rejecting defendant's request for BWS expert to bolster her credibility). Does the right to an expert mean the right to an expert of choice? See State v. Aucoin, 756 S.W.2d 705 (Tenn. Crim. App. 1988) (rejecting request to pay for BWS expert of defendant's choosing after she rejected offer of court-appointed doctor). See generally Laura D. Warren, Comment, The Indigent Defendant's Toolbox: Debating the Addition of the Battered Woman Syndrome Expert, 69 U. Chi. L. Rev. 2033 (2002).

5. *Recognizing abuse.* Attorneys face special challenges when the client has been a victim of domestic violence. The client may be reluctant to discuss past or present acts of abuse or she may not recognize the actions of her abuser as acts of domestic violence. In addition, some attorneys may not consider domestic violence as an issue in some types of cases, such as nonfamily law claims. Because domestic violence can arise in different situations, the ABA recommends that attorneys develop basic checklists for screening for abuse. See ABA Commission on Domestic Violence, Tools for Attorneys to Screen for Domestic Violence (2005), http://www.abanet .org/domviol/screeningtoolcdv.pdf.

6. *Malpractice liability.* Does it constitute malpractice for a lawyer to fail to recognize the signs of abuse in a client? Would this standard be breached if a lawyer did not properly screen a client for domestic violence? If an attorney puts a client in danger of *further* abuse, such as by failing to seek a civil protective order or pursuing spousal support, even if the client does not request such action?

What steps can an attorney take to avoid malpractice regarding issues of domestic violence? New York enacted legislation requiring all attorneys who represent children to take part in domestic violence training. See Robert C. Mangi, Strategies for Family Law in New York, 2010 WL 1635147 (Apr. 2010), at *1. Should other states adopt similar laws? On lawyers' responsibilities to address domestic violence in the practice of law, see generally John M. Burman, Lawyers and Domestic Violence: Raising the Standard of Practice, 9 Mich. J. Gender & L. 207 (2003); Margaret Drew, Lawyer Malpractice and Domestic Violence: Are We Revictimizing Our Clients?, 39 Fam. L.Q. 7 (2005).

How can nonattorney victim advocates protect themselves from liability for unauthorized practice of law? See ABA Model R. Prof. Cond. 5.5; Margaret F. Brown, Domestic Violence Advocates' Exposure to Liability for Engaging in the Unauthorized Practice of Law, 34 Colum. J.L. & Soc. Probs. 279 (2001).

7. *Planning for safety.* In addition to representing the client in domestic violence-related matters, the attorney may have an obligation to plan for the client's safety. Margaret Drew, former Chair of the ABA Commission on Domestic Violence, elaborates:

> Safety planning does not begin or end with obtaining a civil protection order. For example, one must consider whether or not it is safe for the client to seek such an order. What plan does your client have to minimize her risk of abuse? What resources does your client have available to her should the partner or former partner attempt further abuse of her or the children? What referrals has the lawyer's office made to provide the client with assistance on safety issues? Safety concerns may encourage some types of legal action and discourage others.

Drew, supra, at 13. How can a domestic violence advocate help her client plan for safety? What kinds of legal actions might help a domestic violence victim stay safe? Which may jeopardize her safety?

8. *Student representation.* Some legal scholars and clinical professors advocate for the use of students to represent victims of domestic violence through clinical programs. What are the merits and detriments of representation by students in domestic violence clinics? See Jayashri Srikantiah & Jennifer Lee Koh, Teaching Individual Representation Alongside Institutional Advocacy: Pedagogical Implications of a Combined Advocacy Clinic, 16 Clinical L. Rev. 451 (2010).

2. Ethical Issues of Representing Victims of Domestic Violence

■ LEIGH GOODMARK, GOING UNDERGROUND:
THE ETHICS OF ADVISING A BATTERED WOMAN
FLEEING AN ABUSIVE RELATIONSHIP
75 UMKC L. Rev. 999 (2007)

In her novel *Black and Blue*, Anna Quindlen tells the story of Fran Benedetto, an emergency room nurse battered by her husband, a police officer. After one particularly vicious beating, Fran flees her home with her son Robert and goes into hiding. Fran Benedetto of New York City becomes Beth Crenshaw of Lake Plata, Florida, with the assistance of an unnamed organization that aids battered women. . . . After leaving New York, Fran is not permitted to contact her sister, and Robert is forbidden to ever call his father; the organization requires them to essentially disappear. "Secrecy . . . was the hallmark of [the] organization. No stray piece of paper, no phone number, no newspaper clipping, could give [the] volunteers away as they spirited women out of their own homes and into the anonymous America where Robert and I were now living." . . .

Fran never consulted an attorney about going underground. . . . I have sometimes wondered what I would have told Fran had she sought my counsel. The question is not so far-fetched. Although some domestic violence agencies disavow the idea of an "underground railroad" for battered women, it is undeniable that women flee from their abusers and attempt to keep their whereabouts hidden. . . .

COMMUNICATION AND CONFIDENTIALITY

. . . Safeguarding client confidences is particularly important for clients who have gone underground. Rule 1.6 generally precludes lawyers from disclosing information relating to the representation of the client, permitting (but not requiring) lawyers to disclose confidential information in certain situations. Comment 2 to Rule 1.6 notes the importance of confidentiality to the development of trust between lawyer and client. Battered women going underground may literally be trusting their lawyers with their lives; safeguarding information the lawyer has about the client's whereabouts may prevent that client from being killed. The comments to the Rule stress the need to guard confidential information closely and take precautions to ensure that such information is not inadvertently disclosed. . . .

CLIENT COUNSELING AND CRIMINAL BEHAVIOR

Rule 1.2(d) states, "[a] lawyer shall not counsel a client to engage, or assist a client, in conduct that the lawyer knows is criminal or fraudulent, but a lawyer may discuss the legal consequences of any proposed course of conduct with a client and may counsel or assist a client to make a good faith effort to determine the validity, scope, meaning or application of the law." Though the prohibitions of Rule 1.2(d) must be balanced against the duties outlined by Rule 2.1, which requires a lawyer to provide "candid advice" and enables the lawyer to think about the "moral, economic, social and political factors . . . that may be relevant to the client's situation," Rule 1.2(d) seems to trump. . . .

Although there are few cases on point, the conduct of attorneys advising battered mothers who flee with their children has been closely scrutinized under Rule 1.2(d). While "simply counseling a client on the potential ramifications of interstate flight from abuse should not trigger disciplinary consequences," lawyers who provide assistance to fleeing clients or counsel clients to violate court orders on custody and visitation have been disciplined and even disbarred.

In People v. Chappell [927 P.2d 829 (Colo. 1996)], for example, a lawyer represented the mother in a child custody case in which mutual restraining orders prevented either parent from removing the child from the state. After learning that the custody evaluator would recommend awarding custody to the father, the lawyer told the mother that the court would most likely follow the evaluator's recommendation. The lawyer advised the client "as her lawyer to stay, but as a mother to run." The attorney gave the client information about the "network of safehouses for people in her situation"—presumably, battered women. The wife left Colorado for two weeks, moving into a battered woman's shelter when she returned.

In her absence, the court awarded custody of her son to the father. At a prenatal visit for her unborn child, the mother was discovered and physical custody immediately given to the father. The mother later pled guilty to violation of a child custody order, a felony in Colorado. In a subsequent disciplinary hearing, the attorney was found to have violated Rule 1.2(d)'s prohibition on counseling a client to engage in a criminal or fraudulent act. The attorney's actions not only precipitated her disbarment, but also resulted in a felony conviction and a loss of custody for her client.

ENTERING INTO AND WITHDRAWING FROM REPRESENTATION

Before undertaking the representation of a battered woman who is considering going, or has gone, underground, the lawyer should think carefully about whether she can meet her ethical obligations. If she is not competent, if she cannot provide candid counsel, or if she believes that providing representation will require her to violate the rules of professional conduct or other laws, she should not undertake the representation. . . .

For the fleeing battered woman, building an attorney-client relationship means trusting the lawyer with information that could cost the client her life. While Rule 1.16 lays out the circumstances under which a lawyer can ethically withdraw from a case (which may be distinct from state law setting the conditions under which a lawyer can withdraw from representation), withdrawal may be quite harmful for the client. Not only does the client have to find another attorney (which, given the paucity of legal resources for battered women, particularly in matters other than advocacy around protective orders, may be impossible), but she has to develop a trusting relationship with that attorney, which may take time that she cannot invest. She also has to enlarge the number of people who know where she is by at least one (and possibly more if the attorney's staff has access to her information), further jeopardizing her ability to remain hidden. . . .

THE ATTORNEY'S ETHICAL OBLIGATIONS TO OTHERS

The attorney representing a battered woman who goes underground must consider not only her ethical obligations to her client, but also to third parties. Rule 3.3

precludes a lawyer from offering evidence to a tribunal that a lawyer knows to be false. Similarly, pursuant to Rule 4.1, a lawyer may not make a false statement of material fact to a third person. The lawyer must decide how to respond when asked by the court on the record to verify the client's current address, or what information to disclose to the creditor who demands to know whether "Cathy Gordon" is the name the client is currently using, though it is not her given name. Certainly the lawyer's duty to maintain the client's confidences is paramount so long as the party making the request is not entitled to such information by law. But when disclosure is required by law, the attorney faces a dilemma: assert confidentiality and endanger yourself (your professional reputation, your standing with the court) or disclose the information and endanger your client.

It may seem that the safest posture, as criminal defense lawyers in movies have long believed, is ignorance. Just as criminal defense lawyers sometimes believe they are better off not knowing their client's version of the facts (lest the client admit to the crime), it may seem best for the lawyer representing an underground client to know as little as possible about the client's identifying information. The lawyer cannot knowingly offer false evidence or make a false statement of material fact if the lawyer does not know what the truth is. The problem with such a strategy, however, is that avoiding essential information about the client's case may undermine the attorney's ability to provide competent representation. Rule 1.1 defines competence as requiring "thoroughness and preparation." Fact investigation is certainly central to both thoroughness and preparation; deliberately avoiding certain facts could preclude the lawyer from performing competently. Even avoiding knowledge of the client's current address could have serious implications for the competency of representation—for example, if a legal action was filed in an inappropriate venue because of the lawyer's decision to refrain from ascertaining the client's exact whereabouts.

A similar question involves the attorney's duty under Rule 3.4 to refrain from obstructing access to evidence or concealing materials with evidentiary value. The attorney's unwillingness to disclose the whereabouts of a client could constitute an unlawful obstruction of access to evidence. Certainly the opposing party is deprived of the opportunity to inquire into relevant facets of the client's life as a result of the refusal to provide access to the client. The client cannot be personally served or deposed; her neighbors, employment, friends and finances all remain hidden. Particularly in a custody battle, where information about the child's adjustment to home, school and community is essential to establish the child's best interests (the standard ultimately governing the court's decision), strong arguments could be made that denial of access to information unfairly prejudices the opposing party's case. Unfair and unlawful are two different standards, however; the attorney representing the underground client must stand firm against disclosure so long as doing so is not unlawful.

THE ETHICS OF COUNSELING WOMEN TO USE THE LEGAL SYSTEM

So, if Fran Benedetto had entered my office and asked about her options, what would I have told her? That going underground raises a host of legal issues. That taking her son, Robert, would significantly complicate the legal landscape. Given my professional ethical obligations, I could not advise her to withhold her son, as that might be tantamount to counseling her to commit a crime, although I could describe the potential consequences of doing so. But could I, in good conscience, have urged her to turn to the legal system instead of fleeing? Fran had not sought a restraining order, had not filed for custody or divorce. I would certainly have had a professional ethical obligation to counsel her about these options. But I think I would have had a personal ethical obligation to tell her about the many pitfalls that could await her within the system as well. The duty to give candid advice necessarily includes the duty to give full advice—to engage the client in a comprehensive discussion of the risks and benefits of all her potential choices so that her decision is an informed one. . . .

We could have started by discussing her husband, Bobby. I would have asked whether she believed that Bobby's violence could be curbed through court action and if she would consider bringing criminal charges against Bobby. We could discuss the likelihood of conviction and imprisonment as well as the effect of his father's imprisonment on her son and on her relationship with her son. If she felt uncomfortable engaging the criminal system, we could talk about the civil system instead. We would discuss whether she believed Bobby would abide by the terms of a protective order, whether Bobby, a police officer, respected the law sufficiently that violating a court order would deter him from further violence. We would have to consider whether Bobby's fellow officers would actually enforce her court order if she needed their assistance. Some abusers make threats about what will happen if their victims turn to the legal system; had Bobby ever made such threats? Fran would surely have known that Bobby's job would be in jeopardy if she filed criminal charges or sought a restraining order; we would need to discuss the impact Bobby's losing his job would have on her safety as well as her economic viability. We would have come back again and again to the same question: could the legal system keep Fran Benedetto safe? . . .

◼ ABA, COMMISSION ON DOMESTIC VIOLENCE, STANDARDS OF PRACTICE FOR LAWYERS REPRESENTING VICTIMS OF DOMESTIC VIOLENCE, SEXUAL ASSAULT AND STALKING IN CIVIL PROTECTION ORDER CASES (2007)

. . . The goals of the Standards of Practice are: (1) to improve the quality of legal representation of victims of domestic violence, sexual assault and stalking; (2) to enable lawyers to effectively, ethically, and holistically represent victims in civil protection order cases; and (3) to raise awareness about the need for high-quality representation for victims of domestic violence, sexual assault and stalking in civil protection order cases. . . .

III. ETHICAL DUTIES OF LAWYERS REPRESENTING DOMESTIC VIOLENCE SEXUAL ASSAULT OR STALKING VICTIMS

Lawyers are bound by their jurisdiction's ethics rules in all matters. In order to most effectively discharge their ethical obligations, lawyers representing victims of domestic violence, sexual assault and stalking should comply with the standards of practice identified here.

A. Competent Knowledge of Law
1. Knowledge of Civil Protection Order Law

Before representing a client in a civil protection order case, the lawyer should have competent knowledge of the civil protection order laws in the relevant jurisdiction(s).

2. Knowledge of Related Legal Issues

The lawyer should screen for related legal issues arising from the incidence of domestic violence, sexual assault or stalking. If the lawyer is not competent or available to represent the client in related matters, the lawyer has a duty to refer the client to competent counsel.

B. Competent Knowledge of Domestic Violence, Sexual Assault and Stalking

Before representing a client in a civil protection order case, the lawyer should have competent knowledge of the dynamics of domestic violence, sexual assault and/or stalking.

In particular, the lawyer should understand the potential risk of escalated violence due to litigation, and how the experience of domestic violence, sexual assault and/or stalking may affect the client-lawyer relationship, including the process of establishing rapport with and gathering information, evidence and case direction from the client.

C. Culturally Competent Representation

The lawyer should be aware of the culture of the client and of how violence is understood within that culture.

In particular, the lawyer should understand how the culture of the client may affect client-lawyer communication and trust, identification and presentation of evidence, and remedy selection.

D. Effective Client Communication

1. Communication with Clients

The lawyer should always personally consult with the client prior to representation and prior to court proceedings for a private and meaningful exchange of case-related information.

2. Physical Access to Direct Legal Representation

All clients should have comparable access to the lawyer. When working with clients with physical and/or mental disabilities, the lawyer is obligated to ensure that the appropriate accommodations are in place.

3. Interpreters and Other Language Resources

When the client is not proficient in English or is deaf or hard of hearing, the lawyer should ensure a neutral, professional, qualified interpreter is available for all client meetings and court proceedings.

4. Confidentiality and Third Party Privilege Issues

The lawyer should inform the client that ordinarily, communication exchanged between the lawyer and client is protected by the attorney-client privilege. The lawyer should advise the client about the applicable rules and laws regarding confidentiality of communications with third parties (e.g. advocates, interpreters, counselors, personal care attendants, legal guardians, support persons) and any effect of these parties' presence on attorney-client privilege.

E. Client Safety

1. Lethality Assessment and Safety Planning

The lawyer should ensure that comprehensive lethality assessment and safety planning occur with the client.

2. Sensitivity to Effects of Trauma

Lawyers should be sensitive to the effects of trauma in their clients, and aware of the effects of vicarious trauma on themselves and their staff.

F. Scope of Representation

1. Client-Centered Representation

The lawyer should advise the client about legal options and consequences, but must ultimately defer to the client regarding legal decisions.

2. Legal Capacity and Duty of Loyalty

The lawyer should determine whether the potential client has the legal capacity to enter into and/or sustain the client-lawyer relationship pursuant to the rules of the jurisdiction, and communicate this to the client. Once the client-lawyer relationship is established, the lawyer must refrain from divulging case-related information gained in interviewing or representing the client to unauthorized third parties.

3. Scope of Representation, Case Closing and Withdrawal

The lawyer should be clear about his or her role in the client's legal matters, including communicating to the client the limits of the lawyer's role and the anticipated time the lawyer will fulfill that role.

4. Coordination with Allied Professionals; Holistic Representation

The lawyer should refer the client to suitable non-legal professionals for support, advocacy and treatment when necessary and seek to holistically represent the client.

IV. PROCEDURES

A. Office Intake Procedures

Intake for victims of domestic violence, sexual assault and/or stalking should be conducted by personnel trained to work sensitively with this client population. Intake should include, at a minimum, a conflict check, a safety assessment, and identification of any accommodations required by the client.

B. Basic Procedural Obligations of the Lawyer

1. The lawyer should obtain an interpreter if necessary, advise the client regarding confidentiality of communication, and establish the limits of the lawyer's role.

2. The lawyer should create and maintain a trusting relationship with the client.

3. The lawyer should strive to document every aspect of the case as it progresses, taking written notes of client interviews, witness interviews and other case developments, and collecting other relevant written documentation in the file.

4. The lawyer should interview and counsel the client about the client's goals and desires, review the file and any other information that the client has provided, and help the client determine whether obtaining a civil protection order is the best remedy.

5. The lawyer should advise the client about the civil court system, the proceedings at hand and the lawyer's responsibilities. Additionally, the lawyer should understand the basic criminal procedure for a misdemeanor and felony domestic violence, sexual assault or stalking case so as to inform the client how each case is different if they are occurring simultaneously. If relevant, the lawyer should also understand the basic procedures of child and/or adult protective services so as to

inform the client about what to expect if she has a case pending with either agency.

6. The lawyer should inform the client of all relevant available remedies and make sure the client understands the legal implications of not seeking the civil protection order (i.e., whether the civil protection order will be dismissed with or without prejudice, etc.). The lawyer should assist the client with a plan for self-sufficiency and seek economic remedies, where permitted, through the legal process.

C. Pre-hearing Responsibilities

1. The lawyer should interview the client to identify case theory, strategy and evidence; engage in appropriate discovery when permitted and defend against inappropriate discovery requests; and gather and investigate evidence as appropriate.

2. The lawyer should identify potential related legal issues and consequences for the client, such as inter-jurisdictional enforcement of the order, effect of the order on current or future immigration status, intersection of the civil proceeding with criminal prosecution, and crime victim rights.

3. The lawyer should timely file all pleadings, motions, briefs and responses; identify, subpoena and prepare witnesses, including potential expert witnesses; prepare the cross-examination of respondent, including the gathering of respondent's written admissions, criminal history and police reports involving both parties; research applicable legal issues; and advance legal arguments.

4. If there are children involved and the law of the jurisdiction permits it, the lawyer should discuss with the client her wishes regarding temporary custody and visitation, keeping in mind jurisdictional issues. The lawyer should carefully consider the pros and cons of having the children offer witness testimony, in light of current law and scholarship on childhood development.

5. If the client has privacy concerns, the lawyer should consider how protecting her privacy will affect the case progression and continue to discuss the issue with the client.

6. If the respondent is unrepresented by counsel, the lawyer should consider how this may affect his or her ability to negotiate, conduct the hearing, protect the client during cross-examination, and keep the lawyer and the client safe in the courthouse.

7. The lawyer should prepare a specific, enforceable proposed order that both protects the client and holds the respondent accountable.

8. The lawyer should be cognizant of the client's rights in other forums such as immigration, tribal or criminal justice, and when appropriate, the lawyer should coordinate with those systems.

9. The lawyer should become familiar with the practices of the judge or hearing officer on the case, as well as any local procedural rules or standing orders, and plan for safety at court.

D. Hearings

The lawyer should participate actively in all court proceedings on issues within the scope of the lawyer's representation of the client.

1. The lawyer should prepare for and attend all hearings with the client, using creativity and skill in presenting the evidence. Specifically, the lawyer should prepare and make all appropriate motions, responses and evidentiary

objections; prepare, present and cross-examine witnesses and exhibits; and seek every appropriate remedy the client is entitled to under the law, subject to the client's direction.

2. The lawyer should make/protect a record for appeal, ensuring that the court makes specific findings on the record, if possible.

3. The lawyer should seek to ensure that the courtroom is safe for the client and the lawyer, including preparing for litigating against a pro se respondent.

4. The lawyer should consider a negotiated settlement only when it is in the best interest of the client, keeping in mind the danger of mutual orders and the importance of legal findings for inter-jurisdictional enforcement.

E. Post-hearing Responsibilities

Ethical representation does not end with the hearing. At a minimum, the lawyer should ensure that the client understands the outcome of the proceedings, discuss implementation and any alternative legal options, and, when the client-lawyer relationship has ended, clearly communicate that fact to the former client.

1. The lawyer should seek to ensure that the order is clear and accurate and that the client understands all provisions of the order, including its expiration date (if any) and the requirements for renewal or extension. The lawyer should also advise the client about how to modify the order and the availability of civil and criminal contempt proceedings.

2. The lawyer should ensure that the order is served on the respondent and that the client is prepared to respond safely and effectively to violations by the respondent.

3. If the hearing does not result in the issuance of a safe and effective protection order, the lawyer should discuss with the client the process for appeal, rehearing and/or modification.

4. The lawyer should always communicate with the client about case closing procedures, including withdrawal, and implications.

3. *Effective Representation in Practice*

■ **SARAH M. BUEL, EFFECTIVE ASSISTANCE OF COUNSEL FOR BATTERED WOMEN DEFENDANTS: A NORMATIVE CONSTRUCT**
26 Harv. Women's L.J. 217, 218, 225-229 (2003)

. . . Lawyers are obligated to provide their clients informed, competent representation, yet the handling of battered defendants' cases too often fails to satisfy this standard. . . .

. . . A lawyer may be ineffective because she is disconnected from her client and does not know how to reframe the attorney-client relationship. The battered defendant can discern cues from her lawyer regarding her competence as a witness and the lawyer's judgment about the defendant's entrapment in the abuse. Domestic violence expert Dr. Evan Stark cautions lawyers to:

[R]emember that if she is defined only as a victim, albeit a victim deserving defense, the battered woman will act like a victim in court, responding defensively to her abuser and outwardly buying into her misrepresentation as a woman without choice[,] while inwardly seeking ways to survive it by employing the same defensive maneuvers in court she has used at home.

However, in representing battered defendants, even experienced defense lawyers often fail to listen effectively and support the battered client throughout the legal process.

The social disparity in life circumstances between counsel and the battered defendant may make it difficult for an effective relationship to develop, thereby hampering representation. Traditional theories of representation often relegate clients to the periphery of a case. A battered defendant who has often been denied even the right to speak by the abuser, needs her lawyer to accurately present her voice in court. Counsel should encourage a battered client to find her voice and center case strategies upon it. Representation of battered defendants might be radically transformed by altering the typical approach to litigation.

. . . [I]nquiries into the details of abuse are essential for developing a defense strategy for battered women. Moreover, where race, class, and gender issues intersect, counsel must be cognizant of these particularized influences shaping their clients' behavior. Counsel must be prepared to educate the court and jury about these issues and their relevance to the defense. . . .

Discerning client voice is not an easy task; it requires respecting clients' autonomy and dignity. Lawyers who lack training in domestic violence dynamics or who are unable to empathize with the severely limited options battered defendants face are often quick to judge their clients. . . . Lawyers should make a point to reinforce that their clients did not deserve to be abused and make every effort to assist them in obtaining counseling. . . .

Without adequate knowledge about the devastating impact of psychological abuse, counsel tend to minimize its importance in crafting defenses. If a lawyer downplays the significance of abuse, a battered client may feel silenced, to the detriment of case presentation. For example, Betty Lou Beets, convicted of killing her husband, described the mental torture her husband had inflicted on her to her court-appointed lawyer, but he indicated that only physical abuse was relevant. Beets's husband would frequently force her to undress and then stand naked before him for hours while he told her how fat, unappealing, and repulsive she was. He would continue the barrage of humiliating ridicule and criticism for days on end. Coupled with a history of childhood and prior relationship violence, Beets felt the emotional abuse was the most painful and crippling for her.

A conceptual breakthrough in what constitutes acceptable practice is essential. Presently, ethical obligations of lawyers do not demand focus on the harm of abuse; decisions are instead justified under the guise of "case strategy." In Humiston v. Alarcon, [229 F.3d 1157 (9th Cir. 2000)], the Ninth Circuit found that the defense attorney made a suitable strategic decision not to provide evidence of BWS because the appellant denied taking part in the murder for which she was charged. Deferring to counsel's tactical decisions, the court determined that the lawyer's conduct was competent and upheld the jury's conviction. However, as case analysis will show, it is precisely this seemingly irrational behavior of abuse victims that BWS seeks to explain. Had counsel and the court been better informed regarding the beneficial uses of BWS testimony, a more equitable disposition may have resulted. . . .

■ **JOAN S. MEIER, NOTES FROM THE UNDERGROUND: INTEGRATING PSYCHOLOGICAL AND LEGAL PERSPECTIVES ON DOMESTIC VIOLENCE IN THEORY AND PRACTICE**
21 Hofstra L. Rev. 1295, 1333-1337, 1342-1349 (1993)

[The author explains below her techniques of integrating psychology into legal practice and also provides examples derived from teaching in a legal clinic at George Washington University, National Law Center's Domestic Violence Advocacy Project.]

The need for interpersonal skills is especially great in the representation of battered women, which can pose particular challenges to lawyers' capacity for empathy and powers of psychological understanding. . . .

Competent legal interviewing and counseling requires fundamental human and intellectual skills, such as empathy, connection, clarity and focus. To be effective counselors, lawyers also need human and professional judgment to discern what the client wants/needs from the lawyer, e.g., advice or direction, and to determine how to advise her without usurping her autonomy and decisionmaking. While to some extent these "human skills" may be intuitive and a function of individual personality, a grasp of certain psychological concepts can be very helpful in developing these sensitivities. [E]very lawyer-client interaction is shaped by human motivation and the needs of both lawyer and client. To cultivate the full and open communication which is necessary for effective representation, lawyers should understand the potential psychological obstacles to communication such as ego threats, role expectations, and the impact of trauma, among others; as well as psychological facilitators of communication, including empathic understanding, fulfillment of expectations, and affirmation, among others.

Perhaps the single most important psychological ingredient to developing an effective lawyer-client bond, is empathic understanding on the part of the lawyer. People consulting lawyers are often in distress, most obviously in family law and domestic violence cases. Even the need to consult or depend on an "expert" can be in itself disturbing. The confidentiality of lawyer-client communications also invites greater confidence, and hence greater intimacy and vulnerability. Empathy from the lawyer is critical to ease communication for the client, maximize trust, and avoid disruptions in the lawyer-client relationship and joint decisionmaking.

In essence, empathic understanding requires recognition of the importance of people's feelings in affecting what they say or do, and how and when they say or do it. This includes the knowledge that people's feelings are often not articulated directly but are conveyed through nonverbal cues such as body language, or through what people do not say (or do). Once the client's feelings are recognized (or inferred), empathy is expressed by active listening, including the explicit acknowledgement of the client's feelings, whether stated or unstated. . . .

Similarly, a classic instance of the need for empathic expression by lawyers was revealed in [the following account]: In this case, after the client finished a ten-minute harrowing description of the single instance of violence she had experienced from her former lover, there was complete silence. Then one of the students inquired as to the type and size of the knife used in the attack. This instance was painful to hear on the tape, as the story seemed to cry out for an expression of human sympathy or horror. The lack of such an expression is not a reflection of unfeeling students. Their non-response may have been a function of a sub-conscious need to distance themselves from the horror of the client's story. It may also have been a reflection of an attempt to "act like a lawyer" by clinically investigating the facts. If so, this story demonstrates the importance of the clinical experience for helping students unlearn two years of learning to think and act "like lawyers," and teaching them the importance of acting "like a human being" while being a lawyer. . . .

PSYCHOLOGY IN THE REPRESENTATION OF BATTERED WOMEN

In the representation of battered women, there are certain issues which regularly arise, which pose a challenge to lawyers' counseling and psychological skills. In essence, in dealing with domestic violence, available legal remedies are frequently inadequate and never ideal. Because the fear of retaliation hovers over virtually any action they may take, battered women are often (understandably) ambivalent about what to do. Moreover, . . . being subjected to chronic violence, and society's failure to intervene to stop it, can be so demoralizing and disempowering that some clients feel that nothing will help while everything may hurt.

This context gives rise to the need for particular sensitivity and skill in counseling battered women with respect to at least two issues: (1) identifying and coping with client ambivalence; and (2) assessing dangerousness and providing strategic counseling. . . .

A. BATTERED WOMEN'S AMBIVALENCE

[When representing battered women, we need to] confront and examine many of their and society's assumptions about the meaning and context of their clients' experiences. These issues very often converge around the problem of clients' ambivalence about pursuing legal action.

[A]t some point . . . students working with women in civil protection order cases experienced a client's withdrawal, disappearance, or backing off of all or some part of the initially intended legal action. This phenomenon—and the challenge it poses for would-be service providers—has not been satisfactorily addressed by advocates for battered women, in part because they are reluctant to contribute to society's tendency to blame battered women's ambivalence for the system's failures to take action.

[I]it is my view that the ambivalence of these women is largely a response to society's persistent messages to the victim that (a) her experiences of domestic violence are trivial, (b) her allegations are untrue, (c) the violence is her fault, and (d) there is nothing that can be done. In short, battered women's ambivalence about their situation and choices is simply a direct reflection of society's own ambivalence about domestic violence.

Nonetheless, there is also a discernible and genuinely personal component of many battered women's ambivalence about taking legal action: In many cases they love the man, don't want to hurt him, and are reluctant to give up the relationship. Putting aside many socio-economic reasons why many women attempt to make their relationship work, women's personal ambivalence may also be explainable by several psychological phenomena. For instance, a woman may love her abuser because he has only hit her once and they have had an otherwise loving relationship, because they have had children together, because he is the first man who has ever loved her, or for any number of other "normal" reasons to love someone. Battered women may also develop greater dependency on their abusers as a result of the batterer's abuse and forced isolation. In especially severe hostage-like cases, a woman may develop a kind of "traumatic bonding" in which the batterer's threats to harm and the victim's isolation and inability to escape, in conjunction with occasional kindnesses from her "captor," makes her more psychologically as well as physically dependent upon him.

Ambivalence about pursuing legal action can also stem from other very realistic concerns: Some women may correctly fear retaliation by the abuser, based on their knowledge of the abuser's personality and psychology. Others who are suffering from PTSD may avoid talking to their legal representatives, miss appointments, or avoid going to court because they cannot bear to re-invoke the traumatic experiences by talking and thinking about them.

Because social understanding of the psychology of domestic violence is limited, inexperienced lawyers often either fail to register signs of their clients' ambivalence, or react critically to those signs they do notice. Either of these responses can be damaging to their ability to represent their client. For example, a lawyer may push a case forward when it is not in the client's best interest, because the lawyer fails to identify and appropriately weigh the client's fear of retaliation, where the client has stated that she wants to go forward. Alternatively, a lawyer may feel critical of a client's ambivalence, because she feels that battered women need to take action against their abusers, and that their ambivalence is a form of self-destructiveness. The lawyer's feelings may well be sensed by the client even when they are not expressed directly; this will make some clients even less direct and open about their feelings, or more likely to say whatever they think their lawyer wants to hear. In [one] case, the client sensed the students' criticism of her own ambivalence about taking legal action, and suddenly became unreachable by telephone. Eventually, when the students sent a more empathic and non-judgmental message to her neighbor (whose phone she used), stating that the students were perfectly comfortable with whatever the client wanted to do, the client miraculously materialized on the other end of the telephone and informed them that she did not currently want to proceed.

In short, it is critical that [we provide an understanding of] the sources of battered women's ambivalence, and assist the students in developing their abilities to read between the lines of what their clients may tell them explicitly, i.e., to hear the meta-message. Basic psychological concepts, such as the nature and reasons for human ambivalence in these contexts, the phenomenon of "denial," and the nature and effects of PTSD, can be very helpful. Ultimately, students' ability to empathize with the ambivalence inherent in their clients' situations, will most likely determine their capacity to assist those clients.

B. ASSESSING DANGER AND PROVIDING STRATEGIC COUNSELING

Given the possible ambivalence of many battered women, as well as the usual confusion and misinformation plaguing many laypeople concerning the legal system, lawyers for battered women often need to play a relatively affirmative counseling role, which may not come naturally. . . . Such counseling might include providing the client with some perspective on her situation, e.g., assuring her that it is not her fault, that her experiences are not uncommon, and that without significant social or legal intervention the cycle of violence is likely to continue. This type of feedback seeks to reduce the client's sense of fault and inadequacy which an abusive relationship fosters, to strengthen her morale and to support her tentative decision to take action.

However, a crucial dimension of client counseling for any service provider in this field is the danger assessment. In seeking to help a woman who has been chronically violently attacked by someone in a close relationship to her, every step considered must include an assessment of whether it will increase or decrease the danger she faces. This assessment requires a degree of fine-tuned, nuanced comprehension of the client's situation which is often not intuitively grasped by new lawyers.

The danger assessment is complicated by the fact that many people's assumptions about the nature of abusive relationships vastly over-simplify the reality. This was illustrated in [a class session in which we were discussing] the availability of ex parte "temporary protection orders" ("TPOs") which may be obtained on an emergency basis without notice to the respondent, when the petitioner fears imminent danger from him. In the midst of our discussion of the legal proof required to obtain a TPO, one student asked "why wouldn't you always get a TPO? Wouldn't these women always be in imminent danger?" The simple answer is "(n)o, women in these relationships are not always in imminent danger; they are not beaten 24 hours a day, 7 days a week; in fact, abusers are people; they are sometimes nice." However, I found it harder than I expected to answer this question. This was because the articulation of the question itself suggested a host of (inaccurate) assumptions about who batterers and their victims are, how and when the abuse occurs, and what life is like for such people. Assumptions such as these are widespread.

Adequate education about the psychosocial context of domestic violence is essential to give the student-lawyer a more accurate basic framework of assumptions within which to assess the information provided by the client. At a minimum, understanding of the "cycle of violence" tells us that violence does not occur twenty-four hours a day. A more in-depth understanding might entail education about what is known about abusers, including their ability to be charming, appealing, and needy, and recognition that abusive relationships are, like all relationships, complex, and held together by a web of connections.

A reasonably accurate perception of the client's situation is vital to a lawyer's ability to help the client assess the degree of danger she is in, and decide what—if any—action to pursue. In determining whether a TPO, a CPO, possible criminal prosecution, or no legal action is preferable, lawyers and clients must differentiate between imminent and non-imminent danger, and identify what kinds of events may trigger violence. If the client fears legal action will provoke more violence, the lawyer and client must decide if protection can be found, or if the risk is not worth the potential gain. Lawyers must also assist clients in assessing whether the degree of danger suggests that the client's first priority should be fleeing to a shelter, out of state, etc. Alternatively, the lawyer can explain to the client why legal action is often beneficial, and give the client some hope, which she undoubtedly needs. In short, because many battered women have been living entrapped in fear for some time, the lawyer's support and outside perspective can be very helpful in helping the client break through the fears and make constructive decisions about strategy.

Finally, while providing the client with some perspective on the utility of legal interventions—and likelihood of future violence—lawyers must be able to walk the fine line between "counseling" the client and "deciding" for her. One must be able to go beyond clients' often self-protective quick answers, and offer competing perspectives, but at the same time clearly communicate that the decision on how to weigh all the competing factors is the client's to make. This type of in-depth, nuanced counseling may be more than is reasonable to expect most students to achieve quickly. Experience is undoubtedly needed to learn to recognize and entertain simultaneously many overlapping, potentially conflicting, and uncertain options and outcomes. Psychosocial education about domestic violence and interpersonal counseling skills can provide an intellectual foundation and some rudimentary skills; over time, experience must supply the rest. . . .

■ DEBORAH M. GOELMAN, SAFETY PLANNING

in The Impact of Domestic Violence on Your Legal Practice 11-15
(ABA Commission on Domestic Violence 1996)

Safety planning is critical when representing a client who has been battered or threatened by an intimate partner. Evidence has shown that the danger of violence, including the risk of death, escalates when a domestic violence survivor attempts to leave a batterer. Seeking legal assistance is a step towards independence which threatens a batterer's sense of control and may further endanger a survivor. If you represent a client who is planning to leave or to take any legal or financial steps to separate from a batterer, you must alert your client to the increased likelihood of violence. It is also crucial to conduct ongoing safety planning with a client who continues to live with a batterer. Take precautions when contacting your clients, and address their safety concerns by helping to develop comprehensive safety plans which include survival strategies at home, at the workplace, and in court.

CONTACT WITH YOUR CLIENT

- Ask for your client when you call and speak only to your client about the case. Do not leave messages with other family members or on an answering machine or voice-mail until your client has told you this is safe. If questioned by family members, do not indicate that you are a lawyer; rather, give an innocuous reason for the call, such as taking a survey.
- Always ask your client first if it is safe to talk and whether you should call the police. The batterer may be present, even if the batterer no longer lives in the same home. Develop a system of coded messages to signal danger or the batterer's presence.
- Block identification of your number when calling your client by dialing *67 or the equivalent in your area. This prevents a batterer from using "caller ID" to discover that your client is seeking legal assistance.
- Keep your client's whereabouts confidential. Do not disclose your client's addresses, telephone numbers, or information about the children without your client's permission, including during discovery. Batterers often track down their former partners through third parties, such as court personnel or social service providers.
- Send mail to your client only when your client has advised you that it is safe. If a new client fails to attend appointments or return your calls, write your

client a simple letter requesting a response without disclosing your identity as a lawyer (do not use letterhead).

- Remind your client to have an explanation for legal appointments and to limit the children's knowledge to prevent the batterer from finding out about legal actions or an upcoming separation ahead of time.
- Inform your client of legal developments in advance, particularly when a batterer is about to be served or when a hearing is approaching, so that your client may take extra safety precautions.
- If your client fails to respond to your calls, make extensive (but confidential) efforts to confirm that your client is safe. If your client has decided to drop the case, try to verify that your client has not been threatened or coerced.
- Develop a referral list including the national domestic violence hotline, local shelters, domestic violence programs, batterers' intervention programs, and children's programs. Make referrals to clients and give them copies of the referral list if they have safe places to keep the copies. Allow clients to use your phone if necessary or initiate calls at your client's request.

SAFETY AT HOME

Advise your client to take the following preventive measures:

- Make the home as safe as possible by changing the locks, adding dead bolts, and obtaining an apartment that is not on the first floor. Remove sharp objects and weapons from sight. Keep a telephone in a room that locks from the inside. If possible, purchase a cellular phone and keep it in a pocket or in an accessible hiding place; pre-program 911 or the number of a safe friend or relative into the phone's directory.
- Plan and practice an escape route out of the home and a safety plan for the children. Teach the children not to let the batterer in the home (unless the batterer has a legal right to be there). Prepare the children to respond to a batterer who comes to their school or day care center; if a protection order includes provisions about the children, give a copy to the children's school or childcare facility.
- Keep a bag packed and hidden in a safe place at home (or locked in a car trunk with only one key), or with a safe relative or friend, in case of flight. It should include: money for phone calls, transportation, and one month's expenses, clothing, diapers, court documents, passports, identification (social security, driver's license, welfare identification, family photographs), birth certificates, school and medical records, necessary medicines, credit cards, checkbooks, work permits, green cards, lease/mortgage payments, insurance papers, bank books, telephone/address books, car/house keys, and ownership documents for car/house.
- Make extra copies of protection orders and keep them in safe places. Attach a copy of the interstate protection order provisions of the Violence Against Women Act and proof of service to each protection order to minimize enforceability problems in other states. Show the orders to police officers to improve their response.
- Show neighbors a picture of the batterer and/or the batterer's vehicle so they can screen visitors and call the police if necessary. Batterers often gain

access to apartment buildings by pretending to be someone else or by following tenants indoors.

- Develop signals for neighbors and friends to call the police, such as banging on the floor or wall. If possible, arrange to have a relative or friend call every day at an appointed time.
- Enroll in a reliable self-defense course and regularly practice these skills.
- Trade cars with a friend or relative. Batterers often locate former victims by identifying their vehicles.
- Be aware that motor vehicle records, including addresses, may be available to the public. Most Departments of Motor Vehicles will permit drivers to use a number other than their social security number for identification purposes and will keep information confidential upon request.
- Obtain a private or unlisted telephone number, and be selective about revealing a new address. Batterers have located victims through friends, relatives, co-workers, court or social services documents, the post office, and private investigators.
- Use the block code when making telephone calls. Use an answering machine or call trace when receiving calls to collect evidence of harassment or protection order violations.
- Alter routines—change transportation routes or timing (including picking up children form school) so that the batterer cannot locate you.

Advise your client to take the following steps if the batterer becomes violent or threatening:

- Call the police at 911 (or the equivalent) and ask for the dispatcher's name. When the police respond, obtain the officer's name and badge number.
- File criminal charges if the batterer commits a crime or violates a protection order. Filing criminal charges and following through is one of the most effective ways to deter future violence.
- Seek medical treatment if injured by the batterer. Photograph all injuries.
- Record all contact with the batterer in a diary.

SAFETY AT WORK

- Arrive in court before your client so that your client is not alone with the batterer. If this is impossible, advise your client to wait near a security guard or a bailiff. Be aware that batterers often physically assault, repeatedly harass, or emotionally coerce victims in court.
- Sit at a physical distance from the batterer when you talk to your client or wait for the case to be called. Always position yourself between the batterer and your client. Batterers control and threaten their former victims simply by using body language.
- Do not permit the batterer to speak to your client. Even if you are present you may be unaware that the batterer is threatening your client. Discuss any settlement negotiations with the batterer (or the batterer's lawyer if represented by counsel) and then report back to your client.

- Take the same precautions with the batterer's family members. In domestic violence cases, it is not uncommon for the batterer's family members to physically assault or verbally abuse the victim in court. Safeguard children if the batterer or family members insist on holding them.
- Make certain that your client is safe when exiting the courthouse. Batterers often stalk victims to discover where they live, or to punish victims for taking legal action.

OTHER SAFETY CONCERNS

- Assess the batterer's lethality. Your client has an increased risk of being severely assaulted or killed by the batterer if the batterer possesses weapons, abuses drugs or alcohol, stalks your client, or has threatened homicide or suicide.
- Advise your client to stay at a shelter, or with friends or relatives, if your client fears that the batterer will assault or kill her. When your client has children, make certain that you have examined existing court orders and statutes to determine how flight may affect a custody case.
- Under certain circumstances, it may be necessary for a client to disappear completely. Assist your client to change names and social security numbers if necessary.
- Be aware of your safety. Most batterers seek to control their former or current partners, rather than their lawyers, and many batterers appear to be well-behaved in court. Nevertheless, some lawyers representing victims of domestic violence have been threatened by batterers or their family members. Take precautions if a problem arises.

B. MEDIATION

Many states provide for mediation as a form of alternative dispute resolution. The following materials explore whether mediation poses special dangers for victims of domestic violence.

■ ADOLPHSON v. YOURZAK
2008 WL 4628722 (Minn. Ct. App. 2008)

MINGE, Judge.

. . . Appellant Susan Yourzak (mother) and respondent Erik Adolphson (father) were married on August 6, 1994. The parties have a minor child, L.A.Y., born on July 28, 1999.

The parties had a difficult marriage. An incident on June 22, 2006, led to claims of abuse and an order for protection (OFP). The record indicates that on that date father confronted mother after she lit a bonfire in the parties' backyard. During the course of the dispute, father threw items that struck mother. Father contacted police about the fire. Police responded and filed a report detailing the incident, noting that the criteria for domestic assault had not been met. Nonetheless, on July 14, 2006, mother requested an OFP. On July 27, 2006, father initiated this dissolution action. Following an evidentiary hearing in August 2006, a referee found that father committed domestic assault, issued the OFP against father for one year, and entered an interim order in the dissolution action.

The parties entered into a marital termination agreement resolving all issues except legal custody of L.A.Y. . . . Following a hearing, the district court granted joint legal custody of L.A.Y. and ordered that the parties participate in modified mediation to resolve any future issues regarding custody and parenting time. This appeal followed. . . .

The [issue here] is whether the district court erred in ordering modified mediation. The statute provides that a victim of domestic abuse cannot be required to engage in mediation. Minn. Stat. §518.091, subd. 1 (2006); cf. Minn. Stat. §518.1751, subd. 1a (party cannot be required to use a parenting-time expeditor if there has been domestic abuse).

Mother objects to the district court's finding that she was willing to participate in "modified mediation" with father and ordering such mediation. Mother points out an OFP [Order for Protection] was issued against father. This order states that mother is a victim of domestic abuse. However, at the custody hearing, father's counsel sought to elicit testimony from mother that she was willing to participate in some type of dispute-resolution process as long as she did not have to be in the same room with the father to discuss matters. Mother stated that she was aware that mediation did not necessarily require her to be in the same room as father. But when mother was directly asked whether she would be willing to use this form of dispute resolution, her attorney objected on relevancy grounds, and the district court sustained the objection. There is nothing in the record to support a finding that mother is willing to participate in mediation of any form. Moreover, the custody and parenting-time evaluation provided to the district court in this case noted that there were "currently no known methods to resolve disputes other than litigation."

Given statutory and rule-related limits on mediation in cases where abuse has occurred and the error the district court made in finding that mother had agreed to engage in "modified mediation," we conclude that the district court erred in ordering mediation and reverse that part of its order. Because on this record we conclude that provisions for court monitoring of disputes between the parties may be appropriate or the parties may agree upon a method of their choosing, we remand for further consideration of the subject of resolving disputes. . . .

■ JESSICA PEARSON, NAT'L INST. OF JUSTICE, DIVORCE MEDIATION AND DOMESTIC VIOLENCE 1-6 (1997)

available at https://www.ncjrs.gov/pdffiles1/nij/grants/164658.pdf

. . . As the popularity of mediation grew during the 1980s, an important source of dissent also emerged. Advocates for battered women and feminist scholars raised concerns about issues such as gender-related power imbalances and, particularly, the impact of mediation on victims of domestic abuse. While the strongest criticisms have been directed toward the practice of mandating abused women to participate in mediation, some advocates object to the use of mediation when there has been any domestic abuse. They feel that advocacy and attorney-assisted negotiation are the preferred means to handle cases involving domestic abuse. . . .

Feminists and battered women's advocates have raised many important objections to the use of mediation where there has been domestic abuse. One concern is that mediation decriminalizes domestic abuse and encourages a conciliatory approach that does not hold the abuser accountable for his behavior. If abusers are allowed to participate in a conciliatory process, they may learn that there are no adverse consequences to their violence. Not only might abusers avoid accepting responsibility, but victims might be made to feel partially to blame. As a private process, mediation may shield abusers from the public opprobrium they are more apt to receive in the criminal process. Indeed, a major risk of mediation is that it will undermine the great strides that the women's movement has made in defining domestic abuse and treating it in the justice system.

Another concern has to do with safety. There are inherent risks in an intervention that allows a violent spouse to know the time and place his partner will be present for mediation. Nor can the victim be safeguarded from future abuse. Mediators can not fully understand the dynamics of abuse and predict future violence between men and their victims or build in ways to protect victims. Even when they are in writing, mediated agreements do not always provide a victim with protection. Nor are they enforceable by the courts when there is noncompliance.

> Since the mediation process is not designed to deter violent behavior or to protect victims, its use is particularly perilous for battered women. Protection of one's safety should be considered too important to entrust to any other but the legal system, which has the power to remove the batterer from the home, to arrest when necessary, and to enforce the terms of a decree if a new assault occurs.

[Mary Pat Treuthart, All That Glitters Is not Gold: Mediation in Domestic Abuse Cases, 30 Clearinghouse Rev. 243, 246 (1996).]

Women's advocates also take issue with the notion that mediation can occur with parties who have unequal bargaining power. They contend that domestic violence always introduces power imbalances that may render mediation inherently unfair. Fear factors may make it difficult for a victim to face her abuser and negotiate an agreement that meets her needs. A victim may seem willing to participate in mediation because she believes she has no other option. Advocates argue that a victim and abuser can never negotiate on an equal footing, even with the assistance of skilled mediators. Because victims run the risk of giving up too much, a consensual or collaborative decisionmaking process should be avoided.

> It is not possible to provide a non-adversarial means of settling disputes in a neutral environment when one party is using overt or covert intimidation.

[Mildred Pagelow, Effects of Domestic Violence on Children and Their Consequences for Custody and Visitation Agreements, 7 Mediation Q. 347, 354 (1990).]

Many mediation critics are troubled by the conjoint and compromising nature of the mediation process. They feel that mediation may discourage abused women from expressing anger thereby denying them its benefits including the "potential to teach, heal and energize." They maintain that mediators favor joint custody arrangements, that often run counter to what is best for the victim and children. Mediation may also erode their financial status and deprive them of the economic advantages they have won through divorce litigation.

Finally, feminists and advocates for battered women are concerned about the caliber of court-based and community-based mediation programs and the ability of staff to properly screen and handle cases with domestic abuse. Public programs are often under pressure to handle large numbers of cases in short amounts of time. Community programs may rely on volunteer mediators who have only minimal amounts of training. These conditions make it inappropriate and potentially dangerous for mediation programs to handle cases with domestic violence.

The concerns expressed by advocates for abused women and feminist scholars are important and must be seriously considered. Indeed, there is compelling evidence that spousal abuse is present in at least half of custody and visitation disputes referred to family court mediation programs. There is also evidence that many women will continue to be subjected to abuse after separation and many experts in the field of domestic abuse contend that violence escalates when the woman tries to leave the relationship. . . .

[In response to these criticisms,] legislation exempting battered women from mediation has been enacted in numerous states. Indeed, with the exception of West Virginia and Arizona, all states with mandatory divorce and child custody mediation provide a domestic abuse exemption (e.g., California, Delaware, Hawaii, Maine, Nevada, New Mexico, North Carolina, Oregon, South Dakota, Utah, Wisconsin). Similarly, many states (Colorado, Florida, Illinois, Iowa, Louisiana, Maryland, Minnesota, Montana, Nebraska, New Hampshire, North Dakota, Ohio, Virginia, Washington), but not all (Alaska, Connecticut, Kansas, Michigan, New York, Rhode Island), with discretionary mediation also include a provision exempting parties with a domestic abuse situation. . . .

Most mediators and their supporters believe that there are mechanisms such as screening, individual caucusing, and the use of advocates in mediation sessions, which can help mitigate safety and fairness concerns in domestic violence cases. They argue that techniques such as these can allow abuse victims to experience the benefits of mediation. According to mediation advocates, the appropriateness of mediation and its format depends upon the type of domestic violence in the relationship. Relationships differ with respect to the history and nature of violence and the degree of power each partner possesses. [T]here is a continuum of family violence, and a wide variety of families function at different positions of the continuum. [Some scholars] identify major profiles of violent relationships and argue that each requires different types of intervention at separation and/or divorce. [M]ediation supporters contend that [mediation] is sometimes useful to: help a victim communicate safely with her abuser about stopping the violence; help an abuser and a victim explore treatment options; and help a family arrive at visitation arrangements that control the abuser's contact with the victim.

The limited divorce mediation research conducted to date with victims of domestic violence seems to confirm that many cases can be effectively mediated. For example, a comparison of 49 abuse cases and 61 nonviolent cases mediated in Hawaii revealed a higher agreement rate among the abuse cases. An Australian study of satisfaction with mediation found no differences between clients of both sexes with domestic violence and their non-violent counterparts. Finally, a Canadian comparison of mediation and lawyer-represented divorce clients found statistically comparable levels of harassment and post-processing abuse in both samples of cases along with identical rates of compliance and re-litigation.

Feminists and advocates for battered women differ in their assessments of mediation. While some favor voluntary mediation, most strongly oppose requiring victims to mediate, and a few have gone so far as to insist that women who have been abused *cannot* be allowed to mediate. On point is an Alaska pilot mediation project which was legislatively prohibited from serving abused and formerly abused women. This prohibition resulted in the elimination of more than 60 percent of prospective users. The program staff concluded that:

> Many of the women who were excluded believed that the prohibition (against mediating) was damaging, rather than helpful to them. While women's advocates perceived the potential risks of mediation to outweigh any possible benefits, the victims often believed first, that they should be the ones to make that choice and second, that in their own cost-benefit assessment the services offered by the pilot mediation project were valuable enough to overcome the risks as they perceived them.

[Susanne DiPietro, Alaska Child Visitation Mediation Pilot Program: Report to the Alaska Legislation 24 (1992).]

The Alaska project operated in a system where free or low-cost legal advocacy was not readily available, as is true in virtually all American communities. Thus, it is impossible to tell whether battered women would have opted to mediate had other similarly priced legal interventions been available.

One area of consensus between mediators and advocates for abused women is the conviction that mediation must be designed to try to ensure the safety of battered women and children. To accomplish this, both groups support the need for adequate training of mediators and the practice of screening all couples referred to mediation for domestic abuse. . . .

■ **ALEXANDRIA ZYLSTRA, MEDIATION AND DOMESTIC VIOLENCE: A PRACTICAL SCREENING METHOD FOR MEDIATORS AND MEDIATION PROGRAM ADMINISTRATORS**
2001 J. Disp. Resol. 253, 253-254, 256-261, 268-269 (2001)

As the popularity of court-ordered mediation for custody disputes increases, the need for an effective way to address cases involving domestic violence becomes more critical. The ongoing debate over *whether* cases involving domestic violence should be mediated, while relevant, amounts to an exercise in futility. Courts across the country are permitting, and even mandating, such cases be mediated, often unaware that domestic violence is even present. Further, this debate begs the question of how mediators and mediation program administrators should handle such cases that will inevitably come through their doors. . . .

As more and more jurisdictions implement mediation alternatives for family cases, the need for effective screening methods becomes a critical linchpin to ensure the process and potential outcome are fair, voluntary, and do not further endanger victims of domestic violence, the children involved, or the mediator. Nonetheless, the present state of screening nationwide paints a dismal picture. The most recent study of mediation programs found that while eighty percent of mediation programs utilized by family courts do some form of screening for domestic violence, usually in the form of written or oral questions, the mean number of questions relating to domestic violence is only 3.53. . . . [S]uch a shortfall in screening represents "a serious shortcoming and raises questions about the comprehensiveness and adequacy of screening in general." . . .

[The author presents below the primary criticisms against the use of mediation in cases of domestic violence and then offers her response.]

1. UNEQUAL BARGAINING POWER

[The mediation process] assumes each party will participate equally to arrive at a mutually beneficial result. In an abusive relationship, however, mutual participation may be very difficult for a victim because the abuser may have consistently silenced him/her throughout the relationship and the victim may fear retribution if true needs are expressed. If one party fears the other, it is unlikely that party can mediate on equal bargaining ground. Critics argue that, in relationships in which the imbalance of power is great or unrecognized, such as in cases involving domestic violence, equality of participation and fairness are not only compromised, but the process may, in fact, present a danger of physical harm to the victim.

Victim advocates argue that a fundamental inequity in power, control and decision-making exists in relationships involving domestic abuse. . . . Once the balance of power is so greatly altered, critics argue that victims' fears of violent retribution may prevent them from asserting their own interests, thus removing an important element of mediation. Finally, critics caution that merely implementing safety precautions does not remove the "psychological terrorism" that may be perpetuated with a look, movement or word during the mediation.

2. PROCESS FLAWS

A. LACK OF APPROPRIATE MEDIATOR TRAINING

Another criticism focuses on the present lack of widespread domestic violence training available to mediators. Such a flaw potentially renders mediation of such cases either futile or actually dangerous. For example, because mediation is designed to assist the parties to resolve conflict, an untrained mediator may attribute the abuse to conflict. However, in cases involving a history of domestic violence, the conflict is only the pretext for abuse, which really stems from a need to dominate and control. Thus, an untrained mediator attempting to resolve the conflict may, in fact, ignore the real problem. Or, critics fear that mediators may be cornered into a position of mediating the occurrence of abuse, which inappropriately assigns responsibility to both the victim and the abuser.

B. FAILURE TO PROTECT VICTIMS AND HOLD ABUSERS ACCOUNTABLE

Finally, writers such as Karla Fischer, Neil Vidmar and Rene Ellis [in The Culture of Battering and the Role of Mediation in Domestic Violence Cases, 46 SMU L. Rev. 2117 (1993)] argue there is a false assumption among mediators that mediation can protect a battered woman from future abuse, when such protection is highly unlikely. Further, some argue that mediation cannot overcome the long-standing effects of an abusive relationship within the context of such a brief encounter. Regardless of the power balancing techniques the mediator uses, critics argue that believing such techniques will actually reduce the power imbalance and ensure a safe and fair settlement is absurd because it presumes that mediators, in a brief amount of time, are able to accomplish what takes trained psychologists years to accomplish working with violent offenders, and with abuse victims. Not only is this transformation unlikely, critics argue that such false assumptions may, in fact, greatly increase the risk of danger to the victim with this type of intervention by an untrained mediator.

In a related argument, not only does mediation fail to stop the violence, but the future focus of standard mediation styles, rather than a focus on past behavior, actually absolves the abuser of accepting responsibility for past behavior. The perpetrator may be excused for his actions under this model and further, critics argue, this may be perceived by the victim as the mediator condoning the behavior, thus jeopardizing mediator neutrality.

3. FLAWS OF THE CRITICISMS

Two vital flaws in the critics' arguments flow from a misunderstanding of the theory of mediation, and an inaccurate comparison to an idealistic litigation model.

1. MISUNDERSTANDING THE GOALS OF MEDIATION

An example of the first flaw can be found in Fischer, Vidmar and Ellis' article, The Culture of Battering and the Role of Mediation in Domestic Violence Cases, which compares the ideologies of mediation, as they perceive them, with the culture of an abusive relationship to illustrate the incompatibility of the two.

However, of the eight comparisons, three of them are based on practices not taught in standard mediation training programs, such as the concept that batterers need to be coerced into mediation and a belief that a written agreement will end the present violence or end future violence. Three of the other problems discussed would be overcome by basic mediator training: an inaccurate view that abuse arises out of conflict, a false assumption that each party automatically participates equally in the process, and a false belief that private caucusing will necessarily encourage victims to reveal their real needs.

Their final two criticisms address mediation's future focus and, thus, its failure to punish the abuser, and mediation's avoidance of blame and fact-finding. Both of these arguments also suffer from the same flaw of failure to understand the goals and purpose of mediation. Most family mediation programs do not purport to be able to end the violence in an abusive relationship nor do they set about attributing blame to either party. Mediation is not advertised as a panacea for deep rooted psychological, chemical, or other problems. Rather, mediation is designed as an *alternative* to present conflict resolution models, specifically litigation, which leads to the second flaw in the critics' arguments.

2. INCOMPATIBLE COMPARISONS

The second mistake critics make is comparing the best possible litigation scenario (where truth is found and justice served) to the worst possible mediation scenario for cases involving domestic violence (joint sessions with an untrained mediator). When compared to a more realistic picture of family law litigation, however, mediation compares well to litigation, which truly fails battered spouses.

First, the idealistic view of litigation ignores the reality that the judicial system continually neglects victims by failing to provide legal representation. It is, for example, unrealistic to compare mediation to an attorney-represented litigation since litigants lack representation in forty to ninety percent of divorce cases. Secondly, women in the litigation setting can be seriously disadvantaged by evidence of frequent moves (to escape the violence), perceived abandonment of the children, or an apparently uncooperative attitude. The adversarial process also fails to protect children from violent homes, particularly where the abuser has not physically harmed the children.

Litigation also tends to increase hostility, threats, blaming and fear, while doing nothing to improve parties' communication skills or otherwise empower the parties. Despite arguments that mediation may make the victim feel guilty or unacknowledged, the courtroom often creates an even greater risk of victim humiliation, discredit and loss of control. Finally, while many critics argue mediation's future focus excuses the batterer's actions, litigation in fact encourages the abuser to deny past behavior.

Mediation, on the other hand, offers several advantages not available in the litigation context. For example, a long divorce proceeding may not meet the needs of parties in a violent relationship, and mediation may offer quicker results and may also address any immediate or unexpected needs. Additionally, criticisms leveled against mediating cases involving domestic violence ignore the reality that parents will inevitably have future contact over parenting issues, since the likelihood of termination of parental rights in abuse cases is extremely rare. The adversarial litigation model, with a focus on attributing blame and a win-lose outcome, does little to foster conciliatory relations between the parents. Further, while litigation is rigid in its structure and rules, mediation programs vary widely and can be structured to address the issues that arise in the separation of relationships involving domestic violence. In fact, one of the earliest advantages of mediation included its dynamic potential to be shaped to meet the needs of the clients. As a final note, although scholars may be greatly concerned with the mediation model, at least one study indicated process satisfaction rates among domestic violence victims are higher with mediation than with attorney-negotiated settlements.

While critics may argue that mediation is never appropriate for cases involving domestic violence, the more common approach is to assess power issues on a case-by-case basis paying particular attention to: duration, severity, frequency, onset, abuse of alcohol or drugs, psychiatric disorder, and other family dysfunction.

Research in 1990 by mediators Stephen Erickson and Marilyn McKnight [Mediating Spousal Abuse Divorces, 7 Mediation Q. 377, 385 (1990)] concluded, based on more than 1,400 cases, half of which involved emotional or physical abuse, that mediation can be successful in such cases if special precautions are taken, including the use of a highly experienced mediator. However, even Erickson and McKnight acknowledge certain cases are inappropriate for mediation. Those include cases in which: the abuser discounts the other party and refuses to acknowledge the other's worth; abuse is ongoing during the mediation period; where either party insists upon carrying weapons or abusing substances; or either party violates the ground rules the mediator implements to ensure safety and power balance. . . .

Given the flaws in the current criticisms regarding mediation of cases involving domestic violence, and after comparing mediation to the present litigation model, it is clear that, at least in some cases, mediation of such cases may be a more fair process with a greater likelihood of a desirable outcome. This leads to the question of which cases are appropriate for mediation and, if appropriate, how should those cases be handled. . . .

DEFICIENCIES OF SCREENING MECHANISMS

[The author explains that various mechanisms exist to determine which cases are appropriate for mediation (that is, statutory exemptions, judicial exemption, and screening that is limited to whether prior criminal or civil orders of protection exist). Important differences also exist concerning the identity of the person screening (that is, judge, court clerk, attorney, mediator); and the safety measures that are implemented for mediating such cases.]

[D]omestic abuse screening rules vary greatly. . . . In those states that do have screening mechanisms, the processes often suffer from serious flaws. First, the training and screening requirements imposed upon judges are based on an unlikely pattern of assumptions: that judges will review the case file before the case is referred to mediation, that the battered party will come forward with allegations of abuse, and that the judge will then conduct an evidentiary hearing. This process is extremely unlikely in most courts, where cases are often sent to mediation before any judicial intervention occurs.

A second flaw of many of the screening mechanisms is that they require one of the parties to come forward before mediation and make an allegation of domestic violence. [M]any victims may not consider their relationship abusive, may minimize the abuse, or may fear retribution if they come forward.

Further, the likelihood is even more remote that the abuser will make an affirmative motion to the court that violence is present. Therefore, placing the burden on the parties is both ineffective and unrealistic. Finally, none of the states impose a comprehensive structure of screening that encompasses all the necessary elements for effective and safe mediation of cases involving domestic violence. . . .

Thus the responsibility for addressing these matters falls squarely on the shoulders of the mediator, and the mediation program administrators. . . . The foregoing discussion clearly indicates that relatively few states have detailed rules regarding the appropriate screening of potential mediation cases. Given this lack of guidance, it is imperative that the family mediator not only accept responsibility for being a key factor in the process, but also implement a protocol that becomes part of the preparation for every family mediation. While no screening or safety protocol can be perfect, training and experience can increase the likelihood that the mediation process is beneficial, voluntary, and safe. . . .

■ ASSOCIATION OF FAMILY AND CONCILIATION COURTS, MODEL STANDARDS OF PRACTICE FOR FAMILY AND DIVORCE MEDIATION (2000)

[The AFCC Model Standards stem from the efforts of prominent mediation organizations and mediators to develop a code of conduct for mediators to take into account in confronting common issues that arise in divorce and family mediation.]

STANDARD X

A family mediator shall recognize a family situation involving domestic abuse and take appropriate steps to shape the mediation process accordingly.

As used in these Standards, domestic abuse includes domestic violence as defined by applicable state law and issues of control and intimidation.

A mediator shall not undertake a mediation in which the family situation has been assessed to involve domestic abuse without appropriate and adequate training.

Some cases are not suitable for mediation because of safety, control or intimidation issues. A mediator should make a reasonable effort to screen for the existence of domestic abuse prior to entering into an agreement to mediate. The mediator should continue to assess for domestic abuse throughout the mediation process.

If domestic abuse appears to be present the mediator shall consider taking measures to insure the safety of participants and the mediator including, among others:

- establishing appropriate security arrangements;
- holding separate sessions with the participants even without the agreement of all participants;
- allowing a friend, representative, advocate, counsel or attorney to attend the mediation sessions;
- encouraging the participants to be represented by an attorney, counsel or an advocate throughout the mediation process;
- referring the participants to appropriate community resources;
- suspending or terminating the mediation sessions, with appropriate steps to protect the safety of the participants.

The mediator should facilitate the participants' formulation of parenting plans that protect the physical safety and psychological well-being of themselves and their children.

Standard XI

A family mediator shall suspend or terminate the mediation process when the mediator reasonably believes that a participant is unable to effectively participate or for other compelling reasons.

Circumstances under which a mediator should consider suspending or terminating the mediation, may include, among others:

- the safety of a participant or well-being of a child is threatened;
- a participant has or is threatening to abduct a child;
- a participant is unable to participate due to the influence of drugs, alcohol, or physical or mental condition;
- the participants are about to enter into an agreement that the mediator reasonably believes to be unconscionable;
- a participant is using the mediation to further illegal conduct;
- a participant is using the mediation process to gain an unfair advantage;
- if the mediator believes the mediator's impartiality has been compromised in accordance with Standard IV [requiring that the mediator conduct mediation in an impartial manner and disclose any bias and conflicts of interest].

If the mediator does suspend or terminate the mediation, the mediator should take all reasonable steps to minimize prejudice or inconvenience to the participants which may result.

■ AMERICAN LAW INSTITUTE, PRINCIPLES OF THE LAW OF FAMILY DISSOLUTION (2002)

§2.06 Parental Agreements

(1) The court should order provisions of a parenting plan agreed to by the parents, unless the agreement

    (a) Is not knowing or voluntary, or

    (b) would be harmful to the child.

(2) The court, on any basis it deems sufficient may conduct an evidentiary hearing to determine whether there is a factual basis under Paragraph (1) to find that the court should not be bound by an agreement. If credible information is presented to the court that child abuse as defined by state law or domestic violence as defined by §2.03(7) has occurred, the court should hold a hearing and, if the court determines that child abuse or domestic violence has occurred, it should order appropriate protective measures under §2.11 [permitting courts to impose general restrictions such as restraints on communication, substance abuse in the presence of children, supervised visitation, completion of treatment programs for substance abuse or domestic violence, or "any other constraints or conditions that the court deems necessary to provide for the safety" of family members].

(3) If the court rejects an agreement in, whole or in part, under the standards set forth in Paragraph (1), it should allow the parents the opportunity to negotiate another agreement.

§2.07 Court-Ordered Services

. . . (2) A mediator should screen for domestic violence and for other conditions or circumstances that may impede a party's capacity to participate in the mediation process. If there is credible evidence of such circumstances, the mediation should not occur, unless reasonable steps are taken both

    (a) to ensure meaningful consent of each party to participate in the mediation and to any results reached through the mediation process; and

    (b) to protect the safety of the victim. . . .

■ NAT'L COUNCIL OF JUVENILE & FAMILY COURT JUDGES, MODEL CODE ON DOMESTIC AND FAMILY VIOLENCE (1994)

available at http://www.ncjfcj.org/images/stories/dept/fvd/pdf/ modecode_fin_printable.pdf

Sec. 407. Duty of mediator to screen for domestic violence during mediation referred or ordered by court.

1. A mediator who receives a referral or order from a court to conduct mediation shall screen for the occurrence of domestic or family violence between the parties.

2. A mediator shall not engage in mediation when it appears to the mediator or when either party asserts that domestic or family violence has occurred unless:

    (a) Mediation is requested by the victim of the alleged domestic or family violence;

    (b) Mediation is provided in a specialized manner that protects the safety of the victim by a certified mediator who is trained in domestic and family violence; and

(c) The victim is permitted to have in attendance at mediation a supporting person of his or her choice, including but not limited to an attorney or advocate.

Sec. 408(A). Mediation in cases involving domestic or family violence.

[The Model Code provides alternative sections concerning mediation in cases involving domestic or family violence. Both of the sections provide directives for courts hearing cases concerning the custody or visitation of children, if there is a protection order in effect and if there is an allegation of domestic or family violence. Neither of these sections prohibits the parties to such a hearing from engaging in mediation of their own volition. For the majority of jurisdictions, section 408(A) is the preferred section. For the minority of jurisdictions that have developed mandatory mediation by trained, certified mediators, and that follow special procedures to protect a victim of domestic or family violence from intimidation, section 408(B) is provided as an alternative.]

1. In a proceeding concerning the custody or visitation of a child, if an order for protection is in effect, the court shall not order mediation or refer either party to mediation.

2. In a proceeding concerning the custody or visitation of a child, if there is an allegation of domestic or family violence and an order for protection is not in effect, the court may order mediation or refer either party to mediation only if:

(a) Mediation is requested by the victim of the alleged domestic or family violence;

(b) Mediation is provided by a certified mediator who is trained in domestic and family violence in a specialized manner that protects the safety of the victim; and

(c) The victim is permitted to have in attendance at mediation a supporting person of his or her choice, including but not limited to an attorney or advocate.

Sec. 408(B). Mediation in cases involving domestic or family violence.

1. In a proceeding concerning the custody or visitation of a child, if an order for protection is in effect or if there is an allegation of domestic or family violence, the court shall not order mediation or refer either party to mediation unless the court finds that:

(a) The mediation is provided by a certified mediator who is trained in the dynamics of domestic and family violence; and

(b) The mediator or mediation service provides procedures to protect the victim from intimidation by the alleged perpetrator in accordance with subsection.

2. Procedures to protect the victim must include but are not limited to:

(a) Permission for the victim to have in attendance at mediation a supporting person of his or her choice, including but not limited to an attorney or advocate; and

(b) Any other procedure deemed necessary by the court to protect the victim from intimidation from the alleged perpetrator.

Notes and Questions

1. *Family law mediation: background and benefits.* Dissatisfaction with the adversary system led to the growth of mediation. Mediation is a form of alternative dispute resolution in which a neutral third party (the mediator) helps the two parties to

resolve their issues. Unlike arbitration or the adversarial system, the two parties reach their own agreement—the third party does not decide the issues for them. Among the benefits of mediation are: It facilitates settlement, relieves congested court dockets, saves litigation costs, and prevents relitigation. Mediation is also seen as empowering parties by giving them the responsibility for devising an agreement. H. Jay Folberg, Divorce Mediation—A Workable Alternative, in Alternative Means of Family Dispute Resolution 11, 13 (Howard Davison et al. eds., 1982). Mediators come from many fields, including law, mental health, and social welfare. Some divorce mediators addresses all divorce-related issues: property division, spousal support, custody/visitation, and child support. Some mediators, especially those who work in public court settings, limit their practice to child custody issues.

2. *Mandatory mediation.* In 1981, California became the first state to mandate mediation in all custody and visitation disputes (Cal. Fam. Code §3170). Ten other states (Delaware, Hawaii, Idaho, Kentucky, Maine, Nevada, North Carolina, Oklahoma, South Dakota, and West Virginia) soon followed. Alana Dunnigan, Comment, Restoring Power to the Powerless: The Need to Reform California's Mandatory Mediation for Victims of Domestic Violence, 37 U.S.F. L. Rev. 1031, 1031 n.3 (2003). Today, nearly every state has some form of mediation for domestic disputes, although mediation in most states is at the court's discretion. Id. at 1031.

3. *Different views.* A longstanding criticism of academics, legislators, and judges is that mediation poses special dangers for battered women. See Jane Murphy & Robert Rubinson, Domestic Violence and Mediation: Responding to the Challenges of Crafting Effective Screens, 39 Fam. L.Q. 53, 55 (2005). What are these dangers, according to the above excerpts?

Three views exist regarding the role of domestic violence in mediation: (1) mediation is never appropriate; (2) mediation is appropriate provided that procedural and substantive safeguards exist; and finally, (3) the choice of mediation should be left to the victim who is most knowledgeable about her specific circumstances. Id. at 53-54. Based on the above excerpts and *Adolphson*, which view do you find most compelling?

4. *Model laws.* Several model laws address the role of domestic violence in mediation. The Association of Family and Conciliation Courts (AFCC) and the American Bar Association collaborated in 2001 in the adoption of Model Standards of Practice for Family and Divorce Mediation (hereafter Model Standards), available at http://www.afccnet.org/resources/resources_model_mediation.asp. These Model Standards define domestic violence, require domestic violence training for mediators, provide for screening (prior to entry into mediation and throughout the mediation process), and set forth steps to ensure participants' safety during mediation. The Model Standards also recognize that some cases are not suitable for mediation.

The American Law Institute Principles of the Law of Family Dissolution adopt the view that cases of domestic violence should be identified by courts and also that mediation should be used only when both parties agree. ALI Principles §§206, 207.

In addition, the National Council on Juvenile and Family Court Judges' Model Code on Domestic Violence and Family Violence addresses the duty of the mediator to screen for domestic violence. The Model Code also provides directives for courts hearing cases concerning custody and visitation if there is a protection order in effect and if there is an allegation of domestic violence. Seven states have adopted section 408 of the Model Code. ABA Commission on Domestic Violence, Mediation in Family Law Matters Where DV Is Present (Jan. 2008), http://www.abanet.org/

domviol/docs/Mediation_1_2008.pdf (explaining that the Model Code was adopted by Alabama, Alaska, Delaware, Hawaii, New Mexico, Oklahoma, and Tennessee).

Evaluate the above approaches. What are the advantages and disadvantages of each approach? How well does each approach address the issues of mediators' credentials and training about domestic violence? Screening? Safety issues?

5. *Pro se litigants.* Family law mediation in cases of domestic violence must take into consideration the prevalence of pro se litigation in family law. For example, whereas only 1 percent of litigants in California divorce cases were pro se in 1971, that number approached 75 percent by 2000. Drew A. Swank, In Defense of Rules and Roles: The Need to Curb Extreme Forms of Pro Se Assistance and Accommodation in Litigation, 54 Am. U. L. Rev. 1537, 1540 (2005) (citing research).

Mediation proceeds on the assumption that both parties have legal advisors in the background who provide them with advice so that each party is fully informed about the law and the consequences of decisions. Commentators explain some of the negative implications in the mediation context for parties who are pro se:

> [M]ediators do not generally have the authority to force parents to produce evidence. . . . Although there are usually no legal advisors involved in the actual mediation sessions, the mediator can generally rely on the parents' individual lawyers to obtain the evidence necessary for clients to make decisions concerning the range of issues decided in mediation. In the case of most self-represented litigants, however, there is no one providing legal advice before, during, or after mediation. In addition, there are no requirements that the parties be informed of the law or the practices in the local courts concerning the issues the disputants are discussing. Therefore, the parties are reaching decisions without knowing what might be available to them if the case were litigated.

Connie J. A. Beck & Bruce D. Sales, A Critical Reappraisal of Divorce Mediation Research and Policy, 6 Psychol. Pub. Pol'y & L. 989, 994 (2000). How do these implications apply in the context of domestic violence? Is the issue of power imbalance magnified if one party is represented whereas the other party proceeds pro se?

6. *Exemptions to mandatory mediation.* New Mexico was the first state to exempt victims of domestic violence from mandatory mediation in 1978. N.M. Stat. Ann. §40. Today, most states that regulate mediation provide an exemption for domestic violence. See ABA, Commission on Domestic Violence, Mediation in Family Law Matters Where DV Is Present, supra. What circumstances should trigger the exemption? See, e.g., Ala. Code §6-6-20(d) (allegations of domestic violence); Fla. Stat. §44.102(c) (a finding of "a history of domestic violence that would compromise the mediation process"); Ind. Code §34-26-5-15 (existence of civil protective order). What are the benefits and shortcomings of each approach to exemptions?

The Minnesota statute at issue in *Adolphson* provides that "if you are a victim of domestic abuse or threats of abuse as defined [by state law], you are not required to try mediation. . . ." Minn. Stat. §518B.01. How did the court apply the statute? The appellate court in *Adolphson* affirmed the trial court's award of joint custody despite the existence of the order of protection. The trial court, after considering the police report and the parties' credibility, concluded that there did not appear to be a pattern of domestic abuse and, based on the custody evaluator's report, there was no evidence that the couple's child was affected by the incident that led to the OFP. Why, then, did the appellate court exempt the mother from mediation?

7. *Modified mediation.* The mother in *Adolphson* objected to the trial court order that she attend a *modified* mediation, in which she would meet separately with the mediator in order to prevent her from having to undergo face-to-face contact with her abuser. Why did the appellate court determine that modified mediation was inappropriate?

States have a variety of modified or "special rules" mediation. What do the model laws above provide? Do these modifications ensure that mediation reaches a fair and safe outcome for both parties? See generally Murphy & Rubinson, supra.

8. *Special procedures.*

a. *Opting-in.* In *Adolphson,* the court presented the mother with the option of "opting-in" to mediation and also participating in a mediation procedure that did not require her to be in the same room as the father. A number of state codes and model laws provide that where a history of domestic violence is alleged, the victim must "opt in" to mediation. Mary Adkins, Moving Out of the 1990s: An Argument for Updating Protocol on Divorce Mediation in Domestic Abuse Cases, 22 Yale J.L. & Feminism 97, 123 (2010). Under this procedure, the judge may not refer or order the parties to mediation unless the victim requests mediation. What are the advantages and disadvantages of this protective procedure? How does this method address the preceding criticisms of mediation for victims of domestic violence? See id. at 123-124.

b. *Caucusing and shuttling between partners.* Caucuses involve separate meetings with each of the parties. The purpose is to solicit information that a party may not feel comfortable disclosing in a joint session. Shuttle mediation involves the mediator moving between the parties who are in different locations. This avoids the necessity of the victim meeting the abuser face-to-face. Rene L. Rimelspach, Note, Mediating Family Disputes in a World with Domestic Violence: How to Devise a Safe and Effective Court-Connected Mediation Program, 17 Ohio St. J. on Disp. Resol. 95, 107 n.60 (2001). What are the advantages and disadvantages of these procedures? How does each method address the criticisms of mediation for victims of domestic violence?

9. *Evidence of domestic violence. Adolphson* applies a relatively high standard of proof to determine whether or not to require mediation in a case of domestic violence, using the existence of an Order for Protection (OFP) to trigger the denial of mandatory mediation. OFPs usually require an affidavit from the victim that domestic violence, as defined under the state statute, has occurred within a certain time period and that the victim fears future acts of violence against her. In contrast, some courts have allowed a mere claim of domestic violence to suffice as proof for purposes of rejecting mediation. See, e.g., Hilliker v. Miller, 2006 WL 1229633, *4-5. (Minn. Ct. App. 2006). Which approach is preferable? What are the advantages of a low evidentiary burden in deciding the appropriateness of mediation? The disadvantages? How significant is it that traditional litigation remains available to the parties if mediation is denied?

In some states, like Texas, a party may request a hearing on the claim of domestic violence. The parties will only be sent to mediation if, after a hearing, the court finds that the original objection to mediation is not supported by a preponderance of the evidence. See Tex. Fam. Code §153.0071(f); In re E.B.L.G., 2009 WL 3126406 (Tex. App. 2009) (dismissing appeal on procedural grounds where parties were sent to arbitration despite allegations of family violence). See also ALI Principles §2.06 (requiring that the court hold a hearing after there is "credible information" of domestic violence and before the court orders "appropriate protective measures"). Compare these methods to those of *Adolphson* and *Hilliker*. Which is preferable?

10. *Physical violence versus coercive control. Adolphson* involves allegations of physical violence about which the trial court expresses skepticism. As we have seen, domestic violence encompasses a broad range of physical, sexual, and psychological abuse. Thus, state variations in defining "domestic violence" play a significant role in outlining the scope of the exemption. Although most states define domestic violence as physical harm or the threat of physical harm, some states define domestic violence more broadly. See, e.g., Haw. Rev. Stat. §586-1 ("extreme psychological abuse"); Mich. Comp. Laws §400.1501 (acts that "would cause a reasonable person to feel terrorized, frightened, intimidated, harassed, or molested"); N.C. Gen. Stat. Ann. §50B-1 (acts that inflict "substantial emotional distress"). What impact do these various definitions have on the court's decision to order mediation? See generally Connie J. A. Beck & Chitra Raghavan, Intimate Partner Abuse Screening in Custody Mediation: The Importance of Assessing Coercive Control, 48 Fam. Ct. Rev. 555 (2010).

11. *Criticism of mandatory mediation.* Mandatory mediation in cases of domestic violence has faced particularly vehement criticisms. As one commentator explains:

> Major criticisms include: (1) The private nature of mediation and lack of a record tend to perpetuate the idea that spousal abuse is a private family matter rather than a public problem. (2) In treating spousal abuse as a private family matter, mediation decriminalize it and subverts the legal rights of and protections for women. (3) Mediation is oriented to the present and future and thus may minimize the past behavior of the parties. (4) Complex dynamics of fear and learned helplessness make it unlikely that the victim can face the abuser and negotiate an agreement to meet the victim's needs. (5) Sex role expectations place women at a disadvantage in mediation; those who conform to the traditional female role of peacemaker may assign their own needs and interests a lower priority than the interests of other family members. (6) The victim receives less protection from future abuse, because courts do not always enforce mediated agreements. (7) Mediation discourages the expression of anger, which can have a powerful liberating effect on a woman. (8) Mediation of spousal abuse disputes lacks funding, expertise, and personnel.

Luisa Bigornia, Alternatives to Traditional Criminal Prosecution of Spousal Abuse, 11 J. Contemp. Legal Issues 57, 61 (2000). Does "modified mediation" address these criticisms? If so, how? Should domestic violence victims always be given the option of mediation?

Some scholars criticize mandatory mediation's exemption for domestic-violence victims for its refusal to allow victims the option of mediation. See, e.g., Adkins, supra. Adkins points out that requiring a victim of domestic violence to litigate instead of mediate, as many state statutes do, may harm her financial interests, her interest in regulating the traumatic process of a courtroom proceeding, and her sense of safety. Id. at 125. Does litigation present more harm than mediation for survivors? Why or why not?

12. *Screening for domestic violence.* As the excerpts reveal, screening is critically important to identify cases of domestic violence. Although commentators agree

about the importance of screening, "there is little consensus as to exactly how this should be accomplished." Nancy Ver Steegh, Yes, No, and Maybe: Informed Decision Making about Divorce Mediation in the Presence of Domestic Violence, 9 Wm. & Mary J. Women & L. 145, 194 (2003). Some states provide for screening for domestic violence as a part of intake procedures. These screening procedures may require parties to fill out a questionnaire or the judge may review the case file before referring the parties to mediation. However, such screening processes can easily miss the presence of domestic violence. What explains this problem, according to the above excerpts?

When a state does not provide for a screening procedure or the intake process fails to identify domestic abuse, the mediator should screen for domestic violence. This screening process can also be ineffective. Why? See also Alison E. Gerencser, Family Mediation: Screening for Domestic Abuse, 23 Fla. St. U. L. Rev. 43, 60 (1995). What kind of questions can mediators ask to elicit information about potential domestic abuse? One family court mediator suggests that the mediator should begin with open-ended questions about how the parties feel about negotiating with their spouse, then move to issues of fear, and finish with specific questions about abuse. Alexandria Zylstra, Practical Screening Method for Mediators and Mediation Program Administrators, 2001 J. Disp. Resol. 253, 272 (2001). How effective do you think this method would be?

Who should conduct the screening? The judge, court clerks, mediators, lawyers? What are the advantages and disadvantages of leaving the task of screening to the various personnel? See generally Stephen R. Arnott, Screening for Domestic Abuse: What You Don't See, May Be What You Get, 66 Bench & B. Minn. 25, 27-28 (2009) (advocating that lawyers screen for domestic violence even when a client fails to mention the issue).

13. *Good faith.* Some courts and state legislatures refer to an obligation to mediate "in good faith." That is, parties should approach mediation with some minimum level of "well-intentioned participation," to prevent mediation from becoming a mere roadblock on the road to litigation, in which one or both parties simply exploit the procedure to gain additional discovery or to achieve a fraudulent agreement. Megan G. Thompson, Comment, Mandatory Mediation and Domestic Violence: Reformulating the Good-Faith Standard, 86 Or. L. Rev. 599, 604 (2007). How should a court define good faith for mediation in the context of domestic violence?

14. *Domestic violence and parenting plans.* Domestic violence may also play a role in mediation of parenting plans. Many states provide that parents seeking custody must file a parenting plan (that is, a written agreement specifying custodial respon-sibilities) and provide for the appointment of "parenting coordinators" to assist in creating and implementing such agreements. See Katherine T. Bartlett, U.S. Cus-tody Law and Trends in the Context of the ALI Principles of the Law of Family Dissolution, 10 Va. J. Soc. Pol'y & L. 5, 6-7 (2002) (explaining that about half the states have such provisions). Some of these statutory provisions address the role of domestic violence. See, e.g., Fla. Stat. §61.125(3) (prohibiting court-ordered refer-ral to parenting coordinator, absent parental consent, in cases involving "a history of domestic violence"); Wash. Rev. Code §26.09.191(1) (holding that mutual decision-making is not required under a parenting plan where a parent has engaged in domestic violence).

In Hendershott v. Westphal, 253 P.3d 806 (Mont. 2011), a divorcing wife, who alleged that her husband had been emotionally abusive, appealed the denial of her petition to amend the couple's parenting plan by striking the provision that called for mandatory mediation. She alleged that her husband had been emotionally abusive. A state statute exempted cases involving domestic violence from family law mediation if the court had reason to suspect that a party had been "physically, sexually or emotionally" abusive. The husband argued that the statute conflicted with another state statute that invoked the court's discretion to order mediation specifically of parenting plans but contained no domestic violence exception. Reversing the denial to strike the mandatory mediation provision, the appellate court broadly interpreted the domestic violence exception. Domestic violence in parenting plans is also discussed in Chapter 12, Section C.

The American Law Institute also addresses domestic violence in parenting plans, recommending that parenting plans have affidavits that include "limiting factors" such as domestic violence and that the court "have a process to identify cases in which there is credible information" that domestic violence has occurred. ALI, Principles of the Law of Family Dissolution: Analysis and Recommendations §2.05(2)(f), (3) (2002). See generally Peter G. Jaffe et al., Toward a Differentiated Approach to Parenting Plans, 46 Fam. Ct. Rev. 500 (2008) (advocating a differentiated approach to developing parenting plans when domestic violence is alleged).

15. *Collaborative law.*

a. *Background.* Collaborative law is a voluntary form of alternative dispute resolution, in which the parties and their attorneys sign a binding agreement to use cooperative techniques without resort to judicial intervention except for court approval of the parties' agreement. Attorneys are prohibited from participating in contested court proceedings for their clients. That is, if the parties are unable to reach an agreement through collaborative law procedures, their attorneys must withdraw from representation. Like mediation, collaborative law promotes problem solving by the parties and permits solutions not possible in the adversarial system. See generally Norma Levine Trusch, Understanding Collaborative Family Law: Leading Lawyers on Navigating the Collaborative Process, Working with Clients, and Analyzing the Latest Trends, Aspatore (Feb. 2011), 2011 WL 587393, at 3-4.

The ABA Standing Committee on Ethics and Professional Responsibility and several state bar ethics committees (that is, Kentucky, Maryland, Minnesota, Missouri, New Jersey, North Carolina, Pennsylvania, and Washington) have expressly approved the use of collaborative law. Texas became the first state in 2001 to enact legislation providing for resolution of family matters by collaborative law procedures. See Tex. Fam. Code §§6.603, 153.0072. Currently, three other states have enacted collaborative law statutes—California, North Carolina, and Utah. NCCUSL, Collaborative Law Act: Summary, available at nccusl.org (last visited May 13, 2011).

b. *Role of domestic violence in collaborative law.* Collaborative law practitioners disagree as to whether the collaborative process is appropriate for victims of domestic violence. On the one hand, where both parties are committed to the collaborative law process and acknowledge past acts of domestic violence, the process can draw on an interdisciplinary team (including coaches and specialists) to address the family's needs while creating a safe space for negotiation. On the other hand, where acts of violence are continuing or where one spouse fears or is intimidated by the other, the collaborative process may not provide sufficient safety protocols to protect the victim, and may reach a result that is coercive rather than one that satisfies the needs of both parties. See generally John Lande & Forrest S. Mosten, Collaborative Lawyers' Duties to Screen the Appropriateness of Collaborative Law and Obtain Clients' Informed Consent to Use Collaborative Law, 25 Ohio St. J. on Disp. Resol. 347 (2010) (summarizing both sides of the argument); Ellen Abbott, Should I or Shouldn't I: An ADR Provider's View of Referring Victims of Domestic Abuse to Mediation, Collaborative Law and Early Neutral Evaluation, 16 Fam. L. F. (Fall 2007), at 70. Should collaborative law be used in cases of domestic violence? Why or why not? If so, in all cases of domestic violence? Or, in only some circumstances?

c. *Uniform act.* The Uniform Collaborative Law Act (UCLA), completed by the Uniform Law Commission in 2009 and amended in 2010, standardizes features of collaborative law practice. The Act promotes the use of collaborative law as an option for interested parties and their lawyers. One commentator describes the UCLA approach in cases of domestic violence:

> The UCLA starts with the premise that a collaborative law process should not be used in cases involving coercive or violent relationships. Under section 15(c), if the lawyer "reasonably believes" that there is a history of a coercive or violent relationship, the lawyer may not start or continue with the collaborative law process unless certain requirements are met. The collaborative lawyer may proceed if the prospective party so requests, but only if the lawyer "reasonably believes that the safety of the party or prospective party can be protected adequately during a process."
>
> Thus, the UCLA requires the collaborative lawyer to make reasonable inquiry concerning whether the parties have a history of coercion or violence. The collaborative process should generally not proceed if the lawyer "reasonably believes" that such a history exists. However, in an effort to promote autonomy and choice, the prospective party can, with informed consent, request to participate. In addition to facilitating an informed decision, the lawyer must form an independent judgment— he or she must "reasonably believe" that the collaborative law process can be safely completed. . . .

Nancy Ver Steegh, The Uniform Collaborative Law Act and Intimate Partner Violence: A Roadmap for Collaborative (and Non-Collaborative) Lawyers, 38 Hofstra L. Rev. 699, 731 (2009). See also Nanci A. Smith, Empowering Clients with Collaborative Family Law, Aspatore, (Feb. 2011). How well does this approach address mediation in the context of domestic violence?

C. SPECIALIZED DOMESTIC VIOLENCE COURTS

In the 1990s, increased public attention to the problem of domestic violence resulted in criticisms of the criminal justice system for its failure to demand accountability from domestic violence perpetrators and to provide help to victims. In response, many jurisdictions established specialized domestic violence courts. What are the characteristics of these courts? How do they address the shortcomings of the traditional legal system? The following excerpts address these questions.

■ **JUDGE AMY KARAN ET AL., DOMESTIC VIOLENCE COURTS: WHAT ARE THEY AND HOW SHOULD WE MANAGE THEM?**
50 Juv. & Fam. Ct. J. 75, 75-78, 83-84 (1999)

. . . As domestic violence cases have become the fastest growing portion of their domestic relations caseload, court are struggling to keep pace with profound institutional changes in how the criminal justice system, legislatures, and communities respond to domestic violence. . . .

Three major challenges to establishing effective case management systems for cases involving domestic violence are jurisdictional limitations; lack of capacity to identify, link, and track cases; and the need to coordinate the court's operations with the initiatives and resources of other agencies and the community. First, domestic violence potentially can be an issue in a variety of cases that span different jurisdictions within the court system, including civil protection orders, misdemeanor and felony prosecutions, divorce, child custody and support, and dependency and juvenile delinquency. Second, the majority of state courts lack a consistent method for identifying and flagging cases where domestic violence is present in criminal and civil caseloads. They also lack data systems that can track the various case types that may be related to an individual domestic violence case. Third, the scope of domestic violence cases extends beyond the courtroom as the court interacts with other components of the justice system, social services systems, and community service providers that offer an array of programs and services addressing the complex problems encountered by domestic violence victims, perpetrators, and their families.

A growing number of courts have instituted a variety of special systems and procedures to help address these challenges. . . . [These courts have] specialized processing practices for domestic violence cases, including, for example, centralized intake processes, separate calendars for civil protection order petitions and criminal domestic violence cases, and domestic violence units. This trend toward specialized court management of domestic violence cases has been accompanied by the designation of these courts as domestic violence courts. [The term *domestic violence court*] is handy for conveying the idea that the court recognizes the distinct nature of domestic violence cases and the need for special attention to them. . . .

THE POTENTIAL BENEFITS OF DOMESTIC VIOLENCE COURTS

Domestic violence courts hold great promise to improve the responses of the judicial system to individual domestic violence victims. For example, many domestic violence courts include specialized intake units that orient victims to court procedures, provide more extensive legal assistance for victims, and refer them to court-related or community-based assistance programs. Specialized intake units also can facilitate the coordination of case management by linking the present case to any related case currently pending or filed subsequently. Some courts may not have an intake unit, but they coordinate case processing through a case manager or other staff assigned to search court files for related cases and to coordinate the schedule or court hearings for these cases.

Another common feature of domestic violence courts is the dedication of one or more calendars for domestic violence matters, including ex parte protection order petitions, hearings on final protection orders, and proceedings in criminal cases. The availability of a central location for hearing domestic violence cases provides greater access to the judicial process, which is particularly valuable to victims seeking protection orders because the vast majority of these litigants proceed without counsel. Dedicated calendars also promote the use of uniform procedures by judges and court staff. Another advantage of dedicated calendars is that they facilitate case management for prosecutors and defense counsel. Counsel can handle higher caseloads and adhere to the court's scheduling more easily if all the cases are heard in one or more dedicated courtrooms.

Perhaps the most significant characteristic of a domestic violence court is the designation of specialized judges or teams of judges to hear domestic violence cases exclusively or as their primary assignment. Specialized judges have an opportunity to develop expertise in domestic violence issues and to improve their skills in adjudicating cases where one or both parties do not have counsel. Specialized judges also are better able to monitor the behavior of abusers and their compliance with court orders, including the terms of protection orders and orders to batterer intervention programs. Greater judicial oversight of perpetrator behavior and imposition of significant sanctions for violations of court orders should be the hallmark of a domestic violence court.

Finally, the court's focus on domestic violence emphasizes to the community both the seriousness of domestic violence and the dedication of the justice system to addressing the problem. . . . It also should encourage the other components of the criminal justice system and community-based services to collaborate in a systems approach to reducing domestic violence.

To achieve optimum benefits for victims and courts, many practitioners advocated an integrated approach for domestic violence courts that combines both the protection order and criminal calendars within the court's jurisdiction as well as employing various methods of coordination with intake and other processes. . . .

The nature of domestic violence cases and available research indicate the necessity for coordinated case processing and monitoring by all involved units of government and community service providers. However, until very recently, this has not been the practice in most communities. Although legal issues and remedies intertwine, these cases are typically adjudicated in separate courts before different judges and involve several criminal justice and community advocacy agencies with little or no coordination.

The following case scenario illustrates the complexity of domestic violence cases. The victim is raped and beaten by her boyfriend in the presence of their four-year-old child, who has also been beaten by the boyfriend. The boyfriend has a gun and flees. The victim's 14-year-old son, by her estranged husband, chases after the boyfriend and stabs him in the leg with a kitchen knife. The [female] victim files a criminal complaint and requests an emergency protection order and child support. A warrant is issued; city police arrest the boyfriend, who is charged with a felony. Bond is set. The boyfriend posts bond, is released, and files a criminal complaint against the victim's son who is arrested by the county police. Child protective services files an abuse case against the boyfriend, and the victim's estranged husband files for divorce and custody of their 14-year-old son.

In the majority of jurisdictions across the United States, disposition of the cases arising from this scenario could involve numerous judges, a family court, a court of limited jurisdiction, a court of general jurisdiction, a series of prosecutors and victim advocates from different prosecutors' offices (felony, misdemeanor, and juvenile), various law enforcement departments, child protective services, numerous state and local advocacy agencies, various treatment providers, and state and community advocacy groups. Data relating to case histories and disposition could be entered into several different court data systems and numerous other data systems maintained by law enforcement, prosecution, child protective services, and other agencies involved in the case. Case coordination among and within the various agencies and courts involved most likely would be limited or non-existent [Changes are gradually occurring.].

. . . [T]he door to the courthouse in most jurisdictions is still a revolving one. . . . Within the last few years, [however, in many jurisdictions] the court, the criminal justice components, and the community have combined their collective resources to create a system where each component has a carefully defined role and each faithfully executes its responsibilities to safeguard its citizens. . . . Experimentation with specialized processes for domestic violence cases continues to gain momentum in jurisdictions across the country, and the concept of a domestic violence court is becoming a reality. . . .

■ **ALLISON CLEVELAND, SPECIALIZATION HAS THE POTENTIAL TO LEAD TO UNEVEN JUSTICE: DOMESTIC VIOLENCE CASES IN THE JUVENILE AND DOMESTIC VIOLENCE COURTS**
6 Mod. Am. 17, 17-20 (2010)

. . . "Domestic violence courts," as the name implies, are specialized courts that adjudicate cases involving domestic violence. The Violence Against Women Act ("VAWA") (Title IV of the Violent Crime Control and Law Enforcement Act of 1994) routed substantial funds into the nation's court systems and other areas of criminal justice to demand more accountability from domestic violence perpetrators and to provide help and safety to victims. Beginning in the 1990s, courts nationwide began to allocate special court sessions and other procedural resources for domestic violence cases. These "domestic violence courts" were deemed necessary, in part, to handle the growing number of domestic violence cases as arrests for partner abuse became mandatory and as district attorneys faced increasing pressure to prosecute such crimes. There are currently more than 300 courts with special procedures in place to handle domestic violence matters. The goals of specialized domestic violence courts around the country have been relatively uniform and include protecting and empowering domestic violence survivors in addition to holding perpetrators accountable. Improving case management efficiency is also often cited as a goal.

Domestic violence courts vary greatly in structure. Some domestic violence courts may hear only requests for civil restraining orders, while others may adjudicate all issues—such as restraining orders, criminal charges, and divorce and custody issues—for a single family when domestic violence is involved. The term "domestic violence court" can encompass anything from specialized intake processes to an actual separate court system dedicated to domestic violence cases. For example, in 1987, the Quincy District Court in Quincy, Massachusetts, began its Domestic Violence Prevention Program, a procedural system designed to efficiently address domestic violence cases. Although not a separate court, the program integrated a network of judges, clerks, police officers, prosecutors, perpetrators' intervention programs, and other agencies to streamline the system in which victims and perpetrators of domestic violence would have their problems addressed. In 2001, Massachusetts instituted its first (and only) domestic violence court in Dorchester.

Generally, domestic violence courts will, at a minimum, hold specialized sessions for restraining orders and other civil matters involving intimate partner violence. Special attention will also be afforded to victims. Elena Salzman describes what a victim can expect in the Quincy District Court:

> When a woman comes to the Quincy District Court seeking a restraining order, her first contact will likely be with a domestic abuse clerk in the Restraining Orders Office. The Quincy Program innovators felt that the establishment of a separate restraining orders office would be more conducive to providing the one-on-one assistance women need to fill out the proper paperwork. . . . A woman entering the court is often confused, scared, and uncertain. The clerks help provide the security a woman needs to embark on the intimidating process of requesting a restraining order.
>
> Many of the domestic abuse clerks in Quincy are volunteer interns from law schools and social work programs at local universities. Their duties include disseminating: a sheet listing the critical information the woman should provide to the assisting clerk; a sheet detailing procedures on how to file a drug/alcohol petition; and an informational brochure entitled "Help and Protection for Families Experiencing Violence in the Home," which includes a list of emergency resources.
>
> After the initial intake procedure, domestic abuse clerks refer the woman to the daily briefing sessions hosted by the District Attorney's Office. During these sessions, women not only receive information about referral services and their legal rights, but they also receive emotional support. After the briefing, a clerk accompanies a woman to the courtroom for her emergency hearing, which is usually conducted ex parte, without the batterer or his counsel present. Often the clerk will stand with the woman before the bench to provide moral support.

Domestic violence courts have received widespread praise for reducing case filings related to violence between intimate partners. Victims also appear to be generally satisfied with their court experiences and the adjudication process. However, specialized domestic violence courts are not without critics. Some argue that such courts are victim-oriented and focus so heavily on holding perpetrators accountable that there is a bias in favor of alleged victims. The criminal defense bar has been especially concerned, complaining that "judicial education about family abuse and extended tenure on a calendar devoted to such cases creates a pro-victim, anti-defense bias."

I interviewed a local Boston defense attorney who represents alleged abusers. She strongly echoed the sentiment that Dorchester Domestic Violence Court judges are "much harder" on defendants than their district court counterparts, often denying bail or setting bail much higher than defendants can afford. In her opinion, this placed an unreasonable burden on defendants and resulted in differential treatment across courts. It is perhaps unsurprising that a local prosecutor in the Suffolk County Domestic Violence Unit held a different opinion. Domestic violence courts, she reasoned, appropriately recognize the danger that perpetrators of domestic violence pose to victims and to society-at-large. In her view, the seriousness with which domestic violence crimes have been treated in these specialized courts is a model for the district courts to follow.

Internal criticism also exists. Domestic violence judges themselves have cited increased workloads and emotional burnout as disadvantages of specialization. Externally, some have expressed concern that domestic violence courts usurp the power of the legislature by enforcing court-made domestic violence policy.

Finally, confusion sometimes arises where district court domestic violence programs lack jurisdiction over certain matters, resulting in conflicting orders between courts. Massachusetts, for example, solved this problem by giving the Dorchester Domestic Violence Court jurisdiction over criminal and civil matters in domestic violence cases.

The Importance of Specialized Knowledge in Domestic Violence Cases

Domestic violence cases can present special problems to judges. Because domestic violence is common and likely to be relevant to many legal actions, it is advisable that judges and court staff receive specialized training. Because decisions about custody are among the most important decisions made in the judicial system, and there is a strong probability that domestic violence will be considered as a factor in those decisions, training in domestic violence is especially important for judges who make decisions regarding custody and visitation. Most states require the court to consider domestic violence issues when awarding custody and visitation rights. Without knowledge of the particular dynamics of each situation involving intimate partner violence, judges may be misled by information received in court. Victims of domestic violence often make poor witnesses. The trauma experienced by victims may manifest itself as nervousness, timidity, and body language that may be perceived as suspect or deceptive by the judge. In addition "[w]ithout . . . understanding of the dynamics of intimate partner violence, a judge may question the ability of an individual to tolerate such severe acts of violence. . . . As a result, a judge may question the actual level of violence or the victim's motives if she remained in the abusive relationship. . . ." Abusers, on the other hand, are often confident and self-controlled, giving an appearance of reliability and truthfulness in court. Despite appearances, abusers can be, and often are, "master manipulators." Domestic violence includes "tactics [that] are more than physical violence and include a penumbra of threats and actions to induce fear, humiliation, social isolation and resource deprivation. Batterers cast aspersions on the moral character, parenting and mental health of battered women to discredit them with those who might intervene." Moreover, although a batterer may appear calm and trustworthy on the stand, he likely still presents a danger to his victim, even when they no longer reside in the same home. Indeed, the most dangerous period for an abused woman is immediately after separation, when her abuser may—in a panic—take desperate measures to regain control.

Victims may also not be seen in a favorable light when a judge evaluates the best interests of the child for custody purposes. Best interest factors focus on the stability and security of the child's environment, putting domestic violence victims at a disadvantage. Victims are often dependent on their abusers for housing, income and other forms of support. Consequently, separation from her batterer may leave a mother without immediate access to a job and financial resources. . . .

Taken together, these patterns are not intuitive. Special knowledge on the part of judges and others in the criminal justice system is therefore needed to effectively address the special problems of families affected by domestic violence. . . . [B]ecause judges in domestic violence courts have specialized knowledge regarding domestic violence, they are much more likely to grasp the patterns and complexities involved where violence occurs in the home. . . .

■ ROBYN MAZUR & LIBERTY ALDRICH, WHAT MAKES A DOMESTIC VIOLENCE COURT WORK? LESSONS FROM NEW YORK
42 Judges' J., 6-9, 41-42 (Spring 2003)

. . . As domestic violence courts spread across the country, many jurisdictions are beginning to wrestle with questions about how to administer these courts effectively. . . . Based on the collective experience of the New York State domestic violence courts—misdemeanor, felony, and integrated—several core principles have emerged. . . .

VICTIM SERVICES

Complainants in domestic violence cases have unique needs and concerns. Unlike typical assault victims, they are often dependent on their assailant for economic assistance, have children together with him, or are even living with his family. They may also be threatened by the defendant or his family during the course of a case. These factors and others greatly complicate domestic violence cases and make the prompt and effective provision of social services to victims of paramount importance. [The authors make the following suggestions.]

- **Provide victims with immediate access to advocates.** Victim safety is the true cornerstone of domestic violence courts. Every victim should be given immediate access to an advocate who can provide safety planning and explain court procedures. Comprehensive victim advocacy should include long-term services as well as access to counseling, job training, immigration services, child services, and other programs aimed at improving self-sufficiency. A victim should remain paired with her advocate throughout the pendency of the case (i.e., from police response through post-disposition). . . .

- **"Frontload" social services.** Advocates should make linkages with social service agencies, emergency shelter, food, and civil legal services. This makes sense in human terms (providing people in crisis with help as soon as possible) and in terms of improving court outcomes. Studies have shown that when victims receive assistance early in the court process, they are much more likely to remain engaged in their cases. Victims are more likely to follow through with a case when they clearly understand the legal process.

- **Keep victims informed.** In addition to providing general information and referrals, advocates should provide victims with up-to-date information on their cases. This reduces the burden on the victim to constantly reappear in court to find out the status of her case, and ultimately reduces her chances of being placed in further danger. It also gives the victim the feeling that the system cares about her welfare; this may, in turn, persuade the victim to do all she can to participate in the prosecution.

- **Schedule cases promptly.** Another way to enhance victim safety is to schedule domestic violence cases promptly so that victims can get an order of protection quickly. The longer the victim must wait for legal action, the longer she is at risk. The sooner a case can be heard, the sooner assistance can be provided. In Westchester County, for instance, felonies are transferred immediately to the domestic violence court after the initial filing of an indictment. . . .

- **Create "safe places" within the courthouse.** Court planners should recognize the need for victim safety and provide security and comfort for victims accordingly. Design elements can include providing private space to speak with advocates and separate waiting areas near the victim services office. The Bronx Misdemeanor Domestic Violence Court, in fact, has a separate safe waiting area in the victim services office. The waiting area is staffed by victim advocates; victims are escorted to and from the courtrooms when they need to testify.

JUDICIAL MONITORING

Domestic violence courts seek to take advantage of the coercive and symbolic authority of judges. There is good reason for this: research indicates that ongoing judicial monitoring may be the most effective technique to reduce domestic violence recidivism. Monitoring ensures that repeat offenses will not be tolerated and ensures that the full weight of the judge's authority is directed at stopping the violence.

- **Assign a permanent judge.** Assigning a single judge to handle criminal domestic violence cases from arraignment through sentence and compliance helps ensure consistency. It also helps the judge become well-versed in responding to the special issues presented by domestic violence. Having a single judge preside from the beginning to the end of a case also helps the judge make more informed decisions. The judge's ability to hold a defendant accountable is compromised when the defendant has more information than the court and can "play" the system.

- **Supervise defendants continuously.** Domestic violence courts should use intensive judicial supervision from arraignment through disposition. For defendants whose sentences include probation, judicial monitoring should continue post-disposition as well. Intensive monitoring can come in many forms. In felony-level cases, a judge can require defendants to appear in court every two weeks while a case is pending to ensure that they have enrolled in a batterers' treatment program (often a condition of bail) and to ensure that they are refraining from contact with the victim. Later, judges can use similar techniques to ensure compliance with the sentence. Frequent reporting means that if a violation of a sentence does occur, the court is in a position to respond immediately.

- **Explore new methods of judicial monitoring.** Courts should always look for ways to enhance judicial monitoring. Curfews, phone check-ins, and ankle monitors are all techniques that courts have explored. . . .

- **Dedicate additional staff and resources for monitoring. . . .** In New York's domestic violence courts, judges rely on case managers to keep track of victim needs and violations by defendants. Case managers can assist the judge by staying in constant contact with off-site partners and tracking defendant compliance with court orders.

- **Create a separate compliance docket if there is high volume.** Particularly in busy courthouses, it may make sense to create a separate "compliance courtroom" in which a judge is assigned to monitor offenders' compliance after imposition of the sentence. The compliance judge can quickly identify violations and refer the case back to the sentencing judge as necessary. . . .

ACCOUNTABILITY

It is common for both the complaining witness and the defendant in a domestic violence case to believe that the victim brought the violence on herself. The court can respond to this by making sure that defendants understand that they are directly accountable to the judge for their behavior towards the complainant and their compliance with court orders. Domestic violence courts can encourage another kind of accountability as well, holding government and nonprofit partners accountable for serving victims and monitoring defendants in the most effective manner possible.

- **Build strong relationships with service providers.** Information is crucial to any effort to promote accountability. Strong relationships with service providers, such as batterers' intervention programs and substance abuse treatment providers, ensure that when a defendant is noncompliant, the court is notified right away and can act accordingly. . . .

COORDINATED COMMUNITY RESPONSE

To combat domestic violence, all segments of a community have to work together to send a consistent message that violence is not acceptable. Domestic violence courts can play a critical role in raising public consciousness and convening disparate partners to improve interagency communication.

- **Create strong linkages with a wide range of partners.** Because of its complexity, domestic violence inevitably involves a variety of local systems, agencies, and individuals. Recognizing this, domestic violence courts should aspire to expand the range of organizations that are involved in the court's efforts. Partnerships between the domestic violence court and the many agencies that provide victim assistance/advocacy and defendant monitoring help to strengthen the message to the defendant—and to the community—that domestic violence is not tolerated.

- **Convene regular meetings with criminal justice and social service partners.** Interagency collaboration is crucial to ensuring communication, consistency, and continuing education about the court and domestic violence. The domestic violence judge can be a catalyst, providing leadership to the collaboration. Judges should invite all of the court's partners—representatives from the prosecutor's office, the defense bar, court officers, victim advocates, resource coordinators, batterers' intervention programs, and probation—to participate in regular meetings. The meetings create an opportunity to clarify and understand the court's expectation of everyone's roles. Partner meetings can also focus on strengthening outreach to underserved communities and devising preventive education models. . . .

- **Provide court personnel and partners with domestic violence education and training.** Domestic violence courts can continually educate and update staff and partners by scheduling regular court-sponsored trainings. In New York's domestic violence courts, trainings have been held on a variety of topics featuring a wide range of both local and national experts. Trainings have ranged from "Domestic Violence 101" presentations held during Domestic Violence Awareness month to more in-depth day-long presentations focused on specific issues such as the overlap of child maltreatment and domestic violence. The goals of these trainings are really twofold—to provide ongoing support and reinforcement on domestic violence issues to court personnel and partners as well and to highlight the court's commitment to handling domestic violence cases in an educated and serious manner.

OBSTACLES

Creating a domestic violence court is not without its challenges, of course. A domestic violence court is, by its nature, a collaborative enterprise requiring the buy-in of numerous agencies including court administrators, judges, prosecutors, victim advocates, and, where possible, the defense bar. Each of these stakeholders will have their own concerns. Addressing as many of these issues up front will help prevent problems down the road. . . .

DEFINING SUCCESS

Many domestic violence advocates are hesitant to embrace the idea that domestic violence courts are "problem-solving courts." There are substantial differences between domestic violence courts and other problem-solving courts. Many of these differences stem from how success is measured and to whom services are offered. Drug courts can easily look to see whether defendants are successfully completing their court-mandated drug-treatment programs. But domestic violence courts are not targeted at "rehabilitating" defendants. Indeed, services are offered primarily to help victims achieve independence. The primary "service" offered to defendants is batterers' programs. But in New York domestic violence courts, batterers' programs are used by domestic violence courts primarily as a monitoring tool rather than as a therapeutic device. . . .

Other methods of measuring recidivism present substantial challenges. First, one might turn to the victims to track re-offending. After all, they are not defendants—they aren't fingerprinted and the court has no legal hold on them. Moreover, many victims are loath to "re-live" their victimization participating in follow-up studies. As a result, it is often difficult to track victims over the long haul. For the same reasons, it can also be difficult to find out whether domestic violence courts are meeting victims' service needs.

Without victim information, researchers may be forced to use official records, which track only arrests and not unreported offenses, to try to understand the courts' impact on recidivism. . . .

But more is needed. Because it is difficult to identify a single standard for defining success, it has been difficult to show whether or not these specialized courts

are making a difference. This debate echoes the debate over whether or not batterers programs have an impact on either recidivism or safety. As more research is
being done in this area, domestic violence courts will have to modify their procedures to ensure that they are consistent with the best practices in the field.

FUNDING

Finding funding, both initially and for ongoing support, has proven to be an
obstacle to wider implementation of domestic violence courts. Although the federal
government provided a tremendous incentive to launch these specialized courts,
they cannot be expected to provide funding over the long term. . . .

Notes and Questions

1. *Problem-solving courts.* Several jurisdictions have established specialized
domestic violence courts. The creation of these courts stemmed from the recognition of the shortcomings of the traditional legal system in addressing domestic
violence. The objective of these specialized courts was to consolidate judges, prosecutors, court personnel, and other resources into a central system to provide a
more effective response to domestic violence. Betsy Tsai, Note, The Trend Toward
Specialized Domestic Violence Courts: Improvements on an Effective Innovation,
68 Fordham L. Rev. 1285, 1287 (2000). Domestic violence courts are a type of
"problem-solving court," similar to drug courts and mental health courts, that
were formed to target specific issues. Problem-solving courts share similar goals
(that is, the reform of traditional approaches of dealing with problem offenders;
active judicial monitoring; collaboration between the local community, victims, and
offenders; and nontraditional roles for judges). See Greg Berman & John Feinblatt,
Problem-Solving Courts: A Brief Primer, 23 Law & Pol'y 125, 131-132 (2001).
The focus of these courts is on the future, rather than the past:

> Rather than focus on process and precedent, problem-solving justice focuses on
> the outcome. Problem-solving courts are "specialized courts that seek to respond to
> persistent social, human, and legal problems, such as addiction, family dysfunction,
> domestic violence, mental illness, and quality-of-life crime." These courts adapt their
> processes to suit the sources of the problems, which are driving the actions that bring
> the wrongdoer to court in the first place. The focus is on the individual, and the courts
> provide particularized responses designed to change that specific offender's future
> behavior.

Kathryn C. Sammon, Therapeutic Jurisprudence: An Examination of Problem-
Solving Justice in New York, 23 St. John's J. Legal Comment 923, 924-925 (2008).
Is the application of "problem-solving" approaches to domestic violence courts
appropriate given the lack of consensus on a proven effective "treatment" for
domestic violence? See Mandy Burton, Judicial Monitoring of Compliance: Introducing "Problem Solving" Approaches to Domestic Violence Courts in England
and Wales, 20 Int'l J.L. Pol'y & Fam. 366, 369-370 (2006).

2. *First domestic violence court.* The first domestic violence court was established in
Brooklyn in 1996, and became the model for 30 specialized courts in New York alone.

That state's use of domestic violence courts evolved to create integrated domestic violence "parts" (that is, divisions) of criminal courts. Judge Amy Karan, who presides over a similarly structured integrated Florida domestic violence court (and author of one of the above excerpts), explains some of the purposes of these courts:

> Our goal is that people won't have to tell their story 10 different places. Previously, a victim of domestic violence might have to tell her story to the police, then to the intake counselor and then to the prosecutor and then to the domestic violence judge and then to the criminal judge and then to the divorce judge, and if children were involved in dependency, to the dependency judge. We've tried to consolidate that so that the system is easier to navigate. We can consolidate your services and consolidate your court appearances so that one or two judges at the most are handling all of your issues. It's more effective for all parties concerned.

Interview by Carolyn Turgeon with Amy Karan, Judge, Domestic Violence Court, Miami, Florida (Jan. 2005), http://www.courtinnovation.org/index.cfm?fuseaction=Document.viewDocument&documentID=334&documentTopicID=23&documentTypeID=8. More than 300 courts now use these specialized approaches. Rebecca Hulse, Privacy and Domestic Violence in Court, 16 Wm. & Mary J. Women & L. 237, 270 (2010).

3. *Characteristics.* Specialized case management of domestic violence cases reflects certain characteristics, including: intake units for protection order cases; service referral processes; case coordination mechanisms to identify, link, and track cases involving the same parties or their children; specialized calendars for protection orders and/or criminal cases; specialized judges to hear domestic violence cases; judicial review calendars or other mechanisms to monitor compliance with court orders; and data systems for improved case coordination, decisionmaking, and compliance monitoring. Susan Keilitz, Nat'l Inst. of Justice, Specialization of Domestic Violence Case Management in the Courts: A National Survey 4 (2004), available at https://www.ncjrs.gov/pdffiles1/nij/199724.pdf. How do domestic violence courts remedy the limitations in practices and procedures of traditional court handling of domestic violence cases?

4. *Types of specialized courts.* There are two main types of domestic violence courts: criminal and integrated. Criminal domestic violence courts address either felony or misdemeanor domestic violence prosecutions. These types of courts centralize the intake process, expedite trial proceedings, provide advocates for victims, create safe places in the courtroom for victims, assign a single judge for the duration of the proceedings, continuously monitor defendants to ensure compliance with the terms of their bail or probation, have specialized staff and prosecutors trained in domestic violence issues, and promote a coordinated community response involving the local community and family in determining an appropriate solution for the batterer. See Tsai, supra, at 1300-1302.

Integrated domestic violence courts combine the civil and criminal aspects of domestic violence into a single, unified court. Thus, these courts have many of the same attributes of criminal domestic violence courts, while also providing additional social services to victims, aiding in the protective order process, emphasizing a therapeutic approach (such as batterer treatment programs) in lieu of traditional incarceration, and, in some courts, even requiring counseling for the children who witnessed domestic violence in their homes. See Tsai, supra, at 1302-1304. Some integrated domestic violence courts also adjudicate child custody, dissolution, and juvenile dependency where there are allegations of domestic violence. Center for Court Innovation, The Center for Court Innovation—Domestic Violence Courts: What Are They?, http://www.courtinnovation.org/index.cfm? fuseaction=page .ViewPage&PageID=600&currentTopTier2=true (last accessed July 17, 2011).

Do Mazur and Aldrich's suggestions for creating and improving domestic violence courts apply to both criminal and integrated courts? What aspects might fare better in one type of court rather than the other? What gaps would continue to exist between the courts and how could they be addressed?

5. *Benefits of specialized domestic violence courts.* Specialized domestic violence courts have a number of benefits, including: coordination of cases and consistent orders in different cases involving the same parties; comprehensive relief for victims at an earlier stage of the judicial process; advocacy services that encourage victims to improve their well-being; enhanced understanding by judges of how domestic violence affects victims and their children; consistent procedures, treatment of litigants, rulings, and orders; increased availability of mechanisms to hold batterers accountable for the abuse; improved batterer compliance with orders; greater confidence on the part of the community that the justice system is responding effectively to domestic violence; and better system accountability. Keilitz, supra, at 3-4.

What are the disadvantages of these courts? What criticisms are identified by the above excerpts? A student commentator adds the concern that the multidisciplinary approach (involving numerous parties with a variety of perspectives and goals) has the potential for creating conflict in the implementation of interventions to further diverse objectives. The dual focus (victim safety and offender accountability), she contends, may create discord within the coordinated system when agencies and individuals struggle to balance conflicting role expectations with new policy goals. Tsai, supra, at 1310-1312. Another student commentator points out that the biggest problem of a coordinated response is:

> the distrust and competing agendas of the different players (i.e., child advocates and domestic violence advocates). Compromise can be hard when each agency has opposing ideological perspectives. For example, domestic violence advocates may focus more on the rights of the mother as a parent while children's advocates focus on getting the child into a stable placement as quickly as possible, even if that means removal from the mother.

Linda Quigley, Note, The Intersection between Domestic Violence and the Child Welfare System: The Role Courts Can Play in the Protection of Battered Mothers and their Children, 13 Wm. & Mary J. Women & L. 867, 891 (2007).

6. *Jurisdiction.* The creation of New York domestic violence courts faced legal challenges. In People v. Fernandez, 897 N.Y.S.2d 158 (N.Y. 2010), a criminal defendant was charged with harassment of his former girlfriend. When his case was transferred from criminal court to the Integrated Domestic Violence (IDV) Parts of the New York Supreme Court, he argued that the integrated domestic violence court lacked jurisdiction over misdemeanor domestic violence offenses because the integrated court was assigned cases without either a superior court information or a grand jury indictment as required to implement the constitutional rights of the accused. The court rejected the defendant's argument that the transfer infringed on his rights, reasoning that the state constitution provided the chief judge with authority to regulate court practice and procedure. See also

Holsman v. Cohen, 667 So. 2d 769 (Fla. 1996) (holding that domestic violence courts could adjudicate multijurisdictional crimes); In re Report of Comm'n on Family Courts, 646 So. 2d 178 (Fla. 1994) (acknowledging the creation of domestic violence-specific courts by administrative regulation).

How does domestic violence challenge the jurisdictional divide between traditional civil and criminal proceedings? Do specialized domestic violence courts raise due process issues by a focus on individualized remedies that detract from equal treatment? See Rekha Mirchandani, What's So Special about Specialized Courts? The State and Social Change in Salt Lake City's Domestic Violence Court, 39 Law & Soc'y Rev. 379, 408-413 (2005).

7. *Components.* What are the key elements of a domestic violence court? Professor Emily Sack identifies the following components: (1) early access to advocacy and services such as crisis assistance, referrals to long-term counseling, job training, immigration services, or housing referrals; (2) coordination of community partners including court staff, police, drug treatment services, and batterer intervention programs; (3) a victim- and child-friendly court with separate entrances for victims and defendants, metal detectors, security officers in the courtroom, and secure day care centers; (4) specialized staff and judges trained in domestic violence law as well as the dynamics of abuse; and (5) even-handed treatment in the courtroom, allowing counsel to all parties and a fair judicial demeanor; (6) leveraging the judge's role to coordinate partners, protocols, and programs to benefit the victim; (7) an integrated information system providing all of the relevant information and background on the case and people in a single, secure place; (8) evaluation and accountability to obtain feedback and improve the court's and the community's response; (9) protocols for evaluating the risks of re-abuse or homicide in a given domestic violence scenario; (10) ongoing training and education; (11) compliance monitoring to ensure abusers are holding to the court-ordered conditions; and (12) sentencing models to guide a uniform and appropriate response to a domestic violence case while promoting the abuser's accountability. Emily Sack, Creating a Domestic Violence Court: Guidelines and Best Practices 9-23 (2002), available at http://www.futureswithoutviolence.org/user-files/file/Judicial/FinalCourt_Guidelines.pdf. How do these recommendations compare with those made in the above excerpts? How do these components benefit the victim of domestic violence? The abuser? The community? The court system?

8. *Therapeutic jurisprudence.* Domestic violence courts originate from the perspective of "therapeutic jurisprudence." Therapeutic jurisprudence is an interdisciplinary perspective based in mental health law. The term stems from the principle that "law is a social force that has inevitable (if unintended) consequences for the mental health and psychological functioning of those it affects." Dennis P. Stolle et al., Integrating Preventive Law and Therapeutic Jurisprudence: A Law and Psychology Based Approach to Lawyering, 34 Cal. W. L. Rev. 15, 17 (1997). Therapeutic jurisprudence takes into account the social, psychological, and emotional well-being of the accused in determining a resolution that will promote rehabilitation. Therapeutic jurisprudence is implemented through expanded sentencing guidelines (such as allowing judges to send the abuser to batterer intervention programs rather than mandating a strict jail sentence), asking open-ended investigatory questions (such as asking the defendant if there is anything she/he would like to tell the judge before the ruling), and exploring *why* a batterer committed a crime rather than *what* the crime is. Do you agree that this is the appropriate legal response to abusers?

See generally Rekha Mirchandani, Beyond Therapy: Problem-Solving Courts and the Deliberative Democratic State, 33 Law & Soc. Inquiry 853 (2008); Catherine Shaffer, Therapeutic Domestic Violence Courts: An Efficient Approach to Adjudication, 27 Seattle U. L. Rev. 981 (2004); Carrie J. Petrucci, Respect as a Component in the Judge-Defendant Interaction in a Specialized Domestic Violence Court that Utilizes Therapeutic Jurisprudence, 38 Crim. L. Bull. 263 (2002).

9. *Effectiveness.* How effective are domestic violence courts in addressing domestic violence? The few existing studies reveal mixed results. One study reports that, five years after one specialized court was implemented, the percentage of protective orders increased by 11 percent, the rate of dismissal of cases decreased by half, and conviction by guilty pleas became more common, thereby saving the court money and time. Anat Maytal, Note, Specialized Domestic Violence Courts: Are They Worth the Trouble in Massachusetts, 18 B.U. Pub. Int. L.J. 197, 210 (2008) (citing Lisa Newmark et al., Urban Institute Justice Policy Center, Specialized Felony Domestic Violence Courts: Lessons on Implementation and Impacts from the Kings County Experience (2001), available at http://www.courtinnovation.org/_uploads/documents/SpecializedFelonyDomesticViolenceCourts.pdf). Another study reports that, after the domestic violence court was established, arrests for domestic violence increased while rearrests for abusers decreased. Angela R. Gover et al., Combating Domestic Violence: Findings from an Evaluation of a Local Domestic Violence Court, 3 Criminology & Pub. Pol'y 109 (2003).

In contrast, another study reveals that judges in domestic violence courts are just as likely to implement the law half-heartedly as their civil court counterparts. See Deborah M. Weissman, Gender-Based Violence as Judicial Anomaly: Between "The Truly National and the Truly Local," 42 B.C. L. Rev. 1081, 1128 (2001) (noting that one domestic violence court witnessed a *decrease* in the issuance of protective orders). Thus, although some victims report increased satisfaction with domestic violence courts, the effectiveness of these courts in terms of preventing recidivism is unknown.

10. *Monitoring.* A central feature of the domestic violence courts is judicial monitoring of the abuser to ensure compliance with the terms of his sentence. Offenders must appear regularly before a judge to verify compliance with the order. Studies on mandatory compliance hearings in domestic violence courts have shown that such judicial accountability substantially increases the number of abusers who complete batterer intervention programs and also that those who complete the programs are considerably less likely to be rearrested for assault than those who do not. See Edward W. Gondolf, Mandatory Court Review and Batterer Programme Compliance, 15 J. Interpersonal Violence 428 (2000); Carolyn Turgeon, Bridging Theory and Practice: A Roundtable on Court Responses to Domestic Violence, 1 J. Ct. Innovation 345, 349 (2008).

11. *Language barriers.* Language barriers often prevent non-English-speaking victims of domestic violence from seeking protection from the courts. What role can domestic violence courts play in helping non-English-speaking victims to receive the services they need for protection from future abuse? See Nancy K. D. Lemon, Access to Justice: Can Domestic Violence Courts Better Address the Needs of Non-English Speaking Victims of Domestic Violence, 21 Berkeley J. Gender L. & Just. 38 (2006) (arguing that domestic violence courts have the potential of improving services to non-English-speaking victims).

XV

Social Services

A. SHELTERS

1. Constitutional Issues

■ **WOODS v. HORTON**
84 Cal. Rptr. 3d 332 (Ct. App. 2008)

MORRISON, J.

Plaintiffs are five individuals [four men and the daughter of one of these men] who have suffered domestic violence or who are suing as taxpayers to prevent the illegal expenditure of state money, or both. David Woods alleged he had been married to Ruth Woods since 1981. [S]he was physically violent to him, repeatedly hitting him and attacking him with weapons and objects. In 1990 and continuing through 2003, Woods decided he and his daughter, also a plaintiff, should leave to escape the violence. He called WEAVE (Women Escaping a Violent Environment), a domestic violence service provider, and was told WEAVE did not accept men. Woods and his daughter returned to the house and the violence continued. Woods alleged the violence may continue and he still needs services. Woods's daughter alleges she was injured by the denial of services to her father, which forced her to witness and be subjected to continued violence.

Gregory Bowman alleged he is a taxpayer in California. He alleged that his former girlfriend repeatedly assaulted him. On May 11, 2005, he received threats from the girlfriend, who gave him a black eye. He reported the incident to the police. On several occasions during that time, Bowman needed domestic violence services. He requested them from numerous state-funded programs, but was frequently denied services because he was a man. . . . Bowman alleged his former

777

girlfriend stabbed him, and she was arrested and charged with assault with a deadly weapon and domestic assault. She and others continued to threaten and harass Bowman, including smashing his windshield, stealing his license plates and leaving a suspicious package in his car. Bowman alleged he still needs domestic violence services and is denied them based on his gender.

Patrick Neff alleged that from 2001 through 2004, his former girlfriend repeatedly assaulted him and he needed to get out of the house and receive counseling and legal advice. . . . He repeatedly called the Domestic Violence and Sexual Assault Coalition (DVSAC) but was told they do not help men. In 2001, the violence exploded and Neff was arrested and charged and he pled no contest to domestic violence. He maintains his innocence and alleged he still needs domestic violence services. . . .

Plaintiffs challenge a number of statutory provisions that have gender-based classifications [and petition for injunctive and declaratory relief]. In particular, they challenge programs that provide benefits for women and their children, but not men and their children. They contend these gender-based classifications violate equal protection. . . .

Plaintiffs challenge two statutory programs providing grants to those providing services for victims of domestic violence. The first is a comprehensive shelter-based grant program to battered women's shelters to be administered by the Maternal and Child Health Branch of the State Department of Health Services (Cal. Health & Safety Code §124250.) The program provides grants to battered women's shelters that provide services in four areas: emergency shelter to women and their children, transitional housing programs to assist in finding housing and jobs, legal and other types of advocacy and representation, and other support services. The statute defines domestic violence as occurring only against women. "'Domestic violence' means the infliction or threat of physical harm against past or present adult or adolescent female intimate partners, and shall include physical, sexual, and psychological abuse against the woman, and is part of a pattern of assaultive, coercive, and controlling behaviors directed at achieving compliance from or control over, that woman." The statute speaks in gender specific terms; services are to be provided to "women and their children."

The second program is the Comprehensive Statewide Domestic Violence Program administered by the Office of Emergency Services (OES) (Cal. Penal Code §13823.15). . . . The OES provides financial and technical assistance to local domestic violence centers in implementing a variety of services, including 24-hour crisis hotlines, counseling, emergency "safe" homes or shelters, emergency services, counseling, and advocacy. Priority is given to "emergency shelter programs and 'safe' homes for victims of domestic violence and their children."

The language of Penal Code §13823.15 is gender neutral, referring to "victims of domestic violence" rather than women, except in subdivision (f), which addresses the funding process for grants to domestic violence shelter service providers. For purposes of that subdivision, domestic violence is defined as "the infliction or threat of physical harm against past or present adult or adolescent female intimate partners, including physical, sexual, and psychological abuse against the woman, and is a part of a pattern of assaultive, coercive, and controlling behaviors directed at achieving compliance from or control over that woman." . . .

In support of [their petition], plaintiffs offered declarations from several doctors in psychology and sociology and other experts in domestic violence attesting that men suffered from domestic violence as well as women and were in need of domestic violence services. The declarants stated studies showed women used violence in intimate relationships at about the same rate as men, although women suffered greater injuries. Denying services to abused men puts their children in danger. . . .

Dr. Steinberg, the public health medical administrator for DHS, declared that all shelters receiving grants from OES offer gender-neutral services. Of the agencies funded by DHS, 85 percent offer services to men, as well as women. Research showed women have a greater need for shelters than men and there were insufficient resources to provide for all domestic violence victims. . . .

Legislative findings indicated the problem of domestic violence against females was increasing and existing services were underfunded and certain areas underserved. The court found ample support for these findings, as women were more likely to be victims and sustain more severe injuries. . . .

The trial court's reasoning [in denying plaintiffs' petition] is that since more women are victims of domestic violence, and since they suffer more severe injuries, men are not similarly situated for purposes of domestic violence. As plaintiffs argue, this analysis improperly views equal protection rights as group rights, rather than individual rights, and permits discrimination simply because fewer men than women are affected. The trial court recognized that plaintiffs established, through declarations and journal articles, "that men experience significant levels of domestic violence as victims[.]" These men, therefore, are similarly situated to women as to the need for domestic violence services. The trial court erred in finding the similarly situated prerequisite had not been met for the domestic violence programs. . . .

Plaintiffs contend the challenged programs do not survive strict scrutiny analysis because the gender classifications are unnecessary and there are gender-neutral alternatives available. . . . [According to California law, a classification based on gender requires evaluation pursuant to strict scrutiny, requiring that the classification be justified as necessary to a compelling state interest.] The Attorney General contends there is a compelling state interest in funding domestic violence programs only for women and cites the legislative findings. . . .

The greater need for services by female victims of domestic violence does not provide a compelling state interest in a gender classification. [E]qual protection is not concerned with numbers. . . . Arguing that a group of people (here male victims of domestic violence) is too small in number to be afforded equal protection is simply arguing "that the right to equal protection should hinge on 'administrative convenience.'" Administrative convenience is an inadequate state interest under a strict scrutiny analysis. Plaintiffs and defendants agree domestic violence is a serious problem for both women and men, and programs funded under Health and Safety Code §124250 and Penal Code §13823.15 offer a variety of services, primarily shelter but also counseling and other support services. Defendants fail to show a compelling state interest in providing funding only to those programs that provide these services to women only.

Even if there were a compelling state interest, defendants do not show the classification is necessary, rather than convenient, and no gender-neutral alternative is available. Most of the programs funded by DHS and all of the programs funded by OES offer services on a gender-neutral basis, showing the classification is not necessary. There is an alternative; most statutory definitions of domestic violence are gender neutral. . . . The gender classifications in Health and Safety Code §124250 and Penal Code §13823.15, that provide state funding of domestic violence programs that offer services only to women and their children, but not to men, violate equal protection.

We turn now to the question of the appropriate remedy for the violation of equal protection due to the gender classifications in the challenged domestic violence programs. . . . Both plaintiffs and the Attorney General agree that reforming Health and Safety Code §124250 and Penal Code §13823.15 to provide funding for victims of domestic violence regardless of gender would be preferable to invalidating the statutes. . . . Accordingly, both Health and Safety Code §124250 and Penal Code §13823.15 are reformed. . . . In reforming the statutes that provide funding for domestic violence programs to be gender-neutral, we do not require that such programs offer identical services to men and women. Given the noted disparity in the number of women needing services and the greater severity of their injuries, it may be appropriate to provide more and different services to battered women and their children. For example, a program might offer shelter for women, but only hotel vouchers for a smaller number of men. The judgment is reversed. . . .

Notes and Questions

1. *Roots of the shelter movement.* The first battered women's shelter (called a "refuge") opened in England in 1971. The movement that led to the establishment of shelters began in the London suburb of Chiswick, when residents organized a march (consisting of 500 women, children, and a cow) to protest the loss of government funding for milk for schoolchildren. R. Emerson Dobash & Russell Dobash, Violence Against Wives: A Case Against the Patriarchy 1 (1979). The resulting sense of solidarity, fueled by the efforts of Chiswick feminist Erin Pizzey, led to the establishment of a local neighborhood center (called the "Chiswick's Women's Aid") that offered child care and a refuge for homeless women. As the center's clientele realized the centrality of battering in their lives, the group's focus shifted to wife beating. Pizzey used her media contacts (acquired through her BBC journalist-husband) to launch the social movement that led to the establishment of similar refuges throughout England. Elizabeth Pleck, Domestic Tyranny: The Making of American Social Policy Against Family Violence from Colonial Times to the Present 188 (2004) (explaining that Pizzey supplied the media with "a steady stream of horrible accounts about violent treatment of women and demonstrated the need for battered women's refuges by showing the large numbers of women who flocked to Chiswick"). See also Erin Pizzey, Scream Quietly or the Neighbors Will Hear You (1978).

2. *First American shelters.* As news of the English refuge movement reached this country, the first American shelters opened. The St. Paul, Minnesota, shelter, established in 1974, became the popular model. Pleck, supra, at 189-190 (explaining that their services included: a 24-hour crisis hotline; emergency housing; child care; assistance with medical, welfare, and legal issues; and a support group). In 1976, a survey listed 20 American shelters. Id. at 190. By 2008, 2,000 shelters existed. Eleanor Lyon et al., Nat'l Inst. of Justice, Meeting Survivors' Needs: A Multi-State Study of Domestic Violence Shelter Experiences 21 [hereafter Meeting Survivors' Needs], available at https://www.ncjrs.gov/pdffiles1/nij/grants/225025.pdf.

3. *Anglo-American early difference in emphasis.* The British battered women's movement, stemming from its community-based orientation, emphasized housing and social services. In contrast, American efforts, stemming from liberal feminists' concern with equal rights, emphasized criminal law reform. R. Emerson Dobash & Russell P. Dobash, Response of the Movements, in Women, Violence and Social Control: Essays in Social Theory 169, 177 (Jalna Hanmer & Mary Maynard eds., 1987). The roots of the battered women's movement are explored further in Chapter 1.

4. *Booth v. Hvaas: the first challenge.* The first case to challenge state funding to battered women's shelters as a violation of men's equal protection rights was filed in 2000 by male Minnesota taxpayers. Plaintiffs sought a declaratory judgment that the state statutory scheme for dispersing state and federal funds violated equal protection by providing funding to battered women but not battered men. Booth v. Hvaas, 2001 WL 1640141 (D. Minn. 2001), aff'd 302 F.3d 849 (8th Cir. 2002); cert. denied, 537 U.S. 1108 (2003). The district court held that the plaintiffs lacked standing to challenge state expenditures because plaintiffs had suffered no injury. The district court dismissed the case with prejudice, and the Eighth Circuit Court of Appeals affirmed. Other gender discrimination cases were similarly dismissed on standing grounds. See Blumhorst v. Jewish Family Servs., 24 Cal. Rptr. 3d 474 (Ct. App. 2005); Hageman v. Stanek, 2004 WL 1563276 (Minn. Ct. App. 2004). Because *Booth* was decided on standing grounds, Woods v. Horton was the first case to address the merits of the equal protection claim.

5. *Fathers' rights movement.* Many commentators view the gender-based funding cases (such as *Woods*) as a backlash against feminist efforts to recognize domestic violence as a gender-based crime. See, e.g., Molly Dragiewicz, Equality with a Vengeance: Men's Rights Groups, Battered Women, and Antifeminist Backlash (2011); Julie Goldscheid, Domestic and Sexual Violence as Sex Discrimination: Comparing American and International Approaches, 28 T. Jefferson L. Rev. 355, 373-378 (2006).

Plaintiffs in the first case to challenge state funding of battered women's shelters (*Booth*, supra, in Minnesota), were all members of fathers' rights groups. Their challenge originated in an activist agenda "to eliminate what its members consider to be pro-women or anti-men laws." Shannon M. Garrett, Battered by Equality, Could Minnesota's Domestic Violence Statutes Survive a "Fathers' Rights" Assault?, 21 Law & Ineq. 341, 343 n.14 (2003). The fathers' rights law reform campaign was launched initially in the 1970s when members lobbied for joint custody to abrogate the maternal preference. Pamela Laufer-Ukeles, Selective Recognition of Gender Difference in the Law: Revaluing the Caretaker Role, 31 Harv. J. L. & Gender 1, 18 (2008). According to commentators, although the fathers' rights campaign rhetoric was characterized by "moderate-sounding goals of ensuring equal protection for fathers," the agenda involved the pursuit of "much broader and more radical attacks on domestic violence, divorce, custody, and child support laws by arguing that these laws discriminate against men." Garrett, supra, at 341. See also id. at 346 (noting that the plaintiffs' motion papers in *Booth* stated that the "purpose of this suit is to cut off the main source of public money which fuels sexist bias against men in our family court system"). For discussion of the role of the fathers' rights movement in *Booth*, see Dragiewicz, supra. See also Jan Kurth, Historical Origins of the Fathers' Rights Movement, in Domestic Violence, Abuse, and Child Custody 4-1 to 4-28 (Mo Therese Hannah & Barry Goldstein eds., 2010).

6. *Constitutional issues: gender discrimination. Woods* involved a facial challenge, based on state equal protection guarantees, to two California statutes that provided funding for domestic violence programs. Because the California constitution applies strict scrutiny to gender discrimination, plaintiffs had to show that, *as individuals,* they were similarly situated to the distinguished class; then, the burden shifted to the state to show that any facial distinctions based on gender survived strict scrutiny. Did plaintiffs in *Woods* satisfy their burden of proof? Did the defendants demonstrate that state funding laws serving only female victims were necessary to serve a compelling state interest? What evidence did defendants present? Why was that evidence not sufficient to uphold the statutes? What did the trial court rule? What did the appellate court decide?

7. *Criticism.* One commentator notes that the importance of *Woods* is its highlight on "the limits of formal equality review of laws that confer benefits upon women. Specifically, in its formal equality review, the court failed to sufficiently consider the gendered nature of domestic violence and the social and political context in which violence against women occurs." Molly Dragiewicz & Yvonne Lindgren, The Gendered Nature of Domestic Violence: Statistical Data for Lawyers Considering Equal Protection Analysis, 17 Am. U. J. Gender Soc. Pol'y & L. 229, 230-231 (2009). Do you agree? What are the implications of *Woods* for the law's response to domestic violence? For additional discussion of *Woods,* see Amanda J. Schmesser, Note, Real Men May Not Cry, But They Are Victims of Domestic Violence: Bias in the Application of Domestic Violence Laws, 58 Syracuse L. Rev. 171 (2007).

8. *Remedy.* To remedy the equal protection violation, *Woods* reformed the statutes. What injury did plaintiffs suffer? Does reformation adequately redress that injury? For example, does the receipt of a hotel voucher rather than shelter services (as the court suggests) address these needs? Why does the offer of different services to male and female clients survive constitutional scrutiny?

9. *Funding.* From what sources do domestic violence shelters receive funding? What are the advantages and disadvantages of the various funding sources and funding models?

a. *State funding.* Some states, like California in *Woods,* provide funding through laws that dedicate a portion of the state budget to that purpose. What problems does this approach entail? See, e.g., James Rufus Koren, State Budget Leaves No Funding for Domestic Violence Shelters, San Bernardino Cty. Sun, May 19, 2010, available at 2010 WLNR 10309923 (noting the instability of such funding); Andria Simmons, Domestic Violence Shelters Strapped, Atlanta J. & Const., Mar. 25, 2010, at A1 (lamenting budget cuts that eliminate shelter funding).

In many states, marriage license fees or dissolution filing fees include a statutorily designated amount for funding shelters. Florida was the first state to impose such a fee on marriage licenses in 1978. Fla. Stat. §741.01. See also Ala. Code §30-6-11; Ariz. Rev. Stat. §36-3002 (court fees); Ill. Comp. Stat. ch. 20 1310/§3.2 (marriage and court fees); Or. Rev. Stat. §21.111 (court fees). See also Pleck, supra, at 190.

Do marriage license fees or the imposition of court filing fees/costs to fund domestic violence programs raise constitutional issues? For example, do the fees violate the right to marry? Does it violate equal protection if the fees are paid by some (married) persons who will never take advantage of domestic violence services while, at the same time, other persons who do benefit from services (that is, unmarried persons) do not pay the fees? Compare Browning v. Corbett, 734 P.2d

1030 (Ariz. Ct. App. 1987) (upholding court fees against an equal protection challenge), and Villars v. Provo, 440 N.W.2d 160 (Minn. App. 1989) (same); with Boynton v. Kusper, 494 N.E.2d 135 (Ill. 1986) (invalidating a marriage license fee as an infringement on the fundamental right to marry). See also Fent v. State ex rel. Dept. of Human Servs., 236 P.3d 61 (Okla. 2010) (invalidating court fees as a violation of statutory mandate to limit funds to programs that provide "open access to courts," reasoning that abuse-prevention programs were not related to the maintenance of court system); D'Antoni v. Commissioner, N.H. Dept. of Health & Human Servs., 917 A.2d 177 (N.H. 2006) (upholding fees based on separation-of-powers challenge).

b. *Federal funding.* In 1984, Congress enacted the first federal legislation, the Family Violence Prevention and Services Act, Pub. L. No. 98-457, 98 Stat 1749 (codified as amended at 42 U.S.C. §10401-11412), that funded domestic violence shelters. The bill, authorizing the expenditure of $6 million, was passed seven years after similar legislation had been proposed. Pleck, Domestic Tyranny, supra, at 198. Also in 1984, Congress enacted the Victims of Crime Act (VOCA), Pub. L. No. 100-690, 102 Stat. 4420 (codified as amended at 18 U.S.C. §§10601 et. seq.). Although VOCA initially excluded domestic violence victims (because eligibility requirements precluded family members of an offender from recovering), Congress subsequently amended VOCA to require states to allow compensation funds to domestic violence victims. Anti-Drug Abuse Act of 1988, Pub. L. No. 100-690, §7125(c)(1), 102 Stat. 4181, 4422 (1988) (amending 42 U.S.C. §10602(b)).

Currently, the federal government provides funding for domestic violence shelters pursuant to the Family Violence Prevention and Service Act (FVPSA), 42 U.S.C. §§10401-10421, and VAWA. FVPSA, reauthorized in 2010, authorizes grants to agencies to develop collaborations between child protective service entities and domestic violence prevention entities to provide safety to the victim and children and services to children exposed to domestic violence "that also support the caregiving role of the non-abusing parent." 42 U.S.C. §5106. VAWA's Subtitle B (entitled "Safe Homes for Women") helps subsidize the operating costs of shelters. Pub. L. No. 103-322, 108 Stat. 1925 (codified as amended in scattered sections of U.S.C.). Pending VAWA 2011 provisions reauthorize shelter funding.

c. *Private donations.* Federal funding constitutes only a small portion of shelter budgets. Thus, shelters have to rely on volunteers and private donations. Kristin Bumiller, Freedom from Violence as a Human Right: Toward a Feminist Politics of Nonviolence, 28 T. Jefferson L. Rev. 327, 342 (2006). See also Woman's Club Helping Out Domestic Violence Shelters, St. Petersburg Times (Aug. 7, 2009); Verizon Drive Will Aid Domestic Violence Shelters, Patriot Ledger (Nov. 14, 2008), at 10; Domestic Violence Shelters Nationwide to Receive $3 Million Cash Infusion during Economic Downturn, Women's Health Weekly, Oct. 9, 2008, at 440. What difficulties does such reliance pose?

Problem

The Family Protection Services Board, a public entity in West Virginia, is responsible under the state Domestic Violence Act for establishing and enforcing licensing standards and also providing funding for domestic violence shelters by distributing proceeds from a special state revenue fund. The Board recently passed a regulation requiring shelters to be licensed by the Board in order to provide services. To obtain a license, the shelter must (among other regulations) require employees to undergo special training, and have a written process for obtaining alternative lodging in the event the shelter is unable to accommodate "special needs populations," including adolescent or adult males.

Men and Women Against Discrimination (MAWAD), a nonprofit group organized to ensure fairness based on gender, sues the Board, contending that several of its regulations discriminate on the basis of gender and infringe on MAWAD's free speech. Specifically, MAWAD asserts: (1) the licensure regulations discriminate against male victims of domestic violence because men are treated as a "special needs population" for whom alternative lodging may be sought; (2) the regulations discriminate on the basis of gender because they require employees to undergo training that includes the "understanding that domestic violence is deeply rooted in historical attitudes towards women and is intergenerational"; and (3) the Board's rule requiring one-third of a family protection program's direct service providers to be licensed "domestic violence advocates" violates MAWAD's free speech because such certification is available only through a private organization, the West Virginia Coalition Against Domestic Violence ("the Coalition"), and by delegating certification authority to the Coalition, the Board deprives MAWAD of "an opportunity for free expression of their speech, thoughts and ideas relative to domestic violence," thereby constituting an unlawful prior restraint upon plaintiff's right of free speech.

What result? See Men & Women Against Discrimination v. Family Protection Services Bd., 2011 WL 2119028 (W. Va. 2011).

2. Confidentiality

Shelter Sues for Breach of Confidentiality

The location of domestic violence shelters is kept confidential in order to protect the shelter residents. Jewish Family Service of Los Angeles is a 30-bed shelter for battered women that provides 30-day stays for battered women, as well as counseling and assistance in securing restraining orders against abusers. The shelter was forced to close and to move its residents after Pacific Bell printed the shelter's confidential address in its White Pages telephone book.

The agency discovered the problem when a woman appeared at the shelter looking for her daughter-in-law. According to Tracy Hutchinson, director of the agency's Valley-based Family Violence Project, "That's considered a threat, because batterers often use their family members to try and find the women." The visitor told shelter staff that she had found the address in the phone book. "We were horrified," said Ms. Hutchinson, "because the address is in every phone book we saw." "Even 411 [directory assistance] was giving it out."

According to a complaint filed by the agency in Los Angeles Superior Court, the shelter had informed the phone company *not* to list its address or even to print it on its bills. Bills were sent to an office address rather than the shelter location. Stemming from concern about the security breach, the shelter immediately transferred all residents (11 women and their children) to other agencies. The agency also was forced to relocate to a new site. The agency files suit, seeking reimbursement for the costs associated with the move. See Sue Fox, Shelter for Abused Women Sues PacBell, L.A. Times, May 4, 2000, at B5.

■ **FRIGM v. UNEMPLOYMENT COMPENSATION BOARD OF REVIEW**
642 A.2d 629 (Pa. Commw. Ct. 1994)

KELTON, Senior Judge.

Claimant Bonnie Frigm petitions for review of [an] order of the Unemployment Compensation Board of Review, in which the Board affirmed the decision of the Referee to deny Claimant benefits due to willful misconduct under Section 402(e) of the Unemployment Compensation Law. . . .

Claimant last worked for Employer, Access-York, as a Child Play Therapist. . . . Employer operates a battered women's shelter and requires confidentiality from its employees. Claimant was aware of Employer's confidentiality rule [prohibiting disclosure of confidential information with respect to the identities and plans of clients]. In November 1992, a newspaper reporter, who had knowledge of intimate details of one of Employer's clients, contacted Employer. . . . The Board found that on November 13, 1992, Claimant admitted to Employer that she had given confidential information concerning the client to the reporter [because] Claimant had been concerned with Employer's handling of the client's case. . . . Employer discharged Claimant for a breach of confidentiality. . . .

The Bureau of Unemployment Compensation Benefits and Allowances issued a determination denying Claimant benefits for willful misconduct [holding that Claimant failed to establish good cause for her work-rule violation]. On appeal to this Court, Claimant argues that there is insufficient evidence in the record to support the Board's finding that she breached Employer's confidentiality rule. Specifically, Claimant asserts that she gave the reporter only limited information, containing nothing confidential. In the alternative, Claimant contends that her breach of the confidentiality rule was justified because it was in the best interest of the client and the client's child. Further, Claimant argues that a denial of benefits violates her right to free speech. . . .

Under Section 402(e) of the Act, a claimant who is discharged for willful misconduct connected with his or her work is ineligible for unemployment compensation. . . . Employer's policy, of which Claimant was aware, prohibited disclosure of confidential information with respect to the identities and plans of clients. The policy did, however, permit disclosures necessary to accomplish a service plan or for a life-saving emergency.

Claimant does not dispute the reasonableness of Employer's policy. Claimant maintains that she did not reveal any information to the reporter which she considered confidential. Employer's Executive Director, however, testified as follows:

[Referee]:   Let me ask you, ma'am, to present any statements that you might have come here, today, to mention, as to why [Claimant] is no longer with [Employer]. . . .

[Witness: Employer]:   I received a phone call from a reporter, who proceeded to talk about a lot of situations, very intimate details, about a woman and her children who are in our shelter. And I was extremely surprised to hear that information because confidentiality is our chief issue, pretty much, in the shelter, among employees and staff. And the reporter proceeded to tell me a great deal of very intimate information about a woman and her child, and questioned me as to why we chose to take certain actions in regards to dealing with this woman and her child. . . .   When I did speak to [Claimant the next morning] . . . she told me that she wanted to tell me that she had called the reporter and had given her the information. . . . [M]y concern was that if the batterer read the details, he may, just may, not necessarily would, but may recognize that that was his wife and children that he was trying to find. . . .

Due to confidentiality concerns, the Executive Director refused to specify any of the details concerning the client which Claimant allegedly disclosed to the reporter. The Executive Director's testimony reveals, however, that, although Claimant had not revealed the client's name, Claimant had revealed sufficient information to enable the client's batterer to identify the client and her location. Thus, a determination of whether Claimant revealed confidential information depends, first, upon the Board's credibility determination, and second, upon whether the evidence was sufficient to permit the Board to infer that it was Claimant who disclosed the information concerning the identity and location of the client to the reporter.

The Board resolved conflicts in the testimony in favor of Employer and found the Executive Director's testimony credible. . . . We conclude, therefore, that the above evidence was sufficient to permit the Board to infer that it was Claimant who disclosed to the reporter factual details which would allow the identification of a specific agency client and her child. Therefore, we conclude that the Board did not err in finding that Claimant breached Employer's confidentiality rule. [W]e are not persuaded by Claimant's argument that her disclosure of confidential information was warranted when, as the Executive Director indicated, the publication of such information could have jeopardized the safety of the client and her child.

We turn, therefore, to Claimant's argument that a denial of unemployment compensation violates her right to free speech as guaranteed by the first amendment of the United States Constitution. A state's denial of unemployment compensation benefits cannot be based on an individual's exercise of his/her first amendment rights absent a compelling State interest. Where, as here, a claimant is discharged by a private employer, we are required to balance the claimant's interest in commenting upon a matter of public concern and the State's interest in protecting the unemployment compensation fund by disqualifying those individuals whose unemployment is due to willful misconduct.

We must first, therefore, determine whether Claimant's speech is entitled to first amendment protection. Although Claimant's alleged motivation in contacting the reporter was to improve the agency's handling of the client's case, we believe that the furnishing of confidential information concerning the identity and location of a specific battered woman seeking shelter is not a matter of general public concern. To the contrary, the societal interest is in the protection of such persons from further potential abuse. Therefore, we conclude that here a denial of benefits does not infringe upon Claimant's first amendment rights. . . .

[Employer's Personnel Policy] provides that a serious offense may warrant immediate discharge. We believe that Employer reasonably considered Claimant's breach of confidentiality in this case a serious offense; therefore, we find that Employer acted in compliance with its disciplinary policy in discharging her. . . .

■ GA. CODE ANN. §19-13-23. DISCLOSURE OF LOCATION OF FAMILY VIOLENCE CENTER

(a) Any person who knowingly publishes, disseminates, or otherwise discloses the location of a family violence shelter is guilty of a misdemeanor.

(b) This Code section shall not apply to:

(1) Confidential communications between a client and his or her attorney; or

(2) Instances when such publication, dissemination, or disclosure is authorized by the director of the shelter.

■ KELLY WHITE, A SAFE PLACE FOR WOMEN: SURVIVING DOMESTIC ABUSE AND CREATING A SUCCESSFUL FUTURE
130-131, 180-181 (2011)

For the most part, each shelter operates as a private, nonprofit corporation, governed by a local independent board of directors, and with its own policies and procedures, yet the programs also operate as a network, maintaining a loose web of services and attempting to create safe places for battered women and their children across the country. When it was apparent that Estrella, [a] woman who was shot five times as she tried to escape her husband, could not be kept safe in Dallas, her home community, she was transferred to SafePlace in Austin in hopes that her husband wouldn't be able to find her there. Such transfers happen every day across communities, states, and the nation.

Many years ago I hid a woman's car, a distinctive make and model, in my home garage. She and her three children had been moved multiple times between shelters and across several states in an attempt to thwart the efforts of her drug-dealer husband to locate them and make good on his promise to their son to "cut off your mother's head and bury it in the backyard if she ever tries to get away." She had given up all contact with her family and friends, fled to a city she had never visited and where she knew no one, dyed her hair and that of her children, changed all of their names, and disappeared into a totally new and different world. Her preadolescent children lived in fear that their father would discover their new names and where they had run to. . . . Her situation was so dangerous that police officers even advised us that they probably could not keep her safe. . . .

Traditionally, battered women's shelters have relied on the secrecy of their locations as their first line of safety; if a batterer doesn't know where the shelter is located, then he won't be able to find his wife. Even residents were held to an incredibly high standard of secrecy, jeopardizing their continued stay at the shelter if they told anyone of its location without prior permission. . . .

Notes and Questions

1. *Separation abuse.* Leaving an abuser does not mean the violence will suddenly stop, as we have seen (discussed in Chapter 2). Victims of domestic violence remain at higher risk in the post-separation period. What are the implications of this dynamic for shelter providers?

2. Frigm: *Holding.* *Frigm* concerns whether an employee was discharged for "willful misconduct" that would render her ineligible for unemployment compensation. Frigm's misconduct allegedly consisted of a breach of her employer's confidentiality policy. What was that policy? How did Frigm violate it? What was her motivation in doing so? Frigm, according to her testimony, was motivated by concern about the particular shelter resident rather than a desire to do harm. For purposes of discharge for "willful misconduct," should an employee's motive matter? Why or why not? What were Frigm's legal arguments? What was the employer's response? What did the court rule?

3. *Disclosure.* Both federal law and state law require shelters to maintain confidentiality. See Family Violence Prevention and Services Act, 42 U.S.C. §§10401-10413; Mo. Rev. Stat. §455.220(1)(5) (prohibiting a shelter from releasing information that would identify a victim, including her name, former residences, employment, physical description, abuser's identity, and services provided). Disclosure under strict confidentiality policies may occur only under limited circumstances under state and federal law. What might those circumstances be?

For example, may a shelter disclose information in response to requests regarding law enforcement? Compare State ex rel. Hope House, Inc. v. Merrigan, 133 S.W.3d 44 (Mo. 2004) (holding that shelter's records were not subject to mandatory disclosure in response to juvenile officer's petition alleging child abuse); and In re Grand Jury Subpoena Duces Tecum Directed to Keeper of Records of My Sister's Place, 2002 WL 31341083 (Ohio Ct. App. 2002) (holding that statute limiting disclosure only to the public children services agency does not allow state to gain information via grand jury subpoena), with People v. Ramsey, 665 N.Y.S.2d 501, 501 (Sup. Ct. 1997) (ordering counseling service to disclose victim's contact information for use in criminal trial against abuser). For a Freedom of Information Act request? See Domestic Violence Servs. of Greater New Haven, Inc. v. Freedom of Information Comm'n, 704 A.2d 827 (Conn. App. Ct. 1998) (finding that the fact that the agency received funding from government sources did not mean that organization was a "public agency" within the meaning of the Freedom of Information Act).

4. *Remedy for breach.* Does a victim have any remedy if a shelter breaches her right of confidentiality? See, e.g., McDade v. West, 223 F.3d 1135 (9th Cir. 2000) (finding in favor of plaintiff-victim in a section 1983 claim against ex-husband's new wife who illegally obtained plaintiff's shelter address in order to serve custody papers); Thompson v. Branches-Domestic Violence Shelter of Huntington, Inc., 534 S.E.2d 33, 40 (W. Va. 2000) (finding that negligence claim against shelter for breach of confidentiality was barred by statute of limitations).

5. *Identity confidentiality.* What happens when a victim of domestic violence must leave the cloak of confidentiality provided by the shelter, for example to move to another location? In an effort to mitigate the risks that victims face in leaving their abusers, many states have enacted statutes that help victims of domestic violence to change their name or address, and keep those records confidential. See, e.g., Wash.

Rev. Code §40.24.030 (establishing the nation's first comprehensive "address confidentiality program," which allows survivors to acquire a "substitute" address for official state purposes. To date, 35 states have similar programs. What are the benefits and limitations of these programs? See Kristen M. Driskell, Note, Identity Confidentiality for Women Fleeing Domestic Violence, 20 Hastings Women's L.J. 129 (2008).

How might the presence of children complicate the operation of these programs? See Catherine F. Klein et al., Border Crossings: Understanding the Civil, Criminal, and Immigration Implications for Battered Women Fleeing Across State Lines with Their Children, 39 Fam. L.Q. 109 (2005); Lauren E. Parsonage, Caught Between a Rock and a Hard Place: Harmonizing Victim Confidentiality Rights with Children's Best Interests, 70 Mo. L. Rev. 863 (2005). The issue of name changes is explored in Chapter 11.

Problem

Brenda, an employee of a domestic violence shelter, notices that a shelter resident shows alarming symptoms of a drug overdose. Brenda calls 911. While she is waiting for an ambulance, David Rothe arrives. Rothe, who is wearing a state police uniform, comes to the shelter door, identifies himself as a police officer, and claims that he is there is response to the 911 call. Brenda refuses to let him in or give him any information because he is not accompanied by the ambulance. She tells Rothe that shelter policy specifies that no one, including law enforcement personnel, may enter the building (except clients).

Brenda is suspicious as whether Rothe really is a police officer given prior incidents of resourceful batterers attempting to locate their partners at the shelter. Rothe, growing increasingly frustrated, tells Brenda in no uncertain terms that he needs to gain access to the shelter to investigate a possible crime and that if she continues to bar his entry, he will place her under arrest. When she again refuses, he roughly pushes her aside to gain entry and places her under arrest her for obstruction of justice. Brenda files an action for assault and battery, false arrest, gross negligence, and a violation of her constitutional rights under 18 U.S.C. §1983 for being a victim of an unlawful arrest under color of law. What result? Brooks v. Rothe, 577 F.3d 701 (6th Cir. 2009).

3. What Services Do Shelters Provide?

■ SAFE HORIZON, TOUR A DOMESTIC VIOLENCE SHELTER*

http://www.safehorizon.org/index/get-help-8/dealing-with-domestic-violence-35/tour-a-domestic-violence-shelter-3.html (last visited July 7, 2011)

Shelters are not only four walls and a roof. Once a battered woman has dealt with the immediate issues of safety and survival, she begins to address her long-range emotional and practical needs. . . . The focus in the shelter is on stabilizing

*Safe Horizon has 57 locations serving children, adults, and families throughout New York City.

[women's] lives, helping them understand their options, and increasing their ability to achieve their goals. Shelters might offer individual and group counseling sessions with a social worker or therapist to allow a woman to talk about her experiences and sort through her feelings.

In the Safe Horizon shelters, many of the women are focused on moving into permanent housing and getting jobs to support their children. In some of the transitional shelters, there is a housing specialist on staff to assist women in locating a permanent residence. To make the transition easier once they do find housing, shelter staff members work with women to acquire independent living skills such as financial management and household management, as well as cooking and cleaning skills. . . .

Although shelter life may seem serious because of the difficult situations that many of the women have fled, not all of the focus is on the past. Shelter residents are also concerned with developing the friendships and social connections that their abusers have prevented them from having. . . . Even though not all children from violent homes have been abused, all have undergone the traumatic experience of witnessing abuse. A Safe Horizon Children's Specialist works with staff in all of Safe Horizon's Shelter programs to develop age appropriate counseling and play therapy groups. They also facilitate these groups and provide individual sessions with children as needed.

Ongoing support groups (in English and Spanish) offer a peer-focused educational environment that helps women understand that they are not alone and are surrounded by women who have survived similar circumstances. Support groups enable women to learn from each other, build trust and a sense of community, and are a valuable tool for women to establish or re-establish independent lives.

The Job Readiness Resource Center provides a training program and resource center specifically designed for emergency domestic violence shelter residents that focuses on successfully moving toward securing an economically sound, satisfying, and enduring professional position in the work force. The resource center offers tools for building job readiness such as a computer lab, job postings and resources for area training programs and much more. The Job Readiness Training Manager [conducts] workshops in each of our seven (7) shelter programs and offers intensive training at the resource center that incorporates computer training, interviewing, resume building, financial planning and special presentations to prepare domestic violence shelter residents for the workforce.

■ **KELLY WHITE, A SAFE PLACE FOR WOMEN: SURVIVING DOMESTIC ABUSE AND CREATING A SUCCESSFUL FUTURE**
186-188 (2011)

. . . Despite repeated efforts to get away from her abusive husband [including eleven stays at the shelter in nine years], Susan always ended up returning to him because she simply could not support herself and her son on her own. However, during her eleventh stay at the shelter, SafePlace was preparing to open its new supportive-housing apartment community. Susan and her son were the first clients admitted to the program, and to this day I know of no better example of the importance of comprehensive services beyond shelter.

Susan and her son moved out of the emergency shelter and into a two-bedroom apartment within hours of our receiving a certificate of occupancy. Each building was filled with families within days. Local churches and other organizations adopted families and helped to provide them with furniture, linens, and housewares. . . .

Susan was delighted with her new home, and her joy was infectious and apparent to everyone. She regularly allowed interested donors and groups to tour what she considered her palace. . . . [One visitor to the facility asks Susan how she supports herself financially. Susan responds cheerily, "I get $170 a month in public assistance for myself and my son."] Despite these hardships Susan was extraordinarily rich in spirit and will. Within weeks she had successfully completed a course for her high-school general equivalency diploma (GED) and passed the test. She then enrolled in classes at the community college located across the street from her apartment. . . . She energetically participated in life skills training and counseling, as did her son. When her son made the honor roll at his new school, for the first time ever, he proudly presented the certificate to his SafePlace counselor, and said, "We did this together."

Susan and her son stayed in supportive housing for eighteen months. When they moved, it was into another apartment where Susan was hired as the manager. She continued her studies at the community college. Not only was she able to live free from the beatings she had endured so regularly in marriage, her son was also able to break the cycle of abuse for future generations.

As Susan's story so perfectly demonstrates, for many women and children emergency shelter is simply not enough. In order to become truly independent economically and emotionally, women need legal services, transitional and permanent housing, child care, education, job training, life skill straining, and therapeutic counseling. Particularly for women living in poverty, stopping physical violence is not always their number one priority. They say, "I can deal with the violence, but I'm not going to put my kids on the street." Rather than just offering a formula for leaving an abusive relationship, we should be asking what services women need in order to become economically secure. . . .

■ **ELEANOR LYON ET AL., NAT'L INST. OF JUSTICE, MEETING SURVIVORS' NEEDS: A MULTI-STATE STUDY OF DOMESTIC VIOLENCE EXPERIENCES, SUMMARY OF FINDINGS 1-3 (2009)**

[hereafter Lyon et al., Summary of Findings], available at http://www.vawnet.org/Assoc_Files_VAWnet/MeetingSurvivorsNeeds-ResearchInBrief.pdf

[D]omestic violence shelters serve a critical need for people who have experienced abuse, which many survivors described as lifesaving. Respondents reported that if the shelter did not exist, the consequences for them would be dire: homelessness, serious losses including loss of their children, actions taken in desperation, or continued abuse or death. . . . [Research findings below are based on a survey of approximately 3,500 shelter residents in 8 states from 2007-2008.]

Shelters Have Capacity to Meet a Range of Needs

- More than four in five shelters (82 percent) allow survivors to stay more than 30 days and 34 percent allow a stay of more than 60 days.
- Nearly all shelters in the study (98 percent) have the capacity to accommodate residents with disabilities.
- More than four in five shelters (82 percent) have staff members who speak at least one language other than English.
- The most common types of advocacy offered by shelters are: housing (offered by 95 percent of shelters in the survey), civil court (82 percent), criminal court (81 percent), health (81 percent), TANF/welfare (80 percent), child protection (79 percent), job training (78 percent), immigration issues (76 percent) and divorce/custody/visitation issues (73 percent).
- The most common types of shelter services are: support groups (offered by 97 percent of shelters in the survey), crisis counseling (96 percent), individual counseling (92 percent), parenting classes (55 percent), counseling for children (54 percent) and child care (50 percent).

Shelters Serve Diverse Survivors

- More than three in four survivors (78 percent) reported that they had children under the age of 18, and 68 percent had minor children with them at the shelter.
- Most survivors (70 percent) were 25 to 49 years old. One in five was younger than 25.
- More than half (52 percent) of the survivors were white, 22 percent were African American and 12 percent were Hispanic/Latino/a.
- Nearly all survivors surveyed were women (99.6 percent). Thirteen men were a part of the survey. . . .
- More than nine in ten (93 percent) survivors identified themselves as heterosexual.

4. Benefits of Advocacy Services

■ DEBORAH EPSTEIN, PROCEDURAL JUSTICE: TEMPERING THE STATE'S RESPONSE TO DOMESTIC VIOLENCE

43 Wm. & Mary L. Rev. 1843, 1890-1892 (2002)

. . . How can the criminal justice system maximize battered women's ability to engage in optimal decision making? Recent research indicates that one important strategy is to offer victims extensive legal and non-legal advocacy services. Such advocacy includes: providing information about and access to a wide range of social services; strengthening victims' emotional support network; providing information about the civil and criminal justice systems; and safety planning.

Advocacy services can increase a victim's perceptions of social support, improve her mental health, and increase her physical and psychological safety. In a recent study, college students were trained to provide intensive, non-legal advocacy services to battered women leaving a shelter. Advocates helped women access community resources such as housing, employment, legal assistance, transportation, child care, health care, and counseling for their children. After ten weeks, women in the advocacy group reported improvements in social support, greater effectiveness in obtaining necessary resources, less depression, fear and anxiety, and a better quality of life than those in the comparison group. Most importantly, these women experienced less physical and psychological abuse, and those who wished to end their abusive relationships were significantly more effective in doing so.

Such advocacy services can, in turn, increase the degree to which victims are willing to cooperate with the criminal justice system. In one study, survivors with better access to tangible support were approximately twice as likely to voluntarily participate in the prosecutions of their intimate partners.

Advocates also can reverse a victim's sense of social isolation and improve her sense of emotional well-being. Such assistance is particularly important for battered women, whose support networks often are methodically undermined during an abusive relationship. In a recent evaluation of law school domestic violence clinics, battered women reported that their student advocates actively worked on their behalf to repair such relationships as they talked to family and friends during pretrial investigation. The victims reported an increased sense of emotional support that was significantly greater than that among women who did not receive similar intensive advocacy services. In addition, women in the advocacy group reported substantially lower levels of physical and psychological re-abuse, despite the fact that they had similar amounts of contact with their abusive partners during the study period. . . .

To appropriately encourage victim participation in criminal litigation, prosecutors' offices should provide comprehensive advocacy services and referrals from the moment a case is filed, either within their own office or through referrals to private advocacy groups. These services should include drug and alcohol counseling, psychological assistance, support groups, child care services, referrals to shelters, and economic assistance through state crime victims' compensation funds. . . .

Notes and Questions

1. *Types of shelters.* Victims of domestic violence often need emergency shelter and transitional housing. Emergency shelters offer services for a short period, usually four to six weeks. Transitional housing programs, generally operated in conjunction with crisis shelters, permit residence from four to nine months. See Karen Nutter, Note, Domestic Violence in the Lives of Women with Disabilities: No (Accessible) Shelter from the Storm, 13 S. Cal. Rev. L. & Women's Stud. 329, 336 (2004). Are these two types of housing sufficient to help victims get back on their feet? How can programs help victims transition better into permanent housing?

2. *Shelter services.* Early shelter programs emphasized the fulfillment of housing needs. However, as clients' needs were identified, shelters offered a broader range of services. According to the above excerpts, what services do most shelters offer? How might services differ for clients who are mothers? For male clients?

3. *Unmet needs.* What additional services might be beneficial? The most prominent unmet needs, according to shelter residents are mental and physical health needs, housing, educational and economic help, and substance abuse treatment.

Lyon et al., Summary of Findings, supra, at 3. See also Dawn M. Johnson & Caron Zlotnick, HOPE for Battered Women with PTSD in Domestic Violence Shelters, 40 Prof. Psychol. 234 (2009) (describing treatment of post-traumatic stress disorder at shelters). One longstanding complaint of shelter clients is that many shelters do not accommodate teenage boys. See Jane K. Stoever, Freedom from Violence: Using the Stages of Change Model to Realize the Promise of Civil Protection Orders, 72 Ohio St. L.J. 303, 325 n.93 (2011). What explains this problem? How can it be resolved?

4. *Client characteristics: race, ethnicity, sexual orientation.* What is the racial and ethnic composition of shelter clientele? According to the NIJ Meeting Survivors' Needs study, the racial composition of shelter clientele is overwhelmingly white—despite the fact that victims of color tend to be overrepresented in terms of actual rates of domestic violence. Eleanor Lyon et al., Nat'l Inst. of Justice, Meeting Survivors' Needs: A Multi-State Study of Domestic Violence Experiences, Final Report 50 (2008) [hereafter Lyon et al., Final Report], available at https://www.ncjrs.gov/pdffiles1/nij/grants/225025.pdf. What might explain this disparity?

Early empirical research on shelter-related problems documented considerable problems facing victims of color and lesbian survivors. See, e.g., Kimberle Crenshaw, Mapping the Margins: Intersectionality, Identity Politics, and Violence Against Women of Color, 43 Stan. L. Rev. 1241 (1991) (criticizing that some shelters admit only English-speaking women); Lydia Walker, Battered Women's Shelters and Work with Battered Lesbians, in Naming the Violence: Speaking Out about Lesbian Battering 73 (Kerry Lobel ed., 1986) (reporting that some shelter workers believe violence does not occur between female partners). Are these problems still present, based on the above excerpts?

The NIJ report, Meeting Survivors' Needs, reveals a high level of client satisfaction about the treatment of persons of different races and sexual orientation. For example, 97 percent of those who identified as lesbian/gay, bisexual, or "other" sexuality agreed or strongly agreed that their sexual orientation was respected. Similarly, 97 percent of those who identified as people of color agreed or strongly agreed that their racial background was respected. Lyon et al., Final Report, supra, at 15.

5. *Duration of stay.* The median stay in shelters is 22 days. Lyon et al., Final Report, supra, at iv. Do you think this period is sufficient? Are women with children more or less likely to stay longer than those women without children? Why?

6. *Multiple stays.* As Susan's story reveals, some victims experience multiple stays at emergency shelters. What explains this phenomenon?

7. *Conditions on occupancy.* Shelters sometimes require clients to participate in services. If clients refuse, can they be evicted? See Serreze v. YWCA of Western Mass., Inc., 572 N.E.2d 581 (Mass. App. Ct. 1991) (holding that a statute protecting tenants from eviction applied to clients who refused to attend counseling services, despite policy making their participation a requirement of occupancy). Note also that VAWA 2005 provided that domestic violence service providers that receive federal funding cannot condition the receipt of benefits for housing assistance on the participation of clients in support services. 42 U.S.C.A. §13975.

8. *Legal services.* The American battered women's movement has always emphasized the importance of providing for survivors' legal needs. How can shelters best address their clients' need for legal assistance? For example, should shelters make private referrals? Hire their own legal staff? If shelters hire their own lawyers, should these staff members be *women* lawyers? Why or why not? Some law schools offer

clinics, in coordination with local shelters, to address the needs of victims and the high cost of legal services. What challenges might such models face? See Ashley E. Lowe, Community Collaboration: A Blended Domestic Violence Clinic, 10 T.M. Cooley J. Prac. & Clinical L. 375 (2008) (describing challenges).

9. *Accessibility: victims with disabilities.* Shelters accommodate a large number of persons with disabilities. For example, according to the Meeting Survivors' Needs Study, 20 percent of residents had some sort of disability. Lyon et al., Final Report, supra, at 49. If a shelter fails to accommodate persons with disabilities, does the shelter violate the Americans with Disabilities Act (ADA) of 1990, Pub. L. No. 101-336, 104 Stat. 327 (codified as amended at 42 U.S.C. §§12101-12213), that prohibits discrimination in public accommodations? See ADA, Title III, 28 C.F.R. §36.102 (2002).

Many shelters are located in older buildings, making it costly to provide necessary accommodations for disabled persons (that is, ramps, wide doorways, and lower counters). Nutter, supra, at 344. Does a shelter violate the Act if the inability to accommodate clients stems from funding constraints? How can shelters better accommodate the needs of their disabled clients? See generally Doug Jones, Domestic Violence Against Women with Disabilities: A Feminist Legal Theory Analysis, 2 Fla. A & M U. L. Rev. 207 (2007); Nutter, supra; Jane K. Stoever, Stories Absent from the Courtroom: Responding to Domestic Violence in the Context of HIV and AIDS, 87 N.C. L. Rev. 1157 (2009).

10. *Overcrowding.* A perennial problem for shelters is overcrowding, leading many shelters to turn away clients. In one state, almost one in four victims of domestic violence who sought emergency shelter in 2008 was turned away for this reason. Lori Stahl, Not All Seeking Shelter Find It, Dallas Morning News, Dec. 20, 2009, at B1. According to the NIJ report, Meeting Survivors' Needs, the average capacity of participating shelters was 25 beds. Lyon et al., Final Report, supra, at 43. The average number of adults that each shelter accommodated in one year was 130, and the average number of sheltered children was 114. Id. What can be done to improve capacity? How might the economy affect occupancy-related issues? See also Arlene Martinez, More Children in Valley Homeless Shelters, Report Says: Domestic Violence, Lack of Affordable Housing Are the Top Causes, Allentown [Pa.] Morning Call, Apr. 29, 2008, at B3.

Problem

Safety First is a non-profit organization in the State of Blackacre that provides services to victims of domestic violence who are primarily immigrants. The agency provides extensive counseling services, transitional housing, legal services, and transportation services. It also furnishes referrals for shelters, legal services, medical agencies, and housing organizations. One of its services is the provision of assistance with clients' legal problems. Safety First currently is seeking to hire a lawyer to help with clients' legal needs. The agency places a "Help Wanted" advertisement in a local newspaper, advertising the position. Robert Jones submits an application and resume. Safety First reviews his application and informs him that it was not going to interview him because he is male and they "prefer a female legal advocate." Jones files a charge of employment discrimination in federal court, alleging that he has been discriminated against because of his gender in violation of Title VII.

Title VII prohibits employment discrimination on the basis of religion, sex, or national origin. Title VII contains a bona fide occupational qualification (BFOQ) defense for employers. The BFOQ defense provides that, in some circumstances, the characteristics of religion, sex, or national origin may be bona fide occupational qualifications that are "reasonably necessary to the normal operation of that particular business or enterprise." 42 U.S.C. §2000e-2(f). Examples of bona fide occupational qualifications are a mandatory retirement age for airline pilots for safety reasons, or advertisement seeking male models by manufacturers of men's clothing.

Safety First initially argues that subject matter jurisdiction is lacking because it was not an "employer" within the meaning of Title VII for the reason that it is not "engaged in an industry affecting commerce." Second, Safety First claims that its requirement that the employee is a woman is a bona fide occupational qualification for the position because of the nature of the agency's business. What result? See Johnson v. Apna Ghar, 330 F.3d 999 (7th Cir. 2003).

B. BATTERERS' INTERVENTION PROGRAMS

1. Court-Ordered Treatment

■ D.O.H. v. T.L.H.

799 So. 2d 714 (La. Ct. App. 2001)

This is the second time this custody dispute has been appealed. [In the previous case, the trial court judge awarded joint custody based on the best-interests standard, despite finding that the father committed domestic violence. The trial judge designated the father as primary custodial parent during the academic year and the mother during the summer, reasoning that it was important to keep the children together (in light of the fact that the oldest daughter wanted to remain with her father in order to continue her school sports). Reversing, the appellate court applied the rebuttable presumption statute and awarded sole custody to the mother. Hicks v. Hicks, 733 So. 2d 1261 (La. Ct. App. 1999).

After the father completed an anger management program, as required by statute, he filed another motion for custody. The parents stipulated to having the oldest child live with the father, and the trial court awarded sole custody of the two youngest children to the father. The mother appealed. The mother's first assignment of error concerns the treatment program that the father attended pursuant to this court's remand in the earlier appeal.] She argues that the father has not completed a valid treatment program as defined by the Family Violence Relief Act.

According to Louisiana Revised Statute §9:364(A), once it is proven that a parent has a history of family violence, the "presumption shall be overcome only by a preponderance of the evidence that the perpetrating parent has successfully completed a treatment program as defined in R.S. §9:362 [that is,] "a course of evaluation and psychotherapy designed specifically for perpetrators of family violence, and conducted by licensed mental health professionals."

When the [Office of Community Services (OCS)] entered the case after our remand in 1999, it obtained evaluations from Dr. John C. Simoneaux and Dr. Rick Adams, both of whom are clinical psychologists licensed by the State of Louisiana.

The mother argues that Dr. Rick Adams was not qualified to conduct the statutorily required treatment program. . . .

As a clinical psychologist, Dr. Adams testified that he had had training in the area of evaluation of perpetrators of family violence. Although he had worked more with perpetrators of physical abuse of children by parents rather than with spousal abuse, he stated that he had to train parents to address their problems with self-control and how to handle the situations. In this case the father was referred to Dr. Adams by the OCS for anger management training.

Dr. Adams explained that his treatment of the father consisted of exposing him to anger management techniques and strategies for controlling his anger. Dr. Adams met with the father for an initial evaluation and there were six subsequent sessions. During these sessions Dr. Adams went through the tactics that people use for controlling themselves and for identifying risk situations for loss of control, in addition to anger reducers and tactics for managing anger. Dr. Adams found the father to be completely cooperative during these sessions.

Although Dr. Adams admitted he did not know the specific details of the spousal abuse for which the father was receiving treatment, Dr. Adam's psychotherapy assessment indicates that he knew that the father had been physically abusive to his ex-wife, with no indication that he had abused the children. He testified that six anger management training sessions were sufficient to expose the father to the basic principles of anger management.

As a licensed mental health professional, Dr. Adams met the statutory requirements of Louisiana Revised Statute §9:362(7) and he was the one who conducted the course of psychotherapy which was administered. [Dr. Simoneaux initially completed a forensic evaluation to determine the father's treatment needs. Dr. Simoneaux's report explained that his recommendation of counseling was due to spousal abuse of the mother, indicating that he was aware of the facts.] The attack the mother has made on the course of evaluation and psychotherapy included questioning whether the course was, in the statutory language, "designed specifically for perpetrators of family violence." She offered neither expert witness testimony nor other evidence regarding the standard for meeting the program for treatment as defined by the statute. . . .

Although none have been suggested by the evidence nor the mother's brief, we recognize that there may be a number of psychotherapy programs available for spousal abusers, and that there may be differences amongst both lay and professional opinions as to which is most effective. Our task on this appeal is not to decide which is the best program, but to determine whether, on these facts in this case, the trial court's approval of this program as having met the statutory standard, was an abuse of discretion. We find that the father received a proper treatment program as defined by Louisiana Revised Statute §9:362(7). Dr. Adams knew that he was treating the father for spousal abuse and his treatment consisted of helping him to learn anger management. We note that the father has since remarried, and his present wife testified that he has exhibited no abusive behavior towards her. There has never been any concern that he abuses the children. We find no error in the trial court's ruling.

WOODARD, J., dissenting.

. . . The instant case is one of egregious spousal abuse: Mr. D.O.H. beat Ms. T.L.H.C. so severely with a broom stick that her own mother did not recognize her . . . ; [he] gave [her] a black eye . . . ; [he picked her up] with a two by four under her neck and threw her off the porch; [he] beat [her] in the belly so severely that it caused her to miscarry their child; [he] raped her on numerous occasions; [he] squeezed her hand so hard, the ring, which she was wearing, almost broke and left an indentation in her finger; [he] threw her into a chair which caused her to hit her head against the fish tank. . . .

When the Louisiana Legislature passed the Post-Separation Family Violence Relief Act in 1992, [it set strict criteria for how child custody and visitation proceedings should be handled when there is a history of domestic violence, and required the perpetrator to complete specific therapy programs as a condition for access to children.] [I]t requires the perpetrator of family violence to prove that: (1) he has successfully completed "a course of evaluation and *psychotherapy* designed specifically *for perpetrators* of family violence," (2) "conducted by licensed mental health professionals," having (3) "*current* and demonstrable training and experience working with perpetrators and victims of family violence," and (4) *he no longer poses a danger*[21] (emphasis added.) This implies that the batterer must undergo meaningful *psychotherapy*, which is *effective* in changing his behavior. While the legislature did not provide the details of its intended programs, there are many highly respected ones to choose from as models. None of them are mere "exposures" to the basic principles of anger management.

Anger management sessions are not a substitute for psychotherapy. Many experts in the psychological community criticize the use of anger management programs, as a form of batterer intervention, because they fail to address the batterer's real problem. For example, various anger management programs, simply, teach batterers to recognize signs of anger and to implement relaxation and stress management techniques, as well as communication skills. Anger management is also criticized because it *embodies the false assumption that spousal abuse is based on uncontrollable anger, rather than on anger being the batterer's device to control* women. Significantly, anger management, erroneously, implies that the victim provokes the anger and abuse, which is counter-productive to changing the batterer's attitude and harmful behavior, since anger management misplaces the responsibility for the problem and gives the batterer validation for his aberrant behavior. . . .

All batterer intervention should acknowledge that violence against women is a learned behavior, and that batterers use violence to maintain *control* over their partners. Thus, *intervention should focus on learning nonviolence and the appropriate sharing of power and communication within the relationship*; identify, confront, and change all forms of abusive and controlling behaviors; discuss the impact that violence has on the victim; *confront the denial and minimizing of abuse*—the program must emphasize that the batterer is *solely* responsible for the abuse and that abuse is a willful choice that is never justified; identify cultural and social sources of attitudes toward women that contribute to abusive behavior. In other words, the intervention method must actively challenge and modify inappropriate behavior and attitudes towards women and control.

Generally, intervention programs include intake, encompassing a *complete* history of abuse, which neither Dr. Simoneaux nor Dr. Adams had, and an ongoing lethality assessment, neither conducted (emphasis added). . . . Also, *group intervention is the preferred format* cited in 90 percent of the standards; overwhelmingly,

---

21. La. R. S. §9:365.

individual intervention is regarded as inappropriate. Most nationwide standards for batterer intervention programs, as of 1997, suggest a minimum of 24 to 26 weeks. Mr. D.O.H. received *individual* anger management training for one hour per session, for a total of six sessions—*far from the 24 to 26 week minimum standard.*

Facilitators should be licensed or certified mental health service providers; completed at least 20 hours of victim-centered training; have training and experience at facilitating psycho-educational groups; have completed a nationally recognized training program in providing batterer intervention services (e.g. the Duluth Model or EMERGE),* which specifically addresses the dynamics of domestic violence within the context of power and control, the effects of domestic violence on victims and their children, the nature of domestic violence, the role of the facilitator, lethality assessment, teaching alternatives to violent and controlling behavior, and *avoidance* of *facilitator collusion with batterers.* . . .

The majority notes that "[a]lthough none have been suggested by the evidence nor the mother's brief, we recognize that there may be a number of psychotherapy programs available for spousal abusers, and that there may be differences amongst both lay and professional opinions as to which is most effective. Our task on this appeal is not to decide which is the best program, but to determine whether, on these facts in this case, the trial court's approval of this program as having met the statutory standard, was an abuse of discretion." Indeed, the court's task is not to decide which program, *among all the effective models,* is the best; however, . . . the court must decide whether the "program" *was effective in producing the result that Mr. D.O.H. would no longer pose a danger,* which Dr. Adams could not say was the case. Nor did Dr. Simoneaux or Dr. Adams provide any of the standard criteria for credentials or programs or address Mr. D.O.H.'s real psychological problems as a batterer. . . .

Specifically, the record establishes Dr. Adams as a clinical psychologist with considerable experience in child psychology, learning disabilities, and parental training. However, he has no significant experience regarding the physical abuse of intimates, save a rotation during an internship more than 19 years ago, and he never completed any specialized work in this area. By his own admissions, he was not qualified, under the Act, to handle this case. . . . In addition to having inadequate credibility, under the Act, Dr. Adams admitted to the impotency of his sessions. He testified that: these sessions were limited in scope to "exposing" Mr. D.O.H. to the basic principles of anger management; he *did not administer psychotherapy to Mr. D.O.H.;* his sessions *were not designed for perpetrators* of family violence; he was not familiar with the Act; he had no knowledge of the content of the OCS' report; he did not know the severity, nature, and extent of Mr. D.O.H.'s domestic violence; he only knew what Mr. D.O.H. told him, which was that he did not have a problem.

Essentially, Dr. Adams conceded these sessions were not designed to deal, or capable of dealing, with the deeply rooted psychological problems which Mr. D.O.H., obviously, possesses, as a batterer. . . . He explained that Dr. Simoneaux, ultimately, determined what Mr. D.O.H. needed, but we find no evidence in Dr. John C. Simoneaux's psychological evaluation that he was aware of the details, nature, or severity of Mr. D.O.H.'s pattern of violence either, contrary to the majority's assertion. Furthermore, Mr. D.O.H. presented no evidence to indicate that Dr. Simoneaux possesses the requisite statutory credentials to deal with spousal abuse and, therefore, make appropriate treatment recommendations, under the Act. . . .

*[EMERGE is a model of batterer intervention based on a Massachusetts-certified program. *Ed.*]

What is strikingly significant and indicative of the sessions' lack of any positive impact on or change in Mr. D.O.H. is his continued denial and refusal to acknowledge even that he has a problem, and, therefore, his refusal to accept responsibility and to be accountable for his violence. Mr. D.O.H. has minimized or denied his abuse throughout—even when there was objective evidence proving it—from the original 1998 custody trial, in his interview with Dr. Simoneaux, through his anger management sessions, and at the June 26, 2000, custody hearing, where he was suppose to enter evidence, essentially, of his "reform," which necessitates an acknowledgment of previous wrong doing.

Yet, at that hearing, Dr. Adams portrayed Mr. D.O.H. as having been cooperative. And, Mr. D.O.H. portrayed himself as having been the perfect husband and father, who did not have and never did have an "anger problem." In fact, he especially wanted the court to know that he would never even say anything disparaging to his children about their mother because it "would disrespect his children," yet, apparently to him, giving their mother a black eye and other abuse would not disrespect the children. This is interesting thinking, to say the least, which was, apparently, undaunted by six anger management sessions. . . .

Without further inquiry or evidence, *on its face*, it is apparent that Mr. D.O.H. has not carried his prima facie burden of proving his compliance with the Act's requirements and intent. His six sessions of "exposure" to the basic principles of anger management were merely "cosmetic" and far from adequate to satisfy the strict, specific, statutory mandate. . . .

2. *Effectiveness*

■ SHELLY JACKSON, NAT'L INST. OF JUSTICE, BATTERER INTERVENTION PROGRAMS: WHERE DO WE GO FROM HERE?

2, 9-12, 19-21, 26-27 (2003) available at https://www.ncjrs.gov/pdffiles1/nij/195079.pdf

More than 35 [Batterer Intervention Program (BIP)] evaluations have been published. Early studies, which used quasi-experimental designs, consistently found small program effects; when more methodologically rigorous evaluations were undertaken, the results were inconsistent and disappointing. Most of the later studies found that treatment effects were limited to a small reduction in reoffending, although evidence indicates that for most participants (perhaps those already motivated to change), BIPs may end the most violent and threatening behaviors. The results, however, remain inconclusive because of methodological flaws in these evaluations. . . .

[This report discusses the findings of studies of two batterer intervention programs. The Broward County (Florida) experiment randomly assigned convicted batterers to an experimental group of men who were sentenced to 26 weeks of group counseling at a batterer intervention program and a year of probation, and also a control group of batterers sentenced to 1 year of probation only. The Brooklyn (New York) Study focused on batterers who consented to enter a batterer intervention program for either 8 or 26 weeks, and compared these to batterers assigned to a community service program.]

THE BROWARD STUDY: FINDINGS

OFFENDER ATTITUDES

[Men in experimental and control groups were compared at adjudication and six months later. By the second interview, men had completed 85 percent of the counseling sessions.]

There was no difference between groups initially or over time in their views of the proper roles of women, whether battering should be considered a crime, or whether the State had a right to intervene. Both groups also reported the same likelihood of beating their partners again.

The only change noted in all of these comparisons was a small but significant change in men's views of their partners' responsibility for the offense that led them to court. Over time, those in the control group viewed their partners as increasingly responsible. In contrast, in the 6 months after adjudication, those in the experimental group saw the woman as slightly less responsible. Even so, however, the men in the experimental group still viewed their partners as "somewhat" to "equally" responsible for the incident.

Several studies indicate that batterers hold more traditional views than nonbatterers about women and their proper roles. BIPs are based on the premise that teaching men that it is wrong to exert verbal, physical, or sexual control over their partners will lead to changes in their beliefs that will ultimately produce changes in their behavior. The results of these analyses seem to indicate, however, that men directed by courts into BIPs . . . did not change their beliefs about the legitimacy of battering, their responsibility for these incidents, and the proper roles for women. . . .

OFFENDER SELF-REPORTED LIKELIHOOD TO ENGAGE IN ABUSE

Thirty percent of the men reported taking what the [revised Conflict Tactics Scale] defines as a minor abusive action (including grabbing and slapping) against their partners within 6 months after adjudication. Thirty-two percent of the women reported such an incident within the same period. Eight percent of the men reported engaging in more severe physical abuse (using a knife or gun, choking, or beating up their partner), compared with 14 percent of the women who reported being victims of such abuse. . . .

OFFICIAL MEASURES—REARRESTS

Twenty-four percent of men in both the experimental and control groups were rearrested at least once during their year on probation. . . . [A]ttending domestic violence classes and the interaction between group assignment and treatment received were significant in predicting rearrests, as were employment and age. Employment was the most important factor accounting for variation in rearrests. These findings lead to two primary conclusions. First, batterers who are assigned to treatment and fail to attend most or all of the sessions are more likely to be rearrested than similarly situated men who are not ordered to attend counseling. Second, lack of steady employment is more important than nonattendance in predicting rearrest. . . .

POLICY IMPLICATIONS

The results of this study show that counseling had no clear and demonstrable effect on offenders' attitudes, beliefs, or behavior. Evidence of severe physical abuse still existed, even at 6 and 12 months after sentencing. . . .

THE BROOKLYN EXPERIMENT: FINDINGS

TREATMENT EFFECTS ON BEHAVIOR

[Batterers were assigned to 8-week groups and 26-week groups. Batterers were far more likely to complete the shorter course of treatment.] Researchers expected that men assigned to the 8-week group would have a lower reoffense rate than men assigned to the 26-week group because a larger proportion of them completed the program. Only the 26-week group, however, had significantly fewer criminal complaints than the control group at 6 and 12 months after sentencing: The 8-week group and the control group were virtually indistinguishable. . . .

Even when defendants' age, ethnicity, marital status, employment status, and arrest history were factored in, the 26-week group had fewer complaints of new crimes against their battering victims than the 8-week and control groups. In addition, reports of criminal complaints showed that those in the 26-week group went significantly longer before battering again.

TREATMENT EFFECTS ON ATTITUDES

Researchers also looked at measures of cognitive change in batterers, including conflict resolution skills, beliefs about domestic violence, and internal versus external control. . . . [T]here is no basis for claiming that treatment changed batterers' attitudes or ways of dealing with conflict.

POLICY IMPLICATIONS

Does batterer intervention modify attitudes and behavior in a relatively lasting way, or does it simply suppress violent behavior for the duration of treatment? The results of this study do not support the view that treatment leads to lasting changes in behavior. Were that true, the men in the 8-week group (who finished their treatment long before the follow-up period expired) ought to have been no more violent than their counterparts in the 26-week program (who were in treatment for most of the follow-up period). That is not what this study showed. Nor was any evidence found that treatment altered batterers' attitudes toward spouse abuse, which further suggests that treatment brought about no permanent changes.

The results of this study thus support the view that batterer intervention merely suppresses violent behavior for the duration of treatment. Since, however, the study was not designed to test the validity of various treatment models, the results cannot be seen as conclusive. Moreover, they are at odds with results of other studies that found no difference in reoffense rates according to length of treatment. Many batterer programs are adopting longer treatment models, but there is substantial pressure from the defense bar and economics to keep time in treatment to a minimum. Thus, the question of whether treatment works only as long as men attend counseling is crucial to intelligent policy formulation. . . .

POLICY IMPLICATIONS AND FUTURE DIRECTIONS

Although interventions are proliferating, there is little evidence that they work. This raises important policy questions:

- Do batterer intervention programs waste valuable resources?
- Do they create a false sense of security in women who are led to believe that their batterer will reform?
- Is it prudent to mandate batterers to BIPs when there is little evidence that they work?

. . . The field of batterer intervention is still in its infancy, and much remains to be learned. Rather than asking whether BIPs work, a more productive question may be which programs work best for which batterers under which circumstances. . . . As BIPs are a relatively new response to a critical social problem, it is too early to abandon the concept. It is also too early to believe that we have all the answers. Research and evaluation . . . will continue to add to our growing knowledge of responses to battering, including batterer intervention programs.

Notes and Questions

1. *Batterer intervention programs: background.* The legal system turned to batterer treatment programs in the 1970s as a sentencing option to improve the prosecution of domestic violence cases. Melissa Labriola et al., Nat'l Inst. of Justice, Court Responses to Batterer Program Noncompliance: A National Perspective iii, 1 (2007), available at https://www.ncjrs.gov/pdffiles1/nij/grants/230399.pdf. Many early batterers' intervention programs were patterned on mental health models and programs for substance abusers. David Adams, Treatment Programs for Batterers, 5 Clinics in Fam. Practice 159, 161 (2003). However, battered women's advocacy contributed to the development of treatment standards and programs that were specially designed for batterers. Andrew R. Klein, The Criminal Justice Response to Domestic Violence 221 (2004). By 1980, 80 batterer treatment programs existed nationwide. Id. The development of the Duluth model in 1980 triggered a proliferation of batterer treatment programs (discussed in Chapter 2). Id. at 222. Currently, more than 2000 such programs exist. Labriola, supra, at 1.

2. *State mandated intervention.* Colorado was the first state in 1987 to mandate treatment for domestic violence offenders. Klein, supra, at 222. Other states soon followed. Many states mandated participation in batterer treatment programs as a condition of probation or a suspended sentence, court diversion, civil protection orders, and awards of child custody/visitation. Id. at 225. See, e.g., Edward F. v. Superior Court, 2008 WL 616248 (Cal. Ct. App. 2008) (ordering batterer treatment to avoid termination of parental rights).

3. *State standards.* Louisiana, similar to many states, has standards for its batterer intervention programs. How does the state statute define the recommended treatment and qualifications of therapists? Currently, 45 states and the District of Columbia have standards and/or regulations that address batterers' treatment. Roland D. Maiuro & Jane A. Eberle, State Standards for Domestic Violence Perpetrator Treatment: Current Status, Trends, and Recommendations, 23 Violence & Victims 133,

134 (2008). Many state standards are far more detailed than those of Louisiana. For example, a majority of states require batterer intervention programs to conduct assessments of the risk of danger and lethality assessments. Id. at 141. The trend is for more explicit attention to relevant risk factors. Id. (Although the dissenting judge in *D.O.H.* refers to the requirement that an abuser "no longer poses a danger" in order to obtain access to children, this requirement is not specified by the state statute.)

4. *Child custody:* D.O.H. *holding.* Many state statutes, similar to that of Louisiana, contain a rebuttable presumption against awarding custody to a perpetrator of domestic violence. What role does court-ordered batterer treatment play in the application of the presumption in Louisiana? Why does the majority in *D.O.H.* conclude that the father's completion of a six-session anger management course overcomes the presumption? Why does the dissent conclude that the father has not met his burden of producing evidence to show that he is no longer a danger to his children? Which view do you find more persuasive?

In the *D.O.H.* case, before the present appeal was decided, the oldest daughter alleged that she had been sexually abused by her mother and her mother's new husband. She also accused the mother's new husband of physical and emotional abuse of the two younger siblings. 799 So. 2d at 716. The trial court referred the matter to the family services department in the mother's jurisdiction. Id. If the charges are substantiated, what role should they play in the custody determination?

5. *Model programs.* The dissent in *D.O.H.* agrees with the mother that an anger management program is not the type of batterer intervention program mandated by the legislature. See also Lundy Bancroft et al., The Batterer as Parent: Addressing the Impact of Domestic Violence on Family Dynamics 229 (2012) ("anger management programs are not appropriate for men who batter" because such programs cannot influence the batterer to recognize the wrongfulness of his conduct, change his distorted perceptions, and develop respectful behavior).

Two common approaches to batterer treatment exist: (1) the Duluth model of group treatment (the prevailing approach) which views the cause of domestic violence as men's power and control over women, and (2) group cognitive-behavioral treatment (BGT) in which domestic violence is regarded as learned behavior that can be "unlearned." The latter approach involves skill training (for example, anger management, communication skills, assertiveness, relaxation techniques) that promotes alternatives to violence. Carla Smith Stover et al., Interventions for Intimate Partner Violence: Review and Implications for Evidence-Based Practice, 40 Prof. Psychol. 223, 224 (2009).

Which treatment approach did the father undergo in *D.O.H.*? Why did the mother argue that this approach was not a "valid treatment program," as defined by statute? The majority contends that there are a "number of psychotherapy programs available for spousal abusers, and that there may be differences among both lay and professional opinions as to which is most effective." Why does the dissent disagree? Whose view is more persuasive?

Another type of treatment, although highly controversial, is couple therapy. A majority of states explicitly prohibit any type of couple sessions or therapy during domestic violence intervention. Maiuro & Eberle, supra, at 139. Why?

6. *Anger management.* Anger management was an early approach to batterer treatment. Klein, supra, at 221 (explaining that anger management replaced the approach of individual counseling but then was superseded by specially designed

programs for batterers). Currently, a number of state standards explicitly disapprove of anger management as "the primary focus or sole explanatory model of domestic violence treatment." Maiuro & Eberle, supra, at 143. One state even prohibits anger management as an intervention. Id. at 143-144. What light does the dissenting opinion in *D.O.H.* shed on why anger management is no longer in vogue?

7. *Length of treatment.* D.O.H. received six treatment sessions of anger management. Many states mandate the length of batterer treatment. State standards range from a minimum of 12 weeks to 1 year or more. Maiuro & Eberle, supra, at 137. The trend is toward longer treatment. "The prevailing rationale is the need to have a longer time to monitor outcome and intervene in cases of recidivism." Id. at 138. The majority of states require 24 to 26 weeks. Id. What evidence does the above excerpt provide that longer lengths of treatment improve outcome? One disadvantage, however, of longer programs is that they report higher dropout rates. Cheryl Hanna, The Paradox of Hope: The Crime and Punishment of Domestic Violence, 39 Wm. & Mary L. Rev. 1505, 1529 (1998). How can programs address attrition rates?

8. *Monitoring.* What does "completion" of a treatment program involve? How are batterers monitored during treatment programs and after release? One problem raised by the dissent in *D.O.H.* is the lack of accountability for a batterer at treatment programs: He simply has to "show up" for class and he is considered treated, even if he fails to participate or change his behavior. Some treatment programs give certificates upon completion. What do such certificates signify? Suppose a batterer misses several treatment sessions. How can a court identify a batterer's noncompliance and promote accountability? Through the use of sanctions, such as jail? What sanctions might be most effective?

States vary in their methods of monitoring offenders' attendance at batterer treatment programs. See Anat Maytal, Note, Specialized Domestic Violence Courts: Are They Worth the Trouble in Massachusetts?, 18 B.U. Pub. Int. L.J. 197, 218 (2008) (reporting that Dorcester, Massachusetts, hired additional police officers to make home visits and conduct verifications with batterer treatment program staff to ensure batterers' attendance, thereby putting batterers on notice they were "subject to spontaneous checks"); Johnna Rizza, Beyond Duluth: A Broad Spectrum of Treatment for a Broad Spectrum of Domestic Violence, 70 Mont. L. Rev. 125, 137 (2009) (discussing different state practices, such as that of Missoula, Montana, that relies on probation officers to report absences).

A central feature of domestic violence courts is judicial monitoring of the abuser to ensure his compliance with the terms of his sentence. Studies on mandatory compliance hearings in domestic violence courts have shown that such judicial accountability substantially increases the number of abusers who complete batterer intervention programs and also that those who complete the programs are considerably less likely to be rearrested for assault than those who do not. See Edward W. Gondolf, Mandatory Court Review and Batterer Programme Compliance, 15 J. Interpersonal Violence 428 (2000); Carolyn Turgeon, Bridging Theory and Practice: A Roundtable on Court Responses to Domestic Violence, 1 J. Ct. Innovation 345, 349 (2008). Given the importance of monitoring abusers' compliance, how can judicial monitoring be improved?

9. *Victim participation.* How much impact should a victim have on whether an abuser is ordered to attend a batterer treatment program? How much impact should a victim have on the kind of treatment program that is ordered? Some victims who

are unwilling to testify against their abusers are more willing to do so when it will help abusers get treatment. Jonathan Schmidt & Laurel Beeler, State and Federal Prosecutions of Domestic Violence, 11 Fed. Sent. R. 159, 160 (1998). Victim participation in the process also occurs when a victim tries to express her dissatisfaction with a court-ordered treatment, as the mother did in *D.O.H.* See also Cooper v. District Court, 133 P.3d 692, 696 (Alaska Ct. App. 2006) (holding that, although victims have the right to be heard before the court in certain types of decisions, they do not have standing to appeal the defendant's sentence). What should be the victim's role in sentencing?

10. *Effectiveness.* Are batterer treatment programs effective? As the above excerpt points out, a growing body of research explores the effectiveness of such programs. What do those studies conclude? One central problem is the different views regarding the appropriate measures of "effectiveness." One commentator elaborates

> Given the ideological struggles in the field of batterer intervention and domestic violence, it is no surprise that an underlying tension for batterer intervention programs is caused by the lack of agreement among major stakeholders about how to define an effective program. The answer hinges to a great degree on what changes we expect in an abuser's behavior in order to deem a program successful.

Bea Hanson, Interventions for Batterers: Program Approaches, Program Tensions, in Handbook of Domestic Violence Intervention Strategies: Policies, Programs, and Legal Remedies 419, 434 (Albert R. Roberts ed., 2002). What should be the goal of an effective treatment program—to stop battering entirely or reduce the violence? Does reducing the violence mean reducing the number of violent incidents and/or lowering the seriousness of the incidents? Is a program effective if physical abuse stops but psychological abuse continues or escalates? Was the batterer's treatment program effective in *D.O.H.*? What are the views of the various parties regarding its effectiveness?

Recidivism is based on various data sources, including offenders' self-reports, victims' self-reports, and rearrest data. What are the shortcomings of reliance on each of those sources? For example, in *D.O.H.*, the court relies on the offender's testimony and that of his present wife. Are both those accounts reliable?

11. *Policy.* Consider the questions posed by the above excerpt. Do batterer intervention programs waste valuable resources? Do they create a false sense of security in women who are led to believe that their batterer will reform? Is it prudent to mandate batterers to batterer intervention programs when there is little evidence that they work?

If there is little evidence to suggest that batterer programs are effective, should they be abandoned? If not, how can services be improved to reduce recidivism and change attitudes about violent behavior toward women? Should alternative approaches be utilized? If so, which? One commentator contends that a batterer intervention program should not be evaluated as an end in itself but rather as a component of a coordinated criminal justice response. Edward W. Gondolf, Theoretical and Research Support for the Duluth Model: A Reply to Dutton and Corvo, 12 Aggression & Violent Behavior 644, 652 (2007). What do you think of this approach to effectiveness?

Table of Cases

Principal cases appear in italics.

A.C., In re, 629
A.R. v. M.R., 450
Abbott v. Abbott, 516, 663, 664
Adair, People v., 346
Adolphson v. Yourzak, 744, 757, 758, 759
Alexander v. Rogers, 614
Alexander, People v., 251
Alexis, People v., 346
Alison C. v. Westcott, 434
Alle, In re Welfare of, 690
Al-Zubaidy, United States v., 398
Anchorage, Municipality of, v. Gregg, 708
Anderson v. Hensrud, 617
Apressos v. Memorial Press Group, 707
Arbaugh v. Board of Educ., 514
Arnett v. Wills, 127
Aucoin, State v., 726

Baehr v. Lewin, 291
Bailey, United States v., 320
Baker v. Baker, 609
Balas, In re, 291
Balistreri v. Pacifica Police Dept., 266
Bandfield v. Bandfield, 516
Banos, People v., 378
Barber v. Barber, 446
Barrett v. Wright, 634
Bay v. Jensen, 653
Bayles, United States v., 545

Board of Trustees of the Univ. of Ala. v. Garrett, 544
Bean, State v., 656
Beattie v. Beattie, 515
Becker v. Johnson, 451
Benitez, People v., 325, 327, 328
Bevan v. Fix, 665, 670, 671, 672
Blackmon v. Blackmon, 460, 465
Blazel v. Bradley, 433
Blumhorst v. Jewish Family Servs., 781
Boblitt v. Boblitt, 581
Bonaparte, State v., 338
Booth v. Hvaas, 781
Borchgrevink v. Borchgrevink, 628
Borrelli, State v., 724
Bouley v. Young-Sabourin, 693, 695
Bouters v. State, 188
Boyle v. Boyle, 465
Boynton v. Kusper, 783
Bozman v. Bozman, 515
Bradley v. State, 272, 273, 274, 275
Bradwell v. Illinois, 15
Branson, State v., 489, 491
Braxton, State v., 139
Brinkman v. Brinkman, 575
Brooks v. Rothe, 789
Brown, People v., 346, 351, 352
Browning v. Corbett, 782
Bruno v. Codd, 265
Brzonkala v. Virginia Polytechnic Inst. & State Univ., 548

Burella v. City of Philadelphia, 128, 267, 268, 269

C.J.K., State ex rel., 685, 689, 690, 691, 692
C.W. v. K.A.W., 640
Cabrera, People v., 352
California v. Johnson, 368
Caplan v. Donovan, 450
Carmichael v. Siegel, 628
Carroll v. United Sates, 220
Carswell, State v., 287, 290, 291, 292
Carter v. State, 135, 138, 139
Carthew v. County of Suffolk, 471
Castle Rock, Town of, v. Gonzales, 258, 264, 266, 267, 268
Cauley, In re Marriage of, 578, 580, 581
Cave v. Cooley, 221
Ceballos, United States v., 322
Celinkski, State v., 202
Charous, In re Marriage of, 630
Chen v. Fischer, 522, 524, 525, 575
Chevalier, People v., 332
Chiles v. Chiles, 504
Christopher S. v. Anne Marie S., 617
Ciesluk, In re Marriage of, 652
Clark v. Office of Pers. Mgmt., 140, 142, 143
Cloeter v. Cloeter, 436, 441
Cloyed, In re Marriage of, 614
Coburn v. Coburn, 353
Colas v. Watermain, 713
Coleman v. Coleman, 525
Commonwealth v. _____. See party name
Cooper v. Cooper, 192
Cooper v. District Ct., 806
Couch v. Couch, 634
Crawford v. Commonwealth, 144, 157, 158
Crawford v. Washington, 147, 156, 353, 364, 384
Crespo v. Crespo, 457, 465, 466
Croll v. Croll, 663
Crop v. Crop, 188
Cruz-Foster v. Foster, 446
Curley, United States v., 400
Curreri, State v., 292
Curtis v. Firth, 521
Cusseaux v. Pickett, 505
Custody of _____. See party name

D.O.H. v. T.L.H., 796, 804, 805, 806
D.W., In re, 690
D'Antoni v. Comm'r, N.H. Dept. of Health & Human Servs., 783
Danaipour v. McLarey, 664
Dando v. Yukins, 719, 723, 724, 725, 726
Dannels, State v., 726
Danny v. Laidlaw Transit Servs., Inc., 701, 707, 708, 711, 712
Daubert v. Merrell Dow Pharm., Inc., 65, 303

Davis v. Bostwick, 515
Davis v. Monroe County Bd. of Ed., 548
Davis v. Washington, 354, 363, 364, 365, 367, 384
Day, People v., 724
Day v. Heller, 173
Dean v. State, 723
Dee v. Dee, 569
Dena Lynn F. v. Harvey H.F., 626
Depos v. Depos, 462, 465, 466
DeShaney v. Winnebago, 266
DesLauriers v. DesLauriers, 615
Desmond v. Desmond, 646, 651, 652
Devine v. Devine, 613
District of Columbia v. Heller, 410, 411
Dixon v. State, 334
Dixon v. United States, 314, 318-319, 320, 321, 322
Domestic Violence Servs. v. Freedom of Information Comm'n, 788
Drew, United States v., 197
Dubay v. Wells, 178
Dulany, State v., 725
Dunn v. Roberts, 726
Dyer v. Dyer, 442, 447

E.B.L.G., In re, 758
E.F.G., In re, 590, 593
Edward F. v. Superior Court, 803
Edwards v. Edwards, 568
Elliott, State v., 188
Ely, Commonwealth v., 322
Ellzey v. Ellzey, 569
Emerson, United States v., 410
European Connections & Tours, Inc. v. Gonzalez, 564
Evans v. Braun, 430, 433, 434, 435
Ex parte _____. See party name

Faasse, United States v., 543
Farrow, State v., 217, 222
Feltmeier v. Feltmeier, 499, 502, 505, 506, 521, 570, 571
Felton, State v., 725
Fent v. State ex rel. Dept. of Human Servs., 783
Fernandez, People v., 774
Fischer, In re Marriage of, 617, 625, 626, 627
Florida Dept. of Children & Families v. F.L., 690
Forman, People v., 465
Fox v. Encounters Int'l, 555, 565, 566
Freeman v. Ferguson, 269
Freeman v. Freeman, 452, 456, 457
Frigm v. Unemployment Comp. Bd. of Review, 785, 788
Frye v. United States, 303
Fulgham v. State, 19, 275
Furnes v. Reeves, 663

G.L. v. M.L., 516
Garcia, People v., 204, 205

Gdowski v. Gdowski, 79, 83, 85
Gideon v. Winwright, 723
Gilbert v. Dept. of Corr., 710
Giles, People v., 375
Giles v. California, 367, *369*, 375, 376, 377
Gill v. Office of Pers. Mgmt., 291
Giovine v. Giovine, 521
Glover v. State, 339
Gluzman, United States v., 399
Gonzalez v. Raich, 543
Gormley v. Judicial Conduct Comm'n, 472
Grand Jury Subpoena Duces Tecum Directed
    to Keeper of Records of My Sister's Place,
    In re, 788
Grant v. Grant, 629
Gross v. State, 273, 274

H.E.S. v. J.C.S., 465
H.L.T., In re, 630
Hackler's Heirs v. Cabel, 275
Hageman v. Stanek, 781
Hall v. Fla. Unemp't Appeals Comm'n, 710
Harden, State v., 305, 311, 312
Harris v. State, 19
Hastings v. Rigsbee, 640
Hauser v. Nebraska Police Standards Advisory
    Council, 128
Havell v. Islam, 582, 585, 586, 587, 588
Hawthorne v. State, 297, 298-300, 301, 302, 303,
    304, 312
Hayes, United States v., 412
Heacock v. Heacock, 575
Heart of Atlanta Motel, Inc. v. United States, 542
Hedgepeth v. Washington Metro. Area Transit, 221
Heiser v. Heiser, 569
Hellickson, State v., 287
Hemenway v. Hemenway, 447, 450, 451
Hendershott v. Westphal, 761
Henry, People v., 199
Herrington v. Comm'r, 200
Hilliker v. Miller, 758
Hodel v. Virginia Surface Mining & Reclamation,
    Inc., 542
Hofman, In re, 22
Holbach, State v., 188
Holifield, People v., 293
Holsman v. Cohen, 775
Homick, United States v., 322
Hope House, Inc., State ex rel., v. Merrigan, 788
Howard S. v. Lillian S., 587
Hunt v. Oklahoma, 368
Hutson v. Hutson, 568

Iamele v. Asselin, 446

J.B. and H.B., In re Marriage of, 291
J.C., In re Guardianship of, 692

J.S. v. J.F., 76
J.S. v. J.F., 435
Jackson v. United States, 197, 199
James M., In re, 616
Jessica D. v. Jeremy H., 435
Jewell v. Jewell, 22
Jewitt v. Jewitt, 505
Johnson v. Apna Ghar, Inc., 796
Johnson, People v., 284, 286, 287
Johnson, State v., 188

K. v. B., 346
K.J. v K.K., 434
Katzenbach v. Morgan, 544, 548
Kealoha, State v., 287
Keller v. Keller, 421, 422, 423
Kelly, State v., 301
Kellogg, State v., 283
Kent v. Green, 607
Khalifa v. Shannon, 652
Kheyfets, People v., 198
Kimel v. Florida Board of Regents, 544
Kinsella v. Kinsella, 576
Krank v. Krank, 615

L. Pamela P. v. Frank S., 173
Lacey v. Village of Palatine, 268
Landeros v. Flood, 514
Langeslag v. KYMN, Inc., 504
Lankford, United States v., 545
Larsen v. Jendusa-Nicolai, 395
Larsen, United States v., 391, 394, 395, 396, 397
Larson v. Dunn, 652
Larson v. State, 725
Lassiter v. Dept. of Soc. Servs., 690, 724
Lawrence v. Texas, 91
Lefebvre v. Lefebvre, 191
Lenahan v. United States, 261, 263, 264
Lewis v. State, 725
Liberta, People v., 340, 345
Logendyke v. Logendyke, 27
Lopez, United States v., 396
Lutgen, In re, 630
Lyman v. Huber, 503

MacManus, In re Marriage of, 581
Mark M., In re, 628
Markman, Commonwealth v., 323
Marquette v. Marquette, 433
Martinez v. Martinez, 466
Mary D. v. Watt, 628
Martin v. State, 724, 725
Massachusetts v. U.S. Dept. of Health & Human
    Servs., 291
Massey, State v., 332

Maxwell v. Maxwell, 662
McBrayer v. State, 726
McAfee, Commonwealth v., 275
McCauley v. McCauley, 629
McClure v. Rehg, 244
McCulloch v. Drake, 505, 506, *572*, 574, 575, 576
McDade v. West, 788
McDonald v. City of Chicago, 410
McGuire v. McGuire, 19, 22, 23
McMaugh v. State, 325
McNair v. McNair, 451
McSwane v. Bloomington Hosp. & Healthcare Sys.,
    508, 511, 512
Meade v. Chambliss, 199
Meeks v. Bergen, 725
Men & Women Against Discrimination v. Family
    Protection Servs., Bd., 784
Metro N. Owners, LLC v. Thorpe, 696
Meredith, In re Marriage of, 104, 442
Meyer v. Nebraska, 684
Meyers v. Sheehan, 617
Michigan v. Bryant, 366
Miller, State v., 334
Miltiadous v. Tatervak, 665
Minton, In re, 200
Moncher v. Maine, 628
Montgomery Cty. Dept. of Soc. Servs v. Sanders,
    653
Moore v. City of Leeds, 365
Mora, People v., 282
Moran v. Beyer, 27, 515
Morris v. Horn, 615
Morrison, United States v., 396, 530, 537-540,
    541-549
Mozes v. Mozes, 662
Mullen v. Phelps, 629
Municipality of _____. *See party name*
Murphy v. Workers' Comp. Appeals Bd., 713
Murray v. State, 330, 332, 333

Nadkarni, In re Marriage of, 193, 195, 196
Nam, State v., 199
Nearing v. Weaver, 265
Neilson ex rel Crump v. Blanchette, 71, 73, 74, 75, 76,
    77
Nicholson, In re, 683
Nicholson v. Scoppetta, 677, 679-682, 684, 685
Nussbaum v. Steinberg, 522

Odden v. Rath, 446
Ohio v. Roberts, 363
Okin v. Village of Cornwall-on-Hudson Police
    Dept, 267
Opinion of the Justices to the Senate, 614
Orr v. Orr, 580
Overberg v. Lusby, 525

P.I. v. Dept. of Children & Families, 690
Pagan v. Board of Review, 710
Paine v. Massie, 304, 725
Parkhurst v. Parkhurst, 441
Parks v. Parks, 615
People v. _____. *See party name*
Perez v. United States, 542
Perry v. Schwarzenegger, 291
Peters v. Peters, 566, 568, 569, 570
Peterson, State v., 725
Pellegrini, State v., 140
Peters-Riemers v. Riemers, 609, 613, 614, 615
Pierce v. Soc'y of Sisters, 684
Planned Parenthood of Southeastern Pa. v. Casey, 174,
    178, 179
Planned Parenthood v. Danforth, 178
Plante v. Engle, 652
Prince v. Massachusetts, 684
Pugliese v. Superior Court, 517, 520, 521

R. V. Ryan, 521
R.A., In re, 564
R.H. v. B.F., 606
R.M.W. v. G.M.M., 434
Rahn v. Norris, 614
Ramsey, People v., 788
Rawson v. Buta, 570
Reiser v. Reiser, 587
Report of Comm'n on Family Courts, In re, 775
Reyes, State v., 450
Reynolds v. Fraser, 714
Richardson, People v., 188
Ringler, In re Marriage of, 615
Rios v. Fergusan, 452
Ritchie v. Konrad, 187
Robertson, In re, 468, 470, 471, 472, 473, 474
Robertson v. United States ex rel. Watson, 472
Robinson v. Cincinnati Metropolitan Hous. Auth.,
    696
Roe v. Roe, 282
Rogowicz v. O'Connell, 473
Roussel v. Roussel, 524, 575
Rufo v. Simpson, 361
Ruprecht v. Ruprecht, 504
Ryan, R. v., 321

S.D. v. M.J.R., 162, 165, 166, *572*
Sacharow v. Sacharow, 594
Saechao, People v., 199
Sandoval v. Mendez, 434
Santiago, People v., 379, 383
Santos, United States v., 322
Santosky v. Kramer, 689
Scally v. Scally, 569
Schultz v. Schultz, 648, 651, 652
Scott v. Hart, 264, 265

Serreze v. YWCA of Western Mass., Inc., 794
Sheridan v. Sheridan, 654
Sherman v. Sherman, 441
Shrader, United States v., 398
Simcox v. Simcox, 656, 663, 664
Simmons v. Simmons, 614
Simmons v. City of Inkster, 269
Simpson, People v., 359
Sinclair v. Sinclair, 444, 447
Singleton, United States v., 339
Sjomeling v. Stuber, 457
Skoien, United States v., 406, 411
Slansky v. Slansky, 525
Smith v. Jones, 446
Smith v. Martens, 186
Smith v. Martin, 167, 169
Smith v. Oklahoma, 725
Smith v. State, 304, 725
Smith, United States v., 725
Sorichetti v. City of New York, 265
South Carolina v. Katzenbach, 544
Sparks v. Deveny, 186
Spence v. Kaminski, 447, 457
Standefer v. United States, 473
State ex rel _____. *See party name*
State v. _____. *See party name*
Stevenson v. Stevenson, 251
St. Luke's Episcopal-Presbyterian Hosp. v. Underwood, 22
Stonehouse, Commonwealth v., 725
Strane, State v., 491
Sturgeon, State v., 629
Sullivan, People v., 199

T.R. v. F.R., 189
Taft v. Derricks, 708
Taylor v. Board of Review, 710
Taylor v. Frye, 630
Taylor, State v., 334, 337
Thomas v. Phone Directories Co., 504
Thompson v. Branches-Domestic Violence Shelter of Huntington, Inc., 788
Thompson v. Thompson, 23, 26, 27, 514, 515, *655*
Thurman v. City of Torrington, 265
Trammel v. United States, 337, 338, 339
Tulintseff v. Jacobsen, 615

Turner Broadcasting Sys., Inc. v. Federal Communications Comm'n, 548
Twyman v. Twyman, 503, 521, 575

United States v. _____. *See party name*
Uttaro v. Uttaro, 486

Valentine, State v., 386
Van Drunen, United States v., 340
Vaughn, Custody of, 602, 606, 607, 608, 615
Villars v. Provo, 783

Walker v. Commonwealth, 345
Wallin, People v., 199
Wallis v. Smith, 173
Wanrow, State v., 303, 304
Ward, State v., 333
Wardeh v. Altabchi, 441
Washington, State v., 651
Weiner v. Weiner, 182, 186, 187
White, United States v., 411
Wickard v. Filburn, 543
William M.M. v. Kathleen M.M., 570
Williams v. Jones, 484, 488
Williams v. Marsh, State ex rel., 442, 465
Williams, United States v., 286
Willis-Marsh v. Wilkerson, 654
Winters, State v., 340
Wissink v. Wissink, 630, 634, 635, 636
Woods v. Horton, 777, 781, 782
Wright v. Bradley, 79
Wu, People v., 328

Yaden, State v., 292
Young, In re, 200
Young v. United States ex rel. Vuitton et Fils S.A., 473

Zelig v. County of Los Angeles, 269
Zetty v. Piatt, 471
Zia, In re Custody of, 607
Zimmerman, State v., 725

Index

ABA. *See* American Bar Association
Abduction
    fleeing from abuse, 646-665, 728-731
    Hague Convention on Civil Aspects of
        International Child Abduction, 656-665
    international child abduction, 656-665
    International Child Abduction Remedies Act,
        660
    International Parenting Kidnapping Act, 664
    lawyers' ethical issues concerning, 728-731
    Uniform Child Abduction Prevention Act,
        655
Abortion and domestic violence. *See also* Birth
        control sabotage; Pregnancy and
        domestic violence
    coerced abortions, 177, 179
    disclosure of plans to partners, 178
    father's interest in fetus, 178
    federal law on, 174-177
    interference with abortion decision, 174-179
    state laws on coerced abortion, 179
    spousal consent and notification,
        174-177, 178
    undue burden standard, 178
    waiting periods, 174-178
Abuse. *See* Child abuse; Domestic Violence;
        Specific types of abuse
Abusers. *See* Offenders
Acquaintance rape. *See also* Teen dating violence
    characteristics of, 541-542
    college sexual assault policy, 540, 541

federal guidelines regarding, 549-550
    liability for, 530-550
    psychological effects of, 542
    Rape Trauma Syndrome, 542
    statistics, 542
Address Confidentiality Program (ACP) 594, 702.
        See also Confidentiality
Adolescents. *See* Age; Child custody; Children's
        exposure to domestic violence; Teen dating
        violence; Youth gangs
Adoption, 690-692
Adoption and Safe Families Act (ASFA),
        690-691
Adoption Assistance and Child Welfare Act, 691
Adultery, 331, 333, 568. *See also* Criminal defenses;
        Jealousy; Provocation
AFCC. *See* Association of Family and Conciliation
        Courts
African-Americans and intimate partner violence.
        See also Race; Racism
    abusers' characteristics, 33
    barriers to seeking help for, 98-100
    community response, 105
    dual or mutual arrest, 225, 229, 233
    mandatory arrest and, 225, 229, 233
    self-defense, use of, 231
    shelter-related issues, 792
    socioeconomic factors. *See* Economic issues;
        Social class
    statistics on, 32, 33, 103
    victims' characteristics, 33, 231

813

Age and intimate partner violence. *See also* Elder abuse; Teen dating violence; Youth gangs
  abusers, characteristics of, 31, 33, 35, 73, 74
  barriers to seeking help, 75, 76, 77
  disclosure of abuse, 75, 85
  elder abuse, 82-86
  gender issues, 31, 35
  harassment, 73, 74
  representation of victims, 75
  restraining orders, 72, 73, 74, 75, 76, 78
  statistics, 31, 33, 35
  stereotypes, 84
  teen dating violence, 71-79
  victims' characteristics, 29-33, 35, 73, 74
Aid to Families with Dependent Children (AFDC), 114. *See also* Personal Responsibility and Work Opportunity Reconciliation Act
AIDS/HIV, 90, 93-95
Alcohol. *See* Substance abuse
ALI. *See* American Law Institute
Alternate dispute resolution. *See* Collaborative law; Mediation
American Bar Association (ABA), 6, 84, 215, 622, 727. *See also* Attorneys; Standards of Practice
American Humane Association, 205. *See also* Pet abuse
American Indian. *See* Native American
American Law Institute (ALI) Principles
  alimony provisions, 580, 581
  child abuse provisions, 754
  custody provisions generally, 606, 634
  domestic violence provisions, 625, 754, 759, 760
  parenting plans, 625, 744, 745, 754, 760
American Medical Association (AMA), 118
Americans with Disability Act (ADA), 64, 710. *See also* Disabled victims
Animal cruelty. *See* Pet abuse
Anger management, 38, 565 *See also* Batterers' intervention programs
Anti-Drug Abuse Act, 783
Antisubordination theory, 53, 547. *See also* Equality
Armed Forces Domestic Security Act, 123
Arrest and domestic violence. *See also* Orders of protection; Police
  arrest rates, 215, 224, 226, 231
  absent offenders and, 214, 221, 222, 230, 267
  deterrent effect of, 215, 223, 233
  discretionary arrest policy, 221
  domestic vs. stranger arrest, compared, 224, 226, 227, 275
  dual or mutual arrest, 225-232
  evolution of policies regarding, 213-216, 275
  factors affecting decision to arrest, 213, 214, 230
  felony vs. misdemeanor, 214, 220
  lawsuits against police for non-arrest, 214, 223, 258-269
  mandatory arrest, 221-228, 230, 234, 266

minorities and, 225, 229, 233. *See also* African-Americans; Asian-Americans; Native Americans
  permissive arrest policy, 221
  police injuries or deaths during, 214, 216
  preferred arrest policy, 221
  primary aggressor, 227, 228-229, 232, 233
  proarrest policy, 221
  proximity to incident, 222
  race and. *See* Race
  self-defense and, 230, 231, 232
  sexual orientation. *See* Sexual orientation
  statistics, 215, 226, 233
  statutory approaches, 221-222
  restraining orders and. *See* Orders of protection
  VAWA, influence of, 223
  violation of restraining orders. *See* Orders of protection
  warrantless, 214, 215, 217-220, 228, 229, 275
Asian Americans and intimate partner violence, 102-103
  attitudes about, 102, 103
  barriers to seeking help, 102, 103
  community response to, 103
  family pressures, 102
  immigration, influence of, 102
  language-related issues, 102
  racism, 103
  religion, influence of, 102
  restraining orders, 103
  self-defense, use of, 231
  stereotypes, 103
  victims' characteristics, 102
Assange, Julian, 173-174
Assault and battery. *See also* Specific types of abuse
  definition, 30, 273, 276-280
  dual or mutual arrest, 225-228, 230, 231, 232
  felony assault, 220, 221, 273
  gender-based differences, 30, 32, 33
  mandatory arrest. *See* Arrest; Mandatory arrest
  misdemeanor assault, 214, 221, 273
  Model Penal Code provisions on, 277
  pregnancy and, 167-170
  primary aggressor, 228, 229, 232, 233
  statistics, 30, 33, 240
  traditional police response to, 213-214
Association of Family and Conciliation Courts (AFCC), 752-753
Asylum, 563-564. *See also* Immigrants
Athletes. *See* Sports
Attachment. *See* Theories of domestic violence; Traumatic bonding
Attorneys. *See also* Professional responsibility; Standards of Practice
  client counseling, 728, 729, 730, 731, 737-741
  client safety, 727, 731, 732-733, 734, 741-744
  conflicts of interest, 75, 640
  GALs, 638, 639, 640

ineffective assistance of counsel, 719-723
representing battered women as criminal
    defendants. *See* Battered Woman
    Syndrome; Criminal defenses; Evidence
representation of children, 75, 638, 639, 640
representing tort victims, 525-529
Attorney General's Task Force on Family
    Violence, 475-480

Background checks. *See* Firearms
Bankruptcy and domestic violence, 199-200, 395.
    See also Economic issues and abuse;
    Financial abuse
Battered spouse waiver. *See* Immigrants; Marriage
Battered Woman Syndrome. *See also* Criminal
    defenses
  admissibility of evidence of, 297-305
  clemency movement, 305
  confrontational vs. nonconfrontational
      homicides, 302, 314
  credibility-related issues, 302
  criticisms of, 304, 313, 314
  diminished capacity, 725
  duress defense and, 322, 324, 325, 724, 725
  early judicial response to, 301
  excessive force, use of, 303
  expert testimony, 43, 297-305, 724-725
  imminence and, 299, 301, 302, 311, 312
  ineffective assistance of counsel and, 304,
      719-724
  insanity defense. *See* Criminal defenses
  jury instructions on, 301, 302, 314, 725, 726
  limitations on use of, 302
  minorities and, 313
  origins of, 301
  provocation. *See* Criminal defenses; Self
      defense; Provocation
  reasonableness, 301, 302, 311, 312
  reasonable woman standard, 303-304
  reliability of evidence of, 300, 301, 305, 306, 307
  scientific evidence, tests of, 303
  self-defense. *See* Self-defense
  statutes on, 304, 305
  stereotypes engendered by, 313
  uses in criminal trials, 301, 302
  victimization paradigm, 313
Battered women. *See* Victims
Battered women's movement
  arrest policy, influence on, 220, 221, 232, 264
  first wave of women's movement, 4-7, 11, 12, 13
  link to other social movements, 4-10, 12
  restraining order, influence on, 486-487
  second wave of women's movement, 7-10, 12,
      14, 514, 780, 781
Batterers' intervention programs
  anger management distinguished, 798, 804, 805
  approaches to, 797, 799, 804, 805

background on, 803
compliance with, 805
condition of child custody, 628, 804
effectiveness of, 800-803, 806
state standards, 803-804
Batterers. *See* Offenders
Battering. *See* Domestic violence
Biden, Joseph (former Senator), 239-242
Biological theories of abuse. *See* Theories of
    domestic violence
Birth control, sabotage of. *See also* Abortion;
    Pregnancy
  abortions, resulting from, 172
  methods of sabotage, 171, 172
  motivations of abusers, 172
  pressure to become pregnant, 171, 172
  pressure to have an abortion, 171, 177, 178, 179
  sexually transmitted diseases, 171
  statistics, 170
  sterilization, 173
  unintended pregnancy, 171, 172
  women's sabotage of birth control, 173
Blackstone, Sir William
  coverture, 16-17
  husband's right of chastisement, 4, 13, 16, 17,
      18, 19, 274,
  married women's legal disabilities, 16-17
  provocation, 332
  role in shaping legal culture, 4
Borderline personality disorder, 48. *See also*
    Theories of domestic violence
Brady Handgun Violence Prevention Act of 1993,
    404, 412, 413
Bureau of Justice Statistics, 31-33

Causes of domestic violence. *See* Theories of
    domestic violence
Centers for Disease Control and Prevention
    (CDC), 29, 39, 66, 67
Chastisement, husband's right of, 4, 5, 7, 13, 18,
    19, 271, 272, 273, 274, 275
Child abuse and neglect. *See also* Child protective
    services; Children's exposure to violence
  child neglect, 677-685
  child sexual abuse, 521-522
  co-occurrence with domestic violence, 41, 43,
      165, 203, 598, 609
  cultural defense, 328
  elder abuse, analogy to, 85
  failure to protect, 677-685
  reporting laws, 85, 86, 513, 514
  representation of victims. *See* Attorneys;
      Standards of Practice
  specialized courts, 762-776
  termination of parental rights, 622, 629, 655,
      684, 685-692
  transgenerational transmission of abuse, 50

Child Abuse Prevention and Treatment Act
    (CAPTA), 514, 638
Child custody. *See also* Visitation
    abandonment, effect of, on custody, 599, 602,
        653
    allegations of abuse, in custody proceedings,
        640
    ALI Principles. *See* American Law Institute
    attorney for child. *See* Attorneys; Professional
        responsibility
    best interests standard, 606, 607
    child's preference, 633, 634, 663
    child's refusal to visit, 630
    custodial interference, liability for, 651, 652
    custody evaluation, 601, 634, 642-645
    failure to protect, 677-685
    fathers' rights movement, 781
    friendly parent doctrine, 641
    guardians ad litem, 637-642
    joint custody, 641, 642, 746
    jurisdiction, 654, 655
    litigiousness of batterers, 117, 598-599
    mediation. *See* Mediation
    modification, 616, 617
    parental alienation, 636
    Parental Alienation Syndrome, 645-646
    parenting plans, 625, 744, 745, 760
    primary aggressor, role of, 233
    protective mothers, effects on, 602, 677-685
    presumption against custody for abusers,
        602-617
    relocation disputes, 653, 654
    representation, 638, 639
    traumatic bonding, 630-633, 635
    termination of parental rights, 622, 629, 655,
        684, 685-692
    visitation. *See* Visitation
Child protective services, 236, 623, 672-692, 783
Child sexual abuse. *See* Child abuse
Children
    abduction, 646-665
    adoption, 690-692
    child abuse. *See* Child abuse
    childhood exposure to abuse. *See* Children's
        exposure to domestic violence
    custody of. *See* Child Custody
    familicide, victims of, 142
    federal crime to solicit for sex, 191
    litigation abuse and, 117, 598-599, 600
    mandatory reporting of abuse, 85, 86
    name change of, 593
    orders of protection and, 71-77, 78
    parent coordinators, 625
    parental alienation, 636
    Parental Alienation Syndrome, 645-646
    pet abuse by, 204
    teen dating violence. *See* Teen dating violence
    traumatic bonding, 630-633, 635

    visitation. *See* Visitation
    youth gangs, 77
Children's exposure to violence, 665-672
    as form of child abuse, 50, 672
    criminal liability, 672
    effects on children, 43, 50, 669, 670
    evolving views of, 670
    intentional infliction of emotional distress, 670,
        671, 672
    post-traumatic stress disorder, 43, 665
    statistics on, 669
    tort liability, 665-672
Chiswick Women's Aid, 780
Choking. *See* Strangulation
Civil protection order. *See* Orders of protection
Civil rights movement, 7
Coercive control, 38, 42, 51, 93, 179-182, 209, 759.
    See also Psychological abuse
Cohabitants and cohabitation, 29, 61, 67, 287-291,
    424, 425, 458, 561, 570, 578, 579, 593
Collaborative law, 761, 762. *See also* Mediation
Collateral estoppel, 524.
College sexual assault policy. *See* Acquaintance
    rape; Rape; Sexual assault
Commerce Clause. *See* Constitutional issues
Community property, 586. *See also* Marriage; Divorce
Confidentiality
    address, 595, 702, 796
    attorneys' duties. *See* Attorneys; Professional
        responsibility
    employment protections, 709, 710
    housing protections and, 696
    medical personnel and. *See* Health care
    of motor vehicle records, 593
    name change and, 590-595
    parental rights, conflict with, 593
    procedures to change identity, 591, 593, 595
    restorative justice and, 257
    safety planning, 727, 731, 732-733, 734,
        741-744
    shelters and, 784-789
    state program protection. *See* Address
        Confidentiality Program
    Social Security numbers, 594, 595
Confrontation Clause. *See* Constitutional issues
Constitutional issues
    Commerce Clause, 392, 393, 396, 530-537, 542,
        543, 544, 545, 547
    Confrontation Clause, 353, 378
    Cruel and unusual punishment, 300
    Double Jeopardy Clause, 393, 394, 396
    Due Process, 74, 268, 285, 286, 291, 433, 431,
        442, 448, 449, 450, 451, 457-460, 464,
        465, 471, 472, 473, 481, 485, 486, 559,
        640
    Equal Protection, 22, 27, 167, 291, 303, 457,
        777-780, 781, 782, 783
    First Amendment, 163, 164, 411

Fourteenth Amendment, 268, 544. *See also* Due
Process; Equal Protection
Fifth Amendment, 321, 393, 466, 564
Sixth Amendment, 147, 354-362, 363-367,
369-378, 375, 723
Nineteenth Amendment, 10
Second Amendment, 410-411
Contempt of court
civil contempt, 467-468, 471
constitutional issues, 472-473
criminal contempt, 467-468, 471, 472, 473
private individual, suit for, 468-474
violation of restraining order, 474-484
Contraception. *See* Birth control sabotage
Counseling. See Batterers' intervention programs
Court Appointed Special Advocate Program
(CASA), 638
Courts, specialized domestic violence, 762-776
Covenant marriage, 577
Coverture, 4, 11, 17, 18, 23, 337
Criminal defenses, 295-334
Battered Woman Syndrome, 297-305. *See also*
Battered Woman Syndrome
cultural defense, 325-330
diminished capacity, 311
duress, 314-325. *See also* Duress
historical background, 295-297
insanity defense, 298, 299, 300, 311
provocation, 273, 330-334
self-defense, 35, 43, 45, 56, 305-314. *See also*
Self-defense
Cultural defense
Battered Woman Syndrome and, 328
Constitutional issues, 328
controversy regarding, 328-329
definition, 327
as mitigation, 327, 328
multiculturalists, 329
parent-child suicides, 328, 329
provocation and, 327
rationales, 327
reform proposals, 329-330
sexual assault and, 166, 330
Custodial interference, 651, 652. *See also* Child
custody
Custody evaluators. *See* Child custody
Cyber harassment, 193-197
barriers to seeking help, 195
constitutional issues, 196
definition, 195
direct vs. indirect, 196
federal legislation, 197
state laws, 197
statistics, 197
teen cyberbullying, 196-197
teen dating violence, 197
tort liability, 196
types of, 195, 196

Cyberstalking. *See also* Stalking
comparison to stalking, 189
criticisms of laws, 190
definition, 189
effectiveness, 398, 399
federal laws, 190-191, 397-400
police training and, 190
psychological effect of, 190
state laws, 190
types of, 189
Cycle of violence, 53-56, 301
acute battering incident stage, 55, 301
contrition, 55, 301
criticisms of, 55-56
definition, 53
escalation of tension stage, 54, 301
evolution of, 53
stages of, 48, 49, 54-55, 301
Walker, Lenore, 53-56, 301

Danger assessment (DA) tool, 59-65. *See also*
Lethality assessment; Risk assessment
Date rape. *See* Acquaintance rape; Teenage dating
violence
Declaration of Sentiments, 5, 13
Death. *See* Homicide; Lethality Assessment; Risk
assessment
Defense of Marriage Act (DOMA), 287-292
Department of Defense, 121
Disabled victims of domestic violence
adult protective services, 96
Americans with Disabilities Act (ADA), 64, 710
barriers to help seeking, 92-93, 97
comparison to non-disabled victims, 92
federal law, 95-96
HIV/AIDS and abuse, 93-95
perceptions of self, 96-97
police response to, 93
poverty, 97
risk for abuse, 92
shelters, 97, 795
state laws, 96
statistics, 95
stereotypes, 96
victims' characteristics, 92-95, 97
VAWA provisions, 95
Divorce
community property, 586
corroboration requirement, 569, 570
covenant marriage, 577
cruelty as ground for divorce, 6, 14, 345, 524,
568, 569, 570
fault, role of, in property distribution, 582-588
fault, role of, in spousal support, 578-582
fault-based grounds, 422, 524
history of, relationship to wife beating, 14, 19
injunctions issued in conjunction with, 422, 423, 424

joinder with tort action, 572-577
legal separation, distinguished, 14, 423
marital settlement agreement, precluding tort
claims, 525
mediation. *See* Mediation
no-fault grounds, 423, 524, 568, 571, 575
religious views about, 109
restraining orders and divorce, 572
spousal support, 22, 23, 578-582
Doctors. *See* Health care
Domestic Abuse Intervention Project (DAIP),
56
Domestic violence. *See also* Offenders; Specific
types of abuse; Victims
age. *See* Age
childhood history of abuse. *See* Child abuse
children's exposure to. *See* Children's exposure
to domestic violence
domestic violence by proxy, 206
dynamics of relationships, 37-47, 601-602
economic costs of. *See* Economic issues
employment. *See* Employment
federalism and, 545, 546
financial issues. *See* Financial abuse
gay male relationships. *See* Sexual orientation
gender, 30, 32, 33, 34, 35
gender equality, issue of, 10-12, 52, 546, 547,
782
history of. *See* Battered women's movement;
Feminism
HIV-related, 68
Immigrants. *See* Immigrants
interstate aspects of, 188-189, 190, 387-400,
481-484
isolation, 37, 42, 199
lesbian relationships. *See* Sexual orientation
lethality assessment, 59-65
litigation abuse, 117, 598-599, 600
locations of, 33
mandatory reporting, 85, 96, 170, 510
military and, 120-124
mutual. *See* Arrest; Orders of protection
myths, 38-41
onset of, 36, 43, 46
pet abuse. *See* Pet abuse
physical health consequences, 66-69, 118
power and control, 116, 171, 209
Power and Control Wheel, 52, 56-58
privacy, 15, 16, 507, 516, 640
professional athletes. *See* Sports
property damage. *See* Financial abuse
psychological abuse. *See* Psychological abuse
race and, 32, 33
rape. *See* Marital rape; Rape; Sexual assault
religion, role of. *See* Religion
sexual assault. *See* Marital rape; Rape; Sexual
assault
shelters. *See* Shelters

substance abuse, 33, 50
theories of. *See* Theories of domestic violence
time of day, 33
transgenerational transmission of, 50
types of, 275, 281
use of third parties, 206-208
warning signs for, 36-38
weapon use during, 227
Domestic violence by proxy, 206
Domestic Violence Leave Act, 709. *See also*
Employment
Domestic Violence Restraining Order System
(DVROS), 475. *See also* Orders of
protection
Double jeopardy. *See* Constitutional issues
Driver's Privacy Protection Act, 188. *See also*
Stalking
Drug abuse. *See* Substance abuse
Dual arrest. *See* Arrest
Due Process. *See* Constitutional issues
Duluth Power and Control Wheel. *See* Power and
Control Wheel
Duress. *See also* Battered Woman Syndrome;
Criminal defenses
Battered Woman Syndrome and, 322
burden of persuasion, 320, 321
burden of proof, 314-318, 319, 320, 321
common law and, 321
elements of defense, 319
imminence requirement, 322
motivations to commit, 324
murder and, 321
necessity defense, distinguished, 320
objective vs. subjective standard, 321, 322
reasonable opportunity to escape, 322
statistics, 324

Economic issues. *See also* Employment;
Financial abuse, Social class
affluent victims. *See* Social class
African Americans. *See* African Americans; Race
costs of domestic violence, 66-69
economic abuse. *See* Financial abuse
homelessness, 700-701
poverty, 97, 99, 100, 103, 113, 115, 115,
116, 120
welfare, 58, 114, 115, 116
Elder abuse
abusers' characteristics, 82
child abuse analogy, 84, 85
conservatorships/guardianships, 83
definition, 83
depression and, 54
disclosure of, 83
Elder Justice Act, 84
federal law, 84
financial exploitation, 84, 84

identification of, 83
older elders, 82
orders of protection, 83
reporting laws on, 85
screening for, 85, 727
Senate Committee hearings on, 86
state law, 85
statistics, 82
stereotypes, 84
types of abuse, 82
victims' characteristics, 82
Elder Justice Act, 84
Emergency dispatchers, 362-363, 364, 368-369
Emotional abuse. *See* Psychological abuse
Emotional distress, intentional or negligent
    infliction of, 499-507, 524, 570, 571, 574,
    670-671. *See also* Tort
Employment and domestic violence. *See also*
    Economic issues; Employment
    discrimination; Social class; Workplace
    violence
  absenteeism from work, 113, 706
  economic-related costs, 706
  employment discrimination, 701-714
  federal law, 708, 709
  interference with, by abuser, 113, 706
  job termination, 701-704
  protective effect of, 113, 116
  state law, 709-712
  statistics, 705, 706
  tort liability of employers, 712-713
  welfare and, 114, 115, 116
  work leaves, related to domestic violence, 708,
    709
  workers' compensation insurance, 713
  workplace violence, 705-706
Equality, 7, 10-12, 52, 53
  antisubordination, 53, 547
  theories of, 52, 53
  women's rights movement and, 7, 10-12, 15, 52,
    53
Equal Protection. *See* Constitutional issues
Evidence
  admissibility of, 297-305
  Battered Woman Syndrome, 297-305
  character evidence, 346-353
  confidential communications privilege, 337,
    338
  Confrontation Clause, 353-378
  cross-examination, 354-363
  Daubert test, 303
  domestic violence exceptions to ban on, 351,
    352, 353
  evidence-based victimless prosecution,
    252, 353
  evidentiary privileges generally, 339
  exception to marital privilege for familial
    offenses, 338-339

exception to marital privilege for fraudulent
    marriage, 339
  excited utterances, 364
  Federal Rules of Evidence, 303, 352, 353, 364,
    365, 377
  forfeiture-by-wrongdoing doctrine, 367,
    369-378
  Frye test, 303
  hearsay, 363, 364, 375
  hearsay exceptions, 363, 364, 367
  heat of passion defense. *See* Provocation
  marital rape exemption, 340-346
  medical diagnosis and treatment exception,
    364, 365
  motive exception, 351, 352
  Nicole Brown Simpson Law, 351
  O.J. Simpson trial, 351
  prior bad acts, 346-353
  propensity evidence, 351
  provocation. *See* Provocation
  rationale for marital privileges, 338
  recantation, 379-386
  reliability of, 303, 363
  scientific tests for admissibility of, 303
  sexual assault exception to ban on, 352
  spousal testimonial privilege, 334-340
  testimonial standard for admission of hearsay,
    353-358, 363, 364, 365, 366, 367
  victim recantation, 136, 139, 302, 378, 243,
    379-386
Evolutionary theory of abuse. *See* Theories of
    domestic violence
Exit from abusive relationship
  announcement of, 149
  escalation of risk during, 39, 156
  financial issues accompanying, 157
  lethality assessment, 61
  making plans for, 157
  misconception that abuse ends at separation,
    597-598
  multiple attempts at, 156
  obstacles to, 39, 151-154
  precipitating factor for murder, 148, 156, 157,
    158
  process of, 159-161
  restraining orders and, 156
  retaliation, 148, 149, 151, 157, 202,
    214, 231
  risk of death and, 157, 158
  safety planning and, 154-156, 157, 160
  "separation assault," 156
  sexual assault and, 156, 157
  stages of leaving, 159-161
  statistics, 44, 148, 156
  threats, 58
  victim's perception of danger, 39, 158
Expert testimony. *See* Battered Woman Syndrome;
    Evidence

Exposure to domestic violence. *See* Children's exposure to domestic violence

Failure to protect, 677-685. *See also* Child abuse; Child custody
Fair Housing Act, 693, 694, 695, 696
Familicide, 142
Family. *See also* Child custody; Divorce; Fathers; Marriage; Mothers
  change in family structure, 12-13, 273
  family dynamics of domestic violence, 37-47, 601-602
  family systems theory, 49-50, 59
  judicial policy of nonintervention in, 19, 23, 27, 274
Family and Medical Leave Act (FMLA), 708, 709
Family annihilation, 142. *See also* Homicide; Murder suicide
Family privacy, 3, 11, 13, 16, 22, 27, 345, 507, 516, 640
Family Violence Option (FVO), 114, 116
Family Violence Prevention and Services Act and the Victims of Crime Act, 270, 783, 788
Family Violence Prevention Fund, 170
Fatalities. *See* Homicide
Fathers. *See also* Child custody; Family; Offenders
  abortion-related issues, 176, 177, 178, 179
  birth control sabotage, 170-174
  custody-related issues. *See* Child custody
  fathers' rights movement, 781
  parenting behavior of batterers. *See* Child custody; Offenders
  visitation. *See* Visitation
Federal Rules of Evidence. *See* Evidence
Federalism, 530-537, 545, 546
Federalization of criminal law, 387-414
Feminism. *See also* Feminists
  backlash against, 781
  first, 4-7, 11, 12, 13, 344, 345
  links to other social movements, 4-10, 12
  Married Women's Property Acts reform, 11, 12, 13, 18, 23, 26, 344
  second wave, 7-10, 12, 14, 514, 780, 781
  theories of equality, 52, 53
Feminist Alliance Against Rape (FAAR), 9
Feminists
  advocacy for battered women, 48, 304
  liberal, 8, 52, 53
  radical, 8, 53, 53
  socialist, 8
  theories of domestic violence, 48, 50, 52-53
Fetal homicide. *See* Homicide
Financial abuse
  bankruptcy-related issues, 199, 200
  barriers to seeking help, 199
  credit-related issues, 199
  elderly and, 82, 83, 84, 85, 86
  jointly-owned property, 197-198, 199
  multidimensional nature, 198

  property destruction, 42, 198, 199
  tax implications, 200
  types of, 199
Firearms. *See also* Brady Handgun Violence Prevention Act; Lautenberg Act; Violence Against Women Act
  background checks, 404, 405, 412, 413
  constitutional right to bear arms, 410, 411
  conviction of misdemeanor crime of domestic violence, 403, 406-409, 410, 411, 412
  effectiveness of federal firearm laws, 413, 414
  databases, federal and state, 404, 405
  evasion of laws, 414
  federal prosecutions, 413
  history of regulation of, 400-405
  Lautenberg Amendment, 128, 402, 410, 413, 414
  official use exemption, 128, 402, 403, 412
  restraining orders and, 401, 402, 409, 410
  VAWA provisions, 400-403, 409, 410, 413
First Amendment. *See* Constitutional issues
Forfeiture-by-wrongdoing doctrine. *See* Evidence
Fourteenth Amendment. *See* Constitutional issues
Freedom of Information Act, 786
Friedan, Betty, 7
Full Faith and Credit. *See* Orders of protection

Gardner, Richard. *See* Parental Alienation Syndrome
Gay partner violence. *See* Sexual orientation
Gender, differences in rates of domestic violence, 31, 32, 33, 34, 35, 73, 302
Gender role socialization, 76, 100, 102, 109
Global Positioning System (GPS), 190, 208, 399, 400
Gonzales, Jessica (Lenahan), 258-264, 268, 269
Green Book Initiative, 682-683
Guardians ad litem, 637-642. *See also* Child custody
Gun Control Act, 401, 402. 410. *See also* Firearms
Gun-Free School Zones Act, 543

Hague Convention on Civil Aspects of International Child Abduction, 656-665
Harassment, 74, 79, 83, 117, 128, 160, 175, 188, 189, 191, 196, 451
  cyber harassment. *See* Cyber harassment
  direct vs. indirect, 196
  First Amendment defense, 196
  law reform movement, 196
  orders of protection and, 189, 191, 451
  stalking distinguished, 188
  textual harassment, 74
  third party harassment, 190, 207-208
Hearsay. *See* Evidence
Health care
  behavioral indicators of domestic violence, 511, 512

costs of domestic violence, 66-69
consequences of domestic violence, 68-69
counseling regarding domestic violence, 69
emergency room visits by victims, 66, 511
federal guidelines for screening and
    counseling, 69, 511
HIV/AIDS, 68
hospital visits by victims, 66
mental health services, use of, 66-67
liability of health care professionals, 507-510
mandatory reporting by professionals, 512-514
mental health issues, 68
screening for domestic violence, 69, 119, 511, 512
VAWA provisions on, 242
Health Insurance Portability and Accountability
    Act (HIPAA), 513
Hearsay. *See* Evidence
History of domestic violence. *See* Battered
    women's movement; Feminism
HIV/AIDS, 93-96
Homelessness, 700-701
Homicide. *See also* Battered Woman's Syndrome;
    Criminal defenses; Specific types of abuse
confrontational vs. nonconfrontational, 302, 314
family annihilators, 142
familicide, 142
fatality review, 85
fetal, 170
gender differences in, 39, 302
lethality assessment, 59-65
murder-suicides, 126, 140-144, 705
police as victims of, 214, 216
suicide by cop, 267. *See also* Suicide
threats of, 40, 58
Homophobia. *See* Sexual orientation
Honor killings. *See* Religion
Housing discrimination and domestic violence,
    693-699. *See also* Homelessness
chronic nuisance laws, 698
eviction, 694, 694, 695, 696, 697
federal law, 693-700
landlords' liability, 695, 697, 698, 699
"one-strike" rule, exception to, 695, 696
sex-based discrimination, 695
state law, 697, 698, 699
statistics, 695
transfer policy, 696, 697
VAWA provisions, 696, 697, 698
voucher program, 696, 697, 699

Illegal Immigration Reform and Immigrant
    Responsibility Act, 560
Immigrants and domestic violence
attitudes about, 100, 101
asylum, 563, 564
barriers to seeking help, 100-102, 104, 776
battered immigrant spouses, 100-102

battered spouse waiver, 557, 559, 561, 562, 565, 566
deportation, 560, 561, 562
federal immigration law on marriage, 561, 562
joint petitioning process for residence, 561
K-1 fiancée visa, 559
marriage fraud, 560, 561
self petition, 559-561
shelters and, 101, 102
support services for abuse victims, 101
visas, special types, 559, 563
VAWA provisions, 242
Immigration and Naturalization Service, 560
Immigration Marriage Fraud Amendments
    (IMFA), 560
Infliction of emotional distress, 499-507, 524, 570,
    571, 574, 670, 671
Inheritance rights, role of domestic violence in,
    589, 590
Insanity defense. *See* Criminal defenses
Insurance discrimination, domestic violence and,
    714-716
Inter-American Commission on Human Rights
    (IACHR), 261, 263-264
International Association of Chiefs of Police, 215
International marriage brokers. *See* Marriage
International Marriage Broker Regulation Act of
    2005 (IMBRA), 562, 563, 564, 565.
    See also Marriage
International Parental Kidnapping Crime Act
    (IPKA), 664
Interspousal immunity. *See* Tort
Interstate Communications Act, 190, 398, 399
Interstate Domestic Violence Act (IDVA), 395-396
Interstate domestic violence crimes, 188-189, 190,
    387-400
Interstate Stalking Punishment and Prevention
    Act, 190, 397, 398
Interstate Communications Act, 190
Intimate partner violence. *See* Domestic violence
Intimidation. *See* Offenders
Islam. *See* Religion
Isolation. *See* Offenders

Jealousy, 157, 330-334
Jewish victims and domestic violence, 105-107.
    See also Religion
Judaism. *See* Religion

Kidnapping, 79, 209, 275, 278, 388, 393, 394, 395,
    396, 397, 414, 651
Ku Klux Klan, 6

Landlords. *See* Housing
Latina, Latino, response to domestic violence,
    100-104

Lautenberg Amendment, 128, 402, 410, 413, 414.
    See also Firearms
Law enforcement. *See* Police; Prosecutors
Lawsuits, civil
    against police, 214, 223, 258-269
    against health care professionals, 507-510
    against offenders, 499-507
Learned behavior, 51-52
Learned helplessness, 53, 54, 156, 301
Lesbian intimate partner violence. *See* Sexual
    orientation
Lethality assessment
    access to weapon, 40
    Danger Assessment Instrument, 60, 62-65
    forced sex, 40
    obsessive jealousy, 41, 157
    risk factors that predict fatalities, 40, 61, 157
    separation, role of, 61
    stalking, 40
    strangulation, 40
    substance abuse, 40
    threats to kill, 40
    validity of, 62
    victims' perception of danger, 62
Litigation abuse, 117, 598-599, 600
Lizzie's Law, 629, 630. *See also* Visitation
Locke, John, 16
Low-Income Housing Assistance Voucher
        Program, 696, 697, 699

Mail-Order Brides Act, 562. *See* Marriage
Major Crimes Act, 415
Male culture of violence, 123, 128, 129, 133
Mandatory arrest. *See also* Arrest; Police
    advantages, 224-225
    criticisms, 225, 229, 234
    dual or mutual arrests, 225-228, 230, 231, 232
    Duluth model, emphasis on, 57, 58
    domestic and stranger arrests, compared,
            213-214, 224, 226, 227, 275
    effect on immigrants and minorities, 225, 229
    felony vs. misdemeanor, application to, 220-221
    gender discrimination and, 225-228
    history of, 221, 265
    prosecution rates and, 252
    restraining orders, application to, 221
    sexual orientation and, 229
    statistics, 226, 227
    unintended effects of, 225-228
    victim's preferences, 225, 233
    VAWA and, 223
Mandatory reporting, by professionals, 85, 96,
            170, 510, 512-514. See *also* Child abuse;
            Domestic violence
Marital property, 582-588. *See also* Marriage;
    Divorce
Marital rape, 162-167, 340-346

common law view, 344
comparison with stranger rape, 166, 345
consent-related issues, 165, 166, 342, 344
co-occurrence of physical abuse, 41, 43, 165,
        598, 609
cultural beliefs of acceptability, 162-165
disclosure of, victims' reluctance, 166
effects of, 166
exemption, 166, 340-346
historical background on law reform, 344
injury from, 66
law reform, 344, 345
Lord Hale's view on consent, 342, 344
marital rape exemption, 22
offenders' motivations for, 165
prevalence, 165
rape-shield laws, 346, 399
rationales for exemption, 344, 345
restraining orders and, 166
separation and, 156, 345, 346
severity, 166
sexual orientation, 94, 346
spectrum of , 166
statistics, 118, 165
substance abuse and, 166
Marriage. *See also* Divorce
    battered spouse waiver, 557, 559, 561, 562,
            565, 566
    battered wives, historical background. *See*
            Battered women's movement; Feminism
    Blackstone's views on, 4, 13, 16, 17, 18, 19, 274,
            332
    covenant marriage, 577
    federal immigration law on, 559-565
    fraud, 560, 561
    husband's right of chastisement, 4, 5, 7, 13, 18,
            19, 271, 272, 273, 274, 275
    immigrant spouse-victims. *See* Immigrants
    international marriage brokers, 555-562
    mail-order brides, 555-566
    marital privilege, evidence, 334-340
    marital rape exemption, 22, 166
    marriage license fees' funding shelters, 782, 783
    necessaries doctrine, 22
    prenuptial agreement, 587
    restraining orders and spouses. *See* Orders of
            protection
    spousal consent and notification of abortion,
            174-179
    visas for fiancée, 559
Married women's common law disabilities,
            16-17
Married Women's Property Acts, 11, 18, 26, 515
Masculinities research, 123, 128-129, 133
Matrimonial Causes Act, 14
Mediation
    benefits of, 747, 751, 756
    controversy about, 745-752, 756

effectiveness of, 747
individual caucusing, 747
mandatory, 756, 757, 759
model laws, 752-753, 754-755, 756-757
modified mediation, 744-745
parenting plans, 744, 745, 760
power imbalance, 746, 749
pro se litigants and, 757
restraining orders, influence of, 758
screening for abuse, 747, 748, 749, 754, 759, 760
suspension of mediation, 753
state law, 747, 757, 758
training, 749
Medical. *See* Health
Megan Meier Cyberbullying Prevention Act, 197
Minnesota Multiphasic Personality Inventory
    (MMPI), 642, 643
Military and domestic violence
    barriers to seeking help, 120, 121
    career consequences of disclosure, 122, 123
    comparison to non-military victims, 120, 121
    deployment, influence of, 120, 122
    disclosure of, 120, 121
    Family Advocacy Program, 122
    gender roles and, 120, 515
    male culture of violence, 123
    masculinities research, 123
    military protective orders (MPO), 122, 123
    military's response, 122, 123
    offenders' characteristics, 120
    rate of domestic violence in, 120
    relocation and, 120
    restraining orders, enforcement on military
        base, 123
    risk factors for, 120
    severity of, 121
    statistics, 120
    support payments for family members, 123
    Uniform Code of Military Justice, 122
    victims' characteristics, 120
Minimization, 58, 488. *See also* Offenders
Minneapolis Domestic Violence Experiment
    (MDVE), 215, 223
Minorities. *See* African-Americans; Asian
    Americans, Latino/Latina; Native
    Americans; Race
Model Code on Domestic and Family Violence,
    232, 446, 621, 653, 754-755, 756
Model Penal Code, 277, 332, 334
Model Standards of Practice for Family and
    Divorce Mediation (AFCC), 752-753,
    754, 755
Mothers, abused. *See also* Child custody
    batterers' denigration of, 42, 45, 54, 598, 600,
        636
    child protective services and, 623, 764, 765, 773
    failure to protect, 677-685
    fleeing with children, 728-731

protective mothers, effects on, 602
restraining orders and, 429
safety planning, 154-156, 157, 160
termination of parental rights. 622, 629, 655,
    684, 685-692
Murder. *See* Homicides
Murderers. *See* Offenders
Murder-suicide, 140-144, 705
    by elderly, 142
    exit as precipitating factor, 140, 142, 144
    family annihilators, 142
    inheritance issues, 140-142, 143
    mental illness, 142
    motivation for, 142
    offenders' characteristics, 142
    police-perpetrated, 126
    prevalence, 142
    slayer disqualification, 143
    statistics, 142
    substance abuse, 142
    types of, 142
    weapon, use of, 142
    workplace violence and, 705
Mutual arrest. *See* Arrest
Mutual protection orders. *See* Orders of
    protection
Myths about domestic violence, 38-41

Name change, 590-595. *See also* Confidentiality
National Alliance to End Homelessness,
    700, 701
National Coalition Against Domestic Violence
    (NCADV), 95, 169
National Council on Juvenile and Family Court
    Judges, 446, 754-755
National Crime Information Center (NCIC),
    404, 482
National Crime Victimization Survey (NCVS), 98
National Domestic Violence Hotline, 170
National Instant Criminal Background Check
    System (NICS), 404, 405, 412
National Intimate Partner & Sexual Violence
    Survey, 29-36
National Institute of Justice (NIJ), 29, 142,
    493, 497
National Organization for Women (NOW), 8, 14, 52
National Violence Against Women (NVAW)
    Survey, 31, 34-36, 66-67
Native Americans and domestic violence
    barriers to seeking help for, 237
    federal Indian law, 414-417
    reluctance to report abuse, 237
    statistics on, 32
    tribal jurisdiction, 415-417
    victims' characteristics, 237
Nicole Brown Simpson. *See* Simpson
Nineteenth Amendment, 10

No-contact orders. *See* Orders of protection
        (criminal)
No-drop policies. *See* Prosecution and prosecutors

Occupational Safety and Health Act (OSHA), 708
Offenders. *See also* Batterers' intervention
        programs
    abortion, interference with decisionmaking,
        170-179
    accountability, 57, 101, 102
    age of, 73, 77
    anger management, 38, 565
    arrest of. *See* Arrest; Mandatory Arrest; Police
    battered women as, 297-330. *See also* Battered
        Woman Syndrome
    batterers' intervention programs. *See* Batterers'
        intervention programs
    belief system of, 44-46
    birth control sabotage. *See* Birth control
        sabotage
    blaming victim, 58, 235, 247-248
    denial, 58, 287
    denigration of partner, 42, 45, 54, 598,
        600, 636
    economic abuse. *See* Financial abuse
    employment. *See* Employment
    entitlement, sense of, 45
    familicide, 142
    favoritism of children by, 598
    fleeing offenders, 222, 267
    gender-related issues, 31, 32, 33, 34, 35
    homicide by. *See* Homicide
    humiliation tactics, 42, 58
    instrumental use of children, 43, 58
    intimidation, 58, 181
    isolation tactics, 37, 42, 199
    manipulation, 44, 235, 246, 247-248,
        621, 641
    marital rape. *See* Marital rape
    minimization, 58, 488
    military. *See* Military
    minimization of abuse, 58
    murder-suicide, 129, 140-144, 705
    parenting of, 597-602
    popularity of, 44, 46
    possessiveness, 45. *See also* Jealousy
    pregnancy-related abuse, 167-170
    property damage, 42
    pet abuse. *See* Pet abuse
    psychopathology. *See* Theories of domestic
        violence
    race. *See* Race
    rape. *See* Marital rape; Rape; Sexual assault
    recidivism, 281, 408, 411, 494, 495,
        776, 801
    retaliation by, 94, 202, 214, 236, 247, 248,
        251, 600

    sexual orientation, issues of. *See* Sexual
        orientation
    social class, issues of
    stalking. *See* Stalking
    substance abuse, 33
    suicide. *See* Murder-suicide; Suicide
    threats, abusers' use of, 40, 58
    typologies of, 51
    undermining of mother, 42, 45, 54, 598, 600,
        636
    victim, self-perception as, 488
    weapons. *See* Firearms
Omnibus Consolidated Appropriations Act, 410
Omnibus Crime Control and Safe Streets Act, 320.
        See also Duress
Online dating, 551-554
Orders of protection (civil)
    adolescents and, 73-75
    advantages of, 424-425
    burden of proof, 457, 465
    conditions on contact, 74, 187, 426, 436-442
    constitutional issues, 258-261, 266, 441, 442,
        465
    contempt for violation of. *See* Contempt
    criticisms of, 428-430
    discovery abuse, 462-466
    divorce-related, 187, 422, 423, 424. *See also*
        Divorce
    Domestic Violence Restraining Order System
        (DVROS), 475
    dual or mutual orders, 484-488
    duration of, 187, 426, 427, 442-447
    effectiveness of, 40, 258-261, 268, 427, 493-497,
        776
    eligible parties, 75, 76, 83, 91, 278, 279, 281,
        282, 286, 290, 292, 425, 430-435
    enforcement problems, 475-480
    escalation factor, 429
    extension and renewal, 446
    ex parte nature of temporary orders, 74, 426,
        433, 465
    fear requirement, 441, 457
    fetus-related, 167-170
    firearm restrictions, 401, 402, 403, 409-410,
        412-413, 426, 478-479
    Full, Faith and Credit in enforcement, 480-484
    history of enforcement, 258-261, 265
    injunctive relief distinguished, 423
    interstate enforcement of, 481-484
    interstate travel to violate a restraining order,
        389-390, 395
    jurisdictional issues, 447-452
    jury trial, 460-462
    mandatory arrest and, 222, 266-267
    military, 122, 123
    no contact orders, criminal, distinguished, 427
    permanent, 40, 74, 187, 426, 476-477
    pet abuse. *See* Pet abuse

for pregnant victims, 167-170
proof of abuse, types of, 74, 75, 83, 426, 427,
    434, 441, 457, 457-460
recent abuse requirement, 457
right to counsel, 465, 721
separation abuse and. *See* Exit from abusive
    relationships
service of process, 427
stalking and, 186-187
statistics, 40, 435
temporary, 40, 74, 426
termination of, 452-457
types of , 74-75, 187, 423, 425, 426
unserved orders of protection, 476, 478
vacating order, 252
victim satisfaction with, 494-496, 497
violation of, by offenders, 74, 222, 248, 427,
    474-480
violation of, by victims, 429, 489-491
violence escalation, triggered by, 158
withdrawal of, by victims, 492
Orders of protection (criminal), 253-254
Oregon Coalition Against Domestic and Sexual
    Violence, 215

Parent coordinators. *See* Child custody
Parental Alienation Syndrome, 645-646. *See also*
    Child custody
Parental Kidnaping Prevention Act (PKPA), 655
Parenting. *See* Child custody
Parenting plans. *See* Child custody
Patient Protection and Affordable Care Act, 69,
    715
Patriarchy, 52, 53, 59, 102
Pence, Ellen, 56
Personal Responsibility and Work Opportunity
    Reconciliation Act (PRWORA), 114
Pet abuse, 201-206, 324. *See also* Domestic violence
animal cruelty laws, 202, 203, 205
barriers to seeking help, 202
characteristics of abusers, 42, 75
comparison of abusers, 202
children's exposure to, 204
constitutional issues regarding, 203
co-occurrence of domestic violence and child
    abuse, 41, 43, 165, 203, 598, 609
definition, 202
forms of, 202
law reform movement, 203
motivation for, 202
police assistance to remove pets, 202
reporting of, 204, 205
restraining orders regarding, 203
shelter-related issues and, 204
state laws on, 203
statistics, 201
statutory approaches, 203

Physical abuse. *See* Domestic violence
Physicians. *See* Health care
Police. *See also* Police-perpetrated abuse
arrests. *See* Arrest
assistance to victims to remove possessions, 202,
    237-238
barriers to seeking help from, 124, 125, 127,
    234-235
deaths/injuries to, from domestic violence, 214,
    216
delay in responding, 213, 215-216
discretion, use of. *See* Arrest
dual or mutual arrest. *See* Arrest
emergency dispatch, 362-363, 364, 368-369
expansion of police powers, 238-239
factors affecting arrest, 214, 215, 216, 217
lawsuits against, 214, 223, 258-269
mandatory arrest. *See* Arrest
masculinities theory and, 128-129
mediation approach to arrest, 215, 216, 224
nonintervention policy, 214, 215, 275
orders of protection and, 258-269
perception of law enforcement role, 216
policy statements, 215
primary aggressor determination, 228, 229, 232
protocols for 911 calls, 363-363
traditional response to domestic violence,
    213-216
training, 190, 214, 227, 269, 270, 276
warrantless arrest, 214, 215, 217-220, 275
victim-blaming by, 213, 214, 215
Police-perpetrated abuse
barriers to seeking help, 124, 125, 127
causes of, 125, 126
community response to, 128
comparison with other abusers, 127, 128
dynamics of, 126
firearm regulation and, 128
male culture of violence, 126, 128, 129
offenders' characteristics, 126, 127
rate of, 125
severity of, 125
shelters' response to, 127
statistics, 125
stereotypes, 127
victims' characteristics, 127
zero tolerance policy, 128, 129
Post Traumatic Stress Disorder (PTSD), 43, 48,
    53, 54, 122, 436, 599, 665
Poverty. *See* Economic issues
Power and control, 120, 125, 171. *See also*
    Psychological abuse
Power and Control Wheel, 54, 56-58
Pregnancy and domestic violence. *See also*
    Abortion; Birth control sabotage
abuse during pregnancy, rate of, 169, 170
age of victims, 169
contraceptive fraud, 173

effects of violence during, 169, 172, 177, 178
father's interest in, 178
federal law, 170, 174-179
fetal homicide, 170
homicide of adult victim during, 169
motivation for inflicting harm during, 169
obstacles to disclosure, 169, 170
orders of protection during, 167-169
protective function of, 169
rates of abuse during, 169
risk factor for abuse, 169
screening for domestic violence during, 170
state law, 169
statistics, 169
teenage victims, 169
Primary aggressor. *See* Arrest
Privacy. *See* Family privacy
Professional responsibility issues. *See also*
        Standards of Practice
advising fleeing victims, 728-731
client counseling, 728, 729, 730, 731, 737-741
client safety, 727, 731, 732-733, 734, 741-744
competence, 730, 735
confidentiality, 728
conflicts of interest, 75, 640
obligations to non-clients, 729-730
obstructing access to evidence, 730
penalties for violation of, 729
representation of teenage victims, 75
withdrawal from representation, 729
Property damage. *See* Economic issues; Financial
        abuse; Pet abuse
Property division post-divorce. *See* Divorce
Prosecution and prosecutors, response to
        domestic violence
advantages of no-drop policies, 246, 249
case attrition, 243
constitutional issues in response to domestic
        violence, 244
criticisms of no-drop policies, 244, 247, 249,
        250, 253
evidence-based prosecution, 252
institutional constraints on prosecution, 250
no-drop policies, 243-253
rates of, 252
reluctance to prosecute violations of orders of
        protection, 479-480
restorative justice and, 254-257
strategies to address victims' non-cooperation,
        243, 252
traditional response, 250
types of discretion to prosecute, 243, 251
victimless evidence-based prosecution, 252, 353
victims' non-cooperation, 243, 245, 246, 247,
        248, 250, 367
Prosecutorial Remedies and Other Tools to End
        the Exploitation of Children Today Act
        (PROTECT Act), 191, 651

Prostitution, 324. *See also* Trafficking
Protective orders. *See* Orders of protection
Provocation. *See also* Criminal defenses
Blackstone on, 332
common law approach, 331
elements of, 332
Model Penal Code, 332, 334
Roman law approach, 331
Psychological abuse
coercive control, 38, 42, 45, 58, 179-182
constitutional issues, 208
control, 44, 45, 58
degradation, 45, 58
disrespect, 45, 58
financial abuse, 58
French law, 208
forms of, 58
intimidation, 58
isolation, 37, 42, 199
orders of protection and, 442
pet abuse, 42, 201-206, 324
property abuse. *See* Financial abuse
shaming, 58
stalking. *See* Stalking
surveillance, 190, 208, 399, 400
threats, 40, 58
Psychologists. *See* Batterers' intervention
        programs; Custody evaluators; Guardians
        ad litem; Mediators
Psychopathology theory of abuse. *See* Theories of
        domestic violence
Public assistance. *See* Economic issues; Personal
        Responsibility and Work Opportunity
        Reconciliation Act; Welfare
Private family paradigm, 22, 23, 27
Public-private dichotomy, 8, 15, 27, 52

Race and intimate partner violence. *See also*
        African-Americans; Asian-Americans;
        Native-Americans
arrest policies and, 225, 229, 233
barriers to seeking help, 99
community response, 99
disclosure of partner violence, 98-99, 100
gender and, 98
homelessness and, 99
mandatory arrest. *See* Arrest
offenders' characteristics, 98, 99, 100
police response to victims, 99, 100, 229
poverty-related issues, 98, 99, 100
reporting of violence, 98, 100
statistics, 98, 99, 100
stereotypes, 99
victims' characteristics, 98, 99, 100
Rape. *See also* Acquaintance rape; Marital rape
        acquaintance; Teen dating violence
anti-rape movement, 9-10, 344, 345

college campuses and, 540, 541, 549
consent issues, 344, 345
criminal liability for, 41
definition, 30
intimate partners, rape by, 30, 41
law reform movement, 9-10, 344, 345
marital. *See* Marital rape
psychological effects of, 542
rape shield laws, 346, 399
Rape Trauma Syndrome, 542
rapists, traits of, 540, 541
same-sex partners and, 346
statistics, 30, 41, 240
Swedish law on, 173-174
tort liability for, 530-550
underreporting of, 541, 542
wives' implied consent, 342, 344
youth gangs, 77
Rape trauma syndrome, 542. *See also* Acquaintance
 rape; Rape; Sexual assault
Reasonable woman standard, 303-304. *See also*
 Battered Woman Standard; Criminal
 defenses; Self-defense
Recidivism. *See* Offenders
Religion and intimate partner violence
clergy, role of, 101, 107, 110
gender roles and, 106, 109
honor killings, 107-109
Islamic/Muslim community, 107-109
Judaism, 105-107
sexism, 106, 107, 108, 109, 110
Representation. *See* Attorneys, Custody evaluators,
 Guardians ad litem; Professional
 Responsibility
Reproductive coercion, 167-179. *See also* Abortion;
 Birth control sabotage; Pregnancy and
 domestic violence
Res judicata doctrine, 522-526, 528, 581. *See also*
 Tort
Restatement of the Law of Torts, 670, 671
Restatement (Second) of the Law of
 Torts, 502, 503, 504, 574, 652-653,
 671, 672
Restatement (Third) of the Law Governing
 Lawyers, 670
Restorative justice, 254-257
Restraining orders. *See* Orders of protection
Retaliation. *See* Exit from abusive relationship
Risk assessment, 59-65, 306-307. *See also* Lethality
 assessment

Same-sex intimate partner violence. *See* Sexual
 orientation
Same-sex marriage, 91
Schaeffer, Rebecca, 188
Security and Financial Empowerment (SAFE) Act,
 709

Self-defense
admissibility of Battered Woman Syndrome
 evidence, 297-305, 725
apprehension of danger, 306-307
castle doctrine, 307, 312
deadly force, use of, 307, 309, 311
duty to retreat, 306-307, 312
dual or mutual arrest and, 225-228, 230, 231,
 232, 233
elements of, 307, 308, 311
force, 303, 304
gender-based meaning of, 231-232
gender bias in law of, 303-304
gender equality view of, 304
imminence requirement, 304, 305, 306, 307,
 308, 309, 311, 312
imperfect self-defense, 311
jury instruction on, 303, 304, 314
objective vs. subjective standard, 303, 304, 306, 312
paradigm shift in law of, 303-304
primary aggressor, 228, 229, 232
reasons why victims fight back, 231, 232
reasonable person, 303-304
reasonableness, 306, 308, 311, 312
reasonable woman standard, 303-304
stereotypes engendered by, 313
Seneca Falls Convention, 13
Separation. *See* Exit from abusive relationship
Services, Training, Officers, Prosecutors (STOP)
 grants, 269, 270
Sexual assault. *See also* Marital rape; Rape
acquaintance rape, 530-541, 549
condoms, 95, 171, 172, 173-174
consent, 42-43, 94
cultural defense, 166, 330
disabled victims, 92
marital rape, 42-43, 118, 162-167
marital rape exemption, 22, 166
marital status and, 41
Nicole's law, 399
physical assault, co-occurrence of, 41, 43
rape shield laws, 399
Rape Trauma Syndrome, 542
statistics, 41, 94
substance abuse, 118
teens, 73
Sexual orientation and domestic violence
barriers to seeking help, 88-89
community response to, 88, 90
compared to opposite-sex partner violence,
 88-89, 90
custody-related issues, 88, 90
disclosure, 88-89
distrust of police, 88-89
dual or mutual arrest, 91, 225-228, 229, 230,
 231, 232
gender, 89
homophobia, 88, 89, 90

legal response to, 88-89
orders of protection, 88
police response to, 88-89
race and, 90
reporting, 89
shelters and, 89
state DOMAs applied to same-sex partner
    violence, 91
statistics, 88, 89
stereotypes regarding, 90
statutes, 91
threats to "out" partner, 88
transgender partners, 88
VAWA, application to, 91
Shelters
British shelters, 780, 781
conditional nature of services, 794
confidentiality of, 784-789
disabled clients and, 97, 795
discrimination by service providers, 794, 795
duration of stay, 794
ethnicity, 794
experiences in, 789-791
funding, 777-784
gender-based challenges to funding, 777-784
housing, emergency and transitional, 700, 701,
    780, 781, 787, 789-793
immigrants and, 102
liability of, 788
location, 784
needs of clients, 700, 701, 791, 792, 793,
    794, 795
origins of movement, 8-9, 780
overcrowding, 701, 795
pet-friendly, 204
race and, 794
services sought and received, 791, 792, 793, 794
sexual orientation and, 794, 795
Simpson, Nicole Brown, 351, 359-362
Simpson, O.J., 351
civil trial, 361
criminal trial, 351, 359-360
evidentiary issues, 359-361
legacy of, 130, 131, 360-361
Skinner, B.F., 50
Slayer disqualification. See Murder-suicide
Social class
comparison of affluent to other victims, 115,
    117
disclosure, affected by, 117
incidence of abuse, affected by, 32, 117
poverty, relationship to domestic violence, 32,
    36, 115
role of, in intimate partner violence, 32, 36,
    115, 116
shelter services and, 117
statistics, 32
types of abuse, 117

universal risk theory, 115
welfare, 114, 115, 116
Sociological theories of abuse. See Theories of
    domestic violence
Specialized domestic violence courts, 762-776
Sports, 130-133. See also Simpson, O.J., 131-133
Spouse abuse. See Domestic violence; Offenders;
    Victims
Spousal support, 22, 23, 578-582
Spousal testimonial privilege, 337-339. See also
    Evidence
Stages-of-change model, 159-161. See also Exit
    from abusive relationship
Stalking, 182-192
constitutional issues, 188
course of conduct requirement, 192, 398
cyberstalking, 189-191. See also Cyberstalking
definitional issues, 30
effectiveness, 189
fear requirement, 186
federal laws, 188, 189
forms of, 186, 187
harassment distinguished, 188
gender and, 186
intent, 186
interstate, 189
offenders, characteristics of, 30-31, 187
penalties, 188, 189
psychological effects, 187
rate of, 31
restraining orders and, 186, 191
risk factor for homicide, 60
severity, 196
state laws, 186, 187
statistics, 30, 31, 60, 186
technology and, 187, 189, 190
victims, characteristics of, 30-31, 187
Standards of Practice
Model Standards of Practice for Family and
    Divorce Mediation (AFCC), 752-753
Standards of Practice for Lawyers Representing
    Children in Custody Cases, 639
Standards of Practice for Lawyers who
    Represent Children in Abuse and
    Neglect Cases, 639
Standards of Practice for Lawyers Representing
    Victims of Domestic Violence, Sexual
    Assault and Stalking in Civil Protection
    Order Cases, 731-735
Standards for Supervised Visitation Practice,
    625
Stanton, Elizabeth Cady, 14
Strangulation
definition, 138
elements of, 139
frequency of attempts, 138
harm requirement, 139
health consequences, 68, 138

intent requirement, 139
likelihood of prosecution for, 139
mutual combat, 139
petechiae, 136, 137
physical indicators of, 138
risk factor for homicide, 138
social, 68
state statutes, 138-139
types of, 138
Substance abuse and domestic violence
factor in arrest, 227
factor in victim's likelihood to seek help, 217
offenders' use of, 33, 118, 119
risk assessment factor, 61, 118
statistics, 33, 118
victims' use of, 33, 118, 227
Suffrage movement, 5, 10, 15
Suicide
elderly, 143
military rate, 122
murder-suicide, 126, 140-144, 705
suicide by cop, 267
teen behavior, 73, 196-197
threats to commit, 58, 63, 566-567
victim's behavior, 63, 68
Supervised visitation. *See* Visitation

Tahirir Justice Center, 560, 564, 565
TANF. *See* Temporary Assistance to Needy
Families, 114-115
Teen dating violence, 71-79
attitudes about, 76, 77, 78
comparison to adult partner violence, 73, 74,
77-78
effects, 73
offenders' characteristics, 73
orders of protection, 71-75, 78
peer influence, 78
professional responsibility issues, 75
representation, 75
signs of, 75
state laws, 75-76
teenage pregnancy, 73
victims' characteristics, 73
youth gangs, 77
Telephone Harassment Act, 190, 398, 399
Temperance movement, 5, 18
Temporary Assistance to Needy Families (TANF),
114, 115
Temporary injunctions. *See* Orders of protection
Temporary restraining orders. *See* Orders of
protection
Termination of parental rights. *See* Child abuse;
Child custody
Theories of domestic violence, 47-59
attachment, disrupted, 48, 49
biological, 47-49, 59

borderline personality disorder, 48
cycle of violence, 48-49, 53-56
evolutionary, 48
family systems theory, 49-50, 59
feminist, 52-53
genetic, 48
head injury, 47-48
learned behavior, 46, 48, 50, 51
learned helplessness, 53, 54, 156
loss of control, myth of, 38
personality disorders, 48
Power and Control Wheel, 56-58
psychopathology, 48-49
social learning theory, 50
sociological, 50-51
Therapeutic justice, 775-776
Thumb, Rule of, 19
Title II, 534
Title VII, 712, 795, 796
Title VIII, 695
Title IX, 417, 530, 548, 549
Tort liability and domestic violence
continuing tort doctrine, 506, 521
domestic violence torts, 504, 505
employers' liability for workplace violence,
712-713
failure to report, liability for, 512
federal tort liability, VAWA, 530-550
infliction of emotional distress, 499-507, 524,
570, 571, 574, 670, 671
interspousal immunity doctrine, 11, 22, 23-27,
514-516
joinder with divorce, 572-577
jury trial, 574, 576
marital settlement agreement, precluding tort
claim, 525
objective standard, 506, 507
physical injury requirement, 504
policy considerations, 500, 501
purposes of tort liability, 503, 672
relevance of insurance, 526, 527, 529
reluctance by victims to sue, 525-529
res judicata, 522-526, 528, 575, 581
Restatement of the Law of Torts, 670, 671
Restatement (Second) of the Law of Torts, 502,
503, 504, 574, 671, 672
statutes of limitation, 517-522, 527, 528
tort liability of police, 268, 269
tort liability and post-divorce property division,
584, 585, 586
traditional tort claims, 502-503
Trafficking, 398, 483, 560, 561, 563
Transtheoretical Model of behavior change, 159
Transgender persons, 88. *See* Sexual orientation
Transgenerational transmission of violence, 50.
See also Theories of domestic violence
Transitional Compensation for Abused Family
Members, 123

Traumatic bonding, 630-633, 635
Treatment programs, 56, 57, 58. *See also* Batterers'
    intervention programs
Tribal culture and abuse, 414-417
Tribal Law and Order Act, 417
TROs. *See* Orders of protection

Unborn Victims of Violence Act (UVVA), 170
Unemployment. *See* Employment
Uniform Child Abduction Prevention Act
    (UCAPA), 655
Uniform Child Custody Jurisdiction and
    Enforcement Act (UCCJEA), 655, 656
Uniform Collaborative Law Act (UCLA), 762
Uniform Marriage and Divorce Act (UMDA), 423,
    581, 606, 607
Uniform Representation of Children in Abuse,
    Neglect, and Custody Proceedings Act,
    639
United States Attorney General's Task Force on
    Family Violence, 475-480
United States Constitution. *See* Constitutional
    issues
United States Department of Education, 541
United States Department of Health and
    Human Services, 69, 716
United States Department of Homeland Security
    (DHS), 559
United States Department of Housing and
    Urban Development, 696
Universal risk theory. *See* Social class
Unmarried couples. *See* Cohabitants

Visas
    K-1 visa, 559
    U-visa, 563
VAWA. *See* Violence Against Women Act
Victim-blaming, 14, 275, 333. *See also* Offenders;
    Police
Victim compensation schemes, 781
Victimization paradigm, 313, 314
Victims. *See also* Offenders; Specific types of abuse
    age, 31, 33, 35
    arrest of. *See* Arrest
    belief systems, 159-161, 235-237
    clemency movement, 305
    as criminal defendants, 297-330
    cycle of violence, 53-56
    denial, 157, 159, 512
    economic dependence. *See* Economic issues
    employment. *See* Employment
    exit from relationship. *See* Exit from abusive
        relationship
    gender-based issues, 30, 31, 32, 33, 34, 35
    health-related issues. *See* Health
    homelessness. *See* Homelessness

    housing. *See* Housing
    identity change. *See* Confidentiality
    immigrants. *See* Immigrants
    learned helplessness of, 53, 54, 156
    marital rape and, 42-43, 162-167
    mediation. *See* Mediation
    minimization, 157
    mothers. *See* Child custody; Mothers
    perception of danger, 158
    post-traumatic stress, 43, 53, 54, 436, 502, 506,
        599, 665
    poverty. *See* Economic issues; Social class
    pregnant. *See* Abortion; Birth control sabotage;
        Pregnancy abuse
    race. *See* Race
    rape. *See* Rape
    reluctance to testify, 379-386
    retaliation, 231
    risk assessment, 59-64
    sanctions on, for failure to cooperate, 253
    sexual assault, 42-43
    self-blame, 43, 45
    self-defense. *See* Criminal defenses; Self-defense
    separation-related issues. *See* Exit from abusive
        relationships
    social class. *See* Social class
    social services. *See* Shelters
    stereotypes, 34, 104
    substance abuse. *See* Substance abuse
    traumatic bonding, 630-633
    undermining of, by abuser, 42, 45, 54, 58, 598,
        600, 636
    victim advocates, 243, 638
    victim-blaming, 139, 235
    welfare, 58, 114, 115, 116
Victims of Abuse Insurance Protection Act, 715
Victims of Crime Act (VOCA), 270, 781
Victims of Trafficking and Violence Protection
    Act, 398, 563
Violence Against Women Act (VAWA)
    background, 14-15, 239, 388
    civil rights remedy, 241, 530-550
    disabled victims, 242
    elderly victims, 242
    firearm provisions, 400-403, 409, 410, 413
    interstate travel to commit domestic violence,
        389, 391-394, 395, 396
    interstate travel to violate an order of
        protection, 389-390
    full, faith and credit provisions, 451, 481-484,
        487
    housing discrimination, 242, 696, 697
    immigrant provisions. *See* Immigrants
    interstate enforcement, 189, 242, 388-400
    mandatory arrest and, 223
    mutual orders of protection, 487
    Native American victims and, 32, 414-417
    objectives of, 239

overview of, 239-242
protection order enforcement, 123, 451
self-petitioning process, 562
sexual assault and, 530-550
shelter funding, 14, 242, 781
stalking, 189, 242, 398
STOP program grant, 269
tort provisions, 530-550
workplace protections, 242
Violence Against Women Act (VAWA) of 2000,
190, 242, 483-484, 563, 699
Violence Against Women Act (VAWA)
Reauthorization Act of 2005, 129, 189,
191, 242, 398, 415, 696, 699, 700
Violence Against Women Act (VAWA)
Reauthorization Bill of 2011, 191, 242,
270, 696, 697, 783
Violent Crime Control and Law Enforcement Act,
128, 401, 409
Visas, 559, 563
Visitation, 617-630. *See also* Child custody
batterers' treatment programs and, 628
child's refusal to visit, 629, 630
confidentiality of records, 629
cost of, 627
danger, posed by, 620-623
federal funding of visitation centers, 627
Lizzie's Law, 629, 630
mediation. *See* Mediation
Model Code on Domestic and Family Violence,
621, 622, 626
modification, 629
monitoring of, 623
parenting plans, 625, 744, 745, 760
programs, 622, 623, 625, 627, 628, 629
purpose, 626
records of, 629
safeguards against harm during, 620-623
supervised, 617-630
supervisors, 627

termination of, 629
unsupervised, 616, 621, 622, 628, 629

Walker, Lenore. *See also* Cycle Theory of Violence;
Theories of domestic violence
Battered Woman Syndrome, 43, 44, 53-56, 301
criticisms of, 55-56
cycle theory of violence, 48-49, 53-56, 301
learned helplessness, 53-54, 301
Warning signs of abuse, 36-38
Warrants
absent offenders and, 214
common law warrant rule, 220
felonies vs misdemeanors, 220
fleeing offenders, 214, 222
probable cause requirement for felony arrest, 220
rationale for rule, 220-221
requirements for issuance of, 214, 220
warrantless arrest policies, 214, 215, 217-220,
228, 275
Weapons. *See* Firearms
Welfare system and domestic violence, 58, 114,
115, 116. *See also* Personal Responsibility
and Work Opportunity Reconciliation
Act
Wife-beating. *See* Domestic violence
Women. *See* Battered women; Feminism; Gender
Women's movement. *See* Battered women's
movement; Feminism
Workplace violence, 242, 245-246, 705-706, 712,
713
World Anti-Slavery Convention, 13

Youth gangs, intimate partner violence in, 77.
See also Age; Teen dating violence

Zero tolerance policy, 128, 129